D0085390

THE PAPERS OF

WOODROW WILSON

VOLUME 69

SPONSORED BY THE WOODROW WILSON
FOUNDATION
AND PRINCETON UNIVERSITY

THE PAPERS OF

WOODROW WILSON

ARTHUR S. LINK, *EDITOR*

PHYLLIS MARCHAND, *INDEXER*

ANNE CIPRIANO VENZON, *INDEXER AND COMPILER*

CONTENTS AND INDEX, VOLUMES 53-68

Volume 69 • 1918-1924

PRINCETON, NEW JERSEY

PRINCETON UNIVERSITY PRESS

1994

CONTENTS

Explanatory Note, ix
Epilogue, xi

Contents

Wilson Materials

Addresses, statements, and press releases, 3
Political correspondence about domestic affairs
From Wilson, 8
To Wilson, 17
Correspondence, reports, memoranda, and aide-mémoire about
diplomatic affairs
Wilson to and by Wilson, 29
To Wilson from, 33
Personal correspondence
From Wilson to, 40
To Wilson from, 51
Interviews and memoranda of conversations with Wilson, 61
Questionnaire, 64
Press conferences, 64
News reports, 64
Writings, 70
"The Document": correspondence and drafts (to, from, and
by Wilson), 70

Collateral Materials

Diplomatic correspondence, reports, memoranda, and aide-
mémoire, 71
Domestic political correspondence, reports, memoranda, and
aide-mémoire, 73
Diplomatic and military correspondence, reports, memoranda,
and aide-mémoire, 85
Personal correspondence, notes, speeches, statements, and
memoranda, 96
Diaries, 104

The Paris Peace Conference

Minutes of Plenary Sessions, 110
Minutes of the meetings of the Council of Ten, 110
Minutes of the meetings of the Council of Four, 110
Minutes of a meeting of the Council of Four and the Council of
Five, 112
Notes of a British-French-Italian meeting, 112
Notes of a meeting of British and French leaders, 112
Minutes of the Supreme War Council, 113
Council of Four: memoranda, reports, and resolutions, 113
Council of Four: notes exchanged with the German delegation,
115
German notes, 115
Allied replies to, 116

Council of Four: notes and correspondence, 116
Minutes of the meetings of the League of Nations Commission, 117
The Covenant of the League of Nations (drafts and text), 118
Wilson's addresses and statements, 118
Wilson correspondence
   From Wilson to, 119
   To Wilson from, 122
Collateral addresses and remarks, 129
Collateral correspondence, 129
Memoranda, reports, aide-mémoire, and position papers, 135
Reparations and categories of damages, 143
Appendixes, 143
Editorial Note, 143
Miscellaneous, 143

Illustrations, 145

Index, 149

EXPLANATORY NOTE

THE sixteen volumes covered by this cumulative table of contents and index begin with the eve of the Armistice of November 11, 1918, and end with Wilson's death on February 3, 1924, and his funeral services three days later. The documents covering these years tell the story of events of momentous importance to the history of the world in the balance of the twentieth century, and, undoubtedly, into the next millennium: the Paris Peace Conference; Wilson's illness in 1919, with its culmination in his devastating stroke on October 2, 1919; the struggle in the Senate over ratification of the Versailles Treaty and the defeat of that treaty; the seeming repudiation of Wilsonian internationalism in the election of 1920; and the efforts of the Harding and Coolidge administrations to find a middle ground in domestic and foreign policies. The last two volumes also chronicle Wilson's activities in retirement and his efforts to lead the Democratic party and the country toward a revival of domestic reform and membership in the League of Nations.

The Table of Contents is divided into two main sections: Wilson Materials and Collateral Materials. Together, they list, under special editorial headings and in alphabetical or chronological order, all the items printed in Volumes 53-68. Correspondence, reports, memoranda, and aide-mémoire by Wilson and to him are arranged alphabetically under the separate categories of political, diplomatic, and personal. A special section on the Paris Peace Conference gives a conspectus of the materials relating to that congress of the nations. Another special section gives a conspectus of materials relating to what Wilson called "The Document"—a platform for the presidential campaign of 1924, in which Wilson expected to run for a third term. All correspondence between March 4, 1921, and Wilson's death is listed under the rubric, "personal." Wilson's addresses, statements, press releases, press conferences, diplomatic correspondence, interviews with him and records of conversations with him, and news reports about him are arranged chronologically under the appropriate heading. Collateral materials are arranged in the same manner as that described for Wilson Materials. Illustrations are listed separately.

The index includes all persons, places, and subjects mentioned in the text and footnotes. All books, articles, pamphlets, poems, newspapers, and magazines mentioned in the text or cited in footnotes are indexed by author and title. Book titles and plays appear in italics; quotation marks are omitted for articles, editorials, and poems. Newspapers are listed under the city of publication; magazines are listed under their titles. Page references to footnotes which carry a

comma between the page number and the "n" cite both the text and the footnote, thus: "186,n2." Absence of the comma indicates reference to the footnote only, thus: "345n1." In both cases, the page number refers to the page on which the textual reference occurs.

Phyllis Marchand prepared the indexes of Volumes 53-68, as she has done for all volumes in the series since Volume 27. Anne Cipriano Venzon consolidated the individual volume tables of contents and indexes for this Volume 69. I have reviewed this volume and checked all the major entries and numerous others for accuracy. Finally, Margaret Douglas Link gave me invaluable help in proofreading this volume and in checking numerous entries.

ARTHUR S. LINK

Princeton, New Jersey
January 8, 1993

EPILOGUE

The Editors of
The Papers of Woodrow Wilson, 1958-1993

Arthur S. Link, Director and Editor, 1958-1993

John Wells Davidson, Associate Editor, 1958-1971

David W. Hirst, Assistant Editor, 1959-1965; Associate Editor, 1965-1979;
Senior Associate Editor, 1979-1989

John E. Little, Editorial Assistant, 1961-1966; Assistant Editor, 1966-1971;
Associate Editor, 1971-1992

Thomas Hubbard Vail Motter, Consulting Editor, 1964-1967

William M. Leary, Jr., Assistant Editor, 1967-1968

Jean MacLachlan, Contributing Editor, 1967-1972

Milton Halsey Thomas, Consulting Editor and Indexer, 1968-1977

John M. Mulder, Editorial Assistant, 1971-1973; Assistant Editor, 1973-1974

Sylvia Elvin, Contributing Editor, 1972-1978

Edith James, Assistant Editor, 1974-1977

Phyllis Marchand, Indexer, 1977-1992

Manfred F. Boemeke, Editorial Assistant, 1977-1982; Assistant Editor,
1982-1985; Associate Editor, 1985-1991

Thomas J. Knock, Editorial Assistant, 1977-1979

Ann D. Gordon, Assistant Editor, 1978-1979

Margaret Douglas Link, Editorial Assistant, 1978-1988

Anne Cipriano Venzon, Editorial Assistant, 1978-1982; Cumulative Indexer
and Editor, 1982-1993

Fredrick Aandahl, Associate Editor, 1979-1984

Denise Thompson, Assistant Editor, 1983-1988

L. Kathleen Amon, Assistant Editor, 1988-1992

During the life of the Wilson Papers project, my colleagues and I accumulated more obligations than can ever be enumerated to individuals, institutions, foundations, repositories, and agencies.

There is no need to repeat here the story of the organization of the project by the Woodrow Wilson Foundation of New York, which I related in the General Introduction to Volume 1 of *The Papers.* However, I can now reiterate, with far greater emphasis than I employed in that introduction, that it was Raymond B. Fosdick who played the key role in the foundation's decision to devote all its resources if necessary to undertake a comprehensive edition of the Wilson papers.

I dedicate this series to the memory of this great Wilsonian, public servant, and friend. Julie C. Herzog, Executive Director of the Woodrow Wilson Foundation, also supported the project enthusiastically, as did Robert F. Goheen, President of Princeton University, who provided a hospitable academic home for, and invaluable services, to the project. Finally, it would have been impossible to do the work preliminary to the production of volumes without the generous financial start-up support of the Rockefeller Foundation, the Ford Foundation, the Cleveland H. Dodge Foundation, the United States Steel Corporation, the State of New Jersey, John D. Rockefeller 3d, Mrs. Woodrow Wilson, and Bernard M. Baruch.

From the beginning to the end of the project, we have had the unswerving encouragement and support of the members of the Board of Directors of the Woodrow Wilson Foundation. To each of them, whose names (since the reorganization of the board in 1962) are listed below, I extend our heartfelt thanks:

Louise Wright, 1963-1986
Thomas H. Wright, Jr., Secretary, 1974-1993

We owe deep thanks to Princeton University, a co-sponsor of *The Papers of Woodrow Wilson*, for providing us an academic home in the Department of History and for managing, at no cost to the project, all our business affairs. Our thanks for interest and assistance go also to the chairpersons of the History Department, the Deans of the Faculty, and especially the Presidents of the University from 1960 to 1992—Robert F. Goheen, William G. Bowen, and Harold T. Shapiro.

The Librarians of Princeton University—William S. Dix, Richard W. Boss, and Donald W. Koepp—provided us with commodious quarters in Firestone Library from September 1, 1960, to June 30, 1992, and never once intimated that we were about to wear out our welcome; on the contrary, they were always cordial hosts. We would also have been hard up indeed without the daily support of the library's maintenance, reference, archival, manuscripts, and photographic staffs. Our warm thanks go out to all these indispensable servants of students and scholars. Nor do I want to fail to mention the services rendered us by the University Archivists, Milton Halsey Thomas, Earle Coleman, and Ben Primer.

Our documentation and annotation would have been far sparser than it is without the always cheerful and ready responses to our inquiries from literally thousands of heads of manuscript repositories and reference librarians around the world. It would require many pages to list all the helpful friends in such repositories as the Library of Congress, the Public Record Office, the Archives of the German Foreign Office, the libraries of great universities and repositories such as Yale, Harvard, the Hoover Institution, Oxford and Cambridge Universities, the University of North Carolina, the University of Virginia, and in hundreds of public libraries in large cities and small towns. What we call our search file fills the four drawers of a filing cabinet; in addition we made contact with hundreds of librarians by telephone. In not a single case did our request for copies of documents or information fail to evoke a ready response.

That chief initiator, organizer, and supporter of documentary editions relating to the history of the United States, the National Historical Publications and Records Commission, from the beginning gave *The Papers of Woodrow Wilson* its valued imprimatur. Since the income from the endowment of the Woodrow Wilson Foundation was always sufficient to meet the ongoing needs of the Wilson project, we never asked for or received subventions from the commission for annual budgets. However, the commission did provide subventions for

the publication of volumes so long as those subventions were needed. In addition, the commission, very early in the editing of the series, provided us with staff archival members, who assisted us with the ongoing research for documents, beginning with Wilson's assumption of the presidency of the United States. These helpful researchers were Mary Giunta, Sara Jackson, and, particularly, Timothy Connelly.

For the production of handsome and readable volumes we are indebted to the fine cooperation and work of the officers and staff members of Princeton University Press. The two directors of the Press during the life of the project, Herbert S. Bailey, Jr., and Walter H. Lippincott, gave unflagging support and encouragement. P. J. Conkwright, one of the great book designers and typographers of this century, designed and planned the series. Marjorie Putney, Lewis Bateman, Judith May, and Alice Calaprice were our editors at and liaisons with Princeton University Press.

Wilson suffered from cerebrovascular disease from the 1890s until his death, and in chronicling the development of this disease and its impact upon him we have benefited from the counsel of Drs. Edwin A. Weinstein, Norman Geschwind, James F. Toole, and Bert E. Park. We extend our sincere thanks to them for their efforts to see that the facts of Wilson's health history were correctly presented.

People too numerous to mention sent us single Wilson letters or small collections of them. We owe special thanks to Eleanor Wilson McAdoo for making available the correspondence between her parents; to Mrs. Woodrow Wilson, who opened and made available all her correspondence with Woodrow Wilson; and to James Gordon Grayson and Cary Travers Grayson, Jr., sons of Wilson's personal physician, Dr. (Admiral) Cary T. Grayson. Dr. Grayson's diary of the Paris Peace Conference and Wilson's western tour in September 1919 furnish the centerpieces of the documents covering the peace conference and the western tour. Other materials from the Grayson Papers enabled us to chronicle in a clinical manner the progress of Wilson's cerebrovascular disease from 1919 until his death in 1924. Finally, we thank the late Mme. Paul-Joseph Mantoux and her sons, Philippe-Roger Mantoux and Jacques-Adrien Mantoux, for permission to use large portions of M. Mantoux's *Les Délibérations du Conseil des Quatres* in the peace conference series and, with Dr. Boemeke's assistance, to publish *Les Délibérations* as *The Deliberations of the Council of Four (March 24-June 28, 1919)*.

The skill of Clifford P. Gehman, an expert in Graham shorthand, which Wilson used extensively, and of Jack Romagna, an expert in the Gregg reporting system of shorthand, which Wilson's stenographer, Charles L. Swem used, enabled us to recover several thousand pages

of transcripts of Wilson's letters, speeches, memoranda, and press conferences heretofore not transcribed. We are grateful to Mr. Gehman and Mr. Romagna for their notable contributions to history.

Last, but far from least, among the persons who contributed to whatever success *The Papers of Woodrow Wilson* has attained are the members of the Editorial Advisory Committee:

Samuel Flagg Bemis, 1959-1964

Julian P. Boyd, 1959-1965

Katherine E. Brand, 1959-1982

Henry Steele Commager, 1959-1976

Richard W. Leopold, 1959-1992

Arthur M. Schlesinger, Jr., 1959-1992

August Heckscher, 1962-1992

David C. Mearns, 1964-1976

William H. Harbaugh, 1976-1992

John Milton Cooper, Jr., 1977-1992

Betty Miller Unterberger, 1982- 1992

Bert E. Park, 1988-1992

These members, whose service went back to 1959, not only helped us to determine standards of selection and annotation; they also read the first volume with an eye as to whether it met appropriate standards. Several members sent in written critiques, and the full committee discussed the manuscript of the first volume at a meeting in January 1965. The committee met with the editors next on October 13, 1967, for a searching review and discussion of Volumes 1-3 and of the contents of Volumes 4-7. The work of the committee intensified as we approached the period of Wilson's presidency of the United States. A meeting on May 16-17, 1975, focused on principles of selection and annotation for materials relating to the period of the presidency. Moreover, the members of the committee read and critiqued the manuscript of Volume 27, the first of the presidential series, and continued to read and criticize all the manuscripts to the end of the series. And at every new stage in Wilson's career, and every time critical issues needed discussion, the members of the Editorial Advisory Committee gave us their advice generously and candidly.

Now that the task to which I set my hand in 1958 is complete, I hope that readers will indulge me the privilege of saying farewell on my own behalf and on behalf of my colleagues. We hope that we have accomplished the goal that we set before ourselves in 1958: to select, edit, and annotate appropriately the documents and other materials that are essential to a knowledge and understanding of Woodrow

Wilson the human being; the thinker, writer, and scholar; the educational statesman; and the public leader whose actions at home and abroad had a significant impact upon the history of the twentieth century.

I lay down my pen with a feeling of pride in and gratitude to my colleagues over the years, for their contributions were great and indispensable. My wife, Margaret Douglas Link, has sustained and blessed us all. Finally, I give humble thanks to Him who gave me the strength for labors through the years.

ARTHUR S. LINK

Princeton, New Jersey
January 12, 1993

THE PAPERS OF

WOODROW WILSON

VOLUME 69

CONTENTS
FOR VOLUMES 53–68

WILSON MATERIALS

Addresses, statements, and press releases

A statement on the signing of the Armistice, Nov. 11, 1918, **53**: 34

An address to a joint session of Congress, Nov. 11, 1918, **53**: 35

Remarks to state food administrators, Nov. 12, 1918, **53**: 52

A Thanksgiving Proclamation, Nov. 16, 1918, **53**: 95

An announcement of Wilson's intention to head the American delegation to the peace conference, Nov. 18, 1918, **53**: 108

An appeal to the American people in support of the Christmas membership drive of the American National Red Cross, Nov. 26, 1918, **53**: 202

Remarks to members of B'nai B'rith, Nov. 28, 1918, **53**: 239

A press release announcing the appointment of the American peace commissioners, Nov. 29, 1918, **53**: 243

Annual message on the State of the Union, Dec. 2, 1918, **53**: 274

A statement on the pardon of George Webber Mixter and Jesse G. Vincent, Dec. 3, 1918, **53**: 308

An exchange of greetings with the French Foreign Minister at Brest, Dec. 13, 1918, **53**: 380

A reply to the mayor of Brest, Dec. 13, 1918, **53**: 380

A reply to President Poincaré, Dec. 14, 1918, **53**: 386

Remarks to a delegation of French Socialists, Dec. 14, 1918, **53**: 387

An address at the Hotel de Ville in Paris, Dec. 16, 1918, **53**: 404

A statement on the plan for a league of nations advocated by the League to Enforce Peace, Dec. 18, 1918, **53**: 420

Remarks to representatives of the American press in Paris, Dec. 18, 1918, **53**: 421

An address at the University of Paris, Dec. 21, 1918, **53**: 461

A statement on a visit to the American Hospital at Neuilly, Dec. 22, 1918, **53**: 469

A Christmas message to the American people, Dec. 24, 1918, **53**: 491

Remarks at Humes to American soldiers, Dec. 25, 1918, **53**: 505

After-dinner remarks at Buckingham Palace, Dec. 27, 1918, **53**: 522

Remarks in London to Free Church leaders, Dec. 28, 1918, **53**: 530

Remarks to the League of Nations Union, Dec. 28, 1918, **53**: 530

An address at the Guildhall, London, Dec. 28, 1918, **53**: 531

An address at Mansion House, London, Dec. 28, 1918, **53**: 533

Remarks at a stag dinner at 10 Downing Street, Dec. 28, 1918, **64**: 490

4   CONTENTS

Remarks at his grandfather's church in Carlisle, Dec. 29, 1918, **53**:
    541
A luncheon address in Manchester, Dec. 30, 1918, **53**: 548
An address in Free Trade Hall, Manchester, Dec. 30, 1918, **53**: 549
An address to the Italian parliament, Jan. 3, 1919, **53**: 597
Remarks to press representatives in Rome, Jan. 3, 1919, **53**: 599
After-dinner remarks at the Quirinal, Jan. 3, 1919, **53**: 600
Remarks at the Capitol in Rome, Jan. 3, 1919, **53**: 602
Remarks at the Royal Academy of Science in Rome, Jan. 4,1919, **53**:
    608
Remarks in Genoa about Guiseppe Mazzini, Jan. 5, 1919, **53**: 614
Further Remarks in Genoa, Jan. 5, 1919, **53**: 614
Remarks in Genoa about Christopher Columbus, Jan. 5, 1919, **53**:
    615
Remarks at the station in Milan, Jan. 5, 1919, **53**: 616
Remarks at the Royal Palace in Milan, Jan. 5, 1919, **53**: 616
Remarks to the League of Mothers and Widows, Milan, Jan. 5, 1919,
    53: 617
An address at the City Hall in Milan, Jan. 5, 1919, **53**: 617
Remarks at La Scala Opera House, Jan. 5, 1919, **53**: 622
An address at the Philharmonic Club of Turin, Jan. 6, 1919, **53**: 622
A proclamation on the death of Theodore Roosevelt, Jan. 7, 1919, **53**:
    635
An address to the French Senate, Jan. 20, 1919, **54**: 156
Remarks to working women in Paris, Jan. 25, 1919, **54**: 271
Remarks to French Protestants, Jan. 27, 1919, **54**: 282
Remarks to the League for the Rights of Man, Paris, Jan. 28, 1919,
    54: 309
An address to the French Chamber of Deputies, Feb. 3, 1919, **54**: 464
An address to the Third Plenary Session of the peace conference,
    Feb. 14, 1919, **55**: 164
A statement upon leaving France, Feb. 15, 1919, **55**: 197
An address in Boston, Feb. 24, 1919, **55**: 238
Remarks to members of the Democratic National Committee, Feb.
    28, 1919, **55**: 309
A statement about Wilson's alleged intention not to seek a third
    term, March 1, 1919, **55**: 340
An address to a conference of governors and mayors, March 3, 1919,
    55: 389
Two statements upon the adjournment of the Sixty-fifth Congress,
    March 4, 1919, **55**: 408
An address at the Metropolitan Opera House, March 4, 1919, **55**: 413
A statement on progress in formulating the Covenant of the League
    of Nations, March 27, 1919, **56**: 313
Remarks on the Monroe Doctrine, April 11, 1919, **57**: 266
Remarks on the clause for racial equality, April 11, 1919, **57**: 268
A statement in support of Employment Sunday, April 17, 1919, **57**:
    447

A tribute to the memory of Walter Hines Page, April 19, 1919, **57**: 509

A statement inaugurating the Victory Liberty Loan, April 19, 1919, **57**: 509

A statement on the Adriatic question, April 23, 1919, **58**: 5

A memorandum on Japan's claims in Shantung Province, April 30, 1919, **58**: 246

A statement on the labor provision of the peace treaty, May 2, 1919, **58**: 364

A statement on the French security treaty, May 6, 1919, **58**: 489

Special message to Congress, May 20, 1919, **59**: 289

A Memorial Day message, May 28, 1919, **59**: 571

An address at Carnegie Hall, July 8, 1919, **61**: 401

An address to the Senate delivering the peace treaty with Germany, July 10, 1919, **61**: 426

A press release denying an alleged break between Wilson and Senator Gilbert Monell Hitchcock, July 12, 1919, **61**: 469

A congratulatory statement on the contribution made by the sale of White House wool to the 1918 Red Cross War Fund, July 17, 1919, **61**: 505

Remarks to Czechoslovak soldiers, July 18, 1919, **61**: 518

A press release denying Wilson's sole responsibility for the terms of the Shantung settlement at Paris, July 23, 1919, **61**: 603

Message to the United States Senate upon submitting the French security treaty, July 29, 1919, **62**: 27

Message to the United States Senate about protests by members of the A.C.N.P. against the Shantung settlement, Aug. 8, 1919, **62**: 151 (draft), 208

Address to joint session of Congress on the high cost of living, Aug. 8, 1919, **62**: 304

Statement to members of the Senate Foreign Relations Committee on the provisions of the peace treaty, Aug. 19, 1919, **62**: 340

Message to the Governor General of Canada to be placed in the cornerstone of the new Parliament Building in Ottawa, Aug. 25, 1919, **62**: 425

Statement on the railroad crisis, Aug. 25, 1919, **62**: 472 (draft), 496

Remarks to railway shopmen about the demand for a wage increase, Aug. 25, 1919, **62**: 489

Message to railway shopmen about the demand for a wage increase, Aug. 25, 1919, **62**: 493

Labor Day message, Aug. 31, 1919, **62**: 595

Address to the Columbus Chamber of Commerce, Sept. 4, 1919, **63**: 7

Remarks on board the presidential train at Richmond, Indiana, Sept. 4, 1919, **63**: 18

Address in the Indianapolis Coliseum, Sept. 4, 1919, **63**: 19

Luncheon address to the St. Louis Chamber of Commerce, Sept. 5, 1919, **63**: 33

Address at the St. Louis Coliseum, Sept. 5, 1919, **63**: 43

Address in Convention Hall in Kansas City, Sept. 6, 1919, **63**: 66

Address in the Coliseum in Des Moines, Sept. 6, 1919, **63**: 76

Address in the Auditorium in Omaha, Sept. 8, 1919, **63**: 97

Address in the Coliseum in Sioux Falls, South Dakota, Sept. 8, 1918, **63**: 107

Address at St. Paul to a joint session of the legislature of Minnesota, Sept. 9, 1919, **63**: 125

Address in the Minneapolis Armory, Sept. 9, 1919, **63**: 131

Address in the St. Paul Auditorium, Sept. 9, 1919, **63**: 138

Address at Bismarck, North Dakota, Sept. 10, 1919, **63**: 153

Address from the rear platform at Mandan, North Dakota, Sept. 10, 1919, **63**: 162

Address in the Billings, Montana, Auditorium, Sept. 11, 1919, **63**: 170

Address in the Marlow Theater in Helena, Montana, Sept. 11, 1919, **63**: 180

Address at Coeur d'Alene, Idaho, Sept. 12, 1919, **63**: 212

Address in the Spokane Armory, Sept. 12, 1919, **63**: 224

Remarks in the Tacoma Stadium, Sept. 13, 1919, **63**: 240

Address in the Tacoma Armory, Sept. 13, 1919, **63**: 241 (notes); Sept. 13, 1919, **63**: 241 (address)

After-dinner remarks in Seattle, Sept. 13, 1919, **63**: 253

Address in the Seattle Arena, Sept. 13, 1919, **63**: 254

Luncheon address in the Portland Auditorium, Sept. 15, 1919, **63**: 277

Address in the Portland Auditorium, Sept. 15, 1919, **63**: 283

Luncheon address in San Francisco, Sept. 17, 1919, **63**: 310 (notes), 311 (address)

Address in the San Francisco Civic Auditorium, Sept. 17, 1919, **63**: 322 (notes), 323 (address)

Luncheon address in San Francisco, Sept. 18, 1919, **63**: 341

Address in the Greek Theater in Berkeley, California, Sept. 18, 1919, **63**: 350

Address in the Oakland Municipal Auditorium, Sept. 18, 1919, **63**: 352

Address in the San Diego Stadium, Sept. 19, 1919, **63**: 371

After-dinner speech in San Diego, Sept. 19, 1919, **63**: 382

After-dinner speech in Los Angeles, Sept. 20, 1919, **63**: 400

Address in the Shrine Auditorium in Los Angeles, Sept. 20, 1919, **63**: 407

Remarks in Sacramento, California, Sept. 22, 1919, **63**: 426

Address in Reno, Nevada, Sept. 22, 1919, **63**: 428

Remarks in Ogden, Utah, Sept. 23, 1919, **63**: 448

Address in the Tabernacle in Salt Lake City, Sept. 23, 1919, **63**: 449

Address in the Princess Theater in Cheyenne, Wyoming, Sept. 24, 1919, **63**: 467

Address in the Denver Auditorium, Sept. 25, 1919, **63**: 490

Address in the City Auditorium in Pueblo, Colorado, Sept. 25, 1919, **63**: 500

Statement on the threatened coal miners' strike, Oct. 25, 1919, **63**: 599 (draft)

Message vetoing the Volstead bill, Oct. 27, 1919, **63**: 601

Thanksgiving Proclamation, Nov. 4, 1919, **63**: 613

Armistice Day statement, Nov. 11, 1919, **64**: 7

Draft of a statement rejecting all reservations to the peace treaty, Dec. 2, 1919, **64**: 65

Annual Message on the State of the Union, Dec. 2, 1919, Tumulty draft, **64**: 73; message sent, **64**: 106

Draft of a statement on the need to ratify the peace treaty, Dec. 2, 1919, **64**: 118

Statement on the bituminous coal strike, Dec. 9, 1919, **64**: 154

Statement rejecting compromise on reservations, Dec. 14, 1919, **64**: 218

Executive Order establishing the working hours for per-diem federal employees, Dec. 23, 1919, **64**: 218

Proclamation relinquishing federal control of railroads and transportation systems, Dec. 24, 1919, **64**: 228

Press release establishing March 1, 1920, as the date for relinquishing federal control of the railroads, Dec. 24, 1919, **64**: 228

Jackson Day message, Tumulty draft, Jan. 6, 1920, **64**: 247; Wilson redraft, Jan 7, 1920, **64**: 252; Jackson Day letter, Jan. 8, 1920, **64**: 257

Convocation of the first meeting of the League Council, Jan. 12, 1920, **64**: 272

Press release on the letter by Viscount Grey, Feb. 5, 1920, **64**: 363

A press release on the need of the Democratic party to endorse the Versailles Treaty without the Lodge reservations, May 10, 1920, **65**: 263

A model plank on the League of Nations, May 24, 1920, **65**: 319

A message to Congress requesting authority to accept a mandate for Armenia, May 24, 1920, **65**: 320

Memorial Day message, May 25, 1920, **65**: 325

A message to Congress vetoing the Knox Resolution, May 27, 1920, **65**: 328

A message to the House of Representatives vetoing the budget bill, June 3, 1920, **65**: 362

Notes for an acceptance speech and a list of Cabinet members of a third administration, c. June 10, 1920, **65**: 382

A statement on the League of Nations, June 17, 1920, **65**: 424

On the presidential election being a national referendum on U.S. membership in the League of Nations, Oct. 3, 1920, **66**: 181

A proclamation on the observance of Armistice Sunday, Oct. 6, 1920, **66**: 204

A campaign statement on the importance of U.S. membership in the League of Nations, Oct. 27, 1920, **66**: 277

A dedication for the Yearbook of the United States Naval Academy,
    Class of 1921, Nov. 5, 1920, **66**: 325
A Thanksgiving Proclamation, Nov. 11, 1920, **66**: 351
An Annual Message on the State of the Union, Dec. 17, 1920, **66**: 484
A statement on Chinese famine relief, Dec. 9, 1920, **66**: 495
A message vetoing an amendment of the Transportation Act of 1920,
    Dec. 30, 1920, **67**: 12
A message vetoing a bill for resumption of the activities of the War
    Finance Corporation, Jan. 3, 1921, **67**: 18
A message vetoing a bill to favor a private gun club, Feb. 3, 1921, **67**:
    112
A message vetoing a bill to end enlistments in the Regular Army,
    Feb. 5, 1921, **67**: 117
A message vetoing an emergency tariff bill, March 3, 1921, **67**: 191
A message to the Jefferson Dinner of the National Democratic Club
    of New York, April 9, 1921, **67**: 253
A message to Democrats of Akron, Ohio, April 11, 1921, **67**: 255
A foreword to a book by Alexander Thomas Ormond, July 5, 1921,
    67: 349
Unpublished statements on the Treaty of Berlin, Sept. 25, 1921, **67**:
    394; Oct. 20, 1921, **67**: 428
An unpublished statement on his inability to follow the unknown
    soldier to Arlington National Cemetery, Nov. 9, 1921, **67**: 448
Planks assembled for a draft, April 5, 1922, **67**: 589
Announcement of the dissolution of Wilson & Colby, Dec. 13, 1923,
    68: 231
A birthday toast to Sallie White Bolling, Jan. 7, 1923, **68**: 266
Some of Wilson's favorite limericks, Oct. 27, 1923, **68**: 457; Jan. 18,
    1924, **68**: 533
A radio address, Nov. 10, 1923, **68**: 466
A tribute to Frank Irving Cobb, Jan. 7, 1924, **68**: 520

Political correspondence about domestic affairs

From Wilson to

    Joshua Willis Alexander, Oct. 1, 1920, **66**: 175
    The American Legion, Aug. 3, 1920, **66**: 6
    Magnus Washington Alexander, Aug. 30, 1919, **62**: 583 (draft)
    George Weston Anderson, Nov. 18, 1918, **53**: 110
    The Anthracite Wage Scale Committee, May 21, 1920, **65**: 312;
        Aug. 27, 1920, **66**: 69

    Newton Diehl Baker, Nov. 14, 1918, **53**: 83; Nov. 16, 1918, **53**: 97;
        Dec. 2, 1918, **53**: 287; March 24, 1919, **56**: 244; June 10, 1919,
        60: 375; July 31, 1919, **62**: 69; Aug. 1, 1919, **62**: 97 (2); Aug. 22,
        1919, **62**: 461; Sept. 16, 1919, **63**: 301; May 9, 1920, **65**: 261; May
        13, 1920, **65**: 285; May 15, 1920 (2), **65**: 289, 290; June 11, 1920,
        65: 385; June 14, 1920, **65**: 396; June 24, 1920, **65**: 449; Sept. 17,

1920, **66**: 120; Oct. 5, 1920, **66**: 192; Nov. 17, 1920, **66**: 383; Nov. 23, 1920, **66**: 414; Nov. 27, 1920, **66**: 425; Dec. 18, 1920, **66**: 532

William Brockman Bankhead, Feb. 27, 1919, **55**: 302

Antonio Rafael Barcelo, Dec. 2, 1918, **53**: 286

Allen E. Barker, Feb. 14, 1920, **64**: 426

Julius Howland Barnes, April 15, 1919, **57**: 375; July 19, 1919, **61**: 549; July 30, 1919, **62**: 57; Oct. 22, 1919, **63**: 589

Robert McKinney Barton, June 21, 1920, **65**: 440

Bernard Mannes Baruch, Nov. 30, 1918, **53**: 249; April 1, 1919, **56**: 520; Aug. 29, 1919, **62**: 554; Sept. 17, 1919, **63**: 336

Elizabeth Merrill Bass, Nov. 19, 1918, **53**: 129; Aug. 21, 1919, **62**: 437; Nov. 10, 1919, **64**: 3

William Shepherd Benson, Oct. 21, 1920, **66**: 252; Dec. 3, 1920, **66**: 464

Thomas Walter Bickett, June 24, 1920, **65**: 450

Tasker Howard Bliss, March 29, 1919, **56**: 425

Edward William Bok, Feb. 27, 1919, **55**: 303

Evangeline Cory Booth, May 18, 1920, **65**: 297

Rolland Barr Bradley, Oct. 23, 1920, **66**: 262

Charles Hillyer Brand, Nov. 22, 1918, **53**: 163

Thomas T. Brewster and John Llewellyn Lewis, Aug. 10, 1920, **66**: 27

Robert Somers Brookings, Nov. 26, 1918, **53**: 205; Jan, 13, 1919, **54**: 52; Feb. 28, 1919, **55**: 329

Herbert Bruce Brougham, Aug. 27, 1919, **62**: 526

Louis Brownlow, Sept. 16, 1919, **63**: 302

William Jennings Bryan, Nov. 22, 1918, **53**: 161

Benjamin Franklin Buchanan, Aug. 22, 1919, **62**: 462

Albert Sidney Burleson, Nov. 12, 1918, **53**: 55; Nov. 27, 1918, **53**: 214; Dec. 2, 1918, **53**: 289; Feb. 28, 1919, **55**: 327; March 24, 1919, **56**: 245; April 21, 1919, **57**: 577; April 28, 1919, **58**: 215; May 7, 1919, **58**: 531; Aug. 22, 1919, **62**: 461; July 13, 1920, **65**: 510; Sept. 4, 1920, **66**: 99

Theodore Elijah Burton, Feb. 25, 1919, **55**: 255

James Campbell Cantrill, Sept. 2, 1919, **62**: 615

Carrie Clinton Lane Chapman Catt, June 6, 1919, **60**: 247; Feb. 10, 1920, **64**: 396

Francis Edward Clark, July 31, 1919, **62**: 81; Aug. 21, 1919, **62**: 436

John Hessin Clarke, Nov. 18, 1918, **53**: 120

Walter Irving Clarke, Aug. 11, 1919, **62**: 251; Aug. 15, 1919, **62**: 313

Grosvenor Blaine Clarkson, Aug. 8, 1919, **62**: 223

Ira Clemens, Aug. 5, 1920, **66**: 10

Various coal operators and United Mine Workers officers, March 19, 1920, **65**: 104

Bainbridge Colby, Nov. 18, 1918, **53**: 111; Nov. 25, 1918, **53**: 95;

Nov. 27, 1918, **53**: 214; Dec. 2, 1918, **53**: 289; Feb. 27, 1919, **55**: 302; April 2, 1920, **65**: 152; April 12, 1920, **65**: 178; April 13, 1920, **65**: 180; April 16, 1920, **65**: 195; April 26, 1920, **65**: 229; May 3, 1920, **65**: 245; May 11, 1920, **65**: 271; June 4, 1920, **65**: 361; Aug. 31, 1920, **66**: 78; Sept. 20, 1920, **66**: 128; Sept. 24, 1920, **66**: 138; Sept. 27, 1920, **66**: 150; Oct. 6, 1920, **66**: 199; Nov. 6, 1920, **66**: 331; Nov. 10, 1920, **66**: 345; Nov. 12, 1920, **66**: 353; Nov. 20, 1920, **66**: 402

John Collins and Others, Oct. 11, 1920, **66**: 217

William Byron Colver, Aug. 5, 1919, **62**: 166; Sept. 16, 1919, **63**: 301; Sept. 21, 1919, **63**: 425; Oct. 18, 1920, **66**: 241

Calvin Coolidge, Nov. 5, 1919, **63**: 615

James Middleton Cox, July 6, 1920, **65**: 499; Oct. 22, 1920, **66**: 257; Oct. 29, 1920, **66**: 290; Nov. 5, 1920, **66**: 321

George Creel, March 20, 1919, **56**: 124; June 5, 1920, **65**: (draft), 375

Homer Stillé Cummings, June 12, 1920, **65**: 393; June 15, 1920, **65**: 397; June 24, 1920, **65**: 450; June 29, 1920, **65**: 477; July 2, 1920 (2), **65**: 489 (2); July 4, 1920, **65**: 495; July 5, 1920, **65**: 497; July 10, 1920, **65**: 507

Albert Baird Cummins, Aug. 5, 1919, **62**: 163; Aug. 8, 1919, **62**: 223

Josephus Daniels, Nov. 16, 1918, **53**: 98; Nov. 18, 1918, **53**: 113; Nov. 19, 1918, **53**: 128; Nov. 25, 1918, **53**: 195; Dec. 7, 1918, **53**: 334; Jan. 27, 1919, **54**: 303; Jan. 31, 1919, **54**: 408; Oct. 7, 1919, **63**: 556; Aug. 7, 1920, **66**: 17; Aug. 20, 1920, **66**: 56; Aug. 23, 1920, **66**: 59; Aug. 28, 1920, **66**: 71; Oct. 9, 1920, **66**: 213; Nov. 5, 1920, **66**: 324; Nov. 11, 1920, **66**: 348; Dec. 15, 1920, **66**: 511; Dec. 17, 1920, **66**: 527

Norman Hezekiah Davis, May 6, 1919, **58**: 491; June 8, 1920, **65**: 381; Dec. 9, 1920, **66**: 497; Dec. 11, 1920, **66**: 500

Henry Pomeroy Davison, April 16, 1919, **57**: 422

William Edward Dodd, June 17, 1920, **65**: 423; Oct. 1, 1920, **66**: 175; Oct. 25, 1920, **66**: 266

Cleveland Hoadley Dodge, Feb. 27, 1919, **55**: 303; April 19, 1920, **65**: 202

Hugh Manson Dorsey, July 15, 1919, **61**: 480

Thomas Alva Edison, Nov. 18, 1920, **66**: 387

Edward Irving Edwards, Nov. 5, 1919, **63**: 615

Alfred A. Elmore, March 31, 1919, **56**: 485

Friedrich Johannes Hugo von Engelken, Nov. 18, 1918, **53**: 113

John Jacob Esch, Aug. 1, 1919, **62**: 98; Aug. 5, 1919, **62**: 163

Robert Ewing, Dec. 2, 1918, **53**: 287

Albert Bacon Fall, Aug. 20, 1919, **62**: 417; Dec. 8, 1919, **64**: 152

Members of the Federal Electric Railway Commission, Aug. 27, 1919, **62**: 532

Scott Ferris, Aug. 5, 1920, **66**: 10
Joseph Wingate Folk, Nov. 15, 1918, **53**: 84
Rudolph Forster, Nov. 22, 1918, **53**: 160; Sept. 19, 1919, **63**: 392
Raymond Blaine Fosdick (not sent), Jan. 29, 1921, **67**: 97
Philip Albright Small Franklin, Nov. 18, 1918, **53**: 113; Nov. 22,
    1918, **53**: 164; Nov. 25, 1918, **53**: 196
Julius Edgar Frazier and Milton Burr, March 2, 1920, **65**: 36
William Little Frierson, June 24, 1920, **65**: 450
Alvan Tufts Fuller, March 1, 1919, **55**: 343

Charles Mills Galloway, Feb. 28, 1919, **55**: 330; March 25, 1919,
    56: 280; May 2, 1919, **58**: 360; Aug. 5, 1919, **62**: 164; Aug. 11,
    1919, **62**: 251
Helen Hamilton Gardener, Nov. 18, 1918, **53**: 114
Harry Augustus Garfield, Dec. 3, 1918, **53**: 307; Dec. 7, 1918, **53**:
    333; Dec. 13, 1919, **64**: 185; May 31, 1920, **65**: 343
Finis James Garrett, March 1, 1921, **67**: 176
John Work Garrett, Aug. 21, 1919, **62**: 435
Peter Goelet Gerry, Nov. 18, 1918, **53**: 114; April 17, 1919, **57**: 446
James Cardinal Gibbons, July 25, 1919, **61**: 628
Frederick Huntington Gillett, Aug. 1, 1919, **62**: 98; Aug. 6, 1919,
    62: 171
Carter Glass, Jan. 28, 1919, **54**: 332; Feb. 7, 1919, **54**: 555; Feb. 25,
    1919, **55**: 256; Feb. 26, 1919, **55**: 279; March 1, 1919, **55**: 342;
    March 18, 1919, **56**: 83; March 28, 1919, **56**: 397; April 4, 1919,
    56: 623; April 21, 1919, **57**: 577; April 23, 1919, **58**: 47; May 25,
    1919, **59**: 478; July 19, 1919, **61**: 549; Aug. 8, 1919, **62**: 222; Aug.
    14, 1919, **62**: 281; Sept. 17, 1919, **63**: 336; Nov. 17, 1919, **64**: 52;
    Jan. 28, 1920, **64**: 339; May 28, 1920, **65**: 333; June 11, 1920, **65**:
    385; June 14, 1920, **65**: 396; Sept. 29, 1920, **66**: 168
Edward Field Goltra, April 16, 1919, **57**: 424
Samuel Gompers, Nov. 27, 1918, **53**: 220; June 3, 1919, **60**: 111;
    Sept. 3, 1919, **62**: 623
Edward A. Gowen, Dec. 23, 1920, **66**: 546
E. F. Grable *et al.*, Feb. 5, 1921, **67**: 119
Thomas Watt Gregory, Dec. 2, 1918, **53**: 289; Jan. 11, 1919, **53**:
    715; Feb. 5, 1919, **54**: 503; Feb. 26, 1919, **55**: 276
James F. Griffen, Aug. 2, 1920, **66**: 3
Solomon Bulkley Griffin, Nov. 11, 1920, **66**: 349

Charles Sumner Hamlin, Aug. 15, 1919, **62**: 313
Norman Hapgood, Dec. 2, 1918, **53**: 287
Warren Gamaliel Harding, July 29, 1919, **62**: 29; Jan. 22, 1921,
    67: 83; Feb. 17, 1921, **67**: 143
William Procter Gould Harding, July 25, 1919, **61**: 625
Frank J. Hayes, Nov. 15, 1918, **53**: 83
Joseph Francis Heney, July 31, 1919, **62**: 69
Walker Downer Hines, Feb. 26, 1919, **55**: 277; April 18, 1919, **57**:
    470; May 3, 1919, **58**: 420; May 26, 1919, **59**: 523; Aug. 7, 1919,

62: 192; Aug. 11, 1919, **62**: 249; Sept. 16, 1919, **63**: 300; April 22, 1920, **65**: 219; May 18, 1920, **65**: 296

Gilbert Monell Hitchcock, April 18, 1919, **57**: 469; June 7, 1919, **60**: 287; Nov. 11, 1919, Tumulty draft, **64**: 15; Nov. 17, 1919, Wilson's revised draft, **64**: 51; Tumulty draft, Jan. 26, 1920, **64**: 278; letter sent, **64**: 329; March 23, 1920, **65**: 116; "nullifier" letter; first draft, Feb. 28, 1920, **65**: 7; revised first draft, Feb. 28, 1920, **65**: 11; Tumulty redraft, March 1, 1920, **65**: 25; Wilson redraft, March 1, 1920, **65**: 30; penultimate draft, March 5, 1920, **65**: 49; final version, March 8, 1920, **65**: 67

Richard Hooker, Nov. 29, 1918, **53**: 243

Herbert Clark Hoover, March 28, 1919, **56**: 372; March 29, 1919 (2), **56**: 426, 427; April 1, 1919, **56**: 520; April 14, 1919, **57**: 346; April 16, 1919, **57**: 407; June 10, 1919, **60**: 359

Edward Mandell House, Aug. 29, 1919, **62**: 576

David Franklin Houston, March 12, 1919, **55**: 483; March 31, 1919, **56**: 485; Feb. 2, 1920, **64**: 349; May 3, 1920, **65**: 245; Sept. 1, 1920, **66**: 82

Cordell Hull, Nov. 16, 1918, **53**: 99

Edward Nash Hurley, Jan. 24, 1919, **54**: 256; March 1, 1919, **55**: 341; March 3, 1919, **55**: 394; July 10, 1919, **61**: 440; Aug. 2, 1919, **62**: 114; Dec. 9, 1920, **66**: 497

Members of the Industrial Conference, Oct. 6, 1919, **63**: 554; Oct. 20, 1919, **63**: 584

Members of the public group of the Industrial Conference, Nov. 4, 1919, **63**: 612

Bert Mark Jewell, Aug. 7, 1919, **62**: 194; Sept. 1, 1919, **62**: 610; April 21, 1920, **65**: 216

Bert Mark Jewell and Others, Feb. 13, 1920, **64**: 420; Feb. 28, 1920, **65**: 14

Robert Underwood Johnson, Aug. 14, 1919, **62**: 291

Samuel M. Johnson, Jan. 5, 1921, **67**: 28

William David Johnson, Jr., Nov. 5, 1920, **66**: 325

Herman Henry Kohlsaat, Nov. 22, 1918, **53**: 164

Arthur Bernard Krock, Jan. 30, 1919, **54**: 389

Thomas Erby Kilby, Feb. 28, 1919, **55**: 327; July 12, 1919, **61**: 464

Thomas William Lamont, June 7, 1919, **60**: 276; June 10, 1919, **60**: 380; June 17, 1919, **60**: 641; June 23, 1919, **61**: 104; June 27, 1919, **61**: 290; July 17, 1919, **61**: 506; Aug. 1, 1919, **62**: 100; Aug. 21, 1919, **62**: 432; Aug. 29, 1919, **62**: 560; Sept. 19, 1919, **63**: 388; Oct. 4, 1920, **66**: 185; Nov. 29, 1920, **66**: 443; Dec. 18, 1920, **66**: 532; Jan. 5, 1921, **67**: 27; Jan. 30, 1921, **67**: 105; Feb. 25, 1291, **67**: 169

Franklin Knight Lane, Jan. 7, 1919, **53**: 636; March 31, 1919, **56**:

486; Aug. 2, 1919, **62**: 114; Oct. 23, 1919, **63**: 591; Feb. 7, 1920, **64**: 374; Feb. 11, 1920, **64**: 405; Feb. 29, 1920, **65**: 22

Franklin Knight Lane, William Cox Redfield, and William Bauchop Wilson, Jan. 31, 1919, **54**: 409

Robert Lansing, Jan. 24, 1919 (2), **54**: 256 (2); Feb. 1, 1919, **54**: 426; Feb. 13, 1919, **55**: 149; Feb. 10, 1919, **55**: 547; May 21, 1919, **59**: 346; May 24, 1919 (2), **59**: 470, 471; June 3, 1919 (2), **60**: 83, 100; June 10, 1919 (2), **60**: 358, 374; June 12, 1919, **60**: 484; June 17, 1919 (2), **60**: 640, 641; July 25, 1919, **61**: 630; Aug. 4, 1919 (4), **62**: 142, 147, 148, 149; Aug. 14, 1919, **62**: 281; Feb. 7, 1920, **64**: 383; Feb. 11, 1920, **64**: 404; Feb. 13, 1920 (2), **64**: 413, 414

William Granville Lee, May 16, 1919, **59**: 203

Russell Cornell Leffingwell, Feb. 4, 1920, **64**: 361

John Llewellyn Lewis, Dec. 11, 1919, **64**: 179; Aug. 2, 1920, **66**: 4

Librarians of the United States, Aug. 21, 1919, **62**: 436

William C. Liller, July 20, 1911, **64**: 515

Samuel McCune Lindsay, Feb. 13, 1919, **55**: 157

Henry Cabot Lodge, July 18, 1919, **61**: 519; July 19, 1919, **61**: 548; July 25, 1919, **61**: 623; Aug. 8, 1919, **62**: 219; Aug. 14, 1919 (2), **62**: 272 (draft), 276; Aug. 15, 1919, **62**: 310; Aug. 28, 1919, **62**: 535; Sept. 3, 1919, **62**: 624

Breckinridge Long, Feb. 26, 1919, **55**: 279; Feb. 3, 1920, **64**: 352; June 8, 1920, **65**: 381

Frederick Henry Lynch, March 20, 1919, **56**: 120

William Gibbs McAdoo, Nov. 16, 1918, **53**: 99; Nov. 21, 1918, **53**: 150; July 15, 1919, **61**: 480; Aug. 1, 1919, **62**: 99; Aug. 8, 1919, **62**: 224; Oct. 4, 1920, **66**: 184; Oct. 12, 1920, **66**: 224; Oct. 20, 1920, **66**: 250

Samuel Walker McCall, Feb. 28, 1919, **55**: 328; Sept. 10, 1920, **66**: 110

William Frank McCombs, July 23, 1912, **64**: 521; Aug. 5, 1912, **64**: 522, Aug. 6, 1912, **64**: 522; Aug. 14, 1912, **64**: 522; Aug. 23, 1912, **64**: 523; April 5, 1913, **64**: 523; April 20, 1913, **64**: 523; Sept. 9, 1913, **64**: 524

Vance Criswell McCormick, Nov. 22, 1918, **53**: 164; March 28, 1919, **56**: 372; April 15, 1919, **57**: 374; April 16, 1919, **57**: 423; Aug. 1, 1919, **62**: 100

James Edward McCulloch, Aug. 4, 1919, **62**: 128; Aug. 15, 1919, **62**: 313

Porter James McCumber, Sept. 1, 1919, **62**: 611

Grenville Stanley Macfarland, Nov. 27, 1918, **53**: 221; Nov. 29, 1918, **53**: 245

Gavin McNab, Nov. 18, 1918, **53**: 116

Charles Linza McNary, July 16, 1919, **61**: 492

James Robert Mann, Dec. 3, 1918, **53**: 308

Wilbur W. Marsh, Sept. 17, 1920, **66**: 122

Thomas Riley Marshall, Jan, 7, 1919, **53**: 636; Sept. 8, 1919, **63**: 117

Thomas Staples Martin, Jan. 28, 1919, **54**: 332
Thomas Staples Martin and Swagar Shirley, Jan. 10, 1919, **53**: 709
Royal Meeker, Aug. 8, 1919, **62**: 224; Aug. 29, 1919, **62**: 559
The Members of the House Foreign Affairs Committee, Feb. 14, 1919, **55**: 184
Edwin Thomas Meredith, June 14, 1920, **65**: 396; July 19, 1920, **65**: 530
Paul Henry Merrit, July 12, 1919, **61**: 464
Carl E. Moore, Aug. 3, 1920, **66**: 5
H. Arthur Morgan, Feb. 13, 1919, **55**: 157
Henry Morganthau, Feb. 28, 1919, **55**: 329
Frank Morrison, Nov. 22, 1918, **53**: 165; Nov. 27, 1918, **53**: 216; Feb. 26, 1919, **55**: 280
Robert Russa Moton, Jan. 1, 1918, **53**: 579; Aug. 12, 1919, **62**: 260
John J. Mulvena, June 1, 1920, **65**: 351
Philip Murray and others, Sept. 9, 1920, **66**: 107
Henry Lee Myers, Nov. 20, 1918, **53**: 141; Sept. 11, 1919, **63**: 197

George William Norris, July 19, 1919, **61**: 548; Sept. 11, 1919, **63**: 197; March 6, 1920, **65**: 63

Lee Slater Overman, Feb. 9, 1919, **55**: 37; June 19, 1920, **65**: 433

Lemuel Phillips Padgett, Feb. 5, 1919, **54**: 501
Thomas Nelson Page, June 14, 1919, **60**: 566; Aug. 29, 1919, **62**: 561
Alexander Mitchell Palmer, Nov. 20, 1918, **53**: 141; Nov. 22, 1918, **53**: 165; Nov. 27, 1918, **53**: 214; March 12, 1919, **55**: 482; June 4, 1919, **60**: 145; Aug. 1, 1919, **62**: 98; Aug. 11, 1919, **62**: 250; Aug. 28, 1919, **62**: 536; Aug. 29, 1919, **62**: 555; April 22, 1920, **65**: 218; June 21, 1920, **65**: 441; July 31, 1920, **65**: 567; Sept. 9, 1920, **66**: 103; Sept. 16, 1920, **66**: 117; Sept. 29, 1920, **66**: 167; Oct. 4, 1920, **66**: 184; Oct. 14, 1920, **66**: 229; Nov. 18, 1920, **66**: 386; Dec. 30, 1920, **67**: 12; Jan. 3, 1921, **67**: 22; Jan. 15, 1921, **67**: 62
John Milliken Parker, May 18, 1920, **65**: 295
Graham Patterson, Nov. 8, 1920, **66**: 338
John Barton Payne, Aug. 11, 1919, **62**: 249; Aug. 14, 1919, **62**: 291; Aug. 21, 1919, **62**: 448; Feb. 29, 1920, **65**: 23; March 6, 1920, **65**: 64; Feb. 1, 1921, **67**: 110
William Phillips, Sept. 16, 1919, **63**: 304; March 6, 1920, **65**: 63
Key Pittman, Nov. 12, 1918, **53**: 53; Nov. 13, 1918, **53**: 68; Nov. 18, 1918 (2), **53**: 116 (2)
Frank Lyon Polk, June 6, 1919, **60**: 246; Feb. 24, 1920, **64**: 464; March 19, 1920, **65**: 108; April 15, 1920, **65**: 190; April 17, 1920, **65**: 197; April 28, 1920, **65**: 232; June 3, 1920, **65**: 355
Atlee Pomerene, Aug. 14, 1919, **62**: 286
Edward William Pou, Aug. 24, 1920, **66**: 60

CONTENTS 15

Presidents of the railroad brotherhoods, June 24, 1920, **65**: 451

James Henry Preston, Feb. 23, 1919, **55**: 232

Members of the Railroad Labor Board, April 15, 1920, **65**: 189

Henry Thomas Rainey, Nov. 11, 1920, **66**: 348

Joseph Eugene Ransdell, Nov. 18, 1918, **53**: 117; Jan, 23, 1919, **54**: 228; Sept. 1, 1919, **62**: 610

Albert Rathbone, Sept. 3, 1919, **62**: 624

William Cox Redfield, Nov. 12, 1918, **53**: 55; Nov. 26, 1918, **53**: 206; Feb. 13, 1919, **55**: 156; March 1, 1919, **55**: 343; April 16, 1919, **57**: 423; April 18, 1919, **57**: 470; April 21, 1919 (2), **57**: 577, 578; July 25, 1919, **61**: 623; Aug. 2, 1919, **62**: 115; Aug. 5, 1919, **62**: 163; Aug. 8, 1919, **62**: 222; Sept. 1, 1919, **62**: 610

Edgar Rickard, March 3, 1919, **55**: 393

Albert Houston Roberts, June 23, 1920, **65**: 445; June 26, 1920, **65**: 468; Aug. 19, 1920, **66**: 54

Henry Mauris Robinson, April 28, 1919, **58**: 202; May 6, 1919, **58**: 498; Dec. 19, 1919, **64**: 206

Joseph Taylor Robinson, Feb. 25, 1921, **67**: 168

Walter Stowell Rogers, Sept. 30, 1920, **66**: 171

Franklin Delano Roosevelt, Aug. 22, 1919, **62**: 460; July 6, 1920, **65**: 500; July 26, 1920, **65**: 548; Aug. 30, 1920, **66**: 77

Daniel Calhoun Roper, Nov. 14, 1918, **53**: 71

Leo Stanton Rowe, Nov. 16, 1918, **53**: 100

Secretary of Local 78 of the Brotherhood of Painters, Decorators, and Paper Hangers, Aug. 29, 1919, **62**: 561

Jared Young Sanders, April 10, 1920, **65**: 165

San Francisco Labor Council, Sept. 16, 1919, **63**: 303

John Nevin Sayre, Dec. 3, 1918, **53**: 307; March 3, 1919, **55**: 395; July 15, 1919, **61**: 480

The Senate and House of Representatives, July 18, 1919, **61**: 517

Senators opposed to the peace treaty, Dec. 17, 1919, **64**: 199

John Charles Shaffer, Aug. 27, 1919, **62**: 525

William Graves Sharp, Dec. 21, 1918, **53**: 463

Anna Howard Shaw, Nov. 18, 1918, **53**: 118; Feb. 26, 1919, **55**: 281; Feb. 27, 1919, **55**: 299

Morris Sheppard, Nov. 16, 1918, **53**: 100

Joseph Swagar Shirely, Feb. 25, 1919, **55**: 256; Feb. 26, 1919, **55**: 277

William Harrison Short, Feb. 2, 1919, **55**: 186; Feb. 19, 1919, **55**: 208; April 16, 1919, **57**: 424

Jouett Shouse, Nov. 12, 1918, **53**: 54; April 12, 1920, **65**: 177

Furnifold McLendel Simmons, March 11, 1920, **65**: 82 (draft)

John Humphrey Small, Dec. 2, 1918, **53**: 288

Alfred Emanuel Smith, Nov. 26, 1918, **53**: 206

Ellison DuRant Smith, Nov. 27, 1918, **53**: 215

Selden Palmer Spencer, Oct. 5, 1920, **66**: 191; Oct. 6, 1920, **66**: 198

John Spargo, Aug. 29, 1919, **62**: 559; Dec. 27, 1920, **67**: 7

Grant Squires, Nov. 12, 1918, **53**: 55; Nov. 20, 1918, **53**: 142; Jan. 14, 1919, **54**: 57

Dan Voorhees Stephens, Nov. 13, 1918, **53**: 67

John Appleton Stewart, Sept. 14, 1920, **66**: 115; Sept. 18, 1920, **66**: 123

Edwin Forrest Sweet, Aug. 28, 1919, **62**: 533

William Howard Taft, Feb. 14, 1919, **55**: 187; Feb. 26, 1919, **55**: 281; Feb. 28, 1919, **55**: 328; Aug. 11, 1919, **62**: 250

William Howard Taft and Basil Maxwell Manly, Jan. 10, 1919, **53**: 710

Frank William Taussig, Nov. 22, 1918, **53**: 166; May 12, 1919, **59**: 76; May 16, 1919, **59**: 190; July 19, 1919 (2), **61**: 550 (2); Aug. 1, 1919, **62**: 101

James Henry Taylor, Oct. 13, 1920, **66**: 228

Robert Heberton Terrell, Aug. 1, 1919, **62**: 100

George Carroll Todd, March 3, 1919, **55**: 394

Park Trammell, Jan. 14, 1919, **54**: 56; Jan. 27, 1919, **54**: 302

Joseph Patrick Tumulty, Nov. 27, 1918, **53**: 216; Nov. 30, 1918 (2), **53**: 251 (2); Dec. 3, 1918, **53**: 308; Dec. 16, 1918, **53**: 405; Dec. 20, 1918, **53**: 450; Dec. 24, 1918, **53**: 491; Jan. 7, 1919, **53**: 636; Jan. 9, 1919, **53**: 698; Jan. 10, 1919 (3), **53**: 709, 710 (2); Jan. 13, 1919 (2), **54**: 53 (2); Jan. 14, 1919 (2), **54**: 55, 56; Jan. 25, 1919, **54**: 274; Jan. 30, 1919, **54**: 381; Jan. 31, 1919, **54**: 410; Feb. 5, 1919, **54**: 500; Feb. 7, 1919, **54**: 554; Feb. 9, 1919, **55**: 37; Feb. 14, 1919 (2), **55**: 184, 185; Feb. 20, 1919 (2), **55**: 218, 219; Feb. 21, 1919 (2), **55**: 222 (2); Feb. 22, 1919 (2), **55**: 225, 226; Feb. 23, 1919, **55**: 231; Feb. 25, 1919, **55**: 254; Feb. 26, 1919, **55**: 278; March 1, 1919 (2), **55**: 340, 341; March 7, 1919, **55**: 458; March 21, 1919, **56**: 156; March 22, 1919, **56**: 191; March 26, 1919, **56**: 310; April 17, 1919 (2), **57**: 445, 446; April 21, 1919 (2), **57**: 578, 579; April 24, 1919, **58**: 104; April 25, 1919, **58**: 145; May 3, 1919, **58**: 421; May 6, 1919 (2), **58**: 496, 497; May 7, 1919, **58**: 531; May 9, 1919, **58**: 602; May 12, 1919, **59**: 75; May 13, 1919, **59**: 120; May 16, 1919 (2), **59**: 203 (2); May 20, 1919, **59**: 320; May 23, 1919, **59**: 449; May 24, 1919, **59**: 476; May 25, 1919, **59**: 478; June 2, 1919, **60**: 41; June 3, 1919, **60**: 111; June 5, 1919, **60**: 197; June 6, 1919, **60**: 247; June 7, 1919, **60**: 287; June 14, 1919, **60**: 568; June 16, 1919 (2), **60**: 609, 610; June 17, 1919, **60**: 644; June 23, 1919, **61**: 115; June 24, 1919, **61**: 137; June 26, 1919, **61**: 231; June 27, 1919 (3), **61**: 290, 292, 293; June 28, 1919 (2), **61**: 351, 352; July 3, 1919, **61**: 76; July 4, 1919, **61**: 383; July 6, 1919, **61**: 397; July 17, 1919 (2), **61**: 507, 509; Aug. 21, 1919, **62**: 435; Aug. 28, 1919, **62**: 536; Sept. 1, 1919, **62**: 609; Sept. 15, 1918, **63**: 625; Jan. 19, 1918, **63**: 626; Feb. 3, 1920, **64**: 351; Feb. 26, 1920, **64**: 475; June 15, 1920, **65**: 397; July 12, 1920, **65**: 508; July 30, 1920, **65**: 564; Jan. 17, 1919, **65**: 576; Aug. 27, 1920, **66**: 66; Sept. 2, 1920, **66**: 90; Sept. 24, 1920, **66**: 141; Sept. 26, 1920, **66**: 149; Sept. 27,

1920, **66**: 151; Oct. 6, 1920, **66**: 199; Oct. 12, 1920, **66**: 223; Oct. 20, 1920 (3), **66**: 249 (2), 250; Oct. 28, 1920, **66**: 282; Feb. 15, 1921, **67**: 139; Feb. 25, 1921, **67**: 168

Oscar Wilder Underwood, Feb. 23, 1919, **55**: 231; Feb. 6, 1921, **67**: 121
Members of the United Mine Workers of America, July 30, 1920, **65**: 565
Representatives of the United Mine Workers of America of District No. 1, Aug. 30, 1920, **66**: 76
The United States Senate, June 13, 1919, **60**: 534
The people of Utah, Sept. 23, 1919, **63**: 447

Henry van Dyke, July 17, 1919, **61**: 533; Sept. 2, 1919, **62**: 615

Tom C. Waldrep and Martin Edwin Trapp, Feb. 24, 1920, **64**: 466
Seth M. Walker, Aug. 13, 1920, **66**: 30
Francis Patrick Walsh, Nov. 27, 1918, **53**: 215
Thomas James Walsh, Feb. 26, 1919, **55**: 280; July 19, 1919, **61**: 550
Emory Olin Watson, Sept. 20, 1920, **66**: 129
Henry White, Nov. 22, 1918, **53**: 167
William Allen White, July 17, 1919, **61**: 506
The White House Staff, Nov. 26, 1918, **53**: 205; April 12, 1920, **65**: 177
The people of Wichita, Sept. 26, 1919, **63**: 524
Louis Wiley, Oct. 6, 1920, **66**: 199
John Sharp Williams, Nov. 29, 1918, **53**: 244; Jan. 14, 1919, **54**: 56; July 15, 1919, **61**: 482; July 1, 1920, **65**: 482; Sept. 29, 1920, **66**: 166
John Skelton Williams, Aug. 27, 1919, **62**: 526
Justina Leavitt Wilson, Aug. 8, 1919, **62**: 225
William Bauchop Wilson, Nov. 18, 1918, **53**: 118; April 17, 1919, **57**: 447; April 21, 1919, **57**: 578; Aug. 1, 1919, **62**: 95; Aug. 5, 1919, **62**: 162; Aug. 8, 1919, **62**: 224; Aug. 21, 1919, **62**: 436; Oct. 24, 1919, **63**: 593; Nov. 19, 1919, **64**: 64; July 28, 1920 (2), **65**: 554 (2); July 30, 1920, **65**: 566; Aug. 2, 1920, **66**: 3; Sept. 21, 1920, **66**: 132; Oct. 25, 1920, **66**: 265; Nov. 11, 1920, **66**: 349; Dec. 20, 1920, **66**: 535; March 3, 1921, **67**: 196
A draft by Wilson of interpretive reservations to the peace treaty, Sept. 3, 1919, **62**: 621
Gordon Woodbury, Sept. 3, 1920, **66**: 91; Jan. 7, 1921, **67**: 32

Casper Salathiel Yost, July 15, 1919, **61**: 481

To Wilson from

Joshua Willis Alexander, Dec. 6, 1919, **64**: 142; June 25, 1920, 20**65**: 467

The American Hungarian Press Association, April 1, 1919, **56**: 521
George Weston Anderson, Nov. 14, 1918, **53**: 82
John Crawford Anderson, July 15, 1919, **61**: 479
The Atlantic Congress of the League to Enforce Peace, Feb. 9, 1919, **55**: 37
Stockton Axson, Nov. 27, 1918, **53**: 232

Newton Diehl Baker, Nov. 11, 1918, **53**: 11; Nov. 14, 1918, **53**: 83; Nov. 16, 1918, **53**: 101; Nov. 23, 1918, **53**: 182; Nov. 30, 1918, **53**: 252; Dec. 2, 1918, **53**: 300; Dec. 27, 1918, **53**: 524; Jan. 1, 1919, **53**: 580; Jan. 16, 1919, **54**: 105; Feb. 6, 1919, **54**: 519; March 27, 1919, **56**: 330; May 13, 1919, **59**: 122; May 16, 1919, **59**: 204; July 14, 1919, **61**: 478; July 24, 1919, **61**: 614; July 26, 1919, **62**: 8; Aug. 12, 1919, **62**: 261; Aug. 19, 1919, **62**: 415; Aug. 20, 1919, **62**: 420; Aug. 26, 1919, **62**: 515; Sept. 15, 1919, **63**: 296; Feb. 17, 1920, **64**: 436; March 9, 1920, **65**: 76; March 10, 1920, **65**: 78; March 11, 1920, **65**: 83; March 26, 1920, **65**: 126; March 26, 1920, **65**: 135 (2); April 15, 1920, **65**: 193; April 25, 1920, **65**: 227; May 2, 1920, **65**: 243; May 11, 1920 (2), **65**: 272, 273; May 12, 1920, **65**: 277; May 23, 1920, **65**: 318; June 3, 1920 (2), **65**: 355, 357; June 4, 1920, **65**: 363; June 10, 1920, **65**: 383; June 11, 1920, **65**: 386; June 21, 1920, **65**: 442; June 25, 1920, **65**: 459; July 28, 1920, **65**: 557; Feb. 7, 1920, **65**: 576; Aug. 14, 1920, **66**: 34; Sept. 20, 1920, **66**: 129; Oct. 4, 1920, **66**: 188; Nov. 19, 1920, **66**: 401; Nov. 24, 1920, **66**: 415; Dec. 3, 1920, **66**: 464; Dec. 8, 1920, **66**: 493; Dec. 13, 1920, **66**: 502; Dec. 17, 1920, **66**: 527; Feb. 26, 1921, **67**: 171
Antonio Rafael Barcelo, Nov. 29, 1918, **53**: 246
Julius Howland Barnes, April 18, 1919, **57**: 475; July 16, 1919, **61**: 499; July 24, 1919, **61**: 612; July 29, 1919, **62**: 52; Aug. 7, 1919, **62**: 200
Robert McKinney Barton, June 22, 1920, **65**: 444
Bernard Mannes Baruch, Nov. 11, 1918, **53**: 47; Nov. 18, 1918, **53**: 124; Nov. 19, 1918, **53**: 131; Nov. 27, 1918, **53**: 229; Feb. 11, 1919, **55**: 90; April 15, 1919, **57**: 387
Elizabeth Merrill Bass, Nov. 18, 1918, **53**: 125; Aug. 5, 1919, **62**: 167; Aug. 15, 1919, **62**: 314
William Shepherd Benson, Nov. 27, 1920, **66**: 425
Thomas Walter Bickett, June 28, 1920, **65**: 473
Tasker Howard Bliss, March 27, 1919, **56**: 330
Edward William Bok, Feb. 24, 1919, **55**: 253
Evangeline Cory Booth, May 14, 1920, **65**: 288; May 22, 1920, **65**: 317
Emmet Derby Boyle, Sept. 5, 1919, **63**: 54
Charles Hillyer Brand and Thomas Montgomery Bell, Nov. 20, 1918, **53**: 149
Otto Branstetter, July 26, 1920, **65**: 550
George E. Brennan, Sept. 2, 1920, **66**: 90

Robert Somers Brookings, Nov. 22, 1918, **53**: 68
Robert Somers Brookings and Others, Dec. 17, 1918, **53**: 413
Herbert Bruce Brougham, Aug. 24, 1919, **62**: 481
Louis Brownlow, Sept. 13, 1919, **63**: 264; Sept. 15, 1919, **63**: 295
William Jennings Bryan, Nov. 20, 1918, **53**: 150
Albert Sidney Burleson, Nov. 10, 1918, **53**: 28; Nov. 29, 1918, **53**:
    246; Nov. 30, 1918, **53**: 260; March 28, 1919 (2), **56**: 403, 404;
    April 16, 1919, **57**: 423; April 20, 1919, **57**: 530; April 24, 1919,
    58: 106; April 27, 1919, **58**: 176; May 2, 1919, **58**: 365; May 7,
    1919, **58**: 532; May 13, 1919, **59**: 121; June 10, 1919, **60**: 378;
    June 19, 1919, **61**: 10; July 16, 1919, **61**: 503; July 18, 1919, **61**:
    539; Sept. 13, 1919, **63**: 266; Sept. 22, 1919, **63**: 442; March 1,
    1920, **65**: 29; July 3, 1920, **65**: 492; July 15, 1920, **65**: 512; Sept.
    3, 1920, **66**: 92

Carrie Clinton Lane Chapman Catt, April 5, 1919, **57**: 42; April 1,
    1920, **65**: 151
Thomas Lincoln Chadbourne, Jr., March 3, 1919, **55**: 403
Edgar Erastus Clark, July 29, 1920, **65**: 562
Francis Edward Clark, Aug. 12, 1919, **62**: 263
John Hessin Clarke, Nov. 18, 1918, **53**: 120
Walter Irving Clarke, Aug. 7, 1919, **62**: 202; Aug. 13, 1919, **62**: 270
Grosvenor Blaine Clarkson, Aug. 5, 1919, **62**: 165
Frank Irving Cobb, June 6, 1919, **61**: 644
Alfred J. Colburn, July 20, 1919, **61**: 568
Bainbridge Colby, Nov. 19, 1918, **53**: 134; Nov. 23, 1918, **53**: 187;
    Nov. 26, 1918, **53**: 209; Nov. 30, 1918, **53**: 261; Jan. 30, 1919, **54**:
    394; April 1, 1920, **65**: 149; April 10, 1920, **65**: 174; April 13,
    1920, **65**: 180; April 21, 1920, **65**: 215; April 24, 1920, **65**: 222;
    April 24, 1920, **65**: 225; April 30, 1920, **65**: 238; May 1, 1920, **65**:
    242; May 8, 1920 (2), **65**: 260 (2); June 3, 1920, **65**: 357; June 7,
    1920, **65**: 377; June 18, 1920, **65**: 429; June 19, 1920, **65**: 432;
    July 2, 1920, **65**: 490; July 4, 1920, **65**: 496; July 17, 1920, **65**:
    518; July 20, 1920 (2), **65**: 531 (2); Sept. 1, 1920, **66**: 87; Sept. 18,
    1920, **66**: 125; Sept. 23, 1920, **66**: 136; Sept. 25, 1920 (3), **66**: 144
    (2), 145; Nov. 9, 1920, **66**: 342; Nov. 11, 1920, **66**: 350; Nov. 18,
    1920, **66**: 390; Nov. 19, 1920, **66**: 399
William Byron Colver, Aug. 7, 1919, **62**: 201; Sept. 19, 1919, **63**:
    389
James Middleton Cox, July 6, 1920, **65**: 500; Sept. 28, 1920, **66**:
    159; Oct. 23, 1920, **66**: 262; Nov. 6, 1920, **66**: 333
Charles Richard Crane, Aug. 31, 1920, **66**: 79
George Creel, June 5, 1920, **65**: 374
Homer Stillé Cummings, Aug. 30, 1919, **62**: 587; June 11, 1920,
    65: 386; June 17, 1920, **65**: 424; June 18, 1920, **65**: 429; June 22,
    1920, **65**: 445; June 23, 1920, **65**: 446; June 28, 1920 (2), **65**: 470,
    471; June 30, 1920, **65**: 480; July 1, 1920, **65**: 482; July 2, 1920,
    65: 489; July 3, 1920, **65**: 492; July 10, 1920, **65**: 507

Albert Baird Cummins, Aug. 2, 1919, **62**: 117; Aug. 6, 1919, **62**: 183
Thomas DeWitt Cuyler, Feb. 6, 1921, **67**: 121

Josephus Daniels, Nov. 14, 1918 (2), **53**: 73 (2); Nov. 18, 1918, **53**: 110; Nov. 23, 1918 (3), **53**: 185 (2), 186; Dec. 3, 1918, **53**: 311; Jan. 26, 1919 (2), **54**: 281 (2); Jan. 31, 1919, **54**: 411; Feb. 2, 1919, **54**: 432; Feb. 8, 1919, **55**: 36; Feb. 25, 1919, **55**: 263; March 3, 1919, **55**: 457; March 27, 1919, **56**: 346; July 30, 1919 (2), **62**: 45 (2); Nov. 3, 1919, **63**: 610; Nov. 5, 1919, **63**: 618; June 18, 1920, **65**: 430; Aug. 19, 1920, **66**: 55; Oct. 11, 1920, **66**: 222; Nov. 4, 1920, **66**: 317; Nov. 6, 1920, **66**: 332; Nov. 12, 1920, **66**: 356; Dec. 2, 1920 (2), **66**: 452, 453; Dec. 14, 1920, **66**: 508; Dec. 15, 1920, **66**: 511; Dec. 16, 1920, **66**: 520
Clarence Seward Darrow, July 29, 1919, **62**: 58
Felix Cordova Davila, Feb. 13, 1919, **55**: 158; Feb. 25, 1919, **55**: 264
Norman Hezekiah Davis, April 4, 1919, **56**: 623; April 22, 1919, **57**: 629; April 23, 1919, **58**: 47; April 29, 1919, **58**: 242; May 1, 1919, **58**: 320; May 9, 1919, **58**: 595; July 26, 1919, **62**: 7; Aug. 8, 1919, **62**: 230; Dec. 8, 1920, **66**: 493; Dec. 10, 1920, **66**: 499; Dec. 15, 1920, **66**: 513; Dec. 23, 1920, **66**: 544
Henry Pomeroy Davison, April 13, 1919, **57**: 330
William Rufus Day, Nov. 14, 1918, **53**: 78
Nathaniel Barksdale Dial and Others, Aug. 16, 1920, **66**: 36
Jacob McGavock Dickinson, Feb. 28, 1919, **55**: 339
William Edward Dodd, Sept. 28, 1920, **66**: 165; Oct. 21, 1920, **66**: 255
Cleveland Hoadley Dodge, Nov. 19, 1918, **53**: 134; Feb. 25, 1919, **55**: 265; April 29, 1920, **65**: 234
Leonidas Carstarphen Dyer, June 10, 1919, **60**: 380

Joseph Bartlett Eastman, March 22, 1919, **56**: 194
Thomas Alva Edison, Nov. 15, 1920, **66**: 371
Maurice Francis Egan, March 24, 1920, **65**: 121
Abram Isaac Elkus, June 24, 1920, **65**: 457
John Jacob Esch, Aug. 2, 1919, **62**: 117
Charles W. Erwin, Feb. 1, 1919, **54**: 430

Albert Bacon Fall, Dec. 5, 1919, **64**: 140
Arthur Briggs Farquhar, March 4, 1919, **55**: 439
Scott Ferris, Jan. 22, 1919, **54**: 216
Edward Albert Filene, Feb. 15, 1919, **55**: 199; March 5, 1919, **55**: 447
John Fitzpatrick and Others, Sept. 4, 1919, **63**: 29
Hamilton Foley, Sept. 27, 1920, **66**: 152
John Franklin Fort, Nov. 21, 1918, **53**: 156
Philip Albright Small Franklin, Nov. 20, 1918, **53**: 148; Nov. 21, 1918, **53**: 158

William Little Frierson, June 24, 1920, **65**: 456; Sept. 24, 1920, **66**: 138

Charles Mills Galloway, March 7, 1919, **55**: 460; April 14, 1919, **57**: 348
Charles Mills Galloway and Others, Feb. 26, 1919, **55**: 290
Helen Hamilton Gardener, Nov. 27, 1918, **53**: 216; March 22, 1920, **65**: 115
Frederick Dozier Gardner, June 28, 1920, **65**: 472
Harry Augustus Garfield, Dec. 3, 1918, **53**: 310; March 1, 1919, **55**: 362; March 27, 1919, **56**: 343; Dec. 7, 1919, **64**: 145; Dec. 5, 1919, **64**: 146; Dec. 11, 1919, **64**: 180, 181; Dec. 13, 1919, **64**: 186; May 28, 1920, **65**: 335
Elbert Henry Gary, Aug. 31, 1919, **62**: 596
John Palmer Gavit, Feb. 24, 1919, **55**: 255
James Watson Gerard, July 4, 1920, **65**: 496
James Watson Gerard and Others, Feb. 10, 1919, **55**: 65
Adolph Germer, Feb. 1, 1919, **54**: 426
James Cardinal Gibbons, Aug. 23, 1919, **62**: 479
Peter Goelet Gerry, Nov. 16, 1918, **53**: 103; Jan. 23, 1919, **54**: 230
Peter Goelet Gerry and Others, March 28, 1919, **56**: 397
Frederick Huntington Gillett, Aug. 1, 1919, **62**: 103; Aug. 7, 1919, **62**: 199
Carter Glass, Jan. 7, 1919, **53**: 637; Jan. 15, 1919 (2) **54**: 88, 89; Jan. 30, 1919, **54**: 394; Feb. 5, 1919, **54**: 501; Feb. 11, 1919, **55**: 89; Feb. 28, 1919 (2), **55**: 332, 333; March 1, 1919, **55**: 358; March 3, 1919, **55**: 396; March 15, 1919, **55**: 537; March 27, 1919 (2), **56**: 344, 345; April 4, 1919, **56**: 618; April 11, 1919, **57**: 283; April 15, 1919, **57**: 347; April 17, 1919, **57**: 447; May 1, 1919, **58**: 330; June 3, 1919, **60**: 113; July 10, 1919, **61**: 441; July 11, 1919, **61**: 456; July 31, 1919, **62**: 70; Aug. 13, 1919, **62**: 266; Aug. 15, 1919, **62**: 314; Aug. 25, 1919 (2), **62**: 498, 499; Nov. 15, 1919, **64**: 41; Nov. 18, 1919, **64**: 60; Feb. 2, 1920, **64**: 349; Feb. 9, 1920, **64**: 387; Feb. 12, 1920, **64**: 410; May 27, 1920, **65**: 331; June 12, 1920, **65**: 394; Sept. 29, 1920, **66**: 167
Carter Glass and William Cox Redfield, Feb. 27, 1919, **55**: 306
Edward Field Goltra, April 5, 1919, **57**: 47
Samuel Gompers, Nov. 27, 1918, **53**: 217; April 23, 1919, **58**: 48; June 17, 1919, **60**: 645; June 24, 1919, **61**: 138; June 30, 1919, **61**: 357; July 1, 1919, **61**: 364; July 3, 1919, **61**: 377; July 29, 1920, **65**: 562; Oct. 15, 1920, **66**: 231; Dec. 15, 1920, **66**: 515
Samuel Gompers and Others, Dec. 17, 1919, **64**: 197, Feb. 24, 1920, **65**: 19
James Putnam Goodrich, July 26, 1920, **65**: 547
Edward A. Gowen, Dec. 9, 1920, **66**: 498
Charles Henry Grasty, July 24, 1919, **61**: 615
Thomas Watt Gregory, Nov. 9, 1918, **53**: 12; Nov. 29, 1918, **53**: 245; Jan. 9, 1919 (2), **53**: 705, 706; Jan. 17, 1919, **54**: 125; Feb. 5, 1919, **54**: 503; March 1, 1919 (2), **55**: 345, 346

Matthew Hale, July 18, 1919, **61**: 537

Charles Sumner Hamlin, Aug. 14, 1919, **62**: 301

George P. Hampton, July 29, 1919, **62**: 30; Oct. 18, 1920, **66**: 243

Norman Hapgood, Nov. 18, 1918, **53**: 124; Feb. 26, 1919, **55**: 292; March 4, 1919, **55**: 439; Nov. 9, 1920, **66**: 343

Warren Gamaliel Harding, Feb. 14, 1921, **67**: 134; Feb. 20, 1921, **67**: 149

Frank J. Hayes, Nov. 16, 1918, **53**: 118; April 10, 1919, **57**: 234

Francis Joseph Heney, July 18, 1919, **61**: 538

Walker Downer Hines, Feb. 22, 1919, **55**: 227; Feb. 24, 1919 (2), **55**: 246, 251; Feb. 25, 1919, **55**: 257; March 15, 1919, **55**: 536; March 22, 1919, **56**: 193; March 28, 1919, **56**: 399; April 4, 1919, **56**: 620; April 5, 1919, **57**: 43; April 10, 1919, **57**: 233; April 24, 1919, **58**: 106; May 13, 1919, **59**: 122; July 9, 1919, **61**: 412; July 18, 1919, **61**: 536; July 28, 1919, **62**: 20; July 30, 1919, **62**: 50; July 31, 1919, **62**: 72; Aug. 4, 1919, **62**: 133; Aug. 8, 1919, **62**: 227; Aug. 23, 1919, **62**: 469; Aug. 25, 1919, **62**: 488; Aug. 28, 1919, **62**: 548; Aug. 30, 1919, **62**: 586; Sept. 6, 1919, **63**: 88; Sept. 8, 1919, **63**: 118; Dec. 15, 1919, **64**: 188; Dec. 23, 1919, **64**: 223; Feb. 11, 1920, **64**: 406; Feb. 12, 1920, **64**: 411; Feb. 24, 1920, **64**: 467; March 1, 1920, **65**: 36; April 10, 1920, **65**: 175

Gilbert Monell Hitchcock, March 4, 1919, **55**: 437; April 16, 1919, **57**: 424; Sept. 24, 1919, **63**: 482; Nov. 22, 1919, **64**: 70; Nov. 27, 1919, **64**: 93; Jan. 22, 1920, **64**: 312; Feb. 24, 1920, **64**: 466; March 5, 1920, **65**: 48; March 11, 1920, **65**: 80; March 20, 1920, **65**: 109

Albert E. Hohler and Others, April 16, 1919, **57**: 425

Herbert Clark Hoover, Jan. 14, 1919, **54**: 58; Jan. 22, 1919, **54**: 216; Jan. 23, 1919, **54**: 229; Jan. 25, 1919, **54**: 276; Jan. 27, 1919, **54**: 303; Feb. 12, 1919, **55**: 116; Feb. 24, 1919, **55**: 251; March 18, 1919, **56**: 84; March 19, 1919, **56**: 102; March 25, 1919, **56**: 281; March 31, 1919, **56**: 470; April 8, 1919, **57**: 144; April 18, 1919, **57**: 472; April 25, 1919, **58**: 203; May 2, 1919, **58**: 411; June 9, 1919, **60**: 328; June 24, 1919, **61**: 133; Aug. 3, 1919, **62**: 124

Edward Mandell House, Feb. 20, 1919, **55**: 221; Feb. 26, 1919, **55**: 257; May 15, 1919, **59**: 185; June 24, 1919, **61**: 137; June 25, 1919, **61**: 180; Aug. 29, 1919, **62**: 573; Aug. 30, 1919, **62**: 580; Aug. 31, 1919, **62**: 607; Nov. 24, 1919, **64**: 89; Nov. 27, 1919, **64**: 96

David Franklin Houston, March 3, 1919, **55**: 395; March 19, 1919, **56**: 426; Aug. 8, 1919, **62**: 233; Aug. 13, 1919, **62**: 268; Aug. 14, 1919, **62**: 300; Feb. 2, 1920, **64**: 349; Feb. 26, 1920, **64**: 475; April 30, 1920, **65**: 238; May 10, 1920, **65**: 264; Aug. 24, 1920, **66**: 60; Sept. 7, 1920, **66**: 100; Dec. 2, 1920, **66**: 453; Dec. 17, 1920, **66**: 529

Charles Evans Hughes, Nov. 13, 1918, **53**: 70; March 18, 1919, **56**: 84

Merlin Hull, Feb. 13, 1919, **55**: 158

Edward Nash Hurley, March 24, 1919, **56**: 245; May 2, 1919, **58**:

498; July 10, 1919, **61**: 439; July 31, 1919 (2), **62**: 77, 79; Aug. 28, 1920, **66**: 74
William Levi Hutcheson, Feb. 3, 1919, **54**: 472

Bert Mark Jewell, Aug. 29, 1919, **62**: 567; April 21, 1920, **65**: 216; May 13, 1920, **65**: 285
Bert Mark Jewell and Others, Feb. 14, 1920, **64**: 428
Robert Underwood Johnson, Aug. 11, 1919, **62**: 252
William Hugh Johnston and Others, Aug. 2, 1919, **62**: 118
Jesse Holman Jones, Dec. 3, 1918, **53**: 310

Thomas Erby Kilby, Feb. 28, 1919, **55**: 328
Herman Henry Kohlsaat, Nov. 20, 1918, **53**: 148
Adolph Kraus, July 9, 1919, **61**: 409

Thomas William Lamont, June 5, 1919, **60**: 201; June 10, 1919, **60**: 379; June 11, 1919, **60**: 430; June 13, 1919 (3), **60**: 536, 539, 542; July 11, 1919, **61**: 446; July 25, 1919, **61**: 641; Aug. 25, 1919, **62**: 504; Sept. 10, 1919, **63**: 165; Oct. 1, 1920, **66**: 177; Nov. 26, 1920, **66**: 424; Dec. 3, 1920, **66**: 467; Dec. 7, 1920, **66**: 491; Dec. 14, 1920, **66**: 509; Dec. 15, 1920, **66**: 515; Dec. 31, 1920, **67**: 16; Jan. 21, 1921, **67**: 80; Feb. 21, 1921, **67**: 151
George Mason La Monte, Nov. 12, 1918, **53**: 63
Franklin Knight Lane, Feb. 26, 1919, **55**: 284; March 28, 1919 (2), **56**: 402 (2); July 18, 1919, **61**: 540; Aug. 4, 1919, **62**: 140; Sept. 2, 1919, **62**: 617; Oct. 19, 1919, **63**: 582; Oct. 31, 1919, **63**: 611; Feb. 6, 1920, **64**: 373; Feb. 9, 1920, **64**: 392
Robert Lansing, Nov. 29, 1918, **53**: 245; Feb. 11, 1919, **55**: 92; April 18, 1919, **57**: 469; May 19, 1919, **59**: 282; May 20, 1919, **59**: 313; May 23, 1919 (2), **59**: 450, 451; June 2, 1919, **60**: 42; June 4, 1919, **60**: 155; June 6, 1919, **60**: 241; June 7, 1919 (3), **60**: 287, 288, 289; June 8, 1919, **60**: 298; June 12, 1919, **60**: 485; June 13, 1919, **60**: 534; June 14, 1919, **60**: 566; June 27, 1919, **61**: 290; July 30, 1919, **62**: 65; Aug. 4, 1919 (2), **62**: 149, 152; Aug. 7, 1919, **62**: 203; Aug. 8, 1919, **62**: 236; Aug. 12, 1919, **62**: 260; Aug. 15, 1919, **62**: 322; Aug. 28, 1919, **62**: 534; Sept. 17, 1919, **63**: 337; Oct. 22, 1919, **63**: 588; Nov. 16, 1919, **64**: 41; Nov. 24, 1919, **64**: 91; Dec. 1, 1919, **64**: 103; Dec. 9, 1919, **64**: 167; Dec. 12, 1919, **64**: 183; Jan. 21, 1920, **64**: 310; Feb. 9, 1920, **64**: 388; Feb. 12, 1920, **64**: 408
Clarence Frederick Lea, Nov. 30, 1918, **53**: 262
Russell Cornell Leffingwell, Feb. 4, 1920, **64**: 362
Asbury Francis Lever, March 11, 1919, **55**: 478
John Lewellyn Lewis, Dec. 11, 1919, **64**: 180; July 31, 1920, **65**: 568; Oct. 24, 1920, **66**: 263
Henry Cabot Lodge, July 15, 1919, **61**: 484; July 22, 1919 (2), **61**: 582 (2); Aug. 14, 1919 (2), **62**: 275, 276; Aug. 15, 1919, **62**: 310; Aug. 23, 1919, **62**: 477; Sept. 1, 1919, **62**: 611
Henry Cabot Lodge and Others, June 5, 1920, **65**: 373

Breckinridge Long, Feb. 3, 1920, **64**: 352; June 7, 1920, **65**: 377
Frederick Henry Lynch, March 17, 1919, **56**: 57

William Gibbs McAdoo, Nov. 12, 1918, **53**: 58; Nov. 14, 1918, **53**:
74; Nov. 16, 1918 (2), **53**: 106, 112; Nov. 21, 1918, **53**: 151; Nov.
24, 1918, **53**: 190; Feb. 25, 1919, **55**: 258; May 9, 1919, **58**: 603;
July 11, 1919, **61**: 459; July 31, 1919 (2), **62**: 70, 71; Aug. 6, 1919,
62: 184; Aug. 20, 1919, **62**: 423; Oct. 2, 1920, **66**: 180; Oct. 11,
1920, **66**: 218; Oct. 17, 1920, **66**: 234
Samuel Walker McCall, Feb. 26, 1919, **55**: 292; Aug. 3, 1920, **66**: 8
Vance Criswell McCormick, Nov. 25, 1918, **53**: 202; Feb. 18, 1919,
55: 206; April 1, 1919, **56**: 514; April 2, 1919, **56**: 553; April 9,
1919, **57**: 189; April 17, 1919, **57**: 448; May 8, 1919, **58**: 548;
Sept. 18, 1919, **63**: 363; Nov. 27, 1919, **64**: 95
James Edward McCulloch, Aug. 25, 1919, **62**: 505
James Edward McCulloch and Edwin Courtland Dinwiddie, Aug.
1, 1919, **62**: 106; Aug. 14, 1919, **62**: 292
Porter James McCumber, Aug. 29, 1919, **62**: 565
James Grover McDonald, Aug. 27, 1919, **62**: 530
Grenville Stanley Macfarland, Nov. 25, 1918, **53**: 199
William Douglas Mackenzie, Oct. 22, 1920, **66**: 259
Gavin McNab, Nov. 18, 1918, **53**: 115; Nov. 21, 1918, **53**: 158
Dudley Field Malone, Feb. 28, 1919, **55**: 337
Thomas Riley Marshall, Aug. 7, 1919, **62**: 198
Thomas Staples Martin, July 27, 1919, **62**: 13
Royal Meeker, Feb. 11, 1919, **55**: 91; Aug. 5, 1919, **62**: 165; May 5,
1920, **65**: 248
Edwin Thomas Meredith, Jan. 26, 1920, **64**: 330; June 12, 1920,
65: 394; July 30, 1920, **65**: 567
Montana Grain Growers, May 16, 1919, **59**: 206
Thomas Joseph Mooney, Dec. 1, 1918, **53**: 273
Henry Morgenthau, Feb. 26, 1919, **55**: 288; Feb. 29, 1920, **65**: 20;
March 24, 1920, **65**: 121
Frank Morrison, Nov. 18, 1918, **53**: 119; March 1, 1919, **55**: 364
Frank Morrison and Samuel Gompers, Feb. 25, 1919, **55**: 262
Robert Russa Moton, Aug. 8, 1919, **62**: 233

George William Norris, July 21, 1919, **61**: 570

John A. O'Connell, Sept. 13, 1919, **63**: 268
Michael J. O'Leary, July 26, 1919, **62**: 8
Lee Slater Overman, June 25, 1920, **65**: 466
Lee Slater Overman and William Julius Harris, Oct. 12, 1920, **66**:
224
Robert Latham Owen, Nov. 19, 1918, **53**: 134; July 16, 1919, **61**:
495

Thomas Nelson Page, July 19, 1919, **61**: 559

Alexander Mitchell Palmer, Nov. 20, 1918, **53**: 147; Nov. 25, 1918, **53**: 197; Feb. 28, 1919, **55**: 339; March 27, 1919, **56**: 345; April 4, 1919 (2), **56**: 618, 619; July 1, 1919, **61**: 368; July 18, 1919, **61**: 534; July 30, 1919, **62**: 58; Aug. 4, 1919, **62**: 126; Aug. 12, 1919, **62**: 261; Aug. 14, 1919, **62**: 293; Aug. 29, 1919, **62**: 422; Aug. 21, 1919, **62**: 438; Aug. 22, 1919 (2), **62**: 462, 465; Aug. 27, 1919, **62**: 530; Dec. 11, 1919, **64**: 179; Dec. 22, 1919, **64**: 214; Dec. 23, 1919, **64**: 222; April 15, 1920, **65**: 192; April 19, 1920, **65**: 203; April 20, 1920, **65**: 214; April 22, 1920, **65**: 219; Sept. 14, 1920, **66**: 115; Sept. 30, Dec. 30, 1920, **67**: **67**: 98

John Milliken Parker, May 18, 1920, **65**: 295

Graham Patterson, Nov. 5, 1920, **66**: 327

John Barton Payne, Aug. 8, 1919, **62**: 226; Aug. 16, 1919, **62**: 326; Aug. 27, 1919, **62**: 528; Feb. 28, 1920, **65**: 20

George Foster Peabody, May 29, 1920, **65**: 341

Thomas Gilbert Pearson, Jan. 22, 1921, **67**: 81

William Phillips, March 27, 1919, **56**: 339; Sept. 22, 1919, **63**: 444; March 4, 1920, **65**: 47

Gifford Pinchot, Feb. 3, 1920, **64**: 354

Key Pittman, Nov. 11, 1918, **53**: 50; Nov. 12, 1918, **53**: 60; Nov. 15, 1918, **53**: 93; Aug. 15, 1919, **62**: 310

Frank Lyon Polk, Jan. 3, 1919, **54**: 393; March 1, 1919, **55**: 407; July 14, 1919, **61**: 478; March 13, 1920, **65**: 85; March 15, 1920, **65**: 88; March 19, 1920, **65**: 107; April 16, 1920, **65**: 196; April 27, 1920, **65**: 230; June 1, 1920, **65**: 352; June 15, 1920, **65**: 397

Atlee Pomerene, June 10, 1919, **60**: 380; Aug. 23, 1919, **62**: 477

Manuel Luis Quezon, June 5, 1919, **60**: 199

William Cox Redfield, Nov. 11, 1918, **53**: 48; Nov. 25, 1918, **53**: 201; Feb. 6, 1919, **54**: 520; Feb. 7, 1919, **54**: 556; Feb. 28, 1919, **55**: 336; March 27, 1919, **56**: 342; April 4, 1919, **56**: 619; April 11, 1919, **57**: 280; April 15, 1919, **57**: 376; April 19, 1919, **57**: 510; July 9, 1919, **61**: 411; July 23, 1919, **61**: 609; July 29, 1919, **62**: 31; July 31, 1919, **62**: 80; Aug. 1, 1919, **62**: 103; Aug. 4, 1919, **62**: 129; Aug. 30, 1919, **62**: 586; Oct. 15, 1919, **63**: 573

Paul Samuel Reinsch, July 25, 1919, **61**: 631; July 25, 1919, **61**: 634

Edgar Rickard, Feb. 27, 1919, **55**: 307; March 1, 1919, **55**: 362

Albert Houston Roberts, June 25, 1920, **65**: 460; Aug. 19, 1920, **66**: 54

John Roberts, Sept. 1, 1920, **66**: 132

Henry Mauris Robinson, April 30, 1919, **58**: 269; Jan. 6, 1920, **64**: 246; Feb. 9, 1920, **64**: 393

Joseph Taylor Robinson, Feb. 23, 1921, **67**: 166

Walter Stowell Rogers, Sept. 29, 1920, **66**: 169

Franklin Delano Roosevelt, Aug. 8, 1919 (2), **62**: 231, 232; Aug. 28, 1919, **62**: 546; July 24, 1920, **65**: 544

Leo Stanton Rowe, May 10, 1920, **65**: 270
Charles Edward Russell and Others, March 25, 1919, **56**: 282

J. D. Sanders, Aug. 14, 1919, **62**: 302
Francis Bowes Sayre, Jan. 23, 1921, **67**: 85
John Nevin Sayre, March 1, 1919, **55**: 365; July 7, 1919, **61**: 398;
    Aug. 4, 1919, **62**: 126; June 21, 1920, **65**: 441
Charles Michael Schwab, Feb. 12, 1919, **55**: 117
John Charles Shaffer, Aug. 21, 1919, **62**: 439
William Graves Sharp, Nov. 14, 1918, **53**: 80; Dec. 19, 1918, **53**:
    442; Jan. 16, 1920, **64**: 285; June 28, 1920, **65**: 473
Anna Howard Shaw, Nov. 18, 1918, **53**: 117
Morris Sheppard and Kenneth Douglas McKellar, Nov. 14, 1918,
    53: 78
John R. Shillady, Jan. 8, 1919, **53**: 690; July 21, 1919, **61**: 576
Thetus Wilrette Sims, Dec. 17, 1919, **64**: 195
William Harrison Short, Feb. 9, 1919, **55**: 37; Feb. 15, 1919, **55**:
    198; March 29, 1919, **56**: 427
James Thomson Shotwell, Aug. 1, 1919, **62**: 96
Upton Beall Sinclair, July 21, 1919, **61**: 577; Aug. 11, 1919, **62**:
    250; Sept. 21, 1919, **63**: 425
Alfred Emanuel Smith, Feb. 19, 1919, **55**: 216
Ellison DuRant Smith, Feb. 9, 1919, **55**: 38
John Spargo, Aug. 29, 1919, **62**: 555; July 22, 1920, **65**: 541; Dec.
    22, 1920, **66**: 540
Selden Palmer Spencer, Oct. 5, 1920, **66**: 191
John Louis Spivak, May 28, 1920, **65**: 335
Grant Squires, Nov. 9, 1918, **53**: 20; Dec. 30, 1918, **53**: 554; Jan.
    30, 1919, **54**: 396
Raymond Bartlett Stevens, Aug. 8, 1919, **62**: 226
John Appleton Stewart, Sept. 16, 1920, **66**: 118
Warren Sanford Stone, July 29, 1919, **62**: 31
Warren Sanford Stone and Others, June 3, 1920, **65**: 359
Edwin Forrest Sweet, Aug. 20, 1919, **62**: 423

William Howard Taft, March 1, 1919, **55**: 357; June 28, 1919, **61**:
    353
William Howard Taft and Abbott Lawrence Lowell, Feb. 10, 1919,
    55: 65
Frank William Taussig, Nov. 19, 1918, **53**: 132; May 13, 1919, **59**:
    123; July 17, 1919, **61**: 514
James Henry Taylor, Oct. 12, 1920, **66**: 227
Robert Heberton Terrell, July 28, 1919, **62**: 21
William Oxley Thompson, Aug. 25, 1920, **66**: 64
Joseph Patrick Tumulty, Nov. 12, 1918, **53**: 60; Nov. 14, 1918, **53**:
    77; Nov. 21, 1918, **53**: 156; Dec. 12, 1918, **53**: 371; Dec. 17, 1918,
    53: 413; Dec. 29, 1918, **53**: 542; Dec. 31, 1918, **53**: 570; Jan. 6,
    1919 (3), **53**: 624, 625 (2); Jan. 6, 1919, **53**: 626; Jan. 8, 1919, **53**:

687; Jan. 9, 1919 (5), **53**: 704, 705 (3), 706; Jan. 11, 1919 (2), **53**: 717 (2); Jan. 12, 1919, **54**: 31; Jan. 13, 1919, **54**: 54; Jan. 14, 1919 (2), **54**: 57 (2); Jan. 21, 1919, **54**: 193; Jan. 23, 1919, **54**: 228; Jan. 24, 1919, **54**: 258; Jan. 28, 1919, **54**: 332; Jan. 30, 1919, **54**: 390; Feb. 1, 1919, **54**: 428; Feb. 3, 1919, **54**: 471; Feb. 4, 1919 (2), **54**: 485, 486; Feb. 6, 1919, **54**: 519; Feb. 7, 1919 (3), **54**: 555 (3); Feb. 8, 1919, **55**: 36; Feb. 11, 1919, **55**: 94; Feb. 15, 1919, **55**: 197; Feb. 18, 1919 (2), **55**: 205, 206; Feb. 19, 1919, **55**: 214; Feb. 22, 1919 (2), **55**: 225, 226; Feb. 26, 1919, **55**: 289; March 1, 1919 (4), **55**: 344, 347, 348 (2); March 2, 1919, **55**: 368; March 6, 1919, **55**: 448; March 13, 1919, **55**: 493; March 14, 1919, **55**: 500; March 16, 1919 (2), **55**: 540 (2); March 22, 1919, **56**: 192; March 27, 1919 (3), **56**: 340, 341 (2); March 25, 1919, **56**: 373; March 30, 1919 (2), **56**: 435, 436; April 2, 1919 (2), **56**: 551, 552; April 4, 1919, **56**: 618; April 15, 1919, **57**: 376; April 18, 1919, **57**: 471; April 19, 1919, **57**: 511; April 20, 1919, **57**: 530; April 22, 1919 (2), **57**: 629 (2); April 25, 1919, (2), **58**: 145 (2); April 30, 1919 (2), **58**: 244, 274; May 1, 1919, **58**: 329; May 2, 1919, **58**: 364; May 3, 1919, **58**: 421; May 5, 1919 (2), **58**: 459, 460; May 6, 1919, **58**: 498; May 7, 1919 (2), **58**: 531 (2); May 8, 1919 (4), **58**: 560 (3), 561; May 9, 1919 (2), **58**: 603, 605; May 10, 1919 (2), **59**: 38 (2); May 11, 1919, **59**: 47; May 12, 1919 (3), **59**: 76, 77 (2); May 13, 1919 (4), **59**: 121 (3), 122; May 14, 1919, **59**: 160; May 16, 1919, **59**: 203; May 22, 1919, **59**: 419; May 23, 1919, **59**: 450; May 26, 1919, **59**: 524; June 2, 1919 (2), **60**: 18, 42; June 3, 1919 (2), **60**: 112, 113; June 4, 1919 (5), **60**: 153, 155 (4); June 5, 1919 (3), **60**: 198 (2), 199; June 10, 1919, **60**: 376; June 18, 1919, **61**: 9; June 21, 1919, **61**: 66; June 23, 1919, **61**: 116; June 25, 1919 (5), **61**: 182 (2), 183, 184 (2); June 27, 1919 (2), **61**: 293, 294; June 28, 1919 (5), **61**: 350, 351 (2) 352 (2); July 3, 1919 (2), **61**: 376, 377; July 5, 1919 (2), **61**: 388 (2); July 17, 1919, **61**: 509; July 18, 1919 (2), **61**: 533, 534; July 23, 1919 (2), **61**: 605 (2); July 25, 1919 (3), **61**: 626, 627, 628; Aug. 1, 1919, **62**: 104; Aug. 4, 1919, **62**: 150; Aug. 6, 1919 (2), **62**: 180, 181; Aug. 7, 1919, **62**: 196; Aug. 14, 1919 (2), **62**: 272, 274; Aug. 15, 1919, **62**: 309; Aug. 20, 1919, **62**: 419; Aug. 28, 1919, **62**: 536; Aug. 28, 1919, **62**: 542; Aug. 30, 1919, **62**: 581; Sept. 19, 1919, **63**: 371; Sept. 20, 1919 (2), **63**: 397, 399; Nov. 4, 1919, **63**: 609; Jan. 19, 1918, **63**: 625; Nov. 11, 1919, **64**: 15; Jan. 2, 1920, **64**: 238; Feb. 24, 1920, **64**: 467; Feb. 27, 1920, **64**: 479, 480; March 4, 1920, **65**: 44; March 11, 1920, **65**: 81; March 23, 1920 (2), **65**: 117, 128; April 14, 1920, **65**: 189; April 15, 1920, **65**: 190; April 21, 1920, **65**: 215; May 7, 1920, **65**: 257; May 12, 1920, **65**: 276; May 17, 1920, **65**: 291; May 17, 1920, **65**: 294; June 2, 1920, **65**: 354; June 4, 1920, **65**: 361; June 7, 1920, **65**: 378; June 11, 1920, **65**: 388; June 29, 1920, **65**: 478; July 2, 1920, **65**: 488; July 12, 1920, **65**: 508; July 17, 1920, **65**: 519; July 26, 1920, **65**: 546; July 27, 1920, **65**: 553; Aug. 4, 1920 (4), **66**: 7 (3), 8; Sept. 2, 1920, **66**: 90; Sept. 16, 1920, **66**: 118; Sept. 24, 1920, **66**: 138;

Sept. 24, 1920, **66**: 141; Sept. 26, 1920, **66**: 148; Sept. 30, 1920, **66**: 172; Oct. 1, 1920, **66**: 175; Oct. 4, 1920, **66**: 187; Oct. 6, 1920, (4), **66**: 200 (2), 204, 205; Oct. 7, 1920, **66**: 208; Oct. 10, 1920, **66**: 214; Oct. 18, 1920, **66**: 242; Oct. 19, 1920 (2), **66**: 246, 248; Oct. 20, 1920, **66**: 249; Oct. 21, 1920, **66**: 254; Oct. 22, 1920, **66**: 258; Oct. 25, 1920, **66**: 267; Oct. 28, 1920, **66**: 289; Dec. 16, 1920, **66**: 521

Oscar Wilder Underwood, Nov. 21, 1919, **64**: 69; Feb. 7, 1921, **67**: 123; Feb. 22, 1921, **67**: 159
William David Upshaw, April 19, 1919, **57**: 511

Henry van Dyke, July 13, 1919, **61**: 475
Carl Schurz Vrooman, Feb. 15, 1921, **67**: 139

Lillian D. Wald, Aug. 27, 1919, **62**: 527
Seth M. Walker, Aug. 14, 1920, **66**: 35 Fe
Francis Patrick Walsh, Sept. 19, 1919, **63**: 389
Francis Patrick Walsh and Others, March 24, 1919, **56**: 245
Thomas James Walsh, Feb. 25, 1919, **55**: 262; July 17, 1919, **61**: 512; Aug. 12, 1919, **62**: 262
Emory Olin Watson, Sept. 17, 1920, **66**: 120
Harry Andrew Wheeler, Nov. 9, 1918, **53**: 18
Henry White, Nov. 20, 1918, **53**: 147
The White House Staff, Aug. 28, 1919, **62**: 535
Louis Wiley, Oct. 4, 1920, **66**: 188
Enoch Williams and others, Aug. 30, 1920, **66**: 75
John Sharp Williams, Jan. 15, 1919, **54**: 90; July 9, 1919, **61**: 410; Sept. 25, 1920, **66**: 147
John Skelton Williams, Aug. 26, 1919, **62**: 517
William Bauchop Wilson, Nov. 21, 1918, **53**: 154; Feb. 26, 1919 (2), **55**: 291 (2); March 5, 1919, **55**: 447; March 11, 1919, **55**: 478; April 19, 1919, **57**: 510; June 11, 1919, **60**: 432; Aug. 4, 1919 (2), **62**: 131, 132; Aug. 30, 1919 (2), **62**: 582, 584; Sept. 5, 1919 (3), **63**: 53, 54, 56; Feb. 28, 1920, **65**: 16; May 22, 1920 (2), **65**: 314 (2); June 2, 1920 (2), **65**: 352, 353; June 3, 1920, **65**: 360; July 29, 1920, **65**: 558; July 30, 1920, **65**: 564; July 31, 1920 (2), **65**: 568, 569; Aug. 27, 1920, **66**: 66; Aug. 30, 1920, **66**: 75; Sept. 9, 1920, **66**: 104; Sept. 18, 1920, **66**: 125; Oct. 23, 1920, **66**: 262; Nov. 10, 1920, **66**: 346; Dec. 16, 1920, **66**: 520; Dec. 18, 1920, **66**: 533; March 1, 1921, **67**: 178
William Bauchop Wilson and William Cox Redfield, May 19, 1919, **59**: 287
Stephen Samuel Wise, July 1, 1919, **61**: 365
Simon Wolf, Sept. 8, 1920, **66**: 102
Gordon Woodbury, Jan. 5, 1921, **67**: 29
William Seaver Woods, July 18, 1919, **61**: 541

Casper Salathiel Yost, July 7, 1919, **61**: 399

*Correspondence, reports, memoranda, and aide-mémoire
about diplomatic and military affairs*

From Wilson and by Wilson

Albert, King of the Belgians, July 26, 1919, **62**: 6

Joshua Willis Alexander, May 11, 1920, **65**: 271

A note to the Allied governments about a program for European
relief, Dec. 15, 1918, **53**: 393

Newton Diehl Baker, Nov. 22, 1918, **53**: 163; Nov. 25, 1918, **53**:
193; Nov. 28, 1918, **53**: 240; Jan. 9, 1919, **53**: 699; March 3, 1919,
55: 391; May 19, 1919, **59**: 281; July 15, 1919, **61**: 479; July 18,
1919, **61**: 524; July 19, 1919, **61**: 547; Aug. 2, 1919, **62**: 116; Aug.
21, 1919 (2), **62**: 433, 434; Sept. 3, 1919, **62**: 622; Sept. 14, 1919,
63: 274; Feb. 7, 1920, **64**: 375; June 12, 1920, **65**: 393; Jan. 30,
1921, **67**: 105; Feb. 14, 1921, **67**: 133

Julius Howland Barnes, Nov. 11, 1919 (2), **64**: 13, 14

George Barnett, Aug. 14, 1919, **62**: 291

Edward Price Bell, Jan. 20, 1919, **54**: 159

Benedict XV, Dec. 24, 1918, **53**: 489; Aug. 15, 1919, **62**: 317

William Shepherd Benson, May 2, 1919 (2), **58**: 354 (2)

Frederick Jones Bliss, March 24, 1920, **65**: 142

Tasker Howard Bliss, Jan. 24, 1919, **54**: 255; April 22, 1919, **57**:
628; June 10, 1919, **60**: 359; June 28, 1919, **61**: 349

British, French, and Japanese members of the Council of Four,
Aug. 1, 1919, **62**: 108

Herbert Bruce Brougham, Dec. 17, 1918, **53**: 412

James, Viscount Bryce, Dec. 17, 1918, **53**: 411

Bainbridge Colby, March 25, 1920, **65**: 125; March 29, 1920, **65**:
141; April 2, 1920, **65**: 153; April 7, 1920, **65**: 155; April 8, 1920,
65: 159; April 16, 1920 (3), **65**: 195, 197, 198; April 17, 1920, **65**:
201; April 22, 1920, **65**: 217; April 23, 1920, **65**: 221; April 26,
1920 (2), **65**: 229 (2); April 28, 1920, **65**: 232; May 3, 1920, **65**:
245; May 9, 1920 (2), **65**: 261 (2); May 29, 1920 (2), **65**: 340, 341;
June 3, 1920, **65**: 355; June 5, 1920 (2), **65**: 372, 373; June 12,
1920, **65**: 392; June 15, 1920, **65**: 397; June 17, 1920, **65**: 421;
June 19, 1920, **65**: 432; July 24, 1920, **65**: 543; Aug. 5, 1920, **66**:
11; Aug. 10, 1920, **66**: 26; Aug. 12, 1920, **66**: 29; Aug. 20, 1920,
66: 56; Aug. 31, 1920, **66**: 78; Sept. 1, 1920 (2), **66**: 82, 86; Sept.
2, 1920 (2), **66**: 89, 90; Sept. 7, 1920, **66**: 100; Sept. 10, 1920, **66**:
110; Sept. 20, 1920, **66**: 128; Sept. 24, 1920, **66**: 139; Sept. 27,
1920, **66**: 150; Sept. 29, 1920, **66**: 166; Oct. 4, 1920, **66**: 183; Oct.
7, 1920 (2), **66**: 207 (2); Oct. 8, 1920 (2), **66**: 209, 212; Oct. 18,
1920 (2), **66**: 236, 238; Oct. 25, 1920, **66**: 265; Nov. 5, 1920 (2),
66: 321, 322; Nov. 8, 1920, **66**: 337; Nov. 9, 1920, **66**: 342; Nov.
12, 1920, (2), **66**: 353 (2); Nov. 13, 1920 (2), **66**: 357 (2); Nov. 20,
1920 (3), **66**: 402 (2), 403; Nov. 22, 1920, **66**: 411; Nov. 26, 1920,

66: 419; Nov. 30, 1920, **66**: 446; Dec. 3, 1920, **66**: 457; March 3, 1921, **67**: 194

The chairman of the joint committee of Congress in charge of welcoming the First Division, Sept. 15, 1919, **63**: 295

The Most Reverend Aluigi Cossio, Aug. 15, 1919, **62**: 317

The Covenant of a league of nations, first Paris draft, Jan. 8, 1919 (2), **53**: 655, 678; second Paris draft, Jan. 18, 1919, **54**: 138; third Paris draft, Feb. 2, 1919, **54**: 441

Richard Crane, Dec. 3, 1918, **53**: 306

George Creel, Nov. 8, 1920, **66**: 337

Josephus Daniels, May 28, 1919, **59**: 576; July 17, 1919, **61**: 505; July 19, 1919, **61**: 548; Aug. 22, 1919, **62**: 460; May 13, 1920, **65**: 284; Aug. 23, 1920, **66**: 59; Nov. 23, 1920, **66**: 414

The Most Reverend Thomas Randall Davidson, Dec. 17, 1918, **53**: 412; Dec. 20, 1918, **53**: 451

Norman Hezekiah Davis, Jan. 8, 1919 (2), **53**: 691 (2); April 2, 1920, **65**: 153; April 12, 1920, **65**: 178; June 23, 1920, **65**: 445; June 24, 1920, **65**: 449; June 25, 1920, **65**: 459; June 26, 1920, **65**: 468; June 30, 1920, **65**: 479; July 3, 1920, **65**: 492; July 4, 1920, **65**: 496; July 7, 1920, **65**: 501; July 19, 1920, **65**: 529; Oct. 15, 1920, **66**: 230; Oct. 18, 1920, **66**: 236; Oct. 19, 1920, **66**: 246; Nov. 3, 1920, **66**: 312; Nov. 5, 1920, **66**: 324; Nov. 23, 1920, **66**: 413; Dec. 3, 1920, **66**: 457; Dec. 7, 1920, **66**: 490; Dec. 9, 1920, (2), **66**: 496, 497; Dec. 15, 1920, **66**: 512; Dec. 22, 1920, **66**: 539; Dec. 23, 1920, **66**: 542; Dec. 24, 1920, **67**: 4; Dec. 27, 1920, **67**: 8; Jan. 7, 1921, **67**: 32; Jan. 8, 1921, **67**: 41; Jan. 10, 1921, **67**: 47; Jan. 13, 1921, **67**: 58; Jan. 20, 1921, **67**: 73

Henry Pomeroy Davison, Dec. 3, 1918, **53**: 306; March 20, 1919, **56**: 119

Cleveland Hoadley Dodge, Aug. 14, 1919, **62**: 285; Dec. 2, 1920, **66**: 451

Ferdinand I, Jan. 30, 1919, **54**: 379

The First Division of the United States Army, Sept. 15, 1919, **63**: 274

Rudolph Forster, Sept. 15, 1919, **63**: 295

Raymond Blaine Fosdick, April 18, 1919, **57**: 458

Andrew Furuseth, Nov. 18, 1918, **53**: 114

George V, Nov. 12, 1918, **53**: 53; Nov. 18, 1918, **53**: 109; July 27, 1919, **62**: 13

A reply to the German government on the question of food relief, Nov. 12, 1918, **53**: 64

James Cardinal Gibbons, Nov. 18, 1918, **53**: 114; Nov. 30, 1918, **53**: 250

Carter Glass, Dec. 23, 1918, **53**: 472; Jan. 1, 1919, **53**: 578; Jan. 9, 1919, **53**: 698; Jan. 11, 1919, **53**: 715

Samuel Gompers, Dec. 2, 1918, **53**: 286; Dec. 24, 1920, **67**: 3; Jan. 24, 1921, **67**: 86

Peter James Hamilton, Feb. 20, 1921, **67**: 75

Norman Hapgood, May 26, 1919, **59**: 512; June 2, 1919, **60**: 34; June 14, 1919, **60**: 568; June 20, 1919, **61**: 40; Aug. 1, 1919, **62**: 101

Warren Gamaliel Harding, Oct. 18, 1920, **66**: 239

Henry French Hollis, Nov. 11, 1918, **53**: 45

Herbert Clark Hoover, Jan. 11, 1919, **53**: 714; April 16, 1919, **57**: 406

Edward Mandell House, Nov. 10, 1918, **53**: 25; Nov. 13, 1918 (2), **53**: 66, 70; Nov. 16, 1918, **53**: 96; Nov. 18, 1918 (2), **53**: 108, 109; Nov. 19, 1918, **53**: 128; Nov. 20, 1918, **53**: 138; Nov. 21, 1918, **53**: 154; Nov. 25, 1918 (2), **53**: 193, 194; Nov. 26, 1918, **53**: 204; Nov. 28, 1918, **53**: 240; Dec. 3, 1918, **53**: 309; Dec. 15, 1918, **53**: 392; Dec. 17, 1918, **53**: 411; March 20, 1919, **56**: 120; Aug. 11, 1919, **62**: 257; Aug. 15, 1919, **62**: 316; Aug. 24, 1919, **62**: 481; Aug. 28, 1919, **62**: 553; Aug. 29, 1919, **62**: 579

David Franklin Houston, Aug. 19, 1920, **66**: 54

Hsu Shih-ch'ang, Jan. 28, 1919, **54**: 331

Paul Hymans, Nov. 17, 1920, **66**: 382; Nov. 29, 1920 (2), **66**: 443, 444

Peter Augustus Jay, Sept. 24, 1919, **63**: 484; Sept. 29, 1919, **63**: 534

Jean–Jules Jusserand, Nov. 16, 1918, **53**: 98

Robert Lansing, Nov. 18, 1918, **53**: 109; Nov. 19, 1918, **53**: 128; Nov. 20, 1918, **53**: 136; Nov. 20, 1918, **53**: 137; Nov. 22, 1918, **53**: 160; Nov. 25, 1918, **53**: 193; Nov. 26, 1919 (2), **53**: 204 (2); Nov. 28, 1918, **53**: 240; Dec. 1, 1918, **53**: 271; Dec. 3, 1918, **53**: 309; Dec. 7, 1918, **53**: 334; Dec. 24, 1918, **53**: 489; Jan. 9, 1919 (3), **53**: 699 (3); Jan. 9, 1919 (2), **53**: 700 (2); Jan. 10, 1919, **53**: 709; Jan. 20, 1919, **54**: 158; Jan. 24, 1919, **54**: 256; Jan. 25, 1919, **54**: 274; Jan. 30, 1919, **54**: 379; Feb. 7, 1919, **54**: 548; Feb. 14, 1919, **55**: 185; March 19, 1919, **56**: 96; March 22, 1919, **56**: 191; March 24, 1919, **56**: 235; March 28, 1919, **56**: 371; April 21, 1919, **57**: 557; May 27, 1919, **59**: 530; May 28, 1919, **59**: 571; June 3, 1919, **60**: 100; June 17, 1919, **60**: 640; June 24, 1919, **61**: 130; June 25, 1919, **61**: 172; Aug. 4, 1919 (3), **62**: 141, 142, 144; Aug. 6, 1919, **62**: 171; Aug. 8, 1919 (3), **62**: 220, 235 (2); Aug. 11, 1919 (2), **62**: 249, 256; Aug. 14, 1919, **62**: 281; Aug. 21, 1919, **62**: 441; Aug. 22, 1919, **62**: 459; Aug. 24, 1919, **62**: 481; Sept. 19, 1919, (3), **63**: 391 (2), 392; Feb. 4, 1920, **64**: 361; Feb. 7, 1920, **64**: 375; Feb. 12, 1920, **64**: 408

David Lloyd George, Nov. 14, 1918, **53**: 71; Nov. 3, 1920, **66**: 307

William Gibbs McAdoo, Nov. 20, 1920, **66**: 408
Fred McAver, Aug. 26, 1919, **62**: 515
Charles James McCarthy, Aug. 22, 1919, **62**: 460
Count Vincenzo Macchi di Cellere, Aug. 21, 1919, **62**: 448
Vance Criswell McCormick, May 16, 1919, **59**: 188
Louis Marshall, Nov. 16, 1918, **53**: 99; Nov. 20, 1918, **53**: 141; Aug.
    14, 1919, **62**: 284
Thomas Garrigue Masaryk, Jan. 10, 1919, **53**: 711
Royal Meeker, Sept. 27, 1920, **66**: 151
David Hunter Miller and James Brown Scott, Jan. 11, 1919, **53**:
    716
Henry Morgenthau, Sept. 24, 1920, **66**: 139
Roland Sletor Morris, April 16, 1919, **57**: 420

Nicholas I, Jan. 9, 1919, **53**: 704
Francesco Saverio Nitti, Sept. 3, 1919, **62**: 625; Sept. 24, 1919, **63**:
    484

Thomas Nelson Page, Jan. 10, 1919, **53**: 711
Sir George Paish, Jan. 11, 1919, **53**: 717
Alexander Mitchell Palmer, Nov. 5, 1920, **66**: 321
John Joseph Pershing, Feb. 13, 1919, **55**: 149; Sept. 3, 1919, **62**:
    622
William Phillips, Sept. 10, 1919, **63**: 166; Sept. 15, 1919, **63**: 297;
    Sept. 20, 1919, **63**: 421; Sept. 23, 1919 (2), **63**: 463, 464; Sept. 28,
    1919 (2), **63**: 532 (2); Sept. 29, 1919, **63**: 534
Raymond Poincaré, Dec,. 24, 1918, **53**: 489
Frank Lyon Polk, Nov. 22, 1918, **53**: 159; Nov. 22, 1918, **53**: 166;
    March 3, 1919 (2), **55**: 393 (2); May 4, 1919, **59**: 148; June 24,
    1919, **61**: 130; Aug. 2, 1919, **62**: 116; Sept. 2, 1919, **62**: 619; Sept.
    13, 1919, **63**: 270; Sept. 21, 1919, **63**: 424; Feb. 19, 1920, **64**: 445;
    Feb. 21, 1920, **64**: 448; Feb. 27, 1920, **64**: 479; Feb. 28, 1920, **65**:
    10; Feb. 29, 1920, **65**: 22; March 4, 1920 (2), **65**: 43 (2); March 8,
    1920, **65**: 72; March 15, 1920 (2), **65**: 87 (2); March 17, 1920 (2),
    65L 91, 92; March 18, 1920, **65**: 98; March 19, 1920, **65**: 107;
    March 23, 1920, **65**: 116
The President of the Senate, July 22, 1919, **61**: 579

Albert Cushing Read, May 28, 1919, **59**: 576
James Brooks Ayers Robertson, July 18, 1919, **61**: 525
Franklin Delano Roosevelt, Aug. 14, 1919, **62**: 290; July 22, 1920,
    65: 540

Juan Luis Sanfuentes Andonaegui, Dec. 4, 1918, **53**: 316
Charles Prestwich Scott, Jan. 11, 1919, **53**: 717
William Sowden Sims, Dec. 27, 1918, **53**: 524

Ras Taffari, July 23, 1919, **61**: 604

Joseph Patrick Tumulty, Nov. 13, 1918, **53**: 67; Dec. 19, 1918, **53**: 440; Dec. 22, 1918, **53**: 469; May 16, 1919, **59**: 189

United States Senate, Feb. 17, 1921, **67**: 144

Eleuthérios Kyrios Vénisélos, Sept. 19, 1919, **63**: 391
Vittorio Emanuele III, Jan. 9, 1919, **53**: 697

Thomas James Walsh, Dec. 3, 1918, **53**: 306
Brand Whitlock, Jan. 10, 1919, **53**: 712
John Sharp Williams, Aug. 2, 1919, **62**: 116; Aug. 12, 1919, **62**: 259
William Bauchop Wilson, Jan. 12, 1921, **67**: 52
Stephen Samuel Wise, Sept. 10, 1920, **66**: 110; Nov. 15, 1920, **66**: 368
Samuel Isett Woodbridge, Sept. 2, 1919, **62**: 616

Empress Zaouditou, July 12, 1919, **61**: 471 (draft); July 23, 1919, **61**: 603

To Wilson from

Albert, King of the Belgians, July 29, 1919, **62**: 29
Joshua Willis Alexander, Sept. 10, 1920, **66**: 111

Newton Diehl Baker, Nov. 22, 1918, **53**: 168; Nov. 23, 1918 (3), **53**: 182, 183, 184; Nov. 26, 1918, **53**: 208; Nov. 27, 1918 (2) **53**: 227, 229; Nov. 30 1918 **53**: 254; Dec. 5 1918 **53**: 322; Dec. 20, 1918, **53**: 451; March 3, 1919, **55**: 399; April 4, 1919, **56**: 576; April 9, 1919, **57**: 189; May 7, 1919, **58**: 569; May 22, 1919, **59**: 409; July 1, 1919, **61**: 366; July 11, 1919, **61**: 457; July 15, 1919 (3), **61**: 485 (2), 487; July 18, 1919, **61**: 530; July 19, 1919 (2), **61**: 547, 560; July 23, 1919 (3), **61**: 610 (2), 611; July 24, 1919, **61**: 615; July 31, 1919, **62**: 82; Aug. 9, 1919, **62**: 240; Aug. 23, 1919, **62**: 478; Aug. 28, 1919, **62**: 545; Aug. 29, 1919, **62**: 562; Sept. 18, 1919, **63**: 61; Feb. 9, 1920, **64**: 389; March 3, 1920, **65**: 43; March 17, 1920, **65**: 99; April 6, 1920, **65**: 154; April 10, 1920, **65**: 165; May 10, 1920, **65**: 270; June 11, 1920, **65**: 387; Sept. 25, 1920, **66**: 146; Oct. 18, 1920, **66**: 236; Jan. 29, 1921, **67**: 97; Feb. 3, 1921, **67**: 112; Feb. 12, 1921, **67**: 131
Ray Stannard Baker, Dec. 18, 1918, **53**: 433
George Barnett, Aug. 13, 1919, **62**: 270
Francisco Aguilar Barquero, Dec. 8, 1919, **64**: 153
Benedict XV, July 28, 1919, **62**: 26
William Shepherd Benson, April 25, 1919 (2), **58**: 141, 142; May 1, 1919, **58**: 319; May 3, 1919, **58**: 408; May 4 1919 **58**: 426; May 7, 1919, **58**: 528; May 8, 1919, **58**: 554; May 12, 1919 (2), **59**: 64, 66; May 31, 1919, **59**: 640; June 6, 1919, **60**: 241
Frederick Jones Bliss, March 29, 1920, **65**: 142

Tasker Howard Bliss, Dec. 23, 1918, **53**: 485; April 9, 1919, **57**: 189; April 18, 1919, **57**: 460; April 21, 1919, **57**: 560; May 9, 1919, **58**: 568; May 29, 1919, **59**: 599; June 25, 1919, **61**: 174; June 26, 1919, **61**: 225; June 28, 1919, **61**: 349

Louis Dembitz Brandeis, Feb. 3, 1920, **64**: 358

British, French, and Japanese members of the Council of Four, July 27, 1919, **62**: 14

Herbert Bruce Brougham, Dec. 16, 1918, **53**: 406

James Viscount Bryce, Dec. 7, 1918, **53**: 335; Jan. 7, 1919, **53**: 644

Albert Sidney Burleson, Nov. 24, 1920, **66**: 415

Manuel Estrada Cabrera, Nov. 18, 1920, **66**: 390

Georges Clemenceau, Sept. 18, 1919, **63**: 367; Sept. 19, 1919, **63**: 393

Georges Clemenceau, Arthur James Balfour, and André Tardieu, Sept. 5, 1919, **63**: 60

Georges Clemenceau and David Lloyd George, Sept. 11, 1919, **63**: 204

Gilbert Fairchild Close, June 6, 1919, **60**: 241

Bainbridge Colby, April 5, 1920, **65**: 156; April 7, 1920, **65**: 158; April 8, 1920 (2), **65**: 160, 162; April 10, 1920 (2), **65**: 167, 169; April 13, 1920, **65**: 181; April 15, 1920, **65**: 190; April 16, 1920, **65**: 196; April 17, 1920, **65**: 201; April 20, 1920 (3), **65**: 212, 213 (2); April 23, 1920 (2), **65**: 221, 222; April 27, 1920, **65**: 231; April 28, 1920 (2), **65**: 232, 233; April 29, 1920, **65**: 234; April 30, 1920 (2), **65**: 236, 237; May 7, 1920 (3), **65**: 252, 254, 255; May 8, 1920 (2), **65**: 259 (2); May 20, 1920 (2), **65**: 305, 312; May 22, 1920 (2), **65**: 315, 316; May 27, 1920, **65**: 330; June 2, 1920, **65**: 353; June 11, 1920 (2), **65**: 388, 389; June 12, 1920, **65**: 394; June 13, 1920, **65**: 395; June 16, 1920, **65**: 399; June 18, 1920 (2), **65**: 430(2); June 19, 1920 (2), **65**: 433, 434; July 16, 1920 (2), **65**: 515, 517; July 18, 1920 (3), **65**: 525, 526, 529; July 20, 1920 (2), **65**: 531, 532; July 23, 1920, **65**: 542; July 28, 1920, **65**: 555; July 31, 1920, **65**: 571; Aug. 4, 1920, **66**: 9; Aug. 5, 1920, **66**: 12; Aug. 9, 1920, **66**: 19; Aug. 18, 1920 (3), **66**: 42, 50, 53; Aug. 26, 1920, **66**: 65; Aug. 28, 1920, **66**: 72; Sept. 1, 1920 (2), **66**: 86, 87; Sept. 3, 1920, **66**: 91; Sept. 6, 1920 (2), **66**: 99, 100; Sept. 13, 1920, **66**: 113; Sept. 18, 1920, **66**: 123; Sept. 23, 1920, **66**: 135; Sept. 25, 1920, **66**: 142; Oct. 2, 1920 (2), **66**: 178, 180; Oct. 4, 1920, **66**: 185; Oct. 21, 1920, **66**: 253; Oct. 24, 1920, **66**: 263; Oct. 28, 1920, (2) **66**: 283, 288; Nov. 6, 1920, **66**: 334; Nov. 8, 192 **66**: 355, 356; Nov. 13, 1920 (3), **66**: 358, 359 (2); Nov. 13, 1920, (2) **66**: 364, 366; Nov. 16, 1920, **66**: 381; Nov. 18, 1920, (2) **66**: 388, 389, 393; Nov. 20, 1920, **66**: 406; Nov. 25, 1920, **66**: 418; Nov. 26, 1920, **66**: 421; Nov. 27, 1920, **66**: 426; Nov. 27, 1920 (3), **66**: 428, 429, 430; Nov. 28, 1920, **66**: 436; Nov. 29, 1920, **66**: 443; Nov. 30, 1920, **66**: 445; Dec. 2, 1920, **66**: 452; Feb. 4, 1921, **67**: 113; Feb. 13, 1921, **67**: 132; March 3, 1921, **67**: 204

Bainbridge Colby and Newton Diehl Baker, April 10, 1920, **65**: 167

Robert Edward Coontz, July 26, 1920, **65**: 548
The Most Reverend Aluigi Cossio, July 28, 1919, **62**: 26
Edward Prentiss Costigan, Dec. 6, 1918, **53**: 328
Charles Richard Crane, Aug. 31, 1919, **62**: 607
Richard Crane, Nov. 30, 1918, **53**: 258
George Creel, Nov. 9, 1918, **53**: 16; Nov. 20, 1920, **66**: 403
Oscar Terry Crosby, Dec. 23, 1918, **53**: 477; Dec. 31, 1918 **53**: 571

Josephus Daniels, Dec. 3, 1918, **53**: 312; May 9, 1919, **58**: 593; July
    17, 1919, **61**: 511; July 23, 1919, **61**: 604; June 11, 1920, **65**: 390;
    July 21, 1920, **65**: 538; Aug. 12, 1920, **66**: 28; Aug. 13, 1920, **66**:
    31; Aug. 20, 1920, **66**: 56; Aug. 24, 1920, **66**: 62; Nov. 21, 1920,
    66: 410
Philippe Sudre Dartiguenave, Aug. 25, 1920, **66**: 63
The Most Reverend Randall Thomas Davidson, Dec. 14, 1918, **53**:
    388
John William Davis, Jan. 14, 1921, **67**: 61
Norman Hezekiah Davis, Feb. 2, 1919, **54**: 431; May 13, 1919, **59**:
    110; Nov. 11, 1919, **64**: 11; Feb. 26, 1920, **64**: 478; March 5, 1920,
    65: 57; March 17, 1920, **65**: 92; March 30, 1920 (2), **65**: 147 (2);
    April 2, 1920, **65**: 153; May 6, 1920, **65**: 250; May 26, 1920, **65**:
    325; June 24, 1920, **65**: 455; June 25, 1920 (2), **65**: 461, 464; June
    28, 1920, **65**: 477; June 30, 1920, **65**: 479; July 1, 1920, **65**: 483;
    July 2, 1920, **65**: 490; July 6. 1920, **65**: 500; July 7, 1920, **65**: 502;
    July 8, 1920, **65**: 503; July 9, 1920, **65**: 505; July 13, 1920, **65**:
    510; July 20, 1920, **65**: 532; July 21, 1920, **65**: 533; Aug. 7, 1920,
    66: 17; Nov. 1, 1920, **66**: 83; Sept. 28, 1920, **66**: 159; Oct. 5, 1920,
    66: 193; Oct. 14, 1920, **66**: 229; Oct. 16, 1920, **66**: 233; Oct. 18,
    1920, **66**: 241; Oct. 30, 1920 (2), **66**: 294, 295; Nov. 2, 1920 (3),
    66: 302, 304 (2); Nov. 5, 1920, **66**: 326; Nov. 15, 1920, **66**: 377;
    Nov. 22, 1920, **66**: 412; Nov. 26, 1920, **66**: 423; Dec. 1, 1920, **66**:
    447; Dec. 3, 1920, **66**: 458; Dec. 4, 1920 (2), **66**: 471, 472; Dec. 6,
    1920, (2) **66**: 480 (2); Dec. 8, 1920, **66**: 493; Dec. 10, 1920, **66**: 499;
    Dec. 14, 1920, **66**: 506; Dec. 15, 1920, **66**: 512; Dec. 20, 1920, , **66**:
    535; Dec. 23, 1920, **66**: 543; Dec. 27, 1920, **67**: 8; Dec. 28, 1920,
    67: 10; Jan. 3, 1921, **67**: 23; Jan. 7, 1921 (2), **67**: 32, 33; Jan. 7,
    1921 (3), **67**: 36, 37 (2); Jan. 8, 1921, **67**: 41; Jan. 12, 1921, **67**: 53;
    Jan. 14, 1921, **67**: 60; Jan. 15, 1921, **67**: 63; Jan. 21, 1921 (3), **67**:
    78, 79 (2); Jan. 26, 1921, **67**: 92; Jan. 27, 1921, **67**: 95; Feb. 17,
    1921, **67**: 144; Feb. 19, 1921, **67**: 147
Cleveland Hoadley Dodge, Aug. 10, 1919, **62**: 248; Aug. 19, 1919,
    62: 415; Dec. 1, 1920, **66**: 448

Henry Prather Fletcher, March 1, 1919, **55**: 352; Aug. 18, 1919, **62**:
    332; Aug. 20, 1919, **62**: 450
Raymond Blaine Fosdick, Jan. 14, 1920, **64**: 274
David Rowland Francis, March 1, 1919, **55**: 349
Friedrich Wilhelm Viktor August Ernst, Feb. 10, 1920, **64**: 397
Andrew Furuseth, Nov. 16, 1918, **53**: 107

George V, Nov. 12, 1918, **53**: 53; Nov. 15, 1918, **53**: 85; Dec. 24, 1918, **53**: 491

James Watson Gerard, May 14, 1920, **65**: 287; May 18, 1920, **65**: 298

James Cardinal Gibbons, Nov. 16, 1919, **53**: 102; Nov. 27, 1919, **53**: 231; March 26, 1920, **65**: 138

Giovanni Giolitti, June 24, 1920, **65**: 449

Carter Glass, Dec. 19, 1918, **53**: 441; Jan. 6, 1919, **53**: 626; Sept. 26, 1919, **63**: 518

Samuel Gompers, Nov. 30, 1918, **53**: 257; Dec. 22, 1918, **53**: 490; Dec. 21, 1920, **66**: 537; Jan. 20, 1921, **67**: 73

William Elliott Gonzales, Oct. 8, 1920, **66**: 209

The Right Reverend Charles Gore, Dec. 23, 1918, **53**: 486

Jacob Judah Aaron de Haas, May 28, 1920, **65**: 334

Peter James Hamilton, Jan. 12, 1921, **67**: 55

Norman Hapgood, May 26, 1919, **59**: 517; June 30, 1919, **61**: 359; July 29, 1919, **62**: 34; Aug. 20, 1919, **62**: 427

Warren Gamaliel Harding, Oct. 18, 1920, **66**: 240

Charles Robert Hemphill, June 14, 1920, **65**: 422

Herbert Clark Hoover, Nov. 9, 1918 (2), **53**: 14, 15; Nov. 12, 1918, **53**: 59; Nov. 14, 1918, **53**: 75; Dec. 1, 1918, **53**: 273; Dec. 19, 1918, **53**: 443; Dec. 20, 1918, **53**: 453; Dec. 23, 1918, **53**: 476; Jan. 8, 1919, **53**: 687; April 14, 1919, **57**: 347; May 15, 1919, **59**: 174; Aug. 3, 1919, **62**: 123; Aug. 5 1919, **62**: 166; June 26, 1920, **65**: 468

Herbert Clark Hoover and Henry Morgenthau, July 15, 1919, **61**: 486

Edward Mandell House, Nov. 9, 1918 (3), **53**: 3, 4 (2); Nov. 10, 1918 (2), **53**: 25 (2); Nov. 10, 1918 (3), **53**: 26 (2), 27; Nov. 11, 1918 (5), **53**: 33, 34, 43, 44 (2); Nov. 12, 1918, **53**: 56; Nov. 13, 1918, **53**: 69; Nov. 14, 1918, **53**: 71; Nov. 15, 1918 (2), **53**: 84, 85; Nov. 16, 1918 (3), **53**: 100, 101 (2); Nov. 17, 1918, **53**: 108; Nov. 18, 1918 (2), **53**: 123 (2); Nov. 19, 1918 (2), **53**: 130 (2); Nov. 20, 1918 (2), **53**: 142, 143; Nov. 21, 1918, **53**: 154 (2); Nov. 22, 1918 (2), **53**: 167, 180; Nov. 23, 1918 (2), **53**: 181 (2); Nov. 24, 1918, **53**: 189; Nov. 24, 1918, **53**: 190; Nov. 25, 1918, **53**: 196; Nov. 27, 1918, **53**: 221; Nov. 27, 1918 (3), **53**: 222, 225, 226; Nov. 28, 1918, **53**: 241; Nov. 30, 1918, **53**: 251; Dec. 1, 1918 (2), **53**: 272, 273; Dec. 2, 1918, **53**: 290; Dec. 4, 1918, **53**: 316; Dec. 6, 1918, **53**: 324; Dec. 9, 1918, **53**: 344; Dec. 10, 1918, **53**: 359; Dec. 12, 1918, **53**: 372; Dec. 13, 1918, **53**: 381; Dec. 25, 1918, **53**: 507; Jan. 8, 1919, **53**: 687; April 25, 1919, **58**: 138; June 5, 1919, **60**: 192; June 27, 1919, **61**: 286; July 30, 1919, **62**: 60; Aug. 6, 1919, **62**: 187; Aug. 9, 1919, **62**: 243; Aug. 11, 1919, **62**: 254; Aug. 18, 1919, **62**: 333; Aug. 20, 1919, **62**: 425; Aug. 21, 1919, **62**: 451; Aug. 26, 1919, **62**: 525; Sept. 3, 1919, **62**: 625; Sept. 13, 1919, **63**: 271; Sept. 15, 1919, **63**: 299; Sept. 20, 1919, **63**: 421; Sept. 30, 1919, **63**: 537

Hsu Shih-ch'ang, Jan. 21, 1919, **54**: 194

Edward Nash Hurley, Nov. 9, 1918, **53**: 9; Nov. 28, 1918, **53**: 271;
    Dec. 12, 1918, **53**: 372; Dec. 20, 1918, **53**: 454; Dec. 23, 1918, **53**:
    480; Jan. 20, 1919, **54**: 171
Paul Hymans, Nov. 16, 1920, **66**: 380

Peter Augustus Jay, Aug. 31, 1919, **62**: 605; Sept. 23, 1919, **63**:
    464; Sept. 25, 1919, **63**: 515
Douglas Wilson Johnson, Feb. 6, 1920, **64**: 368
Robert Underwood Johnson, March 17, 1920, **65**: 93; March 29,
    1920, **65**: 198; May 20, 1920, **65**: 299; Nov. 5, 1920, **66**: 322; Dec.
    6, 1920, **66**: 481

Thomas William Lamont, May 12, 1920, **65**: 276
Robert Lansing, Nov. 9, 1918, **53**: 6; Nov. 18, 1918, **53**: 121; Nov.
    20, 1918, **53**: 144; Nov. 21, 1918, **53**: 151; Nov. 25, 1918, **53**: 197;
    Nov. 26, 1918, **53**: 206; Dec. 2, 1918, **53**: 291; Dec. 3, 1918, **53**:
    312; Dec. 23, 1918, **53**: 474; Dec. 28, 1918, **53**: 536; Jan. 9, 1919,
    53: 706; Jan. 15, 1919, **54**: 82; Feb. 5, 1919, **54**: 495; Feb. 11,
    1919, **55**: 93; March 19, 1919, **56**: 101; March 21, 1919 (2), **56**:
    152, 153; March 22, 1919, **56**: 184; March 26, 1919, **56**: 304;
    April 2, 1919, **56**: 548; April 7, 1919, **57**: 94; April 8, 1919, **57**:
    134; April 12, 1919, **57**: 313; April 15, 1919, **57**: 373; April 19,
    1919, **57**: 495; May 26, 1919, **59**: 514; May 27, 1919, **59**: 547;
    May 28, 1919 (2), **59**: 572 (2); May 30, 1919 (2), **59**: 618, 619;
    June 5, 1919, **60**: 180; June 6, 1919, **60**: 240; June 16, 1919, **60**:
    603; June 20, 1919, **61**: 40; July 25, 1919 (2), **61**: 636, 638; July
    28, 1919, **62**: 22; July 29, 1919, **62**: 30; July 30, 1919, **62**: 63;
    Aug. 1, 1919, **62**: 108; Aug. 4, 1919, **62**: 153; Aug. 6, 1919, **62**:
    186; Aug. 7, 1919, **62**: 206; Aug. 11, 1919, **62**: 253; Aug. 14, 1919,
    62: 303; Aug. 15, 1919, **62**: 318; Aug. 16, 1919 (3), **62**: 323, 328,
    330; Aug. 18, 1919, **62**: 332; Aug. 20, 1919, **62**: 425; Aug. 21,
    1919, **62**: 449; Aug. 30, 1919 (3), **62**: 581, 588, 594; Oct. 31, 1919,
    63: 606; Nov. 4, 1919, **63**: 616; Nov. 11, 1919, **64**: 8; Nov. 12,
    1919, **64**: 25; Nov. 14, 1919, **64**: 34; Nov. 21, 1919, **64**: 66; Dec. 2,
    1919, **64**: 117; Dec. 5, 1919, **64**: 127; Dec. 7, 1919, **64**: 148; Dec.
    8, 1919, **64**: 153; Dec. 13, 1919, **64**: 186; Dec. 15, 1919, **64**: 190;
    Dec. 19, 1919, **64**: 210; Dec. 20, 1919, **64**: 212; Dec. 22, 1919, **64**:
    216; Dec. 23, 1919, **64**: 219; Dec. 30, 1919, **64**: 236; Jan. 8, 1920
    (3), **64**: 260 (2), 261; Jan. 12, 1920, **64**: 272; Jan. 19, 1920, **64**:
    298; Jan. 20, 1920, **64**: 307; Jan. 22, 1920, **64**: 313; Jan. 28, 1920,
    64: 340; Jan. 30, 1920, **64**: 344; Feb. 6, 1920 (4), **64**: 367, 371, 372
    (2); Feb. 7, 1920 (2), **64**: 380, 381; Feb. 9, 1920, **64**: 390; Feb. 11,
    1920, **64**: 407
Robert Lansing and Others, Dec. 31, 1918, **53**: 572; March 20,
    1919, **56**: 122
Maksim Maksimovich Litvinov, Dec. 24, 1918, **53**: 492
David Lloyd George, Nov. 19, 1918, **53**: 130; Aug. 18, 1920, **66**:
    42
Prince Georgii Evgen'evich L'vov, Dec. 2, 1918, **53**: 289

James McCarthy, Aug. 24, 1919, **62**: 480

Count Vincenzo Macchi di Cellere, Aug. 22, 1919, **62**: 468

Cyrus Hall McCormick, Jr., Nov. 29, 1918, **53**: 255

Vance Criswell McCormick, Dec. 13, 1918, **53**: 431; May 17, 1919 (2), **59**: 233, 235; June 24, 1919, **61**: 130

James Grover McDonald, March 26, 1920, **65**: 138

Grenville Stanley Macfarland, Dec. 23, 1918, **53**: 487

Peyton Conway March, Aug. 13, 1919, **62**: 271; Aug. 16, 1919, **62**: 323

Louis Marshall, Nov. 14, 1918, **53**: 79; Nov. 16, 1918, **53**: 104; Aug. 8, 1919, **62**: 220

Thomas Garrigue Masaryk, Jan. 2, 1919, **53**: 590

Henry Morgenthau, Sept. 24, 1920, **66**: 140

Roland Sletor Morris, May 22, 1919, **59**: 410

Edgar Young Mullins, June 14, 1920, **65**: 421

Nicholas I, Jan. 7, 1919, **53**: 701

Francesco Saverio Nitti, Aug. 31, 1919, **62**: 605; Sept. 23, 1919, **63**: 464

Robert Latham Owen, July 17, 1919, **61**: 510

Ignace Jan Paderewski, Oct. 12, 1920, **66**: 225

Thomas Nelson Page, Nov. 28, 1918, **53**: 242; Dec. 24, 1918, **53**: 494; Jan. 7, 1919 (2), **53**: 637, 639

Sir George Paish, Dec. 26, 1918, **53**: 514

Alexander Mitchell Palmer, Nov. 8, 1920, **66**: 337

John Barton Payne, Sept. 12, 1919, **63**: 368

John Joseph Pershing, Dec. 26, 1918, **53**: 512; Feb. 10, 1919, **55**: 64

William Phillips, July 21, 1919, **61**: 571; Sept. 5, 1919, **63**: 62; Sept. 6, 1919, **63**: 91; Sept. 8, 1919, **63**: 119; Sept. 11, **63**: 204; Sept. 12, 1919, **63**: 235; Sept. 13, 1919 (2), **63**: 270, 271; Sept. 15, 1919 (2), **63**: 297, 298; Sept. 16, 1919 (3), **63**: 305, 306, 307; Sept. 18, 1919 (2), **63**: 364, 366; Sept. 19, 1919 (3), **63**: 392, 394 (2); Sept. 21, 1919, **63**: 423; Sept. 22, 1919, **63**: 445; Sept. 23, 1919, **63**: 466; Sept. 24, 1919, **63**: 485

Józef Klemens Piłsudski, Nov. 22, 1918, **53**: 163; July 4, 1920, **65**: 493; March 3, 1921, **67**: 204

Raymond Poincaré, Dec. 23, 1918, **53**: 485

Frank Lyon Polk, Dec. 2, 1918, **53**: 292; Feb. 4, 1919, **54**: 474; Feb. 28, 1919, **55**: 330; March 1, 1919 (3), **55**: 350, 351, 357; July 8, 1919, **61**: 406; July 11, 1919, **61**: 455; July 12, 1919, **61**: 465; July 16, 1919, **61**: 494; July 17, 1919 (2), **61**: 505, 510; July 18, 1919 (3), **61**: 525, 527, 528; Aug. 1, 1919, **62**: 110; Aug. 8, 1919, **62**: 238; Aug. 11, 1919, **62**: 257; Aug. 25, 1919, **62**: 511; Aug. 29, 1919, **62**: 574; Aug. 31, 1919, **62**: 603; Sept. 6, 1919, **63**: 91; Sept. 8, 1919, **63**: 120; Sept. 16, 1919, **63**: 306; Sept. 18, 1919, **63**: 364; Sept. 19, 1919, **63**: 393; Sept. 23, 1919, **63**: 465, Sept. 26, 1919 (2), **63**: 524, 525; Jan. 24, 1920, **64**: 323; Jan. 26, 1920, **64**: 331;

Feb. 18, 1920, **64**: 436; Feb. 18, 1920, **64**: 443; Feb. 21, 1920 (2), **64**: 448, 450; Feb. 23, 1920, **64**: 458; Feb. 24, 1920, **64**: 464, 468; Feb. 25, 1920, **64**: 472; Feb. 27, 1920 (2), **64**: 480, 483; Feb. 29, 1920, **65**: 21; March 2, 1920, **65**: 37; March 4, 1920 (2), **65**: 45, 46; March 5, 1920, **65**: 55; March 6, 1920 (3), **65**: 64, 65(2); March 10, 1920 (2), **65**: 76, 77; March 13, 1920, **65**: 84; March 19, 1920, **65**: 106; March 22, 1920, **65**: 111

William Emmanuel Rappard, Nov. 26, 1918, **53**: 209
William Cox Redfield, Nov. 22, 1918, **53**: 169; July 12, 1919, **61**: 465
Franklin Delano Roosevelt, Aug. 9, 1919, **62**: 241; July 21, 1920, **65**: 536; July 22, 1920, **65**: 539
Lord Rothschild, Dec. 29, 1918, **53**: 543

Juan Luis Sanfuentes Andonaegui, Dec. 9, 1918, **53**: 346
Charles Prestwich Scott, Dec. 31, 1918, **53**: 572
William Sowden Sims, Dec. 26, 1918, **53**: 512
Sun Yat-sen, Nov. 19, 1918, **53**: 138

Ras Tafari, July 12, 1919, **61**: 472
Tommaso Tittoni, Sept. 18, 1919, **63**: 365
The Trades Union Congress Parliamentary Committee and the Executive Committee of the Labour party, Dec. 28, 1918, **53**: 535
Joseph Patrick Tumulty, Dec. 11, 1918, **53**: 370; Dec. 18, 1918, **53**: 421; Dec. 19, 1918, **53**: 440; Dec. 31, 1918, **53**: 571; Nov. 11, 1920, **64**: 7; Feb. 25, 1920, **64**: 473; June 25, 1920, **65**: 460; Oct. 26, 1920, **66**: 269

Antoine Velleman and Others, Nov. 29, 1919, **64**: 97
Eleuthérios Kyrios Vénisélos, Dec. 8, 1919, **64**: 157

Francis Patrick Walsh, Aug. 16, 1919, **62**: 324; Sept. 1, 1920, **66**: 88
Thomas James Walsh, Dec. 2, 1918, **53**: 299
Henry White, Feb. 14, 1919, **55**: 187; July 27, 1919 (2), **62**: 11, 206
Brand Whitlock, Dec. 30, 1918, **53**: 552; June 5, 1919, **60**: 192; July 23, 1919, **61**: 609
John Sharp Williams, Aug. 9, 1919, **62**: 241
William Bauchop Wilson, Dec. 4, 1920, **66**: 475; Dec. 28, 1920, **67**: 9; Jan. 11, 1921, **67**: 48
Stephen Samuel Wise, May 5, 1920, **65**: 248; Nov. 12, 1920, **66**: 356
Simon Wolf, Nov. 30, 1918, **53**: 259
Francis Call Woodman, Jan. 18, 1919, **54**: 255

Allyn Abbot Young, Dec. 13, 1918, **53**: 381

Empress Zaouditou, July 12, 1919, **61**: 472

Personal correspondence

From Wilson to

Alvey Augustus Adee, Sept. 9, 1920, **66**: 104

H. Adelman, Nov. 26, 1920, **66**: 421

Edwin Anderson Alderman, Oct. 22, 1920, **66**: 258; April 30, 1921,
    67: 275; Feb. 19, 1922; **67**: 549

Joshua Willis Alexander, March 17, 1921, **67**: 234; Feb. 13, 1922,
    67: 543

Alexandra, the Queen Mother, May 21, 1920, **65**: 314

George Weston Anderson, Jan. 12, 1922, **67**: 518

Neal Larkin Anderson, June 8, 1921, **67**: 307

Marietta Minnegerode Andrews, April 6, 1923, **68**: 320

Charles Edward Bacon, Oct. 18, 1920, **66**: 242

Newton Diehl Baker, Nov. 12, 1918, **53**: 54; Jan. 23, 1919, **54**: 227;
    July 12, 1919, **61**: 462; Aug. 26, 1919, **62**: 515; July 7, 1920, **65**:
    502; June 5, 1921, **67**: 305; Sept. 9, 1921, **67**: 389; Oct. 6, 1921,
    67: 404; Sept. 11, 1922, **68**: 133; Oct. 30, 1922, **68**: 168; Sept. 29,
    1923, **68**: 432; Nov. 25, 1923, **68**: 485

Ray Stannard Baker, Dec. 18, 1920, **66**: 532; Dec. 27, 1921, **67**: 7;
    Jan. 5, 1921, **67**: 27; Dec. 25, 1921, **67**: 494; Nov. 23, 1922, **68**:
    201; Feb. 7, 1923, **68**: 284; March 27, 1923, **68**: 303; April 3,
    1923, **68**: 316; May 10, 1923, **68**: 361; Dec. 4, 1923, **68**: 494; Dec.
    13, 1923, **68**: 499; Dec. 31, 1923, **68**: 514; Jan. 8, 1924, **68**: 524;
    Jan. 29, 1924, **68**: 547 (sent unsigned)

Tallulah James Brockman Bankhead, March 2, 1920, **65**: 37

Bernard Mannes Baruch, Nov. 27, 1918, **53**: 213; Dec. 7, 1918, **53**:
    334; Nov. 10, 1920, **66**: 346; Dec. 10, 1920, **66**: 499; Dec. 20,
    1920, **66**: 535; May 10, 1921, **67**: 282; June 2, 1921, **67**: 301; June
    11, 1921, **67**: 309; Nov. 25, 1921, **67**: 468; Dec. 10, 1921, **67**: 478;
    Aug. 18, 1922, **68**: 116; Nov. 15, 1922, **68**: 191; April 22, 1923,
    68: 346; July 15, 1923, **68**: 391; Sept. 28, 1923, **68**: 431; Oct. 2,
    1923, **68**: 439; Oct. 24, 1923, **68**: 453; Oct. 28, 1923, **68**: 458

John Spencer Bassett, Jan. 12, 1922, **67**: 518; Jan. 2, 1924, **68**: 516

Sylvester Woodbridge Beach, Sept. 9, 1920, **66**: 104; Nov. 11, 1920,
    66: 349; Feb. 9, 1921, **67**: 126; May 2, 1923, **68**: 354

Eduard Beneš, June 28, 1919, **61**: 347

William Shepherd Benson, April 22, 1919, **57**: 628

Fred W. Bentley, May 3, 1922, **68**: 43

Martha McChesney Berry, Nov. 17, 1921, **67**: 459; Jan. 7, 1922,
    67: 507

Anita Eugenie McCormick Blaine, March 12, 1919, **55**: 484; Feb.
    18, 1922, **67**: 548

Emily Jane Newell Blair, April 25, 1922, **68**: 33; Oct. 22, 1922, **68**: 157

Herbert Edward Douglas Blakiston, Nov. 22, 1918, **53**: 162

Tasker Howard Bliss, May 31, 1920, **65**: 343; Sept. 15, 1921, **67**:
    390; Dec. 6, 1922, **68**: 228

Edward William Bok, Aug. 17, 1920, **66**: 40; Sept. 29, 1920, **66**: 168; Nov. 15, 1920, **66**: 369; Dec. 6, 1920, **66**: 479; Jan. 22, 1921, **67**: 83; March 9, 1921, **67**: 230; Feb. 1, 1922, **67**: 539; Nov. 2, 1922, **68**: 170

John Randolph Bolling, June 9, 1919, **60**: 331

William H. Bolling, July 15, 1919, **61**: 482

Helen Woodrow Bones, May 26, 1919, **59**: 526

Edward Booth, Dec. 27, 1918, **53**: 524

Evangeline Cory Booth, Dec. 28, 1920, **67**: 11

William Edgar Borah, Feb. 16, 1922, **67**: 547

Isaiah Bowman, Oct. 10, 1921, **67**: 412

Cyrus Townsend Brady, Aug. 27, 1919, **62**: 526

Clinton Tyler Brainard, March 12, 1919, **55**: 484

Thomas W. Brahany, June 12, 1920, **65**: 393

Louis Dembitz Brandeis, Nov. 12, 1918, **53**: 55; Dec. 29, 1921, **67**: 498; Jan. 25, 1923, **68**: 277; Jan. 29, 1923, **68**: 280

George E. Brennan, June 14, 1921, **67**: 312

Robert Bridges, May 29, 1919, **59**: 604; June 3, 1921, **67**: 302; March 26, 1922, **67**: 574

Jessie Bones Brower, Jan. 27, 1922, **67**: 536

Curtis Brown, Sept. 17, 1920, **66**: 121

Marjorie Brown, Dec. 14, 1920, **66**: 505

Paul Brunett, Feb. 21, 1921, **67**: 150

Elizabeth, Lady Bryce, Jan. 29, 1922, **67**: 538

Albert Sidney Burleson, Nov. 15, 1920, **66**: 369; March 3, 1921, **67**: 196

William Calhoun, Feb. 26, 1922, **67**: 557

Andrew Carnegie, Nov. 13, 1918, **53**: 67

Louise Whitfield Carnegie, Aug. 12, 1919, **62**: 259

Lord Robert Cecil, March 31, 1923, **68**: 310; Oct. 20, 1923, **68**: 450

Thomas Lincoln Chadbourne, Jr., June 12, 1919, **60**: 487; Jan. 21, 1921, **67**: 78

Benjamin Bright Chambers, Sept. 2, 1919, **62**: 616

David Laurence Chambers, Nov. 15, 1920, **66**: 370

Children's Delegation, Nov. 15, 1921, **67**: 457

Elmer Talmage Clark, Oct. 14, 1920, **66**: 229

John Hessin Clarke, Sept. 5, 1922, **68**: 127; Sept. 21, 1922, **68**: 138; Sept. 23, 1922, **68**: 140; Oct. 27, 1922, **68**: 166; Nov. 3, 1922, **68**: 171; Nov. 13, 1922, **68**: 188; Jan. 19, 1923, **68**: 276; April 8, 1923, **68**: 324; May 10, 1923, **68**: 361

Georges Clemenceau, Nov. 18, 1922, **68**: 197; Dec. 12, 1922, **68**: 230

Frank Irving Cobb, July 12, 1919, **61**: 463; March 9, 1921, **67**: 230; Oct. 13, 1921, **67**: 419; Jan. 10, 1922, **67**: 513; Jan. 17, 1922, **67**: 529; July 25, 1922, **68**: 100; July 27, 1922, **68**: 101; Nov. 15, 1922, **68**: 191; Nov. 18, 1922, **68**: 197; March 31, 1923, **68**: 311; June 10, 1923, **68**: 384; Aug. 1, 1923, **68**: 397; Aug. 10, 1923, **68**: 402

Margaret Hubbard Ayer Cobb, Dec. 21, 1923, **68**: 504
John Knox Coit, Aug. 5, 1919, **62**: 164
Bainbridge Colby, Aug. 28, 1920, **66**: 71; Nov. 6, 1920, **66**: 331;
    April 16, 1921, **67**: 259; April 17, 1921, **67**: 260; April 19, 1921,
    67: 262; May 5, 1921, **67**: 277; Sept. 3, 1921, **68**: 385; Oct. 5,
    1921, **67**: 402; Feb. 18, 1922, **67**: 548; Feb. 4, 1922, **67**: 555;
    March 3, 1922, **67**: 563; April 17, 1922, **68**: 26; June 10, 1922, **68**:
    74; June 20, 1922, **68**: 83; Aug. 15, 1922, **68**: 113; Aug. 20, 1922,
    68: 118; Aug. 23, 1922, **68**: 120; Sept. 13, 1922, **68**: 135; Sept. 25,
    1922, **68**: 142; Nov. 24, 1922, **68**: 202; Nov. 29, 1922, **68**: 213;
    Dec. 14, 1922, **68**: 232
W. A. Cole, Sept. 6, 1922, **68**: 128
Varnum Lansing Collins, Nov. 16, 1923, **68**: 477
William Byron Colver, Dec. 10, 1921, **67**: 479
Edwin Grant Conklin, Jan. 16, 1922, **67**: 525
George Crouse Cook, Nov. 15, 1920, **66**: 370
Calvin Coolidge, June 14, 1922, **68**: 76; Dec. 30, 1922, **68**: 259;
    Aug. 7, 1923, **68**: 400
Helen Coughlin, Dec. 3, 1920, **66**: 458
Joe Cowperthwaite, Sept. 3, 1920, **66**: 92; Oct. 5, 1920, **66**: 192
James Middleton Cox, Nov. 16, 1923, **68**: 477
Vernon Allen Crawford, Dec. 20, 1923, **68**: 502
George Creel, Aug. 26, 1920, **66**: 64; Feb. 24, 1921, **67**: 167; March
    2, 1921, **67**: 186; April 9, 1923, **68**: 325; Aug. 28, 1923, **68**: 411
Homer Stillé Cummings, Nov. 29, 1918, **53**: 244; Dec. 22, 1920, **66**:
    540; June 29, 1922, **68**: 92
James Michael Curley, Nov. 23, 1922, **68**: 201
Winterton Conway Curtis, Aug. 29, 1922, **68**: 121
Earl Curzon of Kedleston, Nov. 22, 1918, **53**: 161; Feb. 3, 1919, **54**:
    468; May 27, 1919, **59**: 552
Harvey Williams Cushing, May 18, 1920, **65**: 296

D.C. Heath & Company, Nov. 11, 1918, **53**: 45; July 8, 1920, **65**:
    503
Richard Heath Dabney, Nov. 1, 1920, **66**: 298; Nov. 10, 1920, **66**:
    346
Josephus Daniels, April 15, 1919, **57**: 370; Aug. 13, 1920, **66**: 30;
    March 14, 1921, **67**: 233; May 27, 1922, **68**: 69; March 12, 1923,
    68: 295
The Right Reverend James Henry Darlington, July 12, 1919, **61**:
    463
William W. Davies, July 19, 1920, **65**: 530
Edward Parker Davis, Aug. 1, 1919, **62**: 102; May 26, 1922, **68**: 65
Ellen Duane Davis, Feb. 27, 1919, **55**: 304; Aug. 21, 1919, **62**: 437;
    Nov. 5, 1921, **67**: 442; Nov. 25, 1921, **67**: 468; Dec. 3, 1921, **67**:
    471; April 16, 1922, **68**: 25; Nov. 18, 1923, **68**: 479
Norman Hezekiah Davis, Dec. 16, 1920, **66**: 518; Feb. 1, 1922, **67**:
    539; June 26, 1922, **68**: 85; Nov. 13, 1923, **68**: 189; Nov. 17, 1922,
    68: 196; Dec. 24, 1922, **68**: 242; Jan. 1, 1923, **68**: 262; Jan. 12,

1923, **68**: 274; April 12, 1923, **68**: 333; Nov. 2, 1923, **68**: 461; Dec. 4, 1923, **68**: 494; Jan. 15, 1924, **68**: 530

Frank Miles Day, Oct. 11, 1920, **66**: 217

Harry Kent Day, Oct. 18, 1920, **66**: 242

Francis Xavier Dercum, Aug. 16, 1920, **66**: 36; Sept. 21, 1922, **68**: 138; Dec. 12, 1922, **68**: 229

Joseph Tyrone Derry, Sept. 3, 1919, **62**: 624

Leon Dessez, Jan. 8, 1922, **67**: 508

Goldsworthy Lowes Dickinson, June 3, 1919, **60**: 111

Thomas Dixon, Jr., Aug. 2, 1919, **62**: 115

Armistead Mason Dobie, Feb. 15, 1921, **67**: 138

William Edward Dodd, Sept. 9, 1921, **67**: 389; Nov. 14, 1921, **67**: 456; Sept. 6, 1922, **68**: 128

Cleveland Hoadley Dodge, Nov. 13, 1918, **53**: 68; June 12, 1919, **60**: 488; Nov. 18, 1920, **66**: 388; March 2, 1921, **67**: 186; Aug. 23, 1921, **67**: 375; Dec. 1, 1921, **67**: 470; Feb. 23, 1922, **67**: 554; April 16, 1922, **68**: 25; Aug. 15, 1922, **68**: 112; Aug. 19, 1922, **68**: 117; Nov. 16, 1922, **68**: 195; Oct. 5, 1923, **68**: 445; Dec. 12, 1923, **68**: 498; Dec. 13, 1923, **68**: 513

Cleveland Hoadley Dodge and Others, Jan. 20, 1924, **68**: 534

George Henry Doran, Nov. 26, 1920, **66**: 420

Frank Nelson Doubleday, Nov. 14, 1923, **68**: 474

Sir Eric Drummond, July 27, 1923, **68**: 392; Oct. 2, 1923, **68**: 439

John Foster Dulles, June 27, 1919, **61**: 283

Edward Fitzsimons Dunne, June 14, 1919, **60**: 569

Jessie Kennedy Dyer, Sept. 6, 1920, **66**: 99; Dec. 16, 1920, **66**: 519

Henry van Dyke, March 25, 1919, **56**: 280

Edward Irving Edwards, Dec. 12, 1921, **67**: 483; Nov. 13, 1922, **68**: 188

Charles William Eliot, Oct. 28, 1920, **66**: 281; March 17, 1921, **67**: 234

Edward Graham Elliott, Nov. 11, 1918, **53**: 45

James Daniel Evans, April 11, 1923, **68**: 331

Oscar Ross Ewing, Nov. 19, 1920, **66**: 393

Douglas Fairbanks, Jan. 13, 1919, **54**: 53

Mary Fels Fels, Oct. 30, 1920, **66**: 293

Edward Albert Filene, Nov. 27, 1921, **67**: 469

Henry Burchard Fine, July 27, 1922, **68**: 102

Anna Portner Flood, Dec. 10, 1921, **67**: 478

Hamilton Foley, April 28, 1923, **68**: 351

Rudolph Forster, March 3, 1921, **67**: 197

Raymond Blaine Fosdick, Jan. 20, 1921, **67**: 74; April 28, 1922, **68**: 36; Oct. 22, 1923, **68**: 451; Nov. 28, 1923, **68**: 493

George A. Foster, Aug. 21, 1920, **66**: 57

David Rowland Francis, Jan. 8, 1922, **67**: 509

Glenn Frank, May 29, 1923, **68**: 369

Felix Frankfurter, May 1, 1919, **58**: 317

John William Frazer, Sept. 28, 1922, **68**: 144
James Edward Freeman, July 30, 1923, **68**: 396; Sept. 25, 1923,
    68: 429
Ernst Freund, March 29, 1921, **67**: 248
William Goodell Frost, Dec. 10, 1920, **66**: 499

Alfred George Gardiner, Feb. 14, 1923, **68**: 287
Helen Hamilton Gardener, Nov. 1, 1920, **66**: 298
Harry Augustus Garfield, Aug. 1, 1919, **62**: 101; Nov. 8, 1920, **66**:
    338; Nov. 14, 1923, **68**: 474
John Nance Garner, March 24, 1922, **67**: 572
Finis James Garrett, Oct. 13, 1923, **68**: 448
Elbert Henry Gary, July 15, 1919, **61**: 481
Raoul Gautier, June 30, 1919, **61**: 356
George V, June 3, 1919, **60**: 100
James Watson Gerard, March 22, 1922, **67**: 572; Oct. 2, 1923, **68**:
    440; Dec. 13, 1923, **68**: 499
James Thayer Gerould, March 31, 1923, **68**: 308
Frank Ernest Ghiselli, Dec. 26, 1923, **68**: 506
Charles Dana Gibson, Nov. 19, 1922, **68**: 198
Carter Glass, Dec. 11, 1920, **66**: 500; Sept. 15, 1921, **67**: 390; May
    21, 1922, **68**: 57; June 19, 1922, **68**: 80; Nov. 12, 1923, **68**: 472
Nina Deadrick Glenn, May 18, 1920, **65**: 297
Samuel Gompers, April 29, 1919, **58**: 243
William Elliott Gonzales, Nov. 18, 1923, **68**: 479
Mrs. Samuel W. Gordon, July 13, 1920, **65**: 510
Marie Cook Doughty Gorgas, July 13, 1920, **65**: 510
Sir Ludovic James Grant, Feb. 11, 1919, **55**: 89
Cary Travers Grayson, March 2, 1921, **67**: 185
H. J. Gregory-Allen, Nov. 8, 1920, **66**: 339
Henri Gressitt, Sept. 13, 1920, **66**: 113
Solomon Bulkley Griffin, Nov. 30, 1918, **53**: 251

Granville Stanley Hall, Nov. 2, 1920, **66**: 302
Charles Sumner Hamlin, Sept. 7, 1923, **68**: 420; Oct. 10, 1923, **68**:
    448
Norman Hapgood, Aug. 13, 1920, **66**: 30
The Right Reverend Alfred Harding, Aug. 29, 1919, **62**: 561
Florence Mabel Kling DeWolfe Harding, Aug. 3, 1923, **68**: 398
Warren Gamaliel Harding, Oct. 5, 1921, **67**: 402; Nov. 8, 1921, **67**:
    444; Aug. 1, 1923, **68**: 397
George McLean Harper, June 19, 1920, **65**: 433; Oct. 10, 1921, **67**:
    412
Harper & Brothers, Aug. 26, 1920, **66**: 65
Henry Wilson Harris, Jan. 20, 1919, **54**: 159
Charles Homer Haskins, June 10, 1919, **60**: 360; July 19, 1920, **65**:
    530; Jan. 14, 1921, **67**: 59
Samuel Hayward, Jr., Nov. 15, 1920, **66**: 368
Azel Washburn Hazen, May 9, 1920, **65**: 262

Edith Benham Helm, Dec. 10, 1921, **67**: 479; Nov. 23, 1923, **68**: 481

Jeanie North Henderson, Feb. 17, 1921, **67**: 143

Louisa Patterson Henderson, Dec. 22, 1921, **67**: 493; July 20, 1922, **68**: 98

Robert Randolph Henderson, May 7, 1921, **67**: 281

Stanislaus Vincent Henkels, Aug. 2, 1921, **67**: 362

John Bell Henneman, April 7, 1904, **60**: 646

James King Hewison, May 16, 1919, **59**: 190

Walker Downer Hines, Feb. 21, 1921, **67**: 151

Hamilton Holt, April 22, 1920, **65**: 218; July 12, 1920, **65**: 507; March 3, 1921, **67**: 197; April 25, 1921, **67**: 270; Nov. 5, 1922, **68**: 177; Jan. 1, 1923, **68**: 262; Feb. 10, 1923, **68**: 285

Hamilton Holt and Others, April 7, 1922, **67**: 604

Irwin Hood Hoover, May 3, 1921, **67**: 276

Alice Starke Hotchkiss, Nov. 9, 1923, **68**: 464

Edward Mandell House, March 11, 1920, **65**: 80; June 10, 1920, **65**: 383; Nov. 1, 1920, **66**: 298

David Franklin Houston, March 14, 1921, **67**: 233; Jan. 11, 1922, **67**: 515

Herbert Sherman Houston, Oct. 17, 1921, **67**: 424; Nov. 2, 1921, 440; March 26, 1922, **67**: 574; April 15, 1923, **68**: 334

Sid Houston, May 7, 1921, **67**: 279

Mildred Howells, May 12, 1920, **65**: 276

Charles Evans Hughes, July 15, 1921, **67**: 351

Allen Schoolcraft Hulbert, Feb. 27, 1919, **55**: 303

Mary Allen Hulbert, Sept. 20, 1919, **63**: 419

Cordell Hull, May 4, 1922, **68**: 44; May 6, 1922, **68**: 50; May 23, 1922, **68**: 60; May 25, 1923, **68**: 63; May 30, 1922, **68**: 71; June 27, 1922, **68**: 86; July 14, 1922, **68**: 95; Sept. 12, 1922, **68**: 134; Oct. 13, 1922, **68**: 155; Nov. 9, 1922, **68**: 181; Dec. 14, 1922, **68**: 232; June 25, 1923, **68**: 388

Charles Samuel Jackson, June 21, 1920, **65**: 442

Thornwell Jacobs, March 23, 1920, **65**: 117; June 12, 1920, **65**: 393; April 18, 1922, **68**: 27

John Franklin Jameson, Nov. 20, 1920, **66**: 409; May 11, 1922, **68**: 52; May 13, 1922, **68**: 55; June 2, 1922, **68**: 72

Peter Augustus Jay, June 18, 1920, **65**: 429

Richard Jervis, Feb. 28, 1921, **67**: 174

Ben Johnson, Jan. 5, 1922, **67**: 505

Burton Johnson, Sept. 16, 1923, **68**: 424

Douglas Wilson Johnson, Jan. 15, 1921, **67**: 62; Jan. 5, 1922, **67**: 504

Edgar DeWitt Jones, Jan. 7, 1922, **67**: 507

Jesse Holman Jones, Dec. 9, 1920, **66**: 498; Feb. 23, 1921, **67**: 164; Oct. 4, 1923, **68**: 444; Jan. 4, 1923, **68**: 517

Thomas Davies Jones, Jan. 4, 1924, **68**: 518; Jan. 25, 1924, **68**: 546 (not sent)

Albert Kaufman, Nov. 26, 1923, **68**: 486

Joseph Leland Kennedy, April 23, 1920, **65**: 220; Aug. 16, 1920, **66**: 38

Paul Bentley Kern, Jan. 17, 1922, **67**: 529

James Kerney, Jan. 15, 1922, **67**: 521; Oct. 30, 1923, **68**: 459; Dec. 13, 1923, **68**: 499; Jan. 5, 1924, **68**: 519

Philip Henry Kerr, May 27, 1923, **68**: 68

Albert W. Kette, Jan. 9, 1922, **67**: 510

William Fosgate Kirby, March 3, 1921, **67**: 198

Francis Klapus, Jan. 3, 1923, **68**: 263

Charles Zeller Klauder, Oct. 29, 1920, **66**: 291; Nov. 12, 1920, **66**: 354; Nov. 21, 1920, **66**: 410; Dec. 3, 1920, **66**: 458; Dec. 16, 1920, **66**: 518; Dec. 23, 1920, **66**: 543; Dec. 27, 1920, **67**: 7; Jan. 10, 1921, **67**: 47; Jan. 24, 1921, **67**: 86

Lucian Lamar Knight, July 8, 1922, **68**: 93

Arthur Bernard Krock, Dec. 4, 1920, **66**: 471; April 12, 1922, **68**: 14

Michael Kwapiszewski, Nov. 5, 1922, **68**: 177; Nov. 10, 1922, **68**: 183

The Most Reverend Paul Ladeuze, June 24, 1919, **61**: 129

Thomas William Lamont, Sept. 30, 1920, **66**: 170; Jan. 28, 1921, **67**: 96; July 4, 1921, **67**: 342

Anne Wintermute Lane, May 18, 1921, **67**: 284

George Lansbury, May 1, 1919, **58**: 317

Andrew Bonar Law, Oct. 26, 1922, **68**: 163; May 26, 1923, **68**: 366

Charles H. Leichliter, Sept. 15, 1922, **68**: 137

Benno Lewinson, July 7, 1921, **67**: 346

David John Lewis, July 12, 1922, **68**: 94

James Hamilton Lewis, Jan. 18, 1921, **67**: 70

Louis Lipsky, July 25, 1922, **68**: 100

David Lloyd George, Oct. 5, 1923, **68**: 445; Oct. 27, 1923, **68**: 457

Breckinridge Long, Feb. 25, 1921, **67**: 169; March 28, 1922, **67**: 578; April 4, 1922, **67**: 586; April 11, 1922, **68**: 12; Aug. 7, 1922, **68**: 105

Edgar Odell Lovett, July 27, 1920, **65**: 553; Nov. 26, 1920, **66**: 420; May 26, 1923, **68**: 366

Jorgen Gunnarsson Løvland and Ragnvald Moe, Dec. 14, 1920, **66**: 504

Kazimierz Lubomirski, Oct. 4, 1921, **67**: 400

Frederick Henry Lynch, Dec. 15, 1920, **66**: 512

Eleanor Randolph Wilson McAdoo, March 3, 1919, **55**: 395; Nov. 2, 1920, **66**: 302; Nov. 6, 1920, **66**: 332; March 7, 1922, **67**: 565; Dec. 12, 1922, **68**: 238; Dec. 23, 1923, **68**: 505

William Gibbs McAdoo, May 28, 1919, **59**: 575; Dec. 30, 1920, **67**: 14; Jan. 3, 1921, **67**: 22; June 14, 1922 (2), **68**: 75 (2); Sept. 7, 1922, **68**: 129; Oct. 4, 1922, **68**: 151; Dec. 12, 1922, **68**: 229; Dec. 26, 1922, **68**: 243; Jan. 8, 1923, **68**: 267; Feb. 14, 1923, **68**: 287; March 2, 1923, **68**: 293; Dec. 28, 1923, **68**: 510

William Gibbs McAdoo and Eleanor Randolph Wilson McAdoo, Feb. 26, 1919, **55**: 283
Charles Williston McAlpin, May 28, 1920, **65**: 333
James F. McCaleb, July 8, 1922, **68**: 93
William Faulkner McCombs, **57**: 157
Cyrus Hall McCormick, Jr., July 15, 1923, **68**: 391
Vance Criswell McCormick, June 16, 1921, **67**: 313; July 15, 1921, **67**: 351; April 3, 1922, **67**: 583
Walter Irving McCoy, June 29, 1921, **67**: 330
James Grover McDonald, April 2, 1923, **68**: 315
Katherine MacDonald, Jan. 18, 1922, **67**: 530
Charles Stedman Macfarland, Nov. 18, 1920, **66**: 387; Jan. 7, 1921, **67**: 32
Stephenson Waters McGill, Sept. 27, 1920, **66**: 151
William Douglas Mackenzie, June 22, 1923, **68**: 387
Catharine Milligan McLane, March 19, 1888, **63**: 623
Gavin McNab, Jan. 20, 1922, **67**: 532
Angus Wilton McLean, Nov. 28, 1922, **68**: 212
Richard Irving Manning, May 19, 1919, **59**: 276
Richard William Martin, June 24, 1919, **61**: 129
Thomas Staples Martin, July 16, 1919, **61**: 493
William Joseph Martin, Nov. 2, 1920, **66**: 301
Alice Garrigue Masaryk, April 18, 1923, **68**: 337
Thomas Garrigue Masaryk, May 19, 1923, **68**: 364; Nov. 23, 1923, **68**: 481
H. H. Maughirmalani, Aug. 8, 1919, **62**: 225
Franklin Randolph Mayer, Feb. 11, 1921, **67**: 128
Royal Meeker, June 14, 1922, **68**: 77
Alexander Meiklejohn, Dec. 22, 1920, **66**: 539; June 25, 1923, **68**: 388; July 5, 1923, **68**: 390
Marion Edmund Melvin, March 15, 1922, **67**: 567
Desiré-Félicien-François-Joseph Cardinal Mercier, June 24, 1919, **61**: 130; Sept. 11, 1919, **63**: 197
Edwin Thomas Meredith, June 29, 1921, **67**: 330; Aug. 10, 1921, **67**: 366
E. de Mohrenschildt, March 20, 1919, **56**: 125
Tom Moore, Aug. 12, 1921, **67**: 368
William Blackshear Moore, Aug. 1, 1919, **62**: 102
Moore-Cottrell Subscription Agencies, Oct. 13, 1923, **68**: 449
John Farwell Moors, Sept. 27, 1923, **68**: 430
Josephine Perry Morgan, May 20, 1908, **60**: 646
Henry Morgenthau, Nov. 9, 1918, **53**: 3
Christopher Darlington Morley, Dec. 8, 1921, **67**: 476; March 27, 1922, **67**: 575
Roland Sletor Morris, Feb. 26, 1921, **67**: 171
John R. Mott, Nov. 22, 1920, **66**: 411; Oct. 10, 1921, **67**: 413
Arthur Francis Mullen, June 14, 1921, **67**: 312
Gustavus Myers, April 3, 1923, **68**: 316

Fridtjof Nansen, Nov. 12, 1923, **68**: 472

The Norman Foster Company, Nov. 26, 1918, **53**: 205

Editor of the *New York Times*, April 12, 1922, **68**: 14

Chairman of the Nobel Peace Prize Committee, Jan. 7, 1923, **68**: 266

James Aloysius O'Gorman, June 25, 1921, **67**: 329

Isabella Sheldon Owen Osgood, Oct. 30, 1920, **66**: 293

Salomon Frederick van Oss, June 14, 1919, **60**: 566

Oscar Otto, Feb. 4, 1919, **54**: 473

Robert Latham Owen, Feb. 20, 1923, **68**: 290

Ignace Jan Paderewski, Dec. 23, 1923, **68**: 511

Alice Wilson Page, Dec. 24, 1918, **53**: 491

Thomas Nelson Page, June 4, 1919, **60**: 135; June 8, 1921, **67**: 307

Walter Hines Page, Nov. 26, 1918, **53**: 203

John Carver Palfrey, Feb. 14, 1903, **63**: 624

Alexander Mitchell Palmer, June 17, 1920, **65**: 425; Jan. 7, 1922, **67**: 506; March 27, 1923, **68**: 303

Frank Park, Sept. 20, 1920, **66**: 129

George Foster Peabody, Oct. 30, 1920, **66**: 293; Jan. 25, 1921, **67**: 91; Jan. 9, 1922, **67**: 510

Thomas Dowse Peck, March 22, 1909, **60**: 647

Bliss Perry, Nov. 18, 1920, **66**: 388

John Joseph Pershing, Dec. 23, 1918, **53**: 473; Oct. 15, 1920, **66**: 231; Dec. 27, 1923, **68**: 507

May Randolph Petty, Nov. 27, 1918, **53**: 221; July 25, 1919, **61**: 624

William Phillips, July 12, 1919, **61**: 462

Sir Horace Plunkett, Nov. 18, 1923, **68**: 478

Frank Lyon Polk, Oct. 28, 1920, **66**: 282; Nov. 2, 1920, **66**: 301

Donald C. Price, Jan. 4, 1922, **67**: 502

George Madison Priest, March 3, 1921, **67**: 198

Ralph Pulitzer, July 7, 1920, **65**: 501

The Very Reverend Hardwicke Drummond Rawnsley, March 22, 1919, **56**: 191; April 2, 1919, **56**: 553

Rector and Board of Visitors of the University of Virginia, May 30, 1921, **67**: 299

William Cox Redfield, July 12, 1919, **61**: 462; Feb. 11, 1923, **68**: 286; Dec. 31, 1923, **68**: 515

Edith Gittings Reid, Oct. 16, 1921, **67**: 423

James McDowell Richards, Dec. 8, 1921, **67**: 476

Clarence Self Ridley April 22, 1920, **65**: 219 (postscript), May 9, 1920, **65**: 262

Joseph Taylor Robinson, March 21, 1922, **67**: 569

(Anna) Eleanor Roosevelt Roosevelt, Nov. 11, 1921, **67**: 448

Edith Kermit Carow Roosevelt, Jan. 6, 1919, **53**: 625

Franklin Delano Roosevelt, March 23, 1921, **67**: 240; July 4, 1921, **67**: 341; Sept. 16, 1921, **67**: 392; Jan. 5, 1922, **67**: 504; May 1,

1922, **68**: 39; Dec. 28, 1922, **68**: 246; Jan. 29, 1923, **68**: 280; Dec. 30, 1923, **68**: 513

Daniel Calhoun Roper, Nov. 9, 1922, **68**: 180

Arthur Blythe Rouse, April 1, 1923, **68**: 314

Editor of the *St. Louis Daily Globe-Dispatch*, April 15, 1922, **68**: 24

Eleanor Axson Sayre, Jan. 3, 1921, **67**: 22; March 10, 1922, **67**: 566

Francis Bowes Sayre, Jr., Aug. 31, 1920, **66**: 79; March 10, 1922, **67**: 566; June, 14, 1922, **68**: 77

Jessie Woodrow Wilson Sayre, Nov. 13, 1918, **53**: 68; May 26, 1919, **59**: 526; Aug. 26, 1919, **62**: 516; Sept. 26, 1919, **63**: 521; Oct. 25, 1920, **66**: 266; Feb. 9, 1921, **67**: 125; March 12, 1921, **67**: 231; April 22, 1921, **67**: 267; Sept. 3, 1921, **67**: 385; Oct. 21, 1921, **67**: 428; Jan. 12, 1922, **67**: 519; Sept. 1, 1922, **68**: 122; Nov. 9, 1922, **68**: 180; April 28, 1923, **68**: 351; May 26, 1923, **68**: 366; Aug. 29, 1923, **68**: 412; Sept. 13, 1923, **68**: 422

Auguste Schaffner, March 18, 1919, **56**: 64

Loring Ashley Schuler, Nov. 12, 1920, **66**: 354

Jacob David Schwarz, Oct. 25, 1920, **66**: 265

Charles Prestwich Scott, May 6, 1919, **58**: 491

John W. Scott, April 6, 1921, **67**: 252

William Berryman Scott, Jan. 16, 1922, **67**: 525

Ellery Sedgwick, May 2, 1923, **68**: 354; May 19, 1923, **68**: 364; June 7, 1923, **68**: 374

Louis Seibold, June 14, 1921, **67**: 312; Nov. 12, 1921, **67**: 453; Feb. 5, 1923, **68**: 283; June 10, 1923, **68**: 384

Joseph Ramsey Sevier, Oct. 20, 1923, **68**: 450

William Graves Sharp, April 21, 1919, **57**: 559

Edward Wright Sheldon, Nov. 22, 1918, **53**: 167; Nov. 12, 1920, **66**: 354

Morris Sheppard, March 22, 1923, **68**: 298

Clarence Osborne Sherrill, June 21, 1921, **67**: 323

Charles Howard Shinn, Aug. 29, 1919, **62**: 554

Furnifold McLendel Simmons, Feb. 18, 1923, **68**: 289

Skandinaviska Kreditaktiebolaget, Aug. 6, 1921, **67**: 365

Joe Skidmore, Nov. 18, 1920, **66**: 387

Edmund Munroe Smith, Jan. 5, 1921, **67**: 29

Lucy Marshall Smith, July 19, 1919, **61**: 551

Norman Kemp Smith, Aug. 11, 1919, **62**: 251

Jan Christiaan Smuts, Feb. 9, 1921, **67**: 125; Oct. 1, 1923, **68**: 438

Thomas L. Snow, Feb. 26, 1919, **55**: 282; Oct. 22, 1920, **66**: 257; Nov. 8, 1920, **66**: 338

John Spargo, July 12, 1919, **61**: 463; Nov. 5, 1920, **66**: 325; Jan. 17, 1922, **67**: 529

Charles Millard Starbird, May 7, 1921, **67**: 280

Lawrence Vest Stephens, April 27, 1922, **68**: 35; Oct. 27, 1922, **68**: 166

Harold F. Strong, Feb. 1, 1922, **67**: 539

Duane Reed Stuart, July 27, 1922, **68**: 101

Robert Cummins Stuart, Jr., Nov. 20, 1920, **66**: 409; April 8, 1921, **67**: 254

Helen Marie Quinlan Sullivan, April 15, 1920, **65**: 189

Claude Augustus Swanson, Oct. 10, 1921, **67**: 412; Sept. 25, 1922, **68**: 143; Nov. 4, 1923, **68**: 463

William Ellery Sweet, March 26, 1923, **68**: 301

Charles Lee Swem, March 3, 1921, **67**: 197

Herbert Bayard Swope, Oct. 22, 1920, **66**: 257

Helen Herron Taft, March 13, 1920, **65**: 83

William Howard Taft, March 30, 1922, **67**: 580

Frances L. Talcott, March 2, 1920, **65**: 36

Ida Minerva Tarbell, March 29, 1921, **67**: 247; Feb. 26, 1922, **67**: 557; March 7, 1922, **67**: 565

James Henry Taylor, July 25, 1919, **61**: 624; Nov. 5, 1921, **67**: 442; June 3, 1923, **68**: 370

Rudolf Bolling Teusler, Sept. 16, 1923, **68**: 424

Frederick Ingate Thompson, Aug. 18, 1922, **68**: 116; Oct. 28, 1922, **68**: 167; Nov. 4, 1922, **68**: 175

Samuel Huston Thompson, Jr., Dec. 31, 1923, **68**: 515

Katrina Brandes Ely Tiffany, April 5, 1922, **67**: 587

McLane Tilton, Dec. 27, 1921, **67**: 495; Feb. 28, 1922, **67**: 559

Nancy Saunders Toy, March 3, 1921, **67**: 198; Jan. 13, 1922, **67**: 520; Jan. 19, 1922, **67**: 531; Feb. 13, 1922, **67**: 543

Kate Nichols Trask, Jan. 27, 1921, **67**: 95

South Trimble, Nov. 26, 1920, **66**: 421

Joseph Patrick Tumulty, Jan. 17, 1919, **54**: 125; March 3, 1919, **55**: 392; April 29, 1919, **58**: 243; May 29, 1919, **59**: 604; Feb. 9, 1921, **67**: 126; Sept. 3, 1921, **67**: 385; April 6, 1922, **67**: 602; April 10, 1922, **68**: 10

Henry Allen Tupper, May 12, 1920, **65**: 275

Lyon Gardiner Tyler, Sept. 23, 1919, **63**: 463

Oscar Wilder Underwood, June 21, 1921, **67**: 323

Henry van Dyke, Nov. 3, 1923, **68**: 462

Eleuthéiros Kyrios Vénisélos, April 15, 1922, **68**: 23

Ambrose White Vernon, Oct. 28, 1923, **68**: 458

Williamson Updike Vreeland, Jan. 15, 1922, **67**: 524

Charles Doolittle Walcott, March 19, 1920, **65**: 105; Dec. 4, 1920, **66**: 471

Hugh Campbell Wallace, July 25, 1919, **61**: 624

Charles Warren, Jan. 15, 1900, **63**: 623

Schuyler Nielson Warren, Jr., Oct. 26, 1922, **68**: 163

Editor of the *Washington Post*, April 15, 1922, **68**: 24

Charles R. Webster, Jan. 25, 1924, **68**: 546 (not sent)

James Edwin Webster, May 9, 1920, **65**: 262; Dec. 22, 1921, **67**: 493

Robert S. Weeks, July 7, 1920, **65**: 501
Charles W. Weiser, May 7, 1921, **67**: 279
Thomas Bucklin Wells, Sept. 30, 1920, **66**: 171; July 27, 1923, **68**: 392
John Howell Westcott, Nov. 19, 1918, **53**: 129; Dec. 27, 1921, **67**: 495
Howard Duryee Wheeler, March 18, 1919, **56**: 63
Brand Whitlock, June 10, 1919, **60**: 360; June 25, 1919, **61**: 172
To Whom It May Concern (letter of recommendation for Arthur Brooks), April 28, 1921, **67**: 273
To Whom It May Concern (letter of introduction for John R. Mott), Jan. 9, 1924, **68**: 526
Charlotte D. Wilbur, Jan. 25, 1921, **67**: 91
Louis Wiley, Nov. 8, 1920, **66**: 338
John Sharp Williams, July 12, 1919, **61**: 462; Nov. 15, 1920, **66**: 368; Nov. 14, 1921, **67**: 455; Jan. 12, 1922, **67**: 518; March 2, 1923, **68**: 293
John Skelton Williams, Aug. 17, 1920, **66**: 39; Aug. 18, 1920, **66**: 42
Edith Bolling Galt Wilson, May 14, 1920, **65**: 287; Feb. 14, 1921, **67**: 133; Aug. 17, 1921, **67**: 371; Feb. 15, 1922, **67**: 545; Feb. 16, 1923, **68**: 288; Aug. 28, 1923, **68**: 411; Aug. 29, 1923, **68**: 412; Aug. 30, 1923, **68**: 413; Aug. 31, 1923, **68**: 415; Oct. 20, 1923, **68**: 450
Edwin Clinton Wilson, June 22, 1923, **68**: 387
Margaret Woodrow Wilson, Jan. 30, 1919, **54**: 410; Dec. 12, 1921, **67**: 483; June 21, 1923 (2), **68**: 386 (2); July 15, 1923, **68**: 391; Sept. 23, 1923, **68**: 427; Nov. 17, 1923, **68**: 478
William Bauchop Wilson, Oct. 13, 1920, **66**: 228
Announcement of Wilson's marriage to Edith Bolling Galt, Dec. 4, 1915, **63**: 624
Stephen Samuel Wise, Dec. 17, 1921, **67**: 490; Jan. 22, 1922, **67**: 533; July 12, 1922, **68**: 94
Felexiana Shepherd Baker Woodrow, Dec. 31, 1920, **67**: 16
Marion Woodrow, Feb. 26, 1921, **67**: 171
Lawrence Crane Woods, Dec. 1, 1920, **66**: 447
William Woodward, Oct. 4, 1920, **66**: 185
Robert Wickliffe Woolley, Nov. 5, 1920, **66**: 325; Dec. 14, 1920, **66**: 505

Emily Chapman Martin Yates, Sept. 23, 1923, **68**: 428
Frederic Yates, Feb. 26, 1919, **55**: 282

To Wilson from

Albert, King of the Belgians, June 30, 1919, **61**: 355; Sept. 29, 1919, **63**: 535
Edwin Anderson Alderman, Oct. 17, 1920, **66**: 234; April 19, 1921, **67**: 262; May 22, 1921, **67**: 287; Dec. 29, 1921, **67**: 498
Joshua Willis Alexander, March 3, 1921, **67**: 201

American Historical Association, Jan. 25, 1922, **67**: 534
George Weston Anderson, Oct. 6, 1921, **67**: 405; Jan. 9, 1922, **67**: 511
Herbert Henry Asquith, Dec. 29, 1918, **53**: 542

Newton Diehl Baker, Nov. 11, 1918, **53**: 46; Aug. 21, 1919, **62**: 437; July 7, 1920, **65**: 502; Nov. 3, 1920, **66**: 312; Dec. 24, 1920, **67**: 3; March 4, 1921, **67**: 215; May 29, 1921, **67**: 295; Dec. 22, 1921, **67**: 493; Sept. 13, 1922, **68**: 136; Oct. 26, 1922, **68**: 164; Nov. 23, 1923, **68**: 484; Dec. 23, 1923, **68**: 505
Ray Stannard Baker, Dec. 16, 1920, **66**: 521; Dec. 23, 1920, **66**: 544; Dec. 30, 1920, **67**: 15; Jan. 24, 1921, **67**: 89; Dec. 16, 1921, **67**: 488; Aug. 11, 1922, **68**: 108; Nov. 20, 1922, **68**: 200; Dec. 14, 1922, **68**: 232; Feb. 1, 1923, **68**: 281; March 31, 1923, **68**: 312; May 7, 1923 (2), **68**: 357, 358; Aug. 10, 1923, **68**: 402; Nov. 23, 1923, **68**: 482; Dec. 10, 1923, **68**: 495; Dec. 26, 1923, **68**: 506; Jan. 7, 1924, **68**: 522; Jan. 15, 1924, **68**: 530
Emily Greene Balch, Jan. 9, 1921, **67**: 42
Arthur James Balfour, Aug. 16, 1919, **62**: 331
Bernard Mannes Baruch, Nov. 26, 1918, **53**: 209; Dec. 3, 1918, **53**: 309; Oct. 28, 1920, **66**: 288; Nov. 6, 1920, **66**: 336; Dec. 16, 1920, **66**: 525; May 18, 1921, **67**: 284; Aug. 10, 1921, **67**: 366; Aug. 13, 1922, **68**: 109; Nov. 14, 1922, **68**: 190; April 19, 1923, **68**: 341; May 11, 1923, **68**: 362; June, 6, 1923, **68**: 373; Aug. 17, 1923, **68**: 406; Sept. 29, 1923, **68**: 433; Oct. 24, 1923, **68**: 453
John Spencer Bassett, Jan. 10, 1922, **67**: 514; Oct. 31, 1923, **68**: 460; Jan. 2, 1924, **68**: 516
Sylvester Woodbridge Beach, Nov. 9, 1920, **66**: 344; Feb. 7, 1921, **67**: 123; May 22, 1921, **67**: 287; May 1, 1923, **68**: 352
Robert Jacob Bender, March 13, 1921, **67**: 232
Eduard Beneš and Karl (Karel) Kramář, June 24, 1919, **61**: 136
William Shepherd Benson, April 21, 1919, **57**: 579
Martha McChesney Berry, Nov. 14, 1921, **67**: 456; Jan. 4, 1922, **67**: 503
Anita Eugenie McCormick Blaine, March 4, 1919, **55**: 440; Feb. 15, 1922, **67**: 545
Emily Jane Newell Blair, Oct. 17, 1922, **68**: 156
Tasker Howard Bliss, May 27, 1920, **65**: 331; Sept. 15, 1921, **67**: 391; Dec. 4, 1922, **68**: 222
Edward William Bok, Aug. 13, 1920, **66**: 31; Sept. 20, 1920, **66**: 131; Nov. 18, 1920, **66**: 386; Dec. 3, 1920, **66**: 456; Jan. 19, 1921, **67**: 72; March 9, 1921, **67**: 230; Jan. 25, 1922, **67**: 535; Nov. 1, 1922, **68**: 169; Nov. 3, 1922, **68**: 172
Evangeline Cory Booth, Dec. 24, 1920, **67**: 4
William Edgar Borah, Feb. 18, 1922, **67**: 548
Isaiah Bowman, Oct. 6, 1921, **67**: 404
Cyrus Towne Brady, Aug. 23, 1919, **62**: 479
Louis Dembitz Brandeis, Nov. 11, 1918, **53**: 46; Dec. 28, 1921, **67**: 497; Jan. 25, 1923, **68**: 277; Jan. 25, 1923, **68**: 279

Robert Bridges, June 16, 1919, **60**: 610; March 28, 1922, **67**: 578
Robert Bridges and Others, May 31, 1921, **67**: 300
Marjorie Brown, Dec. 13, 1920, **66**: 503
William Jennings Bryan, Aug. 23, 1923, **68**: 407
Elizabeth, Lady Bryce, Feb. 24, 1922, **67**: 556
Albert Sidney Burleson, Sept. 29, 1919, **63**: 534; March 1, 1921,
     67: 181

Cabinet members, March 3, 1921, **67**: 199
Henry Seidel Canby, July 20, 1919, **61**: 568
David Carb, March 30, 1919, **56**: 432
Andrew Carnegie, Nov. 10, 1918, **53**: 32
Louise Whitfield Carnegie, Aug. 13, 1919, **62**: 271
Lord Robert Cecil, July 1, 1920, **65**: 483; March 29, 1923, **68**: 306;
     Oct. 20, 1923, **68**: 450
Benjamin Bright Chambers, Aug. 31, 1919, **62**: 601
Children's Delegation, Nov. 11, 1921, **67**: 453
Elmer Talmadge Clark, Oct. 9, 1920, **66**: 213
John Hessin Clarke, Sept. 9, 1922, **68**: 130; Sept. 21, 1922, **68**: 139;
     Sept. 25, 1922, **68**: 143; Nov. 10, 1922, **68**: 184; Jan. 17, 1923, **68**:
     275; Feb. 1, 1923, **68**: 281; April 11, 1923, **68**: 332; May 8, 1923,
     68: 359
Georges Clemenceau, Nov. 19, 1922, **68**: 198; Dec. 15, 1922, **68**:
     234
Gilbert Fairchild Close, Jan. 12, 1922, **67**: 519
John Firman Coar, Aug. 10, 1921, **67**: 367
Frank Irving Cobb, March 4, 1921, **67**: 216; March 17, 1921, **67**:
     234; Oct. 17, 1921, **67**: 424; Nov. 8, 1921, **67**: 447; Jan. 9, 1922,
     67: 511; Jan. 16, 1922, **67**: 528; Jan. 19, 1922, **67**: 531; July 20,
     1922, **68**: 99; July 25, 1922, **68**: 100; Aug. 1, 1922, **68**: 104; Nov.
     15, 1922, **68**: 195; March 31, 1923, **68**: 308; June 13, 1923, **68**:
     385; Aug. 7, 1923, **68**: 400
Margaret Hubbard Ayer Cobb, Dec. 27, 1923, **68**: 508
Henry Waldo Coe, March 27, 1922, **67**: 577
John Knox Coit, July 29, 1919, **62**: 42
Bainbridge Colby, Nov. 3, 1920, **66**: 313; Dec. 25, 1920, **67**: 6; Jan.
     27, 1921, **67**: 95; Jan. 31, 1921, **67**: 107; Feb. 22, 1921, **67**: 160;
     March 29, 1921, **67**: 248; April 13, 1921, **67**: 256; April 18, 1921,
     67: 261; May 5, 1921, **67**: 277; June 2, 1921, **67**: 301; June 16,
     1921, **67**: 313; June 20, 1921, **67**: 320; June 29, 1921, **67**: 331;
     July 1, 1921, **67**: 338; July 2, 1921, **67**: 340; July 8, 1921, **67**: 347;
     July 16, 1921, **67**: 354; Aug. 26, 1921, **67**: 379; Aug. 27, 1921, **67**:
     382; Sept. 3, 1921, **67**: 386; Oct. 4, 1921, **67**: 401; Oct. 14, 1921,
     67: 420; Oct. 31, 1921, **67**: 437; Dec. 5, 1921, **67**: 472; Feb. 19,
     1922, **67**: 549; Feb. 23, 1922, **67**: 554; March 2, 1922, **67**: 561;
     March 22, 1922, **67**: 571; April 6, 1922, **67**: 602; May 19, 1922,
     68: 56; June 19, 1922, **68**: 81; Aug. 14, 1922, **68**: 110; Aug. 20,
     1922, **68**: 118; Aug. 22, 1922, **68**: 119; Sept. 2, 1922, **68**: 125;
     Sept. 12, 1922, **68**: 134; Sept. 23, 1922, **68**: 140; Oct. 8, 1922, **68**:

54   CONTENTS

152; Nov. 20, 1922, **68**: 199; Nov. 27, 1922, **68**: 211; Dec. 1, 1922, **68**: 214; Dec. 18, 1922, **68**: 238; Feb. 20, 1923, **68**: 290

George Grouse Cook, Nov. 13, 1920, **66**: 366

Calvin Coolidge, June 19, 1922, **68**: 80; Aug. 4, 1923, **68**: 399

Joe Cowperthwaite, Sept. 22, 1920, **66**: 134

James Middleton Cox, Sept. 4, 1923, **68**: 419; Nov. 13, 1923, **68**: 473

Charles Richard Crane, April 13, 1920, **65**: 185

Elijah Richardson Craven, June 27, 1894, **65**: 572; June 21, 1895, **65**: 572

Vernon Allen Crawford, Dec. 17, 1923, **68**: 500

George Creel, March 12, 1921, **67**: 231; Aug. 27, 1923, **68**: 408

Homer Stillé Cummings, Nov. 28, 1918, **53**: 242; Dec. 20, 1920, **66**: 536; July 15, 1922, **68**: 97

Lord Curzon, Feb. 12, 1919, **55**: 116

Harvey Williams Cushing, May 12, 1920, **65**: 283

Richard Heath Dabney, Oct. 28, 1920, **66**: 289

Josephus Daniels, April 14, 1919, **57**: 331; Aug. 21, 1920, **66**: 58; March 5, 1921, **67**: 229

Martin Luther Davey, April 8, 1921, **67**: 254

Edward Parker Davis, Nov. 28, 1918, **53**: 243; May 26, 1922, **68**: 65

Ellen Duane Davis, Feb. 25, 1919, **55**: 265; Aug. 14, 1919, **62**: 303; Nov. 15, 1921, **67**: 458; Dec. 11, 1921, **67**: 481

Norman Hezekiah Davis, July 11, 1919, **61**: 457; Nov. 3, 1920, **66**: 314; Dec. 8, 1920, **66**: 492; Dec. 14, 1920, **66**: 507; Dec. 23, 1920, **66**: 543; Jan. 29, 1922, **67**: 538; Feb. 2, 1922, **67**: 540; Feb. 3, 1922, **67**: 541; Feb. 14, 1922, **67**: 544; Feb. 22, 1922, **67**: 551; June 23, 1922, **68**: 84; Nov. 9, 1922, **68**: 181; Nov. 15, 1922, **68**: 193; Dec. 28, 1922, **68**: 252; Dec. 30, 1922, **68**: 261; Jan. 11, 1923, **68**: 273; Jan. 25, 1923, **68**: 277; April 9, 1923, **68**: 326; April 19, 1923, **68**: 339; Nov. 2, 1923, **68**: 461; Nov. 4, 1923, **68**: 463; Nov. 11, 1923, **68**: 471; Nov. 26, 1923, **68**: 486; Dec. 10, 1923, **68**: 497; Jan. 7, 1924, **68**: 520; Jan. 15, 1924, **68**: 530

Harry Kent Day, Oct. 15, 1920, **66**: 232

William Delahunty, Aug. 2, 1919, **62**: 122

Frederic Adrian Delano, May 31, 1919, **59**: 642

Francis Xavier Dercum, Dec. 21, 1921, **67**: 492

Joseph Tyrone Derry, Jan. 2, 1924, **68**: 516

Leon Dessez, Jan. 10, 1922, **67**: 514

Goldsworthy Lowes Dickinson, May 20, 1919, **59**: 316

Armistead Mason Dobie, May 7, 1921, **67**: 281

William Edward Dodd, Feb. 22, 1921, **67**: 161; Nov. 8, 1921, **67**: 446; Sept. 3, 1922, **68**: 126; Dec. 29, 1922, **68**: 258

Cleveland Hoadley Dodge, Nov. 11, 1918, **53**: 46; Sept. 29, 1919, **63**: 535; Nov. 8, 1920, **66**: 340; Aug. 18, 1921, **67**: 373; Dec. 1, 1921, **67**: 470; Feb. 22, 1921, **67**: 551; May 25, 1922, **68**: 64; Aug. 16, 1922, **68**: 115; Nov. 15, 1922, **68**: 192; Oct. 2, 1923, **68**: 441; Nov. 9, 1923, **68**: 465; Dec. 10, 1923, **68**: 497

Cleveland Hoadley Dodge and Jesse Holman Jones, Oct. 2, 1923,
  68: 441
Sir Eric Drummond, Sept. 7, 1923, **68**: 420
Jessie Kennedy Dyer, Aug. 31, 1920, **66**: 80; Dec. 13, 1920, **66**: 503
Henry van Dyke, Nov. 10, 1920, **66**: 347
John Foster Dulles, June 28, 1919, **61**: 349
Edward Fitzsimons Dunne, June 12, 1919, **60**: 487

Edward, Prince of Wales, April 24, 1920, **65**: 226
Edward Irving Edwards, Dec. 10, 1921, **67**: 480; Dec. 15, 1921, **67**:
  487
Charles William Eliot, March 12, 1921, **67**: 231
Abram Isaac Elkus, April 20, 1921, **67**: 266
Oscar Ross Ewing, Nov. 18, 1920, **66**: 391

Prince Faisal, July 12, 1919, **61**: 467
Mary Fels Fels, Oct. 26, 1920, **66**: 272
Edward Albert Filene, Nov. 22, 1921, **67**: 461
Henry Burchard Fine, Aug. 1, 1922, **68**: 103
Raymond Blaine Fosdick, Jan. 24, 1921, **67**: 87; Jan. 28, 1921, **67**:
  96; April 25, 1922, **68**: 34; Nov. 27, 1923, **68**: 492
George A. Foster, Aug. 28, 1920, **66**: 71
Glenn Frank, May 29, 1923 (2), **68**: 367 (2)
James Edward Freeman, July 27, 1923, **68**: 395; Sept. 25, 1923,
  68: 429
Ernst Freund, March 29, 1921, **67**: 247
Alfred Hermann Fried, Dec. 16, 1920, **66**: 523
William Goodell Frost and Eleanor Marsh Frost, Dec. 6, 1920, **66**:
  483

Helen Hamilton Gardener, Oct. 30, 1920, **66**: 297
Harry Augustus Garfield, July 29, 1919, **62**: 42; Nov. 2, 1920, **66**:
  305
Finis James Garrett, Oct. 27, 1923, **68**: 457
Elbert Henry Gary, July 8, 1919, **61**: 407
George V, Jan. 20, 1919, **54**: 170; June 3, 1919, **60**: 101
James Watson Gerard, Sept. 29, 1919, **63**: 535; Sept. 28, 1923, **68**:
  431; Dec. 21, 1923, **68**: 504; Jan. 29, 1924, **68**: 547
Carter Glass, June 6, 1919, **60**: 247; Dec. 8, 1920, **66**: 494; Sept. 6,
  1921, **67**: 388; May 23, 1922, **68**: 61; June 16, 1922, **68**: 78; Nov.
  17, 1923, **68**: 478
Lionel Golub, April 27, 1921, **67**: 271
William Elliott Gonzales, Nov. 14, 1923, **68**: 475
Mary Owen Graham, Nov. 10, 1918, **53**: 31
Kent Roberts Greenfield, Nov. 3, 1920, **66**: 314
H. J. Gregory-Allen, Nov. 15, 1920, **66**: 379
Henri Gressitt, Sept. 10, 1920, **66**: 112
Solomon Bulkley Griffin, Nov. 28, 1918, **53**: 241; Oct. 7, 1920, **66**:
  208

Granville Stanley Hall, Oct. 28, 1920, **66**: 290

Charles Sumner Hamlin, Sept. 4, 1923, **68**: 418; Sept. 19, 1923, **68**: 425; Oct. 5, 1923, **68**: 446; Dec. 28, 1923, **68**: 511

Sir Maurice Hankey, Aug. 28, 1919, **62**: 547; Nov. 23, 1921, **67**: 462

Norman Hapgood, Aug. 12, 1920, **66**: 28

Florence Mabel Kling DeWolfe Harding, Aug. 25, 1923, **68**: 407

Warren Gamaliel Harding, Oct. 4, 1921, **67**: 400; Nov. 8, 1921, **67**: 445; Oct. 9, 1922, **68**: 152

William Procter Gould Harding, Aug. 15, 1923, **68**: 405

George McLean Harper, June 17, 1920, **65**: 425; Oct. 8, 1921, **67**: 410

Charles Homer Haskins, June 8, 1919, **60**: 295; Jan. 3, 1921, **67**: 24

Azel Washburn Hazen, May 7, 1920, **65**: 251

Edith Benham Helm, Dec. 5, 1921, **67**: 477; Nov. 23, 1923, **68**: 481

Robert Randolph Henderson, May 5, 1921, **67**: 277

Stanislaus Vincent Henkels, July 28, 1921, **67**: 358

Israel Herman, Sept. 6, 1921, **67**: 388

Walker Downer Hines, Jan. 27, 1921, **67**: 93

Hamilton Holt, July 8, 1920, **65**: 504; July 15, 1920, **65**: 513; March 2, 1921, **67**: 187; April 22, 1921, **67**: 267; May 4, 1922, **68**: 44; Nov. 3, 1922, **68**: 172; Nov. 14, 1922, **68**: 190; Jan. 4, 1923, **68**: 264; Feb. 7, 1923, **68**: 284; Feb. 16, 1923, **68**: 288

Edward Mandell House, May 30, 1919, **59**: 610; Sept. 29, 1919, **63**: 536; March 8, 1920, **65**: 75; June 7, 1920, **65**: 379; Oct. 29, 1920, **66**: 292

David Franklin Houston, March 3, 1921, **67**: 199; May 24, 1922, **68**: 62; Jan. 11, 1923, **68**: 269

Herbert Sherman Houston, Oct. 10, 1921, **67**: 414; Oct. 28, 1921, **63**: 433; April 10, 1923, **68**: 330; April 19, 1923, **68**: 336; May 2, 1923, **68**: 355

Sid Houston, May 5, 1921, **67**: 278

Cordell Hull, Oct. 16, 1921, **67**: 423; May 5, 1922, **68**: 49; May 25, 1922, **68**: 63; May 27, 1922, **68**: 70; June 26, 1922, **68**: 85; July 14, 1922, **68**: 95; Oct. 12, 1922, **68**: 154; Nov. 10, 1922, **68**: 183; Dec. 15, 1922, **68**: 235

Thornwell Jacobs, March 15, 1920, **65**: 86; March 16, 1920, **65**: 89; June 8, 1920, **65**: 381

Charles Samuel Jackson, June 18, 1920, **65**: 431

Peter Augustus Jay, June 17, 1920, **65**: 426

John Franklin Jameson, Dec. 3, 1920, **66**: 467; May 12, 1922, **68**: 53; May 26, 1922, **68**: 65

Ben Johnson, Jan. 10, 1921, **67**: 513

Douglas Wilson Johnson, Jan. 12, 1921, **67**: 57; Jan. 3, 1921, **67**: 501

Evangeline Brewster Johnson, Oct. 23, 1923, **68**: 452

James Weldon Johnson, March 22, 1921, **67**: 570

Edgar DeWitt Jones, Jan. 4, 1921, **67**: 503

Jesse Holman Jones, Dec. 4, 1920, **66**: 474; Feb. 21, 1921, **67**: 152;
     Oct. 5, 1921, **67**: 402; Oct. 2, 1923, **68**: 440; Jan. 9, 1924, **68**: 526
Thomas Davies Jones, Jan. 23, 1924, **68**: 545

Albert Kaufman, Nov. 25, 1923, **68**: 485
Joseph Leland Kennedy, April 19, 1920, **65**: 211
James Kerney, Oct. 31, 1923, **68**: 460; Nov. 3, 1923, **68**: 462; Dec.
     12, 1923, **68**: 498; Jan. 5, 1924, **68**: 519
Charles Zeller Klauder, Nov. 2, 1920, **66**: 305; Nov. 9, 1920, **66**:
     344; Nov. 19, 1920, **66**: 393; Dec. 3, 1920, **66**: 470; Dec. 14, 1920,
     66: 510; Dec. 18, 1920, **66**: 534; Dec. 23, 1920, **66**: 545; Jan. 6,
     1921, **67**: 30; Jan. 22, 1921, **67**: 84; Feb. 14, 1921, **67**: 136; May
     3, 1921, **67**: 276
William Fosgate Kirby, March 1, 1921, **67**: 183
Richard Gillmore Knott, Nov. 23, 1923, **68**: 483
Arthur Bernard Krock, Dec. 1, 1920, **66**: 450

Florence Haskell Corliss Lamont, July 2, 1919, **61**: 369
Thomas William Lamont, Sept. 28, 1920, **66**: 163; Jan. 20, 1921,
     67: 74; Feb. 1, 1921, **67**: 110
Robert Lansing, May 9, 1919, **58**: 601
Eleanor Foster Lansing, Jan. 1, 1918, **53**: 584
Andrew Bonar Law, Oct. 26, 1922, **68**: 163; May 26, 1923, **68**: 366
James Hamilton Lewis, Jan. 13, 1921, **67**: 58
David Lloyd George, Oct. 9, 1923, **68**: 446
Sophie Irene Simon Loeb, Nov. 27, 1923, **68**: 492
Håkon Löken and Others, Dec. 31, 1921, **67**: 17
Breckinridge Long, Feb. 23, 1921, **67**: 164
Edgar Odell Lovett, March 20, 1921, **67**: 235; May 19, 1923, **68**:
     365
Jørgen Gunnarsson Løvland and Ragnvald Moe, Dec. 13, 1920, **66**:
     501
Kazimierz Lubomirski, Sept. 16, 1921, **67**: 392
Alfred Lucking, June 18, 1921, **67**: 316
Frederick Henry Lynch, Dec. 13, 1920, **66**: 502
Maurice F. Lyons, June 4, 1921, **67**: 304

Eleanor Randolph Wilson McAdoo and William Gibbs McAdoo,
     Feb. 17, 1919, **55**: 204; Nov. 3, 1920, **66**: 315; Dec. 25, 1921, **67**:
     5; Oct. 21, 1921, **67**: 429; March 2, 1921, **67**: 562; Dec. 28, 1922,
     68: 254
William Gibbs McAdoo, May 12, 1919, **59**: 77; Nov. 4, 1920, **66**:
     318; June 2, 1922, **68**: 72; Sept. 1, 1922, **68**: 122; Sept. 28, 1922,
     68: 145; Oct. 11, 1922, **68**: 153; Dec. 2, 1922, **68**: 221; Dec. 19,
     1922, **68**: 239; Dec. 30, 1922, **68**: 260; Feb. 24, 1923, **68**: 291; May
     16, 1923, **68**: 363; Oct. 9, 1923, **68**: 446; Oct. 31, 1923, **68**: 460;
     Dec. 20, 1923, **68**: 503; Jan. 18, 1924, **68**: 532
Charles Williston McAlpin, May 26, 1920, **65**: 327; Nov. 5, 1921,
     67: 441

Vance Criswell McCormick, July 17, 1919, **61**: 513
Charles Stedman Macfarland, Nov. 15, 1920, **66**: 378; Jan. 5, 1921,
    67: 29
Stephenson Waters McGill, Sept. 22, 1920, **66**: 134
Frank LeRond McVey, Jan. 27, 1922, **67**: 536; Jan. 28, 1922, **67**:
    537
Richard Irving Manning, May 17, 1919, **59**: 243
William Joseph Martin, Oct. 30, 1920, **66**: 296
Alice Garrigue Masaryk, March 20, 1923, **68**: 296
Thomas Garrigue Masaryk, June 21, 1923, **68**: 386
Franklin Randolph Mayer, Feb. 8, 1921, **67**: 124; Feb. 18, 1921, **67**:
    146
Alexander Meiklejohn, Dec. 5, 1920, **66**: 478; July 2, 1923, **68**: 389;
    Sept. 27, 1923, **68**: 430
Edwin Thomas Meredith, March 3, 1921, **67**: 200; Aug. 6, 1921, **67**:
    365
Desiré-Félicien-François-Joseph Cardinal Mercier, Sept. 10, 1919,
    63: 166; Oct. 3, 1919, **63**: 549
Edwin Thomas Meredith, Nov. 4, 1920, **66**: 318
Edwin Young Mitchell, Aug. 7, 1922, **68**: 105
John Farwell Moors, Sept. 23, 1923, **68**: 427
Henry Morgenthau, Jan. 8, 1923, **68**: 268
Christopher Darlington Morley, March 24, 1922, **67**: 573
Roland Sletor Morris, Feb. 26, 1921, **67**: 170
John R. Mott, Oct. 7, 1921, **67**: 407; Oct. 14, 1921, **67**: 422
Arthur Francis Mullen, June 20, 1921, **67**: 321; June 22, 1921, **67**:
    325; July 11, 1921, **67**: 349
Gustavus Myers, March 31, 1923, **68**: 313

Fridtjof Nansen, Nov. 11, 1923, **68**: 467
The Norman Foster Company, Nov. 21, 1918, **53**: 159
Frank Mason North, Jan. 11, 1919, **53**: 718

William Cardinal O'Connell, Dec. 1, 1918, **53**: 274
John Kelso Ormond, June 29, 1921, **67**: 335
Sir William Orpen, May 20, 1919, **59**: 315
Charles Grosvenor Osgood, Oct. 27, 1920, **66**: 280
Isabella Sheldon Owen Osgood, Oct. 25, 1920, **66**: 268
Robert Latham Owen, Feb. 18, 1923, **68**: 289

Ignace Jan Paderewski, Dec. 27, 1921, **67**: 496; Dec. 27, 1923, **68**:
    507
Thomas Nelson Page, May 5, 1919, **58**: 448; May 26, 1919, **59**: 517;
    June 9, 1919, **60**: 327; June 18, 1919, **61**: 9
Walter Hines Page, Nov. 23, 1918, **53**: 189
Alexander Mitchell Palmer, June 18, 1920, **65**: 431; March 23,
    1923, **68**: 299
Frank Park, Sept. 16, 1920, **66**: 117
John Barton Payne, March 4, 1921, **67**: 215

George Foster Peabody, Oct. 27, 1920, **66**: 280; March 1, 1921, **67**: 183; Jan. 9, 1922, **67**: 510
Bliss Perry, Nov. 15, 1920, **66**: 378
John Joseph Pershing, Dec. 18, 1918, **53**: 432; Dec. 17, 1923, **68**: 500
May Randolph Petty and Calvin H. Petty, July 19, 1919, **61**: 543
William Phillips, July 8, 1919, **61**: 407
Sir Horace Plunkett, Nov. 9, 1923, **68**: 464
Donald C. Price, Jan. 2, 1922, **67**: 499
George Madison Priest, March 1, 1921, **67**: 181
The Princeton Class of 1879, June 16, 1919, **60**: 610
Princeton University faculty members, March 1, 1921, **67**: 182
William Edmund Pulsifer, July 12, 1920, **65**: 509

The Very Reverend Hardwicke Drummond Rawnsley, March 2, 1919, **55**: 387; March 26, 1919, **56**: 310; April 7, 1919, **57**: 98
William Cox Redfield, Feb. 10, 1923, **68**: 285; Dec. 27, 1923, **68**: 508
Clarence Self Ridley, May 7, 1920, **65**: 258; March 2, 1921, **67**: 187
Francis H. Robinson, Feb. 26, 1921, **67**: 172
Joseph Taylor Robinson, March 27, 1922, **67**: 577
Lindsay Rogers, June 5, 1921, **67**: 305
Franklin Delano Roosevelt, March 23, 1921, **67**: 239; June 3, 1921, **67**: 302; June 19, 1921, **67**: 333; July 7, 1921, **67**: 346; July 28, 1921, **67**: 357; Dec. 28, 1921, **67**: 497; April 28, 1922, **68**: 36; Dec. 27, 1922 (2), **68**: 245 (2); Dec. 28, 1922, **68**: 246; April 4, 1923, **68**: 319; Dec. 28, 1923, **68**: 511
Franklin Delano Roosevelt, Cleveland Hoadley Dodge, and Hamilton Holt, April 6, 1922, **67**: 603
Daniel Calhoun Roper, Nov. 8, 1922, **68**: 179
George Roth, Nov. 30, 1918, **53**: 261
Arthur Blythe Rouse, March 29, 1923, **68**: 306

Eleanor Axson Sayre, Jan. 3, 1921, **67**: 18
Francis Bowes Sayre, Feb. 23, 1919, **55**: 234
Francis Bowes Sayre, Jr., Aug. 30, 1920, **66**: 75
Jessie Woodrow Wilson Sayre, Nov. 9, 1918, **53**: 21; Nov. 26, 1918, **53**: 212; Dec. 18, 1918, **53**: 436; Jan. 16, 1919, **54**: 107; Feb. 19, 1919, **55**: 216; May 4, 1919, **58**: 428; Sept. 10, 1919, **63**: 166; Nov. 5, 1920, **66**: 329; Dec. 18, 1920, **66**: 534; Jan. 31, 1921, **67**: 107; March 2, 1921, **67**: 188; Oct. 19, 1921, **67**: 427; Jan. 20, 1920, **67**: 615; Sept. 20, 1922, **68**: 149; April 19, 1923, **68**: 338
Albert George Schmedeman, Dec. 6, 1920, **66**: 477; Dec. 15, 1920, **66**: 517
Jacob David Schwarz, Oct. 22, 1920, **66**: 261
Tom Scott, Oct. 18, 1920, **66**: 245
William Berryman Scott, Dec. 27, 1921, **67**: 496
Henrik Samuel Sederholm, Dec. 13, 1920, **66**: 501
Ellery Sedgwick, May 16, 1923, **68**: 363; June 6, 1923, **68**: 371

Louis Seibold, June 3, 1921, **67**: 303; Nov. 14, 1921, **67**: 456
William Graves Sharp, April 18, 1919, **57**: 475; Nov. 27, 1920, **66**: 431
Edward Wright Sheldon, Nov. 18, 1918, **53**: 126; Nov. 9, 1920, **66**: 343
Charles Howard Shinn, Aug. 22, 1919, **62**: 469
Henry Smith, Dec. 16, 1920, **66**: 524
Edmund Munroe Smith, Dec. 31, 1920, **67**: 17
Norman Kemp Smith, July 13, 1919, **61**: 476
Jan Christiaan Smuts, Jan. 4, 1921, **67**: 26; Oct. 2, 1923, **68**: 440
Thomas L. Snow, Nov. 1, 1920, **66**: 300; Nov. 17, 1920, **66**: 385
John Spargo, Nov. 1, 1920, **66**: 299; Jan. 16, 1922, **67**: 528
Duane Reed Stuart, Feb. 4, 1921, **67**: 115; Aug. 1, 1922, **68**: 103
Robert Cummins Stuart, Jr., April 7, 1921, **67**: 253; April 13, 1921, **67**: 257; April 28, 1921, **67**: 273; May 20, 1921, **67**: 285
Claude Augustus Swanson, Oct. 12, 1921, **67**: 418
Herbert Bayard Swope, Oct. 20, 1920, **66**: 250

Helen Taft, March 10, 1920, **65**: 79
William Howard Taft, March 30, 1922, **67**: 580
Ida Minerva Tarbell, March 23, 1921, **67**: 240; March 5, 1922, **67**: 564
Frank William Taussig, July 24, 1919, **61**: 617; Nov. 5, 1920, **66**: 329
James Henry Taylor, July 22, 1919, **61**: 595
Frederick Ingate Thompson, Nov. 2, 1922, **68**: 170
Samuel Huston Thompson, Jr., March 27, 1923, **68**: 302; Dec. 28, 1923, **68**: 512
Nancy Saunders Toy, Jan. 16, 1921, **67**: 526
Kate Nichols Trask, Jan. 30, 1921, **67**: 106
Joseph Patrick Tumulty, June 6, 1919 (2), **60**: 247, 248; June 24, 1919, **61**: 116; Aug. 3, 1920, **66**: 6; Nov. 6, 1920, **66**: 333; Feb. 9, 1921, **67**: 126; June 16, 1921, **67**: 314; Sept. 6, 1921, **67**: 388; Jan. 25, 1922, **67**: 534; April 6, 1922, **67**: 602; April 12, 1922, **68**: 14; April 13, 1922, **68**: 20
Lyon Gardiner Tyler, Aug. 30, 1919, **62**: 588

Henry van Dyke, Oct. 30, 1923, **68**: 459
Ambrose White Vernon, Oct. 25, 1923, **68**: 456; Nov. 27, 1923, **68**: 491
Milenko Vesnić, Dec. 17, 1920, **66**: 531
Vittorio Emanuele III, Jan. 18, 1919, **54**: 134

Schuyler Nielson Warren, Jr., Aug. 7, 1922, **68**: 106
Charles R. Webster, Jan. 23, 1923, **68**: 545
James Edwin Webster, May 7, 1920, **65**: 258; Dec. 20, 1921, **67**: 491
Robert S. Weeks, July 2, 1920, **65**: 491

John Howell Westcott, Nov. 27, 1918, **53**: 235; Dec. 11, 1921, **67**: 482

Thornton Whaling, Dec. 5, 1921, **67**: 473

Howard Duane Wheeler, March 6, 1919, **55**: 456

Henry White, June 28, 1919, **61**: 347

Brand Whitlock, June 23, 1919, **61**: 105; July 15, 1919, **61**: 489

Louis Wiley, Nov. 5, 1920, **66**: 328; Jan. 8, 1924, **68**: 524

John Sharp Williams, July 10, 1919, **61**: 444; Aug. 17, 1920, **66**: 40; Nov. 12, 1921, **67**: 454; Jan. 16, 1922, **67**: 525; March 1, 1923, **68**: 292

Edith Bolling Galt Wilson, May 14, 1920, **65**: 287; May 24, 1920, **65**: 324; June 5, 1920, **65**: 376; Dec. 25, 1920, **67**: 5; Feb. 16, 1923, **68**: 288; Aug. 27, 1923 (2), **68**: 408 (2); Aug. 28, 1923, **68**: 409; Aug. 29, 1923, **68**: 412; Aug. 30, 1923, **68**: 413; Aug. 31, 1923, **68**: 415; Sept. 3, 1923 (3), **68**: 416 (3); Sept. 4, 1923, **68**: 417

Margaret Woodrow Wilson, Jan. 30, 1919, **54**: 400; Sept. 13, 1923, **68**: 422; Nov. 11, 1923, **68**: 471

William Bauchop Wilson, March 2, 1921, **67**: 186

Stephen Samuel Wise, Dec. 15, 1922, **67**: 487; June 28, 1922, **68**: 87; April 12, 1923, **68**: 333

Caroline Bayard Stevens Alexander Wittpenn, July 12, 1921, **67**: 350

Felexiana Shepherd Baker Woodrow, Dec. 28, 1920, **67**: 11

Lawrence Crane Woods, Nov. 27, 1920, **66**: 433; June 6, 1921, **67**: 306; June 29, 1921, **67**: 334

Robert Wickliffe Woolley, Nov. 3, 1920, **66**: 313

Theodore Wright, Dec. 15, 1918, **53**: 394

Simon Wolf, July 24, 1919, **61**: 617

Frederic Yates, Feb. 4, 1919, **54**: 488

Interviews and memoranda of conversations with Wilson

A memorandum by Robert Lansing about Wilson's plan to attend the peace conference, Nov. 12, 1918, **53**: 65

A memorandum by Robert Lansing about Wilson's decision to head the American delegation to the peace conference, Nov. 18, 1918, **53**: 127

A memorandum by Stockton Axson about a White House conference on the creation of an international Red Cross organization, Dec. 2, 1918, **53**: 301

A memorandum by Isaiah Bowman about a conference between Wilson and the advisory staff of the A.C.N.P., Dec. 10, 1918, **53**: 353

An interview with the correspondent of the London *Times*, Dec. 18, 1918, **53**: 422

A news report of a press conference held by Dr. Grayson, Dec. 19, 1918, **53**: 446

A memorandum by Frank Worthington about an interview with Wilson, Dec. 28, 1918, **53**: 574

A report by Lawrence Grant White of a talk between Wilson and Leonida Bissolati-Bergamaschi, Jan. 7, 1919, **53**: 641

A memorandum of a conversation between Wilson and Gustave Ador, Jan. 23, 1919, **54**: 233

Notes by Arthur Hugh Frazier of a conversation between Wilson and Vittorio Emanuele Orlando, Jan. 30, 1919, **54**: 387

A memorandum by Thomas Garrigue Masaryk about a talk with Wilson on intervention in Russia, June 19, 1918, **54**: 557

A press conference with American newspaper representatives, Feb. 14, 1919, **55**: 16

A memorandum of a conference with Andrea Ossoinack on the question of Fiume, April 14, 1919, **57**: 337

A report by Arthur James Balfour about an interview with Wilson on various problems before the peace conference, April 15, 1919, **57**: 364

A memorandum by William B. Wallace about Wilson's instructions with regard to the Polish-Ukrainian conflict and the situation in Luxembourg, April 15, 1919, **57**: 372

A memorandum by Vi Kyuin Wellington Koo about a conversation with Wilson on world peace and the Far East, April 22, 1919, **57**: 631

A memorandum by Vi Kyuin Wellington Koo about a conference with Wilson on the League of Nations and the question of Kiaochow, Nov. 26, 1919, **57**: 632

A discussion with the American delegation about the terms of the peace treaty, June 3, 1919, **60**: 45

An interview by Salomon Frederik van Oss, June 7, 1919, **60**: 250

A memorandum by Thomas William Lamont about a conference with Wilson on British efforts to control the purchase of raw materials and foodstuffs in Europe, June 13, 1919, **60**: 493

An exchange about the German people with David Lloyd George, June 14, 1919, **60**: 553

A memorandum by Harry Shepard Knapp about an interview with Wilson on the naval policy of the United States, June 17, 1919, **60**: 614

Memorandum by Robert Lansing on Wilson's feelings about the situation in Europe, Aug. 20, 1919, **62**: 428

Memorandum by Cary Travers Grayson on a conference between Wilson and Gilbert Monell Hitchcock about the treaty situation in the Senate, Nov. 17, 1919, **64**: 43

Memorandum by Cary Travers Grayson about Wilson's conference with Albert Bacon Fall and Gilbert Monell Hitchcock, Dec. 5, 1919, **64**: 135

Notes by Edith Bolling Galt Wilson on Wilson's conference with Senators Fall and Hitchcock, Dec. 5, 1919, **64**: 133

Memorandum by Joseph Patrick Tumulty on a conversation with Wilson about the Jackson Day Dinner, Jan. 9, 1920, **64**: 261

Memorandum by Cary Travers Grayson on a conversation with Wilson about the appointment of Bainbridge Colby, Feb. 25, 1920, **64**: 472

Note by Cary Travers Grayson on first meeting Wilson, n.d., **64**: 485

Note by Cary Travers Grayson on becoming Wilson's physician, 1913, **64**: 486

Note by Cary Travers Grayson on Wilson's trip to Pass Christian, n.d., **64**: 486

Note by Cary Travers Grayson describing Wilson taking counsel from others, n.d., **64**: 487

Note by Cary Travers Grayson on western trip, n.d., **64**: 488

Report by Louis Seibold of a White House visit, June 17, 1920, **65**: 401

Report by Louis Seibold of an interview with Wilson, June 17, 1920, **65**: 415

Memorandum by Norman Hezekiah Davis on a strategy to secure Senate consent to the ratification of the Versailles Treaty, April 22, 1920, **65**: 223

Memorandum by Homer Stillé Cummings on a conversation with Wilson about events at the Democratic National Convention, July 26, 1920, **65**: 551

Memorandum by Homer Stillé Cummings about efforts by Bainbridge Colby to secure Wilson's nomination at the Democratic National Convention, July 3 and 4, 1920, **65**: 579

An interview by William Walter Hawkins, Sept. 27, 1920, **66**: 153

Memorandum by Homer Stillé Cummings on a conversation with Edith Bolling Galt Wilson on the Democratic presidential campaign of 1920, Oct. 4, 1920, **66**: 189

Memorandum by Homer Stillé Cummings on a conversation with Wilson about politics, Oct. 5, 1920, **66**: 194

Memorandum by Homer Stillé Cumings on a visit with Wilson after the election, Nov. 6, 1920, **66**: 331

Memorandum by Cary Travers Grayson about Wilson's refusal to shake hands with Senator Lodge, Dec. 6, 1920, **66**: 479

Memorandum by Cary Travers Grayson of a conversation with Arthur James Balfour, Jan. 11, 1922, **67**: 516

Memorandum by Homer Stillé Cummings of a conversation with Wilson about the current political situation, Apr. 25, 1921, **67**: 268

Memorandum by Stockton Axson of a conversation with Wilson on the current and future state of politics, Aug. 1919, **67**: 605

Two last talks with Wilson by James Kerney, March 29, 1924, **68**: 588

Memorandum by Cary Travers Grayson on remarks made by Wilson about people minding their own business, April 15, 1922, **68**: 23

Memorandum by Ida Minerva Tarbell of a conversation with Wilson, May 5, 1922, **68**: 45

Two memoranda by Cary Travers Grayson of conversations with Wilson about the Tumulty incident, May 10, 1922, **68**: 51; May 22, 1922, **68**: 59

Memorandum by Cary Travers Grayson of a conversation with Wilson about leaving Washington for the summer, May 22, 1922, **68**: 58

Memorandum by Homer Stillé Cummings of a conversation with Wilson about the current political situation, June 28, 1922, **68**: 88

Memorandum by Cary Travers Grayson of a conversation with Wilson on his sixty-sixth birthday, Dec. 28, 1922, **68**: 250

Memorandum by Cary Travers Grayson on two visits to Wilson by Stockton Axson, Dec. 28, 1922, **68**: 255

Notes of a conversation with Wilson by John R. Mott, Dec. 20, 1923, **68**: 502

Questionnaire

Pelman Institute of America, Inc., Oct. 21, 1920, **66**: 251

Press conferences

Notes by Walter Edward Weyl, June 27, 1919, **61**: 240

A report of a press conference by Charles Thaddeus Thompson, June 27, 1919, **61**: 246

A report of a press conference at the White House, July 10, 1919, **61**: 417

News reports

"President Expounds League of Nations to Dinner Guests," Feb. 26, 1919, **55**: 268

"President Holds Levee at Capitol," Feb. 27, 1919, **55**: 295

"Wilson Denies Irish Statement," Feb. 28, 1919, **55**: 324

"President Gives Hope to Zionists," March 2, 1919, **55**: 386

"Wilson Won't Meet Cohalan with Irish," March 4, 1919, **55**: 421

The success of the White House flock of sheep, March 23, 1919, **56**: 204

"The Mandate," May 13, 1919, **59**: 105

"Speech made by Mr. Dunne in Belfast, 5th May 1919," May 13, 1919, **59**: 107

"Ovation to the President," July 10, 1919, **61**: 424

"Wilson Greets Callers. Holds Reception in Capitol Room to Discuss Peace Problems," July 10, 1919, **61**: 437

"Did Not Like Shantung Settlement," July 10, 1919, **61**: 438

"Leaves League Fight. Hitchock Takes Rest as Wilson Shows 'Lack of Warmth,'" July 12, 1919, **61**: 468

"Wilson to Consult Congress Members," July 13, 1919, **61**: 474

"Three Hear Wilson. McCumber, Colt and Nelson Are Enlightened on the League," July 18, 1919, **61**: 515

"Wilson Told League Cannot Pass Intact," July 19, 1919, **61**: 544

"Wilsons on Cruise Despite the Storm," July 20, 1919, **61**: 562

"35 To Block League. List of Senators Who Oppose It Offered to the President," July 20, 1919, **61**: 563

"President Wilson Returns Ill, Is Ordered To Bed; All Conferences Off; Norris Declines Invitation," July 21, 1919, **61**: 569; "Wilson Stays in Bed. Weakened, But Not Seriously Ill, Dr. Grayson Reports," July 22, 1919, **61**: 578

"Wilson Says He Decided Shantung. Britain and France Had Him Umpire Claim," July 22, 1919, **61**: 593

"Deny Wilson Power. May Not Appoint Reparation Commissioner, Senators Vote," July 23, 1919, **61**: 596

"Wilson Continues Firm. Tells Senators Smaller Nations Would Oppose Treaty Modifications," July 23, 1919, **61**: 599

"Wilson Discusses Riots With Baker. Feeling Better President Resumes His Treaty Talks With Senators," July 23, 1919, **61**: 599

"Urging Japan to Settle. Wilson Tells Spencer of Hope of Agreement in a Few Days," July 25, 1919, **61**: 619

"Wilson to Withhold French Treaty Till Tour Ends; Lodge Not to Press Request for Its Submission," July 23, 1919, **61**: 622

"Shantung Problem Nearing A Solution. Wilson Hopes Developments Will Come in a Few Days," July 26, 1919, **62**: 3

"President May Yield. Statement From White House Expected on Interpretations," July 27, 1919, **62**: 11

"Talks With 11 Democrats. President Tells Senators European Stability Requires Early Ratification," July 28, 1919, **62**: 16

"Fears Reopening Treaty. President Says Germany Would Probably Make Further Demands," July 30, 1919, **62**: 43

"Seven Republican Senators Prepare Four 'Mild Reservations' to Covenant; Will Urge Them as Basis of Settlement," July 30, 1919, **62**: 66

"New For U.S. First. On League Question 'I Am an American,'" Aug. 1, 1919, **62**: 92

"Food Problem at the Fore. President, Cabinet and Congress Tackling Cost of Living," Aug. 1, 1919, **62**: 94

"Made Part of Treaty. Proposals of 7 Republicans Not Merely Reservations," Aug. 2, 1919, **62**: 112

"Reject Wilson's Proposal. Shopmen Threaten to Paralyze Nation if Demands Are Not Met," Aug. 4, 1919, **62**: 134

"Wilson Takes Personal Control of the Food Situation," Aug. 5, 1919, **62**: 157

"Big Brotherhoods Make Formal Demand for U.S. to Retain the Railroads. Call at White House," Aug. 5, 1919, **62**: 161

"Wilson Sees Obstacle in Strikes," Aug. 5, 1919, **62**: 162

"Wilson Is Using Every War Law to Smash the High Price of Food," Aug. 6, 1919, **62**: 168

"Wilson Asks Hines to Act. Says Railroad Director Has Power to Pass on Shopmen's Wages," Aug. 7, 1919, **62**: 189

"Reports Wilson Bound to Carry Treaty Unaltered," Aug. 15, 1919, **62**: 305

"Jovial Luncheon After Conference," Aug. 19, 1919, **62**: 336

"Offer A Compromise. League Adherents Propose Separate Interpretive Measure," Aug. 21, 1919, **62**: 429

"Wilson Calls A Halt on Railway Wage Increases; Tells Shopmen to Wait," Aug. 25, 1919, **62**: 484

"Wilson Still Deaf to Treaty Changes," Sept. 2, 1919, **62**: 613

"Wilson Begins Hard Week," Sept. 8, 1919, **63**: 96

Wilson's definition of the fundamental principles of the peace treaty, Sept. 10, 1919, **63**: 163

"Wilson Dropped Greatness and Showed His Weariness," Sept. 25, 1919, **63**: 487

A description of Wilson at work, Sept. 25, 1919, **63**: 513

"President is Ill and Cancels His Tour," Sept. 25, 1919, **63**: 522

"Wilson Very Ill, Condition Cause of Real Anxiety," Sept. 27, 1919, **63**: 527

"Push Reservation Wilson Scouted: Republicans Now Favor Compromise which, the President Said, 'Knifes the Treaty,'" Sept. 27, 1919, **63**: 529

"Wilson Sleeping Better and Improving: Allowed to Give a Little Time to Work," Sept. 30, 1919, **63**: 536

"President is Jaded Again, After Another Restless Night," Oct. 1, 1919, **63**: 538

"'Very Sick Man' Says Grayson of President in Late Night Bulletin," Oct. 3, 1919, **63**: 543

"Found Wilson Cheerful, Dr. Dercum Announces," Oct. 3, 1919, **63**: 546

"President is Improving Slightly, Late Report by Dr. Grayson Says," Oct. 4, 1919, **63**: 549

"More Encouraging Day," Oct. 4, 1919, **63**: 550

"Wilson Has Good Day," Oct. 6, 1919, **63**: 552

"Wilson Still Gains," Oct. 7, 1919, **63**: 555

"Wilson Is Improved," Oct. 11, 1919, **63**: 560

"President Needs Long Rest," Oct. 11, 1919, **63**: 561

"Reports Wilson Suffered Shock," Oct. 11, 1919, **63**: 563

"Rumor Busy About Wilson," Oct. 12, 1919, **63**: 564

"Had Slight Retinal Lesion," Oct. 12, 1919, **63**: 567

"President's Condition is 'About the Same,' Says the Latest White House Bulletin," Oct. 13, 1919, **63**: 568

"Wilson's Mind 'Clear' and He Can Act, but Grayson Says Cure Requires Time," Oct. 13, 1919, **63**: 569

"Spent Restless Day," Oct. 15, 1919, **63**: 572

"Good Day for Wilson," Oct. 16, 1919, **63**: 574

"Wilson Told of Vote: Grayson Allows Him to Hear Shantung Clause is Beaten," Oct. 17, 1919, **63**: 576

"President Improves after Setback; Dr. Young, Gland Specialist, Called in," Oct. 17, 1919, **63**: 577

"Dr. H. H. Young Tells of Wilson Jesting," Oct. 17, 1919, **63**: 580

"Wilson Has Best Day," Oct. 19, 1919, **63**: 581

"President Better, Signs Four Bills," Oct. 22, 1919, **63**: 586

"President Maintains His Improvement," Oct. 30, 1919, **63**: 602

"Belgian Royalties See the President," Oct. 30, 1919, **63**: 602

"President Interested in Election Returns," Nov. 4, 1919, **63**: 608

"President Still Gaining," Nov. 8, 1919, **64**: 4

"President Able to Sit Up, Enjoys an Evening Serenade," Nov. 11, 1919, **64**: 6

"Prince Sees Wilson," Nov. 14, 1919, **64**: 31

"President on Porch in Wheeled Chair," Nov. 14, 1919, **64**: 32

"Remarkable Improvements in President in Two Weeks," Nov. 15, 1919, **64**: 37

"President Will Pocket Treaty if Passed as Modified," Nov. 17, 1919, **64**: 45

"President Out on Lawn for First Time Since Return," Nov. 17, 1919, **64**: 50

"President Outdoors Again, Holds Informal Lawn Party," Nov. 18, 1919, **64**: 57

"Hitchcock Called to White House on Treaty Fight," Nov. 24, 1919, **64**: 71

"President Has Thanksgiving Dinner in Bed," Nov. 27, 1919, **64**: 93

"Fails to See Wilson. Hitchcock, at the White House, Waits Vainly for Audience," Nov. 30, 1919, **64**: 99

"President's Health Shows Steady Improvement," Dec. 2, 1919, **64**: 105

"Wilson to See Senators," Dec. 4, 1919, **64**: 120

"Wilson Won't Act on Treaty Now," Dec. 5, 1919, **64**: 126

"Senators See President," Dec. 5, 1919, **64**: 126

"President Jests on Moses Story," Dec. 5, 1919, **64**: 132

"President Makes Proposal to Coal Miners," Dec. 7, 1919, **64**: 142

"Wilson Won't Agree to Lodge Program," Dec. 9, 1919, **64**: 165

"Wilson Walks; Not Paralyzed," Dec. 14, 1919, **64**: 187

"Wilson Reported Much Better; Dercum Stops Regular Visits," Dec. 20, 1919, **64**: 211

"No Third Term Ambition. Wilson Has No Idea of Running Again, Says Palmer," Jan. 10, 1920, **64**: 267

"President's Health Shows Steady Improvement," Jan. 20, 1920, **64**: 307

"Senate Conferees Near Compromise on Resolutions," Jan. 22, 1920, **64**: 311

"Wilson for Peace Prize," Jan. 29, 1920, **64**: 342

"Wilson Narrowly Escapes Influenza," Feb. 3, 1920, **64**: 351

"Wilson Recovered from Cold, is out on Portico in Storm," Feb. 4, 1920, **64**: 361

"Sees President Near Recovery. Improvement Slow, Sure and Steady, Says Dr. Young of Johns Hopkins," Feb. 10, 1920, **64**: 394

"Public Diagnosis Vexes President," Feb. 11, 1920, **64**: 403

"Dercum Won't Talk," Feb. 11, 1920, **64**: 403

"President Shows Old Form in Talk with Railroad Men," Feb. 13, 1920, **64**: 420

"President Will Never Recover, Is View of Dr. Bevan," Feb. 15, 1920, **64**: 432

"Dr. Dercum Declares Mind of President Wilson in Keen, Denying
    Relapse," Feb. 15, 1920, **64**: 433
"Grayson Reports President Still Gaining," Feb. 17, 1920, **64**: 435
"President Wilson Comes Back," Feb. 28, 1920, **65**: 3
"Wilson Rejects Lodge Article X., Senators Learn," Feb. 28, 1920, **65**:
    7
"Wilson Has Ride; First in 5 Months," March 3, 1920, **65**: 41
"President Out Driving in Open Automobile," March 8, 1920, **65**: 67
"President Has Two-Hour Auto Ride," March 14, 1920, **65**: 86
"Wilson Hails Colors in Circus Parade," May 17, 1920, **65**: 290
"President's Prize Sheep Sheared," June 3, 1920, **65**: 354
"Wilson Asks for Movie," June 11, 1920, **65**: 384
"McAdoo Refuses to Enter Race for Presidency; Democrats Likely to
    Accept Wilson Platform," June 18, 1920, **65**: 426
"Wilson Platform Centres on League," June 18, 1920, **65**: 436
"Cox and Wilson Reach Full Accord," July 18, 1920, **65**: 522
"Text of Statement by Cox, Wilson and Roosevelt," July 18, 1920, **65**:
    524
"Wilson Conference Decides on Anti-Lenine, Pro-Russia Policy,"
    Aug. 7, 1920, **66**: 16
"Wilson Urges Article X. as Pledge; Shows Illness in Plea from
    Chair," Oct. 27, 1920, **66**: 273
"President Greets White House Crowd," Nov. 4, 1920, **66**: 316
"Wilson Receives Ovation at Theatre," Feb. 1, 1921, **67**: 111
"Wilson Visits New Home," Feb. 11, 1921, **67**: 127
"Shallow-Minded Visitor Reminds Wilson of Bungalow," Feb. 11,
    1921, **67**: 128
"Wilson Goes to Cabinet Office; Is Photographed with Advisers,"
    Feb. 15, 1921, **67**: 138
"Wilson to Devote his Life to Peace," Feb. 22, 1921, **67**: 158
"President Bids Good-bye to His Cabinet," March 1, 1921, **67**: 175
"Mr. and Mrs. Harding at White House," March 3, 1921, **67**: 189
"Wilson and Colby to Start Law Firm," March 3, 1921, **67**: 245
"Wilson's Exit Is Tragic," March 4, 1921, **67**: 205
"Wilson's Stock of Liquor Is Moved," March 4, 1921, **67**: 214
"Wilson Overcome by Fainting Spell," March 25, 1921, **67**: 245
"Wilson Is a 'Little Weak,'" March 26, 1921, **67**: 246
"Wilson Attends the Theatre," April 23, 1921, **67**: 268
"Wilson Militant and in 'a Happy Mood,' Chairman White Finds in
    Chat on Politics," June 10, 1921, **67**: 308
"Will 'Keep His Ideals Before the Public,' Woodrow Wilson Tells
    Princeton Students," June 12, 1921, **67**: 311
"Wilson Goes to Court to Be Admitted to Bar," June 25, 1921, **67**: 328
"Wilson at His Law Offices for First Time," Aug. 27, 1921, **67**: 380
"Wilson Is Cheered by Theatre Crowd," Aug. 27, 1921, **67**: 380
"Wilson, Stricken 2 Years Ago, Now Puts In Healthy Man's Day,
    Sept. 26, 1921, **67**: 395
"Col. House Calls, Wilson Not at Home," Oct. 13, 1921, **67**: 419

"Wilson Abed with Recurrence of Indigestion," Oct. 29, 1921, **67**: 434

"Wilson Rallies After Attack," Oct. 30, 1921, **67**: 436

"Wilson Shows Improvement," Oct. 31, 1921, **67**: 436

"Wilson Goes to Matinee," Nov. 2, 1921, **67**: 440

"Briand Finds Wilson Out," Nov. 10, 1921, **67**: 449

"Wilson in Tears as 20,000 Acclaim Him World's Hero," Nov. 11, 1921, **67**: 449

"Wilson Receives Visit From Balfour," Nov. 24, 1921, **67**: 465

"Wilson Reaffirms His Confidence in League's Vitality," Jan. 15, 1922, **67**: 531

"Cox Boom Launched on Wilson Keynote of Justice For All," April 8, 1922, **68**: 3

"Doubt Is Cast on Wilson 'Message' to the Cox Dinner," April 11, 1922, **68**: 11

"1,000 Women Cheer at Wilson's Home," April 28, 1922, **68**: 36

"Wilson Sees Nation Moving Forward; Hits at His Foes," Nov. 11, 1922, **68**: 185

"Tiger and Wilson Recall Old Times in Cordial Reunion," Dec. 6, 1922, **68**: 226

"Senate Felicitates Wilson on Birthday," Dec. 28, 1922, **68**: 247

"Cecil Visits Wilson: Sees Harding Today," April 20, 1923, **68**: 344

"Wilson Stronger Physically, Turning Again to Politics," June 10, 1923, **68**: 375

"Harding Kept Grayson within Wilson's Call," Aug. 3, 1923, **68**: 398

"Wilson Is Unable to Attend Harding Funeral: He Is Deeply Affected by President's Death," Aug. 4, 1923, **68**: 399

"Ordeal for Wilson to Attend Funeral," Aug. 8, 1923, **68**: 401

"Washington Crowd Gives Wilson Ovation," Aug. 11, 1923, **68**: 401

"Wilson May Lead Democrats in 1924," Sept. 19, 1923, **68**: 425

"Lloyd George Sees Washington Chiefs," Oct. 25, 1923, **68**: 455

"Wilson Overcome Greeting Pilgrims: Predicts Triumph," Nov. 11, 1923, **68**: 467

"Wilson Is Honored on 67th Birthday: Friends Give Auto," Dec. 28, 1923, **68**: 509

"Wilson Receives Party Committee," Jan. 16, 1924, **68**: 531

"Woodrow Wilson Indisposed; Not Serious Says Doctor," Jan. 30, 1924, **68**: 550

"Wilson Condition Is Causing Anxiety," Jan. 31, 1924, **68**: 551

"Ex-President Woodrow Wilson Dying; Told End Is Near, He Replies, 'I am ready,'" Feb. 2, 1924, **68**: 553

"Woodrow Wilson's Life Slowly Ebbs as Night Passes," Feb. 3, 1924, **68**: 561

"Woodrow Wilson Passes Away in Sleep," Feb. 3, 1924, **68**: 566

"Throng in Prayer at Wilson Home," Feb. 3, 1924, **68**: 570

"Simplicity Marks Service in the Home," Feb. 6, 1924, **68**: 575

"Wilson Buried in Cathedral Crypt with Simple Rites as Nation Mourns," Feb. 6, 1924, **68**: 579

Writings

A foreword to a book of lectures by Alexander Thomas Ormond, **67**:
349
Plans and notes for a book, **68**: 39-42
An inscription in memory of his father, **68**: 52
"The Road Away from Revolution" draft, **68**: 322; text, **68**: 393
Notes and passages for an Acceptance Speech, **68**: 541
Notes and passages for a Third Inaugural Address, **68**: 542

"The Document": correspondence and drafts
(to, from, and by Wilson)

Newton Diehl Baker, Jan. 20, 1924, **68**: 534
Bernard Mannes Baruch, March 2, 1922, **67**: 560; March 10, 1922,
    67: 566; March 16, 1922, **67**: 568; March 21, 1922, **67**: 569; March
    31, 1922, **67**: 582; April 3, 1922, **67**: 583; March 5, 1923, **68**: 294;
    March 12, 1923, **68**: 295; March 22, 1923 **68**: 297; June 13, 1923,
    68: 385
Louis Dembitz Brandeis, June 20, 1921, **66**: 319; June 29, 1921, **67**:
    330; Nov. 6, 1921, **67**: 443; Nov. 8, 1921, **67**: 446; Dec. 5, 1921, **67**:
    472; Dec. 6, 1921, **67**: 475; Dec. 8, 1921, **67**: 477; Jan. 2, 1922, **67**:
    499; Jan. 7, 1922 (2), **67**: 506 (2); Feb. 27, 1922, **67**: 558; March 3,
    1922, **67**: 563; April 9, 1922, **68**: 4; April 11, 1922, **68**: 13; April 17,
    1922, **68**: 26; April 2, 1923, **68**: 315; April 3, 1923, **68**: 316; April 15,
    1923, **68**: 334; April 18, 1923, **68**: 336
Thomas Lincoln Chadbourne, Jr., April 13, 1922, **68**: 19; April 19,
    1922, **68**: 28; April 23, 1919, **68**: 29; April 15, 1922, **68**: 33
Frank Irving Cobb, Dec. 15, 1922, **68**: 234; Dec. 19, 1922, **68**: 239;
    March 27, 1923, **68**: 304; March 28, 1923, **68**: 305; April 18, 1922,
    68: 337; April 19, 1923, **68**: 338
Bainbridge Colby, July 2, 1921, **67**: 339; Oct. 24, 1921, **67**: 430; Oct.
    26, 1921, **67**: 432; Oct. 29, 1921, **67**: 435; March 27, 1922, **67**: 575;
    March 29, 1922, **67**: 579; March 30, 1922, **67**: 581; March 31, 1922,
    67: 582; April 5, 1922, **67**: 588; April 9, 1922, **68**: 4; April 10, 1922,
    68: 10; April 11, 1922, **68**: 13; April 12, 1922 (3), **68**: 16 (2), 17;
    April 13, 1922, **68**: 19; April 19, 1922, **68**: 28; April 25, 1922, **68**: 34
Norman Hezekiah Davis, April 18, 1922, **68**: 27; April 25, 1922, **68**:
    32; May 5, 1922, **68**: 49; May 12, 1922, **68**: 53; May 19, 1922, **68**: 56;
    Nov. 3, 1922, **68**: 172; Nov. 6, 1922, **68**: 178; Nov. 9, 1922, **68**: 182;
    Dec. 12, 1922, **68**: 230; Dec. 16, 1922, **68**: 237; Dec. 21, 1922, **68**:
    241; Dec. 27, 1922, **68**: 244; March 20, 1923, **68**: 296; March 27,
    1923, **68**: 302; March 31, 1923, **68**: 311; April 4, 1923, **68**: 317;
    April 9, 1923, **68**: 325
Henry Jones Ford, Feb. 2, 1922, **67**: 540; Feb. 20, 1922, **67**: 550
David Franklin Houston, Dec. 8, 1921, **66**: 476; Dec. 14, 1921, **67**:
    484; April 25, 1922, **68**: 32; May 1, 1922, **68**: 42; May 3, 1922, **68**:

43; May 30, 1922, **68**: 71; Dec. 22, 1922, **68**: 244; Dec. 30, 1922, **68**: 260

George Foster Peabody, Oct. 11, 1922, **68**: 153; Nov. 25, 1922 (2), **68**: 203, 204

Woodrow Wilson, Oct. 24, 1921, **67**: 430; Oct. 29, 1921, **67**: 435; Nov. 6, 1921, **67**: 443; Dec. 5, 1921, **67**: 472; Jan. 2, 1922, **67**: 499; Feb. 27, 1922, **67**: 558; March 31, 1922, **67**: 582

Drafts and revisions of, and additions to, "The Document," April 9, 1922, **68**: 5; May 12, 1922, **68**: 54; Aug. 7, 1922, **68**: 105; Nov. 25, 1922, **68**: 207; Dec. 2, 1922, **68**: 215; March 31, 1923, **68**: 308; April 4, 1923, **68**: 318; April 15, 1923, **68**: 335

An empowering resolution by Wilson, March 22, 1923, **68**: 298

The final draft of "The Document," Jan. 20, 1924, **68**: 535

COLLATERAL MATERIALS

Diplomatic correspondence, reports, memoranda, and aide-mémoire

A British-French-American proposal for settlement of the Adriatic dispute, Dec. 9, 1919, **64**: 168

An Anglo-French proposal for settlement of the Adriatic dispute, Jan. 9, 1920, **64**: 264

An Anglo-French-Italian agreement for settlement of the Adriatic question, Jan. 19, 1920, **64**: 298

A note by the Yugoslav government protesting against the Anglo-French-Italian agreement on the Adriatic question, Jan. 19, 1920, **64**: 304

Draft by Lloyd George of a telegram from the Supreme Council on the question of trade with Russia, Jan. 20, 1920, **64**: 308

A reply by David Lloyd George and Georges Clemenceau to the American protest against a lack of consultation on the Adriatic question, Jan. 23, 1920, **64**: 318

A protest by the United States Government against the unilateral decisions taken by Great Britain and France on the Adriatic question, Jan. 23, 1920, **64**: 320

A reply by the Yugoslav government to the Anglo-French-Italian proposal for a settlement of the Adriatic dispute, Jan. 26, 1920, **64**: 331

A note by the Supreme Council on the opening of peace negotiations with Turkey, Jan. 30, 1920, **64**: 344

A protest by the United States Government against the Anglo-French-Italian proposal for a settlement of the Adriatic dispute, Feb. 7, 1920, **64**: 375 (draft); Feb. 10, 1920, **64**: 398

A reply by the British and French governments to the American protest against the Anglo-French-Italian agreement on the Adriatic question, Feb. 17, 1920, **64**: 436

A note by the United States Government affirming its opposition to the Anglo-French-Italian agreement on the Adriatic question, Wilson draft, Feb. 19, 1920, **64**: 445; Feb. 23, 1920, **64**: 459, note sent

A note by the British and French governments emphasizing the possibility of the implementation of the Treaty of London as the only alternative to a speedy settlement of the Adriatic dispute, Feb. 27, 1920, **64**: 481

A note to the British and French governments on the Adriatic question, March 2, 1920, **65**: 37

A memorandum by Norman Hezekiah Davis on French policy toward Germany, March 6, 1920, **65**: 60

A memorandum by Norman Hezekiah Davis on the question of continued American representation on the commissions established by the Versailles Treaty, March 5, 1920, **65**: 60

An informal note to the British and French governments on the terms of the Turkish treaty, March 8, 1920, **65**: 73 (draft)

A memorandum by military intelligence officers on the political situation in Germany, March 18, 1920, **65**: 99

A draft by Frank Lyon Polk of a note to the French government on the terms of the Turkish treaty, March 22, 1920, **65**: 112

An informal note to the French goverment on the French occupation of the Frankfurt area, April 10, 1920, **65**: 168

A note from the Supreme Council requesting the United States to accept a mandate for Armenia, May 20, 1920, **65**: 307

A memorandum by the Yugoslav delegation on the Adriatic question, May 22, 1920, **65**: 315

A resolution by the Zionist Organization of America thanking Wilson for supporting the creation of a Jewish homeland in Palestine, May 28, 1920, **65**: 334

Reports by Albert Gleaves on the Japanese occupation of Siberia (excerpts), June 11, 1920, **65**: 391

Memoranda by Norman Hezekiah Davis on conversations with Fernando Iglesias Calderon, July 1, 1920, **65**: 483; July 21, 1920, **65**: 534

A note to the Japanese government on Japan's occupation of northern Sakhalin, July 16, 1920, **65**: 515

Memorandum of a conversation between Ambassador Morris and Ambassador Shidehara, Aug. 5, 1920, **66**: 12

Note by Bainbridge Colby to the Italian government setting forth the policy of the U.S. Government of the nonrecognition of the Soviet government, Aug. 7, 1920, **66**: 18

Aide-mémoire by the Japanese government justifying its occupation of Sakhalin, Aug. 18, 1920, **66**: 51

Memorandum by Norman Hezekiah Davis of a conversation with Roberto V. Pesqueira Morales, Sept. 28, 1920, **66**: 160

Memorandum by Norman Hezekiah Davis of conversation with Fernando Iglesias Calderon, Sept. 28, 1920, **66**: 162

Statement by Bainbridge Colby on the prospects for U.S. recognition of Mexico, Oct. 28, 1920, **66**: 287

Draft by Norman Hezekiah Davis on the anti-Japanese movement in California, Oct. 30, 1920, **66**: 296

Memorandum by Sumner Welles on U.S. policy in the Dominican Republic, Nov. 13, 1920, **66**: 360

Two drafts of a reply to the Council of the League of Nations regarding Armenia, Nov. 27, 1920, **66**: 427

Proclamation inaugurating the United States' withdrawal from the Dominican Republic, Nov. 27, 1920, **66**: 429

Domestic political correspondence, reports, memoranda,
and aide-mémoire

A resolution by the American Federation of Labor opposing mob rule and lynchings, June 30, 1919, **61**: 357

A resolution by the American Federation of Labor demanding the dismissal of Albert Sidney Burleson, July 1, 1919, **61**: 364

Charles Bismark Ames to Joseph Patrick Tumulty, April 10, 1920, **65**: 174

George Weston Anderson to Bainbridge Colby, Nov. 18, 1920, **66**: 390

Mary Anderson to Joseph Patrick Tumulty, Sept. 5, 1919, **63**: 58

Stockton Axson to Joseph Patrick Tumulty, July 11, 1919, **61**: 508

Draft by Newton Diehl Baker of a letter by Wilson on the Army reorganization bill, Feb. 7, 1920, **65**: 578

Newton Diehl Baker to Edith Bolling Galt Wilson, April 15, 1920, **65**: 194

Draft by Newton Diehl Baker of an Executive Order granting amnesty to certain military prisoners, April 15, 1920, **65**: 193

Draft by Newton Diehl Baker of a veto of the Army reorganization bill, June 4, 1920, **65**: 365

Memorandum by Newton Diehl Baker on the water-power bill, June 23, 1920, **65**: 447

Julius Howland Barnes to Joseph Patrick Tumulty, July 30, 1919, **62**: 51

A draft by Bernard Mannes Baruch of a suggested message on the controversy between the Industrial Board and the Railroad Administration, April 15, 1919, **57**: 387

Bernard Mannes Baruch to Cary Travers Grayson, Sept. 9, 1919, **63**: 149

Bernard Mannes Baruch to Joseph Patrick Tumulty, Sept. 9, 1919, **63**: 149

Thomas Walter Bickett to William Howard Taft, Oct. 25, 1918, **53**: 28; Nov. 2, 1918, **53**: 30

Tasker Howard Bliss to Newton Diehl Baker and Peyton Conway March, Dec. 2, 1918, **53**: 300

Richard Martin Boeckel to Hamilton Holt, March 4, 1920, **67**: 616
John Randolph Bolling to Newton Diehl Baker, Jan. 22, 1924, **68**: 544
John Randolph Bolling to Louis Dembitz Brandeis, April 3, 1923, **68**: 316
John Randolph Bolling to Norman Hezekiah Davis, May 10, 1922, **68**: 51
Evangeline Cory Booth to Joseph Patrick Tumulty, May 27, 1920, **65**: 332
Louis Dembitz Brandeis to Norman Hapgood, June 7, 1919, **60**: 285
Albert Sidney Burleson to Joseph Patrick Tumulty, June 25, 1919, **61**: 185; March 5, 1920, **65**: 56; July 17, 1920, **65**: 520
Albert Sidney Burleson to Edith Bolling Galt Wilson, Jan. 28, 1920, **64**: 338; March 23, 1920, **65**: 119
A memorandum by Albert Sidney Burleson on governmental ownership of telephone and telegraph system, Nov. 29, 1918, **53**: 247
Theodore Elijah Burton to Joseph Patrick Tumulty, Feb. 24, 1919, **55**: 278

Fred A. Carlson to Charles Lee Swem, Oct. 6, 1920, **66**: 196
Petition by Chicago citizens for return of American soldiers from Siberia, Aug. 21, 1919, **62**: 433
Maurice Brice Clagett to Rudolph Forster, Aug. 28, 1919, **62**: 547
Maurice Brice Clagett to Joseph Patrick Tumulty, Aug. 28, 1919, **62**: 544; Nov. 11, 1920, **64**: 21
Gilbert Fairchild Close to Newton Diehl Baker, April 22, 1919, **57**: 630
Gilbert Fairchild Close to William Shepherd Benson, Jan. 27, 1919, **54**: 303
Gilbert Fairchild Close to Albert Sidney Burleson, April 17, 1919, **57**: 446
Gilbert Fairchild Close to Rudolph Forster, Aug. 28, 1919, **62**: 534
Gilbert Fairchild Close to Samuel Gompers, May 13, 1919, **59**: 108
Gilbert Fairchild Close to Herbert Clark Hoover, Jan. 24, 1919, **54**: 262; March 19, 1919, **56**: 101
Gilbert Fairchild Close to Eugene Francis Kinkead, March 28, 1919, **56**: 405
Gilbert Fairchild Close to Robert Lansing, April 19, 1919, **57**: 509; Aug. 4, 1919, **62**: 151
Gilbert Fairchild Close to Dudley Field Malone, March 3, 1919, **55**: 407
Gilbert Fairchild Close to Frank Lyon Polk, March 3, 1919, **55**: 406
Gilbert Fairchild Close to Charles Michael Schwab, Feb. 14, 1919, **55**: 188
Gilbert Fairchild Close to Joseph Patrick Tumulty, April 19, 1919, **57**: 509; April 22, 1919, **57**: 630; April 29, 1919, **58**: 243
Gilbert Fairchild Close to the White House Staff, Aug. 27, 1919, **62**: 527; Sept. 2, 1919, **62**: 615

Frank Irving Cobb to Edith Bolling Galt Wilson, Nov. 21, 1920, **64**: 66

Assessment by Frank Irving Cobb of the Wilsonian legacy, March 4, 1921, **67**: 216

William Joseph Hamilton Cochran to Joseph Patrick Tumulty, Sept. 11, 1919, **63**: 198; Sept. 24, 1919, **63**: 483

Bainbridge Colby to Joseph Patrick Tumulty, Nov. 27, 1920, **66**: 434

Draft by Bainbridge Colby of a statement on the unconstitutionality of Section 34 of the Merchant Marine Act, Sept. 23, 1920, **66**: 136

Memorandum by Bainbridge Colby on support of Democratic senators for the Treaty of Berlin, Oct. 14, 1921, **67**: 421

James Middleton Cox to Edith Bolling Galt Wilson, Oct. 21, 1920, **66**: 253

George Creel to Edith Bolling Galt Wilson, Sept. 27, 1920, **66**: 122

Homer Stillé Cummings to Jared Young Sanders, April 8, 1920, **65**: 164

Homer Stillé Cummings to Joseph Patrick Tumulty, April 8, 1920, **65**: 163

Josephus Daniels to Joseph Patrick Tumulty, Nov. 4, 1919, **63**: 610

Josephus Daniels to Edith Bolling Galt Wilson, Oct. 7, 1919, **63**: 557

Norman Hezekiah Davis to Gilbert Fairchild Close, April 26, 1919, **58**: 164

Norman Hezekiah Davis to Joseph Patrick Tumulty, Dec. 1, 1919, **64**: 104

Memorandum by Norman Hezekiah Davis of a conversation with Lord Bryce about Wilson and the Versailles Treaty, Aug. 19, 1921, **67**: 375

A memorandum by the Department of Justice on the case of Roger Nash Baldwin, Nov. 9, 1918, **53**: 12

Albert De Silver to Joseph Patrick Tumulty, Feb. 21, 1919, **55**: 224

John Foster Dulles to Robert Lansing, Aug. 4, 1919, **62**: 148; Aug. 8, 1919, **62**: 237

Charles William Eliot to Joseph Patrick Tumulty, July 2, 1919, **61**: 373; July 21, 1919, **61**: 577

Memorandum by Albert Bacon Fall asking Wilson for detailed explanations of various provisions of the Versailles Treaty, Aug. 19, 1919, **62**: 411

Rudolph Forster to Joseph Patrick Tumulty, Sept. 5, 1919, **63**: 51; Sept. 7, 1919, **63**: 93; Sept. 9, 1919, **63**: 150; Sept. 11, 1919, **63**: 169; Sept. 13, 1919, **63**: 26; Sept. 22, 1919, **63**: 445; Sept. 24, 1919, **63**: 483

Rudolph Forster to Edith Bolling Galt Wilson, Feb. 14, 1920, **64**: 426

Andrew J. Gallagher and Others to Joseph Patrick Tumulty, Sept. 16, 1919, **63**: 302

Memorandum by Harry Augustus Garfield on appointments for a joint conference of mine workers and coal operators, Sept. 5, 1919, **63**: 56

Statement of protest by gentiles and Christians against anti-Semitism, Dec. 22, 1920, **66**: 541

Peter Goelet Gerry to Josephus Daniels, June 1, 1919, **60**: 18

Memorandum by Carter Glass about the effects of delay in ratifying the peace treaty, Aug. 13, 1919, **62**: 267

Draft by Carter Glass of a League of Nations plank for the Virginia Democratic platform, May 17, 1920, **65**: 293

Memorandum by Carter Glass on Wilson's plan to accept the Democratic presidential nomination, June 10, 1920, **65**: 383

Memorandum by Carter Glass on Wilson's choice as chairman of the platform committee of the Democratic National Convention, June 12, 1920, **65**: 395

Memorandum by Carter Glass on a conversation with Dr. Grayson about Wilson's plans to seek a third term, June 16, 1920, **65**: 400

Samuel Gompers to Joseph Patrick Tumulty, June 8, 1919, **60**: 291

Memorandum by Charles Henry Grasty about the results of governmental control of British railroads, Aug. 14, 1919, **62**: 287

Cary Travers Grayson to Bernard Mannes Baruch, Sept. 5, 1919, **63**: 53

Memoranda by Cary Travers Grayson about conversations with Wilson, March 20, 1920, **65**: 108; March 22, 1920, **65**: 110; March 25, 1920, **65**: 123; March 26, 1920, **65**: 125; March 30, 1920, **65**: 145; March 31, 1920, **65**: 149; April 13, 1920, **65**: 179; April 14, 1920, **65**: 186

Memorandum by Cary Travers Grayson on his testimony at the first Cabinet meeting during Wilson's illness, Oct. 6, 1919, **64**: 496

Thomas Watt Gregory to Joseph Patrick Tumulty, March 1, 1919, **55**: 344

Frederick Hale to Charles Evans Hughes, Aug. 28, 1919, **62**: 537

Walker Downer Hines to Joseph Patrick Tumulty, Oct. 24, 1919, **63**: 595; Nov. 11, 1919, **64**: 21; Nov. 12, 1919, **64**: 24; March 17, 1920, **65**: 95

A memorandum by Walker Downer Hines on railroad legislation, Feb. 24, 1919, **55**: 247

Walker Downer Hines to Arthur Orlando Wharton, Aug. 29, 1919, **62**: 570

Memorandum by Walker Downer Hines on the possible increase in coal prices, July 28, 1919, **62**: 21

Memorandum by Walker Downer Hines on the establishment of a railroad wage board, Aug. 6, 1919, **62**: 181

Memorandum by Walker Downer Hines on the provisions of the Plumb plan, Aug. 8, 1919, **62**: 229

Suggestions by Walker Downer Hines about Wilson's remarks to the railway shopmen, Aug. 24, 1919, **62**: 482

Statement by Walker Downer Hines on the strike by railway workers in California, Arizona, and Nevada, Aug. 28, 1919, **62**: 549
Draft by Walker Downer Hines of a message to Congress on the railroad situation, Nov. 11, 1919, **64**: 17
Gilbert Monell Hitchcock to Bainbridge Colby, April 1, 1920, **65**: 150
Gilbert Monell Hitchcock to Cary Travers Grayson, Oct. 20, 1919, **66**: 547
Gilbert Monell Hitchcock to Joseph Patrick Tumulty, Jan. 16, 1920, **64**: 283; Jan. 17, 1920, **64**: 288; Jan. 26, 1920, **64**: 327
Gilbert Monell Hitchock to Edith Bolling Galt Wilson, Nov. 13, 1919, **64**: 28; Nov. 15, 1919, **64**: 37; Nov. 17, 1919, **64**: 50; Nov. 18, 1919, **64**: 58; Jan. 5, 1920, **64**: 244; Jan. 13, 1920, **64**: 273
Proposed substitute reservations to the peace treaty by Gilbert Monell Hitchcock, Nov. 13, 1919, **64**: 29
Compromise reservation on Article X by Gilbert Monell Hitchcock, Jan. 22, 1920, **64**: 313
Hamilton Holt to Joseph Patrick Tumulty, Nov. 27, 1920, **66**: 434
A statement by Herbert Clark Hoover about his relationship with the meatpackers, Jan. 23, 1919, **54**: 229
Joint House and Senate resolution authorizing the convocation of an international labor conference, Aug. 4, 1919, **62**: 131
Edward Mandell House to Edward Wyliss Scripps, May 20, 1919, **59**: 320
Edward Mandell House to Edith Bolling Galt Wilson, Nov. 24, 1919, **64**: 88; Nov. 27, 1919, **64**: 95
David Franklin Houston to Joseph Patrick Tumulty, June 3, 1920, **65**: 358
Draft by David Franklin Houston of a portion of a State of the Union message, Dec. 2, 1920, **66**: 454
Charles Evans Hughes to Frederick Hale, Aug. 28, 1919, **62**: 537
Notes and memoranda by David Franklin Houston about Tumulty's draft of a Jackson Day message, Jan. 27, 1920, **64**: 251
Draft by David Franklin Houston of a message to Congress on American participation in the proposed International Financial Conference, April 30, 1920, **65**: 239
Draft by David Franklin Houston of a message to the House of Representatives vetoing the legislative, executive, and judicial appropriation bill, May 10, 1920, **65**: 265
Reservations to the peace treaty proposed by Charles Evans Hughes, Aug. 28, 1919, **62**: 536

Bert Mark Jewell and Others to the Officers and Members of Railroad Union Locals, Aug. 28, 1919 (2), **62**: 568, 570

Hugh Leo Kerwin to Joseph Patrick Tumulty, July 23, 1920, **65**: 545
Draft by Hugh Leo Kerwin of a telegram from Wilson to the coal miners and operators of Illinois, July 24, 1920, **65**: 545
Hugh Leo Kerwin to Rudolph Forster, Aug. 7, 1920, **66**: 18

William Harmong Lamar to Albert Sidney Burleson, Sept. 3, 1920, **66**: 94

A draft by Thomas William Lamont of an address to the American people on the financial situation in Europe, June 13, 1919, **60**: 540

A draft by Thomas William Lamont of a letter to Henry Cabot Lodge, July 11, 1919, **61**: 448

A memorandum by Thomas William Lamont and Norman Hezekiah Davis on new legislation to be suggested to Congress, June 13, 1919, **60**: 543

Suggestions by Thomas William Lamont for a strategy to win Senate consent to the ratification of the peace treaty, June 13, 1919, **60**: 537

Isaac Landman to Joseph Patrick Tumulty, Sept. 20, 1920, **66**: 130

A memorandum by Franklin Knight Lane on the Smith-Bankhead Americanization bill, Feb. 26, 1919, **55**: 284

Franklin Knight Lane to Alexander Mitchell Palmer, Aug. 21, 1919, **62**: 438

Franklin Knight Lane to Joseph Patrick Tumulty, Oct. 20, 1919, **63**: 582; Oct. 23, 1919, **63**: 591

A suggestion by Franklin Knight Lane for a testimonial to the dollar-a-year-men, July 18, 1919, **61**: 540

Memorandum by Franklin Knight Lane proposing modifications in the provisions of the General Leasing bill, Aug. 14, 1919, **62**: 299

Memorandum by Franklin Knight Lane on certain provisions of the the General Leasing bill, Aug. 21, 1919, **62**: 438

Robert Lansing to Frank Lyon Polk, Jan. 26, 1919, **54**: 282; Jan. 31, 1919, **54**: 411; Feb. 10, 1919, **55**: 547; June 6, 1919, **60**: 246; June 10, 1919, **60**: 374; June 13, 1919, **60**: 534; Nov. 17, 1919, **64**: 54

Robert Lansing to Frank Lyon Polk and John Foster Dulles, Aug. 28, 1919, **62**: 550

Memorandum by Robert Lansing on Wilson's refusal to accept any reservations to the peace treaty, Aug. 11, 1919, **62**: 258

Memorandum by Robert Lansing on the spread of "communistic ideas" in the United States, Sept. 1, 1919, **62**: 612

Memorandum by Robert Lansing on Wilson state of health, Nov. 5, 1919, **63**: 618

Memorandum by Robert Lansing on Wilson's capacity to perform his official duties, Dec. 4, 1919, **64**: 123

Memorandum by Robert Lansing on the implications of Wilson's interview with Senators Fall and Hitchcock, Dec. 5, 1919, **64**: 139

Memoranda by Robert Lansing on his desire to resign from the Cabinet, Dec. 11, 1919, **64**: 179; Jan. 7, 1920, **64**: 255; Feb. 9, 1920, **64**: 385

Memorandum by Robert Lansing on Wilson's refusal to compromise in the treaty fight, Dec. 16, 1919, **64**: 192

Memorandum by Robert Lansing on Wilson's Jackson Day message, Jan. 10, 1920, **64**: 267

Memorandum by Robert Lansing on his resignation, Feb. 13, 1920, **64**: 415

Memorandum by Robert Lansing on the "Frazier affair," Feb. 22, 1920, **64**: 451

Memorandum by Robert Lansing on the Cabinet meetings held during Wilson's illness, Feb. 23, 1920, **64**: 454

A resolution by the League of Free Nations Association on the ratification of the peace treaty, July 11, 1919, **61**: 447

Report by the Washington bureau of the League to Enforce Peace on the prospect of ratification of the treaty, Sept. 12, 1919, **63**: 235

Russell Cornell Leffingwell to Norman Hezekiah Davis, May 9, 1919, **58**: 595

Russell Cornell Leffingwell to Joseph Patrick Tumulty, Aug. 1, 1919, **62**: 104; Sept. 13, 1919, **63**: 267

Ronald Charles Lindsay to the Duke of Devonshire, July 24, 1919, **61**: 618

Ronald Charles Lindsay to David Lloyd George, July 1, 1920, **65**: 488

Henry Cabot Lodge to James Grover McDonald, July 10, 1919, **61**: 448

Reservations to the peace treaty by Henry Cabot Lodge, Nov. 15, 1919, **64**: 38; Jan. 17, 1920, **64**: 289

Substitute reservation by Henry Cabot Lodge on Article X of the Versailles Treaty, March 11, 1920, **65**: 81

Breckinridge Long to Joseph Patrick Tumulty, Sept. 22, 1919, **63**: 444

Breckinridge Long to Edith Bolling Galt Wilson, Feb. 2, 1920, **64**: 350

Abbott Lawrence Lowell to William Howard Taft, Aug. 9, 1919, **67**: 610

Alfred Lucking to Joseph Patrick Tumulty, Dec. 13, 1918, **53**: 382

Frederick Henry Lynch to William Fraser McDowell, April 10, 1920, **65**: 183

William Gibbs McAdoo to Walker Downer Hines, Feb. 25, 1919, **55**: 260

William Gibbs McAdoo to Edward Mandell House, Jan. 7, 1918, **53**: 646

Vance Criswell McCormick to Joseph Patrick Tumulty, Sept. 8, 1919, **63**: 117, Sept. 12, 1919, **63**: 235

A proposal by Vance Criswell McCormick for the relaxation of cable censorship, April 17, 1919, **57**: 449

Program by James Edward McCulloch and Theodore DuBose Bratton for the improvement of race relations, Aug. 25, 1919, **62**: 505

James Grover McDonald to Joseph Patrick Tumulty, Aug. 27, 1919, **62**: 530

William Fraser McDowell to Joseph Patrick Tumulty, April 13, 1920, **65**: 183

Michael J. McGuire to Joseph Patrick Tumulty, Sept. 15, 1919, **63**: 296

Kenneth Douglas McKellar to Albert Sidney Burleson, March 23, 1920, **65**: 120

Draft by William Douglas Mackenzie of a campaign statement on the importance of U.S. membership in the League of Nations, Oct. 22, 1920, **66**: 260

Extract from a speech by William McKinley, Sept. 20, 1919, **63**: 398

Gavin McNab to Joseph Patrick Tumulty, June 12, 1919, **60**: 487

Thomas Riley Marshall to Joseph Patrick Tumulty, July 26, 1919, **62**: 10

Memorandum by Thomas Riley Marshall on the treaty situation in the Senate, Aug. 20, 1919, **62**: 419

Guy Mason to Joseph Patrick Tumulty, Sept. 22, 1919, **63**: 445

Resolution by the Massachusetts Democratic State Committee against American membership in the League of Nations, July 26, 1919, **62**: 8

Jacob Allen Metzger to Robert Lansing, July 29, 1919, **62**: 35

Peter Michelson to Joseph Patrick Tumulty, Aug. 27, 1919, **62**: 531

David Hunter Miller to Gordon Auchincloss, June 14, 1919 (2), **60**: 571 (2); June 25, 1919, **61**: 181; June 26, 1919, **61**: 232; June 27, 1919, **61**: 295

Dwight Whitney Morrow to Thomas William Lamont, June 5, 1919, **60**: 202

James Patrick Noonan and Julia S. O'Connor to Joseph Patrick Tumulty, March 26, 1919, **56**: 311

Timothy O'Brien to Joseph Patrick Tumulty, March 3, 1919, **55**: 407

Alexander Mitchell Palmer to Joseph Patrick Tumulty, Sept. 17, 1920, **66**: 120

Memorandum by Alexander Mitchell Palmer on the developments leading to the introduction of the General Leasing bill, July 30, 1919, **62**: 45

Memorandum by Alexander Mitchell Palmer on efforts to reduce the high cost of living, Aug. 6, 1919, **62**: 171

Memorandum by Alexander Mitchell Palmer about steps taken to control the high cost of living, Aug. 7, 1919, **62**: 197

Memorandum by Alexander Mitchell Palmer suggesting provisions to be incorporated in the General Leasing bill, Aug. 14, 1919, **62**: 294

Suggestions by Alexander Mitchell Palmer for a statement by Wilson about the wage demands of the railway shopmen, Aug. 22, 1919, **62**: 462

Alexander Mitchell Palmer to Joseph Patrick Tumulty, Dec. 22, 1919, **64**: 215; Jan. 19, 1920, **64**: 296; July 29, 1920, **65**: 563

Draft by Alexander Mitchel Palmer of a statement on the threatened railroad strike, April 15, 1920, **65**: 192

John Barton Payne to Joseph Patrick Tumulty, Feb. 1, 1921, **67**: 119

George Nelson Peek to Bernard Mannes Baruch, April 11, 1919 (2), **57**: 282, 283

John Joseph Pershing to Joseph Patrick Tumulty, March 30, 1920, **65**: 146

James Duval Phelan to Joseph Patrick Tumulty, April 5, 1919, **57**: 49

William Phillips to Joseph Patrick Tumulty, Sept. 18, 1919, **63**: 369

Key Pittman to Joseph Patrick Tumulty, Oct. 15, 1919, **63**: 573

A statement by Key Pittman on the treaty situation in the Senate, July 25, 1919, **61**: 627

Key Pittman to Cary Travers Grayson, Dec. 5, 1919, **64**: 127

Frank Lyon Polk to the American Commissioners, March 21, 1919, **56**: 161; June 6, 1919, **60**: 245; June 9, 1919, **60**: 329; June 11, 1919, **60**: 434

Frank Lyon Polk to Robert Lansing, Jan. 20, 1919, **54**: 174; Jan. 24, 1919, **54**: 259; Feb. 3, 1919, **54**: 472; Feb. 10, 1919, **55**: 92; May 20, 1919, **59**: 313; May 23, 1919 (2), **59**: 450, 451; June 2, 1919, **60**: 42; June 5, 1919, **60**: 156; June 6, 1919 (3), **60**: 242 (2), 244; June 7, 1919 (4), **60**: 288, 289, 290 (2); June 9, 1919, **60**: 299

Frank Lyon Polk to Robert Lansing and Edward Mandell House, May 19, 1919, **59**: 282

Frank Lyon Polk to Robert Lansing and Vance Criswell McCormick, Feb. 4, 1919, **54**: 486

Frank Lyon Polk and John Foster Dulles to Robert Lansing, Aug. 4, 1919, **62**: 143

Statement by DeWitt Clinton Poole, Jr., on the Bolshevik goal of world domination, Aug. 7, 1919, **62**: 203

Notes of meetings of the Princeton Class Officers' Association, June 12, 1905, **65**: 572; Dec. 9, 1905, **65**: 574

The *Providence News* to Joseph Patrick Tumulty, April 16, 1919, **57**: 425

A memorandum by Manuel Luis Quezon on Francis Burton Harrison's divorce and remarriage, June 5, 1919, **60**: 200

Statement by the railroad brotherhoods in support of the Plumb plan, Aug. 4, 1919, **62**: 138

Joseph Eugene Ransdell to Joseph Patrick Tumulty, May 17, 1920, **65**: 294

William Cox Redfield to Joseph Patrick Tumulty, Oct. 15, 1919, **63**: 573

Paul Samuel Reinsch to the Department of State, Aug. 4, 1919, **62**: 147

Edgar Rickard to Herbert Clark Hoover, Jan. 3, 1919, **53**: 603

Edgar Rickard and William Anderson Glasgow, Jr., to Herbert Clark Hoover, Jan. 3, 1919, **53**: 604

Henry Mauris Robinson to Edith Bolling Galt Wilson, Feb. 9, 1920, **64**: 392

Elihu Root to Henry Cabot Lodge (excerpts), June 21, 1919, **61**: 66

George Andrew Sanderson to Joseph Patrick Tumulty, June 28, 1919, **61**: 353; July 16, 1919, **61**: 495; July 17, 1919, **61**: 510

Edward Wyliss Scripps to Edward Mandell House, May 16, 1919, **59**: 204

Ellery Sedgwick to Joseph Patrick Tumulty, March 21, 1919, **56**: 162

Whitney Hart Shepardson to Gilbert Fairchild Close, June 15, 1919, **60**: 570

Suggestions by Selden Palmer Spencer for reservations to the Covenant of the League of Nations, July 25, 1919, **61**: 622

Resolution by the Southern Sociological Congress condemning lynching and mob rule, Aug. 1, 1919, **62**: 106

Resolution by the Southern Sociological Congress calling for a conference of governors to adopt measures to prevent lynching and mob rule, Aug. 1, 1919, **62**: 107

Memorandum by John Spargo requesting a general amnesty for persons convicted under wartime emergency acts, Aug. 29, 1919, **62**: 556

Dan Voorhees Stephens to Joseph Patrick Tumulty, Nov. 9, 1918, **53**: 61

Oscar Solomon Straus to Joseph Patrick Tumulty, Feb. 7, 1920, **64**: 384

Oscar Solomon Straus and David Hunter Miller to Gordon Auchincloss, June 24, 1919, **61**: 137

Memorandum by Oscar Solomon Straus of a meeting of representatives of the League to Enforce Peace with Wilson, Aug. 6, 1919, **67**: 607

Claude Augustus Swanson to Albert Sidney Burleson, June 25, 1919, **61**: 186

A proposed amendment by Claude Augustus Swanson to the General Leasing bill, July 30, 1919, **62**: 49

William Howard Taft to Thomas Walter Bickett, Oct. 30, 1918, **53**: 29

Suggestions by William Howard Taft for reservations to the Covenant of the League of Nations, July 23, 1919, **61**: 607

George Carroll Todd to Thomas Watt Gregory, March 11, 1919, **55**: 478

Joseph Patrick Tumulty to Newton Diehl Baker, April 5, 1919, **57**: 49; Sept. 10, 1919, **63**: 164

Joseph Patrick Tumulty to Louis Brownlow, Sept. 9, 1919, **63**: 150; Sept. 15, 1919, **63**: 296

Joseph Patrick Tumulty to Josephus Daniels, Nov. 11, 1919, **64**: 16

Joseph Patrick Tumulty to John Fitzpatrick, Sept. 10, 1919, **63**: 164

Joseph Patrick Tumulty to Rudolph Forster, Sept. 7, 1919, **63**: 92; Sept. 10, 1919, **63**: 164; Sept. 11, 1919, **63**: 198; Sept. 23, 1919, **63**: 447; Sept. 26, 1919 (2), **63**: 522 (2), Sept. 27, 1919, **63**: 531

Joseph Patrick Tumulty to John Llewellyn Lewis, Oct. 28, 1920, **66**: 281

Joseph Patrick Tumulty to Selden Palmer Spencer, Oct. 4, 1920, **66**: 187

Joseph Patrick Tumulty to Andrew J. Gallagher, Sept. 16, 1919, **63**: 303

Joseph Patrick Tumulty to Samuel Gompers, Sept. 5, 1919, **63**: 52; Sept. 10, 1919, **63**: 163

Joseph Patrick Tumulty to Cary Travers Grayson, Jan. 16, 1919, **54**: 106; Feb. 20, 1919, **55**: 218; March 14, 1919, **55**: 529; April 19, 1919, **57**: 511; May 9, 1919, **58**: 606; June 8, 1919, **60**: 291; July 2, 1919, **61**: 372

Joseph Patrick Tumulty to Walker Downer Hines, Aug. 28, 1919, **62**: 543; Oct. 24, 1919, **63**: 595

Joseph Patrick Tumulty to Edward Mandell House, June 25, 1919, **61**: 185

Joseph Patrick Tumulty to Franklin Knight Lane, Oct. 23, 1919, **63**: 591

Joseph Patrick Tumulty to Russell Cornell Leffingwell, Sept. 10, 1919, **63**: 165

Joseph Patrick Tumulty to John Sharp Williams, Feb. 15, 1919, **55**: 198; Dec. 8, 1919, **64**: 156

Joseph Patrick Tumulty to Edith Bolling Galt Wilson, Oct. 27, 1919, **63**: 602; Nov. 4, 1919, **63**: 609; Nov. 11, 1919 (3), **64**: 6, 14, 16; Nov. 17, 1919, **64**: 42; Nov. 21, 1919, **64**: 69; Nov. 22, 1919, **64**: 72; Nov. 25, 1920, **64**: 90; Nov. 27, 1919, **64**: 93; Dec. 1, 1919, **64**: 103; Dec. 8, 1919, **64**: 153; Dec. 18, 1919, **64**: 203, 204; Dec. 22, 1919, **64**: 214; Dec. 23, 1919, **64**: 222; Jan. 6, 1919, **64**: 246; Jan. 15, 1920, **64**: 276; Jan. 16, 1920, **64**: 282; Jan. 17, 1920, **64**: 287; Jan. 30, 1920, **64**: 345; Feb. 3, 1920, **64**: 353, 355; Feb. 9, 1920, **64**: 391; Feb. 10, 1920, **64**: 396; Feb. 13, 1920, **64**: 419; Feb. 24, 1920, **64**: 467; Feb. 25, 1920, **64**: 473; Feb. 26, 1920 (2), **64**: 474, 475; Feb. 27, 1920, **64**: 480; 1920, **65**: 24; March 5, 1920 (2), **65**: 48, 56; March 7, 1920, **65**: 66; March 11, 1920, **65**: 82; March 23, 1920, **65**: 117; March 24, 1920, **65**: 122; March 26, 1920, **65**: 134; March 30, 1920 (2), **65**: 145, 146; April 9, 1920, **65**: 163; April 10, 1920, **65**: 175; April 13, 1920, **65**: 183; April 20, 1920, **65**: 215; June 15, 1920, **65**: 398; July 4, 1920 (2), **65**: 493, 494; July 5, 1920 (2), **65**: 497 (2); July 15, 1920, **65**: 513; July 24, 1920, **65**: 544; July 30, 1920, **65**: 564; Aug. 3, 1920, **66**: 4; Sept. 8, 1920, **66**: 102; Sept. 10, 1920, **66**: 112; Oct. 15, 1920, **66**: 230; Nov. 4, 1920, **66**: 317; Feb. 5, 1921, **67**: 119

Joseph Patrick Tumulty to William Bauchop Wilson, Oct. 6, 1919, **63**: 554; Oct. 24, 1919, **63**: 593

A memorandum by Joseph Patrick Tumulty about the political program of the administration, Nov. 9, 1918, **53**: 23

A draft by Joseph Patrick Tumulty of a proposed statement on the industrial situation, Nov. 14, 1918, **53**: 77

Draft by Joseph Patrick Tumulty of a message to Congress on the State of the Union, March 26, 1920, **65**: 129

Draft by Joseph Patrick Tumulty of a message to the National

Democratic Convention on the Volstead Act, June 24, 1920, **65**: 453

Draft by Joseph Patrick Tumulty on the mandatory retirement of certain civil service employees, July 17, 1920, **65**: 519

Draft by Joseph Patrick Tumulty of a statement on changes made in the League Covenant as shown by the Wilson-Taft cables, Sept. 26, 1920, **66**: 148

Suggestions by Joseph Patrick Tumulty for speeches on the League of Nations and an address on reconstruction, June 4, 1919, **60**: 145

A memorandum by Joseph Patrick Tumulty on the suggestions by William Howard Taft for reservations to the Covenant of the League of Nations, July 23, 1919, **61**: 606

Memorandum by Joseph Patrick Tumulty on Wilson's forthcoming address to Congress on the high cost of living, Aug. 7, 1919, **62**: 196

Memorandum by Joseph Patrick Tumulty on the cost of the war to the Allies and the Central Powers, Sept. 12, 1919, **63**: 221

Memorandum by Joseph Patrick Tumulty on themes for an address by Wilson, Sept. 12, 1919, **63**: 222

Memorandum by Joseph Patrick Tumulty on the attitude of the churches of America toward the League of Nations, Oct. 6, 1920, **66**: 201

Statement by Joseph Patrick Tumulty on the effects of a Republican victory in the November election, Oct. 10, 1920, **66**: 214

A suggestion by Henry van Dyke for an interpretive "proviso" to be added to the Covenant of the League of Nations, July 13, 1919, **61**: 476

Press release by the War Trade Board on the resumption of trade with Germany, Aug. 20, 1919, **62**: 424

Thomas James Walsh to Gilbert Monell Hitchcock, Nov. 18, 1919, **64**: 59

George Wakeman Wheeler to William Gibbs McAdoo, July 8, 1919, **61**: 460

Sherman Leland Whipple to Josephus Daniels, Nov. 22, 1918, **53**: 186

Memorandum by the White House Staff on a proclamation of amnesty for certain military prisoners, April 12, 1920, **65**: 177

Henry Winslow Williams to Joseph Patrick Tumulty, July 15, 1919, **61**: 489

A draft by Henry Winslow Williams of a proposed resolution by the Senate consenting to the ratification of the peace treaty, July 15, 1919, **61**: 491

Edith Bolling Galt Wilson to Albert Sidney Burleson, Jan. 28, 1920, **64**: 336; Jan. 29, 1920, **64**: 343

Edith Bolling Galt Wilson to Josephus Daniels, Oct. 7, 1919, **63**: 558

Edith Bolling Galt Wilson to Rudolph Forester, Feb. 14, 1920, **64**: 426

Edith Bolling Galt Wilson to Harry Augustus Garfield, Dec. 9, 1919, **64**: 167

Edith Bolling Galt Wilson to Carter Glass, Feb. 11, 1920, **64**: 405

Edith Bolling Galt Wilson to Gilbert Monell Hitchcock, Dec. 19, 1919 (2), **64**: 206 (2); Jan. 5, 1920, **64**: 243; Jan. 13, 1920, **64**: 274

Edith Bolling Galt Wilson to Thomas Davies Jones, Dec. 28, 1919, **64**: 232

Edith Bolling Galt Wilson to Robert Lansing, Dec. 2, 1919 (2), **64**: 119 (2); Feb. 9, 1920, **64**: 389

Edith Bolling Galt Wilson to Alexander Mitchell Palmer, Dec. 18, 1919, **64**: 202

Edith Bolling Galt Wilson to Joseph Patrick Tumulty, Nov. 10, 1919, **64**: 4; Nov. 11, 1919, **64**: 16; Nov. 29, 1919, **64**: 97; Dec. 7, 1919, **64**: 145; Dec. 17, 1919, **64**: 198; Jan. 26, 1920, **64**: 330; Feb. 21, 1920, **64**: 448; March 1, 1920, **65**: 28; March 26, 1920 (2), **65**: 128 (2); Oct. 15, 1920, **66**: 230

Edith Bolling Galt Wilson to the White House Staff, Jan. 24, 1920, **64**: 322

William Bauchop Wilson to Joseph Patrick Tumulty, Oct. 21, 1920, **66**: 254; Dec. 23, 1920, **66**: 546

Memorandum by William Bauchop Wilson on the coal mining situation in Illinois, July 29, 1920, **65**: 559

Sir William Wiseman to Arthur James Balfour, July 18, 1919, **61**: 541

Sir William Wiseman to Edward Mandell House, July 19, 1919, **61**: 561

Robert Wickliffe Woolley to Vance Criswell McCormick, May 14, 1919, **59**: 149

Robert Wickliffe Wooley to Joseph Patrick Tumulty, Oct. 1, 1920, **66**: 173

Diplomatic and military correspondence, reports,
memoranda, and aide-mémoire

Carl Ackerman to Edward Mandell House, Jan. 6, 1919, **53**: 628

The American Commissioners to the Department of State, April 12, 1919, **57**: 315

The American Commissioners to Frank Lyon Polk, Jan. 7, 1919 (2), **53**: 645, 650; Jan. 8, 1919, **53**: 690

The American Mission in Paris to John William Davis, Jan. 1, 1919, **53**: 585

Statement by the American Commission on Irish Independence demanding a joint Anglo-American secretariat for the League of Nations, Aug. 16, 1919, **62**: 324

Philip Andrews to William Shepherd Benson, April 25, 1919, **58**: 142; May 2, 1919, **58**: 354; May 4, 1919, **58**: 426; May 7, 1919, **58**: 528; May 8, 1919 (3), **58**: 554, 555 (2); May 12, 1919, **59**: 64

Gordon Auchincloss to Gilbert Fairchild Close, Dec. 18, 1918, **53**: 430; May 22, 1919, **59**: 409
Gordon Auchincloss to Frank Lyon Polk, Dec. 18, 1918, **53**: 437

Newton Diehl Baker to Bainbridge Colby, April 8, 1920, **65**: 160
Newton Diehl Baker to Joseph Patrick Tumulty, Sept. 22, 1919, **63**: 441
Arthur James Balfour to Colville Adrian de Rune Barclay, Dec. 6, 1918, **53**: 324
Arthur James Balfour to Lord Derby, Nov. 13, 1918, **53**: 69; Nov. 15, 1918, **53**: 85; Jan. 2, 1918, **53**: 591
Arthur James Balfour to David Lloyd George, Aug. 4, 1919, **62**: 146
Arthur James Balfour to Tommaso Tittoni, July 28, 1919, **62**: 22
Arthur James Balfour to Henry White, July 28, 1919, **62**: 25
Memorandum by Arthur James Balfour about a proposed settlement of the Adriatic question, Aug. 31, 1919, **62**: 603
Colville Adrian de Rune Barclay to the British Foreign Office, Dec. 4, 1918, **53**: 317
Julius Howland Barnes to Joseph Patrick Tumulty, Nov. 10, 1919, **64**: 5; Nov. 11, 1919, **64**: 12, 13
James Levi Barton to Cleveland Hoadley Dodge, Dec. 1, 1920, **66**: 449
James Levi Barton and William Wheelock Peet to Cleveland Hoadley Dodge, Aug. 29, 1919, **62**: 577
Edward Price Bell to Bainbridge Colby, Dec. 3, 1920, **66**: 460
Edward Price Bell to Lawrence Lanier Winslow, Dec. 31, 1918, **53**: 573
Memorandum by Bernard Mannes Baruch on the request by the German government for food and raw materials, Aug. 16, 1919, **62**: 330
William Shepherd Benson to Philip Andrews, May 3, 1919, **58**: 408
William Shepherd Benson to Mark Lambert Bristol, May 2, 1919, **58**: 409
William Shepherd Benson to John Havens Dayton, May 2, 1919, **58**: 409
William Shepherd Benson to William Sowden Sims, May 2, 1919 (2), **58**: 409, 410
Tasker Howard Bliss to Newton Diehl Baker, Feb. 14, 1919, **55**: 188
Tasker Howard Bliss to Newton Diehl Baker and Peyton Conway March, Nov. 26, 1918, **53**: 208; Feb. 13, 1919, **55**: 150; July 15, 1919, **61**: 485
Tasker Howard Bliss to Robert Lansing, April 19, 1919, **57**: 496
A memorandum by Tasker Howard Bliss on the reinforcement of American troops in North Russia, Feb. 12, 1919, **55**: 190
Isaiah Bowman to Robert Lansing, Aug. 21, 1919, **62**: 452
Mark Lambert Bristol to William Shepherd Benson, May 12, 1919, **59**: 67

Draft minutes of a meeting of the British War Cabinet, Dec. 30, 1918, **53**: 558

Arthur Bullard to Joseph Patrick Tumulty, March 29, 1920, **65**: 143

Memoranda by William Christian Bullitt about the Bolshevik movement in Europe, Nov. 8, 1918, **53**: 6; Nov. 18, 1918, **53**: 121

John Kenneth Caldwell to the Department of State, May 6, 1919, **58**: 495

Henry Campbell to the American Commission, Jan. 28, 1919, **54**: 399

A memorandum by Lord Robert Cecil about the constitution for a league of nations, Dec. 17, 1918, **53**: 415

Austen Chamberlain to David Franklin Houston (extract), Feb. 26, 1920, **64**: 477

Georges Clemenceau to David Lloyd George, Nov. 15, 1918, **53**: 84

Georges Clemenceau to Edward Mandell House, Nov. 9, 1918, **53**: 4; Nov. 10, 1918, **53**: 27; Sept. 13, 1919, **63**: 271

Georges Clemenceau to Frank Lyon Polk, Aug. 25, 1919, **62**: 511

Gilbert Fairchild Close to Gordon Auchincloss, Dec. 18, 1918, **53**: 432

Gilbert Fairchild Close to William Shepherd Benson, May 28, 1919, **59**: 576

Gilbert Fairchild Close to Joseph Clark Grew, Feb. 7, 1919, **54**: 552

Gilbert Fairchild Close to Mohammed Abd Al Kadi, March 20, 1919, **56**: 122

Gilbert Fairchild Close to Robert Lansing, Jan. 25, 1919, **54**: 278

Gilbert Fairchild Close to John Joseph Pershing, Feb. 13, 1919, **55**: 151

Gilbert Fairchild Close to Edith Bolling Galt Wilson, Jan. 19, 1920, **64**: 297

Gilbert Fairchild Close to Francis Call Woodman, Jan. 24, 1919, **54**: 262

Bainbridge Colby to Samuel Gompers, June 11, 1920, **65**: 390

Bainbridge Colby to Hugh Campbell Wallace, April 10, 1920, **65**: 167; June 13, 1920, **65**: 395

Bainbridge Colby to the Ambassadors accredited to the Principal Allied Powers (about Yap Island), Nov. 5, 1920, **66**: 326

Bainbridge Colby to George Creel, Sept. 25, 1920, **66**: 143; Nov. 20, 1920, **66**: 406

Bainbridge Colby to Earl Curzon of Kedleston, Nov. 19, 1920, **66**: 394

Bainbridge Colby to John William Davis, Nov. 13, 1920, **66**: 366

Bainbridge Colby to Norman Hezekiah Davis, Jan. 3, 1921, **67**: 23

Bainbridge Colby to Roberto V. Pesqueira Morales, Oct. 28, 1920, **66**: 283; Nov. 25, 1920, **66**: 418

Bainbridge Colby to Hugh Campbell Wallace, Feb. 21, 1921, **67**: 153

Charles Richard Crane to Prince Georgii Evgen'evich L'vov, Oct. 7, 1918, **53**: 258

Richard Crane to the Department of State, Feb. 18, 1920, **64**: 443
George Creel to Bainbridge Colby, Sept. 25, 1920, **66**: 143; Oct. 26,
    1920, **66**: 270; Nov. 15, 1920, **66**: 371
George Creel to Edith Bolling Galt Wilson, Sept. 30, 1920, **66**: 170;
    Nov. 15, 1920, **66**: 371
Memoranda by Oscar Terry Crosby on various foreign loans, Dec. 23,
    1918, **53**: 478; Dec. 31, 1918, **53**: 571

John William Davis to the Department of State, March 4, 1920, **65**:
    45; April 7, 1920, **65**: 158
John William Davis to Bainbridge Colby, Nov. 28, 1920, **66**: 437;
    Dec. 3, 1920, **66**: 459
John William Davis to Norman Hezekiah Davis, Jan. 12, 1921, **67**: 55
John William Davis to Robert Lansing, Aug. 18, 1919, **62**: 334; Nov.
    24, 1919, **64**: 88; Feb. 7, 1920, **64**: 381
Norman Hezekiah Davis to Carter Glass, May 6, 1919, **59**: 111
Norman Hezekiah Davis to John William Davis, Dec. 3, 1920, **66**:
    460; Jan. 5, 1921, **67**: 62
Norman Hezekiah Davis to Paul Hymans, Dec. 15, 1920, **66**: 517
Clive Day to Elizabeth Dike Day, Dec. 10, 1918, **53**: 348; Dec. 11,
    1918, **53**: 367
Manton Davis to the War Department, March 18, 1920, **65**: 103 (2)
Norman Hezekiah Davis to John William Davis, July 6, 1920, **65**:
    504
Norman Hezekiah Davis to Albert Rathbone, Nov. 11, 1919, **64**: 12
Norman Hezekiah Davis to Joseph Patrick Tumulty, Nov. 14, 1919,
    64: 33; June 23, 1920, **65**: 448; Jan. 3, 1921, **67**: 24
Norman Hezekiah Davis to Paul Hymans, Jan. 15, 1921, **67**: 64
    (draft); Jan. 15, 1921, **67**: 65
Norman Hezekiah Davis' statement to the press on Gen. Crowder's
    mission to Cuba, Jan. 4, 1921, **67**: 25
Norman Hezekiah Davis to Hugh Campbell Wallace, Jan. 8, 1921,
    67: 41
Lord Derby to Arthur James Balfour, Dec. 16, 1918, **53**: 409; Dec. 20,
    1918 (2), **53**: 456, 458; Dec. 22, 1918, **53**: 470; Dec. 24, 1918, **53**:
    498; Jan. 6, 1919, **53**: 633
Lord Derby to Edward Mandell House, Nov. 22, 1918, **53**: 167; Dec.
    23, 1918, **53**: 488; Dec. 25, 1918, **53**: 508
Ellis Loring Dresel to Robert Lansing, Feb. 5, 1920, **64**: 364
Sir Eric Drummond to Sir William Wiseman, Dec. 17, 1918, **53**: 414
William Edward Burghardt Du Bois to Joseph Patrick Tumulty,
    Nov. 27, 1918, **53**: 236
A memorandum by William Edward Burghardt Du Bois about the
    future of Africa, Nov. 27, 1918, **53**: 236

Rudolph Forster to Joseph Patrick Tumulty, Sept. 26, 1919, **63**: 526
Raymond Blaine Fosdick to Sir Eric Drummond, Jan. 19, 1920, **64**:
    306

Raymond Blaine Fosdick to Joseph Patrick Tumulty, Jan. 19, 1920, **64**: 306

Charles Warren Fowler to Joseph Patrick Tumulty, Aug. 29, 1919, **62**: 576

John Charles Frémont to Cary Travers Grayson, May 13, 1919, **59**: 119; May 17, 1919 (2), **59**: 241 (2); May 18, 1919, **59**: 252

A proposal by the French government about the organization and procedure of the peace conference, Nov. 23, 1918, **53**: 293

Hampson Gary to the State Department and the American Commissioners, March 18, 1919, **56**: 154

Sir Auckland Geddes to David Lloyd George, June 4, 1920, **65**: 369

A note by the German government accepting the Armistice terms, Nov. 11, 1919, **53**: 33

Hugh Simons Gibson to Bainbridge Colby, July 18, 1920, **65**: 526

Carter Glass to Norman Hezekiah Davis, May 10, 1919, **59**: 112

Ulysses Grant-Smith to the Department of State, Nov. 21, 1918, **53**: 194

William Sidney Graves to Newton Diehl Baker, Nov. 21, 1918, **53**: 168; Nov. 23, 1918, **53**: 184

William Sidney Graves to the Department of State, Dec. 29, 1918, **53**: 557; March 13, 1919, **55**: 493

William Sidney Graves to Peter Charles Harris, **55**: 399; July 31, 1919, **62**: 83

Cary Travers Grayson to Joseph Patrick Tumulty, Jan. 7, 1919, **53**: 646

Viscount Grey of Fallodon to Robert Lansing, Nov. 14, 1919, **64**: 33

Albert Halstead to Robert Lansing, Aug. 5, 1919, **62**: 167

Ernest Lloyd Harris to the Department of State, May 30, 1919, **59**: 619; July 16, 1919, **61**: 494

Ernest Lloyd Harris to Robert Lansing and Vance Criswell McCormick, June 5, 1919, **60**: 180

Peter Charles Harris to John Joseph Pershing, Nov. 29, 1918, **53**: 291

Herbert Clark Hoover to Joseph Potter Cotton, Nov. 14, 1918, **53**: 76

Herbert Clark Hoover to the Food Administration, Jan. 6, 1919, **53**: 648

Herbert Clark Hoover to Edgar Rickard, Jan. 5, 1919, **53**: 649

A memorandum and a statement by Herbert Clark Hoover and John William Davis about an inter-Allied conference on European relief, Dec. 10, 1918, **53**: 360

A memorandum by Herbert Clark Hoover about a proposed agreement between the United States and the Allies about European relief, Jan. 8, 1919, **53**: 689

Edward Mandell House to Arthur James Balfour, Jan. 1, 1919, **53**: 85; April 19, 1919, **57**: 499

Edward Mandell House to Frank Irving Cobb, Dec. 16, 1918, **53**: 408

Edward Mandell House to Robert Lansing, Nov. 15, 1918, **53**: 85;
    Nov. 22, 1918, **53**: 180; Aug. 15, 1919, **62**: 323
Edward Mandell House to Stéphen-Jean-Marie Pichon, Jan. 1, 1919,
    53: 585
A memorandum by Edward Mandell House about the establishment
    of a commission to consider the financial conditions of Germany,
    Dec. 23, 1918, **53**: 473
Draft by Edward Mandell House of provisions for Class A mandates,
    Aug. 9, 1919, **62**: 243
A memorandum by William Chapin Huntington about the Russian
    situation, Nov. 22, 1918, **53**: 169
Paul Hymans to Bainbridge Colby, Dec. 4, 1920, **66**: 473

A memorandum by the Interparty League for the Restoration of Free
    Russia, Nov. 20, 1918, **53**: 136
A memorandum by Kikujiro Ishii about Japanese troops in Siberia,
    Dec. 30, 1918, **53**: 555

Aide-mémoire by the Japanese government about the restoration of
    Shantung to China, Aug. 22, 1919, **62**: 458
Note to the Japanese government about the policy of the Japanese
    forces in Siberia, Aug. 30, 1919, **62**: 589
A note from the Japanese government about its military policy in
    Siberia, Nov. 20, 1918, **53**: 144
Peter Augustus Jay to Robert Lansing, Sept. 15, 1919, **63**: 297; Oct.
    2, 1919, **63**: 543
Douglas Wilson Johnson to Arthur James Balfour (draft), Feb. 6,
    1920, **64**: 370
Robert Underwood Johnson to the Department of State, May 20,
    1920, **65**: 307
Robert Underwood Johnson to Bainbridge Colby, Nov. 13, 1920, **66**:
    365
Robert Underwood Johnson to Robert Lansing, Jan. 29, 1920, **64**:
    343
Charles M. Johnston to Norman Hezekiah Davis, June 25, 1920, **65**:
    462
Jean-Jules Jusserand to the French Foreign Ministry, March 29,
    1920 (2), **65**: 144 (2)
Jean-Jules Jusserand to Robert Lansing, Nov. 29, 1918, **53**: 292;
    Dec. 1, 1919, **64**: 101
Jean-Jules Jusserand to Frank Lyon Polk, March 13, 1920, **65**: 84

Theodore Porter Kane to William Ledyard Rodgers, March 22, 1919,
    56: 184
Alexander Comstock Kirk to Cary Travers Grayson, Nov. 25, 1919,
    64: 90
Memorandum by Alexander Comstock Kirk about the Japanese
    statement on the Shantung settlement, July 30, 1919, **62**: 63

Harry Shepard Knapp to William Shepherd Benson, June 17, 1919,
  60: 613
Alfred William Fortescue Knox to the British War Office, March 22,
  1919, **56**: 184
J. E. Kunhardt to Samuel Gompers, Dec. 21, 1920, **66**: 538

Robert Lansing to the American Mission, Aug. 1, 1919, **62**: 108
Robert Lansing to Felix Cole, Aug. 30, 1919, **62**: 594
Robert Lansing to John William Davis, Aug. 20, 1919, **62**: 427
Robert Lansing to David Rowland Francis, Aug. 28, 1919, **62**: 589
Robert Lansing to Cary Travers Grayson, Nov. 24, 1919, **64**: 88
Robert Lansing to Edward Mandell House, Nov. 18, 1918, **53**: 127;
  Dec. 8, 1918, **53**: 341; Aug. 21, 1919 (2), **62**: 452 (2)
Robert Lansing to Jean-Jules Jusserand, Dec. 1, 1919, **64**: 102
Robert Lansing to Ignace Jan Paderewski, Jan. 22, 1919, **54**: 217
Robert Lansing to Frank Lyon Polk, Dec. 18, 1918, **53**: 436; Jan. 2,
  1919, **53**: 590; Jan. 11, 1919, **53**: 718; Jan. 20, 1919, **54**: 158; April
  1, 1919, **56**: 519; April 15, 1919, **57**: 374; April 21, 1919, **57**: 557;
  Aug. 6, 1919, **62**: 186; Aug. 9, 1919 (2), **62**: 242 (2); Aug. 12, 1919
  (2), **62**: 264 (2); Aug. 14, 1919, **62**: 304; Aug. 18, 1919, **62**: 334; Aug.
  21, 1919, **62**: 449; Aug. 26, 1919, **62**: 522; Aug. 28, 1919, **62**: 551;
  Aug. 29, 1919, **62**: 579; Aug. 31, 1919, **62**: 595; Sept. 2, 1919, **62**:
  620; Nov. 14, 1919, **64**: 36; Dec. 8, 1919, **64**: 156
Robert Lansing to Joseph Patrick Tumulty, Nov. 22, 1918, **53**: 180;
  Aug. 1, 1919, **62**: 111; Nov. 19, 1919, **64**: 5; Nov. 21, 1919, **64**: 66;
  Nov. 27, 1919, **64**: 94; Dec. 15, 1919, **64**: 187; Jan. 12, 1920, **64**: 273
Robert Lansing to Hugh Campbell Wallace, Jan. 23, 1920, **64**: 320;
  Jan. 29, 1920, **64**: 342; Feb. 6, 1920, **64**: 373; Feb. 10, 1920, **64**: 398
Robert Lansing to Edith Bolling Galt Wilson, Dec. 7, 1919, **64**: 147;
  Jan. 23, 1920, **64**: 316; Jan. 20, 1920, **64**: 343; Feb. 6, 1920, **64**: 366;
  Feb. 9, 1920, **64**: 391; Feb. 11, 1920, **64**: 407
Robert Lansing and Vance Criswell McCormick to Frank Lyon Polk,
  Feb. 9, 1919, **55**: 38; April 16, 1919, **57**: 420; June 25, 1919, **61**: 177
A proposed statement by Robert Lansing on the Russian situation,
  Nov. 21, 1918, **53**: 152
A draft by Robert Lansing of various articles of a constitution for a
  league of nations, Dec. 20, 1918, **53**: 475
Memorandum by Robert Lansing about comments by the Japanese
  press on the Shantung settlement, July 30, 1919, **62**: 63
Memorandum by Robert Lansing on Isaiah Bowman's views of Colo-
  nel House, Aug. 21, 1919, **62**: 454
Ronald Charles Lindsay to Robert Lansing, Aug. 16, 1919, **62**: 331
Maksim Maksimovich Litvinov to Ludwig Meyer, Jan. 10, 1919, **53**:
  712
David Lloyd George to Viscount Grey of Fallodon, Nov. 14, 1919, **64**:
  33
David Lloyd George to Edward Mandell House, Nov. 25, 1918, **53**:
  197

Thomas Francis Logan to Edward Nash Hurley, Dec. 23, 1918, **53**: 480

Breckinridge Long to Robert Lansing, Aug. 14, 1919, **62**: 282

Breckinridge Long to Joseph Patrick Tumulty, July 12, 1919, **61**: 470; July 17, 1919, **61**: 514; Dec. 29, 1919, **64**: 234

Memorandum by Breckinridge Long on a conversation with Katsuji Debuchi about a Japanese statement on the future of Shantung, July 29, 1919, **62**: 40

Kazimierz Lubomirski to Bainbridge Colby, Aug. 4, 1920, **66**: 9

William Gibbs McAdoo to Edith Bolling Galt Wilson, Nov. 17, 1920, **66**: 383

Vance Criswell McCormick to Frank Lyon Polk, May 16, 1919, **59**: 188; May 17, 1919, **59**: 236

Newton Alexander McCully to William Sowden Sims, Feb. 9, 1919, **55**: 39

Grenville Stanley Macfarland to Joseph Patrick Tumulty, Dec. 23, 1918, **53**: 487

Edward Fenton McGlachlin, Jr., to Peyton Conway March, Sept. 16, 1919, **63**: 361

A memorandum by Peyton Conway March about the number of American troops in Europe, Nov. 25, 1918, **53**: 200

Ludwig Christian Alexander Karlovich Martens to Robert Lansing, March 25, 1919, **56**: 548

A memorandum by Charles Edward Merriam about the policy of the Vatican, Nov. 9, 1918, **53**: 16

A note to the Mexican government on the murder of American citizens in Mexico, July 18, 1919, **61**: 527

Memorandum by David Hunter Miller on the form of mandate for Togoland, Aug. 27, 1919, **62**: 532

Ransford Stevens Miller to Robert Lansing, Nov. 26, 1918, **53**: 207

Ira Nelson Morris to Joseph Patrick Tumulty, March 2, 1920, **65**: 40

Roland Sletor Morris to the Department of State, Dec. 30, 1918, **53**: 555; April 12, 1919, **57**: 313; May 6, 1919, **58**: 494; July 21, 1919, **61**: 571

Roland Sletor Morris to Frank Lyon Polk, May 17, 1919, **59**: 235

Thomas Bentley Mott to Edward Mandell House, Nov. 10, 1918, **53**: 27

Robert Henry Murray to Henry Morgenthau, Sept. 21, 1920, **66**: 133

A memorandum on proposed remarks by Dedjazmatch Nadao at the intended White House reception of the Ethiopian Mission, July 12, 1919, **61**: 473

Ignace Jan Paderewski to Edward Mandell House, Jan, 4, 1919, **53**: 611

Ignace Jan Paderewski to Robert Lansing, Jan. 21, 1919, **54**: 195

Sir George Paish to Edward Mandell House, Aug. 11, 1919, **62**: 256

John Joseph Pershing to Newton Diehl Baker and Peyton Conway March, July 19, 1919, **61**: 547; Aug. 13, 1919, **62**: 271

Roberto V. Pesqueira Morales to Bainbridge Colby, Oct. 28, 1920, **66**: 285

Marc Peter to Guiseppe Motta, May 28, 1920, **65**: 338

William Phillips to the American Commissioners, April 4, 1919, **56**: 606

William Phillips to Peter Augustus Jay, Oct. 9, 1919, **63**: 560

William Phillips to Robert Lansing, March 25, 1919 (2), **56**: 548, 551; Sept. 8, 1919, **63**: 119

William Phillips to Robert Lansing and Vance Criswell McCormick, June 16, 1919 (2), **60**: 608, 609; June 20, 1919, **61**: 41

William Phillips to Frank Lyon Polk, Sept. 9, 1919, **63**: 151

William Phillips to Joseph Patrick Tumulty, Dec. 8, 1919, **64**: 157

Stéphen-Jean-Marie Pichon to Edward Mandell House, Nov. 21, 1918, **53**: 154

Stéphen-Jean-Marie Pichon to Jean-Jules Jusserand, Dec. 9, 1918, **53**: 345, 346

A statement by Key Pittman on the signing of the Armistice, Nov. 11, 1918, **53**: 51

Frank Lyon Polk to the American Commissioners, March 22, 1919, **56**: 187; April 19, 1919, **57**: 512; May 6, 1919, **58**: 494; May 12, 1919, **59**: 72; May 27, 1919, **59**: 550

Frank Lyon Polk to Edward Mandell House, Sept. 5, 1919, **63**: 59

Frank Lyon Polk to Robert Lansing, Dec. 2, 1918, **53**: 291; Dec. 7, 1918, **53**: 335; Dec. 8, 1918, **53**: 342; Dec. 9, 1918, **53**: 345; Dec. 16, 1918, **53**: 408; Dec. 23, 1918, **53**: 463, 466; Dec. 30, 1918, **53**: 555; Jan. 3, 1919, **53**: 605; Jan. 6, 1919 (3), **53**: 627, 628, 632; Jan. 11, 1919, **54**: 83; Jan. 24, 1919, **54**: 261; March 7, 1919, **56**: 101; May 27, 1919, **59**: 547; May 30, 1919 (2), **59**: 618, 619; June 6, 1919, **60**: 240; Aug. 3, 1919, **62**: 123; Aug. 7, 1919, **62**: 207; Aug. 9, 1919, **62**: 248; Aug. 15, 1919 (3), **62**: 318, 319, 320; Aug. 16, 1919, **62**: 328; Aug. 19, 1919, **62**: 416; Aug. 22, 1919, **62**: 456; Aug. 25, 1919, **62**: 510; Aug. 28, 1919, **62**: 553; Aug. 13, 1919, **62**: 603; Nov. 14, 1919, **64**: 35; Nov. 26, 1919, **64**: 91; Dec. 2, 1919, **64**: 117; Dec. 7, 1919, **64**: 150; Dec. 9, 1919, **64**: 168

Frank Lyon Polk to Robert Lansing and Vance Criswell McCormick, March 13, 1919, **55**: 493; March 21, 1919, **56**: 159; May 17, 1919, **59**: 234; June 27, 1919, **61**: 288

Frank Lyon Polk to William Phillips, Sept. 10, 1919, **63**: 166; Sept. 12, 1919, **63**: 235

Frank Lyon Polk to Joseph Patrick Tumulty, Jan. 21, 1919, **54**: 194; Dec. 26, 1919, **64**: 229

Frank Lyon Polk to Hugh Campbell Wallace, Feb. 12, 1919, **64**: 411; Feb. 24, 1919, **64**: 465; March 8, 1920, **65**: 73 (draft) Frank Lyon Polk and Henry White to Robert Lansing, Aug. 4, 1919, **62**: 144

DeWitt Clinton Poole, Jr., to Tasker Howard Bliss, April 21, 1919, **57**: 560

DeWitt Clinton Poole, Jr. to the Department of State, July 25, 1919,
  61: 637
DeWitt Clinton Poole, Jr., to Robert Lansing, Aug. 21, 1919, **62**: 441

William Ledyard Rodgers to the Navy Department, March 21, 1919,
  56: 184
Walter Stowell Rogers to Albert Sidney Burleson, Nov. 24, 1920, **66**:
  416
Leo Stanton Rowe to Norman Hezekiah Davis, June 24, 1920, **65**:
  465; July 9, 1920, **65**: 505
Leo Stanton Rowe to Joseph Patrick Tumulty, Jan. 5, 1920, **64**: 245

A memorandum by William Salmon, M.D., on the relative absence of
  insanity, inebrity, and crime among the members of the A.E.F.,
  July 18, 1919, **61**: 531
Charles Seymour to his family, Dec. 10, 1918, **53**: 356; Dec. 12, 1918,
  53: 377
William Sowden Sims to William Shepherd Benson, Feb. 9, 1919, **55**:
  39
Charles Hayden Smith to the Department of State, July 25, 1919,
  61: 637
Walter George Smith to Cleveland Hoadley Dodge, Aug. 19, 1919,
  62: 416
A memorandum by Jan Christiaan Smuts on the constitution of a
  league of nations, Dec. 26, 1918, **53**: 515
John Frank Stevens to the Department of State, May 6, 1919, **58**:
  494; June 16, 1919, **60**: 608
Lewis Strauss to Gilbert Fairchild Close, Jan. 7, 1919, **53**: 648
A memorandum by Henry Wickham Steed on the Adriatic question,
  Dec. 19, 1918, **53**: 444
Bonaldo Stringher to Vittorio Emanuele Orlando, May 13, 1919, **59**:
  110
Hans Sulzer to Robert Lansing, Nov. 12, 1918, **53**: 63
George Thomas Summerlin to the Department of State, June 23,
  1920, **65**: 446; July 1, 1920, **65**: 485
George Thomas Summerlin to Charles M. Johnston, July 1, 1920,
  65: 486
Charles Lee Swem to Bainbridge Colby, May 20, 1920, **65**: 299
Charles Lee Swem to Edith Bolling Galt Wilson, Oct. 4, 1920, **66**:
  189
A note from the Swiss government requesting the occupation of Vi-
  enna by Entente forces, Nov. 18, 1918, **53**: 127

André Tardieu to Edward Mandell House, Dec. 24, 1918, **53**: 497
A memorandum by André Tardieu on the future operations of the
  inter-Allied councils, Dec. 24, 1918, **53**: 497
Joseph Patrick Tumulty to Rudolph Forster, Sept. 25, 1919, **63**: 515
Joseph Patrick Tumulty to Raymond Blaine Fosdick, Jan. 16, 1920,
  64: 286; Jan. 21, 1920, **64**: 310

Joseph Patrick Tumulty to Robert Lansing, Nov. 4, 1919, **63**: 613;
  Nov. 24, 1919, **64**: 871; Nov. 26, 1919, **64**: 91; Dec. 8, 1919, **64**: 153;
  Dec. 11, 1919, **64**: 182
Joseph Patrick Tumulty to William Phillips, Sept. 6, 1919, **63**: 91;
  Sept. 13, 1919, **63**: 270
Joseph Patrick Tumulty to Edith Bolling Galt Wilson, Nov. 5, 1919,
  63: 615; Nov. 10, 1919, **64**: 4; Nov. 11, 1919, **64**: 10; Nov. 19, 1919,
  64: 65; Dec. 1, 1919, **64**: 103; Dec. 16, 1919, **64**: 190; Dec. 29, 1919,
  64: 233; Jan. 5, 1920, **64**: 245; Feb. 3, 1920, **64**: 358; Feb. 10, 1920
  (2), **64**: 397 (2); March 2, 1920, **65**: 40; March 29, 1920, **65**: 143;
  Sept. 10, 1920, **66**: 112
A memorandum by Frederick Jackson Turner on the role of international political parties in a league of nations, Nov. 30, 1918, **53**:
  264

Statement by Viscount Yasuya Uchida on the restoration of Shantung to China, Aug. 4, 1919, **62**: 154
Aide-mémoire by the United States Government in reply to the Japanese memorandum on the Shantung question, Aug. 25, 1919, **62**:
  508 (draft); Aug. 26, 1919, **62**: 522 (draft)

Eleuthérios Kyrios Vénisélos to Frank Lyon Polk, Aug. 16, 1919, **62**:
  327

Hugh Campbell Wallace to the Department of State, April 10, 1920
  (3), **65**: 170, 171, 172
Hugh Campbell Wallace to Bainbridge Colby, Dec. 9, 1920, **66**: 496
Hugh Campbell Wallace to Norman Hezekiah Davis, Jan. 7, 1921,
  67: 34
Hugh Campbell Wallace to Robert Lansing, Jan. 9, 1920, **64**: 263;
  Jan. 19, 1920 (5), **64**: 298, 300, 303 (3); Jan. 22, 1920, **64**: 314, 315;
  Jan. 23, 1920, **64**: 318; Jan. 26, 1920, **64**: 331; Jan. 28, 1920, **64**:
  341
Henry White to Robert Lansing, July 28, 1919, **62**: 22
Henry White to Henry Cabot Lodge, Jan. 8, 1919, **53**: 692
Edith Bolling Galt Wilson to Norman Hezekiah Davis, Oct. 17, 1920,
  66: 234
Edith Bolling Galt Wilson to Robert Lansing, Nov. 5, 1919, **63**: 617;
  Dec. 1, 1919, **64**: 100; Dec. 8, 1919, **64**: 156; Dec. 23, 1919, **64**: 218;
  Dec. 24, 1919, **64**: 228; Jan. 19, 1920, **64**: 296; Jan. 24, 1919, **64**:
  322; Jan. 27, 1920, **64**: 335; Jan. 31, 1920, **64**: 346; Feb. 3, 1920, **64**:
  352; Feb. 6, 1920, **64**: 366
Edith Bolling Galt Wilson to John Barton Payne, Dec. 23, 1919, **64**:
  218
Edith Bolling Galt Wilson to Joseph Patrick Tumulty, Nov. 24, 1919,
  64: 87; Nov. 29, 1919, **64**: 97
Stephen Samuel Wise to Joseph Patrick Tumulty, Sept. 9, 1920, **66**:
  108
Sir William Wiseman to Arthur James Balfour, Aug. 4, 1919, **62**: 155

Sir William Wiseman to the British Foreign Office, Dec. 15, 1918, **53**: 394

Sir William Wiseman to Sir Eric Drummond, Dec. 16, 1918, **53**: 409

Sir William Wiseman to Edward Mandell House, April 18, 1919, **57**: 464; Nov. 17, 1919, **64**: 53

Personal correspondence, notes, speeches, statements, and memoranda

Stockton Axson to John Grier Hibben, June 11, 1921, **67**: 309

Stockton Axson to Jessie Woodrow Wilson Sayre, Nov. 4, 1920, **66**: 319

Stockton Axson to Edith Bolling Galt Wilson, Feb. 26, 1921, **67**: 172

Newton Diehl Baker to Edith Bolling Galt Wilson, Sept. 28, 1919, **63**: 534

Draft by Ray Stannard Baker of an article about Wilson, Nov. 29, 1920, **66**: 438

Ray Stannard Baker to John Randolph Bolling, Nov. 15, 1922, **68**: 194; April 6, 1923, **68**: 321

Ray Stannard Baker to Edith Bolling Galt Wilson, Aug. 13, 1920, **66**: 33; Aug. 31, 1920, **66**: 81; March 2, 1921, **67**: 188; Feb. 28, 1921, **67**: 559; Nov. 4, 1922, **68**: 176

Arthur James Balfour to Edith Bolling Galt Wilson, Nov. 17, 1921, **67**: 459

Bernard Mannes Baruch to Jan Christiaan Smuts, Sept. 29, 1923, **68**: 433

Tasker Howard Bliss to Mark Sullivan, Dec. 4, 1922, **68**: 223

Edward William Bok to Joseph Patrick Tumulty, Nov. 11, 1920, **66**: 352

John Randolph Bolling to Edwin Anderson Alderman, April 20, 1921, **67**: 265; Jan. 3, 1922, **67**: 501

John Randolph Bolling to the American Historical Association, Jan. 25, 1922, **67**: 534

John Randolph Bolling to George Weston Anderson, Oct. 8, 1921, **67**: 410

John Randolph Bolling to Ray Stannard Baker, Aug. 13, 1922, **68**: 109; Dec. 18, 1922, **68**: 238; April 9, 1923, **68**: 329

John Randolph Bolling to Bernard Mannes Baruch, Aug. 12, 1921, **67**: 368; Dec. 15, 1922, **68**: 236

John Randolph Bolling to John Spencer Bassett, Nov. 3, 1923, **68**: 462

John Randolph Bolling to Louis Dembitz Brandeis, Sept. 6, 1921, **67**: 387

John Randolph Bolling to Brentano's of Washington, Aug. 18, 1921, **67**: 373

John Randolph Bolling to Bessie P. Britt, March 7, 1922, **67**: 565

John Randolph Bolling to William Jennings Bryan, Aug. 25, 1923, **68**: 407

John Randolph Bolling to John Hessin Clarke, Sept. 28, 1922, **68**: 144; Nov. 8, 1922, **68**: 179; Nov. 19, 1922, **68**: 198

John Randolph Bolling to Gilbert Fairchild Close, Jan. 15, 1922, **67**: 524

John Randolph Bolling to John Firman Coar, Aug. 12, 1921, **67**: 368; Aug. 19, 1921, **67**: 374; Dec. 10, 1921, **67**: 478

John Randolph Bolling to Frank Irving Cobb, Oct. 17, 1921, **67**: 424; Oct. 19, 1921, **67**: 427; Jan. 22, 1922, **67**: 533

John Randolph Bolling to Henry Waldo Coe, March 29, 1922, **67**: 579; April 5, 1922, **67**: 587

John Randolph Bolling to Bainbridge Colby, March 30, 1921, **67**: 250; April 6, 1921, **67**: 252; April 19, 1921, **67**: 262; June 19, 1921, **67**: 318; June 20, 1921, **67**: 320; June 22, 1921, **67**: 325; July 1, 1921, **67**: 336; July 4, 1921 (2), **67**: 342, 343; July 9, 1921, **67**: 347; July 28, 1921, **67**: 357; Oct. 18, 1921, **67**: 425; Dec. 6, 1921, **67**: 475; March 22, 1922, **67**: 571; April 7, 1922, **67**: 604; Aug. 15, 1922, **68**: 114

John Randolph Bolling to George Creel, April 2, 1921, **67**: 251; Aug. 4, 1921, **67**: 364; April 26, 1923, **68**: 350

John Randolph Bolling to Homer Stillé Cummings, Oct. 9, 1921, **67**: 411

John Randolph Bolling to William Edward Dodd, Nov. 14, 1921, **67**: 456; Nov. 19, 1921, **67**: 460; Nov. 27, 1921, **67**: 469; Jan. 8, 1921, **67**: 508; April 9, 1922, **68**: 9; May 27, 1922, **68**: 68; Jan. 22, 1924, **68**: 544

John Randolph Bolling to Edward Irving Edwards, Dec. 17, 1921, **67**: 490

John Randolph Bolling to Edward Albert Filene, Nov. 27, 1921, **67**: 469

John Randolph Bolling to Raymond Blaine Fosdick, Jan. 7, 1924, **68**: 520

John Randolph Bolling to James Watson Gerard, Dec. 23, 1923, **68**: 505; Jan. 31, 1924, **68**: 551

John Randolph Bolling to Carter Glass, Sept. 15, 1921, **67**: 390

John Randolph Bolling to Sir Maurice Hankey, Nov. 25, 1921, **67**: 468

John Randolph Bolling to William Procter Gould Harding, Aug. 15, 1923, **68**: 405

John Randolph Bolling to Stanislaus Vincent Henkels, Aug. 2, 1921, **67**: 362

John Randolph Bolling to Thomas Selby Henrey, July 4, 1921, **67**: 341

John Randolph Bolling to Herbert Sherman Houston, May 7, 1923, **68**: 357

John Randolph Bolling to John Melton Hudgins, Feb. 24, 1923, **68**: 291

John Randolph Bolling to Charles Evans Hughes, Nov. 8, 1921, **67**: 444

John Randolph Bolling to Cordell Hull, Oct. 18, 1921, **67**: 426

John Randolph Bolling to John Franklin Jameson, April 17, 1921, **67**: 260; April 22, 1921, **67**: 267

John Randolph Bolling to Jesse Holman Jones, Oct. 7, 1921, **67**: 407

John Randolph Bolling to Albert Kelsey, May 11, 1922, **68**: 52

John Randolph Bolling to Richard Gilmore Knott, Nov. 23, 1923, **68**: 483; Dec. 18, 1923, **68**: 501

John Randolph Bolling to William Lassiter, Oct. 26, 1921, **67**: 432; Oct. 31, 1921, **67**: 439

John Randolph Bolling to Edgar Odell Lovett, March 26, 1921, **67**: 246

John Randolph Bolling to Alfred Lucking, June 21, 1921, **67**: 323

John Randolph Bolling to Thomas H. Lyon, July 27, 1922, **68**: 102

John Randolph Bolling to Maurice F. Lyons, June 6, 1921, **67**: 306

John Randolph Bolling to William Gibbs McAdoo, Jan. 23, 1924, **68**: 545

John Randolph Bolling to Charles Williston McAlpin, Nov. 5, 1921, **67**: 441

John Randolph Bolling to Cyrus Hall McCormick, Jr., Jan. 18, 1924, **68**: 533

John Randolph Bolling to the MacMillan Company, April 16, 1921, **67**: 259

John Randolph Bolling to Alexander Meiklejohn, Sept. 29, 1923, **68**: 433

John Randolph Bolling to Edward S. Morse, Aug. 18, 1921, **67**: 372

John Randolph Bolling to John R. Mott, Oct. 10, 1921, **67**: 413

John Randolph Bolling to the National Association for the Advancement of Colored People, March 22, 1922, **67**: 571

John Randolph Bolling to the News Enterprise Association, Dec. 21, 1921, **67**: 492

John Randolph Bolling to James Aloysius O'Gorman, July 1, 1921, **67**: 336

John Randolph Bolling to John Kelso Ormond, July 9, 1921, **67**: 348

John Randolph Bolling to Alexander Mitchell Palmer, April 4, 1923, **68**: 317

John Randolph Bolling to Maurice Drummond Peterson, Nov. 12, 1921, **67**: 454

John Randolph Bolling to Franklin Delano Roosevelt, July 9, 1921, **67**: 348; Aug. 2, 1921, **67**: 362; Sept. 3, 1921, **67**: 386; April 6, 1923, **68**: 320

John Randolph Bolling to Ellery Sedgwick, June 3, 1923, **68**: 370

John Randolph Bolling to Clarence Osborne Sherrill, June 29, 1921, **67**: 331

John Randolph Bolling to the Skandinaviska Kreditaktiebolaget, Feb. 12, 1921, **67**: 131

John Randolph Bolling to Robert Cummins Stuart, Jr., April 16, 1921, **67**: 259; April 30, 1921, **67**: 275; May 3, 1921, **67**: 276; May 25, 1921, **67**: 288; June 19, 1921, **67**: 318; June 21, 1921, **67**: 324; July 15, 1921, **67**: 352; Oct. 18, 1921, **67**: 425

John Randolph Bolling to Claude Augustus Swanson, Oct. 13, 1921,
    67: 419; Dec. 14, 1921, **67**: 484
John Randolph Bolling to Richard John Walsh, May 31, 1923, **68**:
    369
John Randolph Bolling to Schulyer Nielson Warren, Jr., Aug. 10,
    1922, **68**: 107; Oct. 17, 1922, **68**: 156; Oct. 23, 1922, **68**: 158; Oct.
    30, 1922, **68**: 168
John Randolph Bolling to John Wingate Weeks, Nov. 5, 1921, **67**:
    442
John Randolph Bolling to George White, June 3, 1921, **67**: 302
John Randolph Bolling to Louis Wiley, April 11, 1922, **68**: 11; Jan. 8,
    1924, **68**: 525
John Randolph Bolling to Lawrence Crane Woods, June 8, 1921, **67**:
    307; July 2, 1921, **67**: 340
Brief history by John Randolph Bolling of Wilson's last illness, Jan.
    29, 1924, **68**: 548
Louis Dembitz Brandeis to John Randolph Bolling, Sept. 9, 1921, **67**:
    389
An extract by Louis Dembitz Brandeis from "The Bacchae" by Eurip-
    ides, Nov. 11, 1918, **53**: 47
Brentano's of Washington to John Randolph Bolling, Aug. 26, 1921,
    67: 379

John Hessin Clarke to John Randolph Bolling, Oct. 23, 1922, **68**:
    158; Nov. 3, 1922, **68**: 174; Nov. 17, 1922, **68**: 196
John Firman Coar to John Randolph Bolling, Aug. 17, 1921, **67**: 371;
    Nov. 23, 1921, **67**: 463
Frank Irving Cobb to John Randolph Bolling, Oct. 19, 1921, **67**: 427
Henry Waldo Coe to John Randolph Bolling, April 3, 1922, **67**: 584
Bainbridge Colby to John Randolph Bolling, July 1, 1921, **67**: 337
Calvin Coolidge to Cary Travers Grayson, Feb. 4, 1924, **68**: 573
Calvin Coolidge to Edith Bolling Galt Wilson, Feb. 1, 1924, **68**: 552;
    Feb. 4, 1924, **68**: 574
George Creel to John Randolph Bolling, March 29, 1921, **67**: 249;
    Aug. 3, 1921, **67**: 363; April 24, 1923, **68**: 348
George Creel to William Edward Dodd, April 8, 1921, **67**: 254
Memorandum by George Creel proposing himself as Wilson's liter-
    ary agent, Aug. 13, 1920, **66**: 33
George Creel to Edith Bolling Galt Wilson, Aug. 13, 1920, **66**: 33;
    Aug. 31, 1920, **66**: 81; Feb. 15, 1921, **67**: 141; March 23, 1921, **67**:
    241; April 19, 1923 (2), **68**: 342, 343; April 24, 1923, **68**: 347; May
    1, 1923, **68**: 353; May 3, 1923, **68**: 356

Josephus Daniels to Hamilton Holt, Jan. 7, 1923, **68**: 266
Josephus Daniels to Edith Bolling Galt Wilson, June 15, 1920, **65**:
    398
Edward Parker Davis to Cary Travers Grayson, Feb. 12, 1921, **67**:
    129

Norman Hezekiah Davis to Albert George Schmedeman, Dec. 8, 1920, **66**: 492

Statement by Norman Hezekiah Davis on a national policy to aid the farmers, Dec. 28, 1922, **68**: 253

Statement by Norman Hezekiah Davis on the World Court, April 19, 1923, **68**: 340

Francis Xavier Dercum to Cary Travers Grayson, March 16, 1920, **65**: 90

Willliam Edward Dodd to Dice Robins Anderson, Jan. 16, 1921, **67**: 68

William Edward Dodd to John Randolph Bolling, Nov. 17, 1921, **67**: 459; Nov. 24, 1921, **67**: 466; Jan. 5, 1922, **67**: 505

William Edward Dodd to Virginia Le Roy, Jan. 7, 1921, **67**: 39

William Edward Dodd to Alexander Frederick Whyte, Jan. 9, 1921, **67**: 43

William Edward Dodd to Edith Bolling Galt Wilson, May 10, 1921, **67**: 282; May 29, 1921, **67**: 297

William Edward Dodd to Margaret Woodrow Wilson, Jan. 20, 1921, **67**: 75

Cleveland Hoadley Dodge to Bayard Dodge and Mary Williams Bliss Dodge, Dec. 16, 1920, **66**: 526

Cleveland Hoadley Dodge to Cary Travers Grayson, Feb. 4, 1921, **67**: 116; Feb. 14, 1921, **67**: 136; Feb. 21, 1921, **67**: 156; Feb. 24, 1921, **67**: 167

Cleveland Hoadley Dodge to Jesse Holman Jones, Jan. 2, 1924, **68**: 516

Cleveland Hoadley Dodge to Edith Bolling Galt Wilson, Oct. 2, 1923, **68**: 442; Oct. 4, 1923, **68**: 444

Memorandum by Cleveland Hoadley Dodge and Jesse Holman Jones on the establishment of an annuity for Wilson, Oct. 1, 1923, **68**: 438

George Henry Doran to Joseph Patrick Tumulty, Nov. 4, 1920, **66**: 417

Elisabeth, Queen of the Belgians, to Edith Bolling Galt Wilson, Oct. 3, 1919, **63**: 548

Jesse Frederick Essary to John Randolph Bolling, March 24, 1921, **67**: 243

Raymond Blaine Fosdick to John Randolph Bolling, Jan. 4, 1924, **68**: 517

Helen Hamilton Gardener to Edith Bolling Galt Wilson, Sept. 21, 1921, **67**: 393

Pietro Cardinal Gasparri to Joseph Patrick Tumulty, Oct. 6, 1919, **63**: 555

Cary Travers Grayson to Edward Parker Davis, Feb. 19, 1921, **67**: 148

Cary Travers Grayson to Francis Xavier Dercum, June 8, 1920, **65**: 380

Cary Travers Grayson to Cleveland Hoadley Dodge, May 29, 1920, **65**: 341; Feb. 19, 1921, **67**: 148; Feb. 24, 1921, **67**: 167

Cary Travers Grayson to Harry Augustus Garfield, Oct. 1, 1919, **63**: 538

Cary Travers Grayson to Gilbert Monell Hitchcock, Oct. 23, 1919, **63**: 593

Cary Travers Grayson to Charles Horace Mayo, Feb. 10, 1921, **67**: 542

Cary Travers Grayson to Joseph Patrick Tumulty, Dec. 12, 1918, **53**: 375

Memorandum by Cary Travers Grayson of a conversation with Wilson about delivering his annual message to Congress in person, Dec. 3, 1920, **66**: 456

Harper and Brothers to Joseph Patrick Tumulty, Aug. 29, 1919, **62**: 564

Irwin Hood Hoover to Cary Travers Grayson, Aug. 5, 1920, **66**: 15

Edward Mandell House to Edith Bolling Galt Wilson, Oct. 22, 1919, **63**: 587; Nov. 17, 1920, **66**: 382

Statement by David Franklin Houston on a national economic policy, Jan. 11, 1923, **68**: 269

John Franklin Jameson to John Randolph Bolling, April 19, 1921, **67**: 263

John Franklin Jameson to Helen Jameson, April 17, 1922, **68**: 26

Isaac Thomas Jones to John Randolph Bolling, Sept. 21, 1921, **67**: 393; Oct. 7, 1921, **67**: 408

Thomas Davies Jones to Cleveland Hoadley Dodge, Dec. 30, 1923, **68**: 513

James Kerney to John Randolph Bolling, Oct. 24, 1923, **68**: 454

Franklin Knight Lane to Cary Travers Grayson, Jan. 5, 1920, **67**: 614

Robert Lansing to Frank Lyon Polk, Oct. 1, 1919, **63**: 539; Oct. 14, 1919, **63**: 571

William Lassiter to John Randolph Bolling, Oct. 26, 1921, **67**: 432; Oct. 31, 1921, **67**: 438; Nov. 8, 1921, **67**: 444

David Lawrence to Edith Bolling Galt Wilson, May 18, 1921, **67**: 284; May 20, 1921, **67**: 286; May 26, 1921, **67**: 294

Edgar Odell Lovett to Edith Bolling Galt Wilson, Nov. 21, 1920, **66**: 410

William Gibbs McAdoo to Edith Bolling Galt Wilson, July 17, 1921, **67**: 356

Cyrus Hall McCormick, Jr., to Edith Bolling Galt Wilson, Jan. 13, 1924, **68**: 528
Charles Horace Mayo to Cary Travers Grayson, Jan. 25, 1922, **67**: 535
Emma Guffey Miller to Joseph Patrick Tumulty, June 3, 1920, **65**: 359
Charles Moore to Joseph Patrick Tumulty, Oct. 29, 1920, **66**: 292; Nov. 4, 1920, **66**: 319
Henry Morgenthau to Cary Travers Grayson, March 16, 1922, **67**: 568

Alexander Mitchell Palmer to Roland Sletor Morris, Nov. 3, 1919, **63**: 608
Garo Pasdermadjian to Norman Hezekiah Davis, Dec. 14, 1920, **66**: 507
Thomas Gedney Patten to Joseph Patrick Tumulty, April 11, 1921, **68**: 585
John Joseph Pershing to Edith Bolling Galt Wilson, March 20, 1920, **65**: 108
William Phillips to Frank Lyon Polk, Sept. 30, 1919, **63**: 537
Frank Lyon Polk to William Phillips, Sept. 30, 1919, **63**: 536

William Cox Redfield to Joseph R. Wilson, Jr., Oct. 5, 1921, **67**: 403
James McDowell Richards to Thornton Whaling, Dec. 5, 1921, **67**: 474
R. A. Rogers to Francis Xavier Dercum, Dec. 13, 1919, **67**: 611; Dec. 17, 1919, **67**: 613
Laurence E. Rubel to Joseph Patrick Tumulty, Feb. 11, 1921, **67**: 128
Sterling Ruffin to Edith Bolling Galt Wilson, Aug. 19, 1920, **66**: 55

Tom Scott to Charles Lee Swem, Feb. 15, 1921, **67**: 140
Speech by May Ladd Simonson on the origins of the Woodrow Wilson Foundation, Jan. 4, 1923, **68**: 264
Robert Cummins Stuart, Jr., to John Randolph Bolling, April 27, 1921, **67**: 271; June 16, 1921, **67**: 314; June 23, 1921, **67**: 326; July 4, 1921, **67**: 344; Oct. 11, 1921, **67**: 415

Frederick Ingate Thompson to Cary Travers Grayson, Aug. 10, 1922, **68**: 107
Katrina Brandes Ely Tiffany to Edith Bolling Galt Wilson, Aug. 12, 1921, **67**: 369
Nancy Saunders Toy to Edith Bolling Galt Wilson, March 3,1921, **67**: 189
Joseph Patrick Tumulty to James Kerney, March 3, 1921, **67**: 202
Joseph Patrick Tumulty to Edith Bolling Galt Wilson, Oct. 2, 1919, **63**: 542; June 16, 1920, **65**: 400; Nov. 1, 1920, **66**: 298; Nov. 24, 1920, **66**: 416; Dec. 17, 1920, **66**: 531; March 3, 1921, **67**: 202; June 3, 1921, **67**: 303

Joseph Patrick Tumulty to William Edward Dodd, Aug. 24, 1920, **66**: 62

Statement by Joseph Patrick Tumulty announcing his decision not to accept appointment to the Supreme Court of Customs Appeals, Dec. 17, 1920, **66**: 531

Charles Doolittle Walcott to Edith Bolling Galt Wilson, Dec. 3, 1920, **66**: 469

Richard John Walsh to Edith Bolling Galt Wilson, May 29, 1923, **68**: 368

Schuyler Nielson Warren, Jr., to John Randolph Bolling, Oct. 13, 1922, **68**: 155; Oct. 22, 1922, **68**: 157; Oct. 24, 1922, **68**: 162

Thomas Bucklin Wells to Thomas William Lamont, Sept. 28, 1920, **66**: 164

White House Staff to Calvin Coolidge, Feb. 2, 1924, **68**: 553

White House Staff to Joseph Patrick Tumulty, Jan. 7, 1921, **67**: 38

David C. Williams to Mrs. Baer, June 1, 1920, **67**: 618

Edith Bolling Galt Wilson to Ray Stannard Baker, Nov. 30, 1920, **66**: 446; Oct. 1, 1922, **68**: 150; Nov. 21, 1923, **68**: 480

Edith Bolling Galt Wilson to Bertha Bolling, Jan. 4, 1918, **53**: 611

Edith Bolling Galt Wilson to Sallie White Bolling and Others, Dec. 25, 1918, **53**: 499

Edith Bolling Galt Wilson to Calvin Coolidge, Feb. 4, 1924, **68**: 574

Edith Bolling Galt Wilson to George Creel, Feb. 16, 1921, **67**: 142; April 20, 1923, **68**: 344; April 24, 1923, **68**: 347; May 3, 1923, **68**: 356

Edith Bolling Galt Wilson to William Edward Dodd, June 19, 1920, **65**: 432; May 5, 1921, **67**: 278; May 22, 1921, **67**: 287

Edith Bolling Galt Wilson to Cleveland Hoadley Dodge, Oct. 5, 1920, **66**: 193

Edith Bolling Galt Wilson to her family, Dec. 15, 1918, **53**: 396; Jan. 2, 1919, **53**: 591

Edith Bolling Galt Wilson to Edward Mandell House, Oct. 23, 1919, **63**: 592; Nov. 15, 1920, **66**: 379

Edith Bolling Galt Wilson to Loulie Hunter House, Oct. 17, 1919, **63**: 580

Edith Bolling Galt Wilson to David Lawrence, May 20, 1921, **67**: 285

Edith Bolling Galt Wilson to Henry Cabot Lodge, Feb. 4, 1924, **68**: 574

Edith Bolling Galt Wilson to Breckinridge Long, March 22, 1920, **65**: 110

Edith Bolling Galt Wilson to Cyrus Hall McCormick, Jr., Jan. 13, 1924, **68**: 529

Edith Bolling Galt Wilson to Kate Nichols Trask, May 27, 1920, **65**: 332; Jan. 30, 1921, **67**: 106

Edith Bolling Galt Wilson to Joseph Patrick Tumulty, June 16, 1920, **65**: 400

Edith Bolling Galt Wilson to Henry White, Aug. 4, 1919, **62**: 155; July 15, 1920, **65**: 513; April 6, 1923, **68**: 320
Margaret Woodrow Wilson to Edith Gittings Reid, Oct. 16, 1919, **63**: 575

Diaries

Henry Fountain Ashurst, Nov. 11, 1918, **53**: 35; Dec. 2, 1918, **53**: 305; Dec. 3, 1918, **53**: 313; July 11, 1919, **61**: 445; July 16, 1919, **61**: 492; Oct. 22, 1919, **63**: 586; Nov. 19, 1919, **64**: 62; Jan. 7, 1920, **64**: 252; Jan. 8, 1920, **64**: 256; Jan. 9, 1920, **64**: 263; Feb. 7, 1920, **64**: 384; May 24, 1920, **65**: 323
Ray Stannard Baker, March 8, 1919, **55**: 463; March 13, 1919, **55**: 489; March 15, 1919, **55**: 531; March 20, 1919, **56**: 103; March 21, 1919, **56**: 128; March 22, 1919, **56**: 179; March 27, 1919, **56**: 337; March 28, 1919, **56**: 353; March 29, 1919, **56**: 425; March 31, 1919, **56**: 441; April 1, 1919, **56**: 518; April 2, 1919, **56**: 542; April 3, 1919, **56**: 577; April 4, 1919, **56**: 588; April 5, 1919, **57**: 4; April 6, 1919, **57**: 52; April 7, 1919, **57**: 68; April 8, 1919, **57**: 140; April 10, 1919, **57**: 194; April 11, 1919, **57**: 240; April 12, 1919, **57**: 286; April 13, 1919, **57**: 316; April 18, 1919, **57**: 467; April 19, 1919, **57**: 508; April 20, 1919, **57**: 527; April 21, 1919, **57**: 575; April 22, 1919, **57**: 585; April 25, 1919, **58**: 142; April 26, 1919, **58**: 169; April 28, 1919, **58**: 214; April 29, 1919, **58**: 229; April 30, 1919, **58**: 270; May 1, 1919, **58**: 327; May 3, 1919, **58**: 418; May 4, 1919, **58**: 427; May 5, 1919, **58**: 459; May 7, 1919, **58**: 529; May 9, 1919, **58**: 601; May 17, 1919, **59**: 245; May 19, 1919, **59**: 285; May 20, 1919, **59**: 316; May 21, 1919, **59**: 367; May 23, 1919, **59**: 447; May 26, 1919, **59**: 480; May 27, 1919, **59**: 551; May 28, 1919, **59**: 574; May 29, 1919, **59**: 603; May 30, 1919, **59**: 621; May 31, 1919, **59**: 645; June 3, 1919, **60**: 79; June 5, 1919, **60**: 196; June 7, 1919, **60**: 286; June 9, 1919, **60**: 328; June 10, 1919, **60**: 374; June 11, 1919, **60**: 430; June 12, 1919, **60**: 486; June 13, 1919, **60**: 532; June 17, 1919, **60**: 644; June 20, 1919, **61**: 28, 34; June 21, 1919, **61**: 65, 70; June 22, 1919, **61**: 179; June 26, 1919, **61**: 231; June 27, 1919, **61**: 252; July 1, 1919, **61**: 363; July 4, 1919, **61**: 383; July 9, 1919, **61**: 416; Nov. 5, 1919, **63**: 619; Nov. 18, 1919, **64**: 61; Jan. 23, 1920, **64**: 320; Feb. 3, 1920, **64**: 359; Feb. 4, 1920, **64**: 362; Feb. 5, 1920 (3), **64**: 365, 385, 434; Nov. 28, 1920, **66**: 435; Dec. 2, 1920, **66**: 451; Dec. 16, 1920, **66**: 521; Dec. 21, 1920, **66**: 537; Jan. 19, 1921, **67**: 71; Jan. 22, 1921, **67**: 82; Jan. 27, 1921, **67**: 93; Feb. 12, 1921, **67**: 129; Feb. 28, 1921, **67**: 174; March 1, 1921, **67**: 184; March 20, 1921, **67**: 236; March 22, 1921, **67**: 237; March 24, 1921, **67**: 243; March 25, 1921, **67**: 245; April 13, 1921 (2), **67**: 256 (2); May 18, 1921, **67**: 284; May 25, 1921, **67**: 288; May 29, 1921, **67**: 295; May 31, 1921, **67**: 300; June 2, 1921, **67**: 301; July 29, 1921, **67**: 360; April 4, 1921, **67**: 585; Feb. 10, 1923, **68**: 285; May 3, 1923, **68**: 356

Bernard Mannes Baruch, April 12, 1919, **57**: 287; April 21, 1919, **57**: 574; April 23, 1919, **58**: 28; April 25, 1919, **58**: 119; June 2, 1919, **60**: 20; June 3, 1919, **60**: 73

George Louis Beer, March 30, 1919, **56**: 434; May 17, 1919, **59**: 244; June 1, 1919, **60**: 17

Edith Benham, Dec. 5, 1918, **53**: 319; Dec. 8, 1918, **53**: 341; Dec. 9, 1918, **53**: 343; Dec. 10, 1918, **53**: 357; Dec. 21, 1918, **53**: 459; Dec. 22, 1918, **53**: 468; Jan. 2, 1919, **53**: 588; Jan. 10, 1919, **53**: 707; Jan. 12, 1919, **54**: 34; Jan. 14, 1919, **54**: 61; Jan. 18, 1919, **54**: 148; Jan. 20, 1919, **54**: 175; Jan. 21, 1919, **54**: 196; Jan. 22, 1919, **54**: 217; Jan. 27, 1919, **54**: 307; Jan. 31, 1919, **54**: 414; Feb. 2, 1919, **54**: 432; Feb. 6, 1919, **54**: 521; Feb. 9, 1919, **55**: 40; Feb. 10, 1919, **55**: 66; March 22, 1919, **56**: 181; March 24, 1919, **56**: 244; March 28, 1919, **56**: 354; March 31, 1919, **56**: 443; April 2, 1919, **56**: 540; April 8, 1919, **57**: 140; April 11, 1919, **57**: 241; April 18, 1919, **57**: 468; April 19, 1919, **57**: 502; April 21, 1919, **57**: 576; April 24, 1919, **58**: 102; April 26, 1919, **58**: 168; April 27, 1919, **58**: 172; April 28, 1919, **58**: 187; May 1, 1919, **58**: 328; May 4, 1919, **58**: 421; May 7, 1919, **58**: 530; May 8, 1919, **58**: 534; May 10, 1919, **59**: 35; May 12, 1919, **59**: 74; May 14, 1919, **59**: 159; May 17, 1919, **59**: 246; May 19, 1919, **59**: 254; May 20, 1919, **59**: 319; May 21, 1919, **59**: 369; May 23, 1919, **59**: 420; May 30, 1919, **59**: 620; June 3, 1919, **60**: 84; June 4, 1919, **60**: 118; June 7, 1919, **60**: 285; June 11, 1919, **60**: 388; June 13, 1919, **60**: 533; June 16, 1919, **60**: 582; June 20, 1919, **61**: 30; June 24, 1919, **61**: 135; June 25, 1919, **61**: 180; June 26, 1919, **61**: 188; July 2, 1919, **61**: 370

William Christian Bullitt, Dec. 10, 1918, **53**: 350; Dec. 11, 1918, **53**: 366

Lord Robert Cecil, Jan. 19, 1919, **54**: 152; Jan. 31, 1919, **54**: 408; Feb. 3, 1919, **54**: 460; Feb. 6, 1919, **54**: 514; Feb. 11, 1919, **55**: 80; March 16, 1919, **55**: 539; March 18, 1919, **56**: 81; March 22, 1919, **56**: 178; March 26, 1919, **56**: 297; March 30, 1919, **56**: 435; April 8, 1919, **57**: 142; April 11, 1919, **57**: 247; May 2, 1919, **58**: 360; May 5, 1919, **58**: 444; May 6, 1919, **58**: 463; June 7, 1919, **60**: 255; April 21, 1923, **68**: 345

Homer Stillé Cummings, Feb. 14, 1920, **64**: 427; Feb. 29, 1920, **65**: 24; May 31, 1920, **65**: 344

Josephus Daniels, Nov. 10, 1918, **53**: 32; Nov. 12, 1918, **53**: 65; Nov. 13, 1918, **53**: 70; Nov. 19, 1918, **53**: 135; Nov. 20, 1918, **53**: 150; Nov. 21, 1918, **53**: 159; Nov. 30, 1918, **53**: 264; Dec. 2, 1918, **53**: 301; Feb. 25, 1919, **55**: 266; March 1, 1919, **55**: 367; March 27, 1919, **56**: 338; March 31, 1919, **56**: 482; April 1, 1919, **56**: 518; April 7, 1919, **57**: 92; Oct. 3, 1919, **63**: 548; Oct. 6, 1919 (2), **63**: 552 (2); Oct. 7, 1919 (2), **63**: 555, 557; Oct. 8, 1919, **63**: 559; Oct. 25, 1919, **63**: 598; Nov. 4, 1919, **63**: 612; Dec. 4, 1919, **64**: 122; Dec. 5, 1919, **64**: 141; Dec. 9, 1919, **64**: 166; Dec. 22, 1919, **64**: 216; Dec. 23, 1919, **64**: 222; Feb. 29, 1920, **65**: 21; April 14, 1920, **65**: 186; April

20, 1920, **65**: 212; May 11, 1920, **65**: 270; May 18, 1920, **65**: 298; June 1, 1920, **65**: 351; June 8, 1920, **65**: 380; Aug. 3, 1920, **66**: 4; Aug. 10, 1920, **66**: 25; Aug. 17, 1920, **66**: 39; Aug. 21, 1920, **66**: 58; Aug. 24, 1920, **66**: 60; Aug. 31, 1920, **66**: 78; Sept. 1, 1920, **66**: 82; Sept. 28, 1920, **66**: 159; Nov. 9, 1920, **66**: 341; Nov. 16, 1920, **66**: 380; Nov. 23, 1920, **66**: 413; Nov. 30, 1920, **66**: 445; Dec. 7, 1920, **66**: 484; Dec. 14, 1920, **66**: 504; Dec. 25, 1920, **67**: 5; Dec. 28, 1920, **67**: 9; Jan. 4, 1921, **67**: 25; Jan. 18, 1921, **67**: 70; Jan. 22, 1921, **67**: 81; Jan. 25, 1921, **67**: 90; Feb. 1, 1921, **67**: 109; Feb. 8, 1921, **67**: 124; Feb. 21, 1921, **67**: 150

John William Davis, Oct. 10, 1920, **66**: 216

Lord Derby, Jan. 11, 1919, **53**: 721

Raymond Blaine Fosdick, Dec. 5, 1918, **53**: 321; Dec. 8, 1918, **53**: 340; Dec. 11, 1918, **53**: 365; Dec. 12, 1918, **53**: 371; Dec. 14, 1918, **53**: 384

Cary Travers Grayson, Dec. 3, 1918, **53**: 305; Dec. 4, 1918, **53**: 313; Dec. 5, 1918, **53**: 318; Dec. 6, 1918, **53**: 327; Dec. 7, 1918, **53**: 332; Dec. 8, 1918, **53**: 336; Dec. 9, 1918, **53**: 343; Dec. 10, 1918, **53**: 348; Dec. 11, 1918, **53**: 364; Dec. 12, 1918, **53**: 370; Dec. 13, 1918, **53**: 378; Dec. 14, 1918, **53**: 382; Dec. 15, 1918, **53**: 391; Dec. 16, 1918, **53**: 403; Dec. 17, 1918, **53**: 410; Dec. 18, 1918, **53**: 420; Dec. 19, 1918, **53**: 439; Dec. 20, 1918, **53**: 449; Dec. 21, 1918, **53**: 458; Dec. 22, 1918, **53**: 467; Dec. 23, 1918, **53**: 472; Dec. 24, 1918, **53**: 488; Dec. 25, 1918, **53**: 502; Dec. 26, 1918, **53**: 508; Dec. 27, 1918, **53**: 519; Dec. 28, 1918, **53**: 526; Dec. 29, 1918, **53**: 537; Dec. 30, 1918, **53**: 543; Dec. 31, 1918, **53**: 569; Jan. 1, 1919, **53**: 577; Jan. 2, 1919, **53**: 589; Jan. 4, 1919, **53**: 605; Jan. 5, 1919, **53**: 613; Jan. 6, 1919, **53**: 620; Jan. 7, 1919, **53**: 634; Jan. 8, 1919, **53**: 654; Jan. 9, 1919, **53**: 696; Jan. 10, 1919, **53**: 706; Jan. 12, 1919; **54**: 4; Jan. 13, 1919, **54**: 35; Jan. 15, 1919, **54**: 64; Jan. 18, 1919, **54**: 126; Jan. 19, 1919, **54**: 150; Jan. 20, 1919, **54**: 155; Jan. 21, 1919, **54**: 175; Jan. 22, 1919, **54**: 199; Jan. 24, 1919, **54**: 237; Jan. 25, 1919, **54**: 262; Jan. 26, 1919, **54**: 278; Jan. 27, 1919, **54**: 282; Jan. 28, 1919, **54**: 308; Jan. 29, 1919, **54**: 334; Jan. 30, 1919, **54**: 348; Feb. 1, 1919, **54**: 415; Feb. 2, 1919, **54**: 431; Feb. 3, 1919, **54**: 459; Feb. 4, 1919 (2), **54**: 473, 489; Feb. 6, 1919, **54**: 505; Feb. 8, 1919, **55**: 3; Feb. 9, 1919, **55**: 36; Feb. 10, 1919, **55**: 41; Feb. 12, 1919, **55**: 94; Feb. 13, 1919, **55**: 120; Feb. 14, 1919, **55**: 159; Feb. 15, 1919, **55**: 197; Feb. 16, 1919, **55**: 201; Feb. 17, 1919, **55**: 202; Feb. 18, 1919, **55**: 205; Feb. 19, 1919, **55**: 207; Feb. 20, 1919, **55**: 217; Feb. 21, 1919, **55**: 221; Feb. 22, 1919, **55**: 224; Feb. 23, 1919, **55**: 228; Feb. 24, 1919, **55**: 235; Feb. 25, 1919, **55**: 254; Feb. 26, 1919, **55**: 267; Feb. 27, 1919, **55**: 294; Feb. 28, 1919, **55**: 308; Feb. 28, 1919, **55**: 339; March 2, 1919, **55**: 367; March 3, 1919, **55**: 387; March 4, 1919 (2), **55**: 409 (2); March 5, 1919, **55**: 442; March 6, 1919, **55**: 448; March 7, 1919, **55**: 456; March 8, 1919, **55**: 460; March 9, 1919, **55**: 471; March 10, 1919, **55**: 471; March 11, 1919, **55**: 473; March 12, 1919, **55**: 479; March 13, 1919, **55**: 486; March 14, 1919, **55**: 496; March 15, 1919,

55: 529; March 16, 1919, **55**: 538; March 17, 1919, **56**: 3; March 18, 1919, **56**: 59; March 19, 1919, **56**: 85; March 20, 1919, **56**: 102; March 21, 1919, **56**: 126; March 22, 1919, **56**: 163; March 23, 1919, **56**: 194; March 24, 1919, **56**: 205; March 25, 1919, **56**: 246; March 26, 1919, **56**: 283; March 27, 1919, **56**: 312; March 28, 1919, **56**: 347; March 29, 1919, **56**: 405; March 30, 1919, **56**: 428; March 31, 1919, **56**: 436; April 1, 1919, **56**: 490; April 2, 1919, **56**: 522; April 3, 1919, **56**: 554; April 4, 1919, **56**: 584; April 5, 1919, **57**: 3; April 6, 1919, **57**: 50; April 7, 1919, **57**: 62; April 8, 1919, **57**: 98; April 9, 1919, **57**: 145; April 10, 1919, **57**: 190; April 11, 1919, **57**: 237; April 12, 1919, **57**: 284; April 13, 1919, **57**: 316; April 14, 1919, **57**: 331; April 15, 1919, **57**: 349; April 16, 1919, **57**: 388; April 17, 1919, **57**: 426; April 18, 1919, **57**: 449; April 19, 1919, **57**: 477; April 20, 1919, **57**: 512; April 21, 1919, **57**: 531; April 22, 1919, **57**: 579; April 23, 1919, **58**: 3; April 24, 1919, **58**: 53; April 25, 1919, **58**: 110; April 26, 1919, **58**: 147; April 27, 1919, **58**: 170; April 28, 1919, **58**: 176; April 29, 1919, **58**: 215; April 30, 1919, **58**: 244; May 1, 1919, **58**: 274; May 2, 1919, **58**: 330; May 3, 1919, **58**: 367; May 4, 1919, **58**: 422; May 5, 1919, **58**: 429; May 6, 1919, **58**: 429; May 6, 1919, **58**: 461; May 7, 1919, **58**: 499; May 8, 1919, **58**: 535; May 9, 1919, **58**: 561; May 10, 1919, **59**: 3; May 11, 1919, **59**: 39; May 12, 1919, **59**: 47; May 13, 1919, **59**: 78; May 14, 1919, **59**: 124; May 15, 1919, **59**: 160; May 16, 1919, **59**: 186; May 17, 1919, **59**: 207; May 18, 1919, **59**: 247; May 19, 1919, **59**: 253; May 20, 1919, **59**: 288; May 21, 1919, **59**: 321; May 22, 1919, **59**: 370; May 23, 1919, **59**: 419; May 24, 1919, **59**: 453; May 25, 1919, **59**: 477; May 26, 1919, **59**: 479; May 27, 1919, **59**: 527; May 28, 1919, **59**: 553; May 29, 1919, **59**: 576; May 30, 1919, **59**: 605; May 31, 1919, **59**: 625; June 1, 1919, **60**: 3; June 2, 1919, **60**: 18; June 3, 1919, **60**: 43; June 4, 1919, **60**: 114; June 5, 1919, **60**: 156; June 6, 1919, **60**: 203; June 7, 1919, **60**: 249; June 8, 1919, **60**: 291; June 9, 1919, **60**: 299; June 10, 1919, **60**: 332; June 11, 1919, **60**: 381; June 12, 1919, **60**: 434; June 13, 1919, **60**: 488; June 14, 1919, **60**: 545; June 15, 1919, **60**: 569; June 16, 1919, **60**: 573; June 17, 1919, **60**: 612; July 8, 1919, **61**: 400; July 10, 1919, **61**: 416; Sept. 3, 1919, **62**: 626; Sept. 4, 1919, **63**: 3; Sept. 5, 1919, **63**: 31; Sept. 6, 1919, **63**: 63; Sept. 8, 1919, **63**: 93; Sept. 9, 1919, **63**: 122; Sept. 10, 1919, **63**: 152; Sept. 11, 1919, **63**: 168; Sept. 12, 1919, **63**: 210; Sept. 13, 1919, **63**: 236; Sept. 14, 1919, **63**: 273; Sept. 15, 1919, **63**: 274; Sept. 16, 1919, **63**: 300; Sept. 17, 1919, **63**: 308; Sept. 18, 1919, **63**: 340; Sept. 19, 1919, **63**: 369; Sept. 20, 1919, **63**: 396; Sept. 21, 1919, **63**: 423; Sept. 22, 1919, **63**: 426; Sept. 23, 1919, **63**: 446; Sept. 24, 1919, **63**: 467; Sept. 25, 1919, **63**: 487; Sept. 26, 1919, **63**: 518; Sept. 27, 1919, **63**: 526; Sept. 28, 1919, **63**: 532; April 16, 1920, **65**: 194; April 18, 1920 (2), **65**: 201 (2); April 20, 1920, **65**: 212; April 22, 1920, **65**: 217; May 1, 1920, **65**: 242; May 2, 1920, **65**: 243; May 3, 1920, **65**: 244; May 19, 1920, **65**: 298; May 20, 1920, **65**: 299; June 22, 1920, **65**: 443; July 1, 1920, **65**: 481; July 2, 1920; **65**: 488; July 3, 1920, **65**:

491; July 6, 1920, **65**: 498; July 15, 1920, **65**: 512; July 16, 1920, **65**: 514; July 18, 1920, **65**: 520; July 19, 1920, **65**: 529; Sept. 8, 1920, **66**: 102

Edward Mandell House, Dec. 14, 1918, **53**: 389; Dec. 15, 1918, **53**: 400; Dec. 17, 1918, **53**: 417; Dec. 18, 1918, **53**: 437; Dec. 19, 1918, **53**: 448; Dec. 21, 1918, **53**: 466; Dec. 27, 1918, **53**: 525; Dec. 31, 1918, **53**: 576; Jan. 1, 1919, **53**: 586; Jan. 7, 1919, **53**: 652; Jan. 8, 1919, **53**: 693; Jan. 27, 1919, **54**: 304; Jan. 28, 1919, **54**: 333; Jan. 29, 1919, **54**: 347; Jan. 30, 1919, **54**: 386; Jan. 31, 1919, **54**: 407; Feb. 3, 1919, **54**: 459; Feb. 4, 1919, **54**: 484; Feb. 5, 1919, **54**: 499; Feb. 11, 1919, **55**: 88; Feb. 13, 1919, **55**: 155; Feb. 14, 1919, **55**: 193; March 14, 1919, **55**: 499; March 16, 1919, **55**: 538: March 17, 1919, **56**: 4; March 21, 1919, **56**: 126; March 22, 1919, **56**: 179; March 24, 1919, **56**: 206; March 25, 1919, **56**: 279; March 26, 1919, **56**: 309; March 27, 1919, **56**: 335; March 28, 1919, **56**: 349; March 29, 1919, **56**: 424; April 1, 1919, **56**: 517; April 2, 1919, **56**: 539; April 3, 1919, **56**: 558; April 4, 1919, **56**: 585; April 4, 1919, **57**: 34; April 6, 1919, **57**: 52; April 7, 1919, **57**: 71; April 8, 1919, **57**: 139; April 9, 1919, **57**: 178; April 10, 1919, **57**: 215, April 11, 1919, **57**: 236; April 12, 1919, **57**: 285; April 14, 1919, **57**: 334; April 15, 1919, **57**: 352; April 16, 1919, **57**: 390; April 18, 1919, **57**: 466; April 19, 1919, **57**: 503; April 20, 1919, **57**: 527; April 21, 1919, **57**: 534; April 23, 1919, **58**: 48; April 24, 1919, **58**: 104; April 26, 1919, **58**: 153; April 28, 1919, **58**: 185; May 3, 1919, **58**: 379; May 5, 1919, **58**: 443; May 6, 1919, **58**: 482; May 7, 1919, **58**: 520; May 10, 1919, **59**: 34; May 11, 1919, **59**: 46; May 12, 1919, **59**: 68; May 13, 1919, **59**: 80; May 14, 1919, **59**: 126; May 15, 1919, **59**: 174; May 16, 1919, **59**: 200; May 17, 1919, **59**: 244; May 20, 1919, **59**: 317; May 21, 1919, **59**: 366; May 23, 1919, **59**: 449; May 24, 1919, **59**: 476; May 25, 1919, **59**: 478; May 28, 1919, **59**: 554; May 29, 1919, **59**: 602; May 30, 1919, **59**: 623; May 31, 1919, **59**: 644; June 2, 1919, **60**: 40; June 3, 1919, **60**: 81; June 4, 1919, **60**: 144; June 8, 1919, **60**: 296; June 9, 1919, **60**: 307; June 10, 1919, **60**: 373; June 11, 1919, **60**: 432; June 20, 1919, **61**: 33; June 21, 1919, **61**: 45; June 23, 1919, **61**: 111; June 25, 1919, **61**: 177; June 27, 1919, **61**: 283; June 28, 1919, **61**: 332; July 1, 1919, **61**: 364; Oct. 21, 1919, **63**: 585; Dec. 11, 1919, **64**: 182; Dec. 12, 1919, **64**: 184; Dec. 22, 1919, **64**: 217; Dec. 28, 1919, **64**: 231; Jan. 2, 1920, **64**: 239; Jan. 5, 1920, **64**: 243; Jan. 11, 1920, **64**: 270; Jan. 31, 1920, **64**: 347; Feb. 3, 1920, **64**: 360; Feb. 18, 1920, **64**: 444; March 2, 1920, **65**: 40; March 10, 1920, **65**: 79; March 28, 1920, **65**: 139; May 11, 1920, **65**: 274; June 10, 1920, **65**: 384; June 30, 1920, **65**: 480

Florence Haskell Corliss Lamont, Feb. 12, 1919, **55**: 120

Thomas William Lamont, April 1, 1919, **56**: 502; April 3, 1919, **56**: 580; April 12, 1919, **57**: 287; April 23, 1919, **58**: 26; April 25, 1919, **58**: 121; July 5, 1919, **61**: 386

Robert Lansing, July 27, 1919, **62**: 11; July 29, 1919, **62**: 27; July 30, 1919, **62**: 45; Aug. 5, 1919, **62**: 164; Aug. 6, 1919, **62**: 169; Aug. 7, 1919, **62**: 202; Aug. 11, 1919, **62**: 253; Aug. 13, 1919, **62**: 266; Aug.

15, 1919, **62**: 316; Aug. 21, 1919, **62**: 453; Aug. 22, 1919, **62**: 456; Aug. 25, 1919, **62**: 507; Aug. 27, 1919, **62**: 531; Aug. 29, 1919, **62**: 574; July 25, 1919, **61**: 629; Oct. 3, 1919, **63**: 543; Oct. 7, 1919, **63**: 547; Oct. 6, 1919, **63**: 552, 554, 606; Nov. 6, 1919, **64**: 3; Nov. 7, 1919, **64**: 3; Nov. 14, 1919, **64**: 36; Nov. 17, 1919, **64**: 50; Dec. 9, 1919, **64**: 167; Dec. 29, 1919, **64**: 235; Jan. 13, 1920, **64**: 274; Jan. 15, 1920, **64**: 276; Jan. 16, 1920, **64**: 282; Jan. 19, 1920, **64**: 296; Jan. 21, 1920, **64**: 310; Jan. 23, 1920, **64**: 316; Feb. 3, 1920, **64**: 353; Feb. 6, 1920, **64**: 366; Feb. 7, 1920, **64**: 383; Feb. 9, 1920, **64**: 385, 386; Feb. 10, 1920, **64**: 398; Feb. 11, 1920, **64**: 405; Feb. 13, 1920, **64**: 414; Feb. 14, 1920, **64**: 428; April 14, 1920, **65**: 188; May 29, 1920, **65**: 343

Breckinridge Long, Oct. 7, 1919, **63**: 558; Jan. 11, 1923, **68**: 527

Vance Criswell McCormick, Jan. 14, 1919, **54**: 61; Jan. 21, 1919, **54**: 196; Feb. 2, 1919, **54**: 440; March 2, 1919, **55**: 387; March 22, 1919, **56**: 180; March 28, 1919, **56**: 353; March 29, 1919, **56**: 424; March 31, 1919, **56**: 444; April 1, 1919, **56**: 501; April 2, 1919, **56**: 535; April 3, 1919, **56**: 579; April 4, 1919, **56**: 588; April 10, 1919, **57**: 203; April 16, 1919, **57**: 391; April 21, 1919, **57**: 575; April 23, 1919, **58**: 27; April 25, 1919, **58**: 121; April 28, 1919, **58**: 188; April 29, 1919, **58**: 237; April 30, 1919, **58**: 262; May 14, 1919, **59**: 127; May 15, 1919, **59**: 173; May 19, 1919, **59**: 283; May 22, 1919, **59**: 383; May 23, 1919, **59**: 448; May 30, 1919, **59**: 624; June 3, 1919, **60**: 72; June 4, 1919, **60**: 120; June 5, 1919, **60**: 196; June 9, 1919, **60**: 306; June 11, 1919, **60**: 399; June 13, 1919, **60**: 491; June 23, 1919, **61**: 110; June 24, 1919, **61**: 134; June 26, 1919, **61**: 230; July 1, 1919, **61**: 366; July 4, 1919, **61**: 383; July 5, 1919, **61**: 385

David Hunter Miller, Jan. 30, 1919, **54**: 379; Feb. 2, 1919, **54**: 439; Feb. 11, 1919, **55**: 67; Feb. 12, 1919, **55**: 118; Feb. 13, 1919, **55**: 154; Feb. 14, 1919, **55**: 192; March 17, 1919, **56**: 58; March 18, 1919, **56**: 75; March 22, 1919, **56**: 178; March 24, 1919, **56**: 223; March 28, 1919, **56**: 395; April 7, 1919, **57**: 90; April 10, 1919, **57**: 195; May 3, 1919, **58**: 381; May 5, 1919, **58**: 445; May 6, 1919, **58**: 488; May 12, 1919, **59**: 70; May 13, 1919, **59**: 80; May 14, 1919, **59**: 125; May 18, 1919, **59**: 249; May 29, 1919, **59**: 578

Frank Lyon Polk, March 15, 1920, **65**: 89

Lord Riddell, Nov. 10, 1923, **68**: 421

Charles Lee Swem, May 17, 1920, **65**: 291; July 6, 1920, **65**: 498; July 18, 1920, **65**: 521; July 26, 1920, **65**: 550; Aug. 13, 1920, **66**: 29; Sept. 9, 1920, **66**: 103; Nov. 3, 1920, **66**: 306; Dec. 18, 1920, **66**: 533; Jan. 6, 1921, **67**: 30; Jan. 12, 1921, **67**: 51; Jan. 14, 1921, **67**: 60; Jan. 15, 1921, **67**: 67; Jan. 30, 1921, **67**: 103; Feb. 11, 1921 (2), **67**: 127 (2); Feb. 17, 1921, **67**: 143; Feb. 21, 1921, **67**: 150; Feb. 22, 1921, **67**: 157; Feb. 26, 1921, **67**: 170

William Linn Westermann, May 22, 1919, **59**: 374; June 13, 1919, **60**: 492; June 28, 1919, **61**: 328

Edward Thomas Williams, **57**: 626

Sir William Wiseman, Jan. 19, 1919, **54**: 151; Feb. 3, 1919, **54**: 461; Feb. 7, 1919, **54**: 556

THE PARIS PEACE CONFERENCE

Minutes of Plenary Sessions

Jan. 18, 1919, 3 p.m., **54**: 128
Jan. 25, 1919, 3 p.m., **54**: 264
May 31, 1919, 3 p.m., **59**: 628

Minutes of meetings of the Council of Ten

Jan. 12, 1919, 4 p.m., **54**: 12
Jan. 13, 1919, 4 p.m., **54**: 43
Jan. 15, 1919, 10:30 a.m., **54**: 64; 2:30 p.m., 70
Jan. 16, 1919, 10:30 a.m., **54**: 96
Jan. 17, 1919, 10:30 a.m., **54**: 108; 3 p.m., 115
Jan. 20, 1919, 10:30 a.m., **54**: 155
Jan. 21, 1919, 10:30 a.m., **54**: 179; 3 p.m., 181
Jan. 22, 1919, 3:15 p.m., **54**: 204
Jan. 23, 1919, 10:30 a.m., **54**: 218
Jan. 24, 1919, 12:15 p.m., **54**: 247; 3 p.m., 248
Jan. 27, 1919, 10:30 a.m., **54**: 283; 3 p.m., 291
Jan. 28, 1919, 11 a.m., **54**: 310; 4 p.m., 318
Jan. 29, 1919, 11 a.m., **54**: 334; 3:30 p.m., 341
Jan. 30, 1919, 11 a.m., **54**: 350; 3:30 p.m., 361
Feb. 1, 1919, 3 p.m., **54**: 415
Feb. 3, 1919, 11 a.m., **54**: 461
Feb. 5, 1919, 3 p.m., **54**: 490
Feb. 6, 1919, 3 p.m., **54**: 505
Feb. 12, 1919, 3 p.m., **55**: 104
Feb. 13, 1919, 3 p.m., **55**: 140
March 19, 1919, 3 p.m., **56**: 88
March 21, 1919, 6 p.m., **56**: 148
March 22, 1919, 11 a.m., **56**: 165
March 24, 1919, 4 p.m., **56**: 209
May 1, 1919, 4 p.m., **58**: 298
May 2, 1919, 5 p.m., **58**: 345
May 12, 1919, 4 p.m., **59**: 60
June 17, 1919, noon, **60**: 615

Minutes of meetings of the Council of Four

March 20, 1919, 3 p.m., **56**: 104
March 24, 1919, 3 p.m., **56**: 208
March 25, 1919, 11 a.m., **56**: 249; 3:30 p.m., 252
March 26, 1919, 11 a.m., **56**: 286; 3:30 p.m., 292
March 27, 1919, 11 a.m., **56**: 316; 3:30 p.m., 323
March 28, 1919, 11 a.m., **56**: 355; 4 p.m., 360
March 29, 1919, 3 p.m., **56**: 408

March 31, 1919, 11 a.m., **56**: 448; 3 p.m., 453
April 1, 1919, 11 a.m., **56**: 495; 4 p.m., 506
April 2, 1919, 11 a.m., **56**: 525; 4 p.m., 529
April 3, 1919, 11 a.m., **56**: 560; 4 p.m., 567
April 4, 1919, 11 a.m., **56**: 589; 1 p.m., 597
April 5, 1919, 11 a.m., **57**: 5; 4 p.m., 21
April 7, 1919, 3:30 p.m., **57**: 73; 4 p.m., 79
April 8, 1919, 11 a.m., **57**: 101; 3 p.m., 120
April 9, 1919, 11 a.m., **57**: 242; 3:30 p.m., 161
April 10, 1919, 11 a.m., **57**: 199; 4 p.m., 203
April 11, 1919, 11 a.m., **57**: 242
April 12, 1919, 11 a.m., **57**: 288; 5 p.m., 293
April 13, 1919, 6 p.m., **57**: 318
April 15, 1919, 11 a.m., **57**: 355; 4 p.m., 359
April 16, 1919, 11 a.m., **57**: 391
April 18, 1919, 11 a.m., **57**: 450
April 19, 1919, 11 a.m., **57**: 479
April 20, 1919, 10 a.m., **57**: 514
April 21, 1919, 4 p.m., **57**: 545
April 22, 1919, 11 a.m., **57**: 586; 11:30 a.m., 599; 4 p.m., 610; 4:30 p.m., 615
April 23, 1919, 11 a.m., **58**: 14; 4 p.m., 29
April 24, 1919, 11 a.m., **58**: 57; 4 p.m., 74
April 25, 1919, 4 p.m., **58**: 113; 5:30 p.m., 122; 6:30 p.m., 129
April 26, 1919, 12:15 p.m., **58**: 148; 3 p.m., 153
April 28, 1919, 11 a.m., **58**: 177
April 29, 1919, 11 a.m., **58**: 216; 4 p.m., 235
April 30, 1919, 11 a.m., **58**: 248; 12:30 p.m., 257
May 1, 1919, 11 a.m., **58**: 277; 5:45 p.m., 311
May 2, 1919, 11 a.m., **58**: 333; 4 p.m., 342
May 3, 1919, 10 a.m., **58**: 368; 11:30 a.m., 378; 12:10 p.m., 383; 4 p.m., 390
May 5, 1919, 11 a.m., **58**: 432
May 6, 1919, 11 a.m., **58**: 464; 5:30, 483
May 7, 1919, 11 a.m., **58**: 504; 12 noon, 510
May 8, 1919, 11 a.m., **58**: 536
May 9, 1919, 10:30 a.m., **58**: 563; 11:25 a.m., 566; 4 p.m., 571
May 10, 1919, 11 a.m., **59**: 6; 11:45 a.m., 11; 12 noon, 14; 3 p.m., 21; 4 p.m., 28
May 11, 1919, 12 noon, **59**: 40
May 12, 1919, 11 a.m., **59**: 48; 3:30 p.m., 57
May 13, 1919, 4 p.m., **59**: 84, May 14, 1919, 11:45 a.m., **59**: 128; 12:15 p.m., 130; 4 p.m., 136
May 15, 1919, 11 a.m., (C.F. 14), **59**: 162; 11 a.m., (C.F. 15), 165
May 17, 1919, 11:10 a.m., **59**: 212; 4:15 p.m., 223
May 19, 1919, 11:30 a.m., **59**: 255; 4 p.m., 265
May 20, 1919, 11 a.m., **59**: 297, 309
May 21, 1919, 11 a.m., **59**: 322; 4:15 p.m., 350; 6:15 p.m., 360

May 22, 1919, 11:45 a.m., **59**: 376; 12 noon, 380; 4 p.m., 385; 6:15 p.m., 392

May 23, 1919, 11 a.m., **59**: 420; 11:30 a.m., 424; 4 p.m., 433

May 24, 1919, 11 a.m., **59**: 455; 4 p.m., 461

May 26, 1919, 11 a.m., **59**: 481; 4 p.m., 495; 4:15 p.m., 496

May 27, 1919, 11 a.m., **59**: 531; 11:15 a.m., 532; 11:45 a.m., 538; 4 p.m., (C.F. 36A), 541; (C.F. 37), 542

May 28, 1919, 11 a.m., **59**: 556; 11:45 a.m., 560, 564; 1:45 a.m., 560, 564; 4 p.m., 568

May 29, 1919, 11 a.m., (C.F. 40), **59**: 578; (C.F. 41), 584

May 30, 1919, 4 p.m., **59**: 613; 5:30 p.m., 631, 634

June 2, 1919, 4 p.m., **60**: 22

June 3, 1919, 4 p.m., **60**: 84

June 4, 1919, 4 p.m., **60**: 122; 5 p.m., 130

June 5, 1919, 11:30 a.m., **60**: 157; 4 p.m., 168

June 6, 1919, 11 a.m., **60**: 206, 213; 4 p.m., 218, 225

June 7, 1919, 11 a.m., **60**: 261; 4 p.m., 264

June 9, 1919, 11 a.m., **60**: 311

June 10, 1919, 11 a.m., **60**: 335, 343; 4 p.m., 351

June 11, 1919, 11 a.m., **60**: 389; 4 p.m., 402, 420; 5 p.m., 411; 5:45 p.m., 415

June 12, 1919, 11 a.m., **60**: 436, 462; 4 p.m., 466, 477

June 13, 1919, 11 a.m., **60**: 494, 498; noon, 511; 4 p.m., 518; 5 p.m., 527

June 14, 1919, 11 a.m., **60**: 548; 4 p.m., 550; 4:45 p.m., 553; 6 p.m., 556

June 16, 1919, 11 a.m., **60**: 576; 12:30 p.m., 582; 4 p.m., 583; 5:15 p.m., 591; 5:54 p.m., 593; 6:30 p.m., 598

June 17, 1919, 3 p.m., **60**: 617, 619; 4 p.m., 623, 634

June 21, 1919, 12:30 p.m., **61**: 46; 3:45 p.m., 50; 4 p.m., 59

June 22, 1919, 7:15 p.m., **61**: 70; 9 p.m., 72

June 23, 1919, 9 a.m., **61**: 79; 11 a.m., 82; 12:10 p.m., 88; 4 p.m., 99

June 24, 1919, 11 a.m., **61**: 11 a.m., 120; 11:15 a.m., 123

June 25, 1919, 11 a.m., **61**: 139; 4 p.m., 149

June 26, 1919, 11 a.m., **61**: 191, 203; 4 p.m., 209, 214

June 27, 1919, 11 a.m., **61**: 254; 12 noon, 257; 4 p.m., 271; 4:30 p.m., 280

June 28, 1919, 10:30 a.m., **61**: 307, 309; 11 a.m., 313; 12 noon, 317; 5 p.m., 334; 6 p.m., 342

Minutes of a meeting of the Council of Four and the Council of Five, April 16, 1919, 4 p.m., **57**: 400

Notes of a British-French-Italian meeting, April 21, 1919, 10 a.m., **57**: 536

Notes of a meeting of British and French leaders, June 13, 1919, 4 p.m., **60**: 523

Minutes of meetings of the Supreme War Council

Jan. 12, 1919, 2:30 p.m., **54**: 7
Jan. 13, 1919, 2:30 p.m., **54**: 35
Jan. 22, 1919, 11 a.m., **54**: 199
Jan. 24, 1919, 10:30 a.m., **54**: 238
Feb. 7, 1919, 3:30 p.m., **54**: 525
Feb. 8, 1919, 3 p.m., **55**: 9
Feb. 10, 1919, 3 p.m., **55**: 51
Feb. 12, 1919, 5 p.m., **55**: 104; 6:30 p.m., 178
March 17, 1919, 3 p.m., **56**: 14
March 21, 1919, 3 p.m., **56**: 129

Council of Four: Memoranda, reports, and resolutions

An agreement on a provision binding Austria and Hungary to recognize the frontiers of the successor states, May 10, 1919, **59**: 13
Draft treaty between the Allied and Associated Powers and Poland on the protection of minority rights, May 13, 1919, **59**: 114
A memorandum by Cecil James Barrington Hurst on the insertion of the Covenant of the League of Nations in the Austrian treaty, May 14, 1919, **59**: 141
Resolutions on mandates in Asia Minor, May 14, 1919, **59**: 146
A resolution on the right of withdrawal from the Reparation Commission, May 14, 1919, **59**: 147
Second Report by the Committee on New States on the protection of minorities in Poland, May 15, 1919, **59**: 180
A memorandum by Arthur James Balfour on the problem of Italy and Turkey in Anatolia, May 17, 1919, **59**: 209
A memorandum by Lord Robert Cecil on the Bolshevik reply to the Nansen plan, May 20, 1919, **59**: 300
A draft by the Committee on New States of articles on the protection of minorities in the treaty with Hungary, May 26, 1919, **59**: 509
A note by the Japanese government suggesting the provisional recognition of the Kolchak government, May 27, 1919, **59**: 550
A proposal by André Tardieu for the settlement of the Adriatic question, May 28, 1919, **59**: 559
A resolution on the future of the Klagenfurt Basin, May 29, 1919, **59**: 587
A report by Jules Cambon about talks with the Yugoslav and Czechoslovak delegations on the official name of the Austrian Republic, May 29, 1919, **59**: 587
A skeleton plan by Pierrepont Burt Noyes on the occupation of the Left Bank, May 29, 1919, **59**: 593
A draft by Lord Sumner of a formula for the share of the Austro-Hungarian successor states in the war costs, May 30, 1919, **59**: 611

A memorandum by Jules-Emile Jeanneney on the involvement of the French Army in the Rhenish separatist movement, June 1, 1919, **60**: 9

A note from Aleksandr Vasil'evich Kolchak on the future policy of his government, June 4, 1919, **60**: 141

An intended proclamation by Aleksandr Vasil'evich Kolchak on the democratic program of his government, June 3, 1919, **60**: 180

A note by Vittorio Emanuele Orlando on the boundary between Italy and Yugoslavia, June 5, 1919, **60**: 197

A report by the Committee on New States about the method of appeal to the League of Nations by minorities in Poland, June 6, 1919, **60**: 223

A memorandum by the delegation of the Kingdom of Serbs, Croats and Slovenes on the plebiscite in the Klagenfurt Basin, June 6, 1919, **60**: 233

Supreme War Council Joint Note No. 43 on possible measures to be taken against Hungary, June 7, 1919, **60**: 256

A note by the Supreme Economic Council on the blockade of Hungary and Bolshevik Russia, June 7, 1919, **60**: 281

A note by the Superior Blockade Council on an agreement proposed by Austria for trade with Hungary and Germany, June 7, 1919, **60**: 283

A memorandum by the Italian delegation on the Adriatic question, June 9, 1919, **60**: 308

A report by the Reparation Commission in reply to the German counterproposal on the reparation clauses, June 9, 1919, **60**: 321

A memorandum by the American representatives on the Reparation Commission on a reply to the German counterproposal, June 9, 1919, **60**: 323

A note for the Council of Four by the Inter-Allied Committee on the Left Bank about a plan for the occupation of the Rhineland, June 10, 1919, **60**: 366

A convention for the military occupation of the Left Bank of the Rhine, June 10, 1919, **60**: 368 (draft); June 13, 1919 (2), **60**: 504, (revision by Wilson), 513

A memorandum on relations between the Allied military authorities and the Inter-Allied Rhineland High Commission, June 10, 1919, **60**: 372 (draft); June 13, 1919, **60**: 517

A declaration by the United States, Great Britain, and France on the military occupation of the Left Bank, June 16, 1919, **60**: 575

A memorandum by the Allied and Associated Powers on the reimposition of the blockade against Germany, June 13, 1919, **60**: 523

A draft of a declaration by the Allied and Associated Powers to the Vatican about the status of Catholic missions in former German colonies, June 16, 1919, **60**: 581

A note from Béla Kun about the peaceful intentions of the Hungarian government, June 17, 1919, **60**: 629

A memorandum by Ignace Jan Paderewski on the minorities provi-

sions in the draft treaty between the Allied and Associated Powers and Poland, June 17, 1919, **60**: 629

A memorandum by the Committee on New States on the objections of Ignace Jan Paderewski to the minorities provisions in the draft treaty between the Allied and Associated Powers and Poland, June 21, 1919, **61**: 47

A memorandum by the Committee on Rumanian and Yugoslav Affairs on proposals by Milenko R. Vesnić for plebiscites in the Klagenfurt Basin, June 21, 1919, **61**: 57

A draft by the Committee on New States of a letter to Ignace Jan Paderewski transmitting the treaty between the Allied and Associated Powers and Poland, June 23, 1919, **61**: 93

An agreement by the Allied and Associated Powers to grant Belgian claims for priority in reparation payments, June 24, 1919, **61**: 120

A memorandum by the Allied and Associated Powers on the method of applying the provisions of the Belgian priority agreement, June 24, 1919, **61**: 121

A report by the Commisssion on Baltic Affairs on the effect of the evacuation of the Baltic provinces by German troops on the food supply of the region, June 25, 1919, **61**: 160

A recommendation by the Commission on Baltic Affairs for immediate financial assistance to the Baltic provinces, June 25, 1919, **61**: 161

A proposed statement by the American, British, and French representatives in the Baltic provinces on the policy of the Allied and Associated Powers, June 25, 1919, **61**: 162

A memorandum by Winston Spencer Churchill suggesting a joint operation between Czechoslovak troops and Kolchak's army, June 25, 1919, **61**: 164

A memorandum by Arthur James Balfour on the situation in eastern Galicia, June 25, 1919, **61**: 167

An agreement by Great Britain and the United States to come to the assistance of France in the event of unprovoked aggression by Germany (French security treaty), June 27, 1919, **61**: 281; June 28, 1919, **61**: 311

A proposed declaration by the Chinese delegation on the Shantung settlement, June 27, 1919, **61**: 289

A statement by Theobald von Bethmann Hollweg assuming responsibility for the actions of the German government in 1914, June 28, 1919, **61**: 340

A draft by the Commission on Mandates of provisions for Class B and Class C mandates, July 11, 1919, **61**: 451

Council of Four: Notes exchanged with the German delegation

German notes
Preliminary protest against the peace terms, May 9, 1919, **59**: 13

Repatriation of prisoners of war, May 10, 1919, **59**: 56

Responsibility for the origin of the war, May 13, 1919, **59**: 274
Economic effect of the peace treaty on Germany, May 13, 1919, **59**: 305
Responsibility for the origin of the war and liability for reparations, May 24, 1919, **59**: 488
Observations on the conditions of the peace, May 29, 1919, **59**: 579
Acceptance of the peace terms with reservations, June 22, 1919, **61**: 72
Unqualified acceptance of the peace terms, June 23, 1919, **61**: 79
A request for an extension of the deadline for the signing of the peace treaty, June 23, 1919, **61**: 81
A request for the notification of populations on the eastern frontier about the date of their separation from Germany, June 26, 1919, **61**: 193

Allied replies to
Preliminary protest against the peace terms, May 10, 1919, **59**: 28
German counterproposal on the League of Nations, May 10, 1919, **59**: 28
Repatriation of prisoners of war, May 14, 1919, **59**: 134 (draft); May 15, 1919, **59**: 163 (draft)
Responsibility for the origin of the war, May 16, 1919, **59**: 275
Economic effect of the peace treaty on Germany, May 21, 1919, **59**: 307 (draft), 362
Territorial arrangements of the peace treaty, May 24, 1919, **59**: 458
The Covenant of the League of Nations, June 7, 1919, **60**: 274, (draft); June 12, 1919, **60**: 459
Reparation for damages, June 11, 1919, **60**: 394 (draft), 406
Observations on the conditions of peace, June 12, 1919, **60**: 442
Responsibility for the origin of the war, June 12, 1919, **60**: 451
The Saar Basin, June 12, 1919, **60**: 460
Punitive provisions of the peace treaty, June 12, 1919, **60**: 475 (draft)
A demand for the unqualified acceptance of the peace terms, June 23, 1919, **61**: 76
A denial of an extension of the deadline for the signing of the peace treaty, June 23, 1919 (2), **61**: 78, 82
A warning concerning alleged German plans for intrigues on the eastern frontier, June 25, 1919, **61**: 163
The scuttling of the German fleet at Scapa Flow, June 25, 1919, **61**: 168

Council of Four: Notes and correspondence

Georges Clemenceau to Lu Cheng-hsiang, May 14, 1919, **59**: 144
Georges Clemenceau to Arthur Henderson, May 14, 1919, **59**: 145
A note by Wilson, Lloyd George, and Clemenceau to the Italian gov-

ernment protesting against the landing of Italian troops in Asia Minor, May 17, 1919, **59**: 225

Minutes of a conversation between Wilson, Lloyd George, and Clemenceau, May 26, 1919, 3:30 p.m., **59**: 492

Georges Clemenceau to Józef Klemens Piłsudski, May 21, 1919, **59**: 359 (draft), 360; May 22, 1919, **59**: 392

The Allied and Associated Powers to Aleksandr Vasil'evich Kolchak, May 23, 1919, **59**: 440 (draft); May 24, 1919, **59**: 468 (draft); May 26, 1919, **59**: 543

Georges Clemenceau to Karl Renner, May 27, 1919, **59**: 533

A note by Clemenceau, Wilson, and Lloyd George to Paul Hymans about the Belgian priority agreement, June 24, 1919, **61**: 122

Edgar Karl Alfons Hainel von Haimhausen to Georges Clemenceau, June 25, 1919, **61**: 139

A note to the Polish government on the fighting in eastern Galicia, June 25, 1919, **61**: 158

A note to the Dutch government requesting the surrender of the former German Emperor, June 26, 1919, **61**: 200 (draft); June 27, 1919, **61**: 258

Eduard Beneš to David Lloyd George, June 26, 1919, **61**: 201

Ignace Jan Paderewski to Georges Clemenceau (extracts), June 27, 1919 (2), **61**: 271, 272

A note to the Polish government authorizing the use of General Haller's army in eastern Galicia, June 27, 1919, **61**: 279

A note to Aleksandr Vasil'evich Kolchak about a plan for repatriating and utilizing the Czechoslovak troops in Siberia (draft), June 27, 1919, **61**: 287

Theobald von Bethmann Hollweg to Georges Clemenceau, June 28, 1919, **61**: 340

A note to the Turkish delegation advising it of the unprofitability of extending its stay in Paris, June 28, 1919, **61**: 340

A note from the British and French governments to Italy on Italian claims in the Adriatic and Asia Minor, June 28, 1919, **61**: 343

A note from the American government to Italy on Italian claims to the Dodecanese Islands and in Asia Minor, June 28, 1919, **61**: 346

Minutes of the meetings of the League of Nations Commission

Feb. 3, 1919, 2:30 p.m., **54**: 463
Feb. 4, 1919, 8:30 p.m., **54**: 481
Feb. 5, 1919, 8:30 p.m., **54**: 495
Feb. 6, 1919, 8:30 p.m., **54**: 509
Feb. 7, 1919, 8:30 p.m., **54**: 545
Feb. 8, 1919, 10:30 a.m., **55**: 4
Feb. 10, 1919, 10:30 a.m., **55**: 41
Feb. 11, 1919, 10:30 a.m., **55**: 70
Feb. 13, 1919, 10:30 a.m., **55**: 120, 3:30 p.m., 137
March 22, 1919, 3:30 p.m., **56**: 170

March 24, 1919, 8:30 p.m., **56**: 223
March 26, 1919, 8:30 p.m., **56**: 298
April 10, 1919, 8 p.m., **57**: 218
April 11, 1919, 8:30 p.m., **57**: 248

The Covenant of the League of Nations

Wilson's first "Paris draft," Jan. 8, 1919, **53**: 655
Wilson's second "Paris draft," Jan. 18, 1919, **54**: 138
A draft by the British League of Nations Section, Jan. 20, 1919, **54**:
    160
The Hurst–Miller draft, Feb. 2, 1919, **54**: 433
Wilson's third "Paris draft," Feb. 2, 1919, **54**: 441; Feb. 3, 1919, **54**:
    449
A draft by Wilson of an article on racial equality, Feb. 5, 1919, **54**:
    500
The Covenant of the League of Nations, April 28, 1919, **58**: 188

Wilson's addresses and statements

Address to the Third Plenary Session of the peace conference, Feb.
    14, 1919, **55**: 164
A statement upon leaving France, Feb. 15, 1919, **55**: 197
A memorandum on the establishment of a mandatory system in Tur-
    key, March 25, 1919, **56**: 272
A statement on progress in formulating the Covenant of the League
    of Nations, March 27, 1919, **56**: 313
A proposal for an agreement on the Rhineland question, March 28,
    1919, **56**: 371
A comment on the amendments suggested by André Tardieu to
    Wilson's proposal for an agreement on the Rhineland question and
    a treaty of guarantee for France, April 8, 1919, **57**: 130 (draft);
    April 12, 1919, **57**: 296
A memorandum on the ethnic situation in Italy's northern frontiers,
    April 11, 1919, **57**: 271
A statement summoning the German plenipotenitaries to Ver-
    sailles, April 14, 1919, **57**: 336
A memorandum opposing Italian claims on the Adriatic, April 14,
    1919, **57**: 343
A statement on the Adriatic question, April 21, 1919, **57**: 542
Remarks to a Plenary Session, April 28, 1919, **58**: 199
Remarks at a dinner given in his honor by Sir Thomas Barclay, May
    9, 1919, **58**: 598
Address to the Academy of Moral and Political Science, May 10,
    1919, **59**: 4
After-dinner remarks in honor of Epitacio Pessoa as President-elect
    of Brazil, May 26, 1919, **59**: 520
Remarks at Suresnes Cemetary on Memorial Day, May 30, 1919, **59**:
    606

Remarks at a luncheon at the American legation in Brussels, June 19, 1919, **61**: 16
An address to the Belgian Parliament, June 12, 1919, **61**: 16
Remarks at the City Hall of Louvain, June 19, 1919, **61**: 21
Remarks at the City Hall of Brussels, June 19, 1919, **61**: 23
Remarks at a dinner at the Royal Palace in Brussels, June 19, 1919, **61**: 25
A statement on the peace treaty with Germany, June 23, 1919, **61**: 108 (draft), 108
After-dinner remarks at the Elysée Palace, June 26, 1919, **61**: 189
A press release upon the signing of the peace traty with Germany, June 27, 1919, **61**: 292
A statement upon leaving France, June 28, 1919, **61**: 350
An address to fellow passengers on the *U.S.S. George Washington*, July 4, 1919, **61**: 378

Wilson correspondence

From Wilson to

Jane Addams, April 26, 1919, **58**: 156; May 16, 1919, **59**: 189
Gustave Ador, April 17, 1919, **57**: 430
Avetis Aharonian, May 13, 1919, **59**: 103
Albert, King of the Belgians, Feb. 20, 1919, **55**: 220; June 20, 1919, **61**: 35
The American Commissioners, Feb. 19, 1919, **55**: 208; July 15, 1919, **61**: 479
Emma Alice Margaret Tennant Asquith, April 26, 1919, **58**: 155

Newton Diehl Baker, Jan. 14, 1919, **54**: 55; Feb. 8, 1919, **55**: 27; March 1, 1919, **55**: 341
Newton Diehl Baker and Edward Nash Hurley, March 22, 1919, **56**: 190
Ray Stannard Baker, April 14, 1919, **57**: 336
Arthur James Balfour, April 30, 1919, **58**: 245
Bernard Mannes Baruch, Feb. 5, 1919, **54**: 494; Feb. 14, 1919, **55**: 186; April 26, 1919, **58**: 155
William Shepherd Benson, Jan. 25, 1919, **54**: 273; April 23, 1919, **58**: 43; May 6, 1919, **58**: 492; June 7, 1919, **60**: 276
Robert Woods Bliss, Jan. 30, 1919, **54**: 380; Feb. 11, 1919, **55**: 81
Tasker Howard Bliss, Jan. 17, 1919, **54**: 123; April 9, 1919, **57**: 178; April 18, 1919, **57**: 458; April 22, 1919, **57**: 628; April 23, 1919, **58**: 42; April 25, 1919, **58**: 135; May 20, 1919, **59**: 313; June 7, 1919, **60**: 277; June 16, 1919, **60**: 602 (2)
Isaiah Bowman, April 18, 1919, **57**: 456
The Right Reverend Charles Henry Brent, April 15, 1919, **57**: 371
William Jennings Bryan, March 19, 1919, **56**: 96
James Viscount Bryce, Jan. 16, 1919, **54**: 104

Felix Ludwig Calonder, March 24, 1919, **56**: 234
Lord Robert Cecil, Feb. 1, 1919, **54**: 426; May 2, 1919, **58**: 353
Georges Clemenceau, Feb. 26, 1919, **55**: 279; May 9, 1919, **58**: 584;
    May 23, 1919, **59**: 443; June 1, 1919, **60**: 9

Josephus Daniels, March 1, 1919, **55**: 343; April 15, 1919, **57**: 371
Norman Hezekiah Davis, Feb. 5, 1919, **54**: 493; Feb. 7, 1919, **54**:
    549; April 19, 1919, **57**: 495; May 9, 1919, **58**: 591; June 10,
    1919, **60**: 361
Baron d'Estournelles de Constant, Jan. 24, 1919, **54**: 257

Prince Faisal, Feb. 14, 1919, **55**: 183; April 21, 1919, **57**: 559
Millicent Garrett Fawcett, Feb. 14, 1919, **55**: 183
Ferdinand Foch, May 13, 1919, **59**: 108
Felix Frankfurter, May 13, 1919, **59**: 108; May 16, 1919, **59**: 189
Arthur Hugh Frazier, Feb. 14, 1919, **55**: 185
Andrew Furuseth, April 15, 1919, **57**: 371

James Cardinal Gibbons, May 6, 1919, **58**: 491
Carter Glass, Feb. 19, 1919, **55**: 208; April 5, 1919, **57**: 42
Samuel Gompers, June 20, 1919 (2), **61**: 37 (2)

Charles Homer Haskins, June 4, 1919, **60**: 136
Arthur Henderson, Jan. 24, 1919, **54**: 257
George Davis Herron, April 28, 1919, **58**: 204
Herbert Clark Hoover, Feb. 3, 1919, **54**: 467; Feb. 7, 1919, **54**: 549;
    Feb. 14, 1919, **55**: 186 (2); April 2, 1919, **56**: 543; April 15, 1919,
    57: 370; April 16, 1919, **57**: 406; April 22, 1919, **57**: 627; April 23,
    1919, **58**: 41; April 25, 1919, **58**: 136; May 17, 1919 (2), **59**: 226,
    227; May 21, 1919, **59**: 346; June 3, 1919, **60**: 99; June 6, 1919,
    60: 230; June 25, 1919, **61**: 173
Stanley Kuhl Hornbeck, June 10, 1919, **60**: 358
Edward Mandell House, Jan. 25, 1919, **54**: 271; Feb. 14, 1919, **55**:
    178; Feb. 17, 1919, **55**: 202; Feb. 23, 1919 (2), **55**: 229, 230; Feb.
    27, 1919, **55**: 299; Feb. 28, 1919, **55**: 326; March 3, 1919 (2), **55**:
    392 (2); March 10, 1919, **55**: 472; March 18, 1919, **56**: 63; March
    31, 1919, **56**: 483; April 7, 1919, **57**: 90; April 12, 1919, **57**: 295;
    May 13, 1919 (2), **59**: 104, 105; June 7, 1919, **60**: 277; June 27,
    1919, **61**: 259; July 1, 1919, **61**: 363; July 18, 1919, **61**: 520
Edward Nash Hurley, March 28, 1919, **56**: 374
Paul Hymans, June 24, 1919, **61**: 120

Morris Jastrow, Jr., March 12, 1919, **55**: 484
Douglas Wilson Johnson, June 27, 1919, **61**: 284
Homer Hosea Johnson, March 20, 1919, **56**: 120
Jean-Jules Jusserand, June 27, 1919, **61**: 284

Henry Churchill King, May 29, 1919, **59**: 594
Harry Shepard Knapp, June 14, 1919, **60**: 565
Vi Kyuin Wellington Koo, April 19, 1919, **57**: 495

Thomas William Lamont, March 24, 1919, **56**: 233; June 12, 1919,
    60: 483; July 19, 1919, **61**: 543
George Lansbury, Feb. 14, 1919, **55**: 187; March 18, 1919, **56**: 63
Robert Lansing, Feb. 19, 1919, **55**: 209; Feb. 23, 1919, **55**: 231;
    March 20, 1919, **56**: 119; March 24, 1919, **56**: 235; April 1, 1919
    (2), **56**: 512, 513; April 9, 1919, **57**: 149; April 14, 1919 (3), **57**:
    346 (3); April 16, 1919 (2), **57**: 406 (2); April 19, 1919 (2), **57**: 494,
    495; May 1, 1919 (2), **58**: 316 (2); May 2, 1919, **58**: 354; May 3,
    1919 (2), **58**: 404 (2); May 13, 1919, **59**: 108; May 22, 1919, **59**:
    394; May 26, 1919, **59**: 512; May 27, 1919, **59**: 546; May 29,
    1919, **59**: 594; June 3, 1919, **60**: 99; June 7, 1919, **60**: 276; June
    10, 1919 (2), **60**: 358, 375; June 12, 1919, **60**: 483; June 14, 1919,
    60: 564; June 16, 1919 (2), **60**: 601 (2); June 20, 1919, **61**: 36;
    June 25, 1919 (2), **61**: 170, 172; June 27, 1919, **61**: 284; June 28,
    1919, **61**: 306; June 28, 1919, **61**: 347; July 2, 1919, **61**: 371; July
    25, 1919, **61**: 629
David Lloyd George, Jan. 25, 1919, **54**: 273; Jan. 27, 1919, **54**: 301;
    March 17, 1919, **56**: 56; May 5, 1919, **58**: 446
Robert Howard Lord, May 31, 1919, **59**: 638; June 6, 1919, **60**: 230

Vance Criswell McCormick, April 15, 1919, **57**: 375; June 10, 1919,
    60: 359
Porter James McCumber, April 15, 1919, **57**: 372
Louis Marshall, May 19, 1919, **59**: 276; May 24, 1919, **59**: 471
Sidney Edward Mezes, March 26, 1919, **56**: 303; May 24, 1919, **59**:
    455
David Hunter Miller, Feb. 3, 1919, **54**: 458
Edwin Samuel Montagu, May 19, 1919, **59**: 277

Fridtjof Nansen, April 7, 1919, **57**: 93 (draft); April 18, 1919, **57**: 456
Frank Mason North, Jan. 14, 1919, **54**: 56
Pierrepont Burt Noyes, May 29, 1919, **59**: 594; June 10, 1919, **60**:
    360
Boghos Nubar, Jan. 23, 1919, **54**: 226, Feb. 3, 1919, **54**: 468; Feb.
    11, 1919, **55**: 80

Vittorio Emanuele Orlando, Jan. 13, 1919, **54**: 50; Feb. 27, 1919,
    55: 300; April 22, 1919, **57**: 627

Edwin Brewington Parker, March 24, 1919, **56**: 234
Ignace Jan Paderewski, Jan. 25, 1919, **54**: 278; April 26, 1919, **58**:
    155; June 3, 1919, **60**: 99
Thomas Nelson Page, June 5, 1919, **60**: 176

Nikola P. Pasić, April 24, 1919, **58**: 90; June 10, 1919, **60**: 361
John Joseph Pershing, Jan. 28, 1919, **54**: 331; May 23, 1919 (2),
    59: 443, 444; June 12, 1919, **60**: 483
William Phillips, July 18, 1919 (4), **61**: 520, 523, 524 (2)
Sir Horace Plunkett, March 26, 1919, **56**: 304
Raymond Poincaré, Jan. 16, 1919, **54**: 104; Feb. 13, 1919, **55**: 149;
    May 7, 1919, **58**: 521
Frank Lyon Polk, Feb. 27, 1919, **55**: 300; July 12, 1919, **61**: 461

The representatives of the small nations at Paris, July 12, 1919,
    61: 461
Henry Mauris Robinson, March 30, 1919, **56**: 429; April 21, 1919,
    57: 558; April 23, 1919, **58**: 43; April 28, 1919, **58**: 204
Walter Stowell Rogers, Jan. 31, 1919, **54**: 400
Lord Rothschild, Jan. 13, 1919, **54**: 52

Maguerite de Witt Schlumberger, March 28, 1919, **56**: 374
James Brown Scott, June 2, 1919, **60**: 22
Jan Christiaan Smuts, May 16, 1919, **59**: 187; May 31, 1919, **59**:
    637
Oscar Solomon Straus, April 18, 1919, **57**: 469
Herbert Bayard Swope, Feb. 1, 1919, **54**: 427; Feb. 7, 1919, **54**: 550

Joseph Patrick Tumulty, Jan. 16, 1919, **54**: 105; Jan. 20, 1919, **54**:
    158; March 15, 1919, **55**: 532; March 17, 1919, **56**: 57; April 25,
    1919, **58**: 144; April 30, 1919, **58**: 272; May 2, 1919, **58**: 364; May
    3, 1919, **58**: 420; May 8, 1919, **58**: 560; May 9, 1919, **58**: 601; May
    27, 1919, **59**: 553; June 8, 1919, **60**: 298

Milenko R. Vesnić, April 21, 1919, **57**: 558; June 10, 1919, **60**: 361;
    June 14, 1919, **60**: 565

Henry White, Feb. 1, 1919, **54**: 426; April 17, 1919, **57**: 430; April
    18, 1919, **57**: 457; May 23, 1919, **59**: 444; June 14, 1919, **60**: 564;
    July 25, 1919, **61**: 623
William Allen White, April 2, 1919, **56**: 545
Brand Whitlock, 7 Feb. 1919, **54**: 550; April 16, 1919, **57**: 422
Queen Wilhelmina, Feb. 20, 1919, **55**: 219

To Wilson from

Jane Addams, May 13, 1919, **59**: 117
Jane Addams and Others, April 25, 1919, **58**: 140
Gustave Ador, April 13, 1919, **57**: 329
Albert, King of the Belgians, Feb. 10, 1919, **55**: 63; June 21, 1919,
    61: 61
The American Commissioners and the American Mission in Paris,
    Feb. 23, 1919, **55**: 232; March 28, 1919, **56**: 386; March 31, 1919,

56: 466; April 1, 1919, **56**: 511; April 28, 1919, **58**: 205; June 10,
  1919, **60**: 375; July 16, 1919, **61**: 494
A committee of the American Federation of Labor, May 2, 1919,
  58: 361
Emma Alice Margaret Tennant Asquith, April 24, 1919, **58**: 95

Ray Stannard Baker, Jan. 21, 1919, **54**: 189; Jan. 21, 1919, **54**:
  191; March 21, 1919, **56**: 155
Newton Diehl Baker, Feb. 11, 1919, **55**: 81; Feb. 28, 1919, **55**: 335
Arthur James Balfour, Jan. 17, 1919, **54**: 123; Jan. 20, 1919, **54**:
  173; April 29, 1919, **58**: 228; April 30, 1919, **58**: 246
James Levi Barton and Others, March 12, 1919, **55**: 485
Bernard Mannes Baruch, Feb. 4, 1919 (2), **54**: 479, 480; March 29,
  1919, **56**: 421; April 9, 1919, **57**: 159; April 24, 1919, **58**: 94; May
  7, 1919, **58**: 523; May 8, 1919, **58**: 548; May 17, 1919, **59**: 227
Bernard Mannes Baruch and Others, May 7, 1919, **58**: 526
Edward Price Bell, Jan. 25, 1919, **54**: 275
William Shepherd Benson, Jan. 31, 1919, **54**: 403; Feb. 4, 1919, **54**:
  477; Feb. 7, 1919, **54**: 552; Feb. 8, 1919, **55**: 27; March 14, 1919
  (2), **55**: 515, 522; April 9, 1919, **57**: 180; April 17, 1919, **57**: 442;
  April 28, 1919, **58**: 206; May 5, 1919, **58**: 456; May 16, 1919, **59**:
  197; May 24, 1919, **59**: 473; June 1, 1919, **60**: 16; June 5, 1919,
  60: 193
Howard Sweetser Bliss, Feb. 7, 1919, **54**: 551; Feb. 11, 1919, **55**:
  86; March 10, 1919, **55**: 472
Tasker Howard Bliss, Jan. 15, 1919, **54**: 84; Feb. 6, 1919, **54**: 514;
  Feb. 8, 1919, **55**: 28; March 14, 1919, **55**: 511; March 26, 1919,
  56: 305; March 28, 1919 (2), **56**: 379, 381; March 31, 1919, **56**:
  468; April 1, 1919, **56**: 491; April 8, 1919, **57**: 134; April 11, 1919,
  57: 274; April 16, 1919, **57**: 415; April 18, 1919, **57**: 461; April 20,
  1919, **57**: 526; April 21, 1919, **57**: 559; April 24, 1919, **58**: 95;
  April 29, 1919, **58**: 232; April 30, 1919, **58**: 262; May 1, 1919 (2),
  58: 307, 310; May 19, 1919 (2), **59**: 277, 280; June 6, 1919 (2), **60**:
  235, 237; June 7, 1919, **60**: 255; June 10, 1919, **60**: 363; June 17,
  1919, **60**: 622
William Bramwell Booth, Jan. 31, 1919, **54**: 406
Ion I. C. Brătianu, June 6, 1919, **60**: 233
Sir Robert Borden, March 14, 1919, **55**: 501
Isaiah Bowman and Others, April 17, 1919, **57**: 432
The Right Reverend Charles Henry Brent, April 11, 1919, **57**: 284
William Jennings Bryan, March 19, 1919, **56**: 95
William Christian Bullitt, March 16, 1919, **55**: 540; April 18, 1919,
  57: 459; May 17, 1919, **59**: 232

Felix Ludwig Calonder, March 22, 1919, **56**: 169
Lord Robert Cecil, Jan. 20, 1919, **54**: 160; April 21, 1919, **57**: 568;
  May 4, 1919, **58**: 423; May 17, 1919, **59**: 243
Georgii Vasil'evich Chicherin, Jan. 29, 1919, **54**: 345

Georges Clemenceau, Feb. 28, 1919, **55**: 335; March 17, 1919, **56**: 9; March 31, 1919, **56**: 477; April 17, 1919, **57**: 432; June 1, 1919, **60**: 8; June 7, 1919, **60**: 275
Gilbert Fairchild Close, April 17, 1919, **57**: 440
Charles Richard Crane, July 10, 1919, **61**: 442
George Creel, Feb. 3, 1919, **54**: 470; March 1, 1919, **55**: 363; March 31, 1919, **56**: 486

Josephus Daniels, March 4, 1919 (2), **55**: 424 (2); March 30, 1919, **56**: 430; April 14, 1919, **57**: 347; May 9, 1919, **58**: 593
John William Davis, March 31, 1919, **56**: 473; June 10, 1919, **60**: 363
Norman Hezekiah Davis, Jan. 22, 1919, **54**: 212; Feb. 12, 1919, **55**: 113; April 18, 1919, **57**: 470; May 9, 1919, **58**: 591; May 31, 1919, **59**: 639; June 7, 1919, **60**: 277
Norman Hezekiah Davis and Vance Criswell McCormick, April 4, 1919, **56**: 598; June 11, 1919 (2), **60**: 399, 400
Henry Pomeroy Davison, March 14, 1919, **55**: 526
Clive Day, May 15, 1919, **59**: 171
William Harbutt Dawson, April 5, 1919, **57**: 36
Ellis Loring Dresel, June 5, 1919, **60**: 177

Prince Faisal, Feb. 11, 1919, **55**: 86: March 24, 1919, **56**: 243; April 20, 1919, **57**: 525; July 9, 1919, **61**: 409
The First Jewish Preliminary Conference in Poland, Jan. 21, 1919, **54**: 232
Ferdinand Foch, March 14, 1919, **55**: 502
Felix Frankfurter, April 29, 1919, **58**: 242; May 8, 1919, **58**: 555; May 14, 1919, **59**: 150; May 20, 1919, **59**: 314
Andrew Furuseth, March 26, 1919, **56**: 308

Alfred George Gardiner, Feb. 1, 1919, **54**: 427; Feb. 12, 1919, **55**: 115
Harry Augustus Garfield, March 3, 1919 (2), **55**: 397, 398
Pietro Cardinal Gasparri, March 13, 1919, **55**: 493
James Watson Gerard, March 5, 1919, **55**: 446
Carter Glass, April 5, 1919, **57**: 42
Samuel Gompers, April 12, 1919, **57**: 303; May 1, 1919, **58**: 329
Thomas Watt Gregory, Jan. 14, 1919, **54**: 58

Norman Hapgood, May 28, 1919, **59**: 572; June 7, 1919, **60**: 284
Charles Homer Haskins, Feb. 11, 1919, **55**: 83; March 23, 1919, **56**: 200; March 29, 1919, **56**: 420; March 30, 1919, **56**: 431; April 1, 1919, **56**: 513; April 16, 1919, **57**: 407
George Davis Herron, Jan. 20, 1919, **54**: 174; Jan. 30, 1919, **54**: 382; March 20, 1919, **56**: 121; March 31, 1919, **56**: 473; April 21, 1919, **57**: 569

Herbert Clark Hoover, Jan. 12, 1919, **54**: 29; Feb. 4, 1919, **54**: 477;
  Feb. 6, 1919, **54**: 515; Feb. 11, 1919, **55**: 86; Feb. 12, 1919, **55**:
  117; March 22, 1919, **56**: 193; March 27, 1919, **56**: 339; March
  28, 1919, **56**: 375; March 31, 1919 (2), **56**: 469, 470; April 2, 1919,
  56: 547; April 3, 1919, **56**: 574; April 9, 1919 (2), **57**: 161, 166;
  April 11, 1919, **57**: 271; April 15, 1919 (2), **57**: 367, 368; April 21,
  1919 (2), **57**: 565 (2); May 9, 1919, **58**: 594; May 16, 1919 (2), **59**:
  191, 192; May 21, 1919, **59**: 347; June 2, 1919, **60**: 39; June 4,
  1919, **60**: 136; June 6, 1919, **60**: 230; June 16, 1919, **60**: 606;
  June 21, 1919, **61**: 61; June 25, 1919, **61**: 173; June 27, 1919, **61**:
  284; July 5, 1919, **61**: 389
Herbert Clark Hoover and John Foster Dulles, July 18, 1919, **61**:
  520
Stanley Kuhl Hornbeck, June 25, 1919, **61**: 175
Edward Mandell House, Jan. 18, 1919, **54**: 128; Jan. 19, 1919, **54**:
  150; Jan. 21, 1919, **54**: 178; Jan. 23, 1919, **54**: 228; Jan. 24, 1919,
  54: 263; Jan. 25, 1919, **54**: 271; Jan. 27, 1919, **54**: 302; Jan. 28,
  1919, **54**: 333; Feb. 3, 1919, **54**: 469; Feb. 5, 1919, **54**: 494; Feb.
  14, 1919, **55**: 178; Feb. 16, 1919, **55**: 201; Feb. 17, 1919, **55**: 203;
  Feb. 19, 1919 (2), **55**: 212, 213; Feb. 21, 1919, **55**: 223; Feb. 23,
  1919 (2), **55**: 233 (2); Feb. 24, 1919, **55**: 245; Feb. 25, 1919, **55**:
  256; Feb. 27, 1919 (4), **55**: 283, 304, 305 (2); March 1, 1919, **55**:
  349; March 2, 1919, **55**: 367; March 4, 1919, **55**: 423; March 7,
  1919, **55**: 458; April 9, 1919, **57**: 179; April 16, 1919, **57**: 390;
  April 20, 1919, **57**: 528; April 21, 1919, **57**: 535; April 25, 1919,
  58: 137; April 29, 1919, **58**: 228; May 8, 1919, **58**: 552; May 9,
  1919, **58**: 585; May 14, 1919, **59**: 127; May 22, 1919, **59**: 395;
  May 27, 1919, **59**: 546; June 5, 1919, **60**: 177; June 6, 1919, **60**:
  205; June 7, 1919, **60**: 260; June 11, 1919, **60**: 431; June 12,
  1919, **60**: 485; June 21, 1919, **61**: 46; June 23, 1919 (2), **61**: 107
  (2); June 24, 1919, **61**: 131; July 9, 1919, **61**: 408; July 11, 1919,
  61: 451; July 14, 1919, **61**: 477; July 17, 1919, **61**: 506
Manley Ottmer Hudson, June 16, 1919, **60**: 607
Edward Nash Hurley, Jan. 20, 1919, **54**: 172; April 1, 1919, **56**: 520
Paul Hymans, June 23, 1919, **61**: 106

Morris Jastrow, Jr., March 4, 1919, **55**: 438
Douglas Wilson Johnson, May 9, 1919, **58**: 588; June 1, 1919, **60**:
  16; June 2, 1919, **60**: 34; June 4, 1919, **60**: 121; June 20, 1919,
  61: 41; June 26, 1919, **61**: 227
Jean-Jules Jusserand, June 24, 1919, **61**: 133

Aleksandr Feodorovich Kerenskii and Others, May 14, 1919, **59**:
  150
Robert Joseph Kerner, April 26, 1919, **58**: 156
Philip Henry Kerr, May 13, 1919, **59**: 105; June 27, 1919, **61**: 286
Kim Kyu-sik, May 24, 1919, **59**: 473

Henry Churchill King and Charles Richard Crane, June 20, 1919, **61**: 44

Eugene Francis Kinkead, March 8, 1919, **55**: 468

Louis-Lucien Klotz, March 30, 1919, **56**: 433

Vi Kyuin Wellington Koo, April 17, 1919, **57**: 431; April 30, 1919, **58**: 247; June 27, 1919, **61**: 288

Thomas William Lamont, March 19, 1919, **56**: 98; April 25, 1919, **58**: 139; May 15, 1919, **59**: 175; May 22, 1919, **59**: 384; May 30, 1919, **59**: 611; June 21, 1919, **61**: 68; July 18, 1919, **61**: 528

George Lansbury, Feb. 11, 1919, **55**: 87; March 14, 1919, **55**: 525; March 4, 1919, **56**: 156; April 4, 1919, **58**: 93

Robert Lansing, Jan. 13, 1919 (2), **54**: 54 (2); Jan. 31, 1919, **54**: 400; Feb. 3, 1919, **54**: 469; Feb. 4, 1919, **54**: 474; Feb. 17, 1919, **55**: 202; Feb. 19, 1919, **55**: 209: March 24, 1919, **56**: 238; March 25, 1919, **56**: 257; March 27, 1919, **56**: 331; April 2, 1919, **56**: 547; April 4, 1919, **56**: 603; April 7, 1919, **57**: 95; April 8, 1919, **57**: 131; April 12, 1919 (2), **57**: 292, 298; April 13, 1919 (3), **57**: 326 (2), 327; April 17, 1919, **57**: 440; April 21, 1919, **57**: 560; April 22, 1919, **57**: 597; April 23, 1919, **58**: 44; April 25, 1919, **58**: 136; April 28, 1919, **58**: 206; April 30, 1919, **58**: 267; May 1, 1919 (4), **58**: 296, 297, 318, 319; May 3, 1919 (2), **58**: 404, 405; May 5, 1919 (2), **58**: 453, 455; May 7, 1919 (2), **58**: 522; May 8, 1919 (2), **58**: 552, 554; May 18, 1919, **59**: 251; May 20, 1919, **59**: 314; May 21, 1919 (2), **59**: 348 (2); May 22, 1919 (2), **59**: 393 (2); May 22, 1919, **59**: 399; May 26, 1919, **59**: 513; May 27, 1919 (2), **59**: 547, 549; May 29, 1919, **59**: 595; May 30, 1919, **59**: 620; June 3, 1919 (2), **60**: 101 (2); June 5, 1919, **60**: 178; June 11, 1919, **60**: 429; June 12, 1919, **60**: 483; June 13, 1919, **60**: 532; June 14, 1919, **60**: 567; June 16, 1919 (3), **60**: 602 (2), 603; June 28, 1919, **61**: 334; June 30, 1919, **61**: 357

Robert Lansing and Others, Feb. 19, 1919, **55**: 210; May 26, 1919, **59**: 480; May 27, 1919, **59**: 546; June 23, 1919, **61**: 105

Robert Lansing and Henry White, July 8, 1919, **61**: 404

Marcel Laurent, April 26, 1919, **58**: 164

Li Shengtoo, Wang Yitang, and the Chinese Parliament, March 4, 1919, **55**: 424

David Lloyd George, April 2, 1919, **56**: 545; April 23, 1919, **58**: 8; June 28, 1919, **61**: 223

Breckinridge Long, March 4, 1919, **55**: 436

Lu Cheng-hsiang, April 24, 1919, **58**: 68

Robert Howard Lord, May 29, 1919, **59**: 596; June 5, 1919, **60**: 189

William Edward Lunt and Others, April 4, 1919, **56**: 607

Frederick Henry Lynch, Jan. 25, 1919, **54**: 277

Charles Williston McAlpin, Jan. 31, 1919, **54**: 411

Vance Criswell McCormick, Jan. 21, 1919, **54**: 192; March 23,

1919, **56**: 200; April 12, 1919, **57**: 303; April 26, 1919, **58**: 161; May 13, 1919, **59**: 109; June 7, 1919, **60**: 281

James Grover McDonald, April 26, 1919, **58**: 169

Julian William Mack and Others, March 1, 1919, **55**: 368; March 2, 1919, **55**: 381

Porter James McCumber, March 13, 1919, **55**: 491

Louis Marshall, May 23, 1919, **59**: 445; May 26, 1919, **59**: 514; June 21, 1919, **61**: 63

Louis Marshall and Julian William Mack, May 16, 1919, **59**: 198

Desiré-Felicien-François-Joseph Cardinal Mercier, March 25, 1919, **56**: 258; June 19, 1919, **61**: 21

Sidney Edward Mezes, Jan. 16, 1919, **54**: 91; April 21, 1919, **57**: 572

Sherman Miles, May 22, 1919, **59**: 403

David Hunter Miller, Feb. 3, 1919, **54**: 449; Feb. 13, 1919, **55**: 148; May 5, 1919, **58**: 446; May 13, 1919, **59**: 113; May 15, 1919, **59**: 179; May 28, 1919, **59**: 556

Edwin Samuel Montagu, May 17, 1919, **59**: 238

Henry Morgenthau, June 20, 1919, **61**: 43

Fridtjof Nansen, April 3, 1919, **56**: 575; April 17, 1919 (2), **57**: 437, 438; April 21, 1919, **57**: 569

Nicholas I, April 3, 1919, **56**: 572

Pierrepont Burt Noyes, May 29, 1919, **59**: 593; June 8, 1919, **60**: 295

Boghos Nubar, Jan. 29, 1919, **54**: 346; Feb. 16, 1919, **54**: 516; April 12, 1919, **57**: 302

Vittorio Emanuele Orlando, Feb. 25, 1919, **55**: 301; April 3, 1919, **56**: 566; April 10, 1919, **57**: 232; April 13, 1919, **57**: 317; April 17, 1919, **57**: 431; April 21, 1919, **57**: 562; May 18, 1919, **59**: 250; June 9, 1919, **60**: 307; June 10, 1919, **60**: 361; June 12, 1919, **60**: 484

Ignace Jan Paderewski, May 8, 1919, **58**: 556; May 19, 1919, **59**: 261; May 30, 1919, **59**: 612; May 31, 1919, **59**: 638

Thomas Nelson Page, Feb. 11, 1919, **55**: 83; March 18, 1919, **56**: 64; May 5, 1919, **58**: 449; May 10, 1919, **59**: 33; May 12, 1919, **59**: 67; May 29, 1919, **59**: 601; June 22, 1919, **61**: 77

Nikola P. Pasić, April 23, 1919, **58**: 44; June 8, 1919, **60**: 293

Nikola Pasić and Others, Feb. 11, 1919, **55**: 87

John Joseph Pershing, Jan. 25, 1919, **54**: 275; April 5, 1919, **57**: 36; May 22, 1919, **59**: 401; June 11, 1919, **60**: 430; June 21, 1919, **61**: 61

William Phillips, July 19, 1919 (2), **61**: 554, 559; July 21, 1919, **61**: 573; July 22, 1919 (3), **61**: 583, 584, 587; July 23, 1919, **61**: 629

Jovan S. Plamenatz (Plamenac), May 3, 1919, **58**: 407

Sir Horace Plunkett, March 6, 1919, **55**: 453
Raymond Poincaré, Jan. 15, 1919, **54**: 76
Frank Lyon Polk, Feb. 25, 1919, **55**: 301; March 6, 1919, **55**: 452;
    July 16, 1919, **61**: 493; July 18, 1919, **61**: 522

William Emmanuel Rappard, April 18, 1919, **57**: 464
The representatives of the small nations at Paris, July 12, 1919,
    61: 461
Syngman Rhee (Yi Sung-man), May 24, 1919, **59**: 474
Ahmed Riza, May 24, 1919, **59**: 473
Henry Mauris Robinson, March 24, 1919, **56**: 236; April 4, 1919,
    56: 605; April 19, 1919, **57**: 498; April 27, 1919, **58**: 173; May 4,
    1919, **58**: 423; May 6, 1919, **58**: 492; May 7, 1919, **58**: 527
Walter Stowell Rogers, Jan. 30, 1919, **54**: 381

Marguerite de Witt Schlumberger, Jan. 18, 1919, **54**: 133
Charles Prestwich Scott, April 30, 1919, **58**: 268
Jan Christiaan Smuts, May 14, 1919, **59**: 149; May 16, 1919, **59**:
    198; May 30, 1919, **59**: 616
Oscar Solomon Straus, March 31, 1919, **56**: 484; April 17, 1919,
    57: 445
Charles Lee Swem, March 23, 1919, **56**: 204
Herbert Bayard Swope, Jan. 31, 1919, **54**: 406
Herbert Bayard Swope and Others, Jan. 14, 1919, **54**: 60

William Howard Taft, March 18, 1919, **56**: 83; March 21, 1919, **56**:
    157; March 28, 1919, **56**: 398; May 5, 1919, **58**: 461
William Howard Taft and Abbott Lawrence Lowell, April 10,
    1919, **57**: 233; April 12, 1919, **57**: 315
Vance Thompson, Jan. 24, 1919, **54**: 258
William Monroe Trotter, June 12, 1919, **60**: 486; June 19, 1919,
    61: 27
Joseph Patrick Tumulty, Jan. 13, 1919, **54**: 53; Jan. 14, 1919, **54**:
    57; Jan. 18, 1919, **54**: 132; April 9, 1919, **57**: 188; April 24, 1919
    (2), **58**: 105 (2); April 26, 1919, **58**: 170; April 28, 1919, **58**: 215;
    May 1, 1919, **58**: 329; May 2, 1919 (2), **58**: 361, 363; June 9, 1919,
    60: 331

Eleuthérios Kyrios Vénisélos, March 14, 1919, **55**: 500; April 29,
    1919, **58**: 241
Milenko R. Vesnić, April 26, 1919, **58**: 161; June 6, 1919, **60**: 232;
    June 17, 1919, **60**: 643

Francis Patrick Walsh, June 2, 1919, **60**: 38
Francis Patrick Walsh and Edward Fitzsimons Dunne, May 31,
    1919, **59**: 642; June 6, 1919, **60**: 239; June 13, 1919, **60**: 544
Francis Patrick Walsh and Others, April 16, 1919, **57**: 419
Chaim Weizmann, Jan. 23, 1919, **54**: 231; Jan. 24, 1919, **54**: 258

Walter Linn Westermann and David Magie, May 21, 1919, **59**: 349
Henry White, Jan. 31, 1919, **54**: 402; April 12, 1919, **57**: 301; April
16, 1919, **57**: 416; April 21, 1919, **57**: 567; April 25, 1919, **58**:
138; May 3, 1919, **58**: 410; May 4, 1919, **58**: 424; June 11, 1919,
60: 402; June 13, 1919, **60**: 530; June 24, 1919, **61**: 132; July 15,
1919, **61**: 482; July 19, 1919, **61**: 551; July 20, 1919, **61**: 566; July
21, 1919, **61**: 575; July 22, 1919, **61**: 588
William Allen White, April 2, 1919, **56**: 544; April 29, 1919, **58**: 241
Edward Thomas Williams, April 23, 1919, **58**: 46; April 24, 1919,
58: 70
Stephen Samuel Wise, Jan. 15, 1919, **54**: 90; March 2, 1919, **55**:
368; May 26, 1919, **59**: 516

Saad Zagloul, June 18, 1919, **61**: 8
Skevos Zervos and Paris Roussos, May 2, 1919, **58**: 355

Collateral addresses and remarks

Remarks at a plenary session by Count Ulrich Karl Christian von
Brockdorff-Rantzau, May 7, 1919, **58**: 514
A reply by Vittorio Emanuele Orlando to Wilson's statement on the
Adriatic question, April 24, 1919, **58**: 97

Collateral correspondence

Newton Diehl Baker to Robert Russa Moton, March 3, 1919, **55**: 404
Ray Stannard Baker to Gilbert Fairchild Close, May 15, 1919, **59**:
184
Ray Stannard Baker to Cary Travers Grayson, Jan. 14, 1919, **54**: 59;
May 3, 1919, **58**: 412
Arthur James Balfour to Edward Mandell House, March 28, 1919,
56: 394
Arthur James Balfour to Baron Nobuaki Makino, April 28, 1919, **58**:
183; April 30, 1919, **58**: 246
Colville Adrian de Rune Barclay to Frank Lyon Polk, Jan. 12, 1919,
54: 26
Malvern-Hill Barnum to Tasker Howard Bliss, April 20, 1919, **57**:
526
A draft by Lawrence Bennett of a message to John Foster Dulles,
July 21, 1919, **61**: 573
William Shepherd Benson to Naval Operations, April 7, 1919, **57**: 61
Henri-Mathias Berthelot to Sir Maurice Pascal Alers Hankey, June
21, 1919, **61**: 47
The Big Four to Fridtjof Nansen, April 17, 1919, **57**: 438
Tasker Howard Bliss to Bernard Mannes Baruch, May 22, 1919, **59**:
382
Tasker Howard Bliss to Newton Diehl Baker, April 3, 1919, **56**: 581
Tasker Howard Bliss to Newton Diehl Baker and Peyton Conway
March, March 3, 1919, **55**: 404

Tasker Howard Bliss to Arthur James Balfour, Feb. 19, 1919, **55**: 214
Tasker Howard Bliss to Eleanora Anderson Bliss, April 7, 1919, **57**: 89; May 1, 1919, **58**: 320; June 24, 1919, **61**: 135
Tasker Howard Bliss to Gilbert Fairchild Close, April 17, 1919, **57**: 444; April 18, 1919, **57**: 457
Tasker Howard Bliss to Sir Maurice Pascal Alers Hankey, June 28, 1919, **61**: 341
Tasker Howard Bliss to Francis Joseph Kernan, March 31, 1919, **56**: 469
Tasker Howard Bliss to Robert Lansing, Feb. 7, 1919, **54**: 522
Tasker Howard Bliss to Ignace Jan Paderewski, April 24, 1919, **58**: 101
Sir Robert Borden to Sir Thomas White, April 12, 1919, **57**: 306; April 15, 1919, **57**: 373; May 3, 1919, **58**: 415; May 6, 1919, **58**: 493; May 7, 1919, **58**: 517
Prince Luca Livio Borghese to Vittorio Emanuele Orlando, March 25, 1919, **56**: 275
Isaiah Bowman to Edward Mandell House, April 11, 1919, **57**: 270
Mark Lambert Bristol to William Shepherd Benson, June 1, 1919, **60**: 16; June 5, 1919, **60**: 193
A suggestion by the British government for a note from the Allied and Associated Powers to the various Russian governments, Jan. 12, 1919, **54**: 26
James Viscount Bryce to Robert Lansing, May 22, 1919, **59**: 399
James Viscount Bryce to Henry White, April 25, 1919, **58**: 139; May 22, 1919, **59**: 398
Count Ulrich Karl Christian von Brockdorff-Rantzau to the Allied and Associated governments, April 20, 1919, **57**: 526
William Hepburn Buckler to Robert Lansing, Jan. 18, 1919, **54**: 135
William Christian Bullitt to Gilbert Fairchild Close, Jan. 18, 1919, **54**: 138
William Christian Bullit to Edward Mandell House, Jan. 30, 1919, **54**: 348

Lord Robert Cecil to Norman Hezekiah Davis, June 7, 1919 (2), **60**: 279, 280
Lord Robert Cecil to Edward Mandell House, April 8, 1919, **57**: 143; April 10, 1919 (2), **57**: 216, 217; May 24, 1919, **59**: 475
Lord Robert Cecil to David Lloyd George, June 7, 1919, **60**: 279
Georgii Vasil'evich Chicherin to Ira Nelson Morris, Jan. 19, 1919, **54**: 153
Georgii Vasil'evich Chicherin to Fridtjof Nansen, May 16, 1919, **59**: 193
Viscount Sutemi Chinda to Robert Lansing, April 21, 1919, **57**: 597
Georges Clemenceau to Robert Lansing, July 12, 1919, **61**: 466
Gilbert Fairchild Close to William Shepherd Benson, May 31, 1919, **59**: 641

Gilbert Fairchild Close to William Bramwell Booth, Feb. 1, 1919, **54**: 430

Gilbert Fairchild Close to William Christian Bullit, Jan. 15, 1919, **54**: 91

Gilbert Fairchild Close to the Marquis de Chambrun, Feb. 6, 1919, **54**: 518

Gilbert Fairchild Close to Felix Frankfurter, May 21, 1919, **59**: 349

Gilbert Fairchild Close to George Davis Herron, Jan. 23, 1919, **54**: 232

Gilbert Fairchild Close to Herbert Clark Hoover, Feb. 13, 1919, **55**: 151; May 31, 1919, **59**: 639

Gilbert Fairchild Close to Vi Kyuin Wellington Koo, May 26, 1919, **59**: 513

Gilbert Fairchild Close to Robert Lansing, March 19, 1919, **56**: 96; June 24, 1919, **61**: 127

Gilbert Fairchild Close to Thomas Edward Lawrence, Feb. 21, 1919, **54**: 195

Gilbert Fairchild Close to Marguerite de Witt Schlumberger, Jan, 24, 1919, **54**: 262

Gilbert Fairchild Close to William Monroe Trotter, June 17, 1919, **60**: 641

Gilbert Fairchild Close to Francis Patrick Walsh, May 31, 1919, **59**: 640

Gilbert Fairchild Close to Chaim Weizmann, Jan. 29, 1919, **54**: 347

Gilbert Fairchild Close to Edward Thomas Williams, April 25, 1919, **58**: 144

Gilbert Fairchild Close to Wen Pin Wei, March 22, 1919, **56**: 183

Arthur Latham Conger to Tasker Howard Bliss, May 1, 1919, **58**: 307

Archibald Cary Coolidge to the American Commissioners, April 7, 1919, **57**: 96

Archibald Cary Coolidge to Robert Lansing, March 22, 1919 (2), **56**: 182 (2)

Lord Curzon to Lord Derby, Jan. 23, 1919, **54**: 235

Norman Hezekiah Davis to Lord Robert Cecil, June 7, 1919, **60**: 280

Clive Day and Charles Seymour to the American Commissioners, May 22, 1919, **59**: 405

Ellis Loring Dresel to the American Commission, April 20, 1919, **58**: 45; May 5, 1919, **58**: 453

John Foster Dulles to Bernard Mannes Baruch and Others, May 8, 1919, **58**: 549; July 4, 1919, **61**: 384

John Foster Dulles to the Department of State, July 18, 1919, **61**: 523

Reginald Candler Foster to Robert Howard Lord, May 25, 1919, **59**: 597

David Rowland Francis to Robert Lansing and Others, Feb. 23, 1919, **55**: 234

Felix Frankfurter to Gilbert Fairchild Close, May 22, 1919, **59**: 411

Arthur Hugh Frazier to Edward Mandell House, May 17, 1919, **59**: 239

Pietro Cardinal Gasparri to Edward Mandell House, May 13, 1919, **59**: 118

Hampson Gary to the American Commission, May 1, 1919, **58**: 328

Hugh Simons Gibson to the American Commissioners, May 19, 1919 (2), **59**: 261, 263

Carter Glass to Norman Hezekiah Davis, Jan. 21, 1919, **55**: 115

John R. Gordon to Joseph Clark Grew, June 4, 1919, **60**: 140

Charles Henry Grasty to Cary Travers Grayson, April 5, 1919, **57**: 37

Cary Travers Grayson to William Gibbs McAdoo, April 12, 1919, **57**: 304

Cary Travers Grayson to Joseph Patrick Tumulty, March 13, 1919, **55**: 495; April 6, 1919, **57**: 60; April 10, 1919, **57**: 194; April 11, 1919, **57**: 235; April 22, 1919, **57**: 579; April 25, 1919, **58**: 146; April 30, 1919, **58**: 248; May 1, 1919, **58**: 328

Joseph Clark Grew to Gilbert Fairchild Close, Jan. 15, 1919, **54**: 77; April 25, 1919, **58**: 137; May 12, 1919, **59**: 74; June 3, 1919 (2), **60**: 104, 106; June 4, 1919, **60**: 138; June 5, 1919, **60**: 182

Herbert Clark Hoover to Edward Mandell House, April 19, 1919, **57**: 505

Edward Mandell House to Lord Robert Cecil, April 9, 1919, **57**: 179

Edward Mandell House to Herbert Clark Hoover, April 20, 1919, **57**: 529

Edward Mandell House to David Lloyd George, May 9, 1919, **58**: 588

Edward Mandell House to Roland Sletor Morris, April 21, 1919, **57**: 570

Peter Augustus Jay to the American Mission in Paris, June 23, 1919, **61**: 109

Douglas Wilson Johnson to the American Commissioners, May 22, 1919, **59**: 406

Henry Churchill King to Gilbert Fairchild Close, May 28, 1919, **59**: 573

Henry Churchill King to Edward Mandell House, May 6, 1919, **58**: 493

Alexander Comstock Kirk to Gilbert Fairchild Close, March 29, 1919, **56**: 97; May 31, 1919, **59**: 643

Iurii Veniaminovich Kliuchnikov to Vasilii Alekseevich Maklakov, May 23, 1919, **59**: 436; May 24, 1919, **59**: 462

Louis-Lucien Klotz to Georges Clemenceau, May 16, 1919, **59**: 275

Robert Lansing to Georges Clemenceau, June 26, 1919, **61**: 199

Robert Lansing to Frank Lyon Polk, Jan. 12, 1919, **54**: 28; Feb. 7, 1919, **54**: 549; Feb. 26, 1919, **55**: 293; March 22, 1919, **56**: 183; June 16, 1919, **60**: 606; June 19, 1919, **61**: 27

Robert Lansing to Francis Patrick Walsh, May 22, 1919, **59**: 394 (draft); May 26, 1919, **59**: 513

Thomas Edward Lawrence to Gilbert Fairchild Close, Jan. 21, 1919, **54**: 195

The League to Enforce Peace to Oscar Solomon Straus, April 17, 1919, **57**: 445

Hunter Liggett to John Joseph Pershing, May 22, 1919, **59**: 401

David Lloyd George to Edward Mandell House, May 9, 1919, **58**: 585; May 13, 1919, **59**: 104

Robert Howard Lord to Joseph Clark Grew, April 8, 1919, **57**: 137

Lu Cheng-Hsiang to Sir Maurice Pascal Alers Hankey, May 28, 1919, **59**: 568

David Hunter Miller to Edward Mandell House, April 8, 1919, **57**: 117

David Hunter Miller to Douglas Wilson Johnson, April 6, 1919, **56**: 609

John Pierpont Morgan, Jr., and Dwight Whitney Morrow to Thomas William Lamont, March 19, 1919, **56**: 99

Keishiro Matsui to Viscount Yasuya Uchida, April 22, 1919, **57**: 581

Ira Nelson Morris to Edward Mandell House, Jan. 19, 1919, **54**: 153

Fridtjof Nansen to Herbert Clark Hoover, May 16, 1919, **59**: 193

Fridtjof Nansen to Vladimir Ilyich Lenin, April 17, 1919, **57**: 438

Vittorio Emanuele Orlando to Edward Mandell House, April 10, 1919, **57**: 564

Ignace Jan Paderewski to Edward Mandell House, Jan. 12, 1919, **54**: 32; Feb. 4, 1919, **54**: 480

Thomas Nelson Page to the American Commissioners, Jan. 18, 1919, **54**: 134; March 28, 1919, **56**: 392; April 24, 1919 (3), **58**: 91 (2), 93; April 25, 1919, **58**: 143; April 28, 1919, **58**: 210; April 29, 1919, **58**: 238; May 1, 1919 (2), **58**: 321, 322; May 2, 1919 (3), **58**: 357, 358 (2); May 3, 1919, **58**: 413; May 4, 1919, **58**: 426; May 5, 1919, **58**: 452; May 7, 1919, **58**: 529; June 13, 1919, **60**: 531; June 19, 1919, **61**: 28

Thomas Nelson Page to Edward Mandell House, April 17, 1919, **57**: 434

Thomas Nelson Page to Baron Sidney Sonnino, April 30, 1919, **58**: 271

Nikola Pasić to Georges Clemenceau, April 16, 1919, **57**: 418

William Phillips to the American Mission in Paris, July 11, 1919, **61**: 450

Raymond Poincaré to Georges Clemenceau, April 28, 1919, **58**: 211
Frank Lyon Polk to the American Commissioners, Jan. 15, 1919, **54**: 77; Jan. 17, 1919, **54**: 126; May 28, 1919, **59**: 573; July 11, 1919, **61**: 450
Frank Lyon Polk to Gordon Auchincloss, May 15, 1919, **59**: 172
Frank Lyon Polk to Robert Lansing, Jan. 12, 1919 (2), **54**: 26, 28; March 31, 1919, **56**: 483; May 8, 1919, **58**: 553; June 16, 1919, **60**: 604
Frank Lyon Polk to Breckinridge Long, July 18, 1919, **61**: 556
Frank Lyon Polk to Roland Sletor Morris, April 21, 1919, **57**: 570
Frank Lyon Polk to Henry White, July 18, 1919, **61**: 526

William Emmanuel Rappard to Hans Sulzer, Feb. 13, 1919, **55**: 151
Paul Samuel Reinsch to the Department of State, June 16, 1919 (2), **60**: 604, 605
Paul Samuel Reinsch to Frank Lyon Polk, Jan. 15, 1919, **54**: 77; Feb. 4, 1919, **54**: 474
Nicholas Roosevelt to Royall Tyler, March 23, 1919, **56**: 240

Marquis Kimmochi Saionji to Georges Clemenceau, April 25, 1919, **58**: 128
Charles Prestwich Scott to Edward Mandell House, March 16, 1919, **55**: 545
Charles Seymour to his family, Jan. 30, 1919, **54**: 382; Feb. 8, 1919, **55**: 34; May 14, 1919, **59**: 158; May 31, 1919, **59**: 647; June 3, 1919, **60**: 75
William Graves Sharp to Frank Lyon Polk, April 9, 1919, **57**: 175
Jan Christiaan Smuts to David Lloyd George, May 22, 1919, **59**: 413
Baron Sidney Sonnino to Stéphen-Jean-Marie Pichon, May 5, 1919, **58**: 432
Henry Wickham Steed to Edward Mandell House, April 1, 1919, **56**: 515
Pleasant Alexander Stovall to the American Commissioners, May 10, 1919, **59**: 35
Pleasant Alexander Stovall to the Department of State, March 23, 1919, **56**: 242
Lewis Strauss to Gilbert Fairchild Close, May 16, 1919, **59**: 191

William Howard Taft to Oscar Solomon Straus, March 31, 1919, **56**: 485; April 17, 1919, **57**: 445
William Howard Taft to Joseph Patrick Tumulty, May 5, 1919, **58**: 460
William Monroe Trotter to Gilbert Fairchild Close, June 15, 1919, **60**: 572; June 25, 1919, **61**: 186
Joseph Patrick Tumulty to Cary Travers Grayson, Jan. 16, 1919, **54**: 105; April 5, 1919, **57**: 37l; April 9, 1919, **57**: 177; April 30, 1919, **58**: 273

An Unknown Person to Felix Frankfurter, May 22, 1919, **59**: 411

Francis Patrick Walsh and Edward Fitzsimons Dunne to the American Commissioners, June 13, 1919, **60**: 544
Francis Patrick Walsh and Others to Robert Lansing, May 18, 1919, **59**: 251
Hugh Campbell Wallace to Frank Lyon Polk, April 24, 1919, **58**: 96
Henry White and Tasker Howard Bliss to the Department of State, July 22, 1919, **61**: 585
Brand Whitlock to Gilbert Fairchild Close, April 1, 1919, **56**: 521
Joseph Edward Willard to the American Commissioners, March 28, 1919, **56**: 392
Edith Bolling Galt Wilson to John Randolph Bolling, Jan. 27, 1919, **54**: 304
Edith Bolling Galt Wilson to her family, Feb. 4, 1919, **54**: 487

Memoranda, reports, aide-mémoire, and position papers

A memorandum by Robert Lansing on Wilson's first "Paris draft" of the Covenant of the League of Nations, Jan. 12, 1919, **54**: 3
An extract from the minutes of the Supreme Council of Supply and Relief, Jan. 12, 1919, **54**: 29
A comment by Tasker Howard Bliss on Wilson's first "Paris draft" of the Covenant of the League of Nations, Jan. 14, 1919, **54**: 85
A memorandum by Robert Howard Lord on the situation in Russia, Jan. 16, 1919, **54**: 91
A memorandum by Wilson on publicity at the peace conference, Jan. 17, 1919, **54**: 121
A memorandum by the French delegation on the organization for the discussion of economic questions, Jan. 17, 1919, **54**: 124
A memorandum by Bernard Mannes Baruch on the need to consult American labor leaders on international labor questions, Jan. 20, 1919, **54**: 172
A resolution by the American press delegation in Paris on the need for publicity, Jan. 21, 1919, **54**: 191
A draft by Robert Lansing of a resolution on the principles of the League of Nations, Jan. 30, 1919, **54**: 401
A memorandum by William Shepherd Benson on the freedom of neutral shipping on the high seas during war, Jan. 31, 1919, **54**: 404
A draft by Herbert Clark Hoover and Vance Criswell McCormick of a resolution on the relaxation of the German blockade, Feb. 4, 1919, **54**: 479
A memorandum by Henry White about a conversation with Eleuthérios Kyrios Vénisélos, Jan. 31, 1919, **54**: 402
A memorandum by David Hunter Miller about amendments to the Covenant of the League of Nations, Feb. 11, 1919, **55**: 68

A memorandum by Henry White about the financial needs of Bel-
    gium, Feb. 15, 1919, **55**: 200
A memorandum by Tasker Howard Bliss on the opposition of the
    United States to a military campaign in Russia, Feb. 17, 1919, **55**:
    214
A draft of the naval peace terms, March 4, 1919, **55**: 425
Memoranda by William Shepherd Benson on the naval peace terms,
    March 4, 1919, **55**: 432; March 14, 1919, **55**: 523; March 16, 1919,
    55: 539
A memorandum by the Japanese Government on racial equality,
    March 4, 1919, **55**: 436
A memorandum by Ray Stannard Baker on American public opinion
    on the League of Nations and the peace conference, March 6, 1919,
    55: 449
A memorandum by Sidney Edward Mezes on the Rhineland ques-
    tion, March 11, 1919, **55**: 475
A memorandum by Ferdinand Foch on the Rhineland question,
    March 14, 1919, **55**: 502
A memorandum by Tasker Howard Bliss on the military peace
    terms, March 14, 1919, **55**: 511
A declaration of principles by the United States Naval Advisory
    Staff on the disposition of German and Austrian war vessels,
    March 13, 1919, **55**: 515
A memorandum by Tasker Howard Bliss on the military terms of
    peace with Germany, March 17, 1919, **56**: 6
A memorandum by Georges Clemenceau on the Rhineland question
    and the proposed French security treaty, March 17, 1919, **56**: 10
A memorandum by William Shepherd Benson on the naval terms of
    peace with Germany, March 19, 1919, **56**: 67
A memorandum by David Hunter Miller and James Brown Scott on
    the need for Senate consent to ratification of the preliminary peace
    treaty, March 18, 1919, **56**: 67
A memorandum by Robert Lansing on the need for Senate consent to
    ratification of the preliminary peace treaty, March 19, 1919, **56**: 97
Comments by Elihu Root on the Covenant of the League of Nations,
    March 19, 1919, **56**: 99
A memorandum by Robert Lansing about the fall of the Károlyi gov-
    ernment in Hungary, March 22, 1919, **56**: 182
A memorandum by Robert Lansing on the Rhineland question,
    March 23, 1919, **56**: 201
A proposal by André Tardieu for the creation of a demilitarized zone
    in the Rhineland, March 23, 1919, **56**: 202
A memorandum by Arthur James Balfour opposing the appointment
    of a near eastern commission, March 23, 1919, **56**: 203
A draft by the Commission on Labour Legislation of principles for a
    labor charter, March 24, 1919, **56**: 237
A memorandum by Allen Welsh Dulles on the situation in Hungary,
    March 24, 1919, **56**: 239

A memorandum by Béla Kun on the policy of the Hungarian Soviet government toward the Allies, March 24, 1919, **56**: 242

A memorandum by David Lloyd George on the terms of peace with Germany (the Fontainebleau Memorandum), March 25, 1919, **56**: 259

A memorandum by Vittorio Emanuele Orlando on the situation in Hungary, March 25, 1919, **56**: 275

A memorandum by Ferdinand Foch on means of containing the spread of Bolshevism in Central Europe, March 27, 1919, **56**: 314

A memorandum by Nicholas Roosevelt on the Hungarian revolution, March 27, 1919, **56**: 331

A memorandum by Robert Lansing on the clash between Wilson and Clemenceau over the question of the Saar Basin, March 28, 1919, **56**: 351

A memorandum by Tasker Howard Bliss opposing a military intervention in Hungary, March 28, 1919, **56**: 379

A statement by Charles-Antoine Charpy on the violation by Rumania of the Hungarian armistice, March 28, 1919, **56**: 382

A memorandum by Tasker Howard Bliss on the Hungarian armistice and French plans for a crusade against Bolshevism, March 28, 1919, **56**: 383

A statement by Marcel Cachin on French public opinion about Wilson and the work of the peace conference, March 28, 1919, **56**: 386

A memorandum by William Christian Bullitt on the situation in Russia, March 28, 1919, **56**: 387

A proposal by Charles Homer Haskins and James Wycliffe Headlam-Morley for an agreement on the Saar Basin, March 29, 1919, **56**: 420

A memorandum by Ferdinand Foch on the importance of the Rhine frontier for the security of France, March 31, 1919, **56**: 445

Resolutions by the Council of Four in regard to the situation in Hungary, April 1, 1919, **56**: 465

A memorandum by the Russian Section of the A.C.N.P. about suggestions for a policy toward Russia, March 31, 1919, **56**: 466

A memorandum by Antal, Count Sigray, on the situation in Hungary, March 31, 1919, **56**: 474

Observations by Georges Clemenceau on the Fontainebleau Memorandum, March 31, 1919, **56**: 477

Proposed amendments by Elihu Root to the Covenant of the League of Nations, March 31, 1919, **56**: 483

Proposed amendments by William Howard Taft to the Covenant of the League of Nations, March 31, 1919, **56**: 485

A memorandum by Robert Lansing about the militaristic character of French foreign policy, April 1, 1919, **56**: 487

A memorandum by Dennis Edward Nolan on peace terms acceptable to Germany, March 31, 1919, **56**: 492

A memorandum by Sidney Edward Mezes on alternate plans for settlement of the Danzig question, April 1, 1919, **56**: 505

A memorandum by Archibald Cary Coolidge about the right of national minorities, April 1, 1919, **56**: 511

A memorandum by Charles Homer Haskins about a proposed agreement on the Saar Basin, April 1, 1919, **56**: 514

A memorandum by Henry Wickham Steed about an agreement on the Saar Basin, April 1, 1919, **56**: 516

A memorandum by David Lloyd George in reply to Clemenceau's observations on the Fontainebleau Memorandum, April 2, 1919, **56**: 545

A memorandum by Norman Hezekiah Davis and Vance Criswell McCormick on reparations and categories of damages, April 4, 1919, **56**: 598

A memorandum by Henry Mauris Robinson opposing the reopening of the work of the Commission on Labour Legislation, April 4, 1919, **56**: 603

A memorandum by Robert Lansing and James Brown Scott on reservations to the report of the Commission on Responsibilities, April 4, 1919, **56**: 611

Memoranda by Charles Henry Grasty about the need for Wilson to break the impasse at the peace conference, April 5, 1919 (2), **57**: 38, 40

A memorandum by Charles Homer Haskins and Others about an agreement on the Saar Basin, April 6, 1919, **57**: 54

A memorandum by Gilbert Fairchild Close about the opinion of Bernard Mannes Baruch on the proposed agreement on the Saar Basin, April 7, 1919, **57**: 90

A memorandum by Josephus Daniels about a conference with David Lloyd George on the naval building program of the United States, April 7, 1919, **57**: 91

A memorandum by David Hunter Miller about corrections in the articles of an agreement on the Saar Basin, April 8, 1919, **57**: 118

A memorandum by David Hunter Miller on additional articles for an agreement on the Saar Basin, April 8, 1919, **57**: 119

A memorandum by Henry White about a conversation with Ion O. C. Brătianu on the situation in Rumania, April 8, 1919, **57**: 136

A memorandum by André Tardieu on the American proposal for an agreement on the Saar Basin, April 9, 1919, **57**: 155

A memorandum by the British delegation about an agreement on the Saar Basin, April 9, 1919, **57**: 196

A memorandum by the Japanese delegation about the report by the Commission on Responsibilities, April 8, 1919, **57**: 132

A memorandum by Jan Christiaan Smuts about his mission to Austria-Hungary, April 9, 1919, **57**: 167

A memorandum by the United States Naval Advisory Staff on the future naval policy of the United States, April 9, 1919, **57**: 180

A memorandum by Lord Robert Cecil about a conference with Colonel House on the naval building program of the United States, April 10, 1919, **57**: 216

A British amendment on the Monroe Doctrine to the Covenant of the League of Nations, April 10, 1919, **57**: 218

A memorandum by Francis Joseph Kernan about a proposed armistice between the Polish and Ukrainian armies in Galicia, April 11, 1919, **57**: 275

A memorandum by André Tardieu suggesting amendments to Wilson's proposal for an agreement on the Rhineland question and a treaty of guarantee for France, April 12, 1919, **57**: 295

A memorandum by Vi Kyuin Wellington Koo on China's claim to former German rights in Shantung Province, April 8, 1919, **57**: 298

A memorandum by Arthur Hugh Frazier about a conversation with Ante Trumbić on the Adriatic situation, April 15, 1919, **57**: 369

A report by Arthur James Balfour on the meeting of the Council of Four of April 16, 1919, **57**: 398

An agreement on the Saar Basin, April 16, 1919, **57**: 407

Recommendations by Jan Christiaan Smuts for a policy of the Allied and Associated governments toward Austria and Hungary, April 17, 1919, **57**: 441

A memorandum by William Linn Westermann on near eastern affairs, April 17, 1919, **57**: 443

A memorandum by Michael Idvorsky Pupin opposing Italian claims in the Adriatic, April 19, 1919, **57**: 499

A statement by Herbert Clark Hoover on the Nansen plan and the Bolshevik regime in Russia, April 19, 1919, **57**: 506

A memorandum by Georges Clemenceau about an agreement on the Rhineland question and a treaty of guarantee for France, April 20, 1919, **57**: 525

A memorandum by Herbert Clark Hoover about the political situation in Germany, April 21, 1919, **57**: 566

A memorandum by Frederick Hermann Kisch and James Wycliffe Headlam-Morley on the Danzig question and the Polish frontiers, April 21, 1919, **57**: 572

An outline by the Big Five on the prosecution of war criminals and the trial of the Kaiser, April 9, 1919, **57**: 631

A memorandum by John Maynard Keynes on the rehabilitiation of European credit and the financing of relief and reconstruction, April 23, 1919, **58**: 12

A memorandum by the American representatives on the Reparation Commission on points for decision by the Council of Four, April 23, 1919, **58**: 24

A statement by Herbert Clark Hoover on the alleged purposes of the Nansen plan, April 23, 1919, **58**: 41

A memorandum about a request by Count Macchi di Cellere for an interview with Wilson, April 23, 1919, **58**: 44

A memorandum by Lu Cheng-hsiang on the Shantung question, April 24, 1919, **58**: 68

A memorandum by Robert Lansing about the furor over Wilson's statement on the Adriatic question, April 24, 1919, **58**: 102

A memorandum by Norman Hezekiah Davis on the proposed establishment of credits for Rumania, April 25, 1919, **58**: 136

A memorandum by the French Foreign Ministry about arrangements for the establishment of credits for Rumania, April 25, 1919, **58**: 136

A memorandum by Jean-Etienne-Paul Gout, Edward Thomas Williams, and James William Ronald Macleay on the Shantung question, April 24, 1919, **58**: 72

A memorandum by Robert Joseph Kerner on the political situation in Central Europe, April 26, 1919, **58**: 156

A memorandum by Edward Thomas Williams about a conversation between Robert Lansing and Viscount Sutemi Chinda on Japan's claims in Shantung, April 26, 1919, **58**: 165

Draft clauses on International Labour legislation, April 27, 1919, **58**: 173

A memorandum by Arthur James Balfour about a conversation with the Japanese plenipotentiaries on the Shantung question, April 27, 1919, **58**: 175

A memorandum by Robert Lansing on Japan's claims in Shantung and her membership in the League of Nations, April 28, 1919, **58**: 185

A draft by William Linn Westermann of general clauses governing near eastern mandates, April 28, 1919, **58**: 206

A memorandum by Baron Nobuaki Makino and Viscount Sutemi Chinda about Japan's claims in Shantung, April 29, 1919, **58**: 228

A memorandum by Ray Stannard Baker on the Shantung question, April 29, 1919, **58**: 230

A memorandum by Arthur Latham Conger about an interview with Count Brockdorff-Rantzau, May 1, 1919, **58**: 307

A memorandum by Arthur Latham Conger about interviews with members of the German government, May 1, 1919, **58**: 308

A memorandum by Henry Churchill King and Charles Richard Crane on the division of the Ottoman Empire, May 1, 1919, **58**: 322

A memorandum by David Hunter Miller on a report by the Committee on New States about the rights of minorities, May 3, 1919, **58**: 383

A memorandum by Tasker Howard Bliss on Allied assistance to Rumania, May 3, 1919, **58**: 405

A memorandum by Sir Robert Borden on the week's activities of the peace conference, May 3, 1919, **58**: 416

A memorandum by David Hunter Miller on Wilson's statement about the French security treaty, May 6, 1919, **58**: 490

A proposed press release by Bernard Mannes Baruch and Others on the possibility of oral negotiations with the German delegation, May 7, 1919, **58**: 526

Memoranda of agreement on the distribution of enemy ships, May 8, 1919 (3), **58**: 557, 559 (2)

A suggested formula by Douglas Wilson Johnson for the settlement of the Adriatic question, May 9, 1919, **58**: 589

Memoranda by Ellis Loring Dresel about the possibility of informal talks with the German government, May 14, 1919, **59**: 156; May 17, 1919, **59**: 237

A memorandum by Gordon Auchincloss on the issue of passports to the American Commission for Irish Independence, May 15, 1919, **59**: 172

A memorandum by Thomas William Lamont and Norman Hezekiah Davis about a talk with Wilson on the financial and economic reconstruction of Europe, May 15, 1919, **59**: 176

Memoranda by Henry Churchill King inquiring about the scope of the proposed commission to the Near East, May 15, 1919, **59**: 184; May 22, 1919, **59**: 372

A draft convention by the military representatives of the Supreme War Council for the occupation of the Left Bank of the Rhine, May 11, 1919, **59**: 228

A memorandum by Philip Marshall Brown on the situation in Hungary, May 17, 1919, **59**: 239

A memorandum by Thomas William Lamont about a talk with Wilson on the financial and economic reconstruction of Europe, May 19, 1919, **59**: 283

A memorandum by Bernard Mannes Baruch and Others on possible talks with the German economic experts, May 20, 1919, **59**: 314

A draft by Bernard Mannes Baruch of a press release about talks with the German economic experts, May 20, 1919, **59**: 315

A memorandum by James Viscount Bryce on questions to be settled by the peace conference, May 22, 1919, **59**: 400

A memorandum by William Linn Westermann on Greek demands in Asia Minor, May 29, 1919, **59**: 595

A memorandum by Norman Hezekiah Davis about the German observations on the reparation clauses of the peace treaty, June 1, 1919, **60**: 4

A memorandum by Edward Mandell House on the German counterproposals, June 3, 1919, **60**: 82

A memorandum by Stanley Kuhl Hornbeck on the Shantung decision, June 3, 1919, **60**: 102

A memorandum by Stanley Dunbar Embick about the German observations on the treaty clauses relating to Belgium and Denmark, June 3, 1919, **60**: 105

A memorandum by Charles Homer Haskins about the German counterproposals on territorial questions, June 3, 1919, **60**: 106

A proposal by Douglas Wilson Johnson on the Adriatic question, June 4, 1919, **60**: 137

A memorandum by Charles Seymour about the German counterproposals on German Austria and Upper Silesia, June 4, 1919, **60**: 139

A memorandum by Royall Tyler on the attitude of the German delegation toward signing the peace treaty, June 5, 1919, **60**: 179

A memorandum by Robert Howard Lord about the German counterproposals on Poland and Lithuania, June 5, 1919, **60**: 182

A memorandum by Robert Howard Lord on the question of a plcbiscite in Upper Silesia, June 5, 1919, **60**: 189

A memorandum by Robert Howard Lord on the national sentiment of Poles in Upper Silesia, June 5, 1919, **60**: 190

A memorandum by Herbert Clark Hoover on the revision of the peace treaty, June 5, 1919, **60**: 194

Memoranda by Manley Ottmer Hudson on the method of appeal to the League of Nations by minorities in Poland, June 6, 1919, **60**: 205; June 16, 1919, **60**: 607

A memorandum by Tasker Howard Bliss on the size of the Allied armies of occupation in the Rhineland, June 6, 1919, **60**: 238

A memorandum by Tasker Howard Bliss on Joint Note No. 43 of the Supreme War Council, June 7, 1919, **60**: 259

A memorandum by Norman Hezekiah Davis and Others on the proposed reply to the German counterproposal on reparations, June 11, 1919, **60**: 401

A memorandum by Woodrow Wilson on the possible occupation of Upper Silesia by American troops, June 17, 1919, **60**: 622

A memorandum by Archibald Cary Coolidge on the terms of peace with Austria, June 17, 1919, **60**: 642

A memorandum by Manley Ottmer Hudson on changes in the treaty with Poland, June 19, 1919, **61**: 26

Questions and Wilson's answers on the policy of the United States in the Near East, June 24, 1919, **61**: 128

A memorandum by Woodrow Wilson about future negotiations with the Italian delegation on the Adriatic question, June 25, 1919, **61**: 170

A memorandum by Douglas Wilson Johnson suggesting a policy in regard to the Adriatic question, June 26, 1919, **61**: 227

A memorandum by Lord Milner on the question of mandates, June 27, 1919, **61**: 260

Drafts by Lord Milner of model clauses for Class B mandates, June 27, 1919, **61**: 265

A memorandum by George Louis Beer on Lord Milner's drafts of model clauses for Class B and Class C mandates, June 27, 1919, **61**: 270

A memorandum by Herbert Clark Hoover on Allied plans for the establishment of a permanent international economic organization, June 27, 1919, **61**: 285

A memorandum by Woodrow Wilson on additional suggestions about future negotiations with the Italian delegation, June 28, 1919, **61**: 307

A memorandum by Robert Lansing on the signing of the peace treaty, June 28, 1919, **61**: 321

A draft by Robert Lansing of a statement by the Japanese govern-

ment about the restitution of Shantung to China, June 28, 1919, **61**: 325

A memorandum by Herbert Clark Hoover on the economic situation in Europe, July 5, 1919, **61**: 389

A report by Henry Churchill King and Charles Richard Crane on mandates in the former Ottoman Empire, July 10, 1919, **61**: 442

A memorandum by Breckinridge Long of a conversation with Katsuji Debuchi on the Shantung question, July 19, 1919, **61**: 557

Reparations and categories of damages

A memorandum on reparations by Baron Sumner of Ibstone, March 18, 1919, **56**: 69

A memorandum on reparations by Norman Hezekiah Davis, March 25, 1919, **56**: 270

A memorandum on reparations by Jan Christiaan Smuts, March 31, 1919, **56**: 480

A memorandum by John Foster Dulles about a conference with Wilson on reparations, April 1, 1919, **56**: 498

A memorandum of Anglo-American progress on reparations, April 1, 1919, **56**: 502

First draft of an Anglo-American accord on reparations, April 1, 1919, **56**: 504

Second draft of an Anglo-American accord on reparations, April 2, 1919, **56**: 536

Second draft of categories of damages, April 4, 1919, **56**: 597

Appendixes

From a memoir by Irwin Hood Hoover, **63**: 632

Wilson's Neurologic Illness at Paris (Link, Park, Weinstein, Toole), **58**: 607

Wilson's Neurologic Illness during the Summer of 1919 (Park), **62**: 628

Wilson's Stroke of October 2, 1919 (Park), **63**: 639

Editorial Note

Wilson's Speeches on His Western Tour, Sept. 4, 1919, **63**: 5

Miscellaneous

A poem by William Church Osborn, Jan. 14, 1921, **67**: 59

A poem by Eleanor Axson Sayre, Jan. 31, 1921, **67**: 108

A tribute to Wilson by women of New York, Feb. 14, 1921, **67**: 135

A description of the Woodrow Wilson Award by Franklin Delano Roosevelt, June, 29, 1921, **67**: 334

Two announcements of the establishment of the law firm of Wilson & Colby, July 1, 1921, **67**: 338; Aug. 18, 1921, **67**: 372

An inscription on a frieze of a portico in Nice, France, Dec. 11, 1921, **67**: 482

ILLUSTRATIONS

Illustrations appear in the center section of each volume

WOODROW WILSON

Wilson on bridge of U.S.S. *George Washington* with Capt. McCauley, **53**

Talking with reporters on the U.S.S. *George Washington* (John F. Nevin, Robert J. Bender, Lionel Probert), **53**

With Raymond Poincaré, **53**

Reviewing and meeting troops with General Pershing on Christmas Day, 1918, **53**

Arriving at Dover, **53**

With George V, **53**

In serious conversation with George V, **53**

In the courtyard of Buckingham Palace with a group of American soldiers just released from German prison camps, **53**

With Vittorio Emanuele III, **53**

The American Peace Commissioners (Edward M. House, Robert Lansing, Wilson, Henry White, Tasker H. Bliss), **53**

The opening of the Paris Peace Conference, **54**

The American Commission to Negotiate Peace, **54**

Wilson leaving the American Church in Paris, **54**

Wilson presents the Covenant of the League of Nations to the Third Plenary Session of the Peace Conference, February 14, 1919, **55**

On the bridge as the U.S.S. *George Washington* arrives in Boston Harbor, **55**

In Mechanic's Hall, Boston, February 24, 1919, **55**

Miss Benham, Dr. Grayson, Mrs. Wilson, and the President examining a German gun emplacement at Coincy, March 23, 1919, **56**

On his way to a meeting with the American Commissioners at the Hotel Crillon, **58**

At Longchamps Race Course with Mrs. Wilson, Admiral Grayson, and Bernard M. Baruch, **58**

Entering Suresnes Cemetery, May 30, 1919, **59**

Speaking at Suresnes Cemetery, **59**

Wilson watches a French woman lay flowers on the graves of American soldiers, **59**

Woodrow Wilson, **60**

Wilson and Albert upon the arrival of the presidential party at Adinkerke, June 18, 1919, **61**

At the ruins of Ypres, **61**

"This immortal spot" on the Yser River near Nieuport, **61**

With Brand Whitlock on the battlefield near Nieuport, **61**

With Elisabeth in the trenches at Nieuport, **61**

A royal picnic in the Forest of Houthulst, **61**

At Les Usines de la Providence near Charleroi, **61**
At the harbor of Zeebrugge, **61**
With Cardinal Mercier at Malines, **61**
Amid the ruins of the library of the University of Louvain, **61**
At the Royal Palace in Brussels, **61**
At the Versailles Palace before the signing of the treaty, **61**
The Big Four, **61**
In St. Paul, Minnesota, **63**
En route to the Theater in Bismarck, North Dakota, **63**
At the Tacoma Stadium, **63**
With Reporters and Others, **63**
On Parade in San Francisco, **63**
In the Greek Theater at Berkeley, **63**
At a Reception in San Diego, **63**
In Union Station on His Return to Washington, **63**
Out driving in April 1920, **65**
Touched-up photographs taken during the last days in the White
    House, **67** (2)
Wilson and his Cabinet, February 15, 1921, **67**
On his way to the Capitol, March 4, 1921, with Harding, Cannon,
    and Knox, **67**
In the Armistice Day parade, 1921, **67**
Leaving his home on the arm of Isaac Scott, **67**
Out for a drive in his Pierce-Arrow, **67**
Greeting women from the Pan-American Conference at his home on
    April 28, 1922, **68**
Greeting well-wishers at his home on Armistice Day, 1922, **68**
Out for a drive with Mrs. Wilson, **68**
On a drive on November 12, 1923, **68**
On his sixty-seventh birthday, **68**

COLLATERAL

U.S.S. George Washington, 53
Murat Palace, **53**
Paris Greets Wilson, **53**
The League of Nations Commission, **54**
Georges Clemenceau, **54, 60**
David Lloyd George, **54**
Eleuthérios Vénisélos, **54**
Vittorio Emanuele Orlando, **54**
Lord Robert Cecil, **54**
Arthur James Balfour, **54**
Emir Faisal with Thomas Edward Lawrence and retinue, **54**
Edith Benham and stenographers: Chief Yeoman Nicholas P.
    Schindler and Yeoman 1st Class Francis A. Kennedy, **54**
Ray Stannard Baker aboard *U.S.S. George Washington*, **55**
David Hunter Miller and Major James Brown Scott, **55**

Irwin Hood (Ike) Hoover, **55**
William Christian Bullitt, **55**
Charles C. Wagner, Gilbert Fairchild Close, and Charles Lee Swem,
   55
Sir Maurice Hankey, **56**
Lt. Paul Mantoux, **56**
James Wycliffe Headlam-Morley, **56**
Charles Homer Haskins, **56**
Bernard Baruch, Norman H. Davis, Vance C. McCormick, Herbert
   C. Hoover, **56**
Jan Christiaan Smuts, **56**
Béla Kun, **56**
Louis-Lucien Klotz, **56**
The Inquiry Division Chiefs (Charles H. Haskins, Isaiah Bowman,
   Sidney E. Mezes, James Brown Scott, David Hunter Miller,
   Charles Seymour, Robert H. Lord, William L. Westermann, Mark
   Jefferson, Col. House, George Louis Beer, Douglas W. Johnson,
   Clive Day, William E. Lunt, James T. Shotwell, A. A. Young), **56**
André Tardieu, **57**
Baron Sidney Sonnino, **57**
Baron Nobuaki Makino, **57**
Ignace Jan Paderewski, **57**
Ion I. C. Brătianu, **57**
Eduard Beneš, **57**
Nikola Pašić, **57**
Ante Trumbić, **57**
Vi Kyuin Wellington Koo, **57**
Viscount Sutemi Chinda, **57**
The German delegation before leaving for Versailles (Robert Lei-
   nert, Carl Melchior, Johann Giesberts, Ulrich Karl Christian
   Count von Brockdorff-Rantzau, Otto Landsberg, Walther Adrian
   Schücking), **57**
The German delegation listening to Clemenceau (Schücking,
   Giesberts, Brockdorff-Rantzau, Landsberg, Leinert, and Mel-
   choir), **58**
Robert Lansing and Henry White leaving Trianon Palace after the
   presentation of peace terms to the German delegation, **58**
The Chinese delegation to the Peace Conference (Lu Cheng-Hsiang,
   Wang Cheng-t'ing and Alfred (Saoke) Sze V. K. Wellington Koo),
   58
The Japanese delegation to the Peace Conference (Baron Nobu-
   aki Makino, Marquis Kimmochi Saionji, and Viscount Sutemi
   Chinda), **58**
Cary Travers Grayson, **59, 64, 65**
Ray Stannard Baker and Arthur Sweetser, **59**
Vance Criswell McCormick, **59**
David Hunter Miller, **59**
Edith Benham, **59**

Charles Seymour, **59**
Field Marshal Ferdinand Foch, **60**
Field Marshal Sir Douglas Haig, **60**
Harvest, **60**
German Prisoners of War, **60**
The Council of Ten at the Quai d'Orsay, **60**
The Signing in the Hall of Mirrors, **60**
Cardinal Mercier and Dr. Grayson at Malines, **61**
Elihu Root, **62**
William Howard Taft, **62**
Gilbert Monell Hitchcock, **62**
Henry Cabot Lodge, **62**
Philander Chase Knox, **62**
Key Pittman, **62**
Porter James McCumber, **62**
Selden Palmer Spencer, **62**
Francis Xavier Dercum, **64**
George Edmund De Schweinitz, **64**
Hugh Hampton Young, **64**
Edward Rhodes Stitt, **64**
Harry Atwood Fowler, **64**
Sterling Ruffin, **64**
John Chalmers Da Costa, **64**
Robert Lansing, **64**
Bainbridge Colby, **65**
Joshua Willis Alexander, **65**
John Barton Payne, **65**
Edwin Thomas Meredith, **65**
Albert Baird Cummins, **65**
William Edgar Borah and Hiram Warren Johnson, **65**
The Wilson statue at the University of Texas at Austin, **66**
Bainbridge Colby and Norman Hezekiah Davis, **66**
Homer Stillé Cummings, **66**
James Middleton Cox and Franklin Delano Roosevelt, **66**
Cox on the campaign trail, **66** (2)
Franklin Delano Roosevelt, **66**
Harding on the campaign trail, **66**
The Hardings and the Coolidges, **66**
The house on S Street, **67**
The library in the S Street house, **67**
"The Straphanger" (cartoon), **68**
Carter Glass, Joseph Taylor Robinson, and Cordell Hull, **68**
Hamilton Holt, **68**
Sterling Ruffin, Cary T. Grayson, and Harry Atwood Fowler, **68**
On the way to the interment in the Washington Cathedral, **68**

A.C.N.P.: *see* American Commission to Negotiate Peace

A.E.F.: *see* American Expeditionary Force

A. Mitchell Palmer: Politician (Coben), **54**: 429n1; **60**: 117n2,7; **64**: 354n1; **68**: 299n1

Abbott, Frank Frost, **67**: 182

Abbott, Lyman, **66**: 246n2, 542n1

Abdul Hamid II, **58**: 555n1

Abdul Medjid Effendi, **60**: 212,n9, 218, 261

Abercrombie, John William, **65**: 187n5

Aberdeen and Temair, Marchioness of (Lady Aberdeen): *see* Gordon, Ishbel Maria Marjoribanks

Aborigines Protection Society, **61**: 276,n4, 277, 314

Abraham Lincoln (Charnwood), **54**: 488,n2

Abraham Lincoln (play, Drinkwater), **65**: 404,n5; **66**: 112; **67**: 111

Abrahams, Kate Trenholm, **67**: 213; **68**: 187

Abrams *et al. v.* United States, **68**: 131n8

Abyssinia: *see* Ethiopia

Académie Française, **53**: 420n1, 450,n1, 500

Academy of Moral and Political Science (Paris): WW's address to, **59**: 3, 4-6

Academy of Music (Philadelphia): proposed lecture series at, **66**: 31-32, 40, 382; lectures at, **66**: 24n2, 56, 59, 62; WW on speaking at, **66**: 83-84

Academy of Political Science in the City of New York, **55**: 157n1

Acheson, Archibald Charles Montagu Brabazon, Viscount Acheson, **53**: 547,n3, 570

Acheson, Mildred Carter, Lady Acheson, **53**: 547,n3

Ackerman, Carl William, **53**: 628-32

Acosta, Julio, **64**: 186; **65**: 46, 464, 465-66, 506, 510, 571,n2

Adachi, Mineichiro, **60**: 205,n3, 206

Adalia (now Antalya), Turkey, **54**: 350; **58**: 435, 512; **59**: 41, 42, 43, 55, 101, 147, 226, 250, 268, 269, 270, 373, 375; **61**: 221

Adam, George Jefferys, **53**: 420,n2, 422n1, 422-30

Adamic, Louis, **63**: 238n1, 273n2

Adams, Alva, **63**: 500,n1

Adams, Edward LeGrand, **56**: 96,n1

Adams, Edwin Plimpton, **66**: 182

Adams, Henry, **68**: 20n1

Adams, John Quincy, **66**: 370

Adams, Marion Hooper (Mrs. Henry), **68**: 20n1

Adams-Onís Treaty (1819), **62**: 35-36, 37

Adana (Seyhan) Turkey, **58**: 326, 477n13

Addams, Jane, **53**: 126; **66**: 542n1; **67**: 37n1, 258; on WW's Adriatic statement, **58**: 140-41, 142; **59**: 117, 189, 450n2; WW acknowledges support of, **59**: 15; WW recommends for Nobel Peace Prize, **68**: 266-67,n1

Addis Ababa, Ethiopia, **61**: 406,n1

Address of the President of the United States to the Senate . . . July 10, 1919, **61**: 435n

Addresses of President Taft on Arbitration, **55**: 448,n1

Addresses of President Wilson, **63**: 19n, 42n, 117n, 131n, 138n, 148n, 162n2, 180n, 197n, 221n, 234n, 252n, 388n, 407n, 418n, 427n, 441n, 448n, 463n, 484n, 513n

Addresses of President Wilson, Boston, Mass., February 24, 1919, New York, N.Y., March 4, 1919, **55**: 245n, 421n

Addresses of President Wilson on First Trip to Europe, December 3, 1918 to February 24, 1919, **53**: 463n, 507n, 524n, 534n, 549n, 522n, 603n, 609n, 620n, 624n; **54**: 156n, 273n, 310n

Adee, Alvey Augustus, **54**: 428; **63**: 58,n1; **65**: 247; praised for fifty years of government service, **66**: 102, 104

Adelman, H., **66**: 421,n1

Adelphi College, **68**: 452n2

Adelsberg, Slovenia, **53**: 642; and Adriatic settlement, **66**: 365

Aden, **59**: 88, 102

Adenauer, Konrad, **58**: 226,n4; **59**: 401n4, 433,n2

Adinkerke, Belgium, **61**: 3

Adler, Victor, **53**: 8; **58**: 157n2

"Admiral Grayson—Medical Culturalist" (Winans), **64**: 496n1

Admiral Sims and the Modern American Navy (Morison), **58**: 500n1

Admiral William Shepherd Benson: First Chief of Naval Operations (Klachko), **65**: 270n2

Ador, Gustave, **54**: 233-34, 302; on Geneva as seat for League of Nations, **57**: 329, 430

Adria Company, Fiume, **56**: 569

Adrianople, Turkey, **59**: 400; **61**: 159; **63**: 236

Adriatic Question: Papers Relating to the Italian-Jugoslav Boundary (State Dept.), **65**: 43n2

Adriatic question: *see* Paris Peace Conference—Italy, Adriatic question
Adriatic Sea: Council of Four on tonnage in, **59**: 50-54
Advancing Hour (Hapgood): WW sent copy of, **66**: 28,n1, 30
Adventures in Understanding (R. S. Baker), **68**: 283,n3
Aegean Sea, **62**: 265
aerial navigation, **55**: 256
aerial warfare: and League of Nations Covenant, **59**: 379-80; Pershing on, **60**: 430; WW on not bombing cities, **60**: 483, 491
Aeronautical Commission of Control: *see* Inter-Allied Aeronautical Commission of Control
aeronautics: transatlantic flight, **57**: 447,n1; **59**: 576,n1; **60**: 44,n1,4, 430-31; Council of Four on German counterproposals on, **60**: 550
Afghanistan, **55**: 542; **56**: 321; **59**: 97-98, 326, 337; and Penjdeh incident, **60**: 210n6
Africa, **53**: 690; **54**: 249, 250, 252-54, 318-22; **55**: 7, 171; W.E.B. Du Bois on future of, **53**: 236-38; German colonies in, **53**: 351, 562; Lord Milner on German colonies and mandates, **61**: 261, 262-64, 265; *see also* under names of individual political units such as South Africa, Union of; South-West Africa
African Methodist Episcopal Zion Church, Washington, D.C., **63**: 268n1
African Origins of the Mandates Idea (Louis), **54**: 311n2
Afrique française, **57**: 468n2
After Election (*Springfield*, Mass., *Republican*), **66**: 258,n2
Aftermath of War: Bainbridge Colby and Wilsonian Diplomacy, 1920-1921 (Smith), **64**: 464n1; **66**: 5n2, 19n1, 430n1
Aga Khan III (Aga Sultan Sir Mohammed Shah), **59**: 87,n4, 97, 98, 207n1
Agamemnon, U.S.S., **58**: 141
Agenzia Stefani, **58**: 239,n3
Agoston, Peter, **56**: 275,n1, 276
Agram: *see* Zagreb
Agricultural Discontent in the Middle West, 1900-1939 (Saloutos and Hicks), **68**: 146n2
Agricultural Education Extension bill, **68**: 270
agriculture: use of cereals for beverages, **54**: 193-94; Tumulty on employment ideas in, **54**: 391; illiteracy problem and, **55**: 288; and WW's Annual Message to Congress, **64**: 110; WW on farm loan program, **65**: 63; and WW's Message to Congress, **65**: 132; appeal for federal assistance, **66**: 36-38,n2,3; farmers' organization requests hearing with WW, **66**: 224; prices and politics, **66**: 242-43,n5; and farmers' credit

request, **66**: 243-45; farm prices discussed at Cabinet, **66**: 445; and WW's State of the Union Message, **66**: 489; cattle raisers wish to see WW, **66**: 521; surplus corn offered to China, **67**: 80, 139-40; and WW's veto of Emergency Tariff bill, **66**: 121n2, 191; and The Document, **66**: 560-61, 566-67, 568-69, 582-83, 583-84, 601; **68**: 8, 18, 237, 241, 242-43, 252-54, 270, 272, 540; WW on Muscle Shoals project, **68**: 448-49; *see also* farmers and farming; cotton industry
Agriculture, Committee on (House of Reps.), **53**: 603; **62**: 491n1
Agriculture, Department of, **53**: 603, 604; **62**: 213, 214, 233n1; Houston resigns as Secretary, **64**: 349; E. T. Meredith appointed Secretary of, **64**: 330,n1, 330-31
Aguilar Barquero, Francisco, **63**: 616,n1; **64**: 95, 153, 186; **65**: 465
Aharonian, Avetis, **54**: 517,n1; **56**: 443,n2; **57**: 303,n1; **59**: 103-104; **65**: 287,n2, 302,n6; **66**: 65, 86n1
Ahmed Fuad Pasha: *see* Fuad I
Aidin (now Aydin), Turkey, **59**: 99,n4, 101, 102, 140,n6, 268, 270,n5, 375, 595-96, 613; **61**: 212, 216; **62**: 239-40
aircraft: Supreme War Council meeting on, **56**: 38-43; torpedo and bombing tests and projects, **63**: 441-42,n1,2
aircraft production investigation, **53**: 70, 308,n1, 309n2
Aivali, Turkey: *see* Ayvalik, Turkey
Aix-la-Chapelle, **57**: 395
Akademische Verlagsgesellschaft, **62**: 564-65,n1
Akron, Ohio: WW's message to Democrats in, **66**: 254, 255
Alabama: and Caldwell case, **55**: 327-28, 328; **62**: 465,n1, 530, 536; and woman suffrage, **61**: 464, 479, 537; coal strike in, **66**: 263-65
Alabama, University of, **68**: 171n1
Alabama Power Company, **68**: 448n1, 457
Åland Islands, **57**: 139; **66**: 138n1; **68**: 521
Åland Islands Commission, **67**: 37; suggestions for and appointment to, **65**: 525-26, 531,n1; **66**: 212,n1,2, 229, 230-31, 253, 263, 265, 304; Elkus on decision of, **67**: 266
Alaska: Daniels and Payne visit, **66**: 4,n1
Alaskan Railroad, **63**: 608
Alaya, Asia Minor, **58**: 435
Albania, **53**: 56; **54**: 490,n2, 527; **57**: 112, 427,n7; **58**: 476, 477,n14, 590; **59**: 186, 492, 556, 558, 559, 565; **65**: 38, 315-16; **66**: 45,n6; **67**: 517; Serbian troops in, **60**: 530, 564-65; **61**: 344, 405, 552, 554, 575; and Adriatic question: **62**: 457, 522, 620; **63**: 206, 208, 209, 270, 364; **64**: 171, 175, 266, 299, 300, 302, 315,

319, 331, 334, 369, 377, 400, 437-38, 439, 461-62, 480, 482; memorandum on form of mandate for, **64**: 176-78; WW on, **66**: 307-308; and Corfu incident, **68**: 419n1

Albanian Political Party of America, **58**: 477n14

Albany, N.Y.: Colby wishes to speak in, **67**: 555

Albany, U.S.S., **58**: 495n6; **65**: 284n1

Albany Evening Journal, **67**: 261,n2

Albert, King of the Belgians, **53**: 384, 552-53, 693, 712; **54**: 495, 550; **55**: 86, 220; **56**: 258, 525, 561, 565, 584; **57**: 23; **58**: 593; **60**: 613; **61**: 3n1, 5, 6, 7, 11, 12, 14, 15-16, 25,n2; **62**: 516; **63**: 21, 119, 166, 259, 515, 526, 542; **64**: 455, 490; **65**: 234; on restoration of Belgium, **55**: 63-64; meets with WW, **56**: 554; R. S. Baker on, **56**: 557; **61**: 29-30; House on, **56**: 585-86; presents Belgium's claims, **56**: 589-97; WW on, **61**: 16; WW's toast to, **61**: 16,n1; WW's thank-you to, **61**: 33, 35-36; thanks WW, **61**: 61, 355; wishes to visit U.S., **61**: 609; WW's invitation to visit U.S. and acceptance of invitation, **62**: 6, 29; wishes to bestow honors on WW and other officials, **63**: 307-308; WW cannot accept proposed decoration by, **63**: 392; WW's illness causes change in plans, **63**: 528, 532, 543; get-well wishes to WW, **63**: 535-36; received by WW, **63**: 602-606; two thank-you notes to WW and WW's response, **64**: 30, 51; Grayson on public doubt that WW met with, **64**: 136; birthday wishes to WW, **64**: 230; and visit to WW's sick room, **64**:511n1; photograph of, *see* illustration section, **61**

Albert J. Beveridge: American Nationalist (Braeman), **68**: 44n2

Alberta, University of, **66**: 367n1

Albertini, Luigi, **53**: 619n1

Albona (now Labin, Yugoslavia), **60**: 138; **62**: 456, 457, 603; **63**: 205, 298; **64**: 169, 175, 370

Albrecht-Carrié, René, **54**: 135n3; **56**: 607n1; **57**: 488n10, 517n4; **58**: 55n3, 237n3, 413n2; **59**: 61n6, 125n1; **61**: 584n2; **64**: 169n3

Alby, Henri-Marie-Camille-Edouard, **55**: 179,n2; **56**: 252, 253, 323, 383; **57**: 247; **59**: 213n2, 324, 354, 531,n5; **60**: 265,n11, 617,n2; on Polish-Ukrainian conflict, **59**: 323,n4

Alcock, John William, **57**: 447n1

alcohol: *see* prohibition; taxation

alcoholism: and American Expeditionary Force, **61**: 531, 532-33

Alderman, Edwin Anderson, **66**: 234, 258; **68**: 185-86; and University of Virginia's centennial, **66**: 262-63, 265, 275; on plaque on WW's room at University of Virginia, **67**: 498, 501; WW suggests Axson as faculty member,

66: 549; and WW Foundation, **68**: 249n2

Aldrich, Amey, **67**: 135,n1

Aldrovandi Marescotti, Luigi, Count of Viano, **57**: 435-36,n3, 488n10, 551, 556; **58**: 53-54,n1, 58, 65, 82; **59**: 213, 257, 435; **60**: 213, 286,n1, 315

Alekseev, Mikhail Vasil'evich, **53**: 256, 290,n2

Aleksinskii, Grigorii Alekseevich, **62**: 445-46,n3; **65**: 191,n2

Alençar, Augusto Cochrane de, **65**: 191,n2; **66**: 179,n3

Aleppo, **54**: 506; **56**: 110, 111, 112, 113

Alessio, Albania, **57**: 517

Alexander, Crown Prince of Serbia, **53**: 346,n2; **65**: 94,n1

Alexander, King of Greece, **67**: 10

Alexander, Archibald Stevens (1880-1912), **67**: 350,n3

Alexander, Archibald Stevens (1906-1979), **67**: 350,n3, 351

Alexander, Charles Beatty, **68**: 17-18,n1

Alexander, Charles C., **68**: 298n2

Alexander, Henry Eckert, **66**: 352n1

Alexander, James Strange, **62**: 34

Alexander, Joshua Willis, **53**: 188; **55**: 532,n1, 535; **64**: 193; **65**: 24; **66**: 82n1, 87, 175; appointed Secretary of Commerce, **64**: 142, 317; and railroad situation, **64**: 184; House on appointment of, **64**: 185; and Democratic platform, 1920, **65**: 29; Houston on, **65**: 41; on trading with Russia, **65**: 247, 271; and Jones bill and Merchant Marine Act, **65**: 351, 467; wishes to be appointed to Shipping Board, **66**: 7, 195; on Jones bill, **66**: 60; on European reconstruction and financing of raw materials, **66**: 111; Cabinet farewell, **67**: 199; praises WW and WW thanks, **67**: 201-202, 234; and J. A. Reed, **67**: 543,n1, 579n4, 586; photographs of, *illustration sections*, **65**, **67**

Alexander, Mrs. K., **62**: 434

Alexander, Magnus Washington, **62**: 582, 583, 623,n1; **68**: 548

Alexander, Robert, **53**: 503,n4

Alexander, Roe Ann Richardson (Mrs. Joshua Willis), **67**: 234,n1

Alexander, Will Winton, **62**: 106-107,n2

Alexandra, Queen Mother of England, **53**: 510, 511, 592-93; **64**: 27-28, 28; birthday greetings to WW and WW's thank you, **64**: 235, 237; WW's get-well wished to, **65**: 314

Alexandra Victoria Alberta Edwina Louise, daughter of Duchess of Fife, **53**: 592,n4

Alexandretta (now Iskenderun), Turkey, **56**: 105, 111; **57**: 334; **59**: 139, 334, 344

Alexandropol, Russia, **66**: 422, 437

Alexandroupolis, Greece: *see* Dedeagach, Bulgaria

Alfonso XIII of Spain, **56**: 392,n1

Algeçiras, Act of, **59**: 498,n2; **62**: 39-40, 41
Algeria, **54**: 368
Alice Garrigue Masaryk, 1879-1966; her life as recorded in her own words and by her friends (Mitchell, comp.), **68**: 296n1
Alien Enemy Regulations Modified by the President (*Official Bulletin*), **53**: 469n1
Alien Property Custodian, **54**: 429n1; **58**: 119; **59**: 449,n2; *see also* Palmer, Alexander Mitchell
Aliens and Dissenters: Federal Suppression of Radicals (Preston), **65**: 187n5
Aljibes, Mexico, **65**: 252n1
Aliotti, Baron Carlo Alberto, **66**: 339,n3
All-American Cable Company, **66**: 221
Allen, Corporal, **59**: 621,n2
Allen, Benjamin Farwell, **62**: 627; **63**: 275-76,n4
Allen, Frederick Hobbes, **67**: 251,n1, 252
Allen, Frederick Sturges, **67**: 127,n1
Allen, Henry Justin, **68**: 148n5
Allen, Henry Tureman, **65**: 160-62,n1, 166, 167, 171-72
Allen, J. Wilson, **67**: 212
Allen, James Lane, **67**: 105n3
Allen, William Elby, **60**: 115n7
Allen, William G., **54**: 380n3
Allen, Texas, **66**: 445
Allenby, Sir Edmund (Henry Hynman), **53**: 572; **54**: 506,n6; **55**: 145; **56**: 88, 103, 106, 109, 113, 114-15, 116, 117, 122n2; **57**: 465, 558; **58**: 172, 318; **59**: 139, 345, 369; **61**: 8n1, 157; WW on appearance of, **56**: 88, 104; and Syria, **59**: 632, 633, 635-36, 637
Allen's Synonyms and Antonyms, **67**: 127,n1
Allenstein, Germany (now Olsztyn Province, Poland), **57**: 596; **60**: 88; **66**: 225,n1
Allgemeine Elektrizitäts-Gesellschaft, **53**: 418n3
Allgemeiner Deutscher Schulverein, **60**: 123,n3
Allgemeine Staatslehre (Jellinek), **67**: 247,n3
Alliata, Enrico, **55**: 332,n2
Allied Food Council: *see* Inter-Allied Food Council
Allied Maritime Transport Council, **53**: 223, 226, 373n2, 497; **54**: 30; **55**: 451n7; **56**: 54, 55, 56, 130, 147, 148; **61**: 151,n5; Council of Four on blockade and, **60**: 626-27, 638-39; and *Imperator* controversy, **64**: 8,n1, 34
Allied Naval Armistice Commission, **55**: 203n3
Allied Railway Commission, **55**: 470n2
Allied Supreme Council for Supply and Relief: *see* Supreme Council for Supply and Relief
Allies: want official German communications addressed to them, not to WW,

53: 69-70; and plans for European relief, **53**: 222-25, 360-64, 372-75, 392-93, 453-54, 585, 649, 650, 687, 689-90, 692; T. Roosevelt on WW and, **53**: 314n4; and conferences in London, **53**: 324-27, 336-37, 341; Hurley on shipping and, **53**: 372-75; and Bolsheviks, **53**: 453-54, 627, 706; and proposal to sink surrendered German ships, **53**: 469n1; U.S. loans to, **53**: 477-80; Litvinov on Russia and, **53**: 492-94,n1, 712-14; Ackerman on importance of unified Russian policy by, **53**: 631-32; and war expenses, **54**: 196; agree on commemorative medal for all soldiers, **54**: 246-47; *see also* under names of individual countries
Allizé, Henri, **58**: 508,n8; **60**: 323,n3
All-Russian Provisional Government, **53**: 258n1, 628, 630
All Russia Union of Cooperatives, **61**: 359
Allyn and Bacon Publishers, **66**: 242n1
Almanach de Gotha, **53**: 596n3
Almond, Nina, **59**: 60n3; **60**: 34n2
Almy, Frederic, **56**: 283,n3
Along the Afric Shore: An historic review of two centuries of U.S.-African relations (Howe), **61**: 406n1
Alter, George Elias, **68**: 56n2
Alsace-Lorraine, **53**: 35, 36, 37, 82n1, 92, 292, 293, 296; **54**: 285, 299, 529; **55**: 30, 52, 152, 480, 506, 507; **56**: 266-67, 317n1, 362, 363, 366, 368, 369, 421, 492, 546, 580; **57**: 99, 106, 107, 158, 160, 201-202, 243, 322, 358, 586; **58**: 45, 62, 294; **59**: 51; **60**: 23, 87, 106, 107, 165, 467,n5, 478; **63**: 132; **64**: 200, 248, 249n1; **67**: 269, 270; Germany on, **59**: 581; Haskins on German counterproposals on, **60**: 109-10; draft reply on, **60**: 467,n5
Alsace-Lorraine—Report on the Problem of Alsace-Lorraine (memorandum, Haskins), **56**: 431,n1
Alsberg, Henry Garfield, **61**: 243,n7
Alto Adige, **57**: 488,n1
Alvarado, Salvador, **66**: 142,n1, 372,n2
Alvarez, Walter, M.D., **58**: 636, 639
Alvord, E. M., **65**: 508,n1; **66**: 205,n1, 206
Am Webstuhl der Zeit, **53**: 121n1
Amalgamated Association of Iron, Steel, and Tin Workers, **63**: 301n1
Amalgamated Copper Company, **56**: 476n2
Amalgamated Sheet Metal Workers' International Association, **62**: 569, 573; **64**: 431
Amaral, Silvino Gurgél do, **66**: 211-12,n5
Ambassador Morgenthau's Story (Morgenthau), **53**: 3,n1; **65**: 20,n1
Ambrosius, Lloyd E., **61**: 66n3; **62**: 308n1; **63**: 482n3; **64**: 276n1, 328n2; **65**: 292n1, 328n2
Ameli, Howard Wilmurt, **65**: 574,n23
America, U.S.S., **58**: 141

America and Russia (Sack), **68**: 125

America and the Fight for Irish Freedom, 1866-1922 (Tansill), **56**: 486n1; **67**: 52n1

America as a Mandatory (New York *World*), **59**: 524,n5

American Academy of Arts and Letters, **68**: 581

American Alliance for Labor and Democracy, **65**: 442n2

American Association for the United Nations, **68**: 178n1

American Banking Group, **65**: 259,n1, 277; see also International Banking Consortium

American Bar Association, **56**: 330; McAdoo on California convention of, **68**: 123; WW on, **68**: 129

American Bible Society, **62**: 435n1

American Catholic College, Rome, **55**: 493

American Chamber of Commerce in Paris, **61**: 625n1

American Chamber of Commerce of China: memorandum on Shantung, **60**: 101, 102

American Church of the Holy Trinity, Paris, **53**: 392

American Civil Liberties Union, **65**: 337, 441

American Column and Lumber Co. *et al. v.* United States, **68**: 130-31,n2

American Commission for Irish Independence, **56**: 486n1; **59**: 393, 549,n1; **60**: 239,n1; statement on Irish situation, **62**: 324-26; **63**: 118n2; *see also* Dunne, Edward Fitzsimons; Walsh, Francis Patrick

American Commission on Conditions in Ireland (Committee of One Hundred), **66**: 37,1

American Commissioners Plenipotentiary to Negotiate Peace (Wilson, Lansing, Bliss, House, White): *see* Paris Peace Conference—commissioners

American Commission to Negotiate Peace (A.C.N.P.), **53**: 348n1, 349n5, 350n1, 356n1, 367n1,2, 376n1, 389n1,2, 418n2, 654n1,2; **54**: 7n1, 180, 399n1, 471n2, 473,n1; **56**: 54n14, 75n2,3, 161-62, 221n7, 223n2, 606; **57**: 25n9, 89, 275, 574n1; **59**: 237, 317, 349n1, 403n2; **60**: 573; **61**: 341; and protests from South Tyrol, **59**: 348,n1,2; on discussing Germany's proposals under WW's guidance, **59**: 546, 546-47; WW agrees to meet with commissioners on German proposals, **59**: 594; and Irish issue, **59**: 645, 646; "black book," **60**: 34n3; on reparations, **60**: 45-53; WW discusses German counterproposals with, **60**: 45-71; on Germany's eastern borders, **60**: 53-59; on Rhineland occupation, **60**: 59-63; questions authenticity of Erzberger letter-interview, **60**: 64-65; on getting Germany to sign treaty, **60**: 69-71; various accounts of WW's meeting with, **60**: 76-80, 81; **61**: 32, 33-34; Hornbeck on China signing treaty with reservations, **61**: 176; on international consultation, **61**: 520-22, 587; on setting up commissions as provided by peace treaty, **61**: 585-87; photograph of, *illustration section*, **54**

American Committee for Armenian and Syrian Relief, **62**: 576-77,n1,2

American Committee for Relief in the Near East, **53**: 134-35; **55**: 485, 486n2

American Committee for the Independence of Armenia, **55**: 65, 265n1, 446; **56**: 95; **61**: 486n1; **63**: 304n1; **65**: 287,n1, 298; **68**: 431n1

American Diplomacy and the Narcotics Traffic, 1900-1939: A Study in International Humanitarian Reform (Taylor), **56**: 270n5

American Economic Association, **56**: 427

American Economic Review, **55**: 334n1

American Expeditionary Force, **53**: 403-404; **60**: 489; Pershing's praise of General Staff, **53**: 512-14; psychiatrist's evaluation of men in, **61**: 530, 531-33; *see also* United States Army

American Expeditionary Forces University, **61**: 361n2

American Express Company: returned to private control, **64**: 222,n1, 223

American Farm Bureau Association, **62**: 300n1

American Farm Bureau Federation: and surplus corn, **67**: 80,n1, 139n1, 139-40

American Federationist, **68**: 285,n1

American Federation of Labor, **53**: 195, 257, 490; **54**: 309; **55**: 262, 284; **58**: 329, 361; **63**: 30n1; **64**: 431, 475; **65**: 563; **66**: 5n3; **68**: 179n1, 581; advocates peace commissioner representing, **53**: 119, 155; WW's message to, **60**: 111, 113, 197; and League of Nations and labor clauses, **60**: 645; endorses League of Nations, **61**: 66, 138, 231; on prohibition, **61**: 294; resolution against mob rule and lynchings, **61**: 357-59; requests Burleson's removal, **61**: 364-65; and railroads, **61**: 377; and California telephone workers' strike, **61**: 503-504; and railroad strike crisis, **62**: 122, 134-35, 138, 140, 161, 162, 190, 485, 567; F. D. Roosevelt on Saturday as half day of work, **62**: 232; and steel industry, **62**: 581; and conference on relationship between labor and capital, **62**: 582, 584, 623; and police, **63**: 149-50, 167,n6, 267, 295; and coal situation, **64**: 179-80; and railroads, **64**: 424; and railroad situation, **65**: 16, 19, 215, 216, 285-86; **68**: 129n1; and general amnesty for "political" prisoners, **66**: 120,n1, 231-32, 516; and self-government for Dominican Republic, **66**: 537, 539; **67**: 73

American Financing of World War I (Gilbert), **55**: 334n1

American Geographical Society, **53**: 350n1; **57**: 313n2

American Handbook of Psychiatry, (Arieti, ed.), **58**: 614n13; **62**: 635n21

American Hebrew, **66**: 139,n1

American Heritage, **55**: 488n2; **57**: 532n2; **67**: 289n3

American Historical Association, **68**: 66; WW elected second vice president of, **67**: 505, 508, 514, 518-19, 534; site for 1924 meeting, **68**: 460,n1, 462-63; WW elected president of, **68**: 514, 516

American Historical Association, 1884-1984: Retrospect and Prospect (Link), **67**: 518n1

American Historical Review, **53**: 515n1; **67**: 518n1; editors to meet with WW, **68**: 9, 68

American Hungarian Press Association, **56**: 521

American Indians, **63**: 168

American Institute of Arts and Letters, **68**: 581

American Interests and Policies in the Middle East, 1900-1939 (DeNovo), **68**: 504n1

Americanization bill: *see* Smith-Bankhead Americanization bill

Americanization of Edward Bok: The Autobiography of a Dutch Boy Fifty Years After, **66**: 131-32,n1

American Jewish Committee, **53**: 79-80; **58**: 381n3

American Jewish Congress, **54**: 258n1; **55**: 368, 377, 386; **59**: 150

American Jewish Joint Distribution Committee, **59**: 411n1

American Jewish Relief Committee, **53**: 251n1; **59**: 445; **62**: 531

American Journal of International Law, **56**: 530n4; **68**: 222n1

American Labor party, **55**: 450,n6; of Greater New York, **55**: 450,n6

American Legion, **65**: 154, 325n1; **66**: 5n1,2; WW's message to, **66**: 6; Baruch asks WW to speak before; WW declines, **68**: 341-42, 346

American Legion Weekly, **65**: 325n1

American Liberals in the League of Nations Controversy (Helbich), **55**: 292n1

American Library Association, **57**: 459

American Medical Association, **60**: 569; **64**: 432

American Mercury, **63**: 238n1

American Monthly, **66**: 248n1

American National Bank Building, Washington, D.C., **67**: 321,n3, 348

American National Red Cross, **53**: 135, 306; **54**: 102, 103n7, 515, 549; **55**: 281,n1; **57**: 60; **58**: 198; **60**: 382, 389; **62**: 34n1; **66**: 133n3; **67**: 140n3; WW's appeal, **53**: 202-203; **61**: 581; Axson and Davison on continued work and internationalization of, **53**: 232-35, 301-

305, 695, 707; commission to Russia, **54**: 181n6; and "White House wool," and sheep; **56**: 204; **61**: 505; **64**: 57n1; Mrs. Wilson visits Tent City in France, **56**: 525; and bronze wreath in memory of *Otranto* victims, **61**: 508,n1; WW on Versailles Treaty and, **63**: 262, 357; relief to Ireland and WW's response, and Pétain visit, **65**: 154; and White House sheep, **65**: 354; **66**: 512-13, 518

American Peace Award (Bok Peace Prize), **68**: 452,n2, 497

American Petroleum Institute, **65**: 380n3

American Presbyterian Church in Paris, **53**: 391,n1; **55**: 36,n1

American Protective League, **60**: 7, 115n6

American Railroad Politics, 1914-1920: Rates, Wages and Efficiency (Kerr), **55**: 248n2; **62**: 198n2

American Red Cross: *see* American National Red Cross

American Relief Administration, **62**: 123, 499; in Finland, **59**: 466n6

American Relief Council: and corn, **67**: 139

American Revolution, **63**: 26, 429

American Samoa: escapes influenza epidemic, **62**: 290,n2

American Socialist Society, **55**: 337n1

American Society of Equity, **56**: 427; **62**: 30n1, 623,n1

American Society of International Law, **55**: 339n1

American Telephone and Telegraph Company, **53**: 248, 654n1; **56**: 403; **57**: 530

American Union Against Militarism, **53**: 13

American University, **68**: 76n1, 80, 367

American University Club of China, **60**: 101n1

American University of Beirut, **54**: 551n1; **65**: 142n2

American Views on Fiume (London *Times*), **58**: 410n1

American Women Opposed to the League of Nations, **62**: 566n1

America's Debt to the World (Dawson), **57**: 36,n3

America's Moment: 1918; American Diplomacy at the End of World War I (Walworth), **53**: 544n1

America's Part in the Peace of Europe (R.S. Baker), **68**: 495-96

America's Siberian Expedition, 1918-1920: A Study of National Policy (Unterberger), **53**: 463n1, 556n4

America's World (speech, Redfield), **68**: 285,n1

Ames, Charles Bismark, **62**: 169; **65**: 96,n3, 174-75, 175

Amet, Jean-François-Charles, **59**: 26,n7, 27

Amette, Léon-Adolphe, Cardinal, **56**: 258,n1

Amherst, Mass.: public opinion on League of Nations in, **55**: 449

Amherst College, **55**: 449n1; **62**: 82n2; **66**: 478n1; **67**: 82, 344; and Meiklejohn, **68**: 388-89,n1, 403

Amidon, Samuel B., **65**: 499n1

A. Mitchell Palmer: Politician (Coben), **65**: 187n5

Ammon, S.M.S., **55**: 432

Anaconda Copper Mining Company, **56**: 476n2; **63**: 610n1; **66**: 133n3

Analysis of the High Cost of Living Problem (report), **62**: 165,n1

Anatolia: *see* Paris Peace Conference—Italy, Anatolia

Ancon, Treaty of, 1883, **53**: 316n2, 347

Anderson, Albert Barnes, **63**: 612n1; **64**: 141,n1, 143

Anderson, Arthur Marvin, **65**: 199,n10, 200

Anderson, Benjamin McAlester, **68**: 63,n2

Anderson, Chandler Parsons, **58**: 119,n2, 120; **60**: 290,n2

Anderson, George Weston, **53**: 82, 110; **54**: 58,n2; **56**: 162,n2; on WW resubmitting treaty to Senate, **66**: 3990,n1, 390-91; WW's reply, **66**: 402; on League of Nations, **67**: 405-407, 410; and Four Power Treaty, **67**: 511-12, 518, 525-26

Anderson, J. F., **62**: 568-69, 570-73; **67**: 119-20,n1

Anderson, John Crawford: and suffrage amendment, **61**: 479,n1

Anderson, Mary, **57**: 426; **62**: 97,n9, 314-15, 436, 437; **63**: 56-57, 58-59

Anderson, Neal Larkin, **67**: 307,n1,2

Anderson Overseas Corporation, **62**: 467

Anderson, Thomas Hart, Jr., **65**: 301,n5, 302

Andonaegui, Juan Luis Sanfuentes: *see* Sanfuentes Andonaegui, Juan Luis

Andrássy, Count Gyula (1823-1890), **61**: 94

Andrews, Charles McLean, **66**: 26n1, 59

Andrews, Edward House, **61**: 332,n4

Andrews, Eliza Frances, **67**: 75,n1

Andrews, Fannie Fern Phillips (Mrs. Edwin G.), **57**: 218,n1, 219

Andrews, Marietta Minnegerode (Mrs. Eliphalet F.), **68**: 320-21,n1, 570

Andrews, Philip, **57**: 442,n1; **60**: 335; **63**: 485,n3, 486n7, 525; **66**: 26n1, 59; naval situation in the Adriatic, **59**: 142,n1, 354, 408, 426, 528, 554-55

Anglo-American Preliminary Negotiations for League of Nations (Raffo), **53**: 515n1

Anglo-American relations: *see* Great Britain and the United States

Anglo-American Relations at the Paris Peace Conference of 1919 (Tillman), **56**: 499n3, 530n4; **57**: 142n1; **60**: 4n3

Anglo-Egyptian Relations, 1800-1956 (Marlowe), **56**: 154n3

Anglo-French loan of 1915, **66**: 166n1

Anglo-Persian Agreement, **62**: 334,n1, 427-28

Anglo-Persian Oil Company, Ltd., **62**: 78, 452-53

Anglo-Soviet Accord (Ullman), **65**: 288n3

Anglo-Soviet Relations, 1917-1921: Britain and the Russian Civil War, November 1918-February 1920 (Ullman), **55**: 181n4

Angress, Werner T., **65**: 155n1

Another War Message (*New York Tribune*), **65**: 71n3

Anizy, France, **56**: 198

Ankara (Angora), Turkey, **68**: 504

Annual Report of the Secretary of the Navy for the Fiscal Year . . . 1918, **53**: 311n1

Anschluss movement (Austria-Germany), **55**: 317n3

Anselme, Philippe-Henri-Joseph d', **56**: 527,n1

Answald, S.M.S., **55**: 432

Antalya, Turkey: *see* Adalia

Anthracite Coal Commission, **65**: 314, 352; **66**: 105-108, 217; WW names members to, **65**: 353,n2; majority and minority reports of, **66**: 64,n1; W. B. Wilson on report of, **66**: 66-69; WW on accepting award with minor changes, **66**: 69-70; minority report acceptance urged by United Mine Workers group, **66**: 75; W. B. Wilson on WW standing firm on decision by, **66**: 75, 76-77

Anthracite Wage Scale Committee, **66**: 67, 69-70, 76

anti-lynching bill, **62**: 234n4; **67**: 570, 571

anti-Semitism: and Ford, **66**: 130n1; Landman on, **66**: 130-31; Spargo on, **66**: 540-42; WW on, **67**: 7

Anti-Slavery and Aborigines Protection Society, **61**: 276n4

antitrust laws: and controversy between Railroad Administration and Industrial Board, **57**: 377, 380, 381; Palmer on prosecutions under, **62**: 173-74

Antivari, Montenegro (now Bar, Yugoslavia), **61**: 405

Antoine of Bourbon-Orleans, Prince, **57**: 241n1

Antonescu, Victor, **56**: 253,n4

Antwerp, Belgium, **55**: 326; **57**: 396; **58**: 99; **59**: 289; **60**: 551, 561; **65**: 43, 278, 280, 282

Anxiety in England over League Fight. Maurice Tells of Fear of Its Effect on Anglo-American Friendship. Other Obstacles Serious. General Says Mutual Recognition of Countries' Part in War Would Help Clear Air. (Maurice), **61**: 182,n1

Aosta, Emanuele Filiberto di Savoia, Duke of, **59**: 64,n3; **67**: 8; proposed visit to U.S., **66**: 543-44,n1

Apostolos, Bishop of Rhodes, **58**: 355,n2

Appomattox: Lee's surrender at, **67**: 45

Appropriations, Committee on (House of Reps.), **53**: 260; **54**: 486; **55**: 227, 291; **65**: 265n2; **66**: 528; **67**: 140n3, 505n1; **68**: 63

Appropriations, Committee on (Senate), **55**: 227, 228, 257

Apuntas para la Historiá de la Guerra entra México y los Estados Unidos (J. M. Iglesias *et al.*), **65**: 484n2

Arabi, Ahmed, **56**: 154,n3

Arabs and Arabia, **54**: 350, 360, 414, 455; **55**: 4, 7; **56**: 104-18, 242-43, 273, 323; **59**: 373; **62**: 235, 242, 257; **65**:: 114; Prince Faisal's claims for, **54**: 506-509; **61**: 159; and Zionism, **57**: 326n3

Arbe Island (now Rab Island, Yugoslavia), **66**: 447,n3

Archangel, Russia, **53**: 178-79; **59**: 152; intervention in: *see* Russia—Murmansk and Archangel, intervention in

Archibald Cary Coolidge: Life and Letters (H. J. Coolidge and Lord), **56**: 54n14

Archiwym Polityczne Ignacego Paderewskiego (Janowska, *et al.*, eds.), **59**: 216n5; **61**: 271n2

Arco-Valey, Count Anton, **55**: 423n1

Argentina, **53**: 342; **56**: 170n1; **58**: 198; and wheat situation, **62**: 52, 53; and recognition of Bolivia, **66**: 135, 480; on U.S. in Santo Domingo, **66**: 360; Colby visits, **66**: 430n1; issue of invitation to foreign minister to visit U.S., **66**: 452, 457

Argunov, Andrei Aleksandrovich, **59**: 156,n4

Argyro Castron (Argyrokastron, Greece), **64**: 299, 301, 315

Arias, Desiderio, **66**: 361

Arica, Chile, **53**: 536n1; **66**: 210n2; *see also* Tacna-Arica dispute

Arieti, Silvano, **62**: 635n21

Arizona: and railroad strike, **62**: 548, 549-50; and copper strike, **66**: 125

Arizona, U.S.S., **57**: 579; **58**: 43,n1, 339,n7, 409, 410; **59**: 252, 640,n1, 641

Arkansas: politics in, **67**: 166,n1

Arlington Cemetery, **65**: 289,n1 **68**: 573

Armenia and Armenians, **53**: 180,n1, 420n3, 489, 530n1, 562, 649; **64**: 27, 56, 309, 449-50; **65**: 65, 114, 502; **66**: 482; WW on, **63**: 71, 458; issue of U.S. troops to, **63**: 304, 423, 64, 466; and wheat to, **64**: 13-14; and mandate by U.S., **65**: 73, 91, 112, 235, 299, 305-307, 307-12; and Cilicia, **65**: 74; U.S. recognition of, 221,n1; Gerard on crisis in, **65**: 287-88,n3, 298; WW willing to arbitrate boundary, **65**: 305,n1; Supreme Council's note to U.S. on, **65**: 307-12; and message to American people, **65**: 353, 355; Democratic platform, 1920, on, **65**: 436,n2; and boundary issue, **65**: 496-97, 532; plans for protecting Americans in, **65**: 536-37, 539-40, 548-49; plans for protecting Arme-

nians along Black Sea coast, **65**: 537, 538-39; and Russia, **66**: 21-22; and Greeks of Euxine Pontus, **66**: 29,n1; Lloyd George on, **66**: 47; boundary issue and mediation, **66**: 65, 86,n1, 110, 350, 357, 426-28, 436, 450n2, 480, 517-19; 67: 63-67, 79; Congress' action on, **66**: 421-22,n2; WW's response to League of Nations Council on mediation, **66**: 426-28, 443-44,n1; mention of an alleged unpublished speech on, **66**: 434,n1; loan to, **66**: 448, 449-50, 452,n2, 489-90; Spain and Brazil offer to help, **66**: 457, 480; on gratitude to WW, **66**: 507-508; Lamont on relief funds for, **66**: 509; Gerard on plight of and WW's thanks for help with, **68**: 431-32, 440; *see also* Paris Peace Conference—Armenia and Armenians

Armistice, **57**: 12, 162, 168-69; **59**: 135; renewal of, **54**: 7,n3; **55**: 27, 53, 94, 95-104, 108, 111, 140-41, 202-203; Supreme War Council on, **54**: 7-12; **55**: 51-58; Germany signs, **54**: 108, 121, 172,n3; Great Britain and Italy want more German territory, U.S. opposed to further encroachment, **54**: 499-500; T. H. Bliss on, **54**: 514, 522-25; **56**: 7-8; and Loucheur Report, **54**: 527, 538-45; WW on not altering terms but setting up commission to negotiate, **54**: 530-31, 532-33; **55**: 14, 15, 40-41; Lloyd George on not being bound to renew same terms, **54**: 531-32, 533; additional clauses to, **54**: 541; Benson on naval clauses, **54**: 522-53; and war criminals, **55**: 59-60; and issue of transport of Haller's troops, **56**: 131-38, 142-43, 167,n3, 408n2, 409-10, 462, 464, 496n2, 526-28, 540; WW on occupation of territories and, **56**: 326; and Austria-Hungary, **56**: 462, 463,n12, 464; and Article 46 of peace terms, **58**: 248, 262-63, 266-67, 310-11, 313-14, 315; WW on Italy's occupation of Fiume and, **58**: 439; and reparations, **58**: 470; and Rhineland, **60**: 13; and German troops in Baltic provinces, **60**: 135; and sinking of German fleet at Scapa Flow, **61**: 57n8, 83-84, 85, 102-103, 123, 142-43, 146, 168-70

Armistice Commission, **54**: 9,n5, 10, 214, 219; **55**: 51, 60; **57**: 444, 445; **59**: 255-56; **64**: 150n1; and issue of Polish troops in Danzig, **56**: 88, 142, 143, 145, 169, 209n2

Armistice, The (Bliss), **68**: 222n1, 224,n1

Armistice, 1918 (Rudin), **53**: 626n1; **56**: 463n12

Armistice Day, **66**: 151,n1,2; WW's statement on, **64**: 7; WW's proclamation on, **66**: 204-205; Harding invites WW to participate in ceremony and WW's response, **67**: 400-401, 402, 432, 436, 436-37, 438-39, 439-40; procession plans exclude WW's going to cemetery

and WW objects, **67**: 444, 444-45, 445-46; WW's unpublished statement on reasons for not accompanying unknown soldier to grave, **67**: 448-49; WW's participation and crowd's ovation, **67**: 449-53, 461; Seibold and WW's decision to participate in Armistice Day procession, **67**: 453,n1, 456; WW and Cummings on (1921), **68**: 91-92; pilgrimage to and demonstration at WW's S Street house, **68**:185, 187-88; WW remarks on in 1922, **68**: 186-87, 190, 191, 192, 194, 200, 203, 222; WW's participation in 1921 mentioned, **68**: 379; request for WW to broadcast message on (1923), **68**: 452; WW's radio address on in 1923, **68**: 466-67; WW's remarks to 1923 pilgrimage and comments on, **68**: 467-71, 471, 471-72, 473-74, 491-92; WW on his emotional breakdown during, **68**: 472; WW thanks people for comments on his 1923 speech, **68**: 474, 474-75; Glass thanks WW for note on, **68**: 478; photograph of, *illustration section*, **67**; **68**

Armour, Norman, **63**: 307,n1, 308

Armour Fertilizer Works, **58**: 29n2; **66**: 289n2

arms limitation, **66**: 260, 472-74; **67**: 126,n7; Lloyd George on Spa Conference and Germany, **66**: 43-44,n5; Daniels on, **66**: 453n1; and WW Clubs, **67**: 286; Morgenthau on Republicans and, **67**: 387; Bliss on, **68**: 391; *see also* Paris Peace Conference—arms limitation; demobilization; Conference on the Limitation of Armament

Armstrong, Hamilton Fish, **67**: 426n1

Armstrong, Helen MacGregor Byrne (Mrs. Hamilton Fish), **67**: 135,n1

Army (U.S.): *see* United States Army

Army Appropriation Act (1920), **67**: 97n1

Army Reorganization 1920: The Legislative Story (Boylan), **65**: 355n1, 576n1

Army Reorganization Act (1920), **65**: 335-56,n1, 357, 363-68, 576-77,n1, 578; **66**: 238, 493; **67**: 97n1, 118; Baker on recruiting and army size, **66**: 527, 528; *see also* National Defense Act (1920), National Guard

Arnold, Benedict, **65**: 149

Arnold, Frances Bunsen Trevenen: WW on death of, **68**: 428,n5

Arnold, Julean, **60**: 102

Arnold, Matthew, **54**: 309; **66**: 440,n2; **68**: 428n5

Aron, Commandant, **58**: 148,n3

Arrogant Diplomacy: U. S. Policy toward Colombia, 1903-1922 (Lael), **62**: 5n6

Ars Poetica (Horace), **61**: 361n1

Arthur, Chester Alan, **65**: 414

Ashanti, **58**: 485

Ashbrook, William Albert, **56**: 428,n3

Ashby, Margery Corbett (Mrs. A. B.), **57**: 218,n1, 219

Ashurst, Elizabeth L. Renoe (Mrs. Henry Fountain), **53**: 35

Ashurst, Henry Fountain, **53**: 35, 305, 313; **55**: 351n1; **60**: 245,n2; **63**: 118,n3, 483, 535, 586; on WW's address to Senate, **61**: 445-46; on Bastille Day reception at French embassy, **61**: 492; on Democratic caucus on treaty, **64**: 62-64, 384; on Senate votes on treaty, **64**: 62-64; on Jackson Day message and banquet, **64**: 252, 256, 263; vote on Lodge reservations, **65**: 81n1, 109n1; on Senate and Armenian mandate, **65**: 323-24

Asia Minor: *see* Paris Peace Conference—Asia Minor

Asiatic exclusion law (Calif.), **57**: 240

Asie française, **57**: 468n2

Asquith, Emma Alice Margaret (Margot) Tennant (Mrs. Herbert Henry), **53**: 595,n7; on WW's Adriatic statement, **58**: 95, 155

Asquith, Herbert Henry, **53**: 519n1, 529, 530n1, 530, 542, 544n1, 594; **54**: 177; **55**: 116; **56**: 57, 532; **58**: 18, 397; **59**: 627; **61**: 386, 387

"'Assassin' of Wilson" (Adamic), **63**: 238n1, 273n2

Assembly of the League of Nations: *see* League of Nations Assembly

Assignment: America. De Valera's Mission to the United States (O'Doherty), **61**: 183n2

Assistance to France in the Event of Unprovoked Aggression by Germany. Message from the President of the United States, 66th Cong., 1st sess., **61**: 313n

Assling (now Jesenice), Yugoslavia: *see* Paris Peace Conference— Italy, Assling

"Assling Triangle": *see* Paris Peace Conference—Italy, Assling Triangle

Associated Business Men's Clubs of San Francisco, **63**: 340,n1

Associated Press, **53**: 318; **54**: 60; **55**: 221n1, 409, 409n4; **56**: 350n3, 428n3, 437, 443, 490n1; **57**: 63n1, 312n1; **59**: 68,n3, 554n2; **60**: 243; **61**: 369, 370, 605n1; **62**: 184n1, 252n1, 626; **65**: 494n1; **63**: 52n4, 547n5; **64**: 188n2, 487; **67**: 395,n1, 417, 448, 528; **68**: 282, 519n1

Associated Women's Clubs of San Francisco: Grayson on WW's address to, **63**: 308-309; WW's address to, **63**: 309-10, 311-12

Association of Italian Journalists, **53**: 599n1

Association of Oil Producers in Mexico, **62**: 155n1

Association of Railway Conductors, **62**: 140

Association of Railway Executives, **67**: 119n1

Association of State Farmers' Unions Presidents, **54**: 228n1

Assyrians, **57**: 426,n2

Astor, Nancy Witcher Langhorne Shaw (Lady Astor), **53**: 547,n2; **68**: 37,n2
Astoria Hotel, Paris, **53**: 143
"Astounding Survival of German Dream of World Dominion Comes to to Light in Erzbeger Letter" (Wales), **60**: 28n12
Aswan (Assuan) Dam, **62**: 437,n1
Athens, University of, **55**: 3; **67**: 235n1
Atherton, Gertrude Franklin (Mrs. George H. Bowen), **61**: 294,n4
Atherton, Ray, **61**: 555,n4
Atkinson, Henry Avery, **66**: 502-503,n4
Atkinson, William, **62**: 122, 568-69, 570-73
Atlanta Constitution, **62**: 234n4; **65**: 220, 381n1; **67**: 488
Atlanta Georgian, **67**: 363
Atlanta Journal, **65**: 220; **67**: 363, 364
Atlantic Monthly, **63**: 387n4; **65**: 411,n1; **66**: 164,n2, 290,n3; **67**: 135,n1, 540,n1; **68**: 233; WW on, **65**: 514; WW's essay, **68**: 348n1, 348, 353, 354, 363-64, 369, 370, 371, 384, 387, 392, 393-95
Atlantic Monthly Press: to publish WW's essay, **68**: 370, 371, 374, 384
Atlantic Transport Company, **53**: 111
Atlantica Company, Fiume, **56**: 569
Atterbury, William Wallace, **67**: 119n1
Attitude of the German Industrialists to the International Loan (Coar), **67**: 463-64,n1
Attolico, Bernardo, **59**: 300,n7,8; **60**: 26n11
At Versailles (London *Times*), **58**: 410n1
Atwater, Caleb Huntington, **54**: 383,n1
Aubert, Louis, **53**: 418,n1; **55**: 89, 387; **56**: 424; **57**: 99,n1; **61**: 43
Auchincloss, Gordon, **53**: 180, 372, 391, 394, 422n1, 430, 432, 507, 525, 654, 719; **54**: 151,n2; **55**: 192, 194; **56**: 75, 179, 208, 309, 539; **57**: 90, 93n1, 140, 179, 350, 390, 477, 532; **59**: 71, 83, 204, 409, 449; **60**: 202; **61**: 134, 181, 232, 295, 332; **62**: 202; **65**: 21, 244; **67**: 290, 293, 294; and WW's London *Times* interview, **53**: 418; on WW's meeting with Clemenceau, **53**: 437; Grayson and WW discuss, **57**: 51, 62, 66; on passports for Irish-American delegates, **59**: 172-73; House's influence over, **62**: 454; WW on, **65**: 180
Auchincloss, Janet House (Mrs. Gordon), **53**: 391
Audubon Society, **67**: 81n1, 110
Auflosung des Habsburgerreiches: Zusammenbruch und Neuorientierung im Donauraum, **55**: 317n3
Aufstieg und Verfall des Linksliberalismus 1918-1933: Geschichte der Deutschen Demokratischen (Stephan), **53**: 121n2
Augsburg, S.M.S., **55**: 23, 427; **56**: 28; **58**: 127
Augusta Chronicle, **65**: 220
Augusta, Ga.: and WW's boyhood, **68**: 296, 450-51,n2

Augusta Victoria, German Empress, **53**: 63n1
Au Service de la France (Poincaré), **58**: 280n4
Austen, Jane, **67**: 585
Austin *Daily Texan*, **66**: 369n2
Australia, **53**: 44, 328, 562, 563, 565, 565-66; **54**: 379; **56**: 164; **57**: 87; **58**: 198; and representation at Paris Peace Conference, **54**: 14, 44, 65; territorial claims and mandatory issues, **54**: 250, 251, 251-52, 289, 299-30, 308, 312, 325, 333, 348, 351, 358, 363, 366, 489; **58**: 442, 484, 510; and Japan's racial equality amendment, **57**: 240, 570-71; and Japan's claims, **57**: 603; and wheat situation, **62**: 52, 53; WW on, **63**: 477, 505; and British policy in Far East, **65**: 392
Austria, **54**: 170, **55**: 317,n3; **56**: 240, 347; **57**: 263n6, 346,n1, 368; **58**: 42; **59**: 354; **60**: 133, 549; **61**: 55, 430; **63**: 20, 24; **68**: 62; and Jews, **55**: 383n2; Lammasch on future of, **56**: 257n1; Lloyd George on armistice with, **57**: 320-21; Lansing on Smuts' report on, **57**: 440-42; Keynes on economic rehabilitation plan, **58**: 13; and frontier issue, **58**: 466-67, 467, 537-44, 584; and Italy, **58**: 78, 79, 369-70, 415; Council of Four on inviting to Paris, **58**: 149, 205, 264-65, 283-84, 315-16, 486; Kerner on, **58**: 157, 159-60; and Germany, **58**: 342, 343; 369-70, 415; accepts invitation to come to Paris, **58**: 508; and International Labor Conference, **63**: 62, 91; and Hungary's demands, **64**: 447; children fed in, **65**: 469; trade and exports to, **66**: 74, 101; and International Financial Conference, **66**: 101n1; *see also* Paris Peace Conference—Austrian treaty
Austria From Habsburg to Hitler (Gulick), **58**: 157n2
Austria-Hungary, **53**: 56, 367, 590, 701; **54**: 51, 303; **55**: 140-41, 317n3, 414; **56**: 5-6, 207; **58**: 5-6, 89, 249; **61**: 56; **64**: 440; Bullitt on Bolshevik movement in, **53**: 6-7; and food problem, **53**: 15-16, 689; and French conference plan, **53**: 294, 296; League of Nations Covenant and, **53**: 672, 685; and naval terms, **55**: 21, 26; and war costs, **55**: 211; and Coolidge mission, **56**: 54n14; and Fiume, **56**: 567-72; and Commission on Responsibilities, **56**: 613; Smuts on mission to, **57**: 167-75; dismemberment of, **57**: 343, 484, 542, 543; and Italy, **57**: 488n10; recognition of states formed out of, **59**: 11, 13; and boundary issue, **59**: 48; Lamont on reparations from successor states of, **59**: 384n; and prisoners of war, **59**: 424-28; Bliss on fixed military strength for, **59**: 428-32; Council of Four on religion of new Austrian state and, **59**: 496-500, 500-501; and Italy and reparations, **59**: 611; and

Kun's reply recommending former states meet on liquidation of monarchy, **60**: 312n1, 598; and Serbia and outbreak of the war, **60**: 452; and railroads of former monarchy, **61**: 317-21; WW on, **63**: 10; war costs, **63**: 221, 243, 349; battle deaths, **63**: 222, 243, 349; and annexation of Bosnia and Herzegovina, **64**: 368n1; and war-ending resolution, **67**: 313n1; *see also* Austria

Autobiography of William Allen White, **64**: 62n2

Avezzana, Camillo Romano, **64**: 458,n4; **65**: 157,n2, 158, 162, 196,n1, 338n2; **66**: 19,n1, 19-24, 50,n1, 87n1; successor to, **66**: 339

aviation: *see* aeronautics

Avksent'ev, Nikolai Dmitrievich, **59**: 156,n4

Awakening American Education to the World: The Role of Archibald Cary Coolidge, 1866-1928 (Brynes), **56**: 54n14

Awni, Adb al-Hadi, **54**: 505,n2

Axson, Edward William, **67**: 456,n2

Axson, Isaac Stockton Keith, paternal grandfather of EAW, **67**: 307,n2

Axson, Stockton (Isaac Stockton Keith Axson II), brother-in-law of WW, **58**: 331, 535; **59**: 207n1, 246, 247, 248, 249, 477; **62**: 226n1; **64**: 324, 520; **66**: 4, 15, 102, 420; and Red Cross, **53**: 232-35, 301-305; **58**: 216; **60**: 157, 292, 569; **61**: 31, 78, 397; **65**: 298, 553,n3; **67**: 6,n2, 129, 149, 172-73, 235, 335, 425, 613, 614; **68**: 483, 577,n10, 591; on payment for bronze wreath in memory of *Otranto* victims, **61**: 508,n1; and Brown-King wedding, **66**: 506n1; reassures Jessie of WW's love and health, **66**: 319-20,n1; and Dodd's book, **67**: 75, 76; on WW's health, **67**: 309-11; and WW Clubs, **67**: 416; reads aloud to WW, **67**: 517; WW recommends as faculty member at University of Virginia, **67**: 549; on meetings with WW, **67**: 605-607; **68**: 255-57; and revision of WW's essay, **68**: 348n1

Aydin, Turkey: *see* Aidin

Ayres, Leonard P., **53**: 275n2

Ayvalik (Aivali), Turkey, **59**: 146,n17, 270n5

Azerbaijan, **55**: 542; **58**: 333,n2; **63**: 157, 348, **64**: 309; **65**: 287; **66**: 21

Azores, **53**: 348

Baccelli, Alfredo, **61**: 109,n7

Bachrach, Germany, **57**: 592

Bacon, Charles Edward, **66**: 242,n1

Bacon, Robert: death of, **60**: 155,n1

Bad Homburg, Germany, **65**: 156n1, 158

Baden, Germany, **60**: 585, 587, 588, 618n3

Baden, S.M.S., **61**: 84, 124, 144

Badger, Charles Johnston, **53**: 312,n1, 395,n1

Badger, Richard G., **67**: 81-83, 82

Badoglio, Pietro, **63**: 485,n2

Bagby, Wesley M., **65**: 291n1, 492n1, 499n1; **66**: 208n1

Bagehot, Walter, **53**: 708; **67**: 554

Baghdad Railway, **58**: 92, 334, 344

Baikal, Lake, **58**: 569, 570

Bailey, Thomas A., **64**: 276n1, 328n2

Bailey *v.* Drexel Furniture Co., **58**: 605,n2

Baillie, Hugh, **62**: 627

Bailly-Blanchard, Arthur, **66**: 63,n1, 72,n1

Bakar, Yugoslavia: *see* Buccari, Croatia

Bakarcić, A., **59**: 241n1

Baker, Colonel, **56**: 334,n5

Baker, A. B., **58**: 615n18

Baker, Charles, **67**: 99,n2

Baker, Elizabeth, **68**: 505,n1

Baker, Elizabeth Wells Leopold (Mrs. Newton Diehl), **57**: 427,n13; **65**: 371; **67**: 3,n1, 297, 305, 493, 494; **68**: 133,n2, 137, 505

Baker, George Luis, **63**: 275,n3, 284n1

Baker, Horace, **65**: 189n1

Baker, Irene Noel (Mrs. Philip John), **58**: 444,n2

Baker, James Stannard, **68**: 108n4

Baker, Jessie Irene Beal (Mrs. Ray Stannard), **68**: 577,n7

Baker, Mary Ann Dukehart (Mrs. Newton Diehl, Sr.): death of, **67**: 389,n1

Baker, Newton Diehl, **53**: 35, 59, 65, 83, 128-29, 157n2, 163, 168, 183-84, 184, 208, 240, 287, 300, 322-23, 401, 609, 699, 719; **54**: 55, 227, 432; **55**: 39, 150, 188-92, 218, 235, 299, 341, 404; **56**: 190, 381, 618, 621; **57**: 49, 233, 381, 427, 630; **58**: 141, 593, 613; **59**: 234, 280-81, 449; **60**: 41, 287, 375-76, 567; **61**: 293, 376, 462, 465, 478, 485, 518n1, 646; **62**: 116, 234, 271; **63**: 164, 223, 274, 361, 421, 548, 585; **64**: 7n1; **65**: 99, 212; **66**: 120, 288, 383, 425, 536, 542n1; **67**: 70, 74, 305-306, 494, 508n1, 514; **68**: 123, 168, 277, 484, 485, 545n1, 576; on War Industries Board and state councils of defense, **53**: 11-12, 97; congratulations to WW, **53**: 46, 54; on not issuing army commissions, **53**: 101-102; on von Engelken, **53**: 106; on Poland's request for return of her soldiers, **53**: 182, 193; on not attending peace conference because of McAdoo's resignation, **53**: 182-83; on withdrawing U.S. troops from Siberia, **53**: 227-29; **62**: 433, 478-79; **64**: 219-21; on WW's route to France, **53**: 229; on postwar reconstruction, **53**: 252-54; on Russian situation, **53**: 254-55; requests retrial for Negro soldiers, **53**: 451-52; on modifying censorship of cable lines, **53**: 524-25; informs WW of conditions and issues in U.S., **53**: 580-84; on France's request for retention of U.S. troops, **53**: 584; and enlistment of

Baker, Newton Diehl (*cont.*)
  Polish troops in U.S., **53**: 605; on pork industry and food relief, **54**: 105-106; on investigation of German propaganda in U.S., **54**: 397n1; and conscientious objectors, **54**: 397-94,n4; **61**: 366-68, 615; **62**: 97; **66**: 401; on carpenter's controversy, **54**: 519-20; on sending U.S. troops to Armenia and Turkey, **55**: 27-28, 81-82; on Moton going to Paris, **55**: 335; and Philippine independence mission to U.S., **55**: 391,n1; **66**: 502; and court-martial reviews, **56**: 192, 244, 330-31, 425; and Siberia, **56**: 371-72, 519, 576-77, 606; **57**: 61; and Japan and Russian situation, **57**: 94, 134, 315, 346; on appropriations for education in Porto Rico, **59**: 122-23; on Gay as Shipping Board appointee, **59**: 185n1; on Harrison's divorce and remarriage, **59**: 204; on clemency for illiterate murderers, **61**: 457-59; and need for passenger vessels, **61**: 479-80; on officers serving in emergency ranks, **61**: 485-86; on mission to Armenia, **61**: 486; on Mexico's border raids and U.S. retaliation, **61**: 487-88; WW on Mexican situation, **61**: 524-25; on psychiatrist's evaluation of American Expeditionary Forces, **61**: 530-33; and troops to remain in Rhineland, **61**: 547; on changed attitude in South America toward U.S., **61**: 560-61; and race riots in Washington, **61**: 576n2, 599, 610; on State Department, not War Department, releasing information on Mexico, **61**: 610-11; on naming the war, **61**: 611; **62**: 69; on Taft's comments on WW, peace treaty and fellow Republicans, **61**: 614-15; on Panama Canal Railroad's steamship operation, **62**: 8-10, 97; on Russian situation and Czech troops, **62**: 82; issue of making public report on cost of living, **62**: 165,n1; army officers to aid Hoover's missions, **62**: 240, 249, 303-304; effect of treaty delays on War Department, **62**: 261; on record of two soldiers WW pardoned, **62**: 415, 434-35; on electric railways, **62**: 420-22, 461, 516-17; on Wilson Dam and WW's answer on dams, **62**: 437, 515; on incidents at Fort Leavenworth, **62**: 545-46,n3; on scandal involving U.S. Army colonel, **62**: 562-64, 610-11; Lansing on "industrial democracy" of, **62**: 612-13; and WW's welcome to Pershing, **62**: 622; on Pomerene's concern over reservationists' strategy, **63**: 296; suggested resolution honoring Foch, **63**: 301; on horrors of next war and aircraft bombing projects, **63**: 441-42,n1,2; offers to help EBW to lessen WW's work load, **63**: 534; reaction to WW's no-compromise statement, **64**: 193; and Tumulty's draft letter to Hitchcock on reserva-

tions, **64**: 278n1; on repatriation of Polish Americans in Haller's Army, **64**: 373, 375, 389-90; **65**: 43; Lansing shares news about his resignation with, **64**: 436,n1; rumor of resignation of, **64**: 436,n1; and Cabinet meetings during WW's illness, **64**: 456, 496; on Hitchcock letter, **65**: 76; on commuting death sentences to life imprisonment, **65**: 78-79; **66**: 34-35; on Ladenburg files, **65**: 83,n1, 135-37; and general amnesty proclamation, **65**: 126-27, 177, 193, 194 203-11; Polk and House on appointments and, **65**: 139; on protocol regarding visits of Pétain and Foch, **65**: 154-55; on U.S. troops and military strategy in occupation zone, **65**: 160-62, 165-66, 167; on appointment of Assistant Secretary of War, **65**: 227-28, 557-58; on proposed bonus bill for veterans, **65**: 243-44; and penalty for soldiers carrying concealed weapons, **65**: 261-62,n1; and controversy with Shipping Board, **65**: 270, 277-83, 290; meets with W. S. Benson, **65**: 270n2, 277-83; on resumption of trade with Russia, **65**: 270, 271; on U.S. Army desertion record, **65**: 272-73; on number of criminal offenses in U.S. Army, **65**: 273,n1, 285; and dedication of memorial amphitheater at Arlington National Cemetery, **65**: 289,n1; suggests Pershing visit Brazil and other South American countries, **65**: 318; and WW's Memorial Day message, **65**: 325; on Army Reorganization bill, **65**: 355-56,n1, 357, 363-68, 576-77, 578; Geddes on NDB, **65**: 371; on not attending Democratic National Convention, **65**: 383, 385; on Republican platform, **65**: 386, 396; on sale of locomotives to Estonia, **65**: 387-88; on Creel's expenditures from National Security Defense Fund, **65**: 442-43; on water-power bill, **65**: 447-48, 459; WW wishes Federal Power Commission be headed by, **65**: 449; sends WW suit of cartridge cloth, **65**: 502; message to American Legion, **66**: 5n2, 6; Debs' pardon, **66**: 25; and Crowder and Selective Service Act, **66**: 58,n1; on chaplain's medal, **66**: 129-30; on selling surplus materials to Poland, **66**: 146-47; and Armistice Day proclamation, **66**: 151,n1,2, 204; on Crowell's endorsement of Republicans, **66**: 188, 192; on Cuban situation, **66**: 236-38; praises WW, **66**: 312-13; **67**: 215; WW's praise of and thanks, **66**: 332n1; at Cabinet meeting on treaty, **66**: 342; and Western Union cable, **66**: 412, 484; on Salmon case, **66**: 414, 415; W. Va. miners' strike requires troops, **66**: 445-46,n2; on Benson's request for Hoboken piers and army supply bases, **66**: 464-67; on revised court martial guide,

66: 493-94; issue of recruiting, **66**: 527-29, 532; **67**: 97-98, 105; Christmas greetings and praise of WW, **67**: 3-4; **68**: 246; on veto message for Milk River Valley Gun Club bill, **67**: 112-13; on Dawes, **67**. 124; on ceremony for French unknown soldier, **67**: 131, 133; on Cabinet farewell to WW, **67**: 150, 199; recommends Kirby, **67**: 171-72; on various personalities and situation in Cleveland, **67**: 295-97; and Harvey, **67**: 296-97; on newspapers, **67**: 296; WW's condolences to, **67**: 389; on Four Power Treaty, **67**: 493; as WW's presidential choice, **67**: 606; Clarke and League of Nations and, **68**: 123; *Encyclopaedia Britannica*'s article on, **67**: 133,n1, 136-37; on criticism of himself, **67**: 164; on revelations about Lane, **68**: 164-65, 168; and visit to League of Nations, **68**: 432,n1; sends WW holiday greetings and family news, **68**: 505; and The Document, **68**: 534, 544,n1,8; photograph of, *illustration section*, **67**

Baker, Philip John, **58**: 444,n1,2, 445,n1; **60**: 270n20

Baker, Ray Stannard, **53**: 123; **55**: 479, 496; **56**: 3n3, 4, 103-104, 128, 179, 337, 337-38, 353-54, 393n1, 425, 440, 441, 518, 542-43, 563n3, 577-78, 588-89; **57**: 52, 148, 194-95, 240-41, 266n1, 312, 316-17, 336, 353, 467-68, 503n2, 527-28, 575, 585; **58**: 3, 169, 214, 245, 331, 367, 369, 418-19, 430, 479, 489, 601; **59**: 184, 245-46, 285-87, 316-17, 367-68, 447-48, 480, 551-52, 603-604, 621-23, 645-47; **60**: 17, 196-97, 252, 286, 328-29, 374, 430-31, 532-33, 644; **61**: 34-35, 179, 231, 360, 361, 416; **62**: 607n1; **63**: 6; **64**: 348, 362, 365, 385, 428; **65**: 140; **66**: 306, 531, 542n1; **67**: 71-72, 105n3, 129-30, 288-94, 494-95; **68**: 259n2, 312-13, 402-404, 544n1, 577; and the press and the peace conference, **53**: 411, 438-39, 440; on Italian situation, **53**: 433-36; and publicity, **54**: 59, 189-91, 191-92; and news leak that Paris Peace Conference might relocate, **55**: 88; on public opinion on League of Nations, **55**: 449-52; a personal view of WW, **55**: 463-67, 489-91; on Lloyd George, **55**: 480; on beginning of breach between House and WW, **55**: 488n2; on League of Nations, **55**: 531,n1; **57**: 4-5; suggestions for near eastern commission, **56**: 155-56; on House, **56**: 338; on personalities of Big Four, **56**: 578; on WW's summoning *U.S.S. George Washington*, **57**: 62, 63,n1, 68-71, 140; on Japanese racial equality clause, **57**: 286,n1; on Hoover's statement on Russia, **57**: 508-509; blames House for some difficulties in negotiation with Italy, **57**: 527-28; on Adriatic statement, **58**: 142; on Japanese-Chinese controversy over Shantung, **58**: 142, 143, 214, 229, 230-32, 370-71,n1, 372, 427; on summary of peace treaty and publicity issue, **58**: 412, 440, 459; on Plenary Session at Versailles, **58**: 529-30; on WW's health, **58**: 634; **64**· 320-21, 527, 527-28; **66**: 451; **67**: 237-38, 284, 300-301; **68**: 285; on publicity of WW's message to Congress, **59**: 286; on publishing peace treaty, **59**: 449; on WW's Memorial Day speech at Suresnes Cemetery, **59**: 621-22; on WW's meeting with American delegates, **60**: 79-80; on delays in reply to German counterproposals, **60**: 286, 486, 532-33; on tour of Belgium, **61**: 28-30; on WW as orator, **61**: 30; on Nitti, **61**: 35; on presence of South and Central American delegates at Versailles, **61**: 65-66; on Germany's reservations on signing treaty, **61**: 70; on WW's press conference, **61**: 252-54; on WW, **61**: 383; **62**: 635; **63**: 539n1, 619-22, 642; and second Industrial Conference appointments, **63**: 609, 621; interview with House, **64**: 61-62; his book on WW, **64**: 320, 325, 355; on need for compromise in treaty fight, **64**: 320-22, 326-27, 359-60; EBW on Baker's observation on the need to preserve the spirit of the League, **64**: 335; and WW's tentative decision to resign, **64**: 362n1; visits E. M. House, **65**: 41; reports from Democratic convention, 1920, **65**: 493-94, 496, 497-98, 499, 580; visit with WW reveals a tragic figure, **66**: 435-36, 438-42; EBW on reworking draft article on WW, **66**: 446-47; will not print article, **66**: 450-51; on importance of writing book on Paris Peace Conference, **66**: 521, 521-23, 537-39, 544-45; WW endorses project on peace conference, **66**: 532-33, 533; and *Woodrow Wilson and World Settlement*, **67**: 7, 15-16,n1, 27, 60, 71-72, 82, 89-90, 93-94, 129-30, 184, 188-89, 360-61, 397,n3, 494, 559-60; **68**: 108, 194, 200-201, 232-34, 281-83, 312-13, 403, 496-97, 506-507; Dodd on book project of, **67**: 76-77,n4, 77, 163, 283; on House-WW break, **67**: 129-30, 289-94; continues his work after WW moves, **67**: 174, 236-39; Creel on arrangement WW made with, **67**: 174, 241, 254-55; to get in touch with Creel on financial aspects and serialization of *World Settlement*, **67**: 238-39, 243-45, 249, 251, 256, 363-64, 364-65, 414, 488-91, 560; on WW's loneliness, **67**: 256; on first impression of WW, **67**: 293; on sightseers looking at WW's house, **67**: 295; WW vetoes Hearst offer for serialization, **67**: 364-65; and Houston's career plans, **67**: 433, 434; and Johnson's memorandum on Adriatic question, **67**: 502, 504-505,n1; on visit with WW, **67**: 585-86; on Versailles Treaty as

Baker, Ray Stannard (*cont.*)
campaign issue, **67**: 617; on EBW, **67**:
617; on Lloyd George's claim to authorship of League of Nations resolution,
67: 108, 109; EBW on *World Settlement*, **68**: 150-51, 480; sends EBW
book, **68**: 176; sends WW checks from
royalties and syndication, **67**: 194, 321,
329; suggests WW meet Jean Longuet,
WW refuses, **68**: 200-201; asks WW
permission to use his comments on
World Settlement and WW complies,
68: 233-34, 238; WW praises, **68**: 284,
514-15; willing to assist Palmer on
chemical and dyestuffs case, **68**: 299-
300, 301, 312, 316, 317, 356, 357-58,
361; concern over powerful U.S. economic interests against defeated nations, **68**: 358-59; on Meiklejohn and
educational philosophy, **68**: 403; permission for written interview denied
by WW, **68**: 482, 494, 495, 499; plans
for biography of WW, **68**: 522-24, 524-
25, 530-31; WW promises preference
and exclusive access to his personal papers, **68**: 544n1, 574; photograph of, *illustration section*, **55**; **59**
Baker, Raymond Thomas, **55**: 409,n2; **62**:
336,n1; **67**: 175, 212
Baker, Roger Denio, **61**: 416,n1; **68**: 108n4
Baker, William Gideon, Jr., **62**: 623,n1
Bakhmet'ev, Boris Aleksandrovich, **56**:
160,n1, 161, 551n1; **57**: 139n1, 421,
422; **60**: 196,n1; **63**: 394,n2, 589; **65**:
247
Baku, Russia, **54**: 372n7; **65**: 306, 320,
323, 539
Baku-Batum Railway, **53**: 335
Bakule, Frantisek, **68**: 296n2
balance of trade: and WW's Annual Message to Congress, **64**: 79, 108
Balch, Emily Greene, **54**: 397n1; **58**: 140,
156; on League of Nations, **67**: 42
Baldwin, Roger Nash, **53**: 12-13; **54**:
397n1
Baldwin, Stanley, **68**: 593,n10
Balfour, Arthur James, **53**: 85, 143, 167,
233, 272, 316, 345, 409-10, 414, 418,
457-58, 470, 483n4, 498, 558, 569, 575,
585, 594; **54**: 173, 464n1; **55**: 66, 192,
213, 305, 423; **56**: 57, 103, 108, 122n2,
407, 457, 487, 488; **57**: 465, 467, 533n4,
588; **58**: 21, 22, 62, 131, 132, 133,
174n1, 185, 236, 255, 368-69, 381; **59**:
39, 142, 269, 311, 396, 466n6, 467; **60**:
27, 31, 95, 220, 306, 546; **61**: 78, 80, 81,
118, 127, 148, 157, 160, 195, 220, 238,
239, 257, 308, 309, 313, 526, 541; **62**:
11, 153, 155, 207, 319, 426, 525, 603;
64: 375; **65**: 141; **66**: 212n1; **67**: 297,
454,n1, 459, 554; invites WW to land in
England, **53**: 69; conferences in London, **53**: 324; plans for WW's visit to
London, **53**: 448, 449; meets with WW,
53: 519-20, 525; **54**: 489; **57**: 364-66;

meets with House in Paris, **53**: 576-77,
586-87; House on, **53**: 577; **57**: 35; on
Russian situation and peace conference, **53**: 591; **55**: 204; and Council of
Ten and Supreme War Council meet-
ings, **54**: 5, 9, 10, 16-17, 19, 20, 24, 37,
47, 66, 70, 74, 76, 110, 114, 116, 117-
18, 119, 182, 184-85, 187, 189, 201,
209, 211, 222, 284, 285-86, 287, 288-
89, 289, 311, 323-24, 343, 345, 352,
374, 375, 376-77, 377-78, 421, 422,
505; **55**: 10, 11, 17, 53, 54-55, 56-57, 57-
58, 59, 95, 98, 100, 102-104, 108, 109,
110, 111, 114, 147, 178; **56**: 16, 17, 23,
24, 24-25, 28, 32, 34, 36-37, 37, 44-45,
45, 46; and Adriatic question, **54**: 123;
58: 15, 17, 48, 103; **63**: 91, 92, 207, 208-
209, 210; on Armistice renewal, **55**:
108-109; on woman suffrage, **55**: 146;
WW on rumors of retirement of, **55**:
480; on Poland's boundaries, **56**: 94; on
Syria and Turkey, **56**: 117, 118; on
transport of Polish troops, **56**: 147,
167-68, 169; on leaks to the press, **56**:
150-51; on Palestine question, **56**: 203-
204; on cables, **56**: 210-11, 213-14, 215-
16, 218, 219, 219-20; **57**: 456; **58**: 283,
296, 298, 299, 300-301, 305, 346-49,
351; on Montenegro, **56**: 394-95; on Rumania and Hungary, **56**: 460, 460-61;
and Schelswig, **57**: 111, 363; and
Monroe Doctrine amendment, **57**:
218n1; on peace treaty publicity, **57**:
291, 292, 293; and labor clauses for
peace treaty, **57**: 307, 528,n3; sits in for
Lloyd George at Council of Four meetings, **57**: 349, 357, 358; and Luxembourg, **57**: 354, 355-56; and China and
Japan, **57**: 358-59; on Heligoland, **57**:
359, 360, 361, 362, 363; on German-
Belgian border, **57**: 393-97; report on
Council of Four's activities, **57**: 398-99;
and Germany's use of lethal gas, **57**:
401, 402-404; and recognition of British protectorate of Egypt, **57**: 499, 557;
and Italian claims, **57**: 538, 541-42; on
Japan's claims and Shantung, **58**: 175-
76, 178, 179, 180, 181, 182, 183-84,
186, 217, 220, 224, 225, 226, 228, 245-
46, 246-47; on Italy's return to peace
conference and on Treaty of London,
58: 373; and French security treaty,
58: 479-80, 486-88, 489-90, 490; **61**:
375n4; on Smyrna, **59**: 40, 41, 42, 44,
45, 46; WW on, **59**: 40; on Italy and
Turkey in Anatolia, **59**: 208, 209-12; on
WW, **59**: 477-78; Grayson promotes relationship between WW and, **60**: 3 on
Lloyd George-WW relationship, **60**:
144; Grayson lunches with, **60**: 203-
204; on Hungary, Rumania, and
Czechoslovakia frontier issue, **60**: 522-
23,n19, 529-30, 595; on Asia Minor and
Turkish delegates at Council of Ten,
60: 616, 617; plans for occupation of

Berlin, **61**: 33n2; and Klagenfurt Basin, **61**: 53; and notes on Turkey, **61**: 59-60,n3, 82, 158n13, 159, 252, 314, 338, 341; on sinking of German fleet at Scapa Flow, **61**: 71, 83, 84, 84-85, 86, 103, 103-104; on Jews in Poland and use of Yiddish, **61**: 89, 92; on Bolshevism in Galicia, **61**: 167-68; bids farewell to WW, **61**: 306; at treaty-signing ceremony, **61**: 333; and redraft of note to Italy, **61**: 342n3; and trade with Russia, **61**: 483; on Bulgaria, **61**: 588; and Greek atrocities in Turkey, **61**: 629n1; on Italian situation, **62**: 22-26; and Thrace, **62**: 110, 111, 238, 239; **63**: 60, 120; and disposal of German and Austro-Hungarian ships, **62**: 145, 145-46, 147; and mandates, **62**: 188; and WW and University of Glasgow's Lord Rectorship, **62**: 331-32; **63**: 395-96; and secret treaties, **62**: 365,n27; and Persia, **62**: 428; and International Labor Conference, **63**: 62; desire to adjourn Council of the Heads of Delegations, **63**: 306; and Johnson's letter on Adriatic question, **64**: 367, 370-71; and Armenia, **65**: 302; and Yap Island, **66**: 461; visits WW, **67**: 465-66; Grayson on meeting with, **67**: 516-18; on League of Nations, **67**: 517; on Great Britain's indebtedness, **68**: 106,n1; photograph of, *illustration section*, **54**

Balfour Declaration, **55**: 383, 384, 386; **57**: 326n3; **58**: 555; **59**: 150, 189, 314, 349; **61**: 128, 443; **64**: 358, 361; **65**: 248,n1, 271n1; **67**: 388; **68**: 485

Balkan states, **53**: 57, 598; **54**: 527; **55**: 30, 293, 317; **57**: 486, 488, 489, 515, 520, 542; **58**: 6, 139; **59**: 166, 397; **61**: 295n1, 517, 567; **62**: 253, 265; **63**: 61, 188, 485, 537n1; **65**: 315; and relief, **53**: 650, 689, 709; Miller on Root's comments on Article X and, **61**: 299; and Italy, **61**: 575, 576; Véniselos on, **64**: 162; WW on, **67**: 361; *see also* Albania; Bulgaria; Greece; Montenegro; Rumania; Turkey; Yugoslavia

Balkan Studies, **54**: 403n3

Ball, Lewis Heisler, **64**: 200-201, 336

Ball, M. Margaret, **55**: 317n3

Ballif, E., **57**: 193,n5, 238

Baltic Sea, **53**: 39; **55**: 23-24, 429, 429-30, 434; **56**: 31, 33, 35,n7,8, 36; **58**: 122, 583

Baltic states, **53**: 648; **54**: 92, 94, 103n7; **57**: 392, 398; **58**: 12, 390-91, 403, 594-95; **59**: 303, 312; **60**: 135, 437, 474-75,n21, 22, 482; **61**: 86-88, 153-54, 160-63, 335; **66**: 21; **67**: 8-9; **68**: 512; Lord on establishing a commission on, **57**: 137-39; Lamont on finances, **59**: 176; and food relief, **59**: 346-47, 347; and Russia, **59**: 466,n5; *see also* Estonia; Latvia; Lithuania

Baltimore, Md.: and Lafayette monument in, **55**: 232; WW on his retirement and, **55**: 482; politics and prohibition in, **59**: 38-39,n2; and WW's speaking tour, **62**: 627

Baltimore and Ohio Railroad Company, **63**: 607n1; and outlaw strikers,**65**: 192; **66** 254n1

Baltimore Evening News, **58**: 430n1

Baltimore *Sun*, **58**: 430,n1, 504; **62**: 196, 627; **63**: 275n4, 643; **64**: 394, 395; **66**: 242n1; **67**: 243n1, 356n2, 390, 391; **68**: 99n2, 132; on Wilson's health, **65**: 5; on Lansing's dismissal, **65**: 6; WW reads, **65**: 230

Bamberger, Simon, **63**: 449,n1

Bammate, Haidar, **61**: 331

Banać, Bozo, **59**: 125n1

Banat, The, **54**: 421n7, 424, 425; **56**: 380n2; **57**: 368, 418; **58**: 566, 571; **59**: 130, 171, 487; **61**: 279; **64**: 465; **67**: 375

Bancroft, Edgar, **55**: 187n2

Bandholtz, Harry Hill, **64**: 150n1

Bane, Suda L., **57**: 347n1

Bangkok, **61**: 347n3

Bankhead, John Hollis, **64**: 199n1, 200; 187n5; death of, **65**: 37,n1

Bankhead, William Brockman: and Americanization bill, **55**: 284,n1, 302

Bankhead, Tallulah James Brockman (Mrs. John Hollis), WW's condolences on death of husband, **65**: 37,n1

banking: Lansing on forming commission on foreign trade, **62**: 65-66; and high cost of living, **62**: 314,n2

Banking and Currency Committee (House of Representatives), **60**: 152; **61**: 496n3; **68**: 585, 586; Glass on, **64**: 52

Banking and Currency Committee (Senate), **54**: 485n1; **60**: 152; **68**: 24

Bapst, Edmond-Constant-Valentin, **60**: 605,n6

Baptist National Association: and League of Nations, **66**: 202

Bar, Montenegro: *see* Antivari

Baralt, Luis A., **66**: 211-12,n5

Bar Association of the City of New York, **67**: 340

Barbizon, France: WW visits, **58**: 422, 427; **59**: 248-49

Barbosa, Ruy, **53**: 342,n4

Barcelo, Antonio Rafael, **53**: 246,n1, 286

Barclay, Colville Adrian de Rune, **54**: 27

Barclay, Sir Thomas, **58**: 562n1; and WW's speech, **58**: 562,n1, 598,n1, 634

Bardens, Dennis, **59**: 95n1

Bardes et Poètes Nationaux de la Bretagne Armoricaine: Anthologie Contemporaine des XIX-XX Siècles (d'Erm), **59**: 186,n4

Baring, Evelyn, 1st Earl of Cromer, **55**: 384n4

Baring Brothers and Company, Ltd., London, **59**: 467n7

Bark, Petr L'vovich, **58**: 543,n6, 576

Barker, Allen F., **64**: 425, 426-27,n1
Barkley (laborer at Senate), **67**: 210
Barnaul, Russia, **62**: 87
Barnell, I. H., **54**: 228n1
Barnes, Mrs., **68**: 46
Barnes, George Nicoll, **55**: 178n2, 195,n4; **56**: 605; **57**: 239n5, 306,n2; **58**: 321,n1, 369, 413, 415, 427, 449, 452, 554; **59**: 50, 141, 222, 383,n1, 486; **60**: 23, 24, 520,n14; **66**: 380n1; on Rhineland occupation, **60**: 440,n8, 465, 501, 524, 526
Barnes, Julius Howland, **53**: 15, 60, 604,n1; **55**: 252; **57**: 144, 346,n1, 579; **59**: 206,n1; **62**: 95, 123, 124, 159, 168, 169; **65**: 470; to continue as head of Grain Corporation, **56**: 281-82, 372, 426, 470, 485, 486; **57**: 375, 475; and wheat prices, **56**: 619, 620; **61**: 499-503, 549,n1, 612-14; **62**: 51-57, 200; on trade contracts, **61**: 502-503; WW on wheat proposals of, **62**: 57; Leffingwell's response to wheat proposal, **62**: 104; and flour to Russia, **63**: 589-90; and Poland's request for grain, **64**: 4, 5-6, 12; and wheat to Armenia, **64**: 13-14; and European Children's Relief Fund settlement with Grain Corporation, **65**: 470; and *Washington Herald* and Hoover, **66**: 169
Barnes, William, **67**: 261,n2
Barnes Explains Profits on Grain (*New York Journal of Commerce and Commercial Bulletin*), **61**: 613,n2
Barnett, George, **62**: 270-71,n1, 291; 430,n1; **65**: 430,n1
Barnett, H. J., **58**: 626n74
Barnett, Lelia Montague (Mrs. George), **65**: 430n1
Barney, Samuel Stebbins, **57**: 630,n1
Barnum, Gertrude, **62**: 167,n2, 224, 436, 437,n2; **63**: 57,n4
Barnum, Malvern-Hill, **57**: 526,n1
Barnum, William Henry, **62**: 167,n5
Baron de Hirsch Fund, **59**: 413,n3
Barquero, Francisco Aguilar, *see* Aguilar Barquero, Francisco
Barrère, (Pierre-Eugène) Camille, **54**: 134,n2; **58**: 321,n1, 369, 413, 415,427, 449, 452, 554; **59**: 46-47,n1, 434, 435, 484, 485, 561; **65**: 162n2
Barrett, Charles Simon, **62**: 623,n1
Barrett, John, **65**: 252; **68**: 36n1
Barrie, Sir James (Matthew), **67**: 105n3
Barrows, David Prescott, **61**: 635,n3; **62**: 284,n3
Barter, C., **55**: 508n2
Barthélemy, Marie-Joseph-Raoul-Léon, **54**: 201,n2; **56**: 54; **57**: 276,n4; **61**: 129
Barthou, Louis-Jean, **56**: 542,n1
Bartlett, John Henry, **57**: 445n1
Bartlett, Louis, **61**: 504,n3; **63**: 350,n2
Bartlett, Ruhl Jacob, **63**: 223n1
Barton, James Levi, **53**: 180; **55**: 485-86; **57**: 313n2; **62**: 576,n2, 577-79; and Armenia, **66**: 448, 449-50, 451-52

Barton, Robert McKinney, **65**: 189n1, 286, 440, 444, 451,n1
Barton, Vermont, **68**: 104
Bartosovky, Bohuslav, **68**: 481,n1
Baruch, Annie Griffen (Mrs. Bernard Mannes), **53**: 334,n1; **68**: 320,n3, 325, 576
Baruch, Belle, **68**: 458,n2, 576
Baruch, Bernard Mannes, **53**: 12, 15, 150, 166, 213-14, 252, 334, 413, 413-14, 572, 645, 647; **54**: 35, 127, 230, 386, 494, 556; **55**: 90-91, 117-18, 148, 156, 186, 188, 336; **56**: 396, 435, 437, 443, 444, 448, 453, 498, 501, 502, 520, 553, 579, 580, 588; **57**: 246n3, 316, 513, 531; **58**: 26, 27, 64, 111, 119-20, 121, 249, 262, 535, 549; **59**: 173, 175, 254, 280, 283, 317, 382, 384n1, 495, 624,n1; **60**: 26n11, 118, 196, 230, 333, 399, 538, 569; **61**: 3n1, 151, 177, 178, 230, 366, 374, 383-84, 514; **62**: 8, 222, 222-23,n1, 322, 504; **63**: 551; **64**: 270, 359; **65**: 382, 444; **66**: 382n1; **67**: 105n3, 270, 284, 309, 353, 368-69, 540; **68**: 70, 109, 116, 137, 190-91, 191, 195, 197, 235, 237, 241, 325, 331, 381, 432, 550n1, 556, 576; on cancellation of war contracts, **53**: 47-48; on discontinuance of War Industries Board, **53**: 124, 131-32, 201, 202, 229-31; resigns from War Industries Board, **53**: 132, 249-50; and steel prices, **53**: 205,n1; praise of and good wishes for WW, **53**: 209, 309-10; **66**: 336, 525-26; and Gompers, **54**: 172-73; on war costs, **55**: 210-11; **57**: 479-80, 494; meets with WW, **56**: 197, 432; **57**: 4, 51-52, 574; **60**: 491, 493-94; on economic and financial issues facing Paris Peace Conference, **56**: 421-24; WW on, **56**: 428; on reparations, **57**: 30, 33, 203, 333,n1; **58**: 28-29, 548-49; **59**: 422; **60**: 47, 51-52, 76-77, 93; on Saar Valley, **57**: 90, 159-60, 287-88; and controversy between Railroad Administration and Industrial Board, **57**: 280, 282, 283, 381, 387-88; and story of his son at boarding school, **57**: 429-30; on WW's Adriatic statement, **58**: 94, 155; on duration of economic clauses, **58**: 115, 116; WW visits country residence of, **58**: 170-71, 172; House on, **58**: 482; on financial assistance to Europe, **58**: 523-25; suggests meeting in person with German delegates, **58**: 526; discovers changes made by France, **58**: 535-36; on Meyer, **59**: 161; takes motor ride with WW, **59**: 161-62; opposes military proposal for Rhineland occupation, **59**: 227; on experts discussing economic clauses with Germany, **59**: 314-15; compares Lloyd George to WW, **60**: 18; on Lloyd George and reparations, **60**: 20-22; on German counterproposals on Upper Silesia, **60**: 57, 58; on French-British conflict over peace terms, **60**: 73-75; proposes to confer with Ger-

many on the treaty, **60**: 334, 488; suggestions on reparations for proposed reply to Germany, **60**: 399-400, 400-401; suggestions for Reparation Commission appointment, **61**: 529; on U.S. as recipient of reparations, **62**: 148; on Germany's list of needed materials, **62**: 328, 330; resigns from Advisory Committee of Council of National Defense, **62**: 554,n1; and steel situation, **62**: 581, 582; **63**: 53, 149, 300, 301; on police crisis in Washington, D.C., and labor crisis, **63**: 149-50; appointed to Industrial Conference, **63**: 30,n1, 336, 611; and Ladenburg files, **65**: 83n1, 135-37, 139; Geddes on, **65**: 371; and Democratic convention strategy, **65**: 497, 580; visits WW, **65**: 514,n1; mentioned as ambassador to Great Britain, **66**: 150; receives service award, **66**: 250-51, 257, 288-89; on election results, **66**: 336; WW thanks for kind words, **66**: 346, 535; and reunion of War Industries Board group, **66**: 499; and fund raising for WW's S Street house, **67**: 137,n3, 168; and copper price fixing, **67**: 176-78,n1; beginnings of WW Foundation, **67**: 271n1; WW's concern over health of father, **67**: 282, 284, 301; urges WW to congratulate Ochs and WW's refusal, **67**: 301, 366; WW's condolences on father's death, **67**: 304; and WW Clubs, **67**: 319, 327n6, 328; on chairmanship of Democratic National Committee, **67**: 366; and Coar, **67**: 368, 370, 374, 463, 464; WW's condolences on mother's death, **67**: 468,n1; WW on friendship of, **67**: 478; and The Document, **67**: 560-61, 566-67, 568-69, 582-83, 583-84; **68**: 26-27,n1, 34, 239, 294,n1, 294-95, 295-96, 296, 297-98,n3, 385; visits WW on treaty strategy, **67**: 616; and issue of WW's involvement in politics and making decisions, **68**: 236; advises Margaret Wilson on career, **68**: 296, 373-74, 386, 391; on plans for Democratic weekly newspaper, **68**: 341, 346, 362; Houston asks WW to solicit funds from, **68**: 355; on League of Nations, **68**: 421-22; appeal to Smuts on reparations settlement and League of Nations support, **68**: 431, 433-37; WW endorses appeal made to Smuts, **68**: 438, 439; calls Smuts's speech to WW's attention and WW's response, **68**: 452,n1; to meet with Kerney, **68**: 458, 460, 461, 463; and WW's last illness, **68**: 557, 564-65; as WW's political adviser, **68**: 588, 590, 592; photograph of, *illustration section,* **58**

Baruch, Bernard Mannes, Jr., **57**: 429-30,n18; **60**: 118,n5; **67**: 319,n2, 328, 353; **68**: 362,n1, 363, 373, 406, 576

Baruch, Isabella Wolfe (Mrs. Simon): death of, **67**: 468,n1

Baruch, Simon, M.D., **56**: 428,n1; **57**: 429,n19; WW's concern over health of, **67**: 282,n1, 284, 301; death of, **67**: 304,n1

Barzilai, Salvatore, **57**: 489,n11; **58**: 17,n4, 211

Basel, University of, **57**: 569-70

Basel *National Zeitung,* **59**: 36-37

Basis of the Syrian Claims (*New York Times*), **65**: 142,n3

Basler, Roy P., **65**: 404n5

Basore, John William, **67**: 182

Bass, Elizabeth Merrill (Mrs. George), **64**: 3, 307; on appointing a woman peace commissioner, **53**: 125-26, 129; on appointment suggestion for woman in Labor Department, **62**: 167,n1, 314-16, 437

Bassett, John Spencer, **66**: 275; **67**: 514,n1, 518-19; **68**: 514, 516; on site for meeting of American Historical Association, **68**: 460-61,n1, 462-63

Bataille, Félix-Henri, **57**: 532n4

Batchelder and Snyder Co., **53**: 15n1

Bates, Blanche: *see* Creel, Blanche Bates

Bates, James Leonard, **53**: 636n1; **61**: 534n1; **62**: 297n1, **64**: 354n1, 392n1, 473n1; **68**: 119n2

Battioni, Augusto, **57**: 610,n2; **59**: 257,n4

Battle, Martha Bagby (Mrs. George Gordon), **67**: 135,n1

Batum, Russia, **54**: 372n7; **62**: 285n1; **65**: 288, 320, 323, 538, 540, 548, 549; Senate authorizes warships to, **66**: 421, 422, 437

Bauer, Charles Christian, **68**: 157-58,n1

Bauer, Gustav Adolf, **61**: 76,n5, 77-78; **65**: 100, 101

Bauer, Ludwig, **59**: 36

Bauer, Otto, **55**: 317n3; **57**: 167,n2; **58**: 157,n2, 159

Bavaria, **55**: 423,n1; **56**: 257n1, 543n2; **57**: 55, 103, 104n5, 105, 290-91, 409; **58**: 581; **59**: 8, 433n4, 434n5; **60**: 643; **65**: 101; and food relief, **56**: 498, 543, 574; and issue of credentials of German delegates, **58**: 244, 424-25,n2; and Council of Four's discussion of march on Berlin, **60**: 585, 587, 588, 589, 618n3

Bavarian Peasants League, **57**: 290

Bavarian Soviet Republic: first, **55**: 423n1; **56**: 543n2; **57**: 4,n1; second, **57**: 4n1

Bayard, Thomas Francis, Jr., **68**: 190,n2

Bayern zwischen Monarchie und Diktatur (Schwend), **59**: 433n4

Bayne, Hugh Aiken, **65**: 148, 153, 178

Bayrouth: *see* Beirut

Beach, Morgan H., **67**: 329, 343

Beach, Sylvester Woodbridge, **66**: 104,n1, 344, 349; **67**: 91,n1, 123-24, 126, 287; made pastor emeritus, **68**: 352,n1,2; WW congratulates on retirement, **68**: 354; and WW's funeral, **68**: 576, 578, 582

Beaconsfield, 1st Earl: *see* Disraeli, Benjamin

Beale, Sir John Field, **54**: 230n4
Bean, Rodney, **62**: 627
Beard, Charles Austin, **54**: 397n1; **66**: 542n1
Bearn et de Chalais, Louis-Elie-Joseph-Henry, Prince de, **66**: 39,n2, 50n1, 241,n1, 246
Beasley, Norman, **65**: 436n2
Beatrice (wife of Alfonso; Infanta of Orleans-Bourbon), **57**: 193,n6, 238, 241n1
Beatty, Earl David, **53**: 325, 521, 594,n13; **65**: 302,n7
Beatty, Troy, **66**: 506n1
Beaupoil, Auguste-Félix-Charles de: *see* Saint-Aulaire, Count de
Beauty Magazine, **68**: 449
Bebel, August, **54**: 342,n2
Beck, James Montgomery, **53**: 441,n2; **55**: 337-38,n2; **61**: 373; WW on, **63**: 625
Becker, Carl Lotus, **68**: 68,n3
Beekman, Robert Livingston, **57**: 445n1
Beer, George Louis, **53**: 350,n1, 352n3, 356; **56**: 434; **59**: 126, 200, 244-45, 488; **60**: 17,n1; **62**: 243,n1; on mandates, **61**: 265-69, 270, 283, 332, 408; photograph of, *illustration section*, **57**
beer industry, **59**: 39; Tumulty on repeal of prohibition law and, **58**: 603, 604
Beeson, Paul B., **58**: 617n24
Behind Prison Walls (*World Tomorrow*), **53**: 307n2
Bein, Alex, **55**: 384n4
Beirut (Beyrouth), **54**: 506, 551; **55**: 142; **56**: 107, 114, 115; **65**: 538
Beirut College: *see* Syrian Protestant College
Bel Air Farm, Collington, Md., **65**: 318n1
Béla Kun and the Hungarian Soviet Republic: The Origins and Role of the Communist Party of Hungary in the Revolutions of 1918-1919 (Tokés), **56**: 182n1
Belfast, Ireland, **59**: 107
Belgian Congo and the Berlin Act (Keith), **54**: 311n2; **56**: 268n2
Belgian Relief Commission: *see* Commission for the Relief of Belgium
Belgium, **53**: 36, 37, 92, 293, 296; **54**: 124, 139, 193, 226n1, 264, 283; **55**: 41-42, 62, 66, 86-87, 122, 151, 164, 184, 387, 458, 507; **56**: 14, 77, 122, 524-25, 584, 615; **57**: 111, 357, 359; **58**: 236, 334, 399, 472; **59**: 247; **60**: 99, 146, 157, 429, 528, 557, 558, 580; **61**: 172, 197; **62**: 560; **63**: 232; **65**: 234; and relief plans for, **53**: 76, 223, 280-81, 649, 689; **58**: 320-21, 411, 411-12; and reparations, restoration, and request for loans, **53**: 108, 181, 298, 324; **54**: 55, 211, 223, 283; **55**: 29n2, 30, 31-32, 33, 42, 63-64, 83, 109-10, 200, 220, 305-306, 349; **56**: 251, 252, 440, 441, 493, 496; **57**: 22,23, 24,n7, 34, 87-88,n7, 309; **58**: 25, 113, 114, 139-40, 229, 237, 249, 259, 262,

263, 278-79, 550; **61**: 120, 384, 385; WW's proposed trip to, **53**: 345, 427, 552-53, 693; **54**: 550; **55**: 86, 326, 349; **60**: 360, 485, 536, 609; Crosby on U.S. loans to, **53**: 480; and representation at Paris Peace Conference, **54**: 13, 16,n3, 45, 46, 65, 115; and armed forces, **54**: 238-39; territorial claims in Africa, **54**: 373-74,n9; **61**: 276, 277; and League of Nations, **54**: 462, 463; **58**: 198, 199, 201; WW's greetings to King Albert, **54**: 495; and war costs, **55**: 210; and Rhineland, **55**: 476, 477, 508, 509; **56**: 445-48, 456; **58**: 541, 542; **60**: 368; and House's resolution on German attacks and, **56**: 126n1; and desire to have Brussels site for League of Nations, **56**: 173-74; **57**: 222-26; presents medal to WW, **56**: 521-22; King Albert presents claims to Council of Four, **56**: 589-97; and William II's crimes against, **57**: 122-23, 131-32, 405; and publicity of peace treaty, **57**: 291, 292; and Luxembourg, **57**: 319, 334, 354, 355-56, 364-65, 372n2; and border issue, **57**: 392-97, 399; and The Netherlands, **57**: 395-97; **59**: 289; WW receives medal from workers in, **57**: 422; economic conditions in, **58**: 9, 563; Keynes on, **58**: 14; threatens to leave peace conference, **58**: 229, 237; delegates' requests concerning peace treaty, **58**: 316; Brockdorff-Rantzau on, **58**: 515, 516; **59**: 489; Daniels suggests WW visit, **58**: 593; Lamont on finances and, **59**: 176, 177; Germany on reconstruction in, **59**: 582, 583; and Eupen and Malmédy, **60**: 105-106; Haskins on German counterproposals on, **60**: 107-108; as great manufacturing nation before war, **60**: 140-41; estimate of damages in, **60**: 359n1; and Rhineland High Commission, **60**: 368; Germany's violation of, **60**: 443; French reaction to WW's proposed trip to, **60**: 485; issue of German labor in, **60**: 520,n14; and articles concerning construction of railroad lines and Germany, **60**: 551-52, 561; WW leaves for, **60**: 613; WW on raising legation to embassy status and appoints ambassador to, **60**: 640; **61**: 19, 396, 548, 582; WW's tour of, **61**: 3-8, 10-16, 105-106; Grayson on WW's address to Parliament, **61**: 12-13; WW's remarks at a luncheon in Brussels, **61**: 16; WW's remarks at Brussels City Hall, **61**: 23-24; WW thanks King and Queen, **61**: 35-36; and Commission of Control for Military Clauses, **61**: 59; King Albert thanks WW, **61**: 61, 355; Hymans on settling financial matters and mandates before WW returns to U.S., **61**: 106; and mandates, **61**: 314; **62**: 188-89; position of ambassador to U.S., **61**: 385; and credit extension for wheat, **61**: 501; King Albert to visit U.S., **61**:

609; **62**: 6, 29; **63**: 515, 532; WW on, **63**: 21-22, 45-46, 242-43, 258-59, 427; King Albert wishes to bestow honors on WW and other officials, **63**: 307-308; war costs, **63**: 349; King, Queen, and Prince visit WW in his sickroom, **63**: 602-606; King Albert thanks WW for hospitality and WW responds, **64**: 30-31; invited to first meeting of Council of League of Nations, **64**: 272; and war criminals, **64**: 364n1; on France's action in Germany, **65**: 170, 173; Ambassador to U.S. presents credentials to WW, **65**: 338n2; exports to, **66**: 74, 100-101; financial obligations and reparations, **67**: 144, 145-46; gift of china from, **67**: 270; *see also* Wilson, Woodrow—tour of Belgium

Belgium Under the German Occupation: A Personal Narrative (Whitlock), **61**: 105,n1

Belgrade Armistice of 13 November 1918 (Krizman), **56**: 462n10

Belin, Emile Eugene, **58**: 514; **59**: 232,n1; **60**: 258,n3

Bell, Edward Price, **53**: 573-74; **54**: 159,n1, 275; **66**: 460,n1

Bell, Sir James, **53**: 528,n5

Bell, Johannes, **61**: 302, 303, 323, 330, 331

Bell, Thomas Montgomery, **53**: 149,n1, 163

Belleau Woods, **54**: 278-79; WW on Battle of, **63**: 432, 450, 469

Bellinger, Patrick Niesen Lynch, **60**: 44,n1, 430

Bell Telephone Company: *see* American Telephone and Telegraph Co.

Bell Telephone Securities Company, **67**: 484n1

Beloroussouff, Mr., **61**: 360

Belorussia, **53**: 611n1

Belsk (now Bielsk), **59**: 354

Belts, The (straits): *see* Great Belt: Little Belt

Belz, **59**: 360

Bender, Robert Jacob, **53**: 314,n3, 318, 332, 336, 348, 369, 621,n2; **55**: 160, 221-22,n1, 409; **66**: 153n1; praises WW, **67**: 232-33,n1; photograph of, *illustration section*, **53**

Benedict XV, **53**: 114, 420n3, 489; **54**: 258-59; **59**: 118; and psychological moment for peace, **53**: 17-18; WW requested to visit, **53**: 231-32, 242, 421; WW's meeting with, **53**: 606-607, 646; protests against trial of William II, **62**: 26, 317; get-well wishes from, **63**: 555

Beneš, Eduard, **55**: 34, 35; **57**: 327; **59**: 186, 217-18, 487, 536, 538; **60**: 133, 222, 335, 344, 418n6, 552, 635; **61**: 136-37, 164, 165, 205, 206; **62**: 82n2; **64**: 443; and Czechoslovakia's territorial claims, **54**: 343, 344,n4, 490-93; on arms limitation, **60**: 171-72, 173; at

Council of Four on Czech-Hungarian conflict, **60**: 353, 355-56; agrees to Council of Four's decision on frontiers, **60**: 357; on infractions of articles on minorities, **60**: 595, 596; on transport of Czech troops from Siberia, **61**: 196-97, 201-202, 206; WW on honorary degree from University of Prague, **61**: 347; thanks WW for efforts on behalf of small nations, **61**: 461; photograph of, *illustration section*, **57**

Bengal, **59**: 327, 337

Benham, Edith, **53**: 166, 204, 319, 321-22, 384, 396, 399, 500, 501, 540, 593, 596, 612; **54**: 34, 61-64, 148-49, 217-18, 305, 414-15, 432-33, 489, 521-22; **55**: 40-41, 66-67, 224, 409, 411, 456, 489; **56**: 81, 81n1, 194, 354-55, 443-44, 540-41; **57**: 140-41, 351, 450, 502-503, 513, 533, 576-77; **58**: 168-69, 170, 188, 216, 277, 530-31, 633,n12; **59**: 35, 67n1, 159-60, 207, 246-47, 248, 254-55, 369-70, 420; **60**: 84, 118-19, 204, 249, 285-86, 300, 532, 533-34, 545; **61**: 370-71; **62**: 155; **65**: 514,n3; **67**: 479; **68**: 556; records impressions, **53**: 319-21,n1, 341, 343-44, 357-59, 369-70, 549-61, 468-69, 588-89; **54**: 218; on France's insistence that WW visit devastated areas, **54**: 175; on Gardiner's visit with WW, **54**: 196-98; on France's changes in meeting of WW and working women, **54**: 307-308; on French people wanting WW's peace, **56**: 244; on the Lansings, **57**: 141; on WW's lunch with Marie of Rumania, **57**: 241-42; on servants as spies in Paris White House, **57**: 468-69, 503; on reaction to WW's Adriatic statement, **58**: 102-104; on Plenary Session, **58**: 187; on outing to Baruch's country residence, **58**: 172; on Poincaré's note to Italy, **58**: 328; on Japanese settlement of claims, **58**: 421-22; on plenary conference with Germany, **58**: 534; on WW's health, **58**: 620, 621; on WW's running in 1920, **59**: 74-75; on Soninno's reaction to Vénislos' presence at Council of Four meeting, **59**: 319; on Memorial Day observances in Paris and at Suresnes Cemetery, **59**: 620-21; on WW's meeting with Walsh and Dunne, **60**: 388-89; on Foch's getting tired of waiting and departure before appearance at Council of Four, **60**: 582-83; on Belgian tour, **61**: 30-32; on excitement over news that Germany will sign, **61**: 135; on Poincaré dinner invitation episode, **61**: 180; describes Poincaré dinner, **61**: 188-89; on EBW and marriage, **67**: 477; on WW's health, **68**: 257,n6; on vacation with EBW, **68**: 408n1, 409, 410, 416; on WW's essay, **68**: 410; admiration for WW, **68**: 481, 481-82; photograph of, *illustration section*, **54**; **59**

Bennett, (Enoch) Arnold, **55**: 338

Bennett, Lawrence, **61**: 574,n4; **62**: 322,n2
Bennett, Richard **65**: 404,n6
Benoist, Charles, **64**: 407n1
Benoist d'Azy, Vicomte Denys, **60**: 546,n7
Benoist d'Azy, Vicomtesse Elisabeth de Vogue, **60**: 546,n7
Benoit, Peter, **61**: 14,n9
Benson, Allan Louis, **56**: 245
Benson, Godfrey Rathbone: *see* Charnwood, 1st Baron
Benson, William Shepherd, **53**: 208, 221, 327, 378, 397, 449, 485, 646, 652; **54**: 127, 303, 386; **55**: 21, 39, 40, 112, 343, 424, 498; **56**: 184, 310, 396, 430; **57**: 50, 61, 63,n1, 215, 331, 349; **58**: 3, 63, 112, 339, 492, 528, 554-55, 579; **59**: 28, 64-67, 119, 167, 241, 252, 432, 473, 576, 641; **60**: 16, 19, 44, 335, 613; **61**: 123, 178, 517, 518n1; **62**: 186; **64**: 228,n1; **66**: 206, 382n1; on disposal of German and Austrian war vessels, **54**: 273,n1; **55**: 515-21; and freedom of seas for neutral shipping, **54**: 403-406, 477; on proposed naval clause in peace preliminaries, **54**: 552-54; on naval and military terms, **55**: 27, 425-26, 426, 428, 429, 430, 431, 431-32, 432-36, 522-24, 539; **56**: 4, 67; and shipbuilding program, **56**: 558; **57**: 91, 92, 216; memorandum on naval policy, **57**: 180-88; on Heligoland, **57**: 359, 360, 362, 366; on deportation of Yugoslavs by Italy, **57**: 442-43; and Kiel Canal, **57**: 568; **58**: 122, 123, 124; receives Distinguished Service Medal, **57**: 579, 628-29; on departure of *U.S.S. George Washington*, **58**: 43,n1; on disposition of enemy ships, **58**: 125, 126, 206, 456-57; on transports' sailing dates, **58**: 141; on troop activity in Adriatic and Fiume, **58**: 142, 354, 408, 409, 410, 426; on withdrawing forces from Russia, **58**: 319-20, 354; **60**: 241; on naval action to be taken if peace treaty not signed, **58**: 581-84; on naval terms of Austrian treaty, **59**: 197-98; on situation in Smyrna, **59**: 640-41; on German counterproposals, **60**: 66; and clashes between Greece and Turkey, **60**: 193, 276, 276-77; on blockade, **60**: 565,n1; appointed to Shipping Board, **66**: 252,n1; on takeover of Hoboken piers and other facilities, **65**: 270,n2, 277-83, 290; **66**: 425-26; and International Communications Conference, **66**: 56
Bentinck, Count Godard, **53**: 63n1
Bentley, Fred W., **68**: 43,n1
Berbera, British Somaliland, **59**: 99, 102
Berchtold, Count Leopold Anton John Sigismund Joseph Korsinus Ferdinand von und zu Ungarschitz, Fratting und Pullitz, **56**: 614,n4, 615
Berea College, **66**: 483n1; **67**: 539,n1
Bérenger, Victor-Henry, **61**: 146,n6
Berger, Victor Luit, **65**: 206

Berkeley, California: WW's address in, **63**: 350-52; photograph of WW in, *illustration section*, **63**
Berkeley, Georgia, **61**: 357,n1
Berkeley Daily Gazette, **63**: 350n2, 352n
Berkenheim, Alexander Moiseevich, **57**: 512; **59**: 518n2; **61**: 359,n3
Berlanga, Aguirre, **62**: 450
Berlin, Germany, **53**: 576; **55**: 430; **56**: 38, 90n4; **58**: 572, 573; 618n3; plans for occupation of if Germany refuses to sign, **60**: 584-88, 599, 600, 618,n3; **61**: 33n2
Berlin, S.M.S., **55**: 432
Berlin, Treaty of (1878), **53**: 104; **58**: 461n1; **60**: 173,n2, 577n5; **65**: 315; and Jews, **55**: 373, 373-75, 376
Berlin, Treaty of (1921), **67**: 313n1, 382,n1, 399,n2, 401; WW's unpublished statements on, **67**: 394-95, 428; comments on Senate situation on, **67**: 418, 419, 421-22, 424; Senate consent to ratification, **67**: 422n4; WW on, **67**: 430
Berlin Act (1885), **54**: 311,n2; **56**: 268,n2
Berlin Conference on African Affairs (1884-85), **54**: 311,n2
Berlin *Deutsche Allgemeine Zeitung*, **59**: 68n3
Berlin Kongress 1878. Protokolle und Materialien (Geiss, ed.), **58**: 461n1
Berlin *Kreuz-Zeitung*, **53**: 576n2
Berliner Tageblatt, **53**: 121n2; **56**: 317; **58**: 23; **60**: 311
Bermuda, **55**: 482
Bern, Switzerland, **53**: 354
Bernhardi, Friedrich von, **65**: 415
Bernhoft, Herman Anker, **59**: 472,n1; **60**: 284,n3
Bernstein, Eduard, **59**: 382,n1
Bernstorff, Count Johann Heinrich von, **56**: 317,n1; **59**: 348,n1, 554; **67**: 224; on peace treaty, **58**: 308-309, 313, 314
Berry, George Leonard, **68**: 280n3
Berry, Josephine, **66**: 102-103,n1, 132, 227-28, 229
Berry, Martha McChesney, **67**: 456-57,n1, 459, 503-504, 507-508
Berry, Walter Van Rensselaer: WW and Wallace on, **61**: 625,n1
Berry Schools: *see* Martha Berry Schools
Berthelot, Henri-Mathias, **56**: 252, 305, 383, 384, 385, 581,n1; **58**: 381, 383, 385, 474; **59**: 465, 497; **65**: 143, 144
Berthelot, Philippe-Joseph-Louis, **59**: 562; **60**: 205,n2, 206; **61**: 27, 56; **64**: 35,n3, 263, 303; and Commission on New States and Polish Treaty, **61**: 46, 47, 47-50
Bertram, Adolf Cardinal ("Prince-Bishop of Breslau"): *see* Breslau, Archbishop of
Bertrand, Francisco, **61**: 638-40,n1,2
Bessarabia, **67**: 375; *see also* Paris Peace Conference—Bessarabia
Bethmann Hollweg, Theobald von, **55**: 507; **57**: 625; **58**: 501; **60**: 454; takes

responsibility for war, **61**: 334-35, 340

Between Two Flags: The Life of Baron Sir Rudolf von Slatin Pasha (Brook-Shepard), **59**: 561n8

Bevan, Arthur Dean, M.D.: on WW's health, **64**: 432, **65**: 4; Dercum on comments of, **64**: 435

Beveridge, Albert Jeremiah, **61**: 373; **66**: 542n1; **67**: 298; **68**: 44n2, 47, 49, 56, 148n5

Beyond the Horizon (O'Neill), **65**: 404,n6

Bey, Jamil Mardam, **55**: 145n3

Beyrouth: *see* Beirut

Bialystok, Poland, **54**: 33

Bianchi, Julio, **66**: 506,n2,5,6, 512

Bickett, Thomas Walter, **53**: 28-31; **65**: 473

Biddle, John, **53**: 583,n7

Bielaski, Alexander Bruce, **60**: 115n7

Bielsk: *see* Belsk

Big Four: *see* Clemenceau, Georges; Lloyd George, David; Orlando, Vittorio Emanuele; Wilson, Woodrow

Big Steel and the Wilson Administration: A Study in Business-Government Relations (Urofsky), **57**: 348n2

Bikaner, Maharaja of (Sir Ganga Singh Bahadur), **53**: 594-95,n16; **55**: 146; **59**: 93,n10, 103, 396; **61**: 329,n5

Billings, Montana: WW's arrival and reception in, **63**: 168; WW's address in, **63**: 170-80

Billings, Mont., *Gazette*, **63**: 162n, 163, 168n2, 180n

Billington, Ray Allen, **53**: 264n1

Billy, Edouard de, **56**: 348,n1

Bingham, Robert Worth, **54**: 389,n2; **63**: 256-57,n3

Bingham School, North Carolina, **63**: 256n3

Biow, Milton, **68**: 427,n1

Biow Company, New York, **68**: 373,n1, 422n1

Birch, Helen Louise Barr (Mrs. Thomas Howard), **56**: 585,n1

Birch, Thomas Howard, **56**: 585,n1; **58**: 111-12,n5

Bird, Andrew Reid, **66**: 121,n2

Birdsall, Paul, **56**: 499n3; **57**: 25n9

Birge, Edward Asahel, **61**: 329n3

Birkenhead, Frederick Edwin Smith, 1st Earl of, **64**: 382,n1; **68**: 447,n1, 484,n2; WW on, **68**: 448, 485

Birhenheim, Alexander, **53**: 179

Birkhoff, George David, **67**: 527n4

Birmingham, Ala., **59**: 287

Birmingham Age-Herald, **65**: 6; **68**: 107n1, 170

Birrell, Augustine, **67**: 105n3; **68**: 308

Birth of the German Republic, 1871-1918 (Rosenberg), **59**: 16n6

Bisbee, Arizona, **66**: 125

Bischoffsheim, Raphael-Louis, **60**: 251,n5

Bishop, Carl Whiting, **60**: 604,n1

Bishop, James Bucklin, **67**: 77n5

Bismarck, North Dakota: WW's arrival and activities in, **63**: 152-53; WW's address in, **63**: 153-62; photograph of WW in, *illustration section*, **63**

Bismarck Daily Tribune, **63**: 162n

Bismarck-Schonhausen, Prince Otto Eduard Leopold von, **54**: 252; **56**: 320, 495; **58**: 23, 124, 312; **60**: 123, 453; **61**: 81, 94-95; **65**: 415

Bissolati, Leonida (Bissolati-Bergamaschi), **53**: 433, 609-10, 637, 639, 711,n1; **54**: 135; WW's conference with on territorial settlements, **53**: 641-44

Bistriza, **59**: 559

Bitlis, Turkey, **65**: 74, 309, 321, 322

Bituminous Coal Commission, **64**: 145-46, 206-209, 246,n1; **65**: 559,n1, 560; **66**: 11, 27, 105-106; majority and minority reports of, **65**: 95,n1, 2; WW's statement on report and award of, **65**: 104-105; recommendation for I.C.C., **65**: 117; WW's statement on coal strike, **65**: 565-66

"Black Book" of the Inquiry, **60**: 34n2

Black Horror in the Occupied Region (*New Yorker Staats-Zeitung*), **65**: 341n1, 394-95

Black, Hugh, **59**: 247,n1, 254

Black Hundred (Russia), **59**: 195,n4

Black Jack: The Life and Times of John J. Pershing (Vandiver), **61**: 519n1

Black, Samuel Charles, **62**: 270n1

blacks: *see* Negroes

Black Sea, **60**: 282

Blaine, Anita Eugenie McCormick (Mrs. Emmons), **55**: 440, 484-85; **67**: 137n3; on WW Foundation awards, **67**: 545-47, 548-49

Blaine, Eleanor Gooding (Mrs. Emmons, Jr.), **55**: 440,n2

Blaine, Emmons, Jr., **55**: 440, n1, 484-85

Blaine, James Gillespie, **66**: 210,n4

Blair, Emily Jane Newell (Mrs. Harry Wallace), **68**: 33-34,n1; on Democratic women, **68**: 156-57; WW thanks for her efforts, **68**: 157

Blair, Frances Greenough (Mrs. Arthur Welland), **68**: 425,n1

Blair, James Molesworth, **62**: 90,n13

Blair, Max F., **67**: 182

Blair, Natalie Knowlton (Mrs. John Insley), **67**: 271n1

Blake, Robert, **57**: 6n7

Blakey, Gladys C., **55**: 334n1

Blakey, Roy G., **55**: 334n1

Blakiston, Herbert Edward Douglas, **53**: 162,n1

Blanco, Lucio, **66**: 445

Blanton, Thomas Lindsay, **62**: 138,n5

Blassingame, John W., **66**: 25n1

Bleuler, M., **64**: 525n1

Bliss, Eleanora Anderson (Mrs. Tasker Howard), **57**: 89; **58**: 320; **61**: 135; **68**: 228,n1

Bliss, Frederick Jones, **65**: 141,n1, 142

Bliss, Howard Sweetser, **55**: 81; **56**: 116, 323,n3; on Syrian situation, **54**: 551-52,n1; **55**: 86, 141-45, 472-73; **65**: 141; death of, **65**: 142,n1

Bliss, Robert Woods, **53**: 640,n3; **54**: 380; **56**: 396; **60**: 546,n9

Bliss, Tasker Howard, **53**: 327, 385, 410, 411,n1, 573, 646, 654, 695; **54**: 127, 255, 264, 386, 402, 403, 404, 427; **55**: 58, 112, 160, 179-80, 203, 234, 245; **56**: 124, 149, 153, 208, 235, 304, 330, 381, 396, 409; **57**: 35, 89, 104, 189, 332, 357, 365, 372,n2, 406, 526, 549; **58**: 57, 63n4, 111, 288, 307, 317, 379, 438, 441, 491, 514, 545, 580; **59**: 285, 313, 480-81, 546, 594; **60**: 17n1, 21-22, 264, 316, 530, 594, 602, 625; **61**: 33n2, 46, 105, 111, 115, 128, 135-36, 178, 196, 205, 332, 547, 587; **62**: 207, 404; **63**: 91, 537; **64**: 444, 472; **68**: 222-23,n1, 577; appointed peace commissioner, **53**: 183, 243; on Italy's misuse of U.S. troops, **53**: 208, 485-86; WW on, **53**: 320; **54**: 34; House on, **53**: 402; **57**: 178; on views from Paris, **53**: 609-11; concern over unpreparedness of American peace commissioners, **53**: 719-21; on League of Nations Covenant, **54**: 3, 4,n1, 84-88, 123; on Armistice terms, disarmament, and the Loucheur committee, **54**: 243, 246, 282, 499-500, 514-15, 522-25, 525, 538, 540; on France and Syria, **55**: 4; on sending U.S. troops to Russia, **55**: 28-29, 150, 188-92; on relationship between peace with Germany and the Russian situation, **55**: 214-15; **58**: 568; and W. S. Churchill's Russian initiative, **55**: 232; on proposed military and naval terms, **55**: 404-406, 511-14; and Bullitt mission to Russia, **55**: 540n1; **63**: 337n1; and peace terms, **56**: 4, 491; on issue of Odessa, and supplying Rumanian army, **56**: 305-307, 581-83; on Bolsheviks, **56**: 327-28; on Hungarian revolt, **56**: 379-81, 383-86; and courts-martial, **56**: 425; on armistice between Poles and Ukrinians, **56**: 468-69, 469; **58**: 101-102; on Foch's request regarding Haller's Army, **57**: 134-36, 178; opposes Smuts' military recommendations on Rumania and Hungary, **57**: 274-75; on the Polish-Ukrinian controversy, **57**: 415-16, 444, 451, 461-64, 628; on Luxembourg, **57**: 457-58, 458; on Allied troops in Archangel, **57**: 460-61, 560, 589, 628; on destroying U.S. surplus arms, **57**: 496-98; on WW's Adriatic statement, **57**: 559-60; **58**: 42; on control commissions in Germany, **58**: 95-96, 135; on invitation to Austria to come to Paris, **58**: 205; on Shantung controversy, **58**: 232-34, 270, 320, 327, 328; on Armistice and Article 46 of peace treaty, **58**: 248, 263-64, 267, 310-11, 313, 315; on supplying Rumanian army, **58**: 405-407; at Plenary Session with Germany, **58**: 503-505; on landing Greek troops at Smyrna, **59**: 22, 23, 24, 25; on continuing withdrawal of U.S. troops from France, **59**: 277-79; on the Rhineland, **59**: 280-81, 382-83, 591, 592; **60**: 61-63, 72, 77, 79, 237-39, 277, 364,n2; **64**: 156; on Foch, **59**: 371; **60**: 599; and talk of not signing peace treaty, **59**: 383; and Turkey and mandatory issue, **59**: 397; on military strength of armies of Austria and new states, **59**: 428-31, 432; on withdrawing troops from Archangel, **59**: 599-600,n6; **60**: 241; on Germany's counterproposals on military terms and League of Nations admission, **60**: 66, 235-37; on Hungarian attacks on Czechoslovakia and proposed occupation of Hungary, **60**: 255-56; WW answers on removal of troops from Archangel, **60**: 359; on stopping aid and supplies in areas of continuing conflict, **60**: 363; on Senate request to have spokesmen for Ireland heard at peace conference, **60**: 375; on Hungary, Rumania, Czechoslovakia border issue, **60**: 596; on demobilization and need for troops in Upper Silesia, **60**: 622; on strength of U.S. occupation force, **61**: 174-75; and Poincaré dinner invitation episode, **61**: 180; on U.S. railway troops aiding British in Russia, **61**: 225-26, 349; at Versailles signing ceremony, **61**: 324; on Kun's statement that Rumania has resumed hostilities, **61**: 339, 341; and Syria, **61**: 442; on no more U.S. troops for Europe, **61**: 485; and Shantung settlement, **62**: 150, 151, 164, 208, 630; and Adriatic question, **62**: 456; and Thrace, **62**: 510; on Turkish situation, **64**: 27; recommendation he stay in Paris to represent U.S. government, **64**: 117, 118; supports WW's veto of Knox peace resolution, **65**: 331; WW acknowledges support of, **65**: 343 and Washington Naval Conference, **67**: 309,n1; on disarmament, **67**: 391; on N. D. Baker, **68**: 133n1, 137; on WW and the Paris Peace Conference, **68**: 223-26; WW thanks for letter to Sullivan on Paris Peace Conference, **68**: 228; and WW Foundation, **68**: 249n2; visits Lloyd George, **68**: 455-56; photograph of, *illustration section*, **53**

Bliss, Peacemaker: The Life and Letters of General Tasker Howard Bliss (Palmer), **54**: 522n1

blockade: Council of Four on, **60**: 495-97, 498-500; WW on, **60**: 495, 499, 533, 534, 565, 621, 639; **61**: 244, 251, 418-19, 450,n1; issue of lifting, **61**: 151-52, 257,n3, 523-24, 526-27

Blockade Council: *see* Superior Blockade Council
Bloomhardt, Paul Frederick, **53**: 336,n1, 340
Blücher, Gebhard Leberecht von, Prince of Wahlstatt, **56**: 316, 321
Blue, Victor, **53**: 264,n1
Blue Eagle: From Egg to Earth (Johnson), **66**: 58n1
Blum, John Morton, **57**: 530n1; **63**: 601n1; **65**: 401n1
Blunt, Arthur Stanley Vaughn, **54**: 380n3
Blythe, Samuel George, **53**: 440-41,n1; **65**: 424,n1
B'nai B'rith, **53**: 239-40,n1, 259; **61**: 409n1, 617
Boardman, Mabel Thorpe, **66**: 542n1
Board of Railroad Wages and Working Conditions (Railroad Administration), **62**: 72, 76; **64**: 422
Bobbs-Merrill Company, **66**: 370-71,n1
Bobeng, William G., **62**: 434
Bocas del Toro, Panama, **67**: 382n5
Bochum, Germany, **54**: 530
Boeckel, Richard Martin, **67**: 616-18,n1
Bogen, Boris David, **59**: 411,n1, 412
Bogotá, Treaty of, **62**: 5,n6; **67**: 581n2
Bohemia: *see* Paris Peace Conference—Bohemia
Bohemian Brethren Evangelical Church of Přrelou , Czechoslovakia, **68**: 263n1
Böhm, Vilmos, **56**: 182,n1, 242n4; **58**: 486n3
Bok, Edward William, **55**: 253, 303; **67**: 535, 539, 586; **68**: 498; on WW speaking at Philadelphia Academy of Music, **66**: 31-32, 40; presents autographed autobiography to WW, **66**: 131-32,n1; WW thanks for book, **66**: 168; sends WW reproduction of Kipling's *If* and WW thanks, **66**: 352-53, 386, 456, 479; and lecture series in Philadelphia, **67**: 24n2, 72, 83-84; praises WW and WW thanks, **67**: 230; on U.S. becoming associate member of League of Nations and WW's reply, **68**: 169-70, 170, 172, 173; and American Peace Award, **68**: 452,n2
Bok Peace Prize (American Peace Award), **68**: 452,n2, 497
Bolam, Fred C., **62**: 121, 568-69, 570-73
Boldyrev, Vasilli Georgievich, **53**: 256,n2
Bolivia, **54**: 264; and Tacna-Arica dispute, **53**: 536,n1, 699; **58**: 330-31; **58**: 198; **65**: 190-191, 237, 245; issue of recognition, **66**: 135, 480-81; **67**: 92, 95; Gonzales on, **66**: 210n2, 211
Bolling, Annie Stuart Litchfield (Mrs. Rolfe E.), **68**: 471
Bolling, Bertha, sister of EBW, **53**: 397, 592,n1, 594,n10, 611-13; **54**: 306,n8; **65**: 348,n6, 349, 413; **68**: 256, 257, 277,n5
Bolling, John Randolph, brother of EBW, **53**: 612,n3; **54**: 304-306; **60**: 331; **66**: 92,n2, 189,n1, 216, 344,n1; **67**: 111, 174, 242n6, 243, 244, 265 270, 301n1, 321n1, 363, 368, 371, 373, 379, 381, 394n1, 427, 466-68, 579, 584; **68**: 68, 227, 236, 257, 280,n3, 286n1, 412, 413, 556, 569; and WW's Nobel Prize money, **67**: 52; answers WW's correspondence and is conduit, **67**: 131-32, 246-47, 250, 259, 276, 302, 306, 307-308, 323, 331, 336, 336-37, 340-41, 348-49, 357, 362, 374, 387, 407, 410, 411, 413, 419, 424, 425, 426-27, 441, 444, 454, 456, 459-61, 463-65, 466-68, 469, 469-70, 475, 478, 484, 490, 492, 501, 505-506, 508-509, 524, 534, 565, 571, 587, 604; **68**: 9-10, 11, 51, 52, 68n1, 102,n2, 107, 109, 134n1, 144, 155, 156, 157, 158, 162, 163, 168, 174, 179, 198, 212, 238, 291, 316, 317, 320, 321, 329, 349, 355, 357, 405, 407, 433, 454, 462-63, 501, 505, 517, 520, 525, 410, 531; on R. S. Baker and Creel's project, **67**: 249, 251; on WW's Jefferson Day message, **67**: 252; on WW Clubs, **67**: 259-60, 260, 263, 267, 271, 275, 288, 314-15, 318-19, 324, 326-28, 344-45, 352-54, 386, 415; on plans for WW's admission to Washington bar, **67**: 318; on WW's law office plans, **67**: 320-21, 325, 339, 342-43, 347-48; and WW Foundation, **67**: 348, 372, 399-400, 417-18; on WW not accepting Hearst offer, **67**: 364-65; on WW's delicate position regarding WW Clubs and WW Foundation, **67**: 425-26; and Armistice Day plans, **67**: 432, 442, 444; on digest of Paris Peace Conference, **67**: 456, 459-61; and WW's silence, **67**: 533; Morley on, **67**: 573; personal advice to Colby on various issues, **68**: 114-15; and WW's essay, **68**: 345, 347, 348, 369, 370, 371; on Foley's project, **68**: 350; and *Louisville Post*'s proposal for WW, **68**: 483; memorandum on WW's last illness, **68**: 548-50; Kerney on sheltering of WW by, **68**: 596
Bolling, Richard Wilmer, brother of EBW, **53**: 396,n1, 399, 500, 592; **54**: 305,n4; **65**: 67; **66**: 519n1, 534; **67**: 381,n1; **68**: 577,n6
Bolling, Rolfe E., **67**: 209; **68**: 471, 577,n6
Bolling, Sallie White (Mrs. William) Holcombe, mother of EBW, **53**: 499, 612-13; **65**: 348,n6, 413; **68**: 244, 470, 471, 577,n5; WW's toast to on 80th birthday, **68**: 266,n1
Bolling, William H.: WW on relatives and appointments, **61**: 482,n1
Bolshevik Propaganda: Hearings Before a Subcommittee of the Committee on the Judiciary, **55**: 297n2
Bolsheviks and Bolshevism, **53**: 228, 554, 568, 571, 627, 692 694; **54**: 7n3, 8, 9, 21, 22,n10, 83, 84, 132n1, 136-37, 181, 344, 349, 397,n1, 412; **55**: 105, 161, 180, 181, 182, 183, 189, 202, 213, 233, 297,n2, 338, 350, 403, 488, 494; **56**:

Bolsheviks and Bolshevism (*cont.*)
128, 132, 152, 180, 186, 253-54, 254-55, 290, 317n1, 320, 325, 326, 327, 327-29, 338, 339-40, 347, 409, 413, 425, 443, 512n1; **57**: 105, 192, 310, 311, 508, 509, 522, 550, 575; **59**: 14n3,4, 17, 31, 72,n2, 98, 120, 225, 234, 262, 432, 465, 518, 519,n2, 531, 566, 590, 600n2; **60**: 146-47, 484n1; **61**: 162-63, 165, 201, 202, 455, 494; **62**: 11, 34n1, 64, 82n2, 281, 323-24, 409-10, 499; **63**: 394, 588-89,n1; **64**: 133, 344, 443; **66**: 4-5,n2; **68**: 255; and Germany, **53**: 5, 121-22, 173, 194; **55**: 458n1, 493; **58**: 10, 11, 15, 16, 20, 168n1, 265, 344n4, 363, 403n14, 495n3, 506, 568, 569, 570, 576, 581; Bullitt on European movement of, **53**: 6-9; the Vatican on, **53**: 17-18; and *Labor Defender*, **53**: 20-21,n3; Lansing on WW making statement on, **53**: 151-53; Huntington on, **53**: 169-80; WW on, **53**: 351n2, 352, 355, 365, 574-75,n1; **54**: 245; **55**: 314, 319-20, 471; **56**: 127, 247, 285, 407; **63**: 73, 134, 214; **66**: 154-55, 308; and food situation, **53**: 453-54, 648, 650, 707, 709, 718; **58**: 42; Litvinov as peace negotiator and on Russian situation, **53**: 492-94,n1; Imperial War Cabinet discusses, **53**: 560-61; and Poland, **53**: 611,n1; **54**: 7n3, 33, 201, 336, 338-39, 343, 419; **56**: 50-51, 53; **57**: 278-79, 280, 462, 463; **58**: 326-27; WW on not making statement on, **53**: 709; and representation at Paris Peace Conference, **54**: 27,n2, 53-54, 99-103, 114-15; Lord memorandum on, **54**: 91-95; Noulens on, **54**: 155; British memorandum on, **54**: 173,n1; and Prinkipo Declaration, **54**: 182,n2, 183-88, 415-16; and situation in Archangel, **55**: 93n2; Bliss on, **55**: 214-15; **56**: 384, 385; Francis on, **55**: 235; and Hungary, **56**: 241, 331-34, 460, 461, 474-76; Lloyd George on, **56**: 261; **57**: 428n14, 459n2; Foch on, **56**: 314; Hoover on, **56**: 375-78; **61**: 61-62; Fontainbleau Memorandum, **56**: 266; American commissioners on rights of national minorities in, **56**: 511-12; frontiers discussed at Council of Four, **56**: 597-98; and reparations, **59**: 387, 538; and Czech troops in Siberia, **61**: 201, 202;, 287, 288; Clemenceau on, **56**: 478, 479; Lansing on, **56**: 488, 490; Hungarian Americans urge WW to stop spread of, **56**: 521; and proposed recognition of Lenin, **56**: 551,n1; House on, **57**: 35; Erzberger on, **57**: 75n6; and Baltic states, **57**: 138; **59**: 467n7, 547n2; Smuts on, **57**: 167, 172; and Egypt, **57**: 465, 466; and Italy, **57**: 539; **58**: 529; and Rumania, **58**: 137; Kerner on situation in Central Europe and, **58**: 157, 158, 160; Hoover on Baltic states and, **58**: 594-95; Kerenskii on, **59**: 152, 153, 155-56; reply to Nansen's proposal, **59**: 192-97, 256,

300,n8, 310-11; and Ukrainians, **59**: 216, 265, 323; Lenin on, **59**: 300n8; and Polish-Ukrainian situation, **59**: 351, 352-53, 356, 357; and Jews, **59**: 515; **60**: 39; Glass on foreign exchange and, **60**: 114; Kolchak on, **60**: 142, 144, 180-81; Tumulty's suggestions on, **60**: 150; and blockade issue, **60**: 281-82, 369, 499, 624-26, 636, 638; **62**: 108-10, 424; and Károlyi and Hungary, **60**: 352, 353; Kramář on, **60**: 355; German treatment of in Riga, **60**: 532; Stevens on need for Allied troops to relieve Czechs, **60**: 608, 609; Balfour on Galicia and, **61**: 167-68; Root on, **61**: 297n2; Hapgood on, **61**: 359-60; **66**: 343n2; issue of Allied trade with, **61**: 482-84; importance of U.S. retaining vessels at Archangel, **61**: 525-26, 604,n1; Pittman on, **61**: 626; issue of Allied trade with, **62**: 14; Graves on Siberian situation and, **62**: 84, 85-86; Poole memorandum on, **62**: 203-205, 441-48; Spargo on, **62**: 556, 558, 559; Lansing recommends withdrawal of U.S. troops from Siberia, **64**: 219-21; and Hapgood's resignation, **64**: 234,n1,3,4; Lloyd George on, **64**: 308-309; and Poland, **65**: 65n1, 527,n1; and Germany, **65**: 102; and Sisson documents, **65**: 134n2; and "Palmer raids," **65**: 187,n5; and Armenia, **65**: 287, 306, 323, 539, 549; and lifting of trade restrictions with Russia, **65**: 455-56, 492; and Japan's invasion of Sakahlin, **65**: 515,n1; and Polish-Soviet war, **66**: 16-17,n2, 87n1; U.S. note on nonrecognition of Bolshevik state, **66**: 19-24; and Bessarabia, **66**: 180,n3; and Crimea, **66**: 355,n1; and Armenia, **66**: 480; **67**: 63, 66; *see also* Russia

Bolshevism and the United States (Russell), **60**: 147n4

Bolshevism: The Enemy of Political and Industrial Democracy (Spargo), **66**: 482,n2

Bolzano: *see* Alto Adige

Bon, Ferdinand Jean-Jacques de: *see* De Bon, Ferdinand Jean-Jacques

Bonaparte, Napolean: *see* Napoleon I

Bonaparte, Roland-Napoleon, **58**: 562n1

Bonasi, Adeodate, **53**: 597n1

Bonar Law, Andrew: *see* Law, Andrew Bonar

Bones, Helen Woodrow, first cousin of WW, **53**: 212, 437; **59**: 526-27; **64**: 325; **67**: 536,n3; **68**: 367, 423,n7, 506,n1, 572, 577n10

Bones, James W., **67**: 536n1

Bones, Marion Woodrow (Mrs. James), maternal aunt of WW, **64**: 517,n1; **67**: 536n1

Bonillas, Ignacio, **61**: 527,n1; **64**: 120n1

Bonin, Count: *see* Longare, Count Lelio Bonin

Bonner, Robert Edwin, **65**: 572,n5

Bonomi, Ivanoe, **65**: 304,n13; **66**: 482,n2

Bonsal, Henrietta Fairfax Morris (Mrs. Stephen), **68**: 187,n3

Bonsal, Stephen, **56**: 517,n2; **58**: 521; **60**: 572; **68**: 227

Bonsor, William T., **63**: 303

Bonus March: An Episode in the History of the Great Depression (Daniels), **65**: 243n1

Bonzo, Theodore Valfre di, **53**: 7,n2

Booth, Edward, **53**: 524,n1

Booth, Evangline Cory, **65**: 288, 297, 317-18, 332; **66**: 542n1; **67**: 4, 11

Booth, Susie, **53**: 166, 204, 319, 344

Booth, William Bramwell, **54**: 406-407,n1, 430

Borah, William Edgar, **53**: 367, 469n1; **54**: 259n3; **58**: 244, 410n1, 635; **59**: 451n1, 524n1; **60**: 531; **65**: 42, 71n3, 212, 354n2; **67**: 26n7, 424n1; **68**: 87, 148n5, 306, 346n2, 504; and famine relief bill, **54**: 174n3, 229; **61**: 137, 372, 411, 417, 468, 506n1; **62**: 45, 67, 264, 311, 339-411, 430-31, 440, 504; **63**: 210, 223n1; **66**: 198n1, 340; opposition to League of Nations, **55**: 214, 225, 270; absent from dinner with WW, **55**: 267; and Irish question, **55**: 325-26; and alleged Wall Street peace treaty leak, **60**: 155, 242, 243, 244, 245, 288, 328,n1, 329, 379; and resolution on Ireland being heard at peace conference, **60**: 249,n2, 288-89, 375; on peace treaty, **61**: 626-27; and Senate resolution requesting information on Shantung settlement, **62**: 151,n1; questions WW at Foreign Relations Committee meeting, **62**: 350-51, 353-54, 360-61, 362, 363, 364, 366-67, 368, 376, 379, 382; and reservations, **63**: 296, 482-83; and Mexican situation, **64**: 120; and treaty fight, **64**: 200-201, 244, 328n2, 336, 338; on Grey's letter, **64**: 381,n1; Glass on, **64**: 387; greets WW on motor ride, **65**: 42; on League of Nations, **67**: 471,n1; praises WW and WW's response, **67**: 547,n1, 548; WW on, **68**: 251, 255; amendment to naval appropriation bill, **68**: 278,n1; and *Woodrow Wilson and World Settlement*, **68**: 282; photograph of, *illustration section*, **65**

Borchard, Edwin Montefiore, **65**: 238,n2

Bordeaux, France, **53**: 15

Borden, Sir Robert (Laird), **53**: 339, 567, 568; **54**: 44, 149, 254, 298, 326, 330, 358-59, 366, 366-67, 490,n2; **55**: 501-502,n1; **58**: 119, 121; **64**: 163; **67**: 105n3, 531n1; on League of Nations, **54**: 358-59; memorandum on Paris proceedings, issues, and solutions, **57**: 306-12; and Japan's racial equality resolution, **57**: 373; on duration of clauses, **58**: 114, 116, 117, 118; issue of labor clauses and the Dominions, **58**: 173, 188, 329, 361, 363, 415-18, 467, 468, 469, 481, 497,n3; on French security treaty, **58**: 493-94; on Plenary Session at Versailles and Brockdorff-Rantzau's speech, **58**: 517-20

Bording, Johannes Biorn, **67**: 18

Boret, Victor, **53**: 360,n2

Borgese, Guiseppe Antonio, **53**: 619n1

Borghese, Prince Luca Livio, **56**: 242,n1, 333, 413, 414, 458, 465, 476; on Hungary's desire to reopen negotiations with Allies, **56**: 275-79

Boris III of Saxe-Coburg-Gotha, **66**: 358,n3

Born a Jew (Bogen), **59**: 411n1

Borowy, Pierre, **56**: 442

Borsa, Mario, **59**: 551,n1, 552; **61**: 229,n2; **68**: 506, 514

Borsarelli de Refereddo, Marquis Luigi, **53**: 622,n1; **58**: 93,n1

Boryslaw (Borislaw, Poland), **59**: 597, 598, 599

Bosio, Alice Schiavoni, **57**: 218,n1, 219

Bosnia, **61**: 54; **63**: 372; **64**: 368,n1

Bosnia, S.M.S., **55**: 432

Bosporus, The (straits), **59**: 137, 146, 225, 340; **62**: 552

Boss Kettering (Leslie), **63**: 441n2

Boston, Mass., **55**: 36; **66**: 306; suggested as WW's port of entry, **53**: 581, 626; WW's sailing for and arrival in, **55**: 185, 193-94, 197, 205-206, 218, 218-19, 225, 226, 229, 235-37; WW on retirement and, **55**: 482; Balfour on, **60**: 204; police strike, **63**: 167,n6,7, 265, 267, 302; WW learns of police strike and comments on, **63**: 169, 196, 211, 216; and WW Foundation, **67**: 526-27

"Boston Police Strike of 1919" (Lyons), **63**: 167n6

Boston City Club, **53**: 82n1

Boston Daily Globe, **62**: 626; **65**: 6; **66**: 267n1

Boston Evening Transcript, **53**: 82,n1; **68**: 281

Boston Herald, **55**: 450; **66**: 306

Boston Post, **53**: 82,n2; **62**: 627; **67**: 488

Boston Publishing Company, **55**: 450n2

Botha, Louis, **54**: 149, 252,n3, 253, 296-98, 351n3, 364-66, 377, 417, 419; **59**: 201, 216, 255-56, 287, 323, 324, 325, 627; **60**: 23; **61**: 304; Seymour on, **54**: 383, 384; **58**: 440, 505; and Polish-Ukrainian situation, **59**: 353, 354, 354-55, 355-56, 357, 531; WW on, **63**: 286, 287, 477, 505

Bottomley, Horatio William, **57**: 243,n1

Boué, Amie, **64**: 160,n4

Bouisson, Ferdinand-Emile-Honoré, **53**: 326,n5; **58**: 492,n1

Bourgeois, Léon, **53**: 485, 489; **54**: 151, 188-89, 198, 269-70, 494; **55**: 41, 178n2, 195, 196; **56**: 3, 102, 178; **57**: 285; **58**: 188, 416; **60**: 215, 260, 261; **66**: 212n1; and League of Nations, **54**: 218, 264, 426,n1, 460, 461, 463, 473, 481, 483, 484, 489, 496, 497, 509, 510, 511, 511-12, 522n1, 546, 547; Cecil and

Bourgeois, Léon (*cont.*)
House on, **54**: 387; and League of Nations Commission, **55**: 5, 6, 43, 45, 46, 68, 69, 70, 72-75, 76-77, 79, 80, 120, 123, 124, 126, 155, 156; **56**: 164, 170n1, 175, 175-76, 176, 177, 178, 223-24, 225, 226, 228, 231, 302; **57**: 220, 224, 225, 226, 230, 236, 249, 252, 253, 254, 256, 257, 258, 259, 262, 265, 266; time wasted by, **56**: 165, 206, 440; **58**: 176-77,n2, 186, 187, 214; House on, **57**: 237; and Germany's membership in League of Nations, **60**: 273, 275, 292, 296, 439; and Nobel Peace Prize, **66**: 477, 517
Bourne, Francis Cardinal, **56**: 258,n1
Bowen, William Miller, **63**: 423n2
Bowerman, Charles William, **54**: 257,n2
Bowers, Claude Gerrade, **65**: 520n1; **68**: 260, 267
Bowman, Cora Olive Goldthwait (Mrs. Isaiah), **59**: 158,n1
Bowman, Frank, **66**: 132
Bowman, Isaiah, **53**: 350,n1, 353-56, 356, 378; **54**: 382, 383; **56**: 221, 351n1, 396, 424, 434; **57**: 415; **59**: 158; **62**: 551; on Adriatic question, **57**: 270, 432, 456; **64**: 178,n4, 458,n3; **65**: 111, 116, 140, 502; on Britain's oil interests in Persia, **62**: 452-43; on House's distorted negotiations, **62**: 453, 454-55; book by, **67**: 404-405,n1, 412-13; photograph of, *illustration section*, **57**
Bowman, John Gabbert, **67**: 361,n6
Bowman Gray School of Medicine, **56**: 556n1; **64**: 507n11
Boxer Rebellion, **63**: 329; **64**: 491; Lansing on, **60**: 603-604
Boyana River, **63**: 210; **64**: 177
Boyd, David French, **63**: 557n2
Boyd, Francis Darby, **58**: 638
Boyd, James Edmund, **58**: 605n2
Boyd, Kate, **55**: 266; **67**: 458, 471
Boyden, Roland William: and International Financial Conference, recommended for Reparation Commission, **65**: 92-93, 147, 148; as unofficial representative, **65**: 245n2, 477, n1; **66**: 101n1, 472
Boyer, F. A., **68**: 110-11,n1, 141
Boyer, Francis, **56**: 525
Boyer, Lucien, **57**: 533n4
Boylan Bernard L., **65**: 355n1, 576n1
Boyle, Algernon Douglas Edward Harry, **60**: 613,n1
Boyle, Emmet Derby, **63**: 53, 54, 428,n1
Boyne, Battle of the, **61**: 512n2
Boynton, Charles Homer, **65**: 183,n3, 184
Boy Scouts of America, **59**: 605-606; **66**: 282n1
Bozen (now Bolzano), The Tyrol, **59**: 400
Brabançonne, La, **61**: 13, 14n10
Bradfute, Oscar Edwin, **62**: 300n1; appointed to first Industrial Conference, **63**: 300, n1
Bradley, Rolland Barr, **66**: 262,n1

Brady, Cyrus Townsend: on story about WW and Cleveland, **62**: 479-80,n1, 526
Brady, James Buchanan ("Diamond Jim"), **63**: 579,n2
Brady, John J., **54**: 473,n1
Bragg, Edward S., **65**: 476
Braeman, John, **68**: 44n2
Brahany, Thomas W., **63**: 302,n2, 524, 532; **65**: 393,n1
Brainard, Clinton Tyler, **55**: 341,n1, 484; **67**: 242, 249, 256, 363, 364, 488; **68**: 354
Brainerd, Chauncy Corey, **54**: 106,n3
Braisted, William Clarence, **57**: 333,n4; **60**: 569,n2, 573
Braisted, William Reynolds, **62**: 460n1; **65**: 284n1
Brambilla, Guiseppe, **66**: 364,n1, 447-48,n1
Brand, Charles Hillyer, **53**: 149,n1, 163
Brand, Katherine E., **67**: 453n1
Brand, Robert Henry, **56**: 435,n3
Brandegee, Frank Bosworth, **54**: 408n1; **55**: 270, 275, 388n1; **59**: 524n1; **61**: 372; **62**: 67,n1, 339-411; **63**: 445, 484; **66**: 141n1; **68**: 185,n1, 247; on copies of peace treaty, **60**: 330; questions WW at Foreign Relations Committee meeting, **62**: 378, 380, 383-88, 390-404, 405-406; and Bullitt testimony, **63**: 337n1; and Mexican situation, **64**: 120n1, 152n2; and treaty fight, **64**: 200-201, 328n2, 336, 338; on WW's Hitchcock letter refusing compromise on reservations, **65**: 71n3; and Armenian mandate, **65**: 351n2
Brandeis, Alice Goldmark (Mrs. Louis Dembitz), **64**: 359; **68**: 277,n1, 315
Brandeis, Louis Dembitz, **53**: 46-47, 55, 185; **59**: 314; **60**: 284, 285, 568; **61**: 178; **62**: 427; **65**: 228, 248; **67**: 330, 339-40, 387-88, 389, 446, 477, 560; **68**: 127; on WW's health, **58**: 612-13; and Rev. Matthews, **62**: 456, 574; and second Industrial Conference appointment, **63**: 609, 618; on railroad situation, **64**: 222; on prohibition, **64**: 262; concern for Balfour Declaration, **64**: 358, 361; R. S. Baker meets with, **64**: 359; and Supreme Court, **66**: 392; WW involves in writing The Document, **67**: 319-20,n1, 443, 472, 475, 499, 506, 506-507, 558-59, 563, 579, 581, 582, 588, 594-97; **68**: 4n1, 4-5, 10, 13, 19, 26-27, 534; on Truax and Duplex cases, **67**: 497,n1,2, 498; on Lemke case, **67**: 563,n2; on woman suffrage, **67**: 563,n1; Clarke on, **68**: 130-32,n8, on Pennsylvania mining case, **68**: 277; on "What Is Progress" reference, **68**: 277, 279, 280; and evolution of prohibition statement for The Document, **68**: 305, 315, 316, 334-36, 336, 337, 338, 385
Brandes, Georg, **55**: 370
Branstetter, Otto, **65**: 550,n1

Branting, Karl Hjalmar, **64**: 342; **65**: 40,n2
Bratenahl, George Carl Fitch, **68**: 581,n3
Brătianu, Mme., **57**: 218
Brătianu, Constantin, **54**: 287, 421,n6
Brătianu, Ion I. C., **54**: 421,n6,7; **55** 35, 376; **56**: 254, 305, 581,n3; **57**: 136-37,n1, 192,n3, 427,n9; **58**: 149, 591-92,n1; **59**: 562, 625,n1, 629-30, 635, 648; **60**: 133, 221, 222,n4, 314, 316, 335, 344; **62**: 123n1; **66**: 192, 196; on Austrian treaty and minority rights, **60**: 97,n8, 233-34,n4; at Council of Four on arms limitation, **60**: 170-71; threat of resignation, **60**: 222, 262; on Rumanian-Hungarian border issue, **60**: 351-53, 354, 355, 356, 357, 418,n6, 427, 428, 462, 470, 478; photograph of, *illustration section*, **57**
Bratton, Theodore DuBose, **62**: 106-108,n2, 292, 293, 505-506
Brazil, **53**: 342; **54**: 264; **55**: 154, 164, 184; **57**: 258; **58**: 113, 402n12, 472; **61**: 65; **63**: 232; **65**: 302; and representation at Paris Peace Conference, **54**: 13, 17, 45-46, 65; and League of Nations, **54**: 263, 462, 463; **58**: 198, 199, 201; and retention of seized ships, **58**: 37, 38, 114, 527, 558; debt of, **58**: 565; and shipping, **59**: 390; WW on Pessoa as new president of, **59**: 520-22; and reparations and German tonnage, **60**: 339, 340, 345; invited to first meeting of Council of League of Nations, **64**: 272; and Germany, **65**: 102; and Tacna-Arica dispute, **65**: 191, 195; visit of President of, **65**: 318,n1; and recognition of Mexico, **65**: 463; and recognition of Bolivia, **66**: 135, 480; Gonzales on, **66**: 212; Orlando visits, **66**: 323; on U.S. in Dominican Republic, **66**: 360; Colby to visit, **66**: 430,n1, 431; and Armenian situation, **66**: 457, 480
Breitenstein, Joseph C., **67**: 101
Bremen, Germany, **53**: 8; **56**: 90n4; **60**: 606
Bremerhaven, Germany, **60**: 606
Brennan, George E., **66**: 90,n1; **67**: 312,n1,2, 325, 356, 447,n3; **68**: 496,n1; meets with WW on 1924 campaign, **68**: 425-26
Brenner Pass: WW on, **59**: 574-75
Brent, Charles Henry, **54**: 5n2, 6; **57**: 284, 371; **66**: 503,n2
Brentano's of Washington, **67**: 373, 379
Breslau, Archbishop of (Adolf Cardinal Bertram), **60**: 158,n4, 413,n4, 424
Breslau, Archbishop of (Georg Cardinal Kopp), (1887-1914), **60**: 190,n1
Brest, France, **53**: 229, 240, 292, 346; WW's arrival and remarks in, **53**: 378, 380-81, 396-97; U.S. military camps at, **55**: 64-65, 149, 151; as port of departure and entry for WW, **55**: 160, 197, 487-88
Brest-Litovsk, Treaty of, **53**: 38, 173, 293;

56: 267, 356n1; **58**: 70, 342, 343-44, 390, 403, 425n2, 466; **59**: 491, 492, 584; **61**: 177n2; **66**: 166n1
Brewing and Liquor Interests and German Propaganda: Hearings Before a Subcommittee of the Committee on the Judiciary, Sixty-fifth Congress, Second Session, **54**: 397n1,2; **55**: 297n2
brewing industry, **53**: 443-44, 450; **54**: 58-59, 216, 227; WW signs proclamation permitting non-alcoholic beverages, **54**: 262; and German propaganda in U.S., **54**: 397,n1,2; **55**: 297n2
Brewster, Reginald R., **68**: 153,n1, 166n1
Brewster, Thomas T., **63**: 56,n5; **66**: 27,n1
Briand, Aristide, **53**: 143, 481-82; **58**: 18; **67**: 447, 449
Bridgeport, Conn: and WW Foundation, **67**: 553n1
Bridges, Robert, **59**: 604-605; **65**: 258,n2; **67**: 105n3, 277, 300, 302-303, 573n1, 578; **68**: 137; greetings from WW's Princeton class, **60**: 610
Bridge to France (Hurley), **58**: 202n1
Brief Statement on the Armenian National Claims (Nubar), **54**: 516n1
Briggs, William Harlow, **67**: 127n1
Bright, John, **66**: 536
Bright, John Irwin, **65**: 572,n12
Brighton, H.M.S., **53**: 508, 509, 569
Brigode, Jame, **57**: 218,n1
Brinkley, George A., **54**: 372n7
Brisbane, Arthur, **60**: 568,n2
Brisson, Commodore, **61**: 163,n16
Bristol, Mark Lambert, **55**: 485,n1; **58**: 409; **59**: 66-67,n1, 225n2, 574; **65**: 537,n4, 538, 539-40, 548, 549; **68**: 147n3; on Greek occupation of Smyrna, **59**: 252, 473, 596, 640,n1, 641-42,n1; on clashes between Greece and Turkey, **60**: 193, 276-77; appointed to Interallied Commission of Inquiry, **61**: 630n4; advises evacuation of Crimea, **66**: 355; and protocol regarding King Constantine, **67**: 9,n1
Britain: see Great Britain
Britain and the 'Great Betrayal': Anglo-American Relations and the Struggle for United States Ratification of the Treaty of Versailles, 1919-1920 (Egerton), **62**: 254n2
Britain and the Russian Civil War: November 1918-February 1920 (Ullman), **57**: 459n2; **63**: 588n1
Britain Between the Wars, 1918-1940 (Mowat), **53**: 519n1; **68**: 593n10
Britain's Fleet a Shield of World's Liberties (Bell), **54**: 159,n1
British and Foreign Anti-Slavery Society, **61**: 276n4
British and North Atlantic Steam Navigation Company, **53**: 111
British Embassy Church, Paris, **54**: 380n3
British Favor Lenine (Brown), **56**: 551n1

British Institute of International Affairs,
60: 17n1
British Plans Revealed to the President
. . . (Seibold), 53: 542n1
British Railway Mission in Siberia, 54:
83n3
British Red Cross, 54: 515, 549
Britt, Bessie (Mrs. L. R.), 67: 565,n1
Britt, James Jefferson, 55: 367,n1
Brixen (now Bressanone), The Tyrol, 59:
400
*Broadening Church: a study of theologi-
cal issues in the presbyterian church
since 1869* (Loetscher), 68: 519n1
Broch-Jahansen, Alison, 54: 33n6; 56:
49n10
Brockdorff-Rantzau, Ulrich Karl Christian, Count von, 55: 55,n5; 56: 318; 57:
552, 523, 526, 590; 58: 19,n7, 20, 169,
248, 255, 311, 312, 313, 399, 518; 59:
6n2, 84, 136, 157, 214, 223, 237, 257,
286, 362, 434n5, 577, 627; 60: 4n1,
124, 334, 462, 574-75; on peace terms
and signing treaty, 58: 45-46, 61-62,
307, 310, 314; 59: 12n5; remarks at
Plenary Session, 58: 514-17; various
comments on address at Versailles and
his remaining seated, 58: 502-503,
519-20, 521, 529, 529-30, 534, 572-73;
Council of Four agrees not to reply to
speech of, 58: 536-37, 545; and labor
clauses, 59: 47, 48,n2,3, 132,n5,
421,n3; on prisoners of war, 59: 56-57,
131-32, 134-35, 162-63, 304,n12, 379;
Council of Four on reparations and, 59:
271-72, 370-71; on responsibility and
reparations, 59: 274, 298, 488-92; on
economic effect on Germany of peace
terms, and Council of Four's reply, 59:
305-307, 307-309, 379; on request for
time extension to examine treaty, 59:
322,n2, 324; on private property provision in peace treaty, 59: 420-21,n2;
Council of Four's revised reply to, 59:
455, 458-60; on draft of peace treaty,
59: 579-84; on oral discussions of peace
treaty, 59: 583; compared to Renner,
60: 19; on counterproposals and
whether Germany will sign peace
treaty, 60: 179; photograph of, *illustration section*, 58
Brodie, Donald Melrose, 62: 607n1
Brody, David, 63: 30n1
Broening, William Frederick, 59: 38,n2
Brookings, Robert Somers, 54: 52; 55:
329; 66: 246n2; 68: 269,n1; on steel industry and prices, 53: 168, 205; on resignation of War Industries Board's
price-fixing committee, 53: 314-14; appointed to first Industrial Conference,
63: 300,n1; and copper price fixing, 67:
177
Brookings Institution, 68: 269n1
Brooklyn Army Base, 66: 425, 426
Brooklyn Daily Eagle, 54: 106n3; 62:
626n1; 65: 6

Brooks, Arthur, 53: 166, 204, 319, 344,
569,n1; 61: 231,n2; 66: 379n1; 67: 103,
209, 212; WW's letter of recommendation, 67: 273
Brooks, Aubrey Lee, 65: 467,n3
Brook-Shepherd, Gordon, 59: 561n8
Brotherhood of Blacksmiths and Help-
ers, 62: 121; 64: 424
Brotherhood of Boilermakers, 62: 122;
64: 424
Brotherhood of Electrical Workers, 63:
29n2
Brotherhood of Locomotive Engineers,
62: 31, 135, 140, 198n2, 572; 64: 431
Brotherhood of Locomotive Firemen, 61:
536; 62: 74, 140, 198n2; 64: 198n2, 431
Brotherhood of Maintenance of Way Em-
ployees and Railway Shop Laborers,
64: 426
Brotherhood of Painters, Decorators, and
Paper Hangers of Hoboken, N.J., 62:
561,n1
Brotherhood of Railway and Steamship
Clerks, Freight Handlers, Express and
Station Employes, 62: 74, 135, 140; 64:
431
Brotherhood of Railway Carmen of
America, 62: 122, 570, 573; 64: 431
Brotherhood of Railway Clerks, 64: 425
Brotherhood of Railway Conductors, 62:
198n2; 64: 198n2
Brotherhood of Railway Signalmen of
America, 64: 425, 431
Brotherhood of Railway Trainmen, 59:
203,n1; 61: 536; 62: 74, 76, 140, 198n2,
572; 64: 431
Brougham, Herbert Bruce, 53: 406-407,
412; 62: 526-27; on Plumb plan, 62:
481-82,n1
Broussa: *see* Brusa
Broussard, Robert Foligny: successor to,
53: 23n1
Brower, Jessie Woodrow Bones (Mrs.
Abraham Thew H.), first cousin of
WW, 53: 707,n1, 708; 67: 536,n1
Brown, Arthur, 66: 379n1
Brown, Arthur Judson, 53: 206n2; 65:
183,n3; 66: 275,n9, 276
Brown, Arthur Whitten, 57: 447n1
Brown, Curtis, 66: 121,n1
Brown, Edward Thomas, 68: 564, 576
Brown, Elmer Ellsworth, 68: 548
Brown, George Rothwell, 56: 551n1
Brown, George Stewart, 65: 564n2
Brown, Harry, 54: 473,n1
Brown, James Wright, 62: 607n1
Brown, Jo Baily, 58: 120,n3
Brown, John G., 62: 300n1
Brown L. Ames, 65: 491,n2
Brown, Marjorie, 66: 267n2; wedding in-
vitation to WW, 66: 503; WW sends re-
grets and wedding congratulations, 66:
505-506,n1; wedding of, 66: 506n1
Brown, Mary Celestine Mitchell (Mrs.
Edward Thomas), 66: 266,n2; 68: 556,
564, 576

Brown, Philip Marshall, **57**: 367,n1; **59**: 256, 368; on Hungarian situation, **59**: 239-40

Brown, William Cornelius, **63**: 268,n1

Brown Brothers & Co., **66**: 501

Brown University, **66**: 467; **68**: 159, 388n1

Browne, Arthur, **66**: 519n1

Browning, Sir Montague (Edward), **55**: 203,n3

Browning, Robert, **66**: 267n3, 439,n1; **67**: 173; **68**: 583

Browning, William Stacy, **56**: 305,n1, 307, 385

Brownlow, Louis, **68**: 471; and police situation in Washington, D.C., **63**: 150,n1, 264-65, 295, 302

Bruce, William Cabell, **68**: 94n3, 190,n2; WW on, **68**: 134-35,n1

Bruere (Brewer), Joseph Holmes, **65**: 572,n1

Brum, Baltasar, **59**: 186,n5; **66**: 179,n4, 431n3

Brun, Constantin, **60**: 284,n3

Brunett, Paul, **67**: 150,n1

Brunschvieg, Cecile Kahn (Mrs. Leon), **57**: 218,n1

Brusa (Brussa), Turkey, **59**: 212, 225, 327, 335, 337, 345, 396

Brussels, Belgium, **53**: 552; **54**: 497, 550; **55**: 326, 349; **56**: 589; **61**: 15; discussed as seat of League of Nations, **56**: 173-74, 178; **57**: 194, 222-26, 237; WW hopes to visit, **60**: 360, 573, 581; WW visits, **61**: 7; WW's remarks at City Hall in, **61**: 23-24; WW's remarks at dinner in the Royal Palace, **61**: 25-26; R. S. Baker on tour of, **61**: 29; as site for League of Nations Assembly meeting, **65**: 389, 434, 500, 501, 504; **66**: 50; and International Financial Conference, **65**: 239, 240, 241; **66**: 101n1; proposed reparations conference at, **66**: 471

Brussels Act (1890), **61**: 266, 454

Brussels Agreement, **56**: 498n4, 523n1

Brussels *La Libre Belgique*, **61**: 4n3, 5n5, 16n1, 21n1, 22n1, 25n1,2, 35n1

Brussels *La Nation Belge*, **61**: 16n1

Brussels *L'Etoile Belge*, **54**: 550n1

Brussels *Le Peuple*, **61**: 11n2

Brussels *Le Soir*, **61**: 11n2

Brussels *Le XX Siécle*, **61**: 5n6, 11n2, 22n1

Brussels *L'Indépendance Belge*, **61**: 16n1

Bryan, Elizabeth Baird (Mrs. William Jennings), **68**: 407,n1

Bryan, J. Franklin, **66**: 348n1, 356

Bryan, Jonathan, **65**: 557,n1

Bryan, William Jennings, **53**: 150, 161; **54**: 429; **55**: 65; **57**: 50; **58**: 171; **61**: 469; **65**: 76; **64**: 261,n1; **66**: 333n1, 542n1; **67**: 292; recommended as peace commissioner, **53**: 73; WW on, **53**: 98, 141; **56**: 87-88; **66**: 155; on Armenia, **56**: 95, 96; on League of Nations, **56**: 346,n1; "cooling off treaties," **57**: 250n1; **63**:

66,n7, 67; Lansing compares WW's treaty position to, **64**: 267, 269; Cobb on treaty position of, **64**: 270n2; WW on party leadership and, **65**: 123, 346, 488; and Secretary of State offer, **65**: 242; code name, **65**: 350; and Democratic National Convention, 1920, **65**: 471, 480, 490,n1, 494, 497; votes received in *Literary Digest* poll, **65**: 474n2; Cox on, **65**: 495; on "dry" plank, **65**: 511n3; and Treaty of Berlin, 1921, **67**: 422,n2; and teaching of evolution, **67**: 536n2, 537; **68**: 390,n1; on WW's essay, **68**: 407; Gonzales on, **68**: 475

Bryan Supports League of Nations. Suggests Amendments (*New York Times*), **56**: 346n1

"Bryan-Wilson Split on Treaty" (*Literary Digest*), **64**: 270n2

Bryan treaty, **65**: 255

Bryant, Louise, **55**: 297n2

Bryce, Elizabeth Marion Ashton, Lady, **53**: 594,n8; WW's condolences to, **67**: 538-39,n1; thanks WW for sympathy, **67**: 556-57

Bryce, James, Viscount, **53**: 335, 411-12, 484, 527, 530n1, 644-45; **54**: 104, 176-77; **55**: 338, 379; **56**: 36; **59**: 244; on boundaries for the Tyrol, **58**: 138, 139; suggests demonstration in House of Lords for League of Nations, **59**: 397, 398-99, 444; on establishing commissions on principles of nationality and self-determination of small countries, **59**: 399-401; N. H. Davis discusses treaty and peace conference with, **67**: 375-78; death of, **67**: 538-39,n1, 556-57

Bryn, Kelmer Halvorsen, **55**: 357,n1

Bryn Mawr College, **64**: 485; **68**: 123; and endowment campaign request of WW, **65**: 79, 83, 359

Buccari, Croatia (now Bakar, Yugoslavia), **53**: 445; **58**: 393,n4, 452; **59**: 86, 95, 97, 261, 329, 339; **60**: 212

Buchanan, Benjamin Franklin, **62**: 462,n1

Buchanan, James, **64**: 32

Bucharest, Rumania, **53**: 57

Bucharest, Treaty of (1913), **61**: 566,n3

Bucharest, Treaty of (August 17, 1916), **53**: 38, 293; **56**: 380,n2; 487,n1; **59**: 584; **60**: 530,n1

Bucharest, Treaty of (May 7, 1918), **56**: 267, 356n1

Buckey, Mervyn Chando, **54**: 258,n3, 259; **56**: 64,n1

Buckingham Palace: WW invited to, **53**: 85, 488, 491, 501; receptions, speeches, and meetings at during WW's stay, **53**: 510-12, 521-22, 522-24, 525, 546, 569, 592, 593; Grayson describes dining hall in, **53**: 521

Buckler, William Hepburn, **53**: 588,n1; **54**: 54; **58**: 410; **59**: 194n2; **60**: 492; **61**: 566n1; **62**: 157,n9; on Litvinov interview, **54**: 135-38, 180, 349

Buckley, William Frank, **62**: 155n1
Bucovina, Rumania: *see* Bukovina
Bucquet, Maurice, **57**: 426,n4
Budapest, Hungary, **54**: 184; **56**: 474; **57**:
    168, 367-68; **58**: 264; **60**: 52, 353; and
    Hungarian revolution, **56**: 239, 278,
    326-27; Council of Four on conditions
    in, **59**: 256-57; and Rumania, **59**:
    631,n2; **62**: 123,n1, 167-68,n1, 235n1,
    265-66
Budget, Bureau of the, **67**: 124n1
Budget bill, **65**: 358, 361-63; **66**: 456, 486
Budrum (Bodrum), Turkey, **59**: 55, 226,
    267, 268, 269
Budziszewski, Cora, **63**: 250,n2
Buena Vista, California: and oil reserves
    in, **61**: 534n1
Buenos Aires, **67**: 23,n1
Buenos Aires *La Nacion*, **65**: 530,n1
Buero, Juan Antonio, **58**: 187,n1; **59**: 186
Buffalo, N.Y., **59**: 287; war chest funds
    in, **67**: 88
Buffum, Douglas Labaree, **67**: 182
Bugbee, Newton Albert Kendall, **63**:
    615,n1
Bug River, **61**: 273
Bukharin, Nikolai Ivanovich, **62**: 204,n1,2
Bukovina, **54**: 421; **59**: 566; **60**: 134,n7
*Bulgaren in ihren historischen, ethnogra-
    phischen und politischen Grenzen*, **64**:
    160,n3
Bulgaria, **53**: 56, 293, 294, 296; **55**: 111,
    211; **56**: 5, 207, 613; **57**: 112, 137, 192;
    58: 42, 397, 435, 436, 437, 461n1; **59**:
    93, 102, 103, 166, 167, 205n13, 391,
    467-68; **60**: 133, 548, 582,n5; **61**: 136,
    494; **62**: 531; **67**: 461n1; **68**: 62; and
    food crisis, **53**: 15-16, 649; and League
    of Nations, **54**: 170; and famine relief
    bill, **54**: 174n2, 303; Keynes on eco-
    nomic rehabilitation plan, **58**: 13; and
    peace treaty, **58**: 583; **59**: 380; Bryce
    on, **59**: 400,n1; and Thrace, **62**: 141,
    207, 265, 266, 320, 327-28, 416-17,
    551-53; **63**: 61, 121, 122, 151,n4, 236,
    305; and Bessarabia and Rumania, **62**:
    206-207; and Rumania, **62**: 265, 266;
    war costs, **63**: 221, 243, 349; Lansing
    on proper U.S. role toward, **64**: 68;
    Vénisélos on, **64**: 159-64; and appoint-
    ments, **64**: 205; and Turkish treaty, **65**:
    111-12, 113; and International Finan-
    cial Conference, **66**: 101n1; Colby's
    suggestion for minister to, **66**: 358;
    WW on, **66**: 367; *see also* Paris Peace
    Conference
Bullard, Arthur, **68**: 495; wishes to verify
    French documents on Allied interven-
    tion in Russia, **65**: 143-45
Bullard, Robert Lee, **63**: 362,n1
Bullard, William Hannum Grubb, **53**:
    208,n1; **59**: 97,n2; suggested as mem-
    ber of International Communications
    Conference, **66**: 57,n1, 59
Bulletin de Jour. La Question de Fiume
    (*Le Temps*), **58**: 383,n4
Bulletin de Jour. Les Revendications de
    l'Italie (*Le Temps*), **58**: 393n4
Bullitt, William Christian, **53**: 160, 193,
    356, 366-67, 368; **54**: 91, 138; **56**: 183,
    279-80, 338, 466n1, 46n1, 473; **57**:
    93n1, 503n2, 508-509, **64**: 417; **65**:
    22,n3; on Bolskevik movement in Eu-
    rope, **53**: 6-9, 121-22; on WW's meeting
    with The Inquiry, **53**: 350-52; on with-
    drawing U.S. troops from Archangel,
    54: 348-49; and League of Nations Cov-
    enant, **55**: 67,n2; mission to and report
    on Russia, **55**: 540-45,n1; **56**: 387-91,
    425, 551, 551n1; **59**: 194,n2; **61**:
    478,n1, 509,n1; on Lloyd George's com-
    ments on Russian mission of, **57**: 459-
    60,n2,3; resignation of, **59**: 232-33,
    314, 447; R. S. Baker on, **59**: 287; testi-
    mony before Foreign Relations Com-
    mittee impeaches Lansing's loyalty to
    WW and Lansing's explanation to WW,
    63: 337-38,n1; Lansing on statement
    on treaty, **63**: 541; photograph of, *illus-
    tration section*, **55**
Bullitt Mission to Russia (Bullitt), **56**:
    466n1
*Bullitt Mission to Russia: Testimony be-
    fore the Committee on Foreign Rela-
    tions, United States Senate, of William
    C. Bullitt*, **55**: 540n1; **57**: 459n3; **63**:
    337n1
Bullock, Seth, **65**: 412
Bülow, Bernhard Heinrich Martin Karl,
    Prince von, **54**: 340,n5, 341; **56**: 89; **60**:
    188,n4
Bulwer, Sir Henry (William Henry
    Lytton Earle), **62**: 37
Bun, Ned, **54**: 414,n2
Bunkley, Sally Shelby Williams (Mrs.
    Joel William), **61**: 410,n1
Bunselmayer, Robert E., **56**: 285n1
Burch, Isaac N., **57**: 176n1
Bureau of Education, **55**: 285
Bureau of Fisheries, **62**: 129n2
Bureau of Immigration, **60**: 433
Bureau of Investigation (Department of
    Justice), **60**: 115,n7
Bureau of Mines, **53**: 131
Bureau of War Risk Insurance: *see* War
    Risk Insurance Bureau
Burgess, Ward: appointed to first Indus-
    trial Conference, **63**: 300,n1
Burke, Edmund, **53**: 355; **62**: 637; **67**:
    556, 561, 585; **68**: 541
Burleigh, George William, **65**: 572,n13
Burleson, Albert Sidney, **53**: 24, 28, 55,
    65, 214; **54**: 521; **55**: 327, 330n2; **56**:
    345, 618; **57**: 233, 376, 381, 387; **58**:
    145; **59**: 121, 121-22, 122; **60**: 248; **61**:
    364, 492; **62**: 94, 461; **63**: 585; **64**: 274;
    65: 24, 187, 298, 382; **66**: 341-42; **67**:
    109, 196; on control of cable system,
    53: 148,n1; **58**: 106, 145, 146, 176, 215,
    243, 365; **66**: 484; on ownership of tele-
    phone and telegraph systems, **53**: 246-
    49,n1; **58**: 145, 215, 365-66, 459-60,

531, 532-34, 560-61, 602; and censorship, **53**: 260, 289; **54**: 430,n2, 555; **56**: 245, 373, 374; **57**: 423, 448; and revenue bill and zone-rate revision, **53**: 542,n2; recommends Palmer for Attorney General, **54**. 485; claims of oppressive labor policies of, **55**: 364-65; and telegraph workers situation, **56**: 340-41, 403, 404; and New England telephone strike, **57**: 425, 446, 530,n1, 577; Gompers on labor's grievances against, **58**: 48-53; on telegraph strike, **60**: 378-79; **61**: 10; on chances of treaty's adoption in Senate, **61**: 185; and amnesty issue, **61**: 351; R. S. Baker on WW's loyalty to, **61**: 416; on California telephone strike, **61**: 503-504, 539-40; on strategy for treaty ratification, **63**: 266; on progress of enlisting cotton producers to support treaty, **63**: 442-43; on position of Tennessee's senators on treaty, **63**: 443; offers get-well wishes and informs WW of improving Senate situation, **63**: 534-34; on WW's Annual Message and his ability to perform his duties, **64**: 123-24; and railroad situation, **64**: 184, 457; Lansing on reaction to WW's no-compromise statement, **64**: 193; suggested as delegate to international conference on communications, **64**: 228,n1; and list of senators who hindered treaty ratification, **64**: 338-39, 343; meets with House, **64**: 444-45; and Cabinet meetings during WW's illness, **64**: 457; on Democratic platform of 1920, **65**: 29; on treaty compromise, **65**: 56-57, 81-82; on appointment of postmaster in Nashville, **65**: 119; and Democratic National convention of 1920, **65**: 345, 383, 492, 495,n1, 496, 498, 499, 580; on Retirement Act, **65**: 478,n3, 512, 519, 520; Wilson angered over prohibition plank presented by, **65**: 495,n1, 510-11,n1, 3; on poor health being reason WW not renominated, **65**: 511n3; WW's cold thoughts toward, **65**: 511n2; on Cox, **66**: 25; and Debs' pardon, **66**: 25; and International Communications Conference, **66**: 56; alleged criticism of, **66**: 58n1, 62; on enforcement of postal regulations of Espionage Act and issue of censorship, **66**: 92-93, 94-98, 99; and proposed statue of WW at Univ. of Texas, **66**: 369,n1; proposed Universal Electrical Communication Union, **66**: 415, 416; on appointments, **67**: 25; on Dawes, **67**: 124; praises WW, **67**: 181; Cabinet farewell, **67**: 199; photograph of, *illustration section*, **67**

Burleson and the Call (*New Republic*), **54**: 430n2

Burlingame Treaty, **66**: 137

Burnaby, Minna Field Gibson (Mrs. Algernon Edwyn), **59**: 517,n2

Burner, David, **67**: 45n2; **68**: 179n1

Burnett, Philip Mason, **55**: 29n2; **56**: 271n2, 272n4, 356n1, 433n2; **57**: 203n3, 498n1; **59**: 50n7, 536n1; **60**: 359n1; **61**: 254n2

Burnett Immigration Act (1917), **67**: 179

Burnquist, Joseph Alfred Arner, **63**: 122,n1, 124, 125,n2, 126, 128, 131,n1

Burns, J. M., **62**: 568-69, 570-73

Burns, John, **55**: 338

Burr, Milton, **65**: 36,n1

Burson, W. H., **67**: 379-80

Bursum, Holm Olaf, **67**: 350n1

Burton, Theodore Elijah, **55**: 255, 278; **62**: 228,n2; **65**: 417; **67**: 609

Bury, J. P. T., **65**: 196n1; **66**: 39n3, 44n5, 46n7; **67**: 109n1

Busch, Briton Cooper, **68**: 141n1

Busch, Lily Anheuser (Mrs. Adolphus), **53**: 141-42

Bush, Samuel Prescott, **54**: 521,n2; **57**: 378

business and industry, **55**: 117-18, 156, 188; Tumulty on reassuring, **53**: 77-78; and importance of Smith-Bankhead Americanization bill, **55**: 286-88; WW on labor and, **64**: 84-85, 113-15

Business Antitrust Policy and the Industrial Board of the Department of Commerce, 1919 (Himmelberg), **54**: 521n1

Business History Review, **54**: 521n1

Bussey, Gertrude, **58**: 141n1; **59**: 117n4

Butenko, Colonel, **57**: 314,n5; **62**: 86,n4, 88

Butler, Harold Beresford, **63**: 445-46,n1; **65**: 249,n1

Butler, Nicholas Murray, **53**: 365,n1, 580n2; **55**: 440; **65**: 372; **66**: 246n2, 542n1; and Nobel Peace Prize, **68**: 266n1

Butler, Rohan, **61**: 157n9; **62**: 254n2; **65**: 196n1; **66**: 39n3, 44n5, 46n7; **67**: 109n1

Butler, Smedley Darlington, **58**: 593,n1; **66**: 82,n1

Butler, Lamb, Foster and Pope of Chicago, **68**: 392n1

Buxton, Frances Vail Culver Tredwell (Mrs. Arthur Kennard), **53**: 312-12,n2

Buyuk Menderes River: *see* Maeander River

Byrd, Richard Evelyn, **66**: 167,n1, 172; **68**: 417,n1

Byrnes, James Francis, **68**: 63,n1

Byrnes, Joseph Wellington, **68**: 63,n1

Byrnes, Robert Francis, **56**: 54n14

Cabell, De Rosey Carroll, **61**: 487-88, 525

Cabinet (U.S.): and cost of living, **62**: 94

Cabinet Government in the United States (Wilson), **61**: 363,n1

cables: *see* submarine cables; wireless telegraphy; Cuban American Telephone Company; International Communications Conference on; Western Union Telephone and Telegraph Company, Yap Island

Cabot family, **68**: 595

Cabot, Maud Bonner (Mrs. Francis Higginson), **67**: 135,n1
Cabrera, Flores, **66**: 31n1
Cabrera, Luis, **65**: 487,n4
Cabrera, Manuel Estrada: *see* Estrada Cabrera, Manuel
Cabrini, Angiolo, **56**: 393,n3
Cachin, Marcel, **53**: 345,n1, 387n1; **60**: 118,n1; on change in public opinion toward WW and peace conference, **56**: 386,n1, 386-87
Cadwalader, Wickersham & Taft, **68**: 162n2
Caen, France, **56**: 125n1
Caesar, Julius, **62**: 427
Caffey, Francis Gordon, **59**: 76n1
Cagni, Umberto, **58**: 142,n2
Cahen-Salvador, Georges-Joseph-Ernest, **58**: 235,n2, 236; **59**: 424,n3; **60**: 473,n19
Cairo, **56**: 154-55
Calais, France, **53**: 508; **61**: 4n3
Calder, William Musgrave, **62**: 122; WW meets with on treaty, **61**: 548,n1, 569n1, 570, 593-94, 584-95, 598, 599; and treaty fight, **64**: 94, 200-201, 337
Caldero, Emilio, **53**: 617-18,n1
Calderon, Fernando Iglesias: *see* Iglesias Calderon, Fernando
Calderon, Don Ignacio, **55**: 330,n4
Caldwell, Dean, **68**: 566
Caldwell, Edgar, **55**: 327-28, 328; **62**: 465,n1, 530, 536
Caldwell, John Kenneth, **58**: 495,n2,3; **62**: 334,n3, 427-28
Caldwell, John Lawrence, **53**: 312,n3
Calhoun, Frederick S., **66**: 58n1
Calhoun, John Caldwell, **53**: 267,n2
Calhoun, William, **67**: 557
California, **53**: 115, 636,n1; **56**: 331; and discrimination against Japanese, **57**: 49-50; **66**: 12-16,n1, 53-54, 58, 185-87, 295-96; telephone strike in, **61**: 503-504,n1, 539; and railroad strike, **62**: 548, 549-50; and oil, **62**: 619; California, University of, **61**: 635,n1; **62**: 284n3; **63**: 340n3; WW speaks in Greek Theater at, **63**: 340n1; and IWW case, **65**: 206; McAdoo's move to, **68**: 72-73; and Teapot Dome scandal, **68**: 119n2; politics in, **68**: 146,n1; WW's property in, **68**: 503-504, 510, 532, 545
California Alien Land Act (1913), **66**: 13,n3, 13-14
Calkins, Harriet B., **66**: 151n1
Calles, Plutarco Elías, **66**: 160,n1, 271, 335, 372
Calloway, Fuller Earle: appointed to first Industrial Conference, **63**: 300,n1
Calonder, Felix Ludwig, **57**: 464; on Switzerland as site of League of Nations, **56**: 169-70, 234
Calthorpe, Sir Somerset Arthur Gough: *see* Gough-Calthorpe, Sir Somerset Arthur
Calvin, John, **56**: 121; **57**: 329

Calvin Coolidge: The Quiet President (McCoy), **63**: 167n6
Calymnos, Dodecanese Islands, **58**: 356
Cambon, Jules-Martin, **54**: 283, 490,n2; **57**: 485; **58**: 253, 312; **64**: 163n6; and Poland, **56**: 54, 88,n2, 90, 90-91, 91, 91-92, 93, 142, 144, 165, 166; **59**: 334, 536, 555, 560, 587, 632; **60**: 189,n2, 411, 423, 468; **61**: 566n1,2; and Teschen, **56**: 221; and German and Italian credentials, **58**: 150, 227, 244, 248, 254-55, 279, 280, 281, 282, 311-12, 424, 425; and Kapp *Putsch*, **65**: 159, 236
Cambon, Pierre-Paul, **54**: 318,n2; **56**: 105, 324; **59**: 41; criticizes WW and slow progress of Paris Peace Confence, **54**: 235-36,n1; on Prinkipo Declaration, **54**: 236-37; and Kapp *Putsch*, **65**: 159, 236
Cambridge, Mass., **53**: 436-37; **54**: 107; **59**: 214n3; WW Foundation chapter at, **67**: 520,n1
Cambridge University, **53**: 69
Cameron, Rev. A. I., **62**: 69
Cameroons, The, **54**: 253, 318-22, 325, 373n9; **58**: 484, 485, 486, 510; **59**: 328, 338; **60**: 30; **63**: 422
Caminetti, Anthony, **57**: 378; **65**: 187n5
Campbell, Charles S., **56**: 531n5
Campbell, Henry, **54**: 256n1, 399n1
Campbell, James Edwin, **63**: 7,n1
Camp Dix, New Jersey, **53**: 157,n2
Camp Funston, Kansas, **53**: 307n2
Camp Grant, Illinois, **53**: 451; **65**: 78
Campo Formio, Treaty of, **57**: 482,n3
Camp Pontanezen, Brest, **58**: 593-94
Canada, **53**: 339, 484, 567; **54**: 185, 254; **58**: 198; **61**: 4, 5; and delegates to Paris Peace Conference, **54**: 15, 44, 65; Borden's general memorandum on activities, issues, and solutions in Paris, **57**: 306-12; and labor convention, **58**: 417,n7, 467-69; **61**: 39; and submarine cables, **58**: 302, 304, 350, 351; and Rumanian credits, **58**: 591; on prohibition, **61**: 294; and wheat situation, **62**: 52, 53; U.S. message for cornerstone of Parliament building, **62**: 425; WW on, **63**: 232, 477-78, 505; proposal for Minister from Canada to U.S., **65**: 181-82, 195, 230, 237, 242, 245; and British policy in Far East, **65**: 392; and paper shortage, **66**: 113-14; and U.S. appointment to joint commission, **67**: 168,n1, 196,n1; immigration issue, **67**: 180; and U.S. imports and exports, **67**: 192
Canadian Boundary Commission: Tumulty's suggestion for, **66**: 333-34
Canadian Commission: *see* International Joint Commission of the United States and Canada
Canadian Pacific Railway, **61**: 397,n2
Canby, Henry Seidel, **61**: 568,n1
Candia (Crete), **59**: 92
Candler, Ezekiel Samuel, Jr., **55**: 297,n4
Candler, Norman, **67**: 327,n5, 353

Canfield, Richard A., **54**: 309n2
Canning, George, **63**: 192,n2, 430, 431
Cannon, Joseph Gurney, **60**: 611,n1; **67**: 208,n1, 209; photograph of, *illustration section*, **67**
Canterbury, Archbishop of: *see* Davidson, Most Rev. Randall Thomas
Cantrill, James Campbell, **62**: 615,n1
Cape Cod Canal, **53**: 128-29
Capel, Mr., **53**: 722,n5
Capellini, Rinaldo, **66**: 75
Cape Province, Union of South Africa, **54**: 298
Cape Vincent, N.Y., **66**: 56
capitalism: WW on, **68**: 322-23, 393-94
capital punishment: N. D. Baker on, **66**: 34
Capodistria, Italy, **53**: 445
Caporetto, Italy, **57**: 166
Capper, Arthur, **55**: 450,n5; **61**: 372; **68**: 241,n2; meets with WW on treaty, **61**: 492-93,n2, 516, 545, 563,n2; on WW and Shantung settlement, **61**: 602; WW wishes to answer on Shantung settlement, **63**: 519; and treaty fight, **64**: 94, 200-201, 337; on WW's Hitchcock letter, **65**: 71n3
Capps, Edward, **64**: 297; **67**: 10,n1, 11, 181; and appointment to Greece, **65**: 271, 317
Captains and Kings (Helm), **53**: 319n1; **58**: 633n12
Carb, David, **56**: 432-33,n1
Cardew, Frederic Anstruther, **54**: 380n3
Cardiff, H.M.S., **59**: 66
Cardinal's Prediction Is League Agreement (Cardinal Gibbons), **61**: 627,n1
Carey, Robert Davis, **63**: 467,n1
Caribbean Studies, **66**: 25n1
Caric, Georges, **56**: 490-91,n1
Carinthia: *see* Paris Peace Conference—Carinthia
Carleton College, **68**: 456n1; support of WW and League of Nations at, **68**: 491-92
Carlin, Charles Creighton, **53**: 242,n1
Carlisle, England: WW's personal, not official, visit to, **53**: 457, 524, 537; WW's remarks in his grandfather's church, **53**: 541; WW named citizen of, **64**: 184
Carlson, Anton Julius, **60**: 532n1
Carlson, Fred A.: and Spencer-WW controversy, **66**: 196-97,n1, 198n1
Carlton, Newcomb, **66**: 219
Carlyle, Thomas, **63**: 12
Carnegie, Andrew, **53**: 32, 67, 82; WW on death of, **62**: 259,n1; and Church Peace Union, **66**: 502; foundation of, **67**: 348
Carnegie, Louise Whitfield (Mrs. Andrew), **53**: 32,n1; **62**: 259, 271
Carnegie Endowment for Interntional Peace, **53**: 82,n2; **68**: 159
Carnegie Hall, N.Y., **53**: 142n1, 690; **61**: 371, 376, 401; WW's address in, **61**: 401-404

Carnegie Institution, **66**: 526; **67**: 260, 264; **68**: 116,n3, 117
Carnot, Marie-Françoise-Sadi, **61**: 187,n1
Caroline Islands, **53**: 312n1; **54**: 325; **62**: 348
Carpenter, Alfred Francis Blaneney, **61**: 6n9
carpenters' union: *see* United Brotherhood of Carpenters and Joiners of America
Carr, Bertram, **53**: 537,n1
Carr, E. E., **56**: 283,n1
Carr, Edward Hallett, **60**: 20,n2, 167n17
Carr, Julian Shakespeare, **66**: 112n1
Carranza, Venustiano, **55**: 351, 352, 354, 355; **58**: 380; **61**: 527; **62**: 155, 459; **63**: 165; **64**: 129, 134,n6, 135, 136, 140n1; **65**: 201n1, 486, 487n1, 534; **66**: 140, 160n1; Fletcher on, **62**: 332-33; anti-American campaign of, **62**: 449-51; talk of severing diplomatic relations with, **64**: 120n1, 121; Lansing on, **64**: 210-11,n1, 240, 241, 242; downfall and assassination of, **65**: 252n1
Carrigan, E., **64**: 431
Carso, **53**: 642
Carson, Sir Edward (Henry), **55**: 455,n2, 481; **61**: 512,n1,2,3
Carter, Allen, J., **65**: 134n2
Carter, Andrew Francis, **56**: 4,n1
Carter Glass: A Biography (Smith and Beasley), **65**: 436n2
Carter, John Ridgley, **65**: 199,n9
Carter, William Samuel, **53**: 647,n2; **62**: 470,n1, 471; **64**: 468,n2; **65**: 359
Cartier de Marchienne, Emile-Ernest, Baron de, **58**: 262,n1, 279; **59**: 555,n2; **60**: 485; **61**: 284n1; **65**: 338n2; and reparations, **61**: 384; hopes for U.S. ambassador position, **61**: 385
Carton de Wiart, Adrian, **56**: 49n10, 54; **57**: 276,n5; **59**: 216
Carty, John Joseph, **53**: 654,n1
Casalgiate, Enrico Millo de, **63**: 557n1
Casey, Michael, **63**: 269
Cassandra (Kassandra), Greece, **62**: 605
Cassel, S.M.S., **55**: 432
Cassels, Alan, **68**: 419n1
Castellanos, Furcy, **66**: 384,n2
Castelnau, Noel-Marie-Joseph-Edouard, Vicomte de Curières, **61**: 329,n2
Castenskiold, Henrik de Grevenkop, **60**: 284,n3
Castleman, Mrs. **65**: 345,n2
Castlereagh, Viscount Robert Stewart, 2nd Marquis of Londonderry, **56**: 316, 361
Castoldi, Fortunato, **54**: 490,n2; **64**: 163n6
Castollorizo: *see* Kastellorizo
Castor and Pollux (Rameau, opera), **54**: 305n7; **56**: 62n4
Castua: and Adriatic settlement, **66**: 365
Cathedral of Saint Rombant (Malines, Belgium), **61**: 13,n6

Catholic Church: see Roman Catholic Church
Catholic University of America, **63**: 603
Catron, Peter, **61**: 527
Catt, Carrie Clinton Lane Chapman (Mrs. George William), **53**: 114n1, 126; **54**: 133; **56**: 191; **57**: 42-43; **59**: 203n1; **60**: 155, 204, 247; **61**: 377, 605; **64**: 396; **65**: 151-52; **66**: 30n1; **67**: 393
Cattaro (Kotor), Yugoslavia, **57**: 483; **61**: 405, 552, 553, 554; **63**: 206, 465, 525
Caucasia, **64**: 27
Caucasus: see Paris Peace Conference—Caucasus
Causey, William Bowdoin, **56**: 470n1; **57**: 367
Cavalla, Greece, **64**: 164
Cavallero, Ugo, **55**: 58,n9, 112, 232, 592; **60**: 258, 313, 313-14, 356; **61**: 33n2
Cavell, Edith Louisa, **57**: 22; **61**: 13; **62**: 318
Cavendish, Edward William Spencer: see Hartington, Marquess of
Cavendish, Victor Christian William: see Devonshire, Ninth Duke of
Caviglia, Enrico, **66**: 482,n2
Cavour, Count Camillio Benso di, **53**: 623; **58**: 451
Cecil, James Edward Hubert Gascoyne—4th Marquess of Salisbury, **56**: 435n1
Cecil, Robert Arthur Talbot Gascoyne: see Salisbury, 3rd Marquess of
Cecil, Lord Robert (Edgar Algernon Robert Gascoyne-), **53**: 483, 560, 564, 577; **54**: 188, 352, 380; **55**: 58, 118, 178n2, 195; **56**: 58, 62,n3, 102, 335, 435,n1,2, 586; **57**: 35, 37, 52, 53, 166, 574; **58**: 11, 417, 443, 445, 463; **61**: 144, 198, 207, 208, 310, 314; **65**: 480; **67**: 105n3, 239; **68**: 87, 136, 141, 142, 152, 311, 333, 334, 381, 428; on League of Nations, **53**: 415-17, 558, 568-69, 693; **54**: 150, 151, 152, 160, 189, 196, 197, 218, 228, 264, 386, 387, 407, 408, 426, 459, 460-61, 463, 481, 482, 483, 484, 494,n2, 496, 497, 510, 511, 514, 545-46, 546, 547; **59**: 109, 128, 129, 141, 300,n8, 326, 585-86; **60**: 17n1, 24, 26, 206, 223, 227, 260, 307, 361, 432n1, 464, 580; **62**: 188, 243, 254, 255, 425-26, 532; **65**: 480; **66**: 71; on Russia, **53**: 568; **59**: 127, 310-11; and British draft convention of League of Nations, **54**: 160-70; on meeting with House and WW on League of Nations Covenant, **54**: 460-61; **55**: 538, 539; opinion of WW, **54**: 514; WW on draft of, **54**: 522; and League of Nations Commission, **55**: 4, 42, 45, 46, 70, 71, 78, 80, 120, 121, 122, 124, 125, 139-40, 154, 155, 155-56; **56**: 170,n1, 171, 172, 173, 174, 175, 176, 177, 178, 179, 226, 228, 229, 230, 299, 300, 301; **57**: 219, 220, 221, 222, 224, 226, 227, 228, 229, 230-31, 232, 248, 249, 250, 251, 252, 252-53, 254, 255, 256, 257, 258, 259, 265, 266,

285, 286; on interntional army, **55**: 78, 80; and food for Germany, **55**: 458n1; on League of Nations Covenant, **56**: 75-81,n4, 82, 100, 297; **58**: 423, 444; **60**: 297; on dinner and evening with WW, **56**: 81-82; and cable censorship, **56**: 373, 514-15; on Anglo-American naval building controversy, **57**: 142,n1, 143-44, 178, 179, 179-80, 215, 216-17, 218n1; on Japan's racial equality amendment, **57**: 247, 261, 264, 571; WW on, **57**: 247; **63**: 286, 287 on arranging Plenary Conference on Covenant, **57**: 568-69; WW thanks for League of Nations work, **58**: 353; on Lloyd George's attitude toward WW and the Adriatic statement, **58**: 360,n1; and mandates, **58**: 400, 401; **59**: 475-76,n2; **61**: 107, 259, 265, 270, 283, 408, 477; on blockade issues, **58**: 563, 564, 565; **60**: 627, 639; on Germany's proposals for League of Nations, **59**: 243; and Rhineland Commission, **59**: 592; **60**: 367; on method of appeal to League of Nations, and execution of guarantees, **60**: 224; on Lloyd George, **60**: 255; on League of Nations and Germany's admission, **60**: 272n20, 273, 274, 296, 439; and N.H. Davis' misunderstanding over credit and European reconstruction, **60**: 277-80; and Rhineland proposal, **60**: 364, 365; and League Bureaus, **62**: 455; sends WW volume on Paris Peace Conference, **65**: 483; hopes to see WW, **68**: 306; speaks on League of Nations, **68**: 308, 315,n1, 317, 327-29, 383; WW's greetings to and encouragement on League of Nations issue, **68**: 310; EBW arranges visit for WW and, **68**: 320; on visit with WW, **68**: 344, 345-46; WW's get-well wishes and Lord Robert's response, **68**: 450; photograph of, *illustration section*, **54**
Cecil, Robert Arthur James Gascoyne-: see Cranborne, Viscount
Cecil, Russell L., **58**: 616-17,n24
Cellere, Countess Dolores Cabo Macchi di, **53**: 183,n1, 318, 589
Cellere, Count Vincenzo Macchi di, **53**: 183-84, 318, 332, 507, 589; **58**: 44, 367,n1, 394, 419, 421; **59**: 68, 80, 81, 83, 125, 200, 249, 254-55; **63**: 298n1; meets with Miller, **59**: 71; meets with House, **59**: 244; on coal situation in Italy, **62**: 253,n1, 326, 448-49, 468
Celtic Circle of Paris, **59**: 186
Cemal Pa a, **58**: 555n1; **59**: 411,n2
censorship, **55**: 337; and mail, **53**: 65, 214, 260, 289; Britain and France remove on U.S. press releases, **53**: 100, 109, 154, 180, 241, 285, 355; and government control of cable system, **53**: 148,n1, 164, 165; McCormick and WW on keeping some, **53**: 431-32, 432; modification of telephone and telegraph,

53: 524-25,n1; Bliss on Paris and French newspapers, **53**: 610; Derby on peace conference and, **53**: 723; and Paris Peace Conference, **54**: 105; and *New York Call*, **54**: 430,n1,2; WW on French newspapers, **54**: 467; Tumulty on, **54**: 555; and French press, **56**: 150; issue of U.S. cables and, **56**: 245, 372-74, 514-15; WW urged to veto, **55**: 281,n1, 290; abolition of cable, **57**: 423, 448, 449; WW on Joint Committee on Printing and, **65**: 266; and Burleson and postal regulations, **66**: 92-93, 94-98, 99

Central America: abolition of cable censorship, **57**: 448, 449; and Unionist movement, **65**: 247,n1

Central and South American Cable Company, **66**: 221

Central Bureau of Planning and Statistics, **53**: 131

Central Church of the Disciples of Christ (Detroit), **67**: 503n1

Central Council of the Irish County Association, **66**: 267n2

Central Presbyterian Church of Des Moines, **63**: 92,n1

Central Presbyterian Church of Washington, D.C., **61**: 595n; **66**: 227n1; **67**: 442n1; **68**: 370n1

Central Territorial Committee, **61**: 566n, 567

Central Trust Company of Chicago, **53**: 474n3; **67**: 124n1

Century Association (Club), **67**: 129,n2

Century Magazine, **68**: 390,n2, 499; and WW's essay, **68**: 353, 367,n1, 367-68,n1, 369

Century of Disagreement: The Chamizal Conflict, 1864-1964 (Liss), **66**: 162n3

Century of Struggle: The Woman's Rights Movement in the United States (Flexner), **66**: 54n1

Ceres, H.M.S., **59**: 66, 242

Cerretti, Bonaventura, **53**: 420,n3; **62**: 26,n1

Cespedes y Quesada, Carlos Manuel, **66**: 124,n1; **67**: 32,n1

Cetinje, Montenegro, **53**: 208,n2, 640

Chace, Olive, **67**: 450-51

Chadbourne, Grace Runnion Wassall (Mrs. Thomas Lincoln, Jr.): death of, **60**: 487,n1

Chadbourne, Marjorie Allen Curtis (Mrs. Thomas Lincoln, Jr.), **67**: 78,n1

Chadbourne, Thomas Lincoln, Jr., **60**: 487; **62**: 96; **65**: 382; **67**: 330, 339-40; on Irish issue and Democratic party, **55**: 403-404; appointed to first Industrial Conference, **63**: 300,n1; WW's wedding congratulations to, **67**: 78; and fund raising efforts for WW's S Street home, **67**: 137n3; and The Document, **67**: 319n1, 430, 433, 435, 437, 443, 567, 581, 582; **68**: 13,n1, 19-20, 26-27, 28-29, 29-31, 534; and chairmanship of

Democratic National Committee, **67**: 321n1, 325, 366; N. Y. Bar Association's charges against cause personal difficulties, **68**: 16,n1, 28-29; WW thanks for comments on The Document and solicits financial contribution for Democratic National Committee, **68**: 33

Chafee, Zechariah, Jr., **55**: 347n1; **66**: 92n1

Chagas, João Pinheiro, **54**: 374n10

Chaikovskii, Nikolai Vasil'evich, **53**: 591,n1; **54**: 26; **57**: 139n1; **58**: 265,n5, 266, 506,n6, 507, 574,n5, 575, 576, 577; **59**: 18,n11, 29, 30, 31, 154n3, 436, 550n1; at Council of Four on Russian situation, **59**: 14-21

Chaldeans, **57**: 426,n2

Chalmers, Robert, 1st Baron Chalmers of Northian, **67**: 91,n1

Chamberlain, Adrian, **68**: 454n2

Chamberlain, (Joseph) Austen, **53**: 566,n8; **58**: 8,n1; **60**: 24,n4, 93; **62**: 626; **66**: 49,n11; on cancellation of inter-Allied war debts, **64**: 475,n1, 477, 477-78; and debt negotiations, **65**: 325n1; on League of Nations, **68**: 193; WW on, **68**: 196,n1

Chamberlain, Eugene Tyler, **62**: 9,n1

Chamberlain, George Agnew, **55**: 356,n6

Chamberlain, George Earle, **53**: 581; **54**: 187n3; **61**: 469,n2; strained meeting with WW, **55**: 298

Chamberlain, Joseph, **55**: 384n4,5; **68**: 196,n1; Balfour on stroke of, **67**: 516-17,n1

Chamberlin, William Henry, **60**: 95n2; **62**: 427n1; **63**: 588n1

Chamber of Commerce of New York: *see* New York Chamber of Commerce

Chamber of Commerce of the United States, **62**: 623,n1; and cancellation of war contracts, **53**: 18-20; and railroads, **58**: 108; at Shanghai, **62**: 64; and Plumb plan, **62**: 198n2; and conference on relationship between labor and capital, **62**: 582, 584

Chambers, Benjamin Bright, **62**: 601-602,n1, 616

Chambers, David Laurence, **66**: 370-71,n1

Chambers, Edward, **53**: 647,n3

Chambers, John Whiteclay II, **61**: 366n3; **65**: 355n1, 576n1; **66**: 58n1

Chambrun, Comte Louis-Charles de, **53**: 346,n3; **54**: 518; **65**: 154,n1; **66**: 432,n2

Chamiec, Zygmunt, **56**: 271n3

Chamizal controversy, **66**: 1622,n3

Champ, Edward, **53**: 452

Chan, Loren B., **63**: 426n1, 428n1

Chandler, Charles S., **63**: 428,n1

Chandler, Julian Alvin Carroll, **62**: 106-107,n2

Chang, Hsun, **53**: 138n1

Chang Chia-sen (Carsun Cheng), **57**: 634,n2, 637

Changsha, China, **58**: 166
Chang Tsung-hsiang, **54**: 475,n4; **57**: 600,n3, 601; **58**: 553,n2,3; **62**: 65,n1
Channing, William Ellery, **66**: 483,n5
Chantilly, France, **58**: 265
Chapman, Loring, **62**: 637n24
Character of Woodrow Wilson (Chambers), **62**: 602,n4
Charity Organization Society, **56**: 283n1
Charleroi, Belgium: WW visits, **61**: 10-11,n2, 26, 29
Charles I (Charles Francis Joseph of Austria), **58**: 544, 547, 578
Charles I (of England), **56**: 510; **57**: 126
Charles Albert of Savoy, King of Sardinia, **63**: 514,n4
Charles Edward Russell on the Adjustment of Labor and Capital (articles), **60**: 147n4
Charles (Carol) of Hohenzollern-Sigmaringen, Prince, **62**: 428n2
Charles-Roux, François-Jules, **58**: 91,n1
Charleston, S.C.: race riots in, **61**: 357n
Charles University (Prague), **68**: 296n1
Charlton, Lionel Evelyn Oswald, **68**: 415,n1
Charm of Birds (Grey), **56**: 62n3
Charnwood, Godfrey Rathbone Benson, 1st Baron, **54**: 488,n2
Charoon, Prince, **59**: 186,n1
Charpy, Charles-Antoine, **56**: 379,n1; on Rumanian advance in Hungary, **56**: 382-83
Chase, Benjamin Franklin, **63**: 616n1; **65**: 466,n1, 505-506
Chase, Olive, **68**: 188
Chase, Samuel, **67**: 124
Chase, Stuart, **63**: 389n2
Chase, Perley Morse & Co., **63**: 389n2
Chastellux, François-Jean, Marquis de, **67**: 333,n2
Château Thiery, France, **53**: 314, 352, 467; WW visits, **54**: 278, 279, 305; battle of, **59**: 621; **61**: 427; **62**: 241n1; WW on battle of, **63**: 432, 450, 469
Chatham House Version and Other Middle-Eastern Studies (Kedourie), **56**: 122n2
Chattanooga, U.S.S., **65**: 538, 540, 549
Chattanooga, Tenn., **59**: 287
Chattanooga Times, **67**: 488; **68**: 268n1
Chaumont, France: WW visits Pershing and troops at, **53**: 488, 502
Chauncy, France: WW visits, **56**: 194, 198
Chautauqua Assembly, **65**: 423n2
Chautauqua Literary and Scientific Circle, **65**: 423n2
Chavariat, Corporal, **61**: 321
Cheetham, Sir Milne, **56**: 122n2, 154,n2, 155
Cheliabinsk, Russia, **62**: 82n2, 87
chemical and dyestuffs industry, **64**: 80-81, 109-10; **65**: 132; **66**: 489; and Palmer's case and Germany, **68**: 299-

301,n1,4,8, 303, 303-304, 356, 357-58, 361
Chemical Foundation, **68**: 299,n1
Chemin des Dames, France: WW visits, **56**: 194, 197
Chemnitz, S.M.S., **55**: 432
Ch'en Lu, **54**: 474,n1, 474n2; **58**: 522n1; **62**: 458,n4
Chernoff, Alex, **53**: 137
Cherso (now Cres, Yugoslavia), **57**: 482, 545, 613; **59**: 86, 95, 569, 570; **60**: 138, 207, 211, 212, 213, 214, 217-18, 310; **61**: 171; **62**: 456, 575, 603, 604; **63**: 205, 207; **64**: 264n4, 265; **66**: 364, 365, 377
Chester, Colby Mitchel, **68**: 504,n1
Chesterton, G. K. (Gilbert Keith), **67**: 105n3
Chevy Chase Country Club, **68**: 376,n3
Cheyenne, Wyoming, **63**: 446; WW's arrival and address in, **63**: 467, 467-82
Cheyenne *Wyoming State Tribune*, **63**: 487
Cheyney, Edward Potts, **68**: 514,n2
Cheysson, Pierre, **61**: 256,n4, 257
Chi, Madeleine, **57**: 453n4
Chicago, Ill: appointments in, **55**: 340,n1; race riots in, **61**: 357n1; **62**: 234,n1; request by citizens for return of U.S. soldiers in Siberia, **62**: 433-34, 478-79, 515; railroad strike of 1893, **62**: 122n3
Chicago *Daily Jewish Courier*, **62**: 609n1
Chicago Daily News, **54**: 83; **67**: 488
Chicago Evening Post, **62**: 439n1; **63**: 399
Chicago Federation of Labor, **63**: 30n1
Chicago Great Western Railroad, **65**: 562
Chicago *Herald-Examiner*, **66**: 196
Chicago Law School, University of, **67**: 247n1
Chicago Nipple Manufacturing Company, **68**: 149n6
Chicago, Rock Island & Pacific Railway Co., **65**: 491
Chicago Daily Tribune, **53**: 420; **54**: 60; **57**: 241n3; **61**: 373; **62**: 626; **66**: 196; Paris edition, **60**: 28n12, 64, 65, 402; and publication of peace treaty, **60**: 328,n1, 329, 330, 331; and Franco-American treaty of guarantee, **61**: 375n; on WW's health, **65**: 3, 4
Chicago, University of, **53**: 259; **56**: 283n1; **62**: 452n1; **66**: 165n5, 256; **67**: 459n1, 2; **68**: 259n3, WW Club at, **67**: 416
Chicherin, Georgii Vasil'evich, **53**: 151-52; **54**: 92n1, 136, 137, 181; **56**: 389, 390; **62**: 446,n6, 447; **65**: 288n3; on U.S. troops in Russia and Russia's desire for peace, **54**: 153-54; and Prinkipo Declaration, **54**: 345-46, 415-16; **55**: 161,n1; and Bullitt mission to Russia, **55**: 540n1, 541-42, 545; reply to Nansen's proposal, **59**: 195-97,n5, 300-301,n8
Ch'ien Neng-hsun, **54**: 475,n5
Chiesa, Eugenio, **56**: 444,n1, 502,n2

child labor, **56**: 238; **58**: 174, 362; **61**: 38; **64**: 98n1; and League of Nations, **55**: 69, 146, 172, 175-76; **60**: 150; Tumulty on legislation and suggestions for WW's speech to Congress, **58**: 605,n2; **59**: 291

Child Labor Tax Case, **68**. 131,n3

Children's Relief Fund: *see* European Children's Relief Fund

child welfare, **68**: 492; WW on, **68**: 478-79,n1

Child Welfare Board of New York City, **68**: 478n1

Chile, **56**: 100, 170n1; **58**: 198; and Tacna-Arica dispute, **53**: 316-17,n2, 317-18, 342, 346-47,n1, 536,n1; **55**: 330-31, 393; **65**: 190-91, 195; and Pan-American Union, **65**: 252-53, 261; and recognition of Mexico, **65**: 463; and recognition of Bolivia, **66**: 135; and controversy with Peru, **66**: 209, 210-12,n2; on U.S. in Dominican Republic, **66**: 360

Chilhi Province, China, **66**: 327,n1

Chilton, Henry Getty, **68**: 581

Chimienti, Pietro, **61**: 109,n6

China, **54**: 264; **59**: 108; **62**: 3-4, 11,n1, 17, 63-65; Japan and, **53**: 207, 464; **54**: 290-91, 308, 315-19, 474n1, 474n2, 475-76,n1; **55**: 294; **56**: 189,n8,9; **57**: 298-301, 358, 358-59, 431,n1, 453-54, 554-56, 560-61,n2, 580, 582-85, 597, 597-98, 599-610, 615-26, 634-35; **58**: 198; **61**: 65; **67**: 552; Reinsch on situation in, **54**: 77-82; **61**: 631-34; factional struggle in, **54**: 476,n7; WW on importance of China standing firm regarding Japan, **54**: 548, 549; wants Germany to return Kiaochow, **55**: 424; and opium conventions, **56**: 270n5; consortium for loan to assist, **57**: 626n3; **59**: 514, 546; **61**: 242; **66**: 294-95; and twenty-one demands, **57**: 617-18, 620, 621-22, 636; **58**: 165; and WW's fears because of secret treaty between Japan and England, **58**: 111, 112; WW's sympathy, **58**: 153, 229; sentiment in Peking against settlement, **59**: 522, 552-53; requests Council of Four's minutes on Kiaochow-Shantung issue, **59**: 568-69; organizational protests against Shantung settlement, **60**: 101,n1, 102-104; Hornbeck on Japan, Shantung settlement and, **60**: 102-104, 429,n1, 484, 602-603; serious situation and boycott in, **60**: 603-606; and Shantung settlement, **61**: 36, 249-50, 386, 387, 438; WW on Shantung settlement and, **61**: 237, 593-95; absent from signing ceremony, **61**: 304; resignation of Reinsch and possible successor, **61**: 631-34, 634-36; **62**: 260, 282-84; and Japan's public statement on Shantung settlement, **62**: 154-55; WW's statement on Shantung settlement, **62**: 170; and Japan, **62**: 281; Reinsch and Long on situation in, **62**: 282-84; Long on not raising mission to embassy status, **62**: 458-59; and oil, **62**: 619; WW on historical background of Shantung settlement, **63**: 314-17, 436-40; WW on treaty as hope for, **63**: 427, 461-62; and Lodge reservations, **64**: 39; and appointments, **64**: 206, 296; U.S. concern over renewal of Anglo-Japanese alliance and rights of, **65**: 254-55; and banking consortium, **65**: 255,n4, 259n1, 261, 277; and Japan, **65**: 391; and recognition of Mexico, **65**: 463; offer of surplus corn, **67**: 80; and Nine Power Treaty, **67**: 544n1; delegates to Paris Peace Conference, photograph of, *illustration section*, **58**; *see also* Shantung settlement

China and the United States: and Sun Yat-sen, **53**: 138-40, 197; **66**: 78-79; Hsi Shih-ch'ang and WW on goodwill between, **54**: 194, 331; Koo meets with WW, **57**: 631-34, 634, 637; U.S. position on boycott in China, **60**: 603-605, 606; and suggestion of raising American mission to embassy status, **60**: 603, 640

China Diplomacy, 1914-1918 (Chi), **57**: 453n4

Chinafu, China, **57**: 555, 616

Chinan (Tsinan), China, **58**: 175, 184, 221, 234

Chinan-Tsingtao Railway: *see* Tsingtao-Chinan Railway

Chinda, Iwako, **61**: 189,n8

Chinda, Viscount Sutemi, **54**: 383,n2; **55**: 155; **57**: 249, 257, 354-55, 553-54; **58**: 131, 179; **59**: 488; **61**: 36; **62**: 170, 508n3, 523; and League of Nations Commission, **54**: 218, 426,n1, 463; and article on racial equality, **54**: 485, 500; **57**: 261-62, 286n1, 571; and Japan's claims, **57**: 581, 597, 597-98, 603, 604, 605, 608; **58**: 165-68, 217, 218, 219, 221, 222, 224, 226, 228, 257, 258, 259; at Council of Four meeting on Russia, **59**: 461-62, 462, 463, 464; and mandates, **61**: 252, 276, 277, 283, 363, 408; and Shantung settlement, **62**: 459; and Yap Island controversy, **66**: 309, 461; photograph of, *illustration section*, **57**

Chinese American Citizens Alliance, **60**: 101n1

Chinese Eastern Railway, **53**: 146, 227, 256, 463n1, 556,n4, 633; **54**: 158n1, 412; **55**: 39; **56**: 152, 153, 519; **61**: 571-72, 580; **62**: 590-91; **64**: 220, 221; **66**: 166n1

Chinese Famine Relief Fund: and effort by *Christian Herald*, **66**: 327,n2, 338, 434; **67**: 75,n2, 96, 140,n3; Lamont organizes, **66**: 424, 443, 467, 491-92; WW's statement on, **66**: 495-96, 497; controversy over use of Sugar Equalization Board's profits, **66**: 509-10, 529-

Chinese Famine Relief Fund (*cont.*) 30, 532; and U.S. surplus corn, **67**: 80, 139; Fosdick on funding for, **67**: 87, 88; WW cannot ask Congress for appropriations for, **67**: 105; WW congratulates Lamont on, **67**: 342,n1

Chinese Patriotic Committee, New York, **60**: 101n1

Chinese Press Association of America, **60**: 101n1

Chirol, Sir (Ignatius) Valentine, **60**: 17,n1

Chistopol, Russia, **60**: 95n2

Chita, Russia, **55**: 400; **56**: 185; **61**: 572; **62**: 87

Chitwood, Joseph Howard, **66**: 167,n2, 167-68, 172-73

Choate, Anne Hyde Clarke (Mrs. Arthur Osgood), **67**: 135,n1

Choate, Joseph Hodges, **53**: 527,n1; **66**: 178

Chojnice, Poland, **60**: 25n9

Chopin, Frederic, **59**: 606

Chou Tse-tsung, **58**: 553n3

Christian, George Busby, Jr., **67**: 208; **68**: 48n6

Christensen, Mr., **54**: 154,n4

Christian Herald: and Chinese Famine Relief Fund, **66**: 327,n1, 424, 434, 491

Christian Science, **68**: 68-69,n1

Christian Science Monitor, **64**: 428n1

Christmas: Its Unfinished Business (Crothers), **63**: 387,n4

Christmas Cards I—To Woodrow Wilson (Morley), **67**: 473,n1

Chronicle of a Generation: An Autobiography (Fosdick), **68**: 451n1

Chrysanthos, Archbishop of Trebizond, **59**: 186; **66**: 29n2

The Church and the League of Nations, An Appeal to Christians (Cantuar *et al.*), **53**: 388,n2

Church Peace Union, **65**: 183n3; **68**: 160; requests WW as trustee and WW's refusal, **66**: 502-503, 512

Churchill, George Bosworth, **55**: 449,n1, 450

Churchill, Mabel Harlakenden Hall (Mrs. Winston), **66**: 71,n1

Churchill, Marlborough, **53**: 318; **54**: 349, 474,n1; **55**: 93n2, 495; **61**: 610,n1

Churchill, Winston (American author), **66**: 57,n2

Churchill, Winston Spencer, **53**: 567,n10; **54**: 244, 246, 307; **57**: 150, 460; **60**: 589; **61**: 99, 154, 206; speech on Britain's naval supremacy, **53**: 299,n1, 321; and Russian situation, **55**: 180-81, 182, 183, 202, 203, 208, 230,n2, 323; on Czech troops in Russia, **61**: 164-66; on Siberia, **62**: 89

Chyrov (Khyrov), Eastern Galicia, **57**: 276

Cianflone, Frank A., **54**: 393n3

Cicero, Marcus Tullius, **60**: 305; **67**: 116n2

Cilicia, Turkey, **54**: 517, 518; **56**: 95, 107, 108, 113, 203, 272; **57**: 334; **59**: 331, 341, 401, 633, 636; **61**: 128; **62**: 257; **64**: 449; **65**: 72, 74, 91, 308

Cincinnati Enquirer, **58**: 51; **63**: 552n2

Cincinnati Times-Star, **61**: 607n1

Cingrija, Melko, **59**: 125n1

Citizen Hearst: A Biography of William Randolph Hearst (Swanberg), **53**: 580n2

citizenship: and Smith-Bankhead Americanization bill, **55**: 284-88

City College of New York, **60**: 118

City in Terror, 1919: The Boston Police Strike (Russell), **63**: 167n6

Ciuffelli, Augusto, **60**: 473,n20

civil service; and census bill, **55**: 281,n1, 290; discussed in draft of Annual Message to Congress, **64**: 76-77; and Retirement Act, **65**: 478; and women appointments, **67**: 113,n1; Houston on, **68**: 271

Civil Service Commission, **67**: 113n1: reorganization plans enable WW to ask for members' resignation, **55**: 330,n1,2,3; and Galloway, **55**: 460, 478; **56**: 280; **57**: 348-49; **58**: 360-61; **62**: 164, 251; and appointments to, **64**: 205; and Helen H. Gardener, **65**: 115

Civil War (U.S.), **53**: 266; **55**: 85; **62**: 559; **66**: 204; WW on, **59**: 608; **63**: 145-46, 172, 234; **67**: 28, 225

Claffy, James Henry, **54**: 228n1

Clagett, Maurice Brice, **55**: 409,n5; **62**: 544-45,n1, 547; **63**: 595,n1; **64**: 16,n1, 21, 391n1

Claim of China (pamphlet), **58**: 137,n1

Claremont, France, **56**: 200

Clark, Alice, **68**: 130,n1, 138, 139

Clark, Champ (James Beauchamp), **53**: 25, 35, 135,n1; **54**: 259n2; **55**: 297; **61**: 388,n1; **64**: 185; **65**: 189n2, 350, 373, 397, 430, 492n2, 576, 577; **66**: 479; **67**: 26n6; suggested for Canadian Boundary Commission, **66**: 333-34; death of, **66**: 334n2

Clark, Edgar Erastus, **65**: 562,n1

Clark, Elmer Talmage, **66**: 213,n1, 229

Clark, Francis Edward, **62**: 81-82, 263-64, 436: on support for League of Nations, **61**: 612

Clark, John Bates, **66**: 275

Clark, Victor Selden, **67**: 264

Clarke, Dumont, **66**: 193n3

Clarke, Ida, **68**: 130,n1, 138, 139

Clarke, James Paul, **64**: 524,n3

Clarke, John Hessin, **53**: 120; **66**: 392; **68**: 164, 184-85, 188-89, 282; and Duplex case, **67**: 497n2; Lemke case, **67**: 563n2; WW on resignation of, **68**: 127-28,n1; on Supreme Court situation, **68**: 130-31; on League of Nations, **68**: 131-32,n10; WW's condolences to, **68**: 138; on formation of independent nonpartisan organization for League of Nations, **68**: 139-40, 140, 143-44, 157,

158-62, 162, 171, 173, 174-75, 178n1, 251, 275, 324-25; on his younger sister, **68**: 139; WW on League of Nations plans of, **68**: 144, 145, 166-67, 276; health of, **68**: 171, 174, 179, 184, 188-89, 196, 198, 275, 275, 281, WW on urging unconditional acceptance of League of Nations Covenant, **68**: 179; on Article X and League of Nations, **68**: 279; on difference with WW on League of Nations approach, **68**: 281; on principles of League of Nations Non-Partisan Association, **68**: 332-33; on his speaking tour for League of Nations, **68**: 359-60; WW thanks, **68**: 361; R. S. Baker on support for League of Nations plan of, **68**: 524

Clarke, John Proctor, **67**: 331, 332,n2, 336, 343

Clarke, Walter Irving, **62**: 202,n1, 251, 270, 313

Clarkson, Grosvenor Blaine, **53**: 97,n1; **62**: 223; on publicizing report on cost of living, **62**: 165,n1

Clark University, **66**: 290n1

Claudel, Paul-Louis, **66**: 343n2

Claudon, Joseph-Pierre-Henry, **60**: 11,n10

Claveille, Albert, **58**: 527,n1; **61**: 280,n15, 314, 317-18, 319, 319-20, 320

Claxton, Philander Priestly, **56**: 402,n1; **66**: 134,n3

Clayton, John Middleton, **62**: 37

Clayton, William McK., **53**: 251,n1

Clayton Antitrust Act, **58**: 362, 363, 497n3; WW's veto of extension of Section 10, **67**: 112-13,n1; and Truax and Duplex cases, **67**: 497,n1,2, 498

Clayton-Bulwer Treaty, **62**: 37

Clemenceau, Georges, **53**: 8, 26, 69, 98, 101, 217, 440, 481, 497 499, 566; **54**: 5, 34, 64, 127, 236, 307, 386, 464n1; **55**: 35, 148, 149,n1, 160, 178n2, 196, 211, 306, 423, 458n1, 497, 499; **56**: 3, 165, 209, 330, 543, 583, 588, 589; **57**: 62, 69, 203, 317, 351, 418, 432,n1, 468, 494, 504, 516, 628; **58**: 119, 128, 148, 172, 188, 211, 237, 462, 463; **59**: 2, 237, 246; **60**: 31-32, 129; **61**: 107, 112, 483, 567, 588n4; **62**: 11, 14, 25, 26n3, 153, 603, 606; **63**: 120, 306, 343, 527; **64**: 26, 227, 348; **65**: 481; **66**: 309; **67**: 130, 145, 183n1, 239; **68**: 201, 223n3; on peace conference, **53**: 3-4, 71-72, 83, 142-43; **63**: 299; on Germany and the Armistice, **53**: 4-5, 33, 34; and publication of Armistice terms, **53**: 26-27; and WW at peace conference, **53**: 84, 409, 414; and Allied conferences in London, **53**: 197, 222, 240, 251-52, 316, 324, 336; WW on, **53**: 339, 367; **54**: 198, 489; **55**: 3, 160; **56**: 62, 86, 338, 408, 518, 539, 580-81; **57**: 351, 391; **58**: 168-69; **59**: 173; **60**: 329, 489n1; **67**: 44; and WW's arrival in France, **53**: 383, 384, 390; meetings with WW, **53**: 391-92, 399, 400, 403, 437, 438, 448, 449, 456, 488; **55**:

529-30; **59**: 39; speech on France and peace plans, **53**: 544,n1, 571, 577, 586, 722,n4; discusses League of Nations with House, **53**: 652-53; and British telegram on Russia stopping terrorism and entering peace negotiations, **53**: 722; and Supreme War Council meetings, **54**: 8, 38, 199, 200, 201, 203-204, 238, 239, 525, 528, 533-34, 534-35, 535, 535-36, 537, 537-38; **55**: 9-10, 14, 15, 54, 55, 56, 57, 58, 60, 61, 62, 95, 95-96, 98-102, 104, 105, 106, 107, 109, 110, 111, 180, 181; **56**: 14, 17, 19, 26, 38, 44, 45, 46, 54, 55; and Council of Ten meetings, **54**: 15, 20, 21, 24-25,n14, 47, 48, 49-50, 67, 68, 69, 70, 71, 73, 74, 75, 96-97, 97, 108, 109, 110, 113, 114, 115, 116, 117, 117-18, 119, 120, 181, 182, 183-84,n1, 186, 187, 188, 207, 208-209, 210, 218, 219, 220, 221, 222, 223, 223-24, 224, 225, 248, 254, 283, 284, 285, 286, 287, 289, 290, 291, 301, 311, 314, 315, 318, 322, 328, 330, 331, 335, 343, 344, 345, 350, 357, 361, 367, 368, 369, 372, 373, 375, 417, 421, 423, 425, 461-62, 505; selected president of Paris Peace Conference, **54**: 127, 129-30, 130-31, 264; acceptance speech, **54**: 130-31; Seymour on, **54**: 383, 384; **59**: 647, 648; and request for Greek troops to Ukraine, **54**: 402-403,n3; and China and Japan, **54**: 474n2, 475; Nubar on Armenia and, **54**: 518; on prisoners of war, **55**: 3, 40; **58**: 235; House on, **55**: 195; **56**: 517; **57**: 335; and Russian situation, **55**: 204, 235,n2; House meets with, **55**: 233-34, 458; **56**: 126,n1; **59**: 623; **60**: 296-97; assassination attempt on, **55**: 209, 213, 279, 335, 497; and Rhineland, **55**: 233, 458, 475n2; **56**: 10-14, 60-61, 323-24, 522, 594; **58**: 462,n1,2, 584; and treaty of guarantee, **56**: 10-14, 126,n1, 323-24, 417,n1, 525, 592; **58**: 486-88, 488-89, 490; **61**: 311, 313; on League of Nations being part of peace treaty, **56**: 59, 249-50; on T. Roosevelt coming to France, **56**: 87; meets with WW and Lloyd George, **56**: 85, 102; on Syria and Turkey, **56**: 104, 107, 108, 116-17; and Haller's Army, **56**: 129, 146, 169, 409-13, 485, 496, 497; **57**: 550; on Lloyd George's condemnation of press coverage, **56**: 148-50, 150; and League of Nations amendments, **56**: 178, 179; French people want WW's peace, not Clemenceau's, **56**: 198, 200, 244; on cables, **56**: 216, 220; wastes time, **56**: 246-47, 279, 312, 338, 353, 440, 490, 524; and reparations, **56**: 246, 246-48, 251, 290-92, 316-20, 322-23, 347, 366-67, 368, 417-18, 448-51, 503, 509; **57**: 7, 8, 9, 11, 13, 14, 17, 19, 24-25, 25, 26, 30, 33, 80, 82, 83, 86, 87, 141, 206, 209, 210, 211, 212, 214; **58**: 30; **60**: 344, 345, 346, 347-48, 349, 350, 351; **62**: 148,

Clemenceau, Georges (*cont.*)
149; and question of Polish territory,
56: 312-13, 560; on Saar Basin, **56**:
347, 366-67, 452; **57**: 129, 130, 162,
163, 164, 165, 195, 199, 200, 201, 245;
59: 381, 382; **60**: 436; confrontation
with WW over territorial demands, **56**:
349-50, 350, 353, 353-54, 365-68, 434;
on Hungarian situation, **56**: 414-16,
465, 487, 488; response to Fontainebleau Memorandum, **56**: 477-79; Lansing on, **56**: 489; **57**: 292-93; and plan
for Germany's economic delegation,
56: 523, 528-29; talk of resignation, **56**:
542; WW's warning to, **56**: 554; R. S.
Baker on, **56**: 578; **59**: 623; on Luxembourg and Belgian claims, **56**: 595-97;
57: 355-56, 364-65; and Council of
Four, **57**: 73, 102, 103, 103-104, 104,
105, 120, 121, 358, 359; **58**: 32, 149,
150, 151, 152, 154, 182, 183; on responsibility and punishment, **57**: 122, 123,
124, 126, 127, 128, 631; **60**: 463-64; on
Danzig, **57**: 154, 289, 357; Sharp on,
57: 176-77; on German bonds, debt,
and finances, **57**: 294; on Italian
claims, **57**: 318, 319, 320, 322, 325;
health of, **57**: 332, 489-90, 513, 536-37,
540, 541, 545, 546-47, 548, 576, 611-
14; Orlando on, **57**: 352; and attacks by
French press against WW, **57**: 353-54,
390, 390-91; on Heligoland, **57**: 361,
362; and Russian food relief, **57**: 390,
438-39; on German-Belgian border, **57**:
392, 393; and Germany's lethal gas,
57: 403, 404; on Kiel Canal, **57**: 404;
58: 124; on stipulations to be embodied
in peace treaty, **57**: 525; on Syria, **57**:
589-90; **58**: 134; **59**: 330-31, 336, 340-
41, 345-46, 633; and Koo on China's
claims, **57**: 621, 625; and WW's Adriatic statement, **58**: 3, 42, 103, 142, 237-
38, 239; on Adriatic question, **58**: 15,
16, 17, 18, 19, 58, 59, 76, 77, 78, 80, 81,
82, 85, 86-90, 359,n2, 392-93; **59**: 50,
51, 52, 53; **63**: 204-206, 208, 209, 210,
364, 393, 424, 465, 526, 617n1; on publication of peace treaty, **58**: 22-24, 61-
63; **59**: 212, 213; McCormick on, **58**: 27;
letter to Italy on Fiume, **58**: 86-90, 333-
34, 336-37; on duration of economic
clauses, **58**: 115, 116; on destruction of
submarines, **58**: 127, 128; on Shantung
and Kiaochow, **58**: 130, 133; on Bourgeois, **58**: 176-77, 186, 187; on Klotz,
58: 177, 186; on Pichon, **58**: 186; and
Belgium, **58**: 237, 262; and Orlando's
speech in Rome, **58**: 237,n3; and issue
of Italy's absence from peace conference and Adriatic claims, **58**: 250, 251;
on journalists' presence at Plenary
Session with Germany, **58**: 254; on inviting Austria and Hungary to Paris,
58: 264, 265, 315-16; at May Day celebration, **58**: 275, 277; and Italian credentials, **58**: 279-80, 281, 282; and

Poincaré, **58**: 328; **61**: 326; Grayson
on, **58**: 429; **59**: 39; **60**: 435; makes
changes in League of Nations Cove-
nant, **58**: 430-31, 443, 444, 445; at Plenary Session at Versailles, **58**: 502,
518-19, 520-21, 530; and seized enemy
ships, **58**: 559; and Germany and
League of Nations, **59**: 6, 7; **60**: 94-95,
273, 274, 275, 292, 296, 334, 494; on
plans if Germany refuses to sign
treaty, **59**: 7, 9, 10, 11; **61**: 33,n2; on
Smyrna, **59**: 23, 40, 41, 42, 43-44, 44,
45; Tardieu on, **59**: 46; Council of Four
on Adriatic question, **59**: 86, 88, 89, 90,
91, 92, 93, 95, 96, 99, 100, 101, 102,
103; on blockade of Germany, **59**: 128;
on attending church, **59**: 248; clashes
with Lloyd George on secret treaties
and Syria and Asia Minor, **59**: 321,
331-33, 336, 369-700, 370,n1, 484; on
France and Asia Minor, **59**: 340-41,
341-43, 344, 345-46; and Foch, **59**: 371;
60: 583; wears grey gloves at meetings,
59: 384, 647; on draft message to Kolchak, **59**: 436, 437, 438, 527; and
Rhenish separatist movement, **59**:
443; **60**: 8n3; on peace treaty with Austria, **59**: 483-85; conversation with
WW and Lloyd George on Italy, **59**:
492-94; on Orlando not making a proposal on Adriatic issue, **59**: 508; on
American soldiers buried at Suresnes
Cemetery, **59**: 607,n1; on changes in
peace treaty, **59**: 622-23, 623; on Lloyd
George, **59**: 623,n1; on WW, **59**: 623; on
peace treaty and Council of Four, **60**:
28-30; conflict with Lloyd George, **60**:
40-41, 144, 334; firm on peace terms,
60: 72, 73; House's memorandum to on
reply to Lloyd George, **60**: 82, 82-83; at
Council of Four on Upper Silesia and
plebiscite, **60**: 86, 88, 89, 90, 91, 404,
405-406, 421, 422-23, 424, 425, 426,
427; and Kolchak, **60**: 141; at Council
of Four on arms limitations, **60**: 174-
75; at Council of Four on Adriatic question and Tardieu plan, **60**: 211, 216,
217, 218; on new states and method of
appeal to League of Nations, **60**: 222;
on minorities and Rumania, **60**:
233,n4; on issue of having conversations with Germany to facilitate signing of peace treaty, **60**: 263; seating
plan for Council of Four meetings, **60**:
285; on German conscription, **60**:
296,n4; on Italy meeting secretly with
Germany, **60**: 332; and photograph of
"Big Four," **60**: 333; on Lloyd George's
proposal on German reparations, **60**:
340-42; on occupation of Rhineland,
60: 440, 441, 464, 465, 501-502, 503,
523-27; quotations from, **60**: 445, 458;
on Czech-Rumanian-Hungarian border issue, **60**: 469-500, 523; Pershing
on the French and, **60**: 546-47; without
authorization extends time Germany

has to reply, **60**: 575; on Foch, **60**: 583; on Foch's plans for march on Berlin, **60**: 583-84, 586-87, 588-89, 617-18, 619-21; meets with Pétain on Foch's plan for drive on Berlin, **60**: 617-18; and presence of South and Central American delegates at Versailles, **61**: 65-66; denies Germany time extension, **61**: 82; on sinking of German fleet at Scapa flow, **61**: 84, 85, 85-86, 102, 103, 111, 114, 125, 134, 140-41, 142-43, 143-48, 151; **62**: 144-47,n1; on retaliation against Germany after treaty is signed, **61**: 114-15; gives WW tour of Versailles Palace, **61**: 118; on burning of French flags in Berlin, **61**: 125-26; at treaty signing-ceremony, **61**: 302, 303, 332, 332-23, 330; on U.S. prohibition, **61**: 305; bids WW farewell, **61**: 306, 328; on whether records of Big Four should be made public, **61**: 336, 337, 338; WW on, **61**: 370, 374-75; **63**: 604; on denying Irish delegates hearing at Paris Peace Conference, **61**: 466-67; Grasty compares Congress and WW to Chamber of Deputies and, **61**: 616,n2; and proposed Inter-Allied Commission of Inquiry on Greek atrocities in Turkey, **61**: 629n1; and mandates, **62**: 188, 235, 257, 304, 511-13, 514, 580; and plan for punishment of alleged war criminals, **62**: 318-19, 334, 449,n1; and Thrace, **62**: 327; given Bible by WW, **62**: 435; and Albania, **62**: 457; and Adriatic question, **62**: 575; **64**: 263, 264-66, 298-305, 376, 398; and Constantinople issue, **63**: 60, 61; House on growing enthusiasm for League of Nations by, **63**: 271-72; and issue of French ships contracted for in U.S., **63**: 366-69; issue of troops to Armenia, **63**: 466; Baker on anecdote about WW and, **63**: 621; and Rumania, **64**: 35; on departure of U.S. representatives in Paris, **64**: 102, 117-18, 151; note of Dec. 9, 1919, to Italy on Adriatic question, **64**: 168-78, 323; Wallace on Adriatic proposal of, **64**: 260,n1, 318-20; and Russian situation, **64**: 307; gives ultimatum to Yugoslavia on Adriatic question, **64**: 314; military faction against, **65**: 87, 89; and intervention in Siberia, **65**: 144; and Tardieu's indiscreet articles, **65**: 542,n1; Cobb on, **67**: 227; reaction to WW's Adriatic statement, **67**: 376,n1; mention of visit to U.S., **68**: 109, 116, 190,n3; WW's welcome to and response of, **68**: 197, 198; Bliss on peace negotiations and, **68**: 224; meets with WW, **68**: 226-28; WW's farewell to, **68**: 230; good wishes to WW, **68**: 234; on Italian situation, **68**: 255; Baruch on, **68**: 406; photograph of, *illustration section,* **54**; **61**
Clemenceau (Duroselle), **68**: 190n3
Clemens, Ira, **66**: 10-11,n1

Clemens, Samuel Langhorne: *see* Twain, Mark
Clémentel, Etienne, **53**: 326,n5, 360, 361, 373, 456, 481, 483; **54**: 37,n3, 37-38, 39; **55**: 58, 458n1; **57**: 116; **58**: 64, 115, 117, 119, 424, 492, 527; **59**: 300,n8; **60**: 26n11; **61**: 278n7, 314
Clerk, Sir George Russell, **64**: 101n2
Cleveland, Frances Folsom (Mrs. Grover), **60**: 646,n2
Cleveland, (Stephen) Grover, **62**: 122; **65**: 458, 476; **66**: 317n1; **67**: 183n1; story that WW kept Cleveland "from attending faculty meeting," **62**: 479-80; physical appearance after leaving Washington, **66**: 378
Cleveland, Ohio, **68**: 505: and telephone strike, **61**: 540; Chamber of Commerce, **68**: 277
Cleveland *Plain Dealer*, **62**: 627; **63**: 275; **65**: 475; **67**: 296, 297
Cleveland Railway Company, **62**: 421n2
Clifden, Ireland, **57**: 447n1
Clinical Neurology, **58**: 615n18
Clive, George Sydney, **60**: 14,n14
Clive, Robert Henry, **53**: 561,n4
Close, Gilbert Fairchild, **53**: 166, 204, 318, 319, 430, 431, 648; **54**: 77, 91, 138, 171, 195, 232, 262, 278, 303, 305, 347, 399, 430, 518, 552; **55**: 151, 188, 233n1, 406, 407, 448; **56**: 96, 97, 101, 122, 183, 223, 337, 405, 430, 441, 521-22; **57**: 68, 90, 240,n2, 371, 374, 432n1, 440, 444, 446, 457, 468, 477, 509, 509-10, 630; **58**: 103, 137, 144, 164, 243, 562n1, 598,n1, 618; **59**: 74, 108-109, 184, 191, 349, 350, 409, 411, 472, 513, 573, 576, 639, 640, 641-42, 643-44; **60**: 16, 104, 106, 138, 182, 241, 250n1, 486n1, 570, 572, 641; **61**: 3n1, 127, 186, 231, 416; **62**: 50n1, 151-52, 240, 423, 534, 615; **63**: 526; **64**: 297, 321; **67**: 519-20, 524; resignation of, **64**: 344; on WW's work habits, **63**: 513-14; photograph of: *see illustration section,* **55**
Close, Helen Smith Farrer (Mrs. Gilbert Fairchild), **67**: 520,n3
clothing industry: *see* garment industry
Clouston, Joseph Storer, **67**: 573n1
Cluj University, **56**: 275n1
Clyne, Charles Francis, **62**: 159-60,n1 **65**: 174,n1, 175
coal, **59**: 267; **62**: 160; and Italy, **58**: 202, 203-204, 269; **62**: 252, 253, 291, 326, 448-49; reduction due to Teschen situation, **59**: 218; and Germany, **59**: 364, 377n3, 415, 459-60, 582, 583; and Upper Silesia, **60**: 55-59, 85, 130n4, 156, 185, 412, 423; and reparations, **60**: 401; and prices, **62**: 20-21; WW on situation in Europe, **63**: 156; Germany's obligations concerning, **65**: 60-62; Italy's problem of transporting, **65**: 198-200; and Italy, **65**: 300; and German protocol at Spa, **66**: 44,n5

coal industry, **53**: 83-84, 310-11, 333; **55**: 251, 286-88, 362-63, 397-98, 398; and prices, **56**: 342, 343,n1, 400-402; **57**: 43-47, 234, 282, 383; strike threat creates crisis, **63**: 54-55, 55, 56, 593-94, 595-97; WW's statement on proposed strike, **63**: 599-601; Palmer meets with WW on, **63**: 608,n1; restraining order against strike, **63**: 612,n1; Brandeis on, **63**: 618; **68**: 277,n1; Hines on railroad situation and, **64**: 23; and strike, **64**: 141n1,2,3; WW's proposal to union leaders, **64**: 142-45; Garfield on, **64**: 145-46; Tumulty on WW's statement and Garfield principle, **64**: 153-54; WW on, **64**: 154-55, 206-209; Cabinet action on strike, **64**: 166, 167, 457; **66**: 4; WW thanks union leaders for help in resolving, **64**: 178-80; miners accept WW's proposal, **64**: 179; Garfield's resignation, **64**: 180-82; draft of letter to Bituminous Coal Commission, **64**: 206-209; Hines on discontinuing price controls, **65**: 96-97; WW on ending price-fixing, **65**: 105; WW's message to Anthracite Wage Scale Committee, **65**: 312-13; W. B. Wilson on anthracite crisis, **65**: 314, 352-53; crisis in West Virginia, **65**: 335-37; appointment of Federal Fuel Administrator, **65**: 508,n1; crisis and Strike in Illinois and Indiana, **65**: 545-46, 546-48, 553-54,n1, 558-62, 562,n2; Palmer and WW on price-fixing, 563-64, 567; WW's statement to members of United Mine Workers urging them to return to work, **65**: 565-66; J. L. Lewis urges miners to return to work, **65**: 568-69; WW thanks J. L. Lewis for urging workers to return to work, **66**: 4; and Indiana and Illinois crisis, **66**: 10-11, 18-19,n1; issue of reconvening Joint Scale Committee, **66**: 27, 107-108; W. B. Wilson on differences between anthracite and bituminous coal settlements, **66**: 104-107; Tumulty on transport problems, **66**: 205-206; anthracite operators and miners have joint meeting, **66**: 217; Lewis on Alabama strike, **66**: 263-65; Peabody on, **68**: 203, 205; *see also* Anthracite Coal Commission and Bituminous Coal Commission

Coalition to Continue (London *Times*), **53**: 71n1

Coal Operators Association, **63**: 56n5

Coar, John Firman, **67**: 367,n1, 368, 368-69, 371, 374, 463-65; WW disagrees with views of, **67**: 478

Cobb, Frank Irving, **53**: 72, 408, 440; **55**: 450; **61**: 463; **65**: 44; **67**: 105n3, 419, 420, 513; **68**: 141, 190, 191-92, 197, 311, 337, 402; on remaining independent rather than being paid propagandist, **61**: 644-46; on treaty, **64**: 66, 270n2; interpretive editorial on WW and WW's thanks, **67**: 216-29, 230; numerous requests for editorial required printing it in pamphlet form, **67**: 234-35; and WW Foundation, **67**: 271n1, 327n6; **68**: 249n2; on Treaty of Berlin, 1921, **67**: 424; to meet with WW, **67**: 427; distressed over article on WW and Foch, **67**: 437; on Washington Naval Conference, **67**: 447-48, 511; on WW's policy of silence, **67**: 528, 529, 531; on U.S. entry into League of Nations and WW's response, **68**: 99, 100; on WW and Democratic program, **68**: 100-101, 101, 195-96; on Democratic party program and Missouri primary, **68**: 104; WW asks advice on party leadership and on critical editorial, **68**: 234; on League of Nations, **68**: 239; on The Document and WW's position as party leader, **68**: 239; WW to review The Document with, **68**: 294, 295, 295-96, 534; on development of Brandeis' prohibition statement, **68**: 304-305, 305, 315, 338, 385; on Lord Robert Cecil's speech on League of Nations, **68**: 308; Seibold on, **68**: 371-72; WW advises to take a rest, **68**: 384-85; takes vacation, **68**: 385; WW offers medical advice on exercise, **68**: 397, 400-401; death of, **68**: 504,n1; love for WW, **68**: 508; WW's tribute to, **68**: 520

Cobb, Hubbard H., **61**: 646n4

Cobb, Margaret Hubbard (Mrs. Frank Irving), **64**: 66; WW's condolences to, **68**: 504; thanks WW, **68**: 508

Cobb of "The World": A Leader in Liberalism (Heaton, comp.), **68**: 520n1

Cobden, Richard, **66**: 536

Coben, Stanley, **54**: 429n1; **60**: 117n2; **64**: 354n1; **65**: 187n5; **68**: 299n1

Coblenz, Germany, **53**: 36; **55**: 475, 507; **57**: 335, 591; **58**: 135; and Rhenish separatist movement, **59**: 401n4; **60**: 10n7, 11, 13

Coca-Cola Company, **67**: 327,n5

Cockrell, Francis Marion, **59**: 477n1

Cochran, William Joseph Hamilton, **63**: 151,n3; on situation in Senate and Foreign Relations Committee on treaty reservations, **63**: 198, 483, 483-84

Cockrell, Francis Marion, **65**: 302,n7

Cochrane, William Bourke, **54**: 473; **55**: 476, 547

Cochrane de Alençar, Augusto, **66**: 410,n1

Coe, Henry Waldo, **67**: 577-78, 579, 584, 587

Coeur d'Alene, Idaho: WW's arrival and activities in, **63**: 210-22; WW's address in, **63**: 212-21

Coeur d'Alene Evening Press, **63**: 210n1

Coffman, Edward M., **65**: 576n1

Coffman, Noah Berry, **63**: 241,n1

Cohalan, Daniel Florence, **55**: 406, 407; **56**: 438; **59**: 78; WW calls a "traitor"

and refuses to meet with, **55**: 411-12, 421, 454, 463; **58**: 587n3
Coincy, France, **56**: 195
Coit, John Knox, **62**: 42,n1, 164
Colaert, M., **61**: 5,n6,7
Colburn, Alfred J., **61**: 568
Colby, Bainbridge, **54**: 432; **55**: 302,n1; **60**: 192; **61**: 69, 134; **65**: 24, 41, 85, 88, 107, 108, 140, 141, 148, 149, 152, 153, 154, 155-56, 159, 160, 198, 217, 221, 232, 274, 298, 299, 355, 372-73, 382, 395, 421, 430, 482; **66**: 12, 26, 29, 42, 63, 71, 78-79, 82-83, 102, 109, 162, 199, 207, 209, 322, 337, 390, 542n1, 544; **67**: 54, 147n2, 176n1, 243, 313, 320, 330, 339-40, 386-87, 420, 425, 472-73, 563, 571, 602; **68**: 13, 118, 118-19, 330; and International Mercantile Marine Corporation, **53**: 111, 134, 159, 164, 186, 187-88, 195-96, 209,n1, 214, 261, 289; **54**: 54, 171; and Hog Island report, **53**: 371; possible resignation of, **53**: 626; on development of U.S. merchant marine, **54**: 394-96; **66**: 87, 89, 125, 128, 136-37, 144-45; WW's choice for Secretary of State, **64**: 464,n1; Grayson on WW's decision to appoint, **64**: 372-73; Polk willing to assist, **64**: 472; on Franco-German crisis, **65**: 156-58, 158, 162-63, 167, 167-69; and diplomatic appointments, **65**: 125, 260-61, 316-17; and Syrian situation, **65**: 141; keeping N. H. Davis in State Department, **65**: 153, 174, 178, 180-81, 229; and vacancies in department , **65**: 180-81, 225-26, 229, 238, 245,n1, 317; and Minister from Canada, **65**: 181-82, 195, 237, 242, 245; on Tacna-Arica dispute, **65**: 190-91, 195, 237; and Polk's resignation, **65**: 196, 231; on U.S. representative at San Remo Conference, **65**: 196, 197, 213, 271; and Mexico, **65**: 201, 201-202,n1, 212-13, 221-22, 252, 312, 446; WW on, **65**: 212, 443; and appointment to Teschen Commission, 213-14, 255-57, 272, 317; and appointment to Egypt, **65**: 215, 232; on Armenia, **65**: 222, 305-307, 380, 532; on WW's presence at Cabinet meeting, **65**: 222; and Lloyd George's alleged comments on WW, **65**: 231-32; on Pan-American Union, **65**: 233-34, 252-53, 261; and Kapp *Putsch*, **65**: 236-37; and submarine cable in Canal Zone, **65**: 247; on trading with Russia, **65**: 247; on Druppers' resignation, **65**: 251, 260; on Italy, **65**: 253; on Anglo-Japanese negotiations, **65**: 254; on banking consortium, **65**: 259, 261; on Yugoslavia and Adriatic question, **65**: 259, 315; on appointment to Honduras, **65**: 316, 357-58, 361; on Spa Conference, **65**: 330-31, 340; on French black troops in Germany, **65**: 341, 394-95, 397; on Armenian message, **65**: 353, 355; Geddes on, **65**: 370; on B. Long's resignation, **65**: 377; and Democratic National Convention of 1920, **65**: 386, 393, 424, 429, 432, 446-47, 451, 497, 498; on WW convening League of Nations Assembly, **65**: 388-89, 392, 433-34; on E. Root as U.S. representative to establish World Court, **65**: 399-400; plan to renominate WW, **65**: 492,n1, 493-94, 496, 498, 499, 579-81; WW's attitude toward on return from convention, **65**: 511n2; and Japanese invasion of Sakhalin, **65**: 515-17; on Teschen question, **65**: 517-18, 529, 533; on landing foreign cables on U.S. shores, **65**: 518-19, 531-32; on Åland Islands dispute, **65**: 525-26; on request for WW statement on Poland, **65**: 526, 531; leaning too much on WW, **65**: 529; on indiscreet article by Tardieu, **65**: 542-43, 543; on Cuba, **65**: 555-57; on Britain's intention to recognize Costa Rican government, **65**: 571; on Bolshivism, **66**: 4-5; and Poland's gratitude to WW, **66**: 9, 11,n1; on Polish-Soviet war, **66**: 11n1, 16, 19-24, 155; and Debs' pardon, **66**: 25; and Great Britain and Japan and action in Siberia, **66**: 39,n3; and Japan's occupation of Sakhalin, **66**: 50; on anti-Japanese movement in California, **66**: 53-54, 56, 185-87, 295, 296; and woman suffrage in Tennessee, **66**: 54n1; Jones bill and, **66**: 60; on Armenian boundary dispute and U.S. offer of mediation, **66**: 65, 86, 110, 349-50, 357, 421-23, 426-28, 436-37, 443-44,n1; on sending Knapp to Haiti, **66**: 73, 78, 99, 100,n1; apologizes for orders sending ship to Danzig, **66**: 82, 86-87; on making public Polish correspondence, **66**: 87-88,n1, 90,n1; on MacSwiney appeal, **66**: 91; suggests commission on paper shortage, **66**: 113-14; on not sending Crowder to Cuba, **66**: 123-24, 128, 236; on recognition of Mexico, **66**: 139, 142-43, 283-84, 287-88, 418-19; controversy over Creel and his Mexican involvement, **66**: 143-44, 270-71, 371-77, 403, 404, 406-408, 411; on resignation of Davis, **66**: 144, 150; and sale of surplus to Poland, **66**: 146; WW on, **66**: 155, 331-32,n1; and Russia and gold payment, **66**: 166,n1; on Pershing's proposed visit to South America, **66**: 178-79; on Bessarabia, **66**: 180,n3; and South American trip, **66**: 183-84, 410, 414, 430-31; **67**: 6-7, 23,n1,2, 109; and Åland Islands Commission appointment, **66**: 212, 253, 263, 265; and conflict with Western Union Telegraph Co., **66**: 220, 221, 399-401; asked to investigate France's contact with Lodge and Harding, **66**: 238; suggested as speaker to answer Root, WW says no, **66**: 246-47, 249; on Siamese dignitary's request to see WW, **66**: 288; praises WW, **66**: 313; on Mexican situation and

Colby, Bainbridge (*cont.*)
  U.S. oil interests, **66**: 321-22, 334-35;
  and Thanksgiving Proclamation of
  1920, **66**: 331, 342, 345, 350-52, 353; on
  appointment of Italian ambassador to
  U.S., **66**: 339-40, 342, 381-82; on resubmitting treaty to Senate and WW's response, **66**: 342, 402; on Gary as U.S.
  observer at League of Nations Assembly, **66**: 352, 353; on evacuation of
  Crimea, **66**: 355,n1; and Central American conference, **66**: 356, 357-58; on appointing minister to Bulgaria, **66**: 359-
  60, 367-68, 419-20, 428; and Adriatic
  settlement, **66**: 364-65, 367, 388-89,
  402; acknowledges King George's message, **66**: 366; on Estrada Cabrera of
  Guatemala, **66**: 389-90, 402; on open
  door in Mesopotamia and mandates,
  66: 393-99; on Anatolia, **66**: 429-30; on
  Christian Herald's relief effort in
  China, **66**: 434; on Mexican situation,
  66: 445, 446; **67**: 132-33; on inviting
  Argentine representative to U.S., **66**:
  452, 457; and O'Callaghan case, **67**:
  52n1; returns to Washington, **67**: 95-
  96; and issue of army recruiting, **67**:
  105; and veto of Milk River Valley Gun
  Club bill, **67**: 112-13; on not protesting
  against Allies' reparation demands on
  Germany, **67**: 113-15; on Cabinet tribute to WW, **67**: 150, 199; and Yap controversy, **67**: 153-56, 194-95; asks
  WW's advice on accepting speaking en-
  gagements and issue of "keeping the silence," **67**: 251-52, 554-55, 555-56, 561-
  62, 602-603, 604; WW's Jefferson Day
  message for New York Democratic
  Club, **67**: 252; **68**: 28; to visit WW, **67**:
  301, 549-50,n1; and WW Clubs, **67**:
  315, 327, 328; and The Document, **67**:
  319n1, 430-32, 432-33, 435-36, 575-77,
  579, 588, 598-601; **68**: 4,n1, 10-11, 17-
  19, 26-27, 34, 315; on search for original copy of Versailles Treaty, **67**: 354-
  44, 357; and Panama-Costa Rica border dispute, **67**: 385; on the Treaty of
  Berlin in the Senate, **67**: 421-22; on
  Cobb's reaction to New York *World*'s
  article on Foch and WW, **67**: 437; on
  Chadbourne's personal and legal dilemma, **68**: 16; and Marshal Joffre, **68**:
  26; on loan to Ecuador, **68**: 56-57, 74,
  111-12, 114, 118; on Western Ukraine
  Republic hearing, **68**: 110-11, 118, 119,
  125, 134, 140-41; WW's advice on
  Western Ukraine Republic, **68**: 113-14,
  135-36, 142; Bolling's personal advice
  on specific issues, **68**: 114-15; on defending Sinclair Consolidated Oil Corporation, **68**: 119, 125; thanks WW for
  autographed photograph, **68**: 290; photographs of, *illustration sections*, **65**:
  67; *see also* Wilson & Colby
Colby, Everett: and League of Nations

non-Partisan Association, **68**: 162,n1,
  178n1; WW on, **68**: 163
Colby, Frances Bainbridge, **67**: 548,n2;
  68: 114,n1, 118, 142
Colby, Katharine Sedgwick, **67**: 548,n2;
  68: 114,n1, 118, 142
Colby, Nathalie Sedgwick, **67**: 548,n2;
  68: 114,n1, 118, 142
Colby, Nathalie Sedgwick (Mrs. Bain-
  bridge), **65**: 370; **67**: 257,n1, 259, 260,
  548; **68**: 114,n1, 118, 142, 152
cold storage: and WW's State of the
  Union Message, **66**: 489
Coldwell, Ethel, **60**: 201
Cole, Felix, **61**: 525-26, 604,n1
Cole, Timothy, **67**: 587,n2
Colegrove, Kenneth, **60**: 146n2
Coleman, James H., **57**: 425
Coleridge, Samuel Taylor, **67**: 296
Coletta, Paolo E., **62**: 460n1; **67**: 536n2
Colins, Burgomaster, **61**: 14,n11, 21,n1
Collected Poems (Johnson), **66**: 481,n1
collective bargaining, **56**: 311n1; **66**: 76,
  217, 263-65,n1; and Burleson, **61**: 364;
  and railroad workers, **62**: 119; and first
  Industrial Conference stalemate, **63**:
  582-83, 583n1; WW on, **64**: 85, 114-15,
  424
College of Charleston, **64**: 458n3
College of New Jersey, **64**: 514,n4
Collegiate Anti-Militarism League, **53**:
  13
Colliard, Pierre, **56**: 236n2; **59**: 50,n5
Collier, William Miller, **65**: 233,n1
Collier's, **66**: 170; **67**: 557n1, 564; **68**:
  476,n3; and WW's essay, **68**: 342, 343-
  44, 353, 357, 368
Collins, Varnum Lansing, **68**: 477,n1,3
Cologne, Germany, **53**: 36; **55**: 475,
  507
Colomb, André, **57**: 533n4
Colombia, **56**: 170n1; **58**: 198; **67**: 382n5,
  581,n2, 582; and League of Nations,
  59: 444,n4; and U.S. and Treaty of
  Bogotá, **62**: 5n6; on U.S. in Dominican
  Republic, **66**: 360
*Colombia and the United States, 1765-
  1934* (Parks), **67**: 581n2
*Colonel House in Paris: A Study of Ameri-
  can Policy at the Paris Peace Confer-
  ence 1919* (Floto), **55**: 488n2
*Colonel's Folly and the President's Dis-
  tress* (Grayson), **55**: 488n2; **57**: 532n2;
  67: 289n3
Colonna, Eduardo, **61**: 189n5
Colonna, Maria Giovanna dei Principi
  (Marquise Imperiali), **61**: 189,n5
Colonna, Prospero, **53**: 496, 602n1; **58**:
  91-92, 238,n1, 239
Colorado: Democratic party in, **68**:
  301n2, 302
Colorado coal strike (1914), **64**: 4
Colored World Democracy Congress, **60**:
  486,n1
Colosimo, Gaspare, **57**: 435,n1

Colt, LeBaron Bradford, **60**: 245,n4; **62**: 67, 68, 113; **66**: 141n1; meets with WW on treaty, **61**: 492-93,n2, 515, 526-17; and reservations, **63**: 150, 296, 444, 445; and treaty fight, **64**: 94, 200-201, 337, 339
Columbia, S.C., *Sentinel*, **65**: 219n1
Columbia (S.C.) *State*, **67**: 488
Columbia Theological Seminary, Decatur, Ga., **67**: 474n1; **68**: 500-501,n1
Columbia University, **53**: 367n2, 414n1; **57**: 499n1; **58**: 15; **59**: 320n2; **61**: 374n3; **64**: 367; **65**: 238n1, 372 **66**: 262n1, 275, 343n4, 414n1; **67**: 17n1, 303, 305n1; **68**: 478n2
Columbia University School of Law, **61**: 366n2
Columbus, Christopher, **53**: 613; **68**: 92; WW remarks on, **53**: 615-16, 616
Columbus, Ga., Clearing House Association, **54**: 228n1
Columbus, Ohio: WW's arrival in, **63**: 3; WW's address in, **63**: 7-18
Columbus *Ohio State Journal*, **61**: 373
Colver, William Byron, **53**: 50, 413-14; **62**: 94, 158, 166, 222, 222-23,n1, 322; **63**: 301, 425; on cost of living, **62**: 201-202; on differences with Food Administration, **63**: 389-91; resignation from Federal Trade Commission, **66**: 241,n1; and "alleged interview" with EBW, **67**: 479, 492n1
commerce, **53**: 48-51, 55-56; Colby on development of U.S. merchant marine, **54**: 394-96
Commerce, Department of, **53**: 131, 201, 206, 230; **55**: 256; **62**: 214; Redfield on reducing level of prices, **54**: 520-21; McCormick declines appointment as Secretary of Commerce, **64**: 95
Commercial Telegraphers' Union of America, **58**: 50; **60**: 378n1
Commission for the Relief of Belgium, **53**: 14, 93n2, 296,n1; **58**: 320, 411-12; **59**: 639
Commission of Control for the Military Clauses, **61**: 59
Commission on Czechoslovak Affairs, **56**: 221, 586n1
Commission on Franco-American Affairs of War, **53**: 418n1
Commission on International Labour Legislation, **56**: 236-37,n1, 237-38; **57**: 239n5, 303, 306-307, 528,n1; Fursueth on defeated labor proposals, **56**: 308; Robinson on not reopening convention, **56**: 603-604, 604-605, 605-606; *see also* International Labour Organization
Commission on Baltic Affairs, **59**: 466,n5; report and recommendations of, **61**: 153, 160-63
Commission on Danish Affairs, **60**: 110
Commission on Greek and Albanian Affairs, **61**: 566,n1; **64**: 163,n6

Commission on Interracial Cooperation, **62**: 106n2
Commission on New States: *see* Committee on New States
Commission on Polish Affairs, **56**: 54, 55, 88-95,n3, 165,n2, 260, 395,n1, 434, 472,n2; **57**: 453; **59**: 615; **60**: 54, 189,n1, 221, 421
Commission on Ports, Waterways and Railways: *see* Inter-Allied Commission on Ports, Waterways and Railways
Commission on Prisoners of War, **59**: 424,n3
Commission on Reparation and Damages: *see* Reparation Commission
Commission on Rumanian and Yugoslav Affairs: *see* Paris Peace Conference—Commission on Rumanian and Yugoslav Affairs
Commission on the League of Nations: *see* League of Nations Commission
Commission on the Left Bank of the Rhine: *see* Inter-Allied Rhineland Commission
Commission on the Responsibility of the Authors of the War and on Enforcement of Penalties: *see* Paris Peace Conference—Commission on the Responsibility of the Authors of the War and on Enforcement of Penalties; responsibility for the war
Commission on Training Camp Activities, **61**: 530n2
Committee for Armenian and Syrian Relief, **53**: 134-35
Committee for Near East Relief, **65**: 234,n4
Committee of One Hundred: *see* American Commission on Conditions in Ireland
Committee of Union and Progress (CUP), **58**: 555n1
Committee on Belgian Affairs, **60**: 105
Committee on Committees (U.S. Congress), **55**: 449n1
Committee on New States: *see* Paris Peace Conference—Committee on New States
Committee on Public Information, **53**: 440n1; **54**: 96n2; **55**: 363; **56**: 340,n2; **58**: 531n1; **61**: 644n1; WW praises Creel's work on, **56**: 124; liquidation of **65**: 374-76, 442-43,n3
Committee on the Eastern Frontiers of Germany: *see* Paris Peace Conference—Committee on the Eastern Frontiers of Germany
Commonwealth Steel Company of St. Louis, **67**: 520n2
Communications Conference, International: *see* International Communications, Conference on
Communism and Communists, **60**: 642: and Hungarian revolution, **56**: 239, 277, 332; and Bavaria, **57**: 4n1;

Communism and Communists (*cont.*)
H. Hoover on, **57**: 503n2; **61**: 392; and
Austria, **58**: 205; Lansing on tendency
in U.S. toward, **62**: 612-13; in Russia,
56: 387, 389, 390 391
Communist party: and "Palmer raids,"
65: 187n5
Complications of Pregnancy (Davis), **67**:
458,n5
Comprehensive Textbook of Psychiatry
(Kaplan and Sadock, eds.), **58**: 612n5;
62: 629n4; **64**: 525n2
Compromise (Morley), **67**: 561,n1
Compton, Thomas Foster, **66**: 414,n1
Comrades in Service, **54**: 5,n2, 6
Concerning a League of Nations (Bryce),
53: 335,n3
*Conditions in the Near East: Report of the
American Military Mission to Armenia*,
64: 450,n4
Coney, Edward A., **58**: 51,n4
Conference of Ambassadors: issue of U.S.
withdrawal from, **67**: 33,n1,2, 34,n1,
44; and Corfu incident, **68**: 419n1, 435;
and Memel, **68**: 521; *see also* Council of
the Heads of Delegations
Conference of Governors and Mayors: *see*
Governors and Mayors, Conference of
Conference of Lecturers, **68**: 285n1
Conference of Woman Suffragists of the
Allied Countries and of the United
States, **57**: 218, 219n2
Conference on the Limitation of Arma-
ment (Washington Naval Conference),
67: 360,n3, 437-38, 454n1, 464, 471,n1,
478, 494n1, 511; and Bliss, **67**: 390n1,
391; Cobb on, **67**: 419n1, 447-48, 511;
WW unable to attend opening of, **67**:
444; WW on, **67**: 490, 585; and Hughes
on open-door resolution, **67**: 531n1;
Davis on, **67**: 538, 539, 540, 544-45,n1;
see also Four Power Treaty; Five
Power Treaty; Nine Power Treaty
Confidential Report asked for by Dr.
Brown (Scott), **53**: 206n2
Conger, Arthur C.: interviews German
officials on attitudes toward peace
treaty, **58**: 307-10,n1, 314; **59**: 348n1
Congregational Church: and League of
Nations, **66**: 202
Congress (U.S.): *see* United States Congress
Congressional Directory, **67**: 170, 171, 484
congressional elections of 1922: *see* Elec-
tion of 1922, and under the names of
individual states
Congressional Record, **66**: 198n1; WW
on, **55**: 310,

63d Cong., 2d sess., **66**: 157n6

65th Cong., 2d sess., **53**: 83n1, 116n1

65th Cong., 3d sess., **53**: 308n1, 469n1,
481n1, 542n2, 581n3, 582n5, 625n1,
637n1; **54**: 55n2, 153n1, 174n1,
259n1,2,3, 397n1, 485n1; **55**: 204n1,
312n1, 351n1, 367n1, 388n1, 469n1;
60: 245n9; **66**: 126n1

66th Cong., 1st sess., **55**: 297n2; **59**:
366n1; **61**: 66n3, 297n2, 353n2, 517n1,
568n1, 626n1; **62**: 209n1, 305n1, 542;
63: 3n4, 52n3, 198n1,3,4, 304n1, 389n,
531n4, 557n1, 601n1; **64**: 58n1, 120n1,
126n1

66th Cong., 2d sess., **64**: 120n1, 259n,
284n1, 338; **65**: 80n1, 109n1, 243n1,
265n2, 288n4, 328n2, 329n3, 351n2,
354n2, 363n1; **66**: 113n1

66th Cong. 3d sess., **66**: 386n2, 505n5;
67: 9n1, 12n1, 22n, 97n1,2, 113n1,
144n1, 176n1, 194n

67th Cong., 1st sess., **67**: 355n4, 418n,
422n4; **68**: 298n1

67th Cong., 2d sess., **67**: 577n1; **68**:
57n1, 61, 119n2

Congressional Review, **68**: 496
Congress of Berlin (1878), **58**: 461,n1; **61**:
94, 337
*Congress of Berlin and After, A Diplo-
matic History of the Near Eastern Settlement, 1878-1880* (Medlicott), **58**:
461n1
Congress of Oppressed Nationalities of
Austria-Hungary, **54**: 135,n3
Congress of Vienna, **53**: 425; **54**: 23n13,
312, 314; **63**: 429
Conklin, Edwin Grant, **67**: 181,n1, 525
Connally, Tom (Thomas Terry), **56**:
428,n3; **68**: 471,n5
Connaught and Strathearn, Arthur William Patrick Albert, Duke of, **53**:
509,n2, 526, 533n1, 569, 592, 583,n6,
594n11; photograph of, *illustration section*, **53**
Connecticut: Democratic party in, and
woman suffrage, **65**: 164; **68**: 50, 98
Connell, William Lawrence, **65**: 353,n1;
66: 68
Conner, Valerie Jean, **55**: 365n1; **66**:
263n1
Conquest of Haiti (Seligman), **66**: 25n1
Conquest of Santo Domingo (Gannett),
66: 383n1
Conrad, Joseph, **67**: 105n3
*Conscientious Objector, Introduction
by Newton D. Baker* (Kellogg), **61**:
366n3
conscientious objectors, **53**: 12-13,
307n1,2; **62**: 97, 250, 545n3; release
from Fort Leavenworth, 54: 397-98,n4;
and amnesty issue, **61**: 351-52, 398-99;
N. D. Baker on, **61**: 366-68, 615; **66**:
401, 415; J. N. Sayre on amnesty issue,
62: 126-28; Spargo on amnesty for, **62**:
555-56, 556-59; Sinclair and petition
for amnesty, **63**: 425,n1; Baker on general amnesty for, **65**: 126-27; J. N.
Sayre objects to treatment of, **65**: 441-
42; Hapgood on, **66**: 343

Conscribing Intellect (*Manchester Guardian*), **59**: 519n2

conscription, **53**: 517, 560; and League of Nations Covenant, **54**: 140, 451; Orlando on, **54**: 388-89; and Schenck *v.* U.S., **55**: 347n1; Lloyd George on arms limitation and, **56**: 264; Council of Four on Russia and, **59**: 436, 437, 438; and Army Reorganization bill, **65**: 355n1, 366; and Crowder and Selective Service Act, **66**: 58,n1

conservation, **53**: 230, 280

Consolidated Coal Company (Baltimore), **63**: 56n2

Consolidated Treaty Series (Parry, ed.), **54**: 326n3; **60**: 52,n4

Constant, Paul-Henri-Benjamin-Balluat d'Estournelles de, **61**: 607n3

Constantine I (of Greece), **63**: 61; issue of recognition of, **67**: 9, 10-11,n2

Constantinides, Constantin-Jason G., **66**: 29n1

Constantinople, **53**: 351, 561, 562; **54**: 197, 414, 556; **55**: 27-28; **56**: 118, 180, 511; **57**: 466, 527, 545-46,n2; **58**: 323-24,n3, 436, 438, 475, 508, 322, 459; **60**: 612, 616; **62**: 265, 552, 607, 620,n1; **63**: 59n2, 60-62, 121, 236, 337n1; **64**: 26, 27, 56, 161, 449; **65**: 64, 91, 113; **68**: 141n1, 147; and King-Crane recommendations, **62**: 608; and Thrace, **62**: 320, 416-17; WW on, **63**: 35-35, 188, 342; **65**: 73-74; and mandate issue, **65**: 202, 271; talk of sending U.S. ship to, **65**: 536-37, 538, 540, 549; *see also* Paris Peace Conference—Constantinople

Constitution (U.S.): *see* United States Constitution

Constitutional Government in the United States (Wilson), **62**: 632,n14; **68**: 115

Contarini, Salvatore, **66**: 365,n1

Contested Election Case of Britt v. Weaver: Hearings Before the Committee on Elections No. 3, House of Representatives, Sixty-fifth Congress, Second Session..., **55**: 367n1

Continental Trust Company, **55**: 247n1

Converse College, **67**: 260

Coogan, Jackie (John Leslie), **68**: 506,n1

Cook, George Crouse, **66**: 366,n1, 370

Cook, Jeff, **62**: 415, 434-35

Cook, Sir John, **53**: 560,n1, 568

Cook Archipelago, **54**: 312, 313

Cooksey, George Robert, **57**: 381,n21

Coolidge, Archibald Cary, **56**: 54n14, 182; **57**: 96-97, 367, 416; **59**: 348, 404; **60**: 17,n1; **61**: 566n1; **62**: 206, 320, 457, 510; **63**: 209; **68**: 68,n3; on peace terms with Austria, **60**: 642-43; and Åland Islands Commission, **66**: 253, 263; and WW Clubs, **67**: 253, 257-58,n1,2, 264

Coolidge, (John) Calvin, **55**: 206,n1, 235, 238; **57**: 445,n1; **65**: 415,n1; **66**: 188n1; **68**: 404, 456; and Boston police strike, **63**: 167n6, 169; WW's election congrat-

ulations and Coolidge's response, **63**: 615,n1; **67**: 206, 207-208, 211; WW praises for League of Nations position, **68**: 76,n1; thanks WW for message, **68**: 80-81; on Senate resolution on WW's birthday, **68**: 247, 247-48; WW thanks for letter with Senate resolution, **68**: 259-60; informs WW of Harding's death and invites to participate in funeral, **68**: 399, 400, 401; Cobb on, **68**: 401; and Turkish treaty, **68**: 504; concern over WW's health, **68**: 552, 553; and WW's death and funeral, **68**: 569, 571, 573, 574, 575, 583

Coolidge, Grace Anna Goodhue (Mrs. Calvin), **67**: 208,n2; **68**: 259,n1, 552,n1; at WW's funeral, **68**: 569, 574, 575, 583

Coolidge, Harold Jefferson, **56**: 54n14

Coolidge Mission, **56**: 54,n14, 384n2; **57**: 367n1; **59**: 403n1,3, 404

Coontz, Robert Edward, **65**: 548-49,n1; **66**: 58; **67**: 27n7; and inauguration ceremonies, **67**: 210-11,n4

Cooper, Henry Allen, **55**: 267,n2, 270

Cooper, John Milton, Jr., **67**: 297n1

Cooper, William Knowles, **66**: 121,n2

cooperative system: Tumulty on, **60**: 152

Copeland, Mrs. James William, **68**: 187

Copeland, Royal Samuel, M.D., **68**: 179n1, 190,n1

Copley-Plaza Hotel, Boston, **55**: 226, 236; **62**: 177

copper: WW on export of, **54**: 409-10; and Arizona situation, **66**: 125-28, 132; WW on prices and price-fixing, **67**: 176-78

Coppini, Pompeo, **66**: 369n1,2

Coppo, A., **59**: 68n2

Corbin, David Alan, **65**: 335n1

Corcoran School of Art, **65**: 106n3; **66**: 470,n2

Cordoba, S.M.S., **55**: 432

Cordova Davila, Félix: on appointment of Attorney-General of Porto Rico, **55**: 158-59, 264-65

Corfu, **59**: 7, 11; incident, **68**: 419,n1, 432n1, 435, 451

Cork, Ireland, **54**: 256,n1; **66**: 512-13,n3, 518

corn: and prices, **61**: 500; **66**: 36n3; surplus for Chinese famine relief, **67**: 80, 139; WW on imports and exports of, **67**: 191, 191-92

Cornell University, **53**: 350n1, 367n1; **66**: 199n1, 478,n2; **67**: 235n3; **68**: 68n3

Cornish, New Hampshire, **66**: 57n1; **68**: 415,n2, 417

Cornwall, James Handyside Marshall, **57**: 246,n3

Cornwell, John Jacob, **65**: 336-37,n2

Cornwallis, Kinahan, **56**: 115,n12

Coromilas, Anna Ewing Cockrell (Mrs. Lambros A.), **59**: 477n1; **65**: 302,n7

Coromilas, Lambros A., **57**: 427,n8; **59**: 477,n1; **65**: 302,n7

Corona (yacht), **67**: 373, 375; **68**: 115, 117

Correl, Col., **65**: 491,n2
Correll, John W.: murder of, **61**: 510, 510-11, 525
Corso, Castillo, **61**: 639,n8
Corwin, Edwin Samuel, **66**: 198n1
Cosenza, Italy, **57**: 442
Cosmopolitan Shipping Co., **65**: 282
Cossacks, **53**: 184-85; **55**: 181; **56**: 185; **57**: 314; **58**: 570, 573, 575, 576, 577; **59**: 234; **63**: 559, 560
Cossio, Rev. Aluigi, **62**: 26,n1, 317
Costa, Afonsa Augusto da, **57**: 427,n10
Costa Rica, **53**: 342,n6; **54**: 24, 46, 170; **61**: 251, 254; **65**: 247n1, 510; **67**: 548; Lansing recommends recognizing, **63**: 616; political situation in, **63**: 616n1; issue of recognition of, **64**: 65, 94-95, 153,n1, 186, 204, 229-30, 235, 245, 317; and appointments, **64**: 205, 317; Central American conference in, **66**: issue of recognition of, **65**: 46, 464-66, 505-506, 571; recognition of, **65**: 571,n2, 356, 357-58; and Panama boundary dispute, **67**: 382-84,n5, 385
Costello, John F., **62**: 21, 100; **66**: 310; **67**: 212, 213
Costigan, Edward Prentiss, **53**: 328-32; **62**: 96
cost of living, **55**: 89, 358, 359; **61**: 549n1; **62**: 122, 158; **63**: 46, 125-29, 596, 599; Tumulty on, **59**: 77; **62**: 180-81; Hines on, **61**: 411-13, 415; **62**: 50-51, 72-77; **63**: 119; and condition of railroad workers, **62**: 31,n1, 161-62; McAdoo on Republican House of Representatives addressing issue of, **62**: 71-72; WW, cabinet, and Congress tackling, **62**: 94-95; WW on, **62**: 99, 163; Leffingwell on, **62**: 104, 105-106; and railroad situation, **62**: 118, 120, 136, 137, 139, 193, 195, 470-71, 484-88, 489, 567-73; Redfield on, **62**: 129-31; WW meets with Federal Trade Commission on prices and, **62**: 158-61; WW gives undivided attention to, **62**: 162; issue of making public report on, **62**: 165,n1; Meeker's suggestions on, **62**: 165; WW's address to joint session of Congress on, **62**: 168, 169, 171, 209-10; Palmer's memorandum on and suggested legislation, **62**: 169, 171-80, 179-80; effect of railroad strike on, **62**: 190-91; Houston on, **62**: 197n1; Colver on Reconstruction Research Division memorandum on, **62**: 201-202; WW advises Clarkson not to make report public, **62**: 223; and farmers, **62**: 300; Glass on, **62**: 314; Palmer on railroad situation, **62**: 463; WW's statements and messages on railroad situation and, **62**: 472-76, 490, 494-95, 496-98; and Hines' suggestions for talk to railway shopmen, **62**: 482-84; Tumulty on railway strike and, **62**: 543-44; and WW's Labor Day message, **62**: 595-96, 636;

Gary on steel wages and, **62**: 600; WW's address on indicates memory loss, **62**: 630; WW addresses Minnesota legislature on, **63**: 123; and WW's Annual Message to Congress, **64**: 81, 82, 83, 111; and coal strike, **64**: 141n2, 146-47, 154; and railroad crisis, **64**: 198, 391n1, 406-407, 412, 420-24, 428-30; and railroad strike, **65**: 15, 187,n4, 359; WW on, **65**: 42; and Tumulty's proposed message to Congress, **65**: 129-30, 131; Burleson on, **65**: 212; charges of congressional inaction concerning, **65**: 359, 368; WW on, **67**: 610
Cost of the War 1914-1919: British Economic War Aims and the Origins of Reparations (Bunselmayer), **56**: 285n1
Cottin, Emile, **55**: 209,n1
Cotton, Joseph Potter, **53**: 76, 360,n3
Cotton Futures Act, **68**: 270
cotton industry, **55**: 38, 157, 252-53, 286-87, 297; prices and exportation, **53**: 25, 78-79, 100, 132-33, 149, 163, 164, 166, 202; **54**: 192-93, 228; **57**: 511-12,n2; Houston on, **62**: 269; Burleson on, **63**: 266; issue of federal assistance for, **66**: 36-38, 112n1, 159; WW on, **66**: 159, 380; **67**: 191, 191-92
Cottrell (or Cotterell), C. R., **63**: 273n2
Coucy-le-Château, France: WW visits, **56**: 194, 198
Coughlin, Blakely, **65**: 425,n1, 431, 433
Coughlin, George Harper, **65**: 425
Coughlin, John William, M.D. **55**: 409,n3; **67**: 203; death of, **66**: 458,n1
Coulson, B. J. B., **56**: 221,n6
Council of Defense System and its Relation to Reconstruction Work (Clarkson), **53**: 97,n1
Council (Conference) of Ambassadors, **65**: 142n1
Council of Five: see Paris Peace Conference—Council of Five
Council of Foreign Ministers: see Paris Peace Conference—Council of Foreign Ministers
Council of Four: see Paris Peace Conference—Council of Four
Council of Jewish Women: and League of Nations, **66**: 202-203
Council of National Defense, **53**: 11, 117, 218-20, 252, 287; **57**: 429,n15; **65**: 117, memorandum on cost of living, **62**: 166, 201-202; Baruch resigns from Advisory Committee of, **62**: 554,n1; and Committee on Public Information, **65**: 374
Council of Ten: see Paris Peace Conference—Council of Ten
Council of the Heads of Delegations (successor to the Supreme Council): see under names of individual members and their principal advisers such as A. J. Balfour, G. Clemenceau, J. W. Davis
Council of the League of Nations: see League of Nations Council

Council of the Principal Allied and Associated Powers: *see* Paris Peace Conference—Council of Four
Council on Foreign Relations, **60**: 17n1; **67**: 426,n1; Davis to address on Washington Conference, **67**: 544-45,n1
Country Life, **68**: 449
Courland (Latvia), **56**: 169; **60**: 475
Courrières, France, **56**: 295
Cousse, Edouard-Sylvain, **56**: 115,n13, 116
Covarrubias, Miguel, **65**: 485,n3
Covenant of the League of Nations: *see* League of Nations Covenant
Covenant of the League of Nations (memorandum, Borden), **55**: 501,n1
Covington, Harry Franklin, **67**: 182
Cowan, Sam K., **62**: 42n2
Cowan, Sir Walter Henry, **60**: 267,n16, 269,n17, 270
Cowdray, 1st Baron, **65**: 534,n1
Cowgill, James S., **63**: 63,n1
Cowles, Edward Spencer, **60**: 569,n1, 573
Cowles, Ione Virginia Hill (Mrs. Josiah Evans), **53**: 125,n2; **63**: 407n1, 423,n3
Cowper, William, **68**: 252n2
Cowperthwaite, Joe, **66**: 92,n1, 134-35, 192; death of, **66**: 245
Cox, James Middleton, **66**: 25, 165, 173, 258, 282n1; **67**: 94,n1, 349, 534; **68**: 96, 139, 492, 576; mentioned as presidential candidate, **65**: 346, 383, 435, 440, 480, 498, 499; code name for, **65**: 350; WW on, **65**: 435, 491, 499, 506, 514, 529; votes received in *Literary Digest* poll, **65**: 474n2; W. G. Sharp on prohibition and candidacy of, **65**: 475; balloting at convention, **65**: 492-93,n2; controversy over Glass' statement on, **65**: 494-95,n1; WW congratulates and Cox's reply, **65**: 499, 500; WW meets with, **65**: 513, 520-21,n1, 522-24; commitment to League of Nations, **65**: 520n1, 521, 522; and reservations to Versilles Treaty, **65**: 523,n1; statement of accord, **65**: 524-25; and removal of Cummings as Democratic national chairman, 551-52,n1; advance reviews of speech, **66**: 4; Hapgood on, **66**: 28; campaign of, **66**: 118, 190; WW on, **66**: 156, 157, 158; on using Taft-WW material on League of Nations, **66**: 159,n1, 184; McAdoo campaigns for, **66**: 180-81, 235; Crowell on League of Nations and, **66**: 188,n1; Harding on difference between League of Nations positions, **66**: 208n1; blames recession on U.S. not joining League of Nations, **66**: 242,n1; and Viereck and German Americans, **66**: 248n1, 249; Tumulty on prospects for, **66**: 250; invites WW and EBW to New York meeting, **66**: 253, 257, 262; Tumulty on WW writing praises of, **66**: 289; WW's endorsement

of, **66**: 290-91; election results, **66**: 306n1; WW's post-election message to, **66**: 321; postelection thoughts, **66**: 333; and 1922 campaign, **68**: 3, 18, 476n3; and Jefferson Day dinner brouhaha, **68**: 3, 11, 15, 17, 22, 59, 591; WW on, **68**: 10, 14, 59; on Corfu incident, **68**: 419; on WW's Armistice Day speech, **68**: 473-74; WW thanks for League of Nations support, **68**: 476; *see also* Democratic presidential campaign of 1920
Cox, Sir Percy (Zachariah), **66**: 48,n10
Cox-Roosevelt College Clubs, **67**: 314n1
Cracow, Poland, **56**: 130, 133
Cracow, University of, **55**: 3; and WW's honorary degree, **67**: 392, 400
Craig, Albert M., **54**: 476n7
Craig, Gordon Alexander, **61**: 34n1; **65**: 98n1
Craighead, Edwin Boone, **68**: 176,n1
Craighead, Erwin, **68**: 171,n1, 175, 176,n1
Crallé, Richard K., **53**: 267n2
Cramer, Lucien, **54**: 233
Cranborne, Viscount (Robert Arthur James Gascoyne-Cecil), **56**: 435,n1,2
Cranborne, Viscountess (Elizabeth Vere Cavendish), **56**: 435,n1
Crandall, Samuel Benjamin, **56**: 58,n3, 68
Crane, Charles Richard, **54**: 84; **57**: 468; **58**: 575,n6; **59**: 369, 373,n1, 376, 420, 574, 575, 595; **61**: 44, 442-44; **64**: 262-63, 522,n2; **68**: 381, 409n1, 577; on Prince L'vov's trip to U.S. and Russian situation, **53**: 258, 258-59; and mediation mission, **56**: 180, 272n2, 310, 442; and Syrian mission, **57**: 388, 391, 535; **58**: 172; on division of Turkish Empire, **58**: 322-27; and Japanese claims settlement, **58**: 328; and appointments, **64**: 296, 317, 407-408; offers vacation home to WW, **64**: 425, **65**: 110; appointment of Mrs. Summers, **65**: 185; on Tenney's retirement plans, **66**: 78-79; and *Washington Herald*, **66**: 169; and relief funds for China, **66**: 327n2; and fund raising efforts for WW's S Street home, **67**: 137n3; and Alice Masaryk, **68**: 296n1
Crane, Cornelia Workman Smith (Mrs. Charles Richard), **53**: 259; **66**: 79; **68**: 414,n4
Crane, Ellen Douglas Bruce (Mrs. Richard), **68**: 414,n5
Crane, John Oliver, **68**: 409,n1, 414
Crane, Richard, **53**: 258, 258-59, 306; **55**: 453; **64**: 447; **68**: 409,n1, 414,n5; appointed minister to Czechoslovakia, **56**: 123,n1; **57**: 334, 374; report on Turkey and Syria, **62**: 607-608,n1; on letter from Masaryk urging ratification, **64**: 443,n1
Crane-King Commission: *see* King-Crane Commission

Craufurd-Stuart, Charles Kennedy, **63**: 606,n1; **64**: 3, 88, 90-91, 217, 235, 239; and Miss Ladenburg, **65**: 83n1

Cravath, Paul Drennan, **53**: 76; **66**: 198n1, 246n2, 251; **67**: 551,n1

Craven, Elijah Richardson, **64**: 514,n4

Craven, Hermon Wilson, **55**: 290, 330n2

Cravens, Joseph M., **65**: 546,n3

Crawford, Vernon Allen, **68**: 500-501,n1, 502

Creel, Blanche Bates (Mrs. George), **68**: 326,n1, 577

Creel, George, **53**: 16, 166, 213, 318, 349, 358, 366, 368, 369, 376, 391, 394, 407; **54**: 431, 432; **55**: 363-64, 529; **61**: 644n1; **63**: 625; **66**: 542n1; **67**: 167; **68**: 161, 577; and Lansing, **53**: 402; publicity work of, **53**: 440; on Hungary and its new Prime Minister, **54**: 470-71; WW's praise for, **56**: 124-25; on Ireland, **56**: 486; **60**: 332; on liquidation of Committee on Public Information, **65**: 374-76, 422-43,n2, 3; becomes WW's literary agent, **66**: 33-34, 64, 65, 81, 121, 171; on campaign and WW's Mexican policy, **66**: 122-23,n1; and campaign strategy, **66**: 148, 150; charges of being followed in Mexico, **66**: 321,n1, 337; and Mexican trip, **66**: 133,n2, 150, 170; **67**: 81-82; on Mexico, **66**: 139,n1, 143, 269-71, 283,n1, 371-77, 403-405; on WW's statement on League of Nations referendum, **66**: 175-76; and Pelmanism, **66**: 251n1; Colby answers on Mexican situation, **66**: 406-408, 411; and Sisson Papers, **66**: 478,n2; encourages WW to write, **67**: 141-42, 163-64; bitter about R. S. Baker's exclusive rights to WW's material and reveals publishing situation, **67**: 174, 241-42, 254-55; and Debs' pardon, **67**: 231; works with R. S. Baker on financial aspects of book and serialization project, **67**: 238, 243-45, 249, 256; on Hearst offer for serialization and WW's rejection, **67**: 363-64, 364-65; WW recommends as adviser to League of Nations advocates, **68**: 140; Clarke to meet with, **68**: 140, 142; WW asks advice on his essay, **68**: 325-26; publication of WW's essay, **68**: 342-44, 347, 347-48, 353-54, 356, 356-57, 367; EBW advises waiting before making decision on WW's essay, **68**: 344-45; on Foley's project using WW's speeches, **68**: 349-50, 350, 355, 408; WW on Foley project, **68**: 411,n1

Creighton, James Edwin, **66**: 478,n2

Cres: *see* Cherso

Crespi, Silvio Benigno, **53**: 326,n6, 360, 481; **55**: 58,n8, 113; **56**: 444, 502; **57**: 166, 609; **58**: 64, 77, 78, 252, 263, 379, 426n1, 471; **59**: 110, 125n1, 492, 495, 625; **60**: 26n11, 74, 473,n20, 591; **61**: 109n11, 151, 252, 277, 278n7, 283, 314, 317, 318, 319, 320, 363, 384; on

reparations, **58**: 334-35; **59**: 422; and Klotz, **58**: 341, 368, 397; on Austrian treaty, **59**: 388-89, 389, 536, 539

Creswell, John Andrew Jackson, **55**: 366,n2

Crete, **59**: 92, 102

Crillon Hotel, Paris, **53**: 384, 422, 438, 573; **54**: 199, 463, 473

Crimea, **66**: 355,n1

Crisis, The (periodical), **53**: 236n1

Crispell, Kenneth R., M.D., **62**: 628n1

Crispi, Francesco, **56**: 495,n1

Croatia and Croatians, **53**: 43,n1, 638n1; **55**: 84, 87-88; **56**: 562, 563, 566, 567-72; **57**: 337, 338, 540-41, 543, 549, 613; **58**: 16, 80, 87, 150, 160, 162, 239n4, 374, 392, 393n4, 396; **59**: 215, 380, 557; **61**: 344; **64**: 368n1; and Fiume, **59**: 97; **63**: 486; and Klagenfurt Basin, **60**: 37

Crocker, F. C., **62**: 300n1

Croiset, Alfred, **53**: 459n1

Croisset, Madame de, **60**: 251,n4

Croisset, Francis de, **60**: 250-51,n3

Croll, Morris William, **67**: 182

Croly, Herbert David, **55**: 451; **61**: 240n1; **68**: 315n1; opposes treaty, **60**: 202,n1

Cromer, 1st Earl of: *see* Baring, Evelyn

Cromwell, Oliver, **55**: 383; **58**: 286, 288

Crooks, James B., **68**: 134n1

Crosby, Oscar Terry, **53**: 627; **54**: 88; on foreign loans, **53**: 477-80, 571-72; resignation as Special Finance Commissioner, **53**: 716

Crosley, Walter Selwyn, **54**: 259,n2

Crothers, Samuel McChord, **63**: 387,n4; **67**: 105n3

Crowder, Enoch Herbert, **62**: 545,n2; **65**: 556,n3; **66**: 493,n3; and draft, **66**: 58,n1; mission to Cuba, **66**: 83-85, 123-24, 128; **67**: 24, 26, 32

Crowe, Sir Eyre (Alexander Barby Wichart), **53**: 721; **54**: 490,n2; **56**: 396; **57**: 392; **58**: 236; **59**: 396; **60**: 98, 121, 468, 480; **61**: 43; **63**: 307, 422, 588; **64**: 163n6; and Adriatic question **64**: 168, 178, 323

Crowell, Benedict, **57**: 383; and resignation, **65**: 227, 228,n1; Geddes on, **65**: 371; and Republican endorsements, **66**: 188,n1, 192; WW on, **66**: 192

Crown Prince of Germany: *see* Friedrich Wilhelm Viktor August Ernst

Crum, William Demos, **54**: 176

Cuba, **53**: 571; **54**: 24n14, 65, 115, 264; **56**: 308; **58**: 198; **62**: 9; **66**: 482; **67**: 26,n4; and cable censorship, **57**: 449; and issue of retention of enemy ships, **58**: 402n12, 527, 558; WW on Spanish-American War and, **63**: 184, 434, 455; Crowder mission to, **66**: 83-85, 123-24, 128; **67**: 24-25,n1, 32; sending ships to, **66**: 233, 234, 236; Baker on Army preparation plans for, **66**: 236-38

Cuban American Telephone and Telegraph Company, **66**: 498, 513-14, 544; **67**: 3

Cuba and the United States: and sugar industry, **55**: 252; Colby on political situation and elections, **65**: 555-57

Cuff, Robert Dennis George, **53**: 205n1

Culberson, Charles Allen, **64**: 63; **67**: 166, 572,n1; Hitchcock on, **65**: 109; defeat of, **68**: 298n2

Cullen, Charles C., **67**: 163n3

Culbert, Frederick Paul, **66**: 535-36,n2, 539

Culme-Seymour, Michael, **59**: 25,n6, 26

Culpeper, Va., **55**: 443

Culpeper & Mitchells Presbyterian Church (Culpeper, Va.), **61**: 595n3

Cumberland, Charles Curtis, **64**: 120n1, 128n1; **65**: 252n1

Cummings, C. K., **54**: 27n2

Cummings, Homer Stillé, **53**: 242, 244; **54**: 56, 61, 408-409,n1, 429; **55**: 308, 313; **59**: 39, 160; **60**: 41, 112-13, 115n7; **61**: 350; **62**: 587; **64**: 527; **65**: 24, 28, 333n1, 429, 514, 580; **67**: 411; **68**: 19; suggested as Lansing's successor, **64**: 419, 427-28; on strategy at Democratic National Convention, 1920, **65**: 344-50, 383, 385, 386, 393, 395, 432, 435, 445, 446-47, 450-51, 470-71, 480, 492-93, 496, 497; code for communicating with WW, **65**: 348, 481; WW suggests vice-presidential candidates to, **65**: 397; on Bryan's demands, **65**: 424; on convention and his keynote speech, **65**: 471,n1; WW congratulates, **65**: 477; on League of Nations plank, **65**: 482; on platform getting WW's approval, **65**: 488, 489; WW thanks for message from convention, **65**: 489-90; votes on sixteenth ballot, **65**: 492n2; Burleson excluded from discussions, **65**: 495,n1; and WW's nomination, **65**: 498, 499; mentioned as candidate, **65**: 498; and Democratic chairmanship, **65**: 507, 551-52; on vetoing WW's renomination, **65**: 579-81; suggested for Cabinet position, **66**: 7, 196; visits WW, **66**: 194-96, 331; **67**: 268-70; on campaign, **66**: 189-91, 194-96; congratulates WW on Nobel Peace Prize, **66**: 536; WW thanks, **66**: 540; and WW clubs, **67**: 345, 353, 426; WW calls to conference on The Document, **68**: 26-27,n1; on interview with WW, **68**: 88-92; WW on his running for Senate, **68**: 92-93; on reasons for not running for Senate, **68**: 97-98

Cummings, Marguerite Tutweiler (Mrs. Homer Stillé), **65**: 347,n5

Cummins, Albert Baird, **58**: 109,n3; **61**: 372; **62**: 67, 113, 223; and railroad crisis, **55**: 248, 257; **61**: 414-15; **62**: 98-99,n3, 117, 118, 163, 183-84, 191, 192, 223-24; meets with WW on treaty, **61**: 548,n1, 569, 593-94, 598, 599; and treaty fight, **64**: 94, 200-201, 337; and railroad legislation, **64**: 195,n1, 196, 197; and Indiana plank, **65**: 292n1; photograph of, *illustration section*, **65**

Cummins-Esch bill: *see* Esch-Cummins bill and Act

Cummins railroad bill, **64**: 195,n1, 196, 197

Cunard Line, **53**: 110n1

Cunliffe, Walter, 1st Baron Cunliffe of Headley, **56**: 69n1, 208, 270, 271,n3, 292, 444; **57**: 287; **58**: 27, 113, 424, 469, 579; **59**: 31, 50,n7, 163, 442; **60**: 50,n1, 93, 494

Cunningham, Minnie Fisher, **59**: 203

Curley, James Michael, **68**: 200-201,n1

Current History, **68**: 482,n1, 495, 499, 531

Currie, Archibald A., **64**: 191n2

Curry, George, **53**: 515n1

Curry, Mabel Dunlap (Mrs. Charles), **66**: 343,n1

Curry, Ray Watson, **57**: 626n3

Curtis, Charles, **58**: 413,n1; **61**: 372; **65**: 401n1; and treaty fight, **64**: 200-201, 337

Curtis, Cyrus Hermann Kotzschmar, **67**: 419,n1

Curtis, Edwin Upton, **63**: 167n6

Curtis, Kate Pillsbury (Mrs. Cyrus Hermann Kotzschmar), **67**: 419,n1

Curtis, Lionel George, **60**: 17,n1

Curtis, Lucius Fisher, **55**: 409,n7, 479

Curtis, Winterton Conway, **68**: 121,n1

Curzola (now Korcula), Yugoslavia, **59**: 570; **60**: 309, 310

Curzon, George Nathaniel, 1st Marquess of Kedleston, **53**: 472, 559, 562, 563, 564, 566, 567, 594,n14; **54**: 235-37, 468-69; **55**: 116, 480; **59**: 19, 298, 309, 317, 317-18, 369, 396; **62**: 61, 254,n2, 285n1, 331, 334, 428; **63**: 306; **64**: 263; **65**: 481; **66**: 39n3; and WW and Oxford University, **53**: 27-28, 66, 161-62,n1; **59**: 552-53; Clemenceau on, **59**: 331-33, 341, 342; Lloyd George defends, **59**: 335, 344; reply to Germany on economic effect of peace treaty, **59**: 360, 362-66, 368; and Syria and Turkish Empire issue, **64**: 25-26; and Craufurd-Stuart affair, **64**: 88, 91; and French troops in Germany, **65**: 158-59; and negotiations with Chicherin, **65**: 288n3; and Armenian mandate, **65**: 301-302, 307; and Mesopotamia and open door in mandates, **66**: 393, 394-99, 430; and mandates, **67**: 54, 147n2, 153

Curzon, Grace Elvina Trilla Hinds Duggan, Lady Curzon, **55**: 480,n3; **59**: 68,n1

Curzon, Mary Victoria Leiter, Lady Curzon, **55**: 480,n3

Cushing, Harvey Williams, **58**: 636; **65**: 283-84,n1, 296, 403n3

Cust, Sir Charles (Leopold), **53**: 508,n1, 529, 540, 592, 593; **66**: 435,n2; **67**: 105n3

Cutcheon, Franklin Warner M., **67**: 271n1

Cutler, Burwell Smith, **53**: 50,n2; **61**: 609,n1

Cuyler, Thomas DeWitt, **65**: 36n1; **67**: 119-20,n1, 121-22

Cuzco, Peru, **66**: 209
Cyprus, **59**: 90, 100; **61**: 159
Cyrenaica, **58**: 435n7
Czacza, Poland, **66**: 225
Czechoslovakia and Czechs, **53**: 294, 590, 649, 711; **54**: 124, 264, 372; **63**: 188; **68**: 62, 352; and boundary issue, **62**: 419; Vénisélos on, **64**: 162; and Adriatic question, **64**: 299, 302, 442, 463; minister to, **64**: 443n1; and Hungary's demands, **64**: 447, 465; on Teschen and Teschen Commission, **65**: 56-66, 213-14, 256, 517-18, 533; children fed in, **65**: 469; and U.S. cotton, **66**: 37; and Poland, **66**: 225n2; WW thanks for kind words from, **68**: 263; children's chorus from, **68**: 296-97,n2; WW on, **68**: 337; WW grateful for albums sent by, **68**: 481; *see also* Paris Peace Conference—Czechoslovakia
Czecho Slovakian Jewish Congress, **54**: 258n1
Czechoslovak National Council, **53**: 629
Czech troops in Russia, **53**: 227, 555, 628, 629, 630, 633; **55**: 401-402; **61**: 99, 154-55, 277, 316; **62**: 442-43, 589, 590; issue of repatriation of, **61**: 41, 196-97, 206, 287-88; Churchill on, **61**: 164-66; replacements for, **61**: 494; WW to address, **61**: 514; WW's remarks to, **61**: 518-19; and Packard Report, **62**: 82n2; request and approval of repatriation loan, **63**: 394, 394-95, 421, 518; repatriation of, **64**: 220, 390

D. C. Heath & Company, **53**: 45; and WW's royalties, **65**: 503,n1, 509n1
Dabney, Charles William, **66**: 246n2
Dabney, Richard Heath, **66**: 298, 346,n1; on WW's League of Nations speech, **66**: 289-90
Dabney, Virginius, **67**: 299n1
Da Como, Ugo, **61**: 109,n7
Da Costa, Alfonso Augusto, **58**: 462n1
Da Costa, John Chalmers, M.D., **58**: 54; **62**: 546,n1, 551n1; **64**: 507n11; attends WW in Paris, **63**: 546,n1, 551n1, 567-68
Da Gama, Domicio: *see* Gama, Dominico da
Daghestan, **61**: 331
Dahomey, **54**: 319; **58**: 485
d'Aigremont, Augustin-Michel Du Faing, **59**: 7n3; **60**: 11,n9
Daily Princetonian, **67**: 306,n1, 307
Dairen, China: *see* Talien-wan
Dalmatia: *see* Paris Peace Conference—Italy; Dalmatia
Daly, Marcus, **56**: 476,n2
Damad Ferid Paşa, **59**: 613n1, 614, 631n2, 641n1; **60**: 16,n1, 193,n3, 212
Damascus, **54**: 506; **55**: 4; **56**: 110, 111, 112, 113, 114, 116, 117; French occupy, **65**: 142n1
D'Amelio, Mariano, **57**: 125,n5; **60**:

225,n1, 226; and reparations, **59**: 422,n7
D'Amico, John B., **68**: 95,n1
Damnable Question: A Study in Anglo-Irish Relations (Dangerfield), **66**: 512n3
Damour, Maurice-Joseph, **59**: 186,n7
Dana, Richard Henry, **55**: 330n2
Dangerfield, George, **66**: 512n3
Dania, S.S., **55**: 432
Danielopol, George, **56**: 271n3
Danielou, Charles-Léon-Claude, **65**: 542,n2
Daniels, Addie Worth Bagley (Mrs. Josephus), **53**: 301; **58**: 594; **65**: 398,n1; **67**: 5,n1; **68**: 69,n2; suggested as U.S. representative to international woman suffrage congress, **65**: 151-52,n1; and WW Foundation, **68**: 266
Daniels, Emil, **53**: 121n1
Daniels, Joan Robertson (Mrs. Winthrop More), **67**: 482,n3
Daniels, Jonathan, **63**: 419n1
Daniels, Josephus, **53**: 32-33, 35, 73, 134, 229, 240, 264, 312, 334, 469n1,2; **54**: 392, 393, 519; **55**: 266-67, 343, 367, 424; **56**: 309-10, 338, 345, 396, 440, 441, 518-19, 559; **57**: 92-93; **60**: 18; **61**: 376, 400, 465, 480, 492, 505, 511, 518n1, 548, 645; **62**: 232,n1, 460, 636; **63**: 239, 419n1, 556-57, 598; **64**: 16, 93, 216, 416n2, 486; **65**: 21-22, 284, 289n1, 290, 390, 395, 398, 511n2; **66**: 17, 30, 31, 59, 207n1, 348, 356, 410, 414, 536; **67**: 5, 74, 214; records Cabinet meetings, **53**: 65, 135, 150; **67**: 9, 25-26, 70-71, 90-91, 109, 124, 150; **68**: 266, 576; records War Cabinet meetings, **53**: 70; and three-year naval building program, **53**: 73, 113, 185-86, 282, 311,n1, 395,n1; suggests Bryan as peace commissioner, **53**: 73, 98, 185, 195; on acquisition of Cape Cod Canal, **53**: 128-29; on Republican attitude toward WW's State of the Union message, **53**: 301; and woman suffrage, **54**: 281; on three-year naval program, **54**: 281-82, 303, 411,n1; suggests Cummings for commission on final settlement, **54**: 408-409,n1; on establishing a corporation for concerns of Shipping Board and Emergency Fleet Corporation, **54**: 432; and oil-leasing bill, **54**: 504; on Palmer for Attorney General, **55**: 36, 263-64; on naval terms, **55**: 424-25; on Democratic victory in Pennsylvania, **55**: 457; on Bryan and League of Nations, **56**: 346; on sinking entire German fleet, **56**: 430-31; on Great Britain and U.S. shipbuilding program, **56**: 482; on Anglo-American naval building controversy, **57**: 91-92; praises WW's hope and vision, **57**: 331, 370; on sinking of German fleet, **57**: 347, 371; on WW visiting Belgium, **58**: 593; on WW visiting Camp Pontanezen in

Brest, **58**: 593-94; and first transatlantic flight, **59**: 576,n1; and General Leasing bills, **61**: 534-35,n1; **62**: 45-46, 293; on situation in Archangel, **61**: 604; advises WW on treaty, **62**: 45; and Sims' article on navy, **62**: 546-47; on WW's health, **63**: 548, 552, 555, 556; on U.S. naval forces in Trau and Adriatic region, **63**: 556-57, 557; on Siberian situation and Cossacks, **63**: 559, 560; on threatened coal strike, **63**: 598; and WW's veto of Volstead bill, **63**: 601n1; on appointment suggestions for second Industrial Conference, **63**: 609, 610, 612; on Brandeis' suggestions of postponing appointments to second Industrial Confernce, **63**: 618; on Mexican situation, **64**: 122-23; Cabinet meeting on coal crisis, **64**: 141, 166; and railroad situation, **64**: 184, 457; reaction to WW's no-compromise statement, **64**: 193; Cabinet meeting on railroads, **64**: 222; on General Leasing bill, **64**: 473; and International Mercantile Marine Corporation, **65**: 110-11, 159, 186; on first cabinet meeting since WW's illness and subsequent Cabinet meetings, **65**: 186-87, 212, 230, 247, 270, 298, 351, 380; **66**: 4, 25-26, 39, 78, 159, 341-42, 380, 413, 445-46, 504; on sending ships to Tampico and Veracruz, **65**: 246-47; meets with Benson on Army-Shipping Board controversy, **65**: 270n2, 277-83; Geddes on, **65**: 370; asks WW to send graduation greetings to his son, **65**: 398; on replacement of Marine commandant, **65**: 430,n1; at Democratic convention, **65**: 492, 496, 580; on protecting Armenians along Black Sea coast, **65**: 538-39; and Dominican Republic, **66**: 25, 28; appointment suggestion for Assistant Secretary of the Navy approved by WW, **66**: 55, 56; on International Communications Conference, **66**: 56-57, 62; on Crowder and draft, **66**: 58; on Cabinet discussion of Jones bill, **66**: 60; WW on direct communication from, **66**: 71; and Haiti, **66**: 73, 99, 100; on WW's reaction to sending ships to Danzig, **66**: 82; and Gatewood case, **66**: 213, 222-23; offers Harding ship for Panama Canal trip, **66**: 317-18, 324, 332-33; and award to Edison, **66**: 371,n1; sends WW advance copy of report on navy, **66**: 452-53,n1; on cables, **66**: 484; on revised navy regulations, **66**: 508, 511-12, 520, 527; on Mexican situation, **67**: 81-82; on Dawes, **67**: 124; Cabinet farewell, **67**: 199; praises WW, **67**: 229; WW thanks, **67**: 233; WW thanks for book by, **68**: 69; WW's condolences to, **68**: 295; Armistice Day message, **68**: 491; mentioned as presidential candidate, **68**: 475-76 photograph of, *illustration section*, **67**

Daniels, Mary Cleaves (Mrs. Josephus, Sr.): death of, **68**: 295,n1
Daniels, Roger, **65**: 243n1
Daniels, Winthrop More: on railroad bill, **64**: 475,n1, 480; **65**: 572,n10; and Princeton professorship, **61**: 514; his suggestion for appointment to Egypt, **65**: 202; WW suggests for senatorial seat from N.J., **68**: 459, 592
Daniels, Worth Bagley: WW's graduation greetings to, **65**: 398, 430,n2
Danilo (Prince of Montenegro), **58**: 163
D'Annunzio, Gabriele, **58**: 92,n2; speech in Rome, **58**: 414, 426-27,n1, 450; **66**: 447n3; **68**: 255,n1; occupation of Fiume, **63**: 298,n2, 364-65, 419n1, 486, 516-17; incursion into Dalmatia, **63**: 517,n2
Dantas, Luis Martins de Souza: *see* Souza Dantas, Luis Martins de
Dante Alighieri, **62**: 606
Dante Alighieri (Italian ship), **59**: 120
Danube River, **56**: 36, 268; **58**: 565-66, 583; **60**: 520n11; **65**: 217n1
Danzig: and controversy over orders sending ships to, **66**: 78, 82, 86; Paderewski on, **66**: 226, 227; *see also* Paris Peace Conference—Poland: Danzig
Danzig, S.M.S., **56**: 28; **58**: 127
Dardanelles, **53**: 562; **59**: 137, 146, 225, 340; **61**: 238; **62**: 552; **65**: 73-74, 113; **68**: 141n1
Darling, Frank C., **65**: 21n2
Darlington, Rt. Rev. James Henry, **61**: 463-64,n1,2
Darmstadt, Germany: French troops occupy, **65**: 155n1, 158, 304
Dartmouth College, **55**: 462; **68**: 365n2
Darrow, Clarence Seward, **66**: 542n1; on pardoning Debs, **62**: 58-59, 98, 262
Dartiguenave, Philippe Sudre, **66**: 63, 72,n1, 73
Daugherty, Harry Micajah, **64**: 405n1; **68**: 48n6, 129n1, 299n1
Davey, Martin Luther, **67**: 254,n1
David, Eduard, **53**: 8
David, Jacques-Louis, **53**: 423, 429
David, Ross, **53**: 21
David, Mrs. Ross, **53**: 21
Davidge, Richard W., **65**: 194,n1
Davidson, Dr. M., **54**: 181,n5; **61**: 359; **62**: 448,n10
Davidson, Jo, **67**: 369,n4, 372
Davidson, Most Rev. Randall Thomas, Archbishop of Canterbury, **53**: 388-89,n1, 412, 451, 527, 529, 533n2; **60**: 24,n5; **61**: 144,n5
Davidson College, **65**: 297n1; establishment of WW chair at, **64**: 191-92,n2, 213; college weekly to be dedicated to WW, **67**: 473,n1,3, 474,n1,2; WW on burning of Chambers building, **67**: 473,n3, 474, 476
Davidsonian, The, **67**: 474,n2
Davie, John Leslie, **63**: 352n1
Davie, W. Galsworthy, **66**: 546,n2

Davies, Joseph Edward, **68**: 471
Davies, Norman, **53**: 611n1; **65**: 527n1; **66**: 46n7
Davies, William W., **65**: 530-31,n1,2
Davis, Calvin DeArmond, **61**: 235n4
Davis, David J., **63**: 29-30,n1
Davis, David William, **63**: 210-11, 212
Davis, Edward Parker ("E.P."), M.D., **53**: 212, 243, 436n2; **54**: 107n1; **55**: 265, 266, 410; **62**: 102, 303, 437; **63**: 166, 167, 634; **67**: 108,n3, 373, 458,n5, 468, 481; **68**: 25, 480; visits WW, **65**: 298; and fund raising for S Street house, **67**: 129, 148-49; on WW remaining in Washington, **68**: 65
Davis, Ellen Duane (Mrs. Edward Parker), **62**: 303, 437; **63**: 166; **67**: 149, 442, 458, 468; **68**: 25; on running for the Senate, **67**: 458, 471, 481; WW's get-well wishes to, **68**: 479-80
Davis, Ellen Graham Bassell (Mrs. John William), **53**: 595; **54**: 199; **60**: 157, 204; **65**: 198,n3
Davis, Goode, **67**: 540,n1, 541
Davis, Jefferson, **55**: 366; **66**: 369n1,2
Davis, John William, **53**: 72, 318, 358, 509, 527, 585-86, 592, 595, 688; **54**: 199, 386-87; **56**: 473, 499; **58**: 594,n2, 601; **60**: 81, 157, 203-204; **61**: 529; **62**: 13n1; **63**: 606n1; **64**: 442, 483; **65**: 198,n3, 200, 221, 237, 399, 434, 503n1; **66**: 71, 87, 216-17, 353; **68**: 236, 548; on European relief program, **53**: 360-64; on WW's new grandson, **55**: 265-66, 304; on Rhineland occupation, **60**: 63-64,n8, 363-65; and Armenia, **62**: 285n1; **66**: 437; and Anglo-Persian secret agreement, **62**: 334, 427-28; and conscription in mandates, **62**: 425-26, 532; on Syria and Turkish Empire, **64**: 25,n1, 26; and Crauford-Stuart affair, **64**: 88, 91; and WW's tentative decision to resign, **64**: 362n1; on Borah's comments on Grey's letter, **64**: 380, 381; question of presence at meeting of Premiers, **64**: 382-83, 391; and war crimes, **64**: 407, 408; on Nitti's views on Adriatic question, **65**: 45-46; on British reaction to French invasion of Germany, **65**: 158-59; reports that Lloyd George's comments on WW are unfounded, **65**: 231-32,n1; given suggestions for renewal of Anglo-Japanese alliance, **65**: 254-55; mentioned as presidential candidate, **65**: 346, 488, 497; code name for, **65**: 350; votes received on sixteenth ballot, **65**: 492n2; and Åland Islands dispute, **65**: 526; **66**: 263, 265; and sending Crowder to Cuba, **66**: 123; and Mexico, **66**: 139,n1, 142; proposed resignation of, **66**: 144, 150; WW approves speeches on League of Nations by, **66**: 199; resignation of, **67**: 36, 60-62
Davis, Lewis, **66**: 75
Davis, Mackie Paschall (Mrs. Norman

Hezekiah), **67**: 473; **68**: 54,n1, 56, 231, 237, 312, 339, 450,n1, 461, 472, 497
Davis, Manton, **65**: 99n1
Davis, May, **68**: 339
Davis, Nellie Johnson (Mrs. David William), **63**: 211,n3
Davis, Norman Hezekiah, **53**: 225,n1, 226, 360, 474, 698, 715-16; **54**: 88, 89, 549; **55**: 58, 148, 186, 200, 332, 499; **56**: 208, 250, 295, 353, 385, 396, 424, 437, 444, 448, 498, 501, 502, 509, 535, 579, 580, 581, 582, 587, 588; **57**: 71, 203, 287, 305n1, 333,n1, 609, 629; **58**: 26, 27, 28, 120, 238, 249, 266, 446n1, 447, 497n4, 548, 549, 565, 595; **59**: 110, 112-13, 173, 175, 227, 283, 284n1, 422, 495, 537, 562; **60**: 26, 73,n1, 196, 227, 361, 542; **61**: 3n1, 99, 230, 256, 285, 377, 384, 441, 529; **62**: 222, 222-23,n1, 322; **63**: 268; **64**: 322; **65**: 24, 153, 178, 238, 483, 506; **66**: 39n3, 178, 193, 307n1, 493, 500, 507; **67**: 8, 26, 73, 91, 105n3, 110, 147n2, 169n1, 194n1, 195, 326, 473, 560, 571; **68**: 34, 51, 137, 172, 178-79, 249n2, 296, 381, 450,n1; and European relief, **53**: 585, 626-27; appointed Financial Commissioner at Spa, **53**: 626-27, 645-46, 690-91; on meetings with German representatives, **54**: 212-16; **58**: 526,n1; economic and financial advice, **54**: 431, 493-94, 494; on Italy's loan request, **55**: 210-11; on reparations, **56**: 270-72,n3, 286, 598-99; **58**: 29, 30, 31, 39, 140; **60**: 4-7, 45, 47, 47-48, 50, 50-51, 52, 53, 76-77, 399-400, 400-401; **66**: 471-72; **67**: 70, 113-15, 144-46; **68**: 261-62, 262-63; on supplying Rumanian army, **56**: 305, 206; on Britain's request for additional credit, **56**: 623; and Council of Four on reparations, **57**: 8, 9, 11, 12, 13, 14, 15, 16, 171, 18, 19, 25,n9, 25-26, 26-27, 30, 33, 82, 214, 293-94; on credits and Italy, **57**: 470-71, 495; **58**: 47, 164; **59**: 111-12, 112-13; **61**: 102; **62**: 230-31; on French credits, **58**: 47, 164; on granting credits for Austrian food relief, **58**: 242-43; on funds for Belgian relief, **58**: 320-21, 411; and Rumanian credits, **58**: 491,n2, 591-93; on experts discussing economic clauses with Germany, **59**: 314-15; Hoover and McCormick on peace treaty and, **59**: 384; on Germany's payment for food in gold, **59**: 639-40; on German counterproposals, **60**: 57, 58, 70; meets with WW, **60**: 93-94, 491; at Council of Four on Austrian political clauses, **60**: 218, 219; misunderstanding of Cecil on credit and European reconstruction, **60**: 277-80; and proposed Rhineland High Commission, **60**: 366-67; and Reparation Commission, **61**: 530; **64**: 10, 11-12,n2; **65**: 57-60, 92-93, 147-48, 153-54, 174, 178, 477; advises WW to make public explanation of treaty, **62**: 7-8; suggested as

Assistant Secretary of Treasury, **62**:
70; suggested as Minister to China, **62**:
260; on *Imperator* controversy, **64**: 7,
333; ideas for treaty ratification, **64**:
104-105; on general cancellation of
inter-Allied debts, **64**: 475, 476-77,
478; pursued for State Department position, **65**: 153, 180, 180-81, 225; resigns as Assistant Secretary of the
Treasury, **65**: 147, 381; memorandum
on treaty suggestions, **65**: 222, 223-25,
229; on U.S. participating in Spa Conference, **65**: 250-51, 330, 331; on debt
negotiations, **65**: 325-26; Geddes on,
65: 370; WW on, **65**: 443; on lifting
trade restrictions with Russia, **65**: 445,
455-56, 490, 492; on Giolitti's greeting
to WW and WW's response, **65**: 448,
449; on representation of Yugoslavia
at Spa Conference, **65**: 459, 477; on
Mexican situation and issue of recognition, **65**: 461-64, 468, 533-36; **66**: 270,
271, 303, 312, 373, 403, 407, 412-13,
413; **67**: 81; on recognition of Costa
Rica, **65**: 464-65, 505, 510; on disposition of German cables, **65**: 479; **66**: 220,
221, 423, 484, 499-500, 513-14, 544;
67: 3; and Armenia, **65**: 496-97, 502;
66: 350n1,2, 457, 480, 490, 517-18; **67**:
63-67, 79; on convening League of Nations Assembly, **65**: 500-501, 503-504;
and Japan's invasion of Sakhalin, **65**:
515-17; on Teschen question, **65**: 246-
47,n1; and Polish-Soviet war, **66**: 16;
on meetings with Iglesias Calderon,
66: 17-18, 162-63; on sending mission
to Cuba, **66**: 83-85; **67**: 24,n1, 32; on
meetings with Pesqueira, **66**: 159, 160-
62, 283,n1; and Russia and gold payment, **66**: 166,n1; and Åland Islands
Commission appointment, **66**: 212,n2,
229, 230-31; on sending ships to Cuba,
66: 233, 234, 236; on France approaching Harding, **66**: 241, 246; on Four-
Power Consortium, **66**: 294-95; on
California situation and Japan, **66**:
295-96; on sending banking group to
Mexico, **66**: 302-304; on U.S. representative on Hungarian Commission and
WW's response, **66**: 304, 324; praises
WW, **66**: 314; on Yap Island controversy, **66**: 326-27,n1, 458-64, 493, 496;
on Adriatic settlement, **66**: 377; on
blockade of Fiume, **66**: 447-48; on U.S.
representatives to Permanent Military, Naval and Air Commission and
WW's response, **66**: 472-73, 497; on
recognition of Bolivia, **66**: 480-81; and
committee for relief in China, **66**: 491,
495; on WW's Nobel Prize, **66**: 492,
501n1, 543; and Italian boundary line,
66: 499; on not dismissing Guata-
malan minister, **66**: 506-507, 512; on
Red Cross sending relief to Ireland, **66**:
512-13, 518; and message from Armenian people to WW, **66**: 518; on U.S.

unofficial representative at Aeronautical Commission of Control and WW's
response, **66**: 535-36, 539; WW sends
Sisson Papers to, **66**: 542; on proposed
visit of Duke of D'Aosta, **66**: 543-44; on
Baltic situation, **67**: 8-9; on recognition
of King Constantine, **67**: 10-11n2; and
Colby's South American trip, **67**:
23,n2; on threatened French occupation of Ruhr Valley, **67**: 33; and issue of
U.S. withdrawal from European commissions, **67**: 33, 34-36, 41, 41-42, 47;
on J. W. Davis' resignation, **67**: 36, 60-
62; and O'Callaghan case, **67**: 49,
52n1; on Yap controversy, **67**: 53-55,
58, 79, 147; on labor's statement on Dominican Republic, **67**: 78-79; on recognition of Bolivia, **67**: 92, 95; and WW
Club project, **67**: 353; and search for
Versailles Treaty, **67**: 357; discusses
WW's decision on treaty and the peace
conference with Lord Bryce, **67**: 375-
78; on Washington Conference and its
treaties, **67**: 538, 539, 540, 543-45,
551-53; on Lippmann's article on U.S.
Chinese policy, **67**: 541-42; WW invites
to conference on Democratic politics
and The Document, **68**: 27; works with
WW and Houston on revision of The
Document, **68**: 32, 42, 49, 53-55, 71,
172, 179, 237, 241-42, 244, 252-54,
294n1, 302-303, 311-12, 317, 318-19,
534; WW thanks for work on The Document, **68**: 56, 244, 325; on essay on
League of Nations for Danish foundation and WW's response, **68**: 84,n1, 85;
and issue of U.S. as associate member
of League of Nations, **68**: 181-82, 189,
193; and address to Democratic women
in Philadelphia, **68**: 182, 196, 230-31,
232, 235-36, 243; on making League of
Nations a partisan issue, **68**: 189, 193;
reviews R. S. Baker's *World Settlement*, **68**: 233; WW asks to write
pamphlet on farmer's situation for
campaign, **68**: 242-43; on introducing
legislation for U.S. entry into League
of Nations and WW's response, **68**:
277-79; on League of Nations and
Cecil's suggestion for elimination of
Article X, **68**: 326-29, 333; on World
Court and League of Nations, **68**: 339-
41; and plans for weekly Democratic
newspaper, **68**: 341, 362; Houston asks
WW to solicit funds from, **68**: 355;
meets with Kerney on prospect of WW
running for Senate, **68**: 460, 461, 462,
463; WW's get-well wishes to, **68**: 461;
on WW's Armistice Day speech, **68**:
471-72; and proposed WW manifesto
for 1924 campaign, **68**: 486-91, 494-95,
497; speaks at WW Foundation, **68**:
510; to go to Europe to serve on League
of Nations committee on Memel, **68**:
520-22, 530; as WW's political adviser,
68: 588, 590, 592

Davis, Westmoreland, **64**: 41-42,n1, 52, 60; **68**: 143n1

Davison, Henry Pomeroy: and Red Cross, **53**: 232, 233, 234, 235, 301-305, 306, 695, 719; **55**: 201, 526-29; **56**: 119; **60**: 330,n2, 389; **62**: 34; resignation of, **53**: 707; on Red Cross' search for Director General, **57**: 330, 422-23; and alleged peace treaty leak and proposed Senate investigation, **60**: 379, 382-83, 434, 536

Davitt, Michael, **58**: 586,n1

Dawes, Charles Gates, **53**: 474,n3; **67**: 124,n1; appointed to first Industrial Conference, **63**: 300,n1

Dawson, Claude Ivan, **61**: 510,n2; **65**: 246-47,n1

Dawson, William Harbutt, **57**: 36,n1, 427,n11; **66**: 87,n2

Day, The, New York: *see* New York *Day*

Day, Clive, **53**: 348-49,n1, 350, 356, 367-68, 377; **54**: 490,n2; **56**: 563n3; **59**: 178,n2; **60**: 34; **62**: 206; **64**: 163n6; on Fiume, **56**: 607-609; **57**: 432-33, 456; **59**: 171; on boundary change between Yugoslavia and German Austria, **59**: 405-406; photograph of, *illustration section,* 57

Day, Elizabeth Dike (Mrs. Clive), **53**: 348-49,n2, 367-38

Day, Franklin, **56**: 466,n2

Day, Frank Miles, **66**: 217-18,n1, 232, 233, 242

Day, Harry Kent, **66**: 232-33, 242; **67**: 48,n1

Day, Morgan C., **67**: 311

Day, William Rufus, **53**: 66, 72; **67**: 563n2; **68**: 131; declines being peace commissioner, **53**: 78

daylight-saving law: WW's veto of, **62**: 304-305

Dayton, John Havens, **58**: 409,n1; **59**: 640,n2, 641

Dayton *News*: and Lansing dismissal, **65**: 6

Dayton Wright Aiplane Company, **63**: 441n2

Deák, Francis, **56**: 182n1; **62**: 123n1, 428n1; **63**: 61n2; **64**: 101n2

Dean, F. E., **68**: 121n2

Dear, Joseph Albert, Jr., **68**: 454,n3

Dear, Walter Moore, **68**: 454,n3

Dearborn Independent, **68**: 149; and anti-Semitism, **66**: 102,n1, 130n1

De Billy, Edouard, **59**: 555,n3

De Billy, Katherine (Mrs. Edouard), **59**: 555,n3

De Blanpré, Commodore, **53**: 397,n4

De Bon, Ferdinand-Jean-Jacques, **55**: 16-17,n3, 21, 112, 426,n3, 427; **56**: 32, 37; **59**: 26, 168,n3, 169; **63**: 485-86,n5; on submarine cables, **56**: 211-12, 214, 216; **58**: 283, 298, 301-302, 304, 351; on Heligoland, **57**: 360-61, 361, 363; and Kiel Canal, **58**: 63,n6, 122-23, 124; on sinking enemy ships, **58**: 126, 127, 128,

456,n2, 579; on naval action to be taken if peace treaty not signed, **58**: 581-84; Lloyd George on, **59**: 170

Debreczen, Hungary, **60**: 352, 353, 357

Debs, Eugene Victor, **54**: 397n1; petition for pardon of, **56**: 245, 282-83; **62**: 98, 126n1, 557,n1, 558; **63**: 238n1, 273n2; **65**: 208-209,n 541; WW on, **56**: 310; Palmer denies clemency, **56**: 618; Sinclair pleads for amnesty for, **61**: 577; **62**: 250, 261-62; Darrow's plea for pardon of, **62**: 58-59; complaints on jail condition of, **62**: 422,n1; various appeals for pardon of, **66**: 25, 343,n1, 515-16, 533-34; WW on not granting amnesty, **66**: 535; **67**: 98-102, 157; WW denies pardon to, **67**: 102n8, 186n1; Creel on pardon, **67**: 231; Harding commutes sentence of, **68**: 48,n7; WW on not pardoning, **68**: 48

Debuchi, Katsuji, **53**: 144,n1; **61**: 554-55,n3, 556, 557-59, 629; **62**: 7, 17, 19, 153, 154; and Shantung settlement, **61**: 620,n1; **62**: 40-42

De Caix de Saint Aymour, Robert: *see* Saint-Aymour, Robert de Caix

Decatur, Ga., **68**: 500n1

Decision to Intervene (Kennan), **53**: 629n3

Declaration of Independence, **57**: 500; **66**: 276; WW on, **63**: 360

Declaration of London (1909), **53**: 312n1

Decrais, Louis-Jean, **57**: 101,n4

Decrais, Pierre-Louis-Albert, **57**: 101n4

Dedeagatch (now Alexandroupolis, Greece), **59**: 400; **62**: 320, 327, 552; **63**: 121, 236, 305; **64**: 164; **65**: 112

Deegan, William Joseph, **58**: 52,n6

Deere & Company, **53**: 308n1

Deering, Milliken and Company, **55**: 486n2

Defender of the Faith, Willian Jennings Bryan: The Last Decade, 1915-1925 (Levine), **67**: 536n2

De Forest, Robert Weeks, **53**: 302,n1

Defrance, Jules-Albert, **60**: 212,n8

Degoutte, Jean-Joseph-Marie, **56**: 26, 257,n6; **60**: 296n4; **65**: 155n1, 172

De Haas, Jacob Judah Aaron, **65**: 334,n1

De Kalb, U.S.S., **55**: 434

De la Barra, Francisco Léon, **58**: 380,n2

Delacroix, Léon, **53**: 458,n1; **54**: 473; **55**: 86,n1, 151, 195, 200,n1; **57**: 405,n3

Delafield, Francis, M.D., **61**: 374,n3

De la Huerta, Adolfo: *see* Huerta, Adolfo de la

Delahunty, William, **62**: 122,n1

Delano, Frederic Adrian: on WW's speech at Sursenes Cemetery, **59**: 642,n1

Delanney (Delaney), Marcel-François, **65**: 143, 144

Delaware: and woman suffrage, **65**: 164, 351

Delaware River Shipbuilding Council, **59**: 476n2

Delbruck, Hans Gottlieb Leopold, **53**: 121,n1

Delbrucks 'Mittwochabend' (Ruhlmann), **53**: 121n1

De Léon, José-Marie Quinones: *see* Quinones, José-Marie De Léon

D'Elia, Vittorio, **58**: 355,n3

Délibérations du Conseil des Quatres (Mantoux), **56**: 209n; **61**: 33n2

Delirium: Acute Brain Failure in Man (Lipowksi), **58**: 618n32, 621n51

Della Torretta, Pietro Paolo Tomasi Marchese, **59**: 488,n10; **60**: 130,n4, 189,n2, 412

DeMartel, Damien-Joseph-Alfred-Charles, Vicomte, **60**: 141,n1

De Merode, Jean, **61**: 31,n2

demobilization: *see* World War—aftermath

Democracy and the War (Coar), **67**: 464-65,n3

Democratic Central Committee of the District of Columbia, **67**: 206, 212-13, 213

Democratic National Committee, **53**: 115, 200; **55**: 469; **62**: 167n1, 587,n1; **63**: 151n3; **64**: 522n1,2; **66**: 458n1; **67**: 308, 312n1, 365, 390,n1, 447; **68**: 4n1, 32, 33n1,2, 70, 137n2, 173, 213, 230, 535; and McCormick's resignation, **54**: 56n1, 61; and chairmanship, **54**: 230-31, 408; **65**: 507; **67**: 321n1, 325, 349-50, 366, 480,n1; Cummings named chairman, **55**: 308; WW's remarks to, **55**: 309-24, 456n2; bars J. A. Reed as delegate, **65**: 470n1; Cummings replaced as chairman, **65**: 551-52,n1; speech ceremonies, **66**: 7; WW's contribution to, **66**: 122n1; Tumulty on, **66**: 141; WW on sending briefs to, **66**: 141; WW on using Speaker's Bureau for issues, **66**: 150; WW Clubs' request of list of contributors, **67**: 314, 318-19, 324, 345, 352; Wilson and Colby announcement, **67**: 343; Colby on The Document and, **68**: 17, 19; WW solicits Chadbourne for financial contribution to, **68**: 33; WW sends contribution to, **68**: 154; WW congratulates Hull on 1922 election results, **68**: 181; Hull on WW's thanks to, **68**: 183; members received by WW, **68**: 531-32; resolution endorsing WW's administration, **68**: 532; *see also* Democratic party; Hull, Cordell; Wilson, Woodrow —The Document

Democratic National Convention (1912), **64**: 518n1; **65**: 189n2, 474

Democratic National Convention (1920): Burleson on platform preparation, **65**: 29; Swem on WW's attitude toward possible presidential nominees, **65**: 291; WW's model plank on unqualified ratification of treaty, **65**: 319, 427; Cummings on strategy, plans, and leadership positions at, **65**: 345-50, 386, 450-51; suggestions for Resolutions Committee chairman, **65**: 345, 445, 446-47, 470; and prohibition plank, **65**: 347,n4, 452-55, 510-11,n1,3; Glass accepts Resolutions Committee chairmanship, **65**: 383, 395, 396; issue of N. D. Baker's attendance at, **55**: 385; WW on, **65**: 393, 416, 419-21; Glass leaves for, **65**: 394, 436; Meredith offers help as member of Iowa delegation, **65**: 397, 500,n1; issue of third term for WW, **65**: 400, 426, 427-28, 438-39, 440, 457-59, 493-94, 496; Bryan's demands, **65**: 424; issue of Colby's attendance at, **65**: 429, 432; plank for Armenian mandate, **65**: 436n2; platform focuses on League of Nations, **65**: 436-40, 482,n1, 489,n1; opening of, **65**: 471,n1; sends resolution of appreciation to WW, **65**: 472-73; WW congratulates Cummings on speech at, **65**: 477; Cummings on presidential candidate situation at, **65**: 480; Grayson on WW's reaction to, **65**: 481; Cummings hopes for WW's approval of platform, **65**: 488; proceedings, **65**: 488; WW's favorite candidate, **65**: 488; Colby's plan to renominate WW and subsequent veto, **65**: 490, 496, 579-81; numerous ballots taken, **65**: 491, 492n2, 499n1; and recess motion, **65**: 492-93,n1,2; and Cox-Glass controversy over Glass statement, **65**: 494-95,n1,2; WW on excluding Burleson from intimate political sessions during, **65**: 495,n1; balloting and final choice, **65**: 499n1; Burleson on reason WW not nominated, **65**: 511,n3

Democratic party, **59**: 158; **63**: 26, 228; **66**: 118; Tumulty on program for 1920, **53**: 23-25; and McCormick's resignation, **54**: 56n1, 61; and Russian situation, **54**: 259,n3; Tumulty on selection of Attorney General and, **54**: 428-30; WW on woman suffrage and, **55**: 37; and League of Nations, **55**: 214, 222; McAdoo on railroad situation and, **55**: 259; WW on congressional election results, **55**: 309-11; and Irish situation, **55**: 348, 403-404, 407; **56**: 397-98; and Galloway and Civil Service Commission, **57**: 349; Burleson's effect on, **58**: 50; and woman suffrage, **58**: 273-74; **61**: 480-81, 537; **62**: 615; and prohibition, **58**: 603, 604; and railroad situation, **58**: 605; and publication of peace treaty, **59**: 313; and support of League of Nations Covenant, **59**: 524; Grayson on opposition to League of Nations, **59**: 528-29; Tumulty on, **60**: 112, 113, 148, 153; and issue of publication of peace treaty, **60**: 242-44, 247; W. A. White on League of Nations and, **61**: 506n1; and conflict in Senate over treaty, **62**: 12; WW meets with Democratic senators on early treaty ratification, **62**: 16-20; and reservations issue, **62**: 45, 307-

Democratic party (*cont.*)
309, 614; Pittman on treaty ratification situation in Senate, **62**: 310-12;
Pittman resolution on League of Nations, **62**: 429-32; outlook for ratification of Versailles Treaty, **63**: 151; and
League to Enforce Peace's prediction
on treaty ratification, **63**: 235; WW on,
63: 417-18; **65**: 489-90; **67**: 533; **68**: 46-
47, 195, 201-202, 230, 384; and reser-
vations, **63**: 444-45, 530-31, 586; **64**:
28, 72, 165-66; WW wants each vote
against Versailles Treaty recorded, **64**:
43; caucus and vote on Lodge resolution for ratification, **64**: 62-64; and
Mexican situation, **64**: 120,n1; Lansing on WW and treaty, **64**: 192, 267-
69; and election of Senate minority
leader, **64**: 192, 194, 273, 274,n1;
Hitchcock seeks WW's advice on compromise to avoid split in, **64**: 203; WW's
hope that no proposal for compromise
will come from caucus of, **64**: 206; and
Jackson Day message, **64**: 247, 252,
257; Bryan on treaty ratification and,
64: 261n1; House on treaty position
and, **64**: 270; Hitchcock on bipartisan
meeting on treaty, **64**: 283-84; bipartisan committee addresses Article X and
hopeful of compromise, **64**: 311-12,
312-13,n1; WW's list of senators who
hindered ratification of treaty reviewed by Burleson and Hitchcock, **64**:
336-37, 338-39; House on, **64**: 348; R.
S. Baker on treaty reservations and,
64: 359; senators caucus on treaty, **64**:
384; Glass on Taft reservations and,
64: 387-88,n1; WW on role of regarding
treaty proposals, **64**: 405; Glass on
treaty negotiations and, **64**: 410; Cummings on, **64**: 419n1; Hitchcock fears
Lodge reservations are being supported by more senators from, **64**: 466;
Tumulty on Democratic support for
Lodge reservations, **64**: 479; WW on
himself as Democrat in *1911*, **64**: 515;
and blacks in *1912*, **64**: 522; various
newspapers identified with comment
on Lansing's dismissal, **65**: 3-7; learns
of WW's refusal to ratify treaty with
Lodge reservations, **65**: 7; Burleson on
preparing platform for, **65**: 29; probable Senate vote on Lodge's changed
reservation to Article X, **65**: 80, 81,n1;
and treaty vote, **65**: 109,n1; issue of
third term and leadership of, **65**: 117-
19, 123; Tumulty on treaty strategy of,
65: 122; WW on H. Hoover and, **65**:
149; Hitchcock on treaty strategy and,
65: 150; and issue of Knox resolution
and separate peace, **65**: 257n1; WW on
importance of endorsement and support of treaty without reservations, **65**:
263-64; and Armenian mandate, **65**:
351n2; WW on not wanting to influence candidate choice, **65**: 419, 420;
sends resolution of appreciation to
WW, **65**: 472; W. G. Sharp's predictions
and suggestions, **65**: 473-76; WW on
Bryan and, **65**: 488; statements of accord by Cox, WW, and Roosevelt, **65**:
524-25; Baker on army reorganization
bill and, **65**: 576-77,n1, 578; W. W.
Hawkins on party's failure, **66**: 158;
Cummings on rehabilitation work if
presidency is lost, **66**: 196; and Young
Americans' Democratic League, **66**:
262, 414,n1; and Irish issue, **66**:
267n1,2; Ewing on WW's achievements for, **66**: 391-92; and Irish Americans, **67**: 45,n2, 46; WW on lack of
unity and on Versailles Treaty defeat,
67: 268-69; G. White and WW discuss,
67: 381-82; Colby and Morgenthau on
pressing Republicans on League, **67**:
386-87; and Treaty of Berlin in the
Senate, **67**: 399,n2, 418, 419; and ratification of Treaty of Berlin, **67**: 422n4;
WW's unpublished statement on supporters of Treaty of Berlin, **67**: 428;
and slogan "America First," **67**: 443;
Cobb on WW's silence and, **67**: 531;
and Four Power Treaty, **67**: 552-53,
577,n1; WW on J. A. Reed and, **67**: 578-
79; and strategy for treaty ratification,
67: 616-68; WW on women and, **68**: 33-
34,n2, 155; WW on not having conference of for election program, **68**: 50;
WW proposes to gentrify candidates,
68: 63-64, 70-71, 71; WW and Cummings on program for, **68**: 89; Hull on,
68: 95-96, 97; and Italian Americans,
68: 95n1; Cobb on need for WW to prepare program for, **68**: 100-101, 101,
195-96; plans for weekly newspaper,
68: 137-38,n2, 346, 362; Blair on
women in, **68**: 156-57, 157; and League
of Nations, **68**: 160-167, 178n1, 178,
189, 190, 192, 276, 334; Davis' speech
on history of, **68**: 172, 178,n1, 196-97,
236; Hull to meet with WW on plans
for, **68**: 183; various comments on WW
as leader of, **68**: 191, 239; Peabody's
suggestions for, **68**: 207-11; McAdoo
on, **68**: 222; WW on comeback of, **68**:
234n1, 294; WW's concern over editorial on his involvement in 1924 campaign, **68**: 234-35,n1; WW on duty and
opportunity of, **68**: 267; Houston on accomplishments and goals of, **68**: 269-
73; WW wants to control caucuses in
Congress of, **68**: 298n3; Cobb on prohibition and, **68**: 305; and World Court
issue, **68**: 306, 339, 340, 341; Seibold
on, **68**: 372; Davis on a WW manifesto
for, **68**: 494-95; WW won't issue Davis'
manifesto for, **68**: 494-95; R. S. Baker
on, **68**: 496; final draft of The Document, **68**: 535-41; WW's notes and passages for an acceptance speech, **68**:

541-42; *see also* Democratic presidential campaign of 1920; Wilson, Woodrow—The Document
Democratic party and Democrats in Colorado, **68**: 301,n2, 302
Democratic party and Democrats in Connecticut, **55**: 237,n4; **68**: 50, 98
Democratic party and Democrats in Delaware: and woman suffrage, **65**: 351
Democratic party and Democrats in Georgia: issue of WW's name on primary ballot, **65**: 145-46,n1; Palmer on primary results, **65**: 219-20,n1,2
Democratic party and Democrats in Illinois, **67**: 312,n1, 447,n1; and Chicago organization, **65**: 189n2; **66**: 90n1
Democratic party and Democrats in Indiana, **68**: 44,n2, 49-50, 56
Democratic party and Democrats in Iowa, **67**: 393n1; favorite son, **65**: 291,n1
Democratic party and Democrats in Kansas, **65**: 178; **68**: 75-76
Democratic party and Democrats in Kentucky, **68**: 14
Democratic party and Democrats in Louisiana: and woman suffrage, **65**: 164-65
Democratic party and Democrats in Maine, **68**: 85-86, 112, 113, 114, 118: WW to Young Democrats, **67**: 280
Democratic party and Democrats in Maryland, **59**: 38,n2; **68**: 94-95,n2,3, 98-99, 134-34,n1
Democratic party and Democrats in Massachusetts, **68**: 64, 70, 83,n1, 86, 96,n1, 154; on Irish question, **62**: 8
Democratic party and Democrats in Michigan, **53**: 382n1; **65**: 120n2; and Ford-Newberry case, **67**: 316-17
Democratic party and Democrats in Mississippi, **68**: 93-94,n2,3
Democratic party and Democrats in Missouri, **53**: 84,n1; **57**: 47-49, 424; **65**: 110n1; **68**: 35, 61, 104, 105n1, 105, 126-27; challenge to Senator Reed, **56**: 192n1; and Reed and League of Nations, **59**: 529; and Long, **65**: 377; rejection of Reed as delegate to Democratic convention, **65**: 470,n1; WW on Reed-Long race, **67**: 543,n1; WW on J. A. Reed, **68**: 12,n1, 24, 151; claims of fraud in primary, **68**: 105,n1; McAdoo will not campaign in Missouri, **68**: 147, 151, 153; nominates Reed for senator, **68**: 166,n1
Democratic party and Democrats in Nebraska, **53**: 61-62
Democratic party and Democrats in New Jersey, **53**: 63; **67**: 480, 482; **68**: 154,n3, 460, 590, 595; suggestion that WW run for Senate from, **68**: 454, 588
Democratic party and Democrats in New Mexico, **67**: 350,n1
Democratic party and Democrats in New York, **68**: 3, 15, 56-57, 154,n4; Jefferson Day celebrations in 1921 and 1922, **67**: 251, 253, 257, 602-603
Democratic party and Democrats in North Carolina, **68**: 212,n1, 213
Democratic party and Democrats in North Dakota, **68**: 96,n2
Democratic party and Democrats in Ohio, **65**: 383, 492n2; **67**: 349-50, 510, 534; **68**: 18; Cox on, **65**: 495; and replacement of chairman of Democratic National Committee, **65**: 551,n1; WW's message to Democrats of Akron, **67**: 254, 255
Democratic party and Democrats in Oklahoma: and primary, **66**: 3,n1, 10
Democratic party and Democrats in Oregon: WW's statement to on unqualified ratification of treaty, **65**: 263-64, 274
Democratic party and Democrats in Pennsylvania, **67**: 481; **68**: 25, 56,n2; congressional victory, **53**: 448-49,n1, 457, 458, 495; WW's message to Lehigh Valley group, **67**: 279-80
Democratic party and Democrats in Tennessee, **68**: 61
Democratic party and Democrats in Texas, **58**: 497,n1; **67**: 572,n1; **68**: 298n2
Democratic party and Democrats in Virginia, **68**: 143,n1,2; and League of Nations plank, **65**: 292, 293-94, 331; WW's approval of plank of, **65**: 333; platform for 1924; *see* Wilson, Woodrow—The Document
Democratic presidential campaign of 1920: Hapgood and, **66**: 28, 30; Creel on, **66**: 81; WW's role defined and contribution to, **66**: 118; Tumulty on press release for, **66**: 141; J. S. Williams on WW's health and, **66**: 147-48; issue of WW's consulting with Republicans on treaty, **66**: 148-49; WW on not debating with Harding, **66**: 149-50; WW on, **66**: 156; Woolley concerned over organization of, **66**: 173-74; and League referendum issue, **66**: 175-76, 181-83; Lamont on Harding's statement on Panama Canal tolls and, **66**: 177-78; McAdoo on speaking tour, **66**: 180-81, 234-35; and platform plank on Japanese exclusion, **66**: 186; EBW and Cummings discuss WW's position in, **66**: 190-91; WW and Cummings discuss, **66**: 194-95; and Wilson-Spencer controversy, **66**: 198,n1; WW unable to fill requests for statements on League of Nations, **66**: 223,n1; Tumulty wishes to use information showing WW's use of Root's suggestions on League of Nations, **66**: 230,n1; and depression in agricultural prices, **66**: 242-43,n5; Tumulty on strategy for answering Root's speech and letter from 31 Republicans and WW's response,

Democratic presidential campaign of 1920 (*cont.*)
66: 246-47,n1,2, 249; WW on Harding and France, 66: 246; and German-American controversy, 66: 248,n1, 249,n1; Tumulty urges WW to take part in and WW's answer, 66: 249-50; encouraging reports from Chicago, 66: 258n1; Mackenzie on restoring faith in League of Nations, 66: 259-61; WW endorses Cox, 66: 289, 290-91; Tumulty's feelings on election eve, 66: 298-99; election results, 66: 306n1; W. B. Wilson's campaign speech, 66: 346,n1; treaty mentioned as issue in, 67: 616-18; *see also* Cox, James Middleton; Democratic National Committee; Democratic party; election of 1920
Democratic presidential campaign of 1924: and Jefferson Day speech brouhaha because of Cox and, 68: 3, 10, 14, 59; suggestions for candidates, 68: 3, 475-76,n3, 535,n2; WW as possible candidate, 68: 4,n1, 4-5, 425, 541-42, 542-43; WW on, 68: 10, 167, 180, 181, 192, 195, 213; McAdoo on, 68: 148-49, 222; WW's prediction, 68: 151, 251; League of Nations as issue in, 68: 167, 177, 178n1, 192, 274; Peabody's suggestions for, 68: 207-11; Hull on, 68: 232; and WW's involvement, 68: 234n1, 381, 479, 588-90; Cobb on, 68: 239; WW on railroad brochure for, 68: 287; WW and Brennan discuss, 68: 425-26; Davis on WW's strategy for selecting candidates, 68: 491; WW won't issue Davis' manifesto for, 68: 494-95; R. S. Baker on, 68: 496; WW's notes and passages for an acceptance speech, 68: 541-42; WW's notes and passages for a third Inaugural Address, 68: 542-43; *see also* Wilson, Woodrow—The Document
Democratic Women's Luncheon Club of Philadelphia: mention of N. H. Davis speech to, 68: 178,n1, 182,n2, 196-97
De Mohrenschildt, E., 56: 125
De Mohrenschildt, Ferdinand, 55: 442,n1; 56: 125,n3; 57: 305,n2; 64: 494
De Mohrenschildt, Nona Hazelhurst McAdoo (Mrs. Ferdinand), 55: 442,n1; 56: 125,n1,4,5; 57: 305,n2; 64: 494; 67: 6,n3
Denby, Charles, 61: 635,n1; 67: 306,n4
Denby, Edwin, 68: 147n3
Denial of Illness: Symbolic and Physiological Aspects (Weinstein and Kahn), 58: 634n14
Denijn, Joseph-Guillaume-François, 61: 13,n6, 14
Denikin, Anton Ivanovich, 53: 256,n2, 355, 591; 54: 9, 26, 94, 101; 56: 254, 256, 257, 314; 57: 575n1; 58: 506, 576; 59: 14,n4, 15,n5, 17, 18, 29, 30, 152, 225, 300n8, 301, 311, 312, 426, 465, 550n2; 60: 282; 61: 154, 466,n2; 62:

427,n1; 63: 394; 64: 308, 309; 65: 288,n3; Bolsheviks on, 59: 194, 195
Denizli, Turkey, 59: 595-96
Denmark, 53: 40, 153; 56: 479; 57: 357, 367; 58: 198; 60: 97, 105, 284; 61: 187; appointment of U.S. minister to, 55: 185, 194, 439,n1; 56: 101, 191,n1; 65: 85, 88; and League of Nations Commission, 56: 170n1; and Schleswig, 56: 200,n1, 267; 57: 363-64; 59: 459, 582; 60: 107, 110, 557, 558, 561, 562; appointments to, 57: 334; Keynes on economic rehabilitation plan, 58: 13, 14; and Kiel Canal, 58: 66; and Germany and plebiscite, 59: 472; Hapgood appointed minister to, 59: 512,n1; and credit extension for wheat, 61: 501; resignation of Hapgood, 64: 233-34,n1-4; N. H. Davis' essay on League of Nations for foundation in, 68: 84,n1
Dennis, Edward Guy, 58: 146,n1
Dennis, William Jefferson, 53: 316n2; 66: 210n4
Dennis, John Benjamin, 63: 544,n2, 579
Dennison, Ohio, 63: 3,n2
DeNovo, John A., 68: 504n1
Densmore, John B., 53: 24,n2, 273
Dent, Stanley Hubert, Jr., 53: 25; 66: 126n1
Dent Act, 66: 126,n2
Denton, Francis B., 53: 693n1; 56: 578; 61: 332
Denver, Colorado, 59: 287; WW's arrival in, 63: 467; WW's address in, 63: 487,n1, 490-500
Denver, U.S.S., 61: 640
Denver Post, 63: 489n3, 500n, 515n, 524n
Denver *Rocky Mountain News,* 62: 439n1; 63: 467n2, 487n1, 500n
Denver Times, 62: 439n1
Denvignes, Joseph-Cyrille-Magdalaine, 59: 401,n3,4; 60: 9,n4, 11, 12, 13
Department of: *see under* latter part of the name, such as, Post Office, Department of
De Peretti de la Rocca, Count Emmanuel, 59: 488,n9
De Polignac, Melchior, 60: 546,n6
De Polignac, Nina Crosley, 60: 546,n6
Deportations Delirium of Nineteen-Twenty: A Personal Narrative of an Historic Official Experience (Post), 65: 187n5
DeQuincey, Thomas, 67: 296
Derby, 17th Earl of (Edward George Villiers Stanley), 53: 69, 85, 143, 154, 324, 327, 359, 390, 418, 448; 54: 235; 55: 160; 57: 503, 533n4; 58: 535; 59: 605; 61: 238-39; 64: 318; on WW sitting at peace conference, 53: 409-10, 414; plans for WW's trip to England, 53: 456-68, 488, 498-99, 508; reaction to Lloyd George's not going to France, 53: 458; meets with WW on issues, 53: 470-72; on H. Hoover, 53: 525-26; and Britain's suggestion of peace negotia-

tions with Russia, **53**: 591, 721-23; meets with House, **53**: 633-34; discussed as British ambassador to U.S., **59**: 160-61; interest in horse racing, **61**: 239; and Franco-German situation, **65**: 170-71, 173

Derby, Alice Montagu, Lady Derby, **57**: 503

Dercum, Francis Xavier, M. D. **63**: 539,n2, 543, 544, 546, 550, 551, 561, 578, 581, 582, 634, 642; **64**: 4, 32, 37, 99, 187, 507-508,n11, 509, 510; **65**: 380; **66**: 36; **67**: 103, 611-14, 618; **68**: 138-39; to stop regular visits due to WW's improvement, **64**: 211; declines comments on WW's health, **64**: 433-34, 435; clinical reports on Wilson after stroke, **64**: 500-507; and Grayson's memorandum on WW's illness, **64**: 507n1; **67**: x; on WW's health and suggestions for continued improvement, **65**: 90; thanks for autographed books, **67**: 492,n1; on WW remaining in Washington, **68**: 65; and Pasteur Centennial, **68**: 229

D'Erm, Camille Le Mercier, **59**: 186n4

Dernburg, Bernhard Jakob Ludwig, **58**: 454,n1; **59**: 298,n3, 309, 310, 560,n4

Derry, Joseph Tyrone, **62**: 624-25,n1; **68**: 516

Deschamps, M., **56**: 428,n2

Deschanel, Germaine Brice (Mme. Paul Eugène Louis), **54**: 488,n1; **60**: 546,n2; **61**: 188,n4

Deschanel, Paul-Eugène-Louis, **54**: 464n1, 489; **60**: 117n1, 546,n2

De Schweinitz, George Edmund, M.D., **58**: 631, 636; **64**: 502, 504, 505n11, 508-509, 510; **65**: 380

De Silver, Albert, **55**: 224,n1; **61**: 398-99,n1, 480; **62**: 126,n1

Des Moines, Iowa, **59**: 287; Grayson on WW's arrival and speech in, **63**: 65-66; WW's address in, **63**: 76-88; WW attends church in, **63**: 92

Des Moines, U.S.S., **61**: 604,n1

Des Moines Successful Farming, **64**: 330n1

Des Moines Sunday Register, **63**: 88n

Dessez, Leon, **67**: 508,n1, 514-15

Desticker, Pierre-Henri, **59**: 433,n3

D'Estournelles de Constant de Rebeque, Baron Paul-Henri-Benjamin Balluat, **54**: 257,n1,2

De Strycker, Peter Joseph, **62**: 111,n2

Detroit Free Press, **61**: 373

Detroit Journal, **61**: 373; **66**: 174

Deutscher, Isaac, **54**: 92n2

Deutsche Verfassungsgeschichte seit 1769 (Huber), **53**: 121n1

Deutschland, S.M.S., **55**: 426

De Valera, Eamon, **57**: 419,n2; **59**: 104, 105-106, 251, 366n1, 393,n1, 513, 549n1; **60**: 289, 383, 384, 386, 435, 544; **61**: 183,n2; denied hearing at peace conference, **61**: 466-67

Devereux, John Ryan, **65**: 506,n2

De Vito, Robert, **61**: 109,n8

Devonshire, 9th Duke of (Victor Christian Willian Cavendish), **61**: 618-19,n2; **62**: 425,n1

Devreux, Emilc, **61**: 11, n1

Dewing, Henry Bronson, **67**: 182

De Wolfe, Elsie, **60**: 491,n2

DeWoody, Charles Frederick, **60**: 115n7

Diagne, Blaise, **54**: 126n1

Diagramatic Map of Future South Slav State (Evans), **57**: 539n3

Dial, Nathaniel Barksdale, **67**: 422,n3: on federal assistance for cotton industry, **66**: 36-38,n1, 60-62

Diamandi, Constantin J., **55**: 6; **56**: 176

Diane, Mademoiselle (French soprano), **68**: 404

Diaz, Armando, **53**: 326,n4, 606; **54**: 221, 499; **56**: 103, 110, 327, 382, 409, 583; **57**: 104; **58**: 264, 321, 580; **61**: 204; on demobilization, **54**: 244-45; and Loucheur committee, **54**: 246, 539, 540; on army of occupation, **60**: 364,n2

Díaz, Felix, **58**: 380,n3

Díaz, Porfiro (José de la Cruz Porfiro), **65**: 534; **66**: 335,n2

Diaz, R. Camilo, **61**: 639,n10

Dickinson, Bessie Louise, **60**: 647,n3

Dickinson, Goldsworthy Lowes, **60**: 111-12; on League of Nations, **59**: 316; on WW, **67**: 135-36,n1

Dickinson, Jacob McGavock, **55**: 339,n1

Dickinson, Thomas Herbert, **68**: 175,n2

Dickinson, Willoughby Hyett, **53**: 530n1

Dickson, Edward Augustus, **63**: 423,n3

Dictionary of American Biography, **68**: 134n1

Dieburg, Germany: French troops occupy, **65**: 155n1, 158

Diego-Fernandez, Salvador, **65**: 201,n1

Dietz, Leonora Antoinette Cooke (Mrs. Gould Price), **63**: 94,n1

Dillard, James Hardy, **62**: 106-107,n2

Dillingham, William Paul, **62**: 29,n1, 43-44; and treaty fight, **64**: 200, 202, 337

Dillon, John, **58**: 586,n1

Dimitra, Albania, **60**: 530

Dinwiddie, Edwin Courtland, **62**: 106-107,n1, 292-93

Diplomacy of the Balkan Wars (Helmreich), **60**: 530n1

Diplomacy by Conference (Hankey), **67**: 462,n1, 468-69

Diplomacy, Scandal and Military Intelligence (Egerton), **63**: 606n1; **65**: 83n1

Diplomatic and Consular Appropriation bill, **56**: 122; **67**: 26n6

Diplomatic Dealings of the Constitutionalist Revolution in Mexico (Mexican Foreign Ministry), **62**: 450,n1

Diplomatic Relations between the United States and Japan, 1853- 1895 (Treat), **62**: 359n23

Director General of Relief: *see* European relief

dirigibles, **56**: 42
disarmament: *see* arms limitations
Diseases of the Neopallium (Chapman and Wolff), **62**: 637n24
Disentangled (*New York Tribune*), **67**: 382,n2
Disraeli, Benjamin, Earl of Beaconsfield, **55**: 384n3; **56**: 321; **60**: 209, 215
District National Bank of Washington, **54**: 555n2
District of Columbia: *see* Washington, D.C.
District of Columbia, Committee on (House of Reps.), **63**: 265
District of Columbia, Committee on (Senate): and police strike, **63**: 295, 302
Dix, Edwin Asa, **65**: 572,n18
Dixmunde, Belgium, **61**: 4
Dixon, Thomas, Jr., **62**: 115
Diyarbakir, Turkey, **54**: 506,n4
Djibouti, French Somaliland, **59**: 88, 99, 139
Dmowski, Roman, **53**: 105; **54**: 32n2; **55**: 3, 464; **56**: 151, 508, 508-509; **57**: 247, 263; **58**: 220, 445, 542; **60**: 91; discusses Poland at Council of Ten meetings, **54**: 335-41, 341-43, 345, 356; Seymour on, **54**: 383, 384; and League of Nations Commission, **54**: 509; and Jews, **55**: 370, 373; **58**: 385; on plebiscite in Upper Silesia, **60**: 553-54, 555
Doberitz, Germany, **65**: 98n1, 100
Dobie, Armistead Mason, **67**: 138-39,n1, 281
Dobrudja (Dobruja), **59**: 568; **62**: 206-207, 265
Document, The: *see* Wilson, Woodrow—The Document
Documents on British Foreign Policy, 1919-1939 (Woodward and Butler, eds.), **61**: 157n9; **65**: 196n1, 248n1, 326n3, 527n3; **66**: 39n3, 44n4, 46n7; **67**: 109n1
Dodd, Mattie Johns (Mrs. William Edward), **65**: 432,n2; **67**: 39,n2, 278, 288
Dodd, William Edward, **63**: 6; **65**: 423, 424n1, 432; **66**: 62-63, 266; **67**: 39 40, 43-46; **68**: 9-10, 355; on Progressives and WW-TR relationship, **66**: 165, 175; on Republican support for WW, **66**: 255-56; on WW's leadership role in American Historical Association, impressions of his health, and tragedy of his ordeal at Paris, **67**: 68-69; on his book, *Woodrow Wilson*, **67**: 75, 298-99, 446-47; **68**: 544; on WW's religious background, **67**: 75-76; on disposition of WW's papers, **67**: 76-77, 163-64, 278, 282-83, 287-88; praises WW, **67**: 161-64; urges WW to write, **67**: 163-64, 283; and WW Clubs, **67**: 285; on 1918 meeting of Republicans and on their plans to destroy WW, **67**: 297-98; speech on WW, **67**: 355,n7, 357; WW on book of, **67**: 389, 456; on "digest" of Paris Peace Conference minutes, **67**: 447, 456, 459-61, 466-68, 469-70; and University of

Missouri presidency, **67**: 505-506, 508-509,n1; *American Historical Review* editors to meet with WW, **68**: 9, 68; on politics, especially Missouri primary, **68**: 126-27; thought of running for office endorsed by WW, **68**: 126, 128; on WW and on his own work, **68**: 258-59; and WW Foundation, **68**: 365
Dodecanese: *see also* Paris Peace Conference—Italy; Dodecanese
Dodge, Bayard, **66**: 193,n4,5, 526
Dodge, Cleveland Earl, **60**: 488,n1; **66**: 193,n4,5; **68**: 64,n1
Dodge, Cleveland Hoadley, **53**: 46, 68, 134-35, 180, 302, 707; **55**: 265, 303, 411; **60**: 488; **62**: 415-16; **66**: 193; **67**: 375, 458, 470, 470-71, 554; **68**: 69, 112-13, 115-16, 117, 137, 192-93, 195, 497-98, 498, 591; on Armenian situation, **62**: 248, 285; **66**: 448-50, 451-52; get-well wishes to WW, **63**: 535; WW asks advice on gaining public opinion for Armenian mandate, **65**: 202; on Near East Relief Committee, **65**: 234-35; **68**: 25-26, 465; Grayson gives account of WW's health to, **65**: 341-43; on election results and praise of WW, **66**: 340-41; WW thanks, **66**: 388; and Chinese Famine Relief Fund, **66**: 513, 532; on visit with WW, **66**: 526; on purchase of Pierce-Arrow for WW and WW thanks, **67**: 116-17,n1, 136-37, 148, 156-57, 167, 167-68, 186,n1; on fund raising for S Street house, **67**: 137, 148, 157; and WW Foundation, **67**: 271,n1; **68**: 249,n2, 264, 265, 355, 365; R. C. Stuart, Jr., on, **67**: 373-74; on *Mere Literature and Other Essays*, **67**: 551; greetings on fifth anniversary of entrance into war, **67**: 603-604, 604; on his health, **68**: 64, 115; WW on health of, **68**: 69, 112, 498; and Clarke's League of Nations plan, **68**: 173; WW disagrees with on nonpartisan League of Nations organization, **68**: 177; Houston asks WW to solicit funds from and WW's response, **68**: 355, 357; and trust fund for WW, **68**: 438-39, 440, 441, 441-42, 442-43, 444, 513, 516, 534; WW grateful for generosity and friendship, **68**: 445, 513-14, 534; and WW's Rolls-Royce, **68**: 513-14, 516; and WW-House relationship, **68**: 529
Dodge, Elizabeth, **66**: 193n5
Dodge, Grace, **66**: 193n5
Dodge, Grace Parish (Mrs. Cleveland Hoadley), **53**: 46; **55**: 265, 303; **66**: 193; **67**: 374, 470, 554,n1; **68**: 25,n1, 113, 115, 116, 117, 442, 443
Dodge, Margaret, **66**: 193n5
Dodge, Mary Williams Bliss (Mrs. Bayard, Jr.), **66**: 193n5, 526
Dodge, Pauline Morgan (Mrs. Cleveland Earl), **60**: 488; **66**: 193n5
Dodge, Phyllis Boushall (Mrs. Cleveland Earl, Jr.), **66**: 193n5; **67**: 137n3
Doe *v.* Braden, **62**: 35-36, 37

Doheny, Edward Laurence, **62**: 155n1; **64**: 134; **66**: 321,n1, 322, 335, 413; **67**: 82,n2, 326; WW on, **67**: 353

Doherty, Charles Joseph, **57**: 311,n10, 312; **58**: 417,n7

Dolbeare, Frederic Russell, **65**: 256,n4, 272, 317

Dollar for Dollar (movie), **65**: 348, 349

Dolphin, U.S.S., **65**: 246

Dolsen, Fred R., **66**: 130n1

Dominian, Leon, **57**: 313,n2

Dominican Republic (San Domingo), **54**: 170; **59**: 524n5; **67**: 3, 23,n1, 75, 78-79; anti-American propaganda in, **66**: 25,n1, 28, 31n1; and Snowden, **66**: 73; plan to restore self-government to, **66**: 359-64, 367-68, 383-84, 408-409, 419-20; U.S. proclamation on gradual withdrawal from, **66**: 428, 429; Gompers on independence for, **66**: 537-39; Hamilton on situation in, **67**: 56-57; labor on returning sovereignty to, **67**: 73, 86

Donald, John A., **54**: 394,n1; **66**: 252,n1

Donets Basin, **61**: 62

Donnersmarck, Guido Georg Friedrich Erdmann Heinrich Adelbert, Prince von, Count Henckel, **60**: 86n1

Donnersmarck, Guigotto Karl Lazarus, Prince von, Count Henckel **60**: 86n1

Donovan, Mike, **65**: 412

Doran, George Henry, **66**: 416, 420, 521,n1

Doremus, Frank Ellsworth, **66**: 258,n1

Dorsey, Hugh Manson, **61**: 480-81,n1, 537

Dorten, Hans Adam, **59**: 401n4; **60**: 13,n12, 14, 15, 60n7

Dothey, General, **60**: 365

Douala, Cameroon: *see* Duala

Doubleday, Frank Nelson, **67**: 256; and R. S. Baker's *Woodrow Wilson and World Settlement*, **68**: 176, 233; and WW's Armistice Day speech, **68**: 474

Doubleday, Page and Company, **55**: 290n1; **68**: 233, 350; and *Woodrow Wilson and World Settlement*, **67**: 129,n1, 241, 242, 249, 256, 363; and W. E. Dodd, **67**: 298; H.S. Houston to leave, **67**: 414, 434

Doughty, Sergeant, **56**: 195,n1

Douglas, Stephen Arnold, **56**: 437-38

Dover, England: WW's arrival in, **53**: 509, 569; photograph, *illustration section*, **53**

D'Ovidio, Francesco, **53**: 608n1

Doyle, Arthur Conan, **53**: 521

Doyle, Michael Francis, **59**: 476,n1

draft: *see* conscription

Drafting of the Covenant (Miller), **54**: 387n2, 439n, 492n2; **56**: 170n1, 223n1; **57**: 248n1, 258n5, 286n2; **58**: 417n6; **59**: 243n1

Drafting of the Four Power Treaty of the Washington Conference (Vinson), **67**: 484n1

Dragomerov, Abram Mikhailovich, **53**: 256,n2

Drava (Drave or Drau), **60**: 22,n2

Dream of Fair Women (movie), **65**: 384

Dresden, Germany: and Kapp *Putsch*, **65**: 98n1, 99

Dresel, Ellis Loring, **53**: 418,n2, 419; **56**: 466n3; **60**: 28n12, 277; **65**: 162; **66**: 535,n1,4; **68**: 548; on peace terms and Germany, **58**: 44-46,n1, 453-55; **59**: 156-58, 237-39,n2; on Erzberger letter-interview, **60**: 64-65; on German counterproposals, **60**: 65-66; praises German government and urges offer of League of Nations membership, **60**: 177-78; suggested as U.S. representative in Germany, **61**: 286; concerning list of war criminals, **64**: 364

Drew, Daniel, **68**: 205

Drin River Valley, **64**: 300, 302, 303; **65**: 315

Drinkwater, John, **65**: 404,n5: **66**: 112; **67**: 105n3, 111; beginnings of WW Foundation, **67**: 271n1

Driver, William Raymond, Jr., **57**: 530n1

Drohobycz, Poland, **59**: 597, 599

Droppers, Garrett, **64**: 414n2, 454; **67**: 10; resignation of, **65**: 85, 88, 251,n1, 260, 271

Drum, Hugh Aloysius, **68**: 575,n2

Drummond, Sir (James) Eric, **53**: 409, 414; **58**: 443; **60**: 204, 431; **61**: 477,n1; **62**: 254, 325, 455, 481; **63**: 59, 445; **64**: 274, 275, 306, 452; **65**: 399; **68**: 125, 134, 135, 136, 141, 392, 439, 521; mentioned as Secretary General of League of Nations, **58**: 199, 201, 214, 441; on appointments of Americans to commissions for Danzig and Saar Valley, **62**: 451; Lansing on danger of, **62**: 455; and summoning first meeting of League of Nations Assembly, **65**: 388,n1, 503n1, 504; on League of Nations' progress, **68**: 420-21

Duala, Cameroon, **54**: 319

Dublin, Ireland: offers WW freedom of the city, **54**: 256n1, 399n1, 552; WW unable to visit, **56**: 96

Dublin *Freeman's Journal and National Press*, **58**: 586,n1; **59**: 105-106, 107; **60**: 385

Dubofsky, Melvin, **65**: 187n3

Du Bois, Arthur Wood, **64**: 150n1

Du Bois, William Edward Burghardt, **66**: 542n1; on future of Africa, **53**: 236-38,n1; **54**: 126n1

Dubost, Henri Antoine, **54**: 155, 156,n1; **61**: 188

Dubrovnik, Yugoslavia: *see* Ragusa

Duff, Arthur Allen, **61**: 163,n15

Duffield, Howard, **66**: 302n1

Duffield, Katherine, **66**: 302,n1

Duffield, Katherine Nash Greenleaf, (Mrs. Howard), **66**: 302n1

Duffy, Frank, **65**: 20

Dugan, Raymond Smith, **67**: 182

Duggan, Grace Elvina Hinds (Mrs. Alfred), **55**: 480,n3

Duggan, Patrick Carroll, **65**: 226,n1, 229, 238
Duggan, Stephen Pierce, **67**: 415,n1, 417; **68**: 548
Duisberg, Germany, **54**: 530
Duke, William, **58**: 56
Dulles, Allen Welsh, **56**: 221,n7, 586n1; **61**: 321,n1; on Hungarian situation, **56**: 239-40
Dulles, John Foster, **55**: 35; **57**: 22; **58**: 26, 27, 28, 262, 423, 424; **59**: 299-300, 310; **61**: 230, 254, 321,n1; on reparations, **56**: 498-99, 501, 502, 535, 580, 588; **59**: 422; **62**: 148, 149, 328, 510, 550; on substantive changes in reparation clause, **58**: 549-52; to remain in Paris, **61**: 283, 349; on interim Reparation Commission, **61**: 384-85; **62**: 143-44, 236, 237-38, 322-23, 551,n1; on proposed International Economic Council, **61**: 520-22; on lifting German blockade, and control of dyestuffs, **61**: 523-24; and Reparation Commission appointment, **61**: 528
Dulles, John Heatley, **65**: 572,n3
Dumba, Constantin Theodor, **66**: 39,n4
Du Mont, Frederick Theodore Frelinghuysen, **61**: 117-18,n3
Du Mont, Mary Wolfe (Mrs. Frederick Theodore Frelinghuysen), **61**: 117,n3
Duncan, James A., **63**: 273n2; **65**: 20; **66**: 5,n3
Duncan, John, **57**: 385
Duneka, Frederick A., **64**: 514-15,n1; **66**: 164,n1
Dunker, Mr., **57**: 591
Dunne, Edward Fitzsimons, **56**: 486,n1; **57**: 419,n3, 426, 534,n1; **58**: 505,n2, 585-87, 588; **59**: 34, 104-105, 106, 172, 251, 366-67, 368, 393, 394-95, 513-14, 549n1, 604, 642-43, 646; **60**: 38, 298, 431, 487, 569; **63**: 118,n2; requests Paris Peace Conference investigate Irish situation, **60**: 239,n1; meets with WW, **60**: 383-87; awaits outcome of Borah Resolution, **60**: 544
Dunne, Peter Finley, **64**: 132n1
Duplex Printing Press Company v. Deering, **67**: 497,n2
Dupont, Charles-Joseph, **56**: 118,n19, 129, 134, 145; **59**: 560,n3; **60**: 524; **61**: 99,n1; **62**: 318
Durand, Walter Y., **63**: 389n2
Duren, Germany, **57**: 591
Duroselle, Jean-Baptiste, **68**: 190n3
Düsseldorf, Germany, **55**: 475
Dutasta, Paul Eugène, **54**: 130,n1, 421; **56**: 574,n1; **57**: 401; **58**: 266, 316, 433, 472, 489, 504, 505; **59**: 156-57, 237, 567, 632; **60**: 468,n6; **61**: 78, 104, 148, 149, 186-87, 192, 203, 323, 324, 339; **64**: 118n2; to deliver treaty at Versailles, **60**: 574-75; at treaty signing, **61**: 302, 303
Dutch East Indies: and Japan, **65**: 392
Dutov, Aleksandr Il'ich, **61**: 572,n6

Duval, Marie-Victor-Charles-Maurice, **55**: 112,n4; **56**: 40, 42, 43
Dwight, Harry Griswold, **66**: 65, 350
Dwight W. Morrow Discusses the Proposed Covenant of the League (New York *Evening Post*), **55**: 451,n9
Dyar, Charles Bowker, **59**: 237,n2; **60**: 178
Dyer, Harvey H., **66**: 80, 81
Dyer, Jessie Kennedy (Mrs. Harvey H.), niece of WW, **66**: 519; requests loan from WW, **66**: 80-81,n1, WW unable to give financial aid to, **66**: 99; on WW's Nobel Prize, **66**: 503-504
Dyer, Leonidas Carstarphen: on prohibition repeal, **60**: 380,n1, 536
dyestuffs, **66**: 489; and Germany, **68**: 356, 357-58

Eagan, James, **62**: 434
Eagle, Joe Henry, **55**: 297,n4
"Eagle boats," **54**: 393,n3
Eagle Boats of World War I (Cianflone), **54**: 393n3
Earl, Commodore, **59**: 67
Early History of the Council on Foreign Relations (Shepardson), **60**: 17n1
Early Life of Georges Clemenceau 1841-1893 (Ellis), **57**: 513n1
East Asia: The Modern Transformation (Fairbanks, Reischauer, and Craig), **54**: 476n7
Eastern Galicia: *see* Galicia; Western Ukraine Republic
East Galicia, **62**: 220-22
Eastman, Joseph Bartlett: appointed to Interstate Commerce Commission, **56**: 194,n1
Eastman, Max, **66**: 95
East Prussia: *see* Paris Peace Conference—East Prussia
Eatough, Henry, **57**: 425
Eberle, Edward W., **68**: 581
Ebert, Friederich, **53**: 8, 63,n1, 122, 576n2; **54**: 532; **55**: 55,n4, 99, 458n1; **56**: 494,n1; **57**: 521, 523, 524, 566; **58**: 45, 313; **59**: 10; **60**: 177, 311-12; **61**: 34n1, 418n2; on peace treaty, **58**: 308, 314; **59**: 68,n3
Eckermann, Johann Peter, **67**: 293,n5
Eckhardt, Heinrich von, **56**: 340,n1
Economic Commission, **58**: 114-19, 119; *see also* Supreme Economic Council
Economic Consequences of the Peace (Keynes), **58**: 623n60; **68**: 223n3
Economic Council: *see* Supreme Economic Council
Economic Outlook in Germany (Coar), **67**: 463-64,n1
Ecuador, **54**: 114-15, 264; **58**: 198; **67**: 571; changed attitude toward U.S., **61**: 560-61; issue of loan to, **68**: 56, 74, 111-12, 113-14, 114
Edge, Walter Evans, **53**: 63; **60**: 246,n12; **61**: 548,n1; **62**: 32, 34, 502; **63**: 203; **68**: 346n2, 460; and bill on foreign bank-

ing, **61**: 497; and League of Nations, **61**: 569n1, 570; meets with WW on treaty, **61**: 594, 598, 599; and treaty fight, **64**: 200-201, 337; and prohibition, **68**: 454,n2

Edge bill, **61**: 497,n4; **62**: 502; **63**: 203

Edinburgh, University of, **61**: 362,n4, 476: and WW's honorary degree, **55**: 89,n1

Edirne, Turkey: *see* Adrianople

Edison, Thomas Alva: receives Distinguished Service award, **66**: 371,n1, 387

Editions Bossard (Paris), **53**: 262

Editor and Publisher **62**: 607n1

Edlin, William, **56**: 283,n1

education: and Smith-Bankhead Americanization bill, **55**: 284-88

Education, Bureau of, **62**: 233n1

Education, Department of (proposed): opposition to, **62**: 233,n1

Education and Labor, Committee on (Senate), **63**: 30n1

Education by Violence: Essays on the War and the Future (Canby), **61**: 568,n1

Edward VII (of Great Britain), **53**: 392

Edward Albert Christian George Andrew Patrick David (later Edward VIII, King of Great Britain and Emperor of India), Prince of Wales, **63**: 297,n1, 559; **64**: 28, 42; visit to U.S., **62**: 13,n1, 516; visits WW, **64**: 31-32; thanks EBW and WW for hospitality, **64**: 36-37, 71; WW thanks for New Year's wishes, **64**: 236

Edwards, Agustin, **55**: 331,n5

Edwards, Clarence Ransom, **53**: 503; **55**: 218n1, 235

Edwards, Edward Irving, **67**: 480, 482, 487; **68**: 154,n3, 179n1, 188, 388n1, 454n2; WW's congratulations to, **63**: 615,n1; **68**: 188

Edwards, Julia, **68**: 188

Egan, Maurice Francis, **53**: 194n1; replacement for, **55**: 185; on appointment of Johnson as ambassador to Italy, **64**: 474

Egerton, George William, **53**: 331n3, 515n1; **54**: 522n1; **57**: 142n1; **62**: 254n2; **63**: 606n1; **64**: 355n1

Egypt, **53**: 293; **54**: 254; **56**: 267-68; **57**: 76; rioting in, **56**: 122n2; **58**: 318; **59**: 326; **61**: 159; **62**: 325; **64**: 49; Gary on critical situation in, **56**: 153-55; and Palestine, **57**: 326,n3; U.S. recognition of British protectorate of, **57**: 464-66, 467, 499, 557, 557-58; wishes to be heard at Paris Peace Conference, **61**: 8,n1

E. H. Gary Warns of Industrial Panic, **53**: 77

Ehrenbreitstein, Germany, **60**: 489,n2

Ehrensvard, Count Johan Jacob Albert, **57**: 251,n3

Eighteenth Amendment, **59**: 76n1; *see also* prohibition

eight-hour day, **59**: 291; **62**: 583; F. D. Roosevelt on, **62**: 232

Eight Years with Wilson's Cabinet, 1913-1920 (Houston), **64**: 133n2, 249n1, 475n1; **66**: 307n1; **67**: 159n2, 176n1

Eisenhart, Luther Pfahler, **67**: 182

Eisner, Kurt, **55**: 423n1; **57**: 4n1

Ekaterinburg, Russia, (now Krasnodar or Sverdlovsk), **53**: 629, 630; **59**: 550,n2; **62**: 87

El-Arish, **55**: 384n4,5

Elbe River, **56**: 268; **58**: 122, 123

Elbing, Poland, **56**: 89

Eldridge, Howard E., **68**: 519n1

Election of 1920, **53**: 68; **55**: 443, 448, 457; **58**: 172, 535; **59**: 74; **60**: 611; **61**: 577; Tumulty on program for, **53**: 23-24; WW and third term mentioned, **60**: 41n1, 112-13; WW on possible candidates, **60**: 381; Hines on railroad situation and effect on, **64**: 22; Grayson on, **64**: 135, 325; treaty as campaign issue, **64**: 263, 267, 384; WW not seeking reelection, **64**: 267; Cobb on, **64**: 270n2; Sherman on, **64**: 328n2; and Palmer, **64**: 347; Burleson on, **64**: 445; mentioned, **65**: 71n3; Tumulty on third-term issue, **65**: 117-19; WW on his candidacy, **65**: 123; WW on H. Hoover and, **65**: 149; Geddes on, **65**: 372; W. G. Sharpon, **65**: 473-76; results of, **66**: 306n1; various comments on, **66**: 312-13, 313, 313-14, 314, 314-15, 318, 318-19, 319-20, 328, 336, 340-41, 474-75; WW's message to Cox, **66**: 321; Cox on, **66**: 333; Peabody on, **68**: 210; Mrs. Simonson on, **68**: 264; WW on, **68**: 310; *see also* Democratic National Convention, 1920; Republican National Convention, 1920; Republican presidential campaign of 1920

Election of 1922, **68**: 179n1, 180, 222; WW asks Houston to write policy paper for Democratic candidates in, **68**: 32; Hull on outlook for, **68**: 49-50, 85-86; exchange between Hull and WW on, **68**: 60-61, 63-64, 70-71, 71; WW on type of candidate for Congress, **68**: 63-64; McAdoo on, **68**: 73, 146-49; Wise on, **68**: 87; WW congratulates Hull on, **68**: 181; Peabody on, **68**: 210

Election of 1924, **67**: 319n1, 562n1; WW on, **67**: 585

election laws: WW's inquiry on and Palmer's answer, **64**: 202-203, 214-15

Electrical Workers of America, **64**: 424

electric railways, **59**: 287-88, 320; **62**: 420-22, 516-17; WW on, **62**: 532-33, 533

Elena, Queen of Italy, **53**: 595,n1, 600, 601, 607, 608n1, 638n1, 697, 698; **54**: 134; **56**: 86; **58**: 239; **65**: 303,n11

Elihu Root (Jessup), **66**: 246n2

Elihu Root and the Conservative Tradition (Leopold), **61**: 66n3; **66**: 246n2

Eliot, Charles William, **54**: 58; **64**: 297,n2; **66**: 164,n2, 281-82, 290; **67**: 333n1, 522; suggestions for WW, **61**:

Eliot, Charles William (*cont.*)
577-78; on Ireland, **61**: 578; and Armenia, **65**: 298; on League of Nations and Irish self-determination, **66**: 267,n2; birthday greetings to WW, **68**: 246; and WW Foundation, **68**: 509
Eliot, Samuel A., **67**: 522
Elisabeth (Elisabeth Valerie), Queen of the Belgians, **53**: 384, 712,n1; **56**: 556n1; **61**: 3, 4, 6, 11, 12, 15, 24, 29, 61, 609; **62**: 6, 29, 516; **63**: 21, 119, 166, 515, 526, 535-36, 542; WW's toast to, **61**: 16,n1; WW's thank you to, **61**: 33, 35; WW's welcoming of canceled, **63**: 528; thanks EBW for flowers, sends WW get-well wishes, **63**: 548; received by WW, **63**: 602-606; photographs of, *illustration section*, **61**
Elisabeth (Rumanian princess), **57**: 193,n4, 238
Elkins, Davis: and treaty fight, **64**: 200, 202, 337
Elkus, Abram Isaac, **55**: 289, 290, 411; **59**: 419n1; **67**: 37, 41, 426n1, 602; **68**: 59, 521,n2; encourages WW to run for third term, **65**: 457-59,n1; and Åland Islands Commission, **65**: 531n1; and Åland Island Commission, **66**: 263, 265, 304; **67**: 266; praises WW, **67**: 266
Elliott, Edward Graham, **53**: 45; **63**: 340n3; **68**: 76,n2, 229,n2
Elliott, Margaret Randolph Axson (Mrs. Edward Graham), sister of EAW, **63**: 340n3; **68**: 76n2, 229,n2, 577,n1
Elliott, John Henry, **65**: 189n1
Ellis, Jack D., **57**: 513n1
Ellis Island, **64**: 9
Ellsworth, James William, **62**: 252,n2
Elmer, Ernest E., **57**: 425
Elmer Sperry: Inventor and Engineer (Hughes), **63**: 441n2
Elmore, Alfred A., **56**: 427,n1, 471, 485-86
Elmquist, Charles Emil, **62**: 420,n1
El Paso, Texas, **61**: 487
El Salvador, **56**: 170n1; **65**: 274n1
Elsberry, Terence, **57**: 193n7
Elston, John Arthur, **66**: 151n1,2
Ely, Helen Rutherford, **67**: 481n1
Ely, Matthias Cowell, **68**: 454,n3
Ely, Richard, **65**: 572,n17
Elysée Palace, **53**: 386n1, 390
Emanuele Filiberto (Italian ship), **59**: 65
Embick, Stanley Dunbar, **57**: 415-16,n1; **60**: 104,n1, 105-106
Emergence of Modern First Amendment Doctrine (Rabban), **55**: 347n1; **66**: 92n1
Emergence of Modern Lithuania (Senn), **59**: 18n10
Emergence of the Middle East 1914-1924 (Sachar), **56**: 110n7
Emergency Fleet Corporation, **53**: 112; **54**: 395, 432; **55**: 398n1; **56**: 245; **59**: 160, 204n2; **62**: 226, 248; **65**: 282; **68**: 81n2; and housing projects, **55**: 342; Payne on existing legislation regard-

ing ships, **62**: 528-29; and Morse case, **68**: 73n2
Emergency Shipping Fund, **62**: 226
Emergency Tariff bill, **67**: 121,n2; Underwood on, **67**: 123, 159; WW's veto of, **67**: 191-94; Eliot on WW's veto of, **67**: 231-32
Emerson, George H., **55**: 400,n1
Emerson, Ralph Waldo, **66**: 315
Emery, Frederick Azron, **60**: 245,n1
Emil Georg Von Strauss, S.M.S., **55**: 432
Employees Compensation Commission, **54**: 274
employment and unemployment, **53**: 279-80, 413; **54**: 221-22, 390-94, 500-501,n1, 520-21; and civil service appointments and census bill, **55**: 281,n1; WW on returning servicemen and, **59**: 292; **64**: 80, 190
Employment of Soldiers and Sailors: Statement of Hon. W. B. Wilson, Secretary of Labor, before the Committee on Rules, House of Representatives, Sixty-fifth Congress, Third Session, **55**: 291n1
Employment Service: *see* United States Employment Service
Emporia, Kan., Daily Gazette, **61**: 506n1; **68**: 148n5
Encyclopaedia Britannica: article on N. D. Baker, **68**: 133,n1, 136-37
Endicott, Henry Bradford, **64**: 141,n4: appointed to first Industrial Conference, **63**: 300,n1
End of a Great Illusion (Lippmann), **67**: 541,n1
End of the War, The (Weyl), **61**: 538,n1
End of Innocence (Jonathan Daniels), **63**: 419n1
Engdahl, John Louis, **62**: 557,n1
Engelken, Friedrich Johannes Hugo von, **53**: 106,n1, 113,n1
England: *see* Great Britain
Englehardt, O., **56**: 392,n2
English Review: reviews Baker's *World Settlement*, **68**: 312-13
English-Speaking Union, **56**: 57,n1
Enoch H. Crowder: Soldier, Lawyer, and Statesman (Lockmiller), **66**: 58n1; **67**: 24n1
Enough Ships Already Have Sunk (*New York Times*), **53**: 469n1
Enright, John, **67**: 483n1
Enver Pasha, **58**: 555n1; **59**: 411,n2; **60**: 612
Epernay, France, **53**: 468n1
Epiphany Church of Washington, **68**: 395n1
Episcopal Church: and League of Nations, **66**: 202
Episcopal Theological School of Cambridge, Mass., **67**: 527n4
Epirus, **54**: 463
Epstein, Fritz, **58**: 308n1
Epstein, Klaus, **53**: 32n1; **61**: 34n1, 76n5
Eregli: *see* Heraclea Pontica
Erie, Pa., Times, **65**: 6

Eritrea, **54**: 326n3

Erivan (now Yerevan, U.S.S.R.), **61**: 159; **65**: 288, 309, 310

Ernest, Emile: *see* Marchienne, Baron Cartier de

Ernst, Elldon G., **64**: 416n2

Erskine, William Augustus Forbes, **58**: 369,n4

Ervin, Charles W.: on censorship, **54**: 430,n1

Erwin, James Brailsford, **61**: 487,n2

Erzberger, Matthias, **53**: 32,n1, 33; **54**: 38-39, 238, 241; **55**: 10, 11, 18-19, 202-203; **56**: 493; **57**: 74,n3,4,5, 75,n6, 105; **59**: 237,n2, 554, 577; **60**: 24,n14, 191n1; **61**: 34, 76n5, 141; **62**: 318-19; **65**: 100, 101; on Bolshevism, **57**: 75n6; on peace treaty, **58**: 308,n1, 314; **59**: 348,n1; American delegation question authenticity of letter-interview, **60**: 64-65

Erzerum, Turkey, **65**: 74, 309, 321, 322

Erzingan, Turkey, **65**: 74

Escalier, José Maria, **66**: 135n1

Esch, John Jacob, **61**: 415,n3; **62**: 98, 98-9,n1, 117, 118, 163; and railroad legislation, **64**: 195,n1; and water-power legislation, **65**: 398n1

Esch-Cummins bill and Act (Transportation Act of 1920), **64**: 467,n1, 474, 475n2; **65**: 14,n3, 16, 286, 508; **67**: 12, 13, 122, 550n1; Hines on, **64**: **65**: 14,n3, 16, 286, 508; 468; Houston on, **64**: 480; **66**: 455; W. M. Daniels on, **64**: 480; A.F.L. urges rejection of, **65**: 19-20; Ames on appointing Railroad Labor Board, **65**: 174-75; appointment of board, **65**: 189,n1; and WW's State of the Union Message, **66**: 488

Espionage Act, **53**: 260; **56**: 619; **61**: 497-98; **62**: 58, 126,n1, 499; **68**: 48n6; movement for repeal of, **55**: 224, 337,n1; and amnesty issue, **55**: 344, 345, 346, 347, 365, 482n1; general amnesty for violators of, **65**: 128, 177, 190, 203-11, 273, 276,n1, 418,n3; **66**: 120,n1; impact on postal regulations, **66**: 92-93,n1, 94-98; and Stokes case, **66**: 176-77, 184; and Debs case, **67**: 98, 101-102

Essad Pasha Tpotanii, **57**: 427,n7

Essary, Jesse Frederick, **67**: 243,n1

Essays and Addresses in War Time (Bryce), **53**: 335,n1, 411

Essays, Speeches and Memoirs (Von Moltke; trans. McClumpha *et al.*), **55**: 508n2

Essays toward a Bibliography of Woodrow Wilson, **68**: 308,n2

Essen, Germany, **54**: 42, 240, 246, 528, 530, 540; talk of occupation of, **61**: 115, 126, 127, 144, 146

estate tax, **59**: 293-94

Estonia and Estonians, **53**: 591; **55**: 202; **56**: 35, 468; **62**: 15; sale of locomotives to, **65**: 387-88; children fed in, **65**: 469; **67**: 8; *see also* Paris Peace Conference—Estonia and Estonians

Estrada Cabrera, Manuel, **65**: 247n1; **66**: 389,n1, 390, 506n5; WW on release of, **66**: 402

Ethiopia: mission sent to U.S., **61**: 406,n1, 471-74; Long on mission's visit with WW, **61**: 470-71; WW's notes to Empress Zaouditou and Ras Taffari, **61**: 603, 604

Eulalia, Infanta, **57**: 241,n1,2

Eupen, Germany, **56**: 592; **57**: 392, 393; **60**: 105, 108

Euripides, **53**: 46, 47, 55

European Alliances and Alignments, 1871-1890 (Langer), **58**: 461n1; **60**: 173,n2

Europe and Italy's Acquisition of Libya, 1911-1912 (Askew), **58**: 435n7

European Children's Relief Fund (Hoover Fund), **65**: 468, 70; **66**: 493n1, 509, 529; **67**: 75,n4, 85, 87, 88

European relief: plans for organization and legislation, **53**: 14-15, 15-16, 32-33, 41-42, 102,103, 395, 435, 483n4; and needed congressional appropriations, **53**: 15-16, 75, 273, 309, 578-79, 707, 717-18; German request for food, **53**: 63, 64; H. Hoover on U.S. as trustee for distribution, **53**: 76-77; Hoover's plan for and appointment as Director General of Relief, **53**: 222-25, 271-72, 361, 363, 393, 714; **53**: 476-77, 648-49, 649-50, 650-51, 651, 687-88, 689-90, 692, 698, 699; and Hurley and shipping plans for, **53**: 271-72, 272; Allied meeting on, **53**: 360-64; WW on creation of European relief organization, **53**: 392-93; and Bolshevism, **53**: 453-54, 692, 709; *see also* Commission for the Relief of Belgium; food relief; United States: European relief, credit and postwar reconstruction

European Relief Council, **67**: 96, 97

European Right: A Historical Profile (Rogger and Weber, eds.), **59**: 195n4

European Student Relief, **66**: 411n1

Euskirchen, Germany, **57**: 591

Euxine Pontus, **66**: 29,n1,2

Evans, Sir Arthur (John), **57**: 539n3

Evans, Arthur Mayberry, **54**: 60,n1

Evans, Charles St. Clair, **67**: 519,n1

Evans, Edward J., **63**: 29-30,n2

Evans, Edward Ratcliffe Garth Russell, **61**: 6-7,n9

Evans, Elizabeth Gardiner (Mrs. Glendower), **53**: 126; **65**: 194,n1

Evans, Frank Taylor, **56**: 444,n3

Evans, Hiram Wesley, **68**: 298n2

Evans, James Daniel, **68**: 331,n1

Evans, Laurence, **66**: 394n1; **68**: 431n2

Evans, Marion Griffin, **66**: 386n1

Evanston, Ill., **66**: 256

Everett Hotel, New York, **55**: 472

Everybody's Magazine, **55**: 392n1, 456n1

evolution: WW on, **68**: 121,n2

Ewing, Oscar Ross: praises WW, **66**: 391-92, 393

Ewing, Robert, **53**: 287
excess profits tax, **54**: 502; **55**: 333-34,n1; **59**: 293-94; **65**: 131; **67**: 484, 485, 500; and WW's Annual Message to Congress, **64**: 78, 107-108; **66**: 488
Expansion and Conflict (Dodd), **67**: 76n2
Experiments in International Administration (Sayre), **54**: 107,n3
Eyes of Woodrow Wilson (Marmor), **58**: 611n2
Eyschen, Paul, **56**: 597,n3

Facts About President Wilson's Illness (I. Hoover), **61**: 112n1
Fagalde, Colonel, **65**: 143
Fairbank, Janet Dyer (Mrs. Kellogg), **66**: 165,n4; **67**: 545,n1
Fairbank, John King, **54**: 476n7
Fairbanks, Douglas, **54**: 53; **65**: 400n1; **68**: 240
Fairbanks, Frances Lewis (Mrs. Henry Parker), **66**: 519n1
Fairbanks, Henry Parker, **66**: 519n1
Fairchild, Charles S., **67**: 563n1
Fairchild *v.* Hughes: Brandeis on, **67**: 563,n1
Fairweather, Tom Patterson, **63**: 65n4
Faisal, Prince, **54**: 5, 90,n1, 195; **56**: 112, 113, 114, 115, 117, 323; **57**: 247, 334, 443, 535, 559, 586; **58**: 134; **59**: 139, 331, 341, 636, 637; **61**: 157,n9, 218, 409, 442n1, 443, 524,n1; **64**: 25-26, 449; **65**: 141, 142,n1, 271n1; **66**: 47; on Arab claims, **54**: 505-509,n2,3; **55**: 4, 81, 86, 183; on proposed mideastern commission, **56**: 243-44; thanks U.S. for help, **57**: 525-26; Clemenceau on France and Syria and, **57**: 589-90; Crane on, **61**: 444; congratulations to WW, **61**: 467; photograph of, *illustration section*, **54**
Fall, Albert Bacon, **55**: 267; **58**: 524n1; **60**: 244,n5, 245, 246; **61**: 184,n1, 240, 372; **62**: 336, 431; **67**: 46, 350n1, 390n1; and Mexico, **62**: 155n1; **64**: 120-21,n1, 123, 127-28, 152; **66**: 335, 337, 405,n5,6; questions WW at Foreign Relations Committee meeting, **62**: 335, 339, 357-58, 370, 379, 382-83, 390; asks to submit his questions (memorandum) to WW after Foreign Relations Committee meeting, **62**: 379, 382-83; memorandum of questions on treaty and League of Nations, **62**: 411-15; WW answers questions in memorandum, **62**: 417-19; and Bullitt testimony, **63**: 337n1; and amendments to treaty, **63**: 482,n2,4; meeting with WW during his illness, **63**: 637,n5; meets with WW on Mexican situation, **64**: 129-32, 132-33, 139-40; on WW's health, **64**: 132, 138; EBW's notes on WW's meeting on Mexico with, **64**: 133-35; WW reaction to prayers by, **64**:

133n2; sends WW transcript of report on Mexico, **64**: 140,n1; and Underwood resolution, **64**: 199n1; and treaty, **64**: 200-201, 337; and Honolulu Oil case, **64**: 405n1; and Teapot Dome scandal, **68**: 119n2; and railroad situation, **68**: 129n1; and Dr. Ruffin, **68**: 552
Fall amendments, **63**: 482,n2,4, 483-84
Fall Resolution, **61**: 184n1, 347n1; **64**: 131, 132, 133, 134, 140; WW on, **61**: 240, 247; **64**: 152,n2; Pittman on, **64**: 127-28; Grayson on spirit behind, **64**: 136-37
Fall River, Mass., **55**: 286
Famine Relief Act, **59**: 231,n1
Famine Relief bill, **53**: 637n1; **55**: 116; controversy over and passage of, **54**: 55n2, 57, 174,n1,2, 229, 258, 303, 332, 394, 486
famine relief committee: *see* Chinese Famine Relief Committee
Farhi, Tewfik, **55**: 145n3
Farley, Edwin Wood Thorp, **53**: 509,n3
Farman, Elbert Eli, **59**: 597,n1, 598
Farm Bureaus, **62**: 300
Farm Bureau Through Three Decades (Kile), **62**: 300n1
Farmer-Labor party, **68**: 146,n2, 156n3, 179n1
farmers and farming: agricultural lobby on public referendum, **62**: 30-31; and cost of living, **62**: 300,n1; and WW's veto of repeal of daylight-saving law, **62**: 304-305,n1; loan system for, **68**: 8, 253, 270; *see also* agriculture
Farmers Educational Co-operative Union of America, **56**: 427
Farmers National Council, **56**: 427; **58**: 145,n1; **62**: 30n1; **66**: 243
Farmers National Headquarters, **62**: 30n1
Farmers Nonpartisan League: *see* Nonpartisan League
Farm Loan Act, **65**: 63
Farm Loan Banks: WW and Baruch on statement for The Document, **67**: 560-61, 582-83, 583-84, 601
Farm Loan Board: Norris resigns from, **65**: 63; **66**: 244
Farquhar, Arthur Briggs, **55**: 439-40,n1
Farquhar, Horace Brand, 1st Viscount Farquhar, **57**: 503,n3
Farquhar Defends League of Nations (*York Dispatch*), **55**: 440,n2
Farr, Marcus Stults, **67**: 182
Farrand, Livingston, **55**: 281n1; **66**: 512,n1, 513
Farrar, Geraldine, **53**: 371
Farrell, James Augustine, **58**: 597,n4; **61**: 512,n4; **62**: 598,n1
Farrell, John J., **54**: 473,n1
Farrington, Mr.: and Illinois coal strike, **65**: 545
Farris, Frank, **57**: 47, 48
Fassett, Charles Marvin, **63**: 224,n1

Fatherland, The, **66**: 248n1
Fatio, Robert, **64**: 98
Faunce, William Herbert Perry, **66**: 246n2, 467,n3; **68**: 159,n4; WW on, **68**: 166-67
Fawcett, Millicent Garrett (Mrs. Henry), **55**: 145,n4, 183-84
Fayolle, Marie-Emile, **60**: 9,n3, 11, 13
Federal Censorship: Obscenity in the Mail (Paul and Schwartz), **66**: 92n1
Federal Control Act, **62**: 75, 77; **64**: 22-23, 226
Federal Council of the Churches of Christ in America, **53**: 718,n1; **54**: 56; **66**: 120-21,n1, 129, 378, 387; **67**: 29-30; **68**: 160-61, 531; and League of Nations, **54**: 277-78; **66**: 203
Federal Electric Railways Commission, **62**: 420-22, 461, 516-17; WW on, **62**: 532-33
Federal Farm Loan Act, **65**: 63; **66**: 244; **67**: 569
Federal Farm Loan Banks: *see* Farm Loan Banks
Federal Farm Loan Board, **66**: 244
Federal Highway (Good Roads) Act, **68**: 270
Federal Justice: Chapters in the History of Justice and the Federal Executive (Cummings and McFarland), **60**: 115n7
Federal Power Commission: and N. D. Baker, **65**: 447-48, 459; WW wishes N. D. Baker to head, **65**: 449
Federal Railroad Administration: *see* Railroad Administration
Federal Reserve Act, **61**: 497; **64**: 52, 195; success of as example for League of Nations propaganda, **55**: 367; and Owen's bill for establishing Federal Reserve Foreign Bank, **61**: 495-98,n1,2, 549; Elkus on, **65**: 458; Root on, **66**: 157,n6; Tumulty's fears for if Republican elected, **66**: 215; and Republican charges of depression and, **66**: 242-43; WW on Reed and, **68**: 24; Glass on Vanderlip and, **68**: 78; T. G. Patten on, **68**: 585-87
Federal Reserve Bank of Philadelphia, **65**: 63; Vanderlip on, **68**: 57,n1
Federal Reserve Board, **53**: 716; **59**: 111, 642n1; **61**: 497; **62**: 223, 314,n2, 499; and railroad crisis, **55**: 536; and Fine, **61**: 625,n1; criticism of, **66**: 112,n1; and southern cotton situation, **66**: 112n1, 159; farmers' organization requests hearing with, **66**: 224; W. P. G. Harding's requested and WW's denial of publication of letter to, **68**: 405
Federal Reserve Foreign Bank (proposed), **61**: 495-98,n1,2, 549; **62**: 498; Glass on, **62**: 501-503
Federal Reserve Policy and the Agricultural Depression of 1920-21 (Link), **57**: 511n2; **66**: 36n3, 112n1; **68**: 241n1

Federal Reserve System: Davis on, **68**: 241, 253; Houston on, **68**: 270, 271; W. P. G. Harding on, **68**: 405,n1; Hamlin speaks on, **68**: 416
Federal Trade Commission, **61**: 440; **62**: 213, 214; **65**: 385; **68**: 301n2; and meatpacking report and legislation, **53**: 156-58, 205, 215; WW meets with on price crisis, **62**: 158-61; Palmer on cost of living and, **62**: 174-75; and steel prices, **63**: 89-90, 301; and differences with Food Administration, **63**: 389-91, 425; appointments to, **64**: 205; and coal prices, **66**: 4; Colver resigns from, **66**: 241,n1; and copper price fixing, **67**: 177-78; Houston on, **68**: 270, 271; Palmer on Chemical Foundation case and, **68**: 298
Federal Transportation Board (proposed): *see* Transportation Board
Federal Wage Board (proposed), **62**: 119-20, 181-82, 191
Federal Warehouse bill, **68**: 271
Federal Water-Power Legislation (Kerwin), **65**: 398n1
Federation of Protestant Churches of France, **54**: 282n1
Federzoni, Luigi, **58**: 92,n1
Fedyshyn, Oleh S., **54**: 32n4
Fehrenbach, Konstantin, **59**: 36,n5, 136,n2; **66**: 44n5
Feisal, Prince: *see* Faisal, Prince
Feiss, Paul Louis: appointed to first Industrial Conference, **63**: 300,n1
Feland, Logan, **66**: 31,n1
Fellowship of Reconciliation, **53**: 13, 307n1
Fels, Count Edmund, **53**: 721,n1
Fels, Mary (Mrs. Joseph), **66**: 272,n2, 293
Felton, Samuel Morse, **65**: 562,n2
Fendall, Annie A. Galt (Mrs. Reginald), **53**: 399,n8, 501; **54**: 306,n9
Feng, Yu-hsiang, **53**: 138,n4
Ferdinand I (of Rumania), **57**: 238,n3, 239; **60**: 352, 427, 428; **62**: 428n2; WW's greetings to, **54**: 379-80,n1
Ferdinand VII (of Spain), **62**: 35-36, 37
Ferdinand Humbert Philippe Adalbert, Prince of Udine, **53**: 589,n1
Ferguson, Charles, **68**: 422,n2, 423; WW on, **68**: 427
Ferguson, Homer Lenoir, **53**: 704,n2; **62**: 582
Ferguson, Lenoir, **62**: 623,n1
Ferguson, Walter G., **53**: 166, 319
Fernald, Bert Manfred, **62**: 29,n1, 43, 44; and treaty fight, **64**: 200-201, 337, 338
Ferrais, Maggiorino, **61**: 109,n11
Ferrell, Robert H., **66**: 58n1
Ferrero, Guglielmo, **68**: 506,n1, 507
Ferris, Scott, **53**: 24; **54**: 486, 554; **55**: 263; **58**: 459; **61**: 535; **68**: 18; and General Leasing bill, **54**: 216,n1, 393, 471; **64**: 473, 474; and primary election, **66**: 3,n1, 10,n1

Ferry, Neal J., **65**: 353n1; **66**: 64n1, 67, 69, 70, 76
Fess, Simeon Davis, **67**: 511,n1; **68**: 268,n3
Fethiye: *see* Makri
Fewell, Alexander, M.D., **58**: 631
Fiallo, Fabio, **66**: 25n1
Field, Marshall, **59**: 517n2
Field, W. K., **63**: 56,n3
Fighting for the League (Chan), **63**: 428n1
Figueroa y Torres, Alvaro: *see* Romanones, Count de
Filene, Edward Albert, **55**: 199, 447
Finance Committee (Senate), **53**: 103; **63**: 203n3; **67**: 121n2, 355n2,6; **68**: 97n3; and revenue bill, **55**: 334,n1
Finch, George Augustus, **56**: 75n3
Finck, Hermann, **57**: 533n4
Finding a Way Out: An Autobiography (Moton), **53**: 526n1, 579n1
Fine, Henry Burchard, **58**: 482,n1; **65**: 572,n8, 573; **67**: 105n3, 182; and Federal Reserve Board, **61**: 625,n1; WW's condolences to, **68**: 102; thanks WW for his sympathy, **68**: 103
Fine, John: death of, **68**: 102,n1, 103
Fine, Philena Fobes, **68**: 103,n1
Fine, Philena Fobes (Mrs. Henry Burchard), **68**: 103,n1
Fine Arts Picture Corporation, **65**: 384
Fink, Reuben, **54**: 60,n1
Finland, **53**: 648; **55**: 202, 233, 542; **56**: 35, 31; **57**: 392, 398; **58**: 42; **59**: 16; **60**: 282; **61**: 455n1; **68**: 512; and Russia, **54**: 136-37, 137, 205, 206, 287; **59**: 21, 442, 470, 545; **66**: 16, 21n1, 24; issues of recognition of and representation at Paris Peace Conference, **54**: 287-88; **58**: 177-78, 248, 319; U.S. recognizes, **58**: 404,n2; Kolchak on, **60**: 143; Lansing on recognition of, **64**: 236; and Åland Islands controversy, **65**: 460,n1,2, 525-26; children fed in, **65**: 469; **66**: 138n1; **67**: 266; children fed in, **65**: 469; and Poland, **65**: 527n3
Finland, Gulf of: H. White on trade and, **62**: 14-16
Finley, John Huston, **66**: 119,n2; **68**: 581
Finley, John Miller Turpin, M.D., **68**: 152n1
First Across: The U.S. Navy's Transatlantic Flight of 1919 (Smith), **57**: 447n1; **60**: 44n4
First Amendment in its Forgotten Years (Rabban), **66**: 92n1
First Baptist Church of Washington, **65**: 275n1
First Class Temperament: The Emergence of Franklin Roosevelt (Ward), **67**: 386n2
First Duce: D'Annunzio at Fiume (Leeden), **58**: 92n2; **59**: 119n3; **63**: 298n2, 517n2
First Lady Between Two Worlds: Ellen

Axson Wilson (Saunders), **60**: 647n2; **68**: 527n2
First Methodist Episcopal Church, South, of Pensacola, Fla., **68**: 144n1
First National Bank of Boston, **53**: 716n2
First Presbyterian Church of Augusta, Ga., **68**: 450,n1
First Presbyterian Church of Gastonia, N.C., **64**: 191, 213
First Presbyterian Church of Princeton, **66**: 194n1; **67**: 91n1, 123n2; and Beach, **68**: 352,n1,2, 354; and Van Dyke, **68**: 519,n1
First Presbyterian Church of Seattle, **62**: 456n1; **66**: 17n1
Fischer, Jacob, **65**: 20
Fisher, Herbert Albert Laurens, **59**: 627,n3; **60**: 20,n1, 24; **65**: 55,n2
Fisher, Irving, **62**: 314,n1, 560,n1; **68**: 331
Fisher, Jacob, **65**: 20
Fisher, Walter Lowrie, **53**: 157
Fiske, John, **55**: 216
Fitzgerald, Cecil Bernard, **63**: 254,n1
Fitzgerald, David Edward, **55**: 237,n3,4
Fitzgerald, E. H., **65**: 359
Fitzgerald, John J., **53**: 166, 319
Fitzhardinge, L. F., **54**: 351n3, 363n3
Fitzmaurice, Henry Charles Keith Petty: *see* Lansdowne, Marquess of
Fitzpatrick, John: on steel strike situation, **63**: 20-30,n1, 148-49, 164
Fiume: *see* Paris Peace Conference—Italy; Fiume
Fiume *La Bilancia*, **59**: 241n1
Five Power Naval Limitation Treaty: Davis on, **67**: 544n1; **68**: 307,n4
Flack, Horace E., **66**: 148n2
Flagg, James Montgomery, **65**: 384
Flanders, **61**: 3, 29
Flatt, Mrs. R. B., **68**: 81-83, 83
Fleming, Matthew Corry, **65**: 574,n20
Fleming, Walter Lynwood, **67**: 285,n1
Flensburg, Germany, **57**: 363
Fletcher, Alfred, **60**: 532n1
Fletcher, Banister Flight, **53**: 528n4
Fletcher, Duncan Upshaw, **53**: 159,n1, 187, 188; **55**: 297; **60**: 330,n4; **67**: 522; **68**: 388n1; treaty vote, **65**: 109n1; on federal assistance to cotton industry, **66**: 36-38,n1, 60-62; and Treaty of Berlin, **67**: 354
Fletcher, Henry Prather, **61**: 610-11, 635,n7; **62**: 142, 155; **67**: 354; on situation in Mexico, **55**: 352-56; **62**: 332-33; **64**: 120n1, 121, 134; on Carranza's anti-American campaign, **62**: 450-51; WW on return to Mexico of, **62**: 459; resignation of, **64**: 310,n1, 397, 448; WW on, **65**: 88; relieved of Mexican duties, **65**: 180, 181; on Macias, **65**: 201n1, 213,n1
Flexner, Eleanor, **66**: 54n1
Flinn, Elizabeth Gurley, **54**: 397n1
Flood, Anna Portner (Mrs. Henry De La Warr): WW's condolences to, **67**: 478

Flood, Henry De La Warr, **53**: 570; **54**: 332; **55**: 270; **60**: 245,n6; **61**: 492, 548,n1; and appointments in Virginia, **66**: 167,n1, 168, 173; death of, **67**: 478,n1
floor tax, **54**: 502
Florence, University of, **53**: 433n1
Florida: and W. J. Bryan, **67**: 422
Florida, U.S.S., **66**: 410, 430
Floto, Inga, **55**: 488n2
Flotow, Hans Karl Theodor Ludwig von, **60**: 118,n4
Fly Fishing (Grey), **56**: 62n3
Flynn, Edward P., **56**: 236,n6
Foch, Ferdinand, **53**: 5, 36, 142-43, 290, 291, 320, 325, 326, 402, 529, 652; **54**: 189, 409; **55**: 387; **56**: 109, 110, 248, 383-84; **57**: 104, 290, 291, 296n, 335, 401, 432, 494; **58**: 20, 21, 57, 63, 171, 436, 483, 534, 542, 544; **59**: 46, 108, 159, 214n3, 253n1, 312, 334, 344, 401n1, 443, 591; **60**: 76, 134, 135, 296n4, 356, 472, 481, 496; **61**: 59, 86-87, 123, 196, 207, 208, 335, 587; **62**: 156, 318; **64**: 149,n2; **65**: 61, 145, 302; **67**: 33n1, 35, 71, 447; **68**: 301; meets with WW, **53**: 410; on Germany, **53**: 540; WW on, **53**: 548; wishes retention of U.S. troops, **53**: 584; on Poland and Allied Commission to Poland, **54**: 7,n3, 8, 199, 200-201, 202-203, 419, 420, 544-45; on terms of Armistice renewal, **54**: 7,n3, 21, 35, 38-39, 64, 121, 172, 220, 221, 238, 239, 239-41, 242, 244, 246; proposes medal for all Allied soldiers, **54**: 246-47; Pershing and WW concerned over possible misinterpretation of information given by, **54**: 275, 331, 414; on Allied occupation of enemy territory, **54**: 525-27, 528, 529, 530; Clemenceau on, **54**: 535; and Loucheur committee, **54**: 538; controversy with Clemenceau over German prisoners, **55**: 3, 19, 40; and Supreme War Council meetings on Armistice renewal and peace terms, **55**: 10, 11, 15, 18, 56, 93, 96, 100, 102, 103, 107, 108, 109, 111-12, 202-203; **56**: 15, 16, 20-21, 23, 30, 45, 46; on immediately dictating peace terms to Germany, **55**: 212-13, 230; on the Rhineland, **55**: 502-10; **56**: 445-48, 453, 559; **57**: 131, 494, 504; **59**: 592; **60**: 25, 59, 393, 440,n8, 501-502, 511-12, 599n1; **61**: 547; on Polish situation, **56**: 49-40, 51, 52-53, 55, 314-15, 581; on Odessa and issue of aid to Rumanian army, **56**: 50, 51, 55, 255-57, 314-15, 326-28, 581; **68**: 405; controversy over transport of Haller's troops results in Foch's mission to Spa, **56**: 88, 129, 130, 131, 131-38, 140, 141, 147, 163, 167n3, 168, 209,n2, 315, 324-25, 384, 409-13, 491, 495, 496-97, 523, 525-28; R. S. Baker on, **56**: 128, 441; McCormick on, **56**: 181; on critical issues, **56**: 314-15; Lloyd George on, **56**:

320; Lansing on militarism of, **56**: 352, 488, 489, 490; WW on, **56**: 524, 542; **58**: 462; **59**: 371; **67**: 269, 270-71, 462n2; on German economic delegation's request for German courier, **56**: 528-29, 541; and Hungarian plan, **56**: 583; and passage of Haller's Army, **57**: 74,n3,4,5, 75,n6, 76, 134-36, 178; **58**: 542, 615-16; meets F. H. Hitchcock, **57**: 350; refuses to deliver invitation to Germany, **57**: 494, 504; and Rhineland and clique with Poincaré, **58**: 211, 213, 462,n1,2, 521, 584; and Armistice terms and Article 46 of peace treaty, **58**: 310-11, 313, 315; attacks treaty, **58**: 493-94; Grasty on, **58**: 501; at Plenary Session, **58**: 518; on action to be taken if emergency arises, **58**: 580; on action to be taken if peace treaty not signed, **59**: 7-8, 9, 10, 11; **60**: 583, 584-85, 587-88, 590-91, 617-18, 618,n3, 619-21; **61**: 33n2; and issue of continued withdrawal of U.S. troops from France, **59**: 277-80,n1;and recommended strength of German army, **59**: 429, 431; Council of Four on Foch's command being ready to advance, **59**: 487; moved to tears at Memorial Day ceremony, **59**: 605, 606, 622; and Rhenish separatist movement, **60**: 13; and strength of army of occupation in Rhineland, **60**: 237, 238-39, 364,n2; H. Wilson, Lloyd George and, **60**: 304, 305; modifies line between Hungary and Czechoslovakia, **60**: 356; criticizes Rhineland plan, **60**: 364,n1, 364-65; objects to proposed Rhineland Commission, **60**: 366; and Polish army, **60**: 394; and Baltic provinces, **60**: 498; **61**: 153, 145; Clemenceau on, **60**: 525-26; "tired of waiting," leaves before appearance at Council of Four, **60**: 582-83; on demobilization of troops, **60**: 584; Council of Four on changed attitude of, **60**: 598-99; absent from signing ceremony, **61**: 326; suggested resolution honoring, **63**: 301n1,2; WW's charges of militarism made in Hitchcock letter, **65**: 52, 66, 87, 89; concern that Pétain invitation to U.S. will cause strained relations with, **65**: 154-55; and military action in Germany, **65**: 155n1, 159, 236; Holt on, **67**: 267,n1; WW unable to receive, **67**: 434, 435, 436, 466; editorial on WW and, **67**: 437,n1; Orpen portrait, *illustration section*, **60**
Foch versus Clemenceau: France and German Dismemberment, 1918-1919 (King), **58**: 462n2; **59**: 401n4; **60**: 60n7
Fogazzaro, Antonia, **60**: 5, 123,n4
Foley, Hamilton, **66**: 152,n1; **68**: 330n1, 355, 408, 411,n1; and *Woodrow Wilson's Case for the League of Nations*, **68**: 349-50; WW gives approval of project, **68**: 351

Foley, John J., **66**: 267n2
Folk, Joseph Wingate, **53**: 84
Folwell, William Watts, **67**: 555
Fontaine, (Victor) Arthur (Léon), **59**: 222,n14
Fontainebleau, **59**: 249
Fontainebleau Memorandum, **56**: 259-70,n1, 545n2; **57**: 6n7; Clemenceau's response to, **56**: 477-79
food: Glass on prices, **55**: 89-90, 358; Hoover on price controls, **55**: 251-53; pork prices, **55**: 306-307, 307-308; and prices, **60**: 491; **62**: 158, 213
Food Administration, **53**: 14, 279, 393; **54**: 276-77; **55**: 90; **56**: 282; **57**: 375; **59**: 191; WW's remarks to state administrators, **53**: 52; and provisioning liberated countries, **53**: 59; extension of Grain Corporation's activities, **53**: 476-77; **56**: 281-82, 426; and U.S. surpluses, **53**: 687-88, 689-90, 699; H. Hoover on, **55**: 251-53; **60**: 328; **61**: 133; **62**: 125; pork prices, **55**: 306, 307-308, 343, 362, 393-94, 396, 483; Glass on prices and, **55**: 359-60; Hoover on termination of, **56**: 281-82; and tonnage needed for relief program, **58**: 269; and wheat situation, **62**: 52; differences with Federal Trade Commission, **63**: 389, 390
Food Control Act of 1917: see Lever Food and Fuel Control Act
Food Control Act of 1919, **63**: 562n2, 571, 608; WW on extension of, **64**: 82, 111
food relief: see European relief
Footner, Hulbert, **67**: 575n1
For a New America in a New World (King), **59**: 574,n1
Forbes, Rose Dabney (Mrs. J. Malcolm), **66**: 275,n6; **68**: 248; and WW Foundation, **67**: 271n1, 327n6
Forces at War in Peace Conclave (Grasty), **54**: 132,n1
Ford, Bertha Batory (Mrs. Henry Jones), **67**: 541,n2
Ford, Guy Stanton, **67**: 141; **68**: 68,n2
Ford, Henry, **53**: 382n1; **54**: 393n3; **57**: 66; **60**: 119; **68**: 336n1, 519; and senatorial race, **65**: 120n2; and anti-Semitism, **66**: 102,n1, 130n1; and Newberry case, **67**: 316-17,n1, 323, 324n1; and WW Clubs and WW Foundation, **67**: 326, 353, 585; McAdoo on as presidential candidate, **68**: 148-49; WW on, **68**: 151; and Muscle Shoals project, **68**: 448,n1
Ford, Henry Jones, **53**: 340,n1; **67**: 540-41; on railroads, **67**: 550,n1, 558-59; Brandeis on railroad memorandum, **67**: 563
Ford, Expansion and Challenge, 1915-1933 (Nevins and Hill), **65**: 120n2; **66**: 102n1, 130n1
Ford Motor Company, **53**: 382n1; **67**: 316n1

Fordney, Joseph Warren, **65**: 243n1; **66**: 479; **67**: 121n2; **68**: 97n3
Fordney-McCumber Tariff Act, **68**: 97n3, 179,n2, 179n1, 489
Fordyce, Samuel Welsey, **55**: 409,n4; **67**: 326,n3, 579,n3
Foreign Affairs, Committee on (House of Reps.), **60**: 245,n6; **61**: 548,n1; **62**: 278, 341-42; **67**: 313n1; WW's meeting with, **55**: 82, 184, 194, 198, 221, 267, 268-76; **66**: 149; and Irish issue, **55**: 469n4; and Mexican situation, **61**: 610-11; WW on meeting with, **63**: 287, 288, 319, 326, 376, 510; and purchase of embassy in Italy, **65**: 305; and Armenian mandate, **65**: 351n2
Foreign Policy Association of New York, **68**: 315n1, 328
Foreign Relations, Committee on (Senate), **53**: 50, 110, 337, 481n1, 583,n6; **59**: 366n1, 524,n1; **60**: 536; **61**: 347n1, 353n2, 446, 468, 470, 474, 491, 493, 541-42, 596, 642; **62**: 19; **64**: 54, 277; **65**: 242, 288n4; **67**: 26,n7, 324n1, 377n2; and Irish question, **54**: 472; **55**: 547; **56**: 80; **60**: 239n1; **63**: 118,n2; WW's meeting with, **55**: 82, 184, 194, 198, 221, 267, 268-76, 499; **62**: 264, 275-76, 309n1, 339-411, 423, 438-39, 504-505, 587; **66**: 149, 156,n1; **67**: 188,n1, 189-90; **68**: 46,n2; and Mexico, **55**: 351n1; and WW's testimony before, **58**: 635; and peace treaty leak investigation and issue of treaty publication, **60**: 242, 244, 245n6, 247, 288, 330, 434; resolution asking for all materials concerning League of Nations, **61**: 484,n1; and Reparation Commission appointment, **61**: 519, 544, 582; raising status of Belgian legation, **61**: 548, 582; and distribution of reparation payments, **61**: 582-83,n1; awaits WW's reply to Johnson Resolution on Russia, **61**: 597; and reservations to treaty, **61**: 601, 619; speculates on treaty ratification, **61**: 618-19; WW explains delay in getting materials to, **61**: 623; and proposed Interallied Commission of Inquiry, **61**: 629,n2; and Treaty of Bogotá, **62**: 5,n6; and peace treaty, **62**: 12, 307-308,n2; and reparations, **62**: 148,n2, 149; issue of submission of treaty documents to, **62**: 152, 477-78, 535; and interim Reparation Commission, **62**: 237; and Tumulty's recommendations for letter to Lodge, **62**: 272-74; news report of WW's meeting with, **62**: 335-39; on secret treaties, **62**: 364-65, 375-76; on Article X, **62**: 391-93, 402-403; **63**: 529, 530n4, 531; on French security treaty, **62**: 399-401; Fall's memorandum on questions not asked at meeting with WW and WW's reply, **62**: 411-15, 417-19; and Shantung amendment, **62**: 507n1; and

Johnson amendment, **62**: 614,n2; and WW's health, **62**: 631, 635; **63**: 640; majority report on treaty, **63**: 52,n3; WW on meeting with, **63**: 86, 103, 247, 287, 288, 319, 326, 376, 510; minority report on treaty, **63**: 198,n1; House on appearing before, **63**: 299; Bullitt's testimony before, **63**: 337-38,n1; and Armenia, **63**: 423; **65**: 320, 323, 351n2; and Fall amendments, **63**: 482n2; I. Hoover on WW's meeting with, **63**: 632; and Mexican situation, **64**: 120-21,n1, 123, 125, 127, 128, 136, 152,n1,2; and Lodge resolution on termination of war, **64**: 126n1; Lansing suggests his meeting with, **64**: 148; WW's interview with, **64**: 165, 206; **66**: 149, 156,n1; and Martens investigation, **65**: 187n3; WW seeks information on proposal for minister from Canada, **65**: 195; and Knox peace resolution, **65**: 225,n1, 328n2; and purchase of embassy in Italy, **65**: 305; and Armenia, **65**: 320, 323, 351n2; and Yap controversy, **67**: 54, 58, 79,n1; and Versailles Treaty, **67**: 608, 609n2

Forest Service: and B. M. King, **65**: 530, 567,n1

Formative Period of the Federal Reserve System (W. P. G. Harding), **68**: 405,n1

Forrester, James Joseph, **62**: 140; **64**: 425, 431; **65**: 16, 189n1

Forstall, James Jackson, **68**: 392,n1, 420

Forster, Rudolph, **53**: 160-61; **55**: 481; **62**: 534, 547; **63**: 51-52, 92, 117, 118, 198, 268, 295, 392, 444, 445, 447, 483, 522; **64**: 36, 52; **65**: 83n1, 143; **66**: 293n3; **68**: 576; and railroad situation, **64**: 426; on misinterpretation of WW's remarks on secret treaties, **63**: 93; on outlook for treaty ratification, **63**: 150-51; on Naval Appropriations Act and arbitration statement, **63**: 169-170; on plans for arrival of Albert, **63**: 526; and Lansing's calling of Cabinet meeting, **65**: 139; WW's farewell to, **67**: 197

Forsyth Memorial Hospital, Winston-Salem, N.C., **56**: 556n2

Fort, John Franklin, **53**: 156-58; **63**: 391,n6; **68**: 299,n3,4

Fort Abraham Lincoln, N.D., **63**: 152,n2

Fort Leavenworth, **62**: 545,n3; conscientious objectors released from, **54**: 397-98,n4

Fortnightly Review, **59**: 97n3

Fort Russell, Wy. **63**: 467

Fort Sumner, N.M., **68**: 121n2

Fort Wayne, Ind., **59**: 287

Fortune publique de la France (Théry), **56**: 294n2

Forty-Two Years in the White House (I. H. Hoover), **58**: 622n56; **63**: 539n1

Forum, The, **65**: 257,n2

Fosdick, Raymond Blaine, **53**: 251,n1, 318, 340-41, 365-66, 368, 371; **57**: 458-

59; **61**: 477,n1, 530; **62**: 455; **66**: 542n1; **68**: 159,n2, 161; on European crossing, **53**: 321-22; upset over poor working conditions of labor, **53**: 366-67; on WW's arrival in Paris, **53**: 384-85; appointed Under Secretary of League of Nations, **60**: 290,n5; and conscription in Togoland, **62**: 425-26, 532; resignation as Under Secretary General of the League, **64**: 274-76,n1, 286, 306, 310, 348; on relief funds, **67**: 74, 87-88, 96, 110; and beginnings of WW Foundation, **67**: 271n1; and League of Nations, **68**: 34-35, 36, 521; and WW's educational plans, **68**: 451,n1, 492-93; to meet with WW, **68**: 517, 520

Foster, George A., **66**: 57,n1, 71

Foster, Sir George (Eulas), **57**: 311,n10, 312

Foster, John Watson, **64**: 417n3

Foster, Maximilian, **53**: 440,n1

Foster, Paul Hadley, **65**: 246-47,n1

Foster, Reginald Candler, **56**: 53,n14; **59**: 616, 638; on Polish-Ukrainian situation, **59**: 596-97, 597-99

Foster, William, **67**: 182

Foster, William Zebulon, **63**: 29-30,n1, 149

Fournier, François Ernest, **53**: 721,n1

Foudre (French ship), **59**: 66

Four-Power Banking Consortium (for China), **66**: 294-95

Four Power Treaty, **67**: 484,n1, 494,n1; various comments on, **67**: 493,n1, 511n1, 511-12, 525-26, 541-42, 544n1, 551-53, 557; WW on, **67**: 518, 585; **68**: 46; Senate vote on, **67**: 577,n1

Fourteen Points, **53**: 147,n1, 296, 297; **55**: 30, 31, 32, 33, 210, 211, 468; **56**: 492-93, 559; **57**: 67n5, 88, 118, 164, 177, 273, 274, 302, 309, 370, 499, 500, 501, 502, 513, 515, 516-17,n4, 532, 634; **58**: 55, 98, 112, 142, 164,n1, 185, 393n4, 419n1, 453; **59**: 37, 78, 157, 158, 258, 348n1, 450n2, 480, 489, 504,n12, 524, 583,n3, 617, 623, 640n1, 645; **60**: 455, 471n12; **61**: 345, 386, 387; **63**: 222; **64**: 49; **65**: 71n3, 223-24; **67**: 183n1, 187n1, 226; **68**: 224, 225; **61**: 345, 386, 387; and T. Roosevelt, **53**: 28-29, 30, 30-31, 314n4; Taft on, **53**: 30; Sharp on, **53**: 81; WW on, **53**: 337, 340; **63**: 509; WW on Adriatic question and, **57**: 343; WW reads excerpts from, **57**: 515; Ebert on, **59**: 68,n3; Herron on, **59**: 68n2; and Ottoman Empire, **59**: 375; and Poland and Upper Silesia, **60**: 53, 81, 92, 191, 559, 563; WW on peace treaty and, **61**: 236, 244-45, 251, 253; discussed at Foreign Relations Committee meeting with WW, **62**: 365n27, 376-77; House on, **64**: 348,n2; Sullivan on, **68**: 223n2

Fowle, Charles Warren: on Armenian situatiuon, **62**: 576, 577

Fowler, Dorothy G., **66**: 92n1

Fowler, Harry Atwood, M.D., **63**: 572,n2, 578,n1, 579, 581, 587; **64**: 506; **68**: 553,n1, 555, 556, 557, 560, 562, 563; photograph of, *illustration section,* **68**
Fox, Albert Whiting, **61**: 515-17; **66**: 16-71,n1, 39,n2, 238,n1, 506n5; reports on WW's health, **63**: 543-45, 549-50, 552,n2
Fox, Frank, **54**: 473,n1
Fox, Stephen R., **60**: 486
Foy, Mary Emily, **53**: 125,n1
France, **53**: 36, 108, 296; **54**: 13n2, 55, 124, 264; **67**: 109; and Italy, **53**: 91, 183-84, 434-35; **55**: 164, 184; **58**: 198; **68**: 62, 111, 456; talk of commissioners to peace conference, **53**: 142-43; and reparations, **53**: 181, 298, 324, 336, 340, 610; **55**: 29,n2, 30, 32, 458; **56**: 286-96, 493, 496, 601-603; **57**: 301-10; **66**: 302-303; **67**: 144-46; and Fiume, **53**: 208; **63**: 485-86; wants WW to see devastated areas, **53**: 345; Socialists and labor and WW, **53**: 359, 387-88; and far eastern situation, **53**: 463n1, 464; and League of Nations, **53**: 481-82; and Britain, **53**: 482; and Clemenceau's speech on peace plans, **53**: 544n1, 586; and Bolsheviks and Russian situation, **53**: 719, 722-23; representation at Paris Peace Conference, **54**: 65; plan for economic discussion at Paris Peace Conference, **54**: 124-25; and WW and woman suffrage, **54**: 133, 262; Chamber of Deputies holds luncheon for WW, **54**: 155, 155n2; WW's address to French Senate, **54**: 156-57; WW's tour of devastated areas in, **54**: 174, 257n2, 278-81; and cotton, **54**: 193; Cambon on attitudes in Paris toward WW and Paris Peace Conference, **54**: 235-37; and armed forces, **54**: 238-39; and D'Estournelles de Constant's requests of WW, **54**: 257n2; WW's remarks to working women in Paris, **54**: 271-73, 307, 308; and WW's remarks to the League for the Rights of Man, **54**: 309-10,n1; and colonial question and territorial claims, **54**: 311, 318-22, 333-34, 367-68, 373n9; and League of Nations Commission, **54**: 463; WW's address to Chamber of Deputies, **54**: 464-67; and Japan and China, **54**: 474n2; **57**: 300, 301; EBW on reception after WW's speech to Chamber of Deputies, **54**: 487-88; and Sykes-Picot Agreement, **54**: 506n7; report on army of, **54**: 526; H. S. Bliss on Syria and, **54**: 551; and Syria, **55**: 4; **57**: 443, 444, 589-90; **61**: 443, 444; **66**: 47-48; and Armistice renewal plans, **55**: 94; Clemenceau on devastation in, **55**: 100-102; and cotton imports, **55**: 157; peace terms and pressure for settlement made by, **55**: 162, 189, 213-14, 230,n1; WW's statement on departing from, **55**: 197; and war costs, **55**: 210; House on financial situation of, **55**: 283-83; and Japan, **55**:

294; and Belgium's finances, **55**: 305-306, 349; and Rhineland, **55**: 475-77,n2, 507-509; **56**: 445-46; 522; **57**: 130, 295-96, 296-98; and disposal of enemy warships, **55**: 518-19; and League of Nations as part of peace treaty, **56**: 3,n1; and treaty of guarantee, **56**: 10-14, 126,n1, 323-24, 148n2, 297, 417,n1, 430, 511, 525, 592, 629,n1; **58**: 479-80, 486-88, 488-89, 489-90, 490, 493-94, 531n1, 532, 602; **59**: 524,n3; **61**: 241, 248-49, 253; **62**: 5, 16, 18, 27-29, 43, 44, 258, 355,n22, 363-64, 399-401, 405; and anti-Wilson propaganda, **56**: 59, 128; WW on rank and file of French people, **56**: 86-87; R. S. Baker on WW's impatience with, **56**: 128, 179; various comments on talkativeness, bad behavior, and delays caused by, **56**: 164-65, 181, 206, 279, 353, 354, 522, 541, 542; people want WW's peace, **56**: 198, 200, 244, 432-33; on capture of enemy cables, **56**: 210, 211, 212; **58**: 296-97; and amendments to League of Nations Covenant, **56**: 223-25; WW angry at reparation position of, **56**: 246-48; on mandates, **56**: 274-75; **58**: 326, 510; **59**: 326-36, 336-46, 374; **62**: 188, 256, 277, 425-26, 481, 532, 595; and Rumanian army, **56**: 305-306, 581-82; and Saar Basin, **56**: 312, 420, 424, 431-32, 514, 516, 559; **59**: 377; and Montenegro, **56**: 394-95; **59**: 178n2; exchange between Britain and France on territorial terms in Fontainebleau Memorandum, **56**: 477-79, 545-47; Lansing on militaristic spirit of, **56**: 489; controversy over German economic delegation's request for German courier, **56**: 523-24, 541; and Luxembourg, **56**: 595-97; Glass on credits and, **57**: 42; Haskins on Saar Valley, **57**: 54-59, 114-17, 407-15; territorial claims of, **57**: 69, 99; and Monroe Doctrine amendment to Covenant, **57**: 237; and militarism in eastern Europe, **57**: 279-80; Lansing on attitude of, **57**: 327; and Foch's defiance of Clemenceau's request, **57**: 494, 504; and stipulations to be embodied in peace treaty, **57**: 525; and Adriatic question and Italy's claims, **57**: 531, 536-42; **62**: 575; and Japan's claims, **57**: 615, 619, 620; economic conditions in, **58**: 8-9, 14; public and press reaction to WW's Adriatic statement and relations with Italy, **58**: 54, 91, 97, 103, 121, 164,n1, 359; and credits and supplies to Rumania, **58**: 136-37, 406-407, 591, 592; McCormick on Belgian claims and, **58**: 237; May Day celebration in Paris, **58**: 274-75, 276; and Poincaré's message to Italy, **58**: 280, 282, 357; and Jews, **58**: 285, 287; and recognition of Finland, **58**: 404n1; Benson on naval interests of, **58**: 456-57,n3,4,6; and Savoy, **58**:

473; and new war losses, **58**: 492; and Syrian Commission, **58**: 493; and changes in League of Nations Covenant, **58**: 535-36; WW on, **59**: 6,n3; **67**: 269; **68**: 26, 42, 422, 458, 502; and press coverage of Paris Peace Conference, **59**: 39; Lamont on finances and, **59**: 176, 177; and Germany and coal, **59**: 377n3; and Rhenish separatist movement, **59**: 401,n4; **60**: 8-15; Reparation Commission members from, **59**: 422; and troops in Milan, Italy, **59**: 434-35; and Polish-Ukrainian situation, **59**: 531, 541; Germany on reconstruction in, **59**: 582, 583; issue of German counterproposals, **59**: 626; **60**: 321-23; conflict with Great Britain over German peace treaty, **60**: 40-41, 49, 72, 73, 82; and Luxembourg protocol, **60**: 52n4; Socialist party in, **60**: 118,n1; and alleged private negotiations with Germany on peace treaty, **60**: 179-80; and Turkey, **60**: 212-13, 218; Bliss on strength and cost of army of occupation in Rhineland, **60**: 237-39; and coal, **60**: 320, 448; and German and Austrian tonnage, **60**: 345; **62**: 144-47, 186-87; estimate of damages, **60**: 359n1; and Inter-Allied Rhineland High Commission, **60**: 364, 368, 372; and WW's proposed visit to Belgium, **60**: 485; meeting on occupation between leaders from Great Britain and, **60**: 523-27; and burning of French flags in Berlin, **61**: 125-26, 144, 148, 169; sinking of German fleet at Scapa Flow, **61**: 135; and shipping for colonies, **61**: 149; seeks passenger tonnage from Germany, **61**: 278,n7; and Sudbahn, **61**: 317-21; and supplies to Russia, **61**: 466; lifting blockade of Germany, **61**: 540,n1; on Bulgarian boundaries and western Thrace, **61**: 591-93; and Anglo-Persian agreement, **62**: 334,n1; Glass on foreign exchange and, **62**: 501-502; and Constantinople, **62**: 620n1; **63**: 59n2; WW on French people, **63**: 132; and Shantung settlement, **63**: 193, 413, 438; war costs, **63**: 221, 243, 349; battle deaths, **63**: 222, 243, 349; WW on business interests of, **63**:397; Rappard on WW's views of, **63**: 631; and Reparation Commission chairmanship, **64**: 11; and Rumania, **64**: 35; proposals for Adriatic settlement, **64**: 168-78, 264-66; invited to first meeting of Council of League of Nations, **64**: and war criminals, **64**: 364,n1; **65**: 100,n1; and Palestine, **64**: 373, 449; and WW's position on Adriatic proposals, **64**: 375-80, 398-402, 436-42, 445-46; and demands on Holland for William II, **64**: 407n1; **64**: 436-42; and Turkish treaty, **64**: 449; **65**: 76-77, 229n1; WW's reply to Anglo-French note on proposed Adriatic settlement,

64: 459-63; debt to U.S., **64**: 475,n1; in 1913 WW offers McCombs ambassadorship to, **64**: 523, 524,n1; Davis on attitude of revenge toward Germany, **65**: 60-62; and Cilicia, **65**: 72, 74; WW on Armenia and, **65**: 73, 74-75; Turkish treaty and, **65**: 76-77, 229n1; and German war criminals, **65**: 100,n1; and Kapp *Putsch*, **65**: 103; and Germany, **65**: 106, 107; crisis caused by German occupation of Ruhr Valley, **65**: 155-63, 165-66, 167-69, 172-73, 236-37; and WW's hesitancy to have official U.S. representative at San Remo Conference, **65**: 197; and banking consortium, **65**: 259,n1; **66**: 294-95; Britain on Allied debt negotiations and, **65**: 325n1; report of black French troops terrorizing Germans, **65**: 341,n1, 394-95, 397; Gleaves on Japanese-Russian situation and, **65**: 392; and recognition of Mexico, **65**: 463; issue of cancellation of Allied debts, **65**: 480-81; and Poland, **65**: 527; Lloyd George on Germany and, **66**: 43; and Spa protocols on disarmament and coal, **66**: 43-44,n5; Hurley on trade rivalry with Britain, **66**: 64; Houston on exports to, **66**: 100-101; and Russia and gold payment, **66**: 166,n1; banking interests in Mexico, **66**: 302-303; and Yap Island, **66**: 326, 496; **67**: 153-56, 194n1; and Bulgaria, **66**: 358; Colby on Anatolia and, **66**: 429-30,n1; and King Constantine, **67**: 9, 10; talk of occupation of Ruhr Valley, **67**: 33,n1; Hines on shipping tonnage decision and, **67**: 93; Lamont denies support for Allied debt cancellation, **67**: 151-52,n1; Cobb on disarmament program of, **67**: 447-48; Coar on, **67**: 463; alleged statement by WW on future war and, **67**: 466; Westcott on inscription on WW found in Nice, **67**: 482; and Four Power Treaty, **67**: 484n1; WW on, **68**: 26, 42, 422, 458, 502; and debt obligations, **68**: 106n1, 434-36,n1, 437n3; and Turkish advance in Asia Minor, **68**: 141n1; and Clemenceau's visit to U.S., **68**: 197, 198, 201, 234; R. S. Baker on WW meeting with J. Longuet, **68**: 200, 201; and League of Nations, **68**: 239, 422; and occupation of Ruhr district, **68**: 289, 362; and German chemical industry, **68**: 300, 301; and proposed reservations to Five Power Treaty, **68**: 307,n4; R. S. Baker on translation of *World Settlement*, **68**: 403; *see also* France and the United States; individuals such as Clemenceau, Georges; Foch, Ferdinand

France, Joseph Irwin, **61**: 372; **68**: 134n1, 247; on League of Nations Covenant and Senate's proposed draft resolution, **61**: 490-91; and treaty fight, **64**: 200-201, 337, 338

France and Her Eastern Allies, 1919-1925: French-Czechoslovak-Polish Relations from the Paris Peace Conference to Locarno (Wandycz), **54**: 481n2; **66**: 46n7, 225n2

France and the Naval Treaty (*New York Times*), **68**: 307n4

France and the United States, **53**: 3-4, 26, 98; Sharp's resignation as ambassador, **53**: 80-81, 422-43, 463; French Foreign Office's remarks on peace conference organization, **53**: 86-93; censorship lifted on cable use, **53**: 100, 109, 154, 180, 355; **57**: 448-49; and Italian request that U.S. troops accompany Italy's forces to Austro-Hungarian border, **53**: 124, 167; description of Murat residence offered to WW, **53**: 180-81; Jusserand to accompany WW to France, **53**: 183-84; and relief plans, **53**: 223, 225, 280-81, 585; French wish Gompers to be in Paris, **53**: 245, 292; and preliminary meetings in London, **53**: 251-52; plans for WW's arrival, **53**: 291-92; France's peace conference plan, **53**: 293-98; Costigan's suggestions, **53**: 328-32; and shipbuilding, **53**: 373-74, 455-56; reception and speeches on WW's arrival in Brest, **53**: 378-79, 380-81; WW's arrival in Paris, **53**: 382-84, 384-85, 386-87,n1, 396-97; WW's activities and speeches, **53**: 386-87, 387-88, 398-91, 391-92, 396, 398-99, 400, 403-404, 404-405, 410, 421, 499-501; WW awarded degree at the Sorbonne, **53**: 458-59, 459-60, 461-63; WW visits wounded in Neuilly, **53**: 467, 469; WW visits Pershing and troops on Christmas Day, **53**: 448-49, 502-505, 505-507; and war loans, **53**: 442, 479; France wishes U.S. representatives to remain on inter-Allied councils, **53**: 497; WW returns to Paris from London trip, **53**: 570; House and Clemenceau on, **53**: 652-53; WW on French demands, **53**: 707-708; Wallace named U.S. ambassador to France, **53**: 710; **55**: 194; and Pan African Conference, **54**: 126,n1; anti-Wilson propaganda campaign by French newspapers causes tension between, **55**: 66, 66-67, 88, 152-53, 266, 489-90; **57**: 353-54, 390, 390-91; WW's Paris "White House," **55**: 193, 223, 230-31, 497; **57**: 100; Bliss on, **56**: 385-86; and bill for WW's traveling expenses, **56**: 444, 547-48; **57**: 100, 374; **61**: 138; 1917 French mission to the U.S., **57**: 100,n3; Benham on French servants as spies, **57**: 468-69, 503; and Italian question, **58**: 16; memorandum by American delegates to Reparation Commission, **58**: 25-26; and claims regarding seized ships, **58**: 37, 527-28, 559; and credits, **58**: 47, 47-48, 164; WW places wreath at Lafayette's tomb, **60**: 291-92; WW and Poincaré dinner invitation episode, **61**: 112-14, 115, 119, 132, 173, 178, 179, 180, 187, 188-89, 189-91; and French security treaty, **61**: 280-82, 311-13, 324, 375-76,n1, 420, 421, 423, 434-35, 600, 622; Root favors alliance with, **61**: 297,n3; WW's statement upon leaving France, **61**: 350; WW on security treaty, **61**: 434-35; Bastille Day reception at French embassy, **61**: 492; Grasty compares Senate and WW to Chamber of Deputies and Clemenceau, **61**: 615,n1; WW on security treaty, **61**: 622; **62**: 27-29; controversy over ships ordered by France and not delivered, **63**: 366-69: and issue of departure of U.S. representatives in Paris, **64**: 100, 101-102, 117-18, 148-49, 150-51; Wallace to remain in Paris, **64**: 156-57; relations mentioned in Jackson Day message, **64**: 248; and French press, **64**: 260n1; reaction to Hitchcock letter, **65**: 71n3, 84-85,n1; WW responds to Jusserand's protest against Hitchcock letter, **65**: 87; U.S. seeks verification of documents on Allied intervention in Russia, **65**: 143-45; U.S. states policy regarding invasion of Germany, **65**: 167; Knights of Columbus to present gift to France, **65**: 397n1; and Tardieu's indiscreet articles on treaty negotiations, **65**: 542-43,n1,2, 543,n1,2; France's relationship with Harding questioned, **66**: 238,n1, 239, 240, 241, 246; Wallace on U.S. remaining on European commissions, **67**: 35; and French unknown soldier ceremony, **67**: 131, 133; and Gobelin tapestry, **67**: 270; *see also* French security treaty

Franchet D'Esperey, Louis-Félix-Marie-François, **53**: 326; **54**: 185, 403,n1; **56**: 55, 252, 253, 257, 379, 380, 381, 383, 383, 385, 410; **57**: 108, 442,n2; **58**: 149, 435, 436, 566; **59**: 531; and Montenegro, **56**: 394, 573,n1; **60**: 174-75,n3, 256,n2, 259, 260, 312, 313, 315-16, 351; and dispatch of Greek troops to Turkey, **58**: 510, 512, 513, 514

Francis, David Rowland, **54**: 153, 259-60; **55**: 224, 228n1, 297n1; **57**: 477; **62**: 365n27; **63**: 579; **65**: 143; LaGuardia's attack on, **54**: 259,n2; on Russian situation, **55**: 234-35, 349-50; and University of Missouri, **67**: 509,n1

Francis, Emelie De Mun Smith (Mrs. John D. Perry), **55**: 228,n1

Francis, Jane Perry (Mrs. David Rowland), **67**: 509n1

Francis, John D. Perry, **55**: 228,n1

Francis Ferdinand, Archduke, **56**: 614; **58**: 515; **63**: 19-20,n1, 108, 187, 245, 359-60, 372-73; assassination of, **65**: 27, 33

Francis Joseph I (Emperor of Austria, King of Hungary), **57**: 165

Franck, Ludwig, **53**: 693n1
Franco, Alberto C., **61**: 639,n9
Francqui, Emilie, **53**: 693n1
Frank, Glenn: and WW's essay, **68**: 353, 367,n1, 367-68,n1, 369
Franken, S.M.S., **55**: 432
Frankfurt, Germany: French occupation of, **65**: 155n1, 158, 168, 169, 170, 304
Frankfurt, Treaty of (1871), **56**: 68, 453; **57**: 162,n1; **59**: 491; **60**: 226,n3
Frankfurter, Felix, **56**: 310, 404,n1; **59**: 108, 249, 314, 411, 447; **68**: 148n5; on WW's Adriatic statement, **58**: 242, 317; on eastern Jewry and establishment of Palestine, **58**: 455-56; on peace treaty and Jews, **59**: 189, 349; and Polish Jews, **61**: 178; and Gibson and anti-Semitism, **61**: 365n1
Frankfurter General Anzeiger, **59**: 37
Frankfurter Zeitung, **56**: 591
Franklin, Benjamin, **55**: 242; **65**: 401n1; **67**: 425; **68**: 77
Franklin, J. A., **65**: 359
Franklin, Philip Albright Small, **53**: 111,n2, 113, 148-49, 158-59, 164, 196, 261; **54**: 54; **58**: 202,n1
Franklin D. Roosevelt: The Ordeal (Freidel), **65**: 500n1; **67**: 386n2
Fraser, George Corning, **65**: 574,n21
Frau unter dem Sozilaismus (Bebel), **54**: 342,n2
Frayne, Hugh, **53**: 413-14; **54**: 521,n2; **57**: 379,n10
Frazer, John William, **68**: 144-45,n1
Frazier, Arthur Hugh, **53**: 391, 394, 438, 586, 696; **54**: 386, 387; **55**: 185, 195; **56**: 5, 183,n1,3, 517n1, 539, 586; **57**: 369-70; **58**: 445, 464, 521; **59**: 200, 239; **61**: 332; **64**: 157,n1; controversy over WW's proposed appointment of, **64**: 353, 366, 383-84, 398, 408, 413, 414, 451-54; on WW and Orlando's meeting on League of Nations Covenant, **54**: 387-89; moved to legation in Greece, **65**: 260
Frazier, Julius Edgar, **65**: 36,n1
Frazier, Lynn Joseph, **63**: 153,n1; **68**: 96n2
Frederick II (of Prussia), **55**: 503
Frederick Jackson Turner: Historian, Scholar, Teacher (Billington), **53**: 264n1
Frederick the Great, **60**: 106, 453
Fredericks, John Donnan, **63**: 423,n3
freedom of speech: Gavit on, **55**: 255; Scripps on, **59**: 205; Palmer on amnesty proclamation and, **65**: 203-204; and post office regulations, **66**: 92-93,n1, 94-98, 99; and W. A. White, **68**: 148n5
freedom of the seas, **53**: 10, 39, 93, 297, 308n1, 314n4, 321, 341, 395, 427, 428, 470, 471, 484, 507, 559, 576; **54**: 198, 404-406, 477; **56**: 407; **67**: 82; WW on, **55**: 160, 162; **63**: 384, 627; House on, **62**: 62

Freeman, Frances, **64**: 345-46,n1
Freeman, James Edward, **68**: 395-96,n1, 396; and consecration as Bishop of Washington, **68**: 429-30; and WW's last illness, **68**: 558; and WW's funeral, **68**: 576, 578, 579, 582, 583, 584
Freeman's Journal, **57**: 333
Free Speech in the United States (Chafee), **55**: 347n1; **66**: 345-46,n1
Freidel, Frank, **65**: 500n1; **67**: 386n2
Freikorps, **54**: 93n4; **56**: 90n4, 543n3
Frelinghuysen, Frederick Theodore, **66**: 210n4
Frelinghuysen, Joseph Sherman, **59**: 528,n2; **60**: 246,n11; **61**: 372; **68**: 154,n3, 454,n2, 460
Frémont, John Charles, **59**: 241, 242, 252-53; on conditions in Fiume and Trieste, **59**: 119-20,n1
French, Burton Lee, **56**: 428,n3
French, John Denton Pinkstone, Viscount French of Ypres and of High Lake, **58**: 505,n3; **59**: 105,n1
French Academy: *see* Academie Française
French Communism in the Making: 1914-1942 (Wohl), **60**: 118n1
French Equatorial Africa, **54**: 319
French Revolution, **53**: 574-75; **61**: 111; **63**: 12-13, 429
French security treaty: *see* France— treaty of guarantee
Freshfield, Douglas, **58**: 138, 139
Fresno, Calif., *Republican*, **63**: 309n3
Freund, Ernst, **67**: 247,n1, 248
Frick, Henry Clay, **53**: 587
Fried, Alfred Harmann: and Nobel Peace Prize, **66**: 523-24
Friedheim, Robert Lyle, **59**: 204n2
Friedrich, Stephen, **62**: 428n1; **64**: 101n2
Friedrich-Wilhelm University (Berlin), **59**: 566n1
Friedrich Wilhelm Viktor August Ernst, Crown Prince of Germany, **61**: 194,n5, 195, 204-205, 218, 231, 313; alleged escape of, **61**: 258-59; on Allied demand for German war criminals, **64**: 397
Friendly Road, The: New Adventures in Contentment (D. Grayson [R.S. Baker]), **64**: 61,n1
Friendship Under Stress: U.S.-Swiss Relations, 1900-1950 (Meier), **56**: 75n1
Frierson, William Little, **66**: 117n1; on states' discretion in ratifying suffrage amendment, **65**: 450,n1,2; on punishment in federal prisons, **65**: 456-57; on Wilsonian appointments after March 4, 1921, **66**: 138
Friesland, **57**: 396
Frola, Count Secondo, **53**: 622,n1
Fromageot, Henry-Auguste, **56**: 44,n9, 45, 97, 209; **58**: 153, 432, 466; **59**: 273,n9, 299, 300, 589, 635; **60**: 556, 557, 560, 561; **61**: 83, 140, 145, 146, 160, 275; and sinking of German fleet, **61**: 102

From Dawn to Sunset (Coppini), **66**: 369n2

From Paris to Sèvres: The Partition of the Ottoman Empire at the Paris Peace Conference of 1919-1920 (Helmreich), **66**: 429n1

From Sea to Sea (Kipling), **67**: 573

From the Dreadnought to Scapa Flow: The Royal Navy in the Fisher Era, 1904-1919 (Marder), **61**: 6n9, 57n8

Frondichmann, Maurice C. A., **64**: 98

Frost, Cleveland Cady, **66**: 483,n2

Frost, Eleanor Marsh (Mrs. William Goodell), **66**: 483, 499

Frost, Robert, **66**: 542n1

Frost, William Goodell, **66**: 483,n1, 499

Fry, Sara Margery, **57**: 218,n1, 219

Fryatt, Charles, **56**: 533; **57**: 22; **62**: 318

Frye, S.S., **58**: 28

Fuad I, Sultan of Egypt, **57**: 465,n1, 466

Fuel Administration, **53**: 279; **60**: 120n1, 568; **62**: 20n1, 101; **63**: 56n1, 596, 599; **65**: 97, 561, 563; and Garfield resignation from, **53**: 307,n1; **64**: 181, 181-82, 185, 186

Fuel Oil Supply for the Merchant Marine (report, D. White *et al.*), **62**: 617n2

Fuerst Buelow, S.M.S., **55**: 432

Fugitive Sleuth (Footner), **67**: 575,n1

Fukien, China, **54**: 79; **61**: 555

Fuller, Mr. (of Madison, Wisconsin), **67**: 569,n1

Fuller, Alvan Tufts, **55**: 343,n1; **66**: 355n2

Fuller, Cyril Thomas Moulden, **59**: 22,n2, 23, 24, 25, 26

Fuller, Gertrude Breslau, **56**: 283,n1

Fuller, Joseph Vincent, **59**: 447,n1

Fulton, Sir Forrest, **53**: 531n1

Fulton, John F., **65**: 403n3

Functional Disorders in Brain Damage (Goldstein), **58**: 614n13; **62**: 635n21

Fundamentalist Controversy, 1918-1931 (Furniss), **67**: 536n2

Furlong, Charles Wellington, **59**: 65,n6, 66, 119, 241,n1

Furman, Mrs. A. R., **68**: 572

Furman College, **67**: 271

Furnes, Belgium, **61**: 3

Furnessia, S.S., **68**: 389,n1

Furniss, Norman F., **67**: 536n2

Furuseth, Andrew, **56**: 236,n6,7, 604, 605; **57**: 371; on Seaman's Act, **53**: 107-108, 114; on defeated labor proposals, **56**: 308; League of Nations, **61**: 66

Futile but Significant Alternatives (New York *Evening Post*), **65**: 122,n1

Future, The (Arnold), **54**: 309

Gade, John A., **62**: 448

Gage, Lyman Judson, **63**: 370,n2, 383, 386

Gaiffier d'Hestroy, Edmund-Ferdinand-Félix-Euchariste-Marie-Guillain, Baron de, **58**: 236,n4; **60**: 367,n4

Gajda (Gaida) Rudolf, **53**: 629, 630; **54**: 93n5; **60**: 180,n1, 608n2;; **61**: 166,n22

Galicia: *see* Paris Peace Conference—Galicia

Galindo, Hermila, **62**: 449,n1,2, 450; **64**: 134,n5

Gallagher, Andrew J., **63**: 269, 302-303

Gallagher, Thomas, **55**: 469n4; and Irish Home Rule, **54**: 332n1

Gallagher Resolution on Ireland, **55**: 469n4, 547

Gallatin, Albert (Abraham Alphonse Albert), **56**: 121; **58**: 422,n1

Galleani, Luigi, **64**: 145n1

Gallica (Italian ship), **59**: 242

Gallipoli, **59**: 326

Gallivan, James Ambrose, **68**: 388n1

Galloway, Charles Mills, **64**: 205,n2: urges WW to veto census bill, **55**: 290; and resignation controversy, **55**: 330,n3, 460, 478; **56**: 280; **57**: 348-49; **58**: 360-61; **62**: 164, 251

Galsworthy, John, **55**: 338; **67**: 105n3

Galt, Alexander Hunter, **68**: 471

Galt, Gertrude Bolling (Mrs. Alexander Hunter), **53**: 500; **68**: 471

Galt, Sterling, **53**: 501; **54**: 306,n10

Galveston, U.S.S., **65**: 538

Gama, Domicio da, **53**: 342,n5; on Tacna-Arica dispute, **65**: 191, 195, 237, 245

Gambrell, James Bruton, **65**: 421,n2, 422, 430

Ganem, Cherki, **55**: 145,n3, 162,n2

Ganga Singh Bahadur, Maharaja of Bikaner: *see* Bikaner, Maharaja of

Gannett, Lewis Stiles, **55**: 92,n2, **66**: 383n1

Garay, Narciso, **67**: 382n5

Garbai, Sandor, **56**: 242,n2; **57**: 108,n11, 170

Garbasso, Carlo, **65**: 303,n10

Garcia, Daniel, **65**: 446

Garcia, Julio, **65**: 446

Garden Magazine, **68**: 449

Gardener, Helen Hamilton (Mrs. Selden Allen Day), **67**: 393; and woman peace commissioner, **53**: 114-15, 216-17; on woman suffrage, **53**: 217; on Civil Service Commission appointment, **65**: 115-16; praises WW, **66**: 297, 298

Gardiner, Alfred George, **53**: 634,n1, 708-709,n3; **54**: 431,n1, 433;; **55**: 115-16, 466; **66**: 411n1; **67**: 105n3; **68**: 282, 287; meets with WW, **54**: 175-78, 196, 197, 198, 218, 305; on League of Nations Covenant, **54**: 427-28

Gardner, Frederick Dozier, **57**: 48,n5; **63**: 31,n1, 33, 43; WW sends resolution of appreciation, **65**: 472-73,n1

Gardner, Hiram, **65**: 145n1

Gardner, Lloyd G., **64**: 417n3

Garfield, Belle Hartford Mason (Mrs. Harry Augustus), **53**: 333,n1;; **63**: 539,n3; **66**: 305,n1; **68**: 475,n2

Garfield, Harry Augustus, **53**: 84, 252, 333, 413, 413-14; **54**: 480;; **55**: 294; **57**: 43, 376,n2, 381, 383; **60**: 568; **62**: 42, 101; **63**: 54, 606; **65**: 96; **66**: 542n1; **67**: 434; resignation of, **53**: 307,n1; **64**: 181,

181-82, 185; and coal industry, **53**: 310-11; **55**: 251, 362-63, 397-98; on price conflict between Railroad Administration and Industrial Board, **56**: 343-44,n1; and proposed Industrial Cabinet, **57**: 630; on coal situation and strike, **63**: 54, 55, 56; **64**: 3, 141,n2, 143, 144, 145-46, 153-54, 166, 167, 457; receives detailed account of WW's condition, **63**: 538-39; on coal commission being of an advisory nature, **64**: 180-81, 181-82; praises veto message, **65**: 335; WW acknowledges support of, **65**: 343; praises WW, **66**: 305, 338; and WW's Armistice Day speech, **68**: 474-75

Garfield, James Abram, **63**: 196, 555
Garfield, James S., **61**: 321,n2
Garfield, Lucretia, **53**: 333,n1
Garibaldi, Guiseppe, **53**: 619n1
garment industry: and foreign-born labor, **55**: 286-87
Garner, James W., **56**: 530n4
Garner, John Nance, **55**: 297,n4; **65**: 24; and Culberson campaign, **67**: 572,n1
Garraty, John Arthur, **56**: 161n1; **64**: 328n2
Garrett, Alice Warder (Mrs. John Work), **57**: 388,n1, 391
Garrett, Finis James, **55**: 297,n4; **60**: 199; WW on, **66**: 60,n2; **67**: 176-78; **68**: 577; and Tennessee judgeship, **66**: 386,n1,2; and Muscle Shoals project, **68**: 448-49, 457
Garrett, John Work, **53**: 130,n1; **57**: 388,n1, 391; **60**: 192; resignation of, **62**: 435,n1; **64**: 41,n1
Garrett, Robert, **65**: 572,n15, 573-74, 574
Garrison, Lindley Miller, **66**: 542n1
Garvan, Francis Patrick, **59**: 449,n2; **65**: 226,n2; **66**: 380,n1
Gary, Elbert Henry, **54**: 392; **57**: 348,n2, 379, 382; **62**: 581-82,n1; congratulates WW, **61**: 407; on labor unions and U.S. Steel Corporation, **62**: 596-601; and steel strike, **63**: 30n1, 66, 149; appointed to first Industrial Conference, **63**: 300,n1
Gary, Hampson, **56**: 153,n1, 154-55,n1; **57**: 326n3; **58**: 318,n1; **64**: 413-14,n1, 453; and appointments, **65**: 85, 87, 88; on being observer at League of Nations Assembly and WW's reply, **66**: 352, 353
Gary Dinner System: An Experiment in Cooperative Price Stabilization (Robinson), **57**: 348n2
Gasparri, Pietro Cardinal, **53**: 102,n1, 114, 607,n4; **55**: 493;; **59**: 118; **62**: 26; **63**: 555
Gaston, William Alexander, **68**: 96n1, 153,n2, 190
Gastonia, N. C., **64**: 191,n2, 213
Gates, Caleb Frank, **58**: 323,n1
Gates, Horatio, **65**: 149
Gatewood, Robert, **66**: 213,n1
Gaulois, Le (Paris): *see* Paris *Le Gaulois*
Gaunt, Sir Guy (Reginald Archer): receives Distinguished Service Medal, **58**: 138n1
Gaus, Friedrich Wilhelm Otto, **58**: 311,n2
Gautier, Raoul, **61**: 356-57,n1
Gavazzi, Ludovico, **53**: 616n1
Gavit, John Palmer, **66**: 542n1; on granting amnesty to political prisoners, **55**: 255, 344
Gay, Edward James, **53**: 23n1, 287; **55**: 297, 368; **65**: 257, 361
Gay, Edwin Francis, **66**: 170n1, 274; **67**: 426n1; considered for Shipping Board appointment, **59**: 121,n2, 160, 185,n1; appointed to first Industrial Conference, **63**: 300,n1; and WW Foundation beginnings, **67**: 271n1, 327n6
Gaza, **56**: 110
Gazepe, George Z., **67**: 235n1
Geddes, Sir Auckland (Campbell), **64**: 483-84,n1,2; **66**: 39n3, 114,n2, 308; **67**: 263,n2; WW's concern over appointment of as Ambassador to U.S., **65**: 43-44; Polk on, **65**: 55-56; and Kapp *Putsch*, **65**: 236,n1; opinion on WW's health, politics, and various people, **65**: 369-72; and Armenia, **66**: 422
Geddes, Isabella Gamble Ross, Lady Geddes, **65**: 372,n7
Geiss, Imanuel, **58**: 461n1
Gelber, N. M., **58**: 461n1
Gelderland, **57**: 396
Geldhof, A. E., **62**: 627
Gelfand, Lawrence Emerson, **58**: 632n9; **59**: 349n2; **60**: 34n3
General Board of the Navy, **53**: 312,n1
General Conference of Palestinian Jews, **54**: 258n1
General Deficiency appropriations bill: and railroads, **55**: 257, 258, 388; WW on, **55**: 277; W. B. Wilson on Employment Service and, **55**: 447
General Education Board, **68**: 451n1
General German School Association: *see* Allegemeiner Deutscher Schulverein
General Leasing bill, **54**: 216,n1, 256, 393, 471, 503, 503-504; **61**: 534-35; **62**: 45-50, 292-300; **64**: 473,n1; Swanson amendment, **62**: 49-50; Lane memorandum on objections to, **62**: 438-49
General Louis Botha: A Biography (Meintjes), **54**: 252n3
Geneva, Switzerland, **53**: 4, 416; **55**: 127, 152, 490; and Red Cross, **55**: 527, 528; as seat of League of Nations, **56**: 76, 77, 103, 25; **57**: 194, 222, 224-26, 237, 329, 430, 464; **58**: 190, 200, 41; **65**: 389, 500, 501, 503,n1, 504; **66**: 50; and League of Nations, **63**: 630, 631, 632,n1; proposed reparations conference at, **66**: 471-72
Geneva, University of: WW receives honorary degree from, **61**: 356-57
Geneva Convention, **53**: 235
Genoa, Italy, **58**: 99, 250n5; WW's arrival and speeches in, **53**: 613, 614, 614-15, 615-16
Genoa, University of, **66**: 339n1, 381

Genoni, Rosa, **59**: 117,n3
Gentle Art to Making Enemies, as Pleasingly Exemplified, in Many Instances, Wherein the Serious Ones of this Earth, Carefully Exasperated, Have Been Prettily Spurred on to Unseemliness and Indiscretion, While Oversome by an Undue Sense of Right (Whistler), **61**: 489,n1
Gentlemen Who Cry Peace (New York *Globe and Commercial Advertiser*), **67**: 313,n1
Geographical Review, **57**: 270
George V (of Great Britain), **53**: 384; **54**: 170; **56**: 462,n11, 532;; **59**: 253, 285; **62**: 13,n1; **63**: 527; **64**: 32, 483; **66**: 353,n1, 366; congratulations to WW, **53**: 53-54; invites WW to stay at Buckingham Palace, **53**: 85, 109, 457, 491, 501; as host to WW in London, **53**: 510; **65**: 233; 511-12, 521-22, 526-27, 546, 547, 569, 592, 634; presents Grayson with cuff links, **53**: 529; WW on, **55**: 228; WW birthday greetings and reply, **60**: 100, 101; and Irish situation, **62**: 324, 326; thanks WW for hospitality shown son, **64**: 42; birthday wishes to WW, and WW's thank you, **64**: 230, 231; photograph of, *illustration section*, **53**
George, Alexander L., **58**: 612,n3, 618n30
George Edward Alexander Edmund, Prince, **53**: 593,n5
George, Juliette, **58**: 612,n3, 618n30
George Harvey: 'A Passionate Patriot' (Johnson), **67**: 297n2
George H. Doran Company, **66**: 416,n1, 417
George H. McFadden and Brothers, **56**: 553n1
George Peabody College for Teachers: Axson and, **67**: 310-11,n4
Georges Clemenceau: A Political Biography (Watson), **59**: 173n1; **60**: 118n1
Georges Mandel and the Third Republic (Sherwood), **60**: 118n1
Georges-Picot, François-Marie-Denis, **66**: 358,n2
George Washington (Wilson), **53**: 261-62; **62**: 564-65,n1
George Washington, Fondateur des Etats-Unis (1732-1799) (trans. Roth), **53**: 261-62; **62**: 564n2
George Washington, U.S.S., **53**: 314,n2, 315, 378, 397; **54**: 392;; **55**: 197, 217, 229, 234n1, 412, 442; **58**: 43,n1, 141; **61**: 230, 354; **66**: 366, 370; WW fondly remembers, **55**: 224n1; WW's summoning of and its effect on peace negotiations, **57**: 51, 61, 63-65,n1, 68, 69, 70, 140, 146, 148, 175, 194, 235-36, 302, 312; **67**: 360,n2, 376; returns to U.S. with troops, **57**: 579; WW's address to fellow passengers on Fourth of July, **61**: 378-82, 378, 383; arrival in U.S.,

61: 400-401; search for WW's desk used aboard, **67**: 124, 128, 146-47
George Washington University, **56**: 212n3; **59**: 473n2; **63**: 544n3; **64**: 510; **65**: 233; WW Club at, **67**: 345
George W. Littlefield: Texan (Haley), **66**: 369n2
Georgia, **53**: 149; and woman suffrage, **61**: 480-81, 537; lynching in, **62**: 234; issue of WW's name on primary ballot in, **65**: 145-46,n1; Democratic primary in, **65**: 219-20,n1, 2; concern over state archives in, **68**: 93,n1
Georgia, Russia, **64**: 309; **66**: 21, 437
Gérard, Augustin Grégoire Arthur, **59**: 401n4; **60**: 600,n3
Gerard, James Watson, **53**: 390; **56**: 474, 476; **68**: 414,n1; and Armenia, **55**: 65-66, 446; **62**: 116,n1, 241,n1; **67**: 602; get-well wishes to WW, **63**: 535; on crisis in Armenia, **65**: 287-88, 298; endorses WW accepting nomination, **65**: 496; Stuart wishes to see, **67**: 327-28; Bolling on, **67**: 353; WW unable to autograph photograph for, **67**: 572; on not ratifying Turkish commercial treaty (Lausanne Treaty) and WW's response, **68**: 431-32, 440, 499-500, 504, 505; invites WW to join relief committee for German intelligentsia, **68**: 547-48
Gerard, Mary Daly (Mrs. James Watson), **56**: 476,n3
German Actualities (Coar), **67**: 463-64,n1
German Americans, **53**: 20; **55**: 443, 448; **67**: 45,n2, 46; **68**: 104, 161, 210, 299n1, 303; and vote in Nebraska, **53**: 61, 62; and Von Engelken case, **53**: 106,n1; Baruch on votes of, **66**: 336; and Hitchcock, **67**: 421
German Armistice Commission, **54**: 238n2
German Austria, **55**: 317n3; **57**: 592
German Delegation at the Paris Peace Conference (Luckau), **59**: 136n2
German East Africa, **53**: 38, 236-38, 351, 470-71, 498, 562, 566;; **54**: 249, 253, 330, 370; **58**: 510; **60**: 30; **62**: 188, 189; and Belgium's claims, **54**: 373,n9, 374; **61**: 276, 277, 314; and Portugal's claims, **54**: 374
German language, **60**: 106-107
German Peace Society, **66**: 523n1
German propaganda in the United States, **54**: 396-98,n1; investigation of, **55**: 297n2; and Cohalan, **55**: 411-12; WW on resurgence of, **63**: 110, 143-44, 215, 292, 321, 333, 334, 385, 401, 456-57, 469-70, 501; WW on League of Nations opponents and, **63**: 447n1, 448
German Revolution of 1918: A Study of German Socialism in War and Revolt (Ryder), **56**: 543n2
German South-West Africa: *see* South-West Africa

German-Soviet Relations Between the Two World Wars, 1919-1939 (Carr), **60**: 167n17

German Zionist Organization, **54**: 258n1

Germanos V, Patriarch of Constantinpole, **57**: 426,n6

Germany, **53**: 27, 296, 691; **68**: 62, 226, 456, 477; accepts armistice terms, **53**: 27, 33, 34; food relief and, **53**: 33, 63, 64, 75-76, 102-103, 360, 690; **54**: 174,n2; **56**: 574-75; **57**: 103, 104; Bolsheviks and, **53**: 121-22,n1,2, 173, 194-95; colonies of, **53**: 236-38, 351, 355, 562, 563, 566; **54**: 249-54, 318; **55**: 24; **60**: 471n12,13, 472, 479-80; and French peace conference plan, **53**: 293, 294; League of Nations and, **53**: 352, 622; **54**: 170; **56**: 264; **59**: 3, 6,n2, 243,n1; Foch and, **53**: 410, 540; **55**: 212-13; 503-505; issue of disposal of warships, **54**: 180, 273,n1, 273-74, 505; **55**: 515-21; financial and economic discussions at Trèves, **54**: 212-16; on food payment, **54**: 212-16; and demobilization issue, **54**: 219-21, 238-46, 275, 538, 542-43; and Japan's claims in the Pacific, **54**: 291-92; and Poland, **54**: 336-41, 545; **55**: 203; **56**: 88-95; and repatriation of prisoners, **55**: 3, 10-11; **57**: 75-76; National Assembly at Weimar and postal facilities, **55**: 10, 18; Supreme War Council discusses arms reduction and, **55**: 11-16, 20; and reparations, **55**: 29-34, 210-11; **56**: 250; **60**: 4n1, 26n11; **66**: 471-72; **67**: 70, 109,n1, 113-15; **68**: 434,n3; issue of representation in League of Nations, **55**: 276; and German Austria, **55**: 317n3; proposed military and naval terms with, **55**: 404-406, 425-32, 511-14, 522-24; food crisis in, **55**: 423, 458,n1, 493; **56**: 127; and Bavaria, **55**: 423,n1; and conscription, **55**: 459; and Rhineland, **55**: 475-77; empire of 1914, **55**: 506; WW on peace with, **56**: 5; and passage of Haller's troops, **56**: 118-19, 209n2; and Schleswig, **56**: 200,n1; and Fontainebleau Memorandum, **56**: 259-70; and Russia, **56**: 466; and Mezes on Danzig, **56**: 471-73; Nolan on peace terms acceptable to, **56**: 492-93, 494; and controversy over request for German courier, **56**: 523-24,n1, 528-29, 541; unrest in, **56**: 543n2; Warburg on situation in, **56**: 585; and frontier with Bohemia, **56**: 597-98; and Commission on Responsiblities, **56**: 613; invitation to peace conference, **57**: 318-25, 349-50; Council of Four on lethal gases of, **57**: 400-405; and Saar Valley, **57**: 407-15; **59**: 380-82, 453; credentials issue, **57**: 520-21, 526, 550; **58**: 244, 254-55, 311-12; political situation in, **57**: 521-24, 565-67; German delegation named, **57**: 590-91,n5; and issue of seized ships belonging to, **58**: 37-38, 547, 548; and peace terms, **58**: 45-46, 307-10, 314-15, 453-55; **59**: 3, 12n5, 28,n3, 348,n1; Bliss on commissions of control in, **58**: 95-96; Bryce on the Tyrol and, **58**: 139; Poincaré on need for French occupation of Rhineland until debt paid by, **58**: 211-14; and submarine cables, **58**: 296-97, 345-53; feelings toward WW in, **58**: 332; and delegates to conference from, **58**: 399; **59**: 433-34, 441-42, 463; WW on reparation plan and, **58**: 447-448; Dresel on hopeless financial and industrial situation in, **58**: 454-55; Brockdorff-Rantzau's remarks at Plenary Session, **58**: 514-17; blockade, food relief, and economic issues in, **58**: 564, 565; Council of Four on occupation of Berlin, **58**: 572, 573; Allied plan for action to be taken if peace treaty not signed, **58**: 580-81, 582-83; WW on German scholarship, **59**: 5,n2; press reaction to peace treaty, **59**: 36-37; and prisoners of war, **59**: 47-48, 50, 56-57, 131-32, 134-36, 162-63, 163-65, 272-73; on labor provisions in treaty, **59**: 48n2, 163; various opinions on blockade of, **59**: 109-10, 127-28, 128-30, 173, 191-92, 318; Lamont on reparations and, **59**: 177; Hoover on food relief, **59**: 191-92; and membership in International Labor Organization, **59**: 222-23,n15; on responsibility for the war, **59**: 274-76, 488-92; **60**: 438n1, 443, 451-55, 467-68, 475-76; **61**: 334-35, 340; note on economic effect of peace treaty and Allied reply, **59**: 305-307, 307-309, 309, 362-66; requests time extension to examine peace terms, **59**: 321-22, 348n1, 560, 574, 577; and Rhenish separatist movement, **59**: 401-402,n4; Smuts on peace treaty and, **59**: 413-19; Council of Four on total army force for, **59**: 429, 431, 439; "unofficial" counterproposals revised early by, **59**: 554,n2; on draft of peace treaty, **59**: 579-84; Council of Four on counterproposals of, **59**: 586,n5, 626-27; on financial terms, **60**: 4n1; Davis' recommendations for reparations from, **60**: 4-7; American delegation on reparations and counterproposals of, **60**: 45-53; issue of League of Nations membership, **60**: 21, 22, 50, 62, 64, 69, 77-78, 83, 94-95, 178, 272-75, 292, 307,n1, 380-81, 439, 450, 459-60, 464, 520-21,n14; **61**: 254, 272, 447, 490; **62**: 352,n19, 357-58, 360; American delegation on eastern borders of, and on Polish-Silesian situation, **60**: 53-59; Council of Four on Upper Silesian issue and, **60**: 84-92; and General German School Association, **60**: 123,n3; Seymour on counterproposals on German Austria, **60**: 139; Paderewski on Russia and, **60**: 167-68; Dresel praises government of, **60**: 177-78; Council of

Germany (*cont.*)
Four on relationship of Russia and, **60**: 208-10, 214-15; report on admission to League of Nations, **60**: 274-75; and proposed Austrian agreement on trade with, **60**: 283; project for reply to counterproposals of, **60**: 323-27, 394-9; and army of occupation, **60**: 326-27; and draft convention on military occupation of Rhineland, **60**: 368-72; Council of Four on blockade of, **60**: 495-97, 498-500; and atrocities in Riga, **60**: 532; WW on blockade, **60**: 533, 534, 565; and Czechoslovakia and Belgium and construction of railway lines, **60**: 551-52, 561; Council of Four on time allowed to sign peace treaty, **60**: 560-61; Council of Four and Foch on plans for march on Berlin, **60**: 583-91; Hoover's concern that blockade is being imposed against, **60**: 606, 614; Paderewski on Poles in, **60**: 634; and sinking of fleet at Scapa Flow, **61**: 57,n8, 71, 79, 80, 102-104, 111, 114, 119, 123-27, 140-48, 151, 160, 168-70, 178-79; Allied reply to note on two reservations, **61**: 76-77; new government formed in, **61**: 76,n1, 77; agrees to sign treaty, **61**: 78, 79,n2, 99; and burning of French flags, **61**: 114-15, 169; lifting blockade of, **61**: 151-52, 251, 257,n3, 450; **63**: 266,n1; andPoland, **61**: 163-64; to sign Rhineland Convention and peace treaty simultaneoulsy, **61**: 279; and French security treaty, **61**: 280-82; House suggests U.S. have special representative in, **61**: 286; and Japan, **61**: 495; and credit extension for wheat, **61**: 502; and blockade and issue of dyestuffs, **61**: 523-24, 573-74; Taussig interested in position of ambassador to, **61**: 618; WW on Senate request for information and documents on Japan and, **62**: 208; list of needed food and raw materials, **62**: 328-30; issue of resumption of U.S. trade with, **62**: 423-24; Poole on Bolsheviks and, **62**: 442-43, 446; WW on rehabilitation of, **63**: 36-37; and International Labor Conference, **63**: 62, 91; battle deaths, **63**: 221, 243, 349; war costs, **63**: 221, 243, 349; and China and Shantung settlement, **63**: 411-13, 437, 471, 507; ratification of Versailles Treaty and exchange of ratifications with Allied Powers, **61**: 418,n2; **64**: 101,n1; and issue of protocol, **64**: 148, 149,n2, 150-51; and Allies' demand for war criminals, **64**: 364,n1, 381-82, 397; WW on war crimes issue, **64**: 408; France's attitude on Germany's coal and gold obligations, **65**: 60-62; and Kapp *Putsch*, **65**: 98,n1, 99-100, 103; U.S. evaluation of future political situation in, **65**: 100-103; and war crimes trials, **65**: 100,n1; and Russia, **65**: 102;

occupies Ruhr Valley, **65**: 155-58, 171-72; Britain on allied debt negotiations and, **65**: 326; and Spa Conference, **65**: 326n4; rumor of black French troops terrorizing in, **65**: 397; children fed in, **65**: 469; disposition of cables, **65**: 479; and Spa protocols on disarmament and coal, **66**: 43-44,n5; Lloyd George on Adriatic question in, **66**: 45; issue of trade with, **66**: 74, 100-101, 380; and International Financial Conference, **66**: 101n1; Paderewski on influence of in Poland, **66**: 226-27; and reparations, **66**: 471-72; Hines on shipping tonnage decision and, **67**: 93; Allies demand tax on exports, **67**: 109,n1; and war ending resolution, **67**: 313n1; Coar on situation in, **67**: 367, 371, 463; WW suggests Baruch meet Coar on, **67**: 368-69; Dodge on WW's Armistice reply to, **67**: 374,n3; Treaty of Berlin, 1921, **67**: 382,n1, 394-95, 401; French occupation of Ruhr district, **68**: 289, 362; chemical and dyestuff trust controversy, **68**: 299-301, 303, 303-403, 356, 357-58; R. S. Baker on powerful U.S. economic interests exploiting, **68**: 358-59; and *World Settlement*, **68**: 403, 496; WW on, **68**: 502; Gerard on formation of relief committee for intelligentsia, **68**: 547-48; delegates from, photograph of, *illustration section*, **58**; *see also* Armistice; under names of spokesmen for, such as Brockdorff-Rantzau, Count Ulrich Karl Christian von; Paris Peace Conference—German treaty

Germany and the United States: and disposition of alien property, **53**: 165, 197-98, 214-15,n1; WW for general elections in Germany, **53**: 194, 194-95; WW against sinking of captured German ships, **53**: 469n1

Germany, 1866-1945 (Craig), **61**: 34n1

Germany's Disastrous Prosperity (Coar), **67**: 463-64,n1

Germany's Drive to the East and the Ukrainian Revolution, 1917-1918 (Fedyshyn), **54**: 32n4

Germany's Plots Exposed (Rathom), **67**: 242n5

Germer, Adolph, **54**: 426; **55**: 92; **62**: 557,n1

Gerould, Gordon Hall, **67**: 182

Gerould, Mrs. Charles Walter, **67**: 527n4

Gerould, James Thayer, **68**: 308,n1

Gerry, Mathilde Scott Townsend (Mrs. Peter Goelet), **59**: 124,n2, 159-60

Gerry, Peter Goelet, **53**: 24, 93, 103-104, 114; **57**: 446; **58**: 431;; **59**: 124, 159, 283; **60**: 18; **61**: 437; **62**: 157; **64**: 359; on Democratic National Committee chairmanship, **54**: 230-31; on Irish Home Rule, **56**: 397-98; and reservations on Ireland, **65**: 120n1; and separate peace with Germany, **67**: 399

Gertrud, S.M.S., **55**: 432
Gesammelte Schriften (Rathenau), **53**: 418n4
Gesammelte Schriften und Denkwurdigkeiten (Von Moltke), **55**: 508n2
Geschwind, Norman, M.D., **58**. 636,n3
Gespräche mit Goethe in den Letzten Jahren seines Lebens (Eckermann), **67**: 293n5
Gettysburg Address, **61**: 445
Gettysburg Cemetery, **59**: 621
Gex, French territory, **60**: 96,n6
Ghent, William James, **56**: 283
Gherardi, Walter Rockwell, **53**: 485-86,n1
Ghiselli, Frank Ernest, **68**: 506,n1
Giannini, Amedeo, **61**: 584n2
Gibbon, Thomas Edward, **63**: 423,n3
Gibbons, Herbert Adams, **66**: 198n1
Gibbons, James Cardinal, **53**: 114, 250, 420n3; **55**: 454; **56**: 258;; **58**: 491; **61**: 294; **62**: 111; **64**: 237; **65**: 395, 397; **67**: 30, 37n1; on German food problem, **53**: 102-103; asks WW to visit the Pope, **53**: 231-32; on Benedict XV's views on peace terms, **59**: 118; on League of Nations, **61**: 627,n1; WW thanks for support, **61**: 628-29; hopes for treaty and League of Nations, **62**: 479; on lack of religious freedom in Transylvania, **65**: 138; death of, **67**: 243
Gibbony, Stuart Gatewood: and Morse case, **68**: 73n2
Gibraltar, **53**: 229
Gibson, Charles Dana, **67**: 369n1; **68**: 198,n1, 380; cartoon, *illustration section*, **68**
Gibson, Hugh Simons, **59**: 261, 458; appointed minister to Poland, **56**: 124,n2; **57**: 285, 334, 373; **61**: 365,n1; **63**: 82,n2; **64**: 5,n1, 372,n1; on situation in Poland and Paderewski's position, **59**: 263-65; and situation of Polish Jews, **61**: 178; wishes to return to U.S., **65**: 65, 88-89; on Teschen Commission appointment, **65**: 256,n2; urges WW to make statement on Polish situation, **65**: 526-28; WW refuses, **65**: 531
Gibson, Irene Langhorne (Mrs. Charles Dana), **68**: 198,n3
Gibson, Thomas, **58**: 19,n5, 20, 61, 65; **60**: 179,n1, 180; political situation in Germany, **57**: 521-24,n1
Gidney, James B., **62**: 27n1; **65**: 351n2
Giesberts, Johann, **57**: 590,n5; **58**: 309-10, 518; **61**: 192, 203; photograph of, *illustration section* **58**
Gifford, Edward S., **58**: 631,n1
Gilbert, Cass, **66**: 369n1
Gilbert, Charles, **55**: 334n1
Gilchrist, Huntington, **64**: 275,n3
Gilder, Richard Watson, **55**: 472,n1
Gildersleeve, Basil Lanneau, **64**: 517,n2
Gill, Edgar R., **57**: 425
Gillen, Francis, F., **65**: 258,n1

Gillen, Martin J., **66**: 252,n1
Gillett, Christine Rice Hoar (Mrs. Frederick Huntington), **68**: 560,n6
Gillett, Frederick Huntington, **53**: 692,n2; **55**: 449n2; **61**: 492; **62**: 171, 199; **64**: 416n2; **68**: 560,n6; issue of postponing House of Representatives recess, **62**: 98, 103
Gilman, Charlotte Perkins, **56**: 283
Ginn, Edward, **53**: 82
Giolitti, Giovanni, **57**: 436,n5, 612,n3, 613; **58**: 338; **61**: 109,n3;; **63**: 486,n8; **65**: 102, 304, 448,n1; **66**: 207n1, 323, 381; Lloyd George on, **66**: 43, 45; and Albania, **66**: 45,n6
Giovanna, Elisabetta Antonia Romana Maria, Princess, **53**: 596,n3
Giovine Fiume (Young Fiume), **59**: 119,n3
Girard-Mangin, Major, **57**: 218, 219
Girsa, Vaclav, **53**: 629
Glad Adventure (Sayre), **53**: 21n2
Gladstone, William Ewart, **54**: 176-77; **55**: 321; **57**: 247; **60**: 209-10, 215, 303; WW on, **67**: 45
Glasgow, William Anderson, Jr., **53**: 15, 157, 604; **54**: 31,n1;; **55**: 336,n1, 360; **57**: 381; **63**: 390n4
Glasgow, University of, **59**: 190n3; **62**: 331-32; **68**: 484,n1; WW unable to accept rectorship of, **63**: 395-96
Glass, Aurelia McDearmon Caldwell (Mrs. Carter), **67**: 390,n2
Glass, Carter, **53**: 474, 646, 691, 715-16; **54**: 429, 520, 521;; **55**: 251, 256, 279; **56**: 83, 342, 397, 621; **57**: 471; **58**: 421, 491n1, 496; **59**: 75,n1, 110, 320, 478,n1, 604; **60**: 41, 42, 111; **61**: 549; **62**: 185, 222-23, 224-25, 281; **63**: 421; **64**: 141, 325, 457; **65**: 24, 385, 521, 522-23, 580, 581; **67**: 25n1, 390, 394n1; **68**: 380, 496, 556, 562, 576; appointed Secretary of the Treasury, **53**: 441n1, 587; and foreign loans, **53**: 441-42, 472-73, 477; **55**: 113, 114, 115, 208, 332-33, 342, 396-97; **57**: 42; and food appropriations, **53**: 578-79, 637, 698; on financial representation at peace conference, **53**: 626-27; **54**: 88-89; and food relief and prices, **54**: 89-90; **55**: 89-90, 358-61; and famine relief bill, **54**: 303, 332, 394; and J. S. Williams appointment, **54**: 485,n1; on revenue bill, **54**: 501-502, 555; and railroad appropriation, **55**: 228, 257; and pork prices, **55**: 306-307, 395, 396; on Treasury bonds and certificates, **55**: 333-34; on financial crisis of War Risk Bureau, **55**: 537-38; on controversy between Industrial Board and Railroad Administration, **56**: 344, 345, 618; **57**: 233, 347-48, 376, 378,n5, 381, 382, 383, 387, 446, 577; and British request for additional credit, **56**: 623; and Liberty Loan, **57**: 283, 447-48; **58**: 560; on first trans-

Glass, Carter (*cont.*)
atlantic flight, **57**: 447-48; on additional French credits, **58**: 47, 47-48; and credits for Austrian relief, **58**: 242, 243; on urgent need for appropriation for dependents of servicemen, **58**: 330; and Rumanian credits, **58**: 592-93; and Victory Loan, **59**: 75,n1; and Italian credits, **59**: 111-12, 112-13; **61**: 441, 456-57; **62**: 230; on Bolsheviks and foreign exchange, **60**: 113-14; on WW's income tax, **60**: 247; and peace treaty leak investigation, **60**: 536; recommends Davis as Assistant Secretary of Treasury, **62**: 70; on effect of delay of treaty ratification on Treasury and business, **62**: 266-68; on high cost of living, **62**: 314; on foreign banking and exchange, **62**: 498-99, 499-504; on international financial situation and U.S. Treasury's position, **63**: 200-204, 336; on loan request for repatriation of Czech troops, **63**: 518; and WW's veto of Volstead bill, **63**: 601n1; resigns from Cabinet to accept Senate seat, **64**: 41-42, 50, 52, 60, 349-50; desires to see WW, **64**: 103; and coal situation, **64**: 154n1, 154-55, 166; and railroad situation, **64**: 184; Lansing on reaction of to WW's no-compromise statement, **64**: 193; on urgent need for food relief in Europe, **64**: 330-40,n1; and Democratic caucus on treaty, **64**: 384; on treaty situation and Taft reservation, **64**: 405; concern over ratification with Lodge reservations, **64**: 479; **65**: 81-82; and WW's refusal to accept Lodge reservations, **65**: 7,n1; and Democratic platform, **65**: 29, 488, 489; appointment suggestions for Railroad Labor Board, **65**: 44-45; and concern over rumor that WW will accept Lodge reservations to Article X, **65**: 81-82; House on treaty strategy and, **65**: 274, 275; and League of Nations plank from Virginia plank, **65**: 292, 293-94, 331, 333, 482; mentioned for leadership position at convention, **65**: 345; and Resolutions Committee, **65**: 345, 385, 386, 393, 394, 489; code name for, **65**: 350; mentioned as presidential candidate, **65**: 350; and convention politics and strategy, **65**: 383, 424, 446, 451, 492, 497, 499; on WW's third term, **65**: 383, 400, 499; accepts Resolutions Committee chairmanship, **65**: 395, 396; meets with WW on convention and platform, **65**: 435-36; attends convention as spokesman for WW, **65**: 436-40; votes received on sixteenth ballot, **65**: 492n2; controversy with Cox over alleged statement, **65**: 494-95,n1,2; on W. R. Williams, **65**: 557; and Democratic National Committee, **67**: 390,n1; on Senate situation on separate peace with Germany, **67**: 399,n2; and WW Foun-

dation, **67**: 415; on taxation, **67**: 484; WW asks opinion on Vanderlip's comments on reserve system for Europe, **68**: 57, 61, 78-80, 80; and Armistice Day demonstration, **68**: 468, 469, 470, 472, 478; and WW's last illness, **68**: 565; and Federal Reserve bill, **68**: 585-86; photograph of, *illustration section*, **68**
Glass, Franklin Potts, **65**: 256-57,n5, 261
Glass, Meta, **68**: 478,n2
Gleaves, Albert, **53**: 65,n1; **55**: 412,n8; **58**: 3, 4; **62**: 460n1; **65**: 284,n1, 390, 391-92
Glenn, Nina Deaderick (Mrs. Robert Broadnax); Wilson sends condolences to, **65**: 297
Glenn, Robert Broadnax, death of, **65**: 297,n1; **66**: 333
Glenn, Thomas Kearney, **57**: 378, 379
Globe, Arizona, **66**: 125
Glubczuce, Poland: *see* Leobschutz
Glynn, James Peter, **56**: 428,n3
Glynn, Martin Henry, **63**: 609,n1, 610, 611; **64**: 64n1; **66**: 542n1
Gmund, Austria, **59**: 63
Gneist, Rudolf von, **63**: 623
Goble, Luther E., **53**: 157,n2
Godoy, Emilia G., **66**: 25n1
Goethals, George Washington, **68**: 422,n3
Goethe, Johann Wolfgang von, **56**: 360,n1; **66**: 440; **67**: 293
Goff, Guy Despard, **66**: 252,n1
Goff, John William, **55**: 421,n1, 422
Gold and Iron: Bismarck, Bleichroder, and the Building of the German Empire (Stern), **58**: 461n1
gold reserve: in Germany, **54**: 212, 213
Gold Star Fathers' Association, **68**: 43n1
Golden Stars, and Other Verses, Following "The Red Flower," (Van Dyke), **56**: 280,n2
Goldstein, Kurt, **58**: 614n13; **62**: 635n21
Goliath: The March of Fascism (Borgese), **53**: 619n1
Golitsyn, Vladimir Vasilevich, **53**: 630,n8
Goltra, Edward Field, **57**: 424; **59**: 320; **60**: 568,n5; **67**: 416,n6; on Senator Reed and Missouri politics, **57**: 47-49
Golub, Lionel, **67**: 271,n1
Gomez, Carlos F., **53**: 347n1; **62**: 628n1
Gomez, José Miguel, **66**: 84, 124; **67**: 24n1, 26,n4
Gompers, Samuel, **54**: 304, 515; **55**: 185, 262, 280, 364; **56**: 236n2, 603, 604, 605; **57**: 239n5, 303, 495,n1; **58**: 204, 329, 362, 420, 497; **59**: 203; **61**: 131; **62**: 96, 122; **63**: 52, 65, 148, 265; **65**: 20, 442-43,n2; **66**: 382n1; **68**: 581; on Council of National Defense in reconstruction, **53**: 217-20, 222; suggested as peace commissioner, **53**: 155, 206, 216; French wish to have in Paris during peace negotiations, **53**: 245, 292; and plans for international labor conference, **53**: 275, 286, 408,n1, 436, 466, 489, 490; Baruch recommends as labor consultant, **54**: 172; meets with WW,

54: 309; and N. D. Baker on carpenters' controversy, **54**: 519, 520; on labor's grievances against Burleson, **58**: 48-53; **59**: 108-109; WW's get-well message to **58**: 243; and WW's message to A. F. of L., **60**: 111, 113, 197, 291; on labor clauses and League of Nations, **60**: 645; **61**: 37-40; on labor's endorsement of League of Nations, **61**: 138, 231; and prohibition, **61**: 294; resolution against mob rule and lynchings, **61**: 357-59; requests Burleson's removal, **61**: 354-65; on Plumb plan, **61**: 377,n1; WW on reasons for not writing tribute to, **61**: 541,n1; WW requests representatives from A. F. of L. for conference on labor and capital, **62**: 623; on steel industry and threatened strike, **63**: 29-30,n1, 163; and Washington, D.C., police situation, **63**: 149-50; and threatened coal strike, **63**: 612n1; and First International Labour Conference, **64**: 98n1; on extending government control of railroads, **64**: 197-98; and trade with Russia, **65**: 389; requests meeting with WW, **65**: 562-63; on general amnesty for "political" prisoners, **66**: 120,n1, 231-32, 515-16; on independence for Dominican Republic, **66**: 537-39; **67**: 3, 73, 78-79, 86; and WW Foundation, **67**: 521-22, 523; **68**: 249n2

Gonzales, Alida, **68**: 476,n4, 479
Gonzáles, Pablo, **64**: 134,n7
Gonzales, Robert Elliott, **68**: 476n4
Gonzales, Sarah Cecil Shiver (Mrs. William Elliott), **68**: 476,n4, 479
Gonzales, William Elliott, **68**: 479; on dispute between Peru and Chile, **66**: 209-12,n1; on presidential possibilities and Democratic politics, **68**: 475-76
Gonzáles Flores, Alfredo, **63**: 616,n1
Good, James William, **54**: 259n1; **65**: 363n1
Goode, William T., **62**: 34n1
Goodhue, Francis Abbot, **53**: 716,n2; **54**: 88
Goodman, Mary H., **67**: 56, 75
Goodnow, Frank Johnson, **61**: 294,n5; **66**: 246n2
Goodrich, Chauncey William, **53**: 391n1; **55**: 36n1
Goodrich, James Putnam, **63**: 4,n6; on Indiana coal situation, **65**: 545,n5, 546, 547-48, 554
Good Stories from Oxford and Cambridge and the Dioceses (Henrey), **67**: 341,n2
Goodwin, Clarence Norton, **68**: 123,n3
Goodwin, Nathaniel Carl, **53**: 177,n1
Goold, Herbert Stewart, **66**: 356,n1
Gora, Lower Silesia: *see* Guhrau
Gordon, Charles George ("Chinese Gordon"), **58**: 225,n3
Gordon, Herbert, **59**: 119,n4
Gordon, Ishbel Maria Marjoribanks,

Marchioness of Aberdeen and Temair (wife of John Campbell), **56**: 223n1, 374; **57**: 219
Gordon, John R., **60**: 615,n3; **61**: 278n7; on Germany's counter-proposals on shipping, **60**: 138,n1, 140-41
Gordon: Martyr and Misfit (Nutting), **58**: 225,n3
Gordon, Samuel (Sam), death of, **65**: 510,n1
Gordon-Taylor, William: *see* Taylor, William Gordon
Gore, Charles, **53**: 486-87; **56**: 57,n2
Gore, Thomas Pryor, **60**: 245,n5; **62**: 68, 69; and famine relief bill, **54**: 174n3, 229; and treaty fight, **64**: 94, 200-201, 273, 337, 338; and Oklahoma appointments, **64**: 205; **67**: 62, 70; WW on, **64**: 488; vote on reservation to Article X, **65**: 81n1; **66**: 3; primary fight and defeat, **66**: 3,n1, 10n1
Gorgas, Marie Cook Doughty (Mrs. William Crawford), **65**: 510
Gorgas, William Crawford, **61**: 560-61; death of, **65**: 510,n1
Gorgas, Ala., **68**: 448n1, 457
Gorham Press, **68**: 81
Gorizia, **53**: 445, 642; **57**: 501
Goschen, Sir Edward, **56**: 615
Gotch, John Alfred, **66**: 546,n2
Gotlieb, Bernard, **61**: 409,n1
Goto, Shimpei, **53**: 556; **57**: 600,n4
Gottardi, Ruggero, **60**: 294
Gough, Sir Hubert de la Poer, **61**: 86,n5, 87
Gough-Calthorpe, Sir Somerset (Arthur), **58**: 253; **59**: 23,n4, 24, 25, 26, 227, 43, 44, 45, 54, 242,n4, 270,n5; **60**: 212,n7; and Baltic provinces, **61**: 154
Gould, Ashley Mulgrave, **63**: 264-65,n1
Gould, Jay, **68**: 16n1, 205
Gould, Norman Judd, **55**: 351n1
Gouraud, Henri-Joseph-Eugéne, **59**: 636,n1
Gout, Jean-Etienne-Paul, **54**: 490,n2; **57**: 626,n2; **64**: 163n6
Government by Fraud (New York *World*), **66**: 258n3
Governors and Mayors, Conference of, **55**: 219, 387; **59**: 288; WW's address to, **55**: 389-91
Gowen, Edward A., **66**: 265, 498
Gowen, Robert Joseph, **57**: 453n4
Grable, Edward French, **67**: 119-20,n1
Grabski, Wladyslaw, **65**: 527n3
Grady, Tom **65**: 476
Graf Waldersee, S.S., **64**: 8
Graham, Andrew Jackson, **67**: 1227n1
Graham, Archibald, **53**: 32,n2
Graham, Edward Kidder, **53**: 31
Graham, Eliza Owen Barry (Mrs. Archibald), **53**: 32,n2
Graham, Mary Owen, **53**: 31-32
Graham, Sir Ronald (William), **64**: 407n1
Graham, Samuel Jordan, **59**: 449,n1; **61**: 482,n1

Grain Corporation, **53**: 75; **54**: 276; **59**: 639; **61**: 455, 499, 502-503; **62**: 55-56, 159, 168, 198; **65**: 469-70; **66**: 509, 510, 530; **67**: 140; to continue to function under Barnes, **56**: 281-82, 426, 470-71, 485, 485-86; **57**: 375, 475; Redfield on wheat prices and, **56**: 619; and wheat prices, **61**: 549n1, 612-14,n2; Palmer on, **62**: 171-72; and flour to Russia, **63**: 588-90; and wheat exports, **64**: 13, 14; and European Children's Fund and food relief, **65**: 469-70

Grain Grades Act, **68**: 270

Grain Trade During the World War: Being a History of the Food Administration Grain Corporation and the United States Grain Corporation (Surface), **59**: 206n1

Grand Army of the Republic, **65**: 289n1

Grand Scuttle: The Sinking of the German Fleet at Scapa Flow, The (Van der Vat), **61**: 57n8

Grand Vizier: *see* Damad Ferid Pa a

Grant, Herbert Jeddy, **63**: 449,n1

Grant, Sir Ludovic James, **55**: 89,n1

Grant, Robert, **68**: 82

Grant, Ulysses Simpson, **53**: 248; **54**: 176; **58**: 535; **63**: 453; **67**: 225

Grant-Smith, Ulysses, **53**: 193, 194-95; and Hungary, **66**: 304,n1

Grasmere, England: WW's planned visit to, **66**: 92,n2, 134-35, 192, 245

Grassi, Rear Admiral M., **55**: 112; **58**: 456,n1, 579, 581-84; **61**: 83

Grasty, Charles Henry, **53**: 438,n1, 440,n1; **54**: 132,n1; **55**: 479, 480, 490; **56**: 354; **57**: 62, 146, 194; **58**: 430, 463, 501, 503, 530; **61**: 69, 348; **62**: 202, 627; **67**: 547n1; on American public opinion in Paris, **57**: 37-41; on WW's two decisions that won the war, **58**: 500; makes offer for WW to write editorials for Baltimore *Sun*, **58**: 504; **60**: 532, 533; on peace treaty, **61**: 615-16; compares Senate and WW to Chamber of Deputies and Clemenceau, **61**: 616,n2; on railroad situation, **62**: 287-90, 477

Grattan, Henry, **65**: 498,n1

Graudenz, S.M.S., **55**: 23

Graves, Ernest, **61**: 572,n2

Graves, John Temple, **67**: 522

Graves, Robert Windham, **56**: 116,n15

Graves, William Sidney, **53**: 557, 629, 631, 632; **54**: 158, 261, 413;; **55**: 39; **56**: 235, 576; **57**: 94, 95, 314; **58**: 495, 568, 574; **59**: 134, 148, 449; **60**: 522; **61**: 177,n1; **62**: 116; **65**: 284n1; on situation in Siberia, **53**: 168-69; **55**: 399-403, 493-95; **56**: 184, 185, 186; **65**: 284n1; on executions by Kalmykov, **53**: 184-85; N. D. Baker praises, **55**: 399; and U.S. policy in Siberia, **56**: 152-53; Lansing on, **56**: 304; instructions to, **56**: 371-72,n1, 519n1; and Y.W.C.A. work in Russia, **57**: 60; recommends U.S. support Kolchak, **58**: 569-70; WW

on, **59**: 134, 449; talk of replacing, **59**: 233, 234-35, 281-82, 409-10, 448; Polk on, **59**: 409-10; and troops in Siberia, **61**: 579, 580; on conditions in Siberia, **62**: 83-90; on N. D. Baker, **68**: 137

Gravle, E. F., **65**: 359

Gray, Carl Raymond, **53**: 704,n1

Gray, George, **64**: 141,n4; appointed to Permanent Court of Arbitration, **64**: 216, 273

Gray, Prentiss Nathaniel, **53**: 15,n2, 60

Grayson, Alice Gertrude (Altrude) Gordon (Mrs. Cary Travers), **53**: 612,n2, 646; **54**: 280; **55**: 185, 496, 529; **57**: 236, 388; **60**: 291, 381, 573; **61**: 356, 401; **63**: 619; **64**: 320-21, 325, 493-94; **65**: 514; **66**: 526; **67**: 516; **68**: 109,n1, 285, 564, 572, 577; gives birth to second son, **57**: 305

Grayson, Cary Travers, **53**: 166, 204, 319, 320, 358, 401, 423, 592;; **54**: 35, 59, 61, 64, 105, 106-107,n4, 148, 150, 237, 282, 308-309, 334, 431, 459, 473, 489, 505; **55**: 3, 36, 41, 94, 120, 187, 218, 465, 529, 538; **56**: 81, 103,n1, 441; **57**: 37, 50-52, 60, 62-67, 98-101, 141, 145-47, 177, 190-94, 235-36, 237-40, 284, 304, 316, 331-34, 349-51, 388-90, 426-30, 477, 477-78, 511, 512-13, 531-33, 579, 597-81; **58**: 3-5, 110-13, 147-48, 172, 176, 188, 215-16, 229,n1, 244-45, 248, 330-33, 367-68, 419, 429-31, 461-63, 499-504, 535-36, 561-62; **59**: 3, 39-40, 47-48, 78-79, 119, 124-25, 160-62, 186, 207, 241, 245, 246, 247-49, 252, 253-54, 286, 288-89, 321, 370-72, 419-20, 453-54, 477-78, 479-80, 527-30, 553-54, 576-78, 603,n1, 625-28; **60**: 3-4, 18-20, 43-44, 74, 114-17, 203-204, 249, 291, 291-92, 299-306, 332-35, 381-88, 434-35, 488-90, 532, 545-47, 569, 569-70, 573-75, 612-13; **61**: 32, 70, 77-79, 116-19, 186-88, 231, 235-39, 348, 360-62, 369-70, 376-77, 385, 395-97, 397-98, 569; **62**: 157, 626; **63**: 53, 149, 300, 419n1, 467, 526, 543, 544, 581, 593, 598, 606; **64**: 15, 32, 95, 127-28, 256, 270-71, 320, 324-26, 335, 346, 359, 396, 420, 455; **65**: 83,n1, 179-80, 212, 217, 242, 243, 261, 274, 291, 317, 348, 443-44, 498, 511n2; **66**: 102, 479, 521, 547; **67**: 23, 103, 175, 205, 206, 212, 239,n2, 256, 284, 301, 614; **68**: 23, 107, 109, 285, 400, 410, 457, 509, 577, 591; and sendoff to Europe, **53**: 305,n1; records transatlantic crossing, **53**: 318, 327, 332-33, 336, 336-40, 343, 348, 364-65, 370-71, 375-76; on WW's arrival in Brest, **53**: 378-79; on WW's arrival in Paris, **53**: 382-84; and activities in Paris, **53**: 391-92, 403-404, 410, 420, 449-50, 458-59, 472, 488, 577-78; on WW's Paris meeting with Vittorio Emmanuele III, **53**: 439; on WW's routine day and personal habits and traits, **53**: 446-48; on WW's hospital visit to

Neuilly, **53**: 467; on trip from Paris to Chaumont, **53**: 488-89; on Christmas Day visit with Pershing and troops, **53**: 502-505; on leaving France for England, **53**: 508-12; on receptions and activities in London, **53**: 519-22, 526-29; receives cufflinks from George V, **53**: 529; on stay in Carlisle, **53**: 537-38; on activities in Manchester, **53**: 538-41, 543-46; return to London, **53**: 546-47; on farewell to London and return to Paris, **53**: 569-70; on trip from France to Italy, **53**: 589; on arrival in Italy, **53**: 595-97, 646; on activities in Rome, **53**: 605-608; meets Benedict XV, **53**: 607; on activities in Turin and Modane, **53**: 620-22; on return to Paris, **53**: 634; on meetings and activities in Paris, **53**: 654, 706-707; WW's meeting with Orlando on Italian claims, **53**: 696-97; on first meeting of Supreme War Council at Quai d'Orsay, **54**: 4-5; on meeting of Comrades in Service, **54**: 5-6; on plenary sessions of Paris Peace Conference, **54**: 126-28, 262-63; on WW's speech to French Senate, **54**: 155; on meeting between WW and Gardiner, **54**: 175-78; on Prinkipo Declaration, **54**: 190, 415; on WW's visit to devastated areas in France, **54**: 278-81, 305; on mandate issue, **54**: 348; and leak to press that peace conference may relocate, **55**: 66, 88; on Plenary Session and completion of Covenant, **55**: 159-60; on WW's departure from Paris and arrival in Brest, **55**: 160, 197; on WW's activities during sea voyage to Boston, **55**: 201, 205, 207, 217-18, 221-22, 224-25, 228-29, 235-38; on WW's arrival and activities in Washington, **55**: 254, 294-95, 308-309, 339, 367, 387-88, 409; on WW's dinner meeting with congressional committees, **55**: 267; on WW's activities during return trip to France and his arrival in Brest, **55**: 409-10, 442-46, 448, 456-57, 460-62, 471-72, 473-75, 479-82, 486-89, 495-96; WW's dependence on, **55**: 466; on House-WW relationship, **55**: 488n2; **57**: 532-33; return to Paris, **55**: 496-98; on WW meeting with Lloyd George and Clemenceau on League of Nations being part of peace treaty, **55**: 529-31; chronicles and comments on WW's activities, **56**: 3-4, 59-62, 85-88, 102-103, 126-18, 163-65, 205-206, 246-49, 283-86, 312-13, 347-49, 405-408, 428-29, 436-40, 490-91, 522-25, 584-85; treats WW for nose abscess, **56**: 85, 102; on WW's visit to battlefront, **56**: 194-200; on WW's oratorical style, **56**: 249; tells WW stories of late Senator Ollie M. James, **56**: 348-49; on WW's luncheon with Lady Northcliffe, **56**: 406-408; on King Albert's visit with WW, **56**: 554-56; on WW's "violent illness," **56**: 556-57, 584-85; on WW's health, **57**: 3-4, 304-306; **58**: 626,n73; **60**: 573; **61**: 578, 599; **66**: 320, 451, 526; **67**: 360, 453; **68**: 382; on WW summoning *U.S.S. George Washington*, **57**: 63-65; on visit of Marie of Rumania, **57**: 190-93, 238-39; on WW's "supposed influenza," **57**: 235; on Hitchcock praises, **57**: 332; declines nomination for Distinguished Service Medal, **57**: 333; on Lloyd George's speech in House of Commons, **57**: 449-50; on Adriatic question and Big Three meetings, **58**: 53-56; requests drug urotropine, **58**: 146; on WW's outing to Baruch's country residence, **58**: 170-71; on May Day celebration in Paris, **58**: 274-75; on Japanese claims settlement, **58**: 328; on visit to Barbizon, **58**: 422; on first meeting with Germans at Versailles, **58**: 501-503; fabricates report to put WW's remarks in reasonable context,, **58**: 562n1; suffers from abscess on neck, **59**: 48, 78, 79, 187; **61**: 574; **62**: 628-29,n3; **63**: 537-38, 538-39, 542, 552,n1; on Ireland, **59**: 371-72,n2; on WW's position on Kolchak recognition, **59**: 527; on WW's Memorial Day speech at Suresnes Cemetery, **59**: 605-605; promotes relationship between WW and Balfour, **60**: 3; on events leading to Palmer's appointment as Attorney General, **60**: 6, 115-16,n4; on lunch with Balfour, **60**: 203-204; treats injured victims of automobile accident, **60**: 292; on his entrance to U.S. Navy, **60**: 301-302; on WW's meeting with Walsh and Dunne on Ireland, **60**: 383-87; on dinner party at Wallaces, **60**: 546-47; confesses to WW he's been to the races, **60**: 574; on Foch, **60**: 583; on tour of Belgium, **61**: 3-8, 10-16; King Albert confers Order of Leopold II upon, **61**: 15,n14; on Lloyd George's illness and apology, **61**: 44-45; on Italian crisis, **61**: 45; on Germany's reservations on signing treaty, **61**: 69; on reaction in Paris to signing of treaty, **61**: 78; on being suggested for French Legion of Honor, **61**: 117; on change of French public opinion toward WW, **61**: 138-39; and Poincaré dinner invitation episode, **61**: 180, 187-88; on WW's press conference, **61**: 235-38; interest in horse racing, **61**: 239; on signing ceremony and WW's departure from Paris, **61**: 302-306; on WW's departure from Brest, **61**: 354; aboard *George Washington* returning to U.S., **61**: 354, 355-56; as WW's confidant, **61**: 383; on WW's arrival in New York and Washington, **61**: 400-401; on WW's Senate speech and his bringing peace treaty to Senate, **61**: 416-17; and WW's decision to make cross-country tour for League of Nations, **62**: 507n1; WW's activities

Grayson, Cary Travers (*cont.*)
and speeches in Columbus and Indianapolis, **63**: 3-5; in St. Louis, **63**: 31-33;in Kansas City and Des Moines, **63**: 62-66; on tour in Omaha and Sioux Falls, **63**: 93-96; insists WW conserve his strength, **63**: 96; in Minnesota, **63**: 122-24; in Bismarck, **63**: 152-53; in Billings and Helena, **63**: 168-69; in Idaho and Spokane, **63**: 210-11; in Tacoma and Seattle, **63**: 236-40, 273; in Portland **63**: 274-76; on WW's arrival, activities and speeches in Oakland and San Francisco, **63**: 308-10, 340; notices first signs of break in WW's health, **63**: 338n4; on first test of "voice phone" by WW, **63**: 269-70; in San Diego, **63**: 369-70; in Los Angeles, **63**: 396-97, 423; in Sacramento and Reno, **63**: 426; concern over WW's health, **63**: 446, 488-90; in Ogden and Salt Lake City, **63**: 446; in Cheyenne, **63**: 467; in Denver and Pueblo, **63**: 487-90; WW's illness causes trip cancellation, **63**: 518-20; press statement on trip cancellation, **63**: 520; return to Washington, **63**: 526-27, 527-28, 532-33; bulletins on WW's health, **63**: 527, 568, 574, 576-77, 577-78, 587, 590; **64**: 4, 37, 99, 100, 120, 211, 216, 351, 435, 511n1; emphatic about strict rest for WW, **63**: 533; and question of WW's disability, **63**: 547,n1; skill and devotion prevented earlier breakdown of WW's health, **63**: 550; on WW's improved condition, **63**: 552-53; reports to Cabinet on WW's health, **63**: 554, 555; on WW's mental condition and ability to work, but rest cure is priority, **63**: 569-71; R. S. Baker on, **63**: 620; reaction to WW's stroke, **63**: 634; Park on role of during WW's illness, **63**: 639-46; refuses to comment on report of stroke, **63**: 642; on Hitchcock's interview with WW, **64**: 43-45; and Crauford-Stuart affair, **64**: 88, 90; announces Jenkins' release, **64**: 129-30, 131, 134, 138; on Fall-Hitchcock visit to WW, **64**: 133, 135-39; on Republican rumors on WW's health, **64**: 135-36; and railroad crisis, **64**: 222; on Jackson Day message, **64**: 252; on proposed biography-memoir of WW, **64**: 324-25; and Frazier, **64**: 353, 452; and WW's tentative decision to resign, **64**: 362n1; on Grey's letter, **64**: 365; and Cabinet meetings held during WW's illness, **64**: 386, 455, 456, 457, 496; and Lansing resignation, **64**: 398, 416, 418; Dercum on medical queries being directed to, **64**: 403, 434; on first meeting WW, **64**: 485; WW's wit and humor, **64**: 488-90; wishes McAdoo was in Paris to see WW's physical and political stress, **64**: 492-94; on birth of his son, **64**: 493-94; Seibold's proposal to write article on,

64: 494-95, 495-96; unpublished statement on WW's health history, **64**: 497-99; and diagnosis of and memorandum on WW's illness, **64**: 506, 507-10; on WW's motor rides, **65**: 41, 42, 67, 86, 201; on WW's reaction to treaty defeat, **65**: 108-109, 109n1, 124, 149; on his son's automobile excursions with WW, **65**: 110-11; on WW on third term, and on treaty strategy, **65**: 123-25; House on health bulletins of, **65**: 140; on WW's comments on lack of oratory, **65**: 145; on WW's first Cabinet meeting since illness, **65**: 186,n1; on son's pony ride at White House, **65**: 194; on WW's health, **65**: 298-99, 341-43, 380, 529; concern over third term for WW, **65**: 383, 400, 435; issue of WW's resignation, **65**: 383; Seibold recalls cancellation of WW's western trip by, **65**: 407-408; on WW's health during convention, **65**: 481, 488; concern over balloting at convention, **65**: 491; on WW's future plans, **65**: 506; on WW's attitude toward himself, **65**: 512; receives I. Hoover's report on WW's health and activities, **66**: 15-16; and Daniels, **66**: 71; had urged WW to resign, **66**: 217, 436; R. S. Baker on, **66**: 435, 440; persuades WW not to deliver messsage to Congress in person, **66**: 456-57; and Pierce-Arrow purchase for WW, **67**: 116-17, 136-37, 148, 167, 167-68; and fund-raising for S Street house, **67**: 129, 137, 148, 148-49; WW's shorthand draft and translation of letter of gratitude to, **67**: 185; and inauguration day activities, **67**: 208, 209; accompanies WW to Senate, **67**: 210, 211, 212; and WW's fainting spell, **67**: 245, 246; on Harvey, **67**: 289; delivers liquor to WW, **67**: 312,n1; and WW's recurrence of indigestion and headaches, **67**: 434, 435; on meeting with Balfour, **67**: 516-18; Dr. Mayo's advice to for WW's health, **67**: 535, 542-43; and issue of WW's resignation, **67**: 568; WW's physical therapist on, **67**: 611-12; on Jefferson Day dinner brouhaha, **68**: 51, 59-60; advises WW on summer vacation plans, **68**: 58-59; on birthday visit to WW, **68**: 250-52; on Axson's two visits with WW, **68**: 255-57; and Harding's orders for, **68**: 398-99; at Harding funeral, **68**: 400, 401, 402; EBW on his not staying with WW while she was on vacation, **68**: 413, 416; and WW's financial affairs, **68**: 442, 443; visits Lloyd George, **68**: 455, 456; Long and WW on diary of, **68**: 527-28; on WW and Mrs. Peck (Hulbert), **68**: 527,n1; returns from trip on notification of WW's illness, **68**: 548-49, 550-51, 551-52, 559; bulletins on WW's last illness, **68**: 553, 555, 556, 557, 561, 564-65; emotional reaction to WW's grave con-

dition, **68**: 555, 557, 559-60, 563; and
WW's death, **68**: 566; bulletins on
WW's death, **68**: 567, 567-68, 571-72;
emotion shown when reading death
bulletin, **68**: 568; Coolidge offers assistance to WW's family and, **68**: 573;
photographs of, *illustration sections*,
59; **65**; **68**
Grayson, Cary Travers, Jr., **53**: 305n1;
57: 236, 388; **60**: 291; **61**: 231,n1; **64**:
325,n4, 485n; birth of, **64**: 493-94; first
visit to White House, **65**: 242,n1
Grayson, David (pseudonym): *see* Baker,
Ray Stannard
Grayson, James Gordon, **53**: 305,n1,
646,n1; **57**: 236, 304, 579,n1;; **60**: 291;
61: 231,n1; **64**: 325,n4, 485n, 494; visits Wilson, **65**: 110,n1, 201, 244,
291,n1, 412, 514; has pony ride on
White House lawn, **65**: 194
Graziani, Jean Cesar, **58**: 149,n8
Grazioli, Francesco Saverio, **58**: 528,n1;
59: 64,n4, 65, 66, 119,n4, 241; **66**:
482,n2
Great Belt Strait, **58**: 123, 124
Great Britain, **53**: 312,n4; **54**: 13n2, 55,
159,n1; **55**: 144, 155, 164, 184; **57**: 433;
general election, **53**: 142, 519n1; and
peace conference, **53**: 142-43, 252, 257;
and reparations, **53**: 324, 336, 340,
341; **56**: 251, 285-86,n1, 286-96, 601-
605; **57**: 6-7,n7, 309, 310; **67**: 70, 144-
46; and Russian policy, **53**: 335; **54**:
173,n1; **62**: 34n1; and France, **53**: 482;
on negotiations with Russia, **53**: 591,
718-19, 722-23; and Dominions, **54**: 13-
15, 17, 43-44, 250, 310-11, 322-26, 329-
30, 333-34, 350-51, 362; and issue of
Russian representation at Paris Peace
Conference, **54**: 27,n2, 53-54, 99-103;
British draft convention of League of
Nations Covenant, **54**: 160-70; and
German submarine disposal, **54**: 180,
273,n1, 273-74, 505; on arms reduction
for Germany, **54**: 219-21; and armed
forces, **54**: 238-39; and Ireland, **54**:
256,n1; **55**: 363-64, 453-55; **56**: 398; **58**:
585-87, 588, 602; **60**: 239,n1, 303-304,
331-32, 383-87, 388-89; and 1911
agreement with Japan on Kiaochow,
54: 292; House's suggestions for appointment of British Ambassador to
U.S., **54**: 304; on expense of military occupation, **54**: 370-71; and League of
Nations Commission, **54**: 463; and
Sykes-Picot Agreement, **54**: 506n7; report on army of, **54**: 526; labor problems and Whitley Councils in, **55**:
91,n1, 204n2, 497; **56**: 205-206; and
Italy's request for U.S. loan, **55**: 113,
114; and Russian railroad situation,
55: 150, 187, 189-93, 400-401; and
Prinkipo Declaration, **55**: 180-83; and
war costs, **55**: 210; **58**: 492; **61**: 224; **63**:
221, 243, 349; and French financial sit-
uation, **55**: 283-84; and Japan, **55**: 294;

and Belgian loan, **55**: 305-306; and
League of Nations and U.S. public
opinion, **55**: 339; and Palestine, **55**:
381, 383, 383n2; refuses to ship coal to
U.S. if U.S. ships coal to Italy, **55**: 397-
98; and Rhineland, **55**: 475-77,n2; Benson on U.S. Navy and, **55**: 516-21; **58**:
456-57n3,4,6; British press gives false
reasons for WW's absence from Supreme War Council meeting, **55**: 530-
31; on capture of enemy cables, **56**:
210, 211, 212; and Fontainebleau
Memorandum, **56**: 259-70, 477-79; on
mandates, **56**: 274-75; **58**: 510; **59**: 326-
36, 336-46; **62**: 257, 257-58; and financing Archangel government, **56**: 279n2;
and financing Rumanian army, **56**:
305-306, 581-82; and Montenegro, **56**:
394-95; **59**: 178n2; economic delegates,
56: 523-24; and credit, **57**: 42, 471, 629;
attacks against Lloyd George on reparations, **57**: 145,n1, 147n5; and French
treaty of guarantee, **57**: 148n2, 417,n1,
430, 511, 525, 629,n1; **58**: 486-88, 488-
89, 489-90, 493-94, 531n1, 532; **61**:
280-82; **62**: 28-29; Hoover on sharing
shipping burden for Russian relief, **57**:
161; and Monroe Doctrine amend-
ment, **57**: 215, 218; and China's claims,
57: 300, 301; and Japan's racial equity
amendment, **57**: 373, 571; and troops
in Russia, **57**: 460-61, 560, 589; and
Italian claims, **57**: 536-42; and Japan's
claims, **57**: 610, 615, 616, 619, 620; on
economic relief, **58**: 8; and memorandum by American delegates to Reparation Commission, **58**: 25-26; secret
treaty with Japan, **58**: 111, 112; and
ship reparation agreement, **58**: 37-38;
and Jews, **58**: 285, 286, 287; and submarine cables, **58**: 296-97, 299, 347;
and Rumanian credits, **58**: 591, 592;
and Anatolia, **59**: 374; Reparation
Commission members from, **59**: 422;
and German counterproposals and
issue of treaty revision, **59**: 627;
changed attitude toward peace treaty
causes conflict with France, **60**: 4n3,
18, 40-41, 43, 49, 72, 75, 73, 78, 79, 82;
and public opinion on peace treaty, **60**:
17, 23, 346; and credit plans, **60**:
26n11; WW and American delegation
on peace treaty and, **60**: 71; Hoover on
changed attitude of regarding treaty,
60: 195; and Penjdeh incident, **60**:
210n6; on Germany's counterproposal
on reparations, **60**: 321-23; and German tonnage, **60**: 345-46; estimate of
damages, **60**: 359n1; and Rhineland
High Commission, **60**: 368; recommendations on Saar Valley, **60**: 460-62;
meeting on occupation between leaders from France and, **60**: 523-27; public
opinion on Germany, **61**: 144,n5; and
Irish situation, **61**: 182-83,n1,2, 185,
512; **62**: 254n2, 324-26; and William

Great Britain (cont.)
II's trial, **61**: 199; and supplies to Russia, **61**: 466; issue of lifting blockade of Germany, **61**: 540,n1; on Bulgarian boundaries and western Thrace, **61**: 591-93; protection of merchant marine and navy, **62**: 78; Graves on Siberian situation and anti-American sentiment, **62**: 89-90; and disposal of German and Austro-Hungarian ships, **62**: 144-47, 186-87; and secret agreement with Greece on Thrace, **62**: 238-40; and Irish situation, **62**: 254n2, 324-26; and issue of troop withdrawal from Armenia, **62**: 259, 285,n1, 576-78; WW on voting strength in League of Nations, **62**: 306; **63**: 231-32, 309-10, 320-31, 328-29, 377-78, 414-15, 435-36, 476-77, 491-92, 504-505; and secret agreement with Persia, **62**: 334n1, 427-28; and Syria, **62**: 608; **64**: 25-27; and Constantinople, **62**: 620n1; **63**: 59n2; and Shantung settlement, **63**: 193, 413, 438; battle deaths, **63**: 222, 243, 349; WW on League of Nations Commission representatives from, **63**: 286; honors bestowed on Foch, **63**: 301n1; wishes to adjourn Council of Heads of Delegations, **63**: 306, 391; and issue of ships ordered by France from U.S., **63**: 367-69; and Czech troops in Russia, **63**: 394, 395; WW on business interests of, **63**: 397; troops withdrawn from Fiume, **63**: 485; and Egypt, **64**: 49; presents proposals for Adriatic settlement, **64**: 168-78, 264-66, 370-71, 375; invited to first meeting of Council of League of Nations, **64**: 272; Grey on League of Nations and, **64**: 355n1; and issue of war criminals, **64**: 364,n1, 381-82, 407,n1; and Palestine, **64**: 373, 449; **68**: 100n2; WW's firm position on Adriatic proposals, **64**: 375-80, 398-402, 445-46; response to WW on Adriatic proposals and threat to withdraw treaty, **64**: 436-42; and Turkish treaty, **64**: 449; WW's reply to Anglo-French note on proposed Adriatic setteelement, **64**: 459-63; WW on Armenia and, **65**: 73, 74-75; and German war crimes, **65**: 100,n1; and Kapp *Putsch* and France, **65**: 103, 236-37; and Russia, **65**: 103, 288,n3; and Germany, **65**: 106, 107; and Reparation Commission, **65**: 147; on French occupation of Frankfurt area, **65**: 158-59, 170-71, 172-73; and Wilson and San Remo Conference, **65**: 197; editorial on Turkish treaty and, **65**: 229n1; awarded mandate for Palestine, **65**: 248,n1, 334,n1; and banking consortium, **65**: 259,n1; Gleaves on Japan and, **65**: 391-92; and recognition of Mexico, **65**: 463; and Poland, **65**: 527,n3; and Polish-Soviet war, **66**: 16-17,n1; and Japan and Siberia, **66**: 39,n3; Hurley on trade and, **66**: 74; and Russia and gold payment, **66**: 166,n1;

and banking consortium, **66**: 294-95; banking interests in Mexico, **66**: 302-303; and Yap Island controversy, **66**: 326, 458, 459, 460-64; Colby on Anatolia and, **66**: 429-30,n1; and Greece and King Constantine, **67**: 9, 10; and disarmament, **67**: 26,n7; Dodd on India and, **67**: 43; and Labour party's program, **67**: 373,n1, 379; and Four Power Treaty, **67**: 484n1; Jameson on European attitude toward newly formed U.S. government, **68**: 66-67; Wise on comments on League of Nations in, **68**: 87; and debt obligations, **68**: 106,n1, 107, 434,n1; and oil concessions in Eastern Galicia, **68**: 111; and Turkish advance in Asia Minor, **68**: 141,n1; WW's congratulations to Bonar Law and Law's response, **68**: 163,n1, 163; and German chemical industry, **68**: 300, 301; WW welcomes Lloyd George to the U.S. and his response, **68**: 445, 446; WW's get-well wishes to Lord Robert Cecil and his response, **68**: 450; and Baldwin's defeat, **68**: 593,n10; *see also* Great Britain and the United States; names of individuals, such as Lloyd George, David

Great Britain and the Creation of the League of Nations: Strategy, Politics and International Organization, 1914-1919 (Egerton), **53**: 331n3; **54**: 522n1; **57**: 142n1; **64**: 355n1

Great Britain and the Making of the Treaty of Trianon (Sakmyster), **56**: 462n11

Great Britain and the United States, **53**: 130; **62**: 16; plans for WW's visit, **53**: 44, 69, 109, 418, 427, 448-49, 456-57, 457-58, 488, 507, 508; George V and WW exchange congratulations, **53**: 53-54; George V invites WW to Buckingham Palace, **53**: 85, 109, 491; lifting of censorship, **53**: 100, 109, 241, 355; **57**: 448, 449; Furuseth on Seamen's Act and, **53**: 107; and International Mercantile Marine Corporation, **53**: 110-11, 111-12, 112-13, 113, 159, 186-87, 187-88, 195-96, 196, 209,n1, 261,n1; **54**: 171; and Italy's request for U.S. troops on Austria-Hungary's border, **53**: 124, 167; and relief, **53**: 225; and Irish situation, **53**: 299-300; **60**: 303-304, 331-32; **61**: 293, 438, 439; **62**: 8; comments and concerns over navies of, **53**: 314n4, 314-15, 373, 375, 427, 455, 512; **58**: 206; and Tacna-Arica dispute, **53**: 317-18; Costigan on, **53**: 328-32; Archbishop of Canterbury on League of Nations, **53**: 388-89, 412; and war loans, **53**: 441, 478; and far eastern situation, **53**: 463-64,n1; and colonies, **53**: 470-71, 498; Logan on League of Nations and, **53**: 482-85; WW's arrival in Dover, **53**: 509; WW's arrival activities and speeches in London, **53**: 509-12, 522-24, 526-29, 531-33, 533-34; British

labor organizations support WW, **53**: 535-36; WW visits Carlisle, **53**: 537-38; WW visits Manchester, **53**: 539-41, 543-46, 548-49, 549-52; WW returns to London, **53**: 546-47; Imperial War Cabinet discusses WW's views, **53**: 558-69; WW leaves Britain for Paris, **53**: 569; Worthington on interview with WW, **53**: 574-76; and League of Nations, **53**: 634; Bryce on success of WW's trip, **53**: 644-45; H. Hoover on withdrawal of British food orders, **53**: 687-88; WW angry at British demands, **53**: 707-708; and pork purchases, **54**: 229-30,n4; WW on resolutions of Trades Union Congress and Labour party, **54**: 257; Lynch on solidifying relations between, **56**: 57-58; WW on, **56**: 87; and Egypt, **56**: 154-55; **57**: 464-66, 499, 557, 557-58; House on, **56**: 350-51; and shipbuilding program, **56**: 482, 558-59; and reparations, **56**: 502-503, 504-505, 536-39; Britain requests and WW approves additional credit, **56**: 623; Dawson on, **57**: 36; and naval building controversy, **57**: 91-92, 92-93, 142,n1, 143-44, 178, 179-80, 180-88, 215, 216-17; Daniels plans trip to London, **57**: 92; and Italian question, **58**: 16; and withdrawal of forces from Russia, **58**: 319-20; **60**: 241; and King-Crane Commission, **58**: 325-26; and credit issues of Supreme Economic Council, **58**: 545-46; Irish-American delegation and issue of Ireland's representation at Paris, **59**: 172-73, 251, 318, 366-67, 368, 393,n1, 393-95, 513-14, 549,n1, 642-43, 645, 646; Bryce suggests demonstration in House of Lords for League of Nations, **59**: 397, 398-99; Republican opposition to Britain, **59**: 451-52; origin of Royal Institute of International Affairs, **60**: 17,n1; WW's birthday greetings to George V and reply, **60**: 100, 101; WW fears for relationship because of Irish issue, **60**: 298; WW on Senate action on Irish delegates, **60**: 435; request granted for U.S. railway troops to remain in Russia to aid British, **61**: 225-26, 349; WW's invitation to Edward, Prince of Wales, **62**: 13,n1; and Russian situation, **62**: 34n1; House on relations between, **62**: 60-63; Japan's views of Shantung settlement and role of, **62**: 64-65; and Grey mission to U.S., **62**: 254,n2, 255; and Armenian situation, **62**: 285-86,n1; **66**: 422; comparison of railroad situation in, **62**: 287-90; and secret treaties, **62**: 365-67,n27; lack of ambassador in U.S., **62**: 553; McCumber on objections to treaty concerning, **62**: 565-66; House on Britain's financial situation, **62**: 626; WW to receive the Prince of Wales, **63**: 297,n1; and Crauford-Stuart affair, **63**: 606n1; **64**: 3; and *Imperator* controversy, **64**: 7-10, 33-34;

Prince of Wales thanks EBW and WW for hospitality, **64**: 36-37, 71; concern over Senate action on reservations, **64**: 53; Polk on effect of U.S. delegates leaving Paris, **64**: 151; Lansing on WW not receiving Lord Grey, **64**: 187-88; and Grey's letter on reservations, **64**: 355n1, 380, 381,n1; issue of cancellation of debts, **64**: 475,n1, 476-78; **66**: 25-26, 309-11; Geddes recommended as Ambassador to U.S., **64**: 483-84,n1,2; WW on friendship between, **64**: 491-92; Geddes appointed Ambassador to U.S., **65**: 43-44, 55-56; proposal for Minister from Canada, **65**: 181-82, 237; Prince of Wales on American hospitality, **65**: 226-27; U.S. concern over renewal of Anglo-Japanese Alliance, **65**: 254-55; and debt negotiations, **65**: 325-26,n1; Wilson unable to write letter for National Institute for the Blind, **65**: 430, 432-33; issue of cancellation of Allied debts, **65**: 480-81; Lindsay's report on Democratic National Convention, 1920, **65**: 488; and recognition of Costa Rica, **65**: 571,n2; Lloyd George on inter-Allied indebtedness, **66**: 48-50, and MacSwiney appeal, **66**: 88-89, 90, 91; and U.S. paper shortage and Canada, **66**: 114; and resignation of J. W. Davis, **66**: 144, 150; **67**: 36, 60-62; Colby on Mesopotamia mandates and oil supply, **66**: 393, 394-39; and American Red Cross relief to Ireland, **66**: 512-13, 518; and Sulgrave Manor, **66**: 543n1; J. P. Morgan offers London home for ambassador's residence, **67**: 26,n6; and influence of Irish Americans, **67**: 44-45; Dodd on, **67**: 45-46; and Yap controversy, **67**: 53-55, 58, 153-56, 194n1; issue of Britain's indebtedness, **67**: 91, 151-52,n1, 355,n2,4,6; Colby on demurrage cases, **67**: 339,n2; WW on, **67**: 462n2; *see also* Great Britain

Great Britain and Germany's Lost Colonies, 1914-1919 (Louis), **54**: 363n3

Great Britain and the Twenty-One Demands of 1915 (Gowen), **57**: 453n4

Great Epidemic (Hoehling), **58**: 616n20

"Greatest Failure in all History": A Critical Examination of the Actual Workings of Bolshevism in Russia (Spargo), **66**: 5n2

Great Impersonation (Oppenheim), **67**: 289n1

Great Lakes Division for League of Nations, **55**: 187

Great Madness, The, **55**: 337n1

Great Northern, U.S.S., **58**: 141; **61**: 355

Great Northern Railway, **63**: 124n5

Great Peacemaker: The Diary of James Gallatin, Secretary to Albert Gallatin, 1813-1827, **58**: 422,n1

Great Swine Epidemic, **56**: 56n2

Greece, **53**: 56, 177n1; **54**: 13, 15, 16, 45, 264, 490,n2; **55**: 3, 29n2, 164, 184, 500-501; **56**: 335; **57**: 112, 334, 520, 545-46,n2; **58**: 114, 317, 472, 477, 478, 499; **59**: 137, 140, 146-47, 16, 167, 215, 390, 468; **60**: 134, 577n5, 582n5; **61**: 96; 128, 344, 566-68, 623-24; U.S. loans to, **53**: 479; and reparation claims, **54**: 55, 211, 223, 283; representation at Paris Peace Conference, **54**: 65; and League of Nations, **54**: 263, 462, 482, 495-96, 509; **58**: 198, 199, 201, 241; wishes to send troops to Turkey, **54**: 402-403, 326-27; and troops to the Ukraine, **54**: 402-403,n3; and territorial claims, **54**: 463, 473n1; and Dodecanese Islands, **58**: 355-56; **59**: 39, 42; dispatch of troops to and landing at Smyrna, **58**: 510-14; **59**: 21-27, 42-46, 54-55, 59, 238, 250, 252, 266-67, 473, 640-41,n1,2,3,4; **61**: 44; Council of Four on mandates and, **59**: 89-90; Council of Four on Adriatic question and, **59**: 91-92; and Turkey, **59**: 299; **60**: 193, 276-77; **62**: 235; **68**: 141n1, 146n3; and Anatolia, **59**: 374; Bryce on, **59**: 400; Bliss on fixed military strength for, **59**: 428-32; and landing in Asia Minor, **59**: 493; and Austrian treaty, **59**: 577; Westermann on territorial demands of, **59**: 595-96; and arms limitation, **60**: 170; estimate of damages, **60**: 359n1; and Thrace, **61**: 589-93;; **62**: 110-11, 141-42, 207, 238-40, 265, 266, 320, 327-28, 429, 551-53; **63**: 59n2, 60-62, 121-22, 305, 391-92; **64**: 157-64, 297,n1; issue of agreement between Great Britain and, **62**: 238-40; and Adriatic question, **64**: 171, 299, 301, 315, 369; and League of Nations, **64**: 272; and appointment of minister, **64**: 414,n2, 453, 454; and Smyrna, **65**: 64; and Thrace, **65**: 91, 111, 113; Droppers' resignation and replacement suggestions, **65**: 251n1, 260, 271, 317; and Euxine Pontus, **66**: 29,n1; and Albania, **66**: 308; issue of recognition of King Constantine; **67**: 9, 10-11,n2; and credit arrangements, **67**: 10-11; and Balfour and inter-Allied indebtedness, **68**: 106n1; and Corfu incident, **68**: 419n1, 427, 435, 451

Greece at the Paris Peace Conference (1919) (Petsalis-Diomidis), **64**: 163n5

Greek Americans: Baruch on votes of, **66**: 336

Greek Orthodox Church, **58**: 491n1

Green, Constance McLaughlin, **61**: 576n2; **67**: 505n1

Green, William: and WW's proposal to end coal strike, **64**: 142-45; urges WW to veto Transportation Act of 1920, **65**: 20

Green, William Raymond, **56**: 428,n3

Greene, Evarts Boutell, **66**: 165,n1, 256

Greene, Warwick, **60**: 532n1; **61**: 163,n17;

and commission to investigate pogroms in Poland, **60**: 567, 601

Greene, Sir William (Conyngham), **53**: 463-64,n2; **57**: 610

Greenfield, Kent Roberts: praises WW, **66**: 314-15

Greenlough family, **68**: 425,n2

Greenstone, A., **62**: 434

Gregg Publishing Company, **67**: 197n1

Gregg Writer, **67**: 197n1

Gregory, Thomas Tingey Craven, **57**: 367,n3

Gregory, Thomas Watt, **53**: 264, 289, 308,n1; **54**: 393; **55**: 409, 411, 463; **56**: 58, 75, 98, 179, 244, 396, 619; **57**: 179, 377, 383; **58**: 106; **64**: 64n1, 322; **68**: 380, 471, 577; on Cabinet appointments and resignations, **64**: 184-85; concerned over situation in Washington and WW's ability to serve, **64**: 217, 243, 348; on General Leasing bill, **61**: 534n1; **62**: 46-47, 48; **64**: 473; on Baldwin, **53**: 12-13; and Busch case, **53**: 142; on Hapgood and "political prisoners," **53**: 245-46, 287; resignation of, **53**: 401, 587,n2, 705, 705, 715; successor to, **54**: 52, 125, 410, 428, 429; **55**: 294; on New England support for League of Nations, **54**: 58; and oil-leasing bill, **54**: 471, 503-504; on granting amnesty, **55**: 344, 345-47; WW praises as Attorney General, **55**: 276-77; Grayson on resignation of, **60**: 115,n4; and "slacker raids," **60**: 115n6; and second Industrial Conference, **63**: 611; and Democratic platform, 1920, **65**: 29; on WW not meeting with Cabinet, **65**: 79; and Mexican oil, **66**: 334

Gregory, Warren, **66**: 246n2

Gregory-Allen, H. J.: saga of WW's missing furniture, **66**: 257,n2, 338, 339, 379, 385

Grenville, William Wyndham, Baron Grenville, **68**: 66

Gressitt, Henri, **66**: 112-13,n1

Grew, Joseph Clark, **53**: 57, 389-90,n2, 402, 526; **54**: 77, 135, 399, 552; **56**: 240n1; **57**: 137; **58**: 137; **59**: 74, 447n1; **60**: 38, 104, 106, 138-41, 182, 245, 250n1; and appointments, **64**: 317,n4, 414, 453; suggested for appointment to Denmark, **65**: 85, 88

Grey, Edward, Viscount Grey of Fallodon, **53**: 487, 498, 527,n2, 530n1, 531; **54**: 318; **56**: 57, 105, 324, 439,n3, 457, 593, 615; **58**: 18, 397; **59**: 334; **61**: 386; **62**: 316, 525, 553; **63**: 559; **64**: 157; **65**: 480; **66**: 200; WW and Cecil discuss, **56**: 62,n2; talk of as ambassador to U.S., **62**: 60-61,n1; on Britain's naval building program, **62**: 61; on Great Britain and the U.S., **62**: 61-62; and mission to U.S., **62**: 254,n1, 255; and conscription in mandated territories, **62**: 425-26, 532; House on, **62**: 625-26; and Crauford-Stuart affair, **63**: 606n1;

64: 3, 88, 90, 91, 217; on *Imperator* controversy, **64**: 33; on treaty being killed by Lodge and Republicans, **64**: 44; controversy over WW not receiving, **64**: 187-88, 203, 235, 239, 360; WW charges conspiracy between Lodge and, **64**: 384; Dr. Park on WW's health and, **64**: 527; *see also* Grey's letter on reservations

Grey's letter on reservations, **64**: 355n1; R. S. Baker on, **64**: 359, 362, 385; House on, **64**: 360; effect on WW's tentative plans to resign, **64**: 362n1; press release on White House reaction to, **64**: 363-64; Lansing on, **64**: 365, 366-67, 380; and Jusserand, **64**: 380; Borah on, **64**: 381,n1; Dr. Park on WW's reaction to, **64**: 527; Tumulty on, **65**: 24-25,n1

Grief (statue, St. Gaudens), **68**: 20,n1

Griffin, Frank J., **53**: 370,n2

Griffin, Ida M. Southworth (Mrs. Solomon Bulkley), **53**: 241,n2

Griffin, James F., **66**: 3,n1

Griffin, Solomon Bulkley, **53**: 241, 251; **66**: 208,n1, 349

Griffith, Arthur, **57**: 419n2; **59**: 105-106, 106, 251, 366n1, 393,n1, 513, 549n1; **60**: 289, 544; denied a hearing at peace conference, **61**: 466-67

Grinberg, Suzanne, **57**: 218,n1, 219

Grinnell College, **55**: 486n2

Groat, Carl Diedrich, **55**: 479,n1

Grodno (Poland) Russia, **53**: 611; **54**: 33, 204; **65**: 527n1

Grogan, Edward Ion Beresford, **62**: 90,n12

Gronna, Asle Jorgenson, **62**: 160,n3; **64**: 200-201, 337, 338; **66**: 141n1

Gross, Edwin J., **65**: 418n3

Gross Wartenberg (now Sycow, Poland), **60**: 158

Grotius, Hugo, **67**: 586

Grouitch (Grujić), Slavko Y., **64**: 341,n1; **65**: 253,n4; **66**: 377,n1

Grout, Louise Adams, **56**: 283,n1

Grove City College, **67**: 335n2

Grove Park Inn, Asheville, N.C., **68**: 58n1

Groves, Percy Robert Clifford, **59**: 379,n8

Groves, Robert Marsland, **54**: 541,n4

Growth of American Foreign Policy (Leopold), **61**: 300n6

Grubb, Bird, **67**: 105n3

Grubbs, Frank L., Jr., **65**: 442n2

Gruet, Intendent, **56**: 139,n2

Grujić, Slavko Y.: *see* Grovitch, Slavko Y.

Grunne, Count Guillaume de Henricourt de, **59**: 222,n14

Guadelupe Hidalgo, Treaty of, **62**: 37; **66**: 283n1

Guam, **54**: 379; and Yap Island, **54**: 381

Guaranty Trust Company, **59**: 71, 111

Guardian, The: *see Manchester Guardian*

Guardian of Boston: William Monroe Trotter (Fox), **60**: 486n1

Guatamala: and delegates to Paris Peace Conference, **54**: 65, 115;; **58**: 198; political situation in, **65**: 247,n1; and Mexico, **66**: 270n1; and conference in Costa Rica, **66**: 356, 357-58; and imprisonment of Estrada Cabrera, **66**: 389,n1, 390, 402, issue of not dismissing minister from, **66**: 506-507, 512

Guerra Diplomatica: Ricordi e Frammenti di Diario (1914-1919) (Aldrovandi Marescotti), **57**: 435n3, 551n7

Guerra Libica (1911-1912) (Malgeri), **58**: 435n7

Guerry, William Alexander, **53**: 392,n2, 396

Guffey, Joseph Finch, **65**: 359,n2

Guhrau, Lower Silesia (now Gora, Poland), **60**: 24,n7

Guides to the Evaluation of Permanent Impairment (American Medical Association), **62**: 634,n17; **63**: 644

Guildhall, London: WW's address at, **53**: 527-28, 531-33

Guillaumat, Louis, **56**: 257,n6

Gulick, Charles Adams, **58**: 157n2

Gundomar, S.M.S., **55**: 432

Gutiérrez Guerra, José, **66**: 135n1, 480

Gutiérrez Ponce, Ignacio, **59**: 444n1

Guthrie, Sir Connor, **58**: 202n1

Gyongyos, Hungary, **60**: 257

Haagsche Post, **59**: 245n2; **60**: 250n1

Haakon VII (of Norway), **59**: 612,n1

Haan, William George, **61**: 576, 610

Haas, Jacob Judah Aaron: *see* De Haas, Jacob Judah Aaron

Haase, Hugo, **53**: 7; **59**: 129,n3; **60**: 96,n5, 498; **62**: 318

Habarovsk, Russia: *see* Khabarovsk

Haboczyn, Adelbert, **56**: 442

Habsburg, S.M.S., **55**: 432

Hadji-Mischef, Pantcho, **59**: 400,n1

Hadley, Arthur Twining, **65**: 217,n1

Haffer, Mr., **67**: 411

Hagedorn, Hermann, **68**: 252n2

Hague, The Netherlands, **53**: 32, 67, 354; **63**: 630; suggested as site for League of nations, **56**: 103; **57**: 224

Hague Arbitration Cases (G. G. Wilson, ed.), **54**: 512n3

Hague conferences and convention, **55**: 31, 68, 121; **62**: 38-39; of 1899, **53**: 312n1; **54**: 71, 72-73, 269; **61**: 235n4, 295n1, 300,n6, 301; **62**: 38; of 1907, **53**: 312n1; **54**: 71, 72-83, 269, 286, 511; **59**: 232; **60**: 369, 515; **61**: 169, 295n1, 300,n6, 301; **62**: 38-39

Haguenin, Emile, **59**: 566,n1

Hague Post: *see Haagsche Post*

Hague Tribunal, **55**: 156

Haidar, Rustum, **54**: 505,n2; **55**: 178n2

Haifa, Palestine, **56**: 105

Haig, Charlotte Augusta Astor Drayton (Mrs. George Ogilvy), **64**: 204,n1

Haig, Sir Douglas, **53**: 521, 594; **54**: 244, 532; **56**: 407; **60**: 599; **61**: 204; Orpen portrait, *illustration section*, **60**

Haile Selassie I (of Ethiopia): *see* Ras
Taffari
Haiti, **54**: 65, 115, 170; **58**: 198; **62**: 9; **66**:
25,n1, 31, 63,n1, 82,n1, 82-83; **67**:
23n1; Colby on, **66**: 72-73; sending
Knapp to, **66**: 73, 78, 99, 100,n1;
Lejeune on, **66**: 189n1
Haitian-American Corporation, **67**: 379-
80
Hajibekov, Jeihun Bay, **58**: 333n2
Hajinskii, Mohammad Hasan, **58**: 333n2
Haking, Sir Richard (Cyril Byrne), **57**:
103,n4; **59**: 255,n2
Haldane, Richard Burton, 1st Viscount
Haldane of Cloan, **62**: 60-61,n1, 254,n1
Hale, Edward Joseph, **64**: 205,n9
Hale, Frederick, **55**: 545,n3; **61**: 373; on
reservations concerning League of Na-
tions, **62**: 536-37; and treaty fight, **64**:
94, 200-201, 337, 339; Grayson on atti-
tude toward WW's health, **64**: 135-36
Hale, Matthew, **58**: 274,n3; urges pas-
sage of woman suffrage amendment,
61: 537-38
Hale, Reuben Brooks, **63**: 341,n1
Hale, William Bayard, **68**: 330,n2; R. S.
Baker on relations with WW, **67**:
292,n4
Haley, J. Evetts, **66**: 369n2
Half-Open Door (*New York Times*), **67**:
531n1
Halifax, Nova Scotia; and cables, **58**: 300,
302, 303
Hall, Barton, **65**: 251n1, 260
Hall, Granville Stanley, **66**: 302; on WW
as inspiration for his book, **66**: 290,n1
Hall, James K., **67**: 173,n2
Hall, Mrs. James K., **67**: 173,n2
Hall, Ruth Preble: *see* Smith, Ruth
Preble Hall
Hall, Thomas Cumming, **54**: 397n1
Hall, William Reginald, **53**: 573,n1
Halle, Germany, **56**: 90n4
Haller, József, **54**: 481,n4; **56**: 52, 56, 129,
130, 133, 540; **57**: 74,n3,4,5, 76n6; **59**:
217, 262, 263, 323, 353, 354, 356, 357,
358, 360, 458, 542, 589, 598; army of,
56: 52n13, 56, 129-48, 209n2, 315,
408,n2, 489-90, 490, 494, 496n2, 526,
540; **57**: 74,n3,4,5, 134-36, 178, 280,
462-63, 549-50; **58**: 20-21, 102, 316,
455; **60**: 206, 161; **61**: 274, 279; and
Polish Jews, **61**: 365n1; repatriation of
Polish Americans in Haller's Army, **64**:
372-73, 375, 389-90; **65**: 43
Hall of Mirrors (Versailles Palace), **61**:
118, 302, 322
Halsey, Abram Woodruff: **65**: 246,n1;
WW on death of, **67**: 280-81
Halstead, Albert, **62**: 167-68,n3, 235n1
Hama, Syria, **56**: 110, 111, 112
Hamaker, G. E., **65**: 263
Hamburg, Germany, **53**: 8; **55**: 458n1
Hamilton, Alexander: WW on, **56**: 62; **67**:
358-59

Hamilton, Edward H., **63**: 309n2
Hamilton, John Andrews: *see* Sumner of
Ibstone, Baron
Hamilton, Joseph Gregoire de Roulhac,
67: 68n3
Hamilton, Peter James, **67**: 55-57, 75
*Hamilton Holt: Journalist, International-
ist, Educator* (Kuehl), **68**: 44n1, 99n1,
178n1
Hamlin, Anna, **68**: 409,n2
Hamlin, Charles Sumner: on Grange endorsing treaty ratification, **62**: 301-
302, 313; EBW vacations at home of,
68: 408n1, 409, 410, 412, 414, 415, 416,
417, 418-19; WW thanks, **68**: 420, 448;
on attending theater with WW, **68**:
425; on WW's essay and Lord Birken-
head's speech, **68**: 446-47, 448; birth-
day greetings to WW, **68**: 511
Hamlin, Edward Everett, **68**: 412-13,n1
Hamlin, Harriet G., **68**: 410,n1
Hamlin, Huybertie Lansing Pruyn (Mrs.
Charles Sumner), **68**: 409,n2, 410, 417,
418, 419, 511
Hamlin, Jane, **68**: 410,n1
Hamlin, Katherine Brooks Conrad (Mrs.
Edward Everett), **68**: 413,n11
Hammerstein, Baron Hans von, **56**:
140,n3, 141, 167n3, 168; **57**: 401
Hammond, George, **68**: 66
Hammond, Percy, **57**: 241n3
Hampton, George P., **58**: 145,n1; on
public referendum on treaty ratifica-
tion, **62**: 30-31,n1, 197-98,n1; on need
for short-term farm credit, **66**: 243-
45,n1
Hampton Institute: motto of, **68**: 206
Hampton Roads, Va., **55**: 37, 193
Hanau, Germany: French troops occupy,
65: 155n1, 158
Hancock, John Milton, **53**: 53, 413-14,n2
Hancock, William Keith, **54**: 148n1; **56**:
416n11; **68**: 437n3, 453n1
Hand, Augustus Noble, **59**: 76,n1; **66**:
95,n2
Hand, Learned, **65**: 77; **66**: 95n2
*Hand-Book of Standard American Pho-
nography* (Graham), **67**: 127,n1
Handler, Mr., **60**: 125-26,n7
Handy, Levin Irving, **56**: 437,n1
Handy, Parker Douglas, **65**: 246,n1
Hangchow, China, **58**: 166
Hanger, Grossbrenner Wallace William,
65: 189n1
Haniel von Haimhausen, Edgar Karl Al-
fons, **57**: 520,n7, 526; **58**: 518; **61**:
69,n2, 70n2, 78, 79,n2, 80, 125, 139,
149, 187, 191, 203, 204, 303, 339; asks
for time to study treaty, **61**: 81-82
Hanihara, Masanao, **68**: 581,n1
Hankey, Adeline de Smidt (Lady Hankey), **60**: 300,n1
Hankey, Sir Maurice (Pascal Alers), **54**:
7n1, 401; **55**: 192, 305; **56**: 108, 111,
259n1; **57**: 71, 102, 104, 140, 400n1,

450, 451, 586, 587, 588, 613; **58**: 21, 64, 86, 118, 148, 153, 179, 183, 226, 227, 236, 250, 252, 259, 264, 278, 316, 334, 335, 381, 400, 401, 419, 431, 444, 445, 505, 513, 545, 546; **59**: 30, 31, 101, 139, 163, 270, 271, 336, 362, 370, 558, 562, 569, 584, 591, 644-45; **60**: 285, 300, 403, 496; **61**: 342n3; **62**: 145; **64**: 263; **66**: 46,n7, 54; **67**: 105n3, 195n4, 516; **68**: 502; delivers message to Italian delegates, **57**: 547, 548, 551, 552; on languages of peace treaty, **58**: 120; on Shantung and Kiaochow, **58**: 130, 131, 132; on reparations, **58**: 266; on responsibility clauses and treaty with Austria, **58**: 578; and Council of Four on Smyrna, **59**: 41; on Scala Nuova, **59**: 90; on aerial warfare not mentioned in Covenant, **59**: 379, 380; thanks WW for photograph and confidence, **62**: 547; on visit with WW, **67**: 462,n2

Hankey: Man of Secrets (Roskill), **54**: 12n1; **67**: 462n1

Hankow, China, **57**: 561n2,5; **58**: 256

Hannon, William, **63**: 29-30,n1, 149

Hannover, Germany, **55**: 430; **56**: 38

Hanotaux, Gabriel-Albert-Auguste, **53**: 420,n1

Hans Delbruck als Kritiker der Wilhelminischen Epoche (Thimme), **53**: 121n1

Hans Heinrich XV, Prince of Pless, **60**: 55n1

Hanson, Ole, **59**: 204n2; **63**: 238n1

Hanyehping Company, **57**: 622

Hapgood, Elizabeth K. Reynolds (Mrs. Norman), **67**: 244

Hapgood, Norman, **59**: 245, 447, 480, 572-73; **60**: 34, 284, 568-69; **61**: 40; **62**: 34, 101, 316, 427, 507; **67**: 244; on pardoning "political prisoners," **53**: 124-25, 245, 246, 287; Minister to Denmark, **55**: 185, 194, 439,n1; **56**: 101, 191,n1; **57**: 334; **59**: 512,n1; **60**: 561,n1; on League of Nations, **55**: 292, 451; on Russian situation, **59**: 517-19; **61**: 359-60; resigns as Minister to Denmark, **64**: 233-34,n1; sends WW his book, **66**: 28, 30; on conscientious objectors and release of Debs, **66**: 343

Hapsburgs: WW on, **63**: 358

Hara, Takashi, **53**: 464,n4, 556; **56**: 185; **66**: 13,n4

Harbin, China, **53**: 145; **55**: 495; **61**: 580

Harbord, James Guthrie, **53**: 473,n1; **55**: 398,n3; **56**: 306,n2; **61**: 486,n2, 487; **62**: 27,n1, 166, 248n1, 578; **64**: 27, 450,n3,4; **65**: 532; **66**: 350, 357; **68**: 452n2; and Cuba, **66**: 237, 238

Harbord Mission, **64**: 27

Harcourt, Viscomte Emmanuel d', **53**: 721,n2

Harcourt, Lewis, 1st Viscount Harcourt, **53**: 593n7

Harcourt, Mary Ethel Burns, Lady Harcourt, **53**: 593,n7

Hard, Anne Nyhan Scribner (Mrs. William), **64**: 362,n4

Hard, William, **64**: 362,n4

Harden, Maximilian, **53**: 419; **67**: 299

Harding, Rt. Rev. Alfred, **62**: 561-62,n1

Harding, Charles R., **67**: 474n2

Harding, Florence Mabel Kling De Wolfe (Mrs. Warren Gamaliel), **67**: 83,n1, 140n3, 208, 381, 419; EBW on, **67**: 244; has tea with Wilsons at White House, **67**: 189-90; illness of, **68**: 152,n1, 398; WW's condolences to, **68**: 398, 399; thanks WW for condolence note, **68**: 407; at WW's funeral, **68**: 581

Harding, Samuel Bannister, **67**: 141,n1, 283

Harding, Warren Gamaliel, **53**: 187, 188, 469n1; **59**: 524n1; **60**: 381; 372, 596-97; **62**: 43, 44, 336; **64**: 200-201, 416n2; **65**: 288n4, 546; **66**: 199,n1,2, 200, 272, 282n1, 315, 335, 346n1, 433, 531; **67**: 26,n5, 109, 124, 140n3, 184, 313n1, 394, 419, 511, 578n1, 584; **68**: 346n2; WW invites for talk on treaty, **62**: 29; questions WW at Foreign Relations Committee meeting, **62**: 339, 352, 361-62, 383, 388-90; and Bullitt testimony, **63**: 337n1; and Armenian resolution, **65**: 323; wins presidential nomination, **65**: 415,n1; W. G. Sharp on, **65**: 474, 475; WW on as candidate, **65**: 552; and Panama Canal tolls controversy, **66**: 141,n1, 177-78; WW will not debate, **66**: 141, 150; WW on, **66**: 156, 157; **67**: 70, 71, 176n1; H. Hoover and, **66**: 169; Crowell endorses, **66**: 188,n1; and League of Nations position, **66**: 188,n1, 208,n1, 258n2,3; WW on country's prospects if Harding wins, **66**: 194; Tumulty's statement for WW on national devastation if Republicans are elected, **66**: 214-16; WW investigates reports that France approached, **66**: 238,n1, 239, 240, 241, 246; and Viereck, **66**: 249n1; Creel on Mexico and, **66**: 271, 404-405,n5; elected President, **66**: 306n1; proposed trip to Panama, **66**: 317-18,n1, 324, 332-33; thanks WW for offer of use of *Mayflower*, **66**: 453,n1; Dodd on, **67**: 46; R. S. Baker on, **67**: 71, 237; and Mexico, **67**: 82; WW invites to White House, **67**: 83; inauguration of, **67**: 134, 143, 149, 176n1, 205-12; **68**: 379; meets with Lamont on rumor of cancellation of Allied debt, **67**: 151-52,n1; and Grayson's assignment, **67**: 185n1; has tea with Wilsons at White House, **67**: 189-90; Cobb on, **67**: 216; attends theater, **67**: 381; and Panama-Costa Rica border dispute, **67**: 382n5; and Armistice Day plans, **67**: 400-401, 402, 444-45, 445-46, 452, 453n1; **68**: 91-92; on League of Nations, **67**: 471,n1; on Four Power Treaty, **67**: 494n1; and Colombia, **67**: 581n2; EBW

Harding, Warren Gamaliel (*cont.*) on, **68**: 45; WW on the man and his administration, **68**: 45-46, 88-89, 113, 381; WW on his not meeting with "political prisoners'" families, **68**: 48,n6; and WW's foreign policy, **68**: 57,n3; various comments on administration of, **68**: 115, 147-48, 192, 273, 282-83, 367; and Teapot Dome scandal, **68**: 119n1; and Supreme Court appointment, **68**: 127n1; thanks the Wilsons for concern over wife's illness, **68**: 152; and Permanent Court of International Justice, **68**: 216-17, 306,n2, 309, 313, 332n2, 339, 340, 537; opposes economic conference, **68**: 278n2; Lord Robert Cecil to visit, **68**: 344; WW's get-well wishes to, **68**: 397; consideration for WW's health shown by orders for Grayson, **68**: 398-99; death and funeral of, **68**: 398n1, 399, 399-40, 401-402; photograph of, *illustration section*, **67**

Harding, William Lloyd, **63**: 65n4

Harding, William Procter Gould, **62**: 159, 169, 201, 222-23, 322; and Federal Reserve Board, **61**: 625; on high cost of living, **62**: 314n2; on agricultural price drop, **66**: 242-43; and farmers' credit request, **66**: 243; and publication of Wilson's letters in his book on Federal Reserve System, **68**: 405,n1

Harding and the Soul of America (*Pittsburgh Post*), **66**: 174

Harding Era: Warren G. Harding and His Administration (Murray), **68**: 97n3, 129n1, 152n1

Hardinge of Penshurst, Charles, 1st Baron, **58**: 227, 312; **60**: 546

Hardly Root (*Boston Post*) **53**: 82,n2

Hardwick, Thomas William, **67**: 457,n4; WW on, **68**: 93,n1

Hardy, Charles Talbot, **61**: 278n7

Hardy, Corinne McCombs, **67**: 304

Hardy, Rufus, **53**: 188,n1

Hare, Miss, **59**: 624

Hare, Constance Parsons (Mrs. Montgomery), **67**: 271n1; **68**: 15,n2

Hargus, Samuel O., **66**: 184,n1

Harington, Sir Charles, **68**: 141n1

Harjes, Frederica Berwind Gilpin (Mrs. Henry Herman), **57**: 503,n1

Harjes, Henry Herman, **57**: 503,n1

Harkins, Miss, **64**: 502-503, 506, 507, 509, 510

Harlakenden (Cornish, N.H.), **66**: 57,n1,2, 71; **68**: 415,n2

Harlan, James Shanklin, **64**: 205,n4

Harlan, John Marshall, **56**: 68

Harlan Fiske Stone: Pillar of the Law (Mason), **68**: 299n1

Harmsworth, Alfred Charles William: *see* Northcliffe, 1st Baron

Harmsworth, Esmond Cecil, **58**: 339,n8; **59**: 561,n5

Harmsworth, Harold Sidney, Viscount Rothermere, **59**: 561n5

Harper, Belle Dunton Westcott (Mrs. George McLean), **67**: 410, 411

Harper, George McLean, on Coughlin kidnapping, **65**: 425, 431, 433; **67**: 51, 182; sends family news to WW, **67**: 410-11, 412

Harper, George McLean, Jr., **67**: 411,n5, 412

Harper, Isabel Westcott, **67**: 411,n4, 412

Harper, Robert Newton, **54**: 555n2

Harper, Samuel, **51**: 259

Harper and Brothers, **53**: 262; **55**: 341n1; **64**: 514n1; **67**: 127n1, 242; proposed German translation of WW's *George Washington*, **62**: 564-65; Creel handles offers from for WW's works, **66**: 64,n1, 65, 81, 163-65, 170; requests article from WW, **68**: 392,n1

Harries, George Herbert, **54**: 515,n1; **59**: 237n2

Harriman, Edward Henry, **68**: 205

Harriman, Florence Jaffray Hurst (Mrs. Jefferson Borden), **68**: 156,n2, 470, 576; and WW Foundation beginings, **67**: 271n1, 327n6

Harrington, Emerson Columbus, **61**: 538,n2

Harris, Alvin, **68**: 102n2

Harris, Charles H. III, **64**: 140n1

Harris, Ernest Lloyd, **53**: 629,n3, 630, 631,n10; **55**: 494; **61**: 466,n1, 494; meets with Kolchak, **59**: 619,n4

Harris, Forbes & Co. of Boston, **65**: 491n1

Harris, Frederick, **54**: 5n2

Harris, Henry Wilson, **54**: 159,n1,3; **58**: 111,n4

Harris, Peter Charles, **53**: 291,n1; **65**: 273n1

Harris, Seale, **64**: 487

Harris, Walter Butler, **67**: 182

Harris, William, Jr., **66**: 112-13,n1,3

Harris, William C., **64**: 522,n1

Harris, William Julius, **54**: 88; **64**: 273; **67**: 522-23; and woman suffrage, **58**: 273,n1, 364n1, 497, 535, 601, 606; **59**: 47, 120,n1; **61**: 538; and Senate resolution on WW's birthday, **68**: 247

Harris, Wilson, **67**: 105n3

Harris & Ewing, **67**: 369n2

Harrison, Benjamin, **54**: 176

Harrison, Byron Patton (Pat), **55**: 297,n4; **62**: 18; **63**: 483; **66**: 258; **68**: 3, 17

Harrison, Constance (Cary) H. (Mrs. Francis Burton), **60**: 201

Harrison, Fairfax, **63**: 607,n2

Harrison, Francis Burton, **55**: 391n1; **60**: 287; **66**: 502; consequences of divorce and remarriage, **59**: 204,n1; **60**: 199, 200-201; **61**: 478,n1; Quezon urges Harrison remain as governor-general, **60**: 198-99, 199-200, 201-202

Harrison, Gilbert A., **55**: 441n1

Harrison, Leland, **53**: 319, 376,n1, 389, 403; **54**: 91, 135; **55**: 192; **57**: 312; **58**:

381; **61**: 66,n2; **64**: 263; **65**: 99; and San
Remo Conference, **65**: 213, 301, 302
Harrison, Mabel Judson Cox (Mrs.
Francis Burton), **59**: 204n1; **60**: 200
Harrison, Pat: *see* Harrison, Byron Pat-
ton
Hart (Bill) William Surrey, **65**: 404,n4,
412
Hart, Louis Folwell, **63**: 241,n1
Hartford Seminary Foundation, **66**:
259n1; **68**: 387
Hartington, Edward William Spencer
Cavendish, Marquess of, **56**: 297,n1
Harts, William Wright, **53**: 397,n6, 461,
592, 596, 606, 607; **54**: 307; **55**: 326; **61**:
3n1
Harvard College, **56**: 54n14; **60**: 118n5
Harvard *Crimson*, **67**: 318
Harvard Graduate School of Business
Administration, **59**: 121n2
Harvard Law School, **53**: 436,n2
Harvard Medical School, **59**: 74n1
Harvard Theological Review, **67**: 527n4
Harvard University, **53**: 12, 29, 350n1,
356n1, 433n1; **54**: 107; **55**: 486n2; **56**:
212n3; **59**: 473n2; **62**: 82n2; **63**: 300n1;
64: 297; **65**: 543; **66**: 359n1, 477; **67**:
189n1, 253n2, 305n1, 458n2, 527n4;
68: 68n3, 362n1, 446; Woodrow Wilson
Club at, **66**: 409, 409-10, 467-69; **67**:
258,n2, 264, 285, 416; delegation from
WW Club meets with WW, **67**: 158-59;
and Wilson & Colby announcement,
67: 344
Harvard University Law School, **68**:
159,n1
Harvey, George Brinton McClellan, **61**:
373; **64**: 515; **67**: 292, 447; **68**: 475,
591,n5; on Hapgood, **64**: 234,n3;
speech on League of Nations and
American war effort sets off protests,
67: 289,n2, 297n2, 394,n2, 554; N. D.
Baker on, **67**: 296-97; Dodd on, **67**: 298;
WW on, **67**: 305; **68**: 136,n2
Harvey, Thomas, **65**: 572,n4
Harvey Cushing: A Biography (Fulton),
65: 403n3
Harvey's Weekly, **61**: 373; **64**: 234n3; **67**:
298
Haskell, William Nafew, **61**: 485-86,n1,
486-87; **62**: 166n1, 578-79,n1; **64**:
13,n1, 450,n3; **65**: 536,n3, 548
Haskins, Charles Homer, **53**: 350,n1,
356, 378; **56**: 200, 509, 560; **57**: 287,
288, 392, 586; **58**: 64, 226-27; **59**: 378,
455; **60**: 64, 72, 295-96; **65**: 530,n1;
543,n2; **67**: 163; on Belgium's restoration, **55**: 83; and Saar Basin, **56**: 420,
424, 431-32, 434, 513, 514; **57**: 54-59,
90-91, 106, 107, 117, 161, 195, 200,
202, 246, 325, 407-15; memorandum
on German counterproposals, **60**: 106-
10, 136; WW answers, **60**: 360; and
Åland Islands Commission, **66**: 212,
229, 230-31, 253; and Woodrow Wilson
Clubs, **66**: 469; **67**: 253, 257-58,n1, 260,

263; defends WW's position at Paris,
67: 24,n2; WW thanks, **67**: 59; photo-
graph of, *illustration section* **57**
Haskins, George Lee, **60**: 296,n2, 360
Hassinger, John H., **68**: 143n2
Hastings, Battle of, **67**: 297; WW on, **67**:
305
Hastings, William Wirt, **56**: 428,n3
Hatch, Harold Ames, **55**: 486,n2; **65**: 234-
35,n5
Hatch, William Henry Paine, **67**: 527n4
Hatchet, The, (ship's magazine), **55**:
224,n1
Hatvan, Hungary, **60**: 257
Haugen, Gilbert Nelson, **62**: 491n1; **63**:
562n2
Haunted Bookshop (Morley), **67**: 476n1
Haute-Savoie, France, **60**: 96,n6
Haven, Joseph Emerson, **53**: 621,n1
Hawaii, **54**: 379; and Pearl Harbor Naval
Base, **62**: 460,n1, 480-81
Hawke *v.* Smith, **65**: 445,n2
Hawker, Harry George, **60**: 44,n5
Hawker, Muriel, **60**: 44n4
Hawkins, John Russell, **63**: 268,n1
Hawkins, William Waller: unpublished
interview with WW, **66**: 153-58,n1
Hay, John, **63**: 315, 330, 331, 332, 412,
437, 439, 460, 471, 496, 507
Hay, John Milton, **66**: 102; on Rumania's
treatment of Jews, **55**: 375
Hay-Pauncefote Treaty, **67**: 220
Hayashi, Gonsuke, **61**: 635,n6
Hayes, Frank J., **53**: 83-84; **57**: 234; sug-
gests peace commissioner from labor,
53: 118-19, 154, 156
Hayes, Patrick Joseph, **61**: 627,n3
Hayes, Ralph A., **68**: 545,n1, 546
Hayes, Rutherford Birchard, **66**: 137
Hayes, Will H. (William Harrison), **54**:
230; **56**: 248; **61**: 66,n1, 605, 628; **62**:
71, 440; **63**: 150, 484;**65**: 292n1; **67**: 387
Hayne, Robert Young, **54**: 63; **55**: 460-62
Haynes, Roy Asa, **68**: 454n2
Haynes, Thornwell, **58**: 404n2
Haynes Powder Company, **64**: 206n1
Hayward, Samuel Jr., **66**: 368
Haywood, William Dudley, **65**: 206
Hazen, Azel Washburn, **65**: 251,n1, 262;
67: 105n3, 108n22
Hazen, Majorie Frances Howe (Mrs. Azel
Washburn), **67**: 105n3
Hazen, Maynard Thompson, **67**: 108,n2
Headlam-Morley, James Wycliffe, **56**:
395,n1, 420, 505, 507, 560; **57**: 586; **58**:
64, 152, 226-27, 286, 383, 384, 385,
386; **59**: 298, 455, 534; **60**: 130,n4,
205,n3, 206, 412, 423, 426; **61**: 27; on
Saar Basin, **57**: 54-59, 106, 107, 163,
164, 195, 200, 246, 325; **59**: 378-79,
381; on Danzig, **57**: 572-74; on rights of
Jews in Poland, **59**: 113, 218, 219, 220,
221; and Austrian peace treaty, **59**:
486; on Austria as new or old state, **59**:
496, 497, 497-98, 498, 499; and Upper
Silesia, **60**: 416,n2

health care: WW on veterans and, **66**: 488-89

Healy, Mary A., **62**: 434

Healy, Timothy, **65**: 359

Hearley, John, **53**: 18,n2, 596-97,n5

Hearst, William Randolph, **53**: 314n4, 580,n2; **55**: 194; **57**: 288n1; **61**: 182,n1, 372; **63**: 167n7; **64**: 123,n1; **67**: 45; **68**: 56-57; Creel on serialization offer of, **67**: 363-64

Hearst newspapers, **53**: 200, 580n1; **54**: 83; **56**: 542; **57**: 63n1, 288; **58**: 338; **60**: 388; **63**: 398; opposition to League of Nations, **61**: 372, 538; and Panama Canal tolls controversy, **66**: 177; makes offer for syndication rights of R. S. Baker's book, **67**: 363-64; WW vetoes offer, **67**: 364-65; Baruch on, **68**: 362

Heath, Ferry K., **59**: 466n6

Heath and Co.: *see* D. C. Heath and Company

Heaton, John L., **68**: 520n1

Heberling, S. E., **64**: 424, 431; **65**: 16, 359

Hebrew language, **55**: 372, 382

Hebrew Union College: and fund-raising tour, **66**: 261, 265-6

Hecaen, Albert M., **64**: 527n3

Hecaen, J., **64**: 527n3

Hedjaz, The, **54**: 264; **56**: 112; **58**: 198, 318,n1, 325; **65**: 271n1; and Paris Peace Conference, **54**: 114; Prince Faisal's claims to, **54**: 505-509

Heflin, James Thomas, **55**: 297,n4; **65**: 491,n1, 522

Heim, Georg, **57**: 290,n1, 291; **59**: 433-34,n4,5

Heinemann (publishers), **68**: 282

Heintzleman, Percival Stewart, **56**: 185,n3

Heiser, Colonel: *see* Hiser, Colonel

Helbich, Wolfgang Johann, **55**: 292n1

Helena, Montana: WW's reception in, **63**: 168-69,n5; WW's address in, **63**: 180-97, 265, 267

Helena, Mont., *Daily Independent*, **63**: 169n5, 197n

Helfferich, Karl Theodor, **56**: 287,n1

Helgoland (Heligoland), **53**: 553; **55**: 23, 425, 429, 434, 539; **56**: 3, 31-33, 267; **57**: 111, 349, 357, 359, 359-63, 366-67, 449; **58**: 236-37; **60**: 66; **61**: 197, 207

Helgoland, S.M.S., **55**: 23, 427; **56**: 28; **58**: 127

Hellenism in Southern Russia and the Ukrainian Campaign: Their Effect on the Pontus Question (1919) (Petsalis-Diomidis), **54**: 403n3

Hello, Paris (play), **59**: 627

Helm, Edith Benham (Mrs. James Meredith): *see* Benham, Edith

Helm, James Meredith, **53**: 319n1; **57**: 502,n1; **59**: 74,n2; **65**: 514n3; **68**: 257,n6, 482

Helmreich, Ernst Christian, **60**: 530n1

Helmreich, Paul C., **66**: 429n1, 430

Helms, Birch, **53**: 367,n1, 385

Helt, D. W., **64**: 425, 431; **65**: 16, 359

Henckel, Count: *see* Donnersmarck, Prince von

Henderlite, James Henry, **64**: 191,n3, 213

Henderson, Arthur, **53**: 8, 519n1, 520; **54**: 190, 257; **58**: 94n1; and labor terms in treaty, **59**: 133, 145

Henderson, Charles Belknap, **62**: 18,n1

Henderson, George Francis Robert, **60**: 301,n4

Henderson, Jeanie North (Mrs. Charles R.), **67**: 135,n1, 143

Henderson, Louisa Patterson (Mrs. Robert Randolph), **67**: 277,n2; **68**: 98-99; WW's condolences to, **67**: 493

Henderson, Philip, **55**: 384n3

Henderson, Robert Randolph, **64**: 518,n1; **65**: 258n2; **67**: 277, 281, 300; death of, **67**: 491; WW on death of, **67**: 493, 493-94

Hendrick, Burton Jesse, **67**: 242,n3,4; **68**: 259n2

Heney, Francis Joseph, **62**: 69; on support for League of Nations, **61**: 538-39

Henkels, Stanislaus Vincent, **67**: 357,n1, 357-58,n1, 358-59, 362

Henneman, John Bell, **60**: 646

Hennessy, Michael Edmund, **62**: 626

Henniker, Alan Major, **60**: 520,n7

Hennocque, Edmond, **60**: 314,n5, 356

Henrey, Thomas Selby, **67**: 341,n1,2

Henriquez y Carvajal, Francisco, **66**: 361,n2, 384, 538, 538-39; **67**: 23n1, 56,n1

Henrotin, Frederick, **59**: 348,n1

Henry Cabot Lodge: A Biography (Garraty), **56**: 161n1; **64**: 328n2

Henry Ford and the Jews (Lee), **66**: 102n1, 130n1

Henry White: Thirty Years of American Diplomacy (Nevins), **53**: 147n1

Henry, Marie-Joseph-Léon-Augustin, **58**: 433,n3, 520; **59**: 12, 322,n3, 324, 326; **61**: 71,n4, 72, 78, 302,n1, 303

Henry, William Frederick Albert, Prince, **53**: 593,n5

Henrys, Paul-Prosper, **56**: 462,n10; **58**: 436,n8; **59**: 541, 542

Hensley Resolution, **53**: 716n1

Heraclea, **59**: 250, 261; **61**: 553; *see also* Aivali (Ayvalik), Turkey

Heraclea Pontica (now Eregli), Turkey, **59**: 91,n5, 101, 102

Herald Publishing Company, **55**: 341n1

Herbert, Mr. (Boston lawyer), **67**: 339

Herbert Croly of the New Republic: The Life and Thought of an American Progressive (Levy), **60**: 202n1

Herford, Oliver, **55**: 244; **63**: 350; **66**: 39

Herman, Israel, **67**: 387, 388, 389

Herms, Mary, **55**: 508n2

Herrera y Luna, Carlos, **66**: 389,n1

Herrick, Myron Timothy, **67**: 35

Herron, George Davis, **53**: 122; **54**: 174,

232, 271, 304, 382; **56**: 473-74; **57**: 569-
70; **58**: 204-205, 414, 426; **59**: 68,n2; on
Geneva as seat of League of Nations,
56: 121-22; on Fiume, **63**: 537,n1
Herschell, Richard Farrer, 2nd Baron
Herschell, **53**: 507,n1, 529
Her Social Value (film), **67**: 530
Hertogenwald Forest, **57**: 393, 394, 395
Hervagault, Ernest-Amélie, **53**: 378,n1;
61: 354,n1
Hervé, Gustave, **58**: 539,n4
Herzegovina, **61**: 54; **64**: 368,n1
Herzl, Theodor, **55**: 384n4,5
Hesse, **59**: 401n4
Hewart, Sir Gordon, **55**: 59,n10, 277,n2;
64: 382
Hewison, James King, **59**: 190,n1,3,4
*H. G. Hawker, Airman: His Life and
Work* (M. Hawker), **60**: 44n4
Hibbard, Elbert, **67**: 105n3
Hibben, Jenny Davidson (Mrs. John
Grier), **64**: 521; **67**: 309,n2, 310, 311
Hibben, John Grier, **64**: 213, 519-21; **65**:
572,n9; **66**: 246n2, 542n1; **67**: 115n1,
309-11; **68**: 462; WW on break with, **60**:
119,n7; sends WW desk from Prince-
ton, **64**: 246-47; to receive salary in-
crease, **64**: 519; and Axson, **67**: 309n1
Hicks, John D., **57**: 146n2, 179n1
Hidalgo, Cutberto, **66**: 405n5
Hidden Illness in the White House (Cris-
pell and Gomez), **62**: 628n1
*Hidden Phase of American History: Ire-
land's Part in America's Struggle for
Liberty* (O'Brien), **60**: 383,n2, 487, 569
High Commission: *see* Inter-Allied
Rhineland High Commission
*Higher Realism of Woodrow Wilson and
Other Essays* (Link), **57**: 511n; **66**:
36n3; **68**: 241n1
Hijo *v.* United States, **56**: 68
Hill, David Jayne, **67**: 406
Hill, Edwin Conger, **65**: 120n2; **62**: 627
Hill, Frank Ernest, **65**: 120n2; **66**: 102n1,
130n1
Hill, James Jerome, **63**: 124n5; **68**: 205
Hill, Louis Warren, **63**: 124,n5
Hills, Laurence, **54**: 60; **57**: 63n1, 65n2,
241n3, 333n2, 417n1; **61**: 243,n6; **62**:
573n1
Hillquit, Morris, **54**: 397n1; **65**: 550
*Hilt of the Sword: The Career of Peyton C.
March* (Coffman), **65**: 576n1
Himmelberg, Robert F., **54**: 521n1
Hindenburg, Paul von, **53**: 63n1; **56**: 411;
57: 550; **60**: 304; and war criminals, **64**:
364n1
Hindenburg, S.M.S., **61**: 124, 145
Hines, John L., **67**: 581
Hines, Walker Downer, **54**: 429; **55**: 90,
277; **58**: 104, 329; **59**: 38, 47, 121; **62**:
94, 98, 117, 118, 158, 162, 163, 201,
286n1, 496, 498, 522; **64**: 141, 197, 198,
246, 457, 475n2; appointed Director
General of Railroads, **53**: 647, 648,
710; on railroad situation, **55**: 227-28,

246-50, 251, 257-58, 260-61, 536-37;
58: 106-10; **59**: 122, 523,n2; **61**: 412-15;
on controversy between Railroad Administration and Industrial Board, **56**:
193-94, 342, 345, 399-402; **57**: 233-34,
58: 120, 280, 281, 282, 283, 347, 376,
376-85, 387, 424, 446, 470, 629; on returning railroads to private control,
56: 620-23; **64**: 183, 184, 188-89, 222,
222n1, 223-25; on coal prices, **54**: 43-
47; **62**: 20-21; on labor problems and
railroad strike, **61**: 536-37; **62**: 133-34,
137, 195n1, 570-71; **64**: 391,n1, 396-97,
406-407, 411-13, 420-24, 426, 427; on
cost of living and railroad workers, **62**:
50-51, 72-77; on plan for railroad wage
board, **62**: 181-82; Cummins on Senate
Interstate Commerce Committee's suggestions for, **62**: 183; WW authorizes
action on wages, **62**: 289-92, 192-93; on
Plumb plan, **62**: 227-28,n1, 229-30,
249; and WW's statement on railroad
situation, **62**: 469, 469-71, 472-76, 484,
487, 586; suggestions for talk to railway shopmen, **62**: 482-84; railroad
leaders meet with, **62**: 485; on railroad
wage adjustment, **62**: 488-89, 492-93;
Tumulty on proposed follow-up message to railway shopmen, **62**: 543-44;
suggestions for Labor Day message,
62: 544-45; and statement on railroad
strike in western states, **62**: 548, 549-
50; on steel prices, **63**: 88-91, 118-19,
300-301; and coal strike, **63**: 595-96,
606; **64**: 3, 166; on draft message on
railroads for WW to present to Congress, **64**: 16, 17-21, 21-24; proclamation relinquishing federal control of
railroads, **64**: 226; on WW's response to
labor since railroad bill's passage, **64**:
467-68; on railroad crisis, **65**: 36, 175-
76, 215, 216-17; on coal situation, **65**:
95-98; Tumulty suggests WW thank,
65: 215; as arbitrator of distribution of
portion of German river fleet, **65**:
271n1, 2; **67**: 93, 151; WW's commendation of on retirement, **65**: 219; protests against appointment of new Director-General of Railroads, **65**: 296
67: 93, 151
Hipwood, Charles, **58**: 423,n1, 424; **61**:
151,n4
Hirsch, Baron Maurice de, **59**: 413,n3
Hirsch, J. B., **57**: 241n3
Hirsch, Paul, **59**: 36,n2
Hirst, Francis Wrigley, **62**: 402n41
Hiser (Heiser), Colonel, **60**: 167,n17,
168
Hispanic American Historical Review,
64: 120n1, 140n1
Histoire de l'Affaire Dreyfus (Reinach),
59: 186n8
Historical Journal **62**: 254n2
*History of Albania, From its Origins to
the Present Day* (Pollo and Puto), **66**:
45n6

History of American Presidential Elections, 1789-1968 (Schlesinger and Israel, eds.), **65**: 386n1, 481n3, 436n2, 482n1, 499n1; **66**: 208,n1

History of the American People (Wilson), **67**: 141; WW rejects offer for revision or condensation of, **55**: 341n1, 484; WW presents set to Albert, **63**: 603; sent to Dr. Dercum, **67**: 492

History of the Balkans (Jelavich), **60**: 530n1

History of the Habsburg Empire, 1526-1918 (Kahn), **57**: 263n6

History of the Ottoman Empire and Modern Turkey (Shaw and Shaw), **58**: 555n1

History of the Peace Conference of Paris (Temperley, ed.), **56**: 380n2; **59**: 61n6, 539n4; **62**: 334n1; **65**: 483n

History of the Sufferings of the Church of Scotland from the Restoration to the Revolution (Wodrow), **59**: 190n3

History of the World War (Simonds), **56**: 436n1

History of United States Naval Aviation (Turnbull and Lord), **57**: 447n1

Hitchcock, Frank Harris, **56**: 248-49,n2; **57**: 331-32, 350

Hitchcock, Gilbert Monell, **54**: 153, 259n3, 519; **56**: 80, 101; **58**: 613; **59**: 149, 313, 529, 578; **61**: 116, 184, 417, 422n3, 548,n1, 597, 607n1, 620; **64**: 103, 104n1, 125, 183, 336, 338; **68**: 17, 470; and League of Nations, **55**: 198, 214, 263, 267, 270, 275, 437; **57**: 424-25, 469; **60**: 571; **62**: 12, 18, 113, 275, 432n3, 615, 621,n1, 632; **63**: 6, 106, 117, 118, 296, 443, 593, 606; **65**: 6,24, 195, 238, 242, 275; and Irish question, **55**: 324-26; on clauses in Covenant subject to Republican attack, **59**: 282,n1,2, 471; and issue of publication of peace treaty and proposed Senate hearings, **59**: 451; **60**: 242-44, 244, 245, 330, 379; WW endorses investigations into peace treaty copies, **60**: 287; press reports rift between WW and, **61**: 468-69; WW denies rift with, **61**: 469-70; meets with WW on treaty, **61**: 545; on Republican opposition to treaty, **62**: 68, 90; and meeting with WW on treaty, **62**: 305-308; questions WW at Foreign Relations Committee meeting, **62**: 339, 340, 358, 362, 374, 383, 404-405; and Foreign Relations Committee's minority report, **63**: 198,n1; and Armenia, **63**: 304n1; and Bullitt's testimony, **63**: 337; on reservations, **63**: 363, 447n1, 482-83, 483, 530-31, 541, 586; predicts defeat of Johnson and Shantung amendments, **63**: 482, 571; on WW's health, **63**: 566,n1; 570-71; meeting with WW during his illness, **63**: 637,n5; on need for concessions and compromise for treaty to be ratified, **64**: 3, 29-30, 58-59, 93-94, 165, 244; Tumulty drafts letter to on danger of reservations, **64**: 15; on Lodge reservations, **64**: 28-30, 37-38, 50, 70; on proposed substitute reservations, **64**: 29-30,n1; on interview with WW on treaty, **64**: 43-45, 45-50, 50, 56; on visiting WW after stroke, **64**: 45n1; draft of letter opposing Lodge resolution of ratification, **64**: 51; Lansing's praise of, **64**: 55, 56; WW answers on Lodge resolution, **64**: 58, 59; holds Democratic caucus, **64**: 62-63, 384; to meet with WW on treaty, **64**: 71; House on treaty strategy involving, **64**: 89, 90, 96; list of Republican senators willing to compromise, **64**: 94; WW's failure to meet with on treaty, **64**: 99, 106; and Mexican situation, **64**: 120, 123, 125, 127; on WW shifting responsibility for treaty's fate to Senate, **64**: 126; meeting with WW and Fall on Mexico, **64**: 129-32, 133-35, 139-40; meets with House on Versailles Treaty, **64**: 182-83; fight for minority leadership, **64**: 192, 194, 273, 274,n1; seeks WW's advice on compromise to avoid split in Democratic party, **64**: 203; WW's advice to on treaty, mistake to propose anything, **64**: 206; Tumulty on WW adopting substitute reservations of, **64**: 238; EBW requests WW's earlier memorandum of reservations from, **64**: 243, 244; approves invitations to first meeting of Council of League of Nations, **64**: 272; proposed letter to on reservations, **64**: 276; on bipartisan meetings on reservations, **64**: 283-84, 311, 312-23,n1; sends copy of Lodge reservations to Tumulty, **64**: 285-88; still hopeful of compromise, **64**: 327-28; WW answers on various articles of treaty, **64**: 329-30; mention of WW deferred letter to, **64**: 365; and Taft reservation, **64**: 387; on treaty situation in Senate and fear more Democrats will support Lodge reservations, **64**: 466; Dr. Park on WW's letter to, **64**: 528; on ratification prospects in Senate, urges WW to see Simmons, **65**: 48; on probable Senate vote on changed Lodge reservation to Article X, **65**: 80; Jusserand on peace treaty position of, **65**: 84n1; on Texas court appointment, **65**: 109; and treaty vote, **65**: 109, 140-41; WW thanks for treaty effort, **65**: 116; on sending treaty back to Senate with interpretive reservations, **65**: 150-51; WW on treaty strategy ideas of, **65**: 152; on proposal for Minister from Canada, **65**: 237, 245; on Tacna-Arica dispute, **65**: 237; and Armenian mandate, **65**: 351n2; WW's letter to of March 8, 1920: *see* Wilson Woodrow on treaty situation, **66**: 547; and Treaty of Berlin, **67**: 399, 421, 422,n4, 424, 617; and plans for Versailles Treaty ratification, **67**: 608-

610,n1, 611; *see also* Hitchcock Resolution
Hitchcock letter, **67**: 466
Hitchcock Resolution, **60**: 198, 244, 249, 287, 288, 290, 299
Hitler, Adolf, **66**: 102n1
Hitz, William, **66**: 94-95,n1
Hoag, Clarence Gilbert, **56**: 283,n1
Hobbes, Thomas, **68**: 446, 447, 448
Hobby, William Pettus, **62**: 527, 536
Hoboken, N.J.: and WW's arrival plans, **61**: 376; WW on, **61**: 401; and piers in, **65**: 270, 281-82; **66**: 425-26, 464-67
Hoboken Manufacturers Railroad, **66**: 464-65, 465
Hocking, William Ernest: and WW Clubs, **67**: 253,n2
Hodder, Frank Heywood, **67**: 68n2
Hodgson, Laurence Curran, **63**: 124,n6, 138,n1, 139
Hoehling, A. A., **56**: 556n2; **58**: 616n20
Hoey, Clyde Roark, **66**: 112n1
Hofer, Andreas, **57**: 97; **58**: 138
Hoffman, Adolf, **59**: 36,n3
Hoffman Brewing Company: *see* Jacob Hoffman Brewing Company
Hog Island, **53**: 371, 405, 406
Hohenlohe-Oehringen, Christian Kraft, Prince zu, Duke of Ujest, **60**: 55n5
Hohenlohe-Schillingfurst and of Ratibor and Corvey, Chlodwig Karl Vikton, Prince of, **56**: 361,n3
Hohenzollerns, The: WW on, **63**: 358
Hohler, Albert E., **57**: 425,n2
Holcomb, Marcus Hensey, **65**: 164,n1
Holden, Hale, **65**: 562
Holding Back Peace (New York *World*), **62**: 180,n1
Hole, Ginnie, **66**: 45n6
Holland: *see* Netherlands, The
Hollis, Henry French, **53**: 45; on surplus arms, **57**: 495-96
Hollister, William R., **53**: 24; **54**: 61,n2
Holmes, Lydia Wicliffe, **65**: 294
Holmes, Oliver Wendell, Jr., **67**: 563n2; **68**: 130, 277n1; and Schenck case, **55**: 347n1; and Debs case, **67**: 99-100; and Duplex case, **67**: 497n2; and Truax case, **67**: 497n1
Holmes, Oliver Wendell, Sr., **63**: 252
Holmes, Ralston, **66**: 30n1, 58
Holt, Hamilton, **54**: 277, 278; **62**: 347,n11; **65**: 183,n3, 234-35,n5, 507-508, 513; **66**: 434n1, 503, 542n1; **67**: 318,n1, 367, 426n1, 616; **68**: 49, 198; requests article from WW, **65**: 218,n1; on having WW and Taft as contributors to *The Independent*, **65**: 504-505; meets with WW as pro-League Republican, **66**: 274, 275-76; praises WW, **67**: 187,n1, WW acknowledges praise of, **67**: 197; on editorial on Foch, **67**: 267; WW declines to comment on Foch, **67**: 270-71; and WW Foundation, **67**: 271n1, 327n6, 333, 346, 393n1, 416, 456, 522, 547, 549; on unknown soldier

and WW, **67**: 450, 451; greetings on fifth anniversary of entrance into war, **67**: 603-604, 604; and WW Democracy, **68**: 44,n1, 44; and controversy with Hughes over League of Nations, **68**: 99,n1; to see WW on idea of League of Nations movement, **68**: 155, 156, 157, 158, 162; on continued interest in independent League of Nations movement, **68**: 159, 171, 172-74, 177-78,n1, 190, 192, 251; WW's advice to on independent League of Nations organization, **68**: 163, 164; visits WW on his birthday with WW Foundation delegation, **68**: 248, 250; on origination of WW Foundation, **68**: 262, 264; on WW Foundation's trustee installation, **68**: 284-85, 285, 288, 365; photograph of, *illustration section*, **68**
Holt, Thomas Michael, **66**: 222,n1
Holt, Winifred, **53**: 501,n2; **58**: 449-50,n4
Holy Alliance, **54**: 314
Holywood, Ireland, **61**: 512n2
Home Rule and Conscription (Plunkett), **55**: 455,n3
Homes and 'A Few Well-Placed Fruit Trees': an Object Lesson in Federal Housing (Lubove) **55**: 341n1; **56**: 246n2
Homs, Syria, **56**: 110, 111, 112
Honan Province, China, **66**: 327,n1
Honduras, **54**: 24,n14; **56**: 270n5; **58**: 198; and representation at Paris Peace Conference, **54**: 65, 115; political situation in, **61**: 638-40; and appointments, **64**: 317; resignation of and appointment suggestions for Minister to, **65**: 260-61, 316-17, 357-58, 361
Honolulu, Prince of Wales on, **65**: 226
Honolulu Consolidated Oil Company, **62**: 46-49; **64**: 405n1
Honolulu Oil case, **64**: 392,n1, 405
Hood, Edwin Milton, **55**: 160n1; **63**: 547,n5
Hood, Ellen Gowen, **68**: 182,n2
Hooker, Richard, **53**: 243-44; **62**: 461; **64**: 64n1; **65**: 77: and second Industrial Conference, **63**: 611
Hooper, Thomas Williamson, Jr., **61**: 595,n3
Hoose, Rose Gouverneur, **67**: 213
Hoover, Herbert Clark, **53**: 8, 50, 52, 53n1, 65, 222, 473, 480, 572 573, 645, 693; **54**: 35, 37, 305, 386, 467; **55**: 148, 185, 279; **56**: 306, 381, 520, 543, 620; **57**: 53, 137, 144, 346, 347,n1, 390, 406, 627; **58**: 8, 9, 20, 28, 565, 566; **61**: 33-34, 45, 111-15, 128, 177-79, 252, 259-60, 561-62; **64**: 64n1, 235; **66**: 141n2, 246n2, 282n1; **68**: 346n2, 565, 580; on European relief, **53**: 14-15, 15-16, 26, 56, 57, 59-60, 75-76, 76-77, 223-25,n2, 226, 272, 273, 326, 360-64, 372, 392-93, 395, 482, 585, 648-49, 649-50; **54**: 29-31, 558; **59**: 175, 227, 383, 448; **60**: 80, 356, 432; **61**: 3n1, 87, 110, 335, 487, 499, 614, 646; **62**: 63, 123-24, 248; **63**:

Hoover, Herbert Clark (*cont.*)
44, 389-90, 606; on need for appropriations for food, **53**: 273, 309, 707; on
brewing industry, **53**: 443-44, 450; **54**:
58-59, 216, 262; on Grain Corporation
extending activities, **53**: 476-77; talk of
as presidential candidate, **53**: 449; **54**:
61; **57**: 503n2; **58**: 172; on Bolshevism,
53: 453-54; **56**: 375-78; **57**: 565; Lord
Derby on, **53**: 525-26; on wheat guarantees, **53**: 603, 604; on surplus caused
by withdrawal of Allied food orders, **53**:
687-88; appointed Director General of
Relief, **53**: 714-15; and famine relief
bill, **54**: 174n3, 229-30, 303; on establishment of Relief Administration, **54**:
276-77; against Allies administering
U.S. relief funds or supplies, **54**: 277;
on relaxing economic controls on
enemy, **54**: 477-79; on U.S. supplying
Russian prisoners with food, **54**: 515,
549; on Belgium, **55**: 86-87, 151; **58**:
411-12; on food prices and controls, **55**:
90, 91, 251-53, 308, 359, 360, 361, 396;
and food relief, **55**: 90, 116-17, 117; **56**:
469-70; **57**: 367-68, 368-69, 391, 398;
and food for Germany, **55**: 458n1; **56**:
574-75; on meatpackers, **56**: 84, 101;
and wheat crop, **56**: 102, 281-82, 372;
on tonnage needed for food relief, **56**:
179, 180, 190, 337, 339, 374; on need
for clothing and the powers of the Liquidation Board, **56**: 193, 234; talks of
his resignation, **56**: 281; on termination of Food Administration but continuation of Grain Corporation, **56**:
281-82, 426, 470-71, 485; his work
praised, **56**: 427,n1; on sharing shipping burden to aid Russian food relief,
57: 161; on Nansen's relief proposal
and Bolshevik reply to, **57**: 166-67; **58**:
41; **59**: 192, 197, 226, 300n8; on U.S.
not continuing membership on various
commissions, **57**: 271-74, 370; and
Russian relief, **57**: 440, 512; denuncia-
tion of "Communist" Russia, **57**:
503n2, 503-504,n2, 505-508, 509, 529;
on political situation in Germany, **57**:
565-67; and relief for Austria, **58**: 149,
242; on recognition of Finland, **58**: 177;
requests that wives of reliief workers
be allowed to come to Europe, **58**: 136;
on food crisis and Shipping Board's
lack of cooperation, **58**: 200, 202-203;
and Rumanian credit, **58**: 591; on situation in Baltic states, **58**: 594-95; on
WW's health, **58**: 622, 634,n16; on food
relief, not blockade, for Germany, **59**:
173, 191-92; on food credits, **59**: 174-
75; on coal reduction and Teschen, **59**:
218; on relief to Baltic states, **59**: 303-
304, 312, 346-47, 347, 466n6, 467n7;
on blockade if fighting continues in Poland, **59**: 323, 325; on dissatisfaction
with peace treaty, **59**: 384, 447, 448;
on WW discussing Germany's reply to
peace terms with American commis-

sioners, **59**: 547; on gold from Germany's food payment, **59**: 639; on forming committee to address Jewish problem in Poland, **60**: 39; on German
counterproposals, **60**: 65, 66, 69, 70;
WW answers on Jews and Poland, **60**:
99; on modifying treaty so Germany
will sign, **60**: 136-37, 194-96; on children's relief program, **60**: 230-32; on
appropriations for Food Administration, **60**: 328, 359; meets with WW, **60**:
491, 493-94; on stopping hostilities in
Riga, **60**: 532; calls order to have ships
leave Germany an "absolute positive
blockade," **60**: 606, 614, 615, 626; WW
on Belgium and, **61**: 24; on establishing economic commission in Russia,
61: 61-63; to remain as Food Administrator, **61**: 133; on postwar reconstruction, **61**: 173-74, 284-86; and Armenia,
61: 314; on economic situation of Europe, **61**: 389-95; on proposed International Economic Council, **61**: 520-22;
62: 331; and economic commissions,
61: 586; resignation as Food Administrator, **62**: 125; request for U.S. military personnel for relief missions, **62**:
166, 240, 249, 303-304; Leffingwell on
financial projections of, **63**: 267-68; and
International Labor Conference, **63**:
602; and second Industrial Conference,
63: 611; mentioned as presidential
candidate, **64**: 325; calls on House, **65**:
139; WW on presidential possibilities
of, **65**: 149; Geddes on, **65**: 372; WW on,
65: 444; on European Children's Relief
Fund, **65**: 468-70; and *Washington
Herald*, **66**: 169; and relief funds, **66**:
493,n1, 509, 510; **67**: 85, 87, 88, 96,
97n1; WW on, **66**: 497; **67**: 94; **68**: 305;
and railroad situation, **68**: 129n1; on
League of Nations, **68**: 160; and prohibition, **68**: 305
Hoover, Irwin Hood (Ike), **53**: 166, 204,
319, 344, 423,n2; **56**: 183; **57**: 468,n1;
58: 103, 622,n56, 632,n10; **61**: 112n1;
63: 642; **64**: 180n1; **65**: 291, 405,
511n2; **66**: 15-16, 189; **67**: 208; **68**: 576;
on WW's health, **58**: 636; **60**: 250, 251;
63: 539n1, 632-38; on WW's obsessions
after illness in Paris, **61**: 112n1; compares WW to other presidents, **67**: 150;
WW praises, **67**: 276; photograph of, *illustration section*, **55**
Hoover, (John) Edgar, **65**: 187n5
Hoover, Lou Henry (Mrs. Herbert Clark),
68: 580
Hope, Anthony, **67**: 105n3
Hope, George Price Webley, **53**: 560,n3;
55: 53-54; **57**: 360, 361; **58**: 63,n7, 123,
124, 456,n2, 579; **59**: 28, 168,n2,
347,n2; **60**: 269, 497; **61**: 151; and
naval terms and sinking of ships, **58**:
125-27; on destruction of submarines,
58: 127, 128; and dispatch of Greek
troops to Turkey, **58**: 511,n2, 513, 514;
on naval action to be taken if peace

treaty not signed, **58**: 581-84; on sinking of German fleet at Scapa flow, **61**: 83, 86, 124

Hope, Walter Ewing, **65**: 574,n22, 575

Hopes of World Still Unfulfilled (Sullivan), **68**: 222-23,n2

Hopkins, Ernest Martin, **66**: 246n2; and WW Foundation, **68**: 249n2, 365,n2

Hopkins, Richard Joseph, **68**: 148n5

Hoppin, Eleanor D. Wood (Mrs. Joseph Clark), **68**: 414,n2

Horace, **61**: 361n1; **67**: 498,n2

Horbac, Oleska, **54**: 480n1

Hornbeck, Stanley Kuhl, **53**: 350,n1; **58**: 214,n1, 229, 327; **60**: 429, 604,n3; on Shantung settlement, **60**: 102-104, 602; WW answers on Shantung decision, **60**: 358, 483; on China's wish to sign treaty with reservations, **61**: 175-76

Horodyski, Jan Marie, **54**: 32,n2

Horta, The Azores, **57**: 447n1

Horton, George, **54**: 380,n2

Horvat (Horvath) Dmitrii Leonidovich, **53**: 168, 557; **57**: 575n1; **59**: 619,n2; **60**: 625,n7, 637; **61**: 572n6, 637,n1; **62**: 84-85, 86, 88

Hospice de Saint Jean de Caen, **56**: 125n1

Hotchkiss, Alice Stark, **68**: 464-65,n1

Hough, Theodore, M.D., **67**: 299n1

House, Edward Mandell, **53**: 8, 25-26, 44-45, 66, 69, 85, 100, 108, 127, 128, 130, 154, 193, 213, 240, 241, 336, 359, 384, 389-91, 392, 408, 411, 434, 458, 466, 468, 497, 498, 525-26, 564, 573, 586-88, 588, 611, 628, 646, 687, 693-96, 709; **54**: 3, 32-33, 127, 153, 196, 264, 271, 304, 386-87, 404, 439, 469, 473, 480, 556; **55**: 3, 41, 67, 87, 107, 118, 152, 154, 160, 178, 192, 193-96, 212-13, 256-57, 299, 326, 387, 455, 487-88, 514, 529, 538-39, 545; **56**: 4-6, 56, 58, 60, 62, 63, 75, 80, 99, 101, 120, 122-24, 128, 179-80, 201, 206-208, 271,n2, 272, 279-80, 335-37, 349-51, 351n1, 379,n2, 437, 443, 466n1, 483, 502, 515, 530n4, 539-40, 551n1, 585-88; **57**: 4, 51, 52, 75, 90-91, 136n2, 139-40, 142,n1, 178-79, 179, 179-80, 270, 285-86, 295, 334-35, 352-55, 390, 390-91, 434, 466-67, 499, 517n4, 535, 574; **58**: 103, 137-38, 153, 169, 185-87, 270, 320, 379-80, 382, 444, 445, 482, 493, 552, 624,n63; **59**: 34, 46-47, 70, 70, 118, 159, 185, 200-202, 238, 239, 282, 285,n2, 317-19, 395, 475, 478, 485, 513, 554-55, 560, 578, 603-604, 623-24, 644-45; **60**: 17,n1, 40, 69, 71, 77, 81-82, 144, 197, 205, 260-61, 277, 292, 303, 307, 432, 608; **61**: 33-34, 45, 111-15, 128, 177-79, 252, 259-60, 561-62; **62**: 202, 242, 264, 403, 531, 625-26; **64**: 53, 182-83, 444-45; **65**: 40-41, 139-41; **66**: 292, 298; **67**: 77, 239; **68**: 222, 452n2, 591; on plans for peace conference and WW's decision to attend, **53**: 3-5, 25, 44, 71-72, 84-85, 96-97, 101, 128, 130, 142-43, 159-60, 181-82, 189-90, 190, 196, 226, 243, 400-402, 409; on armistice, **53**: 25, 26, 33, 34; on Italy's territorial demands and use of U.S. troops, **53**: 43,n1, 123-24, 167, 290-91; plans for securing political intelligence and counter-espionage organization at peace conference, **53**: 56-58; on keeping in touch with liberals in France, **53**: 123; on France lifting U.S. press censorship, **53**: 180; on Prince Murat's residence, **53**: 180-81; **55**: 193, 223, 230-31; **57**: 100; **60**: 46, 50, 53; on reparations, **53**: 181; **56**: 499n3; **57**: 7, 8, 14, 15, 16, 17, 18, 18-19, 23, 23-24, 25, 26, 34, 71, 81, 82-83, 204; and Allied conferences in London, **53**: 197, 222, 251, 324-27, 336, 341; on best sailing route for WW, **53**: 221; on European relief plans, **53**: 222-25, 225-26, 271,n1, 272-73, 585; on starting inter-Allied conference, **53**: 316, 334; on WW's plans while in Paris, **53**: 344-45, 372, 381; Wiseman meets with, **53**: 394-96; on meeting with Northcliffe and other activities in Paris, **53**: 417-19; on newspapers and publicity arrangements, **53**: 437-39; on WW's meeting with Clemenceau, **53**: 448-49; Derby on, **53**: 472; WW's visit to London, **53**: 472, 507, 633-34; on sending a financial representative to Paris, **53**: 473-74; advice to WW, **53**: 507; **55**: 221; meets with Balfour, **53**: 576-77; meets with Clemenceau, **53**: 652-54; **57**: 335; **60**: 296-97; and Russia and peace negotiations, **53**: 722-23; advises WW on opening session of Paris Peace Conference, **54**: 128; on League of Nations Covenant and Commission, **54**: 150, 188, 196, 218, 228n1, 386-87, 407-408, 408, 459-60, 461, 463, 484-85, 494-95,n2; **55**: 137, 140, 155-56; **56**: 78, 82-83, 170n1, 298, 303, 335; **57**: 236-37; **58**: 443-44, 445; recommends recognizing Poland, **54**: 178-79; on points for WW's speech on League of Nations, **54**: 262-64; on neutrals and League of Nations, **54**: 302; on Hughes and claims to Pacific islands, **54**: 333; on mandates, **54**: 333-34; **61**: 107, 270, 283, 363-64, 408-409, 451-55, 477, 506; **62**: 187-89, 243-47, 425-26, 481, 511-12, 513, 514, 532, 579; on Smuts draft on colonial question, **54**: 347,n2; on prejudice, **54**: 485; on meeting with T. H. Bliss on Armistice terms, **54**: 499-500; Cecil on, **54**: 514; on rumor that peace conference might relocate, **55**: 88-89; meets with WW on peace terms and instructions, **55**: 193; on being first to use word "covenant," **55**: 194; on Plenary Session, **55**: 195-96; on Red Cross, **55**: 201, 202; on Churchill's Russian initiative, **55**: 203-204, 229-30; on war costs, **55**: 210-

House, Edward Mandell (*cont.*)
11; activities in Paris during WW's absence, **55**: 212-14, 233-34, 245-46, 283-84, 423; on Lloyd George's views on Russian situation, **55**: 233; on starting functioning of League of Nations Covenant and separating from peace treaty, **55**: 304-305,n1; on Italian-Yugoslav situation, **55**: 305; on Belgian loan request, **55**: 305-306; and invitation to Moton, **55**: 335, 341; on WW coming directly to Paris to meet with Lloyd George, **55**: 349; on success of Federal Reserve Act as propaganda for League of Nations, **55**: 367-68; WW's concern over House's plan to start functioning of League of Nations, **55**: 392; on meeting with Lloyd George and Clemenceau, **55**: 458-59; and Rhineland, **55**: 472, 475n1,2; consents to separating League of Nations from peace treaty against WW's wishes, **55**: 488,n2, 529; break between WW and, **55**: 488,n2; **67**: 130; and WW's arrival and meetings, **55**: 499-500; on WW wanting League of Nations as part of peace treaty, **55**: 499; meets with WW and Lord Robert Cecil on League of Nations, **55**: 538, 539; rumors of break between WW and, **56**: 86; presents resolution on future German attacks to Clemenceau, **56**: 126,n1; meets with Bullitt on Russia, **56**: 279-80; on a Russian settlement, **56**: 309; suggestions for mideastern commission, **56**: 310; R. S. Baker on, **56**: 338, 425, 578; **57**: 68-69, 508, 527-28; on Saar Valley negotiations, **56**: 424; on being discouraged, **56**: 441; on "Big Four," **56**: 517-18; on meetings with Benson and Tardieu, **56**: 558-60; substitutes for ill WW at Council of Four meetings, **56**: 556n2, 584, 585-87, 588, 594, 598; on meetings with WW, **57**: 52-53, 72; belittles WW's order summoning *U.S.S. George Washington*, **57**: 65,n2; as "great American Acquiescer," **57**: 65-66, 235, 508, 527; and Clemenceau, **57**: 66; and Italian claims, **57**: 90, 527, 534, 562, 564-65; on inviting Germany to peace conference, **57**: 103, 104, 105; Mrs. Lansing on Lansing and, **57**: 141; on Anglo-American negotiations on naval program, **57**: 178, 179-80, 215, 216-17; on Monroe Doctrine amendment, **57**: 215, 218n1; French press and, **57**: 235, 236; on Hoover's Russian statement, **57**: 503-504,n2, 529; growing rift between WW and, **57**: 508, 527-28, 532,n2; on labor claims for peace treaty, **57**: 528; and Steed, **57**: 532,n2; Japan's racial equality amendment, **57**: 570-71; on WW's Adriatic statement, **58**: 48, 55, 104; suggests Wiseman for Distinguished Service Medal, **58**: 138; on Japan's claims, **58**: 185, 186-87, 228-29, 327; on Austria presenting her position in Paris, **58**: 205; on Italian crisis, **58**: 379-80; on meeting with Msr. Kelley, **58**: 380; on Plenary Session at Versailles, **58**: 520-21; on Irish Americans in Paris on Home Rule issue, **58**: 585, 588; on WW's character, **58**: 628; **61**: 107-108; on WW antagonizing Republicans in Congress, **59**: 34-35; on Adriatic question, **59**: 68, 83, 126, 127, 174, 200-201, 248, 249, 556; suggests himself as member of Council of League of Nations, **59**: 70; and Irish-American delegates' passport controversy and issue of Ireland's representation at Paris, **59**: 104, 105, 173, 366-67,n1,2, 368, 449, 476; has hope of settling Adriatic question, **59**: 126, 127; on blockade of Germany, **59**: 201-202, 318; on Italy, **59**: 244; on amnesty for political prisoners, **59**: 320; and talk of not signing peace treaty, **59**: 383; and Turkey and mandate issue, **59**: 397; McCormick on jealousy of, **59**: 448; on discussing Germany's reply to peace terms under WW's guidance, **59**: 546, 546-47; on reconvening peace conference in Washington, **59**: 603; on WW's speech at Suresnes Cemetery, **59**: 610, 624; on relationship with WW, **59**: 624; on WW not publicizing peace treaty, **59**: 644-45; on issue of Germany's membership in League of Nations, **60**: 77-78; on reasons for not going to St. Germain for presentation of Austrian treaty, **60**: 81-82; memorandum to Clemenceau on reply to Lloyd George, **60**: 82-83; Grayson on suggestions for attorney general from, **60**: 115-16; suggestions for Page's replacement in Italy, **60**: 192; on WW's appearance and personality, **60**: 373; on Senate request to have Irish delegates heard at peace conference, **60**: 375; on suggestions for lawyer for International Court of Justice, **60**: 431, 432; draft reply to German counterproposal on League of Nations, **60**: 439; urges WW to visit Belgium, **60**: 485; evidence of loss of influence with WW, **60**: 492; **61**: 134; on Lansing, **61**: 34, 112; on treaty being ratified with League of Nations Covenant, **61**: 46; on WW's statement on treaty for London *Daily Mail*, **61**: 107-108; on WW and Poincaré dinner invitation episode, **61**: 112-14, 115, 180; on Shotwell, **61**: 131-32; suggests Dresel as U.S. representative in Germany, **61**: 286; at Versailles signing ceremony, **61**: 324; on treaty-signing ceremony and WW's departure for U.S., **61**: 332-33; urges WW meet Senate with conciliatory spirit, **61**: 354-55; on leaving Paris for London, **61**: 477; WW on mandates, **61**: 520; **62**: 235, 256, 257, 316-17; on relations be-

tween Great Britain and the U.S., **62**: 60-63; on Grey's mission to U.S. and League of Nations, **62**: 254-55; requests forecast of treaty ratification, **62**: 323; on Supreme Economic Council's wish to meet in Washington, **62**: 333-34; on appointments of Americans to commissions for Danzig and Saar Valley, **62**: 451; issue of treaty ratification, **62**: 452; Bowman on, **62**: 453, 454-55; on news of "falling out" with WW, **62**: 525,n1, 573-74,n1, 576, 633; urged to remain in Paris until treaty ratified, **62**: 553-54; on WW's speaking tour, **62**: 580-81; to return to Paris from London, **62**: 607, 626; on Lord Grey, **62**: 625; and League of Nations and treaty ratification, **63**: 59; **64**: 88-90, 95-96; on Clemenceau's growing enthusiasm for League of Nations, **63**: 271-72; on adjourning Council of Heads of Delegations and returning to U.S., **63**: 299-300, 537; and Bullitt testimony, **63**: 337n1; on five remaining principal problems, **63**: 421-22; get-well wishes to WW, **63**: 536; **64**: 53-54; ill upon arrival from Paris, **63**: 563n1, 580-81,n2; on WW's health, **63**: 563,n1, 585-86; friction with EBW, **63**: 587-88, 592-93, 621; R. S. Baker on, **63**: 621; **64**: 61-62; **67**: 129-30, 290-94; WW on, **63**: 627; Lansing on, **64**: 57, 193; EBW relays WW's concern over ill health of, **64**: 61; on appointment of Palmer to Cabinet, **64**: 184-85; meets with Gregory and Tyrrell, **64**: 217; on Lansing's concern over WW's inability to perform his duties, **64**: 231; on WW's treatment of Lord Grey, **64**: 239, 360; on strained relations between Lansing and WW, **64**: 347; on visits from Palmer and Gregory, **64**: 347-48; on Grey's letter and friendship, **64**: 360-61; on Lansing resignation, **64**: 444; and Frazier, **64**: 451; and Lansing, **65**: 21; returns unused funds to WW, **65**: 75; on WW not meeting with Cabinet, **65**: 79-80; on Hitchcock letter, **65**: 80; WW thanks, **65**: 80; WW on his "going wrong," **65**: 180; on treaty situation, **65**: 274-75; praises WW **65**: 379; WW sends wishes for good trip abroad, **65**: 383; on situation in Washington and WW's ability to serve, **65**: 384; WW on, **65**: 444; on Lloyd George and Allied debts, **65**: 480-81; EBW returns clothes and receives thank-you from, **66**: 379-80, 382; and lecture series at Philadelphia Academy of Music, **66**: 382n1; **67**: 24n2, 57, 72; and WW Foundation, **67**: 271n1, 327n6; **68**: 249n2; EBW decodes personal message of, **67**: 293-94; finds WW unavailable when pays call, **67**: 419; Hankey on, **67**: 462n2; and U.S. as associate member of League of Nations, **68**: 181-82; McCormick on trying to

reconcile WW and, **68**: 528-29, 529-30; photograph of, *illustration section*, **53**: 57

House, Loulie Hunter (Mrs. Edward Mandell), **53**: 468, 586; **56**: 62, 81, 86; **59**: 602; **62**: 202; **63**: 580-81, 592; **64**: 61; **65**: 80; Benham on, **61**: 189; **66**: 380, 382

House of Representatives (U.S.): *see* United States Congress

housing, **55**: 341-42; **56**: 245-46

Houston, David Franklin, **53**: 11, 65, 587, 603, 604; **54**: 391; **55**: 219, 360; **56**: 102, 471, 620; **62**: 197,n1, 233; **63**: 555, 601n1; **64**: 133n2, 141, 193, 269; **65**: 24, 325,n1, 380, 382; **66**: 54, 82, 159, 307n1, 510; **67**: 70, 71, 109, 144, 540, 571, 611; **68**: 576; on pork prices, **55**: 343, 395-96, 483; WW on personality of, **55**: 482; on continuation of Grain Corporation, **56**: 426, 485; effects of uncertainty of treaty ratification, **62**: 268-70; on farmers and cost of living, **62**: 300; and International Labor Conference, **63**: 602; and coal situation, **64**: 154n1, 154-55, 166; and railroad situation, **64**: 184, 480; on revised draft of Jackson Day message, **64**: 249n1, 250-52; Crane on, **64**: 262; and draft letter from Tumulty to Hitchcock on reservations, **64**: 278n1, 282-83; resigns as Secretary of Agriculture to become Secretary of Treasury, **64**: 330,n1, 349; Leffingwell willing to assist, **64**: 363, 361-62; and Cabinet meetings during WW's illness, **64**: 457; on general cancellation of inter-Allied debts, **64**: 475; visits House and gives opinion of various appointments by WW, **65**: 40-41; recommends Boyden for Reparation Commission, **65**: 92, 92-93; on WW's first Cabinet meeting since illness, **65**: 186n1; on having U.S. delegate at International Financial Conference of League of Nations, **65**: 238-42, 245; draft message for WW, vetoing legislative, executive, and judicial appropriations bill, **65**: 264-69; and aid to Europe, **65**: 298; and legislation for new budget and auditing system, **65**: 358, 361, 362; Geddes on, **65**: 370; on British debt, **66**: 25-26; on not resuming assistance for exports by War Finance Corporation, **66**: 60-62; on exports to Europe, **66**: 100-101; on farm prices, **66**: 445; suggestions for WW's State of the Union Message, **66**: 453-56; on not using Sugar Equalization Board's profits for relief, **66**: 529-30; and War Finance Corporation, **67**: 17, 18n1, 25,n3; on British debt, **67**: 91; and veto of Emergency Tariff bill, **67**: 159n2, 191-94,n1; on last Cabinet meeting and farewell to WW, **67**: 176n1, 199; praises WW, **67**: 199-200; WW thanks, **67**: 233; statement for The Document,

House, Edward Mandell (*cont.*)
  67: 476-77, 484-87, 499-501, 515-16,
  567; as WW's presidential choice, **67**:
  606; and The Document, **68**: 26n1, 32,
  42, 43, 49, 534; **68**: 172, 178-79, 182,
  237, 242, 244-45; to write article for
  candidates on Democratic policies and
  Republican ineptitude, **68**: 32, 51, 53,
  56; on international banking and currency problems, **68**: 62-63; WW thanks
  for work on The Document, **68**: 71-72,
  260; on accomplishments and goals of
  Democratic party and failure of Republicans, **68**: 244,n1, 269-73; mentioned
  as presidential candidate, **68**: 476n3;
  photograph of, *illustration section*, **67**
Houston, Harry R., **62**: 462,n1
Houston, Helen Beall (Mrs. David Franklin), **67**: 477, 485, 571; **68**: 42,n2, 43,
  72, 245, 260
Houston, Herbert Sherman, **55**: 290,n1;
  68: 159,n3, 249n2, 336, 495; beginnings of WW Foundation, **67**: 271n1;
  on his new career plans, **67**: 414, 433-
  34; WW encourages plans of, **67**: 424-
  25, 440-41; WW on *Our World*, **67**: 574;
  68: 334; on *Our World's* promotion of
  League of Nations, **68**: 330-31; and
  WW's essay, **68**: 345, 353; on WW
  Foundation's trustee installation, **68**:
  35-56; requests WW solicit friends for
  money and WW's response, **68**: 355, 357
Houston, Sid, **67**: 278,n1, 279
Houthulst Forest, Belgium, **61**: 4; photograph of, *illustration section*, **61**
Hovannisian, Richard G., **54**: 517n2; **56**:
  443n2; **58**: 111n2; **62**: 27n1; **63**: 304n1;
  64: 450n4; **66**: 29n1
Hovelaque, Mme. (Mrs. Emile-Lucien),
  53: 459,n5
Hovelaque, Emile-Lucien, **53**: 459,n6
Howard, Clarence Henry, **67**: 520,n2
Howard, Sir Esme William, **56**: 49n10;
  59: 219, 323, 325, 466,n4
Howard, Harry Nicholas, **56**: 272n2; **57**:
  313n2; **59**: 373n1; **62**: 607n1; **64**: 425n2
Howard, James Raley, **62**: 300n1; **67**:
  80,n1
Howard, Roy Wilson, **66**: 154,n2
Howard University, **62**: 530n1
Howe, Annie Josephine Wilson (Mrs.
  George Jr.), sister of WW, **64**: 485, 486
Howe, Frederic Clemson, **54**: 397n1; **66**:
  542n1
Howe, Russell Warren, **61**: 406n1
Howells, Mildred, **65**: 276
Howells, William Dean, WW on death of,
  65: 276,n1
Howenstine, E. Jay, Jr., **54**: 521n1
Howland, Charles P., **67**: 271n1
Howland, Jane, **68**: 419,n2
Howland, Leslie Mosby Wallace (Mrs.
  Samuel Shaw), **57**: 429,n17
Howland, Priscilla, **68**: 419,n2
Howland, Samuel Shaw, **57**: 429,n17
Howland, William Bailey, **65**: 218n1

Hsu Shih-ch'ang, **54**: 78,n1, 194, 331,
  474n2, 475,n5; **59**: 573,n2; **60**: 429n2;
  62: 458; **66**: 79n2
Hubbard, Preston J., **68**: 448n1
Huber, Ernst Rudolf, **53**: 121n2
Huber, Max, **58**: 382,n5
Huddleston, Sisley, **57**: 6n7
Hudgins, John Melton, **68**: 291,n1
Hudgins, T. T., **55**: 444,n8
Hudson, Manley Ottmer, **56**: 75n2; **58**:
  445,n3; **60**: 206, 467, 478, 572; **61**: 87,
  88, 89; **64**: 275; **68**: 159,n1, 495; and
  commission to investigate pogroms in
  Poland, **60**: 358,n2, 567, 601; and Pol-
  ish treaty, **60**: 607; **61**: 26-27; on U.S.
  not now being part of additional trea-
  ties with new states, **60**: 607-608
Hudson, Thomas, **53**: 540,n5
Huerta, Adolfo de la, **65**: 252n1, 446,n1;
  462-64; **66**: 17, 133n2, 160,n1, 161,
  283n1, 285, 335, 372, 373, 374; Creel
  on commitments made by, **66**: 270,n1,
  403, 404,n4, 405; on WW, **66**: 270n1
Huerta, Fernando de la, **66**: 163
Huerta, Victoriano, **66**: 339n4; **67**: 219
Hughes, Antoinette Carter (Mrs. Charles
  Evans), **68**: 580
Hughes, Charles Evans, **53**: 35, 70, 135,
  580n2; **55**: 65; **56**: 192, 244; **59**: 419,n1;
  60: 155, 358n2; **61**: 486,n1; **62**: 275,
  385; **63**: 223n1; **65**: 298; **67**: 46, 360n3,
  394, 402,n1, 444, 464, 466, 511, 552;
  68: 346n2, 530, 580, 593; on calling
  extra session of Congress, **56**: 84-85; on
  amendments to League of Nations
  Covenant, **56**: 339; reservations concerning League of Nations, **62**: 537-42;
  WW on, **67**: 71, 268; WW sends copy of
  Versailles Treaty to, **67**: 351-52; and
  Panama-Costa Rica border dispute,
  67: 382n5, 384; and open door resolution, **67**: 531,n1, 541; and League of
  Nations, **68**: 99,n1, 160; and railroad
  situation, **68**: 129n1; and reparations,
  68: 261, 262-63; and Permanent Court
  of International Justice, **68**: 306,n2,3;
  and Turkish treaty, **68**: 504
Hughes, Thomas Parke, **63**: 441n2
Hughes, William, **67**: 203
Hughes, William Morris, **53**: 44, 328,
  367; **54**: 263, 270-71, 347,n2, 348; **55**:
  155, 160, 178n2, 192; **56**: 81, 543; **57**:
  310,n7, 556; **58**: 173, 186, 344, 478; **60**:
  31,n15; **66**: 246n2; **68**: 454; on Australia's territorial claims and mandatory
  issue, **54**: 251, 298-300, 330, 333, 351,
  357-58, 363, 363-64, 366, 372, 378,
  386; leaks information to London *Daily
  Mail*, **54**: 351,n3; on *de facto* recognition of League of Nations, **54**: 358; and
  Imperial War Cabinet discussion, **54**:
  563,n6, 564-66, 568; and Japan's racial
  equality amendment, **57**: 285, 570-71
Hugo, Victor, **61**: 118
Hugh Young, A Surgeon's Autobiography
  (Young), **63**: 578n

Hulbert, Allen Schoolcraft, **63**: 419,n2, 419n1; and War Department's surplus trucks, **55**: 303-304,n1

Hulbert, Mary Allen, **53**: 20n1; **55**: 304; **60**: 647; last meeting with WW, **63**: 419,n1; **68**: 527

Hulett, Miss, **68**: 548-49

Hulett, George Augustus, **67**: 181,n2

Hull, Cordell, **53**: 99,n1; **55**: 263; **67**: 426-27; **68**: 4,n1, 33n2, 50-51, 95, 156,n1, 244, 260, 263, 269, 380, 565, 577; and Democratic National Convention, 1920, **65**: 397, 446, 451, 496, 497, 499, 507, 580; on Versailles Treaty defeat, **67**: 423,n1; and Democratic National Committee, **67**: 480,n1; and The Document, **68**: 13, 17; and WW Democracy, **68**: 44,n1; on Democratic campaign prospects for 1922 elections, **68**: 49-50, 70-71, 85-86, 86, 95-97; on watching economic issues, **68**: 60-61, 63; and WW on selection of candidates, **68**: 63-64, 71; WW and Cummings discuss, **68**: 88; on organizing ethnic voters, **68**: 95-96; on tariff bill, **68**: 97; WW warns about Bruce, **68**: 134-35; thanks WW for check and comments on Democratic prospects, **68**: 154; WW on women and Democratic party, **68**: 155; WW congratulates on 1922 election results and Hull's response, **68**: 181, 183-84; on using Davis' speech for campaign literature, **68**: 232, 252-54; *Leviathan* sailing, **68**: 388,n1; and reception for Democratic National Committee, **68**: 531, 532; photograph of, *illustration section*, **68**

Hull, Merlin, **55**: 158,n1

Hull, William Isaac, **68**: 266n1

Hull-House, Chicago, **58**: 141n1

Hullo Paris (play), **57**: 534n4

Human Neuropsychology (Hecaen), **64**: 527n3

Humbert I (King of Italy), **53**: 605,n2

Humbert, George Louis, **59**: 561n6, 566

Humbert, Prince of Piedmont: *see* Umberto

Humes, France, **53**: 503; WW's remarks to American soldiers at, **53**: 505-507

Humphries, Alexander C., **66**: 246n2

Hungarian Americans: urge WW to stop spread of Bolshevism in Hungary, **56**: 521

Hungarian-Croatian Company for Coastwise Trade, **56**: 569

Hungarian-Croatian Company for Free Navigation, **56**: 569

Hungary and Hungarians, **53**: 6-7, 56, 294; **54**: 170, 202; **55**: 317; **56**: 26; **57**: 103, 346,n1; **58**: 6, 205; **60**: 133, 426; **61**: 245, 430; **63**: 24, 82; **67**: 461n1; and famine relief, **54**: 174n2; **57**: 367-68, 368-69, 391-92, 398; **58**: 566, 571; Creel on, **54**: 470-71; fall of Károlyi

government and soviet revolution in, **56**: 182,n1, 206, 207, 262, 330, 347, 380; A. W. Dulles on situation in, **56**: 239-40; N. Roosevelt on, **56**: 240-41, 331-34; Kun on, **56**: 242-43; Stovall on, **56**: 242; desire to reopen negotiations with Allies, **56**: 275-79, 458-60; Foch on, **56**: 314-15; T. Bliss on Hungarian-Rumanian boundary issue, **56**: 378-81; Rumania's advances in, **56**: 382-83; Smuts mission to, **56**: 413-17, 465; **57**: 73, 77-79, 108-109, 169-71, 273-75; H. Hoover on difficulties with food relief to, **56**: 469-70; Count Sigray on situation in, **56**: 474-76; Lansing on, **56**: 487-89; and Bolshevism, **57**: 75n6; and Rumania, **57**: 136, 169-71, 274-75; **58**: 149; **61**: 205-206; **64**: 351n1; and Fiume, **57**: 337, 341, 342, 484, 485; **59**: 171; Lansing on Smuts' report on, **57**: 440-42; Keynes on economic rehabilitation of, **58**: 13; Kerner on, **58**: 156, 157, 158-59; invitation to come to Paris, **58**: 264-65, 283-84, 315-16, 369-70, 415, 486; Italy angry over invitation to, **58**: 537-44, 584; and peace treaty, **58**: 540, 561-62, 578,n10; **59**: 13, 130-31, 131, 380; and boundary issue, **59**: 55, 60n3, 63-64, 144; **60**: 418-19,n6, 427-28, 462, 469-70,n11, 478, 479, 529-30; Brown memorandum on, **59**: 239-40, 256-57; and blockade, **59**: 376; **61**: 205; **60**: 281-82, 624-26, 636-38; **61**: 205; Bryce on, **59**: 401; and reparations, **59**: 421-22; draft of articles on minorities to be inserted in treaty with, **59**: 509-12; and arms limitations, **60**: 173; hostilities against Czechoslovakia and frontier solution, **60**: 255-56, 256-58, 264-65,n12, 299-300, 312-14,n1, 343-44, 351-57; and proposed Austrian agreement on trade with, **60**: 283; Bliss on stopping aid to, **60**: 363; Council of Four defines boundaries and demands hostilities stop, **60**: 522,n19; Kun's reply to Allied request for armistice, **60**: 594, 595, 596-98; WW on, **61**: 238; and Sudbahn, **61**: 280; issue of Allied trade with, **61**: 483, 484; and Rumanian occupation of Budapest, **62**: 123,n1, 167-68, 235n1, 242, 265-66, 428-29,n1; and trade restrictions, **62**: 424; new government established in, **64**: 101,n2; and Adriatic question, **64**: 256, 299, 300, 332; U.S. position on negotiations with, **64**: 446-48, 464-66; children fed in, **65**: 469; and International Financial Conference, **66**: 101n1; issue of U.S. representative on Allied commission on, **66**: 304, 324; *see also* Austria-Hungary; Paris Peace Conference—Hungarian Treaty

Hungary at the Paris Peace Conference: The Diplomatic History of the Treaty of Trianon (Deák), **56**: 182n2; **62**: 123n1, 428n1; **63**: 61n2; **64**: 101n2

Hungary Between Wilson and Lenin. The Hungarian Revolution of 1918-1919 and the Big Three (Pastor), **53**: 7n3; **56**: 182n1

Hungary in Revolution 1918-19: Nine Essays (Volgyes, ed.), **53**: 7n3; **56**: 182n1

Hunt, Bampton, **57**: 241n3

Hunt, Frazier, **60**: 328,n1, 329

Hunt, George Wylie Paul: and appointments, **64**: 296,n1, 317, 322, 407-408

Hunt, Henry Thomas, **65**: 189n1

Hunt, John Stuart, **57**: 429

Hunt, Theodore Whitefield, **67**: 182

Huntington, Collis Potter, **68**: 205

Huntington, Elizabeth Wainwright Dodge (Mrs. George Herbert), **66**: 193,n3,5; **67**: 373,n1, 375; **68**: 155,n1, 117

Huntington, George Herbert, **66**: 193,n3,5; **67**: 373n1; **68**: 155,n1

Huntington, William Chapin, **53**: 169,n1, 169-80

Hunton, George K., **66**: 275,n10

Hurban, Vladimir S., **55**: 297n2

Hurewitz, Jacob Coleman, **56**: 110n7

Hurley, Edward Nash, **53**: 15, 59, 110, 326, 360, 405, 480, 645; **54**: 35, 127, 386, 394, 395, 432, 519; **55**: 148, 302n1, 341-42, 394, 397, 398; **56**: 236n2; **58**: 202n1, 203, 269, 297; **61**: 465; **62**: 140-41, 466, 467; **63**: 421; **65**: 24; **67**: 295, 326; on Seamen's Act, **53**: 9-11; on European relief and shipping, **53**: 75, 271,n1, 271-72, 272, 372-75; concern over ship building restrictions, **53**: 454-56; suggested as Director General of Railroads, **53**: 704; on International Mercantile Marine Corporation, **54**: 171, 256-57; on agreement with Germany on food exchange for tonnage, **54**: 172; **56**: 190, 339, 374, 520-21; on shipping policy, **55**: 532-35; on disposition of housing facilities, **56**: 245-46; on building foreign ships in U.S. shipyards, **58**: 498-99, 531; resignation of, **60**: 568; **61**: 439-40, 440-41; McCormick on, **61**: 134; and need for passenger-carrying vessels, **61**: 478-80; and Irish situation, **61**: 512; on protecting fuel oil supply for merchant marine and navy, **62**: 77-79, 114; and France's ships, **63**: 366, 367, 367-68; on creating U.S. trade plan, **66**: 74, 82, 100, 101; inferred secret mission to H. Ford, **66**: 130n1; and Chinese Famine Relief Committee, **66**: 497; and WW Club project, **67**: 353

Hurley, Florence Agnes Amberg (Mrs. Edward Nash), **53**: 573,n1

Hurst, Cecil James Barrington, **55**: 119; **57**: 451; **58**: 129, 153, 277,n2, 334, 390, 417, 443n, 445, 465-66, 466, 468, 566, 567, 568; **59**: 141, 144, 534, 555; **60**: 556, 557, 560; **61**: 102, 148, 160, 275; **62**: 402,n41 and League of Nations

Covenant, **54**: 409,n2, 433-39, 439, 459-60,n1, 461; on sinking of German fleet at Scapa Flow, **61**: 83, 84, 85

Hurst-Miller draft of Covenant, **62**: 402

Huse, Henry Mc Laren Pickney, **65**: 536,n2, 537, 548; **66**: 82, 207n1

Hussein (Husayn) ibn Ali al-Hashimi, **54**: 507,n8; **56**: 110,n7, 111, 113, 116,n17; **58**: 318, 325

Huston, Howard, **64**: 275

Huszár, Károly, **64**: 101n2

Hutcheson, William Levi, **54**: 472,n1, 520

Hutchinson, Elijah Cubberly, **62**: 491n1

Hutchinson, James Pemberton, **53**: 467,n1

Hutton, Laurence, **60**: 644

Hu Wei-te, **54**: 474n2

Hyde, James Hazen, **53**: 358

Hyderabad, **53**: 544

Hyland, John F., **53**: 580-81,n2; **55**: 194; **59**: 419n1; **61**: 182,n1, 371,n1, 401

Hymans, Paul, **54**: 505; **55**: 109; **56**: 102, 565; **57**: 220, 222, 319, 405, 485; **58**: 188, 236, 237, 262, 263, 399-400; **60**: 429; **61**: 12, 16,n1, 19, 20, 29, 120; and League of Nations Commission, **54**: 482, 483, 484, 496, 496-97, 546, 547; **55**: 5, 6, 41, 42, 45, 72, 122, 123, 124, 126; **56**: 170n1, 171, 172, 173-74, 175, 176, 178, 226, 228, 229, 229-30, 299-300, 300; **67**: 64, 65, 79, 144, 153; on Brussels as seat of League of Nations, **56**: 173-74; **57**: 222-23, 226, 237; on reparations, **56**: 456-58, 555, 592-93, 595; on German-Belgian border, **57**: 392-97, 399; at Council of Four on construction of railway lines, **60**: 551-52; on financial settlement and Belgian mandates, **61**: 106; Clemenceau on, **61**: 375; sends tribute to WW from League of Nations Assembly, **66**: 380,n1, 382-83; mediator for the Armenian hostilities and U.S. reaction, **66**: 421,n1, 422, 436-37, 457, 480; WW's reply to on Armenian mediation, **66**: 426-28, 443-44,n1; on U.S. representative on arms limitation committee, **66**: 473-74; notified of Morgenthau as mediator, **66**: 517-18

Hynes, John J., **62**: 121; **64**: 424, 431; **65**: 359

Huysmans, Camille, **54**: 190,n2

Idria (now Idrija, Yugoslavia), **62**: 575; **63**: 297; and Adriatic settlement, **66**: 365

If (Kipling), **66**: 369, 386, 456, 479

Iglesias Calderon, Fernando, **65**: 446, 464, 468; **66**: 17-18, 142; N. H. Davis on meetings with, **65**: 483-85, 533-36; **66**: 162-63

Iglesias, José Maria, **65**: 484,n2

Ijuin, Baron Hikokichi, **65**: 302,n8

Illinois, **53**: 24; **58**: 459; and Democratic politics in 1912, **65**: 189n2; coal crisis

in, **65**: 545-46, 553,n1, 554, 558-62, 562,n2; **66**: 10-11, 18-19,n1; Democratic party in, **67**: 447,n1
Illinois Central Railroad, **65**: 562
Illinois Coal Operators Association, **65**: 545, 546
Illinois, University of, **58**: 327n5; **66**: 165
Illinois Agricultural Association, **62**: 300n1
Illinois Irish Historical Society, **60**: 383
illiteracy: in the United States, **55**: 284-88
Imbrie, Andrew Clerk, **65**: 572,n14, 574, 575, 576
immigration: W. B. Wilson on new issues regarding, **60**: 432-33; and Root's reservations, **61**: 181, 233, 234; anti-Japanese movement in California, **66**: 12-16; and O'Callaghan case, **67**: 37-38, 48-51, 52,n1; *see also* under California
Immigration, Committee on (Senate), **67**: 9n1
Immigration Act (1917), **65**: 360, 569; **66**: 475-76, 477; and anarchists, **66**: 97; *see also* Burnett Immigration Act
Immigration and Emigration, International Commission on: W. B. Wilson on representatives to, **65**: 360-61, 569-71; **67**: 9
Immigration and Naturalization, Committee on (House of Reps.), **60**: 433,n1
immigration bill of 1920-21: *see* Johnson immigration bill
Immigration Bureau, (Dept. of Labor): and "Palmer raids," **65**: 187n5; **67**: 37-38
Immigration Service (U.S.), **67**: 180
Impact of Illness on World Leaders (Park), **58**: 607, 614n14, 623n59, 630n93; **59**: 574n1; **62**: 628n1
Impact of Wilson's Neurologic Disease during the Paris Peace Conference (Park), **58**: 611-30; **62**: 628n1
Imperator controversy, **64**: 7-10, 33-34, 52, 65, 212, 218
Imperiali, Marquis Guglielmo, **57**: 364,n2; **58**: 82,n3, 313, 334, 341 369, 391-92, 393,n4, 394, 395, 396, 398, 434, 478; **59**: 41, 211; **60**: 261, 296; **61**: 109,n11, 189; **65**: 162,n3, 302
Imperial Valley Basin, California, **68**: 503
Imperial War Cabinet (Great Britain), **53**: 558-69; **61**: 386
Impressions of Turkey During Twelve Years' Wanderings (Ramsay), **58**: 324,n4
income tax, **54**: 501-502; **55**: 334n1; **57**: 283; 293-94; **65**: 131; and WW's Annual Message to Congress, **64**: 64,n1; WW on, **64**: 84, 113; **66**: 488; and The Document, **67**: 484, 485, 486, 500; Houston on, **68**: 270, 271, 271-72
In Defense of Yesterday: James M. Beck and the Politics of Conservativism, 1861-1936 (Keller), **55**: 338n2

indemnities: *see* reparations
Independent, The, **62**: 347,n11; **65**: 218n1, 513; **66**: 274; **67**: 187,n1, 267, 464n1, 618n1
Independent Presbyterian Church of Savannah, Ga., **67**: 307n1,2
Independent and Weekly Review, **67**: 464,n1
India, **54**: 13, 14, 15, 43, 65, 72, 497; **55**: 125, 184, 499n1; **56**: 109; **57**: 35, 308; **58**: 198, 324,n3, 417,n6, 508; **59**: 93,n10, 97, 103, 202, 207, 253, 326, 337, 371, 396; **61**: 60; **67**: 43; WW receives Maharaja of Kapurthala, **60**: 333; and wheat situation, **62**: 52; WW on, **63**: 478, 505
Indiana, **53**: 24; Republican party in, **65**: 291-92,n1; coal situation in, **65**: 546; coal crisis in, **66**: 10-11, 18-19,n1; McAdoo on political prospects in, **66**: 235; politics in, **68**: 44,n2, 49-50, 50, 56; Democratic women in, **68**: 156
Indiana Federation of Farmers' Associations, **62**: 300n1
Indianapolis, Indiana: WW's arrival and activities in, **63**: 3-4; WW's address in, **63**: 19-20
Indianapolis Daily News, **55**: 472,n2; **61**: 373; **63**: 3n5, 29n; **65**: 546
Indianapolis *Star*, **58**: 51
Indiana University, **67**: 141n1
Indians, American: *see* American Indians
Indio, California, **68**: 503
Industrial Board of the Department of Commerce, **54**: 520-21,n1; **63**: 88,n1; and controversy with the Railroad Administration, **56**: 193-94,n1, 341, 342-43, 343-44, 344, 399, 618; **57**: 52,n1, 233-34, 280-81, 282, 347-48, 374,n1, 376-86, 387-88, 510-11, 629; **58**: 104, 329, 420; WW on, **57**: 374, 423-24, 446, 470, 577, 577-78; **58**: 420; **59**: 38,n1
Industrial Board Precursor of the N.R.A.: Price-Reduction Movement after World War I (Howenstine), **54**: 521n1
Industrial Cabinet (proposed), **56**: 344n2; **57**: 630
Industrial Conference (first): and steel strike situation, **63**: 149,n2, 163; and police situation, **63**: 150, 265, 295; WW on, **63**: 176, 273n2, 300,n1; request for Negro representation at, **63**: 268; WW urges Baruch to accept appointment to, **63**: 336; WW's message to, **63**: 554,n1; Lane on problems at, **63**: 582-83, 583-84, 591-92; WW's interest in during illness, **63**: 590, 591, 591-92; withdrawal of labor from, **63**: 591-92
Industrial Conference (second): appointment suggestions, **63**: 609-12; **64**: 185; and R. S. Baker, **63**: 609, 621; Brandeis suggests postponing appointments to, **63**: 618; WW names new members to, **64**: 64,n1; WW on, **64**: 84, 113; Tumulty on report of, **65**: 152,n2
industrial democracy, **60**: 147,n4

Industrial News, The, **62**: 122n1
Industrial Workers of the World
(I.W.W.), **53**: 13, 20n3; **59**: 204n2; **60**:
354; **66**: 98; and bombings, **60**: 114-
15,n2; and WW's tour of Seattle, **63**:
238,n1; and Negroes, **63**: 268; and railroad strikes, **65**: 187,n3; and amnesty
cases, **65**: 206
Industrie im Besetzem Frankreich (German General Staff), **55**: 61
industry: *see* business and industry;
under names of specific industry such
as cotton industry
In Flanders Fields (McCrae), **66**: 158,n8
Ingerman, Sergius, **53**: 137,n1
Ingersoll, Royal Rodney, **60**: 302,n7
*Innocent Abroad: Belgium at the Paris
Peace Congerence of 1919* (Marks), **56**:
457n8; **57**: 372n2; **60**: 107n1
Innsbruck, Austria, **54**: 245
Inquiry, The, **53**: 213,n1,2, 348n1,3,
349,n1,3,5, 367n1,2, 368, 419; WW's
remarks to, **53**: 350-52, 353-56, 356-57
*Inquiry: American Preparations for
Peace, 1917-1919* (Gelfand), **58**: 632n9;
59: 349,n2
Institute of American Meat Packers, **53**:
15n1
Institute of Information (proposed), **67**:
440,n1
Institute of International Affairs, **60**:
17,n1; **67**: 462n1
Institute of International Education
(N.Y.), **67**: 415n1
Insular Affairs Committee (House of
Reps.), **60**: 198, 199; **66**: 25
Intelligence and National Security, **65**:
83n1
Inter-Allied Aeronautical Commission of
Control, **56**: 48-49, 49; issue of U.S.
representative on, **66**: 535-36,n3,4, 539
Inter-Allied Blockade Council, **56**: 200
Inter-Allied Commission for the Negotia-
tion of an Armistice Between Poland
and the Ukraine: *see* Polish-Ukrainian
Armistice Commission
Inter-Allied Commission of Control in
Germany, **67**: 33n1
Inter-Allied Commission of Inquiry (pro-
posed), **61**: 629-30,n1,2,3
Inter-Allied Commission on Reparations:
see Reparation Commission
Inter-Allied Commission on Mandates in
Turkey, **62**: 607n1
Inter-Allied Commission on Reparations:
see Reparation Commission
Inter-Allied Commission on Teschen: *see*
Paris Peace Conference —Inter-Allied
Commission on Teschen
Inter-Allied Commission on Interna-
tional Ports, Waterways and Railways:
see Paris Peace Conference—Inter-Al-
lied Commission on International
Ports, Waterways and Railways
Inter-Allied Commissions of Control: *see*

Paris Peace Conference —Inter-Allied
Commissions of Control
Inter-Allied Commission to Poland: *see*
Paris Peace Conference —Inter-Allied
Commission to Poland
Inter-Allied Commission to Syria (proposed), **56**: 104, 116, 117, 118, 126,
155-56, 208, 310, 323; **57**: 113, 246-47,
313, 442-44, 468, 525-26, 535, 586; **58**:
133-34, 493, 555; suggestions for
American appointments to, **56**: 155-56,
179, 180, 200, 310, 337, 442; Faisal
grateful for, **56**: 243-44,n1; awaits in-
structions, **56**: 518; and France's delay,
59: 343; discussed at Council of Four,
59: 632-33, 635-37; *see also* King-
Crane Commission
Inter-Allied Committee for War Purchases and Finance, **53**: 716n2
Inter-Allied Conference for the Preliminaries of Peace: *see* Paris Peace Confer-
ence
Inter-Allied Economic Commission: *see*
Supreme Economic Council
Inter-Allied Food Council: *see* Paris
Peace Conference—Inter-Allied Food
Council
Inter-Allied Maritime Transport Coun-
cil: *see* Maritime Transport Council
Inter-Allied Military Mission (Buda-
pest), **63**: 61,n2
Inter-Allied Mission to Constantinople,
64: 158
Inter-Allied Naval Armistice Commis-
sion (London): *see* Paris Peace Confer-
ence—Inter-Allied Naval Armistice
Commission
Inter-Allied Naval Council: *see* Paris
Peace Conference—Inter-Allied Naval
Council
Inter-Allied Purchasing Commissions:
see Paris Peace Conference —Inter-Al-
lied Purchasing Commissions
Inter-Allied Railway Committee, **62**: 85
Inter-Allied Rhineland Commission, **59**:
280-81,n1, 592; **60**: 295, 366; **62**:
581n1; **65**: 89, 171-72; and Noyes' plan
for occupation, **59**: 593-94; Foch criti-
cizes, **60**: 364n1; report of, **60**: 366-68,
440
Inter-Allied Rhineland High Commis-
sion (proposed): *see* Paris Peace Con-
ference—Inter-Allied Rhineland High
Commission
Inter-Allied Technical Board, **58**: 494n1;
59: 438n11
Interchurch World Movement of North
America, **64**: 416,n2
Interim Reparation Commission: *see*
Reparation Commission, interim
Interim Report on Joint Standing Industrial Councils: *see* Whitley Report
Interior, Department of the, **53**: 131, 230,
280; **62**: 101; and General Leasing bill,
61: 535; **64**: 473-74; and Lane's resig-

nation, **64**: 373-74, 374; Robinson declines appointment to, **64**: 392-93; Payne appointed Secretary, **64**: 448; Lane on issues confronting, **65**: 22n1; Payne appointed Secretary, **65**: 64; and water-power legislation, **65**: 447; and Teapot Dome Scandal, **68**: 119,n2

International Alliance for Woman Suffrage, **54**: 133

International Armistice Commission, **53**: 626n1

International Association of Machinists, **62**: 121, 569, 573; **64**: 424, 431; **67**: 119n1

International Association of Railroad Supervisors of Mechanics, **67**: 121n1

international banking consortium for China, **65**: 255,n4, 259,n1, 261, 277; **66**: 294-95

International Bible Society, **55**: 482-83,n1

International Bible Students' Association, **55**: 482n1

International Book Monthly, **68**: 233

International Brotherhood of B.I.S.B. & H. of A., **62**: 569, 573

International Brotherhood of Blacksmiths, Drop Forgers and Helpers of America, **62**: 568, 573; **64**: 431

International Brotherhood of Boilermakers, Iron Ship Builders and Helpers of America, **64**: 431

International Brotherhood of Electrical Workers, **56**: 311, 340, 340-41, 404,n1; **57**: 425; **61**: 503, 504; **62**: 121, 570, 573; **64**: 431

International Brotherhood of Locomotive Engineers, **64**: 198n2

International Celebration Meeting First American Legislative Assembly, the Mayflower Compact, the Pilgrim Fathers, which Mark the Beginning of Free Institutions in America (pamphlet), **66**: 118n1

International College (Smyrna), **59**: 640n3

international commerce: Redfield on, **53**: 48-51, 55-56

International Commission for Air Navigation, **57**: 308

International Commission on Immigration and Emigration: *see* Immigration and Emigration, International Commission on

International Commission on Mandates in former Ottoman Empire: *see* King-Crane Commission

International Committee of Bankers on Mexico, **66**: 160,n2, 302-303

International Communications, Conference on, **64**: 228-29; **65**: 479, 531-32; **66**: 154; Daniels suggests additional U.S. member to, **66**: 56-57; Bullard as new U.S. member, **66**: 59; and disposition of ex-German cables, **66**: 193, 423,

504; Stowell on proposed Universal Electrical Communication Union, **66**: 416

International Conferences on the Rights of Nations, **56**: 215

International Congress of Women (The Hague, 1915), **58**: 141n1; **59**: 117n4

International Congress of Working Women (proposed), **63**: 57, 58-59

International Council of Women, **56**: 374; **57**: 218, 219n2

International Court of Arbitral Justice, **53**: 484

International Court of Justice (proposed): *see* Permanent Court of International Justice

international courts of arbitration: Lansing on, **54**: 469-70

International Economic Council (proposed), **61**: 520-22, 522; **62**: 330, 331

International Financial Conference (proposed, Brussels), **65**: 238-42, 245,n1, 250; **66**: 101,n1, 471-72; **67**: 19, 20

International Harvester Company, **57**: 384n31; **66**: 289n2

International High Commission on Uniformity of Laws Relating to Foreign Trade (Buenos Aires, 1916), **66**: 218, 220, 234

International Jew, The World's Foremost Problem (*Dearborn Independent*) **66**: 102n1

International Joint Commission of the United States and Canada: appointment to, **65**: 378,n3,4; **67**: 168,n1, 196,n1

International Labor Conference (Washington, 1919), **58**: 43n1, 204; **60**: 151; **62**: 96, 131-33, 162-63; **65**: 360; proposed meeting of, **57**: 495n1; and National Women's Trade Union League, **63**: 57, 58-59; admission of German and Austrian delegates, **63**: 62, 91; WW on, **63**: 14, 78, 99, 147, 261-62, 357, 373, 435, 502; concern over postponement of, **63**: 63: 445-46; suggestions for chairman of, **63**: 602; meeting of, greetings from, **64**: 97-98,n1

international labor conference (proposed), **53**: 257, 286, 292, 408,n1, 436, 466, 489-90, 588; and Germany, **59**: 48n3, 222-23,n15, 486

international labor congresses (Leeds, 1916; Bern, 1917, **59**: 49n4; Bern, 1919, **54**: 426; **59**: 48n2, 49n4, 145, 421n3

International Labour Office (League of Nations), **66**: 151,n1, 476; Meeker accepts appointment to, **65**: 248-50

International Labour Organization (I.L.O.): beginnings of, **54**: 172-73, 190, 210-11, 221-22, 309, 438, 457; **64**: 98,n1; and issue of Germany's membership in, **59**: 222-23,n15; **60**: 520-21,n14

International Labour Review, **66**: 151n1
International Law, Committee on (American Bar Association), **68**: 123,n4
International Loan Fund, **66**: 449
International Mercantile Marine Corporation, **53**: 110-11,n1, 112-13, 113, 148-49, 158-59, 159, 164,n1, 186-87, 187-88, 196, 209,n1, 214, 261,n1, 289; **54**: 54, 171, 256; **55**: 367n2
International Navigation Company, **54**: 171
International News Service, **55**: 221n1, 409; **57**: 98, 288n1; **60**: 381; **62**: 627
International Opium Convention, **56**: 270,n5
International Organization, **54**: 311n2
International Petroleum Company, **65**: 485n4, 485-86
International Press Association, **60**: 388
International Press Service, **53**: 318
International Printing, Pressmen and Assistants' Union of North America, **68**: 280n1
International Radio-Telegraphic Conference, **55**: 26, 430
International Red Cross, **53**: 232-35, 303-305; **54**: 233; **55**: 527-28; **58**: 200, 216, 382n5; **59**: 195; **60**: 290n2
international reserve banking system (proposed), **68**: 57, 61, 78-80, 80
International Review, **61**: 363
International Shoe Company of St. Louis, **67**: 578n2
International Studio Magazine, **68**: 449
International Telephone Convention, **59**: 585
International Trading Corporation, **67**: 295
International Woman Suffrage Alliance, **54**: 133; **65**: 151
Interparty League for Restoration of Free Russia, **53**: 136-37
Interstate and Foreign Commerce Committee (House of Reps.), **55**: 246n3, 247; **61**: 415; **62**: 160; and railroad situation, **62**: 98n1, 117, 138; **64**: 19, 20
interstate commerce: WW on, **64**: 82-83, 111-12; **65**: 130-31
Interstate Commerce, Committee on (Senate), **53**: 215; **55**: 246,n3, 247, 248, 257; **58**: 106, 108; **62**: 99n3, 117, 224; and railroad situation, **62**: 183-84, 191, 192, 194; **64**: 18, 20; McAdoo's railroad statement before, **68**: 291,n1
Interstate Commerce Act of 1887, **64**: 196,n3
Interstate Commerce Commission, **57**: 233; **61**: 414; **64**: 445n1; **67**: 540n1; **68**: 199, 271, 459; and railroads, **55**: 246n1, 247, 257-58; **62**: 75, 76, 134, 137, 181, 182; **64**: 20, 24, 197; **67**: 119,n1, 120, 122, 550n1; Eastman appointed to, **56**: 194,n1; Redfield on, **62**: 129-31; Cummins on railroad crisis and, **62**: 183-84; and Plumb plan, **62**: 229-30; Thornton on, **62**: 288, 289-90;

J. S. Williams on railroads and, **62**: 520; and proposed Cummins and Esch railroad bills, **64**: 195n1; appointments to, **64**: 205; and Transportation Act of 1920, **64**: 467n1; coal commission's recommendation for, **65**: 117; and coal situation, **65**: 508, 562,n1, 2, 563; and Woolley's resignation, **66**: 505,n1; and WW's veto message of Section 10 of Clayton Act, **67**: 13; Woodbury desires appointment to, **67**: 25,n1; and The Document, **67**: 550n1, 559, 591-92; and proposed Transportation Board, **68**: 7, 30, 219
Intervention and Dollar Diplomacy in the Caribbean 1900-1921 (Munro), **61**: 640n14,15; **63**: 616n1; **65**: 247n1; **66**: 389n1; **67**: 24n1
Intervention at Archangel: The Story of Allied Intervention and Russian Counter-Revolution in North Russia, 1918-1920 (Strakhovsky), **59**: 550n1
Intervention of German Jews at the Berlin Congress 1878 (Gelber), **58**: 461n1
In the Anglo-Arab Labyrinth: The McMahon-Husayn Correspondence and its Interpretations, 1914-1939 (Kedourie), **56**: 110n7
Intolerable. But—(*Newark Evening News*), **65**: 229n1
Investigation of Strike in Steel Industries: Hearings Before the Committee on Education and Labor, United States Senate, Sixty-Sixth Congress, First Session, **63**: 30n1
Investment Bankers Association, **62**: 623,n1
Ioffe, Adolf Abrahamovich: *see* Joffe, Adolf Abrahamovich
Ionesco, Take, **60**: 228,n6
Iowa, **56**: 331; Democratic politics in, **64**: 330n1; **65**: 291n1, 394; **67**: 393n1; Democratic women in, **68**: 156
Iowa Farm Bureau Federation, **62**: 300n1
Ipek (now Pec, Yugoslavia), **60**: 530
Iraq, **56**: 323
Irby, Adeline Paulina, **64**: 160,n4
Ireland, Merritte Weber, **53**: 302,n4, 707
Ireland, **53**: 179; **54**: 397; and Home Rule issue, **53**: 299-300, 306, 542,n1, 570; **54**: 332-33,n1, 381; **56**: 397-98, 486,n1; **57**: 426, 427, 446, 534; **58**: 585-87, 588, 602; **60**: 155; **61**: 9, 66, 445, 542; Cork and Dublin offer WW freedom of the city, **54**: 256,n1, 399,n1, 552; **56**: 96; Polk on U.S. supporters of freedom for, **54**: 472-73; WW denies making statement on, **55**: 324-26; Tumulty recommends WW meet with delegates on, **55**: 348; Creel on, **55**: 363-64; attempts to make situation an issue at peace conference, **55**: 403, 412, 421-22, 474, 547; **63**: 118,n2, 269, 304, 310; WW meets with delegates on, **55**: 411-12, 421-22;

Sir H. Plunkett on U.S. public opinion and, **55**: 453-55; WW on, **55**: 480-81; **60**: 287; **61**: 243, 291, 438; **63**: 304; and League of Nations, **56**: 79-80, 82; **68**: 239; Lloyd George on, **56**: 438, 443; **60**: 303-304; American spokesmen for wish to be heard at peace conference, **57**: 419; Lloyd George and Irish-American delegates, **59**: 34; Irish-American delegates request safe passage to Paris for Ireland's representatives, **59**: 104-107, 251, 366-67,n1,2, 368, 393,n1, 393-94, 513-14, 549; Irish-Americans and passport controversy, **59**: 106, 172-73; and U.S. Republican threats regarding, **59**: 372,n2; House on delegates and, **59**: 449; House rewrites Lansing's note to delay representatives, **59**: 476; and rights at Paris Peace Conference, **59**: 642-43, 645, 646; Irish-American delegates request hearing for Ireland's representatives, **59**: 645, 646; Walsh seeks interview with WW, **60**: 38; Walsh and Dunne request Paris Peace Conference investigate situation in, **60**: 239,n1; and Senate resolution supporting Irish delegates' appearance before peace conference, **60**: 249,n2, 287, 288-89, 375, 483; Tumulty on public opinion in U.S. on, **60**: 291, 331-32; WW on difficulty caused by Walsh and others, **60**: 298; WW meets with Walsh and Dunne on, **60**: 383-87, 388-89; Lloyd George compares Upper Silesian situation to, **60**: 414, 425; WW on Senate action on, **60**: 435, 601; General Maurice on, **61**: 182,n1; De Valera's visit to U.S., **61**: 183,n2; Tumulty on N.Y. *Evening Post* editorial on, **61**: 185; *Springfield* (Mass.) *Republican* on, **61**: 293; Clemenceau denies delegates hearing at Paris Peace Conference, **61**: 466-67; Walsh on, **61**: 512; and Sir E. Carson, **61**: 513,n1,2,3; Eliot on, **61**: 578; resolution of Massacuhsetts Democrats on, **62**: 8; House discusses with Grey and Haldane, **62**: 61; and Sir E. Grey, **62**: 254n2; American Commission on Irish Independence's statement on, **62**: 324-26; and Article X, **63**: 389,n1; and Gerry's reservation on, **65**: 120n1; Democratic plank on, 1920, **65**: 438; and Creel and National Security Defense Fund disbursements, **65**: 442,n2; **66**: 147,n1,2; WW urged to make appeal for MacSwiney, **66**: 88-89,n1, 90, 91; Cox's position on, **66**: 267,n1; demonstration outside White House, **66**: 442; issue of Red Cross sending relief to, **66**: 512-13, 518

Ireland and Anglo-American Relations, 1899-1921 (Ward), **60**: 249n2; **61**: 183n2; **67**: 52n1

Ireland and the United States: and O'Callaghan case, **67**: 52n1

Ireland's Fight for Freedom, Setting Forth the High Lights of Irish History (Creel), **66**: 33,n1

Irigoyen, Hipolito, **53**: 342,n2

Irish Americans, **55**: 363, 364, 403, 407, 407-408, 421-22, 448, 453, 463, 468, 474, 547; **56**: 341, 397, 438; **57**: 426; **61**: 512,n2, 627; **63**: 389; **65**: 372n6; **68**: 161; WW meets with, **55**: 411-12, 421-22; WW on, **55**: 443; **59**: 604, 645, 646; **60**: 383, 385, 389; and Irish Race Convention, **55**: 407, 411, 421-22, 443, 454, 463, 547; **56**: 486,n1; **57**: 419; and convention's representatives to Ireland, **59**: 104-107, 646; representatives and passport controversy, **59**: 172-73; and delegation's request for safe passage for Irish representatives, **59**: 318, 366-67; and League of Nations, **59**: 524, 604; and public opinion on Home Rule, **60**: 331-32; and De Valera's U.S. visit, **61**: 183n2; and MacSwiney appeal, **66**: 88-89, 90, 91; Baruch on votes of, **66**: 336; Dodd and WW on influence of, **67**: 44-45, 46; and O'Callaghan case, **67**: 52n1; WW and Brennan on, **68**: 426

Irish Fellowship Club of Chicago, **60**: 487, 569

Irish Home Rule Act (1914), **61**: 512n2

Irish Race Convention, **59**: 105, 172, 251, 642, 643; **60**: 383,n1; **63**: 389

Irish Reconstruction Association (Plunkett), **55**: 455n3

Irkutsk, Russia, **55**: 495; **58**: 569; **62**: 87

iron, **63**: 29-39; and prices, **56**: 193-94

Ironside, William Edmund, **54**: 348; **55**: 93n2; **57**: 460,n1, 461, 560, 628; **59**: 599,n1, 600n4; **61**: 166,n23

Iroquois Club (Chicago), **67**: 447,n1

Irreconcilables: The Fight Against the League of Nations (Stone), **55**: 388n1; **59**: 451n1, 524n1; **64**: 328n2

Irvine, Benjamin Franklin, **63**: 283,n1

Irving, M., **57**: 533n4

Irving National Bank of New York, **68**: 79

Isaachsen, Hanna, **67**: 18

Isabella II (of Spain), **57**: 241n1

Is Germany Going to Pieces? (Coar), **67**: 463-64,n1

Is Germany guilty? German White-book concerning the Responsibility of the Authors of the War, **60**: 438-39,n5, 463, 468

Ishii, Kikujiro, **53**: 144, 555, 556n4; **54**: 485; **55**: 436,n1; **58**: 168; **62**: 590; interview with Lawrence, **56**: 187-89

Ishii-Lansing Agreement, **61**: 438, 558

Ishii Looks to End of Race Prejudice (*New York Times*), **56**: 60n1

Ishii's Plea Stirs Western Senators (*New York Times*), **56**: 187n3

Islay, Scotland, **61**: 508n1

isolationism: WW on, **64**: 79, 109

Israel, Fred L., **65**: 386n1, 418n3, 436n2, 482n1, 499n1; **66**: 65n1, 208n1

Issues in Wilson Scholarship: References
to Early 'Strokes' in the Papers of
Woodrow Wilson (George, Marmor,
and George), **58**: 612n3
Istria, **53**: 434, 444, 445, 642; **62**: 606; **64**:
169, 172, 301, 377, 400, 463; *see also*
Paris Peace Conference—Italy; Istria
Italia alla Conferenza Pace (Giannini,
ed.), **61**: 584n2
Italia Irredenta, **53**: 82n1; **58**: 359n1; **64**:
175, 176, 332
Italian Americans, **53**: 670,n1, 601, 613,
621, 624; **58**: 7; **66**: 323n3; **68**: 95n1,
104; Baruch on votes of, **66**: 336
Italian American Treaty of Commerce
and Navigation (1871), **66**: 87n1
Italian Nationalist Association, **58**: 92n1
Italy, **53**: 18, 26, 296, 374; **54**: 13n2, 49,
55, 264; **55**: 61, 87, 157, 164, 184, 203,
294, 397-98; **56**: 108, 540; **57**: 148; **58**:
198; **68**: 62, 422; and Trieste and
Fiume and the Adriatic question, **53**:
43,n1, 66, 123-24, 128, 381, 444-46,
459, 466, 563-64, 609-10, 638, 641-44,
696-97, 699,n1; **54**: 134; **56**: 393,n1,
556, 561-65, 567-72, 601,n1; **59**: 35;
and peace conference, **53**: 91, 92, 143;
and France, **53**: 183-84, 434-35; plans
for reparation commission, **53**: 324; demands of, **53**: 336, 338, 433-36, 575;
R. S. Baker on situation in, **53**: 433-36;
and far eastern situation, **53**: 463n1,
464; and Montenegro, **53**: 638,n1, 639-
41; **56**: 395; **59**: 178n2,3; WW's proposals for, **54**: 50-51; and representation
at Paris Peace Conference, **54**: 65; and
territorial claims and mandates, **54**:
112n2, 326-27,n3, 348, 357; **59**: 147;
62: 18; Vittorio Emanuele III on WW's
visit to, **54**: 134; and Bolshevism, **54**:
184, 185, 186; and Poles, **54**: 200; and
League of Nations Covenant, **54**: 387,
387-89; and League of Nations Commission, **54**: 463; report on army, **54**:
527; Masaryk on, **54**: 557; and reparations, **55**: 29n2; **56**: 252, 601-603; **57**:
309; **58**: 471,n8; **60**: 98, 323; T. N. Page
on, **55**: 84-86; **56**: 64-66; **57**: 434-37; **59**:
33, 67; requests for loans, **55**: 113-15,
208, 332-33, 342; food relief efforts
thwarted by, **55**: 117; Orlando on military terms and, **55**: 140-41; grants
general amnesty, **55**: 301; praise for
WW, **55**: 301-302; and Yugoslavia, **55**:
305; Orlando meets with WW, **55**: 498;
and capture of enemy cables, **56**: 210,
211, 212; and Hungary, **56**: 333; and
newspapers' reporting of peace conference, **56**: 392-94; WW on Fiume and,
57: 60-70, 90; Coolidge on German
South Tyrol and, **57**: 96-97; talk of occupation of Vienna, **57**: 102; and responsibilities for war, **57**: 128; labor
strike in Rome, **57**: 204,n1, 242;
Orlando presses Council of Four to settle Italy's concerns before inviting Ger-

many to peace conference, **57**: 242-43,
289, 317-18, 318-25, 431; **60**: 579-80;
and map prepared by Marinelli, **57**:
270, 271; Ossoinack says Fiume
wishes to be part of, **57**: 337-43; and
statement summoning German delegates to peace conference, **57**: 336;
WW's memorandum on Adriatic claims
of, **57**: 343-45; and Yugoslavia's
claims, **57**: 369-70; Serbia offers to accept WW's arbitration, **57**: 418; Bowman and others' protest against award
of Fiume to Italy, **57**: 432-33; and Germany, **57**: 435-36; reports of deportation of Yugoslavs by, **57**: 442-43; and
credits, **57**: 470-71, 495; **62**: 230; WW
on claims of, **57**: 450, 585; various comments on claims of, **57**: 477-78, 500-
501, 502, 504, 527, 527-28, 531, 533;
Council of Four receives and discusses
claims, **57**: 479-94, 514-20, 545-49,
610-14; meets with Britain and France
on claims, **57**: 536-42; WW's Adriatic
statement, **57**: 542-44, 551, 552-53,
559-60, 611, 613; **58**: 5-8; rejects verbal
proposal brought by Hankey, **57**: 551,
552; Orlando on Dalmatia and, **57**:
562-64, 564-65; threatens to leave
peace conference, **58**: 4, 15-16, 16-17,
53; Lloyd George on economic conditions in, **58**: 8-9; Keynes on, **58**: 14;
and memorandum by American delegation on Reparation Commission, **58**:
25-26; Orlando's reasons for return to
Italy, **58**: 74; Lloyd George and Clemenceau's letter on Fiume, **58**: 86-90,
333-34, 336-37; Page on reaction in
Rome to WW's Adriatic statement and
his fear for Americans' safety, **58**: 93,
143; Bryce on the Tyrol and, **58**: 139;
59: 400-401; Kerner on, **58**: 157, 160;
and coal, **58**: 202, 203-204, 269; **62**:
252, 253, 291, 326, 448, 448-49; comments on "crisis," **58**: 215, 382; Council
of Four on absence of, **58**: 250-52; and
issue of Italian credentials, **58**: 279-82;
Poincaré's message to, **58**: 280, 282,
357; reaction to invitation to Austria
and Hungary to come to Paris, **58**: 334,
369-70, 415; net war losses, **58**: 492;
and Greek troops dispatched to Tur-
key, **58**: 513, 514; **59**: 23, 24, 26, 27, 43-
46; tonnage issue, **58**: 527; **59**: 50-54;
62: 145, 187; news accounts of Italy
getting Fiume called "fiction" by WW,
58: 531-32,n1, 601; Johnson on formula for Adriatic settlement, **58**: 589-
90; and Dodecanese Islands, **59**: 39;
treaty with Austria and Hungary to be
drafted in Italian, **59**: 131; Lamont on
finances and economic situation of, **59**:
176; House on Adriatic question, **59**:
200; landings on coast of Asia Minor,
59: 208, 223-35, 225-26, 246, 250-51,
561; Balfour on Turkey and Anatolia
and, **59**: 209-12; House on, **59**: 244;

WW on Anatolia and, **59**: 374, 375; Reparation Commission members from, **59**: 422; and Austrian treaty, **59**: 425-28, 483-86, 631-32; WW, Lloyd George, and Clemenceau discuss, **59**: 492-94; Orlando and WW on Treaty of London and, **59**: 503-509; and Austrian reparations and lesser nations, **59**: 611, 631-32, 634, 635; and Klagenfurt and Klagenfurt Basin, **60**: 121, 628; **61**: 41-43, 51-55, 57-59; and Slovenes, **60**: 124; and issue of rolling stock, **60**: 226-27; Pašić on Fiume plebiscite vote against, **60**: 293-94; estimate of damages, **60**: 359n1; on advance of Yugoslav troops into Klagenfurt, **60**: 361-62; and Tarvis occupation, **60**: 394; internal crisis in, **60**: 473-74, 481-82, 531; request for Venetian palace in Constantinople, **60**: 593-94; cabinet crisis in, **61**: 28, 45; pro-German influence in, **61**: 28; and restitution of art works, **61**: 47, 57; Page wishes to see WW on, **61**: 77; signs German treaty, **61**: 109n1; and Asia Minor, **61**: 211-14, 217; Council of Four on Fiume and, **61**: 218, 219, 221, 222-23; Johnson on Adriatic question and, **61**: 227-30; and Sudbahn, **61**: 280, 317-21; WW on future dealings with, **61**: 307; Council of Four on dealing with, **61**: 307-308, 309-10; Allied draft warning to, **61**: 342-46; Tittoni encourages settlement of Adriatic question, **61**: 404-405; White rejects Adriatic proposal presented by Tittoni, **61**: 551-54; and Adriatic question, **61**: 575-76; **62**: 456, 574-75, 603, 620, 625; Thrace and Bulgaria, **61**: 589-91; **62**: 141-42, 319-20; and Turkish Empire, **62**: 235; Johnson on economic considerations concerning, **62**: 252-53; Glass on foreign exchange and, **62**: 501-502; WW on, **63**: 11-12, 259; WW on economy of, **63**: 156; war costs, **63**: 221, 243, 349; battle deaths, **63**: 222, 243, 349; and occupation of Fiume, **63**: 298-99,n2; Polk on situation in, **63**: 364-66; **64**: 323-24; Fiume situation causes crisis in, **63**: 464-65, 485-86, 515-17; Britain and France anxious treaty be ratified by, **63**: 465-66; WW on not yielding his position on, **63**: 534; King approves peace treaty with Germany and Austria, **63**: 547n4; and invasion of Trau, **63**: 557n2; information to be given on WW's health, **63**: 560; appointment suggestions and appointment of Ambassador to, **64**: 205, 296, 343-44, 407, 474; and Anglo-French Adriatic proposal, **64**: 263-66, 298-305; and Nitti compromise on Adriatic proposal, **64**: 264,n4; invited to first meeting of Council of League of Nations, **64**: 272; WW on firm position on Adriatic proposals and claims by, **64**: 352-53, 398-402; Lansing on effect

of economic boycott on, **64**: 371; WW's reply to Anglo-French note on proposed Adriatic settlement, **64**: 459-63; debt to U.S., **64**: 475,n1; and Nitti's views on Adriatic question, **65**: 45-46; relations with Germany, **65**: 102, 253; on French invasion of Germany, **65**: 157-58, 158, 162, 171, 173; Yugoslavia on Albania and, **65**: 315; and "Wilson line" boundary, **65**: 373,n1; politics in, **65**: 448-49,n1; and recognition of Mexico, **65**: 463; and Poland, **65**: 527; note to U.S.'s Russian policy, **66**: 19-24; fear of hostilities at Spalato between Yugoslavia and, **66**: 26,n1; Lloyd George on, **66**: 43, 45; and Albania, **66**: 45,n6; Johnson on, **66**: 207n1, 322-23, 481-83; earthquake in, **66**: 323,n2; and Adriatic settlement, **66**: 367; Colby on Anatolia and, **66**: 429-30,n1; naval force blockades Fiume, **66**: 447-48,n3; N. H. Davis on boundary line, **66**: 499; and Adriatic question, **67**: 376-77,n3; and debt obligations, **68**: 106n1, 434n1; WW on situation in, **68**: 255,n1; R. S. Baker on translation of *World Settlement* in, **68**: 403; and Corfu incident, **68**: 419n1, 427, 435; *see also* Italy and the United States; Adriatic question, and under the names of the spokesmen for, such as Orlando, Vittorio; Vittorio Emanuel III; Sonnino, Sidney

Italy and the United States; **53**: 472, 494-96; use of U.S. troops, **53**: 167, 208, 290-91, 485-86, 697,n3; Cellere to accompany WW to France, **53**: 183-84; WW's proposed Italian trip, **53**: 345, 426, 496, 507, 584-85; Vittorio Emanuele III meets with WW in Paris, **53**: 439; Hurley on shipbuilding and, **53**: 455, 456; U.S. loan to Italy, **53**: 479; WW leaves for Italy, **53**: 578, 589; WW's arrival, speeches, and activities in Rome, **53**: 595-97, 597-99, 600-601, 602-603, 605-608, 608-609, 611-13; WW's speeches and activities in Genoa, **53**: 613, 614-15, 615-16; WW's speeches and activities in Milan, **53**: 613-14, 616, 616-17, 617, 617-18, 619-20; WW's activities and addresses in Turin, **53**: 620-21, 622-24; WW's meeting with Bissolati on Italian settlements, **53**: 641-44, 711,n1; success of WW's Italian trip, **53**: 646; WW meets with Orlando on Italian claims, **53**: 696-97; WW thanks Vittorio Emanuele III for his hospitality, **53**: 697-98; abolition of cable censorship, **57**: 448, 449; WW on ties between, **57**: 544, 612; and credits, **58**: 47; **59**: 71, 110-11, 111-12, 112-23; **61**: 441, 456-57; **62**: 230-31; Page on reaction in Rome to WW's Adriatic statement and fear for American's safety, **58**: 91-92, 93, 143; Page meets Orlando on crisis, **58**: 210; Page on danger of continued attacks by Ital-

Italy and the United States (*cont.*)
ian press on WW, **58**: 271-72; Soninno on, **58**: 322; Page on endangered relationship between, **58**: 357, 358, 450; Soninno and Orlando apologize for anti-Wilson press and speeches, **58**: 552; Lansing unhappy about Page coming to Paris, **58**: 554; Miller on friendship between, **59**: 81; T. N. Page's resignation, **59**: 517; **61**: 9, 559; Page on, **59**: 601-602; and the Thomas Nelson Pages, **60**: 118; Page to return to U.S., **60**: 135-36; House's suggestions for Page's replacement, **60**: 192; Whitlock appointed ambassador, **60**: 192, 358, 360, 485; **61**: 290; internal crisis in Italy and anti-Wilson forces in Senate, **60**: 531; WW memorandum on future relations with, **61**: 346; WW on, **62**: 291-92; and coal, **62**: 468; WW on resignation of T. N. Page, **62**: 561; Nitti on, **62**: 605-606; WW to Nitti on Adriatic question, **62**: 625; and crisis in Spalato, **63**: 524-25, 532; and U.S. draft reply on Adriatic question, **65**: 37-39; R. U. Johnson on assuming ambassadorship, **65**: 93-95, 125; hopes U.S. will have representative at San Remo Conference, **65**: 196; coal transport problem, **65**: 198-200, 300; R. U. Johnson urges purchase of embassy in, **65**: 305; Ambassador to U.S. presents credentials to WW, **65**: 338n2; on Giolitti's greeting to WW and WW's response, **65**: 448-49; issue of joint withdrawal of squadron off Spalato, **66**: 26,n1; suggestions for trade with, **66**: 74, 100-101; rumor of visit by Orlando, **66**: 323,n3; and issue of appointment of Italian ambassador to U.S., **66**: 339-40, 342, 381-82; and proposed visit of Duke of D'Aosta, **66**: 543-44; WW on postponing visit of Duke of Aosta, **67**: 8, and U.S. position on mandates, **67**: 154, 155; *see also* Italy; Vatican, The; Adriatic question; Italy
Italy at the Paris Peace Conference (Albrecht-Carrié), **54**: 135n3; **56**: 607n1; **57**: 488n10, 517n4; **58**: 55n3, 237n3, 413n2; **59**: 61n6, 125n1; **61**: 584n2; **64**: 169n3
Iudenich, Nikola Nikolaevich, **58**: 577,n9; **59**: 20,n13, 196
Ivanov-Rinov, Pavel Pavlovich, **53**: 185,n3; **56**: 185,n5, 186,n2, 519n1; **57**: 314,n3, 575n1; **58**: 495n3, 570,n6; **59**: 19,n12, 134, 234, 235-36, 619,n1
I.W.W.: *see* Industrial Workers of the World
Iwaszkiewicz-Rudoszanski, Waclaw Teodor, **57**: 276,n2; **60**: 161,n11
Iyenaga, Toyokichi, **67**: 258,n4
Izmir, Turkey: *see* Smyrna

J. P. Morgan & Company, **53**: 110n1, 484, 627; **55**: 451,n7; **57**: 503n1; **59**: 454; **60**: 155n1, 382; **62**: 155n1

Jack, Archibald, **54**: 83,n3
Jackson (White House employee), **65**: 194,n1
Jackson, Andrew, **54**: 176; **64**: 249; **66**: 317n1; **68**: 260-61, 267, 488, 489
Jackson, Charles Samuel, **63**: 275,n2, 277, 282; **65**: 431,n1, 442; **67**: 409, 417
Jackson, Frederick Huth, **53**: 528n4
Jackson, Philip, **67**: 409
Jackson, Stonewall: Lloyd George on, **60**: 300-301
Jackson Day Dinner, **64**: 261,n1; **66**: 333,n1
Jackson Day Message, **64**: 257-59; **65**: 416; drafts, **64**: 199n1, 252-55, 269,n3, 270; Houston on first revise of, **64**: 249n1, 250-52; Ashurst on 1920 campaign and, **64**: 263; Cobb on, **64**: 270n2; Sharp on, **64**: 285-86; R. S. Baker on, **64**: 321, 359; as indicator of WW's candidacy, **64**: 347; mentioned, **65**: 416
Jacob, J., **59**: 186
Jacob Hoffman Brewing Company, **59**: 76n1
Jacobs, Thornwell, **68**: 27; and WW's honorary degree, **65**: 86,n1, 89-90, 117, 381-82
Jacobs, Travis Beal, **59**: 447n1
Jacquemaire, Madeleine Clemenceau (Mrs. Numa), **64**: 239,n1
Jadwin, Edgar, **64**: 198n1
Jafredson, H. A.: murder of, **65**: 485,n4
James II (of England), **57**: 124
James, Cassie Mason Myers (Mrs. Julian), **66**: 470,n3
James, Edwin L., **67**: 402n1, 531n1
James, George Roosa, **57**: 378; appointed to first Industrial Conference, **63**: 300,n1
James, Ollie Murray, **56**: 348; **67**: 203
Jameson, Helen, **68**: 26
Jameson, John Butler, **53**: 24
Jameson, John Franklin, **66**: 409; **67**: 161; and Woodrow Wilson Clubs at Harvard, **66**: 476-69; **67**: 259-60, 260, 263-65, 267, 274; on WW's health and appearance, **68**: 26; and WW's request for historical information from, **68**: 52, 53, 55; on European attitude toward newly formed U.S. government, **68**: 65-68; *American Historical Review* editors to meet with WW, **68**: 68; WW thanks for historical investigation, **68**: 72
Jameson, Mariette Thompson, **66**: 467,n1
Jamestown Assembly (1619): celebration of, **66**: 115, 119, 123
Jamison, John Martin, **55**: 448n1
Janin, Pierre Thiebaut Charles Maurice (Maurice Janin), **55**: 400; **56**: 304,n1; **60**: 637,n1; **61**: 166,n21
Janowska, Halina, **59**: 216n5; **61**: 271n2
Japan, **53**: 324, 337, 339, 562-63; **54**: 13n2, 24n14, 264, 325; **55**: 164, 184; **56**: 531; **58**: 14, 114, 140, 198, 510; **60**: 420, 426; **61**: 56, 197; and China, **53**: 139, 140, 207, 464; and Russia, **53**: 144-47, 184-85, 227-29; **54**: 83, 84,

158n1, 158-59, 412; **55**: 493-94; **56**: 576; **58**: 568, 569, 570, 573-74,n3, 575, 576; **62**: 34n1; and representation at Paris Peace Conference, **54**: 24, 65; Reinsch on China and, **54**: 78-82; war claims and China, **54**: 289-93, 308-309, 314-16, 317, 318, 347n2, 348, 474,n1, 474,n2, 474-76,n1; and League of Nations, **54**: 206-208, 357, 463; WW on not trusting, **54**: 379; and Yap Island, **54**: 381-82; and resolution on racial equality, **54**: 485, 500; WW's concerns over seeming distrust of peace conference by, **54**: 548, 549; Masaryk and WW on Siberian intervention and, **54**: 557; and racial equality resolution, **55**: 155, 436-37; **56**: 59-60,n1, 80, 81, 164, 187-89,n3; **57**: 239-49, 247, 259-65, 268-70, 285, 286, 286,n1, 354, 373, 570-71; **61**: 234; has separate negotiations with Allies, **55**: 293-94,n1; naval fleet of, **55**: 517, 519, 520; and Korea, **56**: 187,n2; and China on treaties and claims regarding Shantung Province and Kiaochow, **56**: 189,n8,9; **57**: 358, 358-59, 453-54, 531, 554-56, 580, 582-85, 597, 597-98, 615-26, 626, 636; and cable discussion, **56**: 216-17; **58**: 296-98, 305, 352; and Council of Four meetings without presence of, **56**: 416, 525; and International Labour Legislation Commission, **56**: 604, 605; and Russia and railroads, **57**: 94, 421; on responsibility for war and enforcement of penalties, **57**: 132-33, 146, 150; Koo on restitution to China by, **57**: 298-301; presents claims to Council of Four; **57**: 599-610; doesn't wish to be present when China discusses claims, **57**: 608; Twenty-One Demands on China by, **57**: 617-18, 620, 621-22, 636; **58**: 137,n1, 165; issues and comments on Shantung claims, **58**: 68-70, 70-73, 105, 112, 128, 130-33, 142, 153, 165-68, 170, 175-76, 178-82, 183-84, 185, 186-87, 214, 215-16, 216-26, 229, 230-32, 232-34, 257-59, 261; and secret treaty with Great Britain, **58**: 111, 112; WW on settlement of claims, **58**: 244-45, 272-73; Balfour presents WW's suggested proposal on claims to, **58**: 246-47; and Reparation Commission, **58**: 249, 259, 259-60; on enemy prisoners of war, **58**: 260-61; various comments on claims settlement, **58**: 270-71,n2, 273, 320, 327, 328, 363,n1, 421; and recognition of Finland, **58**: 404n2; China's statements on claims settlement proposal, **58**: 419,n1, 427,n1, 522,n1; Benson on naval interests of, **58**: 456-57,n3,4,6; and retention of seized ships, **58**: 527; and peace treaty with Germany, **59**: 12; and Polish treaty and minority rights, **59**: 183; and Siberia, **59**: 234, 235; issue of Kolchak recognition and Siberia, **59**: 421, 461-62, 527, 550-51; **60**: 419, 428; to

have representative on Committee on New States, **59**: 465-66; and Korea, **59**: 474n3, 644n1; and Council of Four representation, **59**: 487-88; wants greater participation in Paris Peace Conference, **59**: 528; and Shantung settlement, **60**: 102, 104, 429, 602-603; **61**: 36, 249-50, 325-26, 386, 387, 438, 583n1; **62**: 3-4, 11,n1, 16-17, 40-42, 63-65; on reparations, **60**: 317, 323; estimate of damages, **60**: 359n1; and peace treaty, **60**: 434; and situation in China, **60**: 603-605; and removal of Czech troops from Russia, **61**: 206, 494, 579, 581; WW on Shantung settlement and, **61**: 237, 593, 594, 619-20, 629; **62**: 170, 171; Lansing tries to persuade to make statement on Shantung so China will sign, **61**: 325-26; and Germany, **61**: 495; Heney on, **61**: 539; and treaties of 1915 and 1918 with China and Versailles Treaty, **61**: 554-55, 556, 557-59; and Cossacks and Chinese Eastern Railway in Siberia, **61**: 571-73; on Bulgarian boundaries and western Thrace, **61**: 591-93; and Siberian railways, **61**: 636,n1; Graves on Siberian situation and, **62**: 87, 88-89; Lansing on public statement on Shantung settlement by, **62**: 153; public statement on Shantung settlement, **62**: 154-55; and mandates, **62**: 188; WW on Senate request for information and documents on Germany and, **62**: 208; and China, **62**: 281; Japan's aide-mémoire on Shantung settlement and future negotiations with China, **62**: 458-59; drafts of U.S. reply to Japan's aide-mémoire, **62**: 508-509, 522-24; McCumber on main objections to treaty concerning, **62**: 566; and U.S. troops in Siberia and railroad situation, **62**: 588, 589-90; war costs, **63**: 349; and Russia and Cossacks, **63**: 559, 560; and Lodge reservations, **64**: 39; invited to first meeting of Council of League of Nations, **64**: 272; and Adriatic question, **64**: 375, 398; and Siberia, **64**: 390-91; and Germany, **65**: 102; and Allied intervention in Russia, **65**: 144; on France's independent action in Germany, **65**: 173; and Anglo-Japanese alliance, **65**: 254-55; agrees to terms of banking consortium, **65**: 259,n1, 261, 277; **66**: 294-95; U.S. concern over occupation of Vladivostok, **65**: 284n1; ambassador to U.S. presents credentials to WW, **65**: 338n2; and recognition of Mexico, **65**: 463; U.S. concern over invasion of Sakhalin, **65**: 515-17; and Great Britain and action in Siberia, **66**: 39,n3; WW on, **66**: 157; and Yap Island controversy, **66**: 308-309, 326, 458, 459, 460, 460-64, 496; **67**: 54, 147,n1, 154-56, 194-95,n1,4; and disarmament, **67**: 26,n7; and Four Power Treaty, **67**: 484n1; and Hughes' open door resolu-

Japan (cont.)
  tion, **67**: 531n1; earthquake in, **68**: 424n1; delegation to Paris Peace Conference, photograph of, *illustration section*, **58**; intervention in Siberia: *see* Russia—Siberia, intervention in; Shantung settlement
Japan and the United States, **53**: 144-47; and Russian railroads, **53**: 463,n1, 555-57,n4, 623-33; and "Gentlemen's Agreement, **56**: 188,n4; and Siberia, **56**: 184-85, 186; and Tientsin uprising, **56**: 184-85,n2, 187; and Ishii-Lansing Agreement, **61**: 438; and public opinion, **62**: 20; decision to withdraw troops from Siberia, **64**: 219-21; treaty of 1898, **64**: 470; and anti-Japanese movement in California, **66**: 12-16,n1, 185-87, 295-96; and "Gentlemen's Agreement" **66**: 12,n1, 13, 14; and occupation of Sakhalin, **66**: 51-53
Japan's Honor and Pride (New York *World*), **58**: 363,n1
Japan Society, **56**: 60n1
Japanese-American Commercial Treaty of 1911, **56**: 188,n5
Japanese-Russian War: *see* Russo-Japanese War
Jassy, Rumania: anti-Semitic demonstrations in, **68**: 333,n1
Jastrow, Morris, Jr., **55**: 438,n1,3, 484
Jaurès, Jean, **57**: 176,n3
Jay, Peter Augustus, **63**: 270, 297, 484-85; **65**: 125,n2, 199,n13, 253, 299,n1, 300, 301, 304; on Italian situation, **61**: 109,n1; meets with Vittorio Emanuele III on Fiume crisis, **63**: 297-98; on crisis in Italy over Fiume, **63**: 515-17; requests and receives information of WW's health, **63**: 543, 560; promoted to Minister to Salvador, **65**: 426, 429
Jay, Susan Alexander McCook (Mrs. Peter Augustus), **65**: 299,n1
Jay Treaty, **60**: 41n1; **66**: 346n1
Jeanes Fund, **62**: 106n2
Jeanneny, Jules-Emile, **59**: 444,n1; **60**: 60n7; on Rhenish separatist movement, **60**: 8,n3, 9-15
Jebel Druse, **56**: 108,n6
Jefferson, Mark: photograph of, *illustration section*, **57**
Jefferson, Thomas, **60**: 246n10; **61**: 361; **63**: 547n1; **66**: 292; **67**: 162, 183n1; WW on, **67**: 252, 253; **68**: 441, 488; effort to purchase and preserve Monticello, **68**: 321; WW supports, **68**: 464-65
Jeffersonian Club, Washington, D.C., **67**: 252n1
Jefferson Day dinner (1922): brouhaha, **68**: 3, 10, 11-12, 14, 14-15, 17-18, 28, 59-60, 591
Jefferson Medical College, **63**: 539n2, 546n1
Jehovah's Witnesses, **55**: 482-83,n1
Jelavich, Barbara, **60**: 530n1

Jellinek, Georg, **67**: 247,n2, 248
Jenkins, William Oscar, **64**: 120n1, 121, 123, 128,n1; Lansing on, **64**: 123, 124; release announced, **64**: 128n1, 129, 133, 134, 138; Grayson on, **64**: 136
Jenkins affair, **64**: 103,n1, 127-28,n1, 127, 129-30, 131, 134, 231; and Lansing, **65**: 22n3
"Jenkins Case and Mexican-American Relations" (Cumberland), **64**: 120n1, 128n1
Jensen, Joan Maria, **60**: 115n6
Jersey City, N.J.: "slacker raids" in, **60**: 115n6
Jersey Railways Advertising Company, **55**: 468n1
Jervis, Richard, **67**: 174,n1
Jesenice, Yugoslavia: *see* Assling
Jessup, Philip Caryl, **61**: 66n3; **66**: 246n2
Jewell, Bert Mark, **62**: 122, 133,n1, 134-35, 136, 137, 140, 194-95, 485, 486, 567, 568-70, 570, 570-73, 573, 610; **65**: 14-16, 36n1, 215,n1, 359; urges railroad workers to return to work, **62**: 190, 191; and Plumb plan, **62**: 198n2; and railroad crisis, **64**: 420-24, 426, 428-31; letter of apology to WW, **65**: 285-86
Jewish Americans, **60**: 623, 624
Jewish Colonization Association, **59**: 413n3
Jewish Daily Courier: *see* Chicago *Daily Jewish Courier*
Jewish National Council for Bukhovina and Eastern Galicia, **54**: 258n1
Jewish National Council of German Austria, **54**: 258n1
Jewish National Council of Russia, **54**: 5n2
Jewish Tribune, **66**: 356, 357n2, 68
Jewish Welfare Board, **54**: 5n2; **57**: 459
Jews, **53**: 124, 297, 572; **54**: 52, 258, 347, 432-33; **55**: 438,n3; **57**: 169; **67**: 386, 387; eastern European, **53**: 67,n1, 79-80, 104-105; **55**: 368-81, 386; **59**: 419; **66**: 108-109, 356-57,n2; WW on, **53**: 67, 99, 141; **59**: 189, 276, 349, 471, 553; **66**: 110; **68**: 486; WW's remarks to B'nai B'rith, **53**: 239-40; and relief work, **53**: 25n1; Wolf on rights of, **53**: 259-60; Rothschild on, **53**: 543; House and Balfour discuss, **53**: 577; in Poland, **54**: 231-23, 545; **55**: 464; **58**: 290-93, 385, 386; **59**: 411-13, 445-46; **60**: 221-22, 228, 266, 287; and Palestine, **55**: 381-85, 386; **57**: 326n3, 406,n2; **58**: 400, 401; **61**: 27, 46, 47-50, 88-92, 97, 272-73; Balfour on Palestine question and, **56**: 203-204; and mideastern mission, **56**: 310; and story about Baruch, **57**: 429-30; Kerner on Hungary and, **58**: 158; Clemenceau on Klotz, **58**: 177, 186; and protection of rights of, **58**: 284-86, 287-88, 381,n3; and Rumania, **58**: 386, 387, 476; Taft on importance of religious freedom, **58**: 461, 560;

Frankfurter on, **58**: 555-56; and issue of minority rights in Poland and eastern Europe, **59**: 113, 116, 179-83,n3,4, 198-200, 218-21n7, 276, 496, 497, 514-16,n1, 553, 645; and Balfour Declaration, **59**: 150, 314, 349; treatment in Russia, **59**: 195,n4; in Galicia, **59**: 354; and League of Nations, **59**: 524, 604; and Polish-Ukrainian situation, **59**: 597, 598; Paderewski defends Poland's treatment of, **59**: 638-39; and proposed commission to investigate pogroms in Poland, **60**: 39, 99, 99-100, 287, 564, 567, 601, 602; and Rumania and peace treaty, **60**: 233-34,n4, 262; Marshall's suggestions for proposed Polish commission on, **60**: 358,n2; opposition in America to pogroms in eastern Europe, **60**: 487,n1; and press claims that WW under dominance of bankers, **60**: 531; and minority issue in Polish treaty, **60**: 623-24; Paderewski on Polish-Jewish relations, **60**: 629-33; and Senate resolution on massacres in eastern Europe, **60**: 640n1; Morgenthau on minority issue in peace treaty, **61**: 43; Marshall on minority rights issue, **61**: 63-64; House on Poland and, **61**: 178; Wise on WW and, **61**: 365; Kraus applauds WW's position on, **61**: 409-10; King-Crane Commission on Syria and, **61**: 443; Wolf praises WW's efforts on behalf of, **61**: 617; Louis Marshall on Jews situation in East Galicia and conflict between Ukraine and Poland, **62**: 220-22; WW to Marshall on, **62**: 284; request WW make statement on condition of Polish Jews, **62**: 531,n1; and Zionist movement in U.S., **62**: 609,n1; and Morgenthau mission and issue of publication of report on, **64**: 198n1, 260,n1,2; and mandate for Palestine, **65**: 248,n1, 334,n1; and anti-Semitism, **66**: 102,n1, 130-31, 540-42; **68**: 333,n1; inferred mission of Hurley to H. Ford, **66**: 130n1; seek and receive WW's endorsement for U.S. fund raising effort, **66**: 261, 265-66; praise WW, **68**: 485; see also Palestine; Zionism

Jiménez, Juan Isidro, **66**: 361,n1

Joachi, Eunjevic, **57**: 426

Joe Tumulty and the Wilson Era (Blum), **57**: 530n1; **63**: 601n1; **65**: 401n1

Joffe (Ioffe), Adolf Abrahamovich, **59**: 35,n1

Joffre, Joseph-Jacques-Césaire, **53**: 384, 459; **55**: 432; **57**: 38, 352; **62**: 156; **67**: 321n1; **68**: 26, 28; and Academie Française, **53**: 420n1, 450,n1,2, 500, 531-32; **55**: 149,n1; and 1917 mission to U.S., **57**: 100,n3; and Lloyd George and H. Wilson on, **60**: 304, 305

John Charles Francis, Prince: death of, **54**: 170n2

John Maynard Keynes (Skidelsky), **60**: 492n4

John Price Jones Corporation, **67**: 415n5

Johns Hopkins Medical School, **68**: 152n1

Johns Hopkins University, **54**: 194n2; **61**: 294, 635n2; **62**: 469n1; **64**: 32, 394, 516n1, 517n2; **65**: 5; **66**: 290n1, 302, 314n1; **67**: 258n4, 285,n1, 335n1; **68**: 68n1, 452n2; and Sir William Osler, **64**: 237n1; and Wilson & Colby announcement, **67**: 344

Johnson, Dr., **67**: 172

Johnson, Albert, **67**: 9,n2

Johnson, Allen, **66**: 315,n3

Johnson, Ben, **67**: 505,n1, 513

Johnson, Burton, **68**: 424,n1

Johnson, Douglas Wilson, **56**: 434,n3; **57**: 270, 456; **59**: 171, 200, 404, 405, 647,n1; **61**: 92,n3, 171, 284, 552, 566n1; **62**: 206, 238,n1, 239, 320, 457, 510, 575n5, 620,n1; **63**: 59n2, 270, 365; **65**: 94, 140, 373; on Adriatic problem, **56**: 563n3, 607-609,n1, 609-11; **60**: 137-38; **61**: 227-30; **63**: 91, 92, 207, 210; **64**: 367, 368-69, 370-71, 371, 402,n1, 446, 458,n3; on Fiume, **57**: 432-33; on formula for Adriatic settlement, **58**: 588, 589-90; on Klagenfurt Basin, **59**: 406-408; **60**: 34-38, 121-22; **61**: 41-43; on Yugoslav-Austrian border issue, **60**: 16,n1; on Thrace and Greece, **63**: 61-62; WW's suggested alterations to Adriatic text of, **64**: 375-80; on lecture at Academy of Music, **67**: 57-58; memorandum on Adriatic question, **67**: 501-502, 504-505,n1; photograph of, *illustration section*, **57**

Johnson, Edwin Stockton, **62**: 17, 19

Johnson, Evangeline Brewster: and broadcast of WW's Armistice Day message, **68**: 452,n1, 458

Johnson, Evan Malbone, **66**: 322-23,n1

Johnson, Hiram Warren, **53**: 583,n6; **58**: 410n1, 635; **60**: 572; **61**: 372, 506n1, 577, 597; **62**: 67, 264, 340, 347, 440; **63**: 223n1, 309n3, 340, 371, 445; **66**: 340; **68**: 146n1, 247, 278n2; Russian resolution of, **54**: 259,n3, 487; **55**: 149,n1; and publication of peace treaty, **59**: 313; and resolution on U.S. troops in Siberia, **61**: 353,n2, 579,n1, 596n1, 597; opposed League of Nations, **61**: 538; questions WW at Foreign Relations Committee meeting, **62**: 361, 363-64, 369, 374-82, 404, 407-408, 410; and amendment to League of Nations Covenant, **62**: 614,n2; WW answers allegations of, **63**: 309, 310; speech attacking League of Nations and Versailles Treaty, **63**: 398,n1, 399; and reservations, **63**: 482-83n4, 484; and Mexican situation, **64**: 120; on WW's health, **64**: 135-36; and treaty fight, **64**: 200-201, 328n2, 336, 338, 387; as presidential possibility, **65**: 235, 243, 372; WW on League of Nations and, **65**: 416; anti-Japanese movement in California, **66**:

Johnson, Hiram Warran (*cont.*)
186; and Spencer's allegations, **66**:
198n1; R. S. Baker on, **68**: 313; photograph of, *illustration section,* **65**
Johnson, Homer Hosea, **56**: 120,n1,2;
and commission to investigate
pogroms in Poland, **60**: 358,n2, 567, 601;
and Morgenthau's mission to Poland,
64: 198n1
Johnson, Hugh, **66**: 58n1
Johnson, Jackson, **63**: 32,n3, 33
Johnson, James Weldon, **66**: 25n1; on
lynching, **67**: 570,n1
Johnson, Katherine McMahon (Mrs.
Robert Underwood), **65**: 94,n2, 198,n1,
200; **66**: 483,n6
Johnson, Lyndon Baines, **68**: 388n1
Johnson, Mary Wright, **67**: 213
Johnson, Robert Arthur, **59**: 29,n5, 30, 148
Johnson, Robert Underwood, **62**: 291-92;
65: 125, 140, 197; **66**: 87n1, 89, 481-83,
543; **67**: 8; **68**: 581; becomes ambassador to Italy, **56**: 280; **60**: 192; **64**: 296,
317, 322, 343-44, 346, 353, 407, 474;
65: 93-95, 125, 299-305; on Italy and
economic consideration, **62**: 252-53; on
WW's health, **65**: 80; on assuming duties as Ambassador to Italy, **65**: 93-95,
125, 299-305; on Italy and coal transport problem, **65**: 198-200; and San
Remo Conference, **65**: 213, 271n1,
302-303; on Italian situation, **66**:
207n1, 322-23; WW on letters of, **66**:
207; and appointment of Italy's ambassador to U.S., **66**: 339-40, 381; and
Adriatic settlement, **66**: 364, 365, 377;
asked if he commented on Adriatic set-
tlement, **66**: 389
Johnson, Robert Wood, **68**: 452n1
Johnson, Roger Bruce Cash, **64**: 521,n2
Johnson, Samuel M., **67**: 28,n1
Johnson, Simeon Moses, **64**: 296,n1
Johnson, Stewart, **53**: 342,n6
Johnson, Walter, **68**: 148n5
Johnson, Warren Forman, **61**: 489,n2;
65: 401n1; **68**: 14,n1, 581
Johnson, William David, Jr., **66**: 325,n1
Johnson, Willis Fletcher, **67**: 297n2
Johnson amendment, **63**: 482, 483, 484,
571
Johnson & Johnson, **68**: 452n1
Johnson immigration bill, **67**: 9,n2, 51;
WW on not approving, **67**: 178-80
Johnson Resolution, **60**: 242n1, 244, 247,
287, 288, 290, 374,n1, 534; **61**: 353,n2,
579,n1, 596n1, 597
John Spargo and Wilson's Russian Policy
(Radosh), **66**: 5n2, 19n1
Johnston, Albert Sidney, **55**: 85
Johnston, Charles M., **66**: 404n4; on
Mexican situation and issue of recogni-
tion, **65**: 461, 462-64, 486-87
Johnston, Robert, **68**: 558,n4, 577
Johnston, William Hugh, **64**: 424, 431;
65: 16, 359; on railroad wage crisis, **62**:
118-22

*Joint Debate on the Covenant of Paris,
World Peace Foundation, League of
Nations,* **56**: 161n1
Jolanda Margherita Milena Elisabetta
Maria, Princess, **53**: 596,n3
Jones, Andrieus Aristieus, **53**: 188; **55**:
297; **60**: 243,n3; **62**: 18, 263; **64**:
359,n1; **67**: 140,n2,3, 350
Jones, Clement, **59**: 309; **61**: 206
Jones, David Benton: and purchase of
Pierce-Arrow for WW, **67**: 116,n5, 137,
168, 186,n1; death of, **68**: 545,n1; WW
on death of, **68**: 546
Jones, Edgar DeWitt, **67**: 503,n1, 507
Jones, Harry William, **54**: 5,n3, 6
Jones, Isaac Thomas, **67**: 399-400,
415n5; and WW Foundation, **67**: 393-
94,n1, 408-10, 417-18, 545,n2
Jones, Jesse Holman, **53**: 526,n1; **54**:
263; **66**: 498; **67**: 173; praises WW, **66**:
474-75,n1; and fund raising efforts for
WW's S Street home, **67**: 151, 402-403;
WW thanks, **67**: 407; **68**: 444, 513, 517-
18, 534; and WW Clubs, **67**: 416; and
trust fund for WW, **68**: 438-39, 440-41,
442, 443, 444, 516, 526, 534; to help
buy Rolls-Royce for WW, **68**: 516
Jones, John Price, **67**: 415n5
Jones, Kennedy, **57**: 6n7, 145n1
Jones, Marvin, **55**: 297,n4
Jones, Mary Gibbs (Mrs. Jesse Holman),
67: 152,n1, 173, 403, 407, 416; **68**:
444,n1, 517, 526
Jones, John Carleton, **67**: 509n2
Jones (Meredith) Ashby, **68**: 196,n1
Jones, Percy L., **56**: 196, 197, 197-98,
244; **58**: 56,n5
Jones, Thomas Davies, **58**: 482,n2; **65**:
382; appointed to first Industrial Conference, **63**: 300,n1; WW offers Cabinet
position to, **64**: 232,n1; and purchase of
Pierce-Arrow for WW, **67**: 116,n4, 137,
168, 186,n1; and fund raising efforts
for WW's S Street home, **67**: 137n3;
and WW Clubs, **67**: 326, 353; to contribute to trust fund and automobile
purchase, **68**: 443, 513, 516; WW grateful for friendship and generosity, **68**:
518, 534; WW's condolences to, **68**: 546
Jones, Thomas Jesse, **53**: 526,n1; **62**:
292,n1
Jones, Thomas Sambola, **61**: 638-
40,n6,11; **64**: 317; resignation of, **65**:
260,n1, 316-17, 358, 361
Jones, Wesley Livsey, **56**: 187n3; **65**:
270,n1; WW invites to White House to
talk about treaty, **61**: 492-93,n2, 516;
and treaty fight, **64**: 94, 200, 202, 337,
339
Jones, William Carey, **63**: 350,n1; **65**:
289n1
Jones bill, **65**: 270,n1, 277-83, 290,
351,n1; Cabinet discusses, **66**: 60; *see
also* Merchant Marine Act of 1920
Jonnart, Célestin-Augustin-Charles, **65**:
61,n2, 62

Joseph of Hapsburg (Joseph August Viktor Klemens), Archduke of Austria, **56**: 462,n11; **62**: 428n1; **63**: 61n2

Jordan, David Starr, **54**: 397n1; **66**: 542n1

Jordan, Richard H., **53**: 321,n1

Jossier, M., **53**: 502n1

Jostens, General, **61**: 3

Jouasset, Georges: and reparations, **59**: 422,n6

Jouhaux, Léon, **56**: 236, 603,n1, 615

Journal of Abnormal and Social Psychology, **65**: 401n1

Journal of American History, **55**: 347n1; **58**: 611, 612n3; **62**: 155n1; **64**: 120n1; **66**: 5n2

Journal of Commerce, **57**: 384-85

Journal of Contemporary History, **53**: 515n1

Journal of Modern History, **55**: 383n2; **57**: 435n4; **65**: 155n1; **67**: 484n1

Journal of Negro History, **61**: 406n1

Journal Officiel de la République Française, Chambre des Députés, Débats Parlementaires, Session Ordinaire, 1918, **53**: 544n1

Journal of Political Economy, **54**: 521n1

Journey Through My Years (Cox), **65**: 520n1

Jovanović, Ljubomir, **59**: 120,n6

Jowett, Benjamin, **61**: 106,n3

Juárez, Mexico, **61**: 487

Judiciary Committee (House of Reps.), **60**: 380

Judiciary Committee (Senate), **62**: 115n1; investigation of German propaganda in U.S., **54**: 397,n1,2; hearings on Bolshevik and German propaganda, **55**: 297n2, 350,n2

Judson, Harry Pratt, **62**: 452,n1

Julian, Venetia: *see* Venezia Guilia

Julich, Germany, **57**: 591

Jung, Guido, **61**: 314,n7

Junkers, **58**: 572-73

Juriga, Ferdis, **57**: 338,n2

Jusserand, Elise Richards (Mme. Jean–Jules), **53**: 35, 184, 318, 459, 468, 502; **55**: 487, 499; **60**: 546, 547; **61**: 114, 362, 492; **62**: 156; **68**: 580

Jusserand, Jean-Jules, **53**: 35, 98, 183-84, 291, 292, 292-93, 318, 332, 345-46, 348, 368, 385, 502, 504, 693, 723; **54**: 175, 306, 498; **55**: 160, 221, 487, 489, 499; **58**: 482; **60**: 546; **61**: 362, 378, 383, 492; **62**: 156; **63**: 366; **64**: 157; **65**: 76; **66**: 46n7; **68**: 580-81; and WW-Poincaré dinner invitation episode, **61**: 112, 113, 114, 115, 119, 133, 173, 180; on WW, **61**: 136; on treaty being killed by Lodge and Republicans, **64**: 44; on need for U.S. delegates to remain in Paris, **64**: 101-102; and Grey's letter, **64**: 366-67, 380; on France's reaction to Hitchcock letter, **65**: 84,n1, 84-85; WW and Polk respond to charges stemming from Hitchcock letter, **65**: 87, 89, Polk's

draft note to on Turkish treaty, **65**: 111-12, 112-15, 116; and Lansing's calling of Cabinet meeting, **65**: 139-40; and Russia, **65**: 143; and French invasion of Germany, **65**: 156-57, 158; consults Lodge, **66**: 238n1; **67**: 33, 236n1, 466; WW on, **68**: 593,n9

Justice, Department of, **53**: 287, 636n1; **62**: 212; and Gregory's resignation, **53**: 705, 706; WW on allocations to, **61**: 291; and cost of living crisis, **62**: 168, 169,173, 174, 175; and "Palmer raids," **65**: 187n5; accused of trailing Creel in Mexico, **66**: 321

Justice Oliver Wendell Holmes, Jr., Zechariah Chaffee, Jr., and the Clear and Present Danger Test for Free Speech (Ragan), **55**: 347n1

Kabinett Scheidemann (Schulze, ed.), **61**: 34n1

Kachaznunim, Hovhannes, **56**: 443,n2

Kadi, Mohammed Abd Hamud, **56**: 122,n1,2

Kahn, Gaston-Camille, **60**: 605,n5

Kahn, Julius, **55**: 438,n3, 484; **59**: 278,n2; **66**: 261; and army reorganization bill, **65**: 576n1; **66**: 528,n1, 532; **67**: 97n1

Kahn, Otto Herman, **68**: 548

Kahn, Robert Lester, **58**: 634n14

Kakoulides (Kakoulidis), Admiral, **59**: 22,n3

Kalijarvi, Thorsten V., **68**: 521n1

Kalmykov, Ivan Pavlovich, **53**: 184,n1, 556,n7; **55**: 401; **58**: 495n3; **59**: 234; **61**: 572,n5

Kamei (Japanese consul), **56**: 185,n3

Kamenev, Lev Borisovich, **54**: 92n1

Kane, U.S.S., **67**: 9

Kane, Theodore Porter, **56**: 184n1

Kaneko, Kentaro, **53**: 556,n5

Kanellopoulos, Efthymios, **59**: 25,n5

Kann, Robert Adolf, **57**: 263n6

Kansas, **53**: 24; Democratic politics in, **65**: 178; **68**: 75-76; and railroad strike, **68**: 148,n5

Kansas, University of, **67**: 68n2

Kansas City, Mo., **68**: 166n1; Grayson on WW's arrival and address in, **63**: 63-64; WW's address in, **63**: 66-75

Kansas City Star, **53**: 28, 30; **63**: 63n2, 75n, 223n2; and Lansing's dismissal and WW's health, **65**: 6

Kansas City Star, Weekly, **64**: 340

Kapp, Wolfgang, **65**: 98,n1

Kapp Putsch, **65**: 98,n1, 99-102, 106, 107, 155,n1, 236-37, 304

Karabagh, Armenia, **65**: 287

Karaghatch (Karagach), **59**: 137-38,n4

Karavongse, Phya Prabha, **64**: 468,n1, 469

Karawanken Mountains, **59**: 405-406, 408; **60**: 35, 36

Karelia, **57**: 139; **59**: 21,n4

Karger, Gustav J., **61**: 607n1; **63**: 51,n1, 150

Karl Liebknecht: Man Without a Country (Meyer), **62**: 557n2

Károlyi, Count Mihály, **53**: 7,n3; **54**: 470-71,n1; **56**: 254; **57**: 77, 78, 169; **60**: 260, 351, 353, 355; fall of, **56**: 182n1, 332, 333, 384, 459, 460-61; and Hungarian armistice, **56**: 379, 382; Count Sigray on events leading to resignation of, **56**: 474

Kars, Russia, **66**: 422

Kaschau, Czechoslovakia: *see* Kosice

Kasemzadeh, Firuz, **58**: 333n2

Kashmir, S.S., **61**: 508n1

Kashubes, **60**: 186,n3

Kass, Maurice, **53**: 137

Kassandra, Greece: *see* Cassandra

Kassubia (Kashubia), Poland, **60**: 186,n3

Kastellorizo (Castollorizo), **59**: 146,n18

Katherine (McAdoo family nurse), **68**: 240

Katherns, Richard Donland, **68**: 36,n1, 39

Kattegat, **56**: 35n7,8

Katz, Friedrich, **56**: 340n1

Kaufman, Albert, **68**: 485, 486

Kaunas, Lithuania: *see* Kovno

Kavalla, Greece, **59**: 21,n14, 22, 27, 54, 59; **62**: 265, 320; **65**: 112; **68**: 513

Kavanagh, Francis Bernard, **67**: 101

Kazan, Russia, **60**: 95n2

Kearful, Francis Joseph, **62**: 48,n2; **64**: 355,n2

Kearney, Belle, **68**: 93n3

Keating-Owen Child Labor Act, **58**: 605n2

Keblinger, Wilbur, **63**: 486,n6

Kedourie, Elie, **56**: 110n7, 122n2

Keen, Edward Leggett, **54**: 60,n1

Keenan, Frank, **65**: 348

Keeney, C. Frank, **65**: 336,n3

Kehl, Germany, **55**: 475; **57**: 592; **58**: 135

Keil, Wilhelm, **59**: 36,n4

Keith, Arthur Berriedale, **54**: 311n2; **56**: 268n2

Kelch, H., **62**: 82n1, 88

Keller, Friedrich von, **57**: 446

Keller, Morton, **55**: 338n2

Kelley, Cornelius Francis, **63**: 610n1

Kelley, Francis Clement, **58**: 380,n2

Kelley, William J., **59**: 320

Kellogg, Frank Billings, **53**: 75; **60**: 43,n2; **61**: 372, 516, 563,n2, 607n1; **62**: 67, 113, 308, 491n1; **67**: 608, 608-609, 609, 611; **68**: 156n3; WW invites to White House to discuss treaty, **61**: 492-93,n2, 545; looks for compromise on treaty, **61**: 600-601; and Article X, **62**: 263; and treaty reservations, **63**: 151, 296, 363, 444, 445; and treaty fight, **64**: 94, 200-201, 283, 291, 283, 291, 337, 338, 339; and Hitchcock letter, **65**: 71n3

Kellogg, Paul Underwood, **62**: 530; **66**: 542n1

Kellogg, Walter Guest, **61**: 366,n3

Kelly, John, **65**: 476

Kelly, William, **63**: 607,n1

Kelsey, Albert, **68**: 52n1

Kelso, James, **67**: 335

Kemal Atatürk: *see* Mustapha Kemal Pasha

Kenan, Edward, **59**: 476n2

Kendall, Calvin Noyes, **67**: 483,n1, 487, 490

Kendrick, John Benjamin, **53**: 157, 636n1; **56**: 398; and treaty fight, **64**: 199n1, 200, 202

Kennan, George Frost, **53**: 629n3

Kennedy, Anderson Ross, **66**: 80n1

Kennedy, Francis A., **59**: 621,n1; photograph of, *illustration section*, **54**

Kennedy, John Bright, **65**: 397n1

Kennedy, Joseph Leland, nephew of WW, **65**: 211, 220-21; asks WW to intervene on his behalf for job promotion, **66**: 38, 39; J. S. Williams on job performance of, **66**: 40-41, 42

Kennedy, Marion Williamson Wilson (Mrs. Anderson Ross), sister of WW, **65**: 211n1; **66**: 80n1

Kennedy, Mary, **65**: 211

Kennedy, Philip Benjamin, **62**: 322,n1

Kennedy, Thomas: protests coal award, **66**: 66-67, 69

Kent, Frank Richardson, **67**: 357,n2

Kent, H.M.S., **62**: 86

Kentucky, **59**: 39; Democratic politics in, **68**: 14, 473-74; Hull to visit, **68**: 86; and woman suffrage, **62**: 615,n2

Kentucky, University of, **67**: 536n1

Kenyon, William Squire, **54**: 259n3; **55**: 257; **61**: 437; **62**: 96,n1, 233; **63**: 198,n4; on corn to famine areas, **67**: 140,n2,3; WW invites to White House to talk about treaty, **61**: 492-93,n2, 545, 563,n2; and treaty fight, **64**: 94, 200-201, 337, 339

Keppel, Frederick Paul, **57**: 60,n3

Kerenskii (Kerensky), Aleksandr Feodorovich, **53**: 6, 179; **54**: 259n2; **59**: 273, 302, 311; **62**: 87-88; on Russian situation and not recognizing Kolchak, **59**: 150-56

Kern, Howard Lewis, **55**: 264,n3

Kern, Paul Bentley, **67**: 529-30,n1

Kernan, Francis Joseph, **54**: 471,n2; **56**: 49n10; **57**: 275, 302, 357, 372, 628; and Polish-Ukrainian ceasefire, **56**: 468,n1, 469; on situation in eastern Europe, **57**: 275-80

Kerner, Robert Joseph, **59**: 403,n3, 404; on political situation in Central Europe, **58**: 156-60,n1

Kerney, James, **65**: 511n2; Tumulty thanks, **67**: 202; WW thanks for birthday greetings, **67**: 521; on WW running for Senate from N.J., **68**: 454; WW's suggestions for senatorial candidate from N.J., **68**: 459; meets with Baruch and Davis on N.J. senatorial candidate, **68**: 460, 461, 462, 463; on WW writing newspaper articles and WW's response, **68**: 498, 499; and Van Dyke-Machen controversy, **68**: 519, 519-20;

last inverview with and impressions of WW, **68**: 588-97; WW thanks for birthday greetings, **68**: 596

Kerr, Kathel Austin, **55**: 248n2

Kerr, Philip Henry, **54**: 349, 384,n5; **55**: 475,n2, 476, 540n1; **56**: 259n1, 434,n2; **58**: 58, 103, 336, 341, 489, 490; **59**: 105, 302, 303, 304, 312, 366n1, 421, 602, 613; **60**: 20,n2, 95, 300, 308, 394, 420, 436, 466, 467, 478, 482, 519; **61**: 286; **63**: 306; **67**: 105n3; **68**: 502; and draft dispatch to Kolchak, **59**: 435, 436, 437, 440-42, 457, 468-70, 481; and responsibility of Germany for war, **60**: 438, 467-68; and Bullitt mission, **61**: 509,n1; and Christian Science, **68**: 68-69;

Kerr Shipping Company, **65**: 282

Kerwin, Hugh Leo, **60**: 248,n2; **65**: 553n1; on coal situation, **66**: 18-19

Kerwin, Jerome G., **65**: 398n1

Kette, Albert W., **67**: 510-11,n1

Kettering, Charles Franklin, **63**: 441n2

Keuchingen, Saar Basin, **58**: 67

Keyes, George Thurman, **55**: 330n2

Keyes, Henry Wilder: and woman suffrage, **58**: 274,n2; **62**: 29,n1; meets with WW on League of Nations, **62**: 92

Keynes, John Maynard, **56**: 208,n1, 270, 357, 444, 453, 498, 499n3, 501, 502, 535, 580; **57**: 79, 109; **58**: 249, 266, 278, 399, 402, 565, 623; **60**: 26n11; **65**: 457-58,n3; **67**: 169,n1; **68**: 223,n3; on rehabilitation of European credit and relief financing, **58**: 12-13,n1; mention of economic rehabilitation memorandum, **58**: 20, 120, 122, 595n2; on enemy ships in U.S. ports, **58**: 289; and reparations, **60**: 93; leaves peace conference, **60**: 315,n6, 494,n4

Khabarovsk (Habarovsk), Russia, **53**: 184; Japanese troops in, **65**: 515-16; **66**: 51-52

Kherson, Russia, **56**: 51,n11

Khoury, Philip Shukry, **61**: 443n1

Kianga territory, **62**: 189

Kiaochow, China, **54**: 289-90, 291, 315, 316, 316-17, 317, 474n1, 474n2 (2 references); **55**: 424; **56**: 267; **57**: 298, 358, 359, 431n1, 453, 454, 554-55, 561,n2, 580, 597, 608, 615-17, 618; **60**: 104, 429, 471,n12, 12; **61**: 237, 242, 249, 250, 325n5, 447, 555, 556; **62**: 19, 154, 458, 508, 509, 522, 523, 524; **63**: 84, 330, 413, 471; Chinda on, **57**: 597-98; **58**: 46, 68-70, 70-71, 72-73, 112, 130-33, 166, 168, 175, 178-79, 181, 185, 214, 215, 216, 231, 233, 247, 256, 261; and Japan's claims, **57**: 599-610; WW meets with Chinese delegates on, **57**: 635-37; and claims settlement, **58**: 270-71,n1, 272, 277

Kiaochow-Chinan Railway, **57**: 616; **58**: 216-26, 222, 228

Kiaochow-Tsinanfu Railway, **58**: 73; **62**: 154

Kiel, Henry William, **63**: 31,n1, 33

Kiel, Germany: mutiny at, **53**: 7, 8

Kiel Canal, **54**: 553; **55**: 24, 108, 430, 434-35, 522-23, 539; **56**: 3, 34-38, 268; **57**: 358, 391,n1, 397-98, 399, 404-405, 457, 567-69,n2; **58**: 63, 65-67, 122-25; **59**: 417; **60**: 520,n13

Kiev, Russia, **54**: 94; **62**: 427n1; **65**: 527n1

Kilby, Thomas Erby, **55**: 327-28,n1, 328; **61**: 464

Kile, Orville Merton, **62**: 300n1

Kimball's Dairy Farmer, **65**: 45n4

Kimber, Rita, **58**: 44n1; **59**: 68n3

Kimber, Robert, **58**: 44n1; **59**: 68n3

Kim Kyu-sik, **59**: 473-75,n1, 644,n2

Kimm, John Kiusic Soho: *see* Kim Kyu-sik

King, Mr. (of Indio, California), **68**: 503

King, Alexander Campbell, **54**: 429; **55**: 478,n1; **64**: 297,n2

King, Benjamin Mandeville, **65**: 530,n1, 567,n1; wedding plans and marriage, **66**: 267n2, 503, 505-506,n1

King, Charles Dunbar Burgess, **61**: 189,n7, 329,n6

King, Frederick Paul, **65**: 572,n16, 574

King, Henry Churchill, **54**: 277; **57**: 535,n2; **58**: 172,n2, 493; **59**: 318,n2, 369,n1, 420, 449, 575, 594-95; **61**: 44; **64**: 429n2; **66**: 542n1; mideastern commission, **56**: 155, 179, 272n2,, 310, 337, 442; on division of Turkish Empire, **58**: 322-27; on Syrian commission, **59**: 184-85; points to discuss with WW regarding Syrian comisison, **59**: 372-74; and commission to Turkey, **59**: 573-74; report on Turkey, **62**: 607-608,n1

King, Jere Clemens, **58**: 462n2; **59**: 401n4; **60**: 60n7

King, Leroy, **59**: 403,n4

King, Marjorie Brown (Mrs. Benjamin Mandeville), **67**: 356,n3

King, Philip, **61**: 374,n1

King, Stanley, **64**: 64n1; and second Industrial Conference, **63**: 611; suggested for various appointments, **65**: 77, 228,n2

King, William Henry, **54**: 397n1; **55**: 351n1; **56**: 187n3, 339; **61**: 437; **62**: 17-18; **68**: 504; and Mexican situation, **64**: 120n1

King-Crane Commission, **56**: 272n2, 310; **57**: 535; **58**: 172, 322-27, 493; **59**: 184-85, 318, 330, 333, 336, 345, 368, 369-70, 370n1, 420, 594-95, 632, 637; **61**: 44, 157,n9, 409,n2, 442-44; **62**: 607,n1; **65**: 142; points to be discussed with WW regarding, **59**: 372-74; report of, **61**: 442-44; **62**: 607-608,n1; **64**: 425n1,2

King-Crane Commission: An American Inquiry in the Middle East (Howard), **56**: 272n2; 313n2; **59**: 373n1; **62**: 607n1; **64**: 425n2

Kingdom of Serbs, Croats and Slovenes: *see* Yugoslavia

King's College, Cambridge, **59**: 316n1

Kingsley, Darwin Pearl, **67**: 464,n2

Kinkead, Eugene Francis, **56**: 405; and Irish issue, **55**: 468-70,n1
Kinsley, Philip, **62**: 627
Kipling, Rudyard, **53**: 521, 594; **67**: 105n3, 405, 573; WW receives gift of poem by, **66**: 352-53,n1, 369, 442, 456, 479
Kipps, Jack, **63**: 238n1, 273n2
Kiraly, Béla K., **56**: 462n11
Kirby, William Fosgate, **55**: 297,n1; **67**: 183, 198; and treaty fight, **64**: 199n1, 200-201, 336, 338, 339; suggested for Tariff Commission, **67**: 166-67,n1; WW on not appointing, **67**: 168-69; N. D. Baker supports appointment of, **67**: 171-72
Kirk, Alexander Comstock, **56**: 58,n2, 97; **61**: 321,n3; **62**: 152-53; **63**: 543,1; **64**: 90; on Korea wanting to be heard at peace conference, **59**: 643-44
Kirk, Clara Comstock (Mrs. James Alexander), **61**: 321,n4
Kirk Kilissa (now Kirklareli) Turkey, **65**: 111, 113
Kisch, Frederick Hermann, **56**: 255,n5; **59**: 353, 354, 357, 465, 531,n5, 541
Kitchener, Herbert Horatio, 1st Earl Kitchener of Khartoum and of Broome, **58**: 440
Kitchin, Claude, **53**: 23-24, 25, 135,n1, 542n2, 717; **55**: 334n1; **65**: 576; and taxation, **67**: 226, 485,n1
Kittrell College, **63**: 268n1
Klaeborg, Hans B., **67**: 18
Klagenfurt: *see* Paris Peace Conference—Yugoslavia; Klagenfurt
Klagenfurt Basin: *see* Paris Peace Conference—Yugoslavia; Klagenfurt Basin
Klaipeda: *see* Memel
Klapus, Francis, **68**: 263,n1
Klatchko, Mary, **65**: 270n2
Klauder, Charles Zeller, **67**: 567n2; on S Street house, **66**: 534; works with WW on plans for mansion, **66**: 232,n1, 291,n1, 305, 344-45,n3, 354-55, 393, 410, 458, 470, 510-11, 518-19, 543, 545-46; **67**: 7, 30-31, 47-48, 84-85, 86-87; shown movies of WW, **67**: 103; end of WW's plan for new home, **67**: 276,n1
Klein, Franz, **58**: 508-509
Klein, Nicholas, **56**: 283n1
Kline, James W., **64**: 424, 431; **65**: 16, 359
Kliuchnikov, Iurii Veniaminovich, **59**: 436,n7, 462
Klofá , Václav Jaroslav, **60**: 314,n4
Klotz, Louis-Lucien, **53**: 442,n3; **54**: 36,n2, 36-37, 39, 39-40, 41, 215, 283; **55**: 51, 54, 60-61, 66, 100,n3, 283, 284, 458n1; **56**: 353, 444, 502; **59**: 271, 275, 422; **60**: 53; **68**: 224,n2; on reparations, **56**: 355, 416, 417, 433,n2, 448-51, 453, 503, 509; **57**: 6, 8, 9, 11, 12, 13-14, 15, 18, 19, 23, 24, 26, 28-29, 29-30, 30, 31, 32, 80, 81, 82, 86, 203, 204, 207, 207-208, 208, 209, 310,n8; **58**: 36, 40, 40-

41; WW on time wasted by, **56**: 441; R. S. Baker on, **57**: 69; House on, **57**: 71; WW on, **57**: 351; Clemenceau on, **58**: 177, 186; and Crespi and reparations, **58**: 334, 335, 341, 368, 397-98; on reparations and successor states of Austria-Hungary, **59**: 387, 388, 389-90
Knabenshue, Paul, **57**: 465,n2
Knapp, Harry Shepard, **53**: 318,n1; **55**: 66,n1; **56**: 444,n2; **57**: 61, 502,n2; **60**: 241,n1; **61**: 124, 630n4; **63**: 525, 532, 557,n2, 558; **65**: 538-39; and blockade, **60**: 565,n1; meets with WW on various issues, **60**: 613-15; Hoover on relief efforts in Armenia and, **62**: 166; and Haiti, **66**: 73,n6, 78, 82, 99, 100; and Dominican Republic, **66**: 362, 383n1
Knight, Mrs., **53**: 369
Knight, Austin Melvin, **56**: 184n1
Knight, Lucian Lamar, **68**: 93,n1
Knights of Columbus, **54**: 5n2; **57**: 459; **59**: 627
Knock, Thomas J., **58**: 364n1
Knocker, R. E., **53**: 509,n3
Knott, Richard Gillmore: proposal for WW to write for *Louisville Post*, **68**: 483,n1, 483-84; WW considering offer of, **68**: 501
Knox, Alfred William Fortescue, **55**: 187, 400, 401; **56**: 184, 186, 304; **59**: 30; **62**: 34n1, 89-90
Knox, John, **56**: 121
Knox, Philander Chase, **53**: 308n1, 481,n1, 580, 625n1; **55**: 263, 270, 388n1, 499; **59**: 451n1, 524n1; **60**: 41n1, 202, 203, 531, 571, 609; **61**: 66n3, 372, 411; **62**: 5n6, 68, 306, 631; **63**: 223n1, 445, 484, 557,n1; **65**: 122n1, 225n1, 257, 371; and inauguration day activities, **67**: 205, 208, 210, 211, 270; and Senate investigation of alleged peace treaty leaks, **60**: 330; questions WW at Foreign Relations Committee meeting, **62**: 339, 354, 355, 356-57, 359,n23, 369, 395-96, 398; on Versailles Treaty, **63**: 3,n4; and Bullitt testimony, **63**: 337,n1; and treaty fight, **64**: 200-201, 328n2, 337, 338; photograph of, *illustration section*, **62**; *see also* Knox Resolution
Knox Resolution (June 1919), **60**: 376-77, 535, 536, 609; **61**: 66,n3, 116, 137, 347n1, 565, 614; Miller on, **60**: 567; WW on, **60**: 613; **64**: 192n1; declaring war at end, 1920, **65**: 122n1, 225n1, 247, 257n1; and Virginia plank on League of Nations, **65**: 293; WW's veto of, **65**: 328-29,n2
Knox Treaty of General Arbitration, **65**: 255
Koblenz: *see* Coblenz
Kogoma, S.M.S., **55**: 432
Kohler, Henning, **59**: 566n1
Kohlsaat, Herman Henry, **53**: 148, 164
Kohn, William, **55**: 450n6
Kojong (Korean emperor), **56**: 187n2

Kolb, Lawrence E., **58**: 618,n29, 621,n51
Kolberg, S.M.S., **55**: 23, 427; **56**: 29; **58**: 127
Kolchak, Aleksandr Vasil'evich, **53**: 136n1, 256, 258n1, 591, 630-31; **54**: 9, 21n8, 26, 94, 101, 173n1; **55**: 399-401; **56**: 254, 255; **57**: 575,n1; **58**: 265, 494, 496,n7, 506-507; **59**: 14,n4, 15, 16, 17, 18, 19-20, 29, 30, 31, 134, 148, 152, 153,n2, 154, 215, 225, 273, 300n8, 301, 311, 312, 572; **60**: 95,n2, 210, 215, 267, 609, 613, 615, 625, 636, 637; **61**: 99, 110, 130, 154, 166, 201, 202, 277, 316, 424, 455, 483, 484, 572,n6, 581; **62**: 15, 34n1, 86, 88, 206, 592, 594; **63**: 394, 421, 559; **64**: 308, 309; **66**: 21n1; and issue of U.S. supporting, **58**: 568, 569, 570, 573-78; extracts from speeches of, **59**: 72-73; issue of recognition of, **59**: 188, 189, 236, 453, 479, 527, 547, 552; **61**: 117; Bolsheviks on, **59**: 194, 195; and Graves, **59**: 234; Council of Four on draft and final dispatch to, **59**: 435-38, 440-42, 468-70, 481, 543-46, 618-19; Chinda on, **59**: 461-64, 465; and Baltic states, **59**: 466n5, 467n7; Hapgood on, **59**: 518, 519,n2; WW on, **59**: 540; and Estonia, **59**: 547n2, 548; meets with Harris and hopes for U.S. aid, **59**: 619; reply on policies of Russian government, **60**: 141-44; proclamation to Russian citizens, **60**: 180-81, 261-62; various comments on reply to, **60**: 203, 222, 388, 419; Council of Four on reply of, **60**: 228-29; Council's reply to, **60**: 435, 466, 486; and aid to, **61**: 40, 41, 130-31, 465, 466; Allies send plan for repatriation of Czech troops in Siberia, **61**: 287-99, and purchasing supplies from U.S., **61**: 288; and Cossacks and Japan, **61**: 571, 572, 573; collapse of government of, **64**: 219
Kolozsar University, **56**: 275n1
Koltchak's Constituent Assembly. Universal Suffrage (*Manchester Guardian*), **61**: 360,n5
Konenkamp, S. J., **56**: 403,n3; **60**: 378n1
Konia (Konya), Turkey, **56**: 108,n5; **58**: 414, 435; **59**: 43, 143, 147, 337, 345
Königgratz, Battle of: *see* Sadowa, Battle of
Königsberg, East Prussia, **54**: 342; **56**: 89, 146, 168, 169, 408n2, 409, 489, 526, 540, 541; **59**: 582; **60**: 187
Koo, Vi Kyuin Wellington, **54**: 473; **55**: 140, 178n2; **56**: 183, 229; **57**: 298, 371, 426,n1, 495, 627; **58**: 229, 553, 553-54; **59**: 528, 568; **61**: 209, 214; and League of Nations Commission, **54**: 426,n1, 464, 483, 494; **57**: 226-27, 229, 250, 256-57; on China's territorial claims, **54**: 308, 315, 316, 317-18; and Japan's anger at, **54**: 474, 475, 548; and Japan's racial equality amendment, **57**: 263; on restitution to China from

Japan, **57**: 298-301; on Shantung Province, **57**: 431,n1; presents China's claims to Council of Four, **57**: 615-25; on Twenty-One Demands, **57**: 617-18, 620, 621-22; meets with WW, **57**: 631-34, 634-37; on WW's compromise on Shantung controversy, **58**: 247; and China's wish to sign peace treaty with reservations, **61**: 176, 288-89; photograph of, *illustration section*, **58**
Koons, John Cornelius, **57**: 530n1; **61**: 504,n2
Kopp, Georg Cardinal: *see* Breslau, Archbishop of (1887-1914)
Korea, **61**: 618; demonstrations for independence from Japan, **56**: 187,n2; wants recognition at Paris Peace Conference, **59**: 473-75,n1, 643-44; Japan on, **66**: 51
Koren, William, **67**: 182
Koritsa, Albania, **62**: 605; **64**: 299, 301, 315, 369
Kornilov, Lavr Georgievich, **53**: 256; **54**: 259n2; **64**: 390n1
Koromilas, Lambros A.: *see* Coromilas, Lambros A.
Korošec, Anton, **53**: 123,n1, 124
Kosha, Phya Bibadh, **59**: 186,n1
Kosice (Kashcau), Czechoslovakia, **60**: 356,n4
Kossuth, Lajos, **56**: 572
Kotlas, Russia, **57**: 461, 560, 589; **59**: 465; **61**: 154, 164, 165, 166, 287
Kotor (Cattaro, Kotoriba), Croatia, **53**: 290, 638,n2
Kourbatoff (Kourbatov), V. Stepan: *see* Zavoiko, Vasili Stepanvich
Kovno (Kaunas), Lithuania, **54**: 204,n3; **56**: 413,n6
Kramář, Karel (Karl Kramartz), **54**: 344,n4, 490,n3, 509; **55**: 34, 35, 45, 70; **56**: 176, 177, 226; **57**: 224, 225, 252, 256, 263; **59**: 186,n6, 217, 630, 632,n4; **60**: 335, 344, 418n6, 428, 470; **61**: 136-37; and Austrian treaty, **59**: 588-89,n7; at Council of Four on Czech-Hungarian conflict, **60**: 354-55; at Council of Four on construction of railway lines, **60**: 551
Kramer, John F., **67**: 214
Krasnodar, Russia: *see* Ekaterinodar
Krasnov, Petr Nikolaevich, **53**: 256,n2; **54**: 94,n7
Krasnovodsk, Russia, **53**: 335
Krasnoyarsk, Russia, **62**: 87
Kraus, Adolf, **53**: 239,n1; applauds WW's efforts on behalf of Jews, **61**: 409-10,n2
Krech, Alvin Wilhelm, **68**: 548
Kermer, J. Bruce, **65**: 507,n1
Krenek, Joseph, **67**: 287n1
Kriz, Edward C., **67**: 321,n2, 325, 344, 348, 357, 360,n1, 411, 427, 496n1
Krizman, Bogdan, **56**: 462n10
Krk, Yugoslavia: *see* Vegalia
Krobatin, Baron Alexander von, **53**: 6,n1

Krock, Arthur Bernard, **54**: 60, 192, 389,n2; **68**: 14; **65**: 506,n3; **68**: 14; praises WW, **66**: 450; WW thanks, **66**: 471; WW's letter of introduction for, **68**: 28
Kruger, Daniel Wilhelmus, **54**: 252n3
Kruger, Staphanus Johannes Paulus (Oom Paul), **57**: 201
Krupenski, Vasilii Nikolaevich, **59**: 235,n1
Krupp Works, **54**: 244, 540
Kruse, Georgia Fleming W., **67**: 250,n1
Kuban, Russia, **56**: 253,n3; **58**: 42; **59**: 186
Kubijovy , Volodymyr, **54**: 480n1; **58**: 505n4
Kuehl, Warren F., **68**: 44n1, 99n1, 178n1
Kuhn Loeb & Company, **66**: 261n2; **68**: 112
Ku Klux Klan, **68**: 298,n2
Ku Klux Klan in the Southwest (Alexander), **68**: 298n2
Kun, Béla, **56**: 182,n1, 239, 241, 242, 277n4, 332, 414n10, 459; **58**: 157, 158, 486n3; **59**: 355, 519n2; **60**: 299-300, 351, 352, 354, 355, 419, 428, 462, 469, 470, 478; **61**: 195-96, 205, 238; **62**: 123n1; Brown on, **59**: 239, 240; on Hungary's position, **56**: 242-43; and Smuts mission, **57**: 77-79, 169, 170; replies to Council of Four's requests to stop hostilities, **60**: 312,n1, 595, 596-98; claims Rumania has resumed hostilities, **61**: 409-10,n2
Kunfi, Zsigmund, **56**: 182,n1, 276,n3, 277, 332-33; **57**: 108,n1, 170
Kunhardt, J. E., **66**: 538-39,n1
Kurdistan, **54**: 369, 370, 372, 455; **55**: 7
Kurland: *see* Courland
Kurtif, Mr., **62**: 88,n7
Ku Wei-chun: *see* Koo, Vi Kyuin Wellington
Kwangchowan, China, **63**: 412,n3
Kwapiszewski, Michael, **68**: 177,n1, 183
Kwidzyn, Poland: *see* Marienwerder

labor, **55**: 185; **57**: 303; **58**: 94n1, 497,n3; **59**: 145; and cancellation of war contracts, **53**: 18-20, 150; requests for peace commissioner to represent, **53**: 118-19, 119, 154-56, 165, 216; plans for international conference on, **53**: 257, 408n1, 436, 489, 490; working hours as peace conference issue, **53**: 366-67, 402; and unemployment, **53**: 413; British labor organizations support WW, **53**: 535-36; and marine workers strike in N.Y. port, **53**: 710; WW's remarks to working women in Paris, **54**: 271-73, 307, 308; and carpenters' controversy, **54**: 472, 519-20; and League of Nations, **55**: 6, 8-9, 9, 172, 450,n6; **61**: 37-40, 138, 231; **64**: 58,n1; and Whitley Councils, **55**: 91,n1; and railroads, **55**: 247, 248; **58**: 109-10; and Smith-Bankhead Americanization bill, **56**: 286-88; and U.S. Employment Service, **55**: 291-92, 478; and Burleson's poli-

cies, **55**: 364-65; **58**: 48-53; WW on restoration to prewar conditions, **55**: 389-91; problems in Great Britain, **56**: 205-206; International Labour Commission's recommendations for peace treaty and League of Nations, **56**: 236-38; Furuseth on defeated proposals on, **56**: 308; proposed telephone and telegraph workers strike, **56**: 311,n1, 340, 340-41, 403, 404; and Railroad Administration and coal prices, **56**: 401-402; Robinson on not reopening labor convention, **56**: 603-604, 604-605; Hines on coal workers, **57**: 45-47; and peace treaty, **57**: 239,n5, 528,n1,2,3; **58**: 173-74, 329; and steel price controversy, **57**: 386; and Saar Basin, **57**: 411; and New England Telephone and Telegraph Co. strike, **57**: 425,n1, 511, 530, 530,n1; WW on Employment Sunday, **57**: 447; WW on clauses for peace treaty, **58**: 43, 364; French workers support WW's Adriatic statement, **58**: 164,n1; May Day celebrations in Paris, **58**: 274-75, 276; Tumulty on, **58**: 329, 361-63, 605; **62**: 197; Borden on articles for peace treaty, **58**: 416-18, 467-49; and issue of building foreign ships in U. S. shipyards, **58**: 460; Council of Four on Brockdorff-Rantzau's note on Germany's views of clauses in treaty on, **59**: 47-48, 48-50, 132, 133, 163, 486; draft reply to Germany on, **59**: 48n3; eight-hour day, **59**: 49,n4; and grievances against Burleson, **59**: 108-109; and Gompers and League of Nations program on, **59**: 203; and WW's special message to Congress, **59**: 290-93; Brockdorff-Rantzau's reply, **59**: 421,n3; shipyard workers' demonstration in Philadelphia, **59**: 476-77,n2; Hines on railroad situation and, **59**: 523n2; **62**: 72-77, 469-71, 472-76; WW's greetings to A.F. of L., **60**: 111, 113, 197; Tumulty on principles in peace treaty on, and suggestions for legislative action, **60**: 150-54; and bombings, **60**: 153; and telegraph strike, **60**: 378-79; **61**: 539-40; and Germany's offer to restore devastated regions, **60**: 520-21,n14, 529; House praises Shotwell on, **61**: 131-32; and American Federation of Labor's resolution against mob rule and lynchings, **61**: 357-59; requests Burleson's removal, **61**: 364-65; and cost of living, **61**: 412-13; and demands by railroad workers, **61**: 536; and railroad crisis, **62**: 98, 98-99, 117, 118-22, 133-34; Delahunty on WW and, **62**: 122; international conference on, **62**: 162-63; WW appeals to regarding strikes, **62**: 218; F. D. Roosevelt on, **62**: 231-32, 232-33; Palmer's memorandum for WW's statement on railroad wage situation, **62**: 462-65; WW's statement on rail-

road situation, **62**: 472-76; WW's Labor Day message, **62**: 595-96; Gary on U.S. Steel Corporation and, **62**: 596-601; proposed conference on capital and, **62**: 596, 623, Lansing on radical propaganda causing future strikes, **62**: 612-13; WW on treaty and, **63**: 14-15, 78, 87, 99, 110, 176, 246, 261-62, 356, 357, 373, 497, 502; suggestions for volunteer speakers, bureau for interpretation of WW's position, **63**: 53, 54; and Women's Trade Union League, **63**: 56-57; and steel strike, **63**: 65-66; relationship between capital and, **63**: 127-28, 146-47, 244; **64**: 86; request for Negro representation at Industrial Conference, **63**: 268; WW meets with labor leaders in Seattle, **63**: 273,n2; WW and leaders in San Francisco, **63**: 296-97, 302-303, 303-304; WW's message to first Industrial Conference, **63**: 554,n1; and coal strike, **63**: 593-94, 595-98, 599-601; and Versailles Treaty, **64**: 49; WW names new members to second Industrial Conference, **64**: 64,n1; and Annual Message to Congress, **64**: 83-86, 113-15; international conference on, **64**: 97-98,n1; coal miners accept WW's proposal, **64**: 179; on extending government control of railroads, **64**: 197-98; Bituminous Coal Commission established, **64**: 206-209; and Executive Order for half days for government employees, **64**: 218; on not delaying resolution of railroad wage issue, **64**: 428-31; Hines on WW's response to railroad situation, **64**: 467-68; WW's statement on Bituminous Coal Commission's settlement, **65**: 104-105; Tumulty's suggestions for Message to Congress, **65**: 152; Railroad Labor Board members appointed, **65**: 189,n1; WW's message to Anthracite Wage Scale Committee, **65**: 312-13; W. B. Wilson on international conference on emigration and immigration, **65**: 569-71; WW on League of Nation's International Labour Office and, **66**: 151,n1; WW on, **66**: 155-56, 194; Tumulty's fears for if Republicans elected, **66**: 215; A. F. of L. requests general amnesty for "political" prisoners, **66**: 231-32, 515-16; reinstatement of outlaw strikers, **66**: 254,n1, 254-55, 262-63, 546; J. L. Lewis on Alabama coal strike, **66**: 263-65; W. B. Wilson's speech on gains of during Wilson presidency, **66**: 346,n1; Gowen's appeal for elderly railroad workers, **66**: 498; and Women's Bureau, **66**: 520; supports self-government for Dominican Republic, **66**: 537-39; **67**: 73, 86; The Document on, **67**: 575-76; **68**: 8, 220, 540; WW on labor people, **67**: 606-607; WW on disputes between capital and, **68**: 89-90; and railroad strike, **68**: 129n1,

148n5; J. H. Clarke on League of Nations and, **68**: 360; *see also* International Labour Organization; strikes; Immigration and Emigration, Commission on
Labor Adjustment Board, **65**: 17
Labor, Department of, **53**: 253, 279; **54**: 392, 500n1; **62**: 96, 213, 214; **63**: 54; and U.S. Employment Service, **55**: 291-92, 447; and mediation finances, **57**: 510, 578; and appointment of women to, **62**: 167n1; Palmer on cooperative stores and, **62**: 177; WW on employment for returning servicemen, **64**: 80, 109; and Mooney case, **64**: 145n1; and Women's Bureau, **66**: 520; and O'Callaghan case, **67**: 37-38, 48-51, 52
Labor and the New Social Order: A Report on Reconstruction by the Sub-Committee of the British Labor Party (*New Republic*), **67**: 373n1, 379
Labor Day message: Hines on, **62**: 544-45, 586, WW issues, **62**: 595-96
Labor Defender, **53**: 20,n3, 55
Labor in Crisis: The Steel Strike of 1919 (Brody), **63**: 30n1
Labor's Solution of the Railroad Problem (Plumb), **55**: 248n2
labor unions: and railroad strike crisis, **62**: 134-40, 161-62, 190, 567-73; **67**: 119-20,n1, 121-22; unrest regarding wages and cost of living, **62**: 158; Hines on strikes and, **62**: 228; WW praises union which voted against wage increase, **62**: 561; and steel industry, **62**: 581-82,n1; Gary on U.S. Steel Corporation and, **62**: 596-601; and steel strike, **63**: 29-30,n1, 148-49; and police situation, **63**: 265, 295, 296; San Francisco Labor Council's resolutions and questions, **63**: 268-70; and coal strike, **64**: 141,n1,2, 155; WW on critical railroad situation and government's request to, **64**: 420-26; WW on railroad wage issue and, **65**: 14-16; and railroad crisis, **65**: 36,n1, 175-76, 451-52; Jewell clarifies position of regarding railroad strike, **65**: 285-86; anthracite coal strike averted, **65**: 314; situation in West Virginia coal fields, **65**: 335-37,n1; protest adjournment of Congress, **65**: 359, 368-69; and Illinois coal strike, **65**: 545-46, 559-60; WW's statement on coal strike, **65**: 565-66; J. L. Lewis urges miners to return to work, **65**: 569; *see also* strikes
Labour party (Great Britain), **53**: 519n1, 535-36; **54**: 257; **67**: 373n1, 379
Labour Year Book, 1919, **55**: 91n1
Lacakwanna Steel Company, **62**: 518-19n1
Ladenburg, Eugenie Marie (May), **65**: 83,n1, 135-37, 139
Ladeuze, Paulin, **61**: 14n12, 22,n1, 129
Ladies' Home Journal, **66**: 354,n1
Ladine people, **57**: 86,n1

Ladrone Islands, **62**: 348

Ladykiller: The Life of Landru, the French Bluebeard (Bardens), **59**: 95n1

Lael, Richard L., **62**: 5n6

Lafayette, Marie-Paul-Joseph-Yves-Roch-Gilbert du Motier, Marquis de, **53**: 391, 396, 400; **54**: 309, 467, 518; **56**: 366; WW on inscription on monument to, **55**: 232; WW places wreath at tomb of, **60**: 286, 291-92; **65**: 397n1

Lafayette College: Hibben to represent Princeton at, **64**: 519-20

La Follette, Robert Marion, **53**: 35; **54**: 259n3; **61**: 372; **65**: 418n3; **67**: 37n1; **68**: 185,n1, 247; and treaty fight, **64**: 200, 202, 337, 338; and Wisconsin judgeship, **67**: 14; and gasoline prices, **68**: 119n3; and Teapot Dome scandal, **68**: 119n2; R. S. Baker on, **68**: 313

Lagosta (now Lastovo, Yugoslavia), **57**: 563n2; **60**: 266; **62**: 604, 620; **63**: 91, 208, 617n1; **64**: 172, 174, 264n2, 265, 301, 302; and Adriatic settlement, **66**: 364, 377

LaGuardia, Fiorello Henry, **58**: 379,n1; **66**: 323,n3; attack on D. R. Francis, **54**: 259n3

Laguna Life Publishing Co., **66**: 387,n1

Laibach (now Ljubljana) Yugoslavia, **58**: 393n4; **60**: 36, 198

Lake Rousseau, Canada, **68**: 424

Lamar, William Harmong, **61**: 504,n2; on second-class mailing privileges, **66**: 94-98

Lamb, Albert Richard, **63**: 580n1

Lamb, Charles, **53**: 425, 534; **63**: 347

Lamb, Frank R., **62**: 627

Lambert, M. E., **67**: 109n1

Lambs, The (actors' club), **68**: 373,n3

Lammasch, Heinrich, **56**: 257,n1; **59**: 12,n7

Lammasch, Marga, **59**: 12,n8

Lammasch, Nora Gemeiner (Mrs. Heinrich), **59**: 12,n8

Lamon, Ward Hill, **55**: 366,n1; **61**: 445

Lamont, Florence Haskell Corliss (Mrs. Thomas William), **55**: 157,n1; **61**: 375; **62**: 433,n2; **63**: 165; **66**: 164,n3, 171; **67**: 28,n1, 110, 151, 169; celebrates birthday, **61**: 363,n2; thanks WW for birthday greetings, **61**: 369

Lamont, Thomas William, **53**: 627, 716; **54**: 88; **55**: 157,n1; **58**: 27, 28, 119-20, 121-22, 249, 263, 423, 446n1, 447, 470, 526, 548, 549; **59**: 185, 283, 422, 495; **60**: 40, 56, 196, 276, 320,n2, 483, 591,n2, 641; **61**: 3n1, 230, 290, 375, 384, 396; **62**: 7,n1, 97, 100, 432-33, 560; **63**: 165, 388; **64**: 183, 270; **66**: 163-64, 170-71; **67**: 105n3, 355, 415n5; **68**: 310, 328, 548; on Root's opposition to League of Nations, **56**: 98-99, 233; and reparations, **56**: 208, 270, 271n3, 353, 424, 437, 444, 448, 498, 501, 502, 579, 580-81, 585, 587; **57**: 14-15, 17, 29, 31, 32, 79, 82, 109, 208, 210, 214, 287; **58**: 26-27, 29, 113, 114, 139-40; **60**: 46, 47, 49, 50, 53, 76-77, 399-400, 400-401; on financial and economic conditions in Europe, **59**: 175-78; on postwar reconstruction and war finance legislation, **59**: 283-85; on experts discussing economic clauses with Germany, **59**: 314-15; on reparations and successor states of Austria-Hungary and Austrian treaty, **59**: 384,n1, 386, 536, 611-12; WW on, **59**: 454; to be representative to meeting with Lloyd George and Loucheur, **60**: 74; suggestions for ratification of peace treaty, **60**: 201, 536-39; and alleged peace treaty leak and proposed Senate investigation, **60**: 379, 380, 382-83, 399, 434, 536; meets with WW, **60**: 491, 493-94; WW praises, **60**: 382, 389; thanks WW for his support concerning treaty leaks, **60**: 430; on U.S. extending credit to Europe, **60**: 539; on new financial legislation, **60**: 542-44; and plans for WW's U.S. speaking tour, **60**: 610; offers help with Republicans on treaty ratification, **61**: 66; WW hopes he can use his influence to help treaty ratification, **61**: 104; suggestions for WW's message to Congress, **61**: 386-88; on resolutions of League of Free Nations Association and WW's reply, **61**: 446, 448-49, 506; appointment suggestions for Reparation Commission, **61**: 528-30; WW on Reparation Commission appointment, **61**: 543-44; on WW addressing Senate on peace treaty rather than making speaking tour, **61**: 641-43; suggested as Minister to China, **62**: 284; offers to make statement on peace treaty, **62**: 504-505; and banking consortium, **65**: 259,n1, 276-77; on International Committee of Bankers on Mexico, **66**: 160n2, 302-304; on refuting Harding's statement on Panama Canal tolls, **66**: 177-78, 185; leader of Chinese Famine Relief Fund, **66**: 424, 443, 467, 491-92, 495, 515; controversy over using Sugar Equalization Board's profits for relief in China, **66**: 509-10, 529-30; WW on no government funds for relief, **66**: 532; on revival of War Finance Corporation and WW's veto, **67**: 16-17, 27-28; on disposition of relief funds, **67**: 74-75, 87, 88, 96, 105, 110; on surplus corn to China, **67**: 80; on Allied debt cancellation, **67**: 151-52,n1, 169; and WW Foundation, **67**: 271n1; WW's congratulations on success of Chinese Relief Fund, **67**: 342

La Monte, George Mason, **53**: 63

Lanciani, Rodolfo Amadeo, **58**: 210,n1

Land and Power: British and Allied Policy on Germany's Frontiers, 1916-19 (Nelson), **55**: 475n2; **56**: 12n1; **57**: 91n6

Landau, Germany, **56**: 360, 361, 364, 366, 368

Landeskunde der Provinz Schlesien (Partsch), **60**: 413,n3
land grant schools, **64**: 4
Landman, Isaac: on anti-Semitism, **66**: 130-31,n1
Land of Gilead, with Excursions in the Lebanon (Oliphant), **55**: 384n3
Landon, Archer A.: appointed to first Industrial Conference, **63**: 300,n1
Landowski, Paul, **54**: 138n1
Landru, Henri Désire, **59**: 95,n1
Landsberg, Otto, **57**: 590,n5; **58**: 311,n2, 518; photograph of, *illustration section*, **58**
Landvoight, William Arnold, **53**: 166,n2, 319
Lane, Anne Wintermute (Mrs. Franklin Knight), **68**: 164n1, 168; WW's condolences to, **67**: 284
Lane, Franklin Knight, **53**: 35, 280, 302, 636, 707; **54**: 390-91, 409-10, 521; **55**: 219, 357; **56**: 618, 621; **57**: 233, 376, 381, 387; **58**: 605; **61**: 492, 646; **62**: 114, 119, 462n2; **63**: 552,n1, 590, 598; **64**: 64n1, 274; **66**: 542n1; on Smith-Bankhead Americanization bill, **55**: 284-88; on educational action on League of Nations, **56**: 402, 486; suggested as Director General of Red Cross, **57**: 330, 422-23; on Fiume, **58**: 239,n4; on employment for returning servicemen, **59**: 292; and General Leasing bill controversy, **61**: 534-35,n1; and testimonial to wartime volunteers, **61**: 540; and naval oil reserves, **62**: 47-49; Hurley's report on fuel oil for shipping, **62**: 140-41; and oil relief legislation, **62**: 293-94, 438; and WW's message to librarians, **62**: 436,n1; on world oil supply and U.S. shipping needs, **62**: 617-19; on problems at first Industrial Conference, **63**: 582-83, 583-84, 591-92; appointment suggestions for second Industrial Conference, **63**: 611; and coal strike negotiations, **64**: 143; and railroad situation, **64**: 184; Lansing on reaction to WW's no-compromise statement, **64**: 193; resignation of, **64**: 204,n1, 232, 373-74, 385, 456; **67**: 614; visits Lansing, **64**: 385; on Honolulu Oil case, **64**: 392, 405; and Lansing resignation, **64**: 418; and Railroad Wage Commission, **64**: 422,n5; and Cabinet meetings during WW's illness, **64**: 456; comments on Interior Department, **65**: 22,n1; WW on his being "leak" in Cabinet, **65**: 186; death of, **67**: 284,n1; revelations made by publication of letters of, **68**: 164-65, 168
Lane Commission: *see* Railroad Wage Commission
Lane, Winthrop D., **62**: 545n3
Lanel, Etienne-Marie-Louis, **66**: 326,n1
Lang, Most Rev. Cosmo Gordon, Archbishop of York, **60**: 24,n5; **61**: 114,n5

Lang, Louis Jay, **67**: 304n2, 364,n2; **68**: 259n2
Lange, Christian, **64**: 342
Langer, William Leonard, **58**: 461n1; **60**: 173n2
Langlet, Jean-Baptiste-Nicolas, **54**: 279,n2
Langrès, France, **53**: 502, 513
Lanier, Reginald Bishop, **67**: 379
Lansbury, George, **55**: 87,n1, 187, 525-26; **56**: 63, 156, 322, 338; **58**: 93-94, 317; meets with WW on labor conditions in Britain, **56**: 205-206; urges publication of Bullitt report on Russia, **56**: 473
Lansdowne, Henry Charles Keith Petty-Fitzmaurice, Marquess of, **55**: 384n4
Lansden, Dick Latta, **66**: 54n1
Lansing, Eleanor W. Foster (Mrs. Robert), **53**: 318, 370, 468, 584-85; **54**: 199; **57**: 581, 627; **58**: 601; **60**: 546; **61**: 321, 327; **62**: 156; **63**: 540; **64**: 156,n1, 229, 385,n2, 455; on her husband's relationship with WW, **57**: 141; WW on, **64**: 417n3
Lansing, Emma Sterling, **53**: 468,n1, 501,n3
Lansing, Katherine Ten Eyck, **53**: 468,n1, 501,n3
Lansing, Robert, **53**: 35, 65, 85, 109-10, 127, 128, 136, 137-38, 138, 144, 160, 180, 193, 204, 206-207, 213, 240, 271, 291, 309, 312-13, 318, 334, 335, 336, 341, 342, 345, 370, 384, 389, 401, 436, 489-90, 555, 590, 605, 627, 648, 695, 699-700, 709, 718-19; **54**: 54, 82-83, 127, 135, 148, 158, 174, 199, 256, 259, 264, 274, 278, 282, 379-80, 404, 426, 464n1, 472, 473, 486, 495, 522; **55**: 59, 83n1, 88n1, 152, 154, 185, 406, 493, 514; **56**: 61, 75, 96, 97, 119, 159, 168, 183, 235, 257, 279, 468, 512,n1, 530n4, 548; **57**: 35, 52, 65, 72, 141, 236, 275, 312, 313, 319, 332, 346, 371, 400, 406, 469, 509, 554, 570, 627; **58**: 3, 44, 227, 236, 248, 312, 316, 318, 430, 453, 455, 522; **59**: 234, 274, 275, 282, 285, 346, 348, 399, 448, 470-71, 512, 513, 524, 530, 571-72, 595, 603, 614; **60**: 21, 42, 83, 99-100, 114, 155, 178, 192, 220, 257, 276, 298, 338, 483-84, 546, 601, 608; **61**: 45, 105, 111, 128, 130, 134, 155, 170, 172, 284, 288, 306, 332, 347, 467, 477, 513, 611, 629, 636; **62**: 4, 11, 12, 17, 19, 22, 27, 30, 45, 111, 141-42, 142, 144, 147, 148, 149, 151-52, 156, 169, 171, 202, 207, 220, 222, 222-23,n1, 249, 253, 256, 266, 281, 316, 328, 330, 332, 333, 334, 404, 425, 441, 449, 456, 481, 507, 511, 522; **63**: 60, 119-20, 120-22, 391, 543, 552, 559; **64**: 3-4, 50, 65, 66, 216, 263-66, 273, 275, 361, 375, 385, 386, 414; **65**: 21, 188, 343; **66**: 542n1; **67**: 397, 460, 608; **68**: 591; on Bullitt memorandum on Bolsheviks, **53**: 6, 121; and food to Ger-

Lansing, Robert (*cont.*)
many, **53**: 63; advises WW not to attend peace conference, **53**: 65-66, 127-28; requests France and Britain lift censorship on U.S. press, **53**: 109; on making a statement on Bolsheviks, **53**: 151-53, 706; on Sun Yat-sen, **53**: 197; appointed peace commissioner, **53**: 243; on France's wish to have Gompers in Paris, **53**: 245; House on, **53**: 390, 391; and Creel, **53**: 402; on League of Nations, **53**: 474-77; on Tacna-Arica dispute, **53**: 536; on status of advisers not assigned to peace conference, **53**: 572-73; and labor conditions and soldiers' return, **53**: 582; cannot accompany WW to Italy, **53**: 584-85; on WW's meeting with American commissioners on League of Nations plan, **54**: 3-4,n1; and Council of Ten meetings, **54**: 16, 20, 23n13, 223; on Russia, **54**: 158-59; **61**: 40; **64**: 307-308,n1; sends good wishes to Poland, **54**: 217; health and appearance of, **54**: 383; **58**: 601; redrafts resolution on League of Nations, **54**: 400-402; instructions to Polk on congressional hearings on Siberian situation, **54**: 411-12; on international courts of arbitration, **54**: 469-70; on China and Japan, **54**: 474, 548, 549; **57**: 298, 454, 582; and German disarmament, **54**: 538; and Supreme War Council meetings, **55**: 12, 183; **56**: 28; sketches during meetings, **55**: 34-35; on Russian railroad situation, **55**: 38-39; and passports for Socialists, **55**: 92; on situation in Archangel, **55**: 93; and H. W. Johnson's Russian resolution, **55**: 149; on Churchill's Russian initiative, **55**: 202-203; on assassination attempt on Clemenceau, **55**: 209; on war costs, **55**: 210-11, 231; and idea of separating Covenant from peace treaty, **55**: 305n1; and Bullitt's mission to Russia, **55**: 540n1; on Gallagher resolution, **55**: 547; on Senate ratification of peace treaty, **56**: 58-59,n4, 97-98; on Hapgood appointment, **56**: 101, 191; on appointing U.S. ministers to Czechoslovakia and Poland, **56**: 122-24; on instructions for Graves and Siberian situation, **56**: 152-53, 184, 304, 371-72, 519; on Egyptian situation, **56**: 153-54; **57**: 557, 557-58; on Rhineland, **56**: 201-202; on submarine cables, **56**: 212-13, 214, 219; **57**: 456; **58**: 283, 296-97, 298, 301, 302, 302, 306, 347; on Hungarian situation, **56**: 238-39, 331, 459-60, 464, 487-88; on Clemenceau-WW confrontation, **56**: 351-52; on French spirit of militarism and its consequences, **56**: 487-90; on France's bill for WW's traveling expenses, **56**: 547-48; on International Labour Convention, **56**: 603, 606; and Y.W.C.A. work in Siberia, **57**: 60; R. S. Baker and WW on, **57**: 68; on Japan and railroad situation in Siberia, **57**: 94-95, 134; and responsibility for war and punishment, **57**: 122, 128, 146n4, 149; gives legal opinion on possible trial of William II, **57**: 131-32; Mrs. Lansing on WW's dislike of, **57**: 141; on publicity of peace treaty, **57**: 291, 292, 292-93; **58**: 404, 404-405; on Palestine, **57**: 326, 406; on Teschen, **57**: 326-27; on eastern Galicia, **57**: 327-28; on Gibson as minister to Poland, **57**: 373; and R. Crane and Czechoslovakia, **57**: 374; on obtaining German process for lethal gases, **57**: 402-404; on Russian assets and operating funds for Trans-Siberian Railway, **57**: 420-22; on Smuts' mission, **57**: 440-42; on Foch's refusal to deliver invitation to Germany, **57**: 494; on selling surplus arms, **57**: 495-96; on China's claims, **57**: 560-61, 597; Matsui on Chinese leanings of, **57**: 585; on WW's Adriatic statement, **58**: 102; on credits for Rumania, **58**: 136, 316-17; and China, **58**: 153; **59**: 108; on Shantung claims controversy, **58**: 165-68, 185, 232, 320, 327, 328, 552-53; on Austria presenting her case in Paris, **58**: 205; on mandates, **58**: 206; **59**: 397; **62**: 187, 235, 242, 304, 531, 574, 579, 579-80, 581, 595, 603; on Montenegro, **58**: 267-68, 354; **59**: 620,n1; recognition of Finland, **58**: 319, 404; and French security treaty, **58**: 487-88; on Irish situation, **59**: 251, 318, 366n1, 393, 393-94, 394-95, 476, 549; has little hope for League of Nations, **59**: 285; and issue of publication of peace treaty, **59**: 313, 450, 471; on Bullitt's resignation, **59**: 314; on protests from South Tyrol, **59**: 348; and talk of not signing peace treaty, **59**: 383, 384, 447; on food relief in Baltic region, **59**: 466n6, 467; on not withdrawing from peace conference because of Adriatic issue, **59**: 480-81; and consortium for Chinese loan, **59**: 514, 546; on WW discussing Germany's counterproposals with American commissioners, **59**: 546, 594; on Kolchak and Russia, **59**: 547, 572, 618, 619; **61**: 177; on Morison's suggestions for Estonia, **59**: 547-48; on Austrian treaty, **59**: 563, 566, 567, 568; on release of final treaties to press, **61**: 27; House on, **61**: 34; and Shantung settlement, **61**: 36, 620,n1, 629; **62**: 40-41, 63-65, 150, 151, 153, 208, 380-81, 458; and presence of South and Central American delegates at Versailles, **61**: 65-66; House and Clemenceau on, **61**: 112; on sinking of German fleet at Scapa Flow, **61**: 141-42; on Netherlands delivering William II, **61**: 199, 200-201, 204; on Whitlock as ambassador to Italy, **61**: 290; and French security treaty, **61**: 311, 313; on treaty-signing ceremony and celebra-

tion, **61**: 321-28; tries to persuade Japan to make statement on Shantung for China's benefit, **61**: 325-26; request for Council of Four's minutes, **61**: 334, 336; on Austrian frontier, **61**: 357, 371; on confidential meeting with Tittoni and his desire for settlement of Adriatic question, **61**: 404-405; on situation in Honduras, **61**: 638-40; on Chinese-Japanese situation, **62**: 63-65; on forming a commission on foreign trade, **62**: 65-66; on WW's position on blockade of Russian ports, **62**: 108-10; on interim Reparation Commission, **62**: 142, 236, 237-38, 322-23; on reparations, and U.S. as recipient, **62**: 148, 149; on why WW cannot deliver all documents on League of Nations to Foreign Relations Committee, **62**: 151; and Bliss letter on Shantung settlement, **62**: 164; and Rumanian occupation of Budapest, **62**: 167-68; and disposal of German and Austro-Hungarian ships, **62**: 186-87; on WW making statement on Bolshevism, **62**: 203; on Bessarabia being given to Rumania, **62**: 206; on WW's uncompromising attitude on treaty reservations, **62**: 258-59; on resignation of Reinsch and selection of successor, **62**: 260; on appearance before Senate Foreign Relations Committee, **62**: 264; on senators' personal animosity toward WW causing treaty delay, **62**: 264; gives Polk U.S. policy on various issues, **62**: 265-66; on U.S. Army to aid Hoover mission, **62**: 303-304; on war criminals, **62**: 318-19; **64**: 381-82, 407, 408; holds meeting on U.S. problems in foreign commerce, **62**: 322; on Poole memorandum on Bolshevism, **62**: 323-24; and Thrace, **62**: 327-28, 416, 551-53; **64**: 181; and secret treaties, **62**: 427-28; on WW's feelings on European situation, **62**: 428-29; on Mexican situation, **62**: 449-50, 459; on uncertainty of timing of U.S. treaty ratification, **62**: 452; on Bowman's views of House, **62**: 453, 454-55; on submitting Rhineland Convention to Senate, **62**: 534; on ratification first then setting up commissions, **62**: 550; urges House to remain in Paris until treaty ratified, **62**: 553-54; on withdrawal of U.S. troops from Russia, **62**: 588-89, 594; **64**: 219-21; on Japan and the United States and Russian situation, **62**: 589-93; on tendency toward Communistic ideas, **62**: 612-13; on Adriatic question, **62**: 619-20; **63**: 557; **64**: 298, 313-14, 340-41, 342, 371-72; on Constantinople, **62**: 620,n1; on WW, **62**: 630-31, 633, 635; **63**: 571; Bullitt testimony, **63**: 337-38,n1, 338n4, 541; Tumulty on resignation plans for, **63**: 337n4; concern over WW's leadership ability, **63**: 540-42, 542, 547,n1, 560; on Senate fight over

reservations, **63**: 541; and Cabinet meetings, **63**: 554, 555, 556; House on desire of to proceed independently of WW, **63**: 585; on Russia's wish to buy flour from U.S., **63**: 588-89; on appointment to transportation commission outlined in peace treaty, **63**: 606-607; and Crauford-Stuart incident, **63**: 606n1; **64**: 3, 88, 91, 235; and recognition of Costa Rica, **63**: 616; **64**: 94-95, 153, 186; EBW as conduit for WW on Adriatic question, **63**: 617; **64**: 335-36, 352-53; on Thanksgiving Proclamation as indicator of WW's poor health, **63**: 619-19; role during WW's illness, **63**: 645; and Poland's grain request, **64**: 4, 5-6; on *Imperator* controversy, **64**: 7-10, 212,n1, 218; on situation in Syria and Turkish Empire, **64**: 25-27; on Rumanian situation, **64**: 34-35, 36; suggests Phillips for Minister to Netherlands, **64**: 41, 103, 204, 205; views on treaty, **64**: 54-57; reason for opposing WW's western tour, **64**: 55; on WW's falling reputation, **64**: 56-57; on continued U.S. involvement in European activities, **64**: 66-68, 87; on Bulgarian treaty, **64**: 67, 68; and issue of withdrawing U.S. representatives in Paris, **64**: 100, 102, 117, 147-49, 156, 156-57; on appointments, **64**: 119, 296, 316-17, 322, 343, 366, 407-408, 413-14; and Jenkins case, **64**: 120n1, 121, 124, 129-30; on Mexican situation, **64**: 120n1, 121, 123, 127, 210-11, 239-42; on question of WW's ability to perform his duties, **64**: 123-25, 453-54; on ending secrecy about WW's health, **64**: 139-40; on Germany not signing protocol, **64**: 147-49; on coal situation, **64**: 167; saga of resignation of, **64**: 179, 255-56, 270, 385-89, 398, 404, 408-10, 414, 415-19; on Cabinet's position on returning railroads to private ownership, **64**: 183-84; on WW seeing Lord Grey before his return to England, **64**: 187-88, 235; on conference on international communications, **64**: 190, 228,n1; memorandum on WW's policy of "no concession and no compromise," **64**: 192-94; on struggle between Hitchcock and Underwood for minority leadership, **64**: 192, 194; on publication of Morgenthau report on Poland, **64**: 198n1, 260; Christmas and New Years greetings to WW, **64**: 229; and Hapgood resignation, **64**: 234,n1; on Grey and Crauford-Stuart affair, **64**: 235; on recognition of Finland, **64**: 236; House on strained relations between WW and, **64**: 243; on dangers of WW's uncompromising position compared to Bryan's, **64**: 267-69; on invitations to first meeting of Council of League of Nations, **64**: 272-73, 275; meets with Tumulty on reservations, **64**: 276; and Tumulty's draft let-

Lansing, Robert (*cont.*)
ter to Hitchcock on reservations, **64**: 278n1, 282; on Turkish treaty negotiations, **64**: 344-45, 382, 391; on Frazier affair, **64**: 353, 383-84, 398, 413, 451-54; on Grey's letter, **64**: 365, 366-67, 380; R. S. Baker on diary of, **64**: 365; on D. W. Johnson's proposal on treaty and Adriatic question, **64**: 367; on repatriation of Polish Americans in Haller's Army, **64**: 372-73, 375, 389; and Balfour Declaration, **64**: 373; on Davis at meeting of Premiers, **64**: 382, 391; on Cabinet meetings during WW's illness, **64**: 383, 384, 454-58, 496; on Japan's interest in Siberia, **64**: 390-91; on WW's firm Adriatic position, **64**: 398-402; WW accepts resignation of, **64**: 404, 414; resignation of prompts inquiries into WW's health, **64**: 432, 433; House on resignation of, **64**: 444; Dr. Park on WW's charges against, **64**: 527; editorial comment on WW's dismissal of, **65**: 3-7; and calling of Cabinet meetings, **65**: 139; House on Polk and, **65**: 139; and Polk's resignation, **65**: 196; on Russian-Lithuanian situation, **66**: 21n1; WW on, **66**: 155, 322; **67**: 60, 238; and Yap Island, **66**: 461; **67**: 194n1; comments on book by, **67**: 60, 235,n3; R. S. Baker on, **67**: 237, 291, 292; photograph of, *illustration section*, 53; **58**
Lansing-Ishii Agreement: *see* Ishii-Lansing Agreement
Lansing to Reveal Paris Peace Story as Wilson Retires (Wile), **67**: 72n1
Lansing, Mich.: Dodd on speaking at, **66**: 256
Laon, France, **56**: 198
La Paix (Tardieu), **65**: 542n1
Lapedatu, Aledandru, **54**: 421,n6
Lapradelle, Albert-Geouffre de, **55**: 154,n1
La Questione Sociale (Paterson, N.J.), **66**: 96
Laramie, Wyo., *Boomerang*, **63**: 482n
Larkin, Miss, **66**: 330; **67**: 615
Larnaude, Fernand, **53**: 345,n1, 459n1; **55**: 118; **57**: 220, 221, 222, 224, 225, 226, 227, 228, 230, 231, 232, 249, 251-52, 254-55, 256, 257, 265, 266, 285; **60**: 476; **61**: 338; and League of Nations Commission, **54**: 218,n2, 426,n1, 463, 510; **55**: 5, 42, 43, 44, 46, 71, 75, 78-79, 79, 120-21, 122, 123, 125, 126, 155; **56**: 171, 174, 174-75, 177, 225, 226, 226-27, 227, 228, 229, 297, 301, 302, 303; and Japan's racial equality amendment, **57**: 262, 264, 265, 269
Laroche, Jules-Alfred, **60**: 468,n10
La Scala Opera House, **53**: 614, 619-20
Lasker, Albert Davis, **68**: 167,n1, 388,n1
Laskey, John Ellsworth, **66**: 103,n2
La Spezia, Italy, **60**: 474, 482
Lassiter, William: and Armistice Day plans, **67**: 432,n1, 438-39, 439-40, 444, 453n1

Lastovo: *see* Lagosta
Latakia, **54**: 506
Latané, John Holladay, **67**: 285,n1
Latest Allied-American Dealing with Lenin (New York *Nation*), **61**: 478,n1
Lathrop, Julia Clifford, **62**: 96; **66**: 542n1
Latin America, **67**: 384, 385; and cable censorship, **57**: 423; and Mexican situation, **61**: 511
Latvia, **59**: 300n8; **61**: 87, 162; **65**: 469, 527n3; **67**: 8; *see also* Paris Peace Conference—Latvia
Laughlin, Irwin Boyle, **56**: 56, 396,n2
Launay, Comte de, **61**: 94
Laura Spelman Rockefeller Memorial Fund, **67**: 140n3
Laurent, Marcel, **58**: 164,n1
Lausanne, Switzerland, **53**: 588; **56**: 76, 77; *see also* Turkish-American treaty
Lauzanne, Stephané, **57**: 148n2
Lavisse, Ernest, **53**: 485,n1
Law and Order Vs. the Miners: West Virginia, 1907-1933 (Lunt), **65**: 335n1
Law, Andrew Bonar, **53**: 300n2, 329, 520, 563, 593n7; **54**: 35, 36, 38 41, 124; **58**: 371, 425,n1; **59**: 58, 213; **60**: 93, 300, 437, 465, 501, 523-24, 526, 527; **64**: 263; **68**: 196, 593n10; on reparations, **57**: 6n7, 7, 145n1, 147n5, 203, 205, 207, 214; **60**: 318; on Irish, **60**: 303-304; on Adriatic question, **60**: 306; and Armenian situation, **62**: 285n1; **63**: 306, 307; WW congratulations to, **68**: 163; and League of Nations, **68**: 167, 193; WW's get-well message to and Law's response, **68**: 366; death of, **68**: 366n1
Law, Isabel, **53**: 593n7
Law, Mary, **53**: 593,n7
Law Quarterly Review, **57**: 128n6
Lawrence, Bishop William, **66**: 246n2
Lawrence, David, **54**: 106, 192; **62**: 285n1; **63**: 238n1, 265; **65**: 401n1; and Ishii interview, **56**: 187-89; WW on, **66**: 307,n3; wishes to clear up misunderstanding with WW, **67**: 284, 285, 286-87, 294-95
Lawrence, Thomas Edward (Lawrence of Arabia), **54**: 90,n1, 195, 595,n2; photograph of, *illustration section*, **54**
Lawrence, Mass., **55**: 286
Lay, Julius Gareche, **62**: 322,n3
Layton, Walter Thomas: on supplying armaments to new states in central and eastern Europe, **59**: 214-15,n3
Lazaro, Ladislas, **56**: 428,n3
Lazarus, Guidotto Karl: *see* Donnersmarck, Prince von, Count Henckel
Lazistan (now Rize, Turkey), **65**: 114
Lea, Clarence Frederick, **53**: 262-64,n1
Lea, Langdon, **61**: 374,n2
Leacock, Stephen, **67**: 105n3
Leaders of Men (address, Wilson), **62**: 623n14
League for the Preservation of American Independence, **59**: 372n2, 451,n1
League for the Rights of Man, **54**: 309-10,n1

League of American Pen Women, **68**: 37
League of Free Nations Association, **55**: 292,n1; **58**: 169; **61**: 448n1, 448-49, 506; **62**: 530-31,n1; **65**: 138-39,n1; Lamont on resolutions of, **61**: 446, 448-49; resolutions of, **61**: 447-48
League of National Ottoman Unity, **59**: 473
League of Nations, **53**: 82, 90, 92, 93, 115, 213n1, 232, 299,n1, 312n1, 324n2, 330-31, 368, 434, 445, 485, 530n1, 599n1; **54**: 47, 71, 73, 112n3, 131, 132n1, 137, 151, 178, 188-89,n5, 354, 408, 552; **56**: 22, 61, 544, 545; **57**: 92, 345, 469; **58**: 6, 104n3, 112, 113, 134, 139, 152, 176, 213, 273, 343, 363n1, 465; **59**: 114, 143, 149, 159, 303, 320n3; **60**: 432n1; **61**: 95-96; **64**: 15; **65**: 514; **68**: 106, 392, 491; Bickett on, **53**: 29, 30; Lloyd George on **53**: 71n1; Sharp on, **53**: 81; Clarke on, **53**: 120; Owen on, **53**: 134; and J. Reed, **53**: 134; endorsed by League to Enforce Peace, **53**: 135,n2; Huntington on Russia and, **53**: 177, 178; W. E. Rappard on neutrals and, **53**: 209-12; Turner on political parties and, **53**: 264-70; and French plan, **53**: 295-96, 297; **56**: 3,n1, 206; Bryan on, **53**: 335,n3; 645; WW on, **53**: 338, 339, 350, 351, 354-55, 355, 356, 388, 394-95, 412, 420, 451, 462, 530, 532-33, 598-99, 618, 621-22, 622; **55**: 160, 255, 272, 313-24, 328-29, 340, 489; **56**: 34, 114; **57**: 606; **61**: 18, 108, 425, 432-34, 480, 481; Hurley on, **53**: 374, 375; Taft on T. Roosevelt's views on, **53**: 392; Archbishop of Canterbury on, **53**: 388, 412; House discusses with various leaders and his advice on, **53**: 390, 401, 417-18, 448, 507, 525, 652-53, 693, 694; Cecil on, **53**: 415-17, 568; Clemenceau on, **53**: 448, 652-53; WW and Derby discuss, **53**: 471-72, 498, 634; suggested draft of articles for discussion, **53**: 474-76; Logan on, **53**: 480-85; Macfarland on, **53**: 487; Smuts on, **53**: 515-19, 609,n1; Imperial War Cabinet on, **53**: 558-59, 565-66; N. D. Baker on reaction in U.S. to, **53**: 580; Vittorio Emanuele III on, **53**: 600n1; Tumulty on sentiment toward, **53**: 625, 626; Bissolati on, **53**: 644; WW's first Paris draft of the Covenant, **53**: 655-86; Scott and Miller draft, **53**: 695,n2; endorsed by Federal Council of Churches of Christ in America, **53**: 718; **54**: 278; misunderstanding about draft preparation, **53**: 720; Lansing on WW's first Paris draft, **54**: 3-4; WW confident of establishment of, **54**: 51, 104, 233-34, 466; New England's support, **54**: 58; T. H. Bliss' comments on WW's first Paris draft, **54**: 85-88, 123; WW's second Paris draft, **54**: 138-48, 439,n2; WW sends second draft to Smuts, **54**: 148n1, 149; House on resolution for commission to prepare Covenant, **54**:

150; Cecil on meeting with WW and Smuts on second Paris draft, **54**: 152; British draft convention, **54**: 160-70; R. S. Baker on publicity for, **54**: 189-91; WW and Gardiner discuss, **54**: 196-97, 198; Council of Ten's draft of preliminary resolutions and discussion of drafting committee, **54**: 206-10; WW and Ador discuss, **54**: 233-34; Cambon on WW and, **54**: 235, 236; House's points for WW's speech on, **54**: 263-64; WW presents Covenant in speech to Plenary Session, **54**: 265-68; comments on and mention of WW's speech on, **54**: 263, 269-71, 304, 406, 427; Lloyd George second's WW's resolution on, **54**: 268-69; Council of Ten on matters to be taken up by, **54**: 286-87; mandatory and trusteeship discussion and, **54**: 293-301, 308, 320, 324-26, 328-30, 333, 352, 353, 355, 356, 356-57, 357, 358-59, 360, 361, 369-70, 386, 489; **55**: 170-72, 176-77, 321-22; **56**: 110, 118, 272-75, 511; **58**: 291, 293, 325, 400, 401, 510; **59**: 345, 376, 475-76,n2; **61**: 260-70, 408, 451-55; and representation of neutrals, **54**: 302; **57**: 265-66; and labor, **54**: 309; **55**: 8-9, 9; **56**: 236n3; House, WW, and Orlando meet on Covenant, **54**: 387, 387-88; Lansing's draft of Covenant, **54**: 400-402; House stresses importance of WW working for, **54**: 407-408; Gardiner's suggestions on, **54**: 427-28; Hurst-Miller draft of Covenant, **54**: 433-39; WW and Miller discuss changes in Covenant, **54**: 439-40; first version of WW's third Paris draft of Covenant, **54**: 441-48, 449-58; WW thanks Miller for copies, **54**: 458; House, WW, and Cecil discuss, **54**: 459-60, 460-61; **55**: 538, 539; WW accepts Hurst-Miller draft as a basis for discussion, **54**: 460, 461, 464; and representation, **54**: 462; and Armenia, **54**: 516, 517; and labor, **55**: 8-9, 9; **56**: 236n3; varied individual and organizational support for, **55**: 37-38, 158,n2, 198-99, 199, 205, 253,n1, 278, 292, 458, 503, 510, 511; **56**: 427; public opinion on, **55**: 38, 197-98, 339, 449-52, 463-64, 540; **56**: 331, 339; **57**: 188-89, 424, 424-25,n1, 427; **58**: 244, 410n1; Taft on, **55**: 65, 82, 257, 281-82, 289, 357-58, 540; **56**: 57, 83, 157-59, 398-99, 485; **58**: 461; **61**: 353; Bullitt on, **55**: 67n2; **59**: 233; Miller on, **55**: 68-70, 118; Cecil on international army, **55**: 80; preamble adopted by commission, **55**: 121; text of Covenant, **55**: 129-37, 164-73; and Switzerland, **55**: 152; WW on freedom of seas and neutrality, **55**: 160, 162; **56**: 407; WW presents and explains Covenant to Plenary Session, **55**: 164-78; Republican opposition to, **55**: 214, 225, 254, 312-13,n1; **59**: 282,n1,2; WW on importance of U.S. support for, **55**: 224-25; sugges-

League of Nations (*cont.*)
tions for winning support for, **55**: 262-
63, 280, 292-93, 337-38, 339, 437, 491,
501-502,n1; WW meets with congressional committees to discuss, **55**: 267,
268-76; and question of surrender of
U.S. sovereignty, **55**: 268, 272-73;
House's activities give rise to idea of
separating the Covenant from the
peace treaty, **55**: 304-305,n1; Lodge's
attack on, **55**: 312-13,n1; WW on one
sentence in Covenant that should be
altered, **55**: 315-16; and Tacna-Arica
dispute, **55**: 330, 331; Fletcher on Mexico and, **55**: 354; House on using Federal Reserve Act fight as model for, **55**:
367-68; and Palestine issue, **55**: 381-
85; WW's concern over House's proposal to start immediate functioning
of, **55**: 392; WW's address at Metropolitan Opera House, **55**: 413-21; and
Japan and racial equality resolution
and clause, **55**: 437, 464; **56**: 59-60,n1,
80, 81, 164, 187,n3, 187-89,n3; **57**: 239-
40, 247, 268-70, 373; **58**: 179-80, 214;
61: 27-28,n2; and Irish issue, **55**: 470,
474; **56**: 79-80, 82; legal opinion on
U.S. membership in, **55**: 478-79; WW
on membership and withdrawal from,
55: 481; WW learns of House's agreement to separate peace treaty and, **55**:
488,n2; idea of separation from peace
treaty disturbs U.S. public, **55**: 493;
Benson on naval terms and, **55**: 515,
516, 517, 521; Davison on Red Cross
and, **55**: 527-29; WW makes clear to
Lloyd George and Clemenceau that
peace treaty must include, **55**: 529-30;
resolution by Plenary Session to include League of Nations in peace
treaty stands, **55**: 531,n1, 532; controversy over League of Nations being included in peace treaty, **56**: 3,n1, 59-60,
207, 263, 348n1; T. N. Page on Italy's
growing opposition to, **56**: 65-66;
Cecil's amendments to Covenant, **56**:
75-81,n4; suggestions and requests for
site selection, **56**: 76-77, 103, 121-22,
169-70, 173-74, 234, 298, 335; and
withdrawal amendment, **56**: 78-79,
301-303; House on amendments to
Covenant, **56**: 82-83; WW urged to convene extra session of Congress for discussion of, **56**: 85-86; Root's opposition
to and suggestions for, **56**: 99, 99-100,
483-84; neutrals meet to discuss, **56**:
102-103; Homer H. Johnson's suggestions for, **56**: 120,n2; New York *World*
poll on, **56**: 156,n1; Lodge-Lowell debate on, **56**: 161,n1; Sedgwick's suggestions for ratification, **56**: 162-63;
Reed's attack on, **56**: 192n1; issue of
Germany's membership in, **56**: 250,
264; **59**: 3, 5,n2, 28,n3, 207n1, 222-
23,n15, 243,n1, 554, 581, 582; **60**: 21,
22, 27, 40-41, 50, 62, 64, 66, 69, 77-78,

83, 94-95, 178, 235-37, 272-75, 292,
307,n1, 334,n3, 380-81, 459-60, 464,
481, 494, 520-21,n14; **61**: 272; **62**: 357-
58, 360; and Fontainebleau Memoran-
dum, **56**: 265-66; and Monroe Doctrine,
56: 297, 335, 398-99; **57**: 142, 193, 215,
218, 233, 236-37, 254-57, 266-67, 315-
16, 331, 332; WW denies delays in
peace conference caused by, **56**: 313;
Bernstorff on, **56**: 317n1; Bryan on, **56**:
346,n1; Lane suggests educational activities on, **56**: 402, 486; shipbuilding
and, **56**: 482, 518-19; Danzig and, **56**:
505, 507, 508; **57**: 151, 594; **59**: 456;
and Saar Basin, **56**: 514, 516; **57**: 113,
114, 115, 117, 118, 119, 120, 129, 161-
62, 163, 196-99, 412-15; **58**: 227; **60**:
109, 448, 461; and war crimes, **56**: 532,
534; McAdoo's suggestions for amendments to, **56**: 552-53; House envisions
first meeting in Washington, **56**: 586;
R. S. Baker on, **57**: 5; endorsed by
woman suffrage associations, **57**: 43;
Goltra on Missouri politics and, **57**: 47,
48-49; Geneva selected as seat of, **57**:
52-53, 194, 237, 329, 434, 464; and
Anglo-American controversy over
naval building, **57**: 142, 144, 180-81,
185-88; and court of international justice, **57**: 251-52; request to have God
mentioned in Covenant, **57**: 283, 371;
and Adriatic question and Fiume, **57**:
352, 353, 354, 433; **58**: 14, 81, 82, 375,
379, 393n4, 452, 532, 589-90; **59**: 34,
71, 72, 80, 82, 83n3, 87, 558, 559, 569;
60: 308; **62**: 456, 457; **64**: 170, 172, 173,
265, 298-99, 300, 302, 305, 319, 331,
332, 333; and Dalmatia, **57**: 467n2;
WW on China and Japan and, **57**: 622-
23; WW meets Chinese delegates to
discuss, **57**: 633, 634; Keynes on economic rehabilitation plan and, **58**: 13;
WW proposed Plenary Session to discuss Covenant, **58**: 22; and Kiel Canal,
58: 66; Orlando on, **58**: 79, 211; and duration of economic clauses, **58**: 114,
115, 116, 117, 118, 119; and International Congress of Women, **58**: 140,
141n1; labor clauses, **58**: 173, 174, 361,
363, 416-18, 467-69, 481; Council of
Four agrees on alterations of clauses in
Covenant, **58**: 182-83; and Shantung
controversy and settlement, **58**: 179-
80, 181, 185, 257, 271n1, 273, 328,
419n1; Covenant adopted by Paris
Peace Conference, **58**: 185-86, 188,
214; text of Covenant, **58**: 188-99;
WW's remarks to Plenary Session on
Covenant changes, **58**: 199-202;
Westermann on, **58**: 207-10; **61**: 331;
and Greece, **58**: 241, 317-18; R. S.
Baker on WW's faith in, **58**: 270-71;
Tumulty suggests tour by WW to promote, **58**: 329; issue of Italy as member, **58**: 344; WW thanks Cecil for work
on, **58**: 353; Montenegro offended at

not being part of creation, **58**: 407-408; Borden's fight for Dominions' rights and, **58**: 416-18,n7; Cecil on Covenant of, **58**: 423; unauthorized changes made in Covenant, **58**: 432, 443-44, 444, 445, 446; London discussed as temporary seat for, **58**: 441; Benson on British naval power and, **58**: 456-57; Covenant to be presented exactly as passed by peace conference, **58**: 463; Brockdorff-Rantzau on, **58**: 517; and French security treaty, **58**: 602; and China, **59**: 133, 145; and peace treaty with Austria, **59**: 141; and Russia, **59**: 151, 154, 155, 300n8, 442, 470, 545; and minority rights, **59**: 179n3, 182, 183, 200, 221,n1, 577, 604, 625-26; and Gompers and labor program, **59**: 203; **60**: 645; opposition to Article X of Covenant, **59**: 282,n1, 524,n1, 604, 640n1; **63**: 150-51, 392, 444, 444-45, 445, 447n1; Lansing holds little hope for, **59**: 285; Dickinson requests article on, **59**: 316; Council of Four's reply to Germany's proposals on, **59**: 325-26,n7, 470-71; and plebiscite and Italy, **59**: 329, 339; no mention of aerial warfare in Covenant, **59**: 379-80; Bryce suggests demonstration in House of Lords for, **59**: 397-99, 444; WW on conscription and, **59**: 436; and Colombia, **59**: 444n4; and League for the Preservation of American Independence, **59**: 451n1; WW on Article X, **59**: 470-71; **61**: 595; **64**: 279-80; **66**: 277-80; House on, **59**: 478; **62**: 61-62, 243-47, 254-55; and peace treaty with Hungary, **59**: 510, 512; Wise to join cross-country trip advocating, **59**: 516; Simonds on, **59**: 524n3; and Estonia, **59**: 547n2, 548; London as city designated for organization of, **59**: 603; WW on Irish Americans and, **59**: 604; WW on, **59**: 608-10; **61**: 245, 250; Senate opposition to, **60**: 41n1, 42-43; WW's proposed speaking tour on, **60**: 43, 112, 113, 145, 568,n5; **61**: 373, 386, 459, 565, 622; **62**: 507n1; WW on it being too late for amendments to Covenant, **60**: 100,n2; Haskins on Eupen and Malmédy and, **60**: 108; Hoover on, **60**: 136; Trumbić on Adriatic question and, **60**: 138; Tumulty's suggestions for WW on, **60**: 145; and limitation of arms in Austrian treaty, **60**: 169, 170, 172, 175; Morrow on Senate and media opposition to, **60**: 202-203; and appeal procedure and minorities, **60**: 205, 221-22, 227-28, 266, 487,n1, 607; Van Oss on WW's commitment to, **60**: 252-53, 254-55,n8; Allied reply to German counterproposal on, **60**: 260-61,n1, 437, 439-40, 450, 459-60; and Fiume, **60**: 265, 310-11; Fosdick appointed Under Secretary General of, **60**: 290n5; and Knox Resolution, 1919, **60**: 376-78, 535, 571; **64**:

192n1; WW on Catholic opposition to, **60**: 389; editorial in *Stars and Stripes* advocating, **60**: 489-90,n2; issue of labor organization membership in and Germany, **60**: 520-21,n14; various comments on not separating Covenant from peace treaty, **60**: 536, 537, 538, 612-13; and Upper Silesia and plebiscite issue, **60**: 555; Lodge on, **60**: 571-72; **62**: 309; Italy's concern over boundary issue not being settled before treaty signed, **60**: 579-80; and labor clauses, **61**: 37-40; and Poland, **61**: 48, 50; Root's strategy concerning reservations, **61**: 66; WW on Senate adoption of entire treaty, **61**: 115-16, 116; labor's endorsement of, **61**: 138, 231; WW on Fiume and, **61**: 171; Miller on Root's reservations, **61**: 181; D. W. Johnson on Adriatic question and, **61**: 229; issue of U.S. withdrawal from, **61**: 232-33, 542, 561, 621; WW on American people being misled about, **61**: 245; and Irish situation, **61**: 291, 512; Smuts on, **61**: 304n3; senators' opposition to, **61**: 347n1, 563; Stephen S. Wise makes trip promoting, **61**: 365; newspapers opposing, **61**: 372; senators opposing reservations unless adopted, **61**: 372; WW on speeches for, **61**: 388; Gary on, **61**: 407; and League of Free Nations Association's resolutions on, **61**: 447-48; Lamont on, **61**: 448-49; Lodge on, **61**: 448; McAdoo's suggestions for WW's tour on, **61**: 459; Wheeler's suggestions for WW's strategy on, **61**: 460; alleged rift between WW and Hitchcock over plans for defense of League, **61**: 468-69, 469-70; H. W. Williams and proposed draft resolution on, **61**: 490-91, 491-92; support from northern and southern Methodist churches, **61**: 511; McCormick on public opinion on, **61**: 513; and Van Dyke, **61**: 533,n1; Heney on, **61**: 538-39; some of WW's advisers urging him not to make tour, **61**: 565; E. F. Clark's support for, **61**: 612; WW thanks Cardinal Gibbons for support of, **61**: 628-29; WW meets with Republican senators on, **62**: 3-6, 12, 29, 90-94; WW urges treaty ratification with Covenant part of, **62**: 18; and WW's comments on French security treaty, **62**: 27-29; Redfield on establishing credits and, **62**: 33; endorsed by League to Enforce Peace, **62**: 70-71; Louis Marshall on East Galicia and, **62**: 221; WW's threat to withdraw from, **62**: 253, 265, 428-29; and Viscount Grey, **62**: 254n2; Polk on France and mandate issue, **62**: 258; Walsh on Article X, **62**: 262-63; endorsed by United Society of Christian Endeavor, **62**: 263-64; Houston on importance of U.S. participation in, **62**: 268; Tumulty on, **62**: 273-74, 275; WW on Lodge's

League of Nations (cont.)
doubts concerning, **62**: 278-80; and American Commission on Irish Independence, **62**: 325-26; suggestion of joint Anglo-American chairmanship and secretariat, **62**: 325-26; and WW's meeting with Foreign Relations Committee, **62**: 342-44, 345-47; WW on withdrawal clause, **62**: 350-53, 621; Fall memorandum on and WW's reply, **62**: 411-15, 417; Marshall on status of and recommendations concerning, **62**: 419-20; Pittman resolution proposes compromise on reservations, **62**: 429-32; Shaffer on, **62**: 440; and Albania, **62**: 522; **64**: 176-78; WW answers Shaffer on, **62**: 525-26; F. Hale on reservations, **62**: 536-37; Hughes' reservations, **62**: 537-42; Spargo on, **62**: 558; McCumber on WW's speaking tour, **62**: 565; "Women of America" opposed to, **62**: 566n1; House on WW's speaking tour on, **62**: 580-81; Wilson's reservations, **62**: 621; Foreign Relations Committee's reservations concerning, **63**: 52n3; WW advocates treaty ratification before start of, **63**: 59; Rumanian situation, **63**: 119n2; and Foreign Relations Committee's minority report on reservations, **63**: 198n1; and Fiume, **63**: 205, 207, 364, 423, 464; Wickersham's position changes, **63**: 223n1; WW on one weakness of, **63**: 232; WW on meaning of, **63**: 255-64; House on Clemenceau's growing enthusiasm for, **63**: 271-72; WW's memorandum answers San Francisco Labor Council's questions on, **63**: 302-303, 303-304; WW on difference between Assembly of and Council of, **63**: 328-29; and Bullitt testimony before Foreign Relations Committee, **63**: 337-38,n1; and Article X and Ireland, **63**: 389,n1; H. W. Johnson on, **63**: 398,n1; effort to compromise Article X, **63**: 529-31,n4; Lansing on WW's monomania concerning, **63**: 541; Rappard's notes of conversation with WW, **63**: 627-31; WW on labor and, **64**: 84, 85, 113-14, 114; Hitchcock's proposed substitute reservations, **64**: 29-30,n1; text of proposed Lodge reservations on, **64**: 38-41; Grey and Jusserand on fate of, **64**: 44; British reaction to Senate reservations, **64**: 53; reservations on labor, **64**: 58,n1; various comments on Article X, **64**: 59, 59-60, 69, 384, 479-80; Underwood's compromise proposal on, **64**: 69-70; House on WW and, **64**: 90; Hitchcock on, **64**: 94; Vénisélos on Constantinople and, **64**: 161-62; Vénisélos on Dedeagatch, **64**: 164; Tumulty on WW's statement on no compromise on treaty, **64**: 190; national referendum on, **64**: 200, 248, 249n1, 251-52, 254, 258-59, 263, 268, 270n2; and Jackson Day

message, **64**: 251, 257; Lansing on, **64**: 269; invitations sent to first meeting of Council of, **64**: 272-73; and Fosdick resignation, **64**: 274-76, 286, 306, 310; WW on withdrawal clause, **64**: 279-80; WW on financial obligations to, **64**: 281; Hitchcock's marked copy of text of Lodge reservations sent to Tumulty, **64**: 288-95; R. S. Baker on, **64**: 326-27, 359-60; Grey on U.S. position and, **64**: 355n1; Lane on, **64**: 374; and The Netherlands, **64**: 407n1; and Anglo-French Adriatic response and Article IX, **64**: 441-42; and Frazier, **64**: 452; and Fiume, **65**: 38; Polk on U.S. representation on proposed commission to Russia, **65**: 77-78; concern over as issue in 1920 presidential campaign, **65**: 118; WW on country not ready for, **65**: 125; and Tacna-Arica dispute, **65**: 190-91, 195, 237; issue of U.S. representation at financial conference of, **65**: 238-42, 245,n1; and International Labour Office, **65**: 248-50; R. Meeker on, **65**: 249-50; WW on as hope of the world, **65**: 263-64; Republican platform plank on, 1920, **65**: 291-92,n1, 386,n1; Virginia plank leads to Democratic plank on, 1920, **65**: 292, 293-94, 319, 331,n1, 333, 427-28, 437, 482,n1; and Armenia, **65**: 307-308, 311, 324; and proposed commission on emigration and immigration, **65**: 360-61; and committee to establish Permanent Court of International Justice, **65**: 399-400, 419; WW on referendum process and, **65**: 416, 417; WW on "thinly veiled" rejection by Republican National Convention, 1920, **65**: 416; WW's note on to be auctioned at Chautauqua, **65**: 423, 424,n1; and Cummings' keynote speech, **65**: 471n1; W. G. Sharp on, **65**: 476; Cox on his commitment to, **65**: 520n1, 521, 522; Cox's position on, **66**: 4, 159, 267,n1; and Lithuania, **66**: 21n1; Bok on, **66**: 32; **68**: 169-70; Lloyd George on, **66**: 48; and International Financial Conference, **66**: 101n1; and Polish-Lithuanian boundary dispute, **66**: 138-39,n1, 145; Republican party's inconsistencies on, **66**: 141,n2; and International Labour Office, **66**: 151,n1; Foley on giving publicity to, **66**: 152; WW on Root and, **66**: 158; Woolley on, **66**: 174; WW's statement on election being referendum on Versailles Treaty and, **66**: 181-83; Crowell on candidates' positions on, **66**: 188n1; WW approves speeches by J. W. Davis on, **66**: 199; Harding on, **66**: 200, 208,n1; Tumulty on churches' attitude toward, **66**: 200-204; WW unable to fill requests for statements on, **66**: 223,n1; France said to approach Lodge and Harding on new association of nations, **66**: 238,n1, 239; letter from 31 Republicans on, **66**:

246,n2; Root attacks Article X, **66**: 246n1,2; Mackenzie on, **66**: 259-61; De la Huerta on, **66**: 270,n1; pro-League Republicans meet with WW, **66**: 273-76; after-election comments supporting, **66**: 312, 323, 325, 326, 327n1, 318-19, 328, 329, 336, 340-41, 347, 474, 483, 524-25; Creel on Mexico and, **66**: 403; WW's concern over Republican direction for, **66**: 447; and Armenia, **66**: 450; and Permanent Military, Naval and Air Commission, **66**: 472-74, 497,n1; Emily G. Balch on, **67**: 42; and Yap controversy, **67**: 53, 55, 147-48; Bok on WW speaking on and WW's response, **67**: 72, 83-84; demonstration for, **67**: 206; Cobb on, **67**: 228-29; Cummins on defeat of, **67**: 269; WW's emotional reaction to question about, **67**: 269; cheered by General Assembly of Presbyterian Church, **67**: 287,n1; Harvey on, **67**: 289n2; WW on its being dead, **67**: 321n1; and *New York Times*, **67**: 366; and International Court of Justice, **67**: 374,n2; State Department and, **67**: 402n1; Anderson on, **67**: 405-407; Filene on, **67**: 461; Coar on, **67**: 463-65; Dessez on, **67**: 515; Balfour on, **67**: 517; WW reaffirms faith in, **67**: 521-22; J. S. Williams on Article X, **67**: 526; Cox's statement on at Jefferson Day dinner, **68**: 3, 59; Fosdick sends WW summary of work of, **68**: 34-35; as campaign issue, **68**: 44n1, 44, 163, 167; Tarbell on, **68**: 46; WW on Senate rejection of, **68**: 46; C. Coolidge on, **68**: 76,n1; issue of Covenant being part of Versailles Treaty, **68**: 84, 85; N. H. Davis' article on for Danish foundation, **68**: 84,n1, 85; WW on full, not associate membership, **68**: 94, 170, 189, 314, 331,n2, 425-26, 439; Cobb on U.S. membership in, **68**: 99; and Holt-Hughes controversy, **68**: 99,n1; Lloyd George's assertions on denounced by R. S. Baker, **68**: 108, 109; and Western Ukraine Republic, **68**: 110-11, 113, 140-41; evolution of Clarke's nonpartisan plans for, **68**: 131-32,n10, 139, 157-58, 158-62, 162, 174-75, 184, 251, 281, 359-60; clergymen's failure on, **68**: 144-45, 160-61; McAdoo on Turkish situation and U.S. defeat of, **68**: 147-48; Warren and Holt on plans for, **68**: 155, 162, 251; Bonar Law on, **68**: 163; WW tries to persuade Holt and Warren to drop nonpartisan plan, **68**: 163-64, 168,n1; WW on plans for promoting public interest in, **68**: 171, 251; Holt on nonpartisan vs. partisan effort, **68**: 172-74; WW on not proposing unconditional acceptance of Covenant, **68**: 179; N. H. Davis on issue of U.S. as associate member of, **68**: 181-82, 193, 341; making Democratic party instrument for, **68**: 189, 190, 193, 211, 272, 336;

WW on *Life* and, **68**: 198; The Document on U.S. membership in, **68**: 217, 310, 537; Davis on introducing legislation for U.S. entry and WW's response, **68**: 273-74, 274; and Republicans on membership issue, **68**: 275,n2; Davis against compromising on, **68**: 278-79; and Sheppard, **68**: 298,n1; Lord R. Cecil on, **68**: 315n1, 345-46; Davis on Republicans' attitude toward joining, **68**: 327; Houston on promotion of, **68**: 330-31, 336; various speaking tours made for, **68**: 359-60, 473-74; Baruch on, **68**: 362, 406, 435, 436-37; Oulahan on WW and, **68**: 381; various favorable comments on, **68**: 420-21, 427-28, 467, 505; WW on effect of his health on fate of, **68**: 422; and Corfu incident, **68**: 427; N. D. Baker visits, **68**: 432,n1; WW thanks Cox for support for, **68**: 477; Davis on a WW manifesto on, **68**: 488, 490-91; and Memel, **68**: 520-21,n1; mentioned as monument to WW, **68**: 566; *see also* Versailles Treaty; Paris Peace Conference; League of Nations Commission; Woodrow Wilson: Western Tour—Themes

League of Nations (McAdoo), **61**: 459,n1, 460

"League of Nations" (T. Roosevelt), **63**: 223n2

League of Nations. A Programme for the Peace Conference . . . 16 December 1918 (Smuts), **53**: 515n1, 609,n1

League of Nations Assembly, issue of summoning first meeting of, **65**: 388-89, 392, 433-34, 500-501; first meeting of, **65**: 503,n1, 504; issue of U.S. observer at, **66**: 352, 353; sends tribute to WW and WW thanks, **66**: 380,n1, 382-83, 432, 433; and Mesopotamia, **66**: 393-94; WW's emotional reaction to question about, **67**: 269; cheered by General Assembly of Presbyterian Church, **67**: 287,n1; Harvey on, **67**: 289n2; WW on its being dead, **67**: 321n1; and *New York Times*, **67**: 366; and International Court of Justice, **67**: 374,n2; State Department and, **67**: 402n1; Anderson on, **67**: 405-407; Filene on, **67**: 461; Coar on, **67**: 463-65; Dessez on, **67**: 515; Balfour on, **67**: 517; WW reaffirms faith in, **67**: 521-22; J. S. Williams on Article X, **67**: 526

League of Nations Association, **68**: 178n1

League of Nations Association of Washington: supportive demonstration in front of WW's new residence, **67**: 206, 212-13, 213

League of Nations Commission, **54**: 262-63, 264; **57**: 248-66, 372; **59**: 522; **62**: 219n2; appointment of, **54**: 188-89,n5, 206-10, 218; chairmanship, **54**: 263, 387; drafting committee named, **54**: 426,n1; meetings of, **54**: 459, 463-64, 473, 481-84, 484, 495-99, 509-13, 545-

League of Nations Commission (*cont.*)
48; and Miller-Hurst draft of Covenant, **54**: 464, 481-84; **55**: 4-9, 41-51, 70-80, 120-36, 136-40, 154; and redraft of Article 3 (small-power representation), **54**: 494-95,n3, 496, 522n1; and Japan's resolution on racial equality, **54**: 500; **57**: 259-65, 570-71; and mandates, **55**: 7-8, 49-50; on international army and peacekeeping, **55**: 73-80; on racial and religious issue (Article 21), **55**: 137-40, 154, 155, 156; prepares report for Plenary Session, **55**: 147-48, 154, 184, 189; WW presents Covenant to Plenary Session, **55**: 164-78; neutrals meet with, **56**: 61, 170,n1; various reports and diaries record meetings of, **56**: 13-65, 178, 178-79, 206, 284-85; on amendments to the Covenant, **56**: 171-78, 223-33, 298-303; WW's statement denying that peace conference delays caused by, **56**: 313; and woman suffrage delegation, **57**: 218-19, 236; on draft of articles *1-10*, **57**: 219,n3, 219-32; and official language, **57**: 220-21; on site of League, **57**: 222-26; on Monroe Doctrine amendment, **57**: 226-32; various comments on meetings of, **57**: 236-37, 239-40, 240, 285; and Japanese amendment on military preparations, **57**: 248-51; on right of passage of troops, **57**: 254; choice of Geneva as site, **57**: 464; WW explains efforts of, **63**: 285-86; photograph of, *illustration section*, **54**

League of Nations Council: and minorities and appeal issue, **60**: 205, 223, 224, 225, 227, 419, 595, 624, 630, 631, 635, 636; **62**: 254, 262-63; WW on, **61**: 250; and French security treaty, **61**: 312; **62**: 29; and mandates, **62**: 243; WW on, **62**: 343; issue of establishment of League bureaus, **62**: 455; and mandate for Armenia, **66**: 426-28; and Armenian border dispute, **66**: 436-37, 443-44, 517-18; **67**: 64, 65; and mandates and Yap controversy, **67**: 53-55, 153-56; and mandate for Palestine, **68**: 100n2; Colby's uncertainty over his presence at Western Ukraine Republic hearing before, **68**: 110, 118, 119, 125, 134, 136; WW on Colby's not postponing appearance before, **68**: 113, 121; and Corfu incident, **68**: 419n1, 432n1; and Memel, **68**: 520-22,n1; *see also* League of Nations

League of Nations Covenant: Yost's suggestions for gaining Republican support for, **61**: 399-400; Van Dyke's suggestions for ratification, **61**: 475-76; W. A. White on, **61**: 508n1; and Article X, **61**: 516-17, 534; WW's strategy for ratification of, **61**: 561-62; Taft's reservations on, **61**: 606, 607-608; *see: also* League of Nations

League of Nations. Draft Reply to the German Proposals, **59**: 325n7

League of Nations Non-Partisan Association, **68**: 178n1, 275,n1, 286n1, 324-25, 332,n1, 452n1

League of Nations Non-Partisan Committee, **68**: 178n1

League of Nations Society, **55**: 278; Tumulty on WW addressing, **55**: 289; **65**: 441

League of Nations Union, **56**: 57; **68**: 159, 162, 310; WW's remarks to, **53**: 530-31,n1; **59**: 316

League of Red Cross Societies, **55**: 528; **59**: 74n1; **60**: 290n1; formation of, **57**: 330

League of Women Voters, **64**: 396; supportive demonstration before WW's home, **68**: 36-39,n1; and League of Nations position, **68**: 332n2

League or War? (Fisher), **68**: 331,n3

League for the Protection of American Prisoners in Germany, **66**: 151n1

League Stops Two Wars (Philadelphia *Public Ledger*), **66**: 138,n1

League to Enforce Peace, **53**: 28-31, 135,n2, 420, 483-84; **55**: 225 288, 290n1; **56**: 427, 484; **61**: 489,n1; **62**: 185; **63**: 94,n3, 223n1, 241n1, 375, 386, 423,n2, 444,n1, 445n1, 490n1, 529; **66**: 165n4, 246n2; supports League of Nations, **55**: 37-38, 186; and Monroe Doctrine amendment to League of Nations Covenant, **57**: 233, 315-16, 445, 469; endorses ratification of League of Nations Covenant, **62**: 70-71; prediction on treaty ratification, **63**: 235; WW on, **63**: 289; meeting with WW on action for Versailles Treaty ratification, **67**: 607-10

League to Enforce Peace (Bartlett), **63**: 223n1

leather industry: and prices, **62**: 174

Leavenworth Prison, **53**: 289; **65**: 441

Lebanon, **54**: 507, 551; **55**: 142, 143; **56**: 107; **61**: 443,n1; and King-Crane recommendations, **62**: 607

Lebedev, Dmitri Antonovich, **60**: 180,n1

Le Breton, Tomas Alberto, **66**: 410,n1

Lebrun, Albert-François, **56**: 457,n7

Lecastro, Victor M., **66**: 25n1

Ledebour, Georg, **53**: 7

Ledeen, Michael Arthur, **59**: 119n3; **63**: 298n2, 517n2

Lederer, Ivo John, **53**: 638n1; **55**: 88n1; **59**: 125n1; **62**: 574n1; **65**: 303n10; **66**: 364n2

Lee, Albert, **66**: 102n1, 130n1

Lee, Algernon, **55**: 92,n1

Lee, Chong-sik, **56**: 187n2

Lee, Robert Edward, **54**: 175; **55**: 85; Lloyd George on, **60**: 301; proposed memorial highway, **67**: 28,n1

Lee, Robert E., grandson of General Lee, **67**: 213

Lee, William Brewster, **65**: 258,n2; **67**: 277, 300, 578,n1

Lee, William Granville, **59**: 203,n1; **62**: 140, 572; **64**: 424, 431 **65**: 16, 359, 451n2

Leeden, Michael Arthur, **58**: 92n2

Leeds, Mrs., **59**: 68,n1

Leeds, Francis Osborne, 5th Duke of, **68**: 67, 68n1

Lee Highway Association (Roanoke), **67**: 28,n1

Leeper, Alexander Wigram Allen, **60**: 129,n8; **61**: 92,n3; **64**: 178,n4, 263,n1

Lefebure, Victor, **68**: 301,n8

Leffingwell, Elmore, **65**: 332

Leffingwell, Russell Cornell, **53**: 252, 473; **57**: 376, 381; **58**: 497n4; **59**: 47; **60**: 539; **61**: 457,n1, 529, 643; **62**: 94, 158; **63**: 165, 267-68; **64**: 475n1; financial assistance for Europe, **58**: 595-97; on wheat situation, **62**: 104-106; willing to defer resignation, **64**: 349-50, 361-62, 362; Geddes on, **65**: 370

Left Bank: see Rhineland

"Legal Basis," **60**: 438,n3

Legendary Life of William S. Porter (O'Connor), **67**: 173n2

Legge, Alexander, **57**: 287,n1; **58**: 120, 597; **59**: 227, 283,n1; **66**: 289,n2

Legionnaire, The: WW's greetings in, **66**: 5,n2, 6

Lehlback, Frederick Reimold, **65**: 478n2

Lehovich, Dimitry V., **59**: 550n2

Leichliter, Charles H., **68**: 137-38,n1,2

Leinert, Robert, **57**: 590,n5; **58**: 518; **61**: 192, 203; photograph of, *illustration section*, **58**

Leipmann, Mr., **58**: 51,n5

Leipzig, Germany, **65**: 100n1

Leiter, Mary Victoria: see Curzon, Lady

Lejean, Guillaume-Marie, **64**: 160,n4

Lejeune, John Archer, **65**: 430,n1; **66**: 82,n1, 189n1; **68**: 581

Lelong, M., **56**: 183n2

Leman, Gérard-Mathieu-Joseph-Georges, **61**: 17,n2

Lemberg, Poland, **59**: 262, 324, 325, 445, 597, 616; **60**: 161, 166

Lemke, William, **67**: 563n2

Lemke v. Farmers Grain Co., **67**: 563n2

Lemnos, **54**: 182,n2, 188

Lemnos, H.M.S., **59**: 67

Lenehan, George F., **65**: 400n1

Lenin, V. I. (Vladimir Ilich Ulyanov), **53**: 124, 172, 173; **54**: 92,n1,2,3, 94, 155,n2, 419; **56**: 337, 338, 425, 459, 548n1, 551n1; **57**: 168; **59**: 78, 518, 519,n2; **62**: 204, 444, 445,n3, 446, 448; **63**: 559; **64**: 234n3; **66**: 154; and Bullitt, **55**: 540n1, 541-42, 545; **56**: 387, 389, 390, 391; rumors of proposed recognition of, **56**: 551,n1; and Nansen, **57**: 165, 438, 440, 503n2, 569n1, 575; reply to Nansen's proposal, **59**: 300-301,n8, 310-11; and Russian debt, **59**: 436,n9

Lenine Reported Ready to Give Up (*New York Times*), **54**: 92n1

Lennon, John Brown, **65**: 545,n2

Lenox, James, **67**: 359

Lenroot, Irvine Luther, **62**: 29,n1, 43, 45, 67, 113, 308; and treaty reservations, **63**: 151, 363; and treaty fight, **64**: 47, 49, 94, 202, 283, 337; R. S. Baker meets with, **64**: 359; and Wisconsin judgeship, **67**: 14

Lens, France, **56**: 295; coal fields, **57**: 159, 160

Lentin, Antony, **56**: 285n1, 482n2; **57**: 6n7; **60**: 4n3; **61**: 144n5

Leobschutz (Glubczyce), Poland, **60**: 139, 158, 468, 480

Leonard, Clifford Milton, **64**: 205,n7

Leopold (Prince of Belgium): visits WW in his sickroom, **63**: 602-606

Leopold II, King of the Belgians, **61**: 7, 15

Leopold, Richard William, **61**: 66n3, 300n6; **66**: 246n2

Leorat, Anne-Henri-Joseph, **53**: 459,n1; **55**: 160; **61**: 188,n1

Lepidi, Joseph-Charles-Philippe-Laurent-Joachim-Antoine-Paul, **60**: 10,n5

Le Rond, Henri Louis Edouard, **59**: 354,n7, 355, 357, 358; **60**: 130,n4, 189n2; **62**: 220,n1, 239; on Upper Silesia, **60**: 412-15, 423

Leroy, Mrs. Virginia, **66**: 165,n4; **67**: 39,n1

Lersner, Baron Kurt von, **58**: 433,n4; **64**: 118n2; and list of war criminals, **64**: 354n1; **65**: 100,n1

Lesh, Albania: see Alessio

Lesina (now Hvar, Yugoslavia), **59**: 570; **60**: 309, 310

Leslie, Stuart W., **63**: 441n2

Lesser v. Garnett, **67**: 563n1

Lesslie, S. S., **65**: 198-99, 200

Le Temps: see Paris *Le Temps*

Letters from the Paris Peace Conference (Seymour), **53**: 544n1

Letters of Franklin K. Lane (A. W. Lane and Wall, eds.), **68**: 164,n1, 168; WW on, **68**: 286

Letters of Theodore Roosevelt (Morison, ed.), **53**: 242n3

Letters on the League of Nations (Fosdick), **64**: 274n1

Letters to Atticus (Cicero), **67**: 116,n2

Lettland (Latvia): see Latvia

Levant Company, Fiume, **56**: 569

Lever, Asbury Francis, **53**: 603; on Galloway and Civil Service Commission, **55**: 478

Lever Food and Food Control Act of 1917 (Lever Act), **62**: 172-73, 491n1; **63**: 562,n2, 612n1; **64**: 23, 141n1; **65**: 105, 130, 417-18, 508n1, 546n1, 563

Levermore, Charles Herbert, **68**: 452n2

Leviathan, U.S.S., **58**: 141; **68**: 388,n1

Levine, Lawrence W., **67**: 536n2

Le Viness, C. T., **67**: 311

Levy, David William, **60**: 203n1

Levy-Alphandery, Leon-Georges-Maxime, **53**: 502,n1
Lewinson, Benno, **67**: 336,n1, 340
Lewis, David John, **66**: 8n1; WW on, **68**: 94-95,n1,2,3, 98-99
Lewis, Garfield, **66**: 75
Lewis, James Hamilton, **54**: 125; **55**: 296-97, 351n1; **59**: 320,n3; on League of Nations situation, **61**: 350,n1; on Osborn's poem on WW, **67**: 58; WW thanks, **67**: 70
Lewis, John Llewellyn, **65**: 312n2, 314, 546n1, 565; **66**: 19,n1, 27, 281; and coal strike, **63**: 612n1; **64**: 141n1, 142-45, 179-80, 180; urges miners to return to work, **65**: 568, 568-69; WW thanks for urging workers to return to work, **66**: 4; on Alabama coal strike, **66**: 263-65
Lewis, Lucy Biddle (Mrs. J. Reece), **58**: 140-41,n1
Leygues, Georges-Jean-Claude, **54**: 10,n7, 39; **55**: 16, 149,n1, 426,n3; **56**: 28, 34-36, 38
Leyland Line, **53**: 111
Liang Ch'i-ch'ao, **57**: 634,n1, 637
Libbey, William Jr., **66**: 378,n4; **67**: 182
Liberator, The (New York), **66**: 93, 95
Liberia: U.S. loans to, **53**: 573; representation at Paris Peace Conference, **54**: 65, 115; **58**: 198; and League of Nations, **68**: 477
Liberty engine, **53**: 308n1
Liberty Loan, **55**: 200, 227, 259, 333; **57**: 283, 376, 447-48, 472, 510, 511; **58**: 560, 595, 596; Fifth, **59**: 75,n1; bonds, **62**: 177; WW on, **63**: 251
Liberty Loan Acts, **63**: 200, 201
Library of Congress, **66**: 319, 468; and WW's papers, **66**: 292-93; Dodd on WW's papers going to, **67**: 77, 282; Jameson on presidential papers being housed in, **67**: 264; and WW's papers, **68**: 544n1
Libre Belgique, La (underground newspaper), **61**: 35n1
Libya, **54**: 326n3
Lida, Poland, **59**: 411, 446
Liebknecht, Karl, **53**: 6, 7, 8, 122; **54**: 93n4; **62**: 557,n2
Liège, Belgium, **61**: 17n2
Liepaja, Latvia: *see* Libau
Life (magazine), **68**: 198,n1,2, 449
Life and Letters of Walter Hines Page (Hendrick), **68**: 259n2
Life of George Lansbury (Postgate), **55**: 87n2
Life of John Marshall (Beveridge), **67**: 298
Life of Laurence Oliphant: Traveller, Diplomat and Mystic (Henderson) **55**: 384n3
Life of Richard Cobden (Morley), **66**: 536,n1
Life of Mr. Justice Clarke: A Testament to the Power of Liberal Dissent in America (Warner), **68**: 130n2, 168n1, 178n1
Life, Work and Rebellion in the Coal

Fields: The Southern West Virginia Miners, 1880-1922 (Corbin) **65**: 335n1
Liggett, Hunter, **59**: 253, 401-402,n1,4, 443, 444; **60**: 9, 10n6, 11, 12, 15; **61**: 61
Ligue des Droits de l'Homme: *see* League for the Rights of Man
Lille, France, **55**: 326; **56**: 251
Liller, William C., **64**: 515,n1
Limburg, Netherlands, **55**: 110; **56**: 593; **61**: 11n2
Limitation of Armament, Conference on: *see* Conference on Limitation of Armament
limitation of armaments: *see* arms limitation
Lincoln, Abraham, **54**: 175, 198; **55**: 365-66, 481; **56**: 437-38; **59**: 621; **60**: 301; **61**: 230, 238, 445; **62**: 559; **63**: 625; **65**: 415, 510n1; **66**: 280, 484; **67**: 111, 135, 162, 183n1, 225, 235, 533n1; **68**: 256, 567; bed of, **64**: 32; WW's 1916 speech on, **67**: 256,n1
Lincoln Legend: A Study of Changing Conceptions (Basler), **65**: 404n5
Lincoln Memorial: R. S. Baker on, **64**: 362
Lincoln Memorial Commission: dedication plans, **67**: 580
Lindley, Francis Oswald, **53**: 335,n1
Lindsay, Florence Field, **59**: 517,n2
Lindsay, Ronald Charles, **62**: 330, 331, 424; **63**: 297,n1, 559; **64**: 475n1; on WW's senatorial conferences, **61**: 619-19,n1; on WW favoring J. W. Davis, **65**: 488
Lindsay, Samuel McCune, **55**: 157,n1; **62**: 96; **66**: 246n2
Lindsley, Henry Dickinson, **58**: 330,n2
Lingle, Thomas Wilson, **67**: 474n2
Link, Arthur Stanley, **57**: 453n4, 511n2; **58**: 635n20; **61**: 469n1; **62**: 5n6; **63**: 66n7; **64**: 324n2; **65**: 182n2, 398n1; **66**: 36n3, 39n5, 112n1, 157n6; **67**: 518n1; **68**: 78n1, 21n1, 405n2, 475n1, 585n4, 587n6
Link, Arthur Stanley, Jr., **56**: 556n2
Linthicum, Richard, **67**: 365; **68**: 137n2
Lionberger, Isaac Henry, **57**: 47,n3; **66**: 252,n1
Liposwki, Zbigniew, **58**: 618n32, 619, 619-20, 621,n51; **64**: 525n1,2
Lippmann, Faye Albertson (Mrs. Walter), **64**: 362,n3
Lippmann, Walter, **53**: 357; **54**: 376n12; **61**: 240n1, 373; **62**: 365n27; **64**: 362; **67**: 541-42; **68**: 305; opposes treaty, **60**: 202,n1
Lipsky, Louis, **68**: 100,n1
Liquidation Board: *see* United States Liquidation Board
liquor: *see* prohibition
Liss, Sheldon B., **66**: 162n3
Lissa (Now Vis, Yugoslavia), **57**: 345,n2, 519; **59**: 91, 201, 329, 339; **60**: 138, 213, 266; **61**: 228; **62**: 457, 575, 604, 620; **63**: 206, 208; **64**: 171, 299, 301, 302, 305, 331, 334, 462

Literary Digest, **57**: 629n1; **61**: 541,n1; **64**: 270n2; **65**: 7n, 71n3; and presidential poll, 1920, **65**: 474,n2

Literary Digest International Book Review, **68**: 233, 261,n2

Lithuania and Lithuanians, **65**: 469, 527n3; **66**: 21,n1; border dispute with Poland, **66**: 138-39, 145; and Memel, **68**: 521,n1; *see also* Paris Peace Conference—Lithuania and Lithuanians

Lithuania Against Poland: An Appeal for Justice (pamphlet), **66**: 21n1

Lithuanian National Council, **66**: 21

Litovtzeff-Polyakoff, C., **66**: 357n2

Little Belt Strait, **58**: 123, 124

Littlefield, George Washington, **66**: 369n1,2

Little Rock, Ark., **63**: 523

Little Strokes (Alvarez), **58**: 636,n10, 639

Litvinov, Maksim Maksimovich, **53**: 492-94,n1, 561, 588,n5, 712-14; **54**: 27n1, 135-38, 154, 180, 180-81, 182,n2, 349; **59**: 194n2; and Bullitt mission to Russia, **55**: 540n1, 541-42, 545

Liverpool, England, **53**: 544

Livonia (Livland), **55**: 202,n2; **57**: 398; **58**: 42; **59**: 16

Lloyd, Demarest, **66**: 267n1

Lloyd, Henry Demarest, **66**: 267n1,2

Lloyd George, David, **53**: 8, 61,n1, 101, 130, 217, 240, 322, 329, 341, 345, 367, 401, 418, 437, 440, 481, 510, 529, 565, 569, 572, 577, 594, 609; **54**: 5, 124, 127, 130, 198, 236, 273-74, 301-302, 380, 417, 464n1, 489; **55**: 62, 66, 81, 88, 180, 204n2, 211, 230,n2, 305, 320; **56**: 3, 12n1, 122n2, 312, 347, 407, 421, 443, 487, 578, 587, 588; **57**: 52, 99, 101-202, 103, 104, 105, 179, 203, 450-51, 466, 468, 516, 517n4, 532n2, 533n4, 627; **58**: 27, 94n1, 119, 138, 147, 214, 462; **59**: 3, 202, 246; **60**: 17, 197, 252; **61**: 188, 238, 239, 313; **62**: 61, 254,n1, 319, 525, 606; **63**: 343, 422; **64**: 348; **65**: 61, 162, 229n1, 350; **66**: 25-26, 54, 200; **67**: 183n1, 462n1; **68**: 47, 141n1, 223, 313, 480; organizes inter-Allied meetings in London, **53**: 197, 222, 252, 324, 336; on Ireland, **53**: 299-300,n2; **55**: 364, 454, 474; **56**: 438, 443; **58**: 585-87, 588; **60**: 303-304, 384, 385, 388-89; **61**: 439; and issue of WW attending peace conference, **53**: 409, 410, 414; and plans for WW's trip to London, **53**: 448, 449; not going to Paris to meet WW, **53**: 457, 458; and British elections, **53**: 519n1, 565, 589, 595; WW meets with in London, **53**: 519-20, 525; and meeting of Imperial War Cabinet on WW's views, **53**: 558-69; and Supreme War Council meetings, **54**: 8, 9,n6, 10, 11, 12, 41, 42, 203, 204, 239-40, 242, 244, 245-46, 528, 529, 530, 531-32, 533, 534, 535, 537, 538; **56**: 15, 16, 19-20, 22, 24, 26, 32, 33, 36, 37, 51, 54, 55; and Council of Ten meetings, **54**: 13, 14, 15, 16 17, 21,

22, 23, 24, 26, 43, 44, 45, 46, 47, 48, 64, 65-66, 68, 69, 71, 72, 73-74, 75, 76, 97, 98, 99-102, 103n7, 108, 109-10, 111, 113-14, 116, 117, 118, 119, 120, 155, 180, 181-82, 182, 183, 184, 185-86, 187, 187-88, 189, 206, 207, 208, 209-10, 210, 210-11, 219, 219-20, 221-22, 224, 225, 248, 285, 286, 289, 290, 294, 300-301, 310, 311, 318, 322-23, 324, 343-44, 356, 373, 415, 418, 421-22, 423, 424, 425, 462, 463, 492, 505, 508; on representation at Paris Peace conference, **54**: 13, 14, 15, 16, 17, 43, 44, 46; and Bolshevik question, **54**: 22, 23, 45, 53-54; angered by *Daily Mail* articles, **54**: 112n3, 377-78; and League of Nations Covenant, **54**: 196, 197, 206-11, 226, 439, 459; on demobilization, **54**: 219-22, 239-40, 242, 244, 245-46; on colonial question, mandatories, and territorial claims, **54**: 249-51, 300-301, 301, 322-23, 324, 329-30, 347,n2, 350-51, 354-55, 366, 366-67, 368, 369-70, 374, 374-75, 375, 375-76, 386; **62**: 185, 235, 257; seconds WW's League of Nations resolution, **54**: 268-69; on disposal of German submarines, **54**: 273n1, 273-74; and withdrawing troops from Archangel, **54**: 349; on military occupation, **54**: 370-73, 372; varied opinions of, **55**: 35, 480, 546; and Russian situation, **55**: 233, 235,n2; **56**: 551n1; WW on, **55**: 266; **58**: 3, 112, 169, 331-32; **64**: 308-309; meets with WW, **55**: 283, 284, 326-27, 349, 423, 497, 499, 529-30; House meets with, **55**: 458; and Rhineland question, **55**: 475n2; pressured to remain in Paris, **55**: 530; **56**: 4-5, 56; and issue of Covenant being part of peace treaty, **56**: 59, 336; meets with WW and Clemenceau, **56**: 85, 102; on Poland, **56**: 90, 91, 92-93, 94, 95, 165, 165-66, 312-13; on Syria and Turkey, **56**: 106, 107, 108, 109, 110-11, 111, 117, 118; on distorted press reports and leaks on peace conference, **56**: 148-49, 150, 151; and Haller's troops, **56**: 129-30, 130, 131, 132, 134, 136, 136-37, 143, 145, 146, 147, 168, 168-69, 409-13, 495, 496, 497, 526, 527, 528; **57**: 550; House on, **56**: 180, 336, 517; **57**: 71, 72, 139, 140; **59**: 602-603; and British labor problems, **56**: 205-206; and reparations, **56**: 208, 209, 246, 251, 285,n1, 287, 287-90, 357, 358-59, 359, 360, 363-64, 368-69, 369-70, 370, 417-18, 448-51, 499,n3, 501, 503, 506; **57**: 6-7,n7, 8, 9-10, 10, 11, 13, 14, 15, 15-16, 17, 17-18, 18, 19, 21-22, 22, 22-23, 24, 26, 27, 29, 30, 31, 32, 80, 81, 82, 85, 87, 88, 141, 165-66, 204-15; **58**: 29, 30, 31, 32, 33, 35, 36, 37, 38, 161,n1; **60**: 20, 21, 264, 306-307, 317-18, 319, 344-45, 345-46, 347, 349, 400, 401, 558, 559, 560; **62**: 148, 149; **67**: 70, 145; and Interna-

Lloyd George, David (*cont.*)
tional Labour Commission, **56**: 236n2,560; on Germany's admission to League of Nations, **56**: 250, 264; on Odessa and Rumania, **56**: 255-57; and Fontainebleau Memorandum, **56**: 259-70; Cecil meets with, **56**: 297; refutes Clemenceau's views, **56**: 320-22; on Rhineland, **56**: 324; **57**: 297; **59**: 590; **60**: 440-41; on Hungary, **56**: 414-16, 460, 462-63, 488; rejects Monroe Doctrine article for Covenant, **56**: 335; WW and House discuss, **56**: 336, 539-40; and Danzig, **56**: 395, 396, 507, 560, 561; **57**: 151, 153, 154, 155, 289-90; WW on changing positions of, **56**: 408; on WW's sense of humor, **56**: 438; Benham on appearance of, **56**: 443; on Saar Basin, **56**: 452; **57**: 106-108, 129, 150, 162, 163, 164, 165, 199, 200, 201, 201-202, 202,243-44, 245, 246; **59**: 377, 378, 379, 380-81, 382; response to Clemenceau on Fontainebleau Memorandum, **56**: 477-79, 545-47; Daniels on U.S. naval program and, **56**: 518-19; **57**: 91, 92, 142,n1, 215; and prosecution of authors of the war, **56**: 530-34; **57**: 121, 122, 123, 124, 124-25, 127, 128, 150, 631; R. S. Baker on, **56**: 578; **58**: 271; **59**: 623; on substitution of House for ill WW, **56**: 584; on Belgian claims, **57**: 589, 590, 591, 592, 593; R. S. Baker and WW on, **57**: 70; on Smuts' mission, **57**: 73; and invitation to Germany to peace conference, **57**: 101-102, 318, 319; attacks against reparations policy of, **57**: 145,n1, 147n5, 148; and Russian food relief, **57**: 165, 438-39; returns to England for vote of confidence, **57**: 242-43, 316, 317, 318, 325, 349; and publication of peace treaty, **57**: 288-89, 291-92, 292-93; **58**: 23-24, 61-63, 254; **59**: 213; on German bonds, debt and finances, **57**: 294; Orlando on, **57**: 352; speech to Parliament, **57**: 428,n14, 449-50; and Russia and Bullitt mission, **57**: 459-60,n2,3; and Italy's claims, **57**: 490-92, 493-94, 518, 519, 536, 538-39, 540, 541, 545-49, 552, 576, 610-14; and Japan's claims, **57**: 554, 555-56, 602-603, 604, 605, 608, 609, 615-26; and situation in Archangel, **57**: 628; **58**: 265, 266; and WW's Adriatic statement, **58**: 3, 42, 103, 142, 153, 360; and Northcliffe, **58**: 5; on plans for rehabilitation of European credit, relief, and reconstruction and WW's response, **58**: 8-12, 446-48; on Adriatic question, **58**: 14, 18, 19, 57-60, 74-86, 80, 82, 83, 84; **59**: 86, 87, 88, 89, 90, 91, 92, 93, 95, 96, 97, 98-99, 100, 101, 102, 103, 569; **63**: 204-206, 207, 209, 364, 393, 424, 465, 617n1; **60**: 208, 209-10, 211, 212, 214, 215, 216, 217, 303, 308; **62**: 603; meets with Orlando, **58**: 53, 57, 58-59; **59**: 257;

concern over Italy's absence, **58**: 77, 250, 251, 252; letter to Italy on Fiume, **58**: 86-90, 333-34, 336-37; and duration of economic clauses, **58**: 114, 115, 116, 117, 118; on Kiel Canal, **58**: 122, 123, 124; on captured enemy ships, **58**: 125-57, 127, 128, 557-58, 559; on Shantung, **58**: 130, 131, 132, 133, 178, 179, 180, 181, 186, 216, 218, 221-22, 222, 223, 224-25; on Syrian commission, **58**: 133-34, 172; **59**: 632, 633; and Belgium, **58**: 140, 237, 262; **59**: 247, and Council of Four, **58**: 148-49, 150, 151, 152, 153, 154; on recognition of Finland, **58**: 177-78; on prisoners of war, **58**: 235; and Orlando's speech in Rome, **58**: 237,n3; on liabilities of war debt, **58**: 252; on inviting Austria's and Hungary's representatives to Paris, **58**: 264-65; Scott on, **58**: 268; on Italian credentials, **58**: 279, 280, 281, 282; on submarine cables, **58**: 283, 299, 301, 303, 303-304, 304-305, 349, 350, 351; on treatment of Jews and minorities, **58**: 285, 286, 287; **59**: 219, 220; interview with Imperiali, **58**: 391-92; Grayson on, **58**: 429; and French security treaty, **58**: 479-80, 486-88, 489-90, 490; at Plenary Session at Versailles, **58**: 502; on plans if Germany refuses to sign treaty, **59**: 9, 9-10; on Russian situation and Kolchak, **59**: 16, 18, 19, 20, 29, 30, 31, 527; on landing of Greek troops at Smyrna, **59**: 21, 22-23, 23, 24, 25, 26, 41, 43, 59, 266, 267, 268, 269, 270, 271; and Irish-American delegation and Home Rule, **59**: 34, 104-105, 105-107, 366-67,n1,2, 394; Tardieu on, **59**: 46; on labor clauses of peace treaty, **59**: 49,n4; on tonnage and reparations, **59**: 50, 51, 52, 53, 54; on blockade of Germany, **59**: 127, 128, 129, 130; on Lord Derby as British ambassador to U.S., **59**: 160-61; on prisoners of war, **59**: 162; on Polish-Ukrainian situation, **59**: 215, 217, 218, 351, 352, 354, 357, 358, 359; on Italians landing on coast of Asia Minor, **59**: 223, 224, 266, 267, 268, 269, 270, 271; on situation in Asia Minor, **59**: 257-61; on Germany's note on economic effect of peace treaty, **59**: 297-98; clashes with Clemenceau on secret treaties, **59**: 321, 370; proposals regarding Asia Minor and Syria cause conflict with Clemenceau, **59**: 326-28, 330, 331, 333-35, 336, 336-39, 340, 341, 343, 344, 346, 369-70, 370,n1, 484; Hoover on, **59**: 384; on reparations for successor states of Austria-Hungary, **59**: 386-87, 387, 388, 389, 390-91; on figures for fixed military forces, **59**: 429, 431; on note to Kolchak, **59**: 436, 437, 438; Republican opposition to, **59**: 451-52; on Austrian treaty, **59**: 482, 483, 486; conversation with WW and Clemenceau on Italy, **59**:

492-94; on Austria as new or old state, **59**: 496, 498, 499-500; speeches of, **59**: 504,n12; **60**: 444, 457-58; on proposals made to Orlando on Adriatic question, **59**: 569; on treaty revision, **59**: 622-23, 623, 627; Seymour on, **59**: 647, 648; and Baruch, **60**: 18; on peace terms, **60**: 23-27; on peace treaty and France's views, **60**: 30; conflict with Clemenceau, **60**: 40, 334; Baruch on peace terms position of, **60**: 73-74; Seymour's disappointment in, **60**: 78-79; WW on, **60**: 80-81, 84, 329, 491, 533, 570; **61**: 112; **63**: 604; **66**: 411n1; **68**: 27, 502; on issue of Upper Silesia and plebiscite, **60**: 85-92, 156, 404, 405, 406, 415, 417, 421, 422, 423, 425, 426, 427, 432, 555, 556, 558; wants changes in Austrian treaty regarding Yugoslavia and Rumania, **60**: 120; on Klagenfurt Basin, **60**: 126, 127, 128, 129; and relationship with Clemenceau and WW, **60**: 144; friction with Paderewski over Poland's position on Upper Silesia, **60**: 159-66; on Poland's lack of gratitude, **60**: 163-64; on arms limitation for Central European states, **60**: 173-74; McCormick on new proposals by, **60**: 196; constant change of position of,**60**: 197; favors Tardieu plan, **60**: 216; on articles 20 and 22 of Austrian treaty, **60**: 219-20; on new states and method of appeal to League of Nations, **60**: 222; Cecil on, **60**: 255; and N. H. Davis-Cecil misunderstanding over credit, **60**: 277-80; seating plan for Council of Four meetings, **60**: 285; on German conscription, **60**: 296,n4; Grayson on dinner with, **60**: 300-306; on WW, **60**: 303; on his love of music, **60**: 305-306; Tumulty on Irish issue and, **60**: 331; on WW in photograph of Big Four, **60**: 333; proposals for German reparation after peace treaty signed, **60**: 336-37; on hot weather, **60**: 381-82; on text concerning German commerce, **60**: 420; on responsibility for the war, **60**: 463-64; on occupation of Rhineland, **60**: 464, 465, 501, 502, 503, 526, 527; on Czech-Rumanian-Hungarian border issue, **60**: 469, 470; on reply to Kolchak, **60**: 477; Lamont on, **60**: 494; on Baltic states, **60**: 497-98; on blockade, **60**: 498-500, 523; on Germany, **60**: 553; accuses WW of "loading dice against Germany," **60**: 559, 563; on Foch's reservations about march on Berlin, **60**: 585, 586, 589-90; on Grayson, **60**: 612; and apology to Grayson, **61**: 44; and presence of South and Central American delegates at Versailles, **61**: 65; reason for refusing Germany's time extension, **61**: 79, 80, 81; on sinking of German fleet at Scapa Flow, **61**: 102, 103, 111, 143-45; **62**: 144-47,n1, 186-87; on U.S. role in postwar reconstruction, **61**:

223-25; at treaty-signing ceremony, **61**: 302, 333; bids farewell to WW, **61**: 305-306; on whether conversations of Council of Four should be made public, **61**: 337, 338; WW on mandates and, **61**: 393-94,n1; on William II, **61**: 396; and reparations, **62**: 148, 149; and Thracian question and Greece's pact with Great Britain, **62**: 238, and Armenian situation, **62**: 248n1, 285n1; **63**: 466; **67**: 64, 65; and Council of the Heads of Delegations, **63**: 299, 306; Baker on anecdote about WW and, **63**: 621; on *Imperator* controversy, **64**: 9, 10, 33, 33-34; and Fiume, **64**: 260n1; and Adriatic proposal, **64**: 263-66, 298-305, 376, 398; Lansing on draft of telegram on Russia, **64**: 307-308; Wallace on Adriatic proposal of, **64**: 318-20; and Palestine, **64**: 358, 449; Borah on Lodge reservations and, **64**: 381,n1; and war crimes, **64**: 382; reply to WW on Adriatic proposals, **64**: 436-42, 481-83; in 1918 hosts stag dinner, **64**: 490n1; Polk's draft reply to on Adriatic question, **65**: 37-39; on France's relations with Germany, **65**: 106; alleged negative comments about WW were never made, **65**: 221, 231-32,n1; supports German representation at San Remo Conference, **65**: 221; on Kapp *Putsch*, **65**: 236; and British debts to U.S., **65**: 325n1; on cancellation of inter-Allied debts, **65**: 480-81; informed of events at Democratic National Convention, 1920, **65**: 488; and Poland, **65**: 527,n3; on Tardieu's indiscreet articles, **65**: 542,n1; on situation in Europe, **66**: 42-50; on need for U.S. participation in world affairs, **66**: 48; on inter-Allied indebtedness, **66**: 48-50; and MacSwiney hunger strike, **66**: 89; WW answers on reparations and debts, **66**: 307-12; and Yap Island, **66**: 326, 460, 464; WW and, **67**: 44, 227, 239; and Britain's indebtedness, **67**: 355,n2,6; reaction to WW's Adriatic statement, **67**: 376n1; Lord Bryce and Davis on, **67**: 378; asserts he proposed League of Nations being part of Versailles Treaty, **68**: 108; resignation of, **68**: 141n1; Bliss on peace negotiations and, **68**: 224; WW welcomes to U.S. and his response, **68**: 445, 446; arrives in Washington and visits WW, **68**: 455-56; and WW's limericks, **68**: 457, 590; and N. D. Baker, **68**: 485; WW on visit of, **68**: 590; photograph of, *illustration section,* **54**; **61**; Orpen portrait, *illustration section,* **60**

Lloyd George, Gwilym, **59**: 602,n2
Lloyd George, Margaret Owen (Mrs. David), **53**: 593,n7, 595; **68**: 456,n1, 480
Lloyd George, Megan Arvon, **59**: 247,n2, 602,n1; **60**: 300; **68**: 456,n1
Lloyd George, Richard, **59**: 602,n2

Lloyd George (Rowland), **56**: 259n1; **68**: 141n1

Lloyd George Against Vengeance Peace (*New York Times*) **53**: 71n1

Lloyd George, Woodrow Wilson and the Guilt of Germany (Lentin), **56**: 285n1, 482n2; **57**: 6n7; **60**: 4n3; **61**: 144n5

Loans to Foreign Governments (Sen. Doc.), **64**: 475n1

Lobez, Colonel, **53**: 459,n2, 460, 461

Lobit, Paul-Joseph-Jean-Hector de, **56**: 332,n1, 470,n1

Lochridge, P. D., **60**: 258

Lockmiller, David A., **66**: 58n1; **67**: 24n1

Lodge family, **68**: 595

Lodge, Henry Cabot, **53**: 82, 110, 185, 199, 301, 469n1, 580, 581, 625,n1, 626, 692, 707; **54**: 237, 474, 499; **58**: 359,n1, 410n1, 413; **60**: 285, 567, 575; **61**: 66n3, 181, 372, 417, 422n3, 446, 468, 492, 493, 534, 562, 577, 596, 605n1, 619, 623; **62**: 3, 5,n6, 45, 68, 113-14, 151-52, 262-63, 266, 281, 306, 313, 440, 631; **63**: 118, 223n1, 296, 333,n3, 380; **64**: 29, 148, 274, 337, 445; **65**: 7, 76, 118, 179, 212, 228, 298, 416; **68**: 179n1, 180, 190, 202, 247, 278n1, 463, 474; and famine relief bill, **54**: 174,n2; and Armenia, **55**: 66; **62**: 116n1; **65**: 7, 76, 118, 179, 212, 228, 298, 416; **66**: 448, 449-50; and WW's meeting with congressional committees on League of Nations, **55**: 267, 269, 270; attack on League of Nations, **55**: 312,n1, 312-13,n1, 367, 388,n1, 437; R. S. Baker on public opposition to, **55**: 449, 450; debate with Lowell on League of Nations, **56**: 161,n1; charges copies of peace treaty circulating in New York, **60**: 155, 156, 242, 243-44, 245, 288, 330; and Hitchcock Resolution, **60**: 198, 249; opposition to peace treaty, **60**: 202, 203; and peace treaty leak investigation, **60**: 434, 536; and press claims that WW under dominance of bankers, **60**: 531; on options open to Senate on Covenant, **60**: 571-72; as editor, **61**: 363; and reservations to peace treaty, **61**: 448, 448-49, 542; **62**: 12, 150, 235, 307-309, 363, 444-45, 445, 447n1; submits resolution asking for all materials related to League of Nations, **61**: 484; controversy with WW over Reparation Commission appointment, **61**: 519, 582; on raising status of Belgian legation, **61**: 614; speculates on treaty ratification, **61**: 618-19; and French security treaty, **61**: 622; requests and receives treaty documents from WW, **62**: 51, 219,n2, 477-78, 535, 611-12, 624; on interim Reparation Commission, **62**: 142, 236; on reparations, **62**: 148, 149, 347-49; Tumulty's suggestions for WW's letter to, **62**: 272-74, 274-75, 309,n1; requests WW meet with Foreign Relations Committee, **62**: 275-76; WW's draft letter to Lodge becomes his statement to Foreign Relations Committee, **62**: 276-78, 340-44; WW on doubts concerning treaty, **62**: 278-80; Hamlin on, **62**: 301-302; WW agrees to meet with Foreign Relations Committee, **62**: 310, 336, 338; questions WW at White House meeting, **62**: 344-46, 347, 348, 349-50, 353, 383, 396, 402, 403, 405, 407, 411; and Shantung amendment, **62**: 507n1; and WW's memory loss, **62**: 629-30, 631; WW's views of, **62**: 636; WW supports his own position with quotations from, **63**: 285, 371, 375; and Bullitt testimony, **63**: 337,n1; and situation in Senate regarding amendments to treaty, **63**: 482, 484; and compromise reservation to Article X, **63**: 529,n2, 531; Grey and Jusserand on treaty and, **64**: 44; will keep Senate in session to dispose of reservations and move for adoption of his resolution for ratification, **64**: 45-50; on preamble, **64**: 46-47; Hitchcock on meeting with on possible compromise, **64**: 58-59; reads WW's letter into *Congressional Record*, **64**: 63; and treaty and political campaign, **64**: 72; and Mexican situation, **64**: 120,n1, 152n2; on WW's health, **64**: 135-36; and Fall resolution, **64**: 136-37, 152n2; Glass on treaty negotiations and, **64**: 193, 410; WW's challenge to concerning treaty, **64**: 200-201; Hitchcock on unyielding position of, **64**: 244; Cobb on treaty position of, **64**: 270n2; Tumulty on, **64**: 277; and bipartisan meeting, **64**: 283; *Springfield Republican* and New York *World* on, **64**: 287,n1,2; and bitter-enders, **64**: 328n2; and Grey's letter, **64**: 355n1; WW charges conspiracy with Grey, **64**: 384; Glass on Taft reservations and, **64**: 387-88,n1; Cummings on, **64**: 419n1; suggestion of letter from Masaryk to, **64**: 443; WW on opposition to Article X by, **65**: 8, 11, 25, 30; comments on Hitchcock letter, **65**: 71n3; Hitchcock on putting Lodge in defensive position regarding treaty, **65**: 150-51; on Minister from Canada, **65**: 242; on Knox's peace resolution and issue of separate peace, **65**: 257,n2, 293-94, 382n2; House on WW and, **65**: 274; and Indiana plank, **65**: 292n1; and Armenian mandate, **65**: 351n2; Geddes on, **65**: 351n2; notifies WW of adjournment of Congress, **65**: 373; on League of Nations in keynote speech at Republican National Convention, 1920, **65**: 388,n1; WW on as advocate of League of Nations, **65**: 417; and Panama Canal tolls controversy, **66**: 141n1, 178; and charges of WW not consulting with Republicans on treaty, **66**: 148, 149; ap-

proached by France, **66**: 238n1; notifies WW of opening of Congress, **66**: 479; WW on boldness of, **66**: 479, 484; WW's "third leg" as excuse for not shaking hands with brings commendation from Glass, **66**: 479, 484, 494-95, 500-501; and Versailles Treaty, **67**: 45, 187n1, 228, 404, 609n2; WW's reply to on Senate adjournment, **67**: 207; and Newberry case, **67**: 316, 317; WW on, **67**: 321n1; and Washington Naval Conference, **67**: 419n1; on Four Power Treaty, **67**: 511,n1; Hull on Democratic campaign and, **68**: 86; and senatorial election, **68**: 96n1; Dodge on, **68**: 497; and WW's death, **68**: 570; EBW requests he not attend WW's funeral, **68**: 574; WW on, **68**: 589; *see also* Lodge reservations, Lodge resolution of ratification

"Lodge Blocks Pact Compromise, Its Friends Insist" (Michelson), **64**: 287n2

Lodge reservations, **64**: 28,n1, 29, 276n1, 384; Tumulty on, **64**: 15; Hitchcock on proposed substitute reservations, **64**: 29-30,n1, 37-38; text of, **64**: 38-41; WW will not accept, **64**: 39,n1, 47-48, 50, 56, 165-66, 387; 14th and 15th rejected by Senate, **64**: 50; House on, **64**: 89; N. H. Davis on, **64**: 105; senators voting for, **64**: 199n1; bipartisan committee on, **64**: 283-84, 311-31, 312-13,n1, 328n2; public opinion poll of college students and faculty on, **64**: 284n1; Hitchcock's marked copy of text of, **64**: 289-95; and Grey's letter, **64**: 355n1; Borah on Grey's letter being affirmation of, **64**: 381,n1; Hitchcock and Tumulty fear more Democrats are supporting, **64**: 466, 479; Dr. Park on WW's health and, **64**: 526; and editorial history of Hitchcock letter, **65**: 7-10, 11-14, 25-28, 30-35, 49-55, 67-71; WW's refusal to accept, **65**: 7; Straus urges WW to accept, **65**: 47-48; Hitchcock's concern over losing Simmons' vote against, **65**: 48; Tumulty on his opposition to reservation to Article X, **65**: 66; probable vote on changed reservation to Article X, **65**: 80,n1; substitute reservation for Article X, **65**: 80,n1; Tumulty on WW and reservation to Article X, **65**: 81-82; WW urges Simmons to stand with Democrats, **65**: 82; treaty vote supporting, **65**: 109n1; McKellar on Article X and, **65**: 120; Hitchcock on Democrats supporting, **65**: 150; Hoke Smith on, **65**: 219, Dodge on, **65**: 234-35; WW on Democratic party and, **65**: 263; and T. J. Walsh's vote on, **65**: 345; Boeckel on, **67**: 616-17

Lodge resolution of ratification: Hitchcock on, **64**: 29, 46, 58-59; Underwood on, **64**: 42; WW's opposition to, **64**: 43, 51, 58; vote on, **64**: 63, Burleson on votes of various senators on, **64**: 338

Lodge resolution on termination of war, **64**: 126,n1

Lodge Warns Against Pacifist Sentimentality in Making Peace Terms (Boston Evening Transcript), **53**: 82,n1

Lodz, Poland, **58**: 563

Loeb, Walter, **58**: 308n1

Loeb, Sophie Irene Simon, **68**: 478-79,n1, 492

Loetscher, Lefferts A., **68**: 519n1

Logan County, West Va., coal strike in, **65**: 335-37

Logan, James Addison, Jr., **57**: 367,n2; **65**: 256,n3, 272

Logan, Thomas Francis, **53**: 480-85

Loir-et-Cher, France, **54**: 255

Loken, Hakon, **67**: 17-18

Lomonosov, Iurii Vladimirovich (George Vladimir Lomonossoff), **56**: 55,n1

London, England, **53**: 4; Allied conferences in, **53**: 197, 222, 252, 324-27, 336, 341; and Costigan, **53**: 328-32; plans for WW's visit, **53**: 498, 507, 508; WW's arrival activities and speeches in, **53**: 509-12, 526-29, 530, 530-31, 531-33, 533-34, 586, 591-95; WW made honorary citizen of, **53**: 527; and Morgan's offer regarding ambassador's residence in, **60**: 83n1; Balfour on, **60**: 204

London Naval Treaty (1930), **67**: 512n4

London, Treaty of, 1915, **53**: 43,n1, 434, 466, 621, 643, 711n1; **54**: 51, 326n3; **55**: 160; and Adriatic question, **57**: 243,n2, 490-91, 501, 504, 513, 514, 516, 520, 534, 536, 540, 548, 551, 576, 585, 613; **60**: 209, 210-11, 271, 308; **62**: 41, 365n27, 367,n30, 375; **63**: 209; Balfour on Adriatic question and, **62**: 23, 25; WW on, **57**: 344, 492-93, 519, 531, 542, 543; threat of enforcement of, **64**: 263-64, 264,n1, 298, 302, 304, 305, 313, 314, 315, 319, 341, 376, 377-78, 398, 400, 439-40, 480-81; WW on, **64**: 462-63; Britain and France answer WW's charges concerning Adriatic question and, **64**: 355n1, 359, 360; and Adriatic question, **65**: 38-39, 46, 315-16; *see also* Treaty of London (April 26, 1915)

London, University of, **56**: 540

London *Daily Herald*, **56**: 63, 473

London *Daily Mail*, **54**: 112n3, 123, 351n3, 377-78; **60**: 599n1; Paris edition, **57**: 63n1, 145, 175, 459n2,3; **58**: 96; **61**: 395n1; **66**: 486; WW's statement on German treaty, **61**: 107, 108n1

London *Daily News*, **53**: 634n1; **54**: 159n1, 175

London *Daily Sketch*, **54**: 159n1

London *Express*, **56**: 128

London *Globe*, **56**: 128

London *Morning Post*, **53**: 711n1; **55**: 547; **57**: 6n7

London Pact (1915): *see* Treaty of London

London *Times*, **53**: 44-45, 71n1, 329n1, 385, 420,n2, 430n, 444nl, 530n1, 544n1, 592n4, 602n1, 617n1; **55**: 371; **57**: 179, 459n2, 532,n2; **58**: 4n5, 237n3, 313n4, 330n1, 410, 562n1; **60**: 44n4; **61**: 191n2, 347,n1, 508n1, 512n2; **62**: 525n1; **63**: 621,n1; **64**: 355n1, 359, 360; **65**: 24n1; **66**: 44n5; **68**: 106n1, 108n1, 299, 453n1, 464,n1; WW interviewed on major issues, **53**: 418, 422-30, 438

London *Weekly Herald*, **55**: 87,n2

London *Westminster Gazette*, 57: 6n7

Lonergan, Augustine, **68**: 98,n2

Long, Andrew Theodore, **58**: 4,n5; **60**: 44,n3

Long, Boaz Walton, **65**: 125, 464,n2, 556,n4

Long, (Samuel Miller) Breckinridge, **55**: 279, 349, 436; **61**: 554; **62**: 152, 154,n1, 281; **63**: 93, 543,n2, 558-59, 606; **64**: 233, 455; **65**: 231; on Ethiopian mission, **61**: 470-71; and WW's speech to Czech troops, **61**: 514, 518n2; on meeting with Debuchi on Shantung, **61**: 557-59; Reinsch on, **61**: 635; on crisis with Japan over Shantung settlement, **62**: 40-42; on Reinsch's resignation and situation in China, **62**: 282-84; on not raising China's mission to embassy status, **62**: 283; on WW's reaction to Bullitt testimony, **63**: 338n4; on situation in Senate on reservations and Article X, **63**: 444-45; on Hapgood's resignation, **64**: 234; suggested for appointment, but declines offer, **64**: 296, 316-17, 322, 350-51; and quest for senatorial seat, **64**: 316-17; withdraws resignation suggestion, **64**: 352; WW pleased he will stay in present position, **64**: 352, 353; Lansing shows resignation correspondence to, **64**: 414; and Frazier, **64**: 452; offers vacation home to WW, **65**: 110; and banking consortium, **65**: 259; resignation of, **65**: 377-78, 381; **66**: 84,n3, 124; praises WW and WW's acknowledgement, **67**: 164-65,n1, 169-70; senatorial race in Missouri against Reed, **67**: 543,n1, 578-79, 586; **68**: 12, 105,n1, 105, 126, 166n1; on intimacy of WW, **68**: 527-28

Long, Christine Alexander Graham (Mrs. Breckinridge), **65**: 110,n2

Long, E. Hudson, **67**: 173n2

Long, Richard Henry, **63**: 615n1

Long, Walter Hume, **53**: 566,n9; **56**: 430,n1, 482, 518; **57**: 91-92,n1, 92, 93, 142

Longare, Count Lelio Bonin, **53**: 390,n3; **58**: 263,n2, 282, 334,n4, 392-93, 395, 396, 398, 478, 479; **60**: 546,n3; **65**: 198,n4

Longatico (now Dolenji Logatec, Yugoslavia): and Adriatic settlement, **66**: 365

Longchamps Racetrack, **61**: 187; WW

visits, **58**: 534, 535, 536; photograph of, *illustration section*, **58**

Longfellow, Henry Wadsworth, **65**: 514

Longley, Harry Sherman, **63**: 76n1

Longuet, Jean, **53**: 387n1; **68**: 200, 201

Longworth, Alice Roosevelt (Mrs. Nicholas), **53**: 580; **67**: 91

Longworth, Nicholas, **61**: 492

Loomis, Elmer Howard, **67**: 182

Lopez Gutiérrez, J. Antonio, **61**: 638,n4

Lopez Gutiérrez, Rafael, **61**: 638,n3, 639-40

Lord, Clifford Lee, **57**: 447n1

Lord, Robert Howard, **53**: 356,n1, 367; **56**: 49n10, 54n14, 97, 119, 434, 466n1, 468, 512n1, 529-30; **57**: 276, 392, 398, 406; **59**: 596-97, 638; **60**: 21,n4, 130,n4, 230, 423, 468; **62**: 206, 220,n1; **65**: 530,n1; on Bolshevik situation, **54**: 91-95; and Poland, **54**: 471n2; **60**: 77; on Teschen, **56**: 220-22; on a Baltic Commission, **57**: 137-39; on Galicia, **57**: 327, 327-28; **59**: 356-57; on issue of plebiscite for Upper Silesia, **60**: 53-56, 57, 59, 72, 189-92, 412, 414, 415-16, 426; Lloyd George on, **60**: 88; on Germany's observations regarding "Eastern Question" (Poland and Lithuania), **60**: 182-89; and Lloyd George, **60**: 255; photograph of, *illustration section*, **57**

Lord Palmerston and the Rejuvenation of Turkey, 1830-41 (Rodkey), **55**: 383n2

Lord Riddell's Intimate Diary of the Peace Conference and After, 1918-1922, **60**: 489n1; **68**: 422n

Loree, Leonor Fresnel, **53**: 716,n2; **54**: 88

Loring, Katherine Alice Page (Mrs. Charles Greeley), **53**: 22

Lorraine, **60**: 60, 165, 320; draft reply on, **60**: 467,n5; *see also* Alsace-Lorraine

Los Angeles, California: WW's arrival and activities in, **63**: 396-97, 423, 523; WW's speeches in, **63**: 400-407, 407-18

Los Angeles *Evening Express*, **63**: 423,n3; **67**: 363, 364

Los Angeles *Examiner*, **63**: 398; **67**: 363

Los Angeles Sunday Times, **63**: 400n1, 407n,n2, 418n

Los Angeles Times, **55**: 205; **63**: 398n1, 423n2,3

Losina: *see* Lussino

Lothringen, S.M.S., **55**: 426

Loubert, Emile, **67**: 382n5

Loucheur, Louis, **54**: 41,n4, 42, 246, 525, 527, 529, 530; **55**: 13-14, 15, 458n1, 499; **56**: 250, 270, 271n2, 286-89, 291-96, 362, 363, 444, 502, 509; **57**: 71, 79, 109, 358, 609; **58**: 27, 28, 31, 32, 33, 35, 40, 64, 65, 113, 114, 119, 122, 148, 238, 249, 266, 469, 470, 471, 472; **59**: 57-58, 215, 422, 495, 562, 625; **61**: 57, 83, 99, 126, 148, 160, 255, 384; **65**: 542; **66**: 44n5; on reparations, **57**: 10, 11, 12-13, 13, 14, 17, 18, 25, 26, 29, 30, 30-31, 31-

32, 32-33, 87, 205; **60**: 26, 73, 391, 579, 591; **61**: 101; on Saar, **57**: 243, 244, 245, on bonds to be issued by Germany, **57**: 293-94; on experts discussing economic clauses with Germany, **59**: 314-15; on Austrian treaty and reparation clauses, **59**: 537, 537-38, 539, 540, 624-25; and Clemenceau, **61**: 375; WW on, **68**: 593,n9

Loucheur committee, **54**: 525, 527-28, 529, 530, 538-45; and reparations, **60**: 50, 93, 196, 264, 317; and proposed Rhineland High Commission, **60**: 366-67, 511; on size and cost of army of occupation, **60**: 367, 368; on Rhineland occupation, **60**: 441, 501, 502, 503, 511-12, 527; on negotiations with Rumania and Serbia on reparations and Austrian treaty, **60**: 591-92,n2

Loudon, John, **54**: 460,n1; **55**: 219, 220; suggests meeting in person with German delegates on economic clauses, **58**: 526

Louis XIV (of France), **57**: 199

Louis XVI (of France), **57**: 126

Louis, William Roger, **54**: 311n2, 363n3

Louise Victoria Alexandra Dagmar, Princess Royal of Great Britain, **53**: 592n2

Louisiana: and woman suffrage, **65**: 163-65, 294-95

Louisville, Ky., **63**: 523

Louisville & Nashville railroad union, **67**: 121n1

Louisville *Courier-Journal*, **54**: 60, 389n2; **59**: 451n1; **62**: 615,n2, 627

Louisville Post: Knott's proposal for WW to write for, **68**: 483-84,n1

Louisville Times, **65**: 506n3; **66**: 450n1,2

Louvain, Belgium, **58**: 551; **61**: 14, 29, 31; WW's remarks at, **61**: 21

Louvain, University of: WW receives honorary degree from, **61**: 14,n1, 231-32, 106, 129; **62**: 111,n2; WW on desecration of, **61**: 21; photograph of, *illustration section* 61

Lovett, Edgar Odell, **65**: 553; requests one of WW's honorary diplomas for Rice Institute, **66**: 410-11, 420; thanks WW for sending Greek honorary degree and invites him to lecture at Rice, **67**: 235-36,n2,3; on installation of trustees of WW Foundation, **68**: 365,n1; WW thanks for note, **68**: 366

Lovett, Mary Ellen Hale (Mrs. Edgar Odell), **67**: 235,n2

Lovett, Robert Scott, **53**: 704,n1; **56**: 400,n3; **57**: 233,n1, 282, 382, 384; **67**: 177,n2

Lovett, Robert Williamson, M.D., **67**: 386n2

Løvland, Jorgen Gunnarssson, **66**: 501, 504-505, 517; **67**: 18

Lowden, Frank Orren, **65**: 354n2

Lowell, Abbott Lawrence, **53**: 29; **54**: 58; **55**: 225n2; **59**: 516; **61**: 365; **65**: 184,n4; **66**: 246n2; **67**: 608, 609; **68**: 360; on League of Nations, **55**: 65, 187, 199; **56**: 161-62,n1; on Monroe Doctrine amendment to Covenant, **57**: 233, 315-16, 331, 332; on WW's strategy for treaty ratification, **67**: 610-11

Lowell, Carlotta Russell, **67**: 135,n1

Lowell, James Russell, **65**: 514; **67**: 4,n1

Lowrie, Walter, **53**: 607,n5

Lowry, Edmund G., **68**: 476n3

Lowther, Claude, **56**: 285n1; **57**: 6n7

Lowther Street Congregational Church, Carlisle, England, **53**: 524,n1

"Loyal Coalition" of Boston, **66**: 267,n1

Lozano, Fabio, **66**: 211-12,n5

Lubeck, Germany, **53**: 8: **55**: 427

Lubeck, S.M.S., **56**: 29; **58**: 127

Lubin, Germaine, **56**: 62,n5

Lubomirski, Prince Kazimierz, **64**: 260,n1; **65**: 272,n2, 338n2; **66**: 9-10, 11,n1, 39,n4, 87n1, 146; **67**: 204; **68**: 183,n2; and WW's honorary degree, **67**: 392, 400

Lubove, Roy, **55**: 341n1; **56**: 246n2

Lucey, Patrick Joseph, **55**: 340,n1

Lu Cheng-hsiang, **54**: 331,n2, 475,n6; **57**: 560,n1, 582,n1, 633,n2; **58**: 68-70, 167-68, 462n1; **59**: 145, 568; **61**: 289,n1; photograph of, *illustration section*, 58

Luckau, Alma, **59**: 136n2

Lucking, Alfred, **53**: 382,n1; **66**: 130n1; **68**: 336,n1; on Newberry case, **67**: 316-17,n1, 323

Lucking, Helfman, Lucking and Hanlon, **53**: 382n1

Luçon, Louis-Henri-Joseph, Cardinal, Archbishop of Rheims, **54**: 279-80,n3, 305

Ludendorff, Erich Friedrich Wilhelm, **57**: 550; **60**: 304; **65**: 102

Luders, Alfred, **57**: 526

lumber industry, **62**: 173

Lunardini, Christine A., **58**: 364n1

Lunatic at Large (Clouston), **67**: 573,n1

Lundgren-Neilson, Kay, **54**: 33n6, 481n4; **56**: 49n10, 395n1; **59**: 216n5; **60**: 189n2

Lunt, Richard D., **65**: 335n1

Lunt, William Edward, **53**: 350,n1, 381; **56**: 563n3; **57**: 433, 456; on Fiume, **56**: 607-609

Lussin, Lussino (now Losinj, Yugoslavia), **57**: 482; **63**: 206; **64**: 171, 175, 299, 302, 331, 334, 462

Lusitania, S.S., **58**: 28; **59**: 300, 310; and reparations, **62**: 348

Lussin: *see* Lussino

Lussino (now Losinj, Yugoslavia), **59**: 201, 557, 570; **60**: 138, 207, 213, 214; **61**: 228; **62**: 457, 575, 604, 620; and Adriatic settlement, **66**: 364, 377

Luther, Martin, **67**: 76

Lüttwitz, Walther Freiherr von, **65**: 98n1, 99, 101

Lutz, Ralph Haswell, **57**: 347n1; **59**: 60n3; **60**: 34n2

Luxembourg, **53**: 619n1; **54**: 149; **55**: 306, 387, 423, 507, 508; **56**: 267, 561, 615; **57**: 110, 319, 334, 354, 355-56, 364-65, 372,n2, 457-58, 458; **59**: 133-34, 421n4, 500, 582; **60**: 52,n4, 549; and Belgium's claims and France, **56**: 595-97; resignation of U.S. Minister to, **62**: 435,n1

Luxemburg, Rosa, **54**: 93n4

luxury tax, **54**: 502; **58**: 605; **60**: 611

Luzzatti, Luigi, **58**: 240n5, 313,n4, 359,n2

Luzzatto, Riccardo, **53**: 619n1

L'vov, Georgii Evgen'evich, **53**: 258,n1, 258-59, 289-90, 306; **54**: 21, 45; **55**: 369; **57**: 139n1; **59**: 14n4, 18,n11

Lvov: *see* Lemberg, Galicia

Lwow: *see* Lemberg, Galicia

Lybyer, Albert Howe, **58**: 327n5

Lympne, England, **65**: 325n1, 363n3

Lynch, Charles F., **68**: 454

Lynch, Frederick Henry, **54**: 277-78; **66**: 502-503,n1, 512, 542n1; and Anglo-American relations and Taft visiting London, **56**: 57-58, 120-21; requests meeting of WW and religious leaders on treaty, **65**: 183, 183-85,n1

Lynch, R. E., **55**: 540n1; **56**: 183

lynching, **62**: 313,n1; and American Federation of Labor's resolution against, **61**: 357-59,n1; Southern Sociological Congress on, **62**: 106-107, 506; WW on, **62**: 128-29, 260; Moton on, **62**: 233-34; WW on, **68**: 102n2

Lyndonia (yacht), **67**: 419

Lyon, Thomas H., **68**: 102,n1,2

Lyon-Caen, Charles-Léon, **59**: 4n1

Lyons, Maurice F., **64**: 521; **67**: 306; on publication of McCombs book, **67**: 304,n2

Lyons, Richard L., **63**: 167n6

Lyttelton, Adrian, **68**: 255n1

M. M. Warburg and Co., Hamburg, Germany, **56**: 523n1

Macada (Queen of Sheba), **61**: 473

McAdoo, Eleanor Randolph Wilson (Mrs. William Gibbs), daughter of WW and EAW, **53**: 213, 469; **55**: 204-205, 283, 395; **56**: 306; **58**: 104; **61**: 99, 185, 423, 516; **63**: 167, 543, 619; **64**: 325; **65**: 243, 439; **66**: 181, 235, 266, 302, 320, 384, 409, 506n1; **67**: 14, 22, 103, 356, 485, 533; **68**: 115, 122, 145, 153, 221, 229, 268, 292, 338, 363, 366, 408, 471, 503, 505-506, 532; arrives at White House, **63**: 549; after election sends love and encouragement, **66**: 315; WW answers, **66**: 332; Christmas and birthday greetings to WW, **67**: 5-6; sends family news and thanks WW for birthday greetings, **67**: 429-30; on love for WW and on her move to California, **67**: 562; WW sends love and welcomes to new home, **67**: 565; home in California, **68**: 72; WW sends Christmas gift to, **68**: 138;

sends birthday greetings to WW, **68**: 254; visit with WW, **68**: 446, 480; summoned to WW's bedside, **68**: 549, 550, 558; and WW's death, **68**: 569; at WW's funeral, **68**: 582

McAdoo, Ellen Wilson, granddaughter of WW, **55**: 205; **64**: 325; **67**: 5,n1, 6, 429, 562, 565; **68**: 72-73,n1, 124, 145, 153, 221, 229, 480, 503, 510, 545; to visit WW, **68**: 446; at Armistice Day demonstration, **68**: 469

McAdoo, Eva Lee Tardy (Mrs. William), **59**: 78,n2

McAdoo, Eva T., **59**: 78,n2

McAdoo, Mary Faith: granddaughter of WW, **67**: 6, 565; **68**: 72-73,n1, 124, 145, 153, 221, 229, 230, 239-40, 268, 480, 503, 510, 545; to visit WW, **68**: 446

McAdoo, Molly Tackaberry Ferguson (Mrs. William Gibbs, Jr.), **68**: 240,n1

McAdoo, Nona Hazelhurst: *see* De Mohrenschildt, Nona Hazelhurst

McAdoo, Sarah (Sally) Fleming, **55**: 409n5; **67**: 356,n4; **68**: 122,n1, 123-24

McAdoo, William (Chief City Magistrate of New York), **59**: 77-78,n1, 575

McAdoo, William Gibbs, **53**: 35, 65, 70, 150, 226, 281, 282, 587 704; **55**: 283, 395, 409n5; **61**: 182, 291, 350, 376, 480, 646; **62**: 99, 224-25, 498-99, 516, 636; **65**: 140, 243, 382; **66**: 234-36, 266, 282n1, 506n1; **67**: 327, 347, 403, 405, 540, 565, 607, 614; resignation of, **53**: 58, 74, 150-51, 151, 182-83, 401, 468; **54**: 429; **58**: 50, 603; **64**: 307, 347, 416n2; **68**: 75-76, 115, 145-49, 229-30, 408, 471; and Hull's sinking-fund plan, **53**: 99; on Von Engelken's loyalty, **53**: 106; and International Mercantile Marine Corporation, **53**: 112-13; on railroads, **53**: 190-93, 646-48; **55**: 258-60, 260-61; **64**: 197; wishes to be a peace commissioner, **53**: 468-69; talk of presidency, **53**: 469; **54**: 61; **67**: 606, 616-17; **68**: 381, 426, 476,n3; successor to, **53**: 441n1; on League of Nations support, **55**: 205; and revenue legislation, **55**: 333, 334n1; death of son-in-law, **55**: 442,n1; **56**: 125; on League of Nations amendments, **56**: 552-53; Grayson on WW's need for, **57**: 304-306; on public opinion on League of Nations, **58**: 104,n3; suggestions for WW on League of Nations strategy, **61**: 459; **67**: 616-17; and Owen's bill for establishing Federal Reserve Foreign Bank, **61**: 495, 496,n2, 497, 498; and woman suffrage, **61**: 537-38; on League to Enforce Peace's resolution endorsing League of Nations, **62**: 70-71; on WW appealing to House of Representatives to remain in session and address taxation and cost of living issues, **62**: 71-72; on prices, **62**: 184-85; on Strong, **62**: 423; at White House during WW's illness, **63**: 543, 544, 550; and WW's health,

63: 586; House on Alexander's appointment and, **64**: 185; and Lane Commission on railroads, **64**: 422n5; Grayson confides in on WW's health problems in Paris, **64**: 492-94; House on treaty plan and, **65**: 274; as presidential candidate, **65**: 291, 346, 383, 480, 492, 498, 499; code name for, **65**: 350; withdraws candicacy, **65**: 401n1, 428, 435,n1, 438-39, 439-40; votes received in *Literary Digest* poll, **65**: 474n2; balloting and votes received at Democratic National Convention, 1920, **65**: 491, 492n2, 499n1; WW on candidacy of, **65**: 498, 499; failure to win nomination, **65**: 511n3; makes campaign trip for Cox and requests League of Nations information, **66**: 180-81, 184-85, 234-35, 302; on Western Union controversy, **66**: 218-22, 235-36; WW answers, **66**: 224, 250; praises WW, **66**: 318-19; on restoring self-government to Dominican Republic, **66**: 383-84, 429; WW answers on Dominican Republic, **66**: 408-409; WW thanks for birthday greetings, **67**: 14; WW's personal note to, **67**: 22; and Mexican oil, **67**: 82; has poison sumac, **67**: 429; and move to California, **67**: 562n1; **68**: 72-73, 122-24; Tumulty on Jefferson Day message and, **68**: 22; and Morse case, **68**: 73,n2; WW on move of, **68**: 75; on American Bar Association convention in California, **68**: 123; WW delighted to hear from, **68**: 129; sends family news, **68**: 145-46, 221-22, 239-40; will not support Reed in Missouri, **68**: 151-52, 153; on election results and Democratic party, **68**: 221-22; sends photos, **68**: 221-22; sends motion pictures, **68**: 239-40; WW thanks for movies of family, **68**: 243; sends birthday greetings and book to WW, **68**: 254, 260-61; WW thanks for book, **68**: 267-68; writes railroad statement at WW's request, **68**: 287, 291-92, 293; to visit WW, **68**: 363, 446, 460; visits WW, **68**: 366; on WW's California property, **68**: 503-504, 510, 532, 545; at WW's funeral, **68**: 583
McAdoo, William Gibbs, Jr., **68**: 240
McAllister, James Gray, **61**: 595,n2
McAlpin, Charles Williston, **54**: 411; **65**: 327n1, 333; **67**: 105n3, 441
McAndrew, James William, **53**: 474,n4
McAver, Fred, **62**: 434, 478-79, 515
McAvoy, Charles D., **65**: 431,n1
McCabe, Charles Martin, **65**: 119,n1
McCabe, David Aloysius, **67**: 182
McCain, William David, **67**: 382n5
McCaleb, James F., **68**: 93-94,n1
McCall, John Etheridge, **66**: 386n1
McCall, Samuel Walker, **55**: 292-93, 328-29; **64**: 64n1; **67**: 512,n3, 526; suggested as peace commissioner, **53**: 25,n1, 66, 72, 82, 199, 245; and second Industrial Conference, **63**: 611; and

Tariff Commission appointment, **66**: 8-9,n1, 10
McCartan, Patrick, **61**: 183n2
McCarthy, Charles James, **62**: 460,n1, 480-81
McCarthy, Florence W., **54**: 256n1
McCauley, Edward, Jr., **53**: 314,n2, 344, 370, 371; **55**: 207, 217, 224; **57**: 63; **61**: 355,n1, 370, 383; photograph of, *illustration section*, **53**
McChord, Charles Caldwell, **57**: 233, 382,n23
McClellan, George Brinton, **67**: 235,n4
McClellan's Own Story: The War for the Union, the Soldiers Who Fought It, the Civilians Who Directed It and His Relations to It and to Them, **67**: 235,n4
McClintic, James, **66**: 223n1
McClumpha, Charles, **55**: 508n2
McClure's Magazine, **68**: 48n5
McClure Newspaper Syndicate, **55**: 341n1; **60**: 147n4; **68**: 354, 498
McCombs, Dorothy Williams (Mrs. William Frank), **65**: 444,n2, 506n1
McCombs, Robert, **64**: 524,n2
McCombs, William Faulkner: WW's condolences to, **67**: 157,n1
McCombs, William Frank, **64**: 521-24; **67**: 292, 460; **68**: 259n2; and French ambassadorship, **64**: 523, 524,n1; WW on, **65**: 444,n1,2; death of, **67**: 157,n1; book on WW, **67**: 304,n1,2, 364,n2
McConnell, Joseph Moore, **67**: 474n2
McConville, H. A., **67**: 121,n1
McCormack, John, **55**: 237
McCormack, Joseph Nathaniel, **65**: 261,n2, 317
MacCormack, William, **63**: 423,n1
McCormick, Annie, **67**: 313,n1, 351, 583
McCormick, Annie Criswell (Mrs. Henry), **67**: 313,n1, 351; death of, **67**: 583,n1
McCormick, Cyrus Hall, Jr., **62**: 303,n3; **64**: 64n1; **67**: 470; **68**: 330, 577; on Russian situation, **53**: 228, 254, 255-57; **55**: 38-39; and Pierce-Arrow for WW, **67**: 116, 137, 148, 168, 186,n1; and fund raising for WW's S Street house, **67**: 129, 137,n3, 148, 168; and WW College Clubs, **67**: 285, 327; and WW Foundation, **68**: 249n2; WW's condolences to, **68**: 391; and trust fund for WW, **68**: 441, 441-42, 443, 513, 516; to contribute to car for WW, **68**: 516; on trying to reconcile WW and House, **68**: 528-29; sent WW's favorite limerick, **68**: 533; WW on gratitude for trust fund, **68**: 534
McCormick, Harriet Bradley Hammond (Mrs. Cyrus Hall, Jr): death of, **67**: 116,n3
McCormick, Joseph Medill, **53**: 365,n1; **57**: 189; **60**: 244,n4; **61**: 372, 506n1; **67**: 35; **68**: 185,n1; Grayson on attitude of toward WW's health, **64**: 135-36; and treaty fight, **64**: 200-201, 336, 338; and bitter-enders, **64**: 328n2

McCormick, Nettie Maria Fowler (Mrs. Cyrus Hall, Sr.), **67**: 137n3; death of, **68**: 391,n1

McCormick, Robert Rutherford, **61**: 373

McCormick, Vance Criswell, **53**: 252, 255, 572, 573, 632, 633, 645; **54**: 35, 90, 127, 196, 261, 386, 411-12, 440, 477, 486, 494, 558; **55**: 29n1, 113, 148, 186, 351, 387, 457, 465n2, 493; **56**: 159, 180-81, 304, 353, 437, 502, 553, 580, 587, 588; **57**: 189, 303, 305,n1, 333,n1, 375, 388, 391, 423; **58**: 26, 28, 120, 279, 423, 470, 548, 549; **59**: 148-49, 160, 173-74, 188, 227, 233, 283, 384n1, 422, 448-49; **60**: 74, 114, 120-21, 196, 281, 359, 399, 491-92, 608, 615, 621; **61**: 3n1, 40, 130, 143, 195, 288, 366, 384; **62**: 6, 70, 100, 222, 222-23,n1; **64**: 347; **65**: 21n1, 24; **67**: 313, 351, 607, 608; **68**: 414, 471, 527,n4; and cotton exportation, **53**: 164, 202; **54**: 192-93; on censorship, **53**: 431-32; **55**: 372, 373, 514-15; **57**: 448-49; resigns as chairman of Democratic National Committe, **54**: 56, 61; **55**: 308; and Attorney General selection, **54**: 429; on Russian railroad situation, **55**: 38-39; **57**: 420-22; offers appointment suggestions, **55**: 206-207; on war costs, **55**: 210-11; on his suggested appointment to mideastern commission, **56**: 200; on reparations, **56**: 424-25, 444, 498, 499, 501-502, 535, 579-80, 598-99; **57**: 22, 23, 26, 85, 86, 87, 88, 203; **58**: 27-28, 140, 161, 237-38; **60**: 49-50, 72-73, 76-77, 306-307, 399-400, 400-401; and controversy between Railroad Administration and Industrial Board, **57**: 374,n1, 381; on Russia, **57**: 575; **59**: 127, 234, 235, 236; on WW's Adriatic statement, **58**: 121; on Plenary Session and adoption of League of Nations Covenant, **58**: 188; on Belgium, **58**: 237-38, 262; on consequences of blockade of Germany, **59**: 109-10, 127-28; on harmony of "Big Four," **59**: 128; on rumor of British and American delegates not signing peace treaty, **59**: 383-84; on Austrian reparation clauses, **59**: 624-25; meets with WW on Kolchak and Russian situation, **61**: 110-11; on recognition of Kolchak and extension of credits to Russia, **61**: 177; on plans for return to U.S., **61**: 230; on college athletics, **61**: 374; on WW's speech aboard *George Washington*, **61**: 383; suggestions for WW's message to Senate, **61**: 385-86; thanks WW for opportunity in Paris, **61**: 513; suggested as Redfield's replacement, **62**: 266; congratulates WW on effect of tour, **63**: 117; on League to Enforce Peace's prediction on treaty ratification, **63**: 235; and treaty reservations, **63**: 363, 392; declines position of Secretary of Commerce, **64**: 95, 185; and strategy at

Democratic National Convention, 1920, **65**: 496, 497, 580, 581; and fund raising efforts for WW's S Street home, **67**: 137n3; WW Clubs and, **67**: 326, 345, 353; WW's condolences to, **67**: 583; and WW's last illness, **68**: 557, 558, 576; photograph of, *illustration section*, **59**

McCosh, James, **59**: 40

McCoshen, Herbert, **65**: 441-42

McCoy, Donald R., **63**: 167n6

McCoy, Walter Irving, **67**: 318,n1, 329, 330

McCracken, John Henry, **66**: 246n2

McCrae, John, **66**: 158n8

McCray v. United States, **68**: 131,n4

McCulloch, James Edward, **62**: 128-29, 313; on race relations, **62**: 106-107,n1, 292-93, 505-506

McCulloch, Roscoe Conkling, **61**: 549n1, 612

McCullough, Joseph Allen, **62**: 106-107,n2

McCully, Newton Alexander, **55**: 39,n1; **58**: 320,n1; **60**: 613,n2, 615; **66**: 21, 355n1

McCumber, Porter James, **57**: 372; **59**: 524n1; **60**: 245,n4; **61**: 137, 417, 425, 597; **62**: 12, 67, 113, 308; **66**: 141n1; **67**: 608; **68**: 97n3; suggestions for passage of League Covenant in Senate, **55**: 491-92,n1; WW invites to White House to talk about treaty, **61**: 492-93,n2, 515, 516; questions WW at Foreign Relations Committee meeting, **62**: 348, 351-52, 354, 355-56, 358-59, 364, 368, 370-72, 375-76, 383, 390, 405; on Shantung settlement, **62**: 370-72; on main objections to treaty, **62**: 565-66; WW thanks for suggestions, **62**: 611; and treaty reservations, **63**: 150, 296, 363, 444, 445, 447, 482; on compromise reservation to Article X, **63**: 529-30,n4; and treaty fight, **64**: 49, 94, 338, 339, 428

McDermott, Walsh, **58**: 617n24

MacDonald, Captain, **54**: 380n3

MacDonald, Francis Charles, **67**: 182

MacDonald, James Grover, **58**: 169; **61**: 448,n1; **62**: 530-31,n1; **65**: 138-39,n1; **68**: 315,n1, 328

MacDonald, Katherine, **67**: 530,n1

MacDonald, (James) Ramsey, **53**: 498, 519n1; **60**: 474, 482; **68**: 593n10

McDonald, William Jesse, **56**: 350,n1

McDonough, Martin, **66**: 75

MacDowell, Charles Henry, **58**: 29,n2; **66**: 289,n2

MacDowell, Mary, **68**: 296n1

MacDowell, William Fraser, **65**: 183,n1; **66**: 121,n2

Macedonia, **64**: 164n8; Bryce on Bulgarian population in, **59**: 400

McElligott, Richard J., **59**: 76n1

McElwain and Company, **65**: 228

McFadden, George, **56**: 553n1, 588; **60**: 290,n1

McFarland, Carl, **60**: 115n7

Macfarland, Charles Stedman, **65**: 183,n3, 184; **66**: 378, 387; **67**: 29-30, 32
Macfarland, Grenville Stanley, **53**: 199-200, 221, 245, 487
McGee, John Franklin, **65**: 508,n1, 509
McGiffert, Arthur Cushman, **65**: 183,n3
McGill, Stephenson Waters, **66**: 134,n1, 151
McGill University, **65**: 55
McGlachlin, Edward Fenton, Jr., **63**: 274,n2, 361,n1, 361-62
McGlynn, Frank, **65**: 404,n5; **66**: 112; **67**: 111
McGrath, Justin, **64**: 123,n1
MacGregor, Genaro Fernandez, **65**: 446
McGuire, Mr. **61**: 117
McGuire, Michael J., **63**: 269, 296-97
Machen, John Gresham, **68**: 519,n1
Machias, U.S.S., **61**: 640
Macias, José Natividad, **65**: 201, 201-202,n1, 212-13
McIlhenny, John Avery, **55**: 290; **57**: 349; resignation of, **55**: 330,n1
McIlvaine, William Brown, **67**: 460,n4
McIlwain, Charles Howard: and WW Clubs, **67**: 253
McIntyre, Frank, **60**: 199
Mack, John Edward, **54**: 90n1
Mack, Julian William, **53**: 67n1, 104, 105; **55**: 386; **58**: 381n3; **59**: 249, 445; **61**: 367; on plight of eastern European Jews, **55**: 368-81; **59**: 198-200; on Palestine, **55**: 381-85
Mack, Karlheinz, **55**: 317n3
MacKay, Clarence Hungerford, **58**: 561,n2, 602
Mackaye, James, **56**: 283,n1
McKean, Frank Chalmers, **63**: 92n1
McKee, Henry Stewart, **63**: 423,n3
McKellar, Kenneth Douglas, **53**: 24; **55**: 297; **56**: 339; **62**: 263; **63**: 443,n3; on cotton situation, **53**: 78-79, 100; and bipartisan meeting on reservations, **64**: 283-84; and Nashville postmastership, **65**: 119; suggestions for treaty ratification, **65**: 120; WW on, **66**: 175; **67**: 94; **68**: 61
McKelvie, Samuel Roy, **63**: 94
McKenna, Joseph, **65**: 204-205,n3
McKenna, Patrick, **68**: 576
McKenna, Reginald, **53**: 483
Mackensen, August von, **60**: 353,n1, 355
MacKenzie-Grieve, Kenneth, **60**: 44n5
Mackenzie, Georgina Mary Muir, **64**: 160,n4
Mackenzie, William Douglas, **68**: 387,n1; on political strategy on League of Nations, **66**: 259-61,n1
McKeown, Thomas Deitz, **61**: 510,n3
McKim, Mead and White, **53**: 639n1
McKinley, William, **56**: 531; **61**: 397; **65**: 417; **66**: 327, 434n1; and China and open door policy, **63**: 211, 315, 330, 332, 397, 412, 437, 439, 460, 471, 473, 496, 507; WW on League of Nations and, **63**: 370; extracts from last speech

of, **63**: 398, 398-99, 407; I. Hoover compares WW to, **67**: 150
McKinstry, Charles Hedges, **53**: 181,n1; **54**: 55
MacLachlan, Alexander, **59**: 640,n3,4
McLane, Catharine Milligan, **63**: 623
McLaughlin, Andrew Cunningham, **67**: 459,n3, 467; **68**: 259,n3
Maclay, Sir Joseph (Paton), **53**: 326, 360,n1, 373, 482; **54**: 171; **55**: 367,n3; **56**: 495
McLean, Angus Wilton, **65**: 507,n2; **68**: 212-13,n1
McLean, N. C., **65**: 553n1
McLean, Edward Beale, **57**: 429; **63**: 552,n2
McLean, George Payne, **61**: 548,n1, 570, 599, 600, 601; **62**: 34; and treaty fight, **64**: 200-201, 336
Macleay, James William Ronald, **58**: 46,n4; **59**: 488,n8
Macleay, Ronald, **58**: 70, 72-73, 180, 253
McLemore Resolution, **60**: 535; **68**: 587n6
McLeod, Miss, **68**: 391, 427
McMahon (M'Mahon), Sir Arthur Henry, **56**: 110n7,11
McManus, George H., **53**: 314,n1; **55**: 412,n8
MacMechan, Virginia, **67**: 556
Macmillan Company, **67**: 259
McMillin, Benton, **53**: 317 n4, 342,n7; **66**: 389,n2, 506n5
MacMurray, John Van Antwerp, **61**: 634, 635; **62**: 284; on Shantung settlement, **61**: 583,n1
McNab, Gavin, **53**: 115, 116, 158; **63**: 309, 340; **66**: 252,n1; **67**: 532-33; on minority rights issue in Poland, **60**: 487; appointed to first Industrial Confernce, **63**: 300,n1; and WW Clubs, **67**: 326, 353
McNab, John E., **65**: 351,n2
McNary, Charles Linza, **62**: 12, 67, 113, 308, 430; **63**: 150; meets with WW on treaty, **61**: 492-93,n1, 516, 545, 563,n2; and reservations on Article X, **63**: 444-45; and treaty fight, **64**: 94, 200-201, 311-12, 337, 338, 339
McNulty, Edward, **54**: 473,n1
Macon Telegraph, **65**: 220
McRae, Hugh, **68**: 45,n1
McReynolds, James Clark, **54**: 428; **60**: 115,n3; **65**: 384,n1; J. H. Clarke on, **68**: 131
McReynolds, Samuel Davis, **68**: 471,n4
McSparran, John Aldus, **68**: 25,n2, 56n2
MacSwiney, Terence Joseph, **66**: 88-89,n1, 90, 91, 512n2
MacVeagh, (Isaac) Wayne, **63**: 555,n1
MacVey, Frank LeRond, **67**: 536,n1, 537,n1
McWilliams, Tennant S., **68**: 171n1
Madame Roland: A Biographical Study (Tarbell), **53**: 123,n1
Maddox, Robert James, **68**: 278n2
Madison, Dolley, **65**: 412

Madero, Francisco Indalecio, **67**: 219
Madison, James, **67**: 218, 358
Maeander River, **59**: 137,n3
Mafalda, Maria Elisabetta Anna Romana, Princess, **53**: 596,n3
Magalhaes, Olyntho de, **57**: 176,n2
Magie, David, **59**: 349,n1, 374-76; **67**: 182; **68**: 255,n3
Maginnis, Samuel Abbot, **66**: 210,n3, 480-81,n2
Magnesia, **59**: 613
Magoun, Jeanne Cassard Bartholow (Mrs. Francis Peabody), **67**: 527n4
Magyars, **59**: 62, 401; **64**: 465; Kerner on, **58**: 157, 158-59; **60**: 124, 355, 356, 598
Mahaffy, Charles A., **68**: 199
Mahany, Rowland Blenerhassett, **65**: 545,n6; **66**: 477
Mahon, Craig, **68**: 277
Mahon, H. J., **68**: 277
Mahon, William D., **65**: 20
Mahoney, Daniel Joseph, **65**: 551,n3
Maier, Charles S., **65**: 326n4
Maikarzel, Nejil Bey, **55**: 145n3
Main, John Hanson Thomas, **55**: 486,n2
Maine: Young Democrats in, **67**: 280; WW Club in Portland, **67**: 302,n2; Democratic party in, **68**: 85-86, 112, 113, 114, 118
Maine, U.S.S., **56**: 437
Mains, Lillian, **63**: 168,n4
Mains, William Lee, **63**: 168,n3, 170
Mainz, Germany, **53**: 36; **54**: 244; **55**: 475, 507; **57**: 335, 592; **58**: 135; **60**: 8
Mair, George Herbert, **58**: 440,n10, 479
Maitri, Phya Kalyan: *see* Sayre, Francis Bowes
Majestic Hotel, Paris, **53**: 143; **56**: 465n1
Major Peace Treaties of Modern History, 1648-1967 (Israel, ed.), **66**: 65n1
Makeague, John, Lord Mayor of Manchester, **53**: 538-39,n1, 540, 541, 545, 546, 548, 549
Making of a Nation: A History of the Union of South Africa (Kruger), **54**: 252n3
Making of a Radical: A Political Autobiography (Nearing), **55**: 337n1
Making Woodrow Wilson President (McCombs), **67**: 304,n2, 364,n1; **68**: 259n2
Makino, Baron Nobuaki, **53**: 556,n12; **54**: 383,n2; **55**: 72, 146, 178n2; **57**: 149, 366, 553-54; **58**: 131, 185, 363n1, 381; **59**: 12, 461; **60**: 103, 483, 486, 500; **61**: 36, 72, 124, 305, 342, 588n4; **62**: 41, 153, 154, 170, 508n3, 523; **67**: 467; and Council of Ten meetings, **54**: 187, 222, 249, 331, 505; and Inter-Allied Commission to Poland, **54**: 204; and League of Nations, **54**: 206-208, 357, 463, 511; on Japan's claims, **54**: 289-90, 290, 290-91, 291, 311, 315, 315-16, 317; **57**: 581, 599-610; **58**: 178, 179, 180, 181, 182, 217, 218, 219, 220, 220-21, 224, 225, 226, 228, 258; on racial and reli-

gious equality, **54**: 485, 500; **55**: 138-39, 155; **57**: 247, 259-61, 264, 265, 269, 286,n1, 571; **58**: 133, 185, 214; **61**: 234; and League of Nations Commission, **56**: 176, 227, 228, 298; **57**: 248, 251, 252; on submarine cables, **56**: 216-17, 220; **58**: 305, 349; and Balfour's proposal on Japan's claims, **58**: 183-84, 246-47; on publishing Kolchak's reply, **60**: 438; on reply to Kolchak, **60**: 463, 466, 477; and responsibility issue, **60**: 474; and blockade decision, **60**: 523; and religious missions, **60**: 577, 578, 594; Lansing on Shantung settlement and, **60**: 602, 603; on Germany's request for time extension, **61**: 80, 81; Lansing tries to persuade to issue statement on Shantung, **61**: 325-26; and Yap Island, **66**: 309, 460, 461; photograph of, *illustration section*, **57**; **58**
Maklakov, Vasilli Alekseevich, **57**: 139,n1; **59**: 14n4, 18,n11, 436,n8
Makri (now Fethiye), **59**: 55, 89, 91, 92, 99, 101, 137,n4, 138, 140, 147, 268, 269
Malagodi, Olindo, **56**: 393,n2
Malatesta, Errico, **66**: 324,n6
Malatia, Turkish Armenia, **63**: 466
Malcolm, Ian Zachary, **58**: 104,n1,2; **60**: 204; **61**: 238,n2
Malgeri, Francesco, **58**: 435n7
Malkin, Herbert William, **58**: 370,n5
Malines, Belgium, **61**: 13, 22, 29, 30-31; photographs of, *illustration section*, **61**
Malloy, William M., **56**: 58n3
Malmédy, Belgium, **55**: 109; **56**: 267, 592; **57**: 392, 393; **60**: 105, 108
Malone, Dudley Field, **55**: 337-38, 407; **67**: 170-71
Mamatey, Victor Samuel, **54**: 135n3
Man and the Hour (book of verses), **62**: 102,n1, 303
Man in His Time (Spivak), **65**: 335n1
"Man in the Moon" (Riley), **67**: 82
Man They Cannot Forget (Tarbell), **67**: 557-58,n1, 564
Mance, Harry Osborne, **61**: 280,n15, 314, 318
Manchester, England: WW's desire to visit, **53**: 457, 458; WW's reception and speeches in, **53**: 538-41, 543-46, 548-49, 549-52
Manchester, University of, **67**: 46n3
Manchester Guardian, **53**: 539, 546, 575n1; **57**: 36, 427; **59**: 519n2; **61**: 7, 360,n5; **62**: 34,n1; **68**: 282
Manchester Ship Canal, **53**: 544
Manchuria, **53**: 463n1; **54**: 79; **57**: 619; **58**: 165; **61**: 438, 555; and banking consortium, **65**: 277; **67**: 544n1
Mandan, North Dakota: WW's remarks in, **63**: 162, 163
Mandate for Armenia (Gidney), **62**: 27n1; **65**: 351,n2
mandates: Colby letter to Lord Curzon on, **66**: 394-99; comments on, **67**: 147,n1, 147,n2, 153-56, 512, 525-26;

see also Paris Peace Conference—mandates; Yap Island

Mandeville, Bernard, **68**: 446, 447, 448

Mangin, Charles-Marie-Emmanuel, **56**: 257,n6; **59**: 401,n2,4, 443; **60**: 8,n2,3, 9, 10, 11, 12, 13, 14, 15, 60n7, 599, 600; **61**: 329,n4

Manion, Edward J., **64**: 411,n1, 424, 426, 431; **65**: 16, 359

Manly, Basil Maxwell, **53**: 705,n1, 710

Manly, Matthias Evans, **55**: 444,n5

Mann, Frank Hurt, **62**: 435n1

Mann, James Robert, **53**: 301; **55**: 449,n2, 469n4; defends WW's peace mission, **53**: 308,n1, 323n1

Mannerheim, Carl Gustav Emil, Baron, **54**: 287,n4, 288

Mannheim, Germany, **55**: 475

Manning, Lelia Bernard Meredith (Mrs. Richard Irvine), **59**: 243,n2

Manning, Richard Irvine, **59**: 243-44,n1, 276

Manning, Vannoy Hartrog, **55**: 286,n2; **62**: 78,n1; **65**: 380,n3

Manning, W. R., **68**: 66

Mansions of England in the Olden Time (Nash), **66**: 546,n2

Manteuffel, Baron Edwin Hans Karl von, **60**: 350,n2

Manton, Martin Thomas, **68**: 248,n1

Mantoux, Paul-Joseph, **54**: 109,n2, 383, 384; **55**: 35; **56**: 14, 15, 208-209n, 209n2, 409,n3, 540; **57**: 104, 195, 453, 521; **58**: 54,n2, 153, 399, 419, 521; **60**: 503; **61**: 33n2, 330; **62**: 145; **66**: 197,n2, 198n1, 212n1,2

Manual of Parliamentary Practice. For the Use of the Senate of the United States (Jefferson), **63**: 547n1

Manufactures, Committee on (Senate), 68: 119n3

Maoris, **54**: 312-13

Mapes, Carl Edgar, **63**: 265,n7

Marburg, Theodore, **66**: 148n2; **68**: 155,n1; declines Shipping Board appointment, **66**: 252,n1, 273

Marburg (now Maribor, Yugoslavia), **59**: 60,n4; **60**: 36

March, Peyton Conway, **53**: 200, 291; **54**: 397n4; **55**: 150,404; **56**: 606; **61**: 293, 517, 518n1; **62**: 271, 323; **63**: 361; **65**: 99, 289n1, 576n1; and Cuba, **66**: 237

Marchienne, Emile-Ernest-Cartier, Baron de: see Cartier de Marchienne, Emile-Ernest

Marchienne-au-Pont, Belgium, **61**: 11n1

Marconi, Guglielmo, **61**: 109,n11, 408; **62**: 457,n1, 575

Marcora, Guiseppi, **53**: 597n1

Marder, Arthur Jacob, **61**: 6n9, 57n8

Marescotti, Luigi Aldrovandi: see Aldrovandi Marescotti, Luigi

Margherita, Queen Mother of Italy, **56**: 86n1; **65**: 303,n11

Margulies, Herbert, **62**: 311n1; **64**: 276n1, 328n2

Maria Francesca Anna Romana, Princess, **53**: 596,n3

Mariana Islands, **53**: 312n1

Mariani, Alessandro, **66**: 19n1

Maria Theresa: and Fiume, **57**: 337

Marie (Marie Alexandra Victoria, Queen of Rumania): visit and lunch with WW, **57**: 190-93, 193,n4, 238, 238-39, 241-42

Marienburg, **57**: 573

Marienwerder, East Prussia (now Kwidzyn, Poland), **56**: 90, 91, 94, 507, 508, 560; **57**: 121, 151, 153, 289, 357, 451, 452, 573, 595; **66**: 225,n1

Marie of Romania: The Intimate Life of a Twentieth Century Queen (Elsberry), **57**: 193n7

Marinelli, Olinto, **57**: 270; **60**: 207,n5, 214

Marine Corps: appointment of commandant, **65**: 430,n1

Marines: see United States Marines

Marion (Ohio) Democratic Club, **67**: 510

Marionette, The (poem, Herford), **66**: 39

Markets, Bureau of, **68**: 271

Markham, Charles Henry, **65**: 562,n2

Marks, Sally, **56**: 457n8; **57**: 372n2; **60**: 107n1

Marlow, John, **56**: 154n3

Marmarice (Marmaris, Marmaras), **58**: 435; **59**: 43, 55, 101, 137,n4, 138, 140, 224, 226, 268, 270

Marmor, Michael F., M.D., **58**: 611n2, 612n3

Marmora, Sea of, **59**: 146

Marne, First Battle of the (1914), **56**: 196

Marot, Clement, **61**: 14,n7

Marquand, Allan, **67**: 182

Marquis, Don, **67**: 105n3

"Marse Henry": An Autobiography (memoirs, Watterson), **54**: 389n2

Marseilles, France, **53**: 221, 229, 240

Marsh, George Perkins, **65**: 305,n14

Marsh, Wilbur W., **65**: 551,n1; **66**: 122

Marshall, Colonel, **56**: 139,n2, 144

Marshall, Archibald, **67**: 105n3

Marshall, Horace Brooks, Lord Mayor of London, **53**: 527n3, 528, 531, 533

Marshall, Laura Siggs (Mrs. Horace Brooks), **53**: 528,n6

Marshall, Louis, **53**: 67n1; **55**: 386; **58**: 381-82,n3; **59**: 604; **62**: 284; on Jews, **53**: 79-80, 99, 104-105, 141; 2155: 368-81; **59**: 198, 200, 514-16,n1; **62**: 220-22; on Palestine, **55**: 381-85; WW answers on Jewish issue, **59**: 276, 471; on atrocities against Jews in Poland, **59**: 445-46; and commission to investigate pogroms in Poland, **60**: 358,n2, 564, 567; on minority rights and need for treaties to be signed concurrently, **61**: 63; on Gibson's appointment to Poland, **61**: 365n1

Marshall, Thomas Riley, **53**: 35, 308n1, 323n1, 582-84,n9, 636; **54**: 59n1, 487; **55**: 204n1; **62**: 10,n2, 198-99; **63**: 117, 265, 542, 555, 563n1, 563, 585, 586; **64**:

Marshall, Thomas Riley (*cont.*)
  49, 63, 231, 348, 416n2, 455, 456, 496;
  65: 120,n3; **67**: 26n6, 324n1; on status
  of treaty and recommendations, **62**:
  419-20; and Lodge reservations, **64**:
  37; on delay in treaty ratification, **64**:
  217; code name for, **65**: 350; and WW's
  health, **65**: 384; WW on Democratic
  Convention of 1920 and, **65**: 393; possible presidential candidate, **65**: 440
Marshall Islands, **62**: 348
Marston, Hunter Sylvester, **53**: 385,n1
Martel, Damien-Joseph-Alfred-Charles,
  Vicomte de, **60**: 141,n1
Martens, Ludwig Christian Alexander
  Karlovich, **56**: 551,n1; **60**: 484,n1, 566-
  57, 641; **65**: 187,n3; **66**: 504; on estab-
  lishing commercial relations between
  Russia and U.S., **56**: 548-50,n1
Martha Berry Schools, **67**: 456-57,n1,
  459, 503-504; WW on anniversary of,
  67: 507-508
Martial (poet), **62**: 302, 313
Martin, Lawrence, **59**: 403,n1; **65**: 532;
  66: 65, 350
Martin, Lucy Day: death of her father,
  64: 24,n1
Martin, Richard William, **55**: 149,n1; **61**:
  129,n1, 188, 303, 324
Martin, Thomas Staples, **53**: 23, 648,
  709, 717; **54**: 55, 174, 231, 332; **55**: 254,
  296, 367, 388; **62**: 13-14; **64**: 104n1;
  and railroad appropriation, **55**: 228,
  257, 258, 277; WW's get well wishes to,
  61: 493; death of, **64**: 24,n1; Glass
  takes Senate seat of, **64**: 52, 60
Martin, William Joseph, **64**: 191-92,n1,
  213; praises WW, **66**: 296-97, 301
Martino, Giacomo de, **54**: 490,n2; **57**:
  435,n2, 436; **60**: 98,n10, 205,n2, 206;
  61: 566n2; **64**: 163n6
Martov, Richard S., **56**: 389,n2
Marx, Karl, **68**: 200, 201
Marx, Richard S., **56**: 556n2
Mary (Victoria Mary of Teck), Queen,
  wife of George V, **53**: 85, 109, 488, 501,
  510, 522, 524, 529, 546, 547, 569, 592,
  595; **54**: 170; **56**: 86; **63**: 559; **64**: 32, 42,
  231
Mary (Victoria Alexandra Alice Mary),
  daughter of George V, **53**: 510, 522,
  569, 592, 593,n5
Mary Queen of Scots, **56**: 510
Maryland: politics and prohibition in, **59**:
  38-39,n2; and woman suffrage, **61**:
  538; Democratic party in, **68**: 94-
  95,n2,3, 98-99, 134-35,n1
Maryland, U.S.S., **60**: 301,n6
Maryland, University of, Medical School,
  64: 515n1
Masaryk, Alice Garrigue: on children's
  choir from Czechoslovakia, **68**: 296-
  97,n1; WW thanks, **68**: 337
Masaryk, Thomas Garrigue, **53**: 259,
  590, 711; **54**: 557; **57**: 78,n8, 109, 167,
  172, 539,n3; **58**: 158; **60**: 313; **62**: 82n2,

428; **64**: 443; **65**: 144; **68**: 263, 296n1;
  and Jews, **55**: 371; WW on, **68**: 337;
  WW's condolences to, **68**: 364; thanks
  WW for condolence note, **68**: 386; WW
  thanks for albums of places named
  after him, **68**: 481
Mason, Alpheus T., **68**: 299n1
Mason, Guy, **63**: 445,n1, 447, 483
Mason, William Ernest, **67**: 176n1
Masons, **66**: 421
Massachusetts, **53**: 82, 581, 626; **58**: 459;
  59: 39; public opinion in, **55**: 449-50;
  Democratic party in, **62**: 8; **68**: 76, 70,
  83,n1, 86, 96,n1, 154,n4, 202; guberna-
  torial election of 1920, **63**: 615,n1; and
  political outlook, **66**: 267; Baruch on
  election in, **68**: 190
Massachusetts Institute of Technology,
  56: 432n1
Masses, The: and mailing privileges, **66**:
  95,n2
Massey, William Ferguson, **54**: 254,n4,
  301, 312-14, 331, 347, 361-63, 366,
  386; **61**: 329,n7
Massigli, René-Lucien-Daniel, **60**: 179,n2
Masson, Jules-Gustave-Hippolyte, **61**:
  354,n1
Masterman, Edward Alexander Dims-
  dale, **66**: 535-36,n3,4
Master of Ballentrae (Stevenson), **62**:
  427,n2
Matewan, West Virginia, **65**: 337,n4
Mather, Samuel, **66**: 246n2
Mathieu, Don Beltran, **55**: 330,n3; **65**:
  252-53,n2
Matsuda, Takeshi, **65**: 259n1
Matsui, Keishiro, **53**: 419,n7; **54**: 26,n16,
  207; **57**: 581-85; **58**: 425,n1; **60**: 546;
  64: 263, 314,n2
Mattapoisett, Mass., **68**: 408n1, 410, 418
Matthews, Rev. Dr. Mark Allison, **62**:
  456,n1, 574; **63**: 273n1; **66**: 17,n1
*Matthias Erzberger and the Dilemma of
  German Democracy* (Epstein), **53**:
  32n1; **61**: 34n1, 76n5
Maude Charlotte Mary Victoria, Queen
  of Norway, **53**: 510, 592,n3, 593
Maude Alexandra Victoria Georgia Ber-
  tha, daughter of the Duchess of Fife,
  53: 592n4
Maud'huy, Louis-Ernest de, **61**: 329,n4
Maughirmalani, H. H., **62**: 225,n1
Maunoury, Michel Joseph, **61**: 329,n4
Mauretania, S.S., **61**: 406
Maurice, Sir Frederick Barton, **61**: 182,n1
Maury, Lucy, **64**: 93
Maury, U.S.S., **58**: 426; **59**: 65, 241,n1
Max, Adolphe-Eugéne-Jean-Henri, **60**:
  613,n3; **61**: 15,n13, 17, 23
Maxa, Prokop, **54**: 153,n2
Maximilian von Baden (Prince Max of
  Baden), **53**: 63n1, 121, 324n2; **58**:
  168n1
Maxwell, William Babington, **67**: 105n3
May, George Oliver, **55**: 306,n1; **57**: 376,
  381

Maycotte, Fortunato, **65**: 487,n1
Mayer, Arno Joseph, **53**: 408n1, 544n1, 711n1; **54**: 309n1, 309n1; **55**: 204n2, 458n1, 540; **56**: 182n2, 259n1, 285n1; **57**: 6n7, 240n1; **58**: 156n1, 237n3, 427n1, 486n3; **62**: 365n27, 428n1
Mayer, Franklin Randolph, **67**: 124-25,n1, 128, 146-47
Mayer, Julius Marshall, **59**: 76n1
Mayer, Wilhelm, **65**: 61,n1
Mayfield, Earle Bradford, **67**: 572n1; **68**: 298,n2
Mayflower, U.S.S., **55**: 444; **58**: 476; **61**: 569; **62**: 156; **63**: 119; **65**: 42; **66**: 15, 324, 410, 414, 453,n1; WW on two-day cruise aboard, **61**: 562-63; WW permits use for training new personnel, **66**: 30,n1, 58
Mayflower Compact: celebration of, **66**: 115, 118-19, 123
May Fourth Movement (China), **58**: 553,n3
May Fourth Movement: Intellectual Revolution in Modern China (Chou Tse-tsung), **58**: 553n3
Maynard, Sir Charles Clarkson Martin, **61**: 226,n2, 349
Maynard, Mila Tupper (Mrs. Rezin Augustus), **56**: 283,n1
Mayo, Charles Horace, M.D., **67**: 310,n3; **68**: 152n1; advice on WW's health, **67**: 535; Grayson thanks for visiting WW and for medical advice, **67**: 542-43
Mayo, Henry Thomas, **53**: 397
Mayo, William James, M.D., **67**: 310,n3, 543,n1; and WW Foundation, **68**: 249n2
Mazurians, **60**: 186-87
Mazzini, Guiseppe, **53**: 613, 614, 615,n2
Mead, Lucia True Ames (Mrs. Edwin Doak), **58**: 140
meat-packing industry, **56**: 84, 101; **62**: 159; and H. C. Hoover and famine relief bill, **54**: 174n3, 229-30; and foreign-born labor, **55**: 286-87
meat-packing legislation, **53**: 156-57, 157, 215
Meda, Filippo, **55**: 332,n1
Medical Clinics of North America, **62**: 637n24
Medical College of Virginia (Richmond), **67**: 299n1
Medici, Lorenzo de, **62**: 427
Medlicott, William Norton, **58**: 461n1; **60**: 173n2
Medora, North Dakota, **63**: 153,n4
Meeker, Royal, **62**: 224: on labor and Whitley Councils, **55**: 91,n1; on price crisis, **62**: 165,n1; Glass on, **62**: 314; on stabilization of dollar's purchasing power, **62**: 559-60,n1; resignation of, **65**: 248-50; and International Labour Office, **66**: 151,n1; WW answers on German-Polish convention on Upper Silesia, **68**: 77
Meersen, Treaty of (820), **60**: 106

Mehdiev, Mir Yaqub, **58**: 333n2
Mehmed VI, **58**: 324,n1; **59**: 209,n6, 211, 253, 259
Mehring, Franz, **53**: 7, 122
Meier, Heinz K., **56**: 75n1
Meiklejohn, Alexander, **66**: 478,n1, 539-40; **67**: 82; **68**: 433; WW praises for his academic stance, **68**: 388-89,n1, 390; thanks WW for visit, **68**: 430; speaks to Princeton faculty, **68**: 462
Meiklejohn, Nannine A. La Villa (Mrs. Alexander), **66**: 478,n3
Meiklejohn Stirring Figure in American College Life (*New York Times*), **68**: 388n1
Meintjes, Johannes, **54**: 252n3
Melamed, Samuel **Max**, **62**: 609n1
Melchior, Carl, **57**: 590; **58**: 19,n6, 62, 169, 399, 578; **59**: 361-62; **60**: 263,n9; photograph of, *illustration section*, **58**
Meleda (now Mljet, Yugoslavia), **59**: 570; **60**: 309, 310
Mêlée Sociale, La (Clemenceau), **59**: 173,n1
Mellett, Lowell, **61**: 369, 370
Mellon, Andrew William, **67**: 355n2,6, 485; **68**: 346n2, 580
Melony, Marie Mattingly (Mrs. William Brown), **55**: 392n1
Melvin, Floyd J., **56**: 283,n1
Melvin, Marion Edmund, **67**: 567-68,n1
Membreno, Alberto, **61**: 638,n2
Memel, Germany (now Klaipeda, Lithuania), **56**: 169, 408n2; **57**: 453,n2; **59**: 580, 582; **60**: 25, 159-60, 187, 437, 522, 578,n10; **68**: 520-21,n1
Memel Statute: Its Origins, Legal Nature and Observation to the Present Day (Kalijarvi), **68**: 521n1
Memorial Day: WW on, **59**: 571; and WW's message on, **67**: 278,n1, 279, 305
Memoirs of Cordell Hull, **53**: 99n1; **67**: 423n1
Memoirs of Herbert Hoover, **58**: 622n56, 634n16; **61**: 455n1
Memoirs of the Peace Conference (Lloyd George), **56**: 12n1
Memorandum on the Shantung Question (MacMurray), **61**: 583,n1
Memorandum, January 2, 1917 [1918] A Suggested Statement of Peace Terms (Mezes, Miller, Lippmann), **54**: 376,n12
Memphis, Tennessee, **59**: 287; **63**: 443, 523
Memphis *Commercial Appeal*, **58**: 51
Memphis Cotton Exchange, **54**: 228n1
Menderes River: *see* Maeander River
Menelik II (of Ethiopia), **61**: 406n1, 471, 472
Menocal, Mario Garcia, **65**: 555,n2, 556; **66**: 83-84, 123-24; **67**: 24n1, 26, 32
Menoher, Charles Thomas, **60**: 430,n1
Mensheviks, **55**: 161n1; **56**: 389
Mentor (magazine), **68**: 450
Meran (now Merano, The Tyrol), **59**: 400

merchant marine (U.S.), **62**: 273, 467; Colby on, **54**: 394-96; Hurley on, **62**: 77-79; and fuel oil supply for, **62**: 78-79, 114, 140-41, 617-19,n2; and statement for The Document, **67**: 475, 487, 593, 597; **68**: 8-9, 30, 216, 220, 540-41

Merchant Marine Act (1920): **65**: 351n1, 467,n2; Colby on honoring commercial treaty obligations, **66**: 87,n1, 125, 136-37; WW on treaty commitments, **66**: 89, 128; Colby praises WW's stand on commercial treaties, **66**: 144-45; and Hoboken piers, etc., **66**: 425, 464-65; *see also* Jones bill

Mercier, Captain, **56**: 116,n14

Mercier, Desiré-Felicien-François-Joseph, Cardinal, **56**: 258-59, 341, 589; **60**: 613; **61**: 7, 17, 29, 31, 130; WW meets, **61**: 13, 14; greetings by, **61**: 21-22; **63**: 166, 197; arrangements for U.S. visit, **62**: 111,n3; get-well wishes, **63**: 549; photograph of, *illustration section*, **61**

Meredith, Edwin Thomas, **65**: 41; **66**: 521, 542n1; **68**: 186, 576; appointed to first Industrial Conference, **63**: 300,n1; appointed Secretary of Agriculture, **64**: 330,n1, 330-31; at Cabinet meeting, **65**: 212; as presidential candidate, **65**: 291,n1; code name for, **65**: 350; Geddes on, **65**: 371; delegate to Democratic National Convention, 1920, **65**: 394, 396; and B. M. King, **65**: 530, 567; praises WW, **66**: 318; recommends veto of Milk River Valley Gun Club bill, **67**: 104,n2; on Cabinet gift and tribute to WW, **67**: 150, 199, 365, 366; praises WW, **67**: 200-201; WW thanks for Cabinet chair, **67**: 330; photograph of, *illustration section*, **67**

Meriwether, Lee, **68**: 24,n1

Merle-Smith, Van Santvoord, **65**: 444,n3

Merle-Smith, Wilton, **65**: 444,n5, 572,n6

Merle-Smith, Zaidee Van Santvoord (Mrs. Wilton), **65**: 444,n4

Mermeix: *see* Terrail, Gabriel

Merriam, Charles Edward, **53**: 16-18,n1; **66**: 165,n5

Merrill, Mr., **67**: 338

Merrill, Bradford, **67**: 363

Merrill, Maud M., **67**: 320-21,n1, 325, 338-39, 343

Merrill, William Pierson, **65**: 183,n3, 184; **66**: 502,n3

Merritt, Henry Paul, **61**: 464,n1

Merry del Val, Rafael, Cardinal, **53**: 242n3

Mersina (now Mersine or Icel, Turkey), **56**: 111; **59**: 91, 100, 101, 137, 140; **61**: 128

Mesopotamia, **53**: 562; **62**: 608; **64**: 449; **65**: 65, 91, 114, 271n1; Lloyd George on, **66**: 48; Colby demands open door in, **66**: 394-99, 430; *see also* Paris Peace Conference—Mesopotamia

Message of the President of the United States Communicated to the Two

Houses of Congress at the Beginning of the First Session of the Sixty-Sixth Congress, **59**: 297n

Message of the President of the United States . . . December 2, 1919, **64**: 116n

Messenger Commercial Cable Co., **58**: 52n6

Meteor, S.M.S., **55**: 432

Methodist Church, Paris, **54**: 380n3

Methodist Episcopal Church: and League of Nations, **61**: 291, 388-89; **66**: 202

Methodist Episcopal Church, South, **61**: 291, 388-89; **66**: 213,n1, 229

Metropolitan, **63**: 223,n2

Metropolitan Museum of Art (N.Y.C.), **66**: 470

Metropolitan Opera House: WW's address on League of Nations at, **55**: 410, 411, 413-21

Metternich, Prince Klemens Wenzel Nepomuk Lothar von, **56**: 361

Mettlach (Saar Basin), **58**: 67

Metz, Germany, **53**: 320

Metzger, Jacob Allen: on whether U.S. can ratify treaty with reservations without resubmission to other governments, **62**: 35-40,n2

Meuse River, **61**: 11n2

Meuse-Argonne campaign, **53**: 513

Mexican Americans, **64**: 140n1

Mexican Constitution, **55**: 353,n1, 355; **64**: 240, 241, 242; and Article 27, **66**: 283n1, 286

Mexican Railway, **65**: 463

Mexican Revolution: The Constitutional Years (Cumberland), **65**: 252n1

Mexico, **61**: 251, 254, 424; **63**: 165; and League of Nations, **54**: 170; and Germany; and Honduras, **61**: 639; WW on, **63**: 195

Mexico and the United States, **53**: 228, 540; **55**: 351-52,n1; **62**: 78, 142; **64**: 122-23, 231, 270; **67**: 81-82,n1; **68**: 411,n2; WW on, **54**: 63; **61**: 524-25; **62**: 459; **64**: 131, 152; Fletcher on, **55**: 352-56; **62**: 332-33; border raids, **61**: 487-88; murders of American citizens in Mexico, **61**: 510, 510-11, 527, 527-28; missionary against U.S. intervention in Mexico, **61**: 511; N. D. Baker on State Department, not War Department, releasing information on, **61**: 610-11; and United Society of Christian Endeavor's resolution on, **62**: 264; and Joint High Commission, **62**: 333n3; Carranza's anti-American campaign, **62**: 449-51; and seizure of foreign-owned oil wells, **64**: 120n1, 134, 210-11,n1; and Senate action concerning, **64**: 120-21,n1; Lansing on WW's health and, **64**: 123, 124, 125; Tumulty's concern over proposed visit to WW by senators on Mexican situation, **64**: 125; Lansing on difference between general situation and Jenkins case, **64**: 127; Fall and Hitchcock meet with WW

on, **64**: 127, 129-32, 132-33, 133-35; Pittman on, **64**: 127-28; and Plan of San Diego, **64**: 140n1; Lansing's proposals for policy toward Mexico, **64**: 239-42; Fletcher resignation, **64**: 310,n1, 397; and Lansing resignation, **64**: 417n3, Tumulty on new Secretary of State and, **64**: 419; Morgenthau appointed Ambassador to, **65**: 20, 88, 121, 138-39, 140; controversy over Mexican Ambassador-designate, **65**: 201, 201-202,n1, 212-13; Colby on possible crisis situation in, **65**: 221-22; concern for Americans in, **65**: 246-47; General Scott's advice on, **65**: 312,n1; issue of recognition of De la Huerta government, **65**: 446,n1, 461-64; WW on postponing decision on, **65**: 468; N. H. Davis on meetings with Iglesias Calderon, **65**: 483-85, 533-36; and Jafredson murder, **65**: 485n2, 485-86; and Summerlin's interview with Obregón, **65**: 486-87; willing to recognize contracts made with previous governments, **66**: 17-18; Creel's involvement leads to special mission to Mexico, its outcome, **66**: 122-23,n1, 133, 143-44, 150, 170, 269-71, 337, 371-77, 403-405; issue of recognition, **66**: 133, 140, 142-43, 150, 160-63, 269-71, 283-88; **67**: 132-33; Murray on Creel's visit to WW on, **66**: 133; Morgenthau on, **66**: 139-40; Davis on meeting with Pesqueira, **66**: 159, 160-62; and oil interests, **66**: 160-61, 321-22, 334-35, 413; Davis on meeting with Iglesias Calderon, **66**: 162-63; WW on if Harding elected, **66**: 194; and international banking group, **66**: 302-303; Wilson against sending Wiseman as representative to Mexico, **66**: 303, 312; Creel on his position and feelings on situation between, **66**: 371-77; Colby answers Creel on, **66**: 406-408; N. H. Davis on lifting arms embargo and WW's response, **66**: 412-13, 413; Colby's response to Pesqueira, recommends commission to formulate treaty, **66**: 418-19; concern over Mexican revolutionary movement planned in U.S., **66**: 445, 446; immigration issue, **67**: 180; Cobb on WW's policy, **67**: 219-20; Colby on law firm and, **67**: 420; and League of Nations, **68**: 477; *see also* Jenkins case

Mexico City *Excelsior*, **65**: 487

Meyer, Eugene, Jr., **54**: 521; **57**: 381, 387; **59**: 161; **60**: 539, 542; **62**: 222-23,n1, 222, 322, 448; **66**: 445,n1; Bass on, **62**: 315-16; **67**: 25,n2,3; suggested for Reparation Commission, **61**: 529

Meyer, Frederick Brotherton, **53**: 530n1

Meyer, Karl, **62**: 557n2

Meyer, Ludwig, **53**: 712,n1

Meyers, J. Edward, **63**: 131,n1

Mezes, Sidney Edward, **53**: 350, 356, 419; **54**: 91, 376n12, 386; **55**: 499; **56**: 207, 303-304, 350, 424; **57**: 467n2; **58**: 206, 236; **59**: 126, 455, 456; **62**: 365n27; **67**: 290, 294; **65**: 497, 502; and Rhineland, **55**: 475n1,2; on Danzig, Poland, and Adriatic questions, **56**: 395-96, 471-73, 505, 607n1; **57**: 572; House's influence over, **62**: 454; photograph of, *illustration section*, **57**

Michalopoulos, C., **68**: 23,n1

Michaux, Daniel W., **67**: 344-45,n1, 352

Michel Du Faing d'Aigremont: *see* D'Aigremont, Augustin Michel De Faing

Michelson, Charles, **64**: 287n2

Michelson, Peter, **62**: 531,n1

Michigan, **53**: 582; Newberry conviction and appeal, **65**: 120,n2

Michigan, University of, **67**: 459,n2

Mid-America, **65**: 355n1

Middle East and North Africa in World Politics: A Documentary Record (Hurewitz, ed.), **56**: 110n7

mideastern commission: *see* Inter-Allied Commission to Syria (proposed)

Midweek Pictorial Magazine, **68**: 449

Midwest Oil Company, **53**: 636n1

Miesthal, Austria, **61**: 59

Milan, Italy, **53**: 435, 507; **54**: 135; **57**: 539; WW's activities and speeches in, **53**: 613-14, 616, 616-17, 617, 617-18, 619-20; French troops in, **59**: 434-35; demonstration for WW in, **68**: 383; photograph of, *illustration section*, **53**

Milan *Avanti*, **57**: 501n2

Milan *Corriere della Sera*, **53**: 616n1, 619n1; **56**: 393

Milan *Il Popolo d' Italia*, **53**: 619n1

Milan *Secolo*, **59**: 551; **61**: 229n2; **68**: 506

Miles, Basil, **62**: 441

Miles, Jeanie Wardlaw (Mrs. Francis Turquand), **53**: 22,n3

Miles, Katherine Wistar Stockton (Mrs. Louis Wardlaw), **53**: 22,n5

Miles, Louis Wardlaw, **53**: 22,n2

Miles, Nelson Appleton, **65**: 289n1

Miles, Sherman, **56**: 517; **59**: 406, 407; **60**: 34, 530; on Fiume, **56**: 563,n2,3; **58**: 268; on Carinthia's self-determination, **59**: 403-405,n1; on Montenegro, **59**: 620,n1

Miles-De Salis Mission to Montenegro, **59**: 178,n5

Milford, Morton Marshall, **62**: 627

Milicz, Lower Silesia: *see* Militsch

Miligan, W. F.: *see* Milligan, W. F.

Military Affairs, Committee on (House of Reps.), **53**: 116n1; **55**: 150; **66**: 528,n1; WW meets with, **58**: 330n1; **59**: 278,n2; and army reorganization bill (1920), **65**: 273, 576n1

Military Affairs, Committee on (Senate), **55**: 150; and army reorganization bill, **65**: 273, 576-77,n1; **67**: 172

Military Intelligence Division (War Department), **54**: 397,n1

Military Inter-Allied Commission of Control, **56**: 47-48, 49
Militisch, Lower Silesia, **60**: 24,n7
milk: WW on imports and exports of, **67**: 191, 191-92
Milk River Valley Gun Club (Montana): bill pertaining to vetoed, **67**: 81, 104n2, 110, 112-13
Millard, Oscar E., **61**: 35n1
Millard, Thomas Franklin Fairfax, **62**: 373,n35, 374
Millen, Ga., **61**: 357n1
Miller, Adolph Caspar, **53**: 50; **54**: 521; **57**: 387; **67**: 302,n1; **68**: 319
Miller, C. W., **67**: 62, 70
Miller, Clarence Benjamin, **54**: 259n2
Miller, David Hunter, **53**: 213,n1, 693, 695,n2, 716; **54**: 4, 151, 365n4, 376n12, 379, 387n2, 389, 494n1,2, 505n3; **56**: 80n6, 82, 99, 170n1, 178-79, 207, 223, 309, 336, 563n3, 607n1; **57**: 29n9, 93n1, 179, 179n2, 246n3, 248n1, 258n5, 286n2, 431n1, 467; **58**: 137n1, 174n1, 183, 185, 199n1, 285, 286, 381-82, 386, 417n6,8, 443, 444; **59**: 68, 70-72, 80, 126, 200, 248, 257, 472n2, 485, 498, 578; **60**: 98, 233n4, 303, 309, 608; **61**: 629,n2; **62**: 186, 264, 365n27; **67**: 72; and League of Nations Covenant, **54**: 407, 408, 459-60,n1, 461; **55**: 67, 118-19, 154; and Hurst-Miller draft, **54**: 433-39, 439-40; and third Paris draft of Covenant, **54**: 449; WW thanks for copies of revised Covenant, **54**: 458; on amendments to Covenant, **55**: 69-70; **58**: 445,n4, 446; on U.S. representatives to Supreme Economic Council, **55**: 148; distributes copies of Covenant, **55**: 192; on need for Senate ratification of preliminary peace treaty, **56**: 58-59, 67-69, 98; on Cecil's amendments to Covenant, **56**: 75-81; on Mezes and Polish situation and Danzig, **56**: 395-96; on Fiume, **56**: 609-11; on Saar Valley, **57**: 90-91, 117-18, 195; and League of Nations Commission, **57**: 221, 285; on protection of minority rights, **58**: 290-91, 383, 384, 385; on French security treaty, **58**: 488-89, 490; meets with Cellere on Adriatic question, **59**: 71-72; on Adriatic question and negotiations, **59**: 80-84,n3, 249-50; on report on minority rights in Poland, **59**: 113, 179; meets with Orlando on Adriatic question, **59**: 125-26, 127; meets with House on Adriatic question, **59**: 556; and Adriatic question, **60**: 310-11; on Senate situation on League of Nations Covenant and peace treaty, **60**: 570, 571,n1, 572; **61**: 137-38; on Root's reservations, **61**: 181-82, 232-35; second memorandum on Root and Article X, **61**: 295-301; appearance before Foreign Relations Committee, **62**: 393, 395, 402,n41; on mandates and Togo-

land, **62**: 533 photograph of, *illistration section*, **57**; 59
Miller, Emma Guffey (Mrs. Carroll), **65**: 359,n1
Miller, Mary Sprague (Mrs. Adolph Caspar), **67**: 302,n1
Miller, Nathan Lewis, **68**: 154; and WW's admission to N. Y. bar, **67**: 248,n1, 261, 262, 555
Miller, Paul Gerard, **59**: 122,n3
Miller, Pierce, **62**: 626
Miller, Ransford Stevens, **53**: 206, 207
Millerand, Alexandre, **60**: 118n1; **64**: 358; **65**: 61, 217n1, 229n1, 542,n2; **68**: 307n4; and Adriatic question, **64**: 314,n1, 426-42, 450, 481-83; and list of war criminals, **64**: 364n1; and Turkish treaty, **64**: 372,n1; Polk's draft reply to on Adriatic question, **65**: 37-39; and German war crimes trials, **65**: 100n1; and French occupation of Germany, **65**: 170, 172, 173, 304; and Kapp *Putsch*, **65**: 236; R. U. Johnson on, **65**: 304; Lloyd George on, **66**: 43; and German protocol on disarmament and coal delivery, **66**: 44n5
Millet, Jean François, **59**: 248
Milligan (Miligan), W. F., **67**: 121n1
Millo di Casalgiate, Enrico, **57**: 562-63,n1,2; **59**: 242,n3
Mills, Ruth Livingston (Mrs. Ogden), **60**: 491,n2
Mills College, **63**: 352n1
Mills of Peace (London *Times*) **57**: 532n2
Milne, Sir George Francis, **53**: 326,n7; **58**: 512,n3; **59**: 30,n6
Milner, Alfred, 1st Viscount, **53**: 367, 568, 713; **54**: 538; **55**: 145; **56**: 105, 108; **58**: 485, 507; **59**: 102, 330-31, 340-41, 627; **61**: 207, 252; **62**: 187-88, 243; **63**: 299, 307, 422; and Supreme War Council meetings, **55**: 13, 14-15, 61-62, 62, 107, 182-83; and mandates, **61**: 259-64, 270, 275-76, 277, 283, 363, 408, 477; **62**: 513
Milner, Gwen, **68**: 240
Milton Academy, **60**: 118n5
Milwaukee Leader, **55**: 92n1
Milwaukee Social Democratic Publishing Co. *v.* Burleson, **68**: 131n8
Mincer, A., **62**: 434
Mincer, Mrs. A., **62**: 434
Mind and Memory (booklet), **66**: 251n1
Mind of One Piece: Brandeis and American Reform (Urofsky), **67**: 319n1
Minden, Germany, **54**: 240, 244
Miner, Randolph Huntington, **65**: 233,n.1, 2
Mineral Point Zinc Company, **64**: 232n1
Mines, Bureau of, **53**: 230
Minneapolis, Minn.: WW's reception in, **63**: 123-24,n3; WW's address in, **63**: 123-24,n1, 131-38
Minneapolis Journal, **63**: 113n, 148n

Minneapolis Morning Tribune, **63**: 123n3,4
Minnesota, **60**: 43; Democratic women in, **68**: 156,n3
Minnesota, University of, **53**: 302n3; **67**: 141, 555; **68**: 68n2
Minnesota, U.S.S., **67**: 25
Minnis, Mr., **58**: 50,n2
Minor, F., **59**: 156,n4
Minor, John Barbee, **67**: 275,n1
Miši, Zivojin, **56**: 462,n10
Miskolsz, Hungary, **60**: 257
Missionary Mind and American East Asia Policy, 1911-1915 (Reed), **57**: 453n4
Mississippi: Democratic senatorial primary in, **68**: 93-94,n2, 3, 128,n1
Mississippi, U.S.S., **58**: 409
Missouri, **53**: 84; and judgeship appointment, **55**: 207; Democratic challenge to Senator Reed, **56**: 192n1; Democratic politics in, **57**: 47-48, 424; League of Nations endorsement, **59**: 220, 320n3; and Reed and League of Nations, **59**: 529; and Long's senatorial campaign, **64**: 350, 352, 353; Democratic politics in, **65**: 110n1, 377; rejects Reed as delegate to Democratic National Convention, 1920, **65**: 470,n1; Democratic party in, **67**: 543,n1; Democratic senatorial primary in, **68**: 12,n1, 24, 35, 61, 104, 105,n1, 126-27, 147, 151, 153, 166,n1; claims of fraud in Democratic party, **68**: 105; McAdoo will not campaign in, **68**: 146-47, 151, 153
Missouri, University of, **68**: 121n1; and presidency and Dodd, **67**: 505-506, 508-509,n1
Missouri Pacific Railroad, **68**: 16n1
Missouri River, **63**: 152
Mr. Harding's Visit to Panama (*New York Times*), **66**: 317,n1
Mr. Jefferson's University: A History (Dabney), **67**: 299n1
Mr. Pim Passes By (Milne), **67**: 571
Mr. Taft's Suggestions (*New York Times*), **61**: 628,n1
Mr. Wilson and the Issue (*Washington Post*), **65**: 71n3
Mişu, Nicolae, **54**: 421,n6; **60**: 335,n2, 344, 427, 478
Mitchell, Allen, **55**: 423n1; **56**: 542n2; **57**: 4n1; **59**: 433n4
Mitchell, Charles Wellman, **64**: 515-19,n1; **67**: 491,n2
Mitchell, Ewing Young, **68**: 105,n1
Mitchell, Florence M. Crowe (Mrs. Charles Wellman), **64**: 515,n2
Mitchell, John, **62**: 97,n7
Mitchell, Harry, **66**: 228
Mitchell, Henry Sewall, **65**: 174
Mitchell, Ruth Crawford, **68**: 296n1
Mitchell, Silas Weir, **55**: 465,n3
Mithouard, Adrien, **53**: 404n1
Mittelhauser, Eugène-Désire-Antoine, **60**: 356,n3

Mittwochabend, **53**: 121n1
Mixter, George Webber, **53**: 308,n1
Mława, Poland, **56**: 89, 93, 94, 95
Mobile, S.S., **64**: 8
Mobile News-Item, **68**: 107n1
Mobile Register, **68**: 107n1, 170, 171,n1
Mochaverol-Memalek, **58**: 21,n8
Modane, France, **53**: 589, 621
Modern Clinical Psychiatry, **58**: 618n29
Modern Medicine (Osler), **58**: 616
Moe, Ragnvald, **66**: 501, 504-505, 517
Moewe, S.M.S., **55**: 432
Mohammedans: *see* Muslims
Moharramov, Mohammad, **58**: 333n2
Mohr, J. P., **58**: 626n74
Mohrenschildt, Ferdinand de: *see* De Mohrenschildt, Ferdinand
Mohrenschildt, Nona Hazelhurst McAdoo de: *see* Mohrenschildt, Nona Hazelhurst McAdoo
Moldavia, **55**: 373
Moldavia, S.S., **53**: 275n3
Molin de Laffaux, **56**: 198
Moline Plow Company, **66**: 289n2
Mollycoddle (film), **65**: 400n1
Moltke, Count Helmuth von (1800-1891), **56**: 320, 453
Moltke, Helmuth Karl Bernhard, Count von, **55**: 508,n1,2
Moment of Truth for Protestant America: Interchurch Campaigns Following World War I (Ernst), **64**: 416n2
Monaco, Albert-Honoré-Charles, Prince of, **58**: 562,n1
Mond, Sir Alfred Moritz, **59**: 627,n3
Mondell, Frank Wheeler, **58**: 603,n1; **62**: 98,n1; **65**: 373
Mongolia, **54**: 79; **61**: 555; **65**: 277
Monmouth (Ill.) *Daily Atlas*, **67**: 294n1
Monnet, Jean-Omer-Marie-Gabriel, **53**: 481,n2; **58**: 121,n1; **59**: 202,n2; **61**: 151,n5
Monod, Wilfred, **54**: 282n1
Monroe, James, **56**: 80; **57**: 231; **63**: 192, 430, 450; **65**: 8, 12, 26, 31
Monroe Doctrine, **53**: 354, 474, 475; **54**: 314; **58**: 195; WW on, **55**: 271, 275, 295, 328-29; **57**: 266-67; **60**: 112, 202, 572; **61**: 300n6, 445, 534; **62**: 4, 113, 432, 440, 540; **65**: 191, 298; **66**: 260; **67**: 225-26; **68**: 279; comments on, **55**: 293, 312n1, 437, 491, 492; and League of Nations, **56**: 80, 82, 156n1, 163, 223n1, 297, 335, 485, 552; **57**: 193, 215, 218, 226-32, 237, 254-57, 265, 285, 424n1, 445; **59**: 282, 316; Taft on, **56**: 83, 158, 159, 398-99; **61**: 606, 607; Root on, **56**: 100; **61**: 66,n3, 181, 233-35, 301; and League to Enforce Peace, **57**: 233, 315-16, 331, 332; WW on, **61**: 437-38; **62**: 278, 342, 621; **64**: 280; Spencer on Senate reservations on, **61**: 620; and Carranza, **62**: 450; Foreign Relations Committee's reservations concerning, **63**: 52n3; Rappard on WW's hope to

Monroe Doctrine (*cont.*)
    extend, **63**: 627; and proposed substi-
    tute reservations, **64**: 30; and Lodge
    reservations, **64**: 39, 291; WW on, **65**:
    8, 12, 26, 31; and Republican platform
    plank, 1920, **65**: 292n1; and Domini-
    can Republic, **67**: 56; *see also* Wilson,
    Woodrow: Western Tour—Themes
Monroe-Pinckney Treaty, **60**: 246n10
Montagu, Edward Samuel, **55**: 499,n1;
    56: 208,n1; **57**: 10, 12, 35, 72; **58**: 402,
    259n1, 270, 444, 448-49, 451, 498, 501,
    502, 535, 580; **59**: 202, 207n1, 277, 396,
    397; **60**: 20,n3; **61**: 60, 83; on U.S. being
    mandatory for Turkey, **59**: 238-39
Montague, James Jackson, **57**: 241,n3
Montague, Margaret Prescott, **65**: 411n9
Montana, **68**: 96; and Milk River Valley
    Gun Club bill, **67**: 81, 104n2, 110, 112-
    13
Montana Grain Growers, **59**: 206
Montdidier, France, **56**: 194, 195, 199
Montenegro, **53**: 208n2, 368, 377, 486,
    639-41,n3, 700, 719n1; **54**: 54; **63**: 210;
    Grayson receives honorary decoration
    from for keeping WW in good health,
    61: 239; and Yugoslavia, **64**: 177; Yu-
    goslavia on, **65**: 315, 316; *see also* Paris
    Peace Conference—Montenegro
Montevedio, Uruguay, **67**: 23n1
Montgomery, Ala., **59**: 287
Montgomery, Ala., *Journal*, **68**: 107n1
Montgomery, George Redington, **58**:
    327n5
Montgomery, Robert Hiester, **53**: 413-
    14,n1
Montgomery, Stuart, **58**: 445,n2; **61**: 332;
    66: 448,n1, 449
Montgomery-Cuninghame, Sir Thomas
    (Andrew Alexander), **58**: 509,n9
Monticello: WW supports effort to pur-
    chase, **68**: 320-21,n1, 464-65
Montigny Le Roi, France, **53**: 503
Montjoie, Germany, **57**: 394
Mooney, Thomas Joseph, **63**: 273n2; **64**:
    145n1; on commutation of his sen-
    tence, **53**: 273-74,n1
Moore, Benjamin, **61**: 332
Moore, Carl E., **66**: 5,n1
Moore, Charles, **66**: 292-93, 319
Moore, Edmund H., **65**: 551,n1; **66**: 118
Moore, Edward Caldwell, **55**: 486,,n2
Moore, Frederick, **57**: 65n2, 241n3; **58**:
    327,n1
Moore, John Bassett, **54**: 429; **65**: 238;
    67: 263; and Permanent Court of Arbi-
    tration, **64**: 216, 273
Moore, Tom, **67**: 368,n1
Moore, William Blackshear, **62**: 102,n1,2
Moore-Cottrell Subscription Agencies,
    68: 449
Moore's Theaters Corp. of Washington,
    67: 368n1
Moors, Ethel Lyman Paine (Mrs. John
    Farwell), **66**: 274,n2; **67**: 189,n2; **68**:
    338,n1, 352, 427, 430

Moors, John Farwell, **60**: 192,n1; **67**:
    189,n2; **68**: 338,n1, 352, 430; and
    beginnings of WW Foundation, **67**:
    271n1; mentioned as senatorial candi-
    date, **68**: 64, 70, 83n1; on Corfu
    incident and League of Nations, **68**:
    427-28
Moraczewski, Jedrzej, **54**: 33n6
*Morale, The Supreme Standard of Life
    and Conduct* (Hall), **66**: 290,n2, 302
Moralia (Plutarch), **66**: 269n2
Moran, William Herman, **61**: 328,n1; **63**:
    515,n1, 531
Moravia and Moravians, **54**: 343, 491,
    492; **56**: 257n1, **60**: 480
Morawetz, Victor, **55**: 248
Mordacq, Jean-Jules-Henri, **59**: 531,n6,
    541; **60**: 619,n1
Moreaux, Dr., **61**: 6,n8
Moresnet, Belgium, **55**: 109; **56**: 267; **57**:
    392, 393; **59**: 459; **60**: 107-108
Morgan, Edith Parson, **67**: 135,n1
Morgan, Edwin Vernon, **53**: 342,n3
Morgan, H. Arthur, **55**: 157,n1
Morgan, John Pierpont, Jr., **56**: 99,n1;
    66: 302; offers to donate his London
    home for ambassador's residence, **60**:
    83,n1, 299; **67**: 26,n2; and peace treaty
    leak investigation, **60**: 330,n2, 379,
    434
Morgan, Josephine Perry (Mrs. Junius
    Spencer), **60**: 646-47
Morgan, Junius Spencer, **65**: 572,n10
Morgan, Pauline: *see* Dodge, Pauline
    Morgan
Morgan and Company: *see* J. P. Morgan
    and Company
Morgenthau, Henry, **53**: 239n1; **55**:
    438n3; **58**: 56, 147-48; **59**: 74, 447, 575;
    60: 39; **61**: 487; **67**: 105n3, 602; **68**: 59,
    355, 381; on WW and Taft together en-
    dorsing League of Nations, **55**: 288-89,
    329; dedicates book to WW, **53**: 3; and
    commission to investigate pogroms in
    Poland and report, **60**: 564, 567, 601;
    64: 198n1, 260,n1,2; on Jews and mi-
    nority issue in peace treaty, **61**: 43,
    178; and Mexico, **65**: 20, 88, 121, 138-
    39, 140; **66**: 112, 133, 139, 140, 150;
    mediator of Armenian controversy, **66**:
    42, 490, 517-18; **67**: 64, 65, 67; and WW
    Foundation, **67**: 271n1; **68**: 249n2, 365;
    on criticizing the Republican party, **67**:
    386-87; requests information from
    Grayson on WW's possible resignation,
    67: 568; and Armistice Day demonstra-
    tion, **68**: 185, 186; on WW not congrat-
    ulating Ochs, **68**: 268
Morgenthau, Josephine Sykes (Mrs.
    Henry), **59**: 74
Mori, Kengo, **61**: 384,n1
Morison, Elting Elmore, **53**: 243n3; **58**:
    500n1
Morison, Samuel Eliot, **59**: 447,n1; on Es-
    tonia, **59**: 547-48,n1,2
Morizot-Thibault, Charles, **59**: 4n1

Morley, Christopher Darlington, **67**: 105n3, 473n1, 476,n1, 575; praises WW, **67**: 573

Morley, John, Viscount Morely of Blackburn, **53**: 529; **55**: 338; **66**: 536n1

Morocco, **53**: 293; **54**: 368; **57**: 76; Act of Algeciras, **59**: 498n2

Morris, Augusta Shippen West (Mrs. Roland Sletor), **59**: 410n3; **67**: 170,n1

Morris, Benjamin Wistar, **66**: 519n1

Morris, Charles Eugene, **65**: 551n2

Morris, Gouverneur, **68**: 67, 68n1

Morris, Ira Nelson, **54**: 153-54; **65**: 40,n1

Morris, Roland Sletor, **53**: 555-56,n4, 629, 631, 632; **54**: 83, 158, 412, 548, 549; **55**: 39, 493; **57**: 134, 570; **58**: 494; **59**: 29,n4, 30, 148, 188, 225, 233, 235, 236, 281, 282, 449, 457-58, 547, 572; **60**: 100, 605; **61**: 110, 494, 638; **62**: 589; **63**: 395, 608; **67**: 170, 171, 551; **68**: 330; WW on, **53**: 343; on Japan and Russian railway situation, **53**: 463-65,n1; on U.S. policy in Russia, **57**: 313-15; negotiates operation of Trans-Siberian Railroad, **57**: 420,n1; and Graves, **59**: 409-10; thanks WW for opportunity to serve in Russia, **59**: 410; Polk on postponing Russian trip of, **59**: 618; issue of sending to Omsk, **60**: 240; **61**: 130-31; on Siberian situation, **61**: 571-73; praised for negotiations with banking consortium, **65**: 276-77; and anti-Japanese agitation in California, **66**: 12-16,n1, 53, 56, 186-87; receives honorary degree, **67**: 335,n3; and WW Foundation, **68**: 249n2

Morrison, Frank, **55**: 280; **62**: 138; **65**: 20; **68**: 581; on peace commissioner from labor ranks, **53**: 119, 165, 216; on preventing unhealthy labor conditions in U.S., **55**: 262; on Burleson's labor policies, **55**: 364-64

Morrissey, Patrick J., **61**: 470,n3

Morristown School, N.J., **54**: 255

Morrow, Charles H., **58**: 569,n4; **61**: 572,n4; **62**: 86n5, 87

Morrow, Dwight Whitney, **53**: 484; **55**: 451,n7,8,9; **56**: 99,n1; **60**: 276, 537; **61**: 68; on Senate and press opposition to League of Nations, **60**: 202-203

Morrow, Ian F., **59**: 16n6

Morse, Charles Wyman, **68**: 73,n2

Morse, Edward S., **67**: 370,n6, 372, 415

Morse, Frank, **57**: 241n3

Morse telegraph, **53**: 248

Mortara, Ludovico, **61**: 109,n7

Morton, Deborah, **67**: 302n2

Moscow, Russia, **53**: 153, 256, 453; **54**: 94, 95; **62**: 427n1; food and health crisis in, **56**: 388

Moseley, George Van Horn, **55**: 180,n3

Moses, George Higgins, **53**: 717; **59**: 451n1; **61**: 372; **62**: 67,n1; **66**: 55,n3; **68**: 185,n1, 247; on Senate reaction to peace treaty, **61**: 564; on Shantung settlement, **61**: 565; questions WW at meeting with Foreign Relations Committee, **62**: 340, 349, 367, 372-73, 411; on WW's health, **63**: 563-64, 564-67, 570, 642; **64**: 132, 135, 136, 137, 138; and Mexican situation, **64**: 120, 128; and treaty fight, **64**: 200-201, 337, 338; and bitter-enders, **64**: 328n2; on Hitchcock letter, **65**: 71n3; and Guatamela, **66**: 506,n3,5, 512

Moslems: *see* Muslims

Mosul, **56**: 107, 108, 109, 110; **59**: 330, 331, 333, 340, 341

Moton, Robert Russa, **53**: 236; **56**: 63; **62**: 67,n1; visits Negro troops in France, **53**: 526,n1, 579,n1; and House's invitation to go to Paris, **55**: 335, 341, 404; on racial tensions and need for anti-lynching statement from WW, **62**: 233-34

Motono, Ichiro, **57**: 610

Mott, John R., **53**: 254-55, 257; **61**: 291, 388; **66**: 411,n1; **68**: 502, 526; requests WW's aid in fund raising for European relief, **67**: 407-408, 413, 422

Mott, Sara Maude Robinson (Mrs. Ernest J.), **63**: 311,n1

Mott, Thomas Bentley, **53**: 27,n1; **59**: 68,n1

Motta, Giuseppe, **65**: 338-40,n1

Motter, Vail (Thomas Hubbard Vail), **67**: 574,n1, 578

Moulin, M., **56**: 116,n16

Moulton, John Fletcher, 1st Baron Moulton, **68**: 299,n7

Mt. Clemens News Bureau, **62**: 627

Mount Holyoke College, **68**: 355n1

Mount Lovcen, **61**: 552, 553

Mount Nevoso (Sneznik), Slovenia, **66**: 364, 365, 377

Mount Vernon: WW's address at (July 4, 1918), **58**: 71

Mount Vernon, U.S.S., **58**: 141

Mourad-Bekian, Khoren, **65**: 353

Movie Weekly, **68**: 450

Mowat, Charles Loch, **53**: 519n1; **68**: 593n10

Mowrer, Paul Scott, **54**: 192

Mudania, Turkey, **68**: 141n1

Mudros to Lausanne: Britain's Frontier in West Asia, 1918-1922 (Busch), **68**: 141n1

Muehlon, Wilhelm von, **56**: 498,n3

Muhammed Ali, **55**: 383n2

Muhlheim, Germany, **56**: 90n4

Muhu (Mukhu) Island, **55**: 545,n1

Muir, Ramsey, **67**: 46,n3

Muldoon, Peter James, **55**: 422,n2

Mullen, Arthur, **54**: 519; meets with WW on future of Democratic party, **67**: 312,n1, 321,n1; on chairmanship of Democratic National Committee, **67**: 325, 349-50

Müller, Hermann, **61**: 187, 192, 203, 302, 303, 323, 330

Mullins, Edgar Young, **65**: 421-22,n1, 422, 430

Mulrine, Andrew A., **65**: 351,n2

Multi-Infarct Dementia and Delirium States (Kilb), **58**: 618n29, 216n51

Mulvena, John J., **65**: 351,n1

Mumm, Baron Walter de (Walther von Mumm), **54**: 280-81,n5

Mumphrey, Devore, **66**: 34-35,n1

Muna, Alois, **58**: 157,n3

Munch, Peter, **68**: 84,n1, 85

München, S.M.S., **55**: 427; **56**: 29; **58**: 127

Munich, Germany, **55**: 423n1

Munro, Dana Gardner, **61**: 640n14,15; **63**: 616n1; **65**: 247n1; **66**: 389n1; **67**: 24n1

Munsey, Frank Andrew, **61**: 372; **67**: 382,n4

Munsey's Magazine, **68**: 373n2

Munson Steamship Company, **65**: 282

Murat, Princess Cecile Ney d'Elchingen, **58**: 534n1; **60**: 546,n5, 547

Murat, 5th Prince, Joachim Napoleon, Prince of Ponte-Corvo, **53**: 154,n1, 398; **58**: 534n1, 535; **60**: 546,n5

Murat Palace, **53**: 383-84, 439, 458; **55**: 193; descriptions of, **53**: 180-81, 423-24, 428-30; photograph of, *illustration section*, **53**

Murch, Herbert Spencer, **67**: 182

Murdock, Victor, **62**: 158; **63**: 391,n6

Murmansk, Russia: *see* Russia—Murmansk and Archangel, intervention in

Murmansk Railroad, **55**: 190

Murphy, Charles Francis, **64**: 521,n1; **65**: 440; **68**: 426,n2, 496,n1

Murphy, Edward, **64**: 97n1, 215

Murphy, Grayson Mallett-Prevost, **61**: 529,n2

Murphy, John A., **62**: 325

Murphy, Joseph E., **53**: 166, 319, 344; **55**: 237

Murphy, Merle Farmer, **57**: 241n3

Murray, George Gilbert Aime, **53**: 47, 330-31, 530n1; **67**: 105n3, 561,n2; **68**: 87, 94

Murray, George Welwood, **67**: 87

Murray, Margaret, **62**: 434

Murray, Philip, **66**: 67, 108n1

Murray, Robert Henry: on Creel's meeting with WW on Mexico, **66**: 133

Murray, Robert Keith, **59**: 204n2; **63**: 167n6; **65**: 187n5; **68**: 97n3, 129n1, 152n1

Muscle Shoals Dam project, **62**: 437,n1; and nitrate plant at, **68**: 448-49,n1, 457

Mush, Armenia, **65**: 74

Muskoka Lake, Ontario, **55**: 282; **68**: 424

Muslims, **62**: 607; *see also* Paris Peace Conference—Muslims

Mussolini, Benito, **53**: 619n1; **68**: 251-52,n1, 255,n1; and Corfu incident, **68**: 419n1

Mussolini's Early Diplomacy (Cassels), **68**: 419n1

Mustapha (Mustafa) Kemal Pasha, **66**: 46; **67**: 63,n1; **68**: 141n1

Mutual Life Insurance Company Building, **67**: 347

My Diary at the Conference of Paris, with Documents (Miller), **53**: 695n1; **54**: 365n4, 379n, 389n, 494n1,2, 505n3; **55**: 67n, n2, 119, 154n, 192n; **56**: 59n, 75n4, 80n6, 81n, 88n3, 223n, 563n3, 607n1; **57**: 25n9, 195, 246n3, 431n1, 467n2; **58**: 137n1, 382n, 417n6,8, 445n4; **59**: 72n, 84n, 126n, 137n4, 243n, 250, 472n2, 556n; **60**: 233n4

My Memoir (E. B. Wilson), **55**: 488; **57**: 532n2; **63**: 419n1, 539n1, 578n1, 606n1; **64**: 133n2, 405n1, 417n3, 507n1; **66**: 291n2, 345n2, 519n1; **67**: 289n3

Myers, Gustavus, **68**: 313-14,n1, 316

Myers, Henry Lee, **53**: 141; **63**: 197, 265; and vote on Lodge resolution, **64**: 63

Myers Resolution, **63**: 265, 295

Mystery of American Politics (New York *World*), **67**: 424n1

Nabokov, Konstantin Dmitrievich, **59**: 41,n2

Naboth's Vineyard: The Dominican Republic, 1844-1924 (Welles), **66**: 359n1

Nachod, Czechoslovakia, **60**: 552

Nacoochee Institute, **62**: 42n1, 164

Nadao, Dedjazmatch, **61**: 406,n1, 470, 473-74

Nagaoka, Haruichi, **60**: 467,n4

Nahma, U.S.S., **58**: 409

Namier, Lewis Bernstein, **59**: 219,n9

Namik, A. Antoine, **57**: 426

Namslau (now Namyslow, Poland), **60**: 158

Namyslow, Poland: *see* Namslau

Nancy, France, **56**: 363

Nansen, Fridtjof, **57**: 4, 53, 354,n1, 503n2, 508, 529, 527; **58**: 41-42; **59**: 192, 226; **68**: 472-73; on food relief for Russia, **56**: 575-76,n1; **57**: 93-94, 165, 166, 437-40, 440, 456, 512; Bolshevik's (Lenin's) reply to, **59**: 256, 300-301,n8, 310-11; praises WW, **68**: 467

Nanssen, Bernhard, **67**: 18

Naples, Italy, **58**: 144

Naples, University of, **53**: 608n1

Napoleon I, **54**: 241; **55**: 109; **56**: 360, 510, 533; **57**: 122, 132; **58**: 171

Napoleonic Wars, **56**: 316

Nash, Joseph, **66**: 546,n2

Nashville Tennessean, **66**: 169n1

Nashville, Tennessee, **65**: 119

Nassau (Bavaria), **59**: 401n4

Nassau, S.M.S., **55**: 23, 427; **56**: 28; **58**: 127

Nassau Club, Princeton, **68**: 462, 595

Natal, Union of South Africa, **54**: 298

Nat Goodwin's Book, **53**: 177,n1

Nation, The: *see* New York *Nation*

National Albanian League of America, **58**: 477n17

National American Woman Suffrage Association, **56**: 191n1; **57**: 43; **60**: 155, 204; **62**: 225n1; **64**: 396n1

National Association for the Advancement of Colored People, **53**: 236n1, 690; **54**: 126n1; **61**: 576,n1; and Shillady case, **62**: 527, 535-36; and anti-lynching bill, **67**: 570,n1, 571

National Association for the Protection of American Rights in Mexico, **62**: 155n1

National Association of Audubon Societies, **67**: 81n1, 110

National Association of Manufacturers, **57**: 385-86

National Association of State Commissioners, **59**: 288

National Bank of Belgium, **53**: 38

national budget system, **66**: 456

National Bureau for the Advancement of Music of New York, **64**: 346n2

National Cathedral: see Washington National Cathedral

National Catholic War Council, **57**: 459

National City Bank of New York, **56**: 160; **57**: 421; **62**: 82n1, 88; **67**: 365n1

National Civil Liberties Bureau, **55**: 224,n1; **61**: 398, 480; and amnesty issue, **62**: 126,n3, 128

National Civil Liberties Union, **53**: 12-13

National Civil Service Reform League, **55**: 330n2

National Coal Operators Association, **57**: 451; **62**: 20; **63**: 56

National Colored World Democracy Congress, **61**: 28

National Committee for Organizing Iron and Steel Workers, **63**: 30n1

National Council of the Evangelical Free Churches, **53**: 530n1

National Council of Woodrow Wilson Clubs: see Woodrow Wilson Clubs

National Defense Act (1916), **66**: 58n1

National Defense Act (1920), **65**: 365n2

National Democratic Club: and Jefferson Day dinner brouhaha, **68**: 3, 10, 11-12, 14-15, 21, 26

National Democratic Convention of 1912, **53**: 241

National Democratic League of Clubs, **64**: 515n1

National Equal Rights League, **60**: 486; **61**: 27-28,n2, 186

National Farmers' Union, **62**: 623,n1

National Gallery of Art (Washington), **66**: 470

National Geographic, **68**: 449

National Gleaner Federation, **62**: 30n1

National Grange, **56**: 427; **62**: 623,n1; endorses treaty ratification, **62**: 301, 313

National Guard, **66**: 58n1; and Army Reorganization bill (1920), **65**: 355n1, 356, 364-65, 366-67

National Independent Political League, **64**: 522,n2

National Industrial Conference (proposed): Tumulty on, **60**: 151, 154: see also Industrial Conferences

National Industrial Conference Board, **62**: 582, 583, 623,n1

National Institute for the Blind, London, **65**: 430, 432

National Italian Democratic League, **68**: 95n1

National Italian Republican League, **68**: 95n1

National League of the Euxine Pontus, **66**: 29n1

National Monticello Association, **68**: 321n1

National Race Congress, **63**: 268,n1

National Security and Defense Fund: see War Emergency Fund

National Theater (Washington), **67**: 111

National Tribune, **67**: 278n1

National Tribune—Stars and Stripes, **67**: 278n1

National Union for Jewish Rights, **59**: 219n8

National Union of French and Belgian Railwaymen, **59**: 186

National Union of Railwaymen of France, **59**: 186

National Union of Women's Suffrage Societies, **55**: 145n4

National War Labor Board, **53**: 705, 716n2; **57**: 510; **60**: 151, 378; **66**: 263n1; and Walsh's resignation, **53**: 215; and strike in N.Y. harbor, **53**: 710; and carpenters' controversy, **54**: 472,n1, 520; and proposed strike by telephone and telegraph workers, **56**: 311n1, 341, 403, 404; dissolution of, **62**: 250-51

National War Labor Board: Stability, Social Justice, and the Voluntary State in World War I (Conner), **55**: 365n1; **66**: 263n1

National Woman's Suffrage Association, **61**: 377

National Woman's party, **54**: 90n1

National Women's Trade Union League, **63**: 56-57, 58-59

Nauen, Germany, **55**: 40, 430; **56**: 38

Nauru (Southwest Pacific atoll), **58**: 484, 510

Nava Cesare, **61**: 109,n5

Naval Affairs Committee (House of Reps.), **53**: 395n1; **54**: 411,n1; **63**: 160,n2

Naval Appropriation Act of 1916, **63**: 160n2, 164, 169-70, 261; **66**: 453n1

Naval Appropriation Bill of 1917, **63**: 164, 177-78

Naval Appropriation Bill of 1918, **63**: 160,n2, 164, 177-78

Naval Appropriation Bill of 1919, **63**: 160n2, 164, 177-78

Naval Appropriation Bill of 1922, **68**: 278n2

Naval Inter-Allied Commission of Control, **56**: 48

naval oil reserves, **53**: 264; **54**: 216,n3; **61**: 534-35,n1; **62**: 45-50, 78-79, 293-300, 438-39; Pinchot on need for Palmer to appeal case concerning oil

naval oil reserves (*cont.*)
fields, **64**: 354-55; and Honolulu Oil case, **64**: 392,n1, 405; and General Leasing Bill, **64**: 473n1; and Teapot Dome scandal, **68**: 119n2; *see also* General Leasing bill

naval peace terms, **56**: 27-38, 67; discussed at Supreme War Council meetings, **55**: 16-17, 20-26; Daniels on, **55**: 424-25; draft of, **55**: 425-32; Benson on, **55**: 432-36, 515-21, 522-24, 539; House, Lloyd George, and Clemenceau discuss, **55**: 458-59

Navigating the Rapids, 1918-1971: From the Papers of Adolf A. Berle (Berle and Jacobs, eds.), **59**: 447n1

Navy (U.S.): *see* United States Navy

Navy, Department of the, **53**: 131, 253; **55**: 537; **56**: 83; **62**: F. D. Roosevelt on labor and wage issue in, **62**: 231-32; WW on Sims' literary plans, **62**: 460; and General Leasing bill, **64**: 473-74; suggestion for Assistant Secretary, **66**: 55, 56; WW on F. D. Roosevelt's resignation, **66**: 77; Woodbury appointed Assistant Secretary, **66**: 91; **67**: 25,n1; McAdoo on laying of cables and, **66**: 220; Daniels report on, **66**: 452-53,n1; and Aeronautic Commission of Control, **66**: 535-36,n1; and Baltic situation, **67**: 8-9; and Grayson's assignment, **67**: 185n1

Neale, Ben M., **57**: 48,n6

Neale, James Brown, **60**: 120,n1, 491,n1

Near-East Relief Committee, **62**: 166; **67**: 139; WW sends contribution to, **68**: 25, 465

Nearing, Scott, **53**: 554; **55**: 337,n1

Neale, James Brown, **60**: 120,n1, 491,n1

Nebraska, **53**: 61-62; and German Americans, **67**: 421; Democratic women in, **68**: 156

Nebraska Farm Bureau Association, **62**: 300n1

Necessity for the League of Nations: The Past and Probable Future Attitude of the United States (N. H. Davis), **68**: 84,n1

Nedjib, **57**: 426

Neely, Matthew Mansfield, **68**: 190,n2

Négociations Secrètes et les Quatre Armistices, avec Pièces Justifications (pamphlet), **68**: 222,n1

Negro Education: A Study of the Private and Higher Schools for Colored People in the United States (Jones), **62**: 292,n1

Negroes, **53**: 340-41, 344, 690; **64**: 522,n2; Du Bois on future of Africa, **53**: 235-38; N. D. Baker requests retrial of accused soldiers, **53**: 451-52; Moton visits troops in France, **53**: 526,n1, 579,n1; and Pan African Congress, **54**: 126; WW on Bolshevism and, **55**: 471; and Senegalese battalion, **59**: 278, 280, 310; and clauses in peace treaty against racial discrimination, **60**: 489;

and equal rights clauses in treaty, **61**: 27-28,n2; and American Federation of Labor's resolution against mob rule and lynchings, **61**: 357-59; race riots in Washington, **61**: 576,n2, 599, 610; **62**: 21-22; Moton on racial situation and lynchings, **62**: 233-34; WW answers Moton, **62**: 260; and Southern Sociological Congress, **62**: 292-93, 505-506; and France and conscription in Togoland, **62**: 425-26, 532, 595; and Shillady case, **62**: 527-28, 535-36; and Caldwell case, **62**: 530,n1, 536; and unorganized labor, **63**: 268; report of black French troops terrorizing Germans, **65**: 341,n1; Baker on army reorganization bill and, **65**: 576

Negro Rural School Fund: *see* Jeanes Fund

Nelles, Walter, **62**: 126

Nelson, Harold I., **55**: 475n2; **56**: 12n1; **57**: 91n6

Nelson, Keith LeBahn, **56**: 12n1; **59**: 401n4, 402n5; **60**: 14n14, 489n2; **65**: 155n1

Nelson, John Edwin, **65**: 24, 378,n4

Nelson, Knute, **54**: 397,n1; **60**: 43,n2; **61**: 372, 425; meets with WW on treaty, **61**: 492-93,n2, 515, 516, 517; and reservations on Article X, **63**: 150, 444, 445; and treaty fight, **64**: 94, 338, 339

Neman River: *see* Neiman River

Neratov, Anatoli Anatolievich, **59**: 15,n5

Netherlands, The, **53**: 40, 121, 153; **54**: 138-39, 479; **55**: 110, **56**: 458; **58**: 198; **60**: 157, 252; **67**: 542; William II in, **53**: 130,n2, 138, 324n2; **57**: 124, 146n4, 149, 631; **59**: 295; **61**: 96; and Belgian claims and restoration, **55**: 83; **56**: 592-93; issue of passage of troops and supplies through, **55**: 178-80; WW thanks Queen Wilhelmina for offer of hospitality, **55**: 219-20; and League of Nations Commission, **56**: 103, 170n1; and opium convention, **56**: 270n5; and German-Belgian border, **57**: 395-97, 399; Keynes on economic rehabilitation plan and, **58**: 13, 14; and Treaty of 1839, **59**: 289; and delivery of William II, **61**: 157, 194-95, 199, 200-201, 204-205, 218, 257-58, 258-59, 313, 395-96,n1; and extension of credit, **61**: 495, 501; and League of Nations membership, **62**: 412, 418; resignation of U. S. Minister to, **62**: 435,n1; Phillips suggested for appointment to, **64**: 41, 103, 119, 204, 205, 296, 317, 322; banking interests in Mexico, **66**: 302

Neu, Charles Eric, **56**: 188n4

Neuilly, France: WW visits wounded in, **53**: 467, 469, 500-501

Neu Yorker Volkszeitung, **53**: 554

Nevada, **53**: 115; and railroad strike, **62**: 548, 549-50; and land reclamation bill, **64**: 4

Nevada Historical Quarterly, **63**: 426n1

Nevin, Blanche, **54**: 107,n2
Nevin, John Edwin, **53**: 314,n3, 318, 332, 336, 348, 364, 369, 376, 621,n2; **54**: 60, 192; **55**: 221,n1, 222, 409, 479, 480; **57**: 65-66,n3, 98-99, 288,n1; **60**: 381, 383, 388; **61**: 360; **62**: 627; **65**: 24, 378,n4; on WW's health and return trip to Washington, **63**: 527-28; photograph of, *illustration section*, **53**
Nevin, John J., **62**: 466
Nevins, Allan, **53**: 147n1; **65**: 120n2, 130n1
Nevoso, Mount (Sneznik): *see* Mount Nevoso
New, Harry Stewart, **59**: 451n1; **60**: 243,n1; **61**: 372; **62**: 29,n1; **63**: 5; **67**: 97n2, 381,n2; **68**: 44,n2, 47, 49, 581; on League of Nations, **62**: 91; questions WW at Foreign Relations Committee meeting, **62**: 340, 360, 369-70, 408-10; and Bullitt testimony, **63**: 337n1; and Mexican situation, **64**: 120; Grayson on attitude of toward WW's health, **64**: 135-36; and treaty fight, **64**: 200-201, 337; and bipartisan meeting on reservations, **64**: 283; hopeful of treaty compromise, **64**: 311-12; and bitter-enders, **64**: 328n2
New, Kathleen Miller (Mrs. Harry Stewart), **67**: 381,n2; **68**: 581
New Age, **67**: 440,n1
New Alliance as a Guarantee of the League (Simonds), **59**: 524,n3
Newark, N.J.: "slacker raids: in, **60**: 115n6
Newark, Ohio, **63**: 3,n2
Newark Evening News, **60**: 151; **65**: 229n1; **66**: 4; **68**: 194
Newberry, Truman Handy, **61**: 372, 492; **65**: 120,n2; **67**: 316-17, 323-24,n1, 323; meets with WW, **61**: 548,n1, 599,n1, 601-602,n2; and treaty fight, **64**: 200-201, 357
Newberry case, **65**: 120n2; **68**: 46, 47
New England: and coal, **66**: 205-206
New England Quarterly, **63**: 167n6
New England Telephone and Telegraph Company: strike and settlement, **57**: 425,n1, 445-46, 511, 530n1; **58**: 49-50
New Era in World Morality (Colegrove), **60**: 146,n2
New Era Movement of the Presbyterian Church, U.S.A. (Black), **62**: 270n1
New Europe: A Weekly Review of Foreign Politics, **57**: 539,n3; **67**: 43n1, 45
New Freedom: A Call for the Emancipation of the Generous Energies of a People (Hale, ed.), **68**: 330,n2
New Granada (now Colombia), **61**: 295n1, 299n4
New Guinea, **53**: 566; *see also* Paris Peace Conference—New Guinea
New Hampshire, **66**: 368
New Haven, Conn., **55**: 237
New Hebrides, **54**: 254, 320
New Jersey, **53**: 24, 63; **58**: 459; **59**: 39; cold storage regulation law, **62**: 179, 215; **64**: 82-83; 112; **65**: 130; WW's interest in election in, **63**: 608, 615,n1; ratifies 19th amendment, **64**: 396n1; WW on process of pardoning in, **66**: 25; T. Roosevelt on *La Questione Sociale* of Paterson, **66**: 96-97; Democratic politics in, **67**: 480, 482; WW on Commissioner of Education in, **67**: 483,n1, 487, 490; Democratic politics in, **68**: 154,n2,3, 454, 459, 460, 590, 595; Republican party in, **68**: 162n1; prohibition issue in, **68**: 454n2; suggestion that WW run for Senate from, **68**: 454; WW's suggestions for senatorial candidates from, **68**: 459
New Jersey Zinc Company, **64**: 232n1
New London, Conn., **55**: 237
Newlands Act, **65**: 447-48
Newman, Jennie E. Bixby (Mrs. Oliver P.), **68**: 187,n3
Newman, Jacob, **67**: 347
Newman, Poppenhusen, Stern & Johnson, **67**: 347n1
New Mexico: Democratic party in, **67**: 350,n1; Democratic women in, **68**: 156
New Mexico, U.S.S., **55**: 207, 217
New Mexico Historical Review, **64**: 120n1
New Orleans, La., **59**: 287; Benson on takeover of bases in, **66**: 425-26
New Orleans *Times Picayune*, **67**: 488
Newport News Shipbuilding Co., **53**: 704
New Republic, **54**: 430n2; **61**: 240n1, 373; **62**: 347,n12; **67**: 373,n1, 379; opposes peace treaty, **60**: 202,n2
New South Faces the World: Foreign Affairs and the Southern Sense of Self, 1877-1950 (McWilliams), **68**: 171n1
Newspaper Correspondents Association, **54**: 191-92
Newspaper Enterprise Association, **66**: 154n2; **67**: 492
newspapers, **53**: 396, 441; press policy for peace conference, **53**: 87, 411, 440, 723; Britain and France lift censorship on U.S. press releases, **53**: 100, 109, 154, 180, 241; and government control of cable system, **53**: 148; and Russian situation, **53**: 175; correspondents invited to Europe with WW, **53**: 314,n3, 376; WW's remarks to American press in Paris, **53**: 421; WW's remarks to press representatives in Rome, **53**: 599-600; France's censorship of her own press, **53**: 610; publicity and censorship issues at Paris Peace Conference, **54**: 27-28,n2, 59-60, 62, 64-65, 65-66, 66-68, 74-76, 96-99,n2, 105, 108-14, 120, 121-22, 158, 191-92; and commission to Poland, **54**: 248-49; W. Hughes leaks information to, **54**: 351,n3; WW on coverage of meetings in Paris press, **54**: 351-52; London *Daily Mail* article angers peace conference delegates, **54**: 377-78; Tumulty on WW inviting correspondents to return with him, **54**: 392; WW

newspapers (*cont.*)
on censorship in France and, **54**: 467;
Creel on WW meeting with correspondents of U.S. dailies, **54**: 471; leak on
possible relocation of peace conference,
55: 66, 88; anti-Wilson propaganda
campaign and French press, **55**: 66, 88,
94, 120, 153, 266, 489-90; **56**: 3, 59,
128; **57**: 353-54; **60**: 575; British labor
Socialist paper backs WW, **55**: 87,n2;
WW meets with correspondents before
Plenary Session, **55**: 161, 195; British
press gives false reasons why WW absent from Supreme War Council meeting, **55**: 530-31; Lloyd George condemns reports of leaks, **56**: 148-49;
New York *World* poll on editorial support for League of Nations, **56**: 156,n1;
and Polish boundary issue, **56**: 166-67;
R. S. Baker gives hint (leaks) on
France's behavior, **56**: 354; Page on reporting of Italian press, **56**: 392-94; reporting extravagant views and delays
caused by France, **56**: 429; editorials
on proposed recognition of Lenin, **56**:
551n1; leaks concerning WW's summoning of *U.S.S. George Washington*,
57: 63-65,n1, 68, 175-76; W. G. Sharp
on French press, **57**: 175-76; Grayson
persuades press not to attack House,
57: 235; and House, **57**: 286; and issue
of peace treaty publicity, **57**: 288-89,
292, 293; Britain leaks information on
invitation to Germany to peace conference, **57**: 316; leaks of reparation
clauses, **57**: 333,n2; statement summoning German delegation to peace
conference released to, **57**: 336; House
on change in French press, **57**: 390,
390-91; and French treaty of guarantee, **57**: 416-17,n1, 430; WW instructs
Hoover not to give Russian statement
to, **57**: 529; issue of treaty publication
and presence of press at Plenary Session with Germany, **58**: 23-24, 253-54,
404, 404-405, 429-30, 459, 479, 490;
French press on Italian crisis, **58**: 96-
97, 121, 238, 239-40, 282; reaction of
Italian press to WW's Adriatic statement and continued attacks on WW by
Italian press, **58**: 143-44, 210, 239,
240, 271-72, 323, 358-59, 413, 451; ac-
cuse WW of entering into secret treaties, **58**: 104n2; and hints of rift between Britain, France, and the U.S.,
58: 371-72; Clemenceau apologizes for
French position on Italy in, **58**: 431;
press release by Council of Four on in-
person meeting with experts to explain
peace terms if Germany wishes it, **58**:
526; WW calls "fiction" news accounts
that Italy gets Fiume, **58**: 531-32,n1,
601; Orlando and Soninno apologize
for anti-Wilson press, **58**: 552; and
Germany, **58**: 579; reaction in Germany to peace terms, **59**: 35-37;

Grayson on French press, **59**: 39; and
WW's message to Congress, **59**: 286,
367; and publication of peace treaty,
59: 313, 346, 448; draft of news release
on experts' meeting with German representatives on economic clauses, **59**:
315; and House on Irish-American
spokesmen, **59**: 366-67; Lloyd George
on, **60**: 335, 344; and problem of publishing German proposals and Allied
reply on same day, **60**: 518, 527; and
Italy's internal crisis, **60**: 531; and
press claims that WW under dominance of bankers, **60**: 531; Tumulty on
importance of WW meeting with his
journalistic supporters, **60**: 611; WW
meets with Belgian correspondents,
61: 11n2; final German treaty released
to, **61**: 27; Page on pro-German influence in Italian press, **61**: 28; underground newspaper in Belgium, **61**:
35n1; WW's comments to London *Daily
Mail* on German treaty, **61**: 108;
French press and public opinion on
WW, **61**: 138-39; various comments
and reports on WW's press conferences
with American correspondents, **61**:
235-38, 240-45, 246-52, 417-24; those
opposed to League of Nations, **61**: 372-
73; report on rift between WW and
Hitchcock, **61**: 468-69; WW denies rift
with Hitchcock, **61**: 468-70; report WW
to be more available to congressman
and senators, **61**: 474-75; Cobb on, **61**:
644-46; correspondents on WW's western tour, **62**: 626-27; Los Angeles papers endorse WW's position, **63**: 423;
opposition papers on trip cancellation,
63: 521; coments on treaty situation in
Senate, **64**: 287n1,2; and Lansing's
resignation, **64**: 415; editorial comments on WW's health and Lansing
dismissal, **65**: 3-7; comments on Hitchcock letter, **65**: 71n3; advance comments on Cox's speech, **66**: 4; Lloyd
George on French press, **66**: 43; press
release on Polish correspondence, **66**:
87-88,n1, 90,n1; Colby on paper shortage, **66**: 114; Rogers on H. Hoover and
Washington Herald, **66**: 169; and serialization of *World Settlement*, **67**: 241-
42, 249, 363-64, 488-90; N. D. Baker
on, **67**: 296; WW on alleged interview
with EBW, **67**: 492; WW reads, **67**:
517-18; WW on, **67**: 574; proposal for
Democratic party weekly, **68**: 137-
38,n2, 341, 346; Thompson on two in
Alabama, **68**: 170-71, 176; Creel
against syndication of WW's essay, **68**:
342-44, 353-54, 357; and *Louisville
Post*'s proposal for WW, **68**: 483-84;
Kerney's offer and WW's response, **68**:
498, 499; leak on WW's illness, **68**: 549;
see also under names of individual
newspapers such as *New York Times*,
Springfield (Mass.) *Republican*

Newton, Byron R., **68**: 388n1
Newton, Charles, **65**: 289n1
New World: Problems in Political Geography (Bowman), **67**: 404,n2
New York (city), **59**: 287: and controversy over committee to welcome returning soldiers, **53**: 580-81; Smith's invitation to WW, **55**: 216; WW on his retirement and, **55**: 482; "slacker raids" in, **60**: 115n6; Balfour on, **60**: 204
New York (state), **59**: 39; WW's admission to bar in, **67**: 261,n1, 331-32; Democratic party in N.Y.State, **67**: 602, 602-603; **68**: 15, 56-57, 154,n4; Jeffferson Day speech brouhaha in, **68**: 15, 17; and Democratic women, **68**: 156, 182; and Federal Reserve bill, **68**: 585-86
New York *American*, **56**: 340; **57**: 241n3; **61**: 372; **62**: 574; **67**: 363, 364n2
New York Association for the Blind, **53**: 501n2
New York Bar Association: and Chadbourne, **68**: 16n1
New York Call, **54**: 430,n1,2; **56**: 283n1; **61**: 243n7; **65**: 335n1; and court case on mailing, **66**: 170,n1
New York Chamber of Commerce: and revival of War Finance Corporation, **67**: 16-17, 28
New York County Lawyers' Association, **67**: 336,n1, 340; WW joins, **67**: 346
New York *Day*, **54**: 60
New York *Evening Post*, **53**: 13,n2, 627; **55**: 451,n8, 480n2; **56**: 161n1, 187, 189n9, 317n1, 551n1; **57**: 63n1, 629n1; **58**: 250n5; **59**: 120n1, 185, 554n2; **60**: 146,n1; **61**: 182; **62**: 627; **63**: 238n1; **64**: 327,n1; **65**: 5-6, 122,n1; **66**: 274; **67**: 26, 382, 473,n1, 476,n1, 617, 618n3; **68**: 57,n3, 222, 223n2; and summary of peace treaty, **58**: 531n1; on Knox Resolution, **60**: 535; WW on, **66**: 170,n1
New York *Evening Sun*, **65**: 4
New York Evening Telegram, **55**: 151,n1
New York *Globe and Commercial Advertiser*, **65**: 3; **67**: 313,n1, 382; **68**: 373
New York Herald, **53**: 421n1; **54**: 60; **55**: 450n6; **56**: 517n2; **57**: 63n1; **59**: 38,n2; **60**: 44n4; **61**: 373, 549n1, 612, 613; **62**: 200; **63**: 273n2; **67**: 382,n3,4; **68**: 371n1
New York Herald (Paris edition), **56**: 3n1; **57**: 175; **58**: 97, 121
New York Journal of Commerce and Commercial Bulletin, **61**: 612n2
New York Life Insurance Company, **67**: 464n2
New York *Maccabean*, **55**: 381n3
New York *Nation*, **55**: 248n2; **56**: 340; **61**: 373, 478,n1; **66**: 25n1; **67**: 37n1; WW on article on Bullitt mission, **61**: 509,n1
New York *Novy Mir*, **53**: 137n1, 554,n3; **56**: 548n1
New York Peace Society, **55**: 278
New York *Review*, **67**: 464n1

New York *Social Register*, **67**: 135n11
New York State child welfare law of 1915, **68**: 478n1
New York *Sun*, **54**: 60; **55**: 480n2; **56**: 3n1, 436n1, 551n1; **57**: 63n1, 65n2, 236, 241n3, 417n1, 511, 532n2; **60**: 331; **61**: 243n6, 372; **62**: 627; **63**: 521; **68**: 373; and reparation clause, **57**: 333,n2; and story of WW-House break, **62**: 573-74,n1
New York Telephone and Telegraph Company, **68**: 452
New York Times, **53**: 71n1, 135n2, 148n1, 209n1, 239n1, 258n1, 299n1 300n2, 307n2, 308n1, 312n1, 314n4, 316n2, 386n1, 395n1, 418n4, 420n1, 420n3, 438, 459n1, 469n1, 576n2, 580n2, 597n1, 599n1, 600n1, 608n1, 611n1, 626n1; **54**: 27n2, 56n1, 60, 90n1, 92n1,2, 132n1, 229n3, 261n1, 280n5, 397n4, 411n1, 464n1, 485n1, 550n1; **55**: 88n1, 145n4, 163n, 197n, 224n1, 275, 276, 299n, 326n, 330n2, 340n, 355n5, 363n1, 386n, 391n,n1, 422n, 438n3, 448n1, 450n6, 480n2, 482n1; **56**: 3n1, 60n1, 161n1, 187n3, 191n1, 192n1, 345n2, 346n1, 348n1, 428n2,3, 490n1, 517n2, 551n1; **57**: 63n1, 67,n5, 146, 148n2, 241n1, 286n1, 345n1, 385,n32, 417n1, 424n1, 425n1, 447n1, 530n1, 629n1; **58**: 60n2, 94n1, 101n1, 168n1, 202n1, 237n3, 239n4, 243n1, 250n5, 330n1, 355n4, 359n1,2, 419n1, 427n1, 430, 492n1, 562n1; **59**: 3, 38,n2, 68n2, 75n1, 76n1, 84n2, 117n4, 120n1, 204n1, 206n1, 278n2, 320n2, 367n2, 419n1, 450n2, 493n1, 524n1, 607n1; **60**: 29n14, 44n4, 114n2, 115n7, 147n3, 332n1, 599n1; **61**: 66n3, 181, 182,n1, 191n2, 243n11, 347n1, 365n1, 395n1, 418n2, 422n3, 426,n1, 464n5, 512n3, 518n1, 568n1, 576,n1, 598n1, 605n1, 615n1, 628,n1, 645n2; **62**: 31n1, 45n, 69, 94n, 95n, 140n, 148n2, 149, n1, 162n, 165n1, 192n, 252n1, 287, 300n1, 305n1, 309n, 339n, 355,n21, 445n3, 460n1, 477, 481n1, 488n, 491n1, 498n, 507n1, 545n3, 561n1, 614n2, 622n1, 627; **63**: 3n4, 18n, 52n3, 75n, 97n, 118n3, 138n, 148n, 152n, 163n, 165n, 180n, 197n, 198n2,3,4, 211n6, 223n1, 238n1, 254n2, 273n2, 275n4, 283n1, 300n1, 309n2, 333n3, 337n1, 376, 482n2,4, 517n2, 531n, 537n, 538n, 547n4, 551n, 564n,n1, 565, 568n, 580n, 581n2, 585n,n1, 587n, 591n, 593n1, 594n2, 599n1, 606n, 608n1, 609n, 612n1, 615n2; **64**: 4n, 6n, 7n, 37n, 57n, 81n5, 93n, 106n, 118n2, 126n, 133n, 141n, 142n2, 145n, 149n2, 152n2, 155n1, 187n, 195n1, 206n1, 234n1,4, 260n2, 261n1, 267n, 307n, 310n, 312n, 330n1, 342n, 351n, 355n1, 360, 381n1, 394, 396n1, 419n1, 420n, 436n1, 444, 464n1, 522n1; **65**: 22n1, 42n, 67n,

New York Times (cont.)
81n1, 86n, 109n1, 120n2, 145n1, 155n1, 248n1, 261n1, 276n1, 291n, 291n1, 294n1, 325n1, 341n1, 351n2, 354n, 354n2, 369n3, 385n, 389n1, 425n1, 428n, 435n1, 440n, 444n1,2, 450n2, 451,n1,2, 471n1, 473n, 482n1, 492n1, 494n1, 510n1, 525n, 542n2, 576n1; **66**: 4n5, 8n1, 12n1, 24n3, 25n1, 45n6, 54n1, 77n1, 89n1, 90n1, 95n2, 110n1, 141,n1,2, 147n2, 172n1, 183n, 184n1, 188n1, 188n2, 192n2, 198n1, 208n1, 239, 246n1, 248n1, 249n1, 265n, 267n1, 270n1, 276n, 277n1, 282n1, 283n3, 292n2, 295n2, 317,n1, 323n2,3, 343n2, 351n1, 371n1, 419n2, 446n2, 458n1, 493n, 505n6, 513n3, 516n1, 542n1; **67**: 23n1, 26n6, 33n1, 52n1, 79n1, 94n1, 112n, 115n1, 121n2, 128n, 138n, 140n3, 151n1, 159, 176n1, 190n, 197n1, 214n, 234, 246n, 253n1, 258n3, 261n1, 268n, 287n1, 309n1, 311n, 327n6, 327, 329n, 355n2,7, 360n3, 364n2, 369n1, 374n2, 382,n1, 382n5, 386n2, 399n2, 402n1, 414, 435n, 436n, 437n, 440n, 448n1, 466n, 471n1, 484n1, 488, 494n1, 523n, 531n1, 544n3, 547n1, 618n1; **68**: 3n, 11,n1, 12n, 16n1, 24n3, 33n2, 35n3, 36n1, 39n, 44n1, 48n6, 57,n4, 73n2, 76n1, 93n4, 99n1, 100n2, 102n2, 105n1, 106n1, 108n1, 122n2, 127n1, 129n1, 132, 147n3, 166n2, 178n1, 188n, 188n2, 228n, 231n, 249n2, 268n1, 275n1, 278n2, 296n2, 307n4, 315n1, 332n1,2, 339n1, 344n, 373n3, 383n, 388n1, 399, 400n, 402n, 404n, 426n, 452n2, 453n1, 454n2, 456n, 467n,n1, 471n, 478n1, 519n1, 524, 532n, 551n1, 552n, 557, 573n, 574n1, 584n; and publication of peace treaty, **60**: 328,n1; on Knox Resolution, **60**: 535; and Franco-American treaty of guarantee, **61**: 375n4; and Plumb plan, **62**: 198n2; on WW's health, **65**: 5; report on reaction to Hitchcock letter, **65**: 71n3; WW on, **66**: 199; praises WW, **66**: 317,n1; WW thanks, **66**: 338; editorial on WW, **67**: 183,n1, announces nationwide tribute to WW, **67**: 271n1; WW on editorial policy of, **67**: 301,n1; Baruch on, **67**: 366; and Jefferson Day brouhaha, **68**: 14, 51

New York Tribune, **54**: 96n2, 114,n4; **56**: 3n1, 436n1,3, 490n1, 551n1; **57**: 63n1, 65n2, 236, 241n3, 629n1; **58**: 327n1; **59**: 524,n5; **60**: 203,n2; **61**: 241n4, 372; **63**: 165, 223n1, 238n1, 273n2, 309n2; **65**: 4, 71n3; **66**: 199n1,2; **67**: 382,n2, 398n

New York University: organizes WW Club, **67**: 271

New York University Law School: WW Club at, **67**: 275

New York World, **53**: 542,n1; **54**: 57-58, 60, 106n1; **55**: 88n1, 409n, 450; **56**: 3n1, 156,n1, 490n1; **57**: 63n1, 316, 417n1, 629n1; **58**: 51, 531n1; **61**: 243n8, 410-11,n2, 422n3; **62**: 180,n1, 543,n2, 627; **63**: 3n3, 267, 273n2, 309n2, 370n2, 564n1; **64**: 261n1, 270,n2, 287,n2; **65**: 71n3, 354n1, 401n1, 405, 415n, 421n, 439; **66**: 39, 250n1, 251, 258,n3, 277n1; **67**: 229n, 242, 261,n1, 363, 364, 382,n1, 424n1, 453n, 461n1, 541,n1, 547n1; **68**: 57n1, 80, 132, 577n6; and Franco-American treaty of guarantee, **61**: 375n4; Cobb on independence of, **61**: 644-46; on Japanese settlement, **58**: 363,n1; on prohibition, **58**: 604; news leaks on peace treaty, **60**: 115; on separate peace and Knox Resolution, **65**: 257,n1; Pulitzer's meeting with WW, **65**: 501n1; and paper embargo, **66**: 114; Cobb's editorial on WW, **67**: 216-29, 230, 234; inquiry on location of original treaty, **67**: 354-55; editorial on Britain's indebtedness, **67**: 355,n6; article on WW and Foch, **67**: 437,n1; WW on, **67**: 529; article on N. D. Baker in *Encyclopaedia Britannica*, **68**: 133n1

New Yorker Staats-Zeitung, **65**: 341n1, 394

New Zealand, **53**: 562; **56**: 164; **57**: 240; **58**: 198, 442, 484, 485, 510; **62**: 188; **63**: 447, 505; and representation at Paris Peace Conference, **54**: 44, 65; territorial claims of, **54**: 250, 251, 254, 289, 312-14, 314, 348, 361-63, 363, 366, 379; and mandates, **59**: 475,n2; and British policy in Far East, **65**: 392

Niagara, S.S., **65**: 252

Nicaragua, **54**: 24, 65, 115; **58**: 198; **59**: 524n5; **65**: 247n1

Nice, France: inscription on WW in, **67**: 482

Nicholas I (of Montenegro), **53**: 368,n3, 377, 638n1, 704; **54**: 18,n4, 54, 179; **56**: 572-74; **58**: 162, 163, 267-68, 354,n1, 508; **59**: 178,n2,3, 222,n12, 620n1; **61**: 239,n3; on Serbian injustices, **53**: 701-704

Nicolai, Valentino, **61**: 14,n8

Nichols, Rose M., **58**: 140-41,n1

Nicholson, George P., **68**: 423,n4

Nicholson, Samuel Danford, **68**: 301n2, 302

Nicolson, Harold George, **59**: 92,n6, 102, 136, 137, 138; **60**: 491-92,n3; **62**: 238,n1, 239

Niedak, Mr., **57**: 526

Niederle, Lubor, **60**: 122,n2

Nielsen, Fred Kenelm, **58**: 120,n3; **66**: 399-400,n1, 484,n1

Nieman River, **56**: 268; **57**: 453,n2

Niessel, Henri-Albert, **56**: 49n10

Nieto, Rafael, **55**: 355,n5

Nieuport, Belgium, **61**: 4, 29; photograph of, *illustration section*, **61**

Nigeria, **54**: 368, 485, 510

Nikolaievsk, Siberia, **65**: 515n1, 516; **66**: 51, 52, 53

Nine Power Treaty: background of and Hughes open door resolution, **67**: 531-32,n1; N. H. Davis on, **67**: 544n1

Nitti, Francesco Saverio, **61**: 35,n2, 45, 60, 109,n2; **62**: 252,n1; **63**: 210, 486, 516, 517, 524; **66**: 207n1; appeals to WW on Adriatic question and WW's reply, **62**: 605-606, 625; protests against occupation of Fiume, **63**: 298-99; plea to WW regarding Fiume and WW's reply, **63**: 464-65, 485-86; and Adriatic question, **64**: 260n1, 263, 264, 304, 313, 318, 376, 398; Adriatic compromise proposal of, **64**: 264,n4; and Anglo-French Adriatic proposal, **64**: 298, 300, 301; Polk on, **64**: 451; on Adriatic settlement, **65**: 45-46, 199; R. U. Johnson on, **65**: 94, 299, 300, 301, 303; on French invasion of Germany, **65**: 157-58, 162; supports German representation at San Remo Conference, **65**: 221; government's fall, **65**: 303n10, 304, 448n1; and note to U.S. on Armenia, **65**: 307-12; Lloyd George on, **65**: 481; **66**: 43

Nixon, Herman Clarence, **67**: 459,n1, 460, 461, 467

Noailles, Louis-Marie de, Vicomte de, (1756-1804), **68**: 67

No Alliance Needed or Advisable (*Washington Post*), **57**: 629n1

Nobel, Alfred, **66**: 523-24

Nobel Peace Prize: in 1909, **54**: 257n1; **67**: 271n1, 333; candidates recommended for, **64**: 342; WW receives for 1919, **65**: 40, 120; **66**: 477-78, 501, 517, 523n1,2, 543; **68**: 265; WW's acceptance messages, **66**: 492-933, 504-505; congratulatory messages, **66**: 503, 523-24, 531, 536; WW praised for receiving, **67**: 17-18; and WW's financial arrangements, **67**: 131-32, 365; WW recommends Jane Addams for, **68**: 266-67,n1

Noble, George Bernard, **55**: 66n2; **56**: 3n1, 149n3; **57**: 63n1, 459n2; **59**: 447,n1; **61**: 332,n10

Noble Concluding Work (*Louisville Times*), **66**: 450n2

No Dealings With the Enemy (*Washington Post*), **56**: 551n1

Noel-Baker, Philip John: *see* Baker, Philip John

Noggle, Burl, **68**: 119n2

Nolan, Dennis Edward, **53**: 57,n3; **56**: 491,n1, 492-93

Nolan, John Ignatius, **62**: 96,n1

Nolan, William Ignatius, **63**: 125,n1

Nollet, Charles-Marie-Edouard, **67**: 33n1

Noma, U.S.S., **58**: 409

Nonpartisan League, **63**: 95, 152, 153n1; **68**: 96n2, 372

Noonan, James Patrick, **56**: 311; **62**: 121, 568-70, 570-73; **64**: 424, 431; **65**: 16, 359

Norbeck, Peter, **62**: 34

Norfolk, Va., **56**: 404n1

Norman Foster Company, **53**: 159, 205

Norris, George Washington, **53**: 106,n2; **65**: 63

Norris, George William, **53**: 61; **60**: 245,n3; **63**: 94, 106, 197, 390,n1; **64**: 338; **68**: 185,n1, 247; WW wishes to meet with on treaty, **61**: 548-49; declines to meet with WW, suggests address to entire Senate, **61**: 569n1, 570, 602; accuses WW of erroneous statement, **63**: 93; and Treaty of Berlin, **67**: 422n4

North, Frank Mason, **53**: 718,n1; **54**: 56-57, 277,n1; **65**: 183,n3, 184

North American Review, **53**: 406

North Carolina: and Britt-Weaver congressional seat, **55**: 367,n1; and woman suffrage, **65**: 164, 433,n1, 450, 466, 473; Democratic party in, **68**: 212,n1, 213

North Carolina, University of, **67**: 68n3

North Carolina, U.S.S., **55**: 217

North Carolina Avenue Methodist Protestant Church, Washington, D.C., **66**: 348n1, 356

North Carolina Farmers' Union, **62**: 30n1

Northcliffe, Alfred Charles William Harmsworth, 1st Viscount, **53**: 417-19, 438, 441, 481; **54**: 304; **55**: 500; **56**: 350n2, 406; **57**: 243, 317, 532n2; **58**: 4-5; and D. Lloyd George, **57**: 148, 449-50; **59**: 561n5; **60**: 423

Northcliffe, Mary Elizabeth Milner Harmsworth, Lady, **56**: 350,n2, 406-407

Northcliffe press, **56**: 542; **57**: 148; **60**: 406, 423

North Dakota: Lemke *v.* Farmers Grain Co., **67**: 563n2; Democratic party in, **68**: 96,n1

North Dakota, U.S.S., **63**: 153,n4

Norton, Robert L., **62**: 627

Nortoni, Albert Dexter, **55**: 206-207,n1; **67**: 563,n2

North Sea, **55**: 429; **56**: 31, 33; **59**: 51

Norway, **53**: 40, 82n1, 153, 312,n4; **54**: 479; **55**: 545; **56**: 170n1, 270n5; **58**: 13, 14, 198; and credit extension for wheat, **61**: 501; and League of Nations membership, **62**: 412, 418

Norway and the United States: and ship settlement, **55**: 357, 394

Norwegian Peace Society: praises WW, **67**: 17-18,n1

Noske, Gustav, **57**: 523,n12; **60**: 177; **65**: 100, 101

Noulens, Joseph, **54**: 102, 104, 155; **56**: 49n10, 50, 52, 88, 129, 132, 139, 142, 143, 144, 145, 146, 147-48, 168, 528; **65**: 143

Novara, Battle of, **63**: 517,n4

Novemberrevolution und Frankreich: Die franzosische Deutschlandpolitik: 1918-1919 (Kohler), **59**: 566n1

Novo-Nikolaevsk, Russia, **62**: 87
No Wonder (*Atlanta Constitution*), **62**: 234n4
Noyes, Pierrepont Burt, **59**: 280,n1, 590; **60**: 366, 511; **64**: 150n1; on Rhineland, **59**: 593-94, 594; **60**: 295; WW answers on Rhineland, **60**: 360
Noyon, France, **56**: 194, 198, 199
Nubar, Boghos, **54**: 226,n1,2, 346, 468; **55**: 80; **57**: 302-303, 427; **66**: 86n1; on Armenia's claims, **54**: 516-18; thanks WW for effort on behalf of small nations, **61**: 461; **65**: 302,n6
Nudant, Alphonse-Pierre, **54**: 545,n7; **55**: 18; **56**: 118, 135, 137, 138, 139, 140, 141, 145, 167n3, 324, 325, 408,n2; **57**: 590; **61**: 87
Nugent, James Richard, **68**: 590,n4, 591
Nugent, John Charles: on WW, **68**: 373-74,n4
Nugent, John Frost, **55**: 297; **62**: 18; **68**: 299,n5
Nuevo Laredo, Mexico, **65**: 252
Nuorteva, Santeri Alexander Fedorovich, **56**: 548,n2, 549; **60**: 484n1
Nuovi Ricordi e Frammenti di Diario per far Seguito a Guerra Diplomatica (Aldrovandi Marescotti), **57**: 435n3
Nuri al Sa'id, **54**: 505,n2; **61**: 329-30,n8
Nutting, Anthony, **58**: 225n3

Oakland, California: WW activities in, **63**: 308; WW's address in, **63**: 340,n3, 352-61
Oakland Tribune, **63**: 340n1, 361n
Oba, Jiro, **61**: 572,n3
Obata, Torikichi, **54**: 474n2; **62**: 458,n3
Oberlin College, **54**: 277; **56**: 155, 310; **57**: 535; **58**: 172; **59**: 369
Obregón, Álvaro, **64**: 134n7; **66**: 160,n1, 161, 270n1, 271, 283n1, 335, 413; Summerlin's interview with, **65**: 486-87; Creel on, **66**: 122, 123, 372, 373, 374, 376, 404, 405; **67**: 82, 132-33; and Harding, **66**: 404-405,n5; rumors of possible overthrow of, **66**: 445
O'Brian, John Lord, **60**: 115n7
O'Brien, Michael Joseph, **60**: 383,n2, 487, 569
O'Brien, Robert Lincoln, **55**: 450,n2
O'Brien, Timothy, **55**: 407-408,n1
Observations of the German Delegation on the Conditions of Peace (document), **59**: 579,n1
O'Callaghan, Donal, **66**: 512-13,n2; **67**: 37-38,n1, 48-51, 52,n1
Occasional Addresses, 1893-1916 (Asquith), **53**: 542,n1
Oceanic Steam Navigation Company, **53**: 111
Ochs, Adolph Simon, **55**: 438n3; **67**: 234,n2; and WW Foundation **67**: 271n1, 327n6; WW on, **67**: 301,n1; Baruch urges WW to congratulate, **67**: 366; Morgenthau on WW not congratulating, **68**: 268,n1; Wiley on WW sending tribute, **68**: 524; WW's reasons for not sending tribute to, **68**: 525
O'Connell, John A., **63**: 268-70, 303
O'Connell, William Henry Cardinal, **53**: 274; **61**: 627,n2; **66**: 542n1
O'Connor, Julia S., **56**: 311, 404,n1
O'Connor, James Francis Thaddeus, **68**: 96,n2
O'Connor, Richard, **67**: 173n2
O'Connor, Thomas Power ("Tay Pay"), **56**: 443,n1; **57**: 350,n1; **61**: 116-17; **65**: 442-43,n2
October Revolution in Hungary: from Karolyi to Kun (Vernes) **53**: 7n3
Oder River, **56**: 268; **60**: 520n11; **65**: 217n1
Odessa, Russia, **54**: 372,n7, 403n3; **56**: 305-306, 314, 325, 329, 384; **58**: 405; **62**: 427n1; issue of transfer of troops from, **56**: 50, 51, 53, 312, 330, 527, 581; relief requests for, **56**: 252-57
O'Doherty, Katherine, **61**: 183n2
OEconomis, Socrates, **66**: 29n1
Office of: *see* under the latter part of the name, such as Public Records, Office of
Official Bulletin, **53**: 148n1, 205n1, 215n1, 308n1, 309n2, 406n1, 469n1, 635n; **54**: 262n1, 397n1; **55**: 189n2, 347n2; **57**: 439n12
Ogden, Rollo, **67**: 618n3
Ogden, Miss: and WW Foundation, **68**: 265
Ogden, Utah: WW's activities in, **63**: 446, 447,n1; WW's remarks in, **63**: 447, 448
Ogden, Utah, Examiner, **63**: 446n2, 447n
Ogden, Utah, Standard, **63**: 447n
Olgethorpe University, and WW's honorary degree, **65**: 86, 89-90, 117, 381-82,n1; WW's letter to be preserved by, **65**: 393
O'Gorman, James Aloysius, **54**: 473; **55**: 547; **65**: 140,n4; and WW's admission to N.Y. bar, **67**: 261, 329, 331-32,n2, 336, 343
Ogulin, Yugoslavia, **59**: 66
O'Hara, Jerome V., **54**: 473,n1
O'Hare, Kate Richards (Mrs. Francis Patrick), **62**: 557,n1, 558; **67**: 99; **68**: 48n6
O. Henry the Man and His Work (Long), **67**: 173n2
O'Hern, Charles Aloysius, **53**: 242,n2, 606,n3; **55**: 493,n1
Ohio: Democratic party and convention politics, **65**: 383, 492n2, 495, 555,n1; and 19th amendment, **65**: 445,n2, 450n2; W. G. Sharp on Democratic politics in, **65**: 473-76; and replacement of Cummings as Democratic National Chairman, **65**: 551,n1; McAdoo on political prospects in, **66**: 235; Democratic party and politics in, **67**: 254, 349-50, 510, 534; WW's message to Democrats of Akron, **67**: 255; Democratic politics in, **68**: 18; Democratic women in, **68**: 156
Ohio Farm Bureau Federation, **63**: 300n1

Ohio State University, **62**: 233; **63**: 7n1; **65**: 353n1

Oil and Gas Lands Bill. Conference Report on the Bill (S 2812) to Encourage and Promote the Mining of Coal, Phosphate, Oil, Gas and Sodium on the Public Domain, **54**: 216n3

oil, oil industry: fields, **53**: 636-37,n1; and supply for U.S. merchant marine, **62**: 114; Britain's interests in Persia, **62**: 452-53; Lane on world oil supply and U.S. shipping needs, **62**: 617-19; and Mexico, **64**: 210-11,n1; **66**: 160-61, 334-35, 375, 376, 404, 413; Colby on Mesopotamia mandate and, **66**: 397-98; and Western Ukraine Republic, **68**: 111, 113; *see also* Jenkins case

oil-leasing bill: *see* General Leasing bill

Oil Producers Association, **66**: 334

Oklahoma, **58**: 459; appointments in, **64**: 205; and woman suffrage, **64**: 466,n1; Democratic primary in, **66**: 3,n1, 10,n1; appointments in, **67**: 62, 70

Oklahoma City, Okla.: and WW's trip cancellation, **63**: 520-21

Oklahoma Farmers' Union, **54**: 228n1

Olav, Crown Prince of Norway, **53**: 592n4

Olcott, Ben Wilson, **63**: 275n1, 283n1

Old Cottages and Farmhouses in Kent and Sussex (Davie), **66**: 546,n2

Oldenburg, S.M.S., **55**: 23, 427; **56**: 28; **58**: 127

Old-Fashioned Democrat to the Editor of the *Indianapolis News*, **55**: 472,n2

Oldfield, William Allen, **55**: 297,n4

O'Leary, Jeremiah A., **55**: 411; **66**: 249n1

O'Leary, Michael A.: on Irish question, **62**: 8,n2

Olesen, Anna Dickie (Mrs. Peter), **68**: 156,n3, 157

Olginsk, Siberia, **56**: 186,n1

Oliphant, Laurence, **55**: 384,n3; **66**: 459,n1

Oliver, William Bacon, **54**: 281,n1

Olivier, Mr., **59**: 186

Olsztyn: *see* Allenstein

Olympia, U.S.S., **58**: 408, 426; **63**: 557n2; **65**: 538

Olympic Games (1920), **65**: 405,n7

Omaha, Nebraska: Grayson on WW's reception in, **63**: 93-94; WW's address in, **63**: 97-107

Omaha *World-Herald*, **63**: 1-7n; **65**: 6; **67**: 488

Omelianovych-Pavlenko, Mykhailo, **57**: 276,n3, 277, 356,n2; **59**: 262,n; **60**: 161,n12

Omsk, Russia, **53**: 136,n1, 137, 168, 258n1, 628; **54**: 101; **60**: 240; **61**: 494; **62**: 87; issue of sending Morris to, **61**: 139-31

Oneal, James, **55**: 92n1; **65**: 550

Onega, Russia, **55**: 190

O'Neill, John Joseph, **62**: 626n1, 627

O'Neill, Laurence, **56**: 96,n2

"One Way with Sedition" (New York *Evening Post*), **64**: 327n1

On Our Way to The League of Nations (H. S. Houston), **67**: 434

open door policy, **54**: 321, 350; **57**: 454, 555, 584, 605, 607; **58**: 184, 326, 484; **60**: 102; **61**: 131, 275, 386, 387; **67**: 531n1, 541-42, 544n1; WW on, **63**: 412, 437, 460, 507; **65**: 255; **66**: 309, 461

open shop: Gary on, **62**: 597-98, 599, 600

Opium as an International Problem: The Geneva Conference (Willoughby), **56**: 270n5

Opium Convention: *see* International Opium Convention

Ophthalmology, **58**: 611n2

Oppenheim, E. (Edward) Phillips, **67**: 289,n1

Orange Free State, **54**: 298

Orange Publishing Company, **55**: 468n1

Orawa, Poland, **66**: 225

Ordeal of Woodrow Wilson (Hoover), **56**: 575n1

Order of Railway Conductors, **64**: 424, 431

Order of Railway Telegraphers, **64**: 411n1, 424, 431

Oregon, **56**: 331; WW's statement to Democrats of, **65**: 263-64, 274; and WW Foundation, **67**: 409

Oregon, University of, **68**: 244n2

Oregon, U.S.S., **63**: 239

Oregon Historical Quarterly, **63**: 276n5

Orel, Russia, **62**: 427n1

Oresund, Strait of, **56**: 35,n8

Organic Law (Porto Rico), **55**: 158, 159

"Organic Mental Disorders: Introduction and Review of Syndromes" (Lipowski), **64**: 525n1, 527n4

Organic Syndromes: Dementia (Wells), **58**: 612n5, 615n17; **62**: 629n4

Organization of American Relief in Europe, 1918-1919 (Bane and Lutz, eds.), **57**: 347n1

Origines et l'oeuvre de la Société des Nations (Munch, ed.), **68**: 84n1

Origins of Teapot Dome: Progressives, Parties and Petroleum, 1909-1921 (Bates), **53**: 636n1; **61**: 534n1; **62**: 297n1; **64**: 354n1, 392n1, 405n1, 473n1; **68**: 119n2

Origins of the International Labor Organization (Shotwell, ed.), **56**: 236n2; **57**: 239n5, 495n1, 528n2; **58**: 417n8; **64**: 98n1

Origins of the TVA: The Muscle Shoals Controversy, 1920-1932 (Hubbard), **68**: 448n1

Oriental Company, Fiume, **56**: 569

Orlando, Vittorio Emanuele, **53**: 4, 123-24, 143, 242, 345, 433, 444, 449, 458, 466, 472, 507, 589, 596, 637, 639, 694, 711; **54**: 5, 49, 352, 359, 505; **55**: 88, 211, 305, 530; **56**: 65, 80, 103, 110, 250, 275, 312, 312-13, 355, 412, 518, 540, 578, 595; **57**: 52, 53, 71, 72, 191, 195,

Orlando, Vittorio Emanuele (*cont.*)
203, 232, 317, 331, 434, 435, 518, 519,
575; **58**: 3, 48, 144, 321, 334, 371, 391,
393, 398, 415, 449, 561; **59**: 11, 35, 68,
71, 110, 127, 130, 200, 208, 319, 367,
456, 478; WW on, **53**: 367; **57**: 90, 513,
575, 576; **60**: 40, 98-99; **61**: 336; **63**:
343; **64**: 263, 315, 348; **65**: 350; **66**: 45;
67: 183n1; meets with WW, **53**: 696;
55: 497, 498, 538; and Supreme War
Council meetings, **54**: 9, 10, 200, 246,
536-37; **55**: 95, 107; **56**: 46; and Adriatic question, **54**: 50-51, 112n3, 123,
134-35; **56**: 561-65; **57**: 107, 178, 342,
364, 467, 468; **59**: 80, 80-84, 125, 127,
174, 244, 503, 506-507, 553, 569-71;
60: 144, 271-72, 286, 307-11; **67**: 376-
77,n1; and Council of Ten meetings,
54: 186, 220, 249, 285, 311, 326-28,
356-57, 369, 420-21, 422-23, 423-24,
425; **55**: 140-41; **59**: 61; on demobilization, **54**: 220, 246, 526-27; and League
of Nations, **54**: 228, 269, 387, 387-89,
426n1, 460, 463, 464, 483, 494,n2, 496,
510, 511, 547; **55**: 4-5, 6, 42, 44, 45, 71,
123, 125, 126; **56**: 59; on mandatories,
54: 326-28, 352, 356-57, 359, 369; Seymour on, **54**: 384, 385; on Rumania, **54**:
422-23, 423-24, 425; and Plenary Session, **55**: 178n2, 195, 196; praises WW,
55: 300, 301-302; on Haller's troops,
56: 56, 497; and withdrawal clause in
Covenant, **56**: 78; and League of Nations Commission, **56**: 176, 226, 228,
229, 230, 298, 301, 302, 302; **57**: 253,
258-59, 265; on submarine cables, **56**:
217-18, 219; and reparations, **56**: 246,
252, 347, 359, 370-71, 451, 510, 598;
57: 17, 82, 86, 208, 455; **59**: 32-33, 387,
389, 390; meets with Colonel House,
56: 309; **57**: 352; on Russia and Bolshevism, **56**: 326, 329; **59**: 20; on Hungarian situation, **56**: 413, 414, 415, 458,
464, 487, 488; House on, **56**: 517; **57**:
35; absents himself from Council of
Four meetings during Yugoslavia's
claims, **56**: 556, 566, 577; R. S. Baker
on, **56**: 578; on occupation of Vienna,
57: 102, 105; on responsibilities and
punishment for the war, **57**: 124, 125-
26, 128, 631; and Danzig, **57**: 151; on
Germany and interdependence of
debts, **57**: 165, 166; on Saar Valley, **57**:
199-200, 201, 202; on site for League of
Nations, **57**: 220, 222, 223; and Monroe
Doctrine, **57**: 228, 229, 230; on Italy's
claims, **57**: 242, 289, 317-18, 318, 431,
478, 479-94, 513, 514, 516-17, 527,
539-40, 541, 542, 610-11, 614; and
Japan's racial equality amendment,
57: 249, 262; and publication of peace
treaty, **57**: 289; Clemenceau on, **57**:
335; and WW's meeting with Ossoinack on Fiume, **57**: 337-43; on Nansen's
food relief proposal, **57**: 438-39; on
Italy's claims, **57**: 478, 479-94, 513,
514, 516-17, 527, 539-40, 541, 542,

610-11, 614; weeps at Council of Four
meeting, **57**: 513, 527, 576; rejects verbal proposal brought by Hankey, **57**:
551, 552; on Dalmatia and false accu-
sations concerning Italy, **57**: 562-65,
627; absent from meeting, threatens to
leave Paris, **58**: 26, 27; and Adriatic
and Italian crisis, **58**: 53, 55-56, 250-
51, 252, 369; reasons for departure for
Italy, **58**: 56, 74-76, 83, 84, 85, 86, 102;
meets with Lloyd George, **58**: 57; Lloyd
George and Clemenceau on plans to
defer trip of, **58**: 57-58, 59; on WW's
Adriatic statement, **58**: 74-76, 97-101;
as leaving for Italy is presented with
Lloyd George and Clemenceau's note
on Fiume, **58**: 86-90; meets with Page
on Italian crisis, **58**: 210, 322; Tumulty
on, **58**: 215; speech in Rome, **58**: 237-
38,n3; Council of Four on Fiume memorandum to, **58**: 371-72, 372; issue of
publication of memorandum to, **58**:
374-75; on D'Annunizio's speech, **58**:
426-27, 450; to return to Paris, **58**: 429,
462; and claims compromise, **58**: 452-
53; reappears at Paris meeting, **58**:
499-500; at Plenary Session at Versailles, **58**: 517-18; apologizes to WW
for anti-Wilson press and speeches, **58**:
552; on tonnage in Adriatic, **59**: 50, 51,
52,53; and Smyrna, **59**: 58, 59; on Italian troops landing on coast of Asia
Minor, **59**: 223-24, 224, 226, 250-51;
absent from Council of Four meeting,
59: 286, 319; **60**: 33; on Austrian peace
treaty, **59**: 425-28, 483, 485-86; on prisoners of war, **59**: 425-28; Clemenceau,
Lloyd George, and WW discuss, **59**:
492; on Treaty of London, **59**: 503, 506-
507, 507-508; on penalties for war
criminals, **59**: 616; WW tells anecdote
to for solution of Adriatic problem, **60**:
116; on arms limitation, **60**: 175-76; on
Adriatic question and Tardieu plan,
60: 197-98, 207; WW on Fiume and **60**:
213; on articles 20 and 22 of Austrian
treaty, **60**: 219, 220; and restitution of
rolling stock, **60**: 226-27; on Klagenfurt
Basin, **60**: 267-69; seating plan for
Council of Four meetings, **60**: 285; WW
on refusal of to accept proposal on
Adriatic question, **60**: 332-33; and photograph of "Big Four," **60**: 333; on Yugoslavia's advance to Klagenfurt
Basin, **60**: 361-62; speech of Oct. 3,
1918, **60**: 445; on internal crisis in
Italy, **60**: 473-74, 481-82; resignation
of, **60**: 473,n20; **61**: 45; returns to Italy,
60: 484; Italy's concern over boundary
issue not being settled before treaty
signed, **60**: 579-809; and cabinet crisis,
61: 28; rumor of U.S. visit, **66**: 323,n3;
photographs of, *illustration sections*,
54; **61**

Ormond, Alexander Thomas, **64**: 521,n1;
67: 335,n2; WW's foreword for book of
lectures of, **67**: 349

Oroville, California, **68**: 221
Orpen, Sir William (Newenham Montague), **59**: 315,n1, 350; and WW's portrait, **60**: 249, 333, 373, 432, 489,n1; **61**: 45; **67**: 369,n5; *see also illustration section*, **60**
Orts, Pierre-Charles-Auguste-Raphaël, **54**: 373-74,n8
Osborn, William Church: poem on WW, **67**: 58-59
Osborne, Lithgow, **53**: 611,n3; **58**: 44n1
Osborne, Thomas Mott, **67**: 129; **68**: 495
Osgood, Charles Grosvenor, **66**: 280-81, 293-94; **67**: 182
Osgood, Isabella Sheldon Owen (Mrs. Charles Grosvenor), **66**: 268-69,n1,3, 293-94
Oskilko, Volodymyr (Walery Oskiltko), **59**: 262,n5, 264-65
Osler, Grace Linzee Revere Gross, Lady Osler (Mrs. William), **65**: 283,n2; WW's condolences to, **64**: 237
Osler, Revere, **65**: 283
Osler, Sir William, **58**: 616, 637; **65**: 283; death of, **64**: 237,n1
Osmena, Sergio, **60**: 200, 201
Ossinack, Andrea, **56**: 565n4; **57**: 337-43,n1
Ostend, Belgium: WW visits, **61**: 5, 6
Ostend *Le Carillon*, **61**: 6n8
Ostfriesland, S.M.S., **55**: 23, 427; **56**: 28; **58**: 127
Otani, Kikuzo, **53**: 556,n6; **55**: 401
Otchiai, Kentaro, **54**: 218,n2, 426,n1
Otranto, Straits of, **53**: 696,n2
Otranto, H.M.S., **61**: 508,n1
Otto, Oscar, **54**: 473,n1
Otto Bauer und die 'Anschlussfrage' 1918/19 (Steiner), **55**: 317n3
Ottoman-American Development Company, **68**: 504n1
Ottoman Empire, **53**: 294; and Young Turk Movement, **58**: 555n1; **65**: 115; *see also* Paris Peace Conference—Ottoman Empire
Ottoman Public Debt Organization, **59**: 396
Oulahan, Richard Victor, **54**: 60, 192; **55**: 160; **56**: 354, 551; **57**: 63n1, 417n1; **61**: 243,n11; news reports on WW's health and activities, **68**: 375-83
Our Field Marshall (Holt), **67**: 267,n1
Our Navy at War (Daniels), **68**: 69,n1
Our World, **67**: 440n1; WW on, **67**: 574; **68**: 330, 331, 334, 336, 355; and WW's essay, **68**: 345
"Outline of Tentative Report and Recommendations Prepared by the Intelligence Section in accordance with instructions for the President and the Plenipotentiaries:" *see* "Black Book"
Outlook, The, **61**: 459n1, 460
Outs Who Want To Get In: How They Are Lining Up to Get a Man to Beat Coolidge (Lowry), **68**: 476,n3
Overman, Lee Slater, **53**: 23; **54**: 397,n1, 555; **55**: 297, 298; **61**: 492; **62**: 18,
115n1, 446n5; and woman suffrage, **55**: 37; on hearings on German and Bolshevist propaganda, **55**: 297,n2; WW urges support of 19th amendment, **65**: 433; on not supporting amendment, **65**: 466-67; request from farmers' organization for hearing with WW, **66**: 224
Owen, Daisey Hester (Mrs. Robert Latham), **68**: 290,n1
Owen, Robert Latham, **53**: 134, 188; **62**: 32, 34, 431; **63**: 203; on establishing Federal Reserve Foreign Bank, **61**: 495-98, 549; on attacks against Americans in Mexico, **61**: 510; Glass on proposal of, **62**: 498-99, 501; and reservations, **64**: 49, 283, 284, 311; and vote on Lodge resolution, **64**: 63; and Oklahoma appointments, **64**: 205; **67**: 62, 70; treaty vote, **65**: 109n1; code name for, **65**: 350; votes received on 16th ballot at Democratic National Convention, 1920, **65**: 492n2; and Treaty of Berlin, **67**: 422n4; Four Power Treaty, **67**: 577n1; on French militarism, **68**: 289; WW thanks, **68**: 290
Oxford, England, **53**: 457
Oxford University, **53**: 162n1, 331n2, 530n1; **55**: 116; **57**: 128n6; **58**: 444n1; **60**: 349n1; **61**: 106n3; **62**: 220n1; WW invited to give Romanes lecture and receive honorary degree, **53**: 27-28, 66, 69, 72, 161,n1, 162,n1; WW unable to deliver Romanes Lecture, **54**: 468-69; and WW's honorary degree, **59**: 552-53,n1; WW on, **60**: 118, 119
Oxnard, California, **63**: 369

Pabst, Waldemar, **57**: 523,n13
Pacific and Far Eastern Questions, Committee on (Washington Conference), **67**: 531n1
Pacific islands, **54**: 289, 290, 291, 299, 308, 333, 348, 361, 379, 381-82, 456; **55**: 8, 50, 171; **56**: 274
Pacific Mail Steamship Company, **55**: 398n1
Pacific Telephone Company: strike, **61**: 504
Packard, Laurence Bradford, **62**: 82n2
Packard Motor Car Company, **53**: 308n1
Pact of London: *see* Treaty of London
Paderewska, Helena de Rosen (Mme. Ignace Jan Paderewski), **61**: 330
Paderewski, Ignace Jan, **53**: 105, 182, 692; **54**: 178, 179, 180n2, 189, 200, 202, 203, 204, 337, 384; **56**: 167n3, 495, 508-509; **57**: 75, 120, 245, 277,n6, 285, 352, 357, 365, 372, 406, 549, 628; **59**: 215, 216, 217, 323, 353, 354, 355, 358, 392, 445, 458,n8, 531, 555, 561; **60**: 39, 91, 99, 133, 222, 285, 287, 358, 394, 419, 428, 479, 564; **61**: 26, 47, 88, 141, 198, 208; **62**: 221; **64**: 5, 198n1; **66**: 138; **67**: 496; Bolshevik activities in Poland, **53**: 611; on situation in Poland, **54**: 32-33,n2,6; **66**: 225-27; be-

Paderewski, Ignace Jan (*cont.*)
comes Prime Minister and hopes for
U.S. recognition of Poland, **54**: 195-96;
U.S. hopes for success for, **54**: 217; WW
recognizes Poland, **54**: 278; on unrest
and invasions in Poland, **54**: 480-
81,n2; on Danzig, **57**: 152-55, 289, 290;
58: 137; Borden on, **57**: 311; meets with
Lansing on Teschen, **57**: 326, 327; and
Poland and Ukrainians, **57**: 444-45,
451, 461-63; **59**: 261-63; **60**: 160; on Poland and peace treaty, **58**: 152; on
Jews in Poland, **58**: 285, 287; makes
grand entrance at Versailles, **58**: 502,
520; on Russia, **58**: 506, 507; Gibson on
position of, **59**: 263-65; WW fears
downfall of, **59**: 356,n9; on Austria returning buildings, properties, forests
of Poland, **59**: 612-13; on Jews in Poland, **59**: 638-39; **61**: 365n1; and Council of Four, **60**: 43, 130, 156, 157-68,
554, 556; **61**: 197; on Memel, **60**: 159-
60; threatens to resign if changes made
regarding Upper Silesia, **60**: 163, 164;
on arms limitation, **60**: 172-73; and minority issue, **60**: 266, 595, 629-34;
Council of Four on memorandum on
minorities, **60**: 634; draft of Allied letter accompanying Polish minorities
treaty, **61**: 93-99; on Poland's concerns
regarding minorities treaty, **61**: 271-
75; greetings to WW, **68**: 507-508; WW
thanks, **68**: 511; photograph of, *illustration section*, 57
Padgett, Lemuel Phillips, 53: 73; 54: 281,
411, 501
Page, Alice Wilson (Mrs. Walter Hines),
53: 22, 491
Page, Carroll Smalley: meets with WW
on treaty, **61**: 548n1, 599, 600, 601;
and treaty fight, **64**: 200, 202, 337
Page, Charles R., 54: 394,n1
Page, Florence Lathrop Field (Mrs. Thomas Nelson), 53: 399, 606; 59: 517,n1;
60: 118, 135, 327,n2; **63**: 382-83,n2;
death of, 67: 307n1
Page, Katherine Alice: *see* Loring, Katherine Alice Page
Page, Logan Waller, 54: 391,n2; 55: 219
Page, Thomas Nelson, **53**: 26, 399, 589,
605, 606, 696; **55**: 493; **58**: 398; **59**: 79,
174, 246; **60**: 118, 192, 492n1; **61**: 9; **63**:
382-83,n1; on WW visiting Benedict
XV, **53**: 242; on Italy and her territorial
claims, **53**: 494-96, 637-38, 639-41,
641-44, 711; **59**: 601-602; on Italian
situation and Adriatic question, **54**:
134-35; **60**: 176; retirement of, **54**: 274,
56: 280; **58**: 448-49; on situation in
Italy and peace prospects, **55**: 83-86; on
growing opposition to WW and League
of Nations plan, **56**: 64-66; on Italian
press, **56**: 392-94; on political situation
in Rome and Italy's Adriatic claims,
57: 434-37; **58**: 321, 322, 357, 358-59,
369, 413-15, 452-53, 529; on France's

reaction to WW's Adriatic statement,
58: 91; reaction in Rome to WW's Adriatic statement causes press attacks on
WW, **58**: 91-92, 93, 143-44, 238-40,
271-72; on meeting with Orlando on
crisis, **58**: 210-11; **61**: 28; on reopening
Adriatic negotiations, **58**: 358; on
Italy's reaction to invitation to Austria
and Hungary to come to Paris, **58**: 415;
meets with Orlando on D'Annunzio's
speech, **58**: 426-27; goes to Paris to see
WW on Italian situation, **58**: 529,
554,n1, 601; **59**: 46, 517; on Barrère,
59: 47; requests leave, **60**: 135; offers to
stay on if needed, **60**: 327-28; on internal crisis in Italy and anti-Wilson
forces in Senate, **60**: 531; WW on selection of new ambassador to Italy, **60**:
566; wishes to see WW on Italian cabinet situation, **61**: 77; resignation of, **61**:
177, 559-60; **62**: 561; on choice for
Italy's ambassador to U.S., **66**: 339-
40,n4; WW's condolences to, **67**: 307
Page, Walter Hines: illness of, **53**: 22,
189; **68**: 259,n2; on WW going to Europe, **53**: 189; resignation of, **53**: 203-
204; death of, **53**: 491,n1, 514; memorial service for and WW's tribute to, **57**:
469, 509; **67**: 130, 242
Paget, Sir Arthur (Henry Fitzroy), **58**:
534n2
Paget, Mary Fiske Stevens, Lady Paget,
58: 534n2; **59**: 68,n1
Pag Island: *see* Pago
Pago (now Pag), Yugoslavia, **57**: 551,
612; **58**: 14, 81, 358, 450, 452; **59**: 83n3,
557, 559, 569; **60**: 308
Painful Loss of Interest (New York
World), **67**: 355,n6
Painlevé, Paul, **58**: 562; **59**: 334
Paish, Sir George, **53**: 514,n1, 717; **62**:
254,n1; on Great Britain, the peace
treaty, and praise of WW, **62**: 256
Palace Theatre (Paris), **57**: 533,n4
Palais Bourbon, **54**: 464n1; EBW's description of, **54**: 487-88
Palestine, **53**: 543, 562, 572, 577; **54**: 52,
225, 231, 258, 360, 455, 508; **55**: 7, 611;
56: 107, 109, 110, 117, 272, 273, 310;
57: 326,n3, 443; **58**: 325, 400, 401,
491n1; **59**: 330, 333, 412, 413; **61**: 128,
442n1; **62**: 427, 609n1; **64**: 26, 358,
449; **65**: 65, 91, 114, 271n1; **68**: 100n2;
as issue for peace conference, **55**: 381-
85; WW on, **55**: 386; **57**: 406,n2; Jastrow on, **55**: 438,n3; Balfour on, **56**:
203-204; Frankfurter on, **58**: 555-56;
and mandates, **59**: 476; **66**: 395, 396;
and King-Crane Commission, **61**: 443;
62: 607; and oil, **62**: 619; Britain
awarded mandate for, **65**: 248,n1,
334,n1; Lloyd George on, **66**: 48
Palfrey, John Carver, **63**: 624,n1
Pallanza, Italy, **65**: 303,n10
Palmer, Alexander Mitchell, **55**: 338,
482-83; **56**: 310, 618; **57**: 281; **58**: 420;

59: 320; **61**: 291, 437; **62**: 94, 98, 159, 169, 200, 536, 555, 630; **64**: 112, 193, 269, 428; **65**: 24, 212, 425, 441; **66**: 117-18, 380; **67**: 214, 617; **68**: 380, 581; and Busch case, **53**: 141-42; and disposition of alien property, **53**: 147-48, 165, 197-98, 214-15,n1, 432; appointed Attorney General, **54**: 31-32, 52, 125, 410, 429,n1, 485; **55**: 36, 193, 206, 263-64, 276, 294, 339, 412; on Rutherford case, **56**: 345-46; on Debs case, **56**: 618; **62**: 58, 126, 250, 261-62, 422; **65**: 24, 212, 425, 441; **66**: 25; **67**: 98-107, 157; review of convictions under Espionage Act, **56**: 619; and controversy between Industrial Board and Railroad Administration, **59**: 38n1; bombings threaten life of, **60**: 114-15,n2, 153; WW thankful for safety of, **60**: 145; and amnesty issue, **61**: 351, 352; **66**: 120,n1; and prohibition, **61**: 351, 352, 368-69, 423; on General Leasing bill controversy, **61**: 534-35,n1; and memorandum on high cost of living, **62**: 171-80, 197-98; and oil relief legislation, **62**: 292-300, 438; memorandum for WW's statement on railroad wage situation, **62**: 462-65; on Caldwell case, **62**: 465, 530; and Volstead bill, **63**: 590, 601n1; and coal strike, **63**: 598, 608,n1, 612n1; **64**: 141, 142-45, 145, 166, 179, 206n1; on rumors about WW's health, **63**: 608; on sedition, **64**: 81,n5; and WW's coal statement, **64**: 154n1, 154-55; WW's inquiry on possibility of referendum on League, **64**: 202-203; on proposed Talcott appointment, **64**: 215-16, 322n1; and railroad crisis and return of ownership, **64**: 222-23; and revision of first draft of Jackson Day message, **64**: 249n1; on WW not seeking reelection, **64**: 267; on judicial appointments and age factor, **64**: 296-97; talk of as presidential candidate, **64**: 347; visits House, **64**: 347; refuses to appeal oil case, **64**: 354-55; on Democratic primary in Georgia, **65**: 145, 219-20; and "raids" and deportations, **65**: 187,n5,6; on WW's health and appearance, **65**: 188; urges meeting of Railroad Labor Board, **65**: 192-93; opposes general amnesty, **65**: 194, 203-11; on E. B. Parker's appointment, **65**: 214, 218-19; Grayson on, **65**: 242; religious reasons for refusing secretaryship of war, **65**: 242; presidential candidate, **65**: 291, 346, 349, 435, 440, 480; code name for, **65**: 350; opinion on budget bill, **65**: 358, 361-62; Geddes on, **65**: 371; on Coughlin kidnapping, **65**: 431; and balloting at Democratic National convention, 1920, **65**: 491, 492n2, 499n1; on price-fixing for coal, **65**: 563-64, 567; and coal prices, **66**: 4; WW inquires if President has powers of magistrate and reply of, **66**: 103, 115-17; on Chitwood

appointment in Virginia, **66**: 167, 172-73,n1; on Stokes case, **66**: 176-77, 184; and Josephine Berry, **66**: 229; and charges of Creel being trailed in Mexico, **66**: 321, 337; on Tennessee judgeship, **66**: 386,n1; and Section 10 of Clayton Act, **67**: 12n1; and Wisconsin judgeship, **67**: 14, 22; on proposed Oklahoma appointments, **67**: 62, 70; Cabinet farewell, **67**: 199; WW's condolences to, **67**: 506; and Chemical Foundation case, **68**: 298-301, 303, 303-304; R. S. Baker willing to assist in research for case, **68**: 312, 317, 356; WW thanks Baker for assisting, **68**: 316, 317

Palmer, Bradley Webster, **58**: 119,n1, 121, 423, 424, 550; **60**: 57-58,n6, 608; **62**: 12,n2, 186

Palmer, Frederick, **54**: 522n1; **67**: 527n4; **68**: 446

Palmer "raids," **65**: 187,n5, 188

Palmer, Roberta Bartlett Dixon (Mrs. Alexander Mitchell): death of, **67**: 506,n1

Palmerston, John Henry Temple, Viscount, **55**: 383n2

Palmstierna, Baron Erik Kule, **65**: 40,n1

Pan African Congress, **54**: 126,n1

Panama, **54**: 65, 115; **58**: 198; **61**: 295n1, 299n4; **67**: 220; Harding's proposed trip to, **66**: 317-18,n1, 324, 332-33; Colby on possibility of visiting, **66**: 430; and Costa Rican boundary dispute, **67**: 382-84,n5, 385; and Colombia, **67**: 581n2

Panama Canal, **57**: 397; **58**: 123; **66**: 317n1; tolls controversy, **60**: 535; **66**: 141,n1, 177-78; N. D. Baker on, **62**: 8, 9; and Borah, **67**: 424n1

Panama Canal Tolls Act: Cobb on WW's repeal of, **67**: 220

Panama Canal Zone: Prince of Wales on, **65**: 226; Baker on transport service to, **65**: 278, 280-81, 282

Panama News Letter, **66**: 152n1

Panama Railroad Corporation, **54**: 432; **65**: 282; and steamship business of, **62**: 8-10, 97; **66**: 465

Pan-American Conference of Women: demonstration before WW's home, **68**: 36-39,n1; photograph of, *illustration section*, **68**

Pan American Financial Conference, Second, **64**: 307; and Costa Rica, **64**: 230, 245

Pan American Federation of Labor: on the Dominican Republic, **66**: 537-38, 538n1, 539; **67**: 73, 78, 86

Pan-American Pact, **59**: 521-22,n2; **62**: 403,n43

Pan-American Petroleum Company, **63**: 552n1

Pan-American Union: new director named, **65**: 233-34; postponement of conference, **65**: 252-53, 261; Rowe thanks WW for his support, **65**: 270

Paneyko, Vasil (Basil Paneiko), **58**: 506,n5; **59**: 351-53, 512,n1
Panjdeh incident: *see* Penjdeh incident
Pan-Pontic Congress, **66**: 29n1
Pantano, Edoardo, **61**: 109,n8
Pan-Touranianism, **65**: 306,n3
Pao-yu T'ang (Mme. Vi Kyuin Wellington Koo), **57**: 632,n1
paper industry: Colby on Canadian embargo and, **66**: 113-14
Papers Concerning the German Peace Treaty, **62**: 209n
Papers of Smedley Darlington Butler, USMC, 1915-1918 (Venzon), **66**: 82,n1
Papers of Thomas Jeffereson (Cullen, ed.), **67**: 163n3
Paracelsus (Browning), **66**: 267n3
Paraguay, **56**: 170n1; **58**: 198; **65**: 102
Paraskevopoulos, Leonidas, **54**: 403,n2
Parc Monceau, Paris, **53**: 430
Pardee, Allena Gilbert, **68**: 154,n1
Pardo y Barreda, José, **53**: 317,n4, 342
Parenzo, Italy, **53**: 445
Pariani, Alberto, **61**: 52,n3, 92,n3
Paris, France, **53**: 57, 143, 328-32; plans for WW's arrival in, **53**: 344-45, 346, 359, 372, 391; WW's arrival reception, activities and speeches in, **53**: 382-84, 384-85, 386-87, 389-91, 391-92, 396, 398, 399, 403-404, 405, 410, 417-18, 421, 439, 458-60, 461-63, 467, 488; WW and socialist delegation in, **53**: 344-45, 359, 387-88,n1; WW made honorary citizen of, **53**: 403, 499; and international labor conference, **53**: 466, 490; WW returns to, **53**: 570; mentioned as seat for League of Nations, **57**: 224; May Day celebration in, **58**: 274-75, 276; Balfour on, **60**: 204; crowds await news of treaty acceptance or rejection, **61**: 78-79; excitement in over news Germany will sign, **61**: 135; celebrations in after signing of peace treaty, **61**: 327-28; photograph of, *illustration section*, **53**
Paris, Treaty of (1815), **53**: 296
Paris, University of, **53**: 485n1; **54**: 218n2; **55**: 241n1; **57**: 36, 513n1; **59**: 4n1; WW receives honorary degree from, **53**: 345, 458, 459,n1, 459-61, 461-63, 484,n5, 500
Paris *Continental Daily Mail*, **58**: 4n6
Paris *Daily Mail*, **53**: 722
Paris *France-Italie*, **58**: 380n4, 282, 357
Paris *Herald*, **55**: 120
Paris *L'Humanité*, **53**: 345n1, 718, 722, 723; **54**: 227n2; **64**: 99n5; **56**: 386; **58**: 97; **60**: 118n; **68**: 200
Paris *L'Illustration*, **67**: 24
Paris *La Lanterne L'Oeuvre*, **58**: 97
Paris *La Liberté*, **57**: 353, 391
Paris *La Libre Parole*, **56**: 3n1
Paris *La Victoire*, **58**: 539n4
Paris *L'Echo de Paris*, **56**: 125; **57**: 353, 391, 505-506; **58**: 97, 103
Paris *Le Figaro*, **57**: 353, 391; **58**: 97
Paris *Le Gaulois*, **53**: 446n; **58**: 97

Paris *Le Journal*, **53**: 446n1; **56**: 150; **57**: 63n1, 303; **58**: 97
Paris *Journal des Débats*, **60**: 575, 644; **65**: 41n3
Paris *L'Illustration*, **65**: 542-43n1,2
Paris *Le Matin*, **57**: 63n1, 148n2, 354; **58**: 97,n1, 473, 474; **60**: 599; **61**: 141; **64**: 341; **65**: 452,n2
Paris *Le Petit Journal*, **57**: 353, 391; **58**: 97
Paris *Le Populaire*, **58**: 97
Paris *Le Temps*, **53**: 379n1, 380n; **56**: 62n4, 150, 317n1, 428n2; **57**: 63n1, 353, 391; **58**: 142, 393,n4, 450; **59**: 4n1, 34, 334, 344
Paris *Oeuvre*, **53**: 446n1; **56**: 3n1

THE PARIS PEACE CONFERENCE

R. S. Baker on importance of having events at recorded from American view, **66**: 521, 521-23, 537,n1; comments on WW's ordeal at, **67**: 15-16,n1, 40,n4, 44, 69, 82, 94, 239, 489-90; R. S. Baker works on book on, **67**: 71-72, 360-61, 489-90, 560; R. S. Baker organizes WW's documents from, **67**: 89-90; House's role during, **67**: 129-30, 239; WW will not write history of, **67**: 158; Cobb on WW's partisan mistake, **67**: 227; and digest of discussions at, **67**: 447, 456, 459-61; Bliss on, **68**: 224-26

preliminaries: House-WW exchange, **53**: 3, 25-26, 43n1, 84-85, 101; site discussed, **53**: 4, 32, 67, 143; comments on reparations, **53**: 38, 181, 351, 353, 563, 707-708; delays in start, **53**: 44, 359, 369, 499, 698; and official language, **53**: 87, 143, 160, 190, 226, 564; **54**: 68-70; Pittman on, **53**: 50, 51; House's plan for intelligence, security, and counter-intelligence organization, **53**: 56-58; WW's decision to attend, **53**: 65, 66, 71-72, 85, 93-94, 96-97,103-104, 108-109, 114, 115, 116, 120, 127-28, 130, 134, 150, 157-58, 213, 242, 284-85, 308n1, 310, 314n4, 323,n1, 400-401, 409, 414, 425-26; **55**: 408-409; French Foreign Office's protocol for, **53**: 86-93; Furuseth on Seamen's Act and, **53**: 107-108, 114; WW on eastern European Jews, **53**: 141; censorship and news coverage plans, **53**: 148, 411, 575; **54**: 24-25,n14,15, 64-68, 96-99,n2, 108-14, 121-22, 191-92; Rappard on neutrals and, **53**: 209-12; and Du Bois on Africa and, **53**: 236-38; meetings in London, **53**: 252, 324-27, 336-37, 341; and international labor conference, **53**: 257, 286; France on procedure of, **53**: 295-96; Navy General Board's recommendations, **53**: 312n1; WW informs The Inquiry of his views on, **53**: 350-52; House on, **53**: 400-402; and labor, **53**: 402, 535-36; and foreign loans, **53**: 441-42, 473; and financial and treasury is-

sues, **53**: 473-74, 626-27, 627; recommendations to coordinate Inter-Allied Councils with, **53**: 645-46; Bliss' concern over American delegation's unpreparedness, **53**: 719-21

commissioners: **54**: 55, 134-35, 304; **56**: 392; **58**: 494, 520; **59**: 35-37, 286-87, 406-409; **60**: 375; **62**: 219,n2; suggestions for and discussion of number of, **53**: 25, 26, 72, 86, 101, 109, 142, 159-60, 165, 183, 185, 190, 196, 199, 206, 216, 226, 254, 295; and Bryan, **53**: 73, 98, 141; Day declines, **53**: 78; suggestion of woman delegate, **53**: 114-15, 125-26, 129, 216-17; WW on not appointing T. Roosevelt, **53**: 117; requests for labor representative, **53**: 118-19, 119, 155-56, 408; H. White appointed, **53**: 147,n1; U. S. commissioners announced, **53**: 243; WW on Republicans and, **53**: 243-44; Bliss as, **53**: 300; **54**: 84-88; **55**: 404, 511; McAdoo's wish to be commissioner, **53**: 468-69; commissioners wish to know status of advisers not assigned to peace commission, **53**: 572-73; WW meets with, **54**: 3-4; **57**: 51, 52, 53; **58**: 430; T. N. Page and, **54**: 134-35; **56**: 143-44, 452-55, 554,n1; on principles of reparation, **55**: 29-34; and issue of League of Nations being separate from peace treaty, **55**: 305,n1; and Moton, **55**: 335; WW on not keeping the League of Nations to the fore, **55**: 498, 531; talk of "preliminary treaty" dropped, **55**: 531; House on, **56**: 208; on Russian policy, **56**: 466-68; on rights of national minorities, **56**: 511-12; recommend Austria present her case in Paris, **58**: 205; upset by Page's decision to come to Paris, **58**: 554,n1; Polk to, **58**: 494; **59**: 72-74, 573; Lansing and R. S. Baker on, **59**: 285; Westermann on Near East issues, **61**: 128-29; issue of departure of U.S. representatives, **64**: 66-68, 87, 100-102, 117-18, 119; photograph of, *illustration section*, **53**

Adriatic Question: *see* Italy

Anatolia: *see* Italy

Armenia and Armenians: *see* mandates

arms limitation, **53**: 517, 559, 657, 667-68, 679-80; **54**: 140, 189,n5, 218-21, 226, 238-46, 264, 402, 427-28, 451, 510, 512; **55**: 11-16, 20, 112, 116, 268-69, 270-71, 275, 404-406, 426-32, 512-15, 516, 521, 539; **56**: 157, 177; **58**: 7, 154, 191, **64**: 60, 281; Council of Ten on, **54**: 218-21; and Fontainebleau Memorandum, **56**: 263-64, 268; Daniels on sinking of German fleet, **56**: 430; **57**: 347; and League of Nations, **57**: 226; Bliss on disposal of surplus arms, **57**: 496-98; Council of Four on, **59**: 429-32, 439-40; **60**: 131-34, 168-76, 464; and Russia, **59**: 442; Germany on,

58: 581; **60**: 235-37, 473,n16; and Germany and League of Nations, **60**: 272-73, 275, 460; WW on, **61**: 419-20; League of Free Nations Association on, **61**: 447-48; House on, **62**: 62; and disposal of German and Austro-Hungarian ships, **62**: 187; Houston on, **62**: 269; and Lodge reservations, **64**: 294

Asia Minor: *see* Italy

Assling and Assling Triangle: *see* Italy

Austria: *see* Austrian Treaty

Bessarabia: *see* Rumania

Bohemia: *see* Czechoslovakia

Bulgaria: and reparations, **59**: 422; fixed military strength for, **59**: 428-29; and credit plans for, **60**: 26n11; and issue of western Thrace and Greece, **61**: 566-69, 589-93, 624

Carinthia: *see* Yugoslavia

Caucasus: *see* Turkey

China at the peace conference: *see* China, China and the United States, Japan, Shantung controversy and settlement

Commission on Rumanian and Yugoslav Affairs, **59**: 404,n7, 405, 406, 406-408,n1; **61**: 50-56, 57-59

Commission on the International Control of Ports, Waterways and Railways, **55**: 110; **59**: 93

Commission on the Responsibility of the Authors of the War and on Enforcement of Penalties, **56**: 530,n3,4, 611-17; **57**: 22,n4, 132-33,n1,2, 139, 140, 146n4, 149, 405, 631; **58**: 277-78, 295-96, 416, 544, 578,n10; **59**: 130-31, 275, 275,276; **60**: 468, 475-76; **61**: 335; Smuts on clauses in peace treaty on, **59**: 416; Brockdorff-Rantzau on responsibilities, **59**: 488-92; Council of Four on civil versus military law, **59**: 614

Committee on New States, **60**: 577; **61**: 46, 47-50; on League of Nations and minority rights and method of appeal, **60**: 205-206, 221-22, 223-25, 623, 624; Hudson on U.S. not now being party to additional treaties with new states, **60**: 607-608; Paderewski memorandum on Poland and minority issue, **60**: 623, 629-34; recommended changes in Polish treaty, **61**: 26-27

Committee on the Eastern Frontiers of Germany, **60**: 522, 548; report of, **60**: 411-15, 415-18; Council of Four on report of, **60**: 221-22, 521-22

Constantinople: see *mandates*

Council of Five: *see* Council of Foreign Ministers

Council of Foreign Ministers, **56**: 347; **57**: 73, 400-405,n1; **61**: 485; **62**: 14, 22; establishes Rhineland Commission,

Paris Peace Conference (*cont.*)
59: 280n1; and Bulgaria's frontiers, 61: 588-93; R. S. Baker on minutes of on chemical and dyestuffs issue, 68: 357-58,n1

Council of Four, 56: 436-37; 57: 67, 73-79, 101-17, 120-30, 149-55, 161-66, 242-47, 288-92, 355-64, 391-98, 400-405, 450-56; 58: 14-24, 57-67, 113-19, 122-28, 129-35, 148-53, 177-83, 216-27, 235-37, 248-57, 257-61, 263-67, 277-96, 311-16, 333-41, 342-45, 432-42, 464-82, 483-88, 504-10, 510-13, 536-48, 571-84; 59: 11-13, 28-33, 48-55, 57-60, 84-94, 130-36, 136-48, 162-65, 165-70, 212-23, 255-68, 265-76, 297-309, 309-12, 322-46, 376-80, 380-82, 385, 386-91, 433-42, 455-60, 461-70, 481-92, 495-96, 496-512, 532-33, 534-38, 538-41, 542-46, 564-68, 568-71, 584-94, 613-16, 631-33, 634-37; 60: 22-33, 84-99, 130-35, 206-13, 218-25, 225-29, 261-75, 311-21, 335-43, 343-51, 351-58, 389-99, 420-29, 436-62, 462-65, 466-76, 477-82, 494-98, 498-503, 511-18, 518-23, 527-30, 556-64, 576-82, 582, 591-93, 593-98, 598-601, 623-40; on Syria and Turkey, 56: 104-19,n1; WW on issues to be addressed, 56: 208-209; on League of Nations being part of peace treaty, 56: 249-50; on Bolshevik question, 56: 252-57, 325-30; Grayson on meetings of, 56: 312-13, 347, 490, 522; and Haller's Army, 56: 408-13, 495-97, 525-28; 57: 74-75, 549-50; 58: 20-21; and Smuts mission to Hungary, 56: 413-17, 458-64, 465; and revictualing of Bavaria, 56: 497-98; on Polish-Ukrainian controversy, 56: 529-30,n2; 57: 415-16; 59: 215-17, 323-25, 350-60, 392-93, 531-32, 541-42; 60: 470-71, 479; House on note taking at, 56: 540; R. S. Baker on meeting and personalities, 56: 577, 578; Bliss on Hungarian situaion and, 56: 583; WW absent from, 56: 585-87; 57: 4; on frontier between Bohemia and Germany, 56: 597-98; and Belgian claims, 56: 589-97; 57: 392-97; House's comments on, 57: 34-36, 53, 71-72; and question of unanimity, 57: 82; talk of inviting Germany to peace conference, 57: 102-103, 318-25; on issue of Germany not signing peace treaty, 57: 104,n5; 59: 6-11; 60: 95-96; list of subjects for consideration by, 57: 109-13; first united decision of, 57: 146,n4; on Russian relief, 57: 165,440; on German debts and reparation, 57: 165-66, 293-95; issue of publishing peace treaty, 57: 288-89, 291-92, 357; 58: 22-24, 61-63, 439-40; 59: 58; 60: 466, 477; criticism of secret sessions, 57: 301-302, 312; on settling Italian claims before inviting Germany, 57: 318-25; invitation to Germany to attend peace conference, 57: 349-50; on Luxembourg, 57: 355-56; on Schleswig, 57: 363-64; Balfour report on, 57: 398-99; on Germany's revealing process for lethal gas, 57: 402-404; talk of secretary for meetings of, 57: 467, 477,n1; and Italian claims, 57: 479-94, 512-13, 514-20, 527, 545-49, 551-53, 610-14; and Japanese claims, 57: 553-56, 599-610; and Chinese claims, 57: 615-26; on blockade, 58: 20, 290; 59: 128-30; 60: 495-97, 498-500; 61: 151-52; on Persia, 58: 21-22; on Plenary Session to discuss League of Nations Covenant, 58: 22; on duration of economic clauses, 58: 114-19, 121; on Kiel Canal 58: 122-25; on destruction of German surface ships and submarines, 58: 125-28, 226-27, 289-90, 547, 548; 61: 83-84, 123-27, 140-48; on language used for peace treaty, 58: 129; on guarantees of execution of peace treaty, 58: 134-35; on recognition of Yugoslavia, 58: 150; 59: 634, 635; on time given to Germany to make observations on peace treaty, 58: 151, 152; and Drafting Committee, 58: 153-54; on recognition of Finland, 58: 177-78; on prisoners of war, 58: 235, 260-61; 59: 131-32, 134-35, 162-63, 163-65, 272-73; 61: 338-39; on taking hostages for breaches of laws of war, 58: 235-36; on Italy's absence from peace conference, 58: 250-52, 279-82; on liability of successor states for Austro-Hungarian war debt, 58: 252-53; 61: 254-56; on presence of journalists at Plenary Session with Germany, 58: 253-54; and draft of articles on China, 58: 255-57, 261; on inviting Austria and Hungary to Paris, 58: 264-65, 315-16; on Russian situation, 58: 265-66, 506-507, 573-78; 59: 29-31, 225, 300-304; on protection of Jews and minorities, 58: 284-86, 287-88, 383-90; 59: 218-21,n7; on postwar occupation of Germany, 58: 288, 566-68; 59: 326-46; 60: 464-65; to inform Italy of meeting with Germans, 58: 312-13; on Armistice and Article 46 of treaty, 58: 313-14, 315; on Italy and violation of Treaty of London, 58: 333-41, 368-78, 393-403; on presentation of treaty to Germany, 58: 433-34, 478-79, 505-506; on French security treaty, 58: 486-88; on not replying to Brockdorff-Rantzau's speech, 58: 536-37; on frontiers, 58: 537-38, 539-44; Supreme Economic Council presents problems to, 58: 563-66; on Germany's objections to peace treaty, 59: 12,n5; hears Chaikovskii on Russian situation, 59: 14-21; on labor issue, 59: 48-50, 222-23; on German counterproposals, 59: 95-96; 60: 374,n1, 394-404, 406-11, 436-37, 467, 477-78, 548-50; McCor-

mick on harmony of "Big Four," **59**: 128; and Balfour memorandum on Italy and Turkey in Anatolia, **59**: 208-12; to be called Council of the Principal Allied and Associated Powers, **59**: 217, 223; on Italian and Greek landings on coast of Asia Minor, **59**: 223-25, 225-26; on Brockdorff-Rantzau's views and reply to, **59**: 271-72, 304,n12, 370-71, 458-60, 580-84; on reply to German note on economic effect of peace treaty,**59**: 297-98, 307-308, 309, 360-66; and Soninno-Vénisélos incident, **59**: 319; on blockade of Poland, **59**: 359-60, 392-93; on two reparation commissions, **59**: 387-88; study maps on "all fours," **59**: 420, 647-48; draft and final dispatch to Kolchak, and reply, **59**: 440-42, 461-64, 481, 543-46; **60**: 228-29, 419; and Kolchak government, **59**: 465; on Baltic provinces, **59**: 466-68,n4,5,6; **60**: 497-98, 500; **61**: 86-88, 153-54; and Italy's insistence on Treaty of London, **59**: 478, 479, 503-509; on China's request for minutes on Shantung-Kiaochow issue, **59**: 568-69; on whether to make substantial changes in treaty, **59**: 622-23; Lloyd George and Clemenceau on positions on German treaty, **60**: 22-23; on Orlando's absence, **60**: 33; on Polish issues and Upper Silesia, **60**: 84-92; on Germany's membership in League of Nations, **60**: 94-95; on reservations of Serbian and Rumanian delegates, **60**: 97,n8; on Czechoslovakia's proposed amendments to Austrian treaty, **60**: 97-98,n9; Paderewski on Upper Silesia and Polish situation, **60**: 156, 157-59; on having conversations with Germany to facilitate signing of peace treaty, **60**: 263; on German and Estonian attack on Petrograd, **60**: 267, 269-70; seating plan for, **60**: 285; and Italy's reply to Adriatic proposal, **60**: 308-11; on conflicts between Hungary, Yugolsavia, and Rumania, **60**: 312-14,n1, 315-16; on Rhineland army of occupation, **60**: 343, 350-51; on Czechoslovakia's, Hungary's, and Rumania's borders, **60**: 351-57, 418-19, 469-70,n11, 478-79, 529-30,595-96; on plebiscite for Upper Silesia, **60**: 404-406, 411-15, 415-18, 421-27, 553-56; on German colonies, **60**: 471,n12,13, 472, 479-80; and Article 325 akin to "dumping," **60**: 520; on issue concerning Belgium and Czechoslovakia and construction of railroad lines, **60**: 550-52; on Foch's plan for march on Berlin, **60**: 583-91, 617-18, 619-21; on religious missions, **60**: 594-95; on changed attitude of Foch, **60**: 598-601; on minority issue in Poland, **60**: 623; **61**: 82-92, 271-75, 634-36; on Bolsheviks and blockade of Poland, **60**: 624-26; impact of blockade on Czechoslovakia and Poland, **60**: 626-27; on issue of blockade of Bolshevik Russia and Hungary, **60**: 636-38, 639; reply to Germany's note on two reservations concerning treaty, **61**: 70-71, 72-76, 76-77; on Germany's request for time extension, **61**: 78-79, 79-81; **61**: 88-92; and China's reservations on peace treaty, **61**: 155; on The Netherlands, William II, and responsibility issue, **61**: 194-95, 204-205, 258-59, 334-35; on Poland if threatened by Germans, **61**: 208-209; and French security treaty, **61**: 280-82; on dealing with Italy, **61**: 307-308, 309-10; and continuing role of Supreme Economic Council, **61**: 314-16; on whether to supply notes of meetings to others, **61**: 335-38; meeting at Versailles on draft of Allied warning to Italy, **61**: 342-46; and Scapa Flow incident, **62**: 144,n1; WW on, **63**: 99, 343; Bullitt on, **63**: 337n1; R. S. Baker organizes minutes of, **67**: 90; and Yap, **67**: 155; and House, **67**: 239; Dodd on minutes of, **67**: 467; successor to, **68**: 135n1; R. S. Baker on minutes of on chemical and dyestuffs issue, **68**: 357-58,n1

Council of Ten, **54**: 7n1; **55**: 83n1, 104, 140-48, 202n1, 230, 458n1; **56**: 97; **57**: 301, 561; **59**: 48, 529, 530; meetings of, **54**: 12-26,n1, 43-50, 64-70, 70-76, 96-104, 108-15, 115-21, 155-56, 179-81, 181-89, 204-11, 218-26, 247-48, 248-54, 283-91, 291-301, 310-18, 318-31, 334-41, 341-45, 350-61, 361-78, 415-25, 461-63, 490-93, 505-509; **61**: 339; on procedure and representation of Paris Peace Conference, **54**: 12-26, 43-50, 64-68; and official language, **54**: 68-74; and publicity and the press, **54**: 74-76, 96-99, 108-14; **56**: 148-52; and Bolshevik question, **54**: 99-104, 155-56, 179-81, 181-88, 204-205, 415-16; comments about WW at meetings of, **54**: 106n1; drafting of agenda for Paris Peace Conference, **54**: 115, 115-21; and League of Nations, **54**: 206-10, 222-26; territorial and colonial questions, **54**: 223-25, 249-54, 293-301, 310-11, 318-31, 350-61, 361-78; and Allied Commission to Poland, **54**: 248-49, 334-41, 341-45, 418-20; on formation of Supreme Economic Council, **54**: 284-86; question of recognition of Finland, **54**: 287-88; Seymour's observations and impressions of, **54**: 382-85; and Rumania's territorial claims, **54**: 421-25; on appointment of various committees, **54**: 461-63; and Greece, **54**: 463, 473n1; and Czechoslovakia's territorial claims, **54**: 490-93; Prince Faisal presents Arab claims to, **54**: 505-509; and proposal on women, **55**: 145-47; on Polish boundaries, **56**: 88-

Paris Peace Conference (*cont.*)
95, 127,n1, 165-67; on passage of
Haller's troops, **56**: 167-69,n3, 209n2;
on submarine cables, **56**: 209-20; **58**:
298-306, 345-53; disbanded, **56**: 205;
on frontiers of Austria and Hungary,
59: 60-64; McCormick on, **59**: 448-49;
reconvening of, **60**: 612; on Turkish
delegates' presentation, **60**: 615-17; to
continue work of Paris Peace Conference, **61**: 277; Bullitt on, **63**: 337n1;
and Greece, **64**: 163

Czechoslovakia, **54**: 345; **55**: 29n2, 164,
184, 243; **56**: 26, 442, 512; **57**: 111, 238,
245, 290, 327, 368, 484, 485, 497,
539n3, 549; **58**: 39, 198, 279, 472, 509;
59: 166, 167, 169, 215; **60**: 133, 134,n7,
146, 226, 607,n3; **61**: 430, 445; delegates to Paris Peace Conference, **54**:
65, 344,n4; **59**: 8, 33, 131, 536, 632n4;
and Russia, **54**: 84, 101, 153, 412; and
Teschen, **54**: 339-40, 343-45, 374, 375,
382, 384, 388, 416-17,n3; **56**: 220-
22,n9; **59**: 218; and League of Nations,
54: 462, 482, 496, 509; Beneš on territorial claims of, **54**: 490-93; and minorities, **55**: 371, 380; **58**: 284, 287, 291,
384, 388; **59**: 515, 516n1, 629-30; WW
appoints minister to, **56**: 122-23,n1;
57: 95,n1, 334, 374; and Hungarian
revolution, **56**: 239, 333-34; Lammasch
on future of, **56**: 257n1; and Fiume, **56**:
570; and boundaries, **56**: 586-87,n1;
59: 63; **60**: 418-19,n6, 427-28, 462, 469-
70,n11, 478, 479, 498; Smuts on, **57**:
171-73; and France and militarism in,
57: 279-80; Keynes on economic rehabilitation of, **58**: 12; Council of Four on
inclusion of as belligerent, **58**: 151;
Kerner on, **58**: 157-58; articles on recognition, **58**: 388; and food relief, **59**:
174; finances and reparations, **59**: 176,
384n1, 538, 539; and Polish-Ukrainian
situation, **59**: 323, 324-25; and prisoners of war, **59**: 425, 426; and military
strength, **59**: 428-32, 439; on title of
Austrian delegation, **59**: 588; Italy on
recognition of, **59**: 631-32; Seymour on
Upper Silesia and, **60**: 139; and arms
limitation, **60**: 171-72; Hungarian hostilities against, **60**: 256-58, 259-60,
264, 264-65,n12, 299-300, 351-57, 594,
595; Hungary's reply on attacks on, **60**:
312-14,n1, 315-16, 596-98; Bliss on
stopping aid to, **60**: 363; and Ratibor,
60: 417, 427, 468, 480; and Leobschutz,
60: 468, 480; Council of Four defines
boundaries and demands hostilities
stop, **60**: 522,n19, 529; and articles
concerning construction of railroad
lines, **60**: 551-52, 561; Clemenceau on
military ability of, **60**: 586-87; Stevens
on need for Allied troops to relieve
Czechs in Russia, **60**: 608, 609; and
issue of blockade, **60**: 626, 627, 638-39;

and war-cost contributions, **61**: 101,
254-56; University of Prague confers
honorary degree on WW, **61**: 136-37;
and Sudbhan, **61**: 280, 317-21

Bohemia, **53**: 8, 56, 224, 296; **54**:
343, 491, 492-93; **55**: 317, 423; **56**: 240,
257n1, 478, 479; **57**: 78, 155, 245, 290,
291-92, 359, 454-55, 549, 632; **58**: 6,
287; **59**: 63, 498, 637; **60**: 171, 172, 357,
528; **61**: 371, 430; **62**: 25; **63**: 10, 11, 24,
82, 186; and Fontainebleau Memoran-
dum, **56**: 266; American commissioners on rights of national minorities in,
56: 511-12; frontiers discussed at
Council of Four, **56**: 597-98; and Poland and Teschen, **57**: 326-27; and reparations, **59**: 387, 538; and Czech
troops in Siberia, **61**: 201, 202

Slovakia, **54**: 491; **55**: 87-88; **56**: 566;
57: 613; **58**: 150, 160, 162; **59**: 380, 404,
408, 542, 543; **60**: 34-38, 122-29, 207-
208, 214

Sudetenland, **61**: 172, 371,n2
Teschen: see Poland

Dalmatia and Dalmatian Coast: see
Italy

Danzig: see Poland

Dodecanese Islands: see Italy

East Prussia: see Germany

Estonia and Estonians, **56**: 35, 468; **57**:
137-38, 392, 398; **58**: 42, 403, 594-95;
59: 16,n7, 17-18, 300n8, 303, 442, 465,
466n6, 545, 563; **60**: 134n9, 282,
474,n21,22, 482, 498, 501, 625; **61**: 87,
154, 163; and Russia, **59**: 470;
Marshall on Jews in, **59**: 515; Morison
and Lansing on, **59**: 547-48,n2; Kolchak on, **60**: 143; and attack on Petrograd, **60**: 267, 269; and Riga, **60**: 532n1

Finland, **57**: 137, 138-39, 392, 398; **58**:
42; **59**: 16; **60**: 282; **61**: 455n1; and Russia, **54**: 136-37, 137, 205, 206, 287; **59**:
21, 442, 470, 545; issue of recognition
of and representa-tion at Paris Peace
Conference, **54**: 287-88; **58**: 177-78,
248, 319

Fiume: see Italy—Fiume

France: Rhineland (left bank), **55**: 151-
52; **56**: 587, 588; **57**: 130-31, 308, 335,
358, 451, 591; **60**: 210, 216; France's
views on, **55**: 233, 245, 458, 498; **58**:
479-80, 486-88, 541, 584; **59**: 277, 310,
313, 589-92; WW on, **55**: 472, 479-80;
56: 81, 371, 498, 580; **60**: 277; memorandum on, **55**: 475-77; and House-
Wilson growing schism over, **55**:
488n2; House on, **56**: 5; Bliss on, **56**: 7;
Clemenceau's views on, **56**: 10-14, 60-
61, 516-17, 559; Balfour on, **56**: 17;
Lansing on, **56**: 201-202; and Fontainebleau Memorandum, **56**: 266; Council
of Four on, **56**: 289, 323-24, 453-58,
522, 593-95; **58**: 441; **59**: 310, 589-92;
60: 25-26, 29-30, 31, 139-40, 343, 393,

440-41, 464-65, 501-503; Foch on, **56**: 445-48; **57**: 131, 494, 504; **58**: 494; **61**: 139-40; WW and Baruch discuss, **57**: 52; France's amendments on, **57**: 295-96, 296-98; and security treaty, **57**: 296, 297, 525; Poincaré on and WW's reply, **58**: 211-14, 521-2; Foch-Poincaré clique, **58**: 462,n2; effect of WW's health on decisions concerning, **58**: 624; Baruch on proposal for military occupation of, **59**: 227; draft convention of proposal for military occupation of, **59**: 228-32; Bliss on military administration of, **59**: 280-81, 382-83; **60**: 77, 237-39; and separatist movement, **59**: 401-402,n4, 443, 444; Smuts on, **59**: 416; Brockdorff-Rantzau on Germany's observations on, **59**: 580; Noyes on, **59**: 593-94; **60**: 295; American delegation on occupation of, and German counterproposals, **60**: 59-63; J. W. Davis on report of commission on occupation of, **60**: 363-65; British and French leaders meet on occupation of, **60**: 523-27; Grayson on resolution of occupation issue, **60**: 545-46; Allied and Associated Powers declaration on, **60**: 575-76, 580; and size of army of occupation, **61**: 198, 547; and French security treaty, **61**: 281-82, 311-13

Rhineland conventions, **60**: 368-72, 504-10, 511-13, 513-18, 519; to be handed to Germany with reply to German counterproposals, **60**: 581; to be published, **60**: 623; signing of, **61**: 278-79, 324; *see also* Inter-Allied Rhineland Commission

Saar Valley, **55**: 387,n2; **56**: 424, 540, 581; **57**: 69, 106, 110, 113, 113-17, 117-21, 284, 308, 325; **58**: 45, 61, 62, 64-65, 67, 227, 454; **59**: 376-79, 401n4, 414, 459; **60**: 25, 27-28, 29, 106, 156, 436, 460-62; **61**: 431; **62**: 19, 410, 414, 418, 419; France's demands for, **56**: 312, 347; Clemenceau-WW confrontation over, **56**: 349, 353-54, 364-68, 434; Tardieu on, **56**: 360-63, 587, 588; **57**: 155-59; Council of Four on, **56**: 364-70, 451-53; **57**: 106-107, 128-30, 150-51, 161-65, 199-202, 243-46; **58**: 227; **59**: 376-79, 380-82, 385, 453; **60**: 441-42; Haskins on, **56**: 420, 431-36, 513, 514; **57**: 54-50, 407-15; Steed on, **56**: 515, 516-17; Lloyd George on, **56**: 546-47; **57**: 106-107; and Baruch, **57**: 90, 159-60, 287-88; Miller on, **57**: 90-91, 195; corrections in articles on, **57**: 118-20; draft proposals for, **57**: 196-99; effect on WW's health of decisions concerning, **58**: 624; Brockdorff-Rantzau on, **59**: 377,n3, 580; American delegation on, **60**: 65-66, 70; House on, **60**: 83; and German counterproposals on, **60**: 108-109, 441-42, 447-48, 467; and U.S. representation on commission on, **62**: 451, 481

Galicia: see Poland

Germany: *East Prussia*, 56: 92, 94, 95, 127, 165,n1; 57: 452, 572, 573, 595; Lord on German counterproposal on, **60**: 186-87

  Rhineland: *see* France
  Rhineland conventions: *see* France
  Saar Valley: *see* France
  Tyrol, The: *see* Italy
  Upper Silesia: *see* Poland

Greece: *Thrace*, **54**: 463; **59**: 400; **61**: 159, 566,n3, 588-93, 623-24; **62**: 141-42, 207, 253, 265, 345n1, 416-17, 429, 514; **63**: 59n2, 60-62, 120-22; Polk on, **62**: 238-40, 319-21, 510; **63**: 235-36; **64**: 449; Vénisélos on, **62**: 327-28; **64**: 157-64, 182; U.S. compromise concerning, **62**: 551-53; Phillips on deferring decision on, **63**: 151; WW's note to Vénisélos on settlement, **63**: 391-92; college professors support unification with Greece, **64**: 297n1; Johnson on western Thrace, **64**: 368

Hungary: *Transylvania*, **54**: 421; **57**: 274, 441; **59**: 401; and Jews, **55**: 371, 373, 376, 378, 380; **60**: 352; and reparations, **58**: 39; **59**: 387; and prisoners of war, **59**: 425, 426; *see also* Hungary and Hungarians

Inter-Allied Commission on International Ports, Waterways and Railways, **55**: 110; **56**: 36, 37; **57**: 567; **58**: 14, 63, 148,n2, 544, 548; **59**: 93, 124, 417, 438, 585; **60**: 448-49, 519, 551; **61**: 56, 59

Inter-Allied Commission on Teschen, **56**: 220-22,n5,9

Inter-Allied Commissions of Control, **59**: 456; **60**: 582, 593

Inter-Allied Commission to Poland, **54**: 204, 471n2, 545; **56**: 49-50,n10, 52-53, 53, 56, 88, 129, 133, 142, 143, 144-45, 167n3, 209n2

Inter-Allied Naval Armistice Commission, **54**: 10-11, 12, 37; **55**: 53

Inter-Allied Purchasing Commissions, **60**: 474

Inter-Allied Rhineland Commission, **59**: 280-81,n1, 592, 593-94; **60**: 295, 364n1, 366-68, 440

Ireland, **54**: 472-73; **55**: 403, 407, 412, 421-22, 443, 453, 468, 469n4, 474, 547; **56**: 397-98, 486,n1; **57**: 419; **58**: 585, 588; **60**: 298, 435; **61**: 512; issue of Irish delegates' appearance at, **60**: 239,n1, 249,n2, 287, 288-89, 375, 383-87, 388-89, 435, 483, 544-45,n2; **61**: 466-67

Istria: see Italy

Italy: *Adriatic Question*, **53**: 66, 444-46, 609-10, 621, 641, 696; **54**: 134-35; **56**: 303n1, 556, 561-65, 566, 567-72, 577, 607,n1; **57**: 111, 334, 336, 343-45, 456, 477-78, 576; **58**: 561; **59**: 34, 35,

Paris Peace Conference (*cont.*)
144, 160, 173-74, 603; **60**: 43, 270-72;
61: 575; **62**: 345n1; **63**: 91-92; **64**: 260-
61, 263-64; and the press, **54**: 112,n3,
123; House on, **57**: 72, 178, 504; **59**: 68,
126, 127, 174, 200-201, 478, 555; Ossoinack presents Italian position, **57**:
337-43; WW's memorandum on Italian
claims, **57**: 343-45,n1, 575, 576; Yugoslavia on, **57**: 369-70; Benson on deportation of Yugoslavs by Italy, **57**: 442-
43; House and WW discuss, **57**: 466-
67,n2; R. S. Baker and WW discuss, **57**:
467-68; Orlando presents Italy's
claims to Council of Four, **57**: 479-94;
Pupin on, **57**: 499-502; Council of Four
on, **56**: 561-65, 567-72; **57**: 514-20, 610-
14; **58**: 14-19, 57-60, 74-90, 263, 333-
41, 392-99 434-38, 476-78, 510-14; **59**:
40-46, 85-94, 94-103, 260-61, 502-509,
556-59, 564-66, 569-71; **60**: 206-12,
265-66, 270-72; WW's statement on,
57: 542-44, 549,n5; **58**: 5-8, 44, 48, 56,
57, 94, 95, 102, 103, 105, 140-41, 142,
164,n1, 169, 170, 215, 241-42, 242;
issue of publication of WW's statement
on, **57**: 551, 552-53, 559-60, 575, 576,
611, 613; **58**: 4, 15, 42, 57, 102, 103;
and Clemenceau and Lloyd George on
WW's statement, **58**: 3-4, 27, 54, 55,
360, 371-72; Big Three meet on, **58**: 53-
56; and Orlando's reply to, **58**: 57, 58,
74-76, 97-101; reaction in France to
WW's statement, **58**: 91, 96-97, 239; reaction in Italy to WW's statement, **58**:
91-92, 93, 143-44, 239, 358; WW acknowledges support for his statement,
58: 155, 156; Kerner on Yugoslavia
and, **58**: 160; Bliss compares to Japan's
claims, **58**: 233, 234; T. N. Page on, **58**:
321, 358, 413-14, 450-51; and troops at
Sebenico, **58**: 354; Lodge on, **58**: 359n1;
France and Britain's letter to Italy on
Treaty of London and, **58**: 377-78; *Le
Temps* offers suggestions on, **58**:
393n4; U.S. public opinion on WW's
statement on, **58**: 410n1; WW updates
Council of Four on troop situation, **58**:
434-39; D. W. Johnson on, **58**: 588,
589-90; **61**: 227-30; conditions in
Fiume and Trieste, **59**: 64-66, 119-20,
241-42; Page's urgent request to see
WW on, **59**: 67; Herron on, **59**: 68n2;
Miller and Cellere discuss, **59**: 71-72,
249-50; Miller's "Definitive Solution,"
59: 83,n3; WW on, **59**: 94-95, 96, 96-97,
329, 339, 552, 574; **60**: 176, 211-12,
217-18, 286; Miller meets with
Orlando on, **59**: 81-84, 125-26,n1, 127;
WW tells stories appropriate to present situation, **59**: 248, 255; **60**: 116;
and Italy's insistence on Treaty of London, **59**: 478, 479, 480; Lansing on U.S.
not withdrawing from peace conference because of, **59**: 480-81; R. S. Baker
on, **59**: 551-52; Tardieu plan, **59**: 556-
59, 569-71; and issue of islands, **59**:
557, 558, 559, 569, 570; and Yugoslavia, **59**: 645; House and Orlando discuss, **60**: 40; Orlando on Tardieu plan,
60: 197-98; Council of Four on Tardieu
plan, **60**: 207-12, 213, 265-66, 267-69,
335; Pasi on Fiume plebiscite, **60**:
293-94; Italy's rejection of proposal on,
60: 303, 307-11, 374; WW on Italy's refusal to accept proposal on, **60**: 332-33;
Jay on, **61**: 109; WW memorandum on,
61: 170-71; H. White rejects Tittoni's
proposal on, **61**: 551-54; Balfour on, **62**:
22-26; Polk on, **62**: 456-57, 574-75; **63**:
204-10, 524-25; **64**: 323-24, 480-81;
WW on settlement, **62**: 522, 603-605,
625; Tittoni's proposal, **62**: 603-605;
Nitti on, **62**: 605-606; Clemenceau and
Lloyd George's recommendations, **63**:
206; Vittorio Emanuele III appeals to
WW for settlement of, **63**: 270, 297-98;
WW's terms for settlement, **63**: 270-71;
Fiume is obstacle in settlement of, **63**:
393; WW on reinforcements for
Spalato, **63**: 532; WW's unyielding position, **63**: 534; **64**: 335-36, 352-53, 398-
402, 445-46; and U.S. naval forces, **63**:
556-57, 557n,2; Italian troops in Trau,
63: 557,n1,2; WW unable to address
issue, EBW tells Lansing to hold decision, **63**: 617,n1; Anglo-French-Ameri-
can proposal on, **64**: 168-78, 264-66,
298-99; and Nitti compromise, **64**:
264,n4; Wallace on Anglo-French proposal, **64**: 300-305, 318-20; Lansing on,
64: 313-14, 340-41, 367, 371-72; and
Yugoslavia's reply to Anglo-French
proposal on, **64**: 331-35; WW's unyielding position on, **64**: 335-36, 352-53,
398-402, 445-46; Lansing conveys
WW's position to Wallace, **64**: 342; D.
W. Johnson on, **64**: 367, 368-69, 370-
71; WW's suggested changes of
Johnson's text on, **64**: 375-80; WW's
decision to withdraw Versailles Treaty
if Anglo-French Adriatic proposals are
accepted, **64**: 402; French and British
replies, **64**: 436-42, 481-83; France and
Britain on WW's threat to withdraw
treaty, **64**: 442; Straus on WW's response to, **64**: 445; WW's reply to
Anglo-French note on, **64**: 459-63;
delay in delivery and publication of
notes, **64**: 473; Britain and France
agree to withdraw previous proposals
and let Yugoslavia and Italy negotiate,
64: 482; Dr. Park on WW's health and,
64: 527; Lloyd George on, **66**: 45; WW
on, **66**: 307-308; R. U. Johnson on, **66**:
322-23; Colby and, **66**: 364-65, 388-89;
WW on settlement, **66**: 367; N. H.
Davis on settlement, **66**: 377; settlement of, **66**: 382, 402; D. W. Johnson
on, **67**: 57, 501-502, 504-505,n1; *see
also* Rapallo, Treaty of; Italy, Italy and
the United States

Anatolia, **54**: 350; **57**: 545,n2, 548; **58**: 326, 436, 474, 477n13; **61**: 128, 212, 216, 240, 344, 345; **66**: 47, 429-30; mandatory issue and, **59**: 88, 89, 92, 98, 99, 101, 102, 140, 202, 257, 258, 259, 327, 328, 330, 331, 337, 344, 371; **64**: 27, 449; **67**: 154; Council of Four on, **59**: 142-44,n7; Balfour memorandum on Italy and Turkey in, **59**: 209-12; WW on, **59**: 335, 340, 345, 374, 375-76

Asia Minor, **54**: 463, 473n1; **56**: 272; **57**: 548; **59**: 45, 91, 102; **60**: 616; **61**: 128, 159; **63**: 60; Italy in, **59**: 208-209, 223-25, 225-26, 246, 250-51, 561, 565; **61**: 553, 554; **62**: 25, 141-42, 238; **64**: 26, 27, 158, 450; Council of Four on mandates or division of, **59**: 257-61, 326-36; **61**: 211-12, 217, 219-23, 342n3; Clemenceau-Lloyd George conflict over mandatories in, **59**: 331-33, 334, 369, 369-70, 370,n1; WW on **59**: 335, 493; **61**: 307, 309, 346; Lloyd George on U.S. being mandatory for, **59**: 336-39; Westermann interview with WW on, **59**: 374-76; Westermann on Greece's territorial demands in, **59**: 595-96

Assling and Assling Triangle, **59**: 61n6, 85, 95, 559, 587, 631,n2; **60**: 121, 198, 207, 211, 216, 268, 310; **61**: 42, 227, 552; **62**: 456, 574, 604; **63**: 206, 208; **64**: 170

Dalmatia and Dalmatian Coast, **53**: 43,n1, 444, 446, 466, 564, 575, 621, 638, 640, 643-44, 696-97; **54**: 112n3, 134; **56**: 393n1, 490n1, 563n3, 607n1; **57**: 111, 321, 369, 437, 477, 504, 534, 537, 627; **58**: 6, 16, 48, 59, 76, 81, 87, 89, 92, 239, 376, 393n4, 396; **59**: 81, 82, 83n3, 85, 86, 91, 95, 125, 201, 375, 506, 508, 553, 558, 565, 569, 645; **60**: 214, 310, 311; **61**: 228, 405, 552, 553, 554, 575; **66**: 26n1, 322; and Fiume, **57**: 340; delegation from, **57**: 426; Mezes-Warrin articles on, **57**: 467,n2; Orlando on, **57**: 482-83, 562-64, 564-65; **58**: 99-100; WW on, **57**: 485-86, 493; **58**: 164n1; Council of Four on, **57**: 538, 539, 541, 545, 552, 612; Bliss compares Italy's claims to Japan's claims, **58**: 233; and Italy's compromise, **58**: 452; D. W. Johnson suggests formula for Adriatic settlement, **58**: 588, 589-90; House on, **59**: 68; Miller and Cellere discuss, **59**: 71, 72; bases of arrangement for settlement, **59**: 559; and Adriatic settlement, **66**: 365

Dodecanese Islands, **58**: 473, 475; **59**: 39, 43, 89, 92, 146, 246, 269, 329, 335, 339, 345; **61**: 307, 309, 342,n3, 345, 346; **63**: 392; reports of Italian atrocities in, **58**: 355-56,n1, 434

Fiume, **55**: 160; **56**: 303,n1, 396, 472, 562-65; **57**: 69, 70, 107, 111, 178, 321, 364, 467, 504, 520, 531, 534, 536-37, 540-41, 545, 548, 551, 552, 576, 581, 581-82, 611; **58**: 14, 15, 18, 19, 48, 53, 58-59, 63, 75-76, 80, 81, 93, 237n3, 239, 263, 321, 358, 374, 375, 376, 377, 396, 398; **59**: 34, 35, 81, 81-82, 91, 95, 96, 98, 125, 126, 173-74, 200, 201, 479, 493, 506, 508, 552, 553, 557, 558, 564; **60**: 265, 308, 310-11; **61**: 191n2, 213, 307, 344; **62**: 23, 574-75, 603, 620; **63**: 91-92, 306-307, 617n1; **64**: 170, 172, 173-74, 264-66,n4, 301, 302, 303, 304, 305, 318n2, 341, 399, 400; **65**: 315, 481; **66**: 322, 323; **67**: 376-77,n2; U.S. recommendations for, **56**: 607-609,n1, 609-11; WW on, **57**: 90, 344, 484-85, 487, 543; **58**: 6, 164n1; **60**: 332-33; **61**: 171, 420; **64**: 376-77, 460-61; case for annexation to Italy, **57**: 337-43; WW and Ossoinack discuss, **57**: 339-40; Orlando on, **57**: 343n1, 480-81, 514; House and WW discuss, **57**: 352, 353, 466-67; case for annexation to Yugoslavia, **57**: 432-33; T. N. Page on, **57**: 434-37; **58**: 369, 427, 452-53, 529; **59**: 67; Council of Four on, **57**: 611, 612-13; **58**: 392, 394n4, 473, 474-75; **59**: 260-61; **60**: 207, 211, 213, 217; **61**: 218, 219, 221, 222-23, 309; Lloyd George and Clemenceau's letter to Italy on, **58**: 86-90; Italian and U.S. naval movements toward, **58**: 142, 148, 338, 408, 426, 528, 554-55; and Serbia, **58**: 397; and Italy's compromise, **58**: 452-53; news accounts on called "fiction" by WW, **58**: 531-32,n1, 601; effect of WW's health on decisions concerning, **58**: 626-27, 627; **63**: 543; House on, **59**: 68; Day on, **59**: 171; "law" making it treason to separate Italy from, **59**: 241,n1, 241-42; Orlando and Lloyd George discuss, **59**: 257-58; composition of commission for, **59**: 557, 558, 564, 569, 570; reports that Italians have taken, **59**: 566; Brandeis endorses WW position on, **60**: 284; WW answers Pasic on, **60**: 361; Italy's desire to settle issue of, **61**: 404-405, 575; Bowman on House's irregular negotiations, **62**: 454-55; Polk's proposal, **62**: 456; WW's position on, **63**: 270, 424, 484-85, 543; invasion of by D'Annunzio, **63**: 298-99,n2, 354-66, 485; ongoing negotiations over, **63**: 364-66; Clemenceau urges WW to agree to Adriatic settlement, **63**: 393; Nitti's plea for, **63**: 464-65; Britain and France advocate Italy be given, **63**: 465-66; crisis in Italy over, **63**: 485-86, 516-17; Herron on WW yielding position on, **63**: 537,n1; Anglo-French proposals for and Yugoslav reply to, **64**: 264-66, 298, 300, 301, 302, 305, 318-20, 331; D. W. Johnson on, **64**: 368, 370-71; Anglo-French reply to WW on, **64**: 437-38, 439; Polk on France's position on, **64**: 450-51; WW on, **64**: WW's ultimatum mentioned, **65**: 3; U.S. draft reply to Britain and France on, **65**: 37-39; R. U. Johnson on, **65**: 94; 460-61;

Paris Peace Conference (*cont.*)
and Adriatic settlement, **66**: 364, 365, 377; Italy's naval blockades, **66**: 447-48,n1

Istria, **54**: 134; **57**: 344, 369, 480, 482; **58**: 83; **59**: 81, 83n3, 95, 201, 244, 249, 484, 505, 506, 551, 552, 559, 569, 570, 645; **60**: 137; **61**: 552, 575; **63**: 206, 270-71, 298, 617n1

Sebenico, **53**: 640,n2; **57**: 488, 551, 611, 612; **58**: 14, 81, 82, 83, 263, 354, 358, 434, 439, 450, 452; **59**: 53, 82, 83n3, 86, 96, 125, 201, 249, 552, 557, 558, 559, 565, 569, 570; **60**: 138, 211, 213, 217, 266, 308, 310, 311; **61**: 228, 575

Smyrna, **54**: 350; **59**: 58-59, 67, 89, 99, 140, 146, 223, 373, 374, 613; **63**: 61; **64**: 449; Italy's activities regarding, results in dispatch of Greek troops to, **58**: 250, 251, 326, 338, 339, 345, 409, 414, 436, 476-78,n13, 510-14; Greek troops in, **59**: 21-27, 54-55, 58-59, 226, 238, 252, 473, 565, 596, 640-41,n1,2,3,4; **61**: 44, 212, 216, 629n1; **62**: 607; Council of Four on, **59**: 40-46; WW on, **59**: 89, 92, 99, 140, 613

Tardieu plan, **61**: 109, 171; Yugoslavia's counterproposals to, **60**: 137-38,n1; Orlando on, **60**: 197-98, 271, 309-10; Council of Four on, **60**: 207-12, 213, 216-17; Lloyd George favors, **60**: 210

Tarvisio and Tarvis Pass, **58**: 589,n2; **59**: 61,n5, 85, 94, 95, 492, 501, 559, 578, 587; **60**: 268, 362, 394; **61**: 206; **64**: 175

Trentino, **54**: 50, 387; **57**: 488n10, 563; **60**: 98

Trieste, **54**: 50, 112n3, 387; **55**: 117, 546; **56**: 393n1, 564, 565, 570, 607; **57**: 178, 342, 344, 480, 537; **58**: 7, 87, 89, 392, 527; **59**: 51, 52, 53, 64-66, 119-20, 171, 387, 537, 539, 566; **60**: 98, 198, 211, 272

Tyrol, The, **57**: 96-97, 111, 541, 614; **58**: 138, 139, 160, 374, 392; **59**: 348,n1, 400-401; **61**: 230, 387-88

Valona, **57**: 345,n3; **58**: 590; **59**: 82, 83n3; **61**: 552, 575; **62**: 367,n29, 604, 620; **63**: 206, 209, 617n1; **64**: 171, 174, 175, 299, 315

Veglia, **59**: 557, 559, 570; **60**: 138, 207, 212, 213, 214, 217; **61**: 171; **62**: 456

Zara, **57**: 483, 488, 551, 611, 612; **58**: 14, 81, 82, 83, 263, 358, 450, 452, 590,n8; **59**: 71, 82, 83n3, 86, 96, 125, 201, 242,n2, 249, 552, 553, 557, 558, 559, 565, 569, 570; **60**: 138, 211, 213, 217, 266, 308, 310, 311; **61**: 171, 228, 552, 553-54, 575

Japan: Kiaochow, **54**: 289-90, 291, 315, 316, 316-17, 317, 474n1, 474n2; **55**: 424; **56**: 267; **57**: 298, 358, 359, 431n1, 453, 454, 554-55, 561,n2, 580, 597-98, 599-610, 615-17, 618; **58**: 46, 68-70, 70-71, 72-73, 112, 130-33, 166, 168, 175, 178-79, 181, 185, 214, 215, 231, 233, 247, 256, 261; **60**: 104, 429, 471,n12, 13; **61**: 237, 242, 249, 250, 325n5, 447, 555, 556; **62**: 19, 154, 458, 508, 509, 522, 523, 524; **63**: 84, 330, 413, 471; WW meets with Chinese delegates on, **57**: 635-37; and claims settlements, **58**: 270-71,n1, 272, 277

Shantung controversy and settlement, **54**: 79, 81, 308-309, 316-17, 325, 474,n2, 474n1, 475; **57**: 354, 366, 453n4, 495,554, 555, 561,n2,3, 580, 581, 597n1, 598, 609, 616, 620, 626; **58**: 46, 68-70, 70-73, 86, 128, 130-33, 142, 143, 153, 165-68, 175, 178-82, 183-84, 185, 186-87, 214, 215-16, 216-26, 228, 230-32, 232-34, 246, 247, 257-59, 261; **60**: 471n12; Koo on, **57**: 298, 299-300, 431,n1, 618; and Japan's claims, **57**: 599, 601; **58**: 46, 68-70, 70-71, 71-72, 86, 112, 128, 130-33, 167, 178, 179, 180, 183-84, 185, 224, 225, 228, 230-32, 246, 259, 261; WW on, **57**: 606; **58**: 272; settlement of claims on, **58**: 270-71,n1, 277, 327, 328; **59**: 35, 573n1,3; Council of Four on, **58**: 130-33, 178-82, 217-26, 257-59, 261; China's statements on settlement, **58**: 419,n1, 427,n1; Reinsch on China's signing peace treaty, **58**: 522n1; effect of WW's health on decisions concerning, **58**: 626-27

Kiaochow: see Japan

Kiel Canal, **54**: 553; **55**: 24, 108, 430, 434-35, 522-23, 539; **56**: 3, 34-38, 268; **57**: 358, 391,n1, 397-98, 399, 404-405, 457, 567-68,n2; **58**: 63, 65-67, 122-25; **59**: 417; **60**: 520,n13

Klagenfurt: see Yugoslavia

Klagenfurt Basin: see Yugoslavia

Latvia, **56**: 468; **57**: 137-38, 392; **58**: 42, 403, 594-95; **59**: 17, 303, 442, 466n6, 470, 515, 545; **60**: 143, 269, 282; **61**: 154, 163; Libau, **56**: 146, 168, 169, 408n2, 413,n5, 489; **58**: 583; **60**: 9, 134,n8, 474n21, 482, 498, 500; **61**: 87, 161, 335

Lithuania and Lithuanians, **53**: 591, 611n1; **54**: 92, 103,n7, 340, 342, 343; **56**: 35, 169, 413, 468; **57**: 137-38, 154, 155, 453; **58**: 403, 594-95; **59**: 16, 17, 18, 181, 263, 412, 442, 466n6, 470, 515, 545; **60**: 143, 159-60, 164, 187, 166-67, 282, 474n22; **61**: 87, 163; atrocities in, **59**: 412, 515; and Jews, **62**: 221

mandates, **54**: 333-34, 348; **61**: 283; Council of Four on, **58**: 288-89, 400-401, 442, 484-86, 510; **61**: 520; House and Cecil on, **61**: 107; memoranda on, **61**: 259-70; commission to study, **61**: 275-77, 408-409, 451-55, 477; and Al-

bania, **62**: 457, 620; and Armenia, **62**: 149; France's attitude toward, **62**: 257, 257-58, 304; and France and Togoland, **62**: 425-26, 481, 595; House on, **62**: 187 89, 243-47, 254; **63**: 422; WW on Turkish Empire and, **62**: 235, 257; and religious freedom, **62**: 244-45; Polk on, **62**: 257-58, 511-14; WW on voting requirements to revoke, **62**: 316; WW and Foreign Relations Committee discuss, **62**: 370, 374-75, 409; and King-Crane Commission's recommendations, **62**: 607-608; and Turkish Empire, **64**: 25, 26, 27; Lansing on abandoning idea of, **64**: 56; WW on, *see* Wilson, Woodrow: western tour—themes, **63**

Armenia and Armenians, **54**: 225, 330, 360, 370, 371, 455; **55**: 7, 80, 243, 265n1, 274, 321-22, 446, 459, 542; **56**: 95, 96, 102, 117, 180, 203, 204, 272, 273; **57**: 302-303, 334, 443; **58**: 42, 111n2, 326, 436, 437; **59**: 401; **61**: 128, 156, 238; and representation at Paris Peace Conference, **54**: 226,n2, 346; Nubar on claims of, **54**: 516-18; issue of U.S. troops to, **55**: 27-28, 82; American Committee for Independence of, **55**: 65-66, 265n1, 446; and mandate issue, **59**: 89, 91, 100, 101, 137, 140, 146, 184, 185, 327, 328, 330, 337, 340, 341, 345, 373, 476, 640n1; WW on, **59**: 103-104, 137, 335, 374, 376; **61**: 240, 246, 253, 424; **62**: 27n1, 149, 235, 242, 257, 285n1, 416, 454, 607; suggestion of Resident Commissioner to, **61**: 314, 339; mission to, **61**: 486, 487; and Turkish invasion of, **62**: 116n1, 248,n1; Hoover on relief efforts in, **62**: 166; reports and advice on situation in, **62**: 576-79; and King-Crane recommendations, **62**: 608

Asia Minor: see Italy—Asia Minor

Constantinople: issue of mandate and Sultan's residence, **59**: 89, 93, 99, 137, 143, 146, 210, 225, 238, 259, 327, 330, 335, 337, 340, 345, 369, 371, 395-97, 476, 519n2; WW on mandate and, **59**: 137, 146, 259, 340, 345, 374, 375, 376; **61**: 238, 240, 246, 253, 624; King-Crane Commission leaving for, **59**: 573-74; Council of Four on, **61**: 156, 157, 211, 215-16; and Thrace issue, **61**: 567, 588-93

Mesopotamia, **54**: 300, 360, 372, 414, 455, 508; **55**: 7, 27, 82, 142; **56**: 104, 106, 108, 117, 272, 273, 274; **57**: 443; **58**: 325; **59**: 327, 332-33, 333, 337, 373; **61**: 156, 443; *see also* mandates

New Guinea, **54**: 296, 350; and Australia's claims, **54**: 250-51, 251, 251-52, 299-300, 308, 325, 348, 363; **58**: 442, 484; *see also* mandates

Samoa, **58**: 442, 484, 510; and New Zealand and territorial claims, **54**: 251,

254, 312, 313, 320, 363; WW on, **54**: 314, 363; and mandates, **59**: 475,n2

South-West Africa, **54**: 249, 250, 252-54,n3, 290, 294-95, 296-98, 325, 328, 361, 365, 456; **55**: 7-8, 50, 171; **56**: 274, **57**: 603; **58**: 196; **61**: 261

Syria, **53**: 649; **54**: 225, 360, 370, 372, 455, 506, 507; **55**: 4, 7, 61, 86, 160; **56**: 102, 103, 104, 126, 272, 273, 274, 546, 587; **57**: 247, 535; **58**: 172; **59**: 337; and Cilicia, **54**: 517; **61**: 156; H. S. Bliss on, **54**: 551-52; **55**: 86, 141-45, 472-73,n1; Council of Four on, **56**: 104-109; **58**: 133-34; **59**: 330-31, 333-34, 336, 343-44, 345, 345-46, 632-33, 635-37; and Palestine, **57**: 326n3; Clemenceau on, **57**: 334-35, 589-90; **58**: 172, 326, 436; **59**: 343; Westermann on, **57**: 443-44, 468; Lloyd George and House discuss, **57**: 466; Prince Faisal thanks WW, **57**: 525-26, 559; and mandates, **59**: 327, 328, 333; **62**: 188, 235, 242, 257; Lloyd George on, **59**: 343-44, 345; Lloyd George-Clemenceau conflict over, **59**: 331-33, 336, 368, 369-70, 370,n1, 484; and King-Crane Commission recommendations on, **62**: 607-608

Montenegro: see Yugoslavia—Montenegro

Ottoman Empire: see Turkey

Poland: Danzig, **54**: 248, 336, 341, 480; **55**: 233-34, 387, 546; **56**: 89, 90, 91, 92, 94, 95, 127, 289, 318, 321; **57**: 107, 110, 121, 151-55, 289, 308, 357, 451, 452, 467; **58**: 28, 45, 62, 137, 385; **59**: 416, 456-57, 579, 582, 589; **60**: 146, 187, 606, 618; **61**: 431-32; and Haller's Army, **56**: 118, 129, 130, 131, 132, 136, 137, 138, 147-48, 167n3, 168, 209n2, 315, 324-25, 385, 408,n2, 409-10, 411, 489, 494, 495, 496,n2, 523, 523, 526, 540-41; **57**: 74n3,5; and Fontainebleau Memorandum, **56**: 266: Mezes on, **56**: 395-96, 471-73; Council of Four on, **56**: 506-509, 560-61; **57**: 151-55, 289-91; **59**: 456-57; **60**: 558, 559, 562, 563; H. Hoover on food relief and, **56**: 547; compared to Fiume, **57**: 481, 485; Danzig-Mława-Warsaw railways, **56**: 165; **57**: 573; draft of treaty articles on, **57**: 572-74, 588, 593-97; Paderewski on, **58**: 152; public opinion in Germany on, **58**: 454; and draft reply to Germany's counterproposals, **60**: 447; *see also* Jews, Poland

Galicia, **54**: 179, 180,n2, 201, 339, 343; **55**: 542; **56**: 51; **57**: 237, 275-80, 327, 328-29, 462; **59**: 262, 265, 411, 458n8, 561, 566, 598, 616, 635; **60**: 59, 479; **61**: 279-80; and Jews, **55**: 370, 371, 378, 378-79; **59**: 419,n1, 445-46, 446, 640n1; and Lemberg, **54**: 32,n3, 339, 480,n1; **55**: 50, 51, 52, 52-53, 55, 96, 119, 130, 131, 255, 314, 325, 326, 384, 468, 469; **57**: 154, 356, 365, 463,

Paris Peace Conference (*cont.*)
549; **65**: 527n3; and Poland, **59**: 263-64; and Ukraine, **59**: 351, 353, 354; Paderewski at Council of Four on, **60**: 160-62; Balfour on Bolshevism in, **61**: 167-68

Teschen, **54**: 339-40, 343, 345, 416-17,n3, 421, 461, 481,n2; **55**: 163; **56**: 220-22,n9, 365, 587; **57**: 111, 245, 290, 326-27; **58**: 28; **59**: 186, 217-18; *see also* Inter-Allied Commission on Teschen

Thorn (now Toruń, Poland), **54**: 199, 200; **56**: 89, 94, 131, 148, 496,n2; **59**: 325

Upper Silesia, **59**: 186, 329, 416, 615, 627; **60**: 20, 21, 24, 43, 72, 80-81, 106, 130n4, 139, 189-92, 230, 297, 314, 423, 521-22; **62**: 272, 415; American delegation on, **60**: 54-59, 67-68; House on, **60**: 82-83; Council of Four on, **60**: 84-92, 436,n1, 558-60, 562, 563; and peace terms, **60**: 130,n5; andLeobschutz, **60**: 139, 480; Lord on German counterproposals on, **60**: 183-85, 197; and plebiscite issue, **60**: 404-406, 411-18, 421-27, 447, 468, 478, 553-56; and Czech frontier issue, **60**: 468, 478; troops for occupation of, **60**: 602, 622, 628; WW on, **63**: 13-14, 98, 186-87

Reparation Commission, **55**: 29n1, 42, 210-11; **57**: 8, 9, 20, 24, 25, 26, 28, 83-84, 203, 213-15, 609; **58**: 29-41, 294, 402n12, 471n8; **59**: 57-58,147-48, 163, 310, 460, 495-96, 585; **60**: 77, 92, 93, 196, 219, 263, 316, 320, 401, 449; **61**: 57; **62**: 148, 267, 328-30; proposed and formation of, **54**: 211, 223, 226, 283, 286, 462; question of unanimity, **57**: 82, 212-13; WW on U.S. sitting in, **57**: 370; memorandum by American representatives, **58**: 24-26; and Belgium, Serbia, and Japan, **58**: 249, 259-60; **59**: 74n1, 304-305,n13, 312; Council of Four on, **58**: 259-60; **59**: 387-88; Hankey on proportions to be set up by, **58**: 266; and agreement on merchant ships, **58**: 424n3, 557-58, 559; and Austria and Hungary, **58**: 542; appointment suggestions, **59**: 161; **61**: 528-30; WW on Germany and, **59**: 362; and Saar Valley, **59**: 378, 381, 382; **59**: 387-88; Germany on, **59**: 581; **60**: 4n1; Lamont on Austrian reparations, lesser nations and Italy, **59**: 611-12; American delegation on, **60**: 45-46, 51-52, 53; and passenger tonnage for France, **61**: 278,n7; interim commission formed, **61**: 384; controversy over WW's right to make appointment to, **61**: 493, 519, 582, 596, 609,n1; WW on, **63**: 36-37, 44; **64**: 281; issue of chairmanship, **64**: 10, 11-12; and Lodge reservations, **64**: 40, 284, 292, 293; Lansing on continuing U.S. unofficial participation in, **64**: 91-92

reparations, **56**: 5, 246, 279, 433,n2, 580-81; **57**: 53,n1, 309-10; **58**: 26-27, 113-14, 469-71,n1; **59**: 177, 460; **60**: 79, 198, 483, 593-94; **62**: 148, 149; WW on, **54**: 55; **55**: 231; **58**: 447, 448; **63**: 9, 36, 44, 171-72; declaration of principles of, **55**: 29-34; and naval terms, **55**: 431; **56**: 429-30,n1; **59**: 50-54; **61**: 86, 144-46, 146-48, 151; House meets with Lloyd George and Clemenceau, **55**: 458; Baron Sumner on, **56**: 69-74; Lloyd George on, **56**: 209, 285-86,n1; **60**: 20, 21, 25, 32, 329, 336-37; Council of Four on, **56**: 250-52, 283, 286-96, 355-71, 417-20, 448-53, 506, 509-10, 601-603; **57**: 5-21, 21-33, 34-36, 79-89, 203-15, 293-94, 333n2; **58**: 15, 29-41, 278-79, 290, 294, 334-35; **59**: 11, 13, 31-33, 50-54, 57-58, 386-91 495-96, 585; **60**: 92-94, 264, 316-21, 333-34, 344-51, 437; **61**: 100-102; and Fontainebleau Memorandum, **56**: 260, 269; N. H. Davis on, **56**: 270-72; Bernstorff on, **56**: 317n1; and Saar Basin, **56**: 420, 424; **57**: 54-59, 196-99, 407-15; **59**: 459-60; Baruch on, **56**: 421-24; **58**: 28-29, 548-49; McCormick on, **56**: 353, 424-25, 444, 501-502, 535; **58**: 27-28, 161,n1; Smuts on, **56**: 480-82; **59**: 414-15; Germany on, **56**: 493, 496; **58**: 481; decision to include pensions in, **56**: 498-99,n3, 501-501, 502; memorandum on Anglo-American accord on, **56**: 502-503, 504-505, 536-39, 579, 579-80, 580-81; Belgium and, **56**: 589-97; **58**: 278-79; **61**: 120-23; text of clauses and categories, **56**: 599-603; and Lloyd George's "moderation" interview, **57**: 6n7; attacks in Britain against Lloyd George's position on, **57**: 145,n1, 147n5; and interdependence of debts, **57**: 165-66; concern over League of Nations because of U.S. position, **57**: 188-89; Britain's plan for economic restoration, **58**: 11-12; Keynes plan for, **58**: 12-14; Poincaré on need for French occupation of Rhineland until reparations paid, **58**: 211-14; Big Three agree on division of, **58**: 290, 294; and Poland, **58**: 470-71; Brockdorff-Rantzau on Germany and, **58**: 516-17, 519; and Austria and Hungary, **58**: 549-52; **59**: 163, 624-25; effect of WW's health on decision concerning, **58**: 623-24; and clause omission in German treaty, **59**: 139, 147-48; and successor states of Austria-Hungary, **59**: 384n1, 538; **60**: 591-92,n2; **61**: 254-56; and cultural and artistic materials included in, **59**: 391; comments on fixing amount versus not fixing amount, **60**: 4-7, 20, 21, 306-307, 316-21; Clemenceau on, **60**: 29; WW and American delegation discuss Germany's counterproposals on, **60**: 45-53, 76-77; McCormick and Baruch meet with French on, **60**: 72-73, 73-74;

McCormick on Lloyd George and Loucheur's proposals, **60**: 196, 336-43; project for reply to German counterproposals on, **60**: 394-99; suggestions by American negotiators for proposed reply to Germany on, **60**: 399-401; reply to German counterproposals on, **60**: 406-11, 449-50; small change in second revise of reply to German counterproposal on, **60**: 579,n12; Senate committee requests information on distribution of, **61**: 582-83,n1; Baruch on U.S. as recipient of, **62**: 148,n2; discussed at Foreign Relations Committee meeting with WW, **62**: 347-48, 358-60, 378-79, 409; *see also* Reparation Commission

responsibility for the war, **57**: 121-28, 146, 149-50, 405, 631; **60**: 549; and German White Book, **60**: 438,n5, 463; Kerr's draft response to German counterproposals on, **60**: 443-46, 519; reply to German counterproposals on, **60**: 451-55; Council of Four on, **56**: 530-34,n3; **58**: 277-78,n3, 295-96, 440; **60**: 463-64, 467-68, 474; Germany on, **61**: 69, 70, 74; issue of delivery of William II for trial, **61**: 199, 200-201, 395-96,n1; Bethmann Hollweg accepts responsibility instead of William II, **61**: 334-35, 340; issue of which culprits to ask for, **62**: 449

Rhineland: *see* France—Rhineland

Rhineland conventions: *see* France—Rhineland Convention

Rumania, **54**: 202, 203, 264, 287, 461; **55**: 164, 184, 202; **56**: 26; **57**: 73, 78, 112, 136, 168, 368, 484-85, 515; **58**: 39, 114, 198, 252, 381, 471, 472, 476; **59**: 144, 166, 215, 401, 613; **60**: 134,n7, 282, 582n5; **61**: 196, 197; and Jews, **53**: 67n1, 79, 104, 260; **55**: 370, 373-76, 379, 380; **58**: 284, 287, 291, 386, 387, 460-61,n1, 476; **59**: 219, 419n1, 515, 516n1, 562, 566, 577, 625-26, 629, 629-30, 634-35; U.S. loans to, **53**: 480; and food crisis in and relief to, **53**: 649, 698; **56**: 253-57, 329, 330; **59**: 174; and representation at Paris Peace Conference, **54**: 16,n3, 17, 65; and Reparation Commission and reparations, **54**: 211, 223, 283, 462; **55**: 29,n2, 30, 32, 33, 317; **57**: 454-55; **59**: 384n1; **60**: 592; **61**: 100, 101, 254-56; and territorial claims, **54**: 374, 375, 376-77, 421-25; WW's greetings to King Ferdinand, **54**: 379-80; and League of Nations Commission, **54**: 462, 482, 495-96, 509; and Article 21, **55**: 154; and Poland, **56**: 50-51,53, 55, 325-26; and Hungary, **56**: 182n1, 239, 276, 332, 334, 379-80, 382-83, 459-60, 487; **58**: 149, 156, 157, 158; **59**: 240, 256-57, 631,n2; **60**: 257, 259-60, 260, 312-14,n1, 315-16, 351-57; **61**: 205-206, 339, 341; issue of U.S. supply-ing army of, **56**: 305-307, 325-26, 330, 379, 581-83; **58**: 405-407; Foch on, **56**: 314-15, 329; Smuts' Hungarian mission and, **57**: 102, 108, 109, 169-71, 171-73; Queen Marie visits WW, **57**: 190-93, 238-39, 241-42; T. H. Bliss on, **57**: 274-75; **59**: 428-32; **60**: 363; and France and militarism in, **57**: 279-80; rehabilitation of economy of, **58**: 12, 136-37, 316-17, 491n1, 591-93; and Poland and Ukraine, **59**: 353, 512n1, 561; and Austrian treaty, **59**: 562; **60**: 97,n8, 130-31,n5; and Plenary Session of rights of small nations, **59**: 644, 645-46; Lloyd George wants changes in peace treaty regarding, **60**: 120; and arms limitation, **60**: 170-71; estimate of damages, **60**: 359n1; and boundary issue, **60**: 418-19,n6, 427-28, 462, 469-70,n11, 478, 479; **61**: 279; Council of Four defines boundaries, demanding hostilities stop, and Hungary's reply, **60**: 522,n19, 529-30, 597-98; U.S. Senate resolution on Jews in, **60**: 640n1; WW on, **61**: 243,n9

Bessarabia, **54**: 287, 421; **57**: 75n6; **59**: 543, 545; **66**: 180,n3; and Jews, **55**: 373, 376, 378, 380; **60**: 143; **62**: 206-207, 266

Transylvania: *see* Hungary

Russia: issue of Russian representation and participation, **53**: 136, 137, 290, 492-94,n1, 591, 718-19; C. H. McCormick on Russian situation and, **53**: 256; Bolshevik question and Paris Peace Conference, **54**: 21-23,n10, 27, 45, 57-58, 99-103; Prinkipo Declaration and Chicherin's reply to, **54**: 181-88, 199, 205-206, 236-37, 345-46, 415, 415-16; **55**: 161,n1; Council of Four on situation in, **58**: 506; **59**: 29-31, 225, 273, 453, 457-58, 462-63; Council of Four and correspondence with Kolchak, **60**: 95,n2, 435, 438, 463, 466, 477

Ukraine, **54**: 33,n5,7, 92, 100, 136-37, 340, 342-43, 403,n3, 480n1; **58**: 539, 543; **59**: 130; and Poland, **57**: 275-80, 328-29, 356, 365, 372, 415-16, 444-45, 451, 461-64; **58**: 101-102, 316, 455, 505-506,n4; **59**: 215-17, 262-63, 265, 323-25, 350-60, 458, 531, 561, 566, 596-97, 597-99, 616; **60**: 160-62, 164, 165,n15, 470-71, 479; and Rumania, **59**: 512,n1; Marshall on Jews in, **59**: 515; and Jews and East Galicia, **62**: 220-21

Saar Valley: *see* France

Samoa: *see* mandates

Sebenico: *see* Italy

Serbia: *see* Yugoslavia

Slovakia: *see* Czechoslovakia

Shantung controversy and settlement: *see* Japan—Shantung controversy

Smyrna: *see* Italy

Paris Peace Conference (*cont.*)
  South-West Africa: *see* mandates
  Sudetenland: *see* Czechoslovakia
  Supreme War Council, **54**: 35-42; **55**:
  40; **56**: 440; **57**: 204; **61**: 198; and European relief program, **53**: 64, 222, 360,
  361; Grayson on, **54**: 4-5, 35, 64; **55**: 94;
  56: 3; on Armistice terms and Russian
  problem, **54**: 7-12; on representation at
  Paris Peace Conference, **54**: 12-26; and
  demobilization, **54**: 221, 238-46; on
  sending troops to Poland, **54**: 199-204;
  and Allied military force in Turkey, **54**:
  371, 378,n13, 417-18; and H. Hoover
  resolution on relaxing export-import
  control on Germany, **54**: 477-79, 558;
  and Loucheur Committee's report, **54**:
  525-45; and Foch-Clemenceau controversy over German prisoners, **55**: 3, 40;
  meetings of, **55**: 9-26, 51-62, 95-104,
  104-13, 178-83; on arms limitations,
  55: 11-16, 20; on naval terms, **55**: 20-
  26; on enforcement and renewal of armistice terms, **55**: 51-58, 95-104, 104-
  12; on war criminals and trials, **55**: 59-
  60; on passage of troops through Holland, **55**: 178-80; on Prinkipo Declaration, **55**: 180-83; British press gives
  false reasons why WW absent from, **55**:
  530-31; on peace terms and treaty, **56**:
  14-56; on Polish situation and boundaries, **56**: 49-56, 127-28, 163, 312-13; on
  transport of Haller's army, **56**: 129-48,
  209n2; T. H. Bliss on Hungarian revolution being caused by decision of, **56**:
  380-81; and Polish-Ukrainian conflict,
  58: 101
  Syria: *see* mandates—Syria
  Tardieu plan: *see* Italy—Tardieu Plan
  Tarvisio and Tarvis Pass: *see* Italy—
  Tarvisio
  Teschen: *see* Poland—Teschen
  Thrace: *see* Greece—Thrace
  Thorn: *see* Poland—Thorn
  Transylvania: *see* Hungary—Transylvania
  Trentino: *see* Italy—Trentino
  Trieste: *see* Italy—Trieste
  Tyrol, The: *see* Italy—Tyrol
  Turkey, **54**: 170, 369, 370, 371, 417-
  418, 455, 506,n7; **55**: 7, 111, 317; **56**:
  5-6, 26, 103, 109, 207, 270n5, 510-11;
  57: 112, 246-47, 321, 465, 546, 548; **58**:
  12, 21, 111n2, 324,n3, 436, 442,
  477n13; **59**: 41, 42, 89, 97, 98, 100-101,
  103, 207n1, 208, 225, 238, 246, 250,
  253, 258, 277, 326, 336-38, 339-40,
  342, 345, 369, 371, 373, 374-75, 376,
  396, 499, 636, 642; **60**: 615, 616, 617;
  61: 59,n3, 60, 82-83, 128, 136, 158-59,
  221-22, 240, 314, 430, 494, 566-67; **65**:
  n1; and famine relief bill, **54**: 174,n2,
  303; question of mandates, **54**: 225,

  355, 360, 369, 370, 371, 378,n13, 379,
  417-18; **55**: 61, 62, 171, 459; **56**: 114,
  117, 272-75; **59**: 253, 318, 370; **61**: 479;
  62: 188, 243, 257, 345n1, 512, 580; and
  Greece, **54**: 402-403, 426-27; **59**: 21-27,
  40-46, 54-55, 58-59, 252, 299, 463, 473,
  595, 640-41,n1,2,3,4; **60**: 193, 276-77;
  Nubar on Armenia's claims and, **54**:
  516-18; issue of U.S. troops to, **55**: 27-
  28, 81, 82; **58**: 473-74, 475; recommendations from American Relief Committee for, **55**: 485-86; Council of Four on,
  56: 104-18; **58**: 510-14; **59**: 90, 142-44,
  146, 147, 225, 258-60, 326-46; **60**: 96-
  97, 261, 494, 612, 615-17; **61**: 59-60,n3,
  82-83, 155-58, 158-60, 210-13, 214-17,
  277-78; WW on, **55**: 414; **56**: 114; **61**:
  238, 338, 341; and Fontainebleau
  Memorandum, **56**: 267; and Commission on Responsibilities, **56**: 613;
  Westermann on mandates, **58**: 207-10;
  King and Crane recommendations, **58**:
  322-27; **62**: 607-608,n1; and Young
  Turk Movement, **58**: 555,n1; **60**: 612;
  naval action to be taken against if
  peace treaty not signed, **58**: 583-84;
  Council of Four on dispatch of Greek
  troops to, **58**: 510-14; commission to,
  59: 93-94, 573-74, 575; Balfour on, **59**:
  209-12; and Asia Minor, **59**: 326; Clemenceau on, **59**: 332; Montagu on
  U.S.being mandatory for, **59**: 238-39;
  Westermann and Magie on, **59**:
  344,n2; H. White on mandatories and,
  59: 395-97; requests delegates be
  heard at Paris Peace Conference, **59**:
  613-14; **60**: 16; and France, **60**: 212;
  and Armenia, **62**: 116n1, 576-79; and
  Thrace, **62**: 416-17; Polk on note to
  France on, **65**: 64-65, 76-77, 111-12,
  112-15; WW on, **65**: 91; WW approves
  Polk's draft to Jusserand on, **65**: 116;
  and Armenia, **65**: 306, 308-10
    Caucasus, **54**: 370; **55**: 61; **56**: 108,
  109; **58**: 333, 437, 438; **59**: 442, 545; **61**:
  213, 217; **62**: 248n1, 285n1, 416, 576-
  79
  Ukraine: *see* Russia—Ukraine
  Upper Silesia: *see* Poland—Upper Silesia
  Valona: *see* Italy—Valona
  Veglia: *see* Italy—Veglia
  Yugoslavia, **54**: 19, 20, 50, 112n3, 124,
  134, 148-49, 170, 197-98, 233, 388; **55**:
  84, 85, 87-88, 243, 305, 380; **57**: 112,
  368, 466; **58**: 6, 12, 15, 17, 39, 76, 92,
  359n1, 509; **59**: 82, 83n3, 85, 119-20,
  166, 167, 171, 613; **60**: 134,n7, 146,
  577n5, 582n5, 607, 643; **61**: 55, 206,
  279; and Italy, **53**: 43,n1, 123-24, 128,
  167, 433, 434, 435-36, 442-43, 459,
  466, 564, 643, 696; **57**: 369-70, 434-35,
  477, 541, 545, 549, 613, 614; **59**: 505,
  587-88, 631-32, 634, 635; **61**: 196, 552;
  and Steed memorandum on Adriatic,

53: 444-46; and Montenegro, **53**: 638n1, 640, 700, 703; **58**: 161-64, 268; **59**: 178n2, 620,n1; and Fiume and Adriatic question, **56**: 393n1, 472, 490,n1, 556, 562-65,n3, 567-72, 607-609,n1; **57**: 337, 338, 340-41, 344, 432-33, 467n2, 499-502; **58**: 88, 89, 160, 239n4, 396, 452, 588, 589-90; **59**: 34, 96-97, 201, 241, 551, 552, 553, 555, 556, 556-59, 569-70, 645; Smuts on, **57**: 171-73; issue of recognition of, **58**: 150, 236; **60**: 16,n1; and boundary issue, **59**: 60-63, 405-406; **60**: 16,n1; and reparations, **59**: 74n1, 305n13, 384n1, 391; **61**: 100, 101; and prisoners of war, **59**: 425, 426; Bliss on fixed military strength for, **59**: 428-32; and minority rights, **59**: 629-30; **60**: 97,n8; Lloyd George wants changes in peace treaty regarding, **60**: 120; and arms limitation, **60**: 169-70; and Hungary and conflicts, **60**: 312-14,n1; and atrocities in Albania, **60**: 530, 565; and Sudbahn, **61**: 280, 317-21

Carinthia, **57**: 501; **59**: 403-405, 501-502, 613, 631,n2; **60**: 16n1, 361n1, 643; S. Miles on, **59**: 403-405; Council of Four on, **59**: 501-502; Yugoslav troops in, **60**: 361, 643

Klagenfurt and Klagenfurt Basin, **59**: 60,n3, 61, 405, 406-408, 501, 542-43, 578, 587, 603, 613, 647; **60**: 21, 22, 34, 121-29, 232-33, 262, 267-69, 310, 315, 361-62, 394, 428, 565, 628, 639-40 682; **61**: 41-43, 50-56, 57-59, 92, 196; discussed at Council of Four, **59**: 542-43; **60**: 122-29, 267-69; **61**: 41, 51-56; WW on, **60**: 22, 207-208, 232-33, 361; **61**: 57-59; D. W. Johnson on, **60**: 34-38, 121-22; **61**: 41-43; Vesnić on proposition for, **60**: 232-33; Yugoslav troops advance into, **60**: 362, 628; **61**: 92, 196

Montenegro, **53**: 704; **54**: 179, 202; **55**: 29n2, 30, 32, 33; **56**: 394-95, 517, 572-74; **57**: 111, 515, 558,n1, 613; **58**: 354, 407-408, 461n1, 507-508; **59**: 145-46, 167, 178,n2, 215, 222,n12; **60**: 134; **61**: 405, 552, 554; Serbian behavior in, **53**: 638,n1, 701-704; and representation at Paris Peace Conference, **54**: 15, 18-21,n5, 65; **58**: 163; Lansing on situation in and on Anglo-American commission to, **58**: 267-68; Miles' recommendations for, **59**: 620,n1

Serbia, **54**: 226n1, 55, 124, 264, 330; **55**: 66, 84, 87-88, 164, 184, 203; **56**: 26, 242n1, 252, 570, 573, 574, 614; **57**: 78, 112, 124, 224, 585, 613; **58**: 8, 39, 42, 113, 150, 162, 198, 252, 374, 461n1, 471, 472; **59**: 53, 119-20, 130, 166, 215, 247, 255, 380, 562, 626; **60**: 134, 173; **61**: 94, 344, 430; and food relief, **53**: 15-16, 648; **59**: 174, 175; finances of, **53**: 572; **58**: 491n1; **59**: 176; and Montenegro, **53**: 638n1, 640, 700, 701-704, 704; **54**: 18-19,n5, 202; **57**: 558; **58**: 162-64, 354, 508; **59**: 178n2,3, 222,n12, 620n1;

and representation at Paris Peace Conference, **54**: 15, 16,n3, 18-19,n5, 45, 65, 115; and Reparation Commission and reparation, **54**: 211, 223, 283; **55**: 29,n2, 30, 32, 33; **57**: 454-55, 515; **58**: 249, 259; **59**: 74n1, 93, 103, 304-305,n13, 312, 387; **60**: 592; and League of Nations, **54**: 263, 462, 464; and Rumania, **54**: 376, 377, 421n7; offers to permit WW to arbitrate boundary dispute with Italy, **57**: 418; and Fiume and Trieste, **57**: 491, 517, 540-41; **58**: 397, 554-55; **59**: 64-66; Bryce on Macedonia and, **59**: 400; and minority rights, **59**: 577, 629; and Austrian peace treaty, **60**: 130-31,n5l; and issue of Hungarian attacks on Czechoslovakia, **60**: 257, 259, 260; Klagenfurt Basin and, **60**: 262; and atrocities in Albania, **60**: 530, 565; and war-cost contributions, **61**: 101, 254-56

Zara: see Italy—Zara

peace terms and treaties (mainly the German treaty, first phase, **55**: 492, 531, 545-46; **56**: 258, 579; **57**: 142n1; **58**: 430, 566-68; **59**: 315; military and naval aviation terms, **55**: 404-406, 425-32; **58**: 38, 125-28, 226-27, 267, 456-57, 557-58, 559; difference between peace terms and Armistice terms, **55**: 95-104; **58**: 262-63, 267, 310-11, 313-14, 315; Foch and Clemenceau on immediately dictating terms to Germany, **55**: 212-13, 233-34; Bliss on, **55**: 214-15, 511-14; **56**: 6-9; **58**: 95-96; WW on, **55**: 230,n1, 320, 529-31; **56**: 284; **57**: 635; **58**: 205; and war costs, **55**: 231; House on, **55**: 245-46; **56**: 207-208; and Rhineland, **55**: 472, 475-77; WW learns of House's agreement to separate League of Nations from peace treaty, **55**: 488n2; Benson on, **55**: 515-21, 522-24; **56**: 67; and Bullitt's mission to Russia, **55**: 540-45,n1; question of Senate ratification of preliminary treaty, **56**: 58-59,n4, 67-69, 75, 97-98; League of Nations to be part of, **56**: 59-60, 249-50; draft of clauses on cables, **56**: 219, 220; and Teschen resolution, **56**: 222; and labor issues and clauses, **56**: 237-38, 604, 605; **57**: 306-307, 528; **58**: 173-74, 329, 364, 416-18; and Fontainebleau Memorandum, **56**: 259-70; and Turkish Empire, **56**: 272-75; Clemenceau and Lloyd George on, **56**: 316-23; Clemenceau-WW confrontation, **56**: 349, 350, 351-52, 353-54, 365-68; WW's stipulations to be embodied in, **56**: 371; Smuts on, **56**: 416n11; **57**: 79; Nolan on terms acceptable to Germany, **56**: 492-93, 494; Mezes on Danzig and, **56**: 505; American commissioners on rights of national minorities, **56**: 511-12; and Polish-Ukranian negotiations, **56**: 529-30,n1; Commission on Responsibility

Paris Peace Conference (*cont.*)
of the Authors of the War, **56**: 530-34,n3,4, 611-17; questions to be examined, **57**: 76-77, 365-66; Council of Four on, **57**: 104,n5, 105; **58**: 151, 152, 432, 433, 434; and time schedule, **57**: 148n2; issue of publication or secrecy, **57**: 288-89, 291-92, 292-93; **58**: 22-24, 61-36, 404, 404-405, 439-40, 479, 484; news leak on reparation clauses, **57**: 333,n1; and responsibilities for the war, **57**: 346,n1; and informing delegates of text of peace treaty, **57**: 357; and drafting committee, **57**: 450-51; Clemenceau on, **57**: 525; and China's suggestions, **57**: 560-61,n2; draft of various articles, **57**: 572-74, 591-97; **58**: 65-67, 255-57; and Japan's claims and China, **57**: 603; attitudes of German officials and public toward, **58**: 45, 307-10, 314-15, 453-55; and Shantung controversy and settlement, **58**: 68-70, 70-73, 167, 168, 261, 271n1; languages treaty to be published in, **58**: 129; on guarantee of execution of, **58**: 134-35; repatriation of prisoners of war, **58**: 235; Article 41 deleted from air terms, **58**: 249; and minority rights, **58**: 284-86, 287-88, 291-93, 383; **59**: 150, 412, 628-30; need for preparation of two treaties because of Italy, **58**: 331, 334, 344, 382; Page on Italian attitudes toward, **58**: 357; and Anglo-French appeal to Italians, **58**: 376-78; R. S. Baker on, **58**: 412, 419; WW angered by French changes, **58**: 430-31; Foch attacks, **58**: 493-94; Reinsch on, **58**: 522n1; proposals for meetings with German delegates, **58**: 526; and French security treaty, **58**: 531n1, 532; J. F. Dulles on, **58**: 549-52; action to be taken if treaty not signed, **58**: 580-84; Miller on, **59**: 71; Irish-American delegates work for Ireland's representation at, **59**: 104-107, 172-73, 251, 318, 393,n1, 549,n1, 640n1, 642-43; and Montenegro, **59**: 178n3; Lansing disappointed by, **59**: 285-86; Bryce on, **59**: 399, 401; and Korea, **59**: 474-75, 643-44; and Italy's insistence on Treaty of London, **59**: 480-81; House on reconvening in Washington, D. C., **59**: 603; to receive representatives from Ottoman Empire, **59**: 642

Austrian treaty, **63**: 13, 82, 111, 372, 457, 493-94, 501-502; **64**: 101, 126, 150; treaty issues and terms concerning, **58**: 508-10, 540, 561-62, 578,n10, 580-81, 583, 584; **59**: 482,n4, 532-33, 534-38; **60**: 114,n1, 494, 521, 522, 532-33, 553, 558, 562, 573, 582, 621; **61**: 95, 134, 136, 258, 313, 420, 588; **62**: 345, 399, 535, 626; **66**: 377; **67**: 313n1; and reparations and successor states of Austria-Hungary, **58**: 31-33, 163, 304,

384, 384n1, 421-22; **59**: 304, 384n1, 386-89, 611-12, 624-25; **60**: 591-92,n2; **61**: 57, 100,n3; and food relief, **58**: 566; Council of Four on, **59**: 13, 130-31, 131, 368, 380, 419, 424-33, 439, 482-86, 496-500, 529-30, 532-33, 534-38, 538-41, 560-64, 566-68, 584; **60**: 220, 593; and boundary issues, **59**: 55, 60-64, 144, 405-406, 578-79; **61**:357; and treaty and League of Nations, **59**: 141; **61**: 579-80; and labor resolutions, **59**: 141; military, naval and air clauses, **59**: 165-70, 419, 428-32, 432, 481-82; Benson on naval terms, **59**: 197-98; R. S. Baker on, **59**: 368; and Klagenfurt Basin, **59**: 406-408; **60**: 34; **61**: 41-43, 51-56, 57-59, 92-93, 628, 640; and prisoners of war, **59**: 424-28, 455-56; whether considered new or old state, **59**: 496-500, 500-501, 532, 534, 535, 536; and minority rights, **59**: 497, 632, 634-35; **60**: 97,n8, 130-31,n5, 233-34,n4; **61**: 63-64; and term "German Austria," **59**: 500, 536, 587-88; and Carinthia, **59**: 501-502; and financial clauses, **59**: 536-38, 538-41; and Adriatic question and, **59**: 559; **61**: 230; "secret" Plenary Session on, **59**: 576, 577; Poland's claims regarding, **59**: 612; Orlando on, **59**: 616; terms submitted to smaller nations, **59**: 625-26; Italy on, **59**: 631-32; and national properties, forests, etc., **59**: 637; and border question, **59**: 647-48; **60**: 16,n1, 97n8; **61**: 172, 357, 371; delivered at St. Germain, **60**: 19; House on reasons for his not attending presentation of, **60**: 81-82; and Czechoslovakia's requests, **60**: 97-98,n9; and Yugoslavia's requests, **60**: 97,n8; Lloyd George on, **60**: 120, 618; and arms limitations, **60**: 131-34, 168-76; and political clauses, **60**: 218-20,n2, 225-26; and restitution of rolling stock (Article 20), **60**: 219-20, 226-27; and proposed trade agreements with Germany and Hungary, **60**: 283; and League of Nations Covenant, **60**: 579-80; A. C. Coolidge on, **60**: 642-43; and credit plans, **60**: 26n11; Seymour on Germany's counterproposals on German Austria, **60**: 139; and issue of trade with Hungary, **60**: 627,n9; Hoover's proposal for economic reconstruction of, **61**: 173-74; and war-cost contributions of Austro-Hungarian successor states, **61**: 254, 256; and Sudbhan, **61**: 280, 314, 317-21; Foreign Relations Committee requests copy of, **62**: 478, 612; Vittorio Emanuele III gives royal assent to, **63**: 547n1; Hitchcock on strategy concerning, **65**: 150-51

Bulgarian treaty, **61**: 95, 136, 245, 417, 494-95, 567; **62**: 345, 399, 626; **63**: 151,n4, 166, 299, 306, 372, 432, 457,

493-94, 502, 502-503; **64**: 67, 68, 87, 101; and reparations, **61**: 100,n3; and boundary issue, **61**: 588-93; and Thrace, **62**: 110-11, 320, 321, 510, 551; Foreign Relations Committee requests copy of, **62**: 478, 535, 612

Czechoslovakian treaty, **60**: 607; **61**: 47

German treaty, final phase and discussions over, comments on and controversy over, **59**: 36-37, 243-44, 286-87, 314-15, 383-84, 447, 448, 450,n2; **60**: 17, 82-83, 102-104, 105-106, 196, 221, 455-59, 519-20,n6,8, 551-52, 571; **61**: 95, 181-82, 185, 186, 232-35, 331-32, 467; **62**: 560; Germany on, **59**: 3, 12n5, 348,n1; Council of Four on, **59**: 7-11, 156-58, 297-98, 307-309, 360-62, 362-66; **60**: 528-29, 550, 576-78, 579-80; **61**: 150; WW on, **59**: 28,n3; and labor clauses, **59**: 48-50,n2,3,4, 421,n3; **61**: 37-40; and prisoners of war, **59**: 56-57, 131-32, 134-36, 162-63, 163-65, 304,n12; **60**: 473,n18; reparation clauses, **59**: 57-58, 139, 147-48, 370-71; issue of publication of, **59**: 58, 202,n1, 212-13, 313, 346, 448, 450-51, 471, 524, 644-45; **60**: 289, 290, 329-30,n1, 374, 466, 477, 527, 534; Scheidemann on, **59**: 84-85,n2; and blockade, **59**: 109-10, 128-30, 201-202; Gasparri on Benedict XV's views on, **59**: 118; Germany wishes oral discussions on, **59**: 124, 583; Smuts on, **59**: 149-50, 187-88, 201, 413-19, 616-18; proposal for military occupation of Rhineland, **59**: 228-32; Bullitt resignation, **59**: 232-33; Germany's request for time extension to examine terms, **59**: 257, 321-22, 322,n2, 324; **61**: 77-78, 79-81, 82, 111; Lansing on, **59**: 285; Brockdorff-Rantzau on economic effect on Germany of, **59**: 305-307; Bryce on, **59**: 398-99; and private property provision, **59**: 420,n2; R. S. Baker and WW discuss, **59**: 447-48, 646-47; and Danzig, **59**: 456-57, 589; and China's reservations concerning, **59**: 573,n1,3; **61**: 155, 175-76, 288-89; WW discusses German counterproposals with American commissioners, **59**: 594; **60**: 45-71, 263; issue of modifying, **59**: 622, 623-24; question of Germany's counterproposals and treaty revision, **59**: 626-27; British shift concerning terms, **60**: 4n3; Davis on, **60**: 4-7; House compares Clemenceau and Lloyd George's views on, **60**: 40-41; and French-British conflict, **60**: 72, 73; question of Germany accepting, **60**: 78, 89-90, 95-96, 136-37, 178, 179, 194-96, 263, 306, 334, 349, 431, 437, 451, 464, 495-97, 498-500, 533, 534, 560-61, 565,n1, 574-75, 583-91, 617-18; **61**: 33n2, 61, 69, 70, 72-76; Upper Silesian issue, **60**: 84-92, 436,n1; and Germany's eastern boundaries, **60**: 130n4; and commerce, **60**: 140-41, 420; Senate investigation of treaty leak, **60**: 155, 156, 198, 242-44, 245, 246-47, 287, 288, 289, 290, 299, 329-31, 379, 380, 382-83, 399, 430, 434, 536; allegations that France is holding private negotiations with Germany, **60**: 179-80; Morrow on Senate views and public opinion on, **60**: 201, 202-203; *New Republic* opposes, **60**: 202,n1; Senate passes Johnson and Hitchcock Resolutions, **60**: 288; and Knox Resolution, **60**: 376-78, 612-13; and military clauses, **60**: 472-73,n16, 480-81; and naval clauses, **60**: 473,n17, 481-82; and responsibility issue, **60**: 474, 475-76; **62**: 318-19, 334; Trotter on lack of racial anti-discrimination clauses in, **60**: 486; WW would rather Germany didn't sign that weaken terms of treaty, **60**: 488; WW on delays, **60**: 532-33; on not separating League of Nations Covenant from peace treaty, **60**: 536, 537, 538; Lamont's suggestions for ratification of, **60**: 537-39; and German religious missions, **60**: 548,n3, 577-79, 581-82; and economic clauses, **60**: 549-50; WW on presenting treaty to Germans when promised and on having time to review revised text and covering note, **60**: 573-74; and Rhineland occupation, **60**: 575-76; **61**: 139-40; issue of Austrian trade, **60**: 627,n9; on minority issue and, **60**: 629-34; **61**: 63-64, 271-75; and equal-rights clause, **61**: 27-28,n2; final form released to press, **61**: 27; issue of Polish treaty being signed simultaneously with, **61**: 27, 43, 63-64; House on ratification with League of Nations Covenant, **61**: 46; and minorities issue, **61**: 63-64, 271-75; Germany on war guilt clause, **61**: 74,n2; Germany accepts, **61**: 78-79, 99, 104; WW's comments to London *Daily Mail* on, **61**: 108; Italy signs, **61**: 109,n11; Clemenceau on, **61**: 114-15, 125; WW on importance of ratification without reservations, **61**: 115-16, 137, 247; **62**: 16-20, 305-309, 335-39, 433; issue of countries signing with reservations, **61**: 155, 240; German delegation named and verified, **61**: 187, 203; issue of delivery of William II, **61**: 199, 200-201; WW on implications of reservations or amendments to, **61**: 240; WW on, **61**: 243-44, 250-51, 253-54; Germany to sign Rhineland Convention along with, **61**: 279; and China's absence from signing ceremony, **61**: 325-26; Dulles on interim Reparation Commission, **61**: 384-85; House on meeting of Mandates Commission, **61**: 408; WW presents treaty to Senate, **61**: 417, 424, 506; WW's press conference on, **61**: 417-24; ratified by Germany, **61**: 418,n2; WW's ad-

Paris Peace Conference (*cont.*)
dress to Senate on, **61**: 426-36; League
of Free Nations Association urges ratification of, **61**: 447; WW discusses with
senators, **61**: 492-93,n2, 515-17,
548,n1, 561-62, 569-70, 593-95, 599-
602, 619-22; Wiseman on WW's progress toward ratification, **61**: 541-
43,n2; WW's position on compromise,
61: 546-47, 600, 601, 607n1; and China
and Japan and Shantung settlement,
61: 554-55, 556, 557-59, 593; Lodge on
not appointing Reparation Commission member, **61**: 582; and China's
rights under, **61**: 583,n3; American
mission on setting up commissions, **61**:
585-87; and Taft, **61**: 605,n1, 606, 607-
608, 614-15; Grasty on, **61**: 615-16;
Spencer presents reservations to WW
on, **61**: 619-22; Pittman on, **61**: 626-27;
Lamont on WW addressing Senate
rather than making speaking tour, **61**:
641-43; Lansing sends authenticated
copy to WW, **62**: 30; and reparations,
62: 148,n1, 149; Great Britain will sign
without U.S., **62**: 239; Sir G. Paish on,
62: 256; Japan on needed ratification
before negotiations on Kiaochow, **62**:
458; Lansing on ratification first then
setting up commissions, **62**: 550, Bible
used at signing ceremony, **62**: 435,n1;
controversy over ratification of, **62**:
560; and Shantung settlement, **62**: 3-4,
41-42, 508-509; Davis advises WW to
make public explanation of, **62**: 7-8;
WW invitation to and meeting with
Republican senators to discuss, **62**:
29,n1, 43-45; agricultural lobby on
public referendum, **62**: 30-31; Metzger
on whether U.S. can ratify treaty with
reservations without resubmission to
other governments, **62**: 35-40; and Article X, **62**: 67, 262-63; Republicans
seek compromise on reservations, **62**:
67-69, 112-14; various comments on effect of uncertainty of ratification, **62**:
180-81, 261, 266-68, 268-70, 272-74,
452; request for documents on, **62**:
219,n2, 477-78, 534; Lansing fears
WW's uncompromising attitude on
treaty reservations, **62**: 258-59; WW
on economic effect of failure to ratify,
62: 276-78, 340-44; Grange endorses
treaty ratification, **62**: 301; and
Pittman, **62**: 310-12, 429-32; House requests forcast on treaty ratification,
62: 323; Fall's questions and WW's
reply, **62**: 411-15, 417-19 T. R.
Marshall on status of treaty and recommendations, **62**: 419-20; McCumber
on main objections to treaty, **62**: 565-
66; W. B. Wilson on importance of ratification, **62**: 584-86; WW won't oppose
interpretive reservations, will oppose
drastic reservation amendments, **62**:
613-14; Wilson's reservations, **62**: 621;

Knox on, **63**: 3n4; WW's concern over
delay in Senate action on, **63**: 17-18,
76-779, 155, 156, 255; WW advises
reading French text if one cannot un-
derstand English, **63**: 48, 85, 103; Foreign Relations Committee majority
and minority reports treaty to Senate,
63: 52,n3, 198,n1,2; WW's ten principles of, **63**: 163; Glass on effect of ratification delay on financial and economic
situation, **63**: 203; Burleson on, **63**:
266, 442-43, 443; Pomerene's concern
over mild reservationists' strategy, **63**:
296; and Bullitt-Lansing exchange and
controversy, **63**: 337-38, 541; public
opinion in California on, **63**: 388; H. W.
Johnson on, **63**: 398,n1; Britain and
France anxious to have Italy ratify, **63**:
465-66; Hitchcock on amendment situation in Senate, **63**: 482-83, 571; Vittorio Emanuele III gives royal assent to,
63: 547n4; reservations needed for ratification, **63**: 586; organization of
transportation commissions as outlined in, **63**: 606-607, 613,n1; and German protocol on disarmament and coal
delivery, **66**: 44,n5; and Article X and
Ireland, **66**: 147n1,2; WW's statement
on election being referendum on
League of Nations and, **66**: 181-83;
Harding on, **66**: 200; failure to ratify
blamed as cause of recession, **66**: 242-
43,n4,5; issue of resubmission to Senate, **66**: 341-42, 390-91; WW on not resubmitting, **66**: 402; The Document on
Senate's failure to ratify, **68**: 6, 216,
537; Lloyd George asserts that he first
proposed League Covenant being part
of, **68**: 108,n1, 109; and Western
Ukraine Republic, **68**: 110; recollections of signing, **68**: 227; Gerard on, **68**:
432; WW on, **68**: 466; and Memel, **68**:
521n1; presentation of treaty to Germans at Versailles, photograph of, *illustration section*, **58**; *see also* League
of Nations; Versailles Treaty

Hungarian treaty, **59**: 13, 380, 509-12;
60: 283, 469-70,n11, 627,n9; **61**: 95,
100,n3, 136, 245, 420; **62**: 345, 535,
626; **63**: 299, 372, 422, 432, 457, 493-
94, 502-503; **64**: 101, 148, 150, 157,
446-48; Foreign Relations Committee
requests copy of, **62**: 478, 612; Wallace's instructions concerning negotiations, **64**: 464-66

Polish treaty, **59**: 299; **60**: 205, 623,n1;
61: 148-49, 198; **62**: 114, 345, 581; and
minority rights, **59**: 180-83; **60**: 223-25,
607, 633-34; **61**: 26-27, 43, 46, 47-50,
63-64, 88-92, 97-98, 271-75; draft of Allied letter to Paderewski accompanying treaty, **61**: 93-99; and Russian public debt, **61**: 256, 257, 258; signing of,
61: 324; Foreign Relations Committee
requests copy of, **62**: 477-78, 534, 611

Rumanian Treaty: **64**: 148, 150, 157
Turkish treaty: **61**: 128, 136, 245, 277-78, 417, 479; **62**: 345, 399, 535, 551, 626; **63**: 299, 372, 422, 432, 457, 493-94, 502, 502-503; **64**: 27, 52, 65, 261, 372,n1, 382; U.S. position on, **61**: 494-95; and Thrace, **62**: 110-11; Foreign Relations Committee requests copy of, **62**: 478, 612; Vénisélos on, **64**: 158: issue of U.S. participation in negotiations, **64**: 344-45, 391, 411, 448-50, 472; and Balfour Declaration, **64**: 358, 373; Polk on terms of, **65**: 64-65, 76-77, 111-12, 112-15; WW on, **65**: 73-75, 91; WW approves note to France on, **65**: 116; *Newark Evening News* on, **65**: 229,n1; and Euxine Pontus, **66**: 29,n1; and Armenia's boundaries, **66**: 65,n1
Versailles ceremony: **61**: 230, 302-305, 321-28, 328-32; and presence of South and Central American delegates at, **61**: 65-66; arrangements for German delegation, **61**: 148; Germany's delegates for, **61**: 148, 149, 192; arrangements for signing, **61**: 178, 192-93, 203, 235-36; and WW's signet ring, **61**: 179; Tumulty on WW preparing congratulatory message on signing, **61**: 184; issue of seals, **61**: 193, 203-204; plans for military parade, **61**: 193, 204; WW's comments on signing of, **61**: 292-93
Yugoslav treaty, **60**: 607

Paris *Petit Parisien*, **57**: 148,n2, 353, 391; **58**: 97
Paris *Tribune*, **55**: 89
Park, Bert Edwin, M.D., **58**: 607, 611, 630n93, 638, 639, 640; **59**: 574n1; **63**: 539n1; impact of WW's neurologic disease, **58**: 611-30; analysis of WW's medical history and stroke of Oct. 2, 1919, **63**: 639-46; diagnosis of WW's illness, **64**: 507n11; on aftermath of WW's stroke, **64**: 525-29
Park, Frank: makes walking cane for WW, **66**: 117, 129
Park, William Lee, **65**: 189n1
Parke, Myrtle N. (Mrs. Francis J.), **67**: 113,n1
Parker, Mr., **67**: 338
Parker, Alton Brooks, **67**: 261; **68**: 581
Parker, Edwin Brewington, **56**: 285n1; **59**: 161,n1; **61**: 529-30,n3; **65**: 214,n1, 218-19; **66**: 289,n2; and U.S. oil interests in Mexico, **66**: 375-76,n6, 404, 408
Parker, Frank, **63**: 362,n1
Parker, John Milliken, **65**: 295, 295,n2
Parks, E. Taylor, **67**: 581n2
Parliamentary Debates, **56**: 285n1; **57**: 6n7, 428n14
Parnassus on Wheels (Morley), **67**: 476n1
Parnell, Charles Stewart, **58**: 586,n1
Parodi, Vittorio Emanuele, **65**: 198,n6
Parry, Clive, **54**: 326n3; **60**: 52n4

Parsons, B. A., **63**: 66,n1
Partsch, Joseph Franz Maria, **60**: 413,n3, 424
Party Battles in the Heyday of Democracy (McAdoo), **68**: 261,n2
Party Battles of the Jackson Period (Bowers), **68**: 260-61,n1, 267
Pascal (Pasquale), August, **65**: 425n1
Pasco, Washington, **63**: 211n6
Pas de Calais coal fields, **57**: 159, 160
Pasdermadjan, Garegin, **65**: 222,n1; **66**: 507-508, 518
Pasha, Cherif (Sherif), **58**: 111,n2
Pašić, Nikola P., **53**: 702,n1; **55**: 87-88; **56**: 102; **57**: 418, 427,n12, 500; **58**: 44, 90, 162, 571; **59**: 74n1, 305n13, 494, 501; **60**: 16,n1, 97,n8, 221; **61**: 206; and reparations, **59**: 93; and Adriatic question, **59**: 96; **64**: 298, 303, 314; **65**: 94; and Austrian treaty, **59**: 588-89,n7; on Fiume plebiscite vote against annexation to Italy, **60**: 293-94; WW answers on Fiume, **60**: 361; thanks WW for effort on behalf of small nations, **61**: 461; and negotiations with Italy on Adriatic question, **65**: 303n10; photograph of, *illustration section*, **57**
Passaic, N.J., **55**: 286
Pass Christian, Miss.: Wilson's visit to in 1913, **64**: 486-87
Pasteur, Louis, **68**: 138-39; WW on, **68**: 229
Pastor, Peter, **53**: 7n3; **56**: 182n1, 462n11
Patchin, Philip Halsey, **53**: 389,n1, 402, 439; **58**: 404,n1
Paterson, N.J., **66**: 96-97
Paterson *Press-Guardian*, **68**: 454
Pathe Exchange, **67**: 150n1
Patricia, S.S., **64**: 8
Patrick, Mason Mathews, **55**: 112,n3; **67**: 585,n1
Patriot, The (Browning), **66**: 439,n1
Pattangall, William Robinson, **68**: 112,n4, 118
Patten, Thomas Gedney: on inception of Federal Reserve Act, **68**: 585-87,n1
Patterson, Graham: appeals for funds for relief in China, **66**: 327,n1, 338, 424, 434
Patterson, James R., **63**: 275n4
Patton, Francis Landey, **64**: 514,n1; **67**: 341
Patton, George Smith, **63**: 423,n3
Patton, George Smith, Jr., **63**: 423n3
Paul, James C. N., **66**: 92n1
Paul S. Reinsch: Open Door Diplomat in Action (Pugach), **61**: 631n1
Pavlenko, Mykhailo Omelianovychi: *see* Omelianovych-Pavlenko, Mykhailo
Payne, John Barton, **63**: 366, 367, 368-69; **65**: 380, 382; **66**: 7, 87, 102; **67**: 113n1; **68**: 576-77; and *Imperator* controversy, **64**: 8, 212, 218; and Honolulu Oil case, **64**: 405n1; appointed Secretary of the Interior, **64**: 448; on General Leasing bill, **64**: 473; resigns from

Payne, John Barton (*cont.*)
Shipping Board to become Secretary of the Interior, **65**: 20, 64; receives Lane's comments on Interior Department, **65**: 22, 23; and Democratic platform, 1920, **65**: 29; and Jones bill, **65**: 270,n1; named Director General of Railroads, **65**: 296,n5,7; Geddes on, **65**: 370; and Federal Power Commission, **65**: 448, 459; and railroad situation, **65**: 451; and Retirement Act, **65**: 478,n2; and coal situation, **65**: 508; trip to Alaska, **66**: 4,n1; on Debs pardon, **66**: 25; on resubmission of treaty, **66**: 342; and Milk River Valley Gun Club bill, **67**:81, 104,n2, 110; on railroad situation, **67**: 119; on Dawes, **67**: 124; Cabinet farewell, **67**: 199; praises WW, **67**: 215-16; photographs of, *illustration sections*, **65**, **67**

Payne-Aldrich Tariff Act, **67**: 486, 500

Peabody, George Foster, **53**: 12, 13,n2, 236; **65**: 341; **66**: 280, 293; **67**: 91-92, 105n3, 107, 460; **68**: 153-54, 203-11, 287, 291, 485; WW on marriage of, **67**: 117; and fund raising efforts for WW's S Street home, **67**: 137n1; praise of WW, **67**: 183; beginnings of WW Foundation, **67**: 271n1; WW's condolences, **67**: 510,n1; on railroads, **68**: 203, 204-205

Peabody, Jeannette Ennis Belo (Mrs. Charles), **67**: 527,n1

Peabody, Kate Nichols Trask (Mrs. George Foster): *see* Trask, Kate Nichols

peace conference: *see* Paris Peace Conference

Peace Conference Day by Day: A Presidential Pilgrimage Leading to the Discovery of Europe (Thompson), **61**: 252

"'Peace' Congress" (poem, Malcolm), **58**: 104,n2

Peace-Making at Paris (Huddleston), **57**: 6n7

Peace Negotiations: A Personal Narrative (Lansing), **56**: 98n1; **64**: 416n1; **67**: 60,n1, 72n1, 235,n3

Peace Parley Within 'Two Steps' of Failure: Leaders Lose Prestige (Simonds), **56**: 436,n3

Peace President (Gardiner), **53**: 634n1

peace treaty: *see* Paris Peace Conference—peace terms and treaties

Peacock, Captain, **55**: 192,n1

Peacock, Robert, **53**: 539, 540

Peale, Rembrandt: appointment to coal commission, **64**: 206, 209n1; and coal commission's majority report, **65**: 95,n1,2, 96, 97

Pearson, Sir Arthur, **65**: 430

Pearson, Weetman Dickinson, 1st Baron Cowdray, **65**: 534n1

Pearson, Thomas Gilbert, **67**: 81,n1

Pebbles on the Shore (Gardiner), **54**: 431,n1

Peck, Mary Allen Hulbert: *see* Mary Allen Hulbert

Peck, Thomas Dowse, **60**: 647

Peck, Willys Ruggles, **61**: 635,n4

Peck, George Nelson, **54**: 521,n2, 556; **55**: 90, 156, 336; **56**: 400,n4; **59**: 38n1; **66**: 289,n2; and controversy between Railroad Administration and Industrial Board, **57**: 282, 283, 378, 379, 380, 381, 382, 384

Peek Committee: *see* Industrial Board of the Department of Commerce

Peel, Sidney Cornwallis, **60**: 591,n3; **61**: 254,n3, 256, 384

Peerless Leaders (Cobb), **67**: 419,n1

Peery, George Campbell, **68**: 143n2

Peet, William Wheelock, **53**: 180,n1; **55**: 486

Pegram, Samuel, **56**: 556n2

Peking, China: reaction to Japanese claims settlement, **58**: 552n1, 553

Peking Missionary Association, **60**: 101n1

Pelagosa (now Pelagruz, Yugoslavia), **59**: 201; **61**: 228; **63**: 206, 208; **64**: 171, 174, 299, 302, 331, 334, 462; **66**: 377

Pellé, Maurice-César-Joseph, **59**: 323,n5; **60**: 259,n1, 313, 356, 419,n7, 478

Pelletier, Joseph C., **67**: 556,n2

Pelman Institute of America, Inc., **66**: 251n1

Pelmanism, **66**: 251n1

Pelogossa: *see* Pelagosa

Pence, Thomas Jones, **64**: 522,n1; **65**: 378,n2; **67**: 203

Pendleton, Ellen Fitz, **68**: 452n2

Penfield, Frederic Courtland, **65**: 298,n2

Penjdeh (Panjdeh) incident, **60**: 210,n6

Pennie, John C., **58**: 120,n3

Pennington, Mabel Vanderpool, **66**: 267,n3

Pennsylvania, **53**: 24; Democratic congressional victory in, **55**: 448-49,n1, 457, 458, 495; on prohibition, **61**: 294; McAdoo on political prospects in, **66**: 235; WW's message to Lehigh Valley Democrats, **67**: 279-80; Democratic politics in, **67**: 481; **68**: 25, 56,n2; Democratic women in, **68**: 156

Pennsylvania, University of, **55**: 438n1; **65**: 233; **68**: 514,n2

Pennsylvania, U.S.S., **53**: 315, 321, 348; **61**: 371

Pennsylvania Coal Company v. Mahon *et al.*, **68**: 277,n1

Pennsylvania History, **64**: 199n1

Pennsylvania Station (New York City), **61**: 376, 377, 401

Penrose, Boies, **53**: 24; **54**: 32,n3; **61**: 372, 506n1; **67**: 210; **68**: 56n2; and famine relief bill, **54**: 174n3, 229; chairman of Finance Committee, **60**: 113,n3; and woman suffrage, **61**: 5; and WW's health, **64**: 135-36; and treaty fight, **64**: 200-201, 337; WW on, **67**: 71,n2; WW uses wheelchair of, **67**: 207, 210; Cobb on, **67**: 424; photograph of, *illustration section*, **67**

Pentimalli, Major, **56**: 332,n3, 333
People's Council of America for Democracy and Peace, **53**: 13; **55**: 337n1
Pepper, George Wharton, **59**: 451,n1; **61**: 373; **68**: 346n2; on League of Nations, **68**: 326-27,n1, 334
Percy, Lord Eustace, **55**: 119, 154, 192; **60**: 17n1
Pergler, Charles (Karel), **61**: 518n1
Perks, Sir Robert William, **53**: 530,n1
Perley Morse & Co., **63**: 389n2
Perm, Russia, **54**: 93,n5, 94; **61**: 165
Perman, Dagmar Horna, **56**: 393n1l, 596n1; **57**: 78n8; **66**: 225n2
Permanent Association of International Road Congresses, **67**: 42, 47
Permanent Court of Arbitration (The Hague), **54**: 511, 512; **56**: 483; **58**: 382n5; appointments to, **64**: 216, 273; and Mexican Constitution, **64**: 240, 241
Permanent Court of International Justice, **54**: 436, 512, 513; **55**: 168; **56**: 228, 232, 483, 499n3; **57**: 251-52; **58**: 192-93, 199n1, 382n5; **59**: 586; **60**: 206, 224-25, 227, 624; **61**: 269, 491; **62**: 38; **63**: 261; **65**: 399-400; **66**: 158,n7; **67**: 374,n2; suggestions for lawyer for organization of, **60**: 431, 432; and mandates, **61**: 453-54, 455; **62**: 247; and E. Root, **65**: 399-400, 419; and Åland Islands controversy, **65**: 525-26; isssue of U.S. membership in, **68**: 160, 306,n2, 332n2, 339-41; The Document on, **68**: 217, 309-10, 537; WW on, **68**: 314; Davis on as partisan issue, **68**: 339-41; Lord Robert Cecil on WW's views on, **68**: 346; Clarke on, **68**: 360
Permanent Interallied Armistice Commission, **53**: 473n2
Permanent League of Nations, **53**: 514n1
Permanent Military, Naval, and Air Commission (League of Nations), **66**: 472-74, 497,n1
Perron, Mr., **67**: 338-39
Perry, Annie Louise Bliss (Mrs. Bliss), **66**: 378,n2
Perry, Bliss, **67**: 554; praises WW, **66**: 378-79,n1, 388; and WW Clubs, **67**: 257n1; beginnings of WW Foundation, **67**: 271n1
Perry, James De Wolf, Jr., **54**: 380,n2
Perry, Lewis, **58**: 428,n1
Perry, Margaret Lawrie Hubbell (Mrs. Lewis), **58**: 428,n1
Pershing, John Joseph, **53**: 130, 167, 181, 208, 290, 291, 339, 352, 375, 378, 385, 397, 399, 403-404, 410, 504, 583, 584; **54**: 149, 179, 467, 515; **55**: 29, 82, 160; **56**: 597; **57**: 365, 401, 526; **58**: 171, 501, 531; **59**: 7n3, 253-54, 313, 369, 591, 600; **60**: 491, 534; **61**: 193, 204, 306, 349; **62**: 166, 240, 323; **63**: 117; **64**: 416n2; **66**: 238; **67**: 210, 225, 462n1; **68**: 93, 468, 469, 507, 528; WW on "glory madness" of, **53**: 320; WW

visits at Chaumont, **53**: 488, 502, 502-503; offers his residence to WW, **53**: 432-33, 473; praises General Staff, **53**: 512-14; and reparation claims, **54**: 55; talk of as presidential candidate, **54**: 61; on German disarmament and demobilization, **54**: 243-44, 244, 245; concern over misinterpretation of Foch's note on German troops, **54**: 275, 331-32, 414; recommends WW view conditions at Brest, **55**: 64-65, 149, 151; and Wood, **55**: 487; on Sorbonne course for American soldiers, **57**: 36-37; and Haller's troops, **57**: 134, 135, 136, 178; has lunch with WW, **59**: 254; and issue of withdrawal of U.S. troops from France, **59**: 277, 279, 280; **60**: 387; and Rhenish separatist movement, **59**: 401-402, 443, 444; on not using bombers, **60**: 430; WW answers on bombing issue, **60**: 483; on Clemenceau and the French, **60**: 546-47; on military plans if Germany refuses to sign, **61**: 61; on Rhineland occupation force, **61**: 174-75, 547; WW on promoting to Chief of Staff, **61**: 293; receives title of General of the Armies, **61**: 517,n1; on troops for Upper Silesia, **62**: 272; WW's welcome home to, **62**: 622; and welcoming parade, **63**: 274n2; WW regrets he's unable to welcome, **63**: 295; thanks WW and EBW for flowers, **65**: 108; wishes to call on WW, **65**: 146,n1; and personal invitation to Pétain to visit U.S., **65**: 154-55; and relations with Foch, **65**: 155; suggestion that he visit South America, **65**: 318; **66**: 178-79; 178-79; sends WW specially inscribed copy of final report, and WW's response, **66**: 231,n1; on N. D. Baker, **68**: 133n1, 137; and Washington Cathedral, **68**: 396; greetings from Paris, **68**: 500; photograph of, *illustration section*, **53**
Pershing, Warren, **57**: 428
Persia, **53**: 153; **54**: 372; **56**: 170n1; **58**: 21-22,n8, 198, 508; **59**: 318,n1; **65**: 74; and secret agreement with Britain, **62**: 334,n1, 427-28; Britain's oil interests in, **62**: 452-53
Persian Relief Commission, **62**: 452
Personal Cordiality Wins Colleagues to President (Swope), **54**: 106,n1
Peru, **54**: 114-15, 264; **56**: 100; **66**: 445; and Tacna-Arica dispute, **53**: 316-17,n2, 317-18, 342, 346-47,n1, 536,n1; **55**: 330-31; **58**: 198; **65**: 190-91, 195; Minister presents credentials to WW, **65**: 338n2; Gonzalez on attempting settlement between Chile and, **66**: 209-12
Pervyse, Belgium, **61**: 4
Pesqueira Morales, Roberto V., **66**: 133n2, 142,n1, 150; Colby to Creel on, **66**: 407, 407-408; **67**: 132-33; N. H. Davis' meeting with, **66**: 160-62; Creel on willingness of to sign protocol agreement, **66**: 270; exchange of letters with

Pesqueira Morales, Roberto V. (*cont.*)
Colby on obligations Mexico is willing to meet and simultaneous press release, **66**: 283-84,n1, 285-86, 287, 335; Creel on letter of, **66**: 373, 374, 375, 376, 403-404,n4; on Fall, **66**: 405n7; Colby's response to, **66**: 418-19

Pessoa, Epitacio da Silva, **55**: 71, 123-24, 124; **57**: 258; **59**: 479-80; **65**: 318,n1; **66**: 179,n4, 324,n5, 431n3; and League of Nations, **54**: 426,n1, 463, 482, 483, 496; WW's remarks on, **59**: 520, 522

Pest, Hungary: *see* Budapest

Pétain, Henri-Philippe-Benoni-Omer-Joseph, **55**: 100, 149,n2; **56**: 110; **59**: 7n3; **60**: 599, 600; **61**: 33n2; Clemenceau meets with on Foch, **60**: 617; **65**: 154

Petchenga, Russia, **55**: 190

Peter I (of Serbia), **53**: 703,n3

Peter, Marc, **65**: 343n1; on WW, **65**: 338-40,n1

Peter Bent Brigham Hospital, **65**: 283n1

Peters, Andrew James, **55**: 194,n2, 206,n1, 225, 226, 235, 237; **56**: 162; **63**: 167n6, 169

Peterson, Maurice Drummond, **67**: 454,n1, 516

Pethick-Lawrence, Emmeline (Mrs. Frederick William), **59**: 117n,1

Petigru, James Louis, **55**: 460-62; **63**: 252,n4

Petition for Political Amnesty, **63**: 425,n1

Petliura, Symon Vasyl'ovich, **54**: 33,n7; **56**: 51-52,n12, 54, 467,n4; **59**: 195; **60**: 161,n8

Petrograd, Russia, **53**: 153, 256, 453; **54**: 94, 95, 101; **55**: 234, 350; **56**: 183; **59**: 21, 465, 466n6, 467; **60**: 282, 625, 636, 637; **61**: 455n1, 483; food and health crisis in, **56**: 388; Estonians' attack on, **60**: 267, 269; and flour, **63**: 588-90,n1

Petrograd *Novaia Zhizn*, **53**: 9,n6

petroleum: *see* oil industry

Petsalis-Diomidis, N., **54**: 403n3; **64**: 163n5

Pettit, Walter William, **54**: 27n2; **55**: 540n1; **56**: 183,n1, 466n1

Petty, Calvin H., **61**: 543

Petty, Mary Randolph (Mrs. Calvin H.), **53**: 221; **61**: 543, 624

Peyton, Harry, **61**: 482,n1

Pezet, Féderico Alfonso, **65**: 338,n2

Pffeifer, Alexandra Carlisle (Mrs. Eugene), **65**: 411

Phelan, James Duval, **54**: 486; **57**: 49-50; **60**: 536; **61**: 469; **67**: 37n1, 91; on parliamentary procedure for treaty vote, **61**: 437; treaty vote, **65**: 109,n1; Geddes on, **65**: 371; and proposed California alien land law, **66**: 186

Phelps Stokes Fund, **53**: 526n1; **62**: 292,n1

Philadelphia, Pa., **53**: 436,n3; **55**: 410-11, 457; and housing, **56**: 245-46; support for WW, **57**: 189; proposed lecture series at Academy of Music, **66**: 31-32, 40, 382n1; war chest funds in, **67**: 88

Philadelphia Academy of Music: and lecture series, **67**: 57, 59, 62, 72; WW lecturing at, **67**: 83-84; and Pasteur Centennial, **68**: 229n1

Philadelphia Democratic Women's Luncheon Club: *see* Democratic Women's Luncheon Club of Philadelphia

Philadelphia *Evening Public Ledger*, **65**: 4-5

Philadelphia *Evening Times*, **66**: 169n1

Philadelphia North American, **61**: 373; **66**: 352n1

Philadelphia Press, **64**: 403n, 434n

Philadelphia *Public Ledger*, **53**: 323n1; **55**: 253,n1; **56**: 340; **57**: 532,n2; **62**: 481n1, 627; **63**: 275n4; **64**: 360; **66**: 138,n1, 145; **68**: 331,n2; on Knox Resolution, **60**: 535

Philadelphia Record, **53**: 394n1; **66**: 174

Philippine Islands, **56**: 114; **63**: 74, 383, 384, 455; effect of Governor General Harrison's divorce and remarriage, **59**: 204; **61**: 478,n1; and oil, **62**: 618, 619; Baker on transport service to, **65**: 278, 280, 280-81; WW on granting independence to, **66**: 490; Harrison thanks WW for independence recommendation, **66**: 502

Philippine Islands and the United States, **57**: 189-90; and mission for independence, **55**: 391,n1; support and praise for Harrison as governor general, **60**: 198, 199, 199-200, 201; and Harrison's divorce and remarriage, **60**: 199-201

Philippines, University of the, **59**: 204n2

Phillimore, Sir George (Walter French), **54**: 152; **62**: 346; **67**: 239

Phillimore Report, **53**: 417; **54**: 188, 196,n1; **62**: 346, 402-403

Phillips, Albert, **65**: 189n1

Phillips, Caroline Astor Drayton (Mrs. William), **64**: 204n1

Phillips, John Sanburn, **68**: 48,n5

Phillips, William, **53**: 183, 317, 319; **56**: 161, 279, 339-40, 402, 550, 606; **57**: 95, 346, 420,n2; **59**: 172; **60**: 608; **61**: 41, 134, 462, 520, 584, 629; **63**: 119, 119-20, 166, 204, 235-36, 271-72, 297, 304, 369, 392, 392-93, 560; **64**: 3, 52, 157, 452; **65**: 181; **68**: 346n2; ascertaining from Kolchak supplies and support needed, **60**: 609; congratulates WW, **61**: 407; on blockade of Germany and dyestuffs trading, **61**: 450n1, 523, 524, 573; on Shantung settlement, **61**: 554-55, 559, 583; on Russian situation, **61**: 571; **63**: 394, 421; on legal aspect of commissions not sanctioned by legislation, **61**: 587-88; Reinsch on, **61**: 635; ascertaining from Kolchak supplies and support needed, **60**: 609; suggested as Minister to China, **62**: 283-

84; and International Labor Conference, **63**: 62, 445-46, 463-64; on Fiume and Adriatic question, **63**: 91-92, 270, 364-66, 485-86, 532, 534; on Thrace, **63**: 151, 305; on occupation of Fiume, **63**: 298-99; on troops to Armenia, **63**: 423, 464, 466; on reservation concerning Article X, **63**: 444; on WW's health, **63**: 537-38; suggested as Minister to The Netherlands, **64**: 41, 103, 119, 204, 205, 296, 317, 322, 407-408; on Lansing and WW, **64**: 243; resigns as Assistant Secretary of State, **65**: 47, 63; resignation mentioned, **65**: 107, 231

Phillips Exeter Academy, **58**: 428n1

Phillipson, Coleman, **56**: 68,n1

Philosophy of Religion: Lectures Written for the Elliott Lectureship at the Western Theological Seminary (Ormond), **67**: 335-36,n2

Phipps, Lawrence Cowle, **61**: 372; and treaty fight, **64**: 200-201, 336

Photoplay, **68**: 449

Physical Culture, **64**: 496n1

Piccioni, Luigi, **60**: 354,n2, 356

Piccolo Mundo Antico: Romanza (Fogazzaro), **60**: 123,n5

Pichon, Mme. (Mme. Stéphen-Jean-Marie), **53**: 721

Pichon, Stéphen-Jean-Marie, **53**: 142-43, 272, 378, 385, 397, 483n4, 585, 652, 721; **54**: 5; **55**: 57, 107, 149,n1, 283, 487, 499; **56**: 86, 103, 347, 498; **57**: 291, 354, 390, 537, 540; **58**: 137, 328, 423; **59**: 46-47, 202, 330, 438; **60**: 212, 213, 218, 220, 352, 546, 547; **64**: 35; on plans for WW's Paris stay, **53**: 345-46; exchanges greetings with WW, **53**: 380; and Russia and peace negotiations, **53**: 722-23; as chairman presides over Supreme War Council meetings, **54**: 7, 8, 10, 11, 12, 12-13, 15, 16, 17, 18, 41, 42, 43, 46-47, 49, 96, 102, 104, 111, 115, 117, 119; on Russian question, **54**: 21, 22-23, 27,n2, 28-29, 57, 287; on technical advisers, **54**: 26; WW on, **54**: 61-62; and Council of Ten meetings, **54**: 66, 67, 70, 71, 72, 74, 76, 189, 211, 284, 287, 287-88, 288, 311, 367; on publicity and press leaks, **54**: 66, 67, 111; **56**: 151; and official language, **54**: 70, 71, 72, 74, 76; and first Plenary Session, **54**: 127; and Commission to Poland, **54**: 248; on recognizing Finland, **54**: 287-88; on recruitment of colonial volunteers, **54**: 367; Seymour on appearance of, **54**: 383; on League of Nations being separate from peace treaty, **56**: 3,n1, 59; on Poland, **56**: 53, 94; on Syria and Turkey, **56**: 106, 107, 108, 109, 110, 111, 112, 118; on transport of Haller's army, **56**: 135, 146-47; on not entering into territorial negotiations with Hungary, **56**: 458-59, 460, 487, 488; Clemenceau on, **58**: 186; on

Italian credentials, **58**: 279, 280, 281, 282; on postponing invitation to Austria and Hungary, **58**: 283-84; and French security treaty, **61**: 311, 313

Pickett, Charles Edgar, **62**: 297n1

Pickett Act (1910), **62**: 16, 297-98,n1

Pickford, Mary, **65**: 384

Picot, Charles-François-Georges, **55**: 160n1; **56**: 115,n10, 116

Pierce, Robert Morris, **68**: 174,n1

Pierce-Arrow: WW's acquisition of: *see* under Wilson, Woodrow—family and personal life

Pierce-Arrow Company, **67**: 116,n1, 148, 157

Pierson, George Washington, **63**: 168n3, 170

Piip, Ants (Antoine), **59**: 18,n9

Pila, Poland: *see* Schneidemuhl

Pilgrims (London club), **53**: 521

Pillars of Society (Gardiner), **53**: 634n2, 708n3; **54**: 178

Pillau, S.M.S., **55**: 23

Piłsudski, Jósef Klemens, **53**: 163n1; **54**: 33,n6, 178, 195, 338; **59**: 217, 264, 354, 355, 357, 358, 359, 362, 392, 531n3, 541; **60**: 161,n10, 167,n16; **61**: 365n1; **64**: 198n1; **65**: 493; **67**: 204; informed of blockade if fighting continued, **59**: 359-60

Piltz, Erasme, **54**: 335,n3, 343

Pinchot, Amos Richards Eno, **54**: 397n1

Pinchot, Gifford, **64**: 474; **68**: 25n2, 56,n2, 179n1; on having Palmer appeal oil case, **64**: 354-55

Pinega, Russia, **55**: 190

Pisa (Italian ship), **59**: 65

Pitney, Mahlon, **53**: 185; and Duplex case, **67**: 497n2; and Truax case, **67**: 497n1

Pittaluga, Vittorio Emanuele, **63**: 485,n1

Pittman, Key, **53**: 24, 50-51, 53, 60, 68, 75, 116, 188; **54**: 230, 231; **55**: 263; **57**: 446; **61**: 184, 437, 469; **62**: 18; **63**: 483; **65**: 351n2; and woman suffrage, **53**: 23, 24; supports WW's principles, **53**: 50-51; and commemorative medals for U.S. servicemen, **53**: 83,n1, 116,n1; and debate over WW's presence at peace conference, **53**: 93-95; on Ireland, **56**: 398; on Knox Resolution, **60**: 535; on peace treaty, **61**: 626-27; on treaty reservations, **62**: 35, 36; on situation in Senate on treaty ratification, **62**: 310-12; questions WW at meeting with Foreign Relations Committee, **62**: 340, 354, 356, 358, 363; compromise reservations on League of Nations, **62**: 429-32,n3, 507n1; on public opinion in Washington and ratification prospects, **63**: 117-18; minority report on reservations, **63**: 198,n1; on Mexican situation and Jenkins case, **64**: 120, 127-28

Pittman resolution, **62**: 429-32,n3, 507n1

Pittsburg Post, **65**: 6; **66**: 174; **67**: 488

Pittsburgh, U.S.S., **63**: 486,n7
Pittsburgh, Pa., **59**: 287; **61**: 11n2
Pittsburgh, University of, **67**: 285,n1, 361, 361,n6
Pittsburgh Coal Company, **63**: 56
Pittsburgh, U.S.S., **65**: 537, 538, 549
Pius X, **53**: 242n3
Plamenatz (Plamenac), Jovan S., **57**: 558n1; **58**: 267,n2, 354,n2, 507,n7, 508; **59**: 178n3; on Montenegro not being part of League of Nations, **58**: 407-408
Plan de Agua Prieta, **65**: 252n1; **66**: 160n1
Plan of San Diego, **64**: 134,n3, 140n1
"Plan of San Diego and the Mexican-United States War Crisis of 1916: A Reexamination" (Harris and Sadler), **64**: 140n1
Plan to Promote the Public Welfare by More Effective Cooperation Between the Government of the United States and Industry (Garfield), **56**: 344n2
Plaschka, Richard G., **55**: 317n3
Platon, Metropolitan of Odessa and Kherson, **61**: 464,n4,5
Platt, Harriet Floyd McAdoo Martin (Mrs. Clayton), **68**: 124,n58
Platt, Thomas Collier, **67**: 364n2
Players' Club, **68**: 161
Pless, Hans Heinrich XV, Prince of, **60**: 55n1
Plimpton, George Arthur, **66**: 246n2; **68**: 388n1
Plumb, Glen Edward, **55**: 248n2; **62**: 138, 198n2, 227n1, 482, 526
Plumb plan, **55**: 248n2; **61**: 377,n1, 414, 414-15; **62**: 135, 136, 161, 191, 198n2, 249, 482; **64**: 21; McAdoo on, **62**: 185,n2; WW learns of, **62**: 227n1; summary of, **62**: 229-30
Plumb Plan League, **62**: 135, 137, 198n2
Plunkett, Charles Peshall, **55**: 266n1; **60**: 44,n4
Plunkett, George Noble, Count, **57**: 419,n2; **59**: 106, 251, 366n1, 393,n1, 513, 549n1; **60**: 289, 383, 544; denied hearing at peace conference, **61**: 466-67
Plunkett, Sir Horace, **56**: 304; **67**: 129; **68**: 464, 478; on Irish situation and U.S. public opinion, **55**: 452, 453-55
Plutarch, **66**: 269n2
Plymouth, England, **57**: 447n1
Podgorica, Montenegro, **53**: 638n1
Podgorica Resolution, **53**: 638n1
Podmaniczky, Baron Tibor, **56**: 241,n4, 332,n2
Poel, Jean van der, **54**: 148n1; **56**: 416n11
Poelcapelle, Belgium, **61**: 4
Pogany, József, **56**: 182,n1, 239, 242
Poincaré, Henriette Benucci (Mme. Raymond), **53**: 292, 384, 387,n2, 398, 403, 410, 419, 459,n3, 500, 577, 592; **54**: 76, 488,n1; **55**: 196, 497; **58**: 504; **61**: 114, 188, 302

Poincaré, Lucien-Antoine, **53**: 459n1, 460,n7, 500
Poincaré, Mme. (Mme. Lucien-Antoine), **53**: 459,n4, 500
Poincaré, Raymond, **53**: 292, 368, 369, 372, 383, 384, 386-87, 390, 401, 403, 410, 456, 457, 459n1, 485, 489, 500, 577, 592, 652; **54**: 5, 49, 464n1; **55**: 149, 160, 196, 497, 499; **56**: 368, 370, 542, 596; **57**: 356, 365; **59**: 371; **60**: 212, 218, 261, 485, 547; **61**: 107, 306, 311; **62**: 156n1, 337; **65**: 542; **68**: 307n4; refuses WW's theater invitation, **54**: 76-77; opens Paris Peace Conference, **54**: 127, 128, 128-29; on Left Bank, **58**: 211-14, 452,n2, 584; message to Italy, **58**: 280,n4, 282, 328, 336, 357; and Foch clique, **58**: **58**: 462,n2; French public opinion on, **58**: 504; WW answers on the Rhineland, **58**: 521-22; and WW and dinner invitation episode, **61**: 112-14, 115, 119, 132, 133, 173, 178, 180, 187; remarks after dinner, **61**: 189,n1; WW pays farewell visit to, **61**: 302; absent from signing ceremony, **61**: 326; and WW's charges of militarism in Hitchcock letter, **65**: 52, 66, 87, 89; and reparations, **65**: 58; WW on, **66**: 331; **68**: 458-59, 474,n2, 502, 593,n11; and German reparations, **68**: 434,n2; photograph of, *illustration section*, **53**
Poindexter, Miles, **55**: 450; **56**: 187n3, 339; **58**: 410n1; **59**: 451n1; **61**: 372, 411; **68**: 185,n1, 247; and WW's health, **64**: 135-36; and treaty fight, **64**: 196, 200, 202, 337; and bitter-enders, **64**: 328n2
Pola, Yugoslavia, **53**: 445, 696,n1; **54**: 112n3; **58**: 7, 87, 142, 392; **59**: 53, 242; **63**: 298; **64**: 174, 175
Poland, **53**: 56, 179, 293, 294, 338, 351, 353, 420n3, 713; **54**: 264, 302; **55**: 3, 29n2, 42, 57, 66, 79, 96, 110, 164, 184, 202, 233, 243, 317, 387, 542; **56**: 26, 35; **57**: 69, 111, 359, 572; **58**: 39, 40, 42, 155, 198, 279, 383, 472; **59**: 50n7, 130, 166, 167, 215, 247, 300n8, 635; **64**: 442, 443; **66**: 16; **68**: 62; and Jews and minorities, **53**: 67n1, 79-80, 104-105, 141, 260; **54**: 231-32; **55**: 380-71, 372-73, 378, 380, 464; **58**: 283, 285, 287, 288, 290-93, 383-90; **59**: 113, 114-17, 179-83, 198-200, 218-21,n7, 411-13, 419n1, 445-46, 471, 496, 497, 515, 516n1, 638-39; **60**: 134, 146, 155, 221-22, 266, 282, 358, 629-33; **61**: 158, 242, 430, 445; **62**: 80; on having her soldiers return home, **53**: 163, 182, 193; **64**: 389-90; and food crisis, **53**: 226, 649, 689, 709; enlistment in U.S. of Polish troops, **53**: 605, 700; and Russia and Bolsheviks, **53**: 611,n1, 692; **54**: 7,n3, 8, 8n5, 32-33,n6, 94, 103,n7, 136-337, 179-80,n2, 337-39; **59**: 442, 470, 471; and representation at Paris Peace Conference,

54: 61, 211; House on recognizing, 54: 178; Paderewski becomes Prime Minister and hopes for recognition, 54: 195-96; question of sending troops to, 54: 199-204, 414; and reparations, 54: 211, 223, 283, 462; 57: 454-55; 58: 28, 471-71; U.S. extends greetings for success, 54: 217; and Germany, 54: 220, 240, 336-41, 533-34; 55: 15, 55, 100, 108, 112, 203; and Inter-Allied Commission to, 54: 204, 248-49, 334-41, 418-20, 471,n2, 545; recognition of, 54: 278, 288; and Prinkipo Declaration, 54: 287; Council of Ten on, 54: 334-41, 341-45; and Czechoslovakia and territorial claims, 54: 343-45, 374, 375, 388; and Teschen and Bohemia, 54: 416-17,n3; 56: 220-22,n9; 57: 326-27; 59: 218; invasions prevent commission to Paris Peace Conference from leaving, 54: 480-81; and League of Nations Commission, 54: 482, 495-96, 509; and Danzig, 55: 233-34, 387, 546; 56: 318-19, 321, 322, 471-72, 505, 507; 57: 151-55, 289-90, 572-74, 593-97; 58: 137, 152-53; Supreme War Council on, 56: 49-56; Foch on, 56: 49-51, 52-53, 314-15; and the Ukraine, 56: 56, 119, 127,n1; 57: 357-58, 365, 372, 444-45, 451, 461-64, 628; 58: 101-102, 316, 455, 505-506,n4; 59: 215-17, 261-63, 323-25, 350-60, 458, 531, 541-42, 560-61, 566, 596-97, 597-99, 616; boundary issues, 56: 88-95, 127, 165-67,n2, 312-13; 60: 28-29, 77, 139, 436,n1, 553; 62: 419; 66: 138,n1, 145; and controversy over transport of Haller's army, 56: 118-19, 129-48, 167-69,n3, 181, 209n2, 408-11, 494, 523; 57: 75,n6, 134-36, 178, 549-50; U.S. appoints minister to, 56: 123-24,n2; 57: 285, 334, 373; and press leaks, 56: 148-52; and Fontainebleau Memorandum, 56: 266; peasants opposed to being part of Czechoslovakia meet with WW, 56: 442-43; 57: 237-39, 290; Clemenceau's response to Fontaineleau Memorandum concerning, 56: 478, 479; H. Hoover on feeding of and Danzig issue, 56: 547; Kernan on, 57: 275-80; and France and militarism in, 57: 279-80; diseases in, 57: 311; Lord on Galicia and, 57: 328; T. H. Bliss on proposed armistice commission for Ukrainian and Polish troops, 57: 415-16; Keynes on economic rehabilitation of, 58: 12; and Kiel Canal, 58: 66; Council of Four on inclusion of as belligerent, 58: 151; and railroads, 58: 384, 389-90; issue of recognition of, 58: 385, 388; recommendations for separate treaty with, 58: 386-87; Taft on importance of religious freedom in, 58: 460-61,n1; Paderewski on, 58: 556-57; 59: 216,n5; 66: 225-27; economic problems in, 58: 563; and Council of Four on reparations, 59: 31, 32, 33; Lamont

on finances and reparations, 59: 176, 384n1; Gibson on situation in, 59: 263-65; drafting committee to review peace treaty with, 59: 299; threat of blockade if fighting with Ukraine continues, 59: 359-60, 392-93; Smuts on frontier of, and German peace treaty, 59: 415-16; and prisoners of war, 59: 425, 426; and fixed military strength for, 59: 428-32, 439; Germany on, 59: 579, 581-82; and Austrian treaty, 59: 612; and Germany's counterproposals and Upper Silesia, 59: 615; 60: 53-59; and issue of plebiscite for Upper Silesia, 60: 24, 130n4, 189-92, 404-405, 411-15, 421, 436n1, 553-56; and commission to investigate pogroms in, 60: 39, 99, 99-100, 287, 567, 601, 602, 641; Council of Four on issues in peace treaty concerning, 60: 84-92; Kolchak on, 60: 143; Paderewski at Council of Four on Upper Silesia and, 60: 156, 157-68; and Ukraine, 60: 160-62, 470-71, 479; and arms limitation, 60: 172-73; Lord on German counterproposals on, 60: 182-89; and Germany's demands for access to the sea, 60: 187-88; and minorities and League of Nations appeal procedure, 60: 205-206, 223-25, 227-28, 487, 607; and draft reply to Germany's counterproposals, 60: 447; and Article 89 of treaty on free transit, 60: 519-20,n6,8; Council of Four on territory taken from Germany, 60: 553-54; Council of Four on territory taken from Poland, 60: 562; and issue of blockade, 60: 626, 627, 638-39; Paderewski memorandum on minorities and peace treaty, 60: 629-34; 61: 271-75; Paderewski on Germans in, 60: 634; U.S. Senate resolution on Jews in, 60: 640n1; 61: 88-92, 97, 178, 272-73, 275; 62: 220-22, 531,n1; 64: 198n1; and war-cost contributions, 61: 101, 254-56; and Germany, 61: 140-41, 163-64, 179, 208-209; Balfour on eastern Galicia and, 61: 167-68; WW on liberation of, 61: 236; Council of Four on supplies for army of, 61: 274-75; peasants wish to be part of, 61: 347; Gibson appointed minister to, 61: 365,n1; Redfield on economic needs of, 62: 33; Poole on threat of Bolshevism in, 62: 444, 448; WW on, 62: 531; 63: 10-11, 13-14, 24-25, 82, 98, 186, 250, 372; 66: 154-55, 308, 337; grain request from, 64: 4-6, 12-13; Vénisélos on, 64: 162; issue of publication of Morgenthau report on, 64: 198n1, 260,n1,2; Gibson to return to U.S., 65: 65,n1, 88-89; requests U.S. representative on Teschen Commission, 65: 65-66, 213-14, 256; Minister presents credentials to WW, 65: 338n2; children fed in, 65: 469; sends greetings to U.S., 65: 493; and Teschen, 65: 517-18, 533; Gibson on situation in,

Poland (*cont.*)
urges WW to make statement, **65**: 526-28; WW will not make statement on, **65**: 531; thanks WW for continued suppport, **66**: 9-10; and Russia, **66**: 11,n1, 24; U..S. note on its Russian policy and, **66**: 19-24; Hurley on trade and, **66**: 74; decision to publish correspondence with, **66**: 87-88,n1, 90,n1; Wise on plight of Jews in, and request for WW statement, **66**: 108-109; WW on plight of Jews in, **66**: 110; and purchase of surplus from War Department, **66**: 146-47; gratitude to and praise of WW, **67**: 204, 496,n1; WW receives honorary degree from University of Cracow, **67**: 392, 400; and Eastern Galicia, **68**: 110, 111; WW presented with Order of White Eagle, **68**: 177, 183; and *World Settlement*, **68**: 496; greetings to WW, **68**: 507-508; WW's good wishes for, **68**: 511; and Memel, **68**: 521; *see also* Paris Peace Conference—*Polish Treaty*; Polish-Soviet War of 1919-1920

Policies and Opinions at Paris, 1919: Wilsonian Diplomacy, the Versailles Peace, and French Public Opinion (Noble), **55**: 66n2; **56**: 3n1, 148n3; **57**: 6n7, 240n1; **61**: 332n10

Policies at Washington (New York *Evening Post*), **68**: 57n3

Polish Americans: Cora Budziszewski in Tacoma, **63**: 250,n2; repatriation of men in Haller's Army, **64**: 372-73, 375, 389-90; **65**: 43

Polish Commissions: *see* Commission on Polish Affairs; Inter-Allied Commission to Poland

Polish National Committee, **53**: 105; and Jews, **55**: 372, 373

Polish Problem at the Paris Peace Conference: A Study of the Policies of the Great Powers and the Poles, 1918-1919 (Lundgreen-Nielsen), **54**: 33n6, 481n4; **56**: 49n10, 495n1; **59**: 216n5; **60**: 189n2

Polish Relief Committee: and corn, **67**: 139

Polish-Soviet War of 1919-1920, **53**: 611n1; **65**: 527n1; **66**: 11n1, 16-17n1, 19, 39, 45-47,n7, 87n1

Polish-Ukrainian Armistice Commission, **58**: 505-506; **59**: 324, 350-51, 353,n4, 354, 354-55

Polish Weekly, **55**: 370,n2

Political Diaries of C. P. Scott, 1911-1928 (T. Wilson, ed.), **53**: 575n1

Political Education of Woodrow Wilson (Kerney), **65**: 511n2

Political Origins of the New Diplomacy, 1917-1918 (Mayer), **62**: 365n27

Political Science Quarterly, **58**: 364n1; **68**: 259n2

Political Situation in India (*Fortnightly Review*), **59**: 97n3

Politics and Diplomacy of Peacemaking: Containment and Counter-revolution at Versailles (Mayer), **53**: 408n1, 544n1, 711n1; **54**: 309n1, 309n1; **55**: 204n2, 458n1, 540n1; **56**: 182n1, 259n1, 285n1; **57**: 6n7, 240n1; **58**: 156n1, 237n3, 427n1, 486n3; **62**: 428n1

Politics and Life Sciences, **62**: 634n17

Politics of Korean Nationalism (Lee), **56**: 187n2

Politics of Provincialism: The Democratic Party in Transition, 1918-1932 (Burner), **67**: 45n2; **68**: 179n1

Politics of the Prussian Army, 1640-1945 (Craig), **65**: 98n1

Politis, Nicholas, **54**: 463,n2; **60**: 222,n5

Polk, Elizabeth Sturgis Potter (Mrs. Frank Lyon), **64**: 57,n1; **67**: 135,n1

Polk, Frank Lyon, **53**: 159-60, 166, 291-92, 292, 335, 345-46, 432 436, 437, 574, 590, 624, 645, 690-91, 716n1, 718, 719, 723n6; **54**: 158-59, 194, 282; **55**: 82, 289, 300, 452; **56**: 183, 187, 519; **57**: 175, 282, 283, 344, 374, 420n1, 420,n2, 442, 484, 570-71; **58**: 96, 423, 553-54; **59**: 148, 188, 189, 204, 236, 281, 282, 372n2, 449, 471, 547, 549-50, 571n1, 573, 578; **60**: 202, 245, 571,n1; **61**: 45, 130, 134, 172, 177, 277, 461, 478, 513, 526-27; **62**: 5n6, 41, 116, 235, 236, 272, 426, 449, 522, 550, 603, 619; **63**: 59, 151, 166, 421, 422, 537, 571, 588, 607; **64**: 5, 11, 234, 235, 243, 249n1, 269, 318, 436; **65**: 10, 22, 92, 98, 148, 153, 154, 181, 338; **66**: 522; **67**: 426n1, 540, 602; **68**: 59, 576; and Tacna-Arica dispute, **53**: 317, 318, 342, 536,n1; **55**: 330-31, 393; and Gompers and international labor conference, **53**: 408, 466; and Russian railways, **53**: 463-64, 555-57, 632-33, 699; **55**: 38, 350-51, 393; and enlistment of Polish troops in U.S., **53**: 605; on Bolshevism, **53**: 627; on Anderson's plea for definite Russian policy, **53**: 628; on Russia, **54**: 26-29; **56**: 152, 153, 159-61; **57**: 512, 575n1; **58**: 494-96; **59**: 72-74; suggested for Attorney General, **54**: 125; on Senate reaction regarding railroads and troop withdrawal from Russia, **54**: 83-84, 259-60, 261, 486-87; on Pan African congress, **54**: 126; on famine relief bill, **54**: 174, 259; and General Leasing bill, **54**: 216, 256, 393; on Irish situation, **54**: 472-73; on China's fears of Japan, **54**: 474-76; and H. W. Johnson's Russian resolution, **55**: 149; on Japan's negotiations with Allies, **55**: 293-94; on Mexican-U.S. relations, **55**: 351-52; on Norwegian ships, **55**: 357; on issuance of passports to Irish groups, **55**: 406, 407, 547; **59**: 172-73; on Graves and Russian situation, **55**: 493; on N. Hapgood appointment, **56**: 101; on Lowell and League of Nations, **56**: 161-62; issue of publication of peace treaty and Senate leak investigation **59**: 313,

450-51, 471; **60**: 155, 156, 242-44, 290, 299, 329-31, 330, 434, 534; on Graves, **59**: 409-10; on Republican opposition to Great Britain, **59**: 451-52; suggests waiting for Kolchak's reply before sending Morris to Russia, **59**: 618-19; on Senate opposition to League of Nations Covenant, **60**: 42; on Morgan's offer regarding ambassador's residence, **60**: 83,n1; and Morris' trip to Omsk, **60**: 240; **61**: 130-31; on deporting Martens, **60**: 484,n1, 567; on serious boycott situation in China, suggests revision of Shantung settlement, **60**: 604-605; suggested as minister to Belgium, **61**: 134; on supplies and food relief for Russia, **61**: 288, 455, 465-66, 528; poor health of, **61**: 396; WW considers for ambassadorial position, **61**: 396; on Ethiopian mission to U.S., **61**: 406; on lifting blockade, **61**: 450; on U.S. representation on Reparation Commission, **61**: 493; on replacements for Czech troops in Russia, **61**: 494; on retaining vessels at Archangel, **61**: 505-506, 525; on murders of Americans in Mexico, **61**: 510, 527; on WW's ability to appoint representatives to international commissions, **61**: 522; and Japan and China and treaties of 1915 and 1918 and Versailles treaty, **61**: 554, 556, 557, 559; and Thrace, **62**: 110-11, 207, 238-40, 319-21, 327-28, 416-17, 510, 551, 553; **63**: 60-62, 120-22, 235-36, 305; on Rumanian occupation of Budapest, **62**: 123, 242, 248; on need for members on interim Reparation Commission, **62**: 143-44; and disposal of German and Austro-Hungarian ships, **62**: 146; on pact between Great Britain and Greece, **62**: 238-40; on mandates, **62**: 257-58, 304, 511-14, 579-80, 595, 620; and Lansing on U.S. policy on various issues, **62**: 265-66; on Adriatic question, **62**: 456-57, 574-75, 603-605; and Constantinople, **62**: 620; and Adriatic question, **63**: 91-92, 204-10, 270, 617n1; **64**: 168-78, 323-24, 331, 352, 402n1, 445-46, 458-59, 473, 480-81; on Rumania, **63**: 119,n2,3; **64**: 34, 35, 36; concern over adjourning Council of Heads of Delegations, **63**: 299, 306, 391; on pressure from Britain and France regarding Fiume, **63**: 424, 465-66; and troops to Armenia, **63**: 466; on severe Italian crisis, **63**: 524-25; and Italy and Spalato, **63**: 532; and WW's health, **63**: 536, 537-38; and *Imperator* controversy, **64**: 10; on situation in Syria and Turkish Empire, **64**: 25-27; Lansing on reasons for opposition to treaty, **64**: 54-57; and American delegates in Paris, **64**: 102, 117-18, 147, 149, 150-51, 156-57; on Germany not signing protocol, **64**: 150-51; on one of the most critical moments in diplomatic history for U.S., **64**: 150; greetings to WW on his return to U.S., **64**: 227; on recognition of Costa Rica, **64**: 229-30; on Morgenthau report, **64**: 260,n1; meets with House, **64**: 270; and redraft of Jackson Day message, **64**: 270; on Fletcher resignation, **64**: 310; on Lansing's resignation, **64**: 398, 415-19; on Turkish treaty negotiations, **64**: 411, 448-50, 464, 472; mentioned as Lansing's successor, **64**: 419; on R. Crane's suggestion for Masaryk message on ratification, **64**: 443; on Hungarian negotiations, **64**: 446-48, 464-66; on France's position on Fiume, **64**: 450-51; and Frazier, **64**: 452; WW informs of new choice for Secretary of State, **64**: 464; on extraterritorial rights in Siam, **64**: 468-72, 479; on Geddes as British Ambassador to U.S., **64**: on extraterritoriality in Siam, **65**: 21,n2; and Adriatic question, **65**: 37, 43; comments on not being appointed Secretary of State, **65**: 41, 139, 225; on recognition of Costa Rica, **65**: 46; on Geddes, **65**: 55-56; on Turkish treaty, **65**: 64-65, 72-75, 76-77, 91, 111-12, 112-15, 116; on appointing U.S. representative to Teschen Commission, **65**: 65-66, 213; on Gibson returning to U.S. **65**: 65,n1; on U.S. representation on proposed commission to Russia, **65**: 77-78; on France's reaction to Hitchcock letter, **65**: 84,n1, 87, 89; suggestions for diplomatic appointments, **65**: 85 87-88, 88-89; on Kapp *Putsch*, **65**: 106 107; on vacancies in State Department, **65**: 107, 108; on Morgenthau appointment, **65**: 140; and Pétain and Foch visits, **65**: 154; on French invasion of Germany, **65**: 158; resignation of, **65**: 190, 196-97, 197, 230-31, 352 355; WW's appearance painful to, **65** 339, 343; relative of recommended for diplomatic post, **65**: 357-58; Geddes on **65**: 371; on leaving WW's service, **65** 397-98; WW's get-well wishes to, **66** 282, 301; and J. W. Davis' resignation **67**: 60, 62; and WW Foundation, **67** 271n1, 327n5; **68**: 249n2; on purpose of Woodrow Wilson awards, **67**: 544n3

Polk, William, **65**: 357

Pollak, Theodora, **53**: 63

Pollo, Stefanaq, **66**: 45n6

Pollock, Sir Ernest (Murray), **58**: 277,n2, 539,n5; **60**: 476,n23; **61**: 150, 338

Pollock, Sir Frederick, **57**: 128,n6

Pollock, William Pegues, **53**: 23; **54**: 519,n1; **65**: 256,n6, 257, 261

Pomerania, **59**: 579; **60**: 25, 162

Pomare, Maui Wiremu Piti Naera, **54**: 312-13,n4

Pomerene, Atlee, **53**: 188; **58**: 605n2; **61**: 437, 492; **62**: 18, 286; **67**: 399; on publication of peace treaty, **59**: 450-51; on not admitting Germany to League of

Pomerene, Atlee (*cont.*)
  Nations, **60**: 380-81; questions WW at
  meeting with Foreign Relations Committee, **62**: 340, 368, 372, 373-74, on
  railroad situation, **62**: 477; on treaty
  reservations, **63**: 198,n1, 198,n3, 296;
  and vote on Lodge resolution, **64**: 63;
  on WW's no-compromise statement,
  64: 192n1; and Democratic caucus on
  treaty, **64**: 483; and Democratic platform, 1920, **65**: 29; code name for, **65**:
  350; and Treaty of Berlin, **67**: 422n4;
  and Four Power Treaty, **67**: 577n1;
  McAdoo on, **68**: 149
Ponape, Caroline Islands, **54**: 292
Ponce de Leon Avenue Baptist Church
  (Atlanta), **68**: 196n1
Pond, George B., **53**: 157n2
Ponta Delgada, The Azores, **57**: 447n1
Ponte-Corvo, Prince of: *see* Murat, 5th
  Prince of (Joachim Napoléon)
Poole, DeWitt Clinton, Jr., **53**: 629,n3,
  630; **55**: 93n2; **56**: 279n1; **57**: 460-
  61,n2, 560, 628; **59**: 72,n2; **62**: 202,
  281, 543; on retaining American vessel
  at Archangel, **61**: 525-26; memoran-
  dum on Bolshevism, **62**: 203-205, 323-
  24, 441-48
Popovitch, Vladimir, **53**: 640,n3
Poree, Yugoslavia: *see* Parenzo, Italy
pork industry, **53**: 687-88, 699; **54**: 105-
  106, 229-30,n4; **55**: 336, 343, 362, 393-
  94, 395-96, 483; **57**: 473; Hoover on, **62**:
  124-25
Porras, Belisario, **67**: 382n5
Port Arthur, China, **63**: 314, 315, 323,
  330, 412, 437, 438, 461, 471, 472, 507
Porter, Miss (of Red Cross), **54**: 280
Porter, Stephen Geyer, **61**: 548,n1; **65**:
  225n1
Porter, William Sidney: *see* Henry, O.
Portier, André-Léon-Marie, **61**: 139,n1,
  140, 149, 155, 158, 196, 198, 338
Portland, Maine: WW Club in, **67**: 302,n2
Portland, Oregon: WW's activities in, **63**:
  274-76; newsmen in automobile accident, **63**: 275-76; WW's addresses in,
  63: 277-83, 283-94
Portland *Oregon Daily Journal*, **63**:
  275, 283n1, 294n; **65**: 431n1; **67**: 409,
  488
Portland *Oregonian*, **58**: 410n1; **63**: 283n
Porto Baross, **64**: 304-305, 332
Porto Rico, **53**: 246, 287; **62**: 9; **67**: 75; and
  appointment of Attorney General of,
  55: 158-59, 264-65; request for appropriations for education in, **59**: 122-23;
  WW on request for educational appropriations, **60**: 375-76; Hamilton on, **67**:
  57
Ports, Waterways and Railways Commission: *see* Inter-Allied Commission
  on Interntional Ports, Waterways and
  Railways
Portsmouth, Treaty of (1905), **63**: 438,
  461, 472, 507

Portugal, **54**: 264, 283; **55**: 43, 121, 164,
  184; **57**: 427,n10; **58**: 113, 114, 119,
  399, 462n1, 472; **67**: 542; and repre-
  senttion at Paris Peace Conference, **54**:
  16-17, 65; and territorial claims, **54**:
  374; and League of Nations, **54**: 462,
  464; and shipping, **59**: 390; and reparations and German tonnage, **60**: 339,
  340, 345; and German East Africa, **61**:
  276, 277, 314; and mandates, **62**: 188,
  189; and inter-Allied indebtedness, **68**:
  106n1
Posen (Poznań), **53**: 351; **54**: 32-33, 200,
  201, 203, 336, 337; **56**: 89; **59**: 581; **60**:
  185, 188
Posen, S.M.S., **55**: 23, 427; **57**: 28; **58**:
  127
Poska, Jaan, **59**: 18,n9
Post, Alice Thacher (Mrs. Louis
  Freeland), **58**: 140, 156
Post, Louis Freeland, **65**: 187n5, 188,
  544,n1, 545; **66**: 542n1; **67**: 52n1
Postal Telegraph Cable Company, **53**:
  248; **56**: 403; **58**: 51, 561n2, 602; **60**:
  379
Post Office Department, **55**: 327, 337;
  and censorship, **53**: 214, 260, 289; **54**:
  430,n2; **56**: 373; and government control of telegraph and telephone system,
  53: 247-48; and reduction of appropriations for war activities, **53**: 260; and
  zone-rate revision, **53**: 542n2; and
  claims of oppressive policies of Burleson, **55**: 364-65; **58**: 48-53; and strike
  by telegraph and telephone workers,
  56: 311,n1, 341, 404,n1; **57**: 425n1; and
  Espionage Act and censorship, **66**: 92-
  93, 94-98, 99
Postgate, Raymond William, **55**: 87n2
*Post-War German-Austrian Relations:
  The Anschluss Movement, 1918-1936*
  (Ball), **55**: 317n3
postwar reconstruction: *see* World War—
  aftermath
Poti, Russia, **65**: 548
Potter, Mark Winslow, **65**: 44-45,n1
Potter, Virginia: and WW Foundation be-
  ginings, **67**: 271n1, 327n6
Pou, Edward William, **55**: 469; recom-
  mends Garrett for judgeship, **66**: 60
Poullet, Prosper-Antoine-Joseph-Marie,
  61: 12,n3, 16n1
Poulson, Zachariah, **67**: 287,n1
Pound, Roscoe, **68**: 452n2
Powderly, Miss, **64**: 509, 510
Powderly, Terence Vincent, **62**: 122,n2
Powell, Thomas Carr, **54**: 521,n2; **57**:
  233,n2, 379, 379-80, 380, 381, 386
*Power and Principle: Armed Intervention
  in Wilsonian Foreign Policy* (Calhoun),
  66: 58n1
Powers Doubt Pact (Fox), **66**: 238n1
Prabandhu, Prince Traidos, **59**: 186,n1
Praeger, Otto, **65**: 512,n1
Prague, Czecholsovakia: U.S. minister
  appointed to, **56**: 122-23,n1

Prague, University of, **60**: 122,n2; WW receives honorary degree from, **61**: 136-37, 347

Pralon, Eugène-Léon, **59**: 263,n8, 531,n2

Pratt, William Veazie, **53**: 318

Pravda, **62**: 204n1

Prekmurje (Prekomurje, Prekumurje, Yugoslavia), **59**: 408; **60**: 16n1

Presbyterian Church, U.S. (southern), **67**: 567n1

Presbyterian Church, U.S.A., **66**: 134,n1, 151; and New Era Movement, **62**: 202, 251, 270, 313; controversy over "modernism" in, **68**: 519n1

Presbyterian Church of America, **68**: 519n1

Presbyterian Church of Staunton, Virginia: and tablet honoring WW's father, **68**: 52,n1

Presbyterian General Assembly, **67**: 287,n1; and League of Nations, **66**: 202

Presbyterian Theological Seminary of Kentucky at Louisville, **67**: 473n1

Present Crisis, The (Lowell), **67**: 4,n1

President and the Peace (W. A. White), **61**: 506-507,n1

Presidential Disability: Past Experiences and Future Implications (Park), **62**: 634,n17

President Grant, U.S.S., **58**: 141

President Wilson, His Problems and His Policy (Harris), **54**: 159,n3

President Wilson's Charge and French Replies (*Literary Digest*), **65**: 71n3

President's Mediation Commission: and Arizona copper situation, **66**: 125-28

President Wilson (Litovtzeff-Polyakoff), **66**: 357n2

President Wilson (*New York Times*), **66**: 317,n1

press: *see* newspapers

Press and American Intervention in Haiti and the Dominican Republic (Blassingame), **66**: 25n1

Pressburg (now Bratislava, Czechoslovakia), **60**: 313

Preston, James Harry, **55**: 232,n1; **59**: 38,n2

Preston, William, Jr., **65**: 187n5

Pretoria, S.S., **64**: 8

Preussische Jahrbucher, **53**: 121n1

Price, Burr, **54**: 60

Price, Byron, **62**: 626

Price, Donald C., **67**: 499, 502-503

Price, Joseph Morris, **66**: 275,n7

Price, Oscar A., **53**: 587, 647,n4; **55**: 409,n6

Price, William Jennings, **67**: 382n5

Price Fixing Committee (War Industries Board), **53**: 132-33, 166, 168; **55**: 91,n1, 329; resignation of, **53**: 413-14; **54**: 52

Price of Vigilance (Jensen), **60**: 116n6

Price, Waterhouse and Company, **55**: 306n1

prices and price-fixing, **53**: 229; **54**: 89-90, 520-21; and cotton, **53**: 25, 79, 132-33, 149, 166; **57**: 511-12,n1; and steel, **53**: 168, 205n1; **62**: 521; **63**: 88-91, 118-19, 301; and coal, **53**: 310-11; **55**: 251; **57**: 43-47; **62**: 20-21; **63**: 55; Glass on reducing food prices, **55**: 89-90, 358-61; Baruch on, **55**: 90-91; H. Hoover on, **55**: 251; **66**: 124-25; and pork industry, **55**: 306-307, 307-308, 336-37, 343, 396; Redfield on steel, **55**: 336-37; and wheat industry, **55**: 360; **56**: 426, 619-20; **57**: 472-74, 475, 578; **59**: 77, 206; **61**: 499-503, 549,n1, 612-14,n2; **62**: 51-57, 94-95, 104-106, 124, 159, 172, 198, 200; controversy between Railroad Administration and Industrial Board on, **56**: 193-94, 342, 343-44,n1, 344, 345, 399-400; **57**: 233-34, 280-81, 282-83, 347-48 376-86, 470; **58**: 329; and cost of living, **59**: 77; WW meets with economic advisers about, **60**: 491, 493; WW on wheat situation, **62**: 57, 212; Meeker's suggestions, **62**: 165; Palmer's memorandum on high cost of living, **62**: 171-80; Palmer on publicity, **62**: 175-76; McAdoo on publishing corporate tax returns as corrective method, **62**: 185; WW's address to joint session of Congress on, **62**: 209-19; WW on foodstuffs, **62**: 212-14; and farm bureaus, **62**: 300,n1; and food, **64**: 82; Garfield on coal settlement and fuel prices, **64**: 146-47; and WW's statement on coal situation, **64**: 154; and coal industry, **65**: 96-97, 105, 563; and copper, **67**: 176-78; and gasoline, **68**: 119n3; *see also* cost of living

Priest, George Madison, **67**: 181,n1, 182, 198

Prince of Our Disorder: The Life of T. E. Lawrence (Mack), **54**: 90n1

Prince of Wales: *see* Edward Albert Christian George Andrew Patrick David, Prince of Wales

Prince of Wales Lake Hotel, Grasmere, England, **66**: 92,n1

Princes Island Invitation: *see* Prinkipo Declaration

Princeton, N.J., **53**: 22

Princeton Alumni Weekly, **65**: 575, 576; **68**: 477n3

Princeton Class Officers Association, **65**: 572-76

Princeton Theological Seminary, **68**: 519n1

Princeton University, **53**: 22n2, 129n1, 343; **54**: 258n1, 306n10, 411; **55**: 216n2; **57**: 367n1; **58**: 428n1, 482n1; **59**: 239, 247, 349,n1, 473n2; **60**: 646; **61**: 476n1, 477, 625,n1; **62**: 102, 252, 601n1; **63**: 340n3; **64**: 97n1, 232n1, 297, 515n1; **65**: 258n1, 271, 327n1, 359n2, 425, 551n1; **66**: 119, 169,n1, 301, 343n1, 343n4, 370n1, 434n1; **67**: 76n3, 141, 235n3, 280,n1, 285n1, 404, 412, 416n6, 550n1, 574,n1; **68**: 17n1, 76n2, 101,n1, 118, 301n2, 386n2,

Princeton University (*cont.*)
392n1, 594; Van Dyke's poem for memorial service at, **56**: 280n1; WW on an unhappy experience while president of, **57**: 353; WW on student days at, **59**: 40; WW unable to attend class reunion, **59**: 604-605,n1; WW on club system, **60**: 118-19; WW's conflict with Hibben, **60**: 118,n7; greetings from WW's class, **60**: 610; request for physician to be in charge of infirmary, **60**: 646-47; WW on, **61**: 361-62, 363; **67**: 82, 525; and Yale football rivalry, **61**: 374; WW's tribute to men in class of 1917 who gave lives in war, **62**: 102,n2; story that WW kept Cleveland from "attending faculty meeting," **62**: 479-80, 526; WW requests that his desk be sent to White House, **64**: 213, 246-47; WW sings "Old Nassau," **64**: 487; Grayson on WW's health at, **64**: 497; and W. M. Daniels, **64**: 514,n1; Witherspoon Gang, **64**: 516n1; **67**: 491,n1; WW host to various class reunions and dinners, **64**: 516, 517, 518; Hibben to receive salary increase, **64**: 519; WW's letters as university president to Hibben, **64**: 519-21; Hibben to resign from various committees, **64**: 520; WW's reasons for not subscribing to endowment fund, **65**: 246; problems of behavior at reunions, **65**: 572-76; WW gives books to library, **65**: 572; WW receives change of title to Professor of Jurisprudence, **65**: 572; architects involved with, **66**: 218,n1, 232; Alexander Hall, **66**: 269,n2,3; Osgood on WW's leadership at, **66**: 281; Van Dyke on cheers for WW at, **66**: 347; and WW's lucky number, **67**: 105,n1; Stuart on, **67**: 115-16; and Greek language, **67**: 115-16,n1; Pierce-Arrow purchased by friends from, **67**: 116n1, 167-68; Long on WW as professor at, **67**: 164-65; faculty praises WW, **67**: 181-82,n2, WW grateful for support from, **67**: 198; WW unable to attend reunion with friends from, **67**: 277, 281; WW Club at, **67**: 306,n1, 311, 315, 334; WW receives students from WW Club at, **67**: 311; L. C. Woods on WW at, **67**: 334-35; and publication of Ormond lectures, **67**: 335-36,n1, 349; WW witticism from, **67**: 341; and Wilson & Colby announcement, **67**: 343, 344; Dodge donation of armchair, **67**: 374,n3; Harper on, **67**: 410-11; and football games, **67**: 458,n2,4; WW as faculty member, **68**: 35, 590-91; WW's "old Princeton chair" and desk, **68**: 88, 250; WW's reminiscences of, **68**: 88, 451n1; WW touched by spontaneous toast by friends from, **68**: 255-56; library issues bibliography of WW's works, **68**: 308,n2; WW on trustees, **68**: 389, 390; and Meiklejohn speech, **68**: 462, 595; WW requests his report on social reorganization of, **68**:

477,n3; WW on lack of freedom of thought at, **68**: 595
Princeton University Press, **67**: 335; **68**: 351n2, 408
Principle of Nationality and Its Applications (Bryce), **53**: 335,n2
Principles and Practice of Medicine (Osler), **58**: 637,n17
Principles of the Democratic party, An Address by the Hon. Norman H. Davis, **68**: 178,n1
Pringle Pattison, Andrew Seth, **61**: 362,n4
Prinkipo Declaration, **54**: 415; **55**: 180-83; **56**: 467, 544; **59**: 194, 302, 518; WW prepares outline of, **54**: 199; WW's text, **54**: 205-206, 261,n1; Cambon on, **54**: 236-37; and Bessarabia, **54**: 287; Archangel's provisional government declines invitation, **54**: 349; Francis on, **55**: 234, 350; Chicherin's answer to **55**: 161,n1, 181; WW on, **55**: 319
Prinkipo Island, **55**: 545
Prinz Frederick Wilhelm, S.S., **64**: 8
prisoners of war, **60**: 473,n18, 481, 522; **61**: 59, 74, 150, 197, 207, 338-39
Prisoners of War Comittee, **60**: 473,n18, 522
Pritchett, Henry Smith, **66**: 246n2
Privileges and Elections, Committee on (Senate), **65**: 354n2
prize courts, **57**: 405
Probert, Lionel Charles, **53**: 314,n3, 318, 332, 336, 348, 369, 376, 621,n2; **54**: 75, 60; **55**: 221,n1; **67**: 395n1; photograph of, *illustration section*, **53**
Problem of Teschen Silesia, **54**: 344
Problems of the Peace (Dawson), **57**: 36,n2
Progressive party, **68**: 56; Dodd on, **66**: 165
progressivism: WW on, **63**: 127, 216
prohibition, **53**: 413; **59**: 47; **61**: 423-24; **65**: 212; H. Hoover on brewing question and, **54**: 58-59, 216; Washington, D.C., and revenue bill and, **55**: 237-38; WW signs amendment, **55**: 489; WW and N. D. Baker discuss, **57**: 429; Tumulty on repealing law on, **58**: 603-604; **59**: 76,n1, 77; and Baltimore politics, **59**: 38-39,n2; WW on repeal of, **59**: 75, 297; and WW's message to Congress, **59**: 286; issue of repeal, **60**: 380, 536; Tumulty on, **61**: 183-84, 294, 351; WW on, **61**: 291; Clemenceau on, **61**: 305; Palmer on, **61**: 369; and peace treaty, **62**: 69; WW and Tumulty discuss, **64**: 262; Tumulty's suggestion for WW's message to Congress, **65**: 132-34; WW's plank (1920) on, **65**: 346-47,n1, 438; Tumulty on repeal of Volstead Act, 452-55; W. G. Sharp on as campaign issue, **65**: 474-75; WW-Burleson controversy over plank on, 1920, **65**: 510-11,n1,3; WW on lifting ban on brewing, **65**: 576; WW's liquor moved to new home, **67**: 214; and The

Document, **68**: 218-19, 310-15, 334-36, 539; Cobb on, **68**: 304-305, 338; WW answers Cobb on, **68**: 305; Brandeis statement for The Document, **68**: 334-36, 336, 337, 385; and New Jersey, **68**: 454n2; Gonzales on Bryan and, **68**: 475

prohibition amendment, **53**: 150n1

prohibition enforcement bill: *see* Volstead bill

Prologue to Nuremburg: The Politics and Diplomacy of Punishing War Criminals of the First World War (Willis), **58**: 278n3; **64**: 364n1; **65**: 100n1

Prophet Armed: Trotsky: 1879-1921 (Deutscher), **54**: 92n2

Prophets, Priests and Kings (Gardiner), **53**: 634n2; **54**: 178; **55**: 466

Proposed Recognition of Lenine (*Washington Post*), **56**: 551n1

Proti , Stojan, **58**: 162,n2

Providence, R.I., **59**: 287; WW's remarks in, **55**: 237,n2

Providence, R.I., *Evening Bulletin*, **67**: 242n5

Providence News, **57**: 425

Providence Journal, **61**: 373; **67**: 242n5

Providence Telegraph Company: and strike, **57**: 425,n1

Provincial Assembly of Shantung, **58**: 71,n2

Provisional Jewish Council of Poland, **54**: 258n1

Provisional Jewish National Council of Ukrainia, **54**: 258n1

Prussia, **53**: 338; **55**: 503-505; **56**: 166; **57**: 409; **59**: 401n4; and Jews, **55**: 372; suffrage in, **59**: 16n6; **60**: 453

Przemysl, Poland, **59**: 323, 324

Psychiatric Aspects of Neurologic Disease (Benson and Blumer, ed.), **64**: 525n1

Psychology of Bolshevism (Spargo), **66**: 5n2

Public Buildings Commission, **65**: 268-69

Public Health Service: and imigration, **67**: 179

Public Lands and Surveys, Committee on (Senate): and Teapot Dome scandal, **68**: 119n2

Public Ledger Forum on the Peace Conference, **67**: 24n2

public opinion: and censorship and Paris Peace Conference, **54**: 60, 105; Borden on League of Nations and, **54**: 358-59; in Great Britain, **55**: 73, 476; **61**: 144; in U.S. on League of Nations, **55**: 38, 65, 73, 76, 80, 175, 197-98, 279, 392, 439, 447, 449-52, 463-64, 493, 500, 540; **56**: 163, 179, 284-85, 331; and return of U.S. troops, **55**: 81, 82; on U.S. troops in Russia, **55**: 82; Plunkett on Irish question and U.S., **55**: 453-54; Tumulty on reviewing courts-martial, **56**: 192; and reparations, **57**: 28-29, 81, 210, 211; Grasty on American views in Paris, **57**: 38-39, 40-41; R. S. Baker on,

57: 52; **64**: 320-21, 326-27, 359; French appalled at Clemenceau and trust WW, **57**: 101; and William II's punishment, **57**: 123, 127, 128; and Monroe Doctrine amendment, **57**: 215, 233; and Japan's racial equality amendment, **57**: 262; WW on Italy and, **57**: 323, 324; and publicity of peace treaty, **58**: 61; in France on sinking German ships, **58**: 126; on Japanese-Chinese controversy, **58**: 230; in Britain on Italian crisis, **58**: 337; in Italy on Lloyd George and Clemenceau's memorandum, **58**: 337, 338; Lloyd George on Europe's feeling of being bullied by U.S., **58**: 372; in Germany, on peace treaty, **58**: 453-55; and German newspapers, **58**: 579; Bullitt on WW and, **59**: 233; WW and Lamont on U.S. and, **59**: 284; in France on mandates for Asia Minor, **59**: 334, 342, 344; WW's concern over delaying return to U.S. and, **59**: 552; on peace treaty, **59**: 577; R. S. Baker on WW's concern over, **59**: 647; Brandeis on in U.S., **60**: 285; in U.S. on Ireland, **60**: 291, 331-32; change in France favors WW, **61**: 138-39; Hitchcock on treaty and, **64**: 126, 244; Lansing on treaty and, **64**: 149, 367; WW on treaty and, **64**: 200; and Jackson Day message, **64**: 248, 253, 258; Lansing on his resignation and, **64**: 415, 419; Polk on Adriatic question and, **64**: 451; Tumulty on treaty and, **64**: 479; and WW's decision to enter into war, **64**: 487-88; WW seeks advice on winning public opinion for Armenian mandate, **65**: 202; on Germany, **67**: 114; N. H. Davis on treaty situation and, **67**: 376, 377, 378; Davis on, **68**: 273, 278; Peabody on, **68**: 207; WW on League of Nations membership and, **68**: 310

public opinion in the United States: and secrecy of peace conference, **57**: 98-99; and effect of summoning *U.S.S. George Washington*, **57**: 177, 302; support of WW, **57**: 189, 302; and Monroe Doctrine amendment, **57**: 315-16; and League of Nations, **57**: 188-89, 424, 424-25,n1, 427; and reparations, **58**: 30; and claims on German ships in U.S. ports, **58**: 37, 38; and WW's Adriatic statement and Italian crisis, **58**: 105, 178, 179, 270; Tumulty on return of cables to private control, **58**: 146; and WW on Japan's claims, **58**: 219-20, 222, 226; and troops to Archangel, **58**: 266; WW's concern over, **58**: 372; WW on good relations with Britain and France, **58**: 375; and labor clauses in peace treaty, **58**: 417; Lamont on peace treaty and, **61**: 641-43; Cobb on, **61**: 645-46; and peace treaty, **62**: 30; WW on treaty and, **63**: 388, 448, 449, 470, 499, 500; WW seeks advice on winning public support for Armenian mandate, **65**: 202

Public Opinion Quarterly, **55**: 292n1
Public Papers of Woodrow Wilson (Baker and Dodd), **63**: 6
Public Roads, Office of (U.S.), **54**: 391,n2
publishing industry: Creel on, **66**: 33-34
Pueblo, Colorado: Grayson on WW's arrival and activities in, **63**: 487-88; WW's address in, **63**: 500-513
Pueblo, Colo., *Chieftain*, **63**: 487n2, 513n
Pueblo Nuevo de Coto, Panama, **67**: 382n5
Puerto Rico: *see* Porto Rico
Puesch, Mrs., **57**: 218
Pueyrredon, Honorio, **66**: 452, 457
Pugach, Noel H., **61**: 631n1
Pulitzer, Ralph, **54**: 132,n1; **66**: 251; **67**: 271n1, 433; WW meets with, **65**: 501,n1
Pulitzer Prize: Seibold's article on WW, **65**: 401n1; **67**: 303,n1; O'Neill's *Beyond the Horizon*, **65**: 404n6
Pulsifer, William Edmond, **65**: 509
Punch, **66**: 158n8
Punishment of Offenders against the Laws and Customs of War (Garner), **56**: 530n4
Pupin, Michael Idvorsky, **57**: 499-502,n1, 585; **58**: 15,n2, 17
Purachatr, Prince, **66**: 288
Pure Food Act, **62**: 179, 215
Puto, Arben, **66**: 45n6
Puvis de Chavannes, Pierre, **53**: 460
P'u-yi, **53**: 138,n3
Pyne, Moses Taylor, **60**: 646

Quai d'Orsay: Grayson's description of, **54**: 4-5
Quartieri, Ferdinando, **59**: 125,n1
Quesada, Castro, **63**: 616
Quezon, Manuel Luis, **55**: 391n1; **57**: 189-90; supports Harrison as governor general, **60**: 198, 199-200, 201, 202
Quigley, Edward T., **57**: 380,n14, 381
Quinby, Henry Cole, **56**: 85,n2
Quinones de Leon, Jose Maria, **53**: 419,n5; **60**: 546,n4
Quiros, Juan Bautista, **63**: 616,n1; **65**: 465

Rabban, David M., **55**: 347n1; **66**: 92n1
race relations, **62**: 234,n1, 313,n1; discrimination, **60**: 482,n1; Southern Sociological Conference's program for improvement of, **62**: 106-107, 128-29, 505-506; Moton on, **62**: 233-34; WW answers Moton, **62**: 260; and Shillady case, **62**: 527-28, 535-36; *see also* Negroes
Race Riot: Chicago in the Red Summer of 1919 (Tuttle), **61**: 357n1; **62**: 234n1
race riots: WW on, **63**: 196
Raciborz: *see* Ratibor
Radcliffe, Sir Percy de Blaquiere, **60**: 296,n1; **66**: 46n7
Radek, Karl, **54**: 92n1; **60**: 167n17
Radosh, Ronald, **66**: 5n2, 19n1
Radović, Andrija, **56**: 395,n1; **59**: 178,n4; **65**: 315,n1

Raffo, Peter, **53**: 515n1
Ragan, Fred D., **55**: 347n1
Ragovsky, G., **59**: 156,n4
Ragsdale, James Willard, **55**: 297,n4
Ragusa (now Dubrovnik, Yugoslavia), **57**: 438, 517; **58**: 452; **60**: 211
Railroad Administration (U.S.), **53**: 164n1; **54**: 520; **58**: 109; **62**: 76-77, 118, 137, 140, 192, 193, 194, 195, 302, 462, 485, 496, 498, 549, 570-71; **64**: 22, 322; and Japan and Russian situation, **53**: 175, 463,n1, 555-57,n4, 632-33, 699; McAdoo's resignation, **53**: 151; and issue of government control, **53**: 190-93, 282-84, 626; relationship of River and Harbor bill, **53**: 288; Tumulty on importance of selection of Director General, **53**: 704; Hines appointed Director General, **53**: 710; in Siberia, **54**: 259-60, 261; **56**: 161; and financial crisis, **55**: 227-28, 231-32, 277, 536, 537; and coal prices, **55**: 251; **57**: 43-47; price controversy with Industrial Board, **56**: 193-94, 341, 342-43, 344, 345, 399-400, 520, 618; **57**: 52,n1, 233-34, 280-81, 282, 283, 347-48, 374,n1, 376-86, 387-88, 423-24, 446, 470, 510-11, 577, 577-78; **58**: 329, 420; **59**: 38,n1; Hines on, **61**: 412-15; **64**: 412-13,n2; and labor problems and proposed strike, **61**: 536-37; and wage issue, **64**: 429
Railroad Control Act, **55**: 257-58
railroad crisis of 1916, **63**: 251,n1
Railroad Labor Board, **65**: 14, 17; **67**: 119-20,n1, 121-22, 550n1; appointment suggestions for, **65**: 44-45, 174-75, 175, 176; **67**: 121n1; members nominated, **65**: 189,n1; Palmer urges meeting of **65**: 192-93; Jewell on, **65**: 216, 285, 286; WW answers Jewell's protest concerning, **65**: 216-17; hopes for prompt wage decision by, **65**: 440, 444; and railroad wage situation, **65**: 451,n1, 452; suggestion for appointment to, and wage issue, **68**: 129n1
railroads, **62**: 163, 547-50; **63**: 54; Russian railroad situation, **55**: 350-51, 393, 400; issue of government ownership, **55**: 246-50, 258-60, 260-61; and needed appropriation, **55**: 257-58, 277, 536-37; Hines on relinquishing government control, **56**: 620-23; and issue of return to private ownership, **58**: 106-10,n2, 603, 605-606; **59**: 122, 296; Hines' solution to problems of, **59**: 523n2; government ownership of, **61**: 366; and Plumb plan, **61**: 377,n1; **62**: 229-30, 481-82; Hines on, **61**: 412-15; labor issues, **61**: 536-37; and Siberian situation, **61**: 571-73, 636-38; and cost of living, **62**: 31,n1, 50-51; urgency warrants no recess of House of Representatives, **62**: 98-99; and wages, **62**: 117, 118-22; Hines on labor issues, **62**: 133-34, 181-82, 488-89; **64**: 396-97; and strike crisis, **62**: 134-40, 161-62,

169, 189-92, 567-73; Senate Interstate
Commerce Committee on, **62**: 183-84;
McAdoo on, **62**: 184-85; WW asks
Hines to act on wages, **62**: 189-92;
WW's messages and statements on,
62: 192-93, 472-76, 489-93, 493-95,
496-98; WW urges workers to return to
job and negotiations to begin, **62**: 193,
194-95; Palmer on, **62**: 198; Tumulty
on, **62**: 273, 274, 543-44; comparison of
U.S. and Great Britain, **62**: 287-90;
Palmer's memorandum for WW's
statement on strike, **62**: 462-65; Hines'
recommendations for WW's statements on, **62**: 469-71, 472-76, 482-84;
Pomerene on, **62**: 477; news reports on
WW's position on, **62**: 484-87; WW on
adjustment of some wages, **62**: 492-93,
498; J. S. Williams on steel trust and,
62: 519; and Hines' suggested Labor
Day message, **62**: 544-45; Hines' statement on strikes in western states, **62**:
548, 549-50; Hines urges WW to make
another statement to help avert strike,
62: 586; WW on, **62**: 610; **63**: 78; **67**:
231n1, 607; W. B. Wilson on nation-
wide campaign to interpret WW's
statement to railroad shopmen, **63**: 53,
54; WW on, **63**: 78; Hines' proposed
message for WW, **64**: 17-21, 21-24; and
WW's Annual Message to Congress,
64: 74-76, 106; controversy over date of
return of railroads to private ownership, **64**: 183-84, 188-89, 195-96, 197-
98, 222, 223-25, 457; Cummins and
Esch bills, **64**: 195n1; proclamation relinquishing federal control of railroads, **64**: 226-27; press release on return of railroads to private ownership,
64: 228; and threatened strike, **64**:
391,n1, 423-24; and wage issue, **64**:
406-407, 411-13, 428-31; WW's request
for noncomplying union to withdraw
strike order, **64**: 426-27,n1; and Transportation Act of 1920, **64**: 467,n1;
Hines on WW's response to labor on,
64: 467-68; handling of crisis indicates
WW's health improvement, **65**: 5; WW
to Jewell on proceeding with wage negotiations, **65**: 14-16; W. B. Wilson on
not linking end of federal control with
new bill, **65**: 16-19; A.F. of L. urges rejection of Esch-Cummings bill, **65**: 19-
20; labor-management negotiations
under way, **65**: 36; Hines' evaluation
of, **65**: 175-76; discussed at first Cabinet meeting since WW's illness, **65**:
186n1, 187,n3; Tumulty's suggestion
to postpone amnesty proclamation because of situation, **65**: 190,n2; union
wishes hearing before Railroad Labor
Board, **65**: 215, 216; WW's reply to
Jewell on unions' demands, **65**: 216-17;
Jewell clarifies unions' position, **65**:
285-86; unions protest adjournment of
Congress, **65**: 359; WW hopes board's
decision will be announced, **65**: 440;

board working on wage problem, **65**:
444; and threatened strike, **65**:
451,n1,2; and Illinois coal situation,
65: 562,n2; issue of reinstatement of
outlaw strikers, **66**: 254,n1, 262-63;
and WW's State of the Union Message,
66: 488; Gowen's appeal for elderly
workers, **66**: 498; W. B. Wilson unable
to reinstate workers, **66**: 546; The Document statement on, **67**: 431, 540-
41,n1, 550,n1, 556, 558-59, 563, 591-
92; **68**: 7, 30, 217, 538; WW answers
unions on management and wage
issue, **67**: 119-20,n1; management answers labor's charges, **67**: 121-22; WW
asks McAdoo to write piece on, **68**: 287,
293; McAdoo on, **68**: 291-92; and Wilkerson temporary injunction, **68**:
129,n1; and W. A. White, **68**: 148,n5;
Peabody on, 68: 203, 204-206, 208-209;
Davis on WW manifesto and, **68**: 489;
see also Sudbahn; Plumb plan; Esch-
Cummins bill and Act; Railroad Labor
Board
railroad wage board (proposed): *see* federal wage board
Railroad Wage Commission (Lane Commission), **64**: 422,n5
Railway Signalmen of America, **62**: 74
Rainey, Henry Thomas: WW on defeat of,
66: 348,n1
Raker, John Edward, **56**: 428,n3
Raleigh *News and Observer*, **64**: 522n1
Ralston, Samuel Moffett, **65**: 545,n4; **68**:
44n2, 49-50, 190,n2, 504; mentioned as
presidential candidate, **68**: 426
Rameau, Jean-Philippe, **54**: 305,n7, **56**:
62n4
Ramirez, José Manuel, **66**: 135n1
Ramsay, Alexander Robert Maule, **53**:
594n12
Ramsay, Sir William Mitchell, **58**:
324,n4
Ramseyer, Christian William, **56**: 428,n3
Randall Cantur: *see* Davidson, Most Rev.
Randall Thomas
Randall Hagner Realtors, **66**: 519n1
Randolph, Harrison, **64**: 458,n3
Randolph-Macon Woman's College, **67**:
68n17
Randrup, Sören Revsgaard, **53**: 630,n6
Rand School of Social Science, **55**: 92n1,
337n1
Rankin, Walter Mead, **67**: 182
Ransdell, Joseph Eugene, **53**: 117, 187-
88; **54**: 228; **55**: 297; **62**: 610-11; treaty
vote, **65**: 109n1; on woman suffrage,
65: 294-95, recommended for Hondu-
ras appointment, **65**: 357, 361; WW on,
65: 361; on Republicans being cause of
recession, **66**: 243,n4,5
Ransome, Arthur, **54**: 137
Rantzau, Count: *see* Brockdorff-Rantzau,
Ulrich Karl Christian, Count von
Rapallo Conference (Nov. 1920), **65**:
303n10
Rapallo, Treaty of, **66**: 364,n2, 365, 499

Rappard, William Emmanuel, **56**: 75,n1; **58**: 382,n4; **61**: 356-57,n2; on neutrals and peace conference, **53**: 209-12; **55**: 151-54, 154; on Rhineland and League of Nations, **55**: 151-52; on French anti-Wilson propaganda, **55**: 153-54; on Geneva as League of Nations seat, **57**: 464; notes on conversation with WW in Nov. 1918, **63**: 626-31

Rarotonga, Cook Islands, **54**: 312

Ras-Orsted Fondet, **68**: 84,n1

Ras Taffari (later Haile Selassie of Ethiopia), **61**: 470, 471, 472-73, 604

Ratelier, Amiel, **62**: 561,n1

Rathbone, Albert, **58**: 595,n1,2; **59**: 111n,1; **60**: 539; **61**: 457,n1; **64**: 10, 11, 12, 475,n1, 477; **65**: 61, 62, 92, 147, 148, 153; **66**: 48, 49; asked to be financial adviser with peace commission in Paris, **62**: 624; and war debt negotiations, **65**: 325-26,n1

Rathdrum, Idaho, **63**: 210n1

Rathenau, Walther, **53**: 418-19,n3,4

Rathom, John, **61**: 373; **67**: 242,n5

Ratibor, Germany, **56**: 598; **60**: 139, 417, 427, 468, 480

Ratibor, Duke of and Prince zu Corvey, Viktor Amadeus, Prince zu Hohenlohe-Schillingsfurst, **60**: 55n5

Ratify! (New York *World*), **65**: 71n3

Ratify the Treaty! (New York *World*), **64**: 270n2

Ratner, Sidney, **55**: 334n1

Rawnsley, Edith Fletcher (Mrs. Hardwicke Drummond), **56**: 311,n1

Rawnsley, Hardwicke Drummond, **55**: 387,n1; **56**: 191, 310-11, 553; **57**: 98

Raymond, Harry Howard, **58**: 202n1

Rea, Cleveland Dodge, **66**: 193n5

Rea, Grace, **66**: 193n5

Rea, James, **66**: 193n5

Rea, James Childs, Jr., **66**: 193n5; **67**: 373n1

Rea, Julia Parish Dodge (Mrs. James Childs), **66**: 193,n5; **67**: 373,n1, 375; **68**: 115,n2, 117

Rea, Ruth, **66**: 193n5

Rea, William Holdship, **66**: 193n5

Reaction to Peace Treaty Divides Advocates in Paris (Stokes), **60**: 146,n1

Read, Albert Cushing, **57**: 447n1; **59**: 576,n1; **60**: 44,n1, 430-31

Reading, Rufus Daniel Isaacs, 1st Marquess, **53**: 72, 271, 326, 360, 361, 372, 373, 482, 509, 566-67, 592, 721; **54**: 37; **58**: 375; **64**: 91; on threat by Republican senator concerning Ireland, **59**: 371-72; on Republican opposition to Great Britain, **59**: 451-52

Reale Accademia dei Lincei Rome: *see* Royal Academy of Science

Reardon, Timothy A., **63**: 269

Reay, William M., **57**: 384,n31

Rebel at Large: Recollections of Fifty Crowded Years (Creel), **65**: 374n1; **66**: 133n2

Reboul, Colonel, **56**: 413,n1

Recasting Bourgeois Europe: Stabilization in France, Germany and Italy in the Decade After World War I (Maier), **65**: 326n4

Rechenberg, Albrecht, Baron von, **56**: 143,n4, 143-44

Recollections of Abraham Lincoln, 1847-1865 (Lamon), **55**: 366n1

Recollections of a Happy LIfe (Egan), **65**: 122,n2

reconstruction: *see* World War—aftermath

Reconstruction Commission (proposed), **53**: 117, 118

Record Publishing Co. of Philadelphia, **53**: 394n1

Red Cross: *see* American National Red Cross; International Red Cross; Russian Red Cross

Red Cross Magazine, **57**: 241n4

Red Dawn: A Drama of Revolution (Dixon), **62**: 115,n1

Redfield, Elise Mercein Fuller (Mrs. William Cox), **68**: 285,n2, 286, 508

Redfield, William Cox, **53**: 128-29, 169; **54**: 52,n4, 556, 557; **55**: 90, 156, 188, 291; **56**: 553,n1; **57**: 233, 347, 374, 387, 407; **58**: 420; **59**: 320; **61**: 462, 492, 498, 623; **68**: 576; on discontent in Republican party, **61**: 411; on need for passenger-carrying vessels, **61**: 465, 479; on international commerce conference, **53**: 48-51, 55-56; and War Industries Board, **53**: 124, 201, 202, 206; and copper exportation, **54**: 409-10; on prices, **54**: 520-21; **55**: 306-307, 308, 336-37, 343, 336; and conflict between Industrial Board and Railroad Administration, **56**: 341, 342-43, 343,n1, 399, 400, 618; **57**: 280-81, 282, 376-86, 423-24, 470, 510-11, 577-78, 629; **59**: 38,n1; on wheat prices, **56**: 619-20; **57**: 472, 473; on electric railways, **59**: 287-88; and steamship business of Panama Railroad, **62**: 9; on foreign trade and credits, **62**: 31-34, 80-81; question of resignation, **62**: 103-104, 266, 586-87, 610; WW on proposed resignation of, **62**: 115; on reducing cost of living, **62**: 129-31, 163; WW on foreign trade, **62**: 222; on his resignation and suggestions for successor, **63**: 573-74; and WW's veto of Volstead bill, **63**: 601n1; N. D. Baker on, **67**: 295-97; recollections of WW's wit and humor, **67**: 403-404; sends WW speech and WW thanks, **68**: 285,n1, 286; birthday greetings to WW and WW's thanks, **68**: 508, 515; and WW Foundation luncheon, **68**: 508, 510n1

Redmond, John Edward, **58**: 586,n1

Red Scare: A Study in National Hysteria: 1919-1920 (Murray), **59**: 204n2; **63**: 167n6; **65**: 187n5

reduction of arms: *see* arms limitation
Reed, James (author), **57**: 453n4
Reed, James Alexander, **53**: 134, 580; **54**: 229; **55**: 270, 279, 450; **58**: 244; **59**: 451n1, 578; **60**: 245,n5; **61**: 372, 411, 469,n1; **62**: 68, 504; **63**: 64, 167,n5,7; **64**: 185, 488; **67**: 355n6; **68**: 185,n1, 239, 242,n4, 247; attacks on WW and League of Nations, **56**: 192,n1; **57**: 47-49,n1, 424; and League of Nations, **59**: 529; and treaty fight, **64**: 49, 63, 94, 200-201, 273, 337; WW on, **65**: 179; barred as delegate to Democratic National Convention, 1920, **65**: 470, 471,n1; and Wilson-Spencer controversy, **66**: 192, 196, 197, 198n1; WW on, **67**: 543,n1, 578-79, 586; **68**: 12, 24, 39, 48, 61, 151, 166; Long-Reed senatorial primary battle, **68**: 12,n1, 35, 104, 105, 126, 147, 153; primary vote, **68**: 105n1, claims of fraud in primary, **68**: 105; McAdoo will not campaign for, **68**: 147, 153
Reed, John, **55**: 297n2; **61**: 359
Reed, Lewis Balcombe, **57**: 381,n20
Reed, Thomas Brackett, **56**: 437
Reed, Waldo, **62**: 466
Reeves, Ira Louis, **61**: 361,n2
Reformed Church at Oratoire du Louvre, **54**: 282n1
Reformers and War: American progressive publicists and the First World War (Thompson), **60**: 147n4
Regan, James, B., **65**: 140,n3
Regensburg, S.M.S., **55**: 23
Regina Elena (Italian ship), **59**: 42
Reid, Edith Gittings (Mrs. Harry Fielding), **63**: 575-76,n1; **64**: 516, 517; **65**: 284,n4; **67**: 423
Reid, Harry Fielding, **64**: 516, 517
Reid, Ogden Mills, **61**: 372
Reid, Whitelaw, **53**: 527,n1
Reims, France: *see* Rheims
Reinach, Joseph Herman, **59**: 186,n8
Reinhart, Aurelia Isabel Henry (Mrs. George Frederick), **63**: 352,n1
Reinke, Walter, **57**: 526
Reinsch, Paul Samuel, **53**: 464; **54**: 194,n1, 474n1, 548, 549; **59**: 317, 573n1,3, 619; **60**: 103, 429,n1, 483, 603, 606; **62**: 260, 281; on Chinese-Japanese problem being solved at Paris Peace Conference, **54**: 77-82; on protests in China on Japanese claims settlement, **58**: 522n1; resignation, **61**: 631-34; **62**: 147, 282; suggestions for his successor, **61**: 634-36; **62**: 282-84
Reis, Jayme Batalha, **54**: 426,n1, 464, 482, 483, 512; **55**: 5, 6, 43, 44, 70, 121, 124; **56**: 174, 175, 299, 302; and League of Nations Commission, **57**: 221-22, 227, 228, 232, 250, 258; House on, **57**: 237
Reischauer, Edwin Oldfather, **54**: 476n7

Relief Administration (U.S. proposed), **54**: 276
Renaudel, Pierre, **53**: 8, 344-45, 387n1
Renner, Karl, **57**: 167,n1; **58**: 157,n2, 159; **59**: 632; on delays in dealing with German Austria, **59**: 482,n4; **60**: 19, 124
Reno, Nevada: Grayson on WW's arrival and activities in, **63**: 426; WW's address in, **63**: 428-41
Rentis (Rendis), Constantine, **54**: 463,n3
reparation: Lloyd George on, **66**: 48-49; WW on, **66**: 309-12; Lamont on importance of settling, **67**: 17; Cabinet on German, **67**: 109,n1; Colby on not protesting Allies' demands on Germany, **67**: 113-15; Germany's obligations to Belgium and other Allies, **67**: 144-46; H. J. Ford on, **67**: 550; Davis to speak on, **68**: 261-62; WW on Baruch's paper on, **68**: 431; Baruch on, **68**: 434-37; Smuts answers Baruch on inter-Allied loan settlement, **68**: 437n3; Smuts recommends meeting on, **68**: 453n1; *see also* Paris Peace Conference—reparations; Ruhr Valley
Reparation at the Paris Peace Conference: From the Standpoint of the American Delegation (Burnett), **55**: 29n2; **56**: 271n2, 272n4, 356n11; **57**: 203n3, 498n1; **59**: 50n7, 536n1; **60**: 359n1; **61**: 254n2
Reparation Commission, **62**: 143, 236, 237-38, 330; search for replacement for Dulles, **62**: 322-23; issue of U.S. representation on, **65**: 57-60, 92-93, 147-48, 153; **67**: 34,n1, 35, 41n2; and Germany's coal obligations to France, **65**: 61-62; and Germany's payment of gold marks, **65**: 62; N. H. Davis wishes to continue on, **65**: 147, 174, 178, 181; WW on payment for first U.S. representatives on, **65**: 178; and attendance at Spa Conference, **65**: 250-51, 477; N. H. Davis on plans for reparations settlement, **66**: 471-72; and Germany, **67**: 144; *see also* Paris Peace Conference-Reparation Commission
Reparation in World Politics: France and European Economic Diplomacy 1916-1923 (Trachtenberg), **65**: 326n4; **67**: 109n1
reparations and Allied debt negotiations, **65**: 325n1
Repogle, Jacob Leonard, **66**: 288-89,n2
Report to the President of the United States on Work Done Toward the Establishment and Maintenance Under the American Flag of a Merchant Marine Adequate to the Needs of American Overseas Trade (Hurley), **62**: 80,n1
Republican Ascendancy, 1921-1933 (Hicks), **68**: 179n1
Republican National Committee, **68**: 332n2

Republican National Convention of 1920, and Indiana plank, **65**: 292n1; Tumulty on Lodge's keynote speech at, **65**: 388,n1; and women's speeches, **65**: 411; and WW on, **65**: 415-16, 419-21

Republican party, **58**: 606; **59**: 158; **60**: 575; **61**: 577; **63**: 26; **66**: 346n1; **68**: 18, 27, 56, 359, 372, 500; position on cables, **58**: 145; and woman suffrage, **58**: 410n1; **61**: 537; and League of Nations, **58**: 410n1; **59**: 524n1, 528-29; and issue of building foreign ships in U.S. shipyards, **58**: 531; House on WW antagonizing, **59**: 34-35; and issues facing Congress, **59**: 47; and tariff, **59**: 121; and opposition to Great Britain, **59**: 372, 451-52; and publication of peace treaty, **59**: 450-51; and Senate opposition to League of Nations Covenant, **60**: 41n1, 42-43, 112; Tumulty on, **60**: 112, 113, 153, 535, 610-11; and 1920 election, **60**: 381; and Knox Resolution, **60**: 535, 612; and League of Nations, **61**: 66, 511; Lamont offers WW his help with senators of, **61**: 68; **62**: 504-505; differing views on treaty ratification, **61**: 137-38; activity in Congress on treaty and proposed declarations of state of peace between Germany and U.S., **61**: 184; WW on effort to have peace declared by Congress, **61**: 290, 290-91; and Irish issue, **61**: 291; and fight against League of Nations Covenant, **61**: 347n1; Taft on WW's strategy and, **61**: 353; Yost's suggestions for gaining support for League of Nations from, **61**: 399-300; Redfield on discontent within, **61**: 411; reaction to WW's Senate appearance and address, **61**: 424-25; Wheeler's advice to WW and, **61**: 460; W. A. White on League of Nations Covenant and, **61**: 506n1; WW meets with senators from on treaty, **61**: 515-17, 548,n1, 561-62, 593-95, 597, 598, 599-602; **62**: 29,n1, 43-45, 90-94; members friendly toward League of Nations still firm on reservations, **61**: 544-47; and Foreign Relations Committee, **61**: 597; and Taft's attempt at treaty ratification, **61**: 605,n1; N. D. Baker on Taft's statement on Republican senators, **61**: 614-15; and Senate opposition to treaty, **62**: 3-5, 7; and reservations issue, **62**: 11-13, 45, 66-69, 112-14, 307-309, 429, 614; McAdoo on, **62**: 71-72, 184; WW on, **62**: 99, 636; and WW's meeting with Foreign Relations Committee, **62**: 335, 336; Shaffer on possible division in, **62**: 440; and situation in Senate regarding reservations, **63**: 150, 235, 363, 445, 482, 529, 531, 541, 586; WW on nonpartisan character of treaty, **63**: 222, 228-29, 247, 248, 257, 288, 386, 417-18; and proposed super cabinet, **63**: 626; and reservations, **64**: 28, 43,

45-50, 71-72, 165-66; Grey and Jusserand on treaty and, **64**: 44; and voting in Senate, **64**: 48; Lansing on personal animosity toward WW driving force against treaty, **64**: 54-55; Underwood on treaty and, **64**: 69-70; Hitchcock on senators willing to compromise on treaty, **64**: 69-70; Polk on issue of departure of U.S. representatives in Paris, **64**: 117-18; and Mexican situation, **64**: 120,n1, 122, 128; Lansing on, **64**: 149; and treaty delay, **64**: 277, 283; bipartisan committee addresses Article X and hopeful of compromise, **64**: 283-84, 311-12, 312-13,n1; W. G. Sharp on, **64**: 285; and bitter-enders, **64**: 328,n2; WW's list of senators who hindered ratification of treaty reviewed by Burleson and Hitchcock, **64**: 336-37, 338-39; Glass on Taft reservation and responsibility of treaty defeat resting with, **64**: 387-8,n1; WW feels treaty proposals should come from, **64**: 405; Cummings on, **64**: 419n1; and blacks in 1912; **64**: 522; Republican newspapers on Lansing's dismissal, **65**: 3-7; probable Senate vote on revised reservation to Article X, **65**: 80, 81,n1; and treaty vote, **65**: 109,n1; WW on treaty defeat and **65**: 116, 418-19; on WW seeking third term, **65**: 118; treaty strategy of, **65**: 122,n1; WW on H. Hoover and, **65**: 149; N. H. Davis on treaty and **65**: 223; and selection of Director-General of Pan-American Union, **65**: 233; Dodge on, **65**: 235; and Indiana plank, **65**: 291-92,n1; and Harding resolution on Armenia, **65**: 323. N. D. Baker on platform of, **65**: 386; platform, **65**: 386,n1; WW on platform, **65**: 396; WW on, **65**: 411; WW flattered by being issue of campaign of, **65**: 415-16; denounced by WW's League of Nations plank, **65**: 437; Cummings on, in keynote speech, **65**: 471n1; and WW as autocrat, **65**: 546; inconsistencies in League of Nations statements, **66**: 141; WW on consequences of Republican victory, **66**: 156; and H. Hoover, **66**: 169; Crowell's endorsement of candidates from, **66**: 188,n1; Tumulty's statement for WW on national devastation if Republicans elected, **66**: 214-16; blamed for recession, **66**: 242-43; Dodd on support for WW from, **66**: 256; pro-League delegation meets wtih WW, **66**: 273-76; N. D. Baker on conservatism and isolationism of, **66**: 312-13; Dodge on, **66**: 340, 341; WW on Dominican Republic and, **66**: 409; N. D. Baker on Army size and, **66**: 527-29; Coar on, **67**: 464; issue of U.S. representatin on European commissions, **67**: 35-36; and Irish Americans, **67**: 45n2; WW on League of Nations and, **67**: 84; WW on, **67**: 94; and

Emergency Tariff bill, **67**: 159; Creel on publication of *World Settlement* and involvement of, **67**: 242; Dodd on meeting of anti-Wilson cabal, **67**: 298; Seibold on, **67**: 313; WW on Newberry case and, **67**: 323-24; and issue of Britain's indebtedness, **67**: 355n2,6; Colby and Morgenthau on making demands of, **67**: 386-87; and Treaty of Berlin, 1921, **67**: 394, 422n4, 428; WW on slogan "America First," and, **67**: 443, 589-90; **68**: 5, 215, 536; and The Document, **67**: 499-501; **68**: 5, 6, 54-55, 215-16, 253, 269-70, 271, 318, 536-41; and Four Power Treaty, **67**: 552-53, 577,n1; Colby on, **67**: 575-76; and Versailles Treaty, **67**: 610-11, 616; WW wishes to study effect on Europe of policies of, **68**: 52, 53, 55; WW on type of candidate from, **68**: 64; McAdoo on Morse case and, **68**: 73; Hull on tariff bill and, **68**: 97; and issue of League of Nations membership, **68**: 160, 178n1, 273, 275,n3, 313, 326-27; and 1922 election results, **68**: 179n1; and World Court, **68**: 306, 339; Davis on WW manifesto and, **68**: 487, 488-90; WW on failure of, **68**: 542; *see also* under names of spokesmen for, such as Lodge, Henry Cabot

Republican party and Republicans in Indiana, **63**: 4; **68**: 44,n2, 49

Republican party and Republicans in Maryland, **59**: 38,n2

Republican party and Republicans in Massachusetts, **55**: 449-50

Republican Party and Republicans in Michigan: **65**: 120,n2; and Newberry case, **67**: 316-17

Republican party and Republicans in Missouri, **53**: 84n1; **57**: 47; **63**: 32; **68**: 147, 166n1

Republican party and Republicans in Nebraska, **53**: 61-62; Republican party and Republicans in New Jersey, **68**: 162n1

Republican party and Republicans in New York: Colby on, **67**: 555

Republican party and Republicans in Pennsylvania, **68**: 56,n2; and congressional seat loss, **55**: 448-49,n1, 457

Republican presidential campaign of 1920: Woolley on tactics of, **66**: 174; and platform plank on Japanese exclusion, **66**: 186; and Wilson-Spencer controversy, **66**: 198,n1; Harding clarifies position on French approaching him and WW's reaction, **66**: 240, 246; on agricultural price decline, **66**: 242-43,n4,5; statement of the 31 Republicans, **66**: 246,n2; and Root's speech attacking League of Nations, **66**: 246,n1; Harding's League of Nations position, **66**: 258,n2,3; election results, **66**: 306n1; McAdoo on, **66**: 318; Holt on, **67**: 187n1; *see also* Harding, Warren Gamaliel; Republican party

Republic of Armenia (Hovannisian), **58**: 111n2; **62**: 27n1; **63**: 304n1; **64**: 450n4; **66**: 29n1

responsibility for the war: *see* Paris Peace Conference— responsibility for the war

"Responsibility of Germany" (document), **60**: 438,n3

Responsibility of the Authors of the War and on Enforcement of Penalties, Commission on the: *see* Paris Peace Conference —Commission on the Responsibility of the Authors of the War and on Enforcement of Penalties

Retirement Act: Tumulty on, **65**: 478,n1,2,3, 519-20; Burleson on, **65**: 512,n1; 519, 520

restitution: *see* reparation

Reuter, Emile, **56**: 597n3; **57**: 457,n3, 458

Reuter, Ludwig von, **61**: 57n8, 142, 144, 145, 146, 168, 169

Reval (Revel), Estonia, **53**: 335,n2; **59**: 18,n8; **60**: 134n9

Revel, Paolo Thaon di, **55**: 21,n6

Revelstoke, John Baring, 2nd Baron, **59**: 467n7

Revenue Act of 1917, **53**: 542,n2; **55**: 334n1

Revenue Act of 1918, **55**: 334,n1; **58**: 605n2; **64**: 77-78, 107; and theater ticket prices, **54**: 227,n2; Glass on provisions of bill, **54**: 501-502; WW signs, **54**: 555; **55**: 237-38; and WW's income tax, **60**: 247

Revenue Act of 1918 (Blakely and Blakely) **55**: 334n1

revenue bill, **53**: 53, 103, 542,n2

Review of Reviews, **68**: 233

Revolution in Bavaria, 1918-1919: The Eisner Regime and the Soviet Republic (Mitchell), **55**: 423n1; **56**: 543n2; **57**: 4n1; **59**: 433n4

Revue de Paris, **53**: 721n1

Reynolds, Stanley Meade, **62**: 627; **63**: 275n4

Rhee, Syngman, **59**: 473-75,n2

Rheims, France: WW visits, **54**: 278, 279-81, 305, 466

Rheims Cathedral, **54**: 278-79

Rheinland, S.M.S., **56**: 28; **58**: 127; **66**: 23, 427

Rhenish Provinces: **65**: 87, 159; *see also* Rhineland; Inter-Allied Rhineland High Commission

Rhine-Danube Canal, **60**: 520,n11

Rhineland, **53**: 36, 37; **55**: 387; **62**: 114, 272, 407-408, 534; and U.S. troops in, **64**: 149, 156; *see also* Paris Peace Conference-Rhineland

Rhineland Commission: *see* Inter-Allied Rhineland Commission

Rhineland conventions: Foreign Relations Committee requests copy of, **62**: 477; sent to Senate, **62**: 534, 581, 611, 624; *see also* Paris Peace Conference—Rhineland conventions

Rhine River, **56**: 201, 268; and passage of troops through Holland, **55**: 178-80; as western military frontier, **55**: 507-10; **65**: 217,n1

Rhode Island, **58**: 459

Rhode Island State Federation of Labor, **57**: 425

Rhode Island Textile Council, **57**: 425

Rhodes, **59**: 269; reports of atrocities by Italians in, **58**: 355-56, 434

Rhodes, Charles Dudley, **53**: 473,n2

Rhodes, Peyton Nalle, **67**: 567n2

Rhodes College, **66**: 134n4

Riano y Gayangos, Juan, **68**: 581,n1

Ribot, Alexandre-Félix-Joseph, **53**: 653; **56**: 596; **57**: 176; **59**: 42,n5, 43, 334; on reparations, **60**: 29,n14; and Rhineland occupation, **60**: 61

Ribot, Mary Burch (Mme. Alexandre Félix Joseph), **57**: 176,n1

Ricci, Vittorio Rolandi, **66**: 339,n1, 381-82, 545

Ricci-Busatti, Arturo, **54**: 218,n2

Rice, Ralph R., **67**: 384

rice industry, **55**: 252-53

Rice Institute (University), **67**: 549; lecture offer to WW, **65**: 553,n2; requests one of WW's honorary diplomas, **66**: 410-11, 420,n1; WW invited to lecture at, declines, **67**: 235-36, 246-47; WW sends one of his honorary degree diplomas to, **67**: 235,n1

Rich, A. J., **54**: 228n1

Richards, Bernard Gerson, **55**: 381,n3, 385, 386

Richards, James McDowell, **67**: 473, 474,n1,2, 476

Richards, John H., M.D., **68**: 252,n2

Richardson, Wilds Preston, **60**: 241,n1, 359; **61**: 226,n3; on maintaining U.S. troops in Russia, **59**: 600,n2,3,4

Richelmy, Agostino, Cardinal, **56**: 258,n1

Richmond, Charles Alexander, **66**: 246n2

Richmond Forging Corporation, **65**: 557n1

Richmond, Indiana, **63**: 3n5; WW's remarks in, **63**: 18-19

Richmond *Times-Dispatch*, **65**: 6

Richmond, Va., **55**: 482; as site of American Historical Association meeting, **68**: 460, 462

Richvaldt, Sudetenland, **54**: 344

Rickard, Edgar, **53**: 14, 252, 273, 603, 604, 649; **56**: 426; **57**: 381; **62**: 123,n1, 124; on pork prices, **55**: 307-308, 336, 362, 393-94; and wheat prices, **55**: 360

Rickert, T. A., **65**: 20

Rickey, Harry Norris, **63**: 444,n1, 445, 447

Riddell, Crockett Morgan, **63**: 241,n1

Riddell, Sir George (Allardice), **54**: 248,n2; **58**: 579,n11; **59**: 55n,8; **60**: 466, 477, 489n1, 518; **68**: 421-22n

Riddick, Carl Wood, **67**: 81,n3

Riddle of the Rhine: Chemical Strategy in Peace and War (Lefebure), **68**: 301,n8

Ridgeway, Ellen Munroe (Mrs. C. Henry), **60**: 546,n8

Ridley, Clarence Self, **59**: 320,n2; **65**: 219,n1, 258, 262; **67**: 187-88,n1

Ridley, Thomas, **64**: 184

Riesenberg, Germany, **56**: 94

Riga, Latvia, **56**: 413; **58**: 594; **61**: 162; military occupation of and atrocities in, **60**: 532,n1

Rijeka: *see* Fiume

Rikaby, Ali Riza el, **56**: 115, 116

Riley, James Whitcomb, **67**: 82,n1

Rinehart, Mary Roberts: and prohibition, **61**: 294

Ringling Brothers Barnum and Bailey Circus, **65**: 290

Rinov, Pavel Pavlovich Ivanov: *see* Ivanov-Rinov, Pavel Pavlovich

Rio de Janeiro, **67**: 23n1

Rio Negro, S.M.S., **55**: 432

Rio Pardo, S.M.S., **55**: 432

Ritter, William McClellan, **54**: 521,n2; **55**: 395,n1; **56**: 342,n1, 400,n4; **57**: 376, 377, 379, 380, 381; **65**: 44

River and Harbor bill, **53**: 288

"Riverside History of the United States" (Dodd, ed.), **67**: 76n2

Rivne (Rovno, Russia), **60**: 161,n8

Riza, Ahmed, **59**: 473

Rizov, Dimitur, **64**: 160,n3

Road Away From Revolution (Wilson), **68**: 326, 384, 387, 393-95, 462; draft of, **68**: 322-24; and Creel's dilemma concerning publication of, **68**: 342-44; EBW on waiting before making decision on, **68**: 344-45; WW revises, **68**: 347-48,n1; publication of, **68**: 348n1; Axson's involvement, **68**: 348n1; *Atlantic Monthly* accepts and sends WW check for, **68**: 354,363-64,n2; and publication choices, **68**: 367,n1, 367-68, 368, 369; inquiry into whether to also publish in book form, **68**: 370, 371; text of, **68**: 383-95; various comments on, **68**: 395, 402-403, 406, 407, 410, 427, 459, 462

Road to Normalcy: The Presidential Campaign and Election of 1920 (Bagby), **65**: 291n1, 492n1, 499n1; **66**: 208n1

Roanoke College, **59**: 473n1

Roanoke Convention: *see* Virginia State Democratic Convention

Robbins, Edmund Yard, **67**: 182

Robbins, Edward Everett, **55**: 448n1

Robbins, Edwin Clyde, **68**: 244,n2, 274

Robbins, Hallet R., **54**: 474,n2

Robbins, Keith, **62**: 254n2

Robert College (Constantinople), **55**: 28, 321, 322; **57**: 303; **58**: 323; **67**: 373n1

Roberts, Albert Houston: and woman suffrage, **65**: 445,n1, 460, 468; **66**: 54, 54-55

Roberts, John, **66**: 132-33,n3

Roberts, John C., **67**: 578,n2, 579, 586

Robertson, James Brooks Ayers, **61**: 510,n2, 510-11, 525
Robertson, John, **66**: 348n1, 356
Robertson, Sir William Robert, **59**: 7n3; **60**: 11n8, 350,n3, 599, 620; **61**: 33n2, 193, 204
Robertson, T. J., **61**: 488
Robins, Margaret Dreier (Mrs. Raymond), **62**: 96,n2, 97, 132, 164,n4, 314, 315, 436; **63**: 56,n2
Robins, Raymond, **53**: 628; **55**: 297n2; **62**: 447,n9
Robinson, Corinne Roosevelt (Mrs. Douglas), **61**: 294,n3; **65**: 411,n10
Robinson, Francis H., **67**: 172,n1
Robinson, Henry Mauris, **53**: 50,n1; **54**: 386,n1; **55**: 148,n1; **56**: 337,n1; **57**: 495n1; **58**: 202-203, 204, 498; **59**: 50, 227; **64**: 64n1; and International Labour Legislation Commission, **56**: 236,n1, 603-604, 604-605; and German ships seized in war, **56**: 429-30,n1; **57**: 498, 558; and labor clauses, **58**: 43, 173-74,n1, 416-17, 497; on ships for food relief, **58**: 269; on ship reparation agreement, **58**: 423-24, 527-28; on total net war losses, **58**: 492-93; and second Industrial Conference, **63**: 611; resignation from Shipping Board, **64**: 205,n5; appointed to coal commission, **64**: 206-209,n1, 246; declines appointment as Secretary of the Interior, **64**: 392-93; concern over ratification with Lodge reservations, **64**: 479; and Coal Commission's majority report, **65**: 95,n1,2, 96, 97
Robinson, Joseph Taylor, **55**: 263; **64**: 524,n3; **68**: 241-42,n3, 242, 380, 504, 570; supports WW, **60**: 568,n1; **61**: 184; and Democratic National Convention, 1920, **65**: 29, 345, 445, 447, 450-51, 471, 492, 494, 496, 497, 580; praises WW, **67**: 166-67; and suggestion of Kirby for Tariff Commission, **67**: 166, 168-69, 171-72; and Fuller letter, **67**: 569; on Four Power Treaty vote, **67**: 577; photograph of, *illustration section*, **68**
Robinson, Maurice H., **57**: 348n2
Robinson, Oliver Prescott, **53**: 629,n5
Rochambeau, Comte de, Jean Baptiste Donation de Vimeur, **56**: 366
Rockaway Beach, Long Island, **57**: 447n1
Rock Creek Park, Washington, D.C.: WW on tree removal in, **65**: 219, 258, 262; WW on golf course in, **67**: 323, 331,n1
Rockefeller, John Davison: foundation of, **67**: 348
Rockefeller, John Davison, Jr., **67**: 140n3; appointed to first Industrial Conference, **63**: 300,n1
Rockefeller Foundation, **53**: 302,n3; **64**: 13; **67**: 348; and yellow fever research, **61**: 560; and Fosdick and WW's educational plan, **68**: 451,n1, 492-94
Rockford, Ill., **53**: 451, 452
Rocky Ford, Colo., **63**: 489-90

Rodd, Sir (James) Rennell, **54**: 134,n2; **58**: 371,n6, 449,n2; **61**: 192,n3, 220
Rode, Ove, **60**: 284,n1
Rodgers, William H., **65**: 545,n3
Rodgers, William Ledyard, **56**: 184,n1, 184-85,n6, 519,n1
Rodkey, Frederick Stanley, **55**: 383n2
Rodman, Hugh, **53**: 397,n2; **62**: 460n1
Rodosto (now Tekirdag, Turkey), **60**: 193,n2
Roewer, George E., Jr., **65**: 550,n2
Rogers, Edward Sidney, **68**: 299,n2
Rogers, Harry Lovejoy, **55**: 397-98,n1
Rogers, John Jacob, **53**: 692,n2; **61**: 492,n1
Rogers, John Middleton, **53**: 509,n3
Rogers, Lindsay: on WW's Memorial Day message, **67**: 305,n1
Rogers, R. A., **67**: 613n1, 619; on WW's health and physical therapy treatment, **67**: 611-14
Rogers, Samuel Lyle, **63**: 573,n2
Rogers, Walter Stowell, **55**: 194,n3; **58**: 352,n5; on cable situation on Yap Island, **54**: 381-82, 400,n1; and International Communications Conference, **64**: 228,n1; **66**: 56, 154; on situation of *Washington Herald*, **66**: 169, 171; and proposed Universal Electrical Communications Union, **66**: 415, 416
Rogger, Hans, **59**: 195n4
Rolin-Jacquemyns, Edouard-Gustave-Marie, **55**: 72,n1
Rolph, James, Jr., **61**: 503,n1, 504; **63**: 308,n1, 323,n1
Roman Catholic Church, **53**: 339, 388; **58**: 491n1; WW urged to visit Pope, **53**: 231-32, 242, 421; WW visits Pope, **53**: 606-607, 646; WW on Irish question and, **59**: 646; and Upper Silesia, **60**: 158,n4, 184, 190, 191,n1, 315, 402, 404; and Poland, **60**: 165; and Harrison's divorce, remarriage, and proposed resignation, **60**: 199, 200-201; **61**: 478; and German missions, **60**: 471-72, 479-80, 578; and draft declaration on German missions, **60**: 581-82; and De Valera's U.S. visit, **61**: 183n2; and Irish situation, **61**: 513n2; Irish Americans and League of Nations, **61**: 627; and labor, **63**: 610, 612; *see also* Vatican, The
Romanes Lecture: *see* Oxford University
Romanones, Alvaro Figueroa y Torres, Count de, **53**: 419,n6, 449-50, 458
Romanovski, Ivan Pavlovich, **53**: 557,n13; **59**: 312,n1
Romanovskii, B.S., **56**: 186,n3, 569,n3, 576,n8
Rome, Italy: WW departs for, **53**: 578, 589; WW's arrival, activities and speeches in, **53**: 595-97, 597-99, 599-600, 600-601, 602-603, 605-607, 608-609; labor strike in, **57**: 240,n1, 242; reaction to WW's Adriatic statement and fear for safety of Americans in, **58**: 91-

Rome, Italy (*cont.*)
83, 143, 148; Benham on demonstrations when WW in, **59**: 246-47
Rome *Avanti*, **58**: 240
Rome *Corriere d'Italia*, **58**: 414
Rome *Epoca*, **58**: 414; **59**: 68n2
Rome *Giornale*, **61**: 109; **64**: 368, 370
Rome *Idea Nazionale*, **58**: 359
Rome *Messaggero*, **58**: 92, 143, 239, 413; **61**: 109
Rome *Osservatore Romano*, **62**: 27,n2
Rome *Popolo Romano*, **58**: 92, 239, 358, 413
Rome *Il Tempo*, **58**: 358, 413,n2, 414; **61**: 109
Rome *Tribune*, **56**: 393
Rome *Vala*, **58**: 92
Ronarc'h, Pierre-Alexis-Marie-Antoine, **61**: 83,n3, 124n2
Ronin, Charles-Eudin, **62**: 334,n2
Roosevelt, Edith Kermit Carow (Mrs. Theodore), **53**: 621, 625
Roosevelt, (Anna) Eleanor (Mrs. Franlklin Delano), **55**: 224; **67**: 135,n1, 302, 392, 448-49, 504; **68**: 39, 280, 320
Roosevelt, Emily Sinkler (Mrs. Nicholas Guy), **67**: 135,n1
Roosevelt, Franklin Delano, **55**: 207, 224, 228n1; **62**: 290; **67**: 94n1, 324; **68**: 319, 320, 381; on Navy Department and labor and wage issue, **62**: 231-32; on Saturday as half day of work, **62**: 232-33; on WW reviewing marine brigade, **62**: 241,n1; and Sims's article on navy, **62**: 460, 546-47; Geddes on, **65**: 371; mentioned as vice-presidential candidate, **65**: 488; WW's congratulations to, **65**: 500,n1; and vice-presidential nomination, **65**: 507; meets with WW **65**: 520-21,n1, 522-24, 525; on protecting Americans in Armenia, **65**: 536-37, 539-40; resignation of as Assistant Secretary of Navy, **65**: 544, 548; **66**: 5, 17,n2, 77; and replacement of Cummings as Democratic chairman, **65**: 551; wishes to see WW but WW unable to see him, **67**: 239, 240, 302; and WW Foundation, **67**: 271,n1, 273, 274, 276, 285, 327,n6, 333-34, 341-42, 346, 348, 352, 386, 393n1, 416, 544n3, 565; **68**: 245-46, 249n2, 365, 509, 510; on WW Award, **67**: 333-34; and naming "the Fund," **67**: 341-42, 346, 348; and Henkels and Washington's Farewell Address, **67**: 357-58; denied request for WW's autograph in book, **67**: 358, 362; stricken with polio, **67**: 386,n2; WW on health of, **67**: 392, 449; sends WW Foundation's birthday greetings, **67**: 497, 504; **68**: 245, 511; greetings on fifth anniversary of entrance into war, **67**: 603-604, 604; and health, **68**: 36, 39; WW thanks, **68**: 246, 513; WW's birthday wishes to, **68**: 280; EBW visits on yacht in Massachusetts, **68**: 410, 415

Roosevelt, Nicholas, **56**: 241,n5; on Hungarian revolution, **56**: 331,n1, 331-34
Roosevelt, Sara Delano (Mrs. James), **67**: 135,n17
Roosevelt, Theodore, **53**: 199, 406, 448, 580, 708,n3; **54**: 176, 198; **55**: 466; **56**: 437; **57**: 349; **59**: 159; **60**: 329; **62**: 21n1; **63**: 94, 438, 473; **65**: 233, 411, 412, 498; **66**: 165, 255, 266, 292, 317n1, 327; **67**: 30, 77,n5, 183n1, 184, 187-88, 219-20, 238, 283, 398, 533n1; **68**: 56, 398, 464n1, 594; and League to Enforce Peace, **53**: 28-29, 29-30, 30-31, 31; WW on not appointing as peace commissioner, **53**: 117,n1; and Pius X, **53**: 242,n3; attack on WW, **53**: 314,n4; and League of Nations, **53**: 382; **63**: 223,n2; death of and WW's proclamation, **53**: 621, 624, 625, 634, 635, 636; **54**: 106; bill to name national park after, **54**: 486, 554; R. S. Baker on extremes and excesses of, **55**: 467; and L. Wood, **55**: 486; **68**: 528; wanted to lead volunteer division in France, **56**: 87; and memorabilia exhibition, **59**: 320,n2; WW compares Lloyd George to, **60**: 570; in North Dakota, **63**: 153,n3; WW quotes from, **63**: 371, 376; on international court, **63**: 509; and W. A. White, **64**: 62; on mail censorship, **66**: 96-97; WW on, **66**: 175; and Dominican Republic, **66**: 383n1; I. Hoover compares WW to, **67**: 150; Dodd on Republican politics and, **67**: 298; unveiling of statue of, **67**: 577-78,n1; WW on administration, **68**: 88-89
Roosevelt in the Kansas City Star: War-Time Editorials by Theodore Roosevelt, with an Introduction by Ralph Stout, **63**: 223n2
Roosevelt's Talks with his Physician (Richards), **68**: 252,n2
Root, Elihu, **53**: 72, 185, 199, 692,n2; **55**: 367, 440; **56**: 233; **60**: 330, 572; **61**: 178, 373, 390, 605n1; **63**: 223n1; **64**: 216; **66**: 141n1, 178, 246n2; **67**: 227; **68**: 346n2, 452n2; on League of Nations amendments, **56**: 99, 99-100, 483-84; suggested for International Court of Justice, **60**: 431, 432; and peace treaty leak investigation, **60**: 434, 536; proposal to accept treaty with reservations, **61**: 66,n3, 137-38; attack on Article X, **61**: 181, 295-301; Miller on treaty objections of, **61**: 232-35, 295-301; WW on reservations of, **61**: 247; and reservations issue, **62**: 68, 308,n1, 309, 385, 504, 540; appointed to Permanent Court of Arbitration, **64**: 273; and Armenia, **65**: 298; and World Court, **65**: 419; suggested for Åland Islands Commission, **65**: 526; WW has no faith in, **65**: 531; and Federal Reserve System, **66**: 157,n6; and League of Nations position, **66**: 158, 258n2,3; and international cables, **66**: 221; Tu-

multy wishes to show that WW incorporated suggestions of into Covenant, **66**: 230,n1; speech of League of Nations attacking Article X, **66**: 246,n1; WW on not answering speech, **66**: 249; and Four Power Treaty, **67**: 553; on League of Nations, **68**: 159-60

Root, Robert Kilburn, **67**: 182

Root-Takahira agreement (1908), **61**: 299,n5

Roper, Daniel Calhoun, **53**: 71; **54**: 429; **65**: 438, 511,n3; **67**: 350, 366, 616,n2; **68**: 179, 180

Rose, Henry Martin, **65**: 323,n1

Rosenberg, Germany, **57**: 153, 595

Rosenberg, Arthur, **59**: 16n6

Rosenthal, B. B., **63**: 269

Rosenwald, Julius, **64**: 64n1: **66**: 261; and second Industrial Conference, **63**: 611

Roskill, Stephen W., **67**: 452n1

Ross, Charles Griffith, **66**: 172n1

Ross, Sir Charles Henry Augustus Frederick Lockhart, 9th Baronet, **53**: 245,n1

Ross, Edward Alsworth: on King-Crane Report, **64**: 425,n2

Rosseter, John Henry, **55**: 398,n1; **58**: 269,n2; **62**: 465,n1

Rossi, Luigi, **61**: 109,n6

Rostock, Germany, **53**: 8

Rostov, Russia, **53**: 335

Roth, Georges, **53**: 261-62

Rothenberg, Morris, **66**: 109

Rothermere, Viscount: see Harmsworth, Harold Sidney

Rothesay Parish Church (Reformed), Bute, Scotland, **59**: 190n1

Rothschild, Lionel Walter, 2nd Baron, **54**: 52; **55**: 383; on Jews and Zionism, **53**: 543,n1

Rotterdam, The Netherlands, **55**: 180; **58**: 99

Rouche, Jacques, **54**: 305,n6

Roumania: see Rumania

Round Table: A Quarterly Review of the Politics of the British Empire, **67**: 462n1

Rouse, Arthur Blythe: on U.S. membership in World Court, **68**: 306-307,n1; WW's response, **68**: 314, 339

Rousseau, Jean-Jacques, **56**: 121; **57**: 329

Roussos, Paris, **58**: 355-56,n1, 435,n6

Rovigno, Italy, **53**: 445

Rowe, Leo Stanton, **53**: 100,n1; **66**: 178-79, 431; **68**: 577; on recognition of Costa Rica, **64**: 245,n1; **65**: 465-66, 505-506, 571; elected Director of Pan-American Union, **65**: 233n1, 234, 252, 270

Rowell, Chester Harvey, **63**: 309,n3, 323,n1; **66**: 252,n1

Rowland, Peter, **56**: 259n1; **68**: 141n1

Rowse, D. C., **66**: 275

Royal Academy of Science, Rome, **53**: 608-609,n1

Royal Dutch Shell Company, **62**: 78

Royal Institute of International Affairs: see British Institute of International Affairs

Rozano, Sergei Nikolaevich, **61**: 572,n6

Rubel, Laurence E., **67**: 128-29,n1

Rublee, George, **60**: 358,n2: suggested for mideastern commission, **56**: 155

Rublee, Juliet Barrett (Mrs. George), **57**: 218, 219

Ruddock, Albert Billings, **64**: 458n3

Rudin, Harry Rudolph, **53**: 626n1; **56**: 463n12

Rudwick, Elliott M., **54**: 126n1

Ruffin, Sterling, M.D. **63**: 544,n3, 550, 551, 553, 556, 578, 579, 634; **64**: 4, 506, 507, 508, 509, 510; **67**: 245; bulletins on WW's health, **63**: 568, 574, 577, 578, 579, 581, 587, 590; **68**: 549, 553, 555, 556, 557, 559, 560, 562, 563, 571, 573; prescribes medication for WW, **66**: 55-56; photograph of, *illustration section,* **68**

Ruggles, James A., **55**: 93n2

Rugia, S.M.S., **55**: 432

Ruhlman, Paul, **53**: 121n1

Ruhr Valley: riots in and German occupation of, **65**: 155n1, 156-63; U.S. position on Franco-German crisis, **65**: 160-62, 165-66, 167-69; Britain's position on, **65**: 170-71; H. C. Wallace on, **65**: 170-73; and French threatened occupation of, **67**: 33,n1, 269; and French invasion of, **68**: 282,n2, 289, 300, 362, 453n1

Rules, Committee on (House of Reps.), **61**: 610; **65**: 43

Rumania, **53**: 38, 56, 293, 296, 650, 692; **55**: 542; **58**: 6, 8, 42; **59**: 176; **61**: 56, 430; **62**: 78, 510; **63**: 24, 61, 82, 119-20,n2,3, 306, 421; **64**: 265, 332; **66**: 172,n1, 180, 187-88, 191-92, 196-97; **67**: 461n1; **68**: 62; and wheat situation, **62**: 52; occupation of Budapest, **62**: 123,n1, 167-68,n1, 265-66; and Bessarabia, **62**: 206-207; WW on invasion of Budapest by, **62**: 235-36, 242, 253, 428-29,n1; Polk on U.S. withholding financial aid from, **62**: 248; approval to withdraw U.S. minister if demands are not met, **64**: 35, 36; and Hungary, **64**: 101n2, 447, 465; Vénisélos on, **64**: 162; Cardinal Gibbons on persecution of Christians in, **65**: 138; and food relief, **65**: 469; and Balfour and inter-Allied indebtedness, **68**: 106n1; anti-Semitic demonstrations in, **68**: 333,n1; see also Paris Peace Conference—Rumania

Rumania at the Paris Peace Conference: A Study of the Diplomacy of Ioan I. C. Brătianu (Spector), **60**: 222n4

Rumanian National Council, **60**: 228n6

Rural Credits Act, **53**: 78

Rush, Richard, **63**: 430

Rush, Thomas E., **67**: 602; **68**: 15,n2, 20

Rush Medical College, **64**: 432

Ruskin College, Oxford, **58**: 444n1

Russell, Albertina Pyne (Mrs. Archibald Douglas), **60**: 646,n2
Russell, Charles Edward, **56**: 245, 282-83, 310; on labor, **60**: 147-48,n4; **66**: 542n1; **67**: 522, 523; appointed to first Industrial Conference, **63**: 300,n1
Russell, Francis, **63**: 167n6
Russell, Theresa Hirschl (Mrs. Charles Edward), **68**: 48n6
Russell Sage Foundation, **62**: 167n3
Russia, **53**: 38, 293, 338; **54**: 34, 47; **56**: 112, 512n1, 615; **58**: 9, 397, 477,n13; **59**: 72-74, 134, 374, 572; **60**: 95,n2, 549; **61**: 40, 154, 424; **68**: 62, 125, 226; Huntington memorandum on, **53**: 169-80; executions by Kalmykov, **53**: 184-85; C. H. McCormick's suggestions for, **53**: 255-57; British Imperial War Cabinet discusses, **53**: 560-61, 568; Britain on peace negotiations with, **53**: 591, 718, 722-23; Ackerman on need for definite policy in, **53**: 628-32; and League of Nations, **53**: 658n1, 672; **57**: 170; Foch on, **54**: 8-9,n4, 19; **55**: 213; **56**: 314-15; and peace negotiations, **54**: 26-29,n1, 153-54; and Poland, **54**: 32-33,n5,7, 337-39; **59**: 114; and Japan, **54**: 83-84, 158n1, 158-59; **55**: 294; Lord memorandum on Bolsheviks, **54**: 91-95; Buckler meets Litvinov on peace prospects, **54**: 135-38, 180-81; and issue of congressional appropriations for railroads in, **54**: 259-60, 261, 412-13, 486-87; and Finland, **54**: 287; **58**: 404; military occupation of, **54**: 371-72,n7; Sykes-Picot Agreement, **54**: 506n7; and railroad situation, **55**: 38-39, 150, 187-88, 393, 400; comments on withdrawing U.S. troops from, **55**: 149,n1, 181-83, 235; Churchill's initiative on, **55**: 202, 203-204, 208, 229-30, 232; T. H. Bliss on, **55**: 214-15; **58**: 568; Lloyd George on, **55**: 233; **56**: 265; Francis on situation in, **55**: 234-35, 350; WW on, **55**: 319-20; **63**: 70, 76-77, 95-96, 134, 145, 152, 161-62, 174-75, 214, 216, 245, 263; and Jews, **55**: 369; Morris on Graves and, **55**: 493-95; Bullitt mission to, **55**: 540-45,n1; **56**: 183, 279-80, 387-91; and Hungary, **56**: 239, 240-41, 242-43, 276; House on, **56**: 309; **63**: 421-22; H. Hoover on establishing relief commission for, **56**: 377; Cachin on peace conference and, **56**: 387; *Springfield Republican* editorial on, **56**: 435-36; suggestions on policy toward by Russian Section of A.C.N.P., **56**: 466-68, 512n1; Lansbury on publishing Bullitt report on, **56**: 473; W. A. White on, **56**: 544, 545; Martens on U.S. establishing commercial relations with, **56**: 548-50; hopes for commercial dealings with U.S., **56**: 551,n1; rumors and editorial comments on proposed recognition of Lenin, **56**: 551,n1; Nansen's food relief program, **56**: 575-

76; **57**: 93-94, 165, 166-67, 437-40, 456, 569; **58**: 41-42; J. N. Sayre on need for Y.W.C.A. work in, **57**: 60-61; and return of prisoners from Germany, **57**: 76; and Baltic states, **57**: 139; **59**: 466,n5; Russian Political Conference, **57**: 139n1; Hoover on sharing shipping burden of food and relief distribution in, **57**: 161, 512; diseases in, **57**: 311; House and Clemenceau on food relief, **57**: 335; Lloyd George on, **57**: 428n14; Lloyd George's statement on Bullitt mission, **57**: 459-60,n2,3; W. G. Sharp on, **57**: 476; Hoover on Bolshevism and, **57**: 503n2, 505-508; Hoover instructed not to give statement to press, **57**: 503-504, 529; McCormick on political and relief situation in **57**: 575; Lansing on states carved out of, **58**: 319; and Germany, **58**: 342-43, 344, 403; question of support and recognition of Kolchak, **58**: 569-70; **59**: 148, 188, 189, 236, 421, 479, 527, 530, 550-51, 552; Chaikovskii on situation in, **59**: 14-21; Lenin's reply to Nansen's proposal, **59**: 192-97, 300n8, 310-12; and Ukraine, **59**: 352; dispatch to Kolchak, **59**: 435-38, 440-42, 468-70, 481; and debt, **59**: 436-37,n9, 462, 543-46; Marshall on Jews in, **59**: 515; Hapgood on, **59**: 517-19; **61**: 359-60; **66**: 28, 343,n2; dispatch to Kolchak, **59**: 543-46; Polk on waiting for Kolchak's reply before sending Morris to, **59**: 618-19; Kolchak's reply on priorities of his government, **60**: 141-44, 228-29; various comments on relationship of Germany and, **60**: 167-68, 208-10, 214-15; and Rumania, **60**: 171; Kolchak's proclamation to citizens of, **60**: 180-81; and Penjdeh incident, **60**: 210,n6; Stevens on need for Allied troops to relieve Czechs, **60**: 608, 609; Phillips on ascertaining from Kolchak supplies and support needed, **60**: 609; support for Kolchak, **61**: 40, 41; Hoover's plan for economic commission for, **61**: 61; McCormick meets with WW on, **61**: 110-11; plan to send Morris to Omsk, **61**: 130-31; and Baltic provinces, **61**: 153; removal of Czech troops from, **61**: 206; WW on blockade and, **61**: 224; and Poland, **61**: 257, 258; desires to purchase supplies from U.S., **61**: 288; and League of Nations membership, **61**: 447, 490; Polk urges sending supplies to, **61**: 465-66; and Bullitt mission, **61**: 509,n1; issue of trade with Bolshevik Russia, **62**: 11; proposed blockade and U.S. response, **62**: 14, 108-10; situation in as seen by *Manchester Guardian* correspondents, **62**: 34n1; and wheat situation, **62**: 52; Poole memorandum on, **62**: 203-205, 441-48; and issue of Bessarabia being given to Rumania, **62**: 206-207, 266; and League of Free Nations Associa-

tion, **62**: 530-31,n3; battle deaths, **63**: 221, 243, 349; war costs, **63**: 221, 243, 349; and China, **63**: 314, 330, 437, 438; and Bullitt's testimony before Foreign Relations Committee, **63**:337,n3; need for aid, **63**: 394; issue of troops to Armenia, **63**: 466; U.S. to send grain to, **63**: 588-90,n1; WW on, **64**: 87, 116; Lansing on situation in, **64**: 307-308,n1; Lloyd George draft telegram on U.S. resuming trade with, **64**: 308-309; Russia and Turkish treaty, **65**: 64, 113; WW on issue of Constantinople and Straits, **65**: 74; Polk on U.S. representation on proposed commission to, **65**: 77-78; concern over Germany's relations with, **65**: 102; and Great Britain, **65**: 103, 288,n3; and Sisson documents, **65**: 134n2; Bullard wants verification of documents on Allied intervention in, **65**: 143-45; issue of trade with, **65**: 247, 270, 271, 445, 490, 492,n1; and Armenia, **65**: 287-88; and Baker's concern over sale of locomotives to Estonia, **65**: 387; and Japan's invasion of Sakhalin, **65**: 515,n1; Gibson on Poland and, **65**: 526-28,n1; and Poland, **66**: 9n1, 11n1; on Polish-Soviet situation and policy toward, **66**: 19-24; Colby on friendship between U.S. and, **66**: 20-21, 22; Lloyd George on, **66**: 45-47; and French note on, **66**: 50n1; Japan on reasons for troops in Vladivostok, **66**: 51; and gold payment in Germany, **66**: 166n1; Huse's concern over "Bolshivik" ships in Baltic Sea, **66**: 207,n1; WW answers Lloyd George on, **66**: 308; and Armenia, **66**: 436, 437; **67**: 64, 65-66; and Sisson Papers, **66**: 542,n1; and Baltic provinces, **67**: 8-9; Four Power Treaty and, **67**: 544n1, 552; *see also* Bolsheviks and Bolshevism; Paris Peace Conference—Russia; Russia and the United States

Murmansk and Archangel—intervention in, **53**: 152, 227, 335, 713-14; **58**: 133, 265-66, 576, 577-78; **60**: 637; **62**: 108; Polk on, **54**: 83; Bullitt on withdrawing U.S. troops from, **54**: 348-49; T. H. Bliss on Britain's request for U.S. troops, **55**: 28-29; situation in Archangel, **55**: 39, 93,n2; U.S. public opinion on, **55**: 82; WW approves sending railway troops to, **55**: 150, 188-92,n2; talk of U.S. troop removal, **55**: 182-83, 189-92; financing qovernment in Archangel, **56**: 279,n1; Bliss on Archangel situation, **56**: 307; and plans of Britain and U.S. **57**: 460-61,n2, 560, 589, 628; and Finland, **58**: 177; Benson on withdrawing forces from, **58**: 319; WW on sending vessels to assist troop removal, **58**: 354; Council of Four on situation in Archangel, **59**: 16, 18; Bliss on withdrawal of troops from Archangel, **59**: 599-600; **60**: 241; U.S. Navy withdraws from Murmansk, **60**: 241; withdrawal of troops from Archangel, **60**: 241; WW on removal of troops, **60**: 359; evacuation of Czech troops in, **61**: 99; U.S. railway troops to aid British in, **61**: 225-26, 349; and U.S. food relief to, **61**: 455,n1; on maintaining some vessels at Archangel, **61**: 505-506, 604,n1; request for retention of U.S. troops in Archangel, **62**: 594; and flour from U.S., **63**: 589

Siberia—intervention in, **53**: 152; **54**: 22,n10, 83, 100-101, 158-59; **58**: 42; **62**: 15, 34n1; **63**: 394; **65**: 144, 145,n1; Japan and, **53**: 144-47, 463-64,n1, 632-63; **54**: 379, 557; **56**: 184-85, 186; **61**: 172; talk of withdrawal of U.S. troops, **53**: 168-69, 227-29; **55**: 182-83; and British policy, **53**: 335; **57**: 460-61,n2; R. Ackerman on need for definite policy in, **53**: 628-32; M. Litvinov on, **53**: 713-14; H. W. Johnson for troop withdrawal, **54**: 259,n3; and congressinal hearings on, **54**: 412-13; W. S. Graves on, **55**: 399-403; and instructions to Graves, **56**: 152-53, 184, 371-72,n1, 519,n1, 576; N. D. Baker on, **56**: 576-77; Phillips on Baker's views on, **56**: 606; J. N. Sayre on need for Y.W.C.A. work in, **57**: 60-61; issues of railroads, military, and U.S. policy, **57**: 94-95, 134, 313-15; operations of Trans-Siberian Railway, **57**: 420,n1, 420-22,n2; and Kolchak government, **58**: 494-96, 569-70, 573-78; **59**: 461-64, 465, 619; **60**: 625, 637; talk of replacing W. S. Graves, **59**: 234-35, 281-82; WW has no regrets on not having Russian policy, **59**: 301-302, 311; Polk on German graves, **59**: 409-10; Phillips on morale in, **60**: 609; Knapp on meeting with WW on troop withdrawal, **60**: 613, 615; troop morale in, **61**: 41; McCormick on, **61**: 110; and repatriation of Czech troops, **61**: 164-66, 196-97, 201-202, 206, 287-88, 316, 494, 629; Johnson's Senate resolution on U.S. troops in, **61**: 353,n2; repatriation of Czech troops leads to request for more U.S. troops, **61**: 485; Long on WW addressing Czech troops, **61**: 514; WW's remarks to Czech troops, **61**: 518-19; need for civilian and medical supplies, **61**: 528, 581; Morris on, **61**: 571-73; WW on maintaining U.S. troops in, **61**: 579-82; and railroads, **61**: 636-38; and Czech troops and Packard Report, **62**: 82,n2; Graves on conditions in, **62**: 83-90; anti-American propaganda in, **62**: 88-89; reason for U.S. intervention, **62**: 108-109; request for return of U.S. soldiers in, **62**: 433-34, 478-79, 515; Poole on, **62**: 443; Lansing on withdrawal of U.S. troops from, **62**: 588-89; and Japa-

Russia (*cont.*)
nese railroad plan, **62**: 589-93; loan request and repatriation of Czech troops, **63**: 394-95, 421, 518; Daniels on, **63**: 559-60; Lansing recommends withdrawal of U.S. troops from, **64**: 219-21; and Japan, **64**: 390-91; U.S. decision to withdraw troops, **64**: 436; and Japan, **65**: 284n1, 391-92, 516; *see also* Czech troops in Russia; Bolsheviks and Bolshevism; Russia and the United States; Russian Civil War
Russia and Constantinople (*Manchester Guardian*), **59**: 519n2
Russia and the United States, **53**: 290, 331-32; and Interparty League, **53**: 136-37; Japan and railroads, **53**: 146, 555-57,n4, 699; question of making statement against Bolshevik terrorism, **53**: 152-53, 627, 706; Macfarland on, **53**: 199-200, 221, 487; and Prince L'vov's visit to U.S., **53**: 258-59; arrest of American Consul Tredwell, **53**: 312-13,n1; Litvinov on Russian situation and peace negotiations, **53**: 492-94,n1, 712-13; U.S. loans to, **53**: 571; U.S. sentiment regarding troops in, **53**: 582-83,n5,6; and financial status of Russian embassy, **56**: 159-61; and Russian rifles being stored by State Department, **59**: 571-72,n1; cancellation of Morris' trip to Omsk, **60**: 240; Polk on deportation of Martens, **60**: 484,n1; issue of lifting trade restrictions, **65**: 247, 270, 271, 389-90, 445, 455-56, 490, 492,n2; Colby-Wilson note on nonrecognition of Bolshevik regime, **66**: 19-25; *see also* Russia
Russia as an American Problem (Spargo), **66**: 5n2
Russia, Bolshevism and the Versailles Peace (Thompson), **53**: 492n1; **55**: 161,n1, 202n1, 540n1; **56**: 466n1, 575n1; **57**: 93n1, 139n1, 459n2,3; **61**: 455n1
Russia from the American Embassy, April 1916-November, 1918 (Francis), **55**: 234n1
Russia in the Shadow (Wells), **66**: 343n2
Russian-American Commercial Treaty (1832), **56**: 188,n6
Russian-American Relations, March, 1917-March 1920: Documents and Papers (Cumming and Pettit, eds.), **54**: 27n2
Russian Bureau, Inc., **54**: 259,n1, 413, 440; **55**: 39, 351; **56**: 161; **64**: 308
Russian Civil War, **53**: 172-77, 184-85; *see also* Bolsheviks and bolshevism
Russian Cooperative Societies, **64**: 308
Russian-Polish War of 1919-1920: *see* Polish-Soviet War of 1919-1920
Russian Political Conference, **57**: 139,n1; **59**: 154,n3; **61**: 40, 41
Russian Quagmire. Counter-Revolutionary Activities. Baltic Peoples' Fears (*Manchester Guardian*), **61**: 360,n7
Russian Railway Service Corps, **53**: 463n1; **54**: 261; **55**: 350; **61**: 580
Russian Red Cross, **59**: 14n3, 195
Russian Revolution (1917), **66**: 20; WW on, **67**: 66; **68**: 322, 393
Russian Revolution, 1917-1921 (Chamberlin), **60**: 95n2; **62**: 427n1; **63**: 588n1
Russian Soviet Government Bureau, **56**: 548n1
Russia's Civil War. Great Britain's Support of Koltchak (*Manchester Guardian*), **62**: 34n1
Russo-Japanese War, **63**: 315, 330, 412, 438, 472-507
Russo-Turkish War (1878), **64**: 161
Ruthenberg, Charles Emil, **67**: 99,n2
Ruthenia and Ruthenians, **57**: 356, 357; **58**: 42; **59**: 597, 598; **60**: 160-61; **61**: 167-68, 243; **64**: 442, 447, 463, 465
Rutherford, Joseph Franklin, **55**: 482n1
Ruutz-Rees, Caroline, **67**: 271n1; **68**: 248
Ryan, John Dennis, **54**: 392; **58**: 597,n3; **61**: 512,n4, 529; **66**: 133,n3; and copper price fixing, **67**: 176-78,n1
Ryan, Martin F., **62**: 122, 568-70, 570-73; **65**: 16, 359
Ryan, Michael J., **56**: 486n1; **57**: 419,n4, 426, 534,n1; **58**: 505,n2, 585-87, 588; **59**: 34, 104-105, 106, 172, 251, 366-67, 368, 393, 394-95, 513, 549n1; **60**: 239n2, 298; **63**: 118n2; **64**: 424, 431
Ryan, Thomas Fortune, **68**: 426,n1
Ryan, William, **67**: 14, 22
Rydal, Ambleside, Westmorland, **53**: 425
Ryder, Arthur John, **56**: 543n2

Saarbrücken, Germany, **56**: 360, 361
Saar Commission (proposed), **60**: 109
Saarlouis, Germany, **56**: 360, 361
Saar Valley, **55**: 387,n2; **56**: 424, 540, 581; **60**: 25, 27-28, 29, 156, 436, 460-62; France's demands for, **55**: 312, 347; **57**: 63n1, 69, 106, 110, 113, 113-17, 117-21, 284, 308, 325; **58**: 45, 61, 62, 64-65, 67, 227, 454; **59**: 376-79, 401n4, 459; **61**: 431; **62**: 19, 410, 414, 418, 419; Clemenceau-WW confrontation over, **56**: 349, 353-54, 364-68, 434; Tardieu on history of, **56**: 360-63, 587, 588; Council of Four on, **56**: 364-70, 451-53; **57**: 106-107, 128-30, 150-51, 161-65, 199-202, 243-46; **59**: 376-79, 385, 453; Haskins on, **56**: 420, 431-32, 513, 514; **59**: 108-109; Steed on, **56**: 515, 516-17; Lloyd George on, **56**: 546-47; and Baruch, **57**: 90, 159-60, 287-88; Miller on, **57**: 90-91, 195; Lloyd George on, **57**: 106-107; corrections in article on, **57**: 118-20; Tardieu on, **57**: 155-59; draft proposals for, **57**: 196-99; effect of WW's health on decisions concerning, **58**: 624; Brockdorff-Rantzau on, **58**: 377,n3, 580; Smuts on, **59**: 414; American delegation on, **59**: 65-66, 70; reply

to German counterproposals on, **59**: 441-42, 447-48, 467; House on, **60**: 83; and U.S. representation on commission on, **62**: 451, 481; and Tardieu's indiscreet article on discussions about, **65**: 542, 543; R. S. Baker organizes WW's documents on, **67**: 89

Saavedra, Bautista, **66**: 135n1; **67**: 92

Saburi, Sadao, **58**: 346,n3; **59**: 12,n6; **60**: 419, 478

Sacco, Nicola, **55**: 343n1

Sacher, Howard Morley, **56**: 110n7

Sack, Arkady Joseph, **68**: 125,n4

Sackville-West, Charles John, **59**: 232,n2; **60**: 258,n4, 316, 475, 500

Sacramento, California: WW's arrival and activities in, **63**: 426; WW's remarks in, **63**: 426-27

Sacramento, U.S.S., **65**: 252

Sacramento Bee, **63**: 427n

Sadler, Louis R., **64**: 140n1

Sadowa, Battle of, **55**: 503

Safe for Democracy: The Anglo-American Response to Revolution, 1913-1923 (Gardner), **64**: 417n3

Safford, Jeffrey Jaeger, **53**: 110n1; **65**: 270n1, 351n1, 467n2

Sage, Russell, **53**: 332

Saint-Aulaire, Auguste-Félix-Charles de Beaupoil, Count de, **59**: 566,n2

Saint-Aymour, Robert de Caix, **57**: 468n2

Sainte Croix, Eugènie-Avril de, **57**: 218,n1, 219

St. Gaudens, Augustus, **68**: 20

St. George's Episcopal Church, Paris, **54**: 380n3

St. Germain, France, **58**: 315; **60**: 19; *see also* Paris Peace Conference—Austrian treaty

St. Gobin, France, **56**: 198

St. Gotthard Railway, **56**: 268

St. Gotthard Tunnel, **56**: 75

St. Jean de Maurienne, Agreement of, **58**: 477,n13; **59**: 41, 42, 374; **61**: 191,n2, 213, 217, 310

St. John de Medua, **57**: 517

St. John's, Newfoundland, **57**: 447n1

St. Joseph, Mo., **63**: 64

St. Joseph, University of (Beirut), **56**: 107,n3

St. Louis, Mo., **53**: 413; **59**: 287; **68**: 166n1; and plans for WW's tour on League of Nations, **60**: 568n5; and telephone strike, **61**: 540; speeches in, **63**: 32; WW's address to Chamber of Commerce in, **63**: 33-42, 198,n1; WW's address in Coliseum, **63**: 43-51; Norris criticizes WW's address in, **63**: 93

St. Louis, U.S.S., **65**: 537

St. Louis Chamber of Commerce: WW's address to, **63**: 32,33-43, 45

St. Louis *Globe-Democrat*, **61**: 399n1; **64**: 42n, 51n; **68**: 24

St. Louis Post Dispatch, **63**: 18n, 29n, 32n, 42n, 51n, 52n4; **66**: 172n1, 188, 246

St. Louis Republic, **63**: 151n3

St. Louis Star, **67**: 488, 578n2

St. Luke's International Hospital (Tokyo), **68**: 424n1

St. Maxence, France, **56**: 195, 199

St. Paul, Minnesota, **59**: 287; WW's reception and activities in, **63**: 122-23, 124,n4; WW's addresses in, **63**: 125-31, 138-48; photograph, *illustration section*, **63**

St. Paul News: and Lansing dismissal, **65**: 6

St. Paul's American Church in Rome, **53**: 607,n5

Saint-Quentin, René-Doynel de, **61**: 92,n3

St. Veit, Austria, **60**: 362

Saionji, Marquis Kimmochi, **57**: 631,n1; **58**: 128, 129, 442; **59**: 487; and dispatch to Kolchak, **59**: 481, 546; photograph of, *illustration section*, **59**

Sakhalin, **67**: 544n1; Japanese occupation of, **65**: 515-17,n1; **66**: 39n3, 50, 51, 53

Sakharov, Konstantin Viacheslavovich, **56**: 186,n3

Sakmyster, Thomas L., **56**: 462,n11

Salandra, Antonio, **53**: 596,n4; **54**: 134,n1; **56**: 271n3

Salem, U.S.S., **65**: 252

Salis, John Francis Charles, Count de, **55**: 493; **56**: 395,n2

Salisbury, 3rd Marquis of (Robert Arthur Talbot Gascoyne-Cecil), **55**: 384n3; **57**: 361

Salmon, Benjamin J., **66**: 401, 414, 415

Salmon, Thomas William: psychiatric evaluation of men in American Expeditionary Force, **61**: 530-33

Salonika, **53**: 648; **54**: 181, 182,n2, 188; **58**: 513, 514; **60**: 135; **64**: 164n8

Saloutos, Theodore, **68**: 146n2

Salt Creek oil field (Wyoming), **53**: 596,n4

Salter, James Arthur, **53**: 373,n2

Salt Lake City, Utah: WW's activities in, **63**: 446, 447,n1; WW's addresses in, **63**: 446,n2, 449-63, 529

Salt Lake Railroad, **62**: 548

Salt Lake City, Utah, **56**: 404n1

Salvador: and Honduras, **61**: 639; and appointments, **64**: 205; Jay appointed minister to, **65**: 125, 426

Salvago-Raggi, Marquis Guiseppi, **58**: 225,n8

Salvation Army, **54**: 5n2, 6; **57**: 459; **67**: 4, 11; WW helps with fund appeal, **65**: 288, 297; and White House sheep, **65**: 317-18,n1, 332, 354

Salvation for Germany (Coar), **67**: 463-64,n1

Salvemini, Gaetano, **53**: 433,n1, 434

Salzburg, Austria, **60**: 643

Samara (now Kuibyshev), **59**: 225

Sambor, Poland (now Russia), **59**: 597

Sammons, Thomas, **53**: 197,n1; **60**: 604,n2

Samne, Georges, **55**: 145n3

Samoa, **58**: 442, 484, 510; and New Zealand and territorial claims, **54**: 251, 254, 312, 313, 320, 363; **58**: 442, 484, 510; WW on, **54**: 314, 363; and mandates, **59**: 475,n2

Samsun, Turkey, **65**: 538, 540, 549

Samuel, Sir Herbert (Louis), **59**: 113,n3; **66**: 48,n9

Samuel, Maurice, **55**: 384n4

Sand (movie), **65**: 412

Sanders, Ivan, **56**: 452n11

Sanders, J. D.: resolution asking railroad strikers to return to work, **62**: 302-303

Sanders, Jared Young, **65**: 163,n1, 164-65, 165

Sanderson, George Andrew, **61**: 353,n1, 495, 510

San Diego, California: WW's arrival and activities in, **63**: 369-70, 523; WW's addresses in, **63**: 371-82, 382-88; Prince of Wales on, **65**: 226; photograph of WW in, *illustration section*, **63**

San Diego, Texas, **64**: 140n1

San Diego *Evening Tribune*, **63**: 382n, 388n

San Domingo: *see* Dominican Republic

San Francisco, California, **56**: 404n1; WW's activities in, **63**: 308-10, 340; Grayson on WW's address in Civic Auditorium, **63**: 309-10,n2; WW's address to Associated Women's Clubs of, **63**: 311-22; WW's address in Civic Auditorium, **63**: 323-36; WW's luncheon address in, **63**: 322-23, 341-50; photograph of WW in, *illustration section*, **63**

San Francisco *Bulletin*, **67**: 363, 364

San Francisco *Chronicle*, **61**: 373; **63**: 336n, 350n; **67**: 488

San Francisco Convention: *see* Democratic National Convention of 1920

San Francisco *Examiner*, **63**: 309n2, 322n, 336n, 350n; **67**: 363

San Francisco Labor Council, **63**: 268-70; requests meeting with WW, **63**: 296-97, 302-303; WW's memorandum answers questions posed by, **63**: 303-304

Sanfuentes, Andonaegui, Juan Luis, **53**: 316-17,n1, 346-47,n1

San Giorgio (ship), **58**: 142, 148; **59**: 66

San José, Costa Rica: Central American conference at, **66**: 356, 357-58

San Marino, **57**: 426, 481

Sanok, Poland, **59**: 262,n7

San Pietro, Italy: and Adriatic settlement, **66**: 365

San Remo Conference, **65**: 196,n2; issue of U.S. attendance, **65**: 196, 197, 213; WW on no U.S. representation if Germany attends, **65**: 221; editorial on, **65**: 229n1; and mandates, **65**: 248,n1, 271n1, 271-72,n1, 299, 321-23, 334,n1; R. U. Johnson on, **65**: 299, 302-303; agreement, **66**: 394n1, 397, 398

San Salvador: changed attitude toward U.S., **61**: 560-61

San Stefano, Treaty of, **53**: 296; **58**: 461n1

Santa Barbara Press, **55**: 205

Santa Catalina Island, **63**: 370

Santa Cruz, S.M.S., **55**: 432

Santa Elena, S.M.S., **55**: 432

Santa Fe, S.M.S., **55**: 432

Santa Fe Railroad, **62**: 548

Santander, Manuel de Freyre y, **55**: 330,n1

Santo Domingo *Las Noticias*, **66**: 31n1

Sapieha, Prince Eustachy Kajetan Wladyslaw, **66**: 87n1

Sardinia, **57**: 442

Sargent, John Singer, **53**: 594,n15; **59**: 320,n2; **62**: 157,n8; **67**: 587,n3; portrait of WW, **60**: 373,n1

Sarre Valley: *see* Saar Valley

Sartorius, Herman U., **65**: 251n1

Sasseville (nurse), **66**: 36

Saturday Evening Post, **53**: 389n2; **65**: 424n1; **68**: 252,n2, 597n

Saudi Arabia, **58**: 318n1

Saulsbury, Willard, **61**: 635,n5; **65**: 440; and woman suffrage, **54**: 228

Saunders, Frances Wright, **60**: 647n2; **68**: 527n2

Savannah Cotton Exchange, **54**: 228n1

Savannah News, **65**: 220

Savannah Press, **65**: 220

Savinkov, Boris Viktorovich, **54**: 22,n9; **57**: 139,n1

Savoia, Emanuele Filberto de: *see* Aosta, Duke of

Savoy, **58**: 473; *see also* Haute Savoy

Savy, Joseph-Jean-Michel, **59**: 65,n5, 66, 119,n4, 120; **63**: 485,n4

Sawyer, Charles Elmer, M.D., **67**: 297,n2, 527,n3; **68**: 398,n1

Saxe, John Godfrey, **62**: 302

Saxony, Germany, **65**: 101

Sayre, Eleanor Axson, grandaughter of WW, **53**: 68; **66**: 329-30; **67**: 18, 22, 103, 553, 566; **68**: 77, 150, 338; poem by, **67**: 108-109; WW on poem, **67**: 125; leaves for Siam, **68**: 423,n8

Sayre, Francis Bowes, son-in-law of WW, **53**: 21, 22, 69, 213,n2, 436-37; **54**: 107; **55**: 216, 234, 366; **58**: 428; **62**: 42,n2, 101; **65**: 441; **66**: 102, 266, 319, 320, 330, 506n1; **67**: 108, 189, 231, 258, 356; **68**: 77, 115, 149; and Siam, **65**: 21n2; on YMCA and use of relief funds, **67**: 85-86; C. W. Eliot on, **67**: 232; **68**: 338,n1, 423,n8, 558,n5; WW encourages to take Siam offer, **68**: 351, 366

Sayre, Francis Bowes, Jr. (Francis Woodrow Wilson Sayre until Feb. 1919) grandson of WW, **53**: 68; **55**: 216; **66**: 75, 79-80; **67**: 23, 553, 615; **68**: 77, 150, 338; on his grandfather, **66**: 329-30; WW answers, **67**: 566; leaves for Siam, **68**: 423,n8

Sayre, Jessie Woodrow Wilson (Mrs. Francis Bowes), daughter of WW and EAW, **53**: 21-22, 68-69, 212-13, 436-37; **54**: 107-108; **55**: 265, 266, 304, 366; **58**: 428; **59**: 526; **62**: 42, 101, 303, 516; **63**: 610; **66**: 102, 266, 504, 506n1, 519, 532; **67**: 86, 103, 189, 231, 356, 470, 519; **68**: 77, 115; awaits birth of third child, **55**: 216-17; gives birth to son, **55**: 234; WW visits in hospital, **55**: 410; on need for Y.W.C.A. work in Siberia, **57**: 60-61; shares family news, **63**: 166-67; **67**: 107-109, 615; **68**: 149-50, 338; notified of WW's canceled trip, **63**: 521; arrives at White House, **63**: 549; and visit of Belgian royalty, **63**: 603, 606; greets Prince of Wales, **64**: 31; reassured by Axson of WW's love, **66**: 319-20; sends WW love and invitation to visit, **66**: 329-31; WW answers, **67**: 125; sends love and good wishes in new home, **67**: 188; C. W. Eliot on, **67**: 232; WW unable to attend grandson's christening, **67**: 267; WW's birthday greetings to, **67**: 385; hopes to visit WW, **67**: 427-28; WW on arrangements if entire Sayre family visits, **67**: 428-29; E. P. Davis on, **67**: 458; makes appearances on behalf of WW Foundation, **67**: 527; on son's birthday, **67**: 553-54; WW on elections, **68**: 180; WW encourages to move to Siam, **68**: 351-52; WW excited by planned visit of, **68**: 366-67; WW's birthday greetings and gift to, **68**: 412, 422; leaves for Siam, **68**: 423,n8; notified of gravity of WW's illness, **68**: 549, 550, 558; and WW's death, **68**: 569

Sayre, John Nevin, **53**: 307,n1, 437; **61**: 480; **62**: 545; on granting general amnesty, **55**: 365-66, 395; **61**: 398-99; **62**: 126-28; on treatment of conscientious objectors, **65**: 441-42; reply to concerns of, **65**: 456-57

Sayre, Woodrow Wilson (grandson of WW), **57**: 60,n1, 61; **62**: 303,n4, 516,n2; **66**: 330,n4; **67**: 23, 108, 566; **68**: 77, 150, 423,n8; Jessie on resemblance to WW, **63**: 167,n4; WW's birthday greetings to, **64**: 451; WW unable to attend christening of, **67**: 267; birthday celebration, **67**: 553

Sazanov, Sergeii Dmitrievich, **54**: 21,n7, 45, 101, 182,n2, 228; **57**: 139,n1, 520,n6; **59**: 14n4, 15,n5, 18,n11; **60**: 95,n4

Schafer v. United States, **68**: 131n8

Scala Nuova (now Kusadasi, Turkey), **59**: 55, 90, 91, 101, 137, 208, 223, 224, 226, 267, 268, 269, 375; **61**: 344

Scapa Flow, **58**: 125, 582; **60**: 497; **61**: 57n8; **64**: 149; sinking of German fleet at, **61**: 71, 114, 119, 123, 135, 140-48, 178-79, 179; and reparation for incident at, **61**: 151; **64**: 118n2; Allied note to Germany on sinking of fleet at, **61**: 168-70; and issue of disposal of Ger-

man and Austro-Hungarian ships, **62**: 144-47,n1, 186-87

Scavenius, Harald Roger de, **54**: 104,n8, 179, 185

Schaffner, Auguste, **56**: 64,n1

Schanzer, Carlo, **61**: 109,n4

Scharnhorst, S.M.S., **55**: 432

Schauffler, William Gray, **59**: 528,n1

Scheidemann, Philipp, **53**: 8, 63n1; **54**: 532; **55**: 55n5, 99, 203, 458n1; **56**: 318; **57**: 521, 522, 523, 566; **59**: 10, 37, 129, 136, 434n5, 566; **60**: 167-68, 177, 311-12; **61**: 28, 32, 76n5; on peace treaty, **58**: 309, 313, 314-15; **59**: 84-85,n2; speech of, **59**: 94; resignation of, **61**: 34,n1

Scheldt (Shelde) River, **55**: 110; **56**: 592-93; **57**: 396; **59**: 289; **61**: 11n2

Scheller-Steinwartx, Robert Richard von, **63**: 254,n2, 333-34,n2

Schenade, Anis, **55**: 145n3

Schenck, Charles T., **55**: 347n1; **62**: 126n1

Schenck v. United States, **55**: 347n1

Schiaffino, Mr., **65**: 487,n3

Schiff, Jacob Henry, **53**: 251n1; **59**: 419n1, 516n1; **66**: 261n2; and peace treaty leak investigation, **60**: 330,n2, 434

Schiff, Mortimer Leo, **66**: 261

Schindler, Nicholas P., **59**: 621,n1: photograph of, illustration section, **54**

Schlanney, Czechoslovakia, **60**: 552

Schlesien: Eine Landeskunde fur das deutsche Volk auf wissenschaftlicher Grundlage (Partsch), **60**: 413n3

Schlesinger, Arthur M., Jr., **65**: 386n1, 418n3, 436n2, 482n1, 499n1; **66**: 208n1

Schleswig, S.M.S., **55**: 432

Schleswig-Holstein, **55**: 506; **56**: 200,n1, 267, 347; **57**: 111, 349, 359, 363-64; **58**: 294; **59**: 28, 377n3, 459, 582; **60**: 97, 107, 110, 284,n2, 557, 558; **61**: 187

Schlumberger, Marguerite de Witt, **56**: 374; **57**: 218, 219

Schmedeman, Albert George, **67**: 18,n2; and WW's Nobel Peace Prize, **66**: 477-78,n1, 492,n2, 505, 517, 543

Schmidt, Harvey W., **67**: 345, 353

Schmidt, Robert, **61**: 303,n2

Schmidt, Julius, **57**: 526

Schmitt, Ernst, **57**: 520,n7, 526

Schneidemuhl (now Pilo, Poland), **60**: 29,n9

Schneidemuhl-Konitz region, **60**: 25,n9, 85-86

Schneiderman, Rose, **57**: 426,n5; **63**: 56

Schucking, Walther Max Adrian, **57**: 590,n5; **58**: 518; photograph of, illustration section, **58**

Schuler, Loring Ashley, **66**: 354,n1

Schulze, Hagen, **61**: 34n1

Schumpeter, Joseph Alois, **57**: 167,n3

Schurman, Jacob Gould, **66**: 199,n1,2, 200, 246n2, 542n1

Schuyler, Roy L., **55**: 401,n2
Schuylkill Railway Company, **68**: 331n1
Schwab, Charles Michael, **55**: 117-18, 188; **57**: 382
Schwabe, Klaus, **53**: 121n1; **55**: 458n1; **56**: 530n4; **58**: 44n1, 308n1; **59**: 554n2, 579n1
Schwaben, S.M.S., **55**: 432
Schwartz, Murray L., **66**: 92n1
Schwarz, Jacob David, **66**: 261,n1, 265-66
Schwarzengreuel in Besetzten Gebeit (*New Yorker Staats-Zeitung*), **65**: 341n1, 394
Schweinitz, George de: *see* De Schweinitz, George Edmund
Schwend, Karl, **59**: 433n4
Scialoja, Vittorio, **54**: 218,n2, 264, 426,n1, 463, 546; **55**: 123; **57**: 125,n5; **61**: 109,n10,11; **62**: 145,n3, 575,n3; **63**: 393, 525, 525-26; **64**: 263, 264, 318, 332n2; **65**: 198,n5, 303,n10; House on, **63**: 422; R. U. Johnson on, **65**: 299-300, 303
Scordia, Prince G. di, **59**: 80,n2
Scorpion, U.S.S., **65**: 538, 540, 549
Scott, Adele C. Reed (Mrs. James Brown), **58**: 445,n6
Scott, Adeline Mitchell, **53**: 22
Scott, Charles Ernest, **53**: 206,n2, 207
Scott, Charles Prestwich, **53**: 539,n4, 546, 575n1, 717; **58**: 268, 491; on Weizmann, **53**: 572; **57**: 36
Scott, Emmett Jay, **62**: 530n1
Scott, Frank Augustus, **54**: 521,n2
Scott, Frederic William, **53**: 164,n1
Scott, Hugh Lenox, **55**: 486; **61**: 543,n2; **67**: 525,n2; on Mexican crisis, **65**: 312,n1; on N. D. Baker, **68**: 133n1, 137
Scott, Isaac, **67**: 360,n5; **68**: 187,n4, 410,n2; photograph of, *illustration section*, 67
Scott, James Brown, **53**: 695,n2, 716; **54**: 4; **56**: 75, 396; **57**: 146n4, 407, 561,n4,5; **58**: 153,n2, 154, 445, 467, 469, 471; **59**: 275, 534, 535, 536, 635; **60**: 21, 22, 476, 561, 562; **61**: 281,n2; **68**: 100, 123,n4; on need for Senate ratification of peace treaty, **56**: 58,n1, 59, 67-69, 98; and Commission on Responsibilities, **56**: 530n4; photograph of, *illustration section*, 57
Scott, John W., **67**: 252
Scott, Mary Blanchard, **67**: 108,n1; **68**: 410,n2
Scott, Sarah Post, **54**: 107,n4; **55**: 216,n2; **67**: 108,n1
Scott, Tom, **66**: 245; **67**: 140
Scott, Thomas Albertson, **59**: 121,n3, 160
Scott, William Berryman, **54**: 107n4; **55**: 216n2; **67**: 108,n1, 182, 496, 525
Scott, William Lawrence, **59**: 159,n1
Scottish Church and University Almanac, 1919, **54**: 380n3
Scottish Presbyterian Church, Paris, **54**: 380n3; **59**: 247

Scribner's Magazine, **65**: 258n2
Scripps, Edward Wyllis: on amnesty, **59**: 204-205,n1, 318-19, 320
Scripps, James, **59**: 204
Scripps-McRae newspapers, **66**: 154n1
Scritti: Letterari con un saggio di Enrico Neucioni (Mazzini), **53**: 615,n2
Screenland, **68**: 449
Scudder, Edward Wallace, **68**: 454,n3
Scudder, Wallace McIlvaine, **68**: 454,n3
Scutari, Albania, **64**: 302, 303, 482; **65**: 38, 316; **66**: 322
Seaboard Air Line, **55**: 247n1
Seamen's Act, **53**: 10-11, 107-108, 110; **56**: 236n6; **60**: 152; **66**: 87
Seattle: Grayson on WW's arrival and activities in, **63**: 237-40, 273; WW attends First Presbyterian Church of, **63**: 273,n1; WW's remarks and address in, **63**: 253-54, 254-64; WW meets with labor leaders, **63**: 273,n2
Seattle General Strike (Friedheim), **59**: 398,n2
Seattle Post-Intelligencer, **63**: 210n1,2, 211n5, 234n, 264n, 273n1
Seattle Times, **63**: 398; **67**: 488
Sebastian, Forest D., **62**: 415, 434-35
Sebenico, Croatia (now Sibenik), **53**: 640,n2; **57**: 488, 551, 611, 612; **58**: 14, 81, 82, 83, 263, 354, 358, 434, 439, 450, 452; **60**: 138, 211, 213, 217, 266, 308, 310, 311; **61**: 228, 575; and Adriatic settlement, **66**: 365
Second Pan American Financial Conference: *see* Pan American Financial Conference, Second
Secret City: A History of Race Relations in the Nation's Capital (Green), **61**: 576n2
Secret War in Mexico: Europe, The United States and the Mexican Revolution (Katz), **56**: 340n1
Sederholm, Henrik Samuel, **66**: 501,n1
Sedgwick, Ellery, **67**: 40,n5; suggestions for League of Nations Covenant, **56**: 162-63; publishes WW's essay, **68**: 353, 354, 363-64, 369, 392; WW thanks, **68**: 364; to also publish essay in book form, **68**: 370, 371, 374
sedition: Palmer's draft bill on, **64**: 81,n5
Seelenfreund, A. B., **53**: 239n1
Seely, Fred L., **68**: 58n1
Segna, **57**: 520
Segre, Roberto, **60**: 313,n3
Seherr-Thoss, Countess (Muriel White), **59**: 398,n2; **62**: 156,n4; **65**: 513,n1, 514
Seherr-Thoss, Count, Hermann Roger Hans Christow, **59**: 398n2; **62**: 156,n4
Seherr-Thoss, Hans Christow, **59**: 398n2; **62**: 156,n4; **65**: 513,n1
Seherr-Thoss, Hermann, **59**: 398n2; **62**: 156,n4; **65**: 513,n1
Seherr-Thoss, Margaret, **59**: 398n2; **62**: 156,n4; **65**: 513,n1
Seibold, Louis, **53**: 542,n1; **54**: 106,n2; **58**: 51,n3; **62**: 627; **63**: 3n3, 370n2; **66**: 112; **67**: 312; **68**: 384; on rumors on

WW's health and desire to write story on Grayson, **64**: 494-95, 495-96; interviews WW, **65**: 401-15, 426, 428; recalls cancellation of WW's western trip, **65**: 407-408; news report of interview with WW, **65**: 415-21; on Pulitzer Prize interview, **67**: 303; on Republican politics, **67**: 313; on WW's Armistice Day decision, **67**: 453,n1, 456; WW's condolences to, **68**: 283; on F. Cobb, **68**: 370-71,n1

Seibold, Louis Philip: death of, **68**: 283,n1

Seizure of Power: Fascism in Italy, 1919-1929 (Lyttelton), **68**: 255n1

Selden, Charles Albert, **56**: 551n1; **58**: 168,n1; **59**: 278n2; **61**: 365n1

Select Classical School (Augusta, Ga.), **62**: 624n1

Selection of Cases and Other Authorities on Labor Law (F. B. Sayre), **68**: 149,n1

Selections from the Smuts Papers (Hancock and Van der Poel), **54**: 148n1; **56**: 416n1; **61**: 304n3; **68**: 437n3, 453n1

Selective Service Act, **53**: 12, 13; **65**: 208-209, 366; **67**: 225; origins of, **66**: 58,n1

Self-Dependence (Arnold), **66**: 440,n2

Seligman, Edwin Robert Anderson, **55**: 438n3; **67**: 271n1

Seligman, Herbert J., **66**: 25n1

Sells-Floto Circus, **65**: 290

Semenov, Grigori Mikhailovich, **53**: 556-57; **55**: 401,n3; **56**: 185,n4; **57**: 575n1; **58**: 495n3, 570,n7; **59**: 234, 619,n3; **60**: 625,n7, 637; **61**: 572,n1, 637,n2; **62**: 86-87, 592,n8

Semipalatinsk, Russia, **62**: 87

Senate (U.S.): *see* United States Congress—Senate

Senator Lenroot of Wisconsin: A Political Biography, 1900-1929 (Marguiles), **62**: 311n1; **64**: 276n1, 328n2

Senegal, **54**: 368

Senn, Alfred Erich, **59**: 18n10

Serbia (Servia) and Serbs, **53**: 43,n1, 56, 76, 296, 444, 649, 699n1; **54**: 55, 124, 264; **55**: 66, 84, 87-88, 164, 184, 203; **56**: 26, 242n1, 252, 570, 573, 574, 614; **57**: 78, 112, 124, 224, 585, 613; **58**: 8, 39, 42, 113, 150, 162, 198, 252, 374, 461n1, 471, 472; **59**: 53, 119-20, 130, 166, 215, 247, 255, 380, 562, 626; **60**: 134, 173; **61**: 94, 344, 430; **62**: 80; **64**: 162, 368n1; and food relief, **53**: 315-16, 648; **59**: 174, 175; **66**: 172,n1, 187-88, 191-92, 196-97, 322; **67**: 517; U.S. loans to, **53**: 572; and Montenegro, **53**: 638n1, 640, 700, 701-704, 704; **54**: 18-19,n5; **57**: 558; **58**: 162-64, 354, 508; **59**: 178n2,3, 222,n12, 620n1; and representation at Paris Peace Conference, **54**: 15, 16,n3, 18-19,n5, 45, 65, 115; and Reparation Commission, **54**: 211, 223, 283; **58**: 249, 259; and League of Nations, **54**: 263, 462, 464; and Rumania, **54**: 376, 377, 421n7; and reparation, **55**: 29,n2, 30-32, 33; **57**: 454-55, 515; **59**: 74n1, 93, 103, 304-305,n13, 312, 387; **60**: 592; offers to permit WW to arbitrate boundary dispute with Italy, **57**: 418; and Fiume, **57**: 491, 517, 540-41; **58**: 397, 554-55; Keynes on rehabilitation of economy, **58**: 12; and credits, **58**: 491n1; Andrews on conditions in Fiume and Trieste, **59**: 64-66; Lamont on finances and, **59**: 176; Bryce on Macedonia and, **59**: 400; and minority rights, **59**: 577, 629; and Austrian peace treaty, **60**: 130-31,n5; and issue of Hungarian attacks on Czechoslovakia, **60**: 257, 259, 260; Klagenfurt Basin and, **60**: 262; and Germany and outbreak of and responsibility for the war, **60**: 452; and atrocities in Albania, **60**: 530, 565; and war-cost contributions, **61**: 101, 254-56; WW on start of war and, **63**: 20, 24, 109, 187-88, 245-46, 259, 360, 372-73; **65**: Bulgaria and, **65**: 114; children fed in, **65**: 469

Serbs, Croats and Slovenes, Kingdom of: *see* Yugoslavia

Sergeant York: His Own Life Story and War Diary (Skeyhill, ed.), **62**: 42n2

Sergeant York and His People (Cowan), **62**: 42n2

Service with Fighting Men: An Account of the Work of the American Young Men's Christian Associations in the World War (Harris *et al.*), **54**: 5n2

Seton-Watson, Robert William, **57**: 529n3

Seven Pillars of Wisdom: A Triumph, (Lawrence), **54**: 90n1

Sevey, Mrs. George B., **68**: 37

Sevier, Joseph Ramsey, **68**: 450-51,n1,2

Sèvres, Treaty of (1920), **66**: 65,n1; **67**: 154

Sèvres, Tripartite Pact of, **66**: 429n1, 430

Sewanee, Tenn., **60**: 646

Sexton Valley, **58**: 589,n1; **59**: 94, 201, 578, 587; **64**: 175

Seyhan, Turkey: *see* Adana

Seymour, Charles, **53**: 348,n3, 349,n4, 350, 351n2, 367, 368, 544n1; **55**: 34-35; **56**: 351n1, 393n1, 530n4, 563n3, 586n1; **58**: 588,n1; **59**: 404, 647-48; **60**: 34; **61**: 54; **62**: 206; **66**: 315; **67**: 24n2, 285; on WW's remarks to The Inquiry, **53**: 356-57, 377-78; observations on Council of Ten meetings, **54**: 382-85; on Fiume, **56**: 607-609; **57**: 432-33, 456; on WW, **58**: 629; **59**: 158-59; on change in frontier between Yugoslavia and German Austria, **59**: 405-406; on Klagenfurt Basin, **59**: 406-407; on WW's meetings with American delegates on German proposals, **60**: 75-79; on German peace proposals in German Austria and Upper Silesia, **60**: 138, 139; photograph of, *illustration section*, **57**; **59**

Seymour, Gladys Marion (Mrs. Charles), **53**: 356n2

Seymour, John Barton, **55**: 91n1

Seymour, John Sammis, **67**: 257,n2

Seymour, Private, **61**: 321

Seymour, Michael Culme-: *see* Culme-Seymour, Michael

Sforza, Count Carlo, **63**: 517,n3; **66**: 43,n3, 207n1, 482,n2; **68**: 506,n1, 507; R.U. Johnson on, **65**: 299,n2, 300; and Adriatic settlement, **66**: 45, 364, 365

Shackleford, Dorsey William, **55**: 267

Shadrinsk, Russia, **62**: 87

Shaffer, John Charles, **62**: 525-26; encourages Republicans to ratify treaty, **62**: 439-40,n1

Shafroth, John Franklin, **54**: 216

Shaftsbury, Earl of, **68**: 447, 448

Shamun, China, **58**: 256-57

Shanghai, China, **58**: 257

Shannon Copper Company, **66**: 126-28

Shansi Privince, China, **66**: 327

Shantung, China, **53**: 207; **54**: 79, 81, 308-309, 316-17, 325, 474,n2, 747n1, 475; **57**: 354, 358, 366, 453n4, 495, 554, 555, 561,n2,3, 580, 581, 597n1, 598, 609, 616, 620, 626; **60**: 471n12; **66**: 327,n1; Koo on, **57**: 298, 299-300 431,n1, 618; and Japan's claims, **57**: 599-610; WW on, **57**: 606; **58**: 272; controversy between Japan and China over, **58**: 46, 68-70, 70-71, 71-72, 86, 112, 130-33, 167, 178, 179, 180, 183-84, 185, 224, 225, 228, 230-32, 246, 259, 261; settlement of claims on, **58**: 270-71,n1, 277; China's two statements on settlement, **58**: 419,n1, 427n1; Reinsch fears China will not sign peace treaty because of settlement concerning, **58**: 522n1; effect of WW's health on decisions concerning, **58**: 626-27

Shantung Amendment, **62**: 507n1; rejected by Senate, **63**: 482,n4; Hitchcock's prediction concerning, **63**: 482, 571; result of Senate vote on brought to WW's bedside, **63**: 576

Shantung Chamber of Commerce and Agriculture, **58**: 71,n2

Shantung Educational Association, **58**: 71,n2

Shantung Industrial Association, **58**: 71,n2

Shantung Railway, **57**: 583, 598, 599; **58**: 165, 167

Shantung settlement, **59**: 35, 573n1,3; **60**: 572; **61**: 155, 209, 214, 420, 445, 534, 543, 554-55, 556, 557-59, 559, 562, 583; **62**: 3-4, 11,n1, 16-17, 18-19, 44, 93; numerous Chinese organizations protest against, **60**: 101,n1, 102-104; Hornbeck on, **60**: 102-104; WW on Hornbeck's recommendations on, **60**: 357, 483-84; China's request regarding, **60**: 429n1; Lansing on, **60**: 602-603; **61**: 36; **62**: 153; Polk suggests revision of, **60**: 605; China on reservations concerning, **61**: 176n1; WW on, **61**: 237, 242, 249-50, 386, 387, 437, 438, 546, 593-95, 603; **62**: 91-92, 616; **63**: 28, 40, 83-84, 94-95, 104-105, 123-224, 193-94, 237, 314-17, 329-32, 411-13, 436-40, 460-61, 470-74, 496, 507; **64**: 280; Koo on signing peace treaty with reservations, **61**: 288-89; causes China's absence from treaty signing, **61**: 325-26; J. S. Williams on, **61**: 410; League of Free Nations Association's resolutions on, **61**: 447; Senate resolution requesting information on and reply to, **61**: 510; **62**: 151; WW and Colt discuss, **61**: 516; Moses on, **61**: 565; Senate reaction to, **61**: 565; Capper on, **61**: 602; WW denies responsibility for, **61**: 603; Spencer presents Senate's reservations on, **61**: 619-20, 621-22; WW wishes to make statement on if Japan will not, **61**: 629; and Reinsch, **61**: 631,n1; attitude on in Japan and China, **62**: 63-65; Tumulty on Bliss letter on, **62**: 150; Lansing's displeasure with Japan's public statement on, **62**: 153; Bliss letter on, **62**: 164; WW's statement on, **62**: 169, 170; WW's message to Senate on, **62**: 208-209; and issue of amendments and reservations to treaty, **62**: 306, 307; WW and Foreign Relations Committee discuss, **62**: 349, 368-69, 370-74, 377, 378, 379-82, 384, 408; and secret treaties, **62**: 364-65; Bowman on House's irregular negotiations on, **62**: 454-55; Japan's aide-memoire on, **62**: 458-59; Lodge's amendment to adopted by Foreign Relations Committee, **62**: 507n1; drafts of reply to Japan's aide-memoire, **62**: 508-509, 522-24; McCumber on, **62**: 566; Swanson on Senate reaction to, **62**: 614; Woodbridge on, **62**: 616n2; and WW's memory loss, **62**: 630; Norris accuses WW of erroneous statement on, **63**: 93, 94; WW's concern over Capper's opposition to, **63**: 519-20; and documents on, **67**: 89, 467

Shaping of the Czechoslovak State (Perman), **56**: 393n1, 586n1; **57**: 78n8; **66**: 225n2

Sharp, Hallie M. Clough (Mrs. William Graves), **53**: 399, 419, 499; **56**: 86; **57**: 476,n1; **66**: 432,n3

Sharp, William Graves, **53**: 25, 101, 384, 399, 419, 472, 499; **55**: 223; **56**: 86, 396, 512n1; **58**: 136-37, 162; resignation of, **53**: 80-81, 442-43, 463, 693, 710; **54**: 57-58; on French press, **57**: 175-77; praises WW, **57**: 475-76, 559; on Russian situation, **57**: 476; on Jackson Day message, **64**: 286-86; predicts elections, **65**: 473-76; on prohibition, **65**: 474-75; on labor, **65**: 476; on U.S. acquiring diplomatic residences abroad, **66**: 431-32

Shashih, China, **58**: 166
Shattuck, S. O., **65**: 294,n1
Shaugnessy, Thomas George, 1st Baron Shaughnessy, **61**: 397-98,n2
Shaw, Albert, **68**: 233
Shaw, Anna Howard, **53**: 125, 126; **54**: 133; on appointing a woman to a reconstruction commission, **53**: 117, 118; on census bill, **55**: 281,n1, 299-300; death of, **61**: 376-77; WW's tribute to, **62**: 255,n1
Shaw, Ezel Kural, **58**: 555n1
Shaw, Gardiner Howland, **60**: 290,n4
Shaw, George Bernard, **67**: 105n3
Shaw, Stanford J., **58**: 555n1
Shaw, Thomas, Baron Shaw of Dunfermline, **53**: 530n1
Shaykh'ul'-Islamov, Akbar, **58**: 333n2
Shea, Joseph Hooker, **53**: 316n1, 342n8, 347,n1
Shea, Timothy, **62**: 140; **64**: 197-98,n2, 420, 424, 426, 431; **65**: 16; on WW's appearance and health, **65**: 5
Sheet Metal Workers, **62**: 121; **64**: 424
Sheldon, Edward Wright, **53**: 126-27, 167; **65**: 382; **66**: 343-44,n1, 354; **68**: 386,n2; and Pierce-Arrow purchase for WW, **67**: 137,n3, 168, 186,n1; and Ecuadoran loan, **68**: 114, 118
Shengto, Li, **55**: 424
Shenkursk, Russia, **55**: 93n2
Shensi Province, China, **66**: 327
Shephardson, Whitney Hart, **56**: 466n1; **57**: 266,n1, 268, 286,n2, 503; **60**: 17,n1, 307, 570-71; **61**: 328,n1, 331, 332, 477,n1
Sheppard, J. I., **56**: 283,n1
Sheppard, Lucius Elmer, **62**: 140; **64**: 197-98,n2, 424; **65**: 16, 359
Sheppard, Morris, **53**: 78-79, 100; **55**: 297; **62**: 69; WW thanks for League of Nations work, **68**: 298
Sherley, Joseph Swagar, **53**: 260, 339, 637n1, 648, 709, 717; **54**: 55,n2, 277, 281, 555; **55**: 256, 257, 277-78, 297, 298; **64**: 21,n1
Sherman, Edward Augustine, **65**: 567n1
Sherman, Lawrence Yates, **53**: 308n1, 365,n1; **61**: 372, 506n1; **63**: 295,n1; and WW's health, **64**: 135-36; and treaty fight, **64**: 200-201, 328n2, 336, 338
Sherman Antitrust Act, **55**: 90, 156; **56**: 345, 618; Palmer on, **62**: 173, 174; **64**: 141n1,2
Sherrill, Clarence Osborne, **67**: 323,n1, 331; **68**: 399-400n1
Sherwood, John M., **60**: 118n1
Sherwood, Sidney, **67**: 311
Shidehara, Kijuro, **53**: 556,n11; **64**: 219,n1; **65**: 338n2, 515,n1; and anti-Japanese movement in California, **66**: 12-16, 53, 56; and Four-Power banking consortium, **66**: 295, 296
Shield, Catherine, **55**: 445,n10
Shields, John Knight, **53**: 23; **62**: 18, 336; and treaty reservations, **63**: 198,n1,

443,n3, 483; and treaty fight, **64**: 49, 200-201, 273, 337, 338; and Mexican situation, **64**: 120; and Armenian mandate, **65**: 351n2
Shiloh Baptist Church, Washington, D.C., **63**: 268n1
Shih, Chao-chi: *see* Sze, Alfred (Soake)
Shillady, John R., **53**: 690; **62**: 527-28, 535-36; on race riots in Washington, **61**: 576
Shimonoseki indemnity, **62**: 359n23
shipbuilding industry, **53**: 374, 454-56; and three-year program, **54**: 411,n1; and labor, **55**: 262; Lloyd George on U.S. and League of Nations, **56**: 482, 518-19; issue of building foreign ships in U.S. shipyards, **58**: 460, 496, 498-99, 531
shipping: and International Mercantile Marine Corporation, **53**: 110-11, 111-13, 113, 186-87; and relief plans, **53**: 271-72; and Britain, **53**: 373; Benson on neutrals and freedom of the seas, **54**: 403-406, 477; Hurley on policy for, **55**: 532-35; Hoover on Russian relief and, **57**: 161; agreement reached on retention of enemy ships, **58**: 289-90, 527-28, 557-58, 559; and tonnage and war losses, **58**: 492; issue of building foreign ships in U.S. shipyards, **59**: 47, 120; Council of Four on tonnage in Adriatic, **59**: 50-54; and WW's special message to Congress, **59**: 293; shipyard workers' demonstration in Philadelphia, **59**: 476-77,n2; Gordon on Germany's counterproposals on, **60**: 140-41; reparations and, **60**: 339-40, 400-401; need for passenger tonnage, **61**: 278,n7, 465, 478-80; fuel for, **62**: 140-41; WW on disposition of merchant ships, **64**: 80
Shipping Act of 1916: Payne on, **62**: 528-29
Shipping Board (U.S.): *see* United States Shipping Board
Shipping Control Committee (Franklin Committee), **58**: 202,n1, 269
Shipstead, Henrik, **68**: 156n3
Short, William Harrison, **55**: 37-38, 186, 198-99, 208; **56**: 427; **57**: 424; **65**: 184,n4; **67**: 608, 609
Shotwell, James Thomson, **53**: 367,n2; **55**: 119; **56**: 236n2; **57**: 239n5, 495n1; **58**: 417n8; **59**: 222; **61**: 328,n1; **62**: 96-97, 132, 133; **63**: 58; **64**: 98n1; **67**: 459n2, 560; and labor clauses for peace treaty, **57**: 528; **60**: 17,n1; House on, **61**: 131-32; photograph of, *illustration section,* **57**
Should the United States Remain Outside the League of Nations? Address Delivered at the Annual Meeting of the League for Permanent Peace (R. S. Baker), **67**: 15-16,n1
Shouse, Jouett, **53**: 54; **65**: 177-78,n1, 435n1, 438

Shvets, Fedir, **54**: 33,n7
Siam, **54**: 264; **58**: 198, 402n12, 442, 472-73; **61**: 65; **65**: 108; **66**: 288; and representation at Paris Peace Conference, **54**: 13, 16, 65, 99; and issue of enemy ships, **58**: 527, 558; White suggests replacing his son as minister to, **61**: 348; and appointments, **64**: 295, 296; and extraterritorial rights issue, **64**: 468-72, 479; **65**: 21,n2; and F. B. Sayre, **68**: 338,n1, 351, 366
Siam: Treaties with Foreign Powers, 1920-1927 (Sayre [P.K. Maitri]), **65**: 21n2
Sibenik, Croatia: *see* Sebenico
Siberia, **54**: 94, 205, 259-60, 261; **59**: 16, 17, 134, 152, 188; and railroad funds, **55**: 350, 351, 393; Bolsheviks on atrocities in, **59**: 195; and talk of replacing Graves in, **59**: 234-35, 409-10; issue of recognition of Kolchak, **59**: 236; Morris on, **59**: 510; intervention in: *see* Russia—Siberia, intervention in
Siberian Railway: *see* Trans-Siberian Railway
Sibert, William Luther, **63**: 362,n1
Siddons, Frederick Lincoln, **68**: 471,n3
Siegfried, Julie Puaux (Mrs. Jules), **57**: 218,n1, 219
Sierra Ventana, S.M.S., **55**: 432
Sifton, Arthur Lewis, **57**: 311,n10, 312; **58**: 417,n7, 518
Signa, **58**: 452
Sigray, Count Antal, **56**: 242,n1,5, 473-74,n1, 474-76
Sigray, Harriot Daly (Mrs. Antal), **56**: 476,n1
Silesia, **54**: 336, 341, 343, 344, 345, 388, 491, 492; **56**: 287, 289, 598; **58**: 45, 61, 62, 385; **63**: 306; **64**: 447; and Jews, **55**: 372; *see also* Upper Silesia
Silzer, George Sebastian, **68**: 588,n2, 590
Simmons, Furnifold McLendel, **53**: 23, 24, 717; **55**: 254, 296; **65**: 109, 238; **68**: 242,n4; on treaty reservations, **63**: 118, 198,n3; **64**: 283, 284, 311; circulating rumor of defection on Article X, **65**: 48, 81-82; WW urges unified Democratic stance against reservations, **65**: 82; and woman suffrage, **65**: 433,n1, 466,n1; on War Finance Corporation assisting cotton industry, **66**: 36-38,n1, Houston answers, **66**: 60-62; WW's get-well wishes, **68**: 289
Simmons, Roger E., **62**: 446,n5, 447
Simms, Dan W., **64**: 141n1
Simo, Matavulj, **57**: 426
Simon, Henry, **54**: 311, 318-22, 324, 325, 328, 384,n4; **58**: 484,n2, 485, 486, 507; **59**: 93,n7; and mandates, **61**: 252, 277, 283, 363, 408
Simonds, Frank Herbert, **56**: 436,n1,3; **59**: 524,n3; **63**: 621,n2; **66**: 198n1
Simons, Walter, **58**: 311,n2, 518; **66**: 44,n4, 45
Simonson, Charles E., **68**: 248, 249n2

Simonson, May Ladd (Mrs. Charles E.), **67**: 271n1, 394, 400; on idea for WW Foundation and women's role in, **68**: 262, 264-66
Simpkin, Marshall, Hamilton, Kent & Co., **67**: 341n2
Simpson, Herman, **56**: 283,n1
Simpson, John A., **54**: 228n1
Sims, Thetus Willrette, **55**: 246,n3; **62**: 198n2; on keeping government control over railroads, **64**: 195-96
Sims, William Sowden, **53**: 358, 378, 397, 524; **55**: 39; **58**: 409,n1, 500, 530-31; **60**: 241n1; **61**: 145, 517; **67**: 242,n4, 321n1; promoted to admiral, **53**: 65; on Britain's naval views, **53**: 512; WW on, **53**: 320, 339; publishes article on navy in the war, **62**: 460,n1, 546-47,n2
Sinaloa, state, Mexico, **65**: 252n1
Sinclair, Earle Westwood, **68**: 125,n2
Sinclair, Harry Ford, **68**: 119n2, 125,n2
Sinclair, Upton Beall, **56**: 283; on political amnesty, **61**: 577; and Eugene V. Debs, **62**: 250, 261-62, 422; on conscientious objectors, **63**: 425,n1
Sinclair Consolidated Oil Corporation, **68**: 119, 120, 125,n2
Sinha, Satyendra Prasanno, First Baron Sinha of Raipur, **59**: 93,n10
Sinn Fein, **53**: 519n1; **55**: 348, 363, 364, 474; **57**: 419n2; **58**: 505; **60**: 414; **61**: 117; **62**: 565; **66**: 267n1
Sino-Japanese Timber Company, **57**: 605
Sino-Japanese Treaty (May 25, 1915), **57**: 453n4, 555,n8, 597n1
Sino-Japanese treaties (1918), **57**: 453n5
Sinnott, Arthur, **66**: 4
Sioux Falls *Daily Argus-Leader*, **63**: 117n
Sir Edward Grey: A Biography of Lord Grey of Fallodon (Robins), **62**: 254n2
Sis, Cilicia, **54**: 517
Sisson Documents, **53**: 492,n2; **66**: 542,n1
Sivas (Swas), Turkey, **60**: 193
Sjoblom, Paul, **58**: 404n2
Skagerrak, **56**: 35n7, 523
Skandinaviska Kreditaktiebolaget, **67**: 131-32, 365
Skeyhill, Tom, **62**: 42n2
Skidelsky, Robert, **60**: 492n4
Skidmore, Joe, **66**: 387,n1
Skinner, Robert Peel, **61**: 406n1
Skomorokhov, P. P., **62**: 594n1
Skoropadski, Pavlo Petrovich, **54**: 32n4
"slacker raids," **60**: 6, 155,n5
Slade, George Theron, **64**: 64n1
Slander of Baker in Encyclopedia Rouses Americans (New York *World*), **68**: 133,n1
Slatin, Rudolf Carl von, **59**: 561-62,n8
Slater Fund, **62**: 106n2
Slaughter, Homer Havron, **55**: 402,n4; **58**: 569,n1
Slavonic and East European Review, **56**: 462n10
Slavs, **53**: 444-46, 642, 643

Slemp, Campbell Bascom, **68**: 143n2
Sloane, William Milligan, **66**: 323,n4
Slobodin, Henry L., **56**: 283
Slonim, Mark L'vovich, **59**: 156,n4
Slosson, Preston William, **57**: 25n9; **67**: 459,n2
Slovakia, **54**: 491
Slovenes, **53**: 43,n1, 294, 638n1; **55**: 87-88; **56**: 566; **57**: 613; **58**: 150, 160, 162; **59**: 380, 404, 408; **60**: 214; and Klagenfurt Basin, **59**: 542, 543; **60**: 34-38, 122-29, 207-208, 214
Slutzky, H., **53**: 137
Slye, John Queen, **53**: 166,n1, 319
Small John Humphrey, **53**: 288; **65**: 378,n1
Small, Robert T., **62**: 627; **63**: 275-76,n4; **64**: 511n1
Smillie, Robert, **56**: 320,n2
Smith, Addison Taylor, **56**: 428,n3
Smith, Alfred Emanuel, **53**: 206; **55**: 411; **61**: 371,n1, 401; **67**: 377n2; **68**: 154, 156, 179n1, 415,n3; invitation to WW to speak on League of Nations in N.Y., **55**: 216, 289
Smith, Amy Kemp (Mrs. Norman), **61**: 476,n3
Smith, Charles Hadden, **61**: 636,n2; **62**: 85,n2
Smith, Charles Stephenson, **58**: 327,n1
Smith, Daniel M., **64**: 464n1; **66**: 5n2, 19n1, 430n1
Smith, Duncan, **67**: 263,n1
Smith, (Edmund) Munroe, **67**: 17,n1, 29
Smith, Ellison DuRant, **53**: 215; **54**: 228n1; **55**: 246,n3, 297, 478; on cotton situation, **55**: 38; appointment suggestions from, **65**: 256, 257, 260-61
Smith, Emily, **68**: 423
Smith, Francis Henry, **67**: 263,n1
Smith, Frederick Edwin: *see* Birkenhead, Baron
Smith, Gene, **58**: 636,n9; **67**: 137n3
Smith, Harry Alexander, **57**: 457,n2, 458
Smith, Henry, **66**: 524-25,n1
Smith, Herbert Stearns Squier, **65**: 574,n19; **67**: 182
Smith, Hoke, **55**: 297; **63**: 483, 535; and Americanization bill, **55**: 284,n1; WW on, **64**: 45; and treaty fight, **64**: 200-201, 273, 274n1, 336, 338; vote on reservation to Article X, **65**: 81n1; and Georgia primary, **65**: 145-46,n1, 219-20,n2; WW on attitude of, **65**: 179; code name for, **65**: 350
Smith, Hubert Llwelllyn, **58**: 29,n1, 64, 118, 119, 148, 285, 286, 293-94, 386; **60**: 263, 420, 520; on reparations, **60**: 402-403
Smith, James, Jr., **68**: 591,n5
Smith, James Ellwood, **63**: 43,n1
Smith, John McMunn, **62**: 96,n1
Smith, Lucy Marshall, **61**: 551; **67**: 173n4, 356
Smith, Marcus Aurelius, **62**: 17, 340; and Foreign Relations Committee's minor-

ity report on reservations, **63**: 198,n1; and Mexican situation, **64**: 120n1; and Armenian mandate, **65**: 351n2
Smith, Mary Randolph, **61**: 551; **67**: 173n4, 356
Smith, Norman Kemp, **61**: 476-77,n1; **62**: 251-52
Smith, Richard K., **57**: 447n1; **60**: 44n4
Smith, Rixey, **65**: 436n2
Smith, Robert Freeman, **55**: 355n5; **66**: 142n1, 160n2
Smith, Ruth Preble Hall (Mrs. Earl Baldwin), **53**: 22,n7
Smith, Walter George, **62**: 248,n1, 415-16
Smith, William Alden, **53**: 582,n5
Smith, William Robert, **53**: 528,n4
Smith-Bankhead Americanization bill, **55**: 284-88,n1, 302
Smith College, **66**: 272; **67**: 514n1; **68**: 460n1
Smither, Harriet, **60**: 647,n3
Smithsonian Institution, **66**: 469n1
Smodlaka, Josip, **62**: 575,n2
Smoot, Reed, **53**: 83; **54**: 471; **61**: 372; **68**: 278n2; and treaty fight, **64**: 94, 200, 202, 337; and general leasing bill, **64**: 473n1; and Committee on Public Information, **65**: 374-75
Smuts, Jan Christiaan, **53**: 560, 589; **56**: 298; **57**: 53, 247; **58**: 149, 156, 158, 265, 417, 623; on League of Nations, **53**: 515-19,n1, 558, 609,n1, 621-22, 655n1, 694; **54**: 3, 87-88, 148n1, 149, 151, 152, 188, 189, 196n2, 218, 228, 301, 407, 426,n1, 459, 460, 463, 484, 494; **55**: 4, 122, 125, 321; **57**: 219, 221; **59**: 198, 240, 256, 287, 495, 623,n1, 627, 637; **60**: 20, 252, 595; **61**: 181, 329; **62**: 346; **63**: 286, 287; **67**: 105n3, 125-26, 228, 239; on territorial claims, **54**: 252, 347,n2; WW on, **55**: 266; **63**: 198,n1; **68**: 589; on Poland and Danzig, **56**: 321, 322; and Hungarian mission, **56**: 415, 416, 463, 464, 465, 488, 517, 554; **57**: 73, 77-79, 101-102, 108-109, 167-75, 274, 440-42; criticism of peace conference proceedings, **56**: 416n11; **59**: 422; on reparations, **56**: 480-82, 499,n3; and Rumania, **57**: 136; on not publishing peace treaty, **58**: 439; objects to German treaty, **59**: 149-50, 201, 383, 413-19, 616-18; WW answers on peace treaty, **59**: 187-88; statement at treaty signing ceremony, **61**: 304,n3; praises WW, **67**: 26-27, 216; WW endorses Baruch's appeal to, **68**: 431, 438, 439; Baruch's plea to on reparations settlement and League of Nations support and reply to, **68**: 433-37,n3; receives WW's message, **68**: 440; speaks on European condition and reparations, **68**: 453,n1
Smyrna (now Izmir, Turkey), **54**: 350; **59**: 58-59, 67, 89, 99, 140, 146, 223, 373, 374, 613; **63**: 61; **64**: 449; **65**: 64, 74,

Smyrna (*cont.*)
114; **68**: 141n1, 147n3; Italy's activi-
ties regarding, results in dispatch of
Greek troops to and landing at, **58**:
250, 251, 326, 338, 339, 345, 409, 414,
436, 476-78,n13, 510-14; **59**: 21-27, 54-
55, 226, 238, 250, 252, 473, 565, 596,
640-41,n1,2,3; **61**: 44, 212, 216, 629n1;
62: 607 Council of Four on, **59**: 40-46;
WW on, **59**: 89, 92, 99, 140, 613
Smyth, Charles Henry, Jr., **67**: 182
Smyth, Nathan Ayer, **58**: 204,n2
Sneznik (mountain), Slovenia: *see* Mount
Nevoso
Snook, Marie B., **66**: 151n1
Snow, Cecil, **66**: 257n1
Snow, Chauncey Depew, **61**: 609,n1
Snow, Thomas L., **55**: 282; **66**: 257,n2,
300-301, 338, 339, 385; **67**: 56,n1
Snyder, May Ross (Mrs. Meredith
Pinxton), **63**: 423,n3
Snyder, Meredith Pinxton, **63**: 407n1,
423,n3
Social Democratic party (Fiume), **60**:
293-94
Socialist party, **53**: 245,n1; **54**: 426; and
passports, **55**: 92; and Deb's candidacy
in 1920, **65**: 541,n3; on amnesty for
wartime prisoners, **65**: 550
Schenck v. United States, **55**: 347n1; in
Italy, **58**: 240; in France, **60**: 118,n1;
and Debs candidacy, **65**: 541,n3; on
amnesty for wartime prisoners, **65**:
550
socialists and socialism: Paris group
wishes to meet with WW, **53**: 344-45,
359; WW's remarks to delegation in
Paris, **53**: 387-88l; and proposed international labor conference, **53**: 408n1;
Tumulty on, **53**: 571; WW on, **67**: 606-
607; Seibold on, **68**: 372
Social Research, **55**: 341n1; **56**: 246n2
Social Outlook in Germany (Coar), **67**:
463-64,n1
Société Chinoise pour la Paix Interna-
tionale, **60**: 101n1
Société des Nations: *see* League of Na-
tions
Society of Free Nations (Morrow), **55**:
451,n8
Society of Sunday Schools of France, **56**:
64n1
Sofia, Bulgaria, **56**: 122
Soisson, France, **56**: 194, 195, 196-97
Sokolov, Boris Fedorovich, **59**: 156,n4
Sokolow, Nahum, **61**: 461,n1
Soldau, Germany, **56**: 94
Solf, Wilhelm, **53**: 32, 419
Solling, S.M.S., **55**: 432
Somaliland, **54**: 326n3; **59**: 88, 90, 92-93,
99, 100, 102
Some Observations on Wilson's Neurol-
ogic Illness (Toole), **62**: 628n1
Some Problems of the Peace Conference
(Haskins and Lord), **65**: 530,n1
Somerville, John Arthur Coghill, **62**: 89-
90,n11

"Something Desperate In His Face":
Woodrow Wilson in Portland at the
"Very Crisis of his Career" (Trow), **63**:
276n5
Sonnino, Sidney, **53**: 85, 143, 272, 324,
345, 433, 434, 449, 459, 466, 472,
483n4, 507, 564, 589, 596, 621, 637-38,
639-40, 696, 700, 711n1; **54**: 127, 130,
134; **55**: 107, 180, 182, 305; **56**: 65, 66,
168, 487, 566; **57**: 289, 291, 431, 485,
519, 520, 576; **58**: 53, 57, 271-72, 322,
391, 413, 415, 449; **59**: 34, 43, 44, 55,
71, 163, 211, 244, 247, 553; **60**: 221,
621; **61**: 33n2, 41, 45, 78, 109n11, 189,
220, 221, 305, 342; **62**: 22; **64**: 368, 370;
66: 45; and Supreme War Council
meetings, **54**: 5, 10, 204, 536, 538; and
Council of Ten meetings, **54**: 17, 19, 20,
21, 97, 97-98, 104, 110, 110-11, 119,
120, 209, 211, 219, 222, 224, 225, 248,
286, 288; **56**: 28, 31, 34, 37, 43; **59**: 60;
and Montenegro, **54**: 19, 20; **58**: 163; on
representation at Paris Peace Conference, **54**: 45-46, 49; on publicity for
peace conference, **54**: 67, 68, 69, 97-98;
on official language, **54**: 72; on Bolsheviks, **54**: 182, 185; WW on, **54**: 198; on
Czechs and Poles, **54**: 375; Seymour on
appearance of, **54**: 383-85; on Rumanian claims, **54**: 424; on press leaks,
56: 151; on Hungary, **56**: 461, 463, 464;
and Italian claims and Adriatic question, **57**: 364, 467, 477, 487-90, 491,
492, 493, 513, 527, 537, 537-38, 539,
540-41; **58**: 79-80, 82, 82-83, 83-84, 85,
250,n5, 251, 369, 370; **58**: 452-53; **61**:
575; on work of Council of Foreign Ministers and upkeep of army in occupied
territory, **57**: 400-402; on obtaining
German process for lethal gas, **57**: 402,
403, 404; T. N. Page on, **57**: 435, 436;
rejects verbal proposal brought by
Hankey, **57**: 551, 552; to leave for Italy,
58: 102; Tumulty on, **58**: 215; to return
to Paris, **58**: 429, 432, 434, 463; at Plenary Session at Versailles, **58**: 517-18;
apologizes to WW for anti-Wilson press
and speeches, **58**: 552; WW on Fiume
and, **59**: 174; on landing of Italian
troops in Asia Minor, **59**: 223, 266, 267,
268, 269, 270, 271, 375, 492; R. S.
Baker on, **59**: 286; on Veniselos' presence at Council of Four meeting, **59**:
319; to replace absent Orlando in negotiations, **60**: 484; and Council of Four's
decision on blockade, **60**: 523; on reparations and Danzig and Upper Silesia,
60: 558, 559; and religious missions,
60: 577, 578, 594; concern over not settling boundary issue before treaty is
signed, **60**: 579-80; request for Venetian palace in Constantinople, **60**: 593-
94; on Committee on New States, and
Poland, **60**: 624,n5; on Klagenfurt
Basin, **61**: 51-55; on Polish Jews and
Yiddish, **61**: 91, 91-92; on sinking of
German fleet at Scapa Flow, **61**: 103;

at treaty ceremony, **61**: 333; on whether conversations of Big Four should be made public, **61**: 336, 337, 338; Clemenceau on, **61**: 375; photograph of, *illustration section*, **57**

Sonora, state, Mexico, **65**: 252n1

Sookine, Jean, **58**: 569,n2, 576,n7

Sorbonne, The: *see* Paris, University of

Soriano, Nazario, **61**: 638,n5

Soroka, Russia, **55**: 190

SOS—Europe to America (Dickinson), **67**: 135n1

Soto, José Maria, **64**: 186; **65**: 46, 465

Soul of the Covenant (Holt), **62**: 347n11

South Africa, Union of, **54**: 44, 65, 250, 252-54,n3, 290, 294, 296-98, 325, 328, 363, 364; **57**: 22, 536, 603; **58**: 198, 442; **62**: 188, 189; **63**: 477, 505

South America, **67**: 109,n2, 384; and cable censorship, **57**: 448, 449; and need for passenger vessels, **61**: 465, 479-80; and Mexican situation, **61**: 511; changed attitude toward U.S., **61**: 560-61; and Germany, **65**: 102; and Pershing's proposed trip to, **66**: 178-79; Colby's trip to, **66**: 183-84, 430-31; **67**: 6-7, 23,n1,2; McAdoo on cable communication and, **66**: 218-20

Southard, Addison, **61**: 473

South Carolina, University of, **68**: 500,n1

South Carolina Exposition (Calhoun), **53**: 267,n2

South Carolina Farmers' Union, **54**: 228n1

South Dakota: and horses to Poland, **62**: 33, 34

Southern Baptist Convention, **65**: 275,n1; WW denies request for letter of introduction of leaders of, **65**: 421-23, 430

Southern Baptist Theological Seminary (Louisville), **65**: 421n1, 423

Southern Methodist University: WW declines to lecture at, **67**: 529-30,n2

Southern Pacific Railroad, **62**: 548; **64**: 354-55; and WW's land in California, **68**: 503

Southern Presbyterian Church: *see* Presbyterian Church, U.S.

Southern Railway Company, **63**: 607n1

Southern Sociological Congress: and race relations, **62**: 106-107,n1,2, 128, 292-93, 505-506

South Pacific islands: and mandates, **61**: 261

South-West Africa (German South West Africa), **54**: 249, 250, 252-54,n3, 290, 294-95, 296-98, 325, 328, 361, 365, 456; **55**: 7-8, 50, 171; **56**: 274; **57**: 603; **58**: 196; and mandates, **61**: 261

Southwestern Baptist Theological Seminary (Fort Worth), **65**: 421n2, 430

Southwestern Interstate Coal Operators Association of Kansas City, **66**: 10n1

Southwestern Political and Social Science Quarterly, **57**: 348n2

Southwestern Presbyterian University (Clarksville, Tennessee), **67**: 567n2

Southwestern Presbyterian University at Memphis, **67**: 567-68,n1,2

Souza Dantas, Luis Martins de, **65**: 302,n9

Soviet-Polish Relations 1917-1921 (Wandycz), **54**: 33n6; **65**: 527n1,2,3

Soviet-Polish War of 1919-1920: *see* Polish-Soviet War

Spa, Belgium, **53**: 63n1, 473n2, 626,n1, 646, 691; **54**: 9,n5, 10, 214; **55**: 458n1; **57**: 74,n3,4,5, 75,n6; Foch mission to on passage of Haller's troops, **56**: 88, 133, 134, 135, 137, 138, 144, 411-12,n4; *see also* Armistice Commission

Spa Conference, **65**: 326,n4; issue of U.S. representation at, **65**: 250, 330-31, 340, 380; issue of Yugoslavia's participation, **65**: 459, 477; Reparation Commission to attend, **65**: 477; and Teschen question, **65**: 518, 529, 532-33; agreement made by Poland at, **65**: 527,n3; Lloyd George on coal and disarmament agreements, **66**: 43-44,n5; and German disarmament, **67**: 33,n1

Spain, **53**: 153, 164, 419, 449-50; **54**: 302; **56**: 170n1, 392; **57**: 265; **58**: 198, 199, 201, 344; **62**: 418; **63**: 232; and German ships in, **58**: 547, 548; and credit extension for wheat, **61**: 501; invited to first meeting of Council of League of Nations, **64**: 272; and French occupation of Frankfurt, **65**: 171; offers help on Armenian conflict, **66**: 457, 480; and International Court of Justice, **67**: 373-74,n2

Spalato (now Split), **56**: 536,n2,3, 570-71; **57**: 483, 488, 611; **58**: 81, 239, 426, 452; **59**: 53, 71, 125, 242, 506; **63**: 525, 532, 557; **66**: 26n1

Spal'vin, Evgenii Genrikovich, **62**: 88,n8

Spanish-American War: peace treaty, **56**: 68; and submarine cable, **56**: 211, 219; and declaration of war, **56**: 437, 531,n5; WW on, **63**: 434, 455

Spanish Flu epidemic: *see* Great Swine epidemic

Spargo, John, **56**: 283; **61**: 463; on amnesty for conscientious objectors, **62**: 555-56, 556-59; appointed to first Industrial Conference, **63**: 300,n1; on pardoning Debs, **65**: 541-42; on Bolshevism, **66**: 5,n2; praises WW, **66**: 299-300; WW thanks for letter of support, **66**: 325; on anti-Semitism, **66**: 540-42; **67**: 7; praises WW and WW thanks, **67**: 528, 529

Spartacist Uprising of 1919 and the Crisis of the German Socialist Movement: A Study of the Relations of Political Theory and Party Practice (Waldman), **54**: 93n4

Spartacus Association (Sparticists), **53**: 7, 121; **54**: 35, 93,n4, 212, 220, 240, 338; **56**: 15, 90n4, 262, 263, 466, 467; **57**: 73, 74, 522; **59**: 35; **65**: 98n1, 100, 101, 155n1

Spaulding, Edward Gleason, **67**: 182

Spector, Sherman David, **60**: 222n4

Speeches of Lord Birkenhead, **68**: 477n1
Spellacy, Nellie Walsh (Mrs. Thomas Joseph), **55**: 228,n1
Spellacy, Thomas Joseph, **55**: 228,n1; **68**: 98,n1
Spencer, Henry Benning, **57**: 45,n1, 233,n2, 379,n11, 381, 382
Spencer, Selden Palmer, **53**: 84n1; **61**: 372; **62**: 3-4,n7, 12, 67, 113; **63**: 296; **64**: 316, 416n2; presents reservations on treaty to WW, **61**: 619-22; and treaty fight, **64**: 94, 200-201, 337, 339; on rumors of WW's health and inability to make decisions, **64**: 124-25; accuses WW of guaranteeing use of U.S. military forces under League Covenant, **66**: 172,n1, 187-88, 191-92; WW denies charges, **66**: 191; Carlson refutes charges made by, **66**: 196-97; controversy comes to a head, **66**: 198,n1; Root on controversy between WW and, **66**: 246,n1; photograph of, *illustration section*, **62**
Speranza, N., **54**: 463,n3
Sperry, Elmer Ambrose, **63**: 441n2
Sperry, Lawrence, **63**: 441n2
Spicer, Sir Albert, **56**: 57
Spinozzi, Augustine, **63**: 587,n2
Spisz, Poland, **66**: 225
Spivak, John Louis: on coal situation in West Virginia, **65**: 335-37,n1
Splain, Maurice, **67**: 329
Split, Yugoslavia: *see* Spalato
Spokane, Wash., **59**: 287; WW's arrival in, **63**: 211,n5,6; WW's address in, **63**: 224-34
Spokane *Spokesman-Review*, **63**: 221n4, 234n
Sprigg, Carroll, **65**: 202n2, 215, 232
Springfield, Ill., **65**: 545
Springfield *Illinois State Register*: and Lansing dismissal, **65**: 6
Springfield (Mass.) *Republican*, **54**: 57-58; **58**: 215; **60**: 41,n1; **62**: 196, 461n1; **63**: 609n2, 611; **64**: 277, 287,n1, 355,n1; **65**: 5, 24, 118,n2; **66**: 208n1, 258,n2, 349; **67**: 488; on Russia, **56**: 435-36; on peace treaty, **58**: 274; on prohibition, **58**: 604; Tumulty's advice on editorial in, **60**: 112-13; on Irish situation, **61**: 293
Sprout, Harold, **57**: 142n1; **62**: 460n1
Sprout, Margaret, **57**: 142n1; **62**: 461n1
Sprunt, James, **68**: 45,n1
Squibb, Charles Fellows, **67**: 350,n2
Squibb, Edward Robinson, **67**: 350n2
Squibb, John, **67**: 350n2
Squibb, Margaret Dodge (Mrs. Charles Fellows), **67**: 350n2
Squibb, Paul, **67**: 350n2
Squires, Grant, **53**: 20-21,n1, 55, 101-102, 142, 554; **54**: 57; on German propaganda in the U.S., **54**: 396-98,n2
Staak, S., **53**: 137
Stacy, Mrs., **53**: 707
Stahlberg, Kaarlo Juho, **64**: 236,n1

Stalin, Joseph (Iosif Vissarionovich Dzhugashvili), **54**: 92n2
Stamboliiski, Aleksandur, **66**: 358,n4
Standard Oil Company, **60**: 152; **68**: 111; in Rumania, **62**: 78; and the *Imperator* controversy, **64**: 212; **67**: 82,n3
Stanislau (now Stanislav, Poland), **59**: 561; **60**: 161
Stanley, Edward George Villiers: *see* Derby, 17th Earl of
Starbird, Charles Millard, **67**: 305
Starbuck, Ellen, **65**: 341,n1
Starling, Edmund William, **53**: 166, 319, 344; **58**: 631,n2; **66**: 103n1; **68**: 576,n4
Starling of the White House, **58**: 631n2; **66**: 103n1
Stars and Stripes (organ of A.E.F.), **60**: 489
State councils of defense, **53**: 11, 97, 135
State Department: and Mexican situation, **61**: 610-11; and League bureaus, **62**: 455; and National Women's Trade Union League, **63**: 57, 58-59; Lansing fears for emergency fund, **64**: 67; Lansing on Phillips' service in, **64**: 103; suggestions for Lansing's successor, **64**: 419; WW's plans for, **64**: 464; and Adriatic question, **65**: 43n2; Phillips' resignation, **65**: 47, 63; Polk's suggestions for vacancies in, **65**: 107; Colby assumes duties, **65**: 125,n1; question of N. H. Davis serving in, **65**: 153, 180-81, 225; and Undersecretary position, **65**: 180-81, 226, 229; permanent appointment for Mrs. Summers, **65**: 185; Polk's resignation, **65**: 190, 196-97, 230-31, 352; and Solicitor position, **65**: 226, 238, 245, 317,n3; Long's resignation, **65**: 377-78, 381; Colby's concern that he's leaning too much on WW for decisions, **65**: 529; WW on protection of Americans in Armenia and, **65**: 540; and sending of ship to Danzig, **66**: 78, 86-87; and Western Union's charges, **66**: 400; Colby defends Mexican position of, **66**: 407-408; and O'Callaghan case, **67**: 37-38, 48-51, 52n1; and League of Nations, **67**: 402n1
State: Elements of Historical and Practical Politics (Wilson): WW on, **53**: 45; **62**: 225; issue of reduced royalties, **65**: 503,n1, 509
state food administrators: WW's remarks to, **53**: 52
Statutes at Large, **53**: 78n2, 150n1, 214n1, 716n1; **65**: 296n5, 398n1, 467n2, 478n1; **66**: 126n1; **67**: 26n6, 104n2; **68**: 97n3
Staunton, Va., **66**: 290
Stavelot, Belgium, **60**: 108
Steck, Charles F., **66**: 121,n2
Stedman, Seymour, **65**: 276n1
Steed, Henry Wickham, **54**: 304; **57**: 459n2, 532,n2, 533; **62**: 525n1, 574,n1; **63**: 621,n1; **67**: 290-91, 294; on Adriatic

difficulty, **53**: 444-46,n1; **56**: 515, 516-17, 542
Steel, Ronald, **60**: 202n1
steel industry: and prices, **53**: 168, 205; **55**: 286-87; price conflict between Railroad Administration and Industrial Board, **56**: 193-94, 341, 342, 399-400; **57**: 233-34, 280-21, 282-83, 347-48, 379, 383-84; WW's concern over possible strike, **62**: 581-82,n1; Gary on labor unions and U.S. Steel Corporation, **62**: 596-601; and strike, **63**: 29-30,n1, 52, 56, 148, 149, 163, 583; **64**: 416n2; and steel rail prices and disclosure issue, **63**: 88-91, 118-19, 300, 301; and breakup of first Industrial conference, **63**: 582-83
Steel Trust: John Skelton Williams on, **62**: 518-22
Stefani, Guglielmo, **58**: 239n3
Steffens, Lincoln, **59**: 447; **61**: 241, 242, 509; and Bullitt mission to Russia, **55**: 540n1; **56**: 183, 473, 551n1
Steigerwald, S.M.S., **55**: 432
Stein, B. M., **58**: 626n74
Steiner, Herbert, **55**: 317n3
Stephan, Werner, **53**: 121n2
Stephens, Dan Voorhees: on Democratic losses in Congress and Nebraska, **53**: 61-62, 67
Stephens, Hubert Durrett, **68**: 93n3, 128,n1
Stephens, Lawrence Vest: on Missouri senatorial race, **68**: 35,n1, 166,n1
Stephens, William Dennison, **57**: 49; **63**: 308,n1; and Mooney case, **53**: 273,n1; and California's anti-Japanese legislation, **66**: 286
Sterling, Thomas, **54**: 397n1; **61**: 372, 548,n1, 599, 601; and treaty fight, **64**: 94, 200-201, 337, 339
Stern, Fritz, **58**: 461n1
Stern, Jacques, **56**: 523
Stettin, Germany (now Szczecin, Poland), **56**: 408n2, 409, 411, 526, 527, 540, 541; **60**: 606
Stettin, S.M.S., **55**: 427; **56**: 28; **58**: 127
Stettinius, Edward Reilly, **68**: 548
Stevens, Horace Paine, M.D., **67**: 527,n2
Stevens, John Frank, **53**: 463n1, 556-57,n4, 632; **54**: 83,n3, 159, 261, 412, 413; **55**: 39, 350, 351, 494, 495; **58**: 573,n2, 575; **59**: 438,n11; **61**: 41, 571, 579-80, 636; **62**: 34n1, 86n5, 590-91; on recognition of Siberia, **59**: 494-95,n1; on situation in Russia and need for Allied trops to relieve Czechs, **60**: 606
Stevens, Raymond Bartlett, **55**: 388n1; **58**: 269,n2; **59**: 185n1
Stevens Commission: *see* Russian Railroad Commission
Stevens Institute of Technology, **68**: 577n9
Stevenson, Mr., **68**: 360
Stevenson, Archibald Ewing, **54**: 397n1
Stevenson, Frances, **60**: 300,n2, 305

Stevenson, Robert Louis, **62**: 427,n2; **66**: 442
Stewart, George E., **54**: 93n5; **57**: 60,n2; **60**: 95n2; **63**: 588n1
Stewart, Harry, **59**: 524n1
Stewart, John Appleton, **66**: 115,n1, 118-19, 123
Stewart, Robert P., **62**: 465,n1; **65**: 441,n2
Stewart, Samuel Vernon, **63**: 169,n6, 180
Stewart, Stella Baker (Mrs. Samuel Vernon), **63**: 169,n7
Still the First Citizen of the World (cartoon), **66**: 450,n2
Stimson, Frederic Jesup, **53**: 342,n1
Stimson, Henry Lewis, **53**: 580n2; **66**: 246n2
Stirling, Walter Francis, **56**: 115,n12
Stitt, Edwards Rhodes, **63**: 544,n1, 550, 551, 553, 556, 568, 574, 577, 578, 579, 581, 587, 590, 634; **64**: 4, 489, 506, 507n1, 507, 508, 509, 510
Stockhammern, Franz Elder von, **58**: 518,n1
stock market: WW on Plumb plan and, **62**: 227n1
Stockbridge, Frank Parker, **64**: 515
Stockton, Charles Herbert, **56**: 212,n3
Stockton, Samuel Witham, **53**: 22n6
Stojanovi , Kosta, **56**: 271n3
Stokes, Edith Minturn (Mrs. Isaac Newton Phelps), **67**: 135,n1
Stokes, Harold Phelps, **60**: 146,n1
Stokes, James Graham Phelps, **56**: 283
Stokes, Rose Harriet Pastor (Mrs. James Graham Phelps), **62**: 126n1, 557,n1; **66**: 176-77, 184; **67**: 99-100
Stone, Albert W., **63**: 513-14,n1
Stone, Harlan Fiske, **61**: 366,n2; **65**: 77; and Chemical Foundation case, **68**: 299n1
Stone, Melville Elijah, **53**: 525; **56**: 350,n3, 437, 440, 441, 443; **62**: 184,n1; advises WW on entry into war, **64**: 487
Stone, Ralph, **64**: 328n2
Stone, Warren Sanford, **62**: 138, 140, 198n1, 572; **64**: 197-98,n1, 424, 431; **65**: 16; on cost of living, **62**: 31,n1; protests adjournment of Congress, **65**: 359
Stone, William Joel, **53**: 84n1
Stone, Ralph, **59**: 451n1, 524n1
Stonewall Jackson and the American Civil War (Henderson), **60**: 301n4
Storck, John, **59**: 447,n1
Storey, Charles Moorfield, **56**: 384,n2
Story, Joseph, **66**: 116
Story of Mrs. Peck: An Autobiography by Mary Allen Hulbert, **63**: 419n1
Stovall, Pleasant Alexander, **53**: 6, 7; **56**: 242; on German and Swiss press reaction to peace terms, **59**: 35-37
Straight, Willard Dickerman, **59**: 605,n1
Straits of Otranto, **58**: 590
Strakhovsky, Leonid Ivan, **59**: 550n1
Stralsund, S.M.S., **55**: 23
Strandmann, Otto, **60**: 269,n18

Straphanger, The (cartoon), **68**: 198,n1; *illustration section*, **68**

Strasbourg, **56**: 363; **60**: 67n10, 110

Strassburg, S.M.S., **55**: 23, 427; **56**: 28; **58**: 127

Stratton, Samuel Wesley, **63**: 573,n2, 621

Straus, Nathan, **59**: 419n1

Straus, Oscar Solomon, **53**: 105; **54**: 8-89; **55**: 195, 200; **57**: 445, 469; **60**: 39; **61**: 181; **64**: 64n1, 141n4, 216, 384; **65**: 183,n3, 184, 184-85; **66**: 141n2, 246n2; **67**: 426n1; **68**: 147; on Taft's amendments for Covenant, **56**: 484-85; on situation in Senate regarding peace treaty, **61**: 137-38; and second Industrial Conference, **63**: 611; appointed to Permanent Court of Arbitration, **64**: 273; on negative effect on treaty of WW's Adriatic reply, **64**: 445; urges WW to accept reservations in order to save treaty, **65**: 47-48; on meeting with WW on treaty, **67**: 607-10

Strauss, Albert, **53**: 627, 716; **55**: 186, 306n1; **56**: 208; **58**: 595n2; **60**: 539; **61**: 529; and recognition of Costa Rica, **65**: 464-65

Strauss, Edith, **58**: 148

Strauss, Lewis, **53**: 647; **59**: 191, 411

Strauss, Manny, **66**: 261,n2

street railways, **62**: 420-22, 461, 516-17; WW on, **62**: 532-33; *see also* electric railways

Strike at Fort Leavenworth (Lane), **62**: 545n3

strikes: marine workers in N.Y. port, **53**: 710; general strike in Seattle, **59**: 204n2; of telephone and telegraph workers, **60**: 248, 331; Burleson on telegraph companies and, **61**: 10; and California telephone and telegraph workers, **61**: 503-504, 539-40; railroad strike, **61**: 536-37; **62**: 161-62, 470, 485, 486, 567-73;548, 549-50, 567-73; 1901 U.S. Steel Corporation, **62**: 597; WW on, **62**: 162, 210, 218; **64**: 86, 115; Hines on railroad employees right to, **62**: 228; WW's concern over possible steel strike, **62**: 581-82,n1; steel, **63**: 209-30,n1, 52, 148-49, 163, 583; Boston police, **63**: 167,n6,7; bituminous coal, **63**: 593-94, 595-98, 599-601; *see also* coal strike, railroads

Stringher, Bonaldo, **55**: 113,n1; on Italian credits in U.S., **59**: 110, 110-11

Stroke: Pathophysiology, Diagnosis, and Management (Barnett, Stein, Mohr and Yatsu), **58**: 626n74

Strong, Agnes Leas Freer (Mrs. Richard), **59**: 74,n1

Strong, Benjamin, **61**: 529; **62**: 423,n1

Strong, Harold F., **67**: 539,n1

Strong, Richard Pearson, **59**: 74,n1

Struggle for Labor Loyalty: Gompers, the A. F. of L., and the Pacifists, 1917-1920 (Grubbs), **65**: 442n2

Struggle for Transcaucasia (1917-1921) (Kazamzadeh), **58**: 333n2

Struj, Poland (now Stry), **59**: 561

Stuart, Sir Campbell, **58**: 4-5n6

Stuart, Charles Kennedy Crauford: *see* Crauford-Stuart, Charles Kennedy

Stuart, Donald Clive, **67**: 182

Stuart, Duane Reed, **67**: 105-106,n1, 125, 182; confirms WW's accuracy in Greek and on his experiences at Princeton, **67**: 115-16; answers WW's question on Greek language, **68**: 101, 103-104

Stuart, Henry Carter, **53**: 413-14; **55**: 91,n3, 396,n2; **63**: 611; **64**: 64n1

Stuart, James Ewell Brown ("Jeb"), **60**: 301,n5

Stuart, Robert Cummins, Jr., **66**: 409-10, 468; **67**: 158,n1; and plans for organization of WW Clubs, **67**: 253,n1, 257-58,n1, 259-60, 260, 275, 285-86, 288, 314-15, 324, 344-45, 352-54, 386; WW congratulates on organizational work at universities, **67**: 254; suggests combining appeal for WW Clubs with the WW Foundation effort, **67**: 271-72, 273-74; WW wishes to keep WW Clubs separate from Foundation appeal, **67**: 276; on continued efforts for national movement for WW Clubs, **67**: 326-28; on competition between WW Clubs and WW Foundation, **67**: 415-17, 425-26

Stuff—and Nonsense: A Book of War Verses (Malcolm), **58**: 104,n2

Stuhm, **57**: 153, 595

Stupid Falsification of the Record (New York *World*), **67**: 424n1

Stuttgart, S.M.S., **55**: 23, 427; **56**: 29; **58**: 127

Stuttgart Neues Tageblatt, **59**: 35

Stuyvesant, Elizabeth Loewnguth de Wassenaer (Mrs. Rutherford), **60**: 491,n2

Styer, Henry Delp, **53**: 184,n2; **55**: 402,n5

submarine cables, **56**: 38, 210-16; **57**: 358, 366, 455-56, 609; **58**: 283, 296-97, 298-306, 345-53, 378-79

submarines: and armistice terms, **54**: 10-12; issue of disposal of German submarines, **54**: 180, 273,n1, 273-74, 505; **58**: 127-28, 457n4, 579; and peace terms, **55**: 22, 26, 425, 426-27, 433, 518; **56**: 29, 30; and treaties, **67**: 512n4

Suds (movie), **65**: 400n1

Sudan, **59**: 326

Sudbahn, **61**: 280, 314, 317-21

Sudetenland; **61**: 172, 371,n2

Suez Canal, **56**: 36; **58**: 123, 124

suffrage: and Washington D.C., **53**: 251,n1; *see also* woman suffrage

sugar: Hoover on, **62**: 125; and prices, **62**: 160; WW on imports and exports of, **67**: 191, 194

Sugar Equalization Board, **53**: 273; **54**: 277; **66**: 509, 529-30

sugar industry: and prices, **55**: 252

Sugrue, Thomas W., **58**: 631n2
Sulgrave Institution, **66**: 115,n1,2, 118n1, 119, 543,n1
Sulgrave Manor, **66**: 543
Suitors and Suppliants: The Little Nations at Versailles (Bonsal), **56**: 517n2
Sullivan, Helen Marie Quinlan (Mrs. Roger Charles), **65**: 189,n1
Sullivan, Mark, **53**: 419; **54**: 192; **68**: 222-23,n2, 223-26, 476, 495; on WW's health and personality, **65**: 5-6; WW on, **68**: 228
Sullivan, Roger Charles, **55**: 340,n1; **65**: 189n2; **66**: 90n1; **67**: 312n1
Sulzer, Hans Adolf, **53**: 63, 64, 127,n1; **54**: 215,n2; **55**: 151; **65**: 338,n3
Summerall, Charles Pelot, **63**: 362,n1
Summerlin, George Thomas, **61**: 528n2; **65**: 107,n1, 446; Colby defends appointment suggestion of, **65**: 181; on Macias as Mexican Ambassador to U.S., **65**: 201n1; on interview with Obregón, **65**: 485, 486, 486-87
Summers, Leland L., **57**: 287,n1; **58**: 120; **66**: 288; on reparations, **60**: 47,n2, 52
Summers, Maddin, **65**: 185
Summers, Natalia Goraynoff (Mrs. Maddin), **65**: 185,n1
Sumner of Ibstone, John Andrew Hamilton, Baron, **56**: 444, 449; **57**: 87, 287; **59**: 275, 422, 495, 611, 624-25; on reparations, **56**: 69-74, 270, 285-86, 286, 292, 535; **57**: 9, 10, 12, 16, 23, 28, 203, 204, 294, 609; **58**: 27, 28, 31, 33, 34, 114, 252; **60**: 336, 337, 338, 339, 345, 349, 391, 392, 403, 494; **60**: 93; on artistic and cultural materials included in reparations, **59**: 391; and reparations, **60**: 93; Nicolson on, **60**: 492
Sumner, William Graham, **68**: 126,n1
Sumners, Hatton William, **56**: 428,n3
Sunderland House (London), **61**: 477,n1
Sundry Civil bill, **61**: 568,n1; **62**: 226
Sun Yat-sen: on Chinese political and military situation, **53**: 138-40,n1, 197
Superior Blockade Council, **60**: 283, 495,n2, 496, 497, 518, 519, 523, 627,n9; **61**: 56, 134, 151-52, 195-96, 257
Supreme Control at the Paris Peace Conference 1919: A Commentary (Hankey), **57**: 400n1
Supreme Council (Inter-Allied Conference of Prime Ministers), **64**: 26, 149, 168, 307; and issue of German tankers, **64**: 34; and Rumania, **64**: 34-35; issue of U.S. representation on, **64**: 67, 67-68, 87, 148; and new Hungarian government, **64**: 101n2; on negotiations on Turkish treaty, **64**: 344; and reparations discussions at Spa, **65**: 250; note to U.S. on mandate for Armenia, **65**: 307-12; and Teschen question, **65**: 517-18; and Western Ukraine Republic, **68**: 110
Supreme Council for Supply and Relief,

54: 29-31, 214, 230n4, 277, 335, 420, 479, 515
Supreme Council of the Principal Allied and Associated Powers: *see* Council of Four
Supreme Court: *see* United States Supreme Court
Supreme Economic Council, **60**: 372: plans for formation of, **54**: 284-86; **55**: 17, 52, 53, 54, 55, 60, 61, 111, 458n1; **56**: 4; **57**: 83, 105, 140; **58**: 8, 545, 546; **59**: 130,n4; **61**: 310; U.S. representatives to, **55**: 148; and plans for blockade if Germany refuses to sign treaty, **59**: 109; and blockade and Hungary and Bolshevik Russia, **59**: 376; **60**: 281-83, 621, 624-26, 636-38, 639; and proposed Austrian agreement on trade with Hungary and Germany, **60**: 283; Hoover's suggestions for coordinated postwar reconstruction efforts, **61**: 284-86; Cecil and WW on continued role of, **61**: 314-16; on international consultation, **61**: 520, 521, 587; Hoover on food relief and, **62**: 123-24; wishes to meet in Washington, **62**: 333-34
Supreme War Council, **54**: 35-42; **56**: 3; **57**: 204; **61**: 198; and European relief program, **53**: 64, 222, 360, 361; Grayson comments on, **54**: 4-5, 35, 64; **55**: 94; on Armistice terms and Russian problem, **54**: 7-12; on representation at Paris Peace Conference, **54**: 12-26; and demobilization, **54**: 221, 238-46; on sending troops to Poland, **54**: 199-204; and Allied military forces in Turkey, **54**: 371, 378,n12, 417-18, 326; and Hoover resolution on relaxing export-import control on Germany, **54**: 477-79, 558; and Loucheur committee's report, **54**: 525-45; and Foch-Clemenceau controversy over German prisoners, **55**: 3, 40; meetings of, **55**: 9-26, 51-62, 95-104, 104-13, 175-83; on arms limitations, **55**: 11-16, 20; on naval terms, **55**: 20-26; Benham reports on, **55**: 40; on enforcement of Armistice terms, **55**: 51-58; on war criminals and trials, **55**: 59-60; Armistice renewal terms and peace terms, **55**: 95-104, 104-12; on passage of troops through Holland, **55**: 178-80; on Prinkipo Declaration, **55**: 180-83; British press gives false reasons why WW absent, **55**: 530-31; on peace terms and treaty, **56**: 14-56; on Polish situation and boundaries, **56**: 49-56, 127-28, 163, 312-13; on transport of Haller's Army, **56**: 129-48, 209n2; Bliss on Hungarian revolution being caused by decision of, **56**: 380-81; time wasted at, **56**: 440; and Polish-Ukrainian conflict, **58**: 101
Suresnes Cemetery (Paris), **64**: 511n1; various comments and observations on WW's speech at Memorial Day obser-

Suresnes Cemetery (Paris) (*cont.*)
vances at, **59**: 605, 610, 621, 621-22,
624, 642; WW's remarks at, **59**: 606-10;
63: 181, 197, 512; **68**: 256,n4; photograph of, *illustration section*, **59**
Surface, Frank Macy, **59**: 206n1
Survey, The, **62**: 545n3
Susac, Croatia: see Susak
Susak (now Rijeka), **53**: 642; **58**: 358,
398-99; **59**: 201; **60**: 138, 213, 218; **62**:
604; **64**: 304, 305, 332
Sussex, S.S., **58**: 28
Suter, Herman Milton, **66**: 169,n1
Sutherland, George, **68**: 119,n1; WW on,
68: 121, 127,n1
Sutherland, Howard, **59**: 451n1; and
treaty fight, **64**: 200, 202, 337; sug-
gested for Tariff Commission, **66**: 8n1
Sutter, Bertha Felice Sophie Kinsky,
Baroness von, **66**: 523n2
Sutter, Charles, **66**: 252,n1
Svegelj, Gustav Gregorin Ivan, **58**: 111,n1
Svehla, Antonin, **54**: 481,n3
Sverdlovsk, Russia: *see* Ekaterinburg
Swanson, Claude Augustus, **53**: 73, 185;
55: 263, 270, 297; **61**: 184, 437, 468,
469, 545; **62**: 17, 19, 45, 263; **65**: 109;
66: 167; **68**: 34, 143, 380, 471, 576; and
woman suffrage, **55**: 368; and League
of Nations resolution, **55**: 388,n1; and
League of Nations Covenant, **60**:
42,n1, 43, 100,n2; and issue of peace
treaty publication, **60**: 242-43, 243,
244, 320; on strategy for WW regarding treaty, **61**: 186; amendments to
General Leasing bill, **62**: 49-50; questions WW at Foreign Relations Committee meeting, **62**: 339, 340, 359, 368,
381, 382; on WW's opposition to treaty
changes, **62**: 613-14; and Foreign Relations Committee's minority report on
reservations, **63**: 198,n1; **64**: 120; and
Treaty of Berlin in Senate, **67**: 412,
418, 419; and WW's request for text of
Four Power Treaty, **67**: 484; WW
thanks for liquor, **68**: 143; WW thanks
for partridges, **68**: 463-64
Swanson, Lulie Lyons (Mrs. Claude Augustus), **68**: 463-64, 471
Swariks, Michael, **53**: 137
Swartz, Edwin M., **66**: 147n1
Sweden, **53**: 40, 153; **54**: 137, 479; **56**:
170n1; **57**: 139; **58**: 13, 14, 198; and
trade with Russia, **61**: 483; and extension of credit, **61**: 495, 501; and League
of Nations membership, **62**: 412, 418;
proposes WW for Nobel Peace Prize,
65: 40; and Åland Islands,   **65**:
460,n1,2, 525-26; **66**: 138n1; **67**: 266
Sweet, Edwin Forrest, **63**: 573,n1, 621;
on resumption of trade with Germany,
62: 423-24,n1; and electric railways,
62: 461, 516, 533
Sweet, Louis Dennison: appointed to Industrial Conference, **63**: 300,n1
Sweet, Richard C., **57**: 477

Sweet, Sophia Fuller (Mrs. Edwin Forest), **63**: 621
Sweet, William Ellery, **68**: 301,n1
Sweet Briar College, **68**: 478n2
Sweetser, Arthur, **57**: 312,n1; **59**: 70n1;
64: 275,n2, 362; photograph of, *illustration section*, **59**
Swem, Charles Lee, **53**: 319, 376; **54**:
305; **57**: 240,n2, 468; **58**: 562n1; **60**:
157; **61**: 3n1, 342n3; **62**: 482n1; **64**:
526; **65**: 7n1, 24, 299, 305, 320n1, 442,
498-99, 520n1; **66**: 103, 189, 196,
277n1, 306-307, 490n3, 491n4; **67**: 30,
39n1, 140, 170-71; **68**: 577; on WW's insistence letters be folded EBW's way,
66: 29-30; on why WW would not write
what happened at Paris, **66**: 533; on
WW and Democratic National Convention, 1920, **65**: 291; and WW's prohibition plank, **65**: 347n4; Cummings on
expertise of, **65**: 349-50; Seibold on,
65: 407; on WW's health, **65**: 521; **67**:
103-104; decodes messages, **65**: 552n6;
on asking wife to join him in Paris, **56**:
204-205; at Foreign Relations Committee meeting, **62**: 339; and WW's western tour, **63**: 5-6, 97; **67**: 189n3; Hoover
on, **63**: 638; and Tumulty's draft letter
to Hitchcock on reservations, **64**:
278n1; on WW's Nobel Prize money,
67: 51-52; on WW's reaction to Lansing's book, **67**: 60; on WW's prejudices
on appointments, **67**: 67-68; on WW 's
reaction to special request for civil
service position, **67**: 113,n1; on WW's
concern over telling lie to Tumulty, **67**:
117; reveals WW's opinions on synonyms, antonyms, and on shorthand,
67: 127; Creel on importance of, **67**:
141; on WW's quip on bad portrait of
himself, **67**: 143; on I. Hoover's comparison of WW to other presidents, **67**:
150; on issue of Debs' pardon, **67**: 157;
WW's farewell note to, **67**: 197; photograph of, *illustration section*, **55**
Swem, Daisy Bunting (Mrs. Charles
Lee), **56**: 205,n1
Swift and Company, **54**: 229
Swiggart, William Harris, **66**: 386n1
Swiss Federal Council, **65**: 338n1
Switchmen's Union of North America,
64: 431
Switzerland, **53**: 153; **54**: 139, 479; **55**:
92, 152, 154; **56**: 170n1, 498; **57**: 102;
58: 13, 198, 473; **61**: 357; **64**: 98, 205;
German finances and, **54**: 215; and
League of Nations and neutrals, **54**:
233-34, 302; and Bolshevism, **53**: 6,
121; mentioned as site for League of
Nations, **56**: 76-77, 103, 121-22, 170,
234; Geneva chosen as seat of League
of Nations, **57**: 194, 222, 224-26, 329,
430, 464; and League of Nations membership, **62**: 412, 418; Rappard's note
on meeting with WW on League of Nations, neutrality and, **63**: 627-31; Long

declines appointment to, **64**: 296, 316-17, 350-51; and Grew, **64**: 317n4; and Frazier affair, **64**: 383-84, 408, 413, 414, 451-54; Gary appointment to, **64**: 453, 454; and appointments, **65**: 85, 87, 88; Minister to U.S. gives impressions of WW, **65**: 338-40; **66**: and banking interests in Mexico, **66**: 302

Swope, Herbert Bayard, **54**: 60, 106,n1, 192, 550-51; **55**: 160; **56**: 354; **57**: 316, 417,n1; **61**: 243,n8, 244, 375n4; **66**: 250-51,n1, 257, 288; **67**: 242; on WW's speech on League of Nations, **54**: 406, 427; and news leak on reparation clauses, **57**: 333

Sycow, Poland: see Gross Wartenberg

Sydorenko, Gregory, **56**: 96,n1, 97; **59**: 350-51, 352

Sykes, Sir Charles, **67**: 327

Sykes, Frederick Hugh, **54**: 539; **55**: 112; **59**: 379,n7

Sykes, Mark, **56**: 115,n11

Sykes-Picot Agreement of 1916, **54**: 506,n7; **55**: 160,n1; **56**: 104, 107, 110, 111, 112, 113; **57**: 443; **59**: 340, 344; **61**: 310, 443; **63**: 466; **64**: 358, 449

Symon, Charles, **62**: 111,n1

Syria, **53**: 649; **54**: 225, 360, 371, 372, 455, 506, 507; **55**: 4, 7, 61, 160; **56**: 102, 103, 104, 126, 272, 273, 274, 546, 587; **57**: 247, 535; **59**: 337; **61**: 156; **62**: 429; **64**: 25-26, 449; **65**: 65, 91, 114, 141; and Cilicia, **54**: 517; H. S. Bliss on, **54**: 551-52; **55**: 86, 141-45, 472-73,n1; Council of Four meeting on, **56**: 104-18; and Palestine, **57**: 326n3; Clemenceau and House discuss, **57**: 334-35; Westermann on, **57**: 443-44, 468; Prince Faisal thanks WW, **57**: 525-26, 559; Clemenceau on France's support, **57**: 589-90; and proposed mission to, **58**: 172; and France, **58**: 172, 326, 436; **59**: 343; and mandates, **59**: 327, 328, 333; **62**: 188, 235, 242, 257; **65**: 142n2, 271n1; and France, **59**: 343; Lloyd George on, **59**: 343-44, 345; Lloyd George-Clemenceau conflict over, **59**: 368, 369-70, 370,n1, 484; Council of Four on commission to, **59**: 632-33; and King-Crane Commission report on, **61**: 442-44; **62**: 607-608; crisis in, **65**: 142,n1; and mandate issue, **65**: 142n2, 271n1; Lloyd George on, **66**: 47-48; see also Inter-Allied Commission to Syria

Syria and the French Mandate: The Politics of Arab Nationalism, 1920-1945 (Khoury), **61**: 443n1

Syrian Commission (proposed): see Inter-Allied Commission to Syria; King-Crane Commission

Syrian Protestant College, Beirut, **54**: 551n1; **55**: 321-22; **65**: 141, 142,n2

Syrkin, Nahum, **53**: 137

Syrovy, Jan, **53**: 629,n4; **60**: 608,n2

Syrzan, Russia, **62**: 87

Szasz, Karoly, **56**: 276,n2; **59**: 239n1

Sze, Alfred (Saoke), **57**: 77n7; photograph of, illustration section, **58**

Szogyeny-Marich, Ladislaus, Count von, **56**: 614,n3

Szterenyi, Jozsef, **57**: 339,n3

T. S. Scott & Company, **59**: 121n3

Tachi, Sakutaro, **59**: 275; **60**: 476,n25

Tacna-Arica dispute, **53**: 316-17,n2, 317-18, 342, 536,n1, 699; **55**: 330,n2, 393; **65**: 237; **66**: 210,n2; and Root on, **56**: 100; issue of submission to League of Nations, **65**: 190-91, 195, 245

Tacna-Arica: An Account of the Chile-Peru Boundary Dispute and the Arbitrations by the United States (Dennis), **53**: 316n2; **66**: 210n4

Tacoma, Washington: Grayson on WW's arrival and activities in, **63**: 236-37; WW's speeches in, **63**: 240-41, 241-52; photograph of WW in, illustration section, **63**

Tacoma, U.S.S., **61**: 640; **65**: 252

Tacoma Ledger, **63**: 241n, 250n2

Tacoma News Tribune, **63**: 252n

Taft, Helen, **64**: 485; **65**: 79, 83

Taft, Helen Herron (Mrs. William Howard), **64**: 485

Taft, Henry Waters, **66**: 246n2

Taft, William Howard, **53**: 135, 301, 344, 377, 382, 420,n1, 580, 625, 705, 710; **54**: 58; **55**: 225,n2, 281-82, 467; **56**: 57, 156, 162; **57**: 469; **58**: 613; **59**: 516; **61**: 66, 116, 356, 628,n1; **62**: 4, 17, 71, 96, 250-51, 385, 636; **63**: 94, 444; **65**: 79n1, 218n1, 412, 505; **66**: 141n2, 263n1, 282n1, 327, 502,n2, 542n1; **67**: 184, 187n1, 188, 190, 227, 297n1, 398, 434, 610; **68**: 123, 126, 131,n6, 398, 401, 569; on Roosevelt and, **53**: 246,n10; League to Enforce Peace, **53**: 28-31; WW on, **53**: 243-44; supports WW, **53**: 323,n1; **58**: 244; and League of Nations, **55**: 37, 65, 187, 199, 257, 282, 315-16, 418, 419, 439, 540; **59**: 529; **60**: 332, 538, 610; **61**: 542, 561; **66**: 202, 258n2,3; and speech at Metropolitan Opera House with WW on League of Nations, **55**: 289, 289-90, 328, 329, 357-58, 411, 413, 448; WW on as presidential candidate, **55**: 448; Lynch on Taft visiting London, but WW disagrees, **56**: 57-58, 120; suggestions for Covenant approved by Senate, **56**: 83, 157-58, 339, 398-99, 484-85; on Monroe Doctrine amendment to Covenant, **57**: 233, 315-16, 331, 332, 445; on religious freedom for Jews, **58**: 460-61, 560; critical of WW's reply to women's peace group, **59**: 450,n2, 479; and publication of peace treaty, **60**: 330-31; suggested for International Court of Justice, **60**: 431, 432; on WW's League of Nations strategy, **61**: 353; attempts to have treaty ratified, **61**: 605-606,n1; memorandum on reservations, **61**:

Taft, William Howard (*cont.*)
607-608; on WW, peace treaty, and fellow Republicans, **61**: 614-15; and reservations, **61**: 627; **62**: 308n1; **63**: 363; WW praises for League of Nations work, **63**: 222, 248; and International Labor Conference, **63**: 602; Grayson's recollections of, **64**: 485; and Lansing dismissal, **65**: 6; WW on, **65**: 498, 551; WW advised to use material showing he consulted with Taft on League Covenant, **66**: 148, 149, 181, 184; Cox wishes to use WW-Taft material, **66**: 159, 184; on Republicans' "numbing" prosperity, **66**: 243,n4; and papers in Library of Congress, **66**: 292; **67**: 77n5; residence while Chief Justice, **66**: 355n2; and Armistice Day parade, **67**: 452; and WW's funeral, **68**: 576

Taft Defends Wilson's Trip: Says Advantages Are Clear; Constitution Confers the Right (Taft), **53**: 323n1

Taft Papers on League of Nations (Marburg and Flack, eds.), **66**: 148,n2

Taft reservation, **64**: 387-88,n1, 405, 411, 445

Taggart, Thomas, **65**: 440,n1; **68**: 496,n1

Taiping Rebellion, **58**: 225,n3

Taiping Rebellion and Western Powers: A Comprehensive Survey (Teng Ssu-Yu), **58**: 225n3

Takeshita, Isamu, **55**: 21n7, 346,n3, 456,n2, 579

Talat, Pa a, **58**: 555n1; **59**: 411,n2

Talbot, Gerald, **59**: 43,n7

Talcott, Charles Andrew, **64**: 97,n1, 215-16, 322,n1; **67**: 52n1; death of, **65**: 36,n1

Talcott, Francis L., **65**: 36n1

Tales of the Phelps-Dodge Family: A Chronicle of Five Generations (P. B. Dodge), **67**: 137n3

Talien-Wan (Darien), China, **63**: 314,n3, 323, 330, 412, 437, 472

Tallents, Stephen George, **61**: 163,n18

Talley, Truman H., **55**: 161; **57**: 63n1

Talleyrand-Perigord, Charles-Maurice de, **68**: 67

Tallinn (Tallin), Estonia: *see* Reval

Tallman, Clay, **53**: 636n1; **62**: 47,n1, 48, 49

Tammany Hall, **64**: 521n1; **68**: 3

Tampico, Mexico, **61**: 510; **65**: 246-47

Tanaka, Giichi, **57**: 134,n1, 313, 314, 315

T'ang Shao-yi, **57**: 632n1

Tansill, Charles Callan, **56**: 486n1; **67**: 52n1

Tarbell, Edmund Charles, **65**: 106,n3; **66**: 542n1

Tarbell, Ida Minerva, **53**: 123,n1, 128; **66**: 542n1; **67**: 491,n3; on WW, **57**: 241,n4; praises WW and WW thanks, **67**: 240-41, 247; editorial on WW, **67**: 557-58,n1; on visit with WW, **68**: 45-48

Tardieu, André-Pierre-Gabriel-Amedée, **53**: 337, 397, 449, 497; **54**: 538; **55**: 11, 13, 14, 160, 209, 245, 283, 284, 350, 387, 458,499; **56**: 12n1, 92, 126, 201, 324, 539, 560, 566; **57**: 35, 65n2, 295, 586; **58**: 227, 236, 370-71, 440, 464, 482, 489, 490, 536; **59**: 139, 140, 330, 331, 333, 334, 336, 422, 455, 478, 495, 564, 605, 635; **60**: 98, 309, 467, 478, 557; **61**: 43, 99, 149, 206, 278n7, 566n1; **62**: 110, 207; **63**: 271, 305; **66**: 44n5; and Rhineland Question, **55**: 475-77,n2; **57**: 295-96,n1; Sharp warns WW of, **56**: 86; on cables, **56**: 218; and Republican party, **56**: 348, 354; on Saar Valley, **56**: 360-63, 424; **57**: 54-59, 106, 128, 129, 151, 155-59, 163, 164, 165, 195, 200, 201, 202, 246, 325; **59**: 378, 382; meets with House, **56**: 559, 587; **57**: 285; and German-Belgian border, **57**: 392-97; and Drafting Committee, **57**: 450; House on, **59**: 46, 554, 555; on Austrian boundary issue, **59**: 60, 61; and Syria, **59**: 340, 341, 343, 345-46; on Turkish Empire, **59**: 371; Adriatic plan (the Tardieu plan), **59**: 555,n1, 556, 559, 564-65, 570, 571; on reparations, **60**: 46, 49-50, 72-73, 73; at Council of Four, **60**: 548-49, 549; and Klagenfurt Basin, **61**: 92-93; and Clemenceau, **61**: 375; Tittoni and, **61**: 554; and Thrace, **62**: 239-40, 321, 327, 553; and Adriatic question, **62**: 575, 603; 63: 60, 120-22, 208-209; indiscreet article by, **65**: 542-43,n1,2; **67**: 24n3; and WW's summoning of *George Washington*, **67**: 360,n2; photograph of, *illustration section*, **57**

Tardieu plan: *see* Tardieu, André P.G.A.; Paris Peace Conference —Tardieu plan

tariff, **59**: 76, 121; suggestions for WW's speech to Congress, **58**: 605; **59**: 123; WW on, **59**: 294-96; and chemical and dyestuffs industry, **64**: 80-81, 109-10; and WW's Annual Message to Congress, **64**: 80-81, 108-109; Tumulty's suggestion concerning, **65**: 132; WW's veto of Emergency Tariff bill, **67**: 191-94; The Document, **67**: 486-87,n1, 500; **68**: 216, 237, 309, 319, 536-37; Davis and Houston to collaborate on policy statement, **68**: 54, 55, 178-79, 182, 253-54; Hull on, **68**: 97,n3; Houston on, **68**: 270, 271; Davis on WW manifesto and, **68**: 489-90; *see* Emergency Tariff bill

Tariff Commission (U.S.), **59**: 121; WW on, **59**: 295-96; Taussig resignation from, **61**: 514, 550, 617-18; T. W. Page appointed to, **61**: 617,n2; appointments to, **64**: 205; suggested appointment of Kirby to, **67**: 166, 168-69, 171-72; Houston on, **68**: 270, 271

Tariff History of the United States (Taussig), **68**: 97n3

Tarvisio (Tarvis), Italy: *see* Paris Peace Conference—Tarvisio

Tarvis Pass: *see* Paris Peace Conference—Tarvis Pass

Tashkent (Taskend), Russia, **53**: 312n1

Tatsumi, Konojo, **56**: 271n3
Taussig, Frank William, **53**: 50, 166, 413-14; **57**: 574,n1; **58**: 111, 118, 119, 120, 605; **59**: 76, 121, 190; **60**: 608; **61**: 99, 100, 377, 385, 617-18; **62**: 101; **64**: 64n1, 205,n6; **66**: 329; **68**: 97n3; on cotton prices, **53**: 132-33; tariff suggestions for WW's message to Congress, **59**: 123; **61**: 386-87, 387-88; on German counterproposal, **60**: 57, 58, 66-67; and nationalization of utilities, **61**: 366,n2; resigns from Tariff Commission, **61**: 514, 550; interested in becoming ambassador to Germany, **61**: 618; and Industrial Conference, **63**: 611
Tauszky, Edmund, **60**: 487n1
taxation, **53**: 103, 281-82; and theater industry, **54**: 227,n2; Glass on, **54**: 501-502; **62**: 502; and Rhine question, **55**: 475-77,n2; and WW's special message to Congress, **59**: 293; McAdoo on Republican House of Representatives addressing issue of, **62**: 71-72; WW on McAdoo's suggestions on corporate taxes, **62**: 224-25; WW on railroad situation and, **62**: 497; and WW's Annual Message to Congress, **64**: 77-78, 107-108; Tumulty's suggestions concerning, **65**: 131; Burleson on, **65**: 212; Glass on, **65**: 437-38; Tumulty's fears for if Republicans elected, **66**: 215-16; Houston on, **66**: 455; and WW's State of the Union Message, **66**: 488; The Document on, **67**: 476-77, 484-87, 499-501, 506, 506-507, 600; **68**: 6, 237, 237-38; Davis and Houston work on statement on, **68**: 244-45, 271-72; Baruch on German debt and, **68**: 436
Taxation and Democracy in America (Ratner), **55**: 334n1
Taylor, Alonzo Engelbert, **53**: 649,n1; **65**: 77, 89
Taylor, Arnold H., **56**: 270n5
Taylor, Clara Sears (Mrs. Eugene Whitman), **64**: 3,n1
Taylor, David Watson, **53**: 264,n1
Taylor, Harry, **62**: 437n1
Taylor, Henry Noble, **62**: 20,n1; **63**: 56,n4
Taylor, James Henry, **61**: 595,n1, 624; **67**: 42,n1; **68**: 370,n1; on Berry case, **66**: 227-28,n1, 228; and WW's funeral, **68**: 576, 582
Taylor, William Gordon, **54**: 488,n3
Teal, Joseph Nathan, **66**: 252,n1
Teapot Dome: Oil and Politics in the 1920's (Noggle), **68**: 119n2
Teapot Dome scandal, **68**: 119-20,n2, 121
Tedesco, Francesco, **61**: 109,n4
Tekirad, Turkey: *see* Rodosto
telegraph system: and government control, **53**: 246-49; and censorship, **54**: 448, 449
telephone and telegraph cable, **66**: 499-500; *see also* International Communications, Conference on
telephone and telegraph companies: and issue of returning lines to private ownership, **58**: 215, 365-66, 532-34, 560-61, 602, 603, 606; **59**: 47, 121, 121-22, 296; issue of rate increases, **58**: 459-60, 531; and strike, **60**: 248; 331, 378-79; **61**: 10, 503-504,n1, 530-40; Burleson on return to private ownership, **60**: 378-79
telephone and telegraph workers: and strikes, **56**: 311n1, 340, 403; **57**: 425,n1, 445-46, 446, 511, 530; **58**: 49-50; settlement of strike, **57**: 530,n1, 577
Telfair County, Ga., **62**: 234n4
Tellini, Enrico, **68**: 419n1
temperance: *see* prohibition
Temperley, Harold William Vazeille, **56**: 380n2; **59**: 61n6, 539n1; **60**: 17n1; **62**: 334n1; **65**: 483n1
Ten Days that Shook the World (Reed), **61**: 359
Teng Ssu-yu (S. Y. Teng), **58**: 225n3
Tennant, Hugh Vincent, **68**: 415,n1
Tennant, John Hunter, **68**: 423,n5
Tennessee: and postmastership in Nashville, **65**: 119; and 19th amendment, **65**: 445,n2, 450,n2, 460; Wilson-Walker exchange on woman suffrage, **66**: 30, 35; ratifies Nineteenth Amendment, **66**: 54,n1, 54-55; judgeship appointment in, **66**: 60,n2, 386,n1; election results, **66**: 306n1; Hull to visit, **68**: 86; Democratic party in, **68**: 561
Tenney, Charles Daniel, **66**: 78-79,n1
Tennyson, Alfred Lord, **68**: 584
Ten Years Near the German Frontier: A Retrospect and a Warning (Egan), **53**: 194n1; **65**: 122,n1
Teodor, Novakovic, **57**: 426
Terachui, Masatake, **53**: 556
Ter-Hakobian, Abraham, **57**: 303,n2
Terhune, Warren Jay, **62**: 290,n2
Termination of War and Treaties of Peace (Phillipson), **56**: 68n1
Terni, Italy, **53**: 435
Terrail, Gabriel, **68**: 222n1
Terrell, Mary Eliza Church (Mrs. Robert Heberton), **58**: 140-41,n1
Terrell, Robert Heberton, **62**: 21-22,n1, 100
Terrible Book, A (book review), **68**: 312-13
Territet, Switzerland, **55**: 152
Territorial Claims of the Government of the Hedjaz (Faisal), **54**: 505n3
Teschen: *see* Paris Peace Conference—Teschen; Inter-Allied Commission on Teschen
Teschen Commission: *see* Inter-Allied Commission on Teschen
Teschen question and Plebiscite Commission, **65**: 517-18, 527n3, 529, 532-33; and appointment of U.S. representative to, **64**: 150,n1; **65**: 65-66, 213-14, 217, 255-57, 272, 317
Test of Labor (New York *World*), **62**: 543,n2
Testerman, Cabbell C., **65**: 337,n4

Teusler, Mary Jefferson Bolling (Mrs. Rudolf), **68**: 424n1
Teusler, Rudolf Bolling, M.D., **53**: 629; **59**: 410,n1; **68**: 424,n1
Texas, **56**: 331; Democratic party in, **58**: 497,n1; **67**: 572,n1; **68**: 298n2; and woman suffrage, **58**: 497-98,n2; **59**: 203,n1; and Shillady case, **62**: 527-28, 535-36; appointments in, **65**: 109
Texas Company, **65**: 214,n1, 218; **66**: 289n2
Texas, University of: memorial gateway, **66**: 369n1
Texas Woman Suffrage Association, **59**: 203
Textbook of Medicine (Cecil), **58**: 616-17,n24
Textile Alliance, **68**: 300
textile workers, **62**: 122
Thailand: *see* Siam
Thailand and the United States (Darling), **65**: 21n2
Thanksgiving Day: WW observes, **64**: 93; WW thanks for turkey, **64**: 97
Thanksgiving Proclamation, **53**: 95-96; **63**: 613-15; **66**: 467,n2; as indicator of WW's illness, **63**: 618-19, 644; Lansing and authorship of, **64**: 231; Colby writes, **66**: 331, 342, 345, 350-52; WW thanks Colby for, **66**: 353
Thaon di Revel, Paolo, **56**: 220,n4; **59**: 168,n4, 169
Thaxter, Roland, **67**: 527n4
Thayer, Harvey Waterman, **67**: 182
Thayer, William Sydney, **63**: 576,n3
Thelen, Max, **65**: 296-97,n3,6,7
theater industry: and taxes, **54**: 227,n2
Theater Magazine, **68**: 450
Thelwall, John Walter Francis, **59**: 298,n3
Theodoli, Marquis Alberto, **61**: 109,n13
Theodore Herzl: A Biography (Bein), **55**: 384n4
Theodore Roosevelt Writes on Helping the Cause of World Peace (*New York Times*), **63**: 509,n2
Théry, Edmond Amedée, **56**: 294,n2
Thewlis, Malford Wilcox, M.D., **58**: 636, 638, 639
Thiers, Louis Adolph, **58**: 212; **61**: 220,n2
Thiery, Raymond Donlé, **57**: 442,n2
Thilly, Frank, **67**: 235,n3
Thimme, Annelise, **53**: 121n1
Thomas, Albert, **53**: 8, 9, 344, 387n1; **65**: 249, 360, 361, 569, 570; **66**: 475, 476; **67**: 9,n1
Thomas, Charles Spalding, **53**: 581; **55**: 316; **60**: 243,n2; **63**: 483; on treaty and reservations, **62**: 17, 19; on WW's no-compromise statement, **64**: 192n1; and treaty fight, **64**: 200-201, 336, 338
Thomas, Evan Welling, **55**: 336,n3
Thomas, Martha Carey, **67**: 271n1
Thomas, Norman Mattoon, **54**: 397,n1
Thomas Jefferson Memorial Foundation, **68**: 321, 464n1
Thommen, Edward, **64**: 98

Thompson, Alexander Marshall, **67**: 285,n1
Thompson, Caroline Margaret Cordes (Mrs. Samuel Huston, Jr.), **68**: 187,n3, 302,n1, 512, 515
Thompson, Charles Thaddeus, **61**: 369-70, 370; notes of WW press conference, **61**: 246-52
Thompson, David O., **62**: 300n1
Thompson, Frederick Arthur, **61**: 369,n1
Thompson, Frederick Ingate, **66**: 252,n1
Thompson, Henry Burling, **66**: 232,n2
Thompson, John Anderson, **60**: 147n4
Thompson, John Means, **55**: 161n1, 202n1, 540n1; **56**: 466n1, 575n1; **57**: 93n1, 139n1, 459n2,3; **61**: 455n1
Thompson, Samuel Huston, Jr., **63**: 391,n6; **65**: 385,n1; **68**: 512, 565; WW explains on "peace without victory," **68**: 515; WW suggests for Senate seat, **68**: 301,n2
Thompson, Vance, **54**: 258-59,n1
Thompson, William Howard, **55**: 297,n3
Thompson, William Oxley, **62**: 233,n1; **63**: 7,n1; **64**: 64n1; **65**: 353,n1; **66**: 64, 69; and Industrial Conference, **63**: 611
Thomson, Valentine, **54**: 91,n1, 138,n1, 271
Thomson, William Montgomerie, **54**: 372,n7
Thorn (Toruń), Poland: *see* Paris Peace Conference—Thorn
Thorn-Danzig railroad line: *see* Danzig-Thorn railroad line
Thornton, Henry W., **62**: 287; comparison of railroad situation in Great Britain and U.S., **62**: 288-89
Thorup, Joseph F., **65**: 251n1, 260
Thrace, **65**: 75, 91, 111-12, 113-14, 116; **67**: 375; *see also* Paris Peace Conference—Thrace
Through Thirty Years, 1892-1922, A Personal Narrative (Steed), **56**: 517n1; **57**: 459n2
Thuringen, S.M.S., **55**: 23, 427; **56**: 28; **58**: 127
Thurman, Albert Lee, **63**: 573,n2
Thvedt, N. B., **67**: 18
Thwaites, William, **55**: 58,n6; **56**: 248,n1, 254, 255; **58**: 288, 390; **59**: 590,n8, 599; **61**: 225-26,n1
Ticino (Swiss canton), **57**: 96
Ticonderoga, U.S.S., **66**: 483n2
Tide of Affairs: The Lost Spirituality of American Politics (Frank), **68**: 367,n1
Tientsin, China, **57**: 561n2,3; **58**: 256; conflict between American and Japanese soldiers in, **56**: 184-85,n2, 187
Tiffany, Katrina Brandes Ely (Mrs. Charles Lewis), **67**: 135,n1, 271n1, 369-70, 372, 400, 565, 587; and WW Foundation, **68**: 249n2, 262, 264, 265, 510
Tiflis, Russia, **54**: 372n7
Tighe, M. F., **63**: 149
Tillman, Seth Phillip, **56**: 499n3, 530n4; **57**: 142n1; **60**: 4n3

Tilsit (now Sovetsk, U.S.S.R.), **60**: 160
Tilsit, Treaty of (1807), **54**: 241
Tilton, McLane, **67**: 495,n1, 559
Timeless Affair: The Life of Anita McCormick Blaine (Harrison), **55**: 441n4
Tims, Margaret, **58**: 141n1; **59**: 117n4
Tinkham, George Holden, **62**: 160,n4
Tinoco Granados, Féderico, **54**: 46,n4; **61**: 639,n9; **63**: 616n1; **64**: 186, 229, 245, 317; **65**: 46, 465-66, 506, 510, 571
Tinoco Granados, Joaquin, **63**: 616n1
Tippy, Worth Marion, **65**: 183,n3
Tirebolu, Turkey, **65**: 74
"'Tired of Waiting': Senator Albert B. Fall's Alternative to Woodrow Wilson's Mexican Policies" (Trow), **64**: 120n1
Tirol, The: *see* Tyrol, The
Tirpitz, Alfred Peter Friedrich von, **57**: 121,n2; **67**: 222; and penalties, **62**: 318
Tisza, Count István, **56**: 242,n3, 254, 414, 459
Tittemore, James Nelson, **62**: 623,n1
Tittoni, Tommaso, **53**: 602n1; **58**: 240,n5, 338; **61**: 60, 109,n6,11, 191,n2, 211, 212, 213, 214, 216, 217, 218, 220, 221, 222, 308, 309, 336, 342n3, 483, 588n4; **62**: 22, 25, 26n3, 156,n6, 207, 253, 264, 319, 606; **63**: 62, 484; **65**: 94; **67**: 440; White on, **61**: 347-48; Clemenceau on, **61**: 375; White meets with on Adriatic question and rejects Italy's proposal, **61**: 551-54; reply to Anglo-French note, **61**: 602,n3; on Thrace, **62**: 110, 141, 239-40; and Fiume and Adriatic question, **62**: 456, 457, 575, 603; **63**: 91-92, 270, 297, 364-66, 393, 424, 465, 517, 525, 526, 617n1; **64**: 174-75, 178, 300, 304; **66**: 467,n2
Titus, Louis: appointed to first Industrial Conference, **63**: 300,n1
Tiumen, Russia, **62**: 87
To an Anxious Friend (W. A. White), **68**: 148n5
Tobin, Daniel J., **65**: 20
Tobolsk, Russia, **62**: 87
Tocqueville, Alexis-Charles-Henri-Maurice-Clérel de, **68**: 40
Todd, Ambrose Giddings, **67**: 334,n2
Todd, Mrs. Erard, **67**: 213
Todd, George Carroll, **53**: 587,n3; and Attorney General position, **54**: 31,n1, 52, 410, 428-30; **60**: 115,n4,6; WW accepts resignation of, **55**: 394; on legal question of U.S. early membership in League of Nations, **55**: 478-79
Togoland, **54**: 253, 311, 318-22, 325; **58**: 484, 485, 486, 510; **59**: 328, 338, 375; **62**: 426, 481, 532, 595; **63**: 422
Tökés, Rudolf Leslie, **56**: 182n1
Tokyo: earthquake in, **68**: 424,n1
Tokyo Asahi, **62**: 64
Tokyo Chuo Koron, **62**: 65
Tokyo Hochi, **62**: 64-65
Tokyo Imperial University, **60**: 476n25
Tokyo Jiji, **62**: 64

Tokyo Yamato, **62**: 65
Toledo, Ohio, *Times*, **58**: 51
Tomasi, Pietro Paolo: *see* Della Torretta, Marchese
Tomsk, Russia, **60**: 608; **62**: 87
Toole, James F., M.D., **58**: 607, 611, 635-38; **62**: 628n1, 634-35; **64**: 507n11
Topchibashev, Ali Marden Bek, **58**: 333n2
Topeka Daily Capital, **61**: 602,n3
To Put Our Unemployed at Work Anew, and to Export Our Surplus Products, America Must Co-Operate with Europe (Filene), **67**: 471n1
To Raise an Army: The Draft Comes to Modern America (Chambers), **65**: 355n1, 576n1; **66**: 58n1
Torre, Andrea, **53**: 599n1
Torres, Elias, **66**: 405n5
Torretta, Marchese della: *see* Della Torretta, Marchese
Toruń, Poland: *see* Poland—Thorn
Tosti, Gustavo, **60**: 476,n24
Tottenham, Francis Loftus, **68**: 415,n1
Touranianism: *see* Pan-Touranianism
Tournai, Belgium, **56**: 589
Toward a New Order of Sea Power: American Naval Policy and the World Scene, 1918-1922 (Sprout and Sprout), **57**: 142n1; **62**: 460n1
Tower, Sir Reginald (Thomas), **66**: 226,n4
Towers, John Henry, **60**: 44,n1, 430
To Whom Are We Responsible? A Memorandum on the Freedom of Teachers (Meiklejohn), **68**: 390,n2
Town and Country, **68**: 450
Townsend, Charles Elroy, **53**: 582-83,n5; **61**: 372; and Versailles treaty, **64**: 94, 200-201, 337, 339
Townsend, Mary T. Scott (Mrs. Richard H.), **59**: 159,n1
Townsley, Chief Ranger, **68**: 122,n2
Toy, Crawford Howell, **67**: 189n1
Toy, Nancy Saunders (Mrs. Crawford Howell), **67**: 105n3, 189,n1, 198, 543-44; WW thanks for birthday greetings, **67**: 520; on WW Foundation's success, **67**: 526-27, 531
Tozzi, Pietro, **57**: 527,n1, 575
Trabson, Turkey: *see* Trebizond
Trachtenberg, Marc, **65**: 326n4; **67**: 109n1
Trade Commission: *see* Federal Trade Commission
Trades Union Congress (Great Britain), **53**: 535-36; **54**: 257,n2
Trading with the Enemy Act, **53**: 147-48, 198, 260, 289, 432; **61**: 418-19, 498; **62**: 424
Tradition and Progress (Murray), **67**: 561,n2
Trammell, Park, **53**: 717; **63**: 483; and woman suffrage, **54**: 56, 274, 281, 302, 555; and treaty fight, **64**: 200-201, 336, 338-39; and Treaty of Berlin, 1921, **67**: 422,n2

transatlantic flight, **60**: 44,n1, 430-31; first, **57**: 447,n1

Trans-Baikal Railway, **61**: 580; **64**: 221; **66**: 51

Trans-Baikalia: Japanese withdrawal from, **65**: 515-16

Trans-Caspian Railway, **53**: 335

Trans-Caucasia, **55**: 61, 62

Transformation of American Foreign Relations, 1865-1900 (Campbell), **56**: 531n5

transit companies: and electric railways, **59**: 287-88

transportation: The Document on having Cabinet position on, **68**: 7, 219, 539-40

Transportation Act of 1920: *see* Esch-Cummins bill and Act

Transportation Board, Federal (proposed), **67**: 559, 591; **68**: 7, 30, 219, 539-40

Trans-Siberian Railway, **53**: 256, 463n1, 555-56,n4, 629n3; **54**: 83n3, 84, 158n1, 412, 487; **55**: 38-39, 187, 350; **56**: 152, 153, 519, 576-77, 606; **57**: 134, 314, 315, 420,n1; **58**: 575; **59**: 438n11; **61**: 571-72, 580-81; **62**: 83-87, 590-91; **64**: 220, 221; and operating funds, **57**: 420-22,n2

Transvaal Province, Union of South Africa, **54**: 298

Transylvania, **53**: 294; **64**: 299, 447; **65**: 138; *see also* Paris Peace Conference—Transylvania

Trapp, Martin Edward, **64**: 466,n1

Trask, David Frederic, **56**: 531n5

Trask, Kate (Katrina) Nichols (Mrs. Spencer), **65**: 332-33

Trask, Kate Nichols (after Feb. 5, 1921, Kate Trask Peabody; Mrs. George Foster Peabody), **67**: 91-92,n1, 95; **68**: 154n1; EBW's congratulations on forthcoming marriage, **67**: 106-107; WW on marriage of, **67**: 117; death of, **67**: 510,n1

Trau (Trogir), Yugoslavia, **57**: 483; **58**: 239, 426, 452; **59**: 506; **63**: 557n1,2

Travels in the Slavonic Provinces of Turkey-in-Europe (Mackenzie and Irby), **64**: 160,n4

Treasury, Department of the, **56**: 397; **58**: 596, 597; and postwar reconstruc-tion, **53**: 14-15; McAdoo's resignation, **53**: 58, 74, 150-51; **62**: 222, 498; and wheat prices, **56**: 619, 620; amd Victory Loan, **59**: 75n1; and Italian credits, **59**: 71, 111, 112, 113; WW on Glass' suggestions, **63**: 336; Glass leaves, **64**: 42, 350; mentioned in Annual Message, **64**: 107; Houston becomes Secretary of, **64**: 349; Leffingwell willing to defer resignation from, **64**: 349-50, 361-62, 362; resignation of N. H. Davis, **65**: 147, 381; Houston on legislation for new budget and auditing system, **65**: 358; suggestions for WW's message to

Congress, **66**: 435-36; Houston on relief funds and, **66**: 529-30

Treat, Charles Gould, **53**: 290,n1, 291, 486,n3

Treat, Payson J., **62**: 359n23

Treaties, Conventions, International Acts, Protocols and Agreements between the United States of America and Other Powers (Malloy, comp.), **56**: 58n3

Treaties, Their Making and Enforcement (Crandall), **56**: 58n3, 68

Treaty of 1839 (Belgian neutrality), **57**: 23, 122, 124, 396; **58**: 550; **59**: 289; **60**: 157; **61**: 11n2; **67**: 145

Treaty of Berlin: *see* Berlin, Treaty of, 1878; Berlin, Treaty of, 1921

Treaty of Bucharest, **55**: 376

Treaty of 1819 (with Spain): *see* Adams-Onís Treaty

Treaty of Frankfurt (1871), **57**: 335; **58**: 23

Treaty of London (April 26, 1915), **53**: 43,n1, 434, 466, 621, 711n1; **54**: 51, 326n3; **55**: 160; **58**: 18-19, 48, 57, 76 77, 89, 97, 279, 280, 369, 370, 371, 380, 391, 398, 413, 473, 475; **59**: 34, 39, 41, 42, 81, 85, 86, 96, 97, 99, 102, 201, 269, 328, 374, 519n2, 578; **60**: 209, 210-11, 271, 308; **61**: 171, 342, 343, 344, 345; **66**: 499; and and Adriatic question, **57**: 243,n2, 490-91 501, 504, 513, 514, 516, 520, 534, 536, 540, 548, 551, 576, 585, 613; **60**: 209, 210-11, 271, 308; **62**: 41, 365n27, 367,n30, 375; **63**: 209; WW on, **57**: 344, 492-93, 519, 531, 542, 543; **58**: 55, 103, 250, 251-52; **61**: 237, 242, 420; **64**: 462-63; WW's Adriatic statement, **58**: 5, 6; and Fiume, **58**: 53, 80, 87, 239n4; Lloyd George on, **58**: 58, 59, 372-73; Orlando on, **58**: 237n3; Lodge on, **58**: 359n1; issue of Italy breaking, **58**: 339-40, 341, 376, 382; and Italy's insistence on execution of, **59**: 478, 479, 480, 480-81, 493, 494, 503, 505, 506, 507, 508, 509, 551, 552, 553; and Italian-Austrian boundary, **59**: 587; Council of Four on Fiume and Italy and, **61**: 219, 221, 222-23; White and Tittoni on, **61**: 553; Balfour on Adriatic question and, **62**: 23, 25; threat of enforcement of, **64**: 263-64, 264,n1, 298, 302, 304, 305, 313, 314, 315, 319, 341, 376, 377-78, 398, 400, 439-40, 480-81; Britain and France answer WW's charges concerning Adriatic question and, **64**: 355n1, 359, 360; *see also* London, Treaty of, 1915

Treaty of Peace with Germany: Hearings before the Committee on Foreign Relations, United States Senate, 66th Cong., 1st sess., **62**: 148n2, 264n1; **63**: 118n2

Treaty of Saint Germain: a Documentary History of Its Territorial and Political Clauses (Almond and Lutz, eds.), **59**: 60n3; **60**: 34n2

Treaty of Versailles: *see* Paris Peace Conference—German Treaty

Trebizond, Turkey, **59**: 186; **65**: 74, 114, 309, 321, 322, 538; **66**: 29n1

Tredwell, Roger Culver, **53**: 312-13,n1

Trenton Evening Times, **68**: 458, 590

Trenton True American, **66**: 352n1

Trieste, **63**: 298, 485; **65**: 315

Treitschke, Heinrich von, **56**: 361,n4

Tremaine, Charles Milton, **64**: 346,n2

Trente, Austria (now Trento, Italy), **54**: 112n3; **59**: 539

Trentino, **53**: 381, 434, 642, 696; *see also* Paris Peace Conference —Trentino

Trepassey, Newfoundland, **57**: 447n1

Trescot, William Henry, **66**: 210,n4

Trèves, Claudio, **53**: 434,n1; **65**: 304,n12

Trèves (Trier), Prussia, **54**: 172, 212; **55**: 52, 212; **59**: 237

Treviso, Italy, **53**: 290

Trial of Scott Nearing and the American Socialist Society, **55**: 337n1

Trial of the Kaiser (Scott), **56**: 530n4

"Trial of the Kaiser" (trans. from *Osservatore Romano*), **62**: 27,n2

Trianon, Treaty of, **66**: 377

Tribute of a Friend (Tumulty), **66**: 292n2

Trier, Germany, **55**: 52, 212

Trieste, **53**: 434, 445, 696; **64**: 174, 299, 301, 370; **65**: 315; *see also* Paris Peace Conference—Trieste

Trimble, South, **64**: 93, 97; **66**: 421,n1

Trinity College, Oxford, **53**: 162n1

Trinkle, Elbert Lee, **68**: 188,n3

Trinkle, Helen Sue, **68**: 188

Tripartite Pact of Sevres, **66**: 429n1

Tripoli, Lebanon, **54**: 506; **59**: 334-35, 344

Tripolitania, **58**: 435n7

Triumph of Ideals; Speeches, Messages and Addresses made by the President between February 24, 1919 and July 8, 1919, **67**: 515,n1

Trotsky, Leon (Leib or Lev Davydovich), **54**: 92,n1,2, 94, 155,n2, 419; **55**: 320; **56**: 242, 337, 390, 548n1, 551n1; **59**: 519,n2; **60**: 168; **62**: 204-205,n2, 365n27; **63**: 559, 588n1; **64**: 234n3; **66**: 154

Trotsky Dictator; Arrests Lenine (*New York Times*), **54**: 92n2

Trotter, William Monroe, **60**: 486,n1; **61**: 186; asks for appointment with WW, **60**: 572-73; WW cannot meet with, **60**: 641; and equal rights clause in Covenant of League of Nations, **61**: 27-28,n2

Troubridge, Sir Ernest (Charles Thomas), **58**: 566,n2

Trow, Clifford W., **62**: 155n1; **63**: 276n5; **64**: 120n1

Truax *v.* Corrigan, **67**: 497,n1

Trumbić, Ante, **55**: 88n1; **57**: 369-70, 481,n2, 500, 545; on Fiume, **56**: 567-72, 577; **58**: 150, 588; **59**: 34, 68n2, 96, 125n1, 126, 174, 200, 630; **60**: 97,n8;

65: 303,n10; **66**: 364, 377; meets with D. W. Johnson on Adriatic problem, **60**: 137-38; **64**: 298, 303-305, 313, 314, 315, 340, 341-42; photograph of, *illustration section* **57**

trusteeships: *see* Paris Peace Conference—mandates

Truth About the Peace Treaties (Lloyd George), **56**: 12n1; **57**: 145n1, 147n5; **60**: 4n3

Truth About the Treaty (Tardieu), **55**: 475n2; **56**: 12n1; **57**: 65n2; **65**: 542n1; **67**: 360n2

Ts'ao Ju'lin, **54**: 475,n3; **58**: 553,n3; **62**: 65,n1

Tserderbaum, Yulii Osipovich: *see* Martov, L.

Tsinan, China, **53**: 207; **58**: 175, 184, 221, 234

Tsinanfu, China, **58**: 72

Tsingtao, China, **53**: 207; **54**: 308; **57**: 298, 299, 371, 555, 561n5, 616; **58**: 69, 70, 71, 72, 166, 175, 221, 224, 228, 233, 234, 246, 257, 259, 271n1, 272; **60**: 104; **61**: 325n5; **62**: 155, 170

Tsingtao-Chinan Raiilway, **57**: 298, 299, 431n1, 554, 555, 601, 609; **58**: 175, 216-17, 259, 261

Tuan Ch'i-jui, **53**: 138-39,n2; **61**: 633,n2

Tucker, Rev. Irwin St. John, **62**: 557,n1

Tumulty, Joseph Patrick, **53**: 12, 28, 60, 67, 180, 216, 236, 305, 308, 370, 371, 375-76, 382, 391, 401, 405, 450, 469, 491,542, 571, 636, 646, 709-10; **54**: 53-54, 57-58, 106-107, 125, 132, 194, 500-501,n1, 554-55; **55**: 162, 184, 194, 198, 222, 229, 254, 278, 279, 324, 340, 347, 392, 407, 409, 410, 411, 448-49, 458, 493, 495, 500, 529, 532; **56**: 57, 156, 162-63, 191, 311, 435-36, 552-53; **57**: 49, 99, 146, 235, 350, 425, 445-46, 471-72, 477, 509, 511, 578, 630; **58**: 104, 145, 176, 243, 248, 270, 328, 420, 496, 560; **59**: 75, 120-21, 189, 203, 447, 449, 450, 476, 478-79, 553, 604; **60**: 41, 42, 111, 112-13, 153-54, 155, 197, 198, 247, 297, 487, 568, 569, 573, 644-45; **61**: 231, 370, 373, 386, 489, 495, 507, 509, 533, 563, 564, 577, 605, 626, 628; **62**: 10, 51, 104, 162, 181, 241n1, 336, 419, 435, 469, 530, 536, 542-43, 576, 609, 626; **63**: 51, 52, 64, 91, 92, 117, 117-18, 150, 163, 165, 198, 221, 235, 264, 268, 296, 302, 369, 371, 444, 447, 483, 490, 514, 552,n1, 556, 582, 606, 625, 626; **64**: 1-4, 7n1, 87, 94-95, 97, 130, 141, 216, 261-62, 270, 286, 327,n1, 351, 353, 355, 366, 384, 386, 397, 420, 459, 473-74, 480, 490, 511n1; **65**: 24, 28, 40, 48, 56, 81-82, 143, 146, 152, 183, 332, 397, 448, 460, 491, 506, 522, 563, 564, 576; **66**: 66, 108, 112, 120, 173, 269, 281, 292, 317, 319, 434, 435, 521; **67**: 24, 38-39, 94, 119, 190, 212, 243, 425, 460, 579n3, 614, 617; **68**: 137, 259n2, 459, 576, 585-87, 591; on a

Tumulty, Joseph Patrick (*cont.*)
program for 1920, **53**: 23-24; on reassuring business and industry on postwar reconstruction, **53**: 77-78; to stay in U.S. and keep WW informed on U.S. views, **53**: 156; on WW's prohibition of grain in soft drinks, **53**: 413; on WW visiting Vatican, **53**: 421; on newspaper policy and peace conference, **53**: 440; warns of Clemenceau-Lloyd George agreement, **53**: 440-41; on Irish Home Rule, **53**: 570; **54**: 332-33, 381; on death of T. Roosevelt, **53**: 624; on U.S. public opinion on League of Nations, **53**: 625; **55**: 197-98, 214, 540; suggests WW return to Boston instead of New York, **53**: 625-26, 698; on government control of railroads, **53**: 626; suggestions for Director General of Railroads, **53**: 704; and Gregory's resignation, **53**: 705, 706; and woman suffrage, **53**: 717; **54**: 228-29, 274, 519, 555; **55**: 368; **58**: 273-74, 364, 606; **60**: 247; **64**: 466,n2; **66**: 30n1; on Attorney General appointment, **54**: 31-32, 52, 410, 428-30, 485; and famine relief bill, **54**: 55, 258; on W. G. Sharp's resignation, **54**: 57; and publicity and censorship of Paris Peace Conference, **54**: 105, 158; on proclamation on brewing industry, **54**: 193-94, 227; on U.S. commercial and economic recovery, **54**: 390-93; on oil-leasing bill, **54**: 471; on parade in Washington for returning soldiers, **55**: 36, 37; plans for WW's arrival in Boston, **55**: 205-206, 218, 218-19, 222, 223, 225, 226, 231; suggests WW address various League of Nations societies, **55**: 289-90; on granting amnesty, **55**: 344, 344-45; recommends WW meet with Irish contingent, **55**: 368; WW on Irish and, **55**: 474; on reviewing court-martial sentences, **56**: 192; on Debs case, **56**: 245, 310, 618; **67**: 157,n1; on telegraphers labor situation, **56**: 340-41; and steel prices, **56**: 341; on abolishing cable censorship, **56**: 373-74; on WW asserting his leadership, **56**: 436; on proposed recognition of Lenin, **56**: 551; on need for WW to take "dramatic action," **57**: 37, 60; on WW summoning *U.S.S. George Washington*, **57**: 177, 194; concern over fate of League of Nations, **57**: 188-89; on railroad situation and the Treasury, **57**: 376; on New England telephone strike, **57**: 511, 530; and controversy between Railroad Administration and Industrial Board, **57**: 629; **58**: 329; **59**: 38,n1; on French security treaty, **57**: 629,n1; denies WW entered into secret treaties, **58**: 104n2; on WW's Adriatic statement, **58**: 105; and Shantung controversy, **58**: 105, 170, 272-73, 273, 329, 363, 364; **62**: 150-51; **63**: 576; WW thanks for support, **58**: 144; on tele-

phone and telegraph lines, **58**: 145-46, 560-61, 602; **59**: 121-22; on Italian crisis, **58**: 215; on labor clauses in peace treaty, **58**: 361-63, 364; and call for special session of Congress, **58**: 421, 498; on increased telephone rates, **58**: 459-69, 531; on building foreign ships in U.S. shipyards, **58**: 460, 531; and news accounts of Italy getting Fiume, **58**: 531-32, 601; and Liberty Loan, **58**: 560; on prohibition law, **58**: 603-604; **59**: 38-39, 76, 77; **61**: 183-84, 294, 351; **64**: 262; suggests topics for WW's speech to Congress, **58**: 605-606; urges quick action on issues facing Congress, **59**: 47; on costof living, **59**: 77; on Gay for appointment to Shipping Board, **59**: 121, 160; on tariff, **59**: 121; on Gompers and labor program of League of Nations, **59**: 203; on demonstration in New York protesting treatment of eastern European Jews, **59**: 419; on Republican opposition to League of Nations Covenant, **59**: 524,n1; on WW's Memorial Day message, **60**: 18; and appointment of Palmer as Attorney General, **60**: 116; suggestions for WW's speeches on return to U.S., **60**: 145-53; on Hitchcock Resolution, **60**: 198; on threatened telephone and telegraph strike, **60**: 248; on Irish situation, **60**: 291, 298, 331-32; **61**: 9, 182-83, 185, 293; on Knox Resolution, **60**: 376-78, 535, 536; on leak investigation on peace treaty, **60**: 536; on not separating League of Nations Covenant from peace treaty, **60**: 536; WW answers on Knox Resolution, **60**: 609; on situation in U.S. and program for WW on his return, **60**: 610-11; on Root's League of Nations strategy, **61**: 66; on issue of treaty adoption without reservations, **61**: 115-16, 116, 137; on plans for WW's arrival in New York, **61**: 182, 350, 371, 376; on Republican efforts for joint congressional resolution declaring state of peace between Germany and U.S., **61**: 184, 290; on WW preparing congratulatory message on treaty signing, **61**: 184; on WW's statement on reservations, **61**: 184; WW answers on variety of issues, **61**: 290-91; suggestions for WW on return to U.S., **61**: 350; on amnesty issue, **61**: 351, 352; list of senators opposing League of Nations unless reservations adopted, **61**: 372; advises WW on addressingSenate alone, **61**: 383, 388; and WW's address to Senate, **61**: 397; on *Nation* article on Bullitt mission to Russia, **61**: 509; on WW making speech clarifying peace treaty and issue of reservations, **61**: 534; and wheat prices, **61**: 549n1; on Catholics and League of Nations, **61**: 627; suggestions for WW's message on cost of living, **62**: 180-81, 196-97; on

U.S. role in world economic situation, **62**: 196-97; draft of letter to Lodge on urgency of treaty ratification, **62**: 272; advises WW make statement on reservations (Lodge letter), **62**: 309,n1; and railroad situation, **62**: 454; and WW's western tour, **62**: 507n1; proposed follow-up message to railway shopmen, **62**: 543-44; on steel situation, **62**: 581-82; and proposed women's international labor conference, **63**: 58-59; on plans for California tour, **63**: 164; and steel strike, **63**: 164; strategy and ideas for WW's speeches, **63**: 164, 222-23, 397-99; on WW's reaction to Bullitt testimony, **63**: 338n4; on answering criticism of WW's opponents, **63**: 399-400; and possible horrors of next war, **63**: 441; plans for Albert's visit, **63**: 515; on trip cancellation, **63**: 519, 522-23; organizes WW's return to Washington, **63**: 522, 531-32; WW discusses treaty with via telephone, **63**: 537; on WW's health, **63**: 539, 539n1, 542, 548, 586, 619; **64**: 99, 100, 125, 455; **66**: 62-63, 451; loyalty to WW indicates he will never certify WW is disabled, **63**: 547,n1, 638; on first Industrial Conference, **63**: 554,n1, 590, 591; WW's unavailability to during illness, **63**: 567, 638; and coal strike, **63**: 593-94, 595-98; and veto message of Volstead bill, **63**: 601n1; appointment suggestions for second Industrial Conference, **63**: 602, 609-12; and reorganization of European transportation, **63**: 613; messages to WW filter through EBW, **63**: 615; on proposed super cabinet, **63**: 625; I. Hoover on WW's illness and, **63**: 637, 638,n6; role during WW's illness, **63**: 638,n6, 645; and EBW as conduit to WW, **64**: 4, 6, 10, 14, 42, 65, 66, 93, 97, 103, 156, 198, 204-205, 233, 245, 246; involvement in WW's Annual Message to Congress, **64**: 6, 16, 72, 90, 123, 125; and *Imperator* controversy, **64**: 7; and wheat to Armenia, **64**: 114; Hitchcock letter, **64**: 15, 238, 276-77,n1, 278-82; **65**: 7n1, 24-25; on railroad crisis and controversy over date of return to private ownership, **64**: 16, 21, 189n1, 222, 222,n1, 228, 391, 396-97, 467; on appointments, **64**: 52n1, 142n2, 296, 330, 448; on U.S. unofficial participation on Reparation Commission, **64**: 91-92; Lansing on political decision making and, **64**: 124; and coal strike negotiations, **64**: 142, 143, 144, 154-55, 206n1; and Mooney case, **64**: 145; and recognition of Costa Rica, **64**: 153, 229-30; on rumors of W. B. Wilson's resignation, **64**: 176; and Thrace, **64**: 181; and treatment of Lord Grey, **64**: 188n1, 235, 239; on WW's statement on no compromise being "body blow," **64**: 190; and draft of WW's challenge to op-position senators, **64**: 199n1; relationship with Lansing, **64**: 243; draft and redraft of Jackson Day message, **64**: 247-49, 259n1, 269,n3, 270; Lansing on as a conduit to WW, **64**: 269; and Fosdick dilemma and resignation, **64**: 274n1, 310; on WW's opportunity to act on treaty, **64**: 287; receives marked copy of Lodge reservations, **64**: 288-95; on requests for WW to participate in fund raising "schemes," **64**: 345-46; R. S. Baker on, **64**: 359, 365; and Frazier affair, **64**: 383, 384, 452; on Fletcher's resignation, **64**: 397; on Lansing's resignation, **64**: 415, 416, 417,n3, 418; suggestions for Lansing's successor, **64**: 419, 427-28; and Cabinet meetings during WW's illness, **64**: 455-56; on possibility of Marshall taking over, **64**: 455; on Adriatic question, **64**: 473; and railroad bill, **64**: 474, 475, 480; on treaty situation in Senate and concern over ratification with Lodge reservations, **64**: 479-80; **65**: 7n1, 24-25; suggestions for new railroad arbitration board, **65**: 44-45; on Article X and suggestions for Hitchcock letter, **65**: 66; and coal situation, **65**: 95, 553; and issue of WW's third term, **65**: 117-18, 435, 493-94, 499; on recommendations of coal commission, **65**: 117; on Democratic party's treaty strategy, **65**: 122; suggested message to Congress, **65**: 128-34; on Volstead Act, **65**: 132-34, 452-55; and Sisson documents, **65**: 134,n1,2; House and Polk on relationship of WW and, **65**: 139; ability to imitate WW's writing style, **65**: 140; on issue of WW's name on ballot in Georgia primary, **65**: 145-46; and woman suffrage, **65**: 163, 294; and railroad situation, **65**: 175, 215, 451-52,n2; on Railroad Labor Board nominations, **65**: 189; on timing of amnesty proclamation, **65**: 190; suggests thank-you note to Hines, **65**: 215; on answering Knox and Lodge on treaty reservations, **65**: 257; on Socialist petition for pardon of Debs, **65**: 276n1; on Democratic platform, **65**: 291-92, 488; on corrupt practices bill, **65**: 354; on budget and audit bill, **65**: 361-62; answer to labor on issue of Congress' adjournment, **65**: 368-69; Geddes on, **65**: 371; suggests J. H. Small for International Joint Commission, **65**: 378; on Lodge's comments on League of Nations at Republican convention, **65**: 388; on water-power bill, **65**: 398; and offer of films for WW, **65**: 400,n1; plans for Seibold interview with WW, **65**: 401n1; Seibold on WW's work routine with, **65**: 406, 408; on Retirement Act, **65**: 478, 519-20; on never seeing Cummings' coded messages to WW, **65**: 481, 552; and WW's alleged statement on

Tumulty, Joseph Patrick (*cont.*)
Cox, **65**: 494-95,n1,2; concern over convention situation and choice of candidate, **65**: 497-98; on appointment of Federal Fuel Administrator, **65**: 508-509; and Burleson, **65**: 511n2; on possible controversy over WW meeting with Cox on a Sunday, **65**: 513; and Illinois coal strike, **65**: 544, 545, 546; on J. L. Lewis' coal statement, **65**: 568n1; on advance newspaper reviews of Cox's speech, **66**: 4; offered but declines appointment to customs Court of Appeals, **66**: 6, 531; campaign involvement and strategy, **66**: 7, 118, 141, 148-49, 149-50, 223, 242-43, 245, 249-50, 258, 289; on appointment of Cummings to Cabinet, **66**: 7-8; on Alexander's wish to be on Shipping Board, **66**: 7, 195-96; on Tariff Commission appointment, **66**: 8; on Anthracite Coal Commissin's decision, **66**: 77n1; and MacSwiney case, **66**: 90; on Berry case, **66**: 102-103; urges WW to take part in campaign, **66**: 118, 249-50, 258; and H. Ford on anti-Semitism, **66**: 130-31,n1; on Polish-Lithuanian border dispute, **66**: 138-39; and Armistice Day proclamation, **66**: 151,n1,2, 204; and Wilson-Spencer controversy, **66**: 172n1, 187-88, 191-92, 197n3, 198n1; on WW's statement on League of Nations referendum, **66**: 175-76; on Harding-Schurman correspondence, **66**: 199-200,n2; on churches' attitude toward League of Nations, **66**: 200-204; on coal transport problems, **66**: 205-206; on Harding's speech rejecting League of Nations, **66**: 208; statement for WW on national devastation if Republicans elected, **66**: 214-16; on Root's speech and statement of the 31 Republicans, **66**: 246-47; on Viereck's statement on German-Americans, **66**: 248,n1, 249; on reinstatement of outlaw strikers, **66**: 254; and Boy Scouts' request, **66**: 282,n1; advises WW to write to Cox, **66**: 289; is confident on election eve, **66**: 298; suggests Champ Clark for appointment, **66**: 333-34; and Kipling poem, **66**: 352-53, 386; and literary request for rights to WW's works, **66**: 416-17, 420; loyalty to WW, **66**: 451; and WW's veto of extension of Section 10 of Clayton Act, **67**: 12n1; WW annoyed at request for condolence, **67**: 30; on taking new photograph of WW and Cabinet, **67**: 126; and coordination of relief effort, **67**: 139n1, 140n3; and appointment to Canadian Commission, **67**: 168,n1; on experience of working with WW, **67**: 202-203; praises EBW, **67**: 202; and inauguration day ceremonies, **67**: 205, 209, 211, 212; successor to, **67**: 208; and Pierce-Arrow accident claim, **67**: 303-304,n1, 385, 388; and WW maintaining silence, **67**: 314, 602; and WW

Clubs, **67**: 315, 345, 352-53; and WW's admission to Washington bar, **67**: 329; and syndicated articles on WW, **67**: 414,n2, 434; book of, **67**: 447; on Jackson Day banquet in Ohio, **67**: 543; and WW foundation, **67**: 547n1; brouhaha over Jefferson Day telegram, **68**: 10, 11-12, 14-15, 20, 21, 28, 51, 59-60, 591; explains and takes responsibility for Jefferson Day message, **68**: 14-15, 20-21; WW's attempt to remove as his secretary, **68**: 527,n4; and WW's last illnesss, **68**: 577, 560, 565; WW suggests as senatorial candidate, **68**: 591-92, 595
Tumulty and Leavenworth: A Case Study in Rumor (Blum), **65**: 401n1
Tumulty, Mary Byrne (Mrs. Joseph Patrick), **57**: 236; Geddes on, **65**: 371,n5
Tupper, Henry Allen, **65**: 275
Turati, Filippo, **58**: 94n1, 240n6, 313,n4
Turin, Italy, **53**: 435, 507, 589; WW's arrival and speech in, **53**: 620-21, 622-24
Turkestan, **53**: 176
Turkey and Turks, **53**: 15-16, 38, 56, 293, 294, 296, 561, 672, 685, 689; **63**: 49, 71, 74, 100, 236; **64**: 26, 27, 344-45, 358, 448-50; **66**: 429n1; Tardieu on Thrace and, **63**: 121, 122; war costs, **63**: 221, 243, 349; Vénisélos on Greece and, **64**: 157-64; and Armenia, **65**: 287, 306, 308-10, 321-22; Egan praises Morgenthau's work in, **65**: 121; Polk on terms of Turkish treaty, **65**: 64-65; and Greeks of Euxine Pontus, **66**: 29n1; Lloyd George on, **66**: 47; and Armenian boundary dispute, **66**: 86n1, 350, 436; **67**: 63-67; army advance in Asia Minor, **68**: 141,n1, 147,n3; WW on situation in, **68**: 142; and League of Nations, **68**: 477; and Chester concession, **68**: 504,n1; *see also* Paris Peace Conference—Turkey
Turkish-American treaty of amity and commerce (Lausanne Treaty), **68**: 431-32,n2, 499-500, 502, 504n1; WW's views on are not for publication, **68**: 499-500, 505
Turkish Empire: and mandates, **62**: 188,n3, 235, 242, 511-14, 580; **64**: 25-27; **65**: 91; *see also* Ottoman Empire
Turkhan Pasha, **59**: 186
Turnbull, Archibald Douglas, **57**: 447n1
Turner, Frederick Jackson, **53**: 264-70,n1; **67**: 76n3, 161, 264, 163; and WW Clubs, **67**: 253, 258,n1,2, 264
Tuscania, S.S., **53**: 275n3
Tuscany: earthquake in, **66**: 323,n2
Tuttle, William M., Jr., **61**: 357n1; **62**: 234n1
Twain, Mark, **65**: 305; **67**: 397, 573
Tweedale, Alonzo, **62**: 466
Twenty-One Demands, **57**: 617-18, 620, 621-22, 636; **58**: 137n1, 165, 221, 245, 258; **61**: 237, 242, 249-50, 556, 557, 558; **67**: 531n1
Tygodnik Polski, **55**: 370,n2

Tyler, David Gardiner, **55**: 444,n6
Tyler, Lyon Gardiner, **55**: 444,n7; **62**: 588; **63**: 463
Tyler, Royall, **56**: 240,n1; **58**: 307,n1; **60**: 178,n1, 256,n2
Tyrol, The, **53**: 6-7, 8, 644, 649, 711n1; **62**: 24, 25; **65**: 481; **67**: 375; see also Paris Peace Conference—Tyrol, The
Tyrrell, Sir William (George), **54**: 386; **57**: 35; **62**: 254n2, 525,n1; **63**: 606n1; **64**: 53, 217

Uchida, Viscount Yasuya, **53**: 463n1, 556; **57**: 314,n2, 582-85, 607,n8; **62**: 154, 170, 171
Ufa, Russia, **56**: 254; **60**: 95n2; **62**: 87; Directorate, **59**: 152,n1
Uganda, **54**: 368
Ughet, Serge, **55**: 351,n2; **59**: 234,n2
Uglian (Ugliano) (now Uljan, Yugoslavia), **62**: 604, 620; **63**: 91, 206, 207, 208
Ukraine, **53**: 56, 713; **54**: 33,n5,7, 92, 100, 136-37, 340, 342-43, 403,n3, 480n1
Ukraine: A Concise Encyclopedia (Kubijovyc, ed.) **54**: 480n1; **58**: 505n4
Ukrainian Republic and Ukrainians, **58**: 539, 543; **59**: 130; Poles and Poland and, **56**: 96,n1, 97, 119, 126-27,n1, 326; and temporary truce with Poland, **56**: 468-69,n1, 469, 529-30,n2; and conflict with Poland, **57**: 275-80, 328-29, 356, 365, 372, 415-16, 444-45, 451, 461-64; **58**: 101-102, 316, 455, 505-506,n4; **59**: 215-17, 216-17, 262-63, 265, 323-25, 350-60, 458, 531, 561, 566, 596-97, 597-99, 616; **60**: 160-62, 164, 165,n15, 470-71, 499; and Council of Four's ultimatum, **59**: 392-93; and Rumania, **59**: 512,n1; Marshall on Jews in, **59**: 515; and Jews and East Galicia, **62**: 220-21
Ukrainian-Polish War in Galicia (Horbac), **54**: 480n1
Ullman, Isaac M., **66**: 246n2
Ullman, Richard Henry, **55**: 184n4; **57**: 459n2; **63**: 588n1; **65**: 228n3
Ulster, Ireland, **62**: 254n2
Umberto (Umberto Nicola Tommaso Giovanni Maria), Prince of Piedmont **53**: 439,n1, 596,n2
Uncertain Friendship: Theodore Roosevelt and Japan, 1906-1909 (Neu), **56**: 188n4
Uncle Sam of Freedom Ridge (Montague), **65**: 411,n9
Underground News: The Complete Story of the Secret Newspaper that Made War History (Millard), **61**: 35n1
Underwood, Oscar Wilder, **63**: 443, 535; **64**: 336, 338; **65**: 238, 275, 373; **66**: 113n1, 479; **68**: 22, 586,n5; mentioned as presidential candidate, **68**: 426; and Bryan, **68**: 475; and railroad appropriations, **55**: 228, 231-32; and issue of copies of peace treaty, **60**: 330; on defeat of Lodge resolution and vote for unconditional ratification, **64**: 42, 63,

63-64; compromise proposal for ratification, **64**: 69-70; and battle for minority leadership, **64**: 192,n1, 194, 273, 274n1; R. S. Baker on treaty views of, **64**: 359; and Taft reservation, **64**: 387; and Democratic platform, **65**: 29; appointment suggestions, **65**: 256, 260-61; on Emergency Tariff bill, **67**: 121, 123, 159; and Newberry case, **67**: 323-24; and Washington Naval Conference, **67**: 419n1; and Treaty of Berlin, 1921, **67**: 420, 421-22,n4, 424; on Four Power Treaty, **67**: 577,n1; mentioned as presidential candidate, **68**: 426
Underwood, William M., **67**: 210
Underwood and Underwood, **67**: 128-29,n1
Underwood bill (on Canadian paper embargo), **66**: 113,n1
Underwood resolution: list of senators voting against, **64**: 199n1
unemployment: see employment and unemployment
Unfinished Business (Bonsal), **56**: 517n2
Unie (now Unije, Yugoslavia), **62**: 604, 620; **63**: 206, 208; **64**: 171, 302, 462
Union Française pour le Suffrage des Femmes, **54**: 133, 262
Union League Club of New York, **56**: 84, 339
Union of American Hebrew Congregations, **55**: 259; **61**: 617; **66**: 261,n1, 266
Union of Russian People, **59**: 195n4
Union of Russian Workers: raids against, **65**: 187n5
Union of South Africa: see South Africa, Union of
unions: see labor unions
Union Station (Washington, D.C.), **61**: 401
Union Sulphur Company, **60**: 138,n1
Union Theological Seminary (New York), **59**: 247n1
Union with Wilson: Ends Wage Demand (New York Times), **62**: 561n1
Unitarian General Conference: and League of Nations, **66**: 202
United Artists Corporation, **65**: 400n1
United Brotherhood of Carpenters and Joiners of America, **54**: 473n1, 519-20
United Brotherhood of Maintenance of Way Employees, **64**: 425
United Brotherhood of Maintenance of Way Employees and Railroad Shop Employees, **62**: 74; **64**: 431; **67**: 119
United Cooperative Associations (Russia), **59**: 518
United Fruit Company, **65**: 510
United Kingdom: see Great Britain
United Methodist Conference of England, **66**: 524n1
United Mine Workers of America, **53**: 84; **57**: 234; **63**: 56n1, 593n1, 596, 597, 599, 600, 612n1; **64**: 141,n1, 143, 207, 208; **65**: 95n1, 314, 559, 560, 565-66; **66**: 19, 27, 217n1; request for peace commissioner representing labor, **53**:

United Mine Workers of America (*cont.*) 118-19; WW's statement on Bituminous Coal Commission's settlement, **65**: 104-105; and West Virginia coal crisis, **65**: 335-37; and representative to Anthracite Coal Commission, **65**: 353; J. L. Lewis urges miners to return to work, **65**: 568; and WW's statement urging return to work, **65**: 568; and award of Anthracite Coal Commission, **66**: 64n1, 68-69; Dist. No. 1 rejects award, **66**: 75. 76; Lewis on Alabama coal strike, **66**: 263-65

United Nations, American Association for the: *see* American Association for the United Nations

United Press, **53**: 318; **54**: 60; **55**: 221n1, 409, 479n1; **59**: 204n1; **62**: 627; **63**: 58; **66**: 153,n1, 154n2

United Society of Christian Endeavor, **61**: 612n1; **62**: 81-82, 263-64

United Spanish War Veterans, **65**: 289n1

United States: war casualties, **63**: 221-22, 223, 243, 349; war costs, **63**: 221, 243, 349

United States: European relief credits and postwar reconstruction: **57**: 347,n1, 406-407; **59**: 173, 639-40; **60**: 26-27,n11, 223; **61**: 177,n1,2; **66**: 493n1; Hoover on, **54**: 29-31, 477-79, 588; **55**: 203-204; **59**: 174-75, 216n5; **60**: 230-32; **61**: 61-63, 173-74, 284-86, 389-95; and U.S. Treasury representatives in Paris, **54**: 88-89; France's plan for economic issues, **54**: 124-25; and cotton industry, **54**: 192-93; **55**: 38; WW concerned over Allied plan for war expenses, **54**: 196; Hoover on not allowing Allies to administer U.S. relief funds, **54**: 277; Tumulty on, **54**: 390-94; N. H. Davis' advice on, **54**: 431; Baruch on, **54**: 480; **57**: 574; Baruch on Davis and Baruch's advice, **54**: 493-94, 494; and Belgium, **55**: 63-64, 200; **58**: 320-21, 411-12; Glass on reducing food prices, **55**: 89-90; and labor and Whitley Councils, **55**: 91,n1, 262; and Italy's requests for loans, **55**: 113-15, 208, 332-33, 342; and U.S. business and industry, **55**: 117-18, 156, 188; WW on, **55**: 161; **59**: 294-95; **60**: 111, 319; **61**: 420-21, 435; **62**: 212, 216-17, 222-23, 276-78, 340-44, 494-95; **63**: 44-45, 499; **65**: 372-73; **66**: 411,n1; and war costs, **55**: 210-11, 231; W. B. Wilson on importance of Employment Service, **55**: 291-92; and foreign loans, **55**: 333, 396-97; WW on disposition of U.S. housing projects, **55**: 341-42; Liquidation Board and clothing needs, **56**: 193, 234-34; and housing, **56**: 245; economic terms for Germany in Fontainebleau Memorandum, **56**: 269-70; and Odessa, **56**: 252-57; and Rumania, **56**: 253-57, 303-307, 314; **58**: 406-407, 591-93; on establishing distribution centers for American exports, **56**: 553,n1; WW on Nansen's proposed commission, **57**: 93-94; and Russia, **57**: 161, 165, 166-67, 575; **61**: 455,n1, 465-66; and U.S. not sitting on various commissions, **57**: 271-74, 370; and Liberty Loan, **57**: 283, 471-72; and Hungary, **57**: 368-69; and credits to Italy and Britain, **57**: 470-71; **61**: 441, 456-57; Lloyd George on, **58**: 8-12; Keynes plan for rehabilitation of European credit, **58**: 12-14; N. H. Davis on granting credits for Austrian relief, **58**: 242-43; H. M. Robinson on tonnage for food relief, **58**: 269; WW's response to Keynes' plan, **58**: 446-47; Supreme Economic Council presents view to Council of Four, **58**: 563-66; Leffingwell on, **58**: 595-57; **63**: 267-68; McCormick on effect of blockade of Germany, **59**: 109-10; Lamont on, **59**: 175-78, 283-85; **60**: 539-42, 542-44; **66**: 509; and Baltic states, **59**: 346-47, 347, 466n6, 467n6; and Germany's payment in gold, **59**: 639-40; Vanderlip on, **60**: 147,n3, 149-50; N. H. Davis-Cecil misunderstanding over credit, **60**: 277-80; Council of Four on Germany's reconstruction, **60**: 402-404, 410; WW meets with economic advisers on food prices and food relief, **60**: 491, 493; Lloyd George on U.S. role in postwar reconstruction, **61**: 223-25; Cecil and WW on continuing role of Supreme Economic Council, **61**: 314-16; and Owen's bill for establishing Federal Reserve Foreign Bank, **61**: 495-98; Barnes on wheat policy and credit extensions, **61**: 499-403; and proposed international economic council, **61**: 520-22; Redfield on foreign credits and transportation needs abroad, **62**: 31-34, 80-81; Lansing on forming commission on foreign trade, **62**: 65-66; and interim Reparation Commission, **62**: 143-44, 236-38; and military personnel for Hoover's relief missions, **62**: 166, 240, 303-304; effect of uncertainty of treaty ratification, **62**: 266-68, 273, 276-78; Glass on, **62**: 499; **63**: 200-204; **64**: 339-40; and transportation commissions appointments, **63**: 613,n1; and Poland's request for grain, **64**: 4-6, 12-13; and wheat to Armenia, **64**: 13-14; and U.S.continued role on Reparation Commission, **64**: 91-93; Houston on inter-Allied debts and, **64**: 475,n1; issue of U.S. delegates to international financial conference, **65**: 238-42; Davis on, **65**: 250; and WW's plea to Anthracite Wage Scale Committee, **65**: 313; issue of Allied debt negotiations, **65**: 325-26,n1-4; Baker on sale of locomotives to Estonia, **65**: 387-88; Hoover on Children's Relief Fund, **65**: 468-70; Hurley on British schemes and responses from Houston and Alexander

on, **66**: 74, 82, 100-101, 111; Harding on, **66**: 200; WW answers Lloyd George on reparations and debts, **66**: 307-12; importance of reparation settlements on, **66**: 472; and WW's veto of revival of War Finance Corporation, **67**: 18-22, 33,n1; issue of U.S. representation at European commissions, **67**: 34-36, 41; and Y.M.C.A., **67**: 85-86; issue of use of United War Work Campaign funds, **67**: 87-88, 96-97; surplus corn offered for relief, **67**: 139,n1, 139-40; and WW's interest in British Labour party program, **67**: 373,n1; Anderson on League of Nations and, **67**: 406-407; Mott's fund-raising plans, **67**: 407-408, 413, 422; and The Document, **68**: 5-6, 54-55, 318; and banking and currency issues, **68**: 57, 62-63; Davis to speak on reparations and inter-Allied debt, **68**: 261-62; Morgenthau on Fess and, **68**: 268; fate of Borah's amendment on, **68**: 278n2; Baruch's plea to Smuts for reparation settlement and League of Nations support, **68**: 433-37,n3; *see also* food relief; League of Nations

United States and East Central Europe, 1914-1918: a Study in Wilsonian Diplomacy and Propaganda (Mamatey), **54**: 135n3

United States and Ethiopia: A Study in American Imperialism (Manheim), **61**: 406n1

U.S. and France Stand Together . . . (Fox), **66**: 39n2

United States and French Security, 1917-1921 (Yates), **56**: 12n1

United States and Revolutionary Nationalism in Mexico, 1916-1932 (Smith), **55**: 355n5; **66**: 142n1, 160n2

United States and the First Hague Peace Conference (Davis), **61**: 235n4

United States and the League (Dickinson), **68**: 175n2

United States and the Republic of Panama (McCain), **67**: 382n5

United States Army, **53**: 47-48, 75, 386, 426, 580,n1; and commemorative medal resolution, **53**: 83,n1; not to issue new commissions, **53**: 101-102; concern over Italy's use of, **53**: 123-24, 485-86, 719n1; Surgeon General, **53**: 302n4; Baker requests retrial for Negro soldiers accused of rape, **53**: 451-52; WW visits wounded in France, **53**: 467, 469; WW reviews troops in Chaumont, **53**: 502-505; WW's remarks to American soldiers at Humes, **53**: 505-507; Pershing praises General Staff, **53**: 512-14; Moton visits Negro soldiers, **53**: 526,n1. 579n1; Baker on retaining U.S. troops in France, **53**: 584; and enlistment of Polish troops, **53**: 605, 700; and demobilization, **54**: 238, 239; **59**: 277-80; Woodman on poor morale and conditions of, **54**: 255-56;

Hoover's relief plans for Russian prisoners and, **54**: 515, 549; in France, **54**: 526; issue of U.S. troops in Turkish Empire, **55**: 27-28, 81-82; conditions at Brest, **55**: 149, 151,n1; welcome-home parade in Washington, D.C., **55**: 294; WW on, **55**: 416-17; and review of court-martial cases, **56**: 192, 244, 330-31, 425; courses offered at the Sorbonne for, **57**: 36-37; and Haller's Army, **57**: 134-36, 178; WW on continued work of Fosdick's group, **57**: 459; Glass on urgent need for appropriation for dependents of servicemen, **58**: 330; Council of Four on withdrawal of and issue of occupation of Berlin, **58**: 571, 572; Daniels on WW visiting Camp Pontanezen, **58**: 593-94; Kahn on universal military training, **59**: 278n2; WW on employment of returning servicemen, **59**: 292; **64**: 80, 109; and Urgent Deficiency bill, **59**: 478n1; and editorial in *Stars and Stripes*, **60**: 489-90,n2; WW willing to recall troops if Foch needs them, **60**: 590; WW on troops to occupy Upper Silesia, **60**: 602; Bliss on troop strengths, **60**: 622; **61**: 485; and strength of occupation force, **61**: 174-75, 547; Britain's request that U.S. railway troops remain in Russia, **61**: 225-26, 349; and Senate resolution on U.S. troops in Siberia, **61**: 353,n2; N. D. Baker on conscientious objectors, **61**: 366-68; N. D. Baker on military justice, **61**: 457-59; **62**: 415; **65**: 78-79, 126-27; **66**: 34-35; and brevet ranks, **61**: 485-86; WW's recommendation for permanent rank of general, **61**: 517,n1; psychiatrist's evaluation of men in, **61**: 530, 531-33; and rehabilitation of disabled soldiers, **61**: 569,n1; and proposed Interallied Commission of Inquiry on Greek atrocities in Turkey, **61**: 629-30,n1,2; Hoover's request for troops, **62**: 166, 240, 303-304; issue of officers receiving compensation from foreign states, **62**: 240; N. D. Baker on effect of treaty delays on, **62**: 261; and troops in Rhineland, **62**: 323; citizens' request for return of U.S. soldiers in Siberia, **62**: 433-34, 478-79, 515; and Caldwell case, **62**: 465,n1, 530, 536; and incidents at Fort Leavenworth, **62**: 545-46,n3; scandal involving U.S. Army colonel, **62**: 562-64, 610-11; and WW's welcome home to Pershing, **62**: 622; WW on, **63**: 74-75, 81, 108, 293-94; battle injuries and deaths, **63**: 223, 243; First Division, **63**: 274, 361-62; issue of troops to Armenia, **63**: 423; Lansing on German protocol issue and use of, **64**: 149,n2; N. D. Baker on commuting sentences for soldiers because of previous trial, **65**: 78-79; Baker on military prisoners and general amnesty, **65**: 126-27; Baker on situation in Germany

United States Army (*cont.*)
  and, **65**: 160-62; Baker on proposed bonus bill for veterans, **65**: 243-33; and harsher penalty for soldiers carrying concealed weapons, **65**: 261-62,n1; on desertion penalties, **65**: 272-73; on criminal offenses in, **65**: 273n1, 285; and dedication of memorial amphitheater at Arlington National Cemetery, **65**: 289,n1; and WW's Memorial Day message, **65**: 325; and Army Reorganization bill, 1920, **65**: 355-56,n1, 357, 363-68, 576-77,n1, 578; and origins of Selective Service Act of 1917, **66**: 58n1; and medal for chaplains, **66**: 120-21, 129-30; and Armistice Day, **66**: 151,n1,2; troops sent to W. Va., **66**: 445-46,n2; issue of Shipping Board taking over Hoboken piers and army supply bases, **66**: 464-67; revised court-martial guide, **66**: 493-94; issue of recruiting, **66**: 527-29, 532; **67**: 97-98,n1, 105, 117-18; WW's unpublished statement on reasons for not accompanying unknown soldier to grave, **67**: 448-49; WW's greeting to soldier who introduced himself, **67**: 508,n1, 514-15
United States Board of Indian Commissioners, **65**: 312n1
United States Chamber of Commerce: *see* Chamber of Commerce of the United States
United States Civil Service Commission: *see* Civil Service Commission
United States Congress, **53**: 103, 626; **54**: 285; **57**: 535; **58**: 119; comments on congressional election results, **53**: 22, 44-45, 62, 63, 68, 115, 116, 200, 401; reaction to WW's reading of armistice terms, **53**: 35, 35-43; and comments on WW's going to peace conference, **53**: 103-104, 108, 128, 313, 323n1; WW's State of the Union message, **53**: 113, 157, 185-86, 251n1, 274-86, 301, 305, 310; and meat-packing legislation, **53**: 156-57, 205, 215; and cotton shipments, **53**: 164; and McAdoo's solution to railroad control dilemma, **53**: 198; and government control of telegraph and telephone system, **53**: 190-93, 247-49,n1; and enemy property, **53**: 198; suggestion of delegate from Washington, D.C. to, **53**: 251n1; and wheat surplus, **53**: 245, 603, 604; Lea on administration and lack of cooperation in, **53**: 262-64; and appropriations for food relief, **53**: 273, 578-79, 637,n1, 707, 709; Baker on sentiments in, **53**: 581; House and WW discuss legislation, **53**: 587-88; and Irish Home Rule, **53**: 636; and three-year naval program, **54**: 281-82; and famine relief bill, **54**: 394; and development of merchant marine, **54**: 395; and Russian railways, **54**: 412, 413; **55**: 39; and oil-leasing bill, **54**: 503; and request for national park

named after T. Roosevelt, **54**: 486; and loans outside the U.S., **55**: 113, 115; WW's plans to meet with foreign affairs committees on League of Nations, **55**: 163, 184, 194, 221, 262-63; question of, **55**: 206, 222, 250, 254, 261, 267, 295, 297-98, 388n1, 409, 537; **56**: 540, 622; **58**: 421, 496, 498, 499, 529, 531; and railroad appropriations, **55**: 248-49, 537; and food and price control, **55**: 251, 252, 253; WW's meeting with representatives of foreign affairs committees, **55**: 267, 268-76; and League of Nations and disarmament, **55**: 268-69, 270; and appropriations for Employment Service, **55**: 291-92; WW on election results, **55**: 309-11; WW on importance of keeping in touch with constituents, **55**: 311-12; and Mexican situation, **55**: 351,n1; kills General Deficiency Appropriations bill, **55**: 388; before adjournment WW praises, **55**: 408; and enemy vessels seized in U.S. ports, **55**: 434; **58**: 289-90, 599; and League of Nations and treaty-making power versus legislative power, **55**: 478-795; Hines on railroads and, **56**: 622-23; **58**: 110; and naval building program, **57**: 91, 92, 216; Italy hopes to appeal to, **58**: 144; and issue of return of telephone and telegraph lines to private owners, **58**: 215, 365, 366, 561; Glass on urgent need for appropriation for dependents of servicemen, **58**: 330; Lloyd George on mention of in peace treaty, **58**: 402,n12; issue of guaranteeing European bonds, **58**: 447, 497n4; WW on sending troops to Turkey, **58**: 474, 475; Tumulty on WW's message to, **58**: 560, 602, 603, 605-606; and loans, **58**: 596; and child labor legislation, **58**: 605,n2; House on WW antagonizing Republicans in, **59**: 34-35; Tumulty on issues to be addressed, **59**: 47; WW's message to, **59**: 76, 123, 124-25, 174, 190, 283, 286, 289-97, 367; and prohibition, **59**: 77; **61**: 351, 352, 369; and request for educational appropriations for Porto Rico, **59**: 122-23; **60**: 375-76; and wheat prices, **59**: 206; WW on plans for financial reconstruction of Europe, **59**: 284; and mandates, **59**: 395-96; and peace treaty, **59**: 447; and aid to Russia, **59**: 463,n2; and Urgent Deficiency bill, **59**: 478n1; and War Finance Corporation, **60**: 26n11; and appropriation for national security and defense, **60**: 42; and J. P. Morgan's offer regarding ambassador's residence in London, **60**: 83n1, 299; WW on appropriations for reconstruction, **60**: 111; Tumulty's suggestions for WW's congressional messages and legislation, **60**: 145, 150, 151-53, 153-54; and Philippines, **60**: 200; and adoption of woman suffrage amendment, **60**: 247;

and appropriations for reconstruction, **60**: 279; and Hitchcock Resolution, **60**: 288; passes Johnson Resolution, **60**: 288; and resolution on Irish appearing at peace conference, **60**: 288-89; WW on issue of publication of peace treaty, **60**: 466; Lamont's proposed financial legislation, **60**: 542-44; Bliss on appropriations for troops in Upper Silesia, **60**: 622-23; WW on raising two legations to embassy status, **60**: 640; **61**: 19; and Republican efforts to have unconditional peace declared by, **61**: 184, 290, 290-91; WW works on message to, **61**: 356, 360-61, 362, 363, 369, 370, 377, 385-86, 386-88; WW unsure if he will address joint session or just Senate, **61**: 370, 376, 383, 386; Hines on railroad question and, **61**: 414-15; and war-making power, **61**: 439, 534; WW to consult with members of more often, **61**: 474-75; and WW's right to appoint representatives to international commissions, **61**: 519, 520, 522,n2; and dyestuffs importation, **61**: 574; and railroad wage crisis, **62**: 50-51, 136, 137, 191, 194; controversy over WW's request for no recess, **62**: 103; Lansing on Congress' view of Allied Russian blockade proposal, **62**: 108, 109; Hoover on protection for producers and consumers, **62**: 124-26; W. B. Wilson on international labor conference and, **62**: 131-32; WW to address on cost of living crisis, **62**: 171; Walsh on Article X, **62**: 262-63; Glass on blindness of toward business situation, **62**: 266-67; and daylight-saving law, **62**: 304-304,n1; WW on League of Nations and, **62**: 343; and appropriation request by Federal Electric Railways Commission, **62**: 420-22, 532-33, 533; and labor reforms, **62**: 583-84; and on war-declaration power of, **63**: 229, 346-47; **65**: 9, 13, 26, 32, 50, 68, 81, 120, 482n1; **66**: 183; and Pershing's welcome, **63**: 295; suggested resolution honoring Foch, **63**: 301,n1,2; and presidential disability, **63**: 562; I. H. Hoover on authorship of WW's message to, **63**: 638; Annual Message to, **64**: 6, 16,n1, 73-87, 89, 106-16; Hines' proposed congressional message for WW on railroad situation and needed legislation, **64**: 17-21, 21-24; concern over WW's ability to perform his duties, **64**: 106, 120, 139, 140; and railroad crisis, **64**: 183-84, 188-89, 195-96, 224, 391n1, 412; and WW's railroad proclamation, **64**: 228; Lansing on sending report on Russian situation to, **64**: 307,n1; and need for food relief in Europe, **64**: 340; and war-making power, **65**: 9, 13, 26, 32, 50, 68, 81, 120, 482n1; N. D. Baker on procedure for ridding departments of unwanted files, **65**: 83, 136-37; WW on

mandate for Armenia, **65**: 91, 320-23; **66**: 421-22, 448, 449-50, 452,n1; Tumulty's suggested message to, **65**: 128-34, 152; issue of U.S. representatives to international financial conference and, **65**: 238-42; Houston's draft message for WW vetoing legislative, executive, and judicial appropriations bill, **65**: 264-69; WW's concern over authority of Joint Committee on Printing, **65**: 265-69; approves Army Reorganization bill, **65**: 355n1; **67**: 118; railroad unions protest adjournment of, **65**: 359, 368-69; WW notified of adjournment of, **65**: 373; and Committee on Public Information, **65**: 374-75; and water-power legislation, **65**: 398,n1; WW on Republican leadership in, **65**: 417-18; WW on Eighteenth Amendment, **65**: 453; Merchant Marine Act's provisions and commercial treaties, **66**: 87, 89, 144-45; WW on W. B. Wilson submitting copper company's claims to, **66**: 132; Tumulty on dangers of Republican control, **66**: 214; Houston on needed fiscal responsibility of, **66**: 455; Grayson persuades WW not to deliver message to Congress in person, **66**: 456-57; WW's State of the Union Message (1920), **66**: 484-90; Milk River Valley Gun Club bill and WW's veto, **67**: 81, 112-13; WW on not asking for appropriations for Chinese Relief Fund, **67**: 105; Cobb on, **67**: 218-19, 226-27; **68**: 99. 100-101; and Wilson & Colby announcement, **67**: 343; Colby on, **67**: 600; The Document condemns, **68**: 6, 217, 537; and E. P. Davis, **68**: 25; comments on 1922 campaigns and elections, **68**: 49-50, 50, 51, 59, 70-71, 71, 73, 85-86, 89, 96, 186, 192; WW on type of candidate for, **68**: 63-64; issue of executive right to places on floor of, **68**: 105-106, 538; results of 1922 elections, **68**: 179n1; and declaration of war power and Article X, **68**: 278; and WW's death, **68**: 569-70; *see also* Election of 1922

House of Representatives: **62**: 163; and WW's trip abroad, **53**: 308n1; and Ireland, **53**: 570; **54**: 332-33,n1, 381; **55**: 469,n4; **59**: 72; and League of Nations, **53**: 636; passes famine relief bill, **54**: 57, 106, 174n1, 303, 332; J. W. Good attacks Russian Bureau, **54**: 259n1; and railroad appropriation crisis, **55**: 227, 232; and census bill, **55**: 290; Britt-Weaver contest, **55**: 367,n1; and General Deficiency appropriation bill, **55**: 447; and Pennsylvania election, **55**: 448-49,n1, 457, 458, 495; approves 19th Amendment, **60**: 155,n1; and prohibition, **60**: 380; Tumulty on importance of WW meeting with his supporters, **60**: 611; Burleson on telegraph

United States Congress (cont.)
   strike and return of lines to private
   ownership, **61**: 10; and WW's speech to
   Senate on Versailles Treaty, **61**: 370,
   388; and WW's recommendations for
   permanent rank of general and admiral, **61**: 517,n1; and Sundry Civil Bill,
   61: 568n1; McAdoo on Republicans and
   cost of living and taxation issues, **62**:
   71-72; McAdoo on WW appealing to
   Republicans to remain in session, **62**:
   71-72; WW requests no recess of, **62**:
   94-95, 98, 102, 117; and wheat prices,
   62: 95; and prices and cost of living, **62**:
   160, 491,n1; joint session to convene,
   62: 199; WW's veto message of Volstead bill and House vote on, **63**:
   601,n1; and Esch bill, **64**: 195n1; and
   Esch-Cummins bill, **64**: 467n1, 468;
   and repatriation of troops in Haller's
   Army, **65**: 43; and Porter peace resolution, **65**: 225n1; and bonus bill for veterans, **65**: 243,n1; vote on legislative,
   executive, and judicial appropriations
   bill and WW on reasons for veto of, **65**:
   265n2, 265-69; passes Knox resolution
   and WW's veto, **65**: 328n3, 328; override of WW's veto fails, **65**: 329n3; and
   Armenian mandate, **65**: 351n2l; and
   Army Reorganization bill, **65**: 355n1,
   365-68, 576-77,n1; vote on and WW's
   veto of budget and auditing bill, **65**:
   362-63,n1; Rainey's defeat, **66**: 348,n1;
   and budget bill, **66**: 486; and immigration bill, **67**: 9,n1; and override of WW's
   veto of War Finance Corporation revival, **67**: 22n3; accepts J. P. Morgan's
   London home for ambassador's residence, **67**: 26n6; bill to stop army recruiting and WW's veto, **67**: 97-98,n1,
   117-18,n2; and Emergency Tariff bill
   and WW's veto, **67**: 121n2, 191-94; WW
   on German reparation to Belgium and
   other Allied financial obligations, **67**:
   144-46; WW on copper price fixing and,
   67: 176-78,n1; and war-ending resolution, **67**: 313n1; and anti-lynching bill,
   67: 570; The Document on, **68**: 6, 217,
   537; McAdoo on political prospects, **68**:
   146-47;results of 1922 election, **68**:
   179n1; and Muscle Shoals project, **68**:
   448-49, 457; see also under name of individual committees, such as Appropriations, Committee on

Senate, **58**: 465n2, 613, 614; **59**: 99; **61**:
   642; **62**: 491; Tumulty's political strategy and, **53**: 24; Pittman supports WW
   on, **53**: 50, 53, 60; Hoover on food appropriations and, **53**: 75-76; Republican attacks on WW, **53**: 308n1; Lodge
   on destruction of enemy ships, **53**:
   469n1; and shipbuilding restrictions,
   53: 454-55, 456; and Russia, **53**:
   583,n6; and railroads, **53**: 646-47; **55**:
   228, 277; and famine relief bill contro-

versy, **54**: 106, 174,n1,2, 229, 230, 258,
   303, 332; controversy over U.S. troops
   in Russia, **54**: 259,n3; **55**: 149,n1,
   204,n1; and development of merchant
   marine, **54**: 394; and German propaganda in the U.S. and brewing interests, **54**: 397n1; Daniels on Cummings
   and, **54**: 408n1; and J. S. Williams' con-
   firmation as Comptroller of Currency,
   54: 485,n1; **55**: 149,n1, 204,n1; debate,
   filibuster, and opposition to League of
   Nations, **55**: 199, 205, 270-71, 274,
   367, 388n1, 439, 465, 538, 539; WW on
   direct election of senators, **55**: 228-29;
   and census bill, **55**: 290; and Ireland,
   55: 324-25; **59**: 372; **60**: 249,n2, 291,
   328, 375, 386-87, 435, 483, 544-45,n2,
   601; **61**: 466-67; and Mexico, **55**:
   351n1; WW on obstruction of legislation by a group of senators, **55**: 408-
   409, 409; and General Deficiency appropriations, **55**: 447; McCumber's
   suggestions for changes in Covenant to
   help passage in, **55**: 491-92; Foch on
   ratification of peace treaty and, **55**:
   514; and peace treaty ratification procedures, **56**: 58,n4, 67-68, 97-98; and
   Monroe Doctrine, **56**: 82, 83, 335, 398-
   99; Taft's suggestions for peace treaty
   approval by, **56**: 83, 398-99; WW urged
   to convene extra session, **56**: 84-85;
   and Hapgood appointment, **56**: 101,
   191; and Lodge on League of Nations,
   56: 161,n1; WW on League of Nations
   as part of peace preliminaries and, **56**:
   249; and WW on withdrawal amendment in Covenant, **56**: 302; and French
   treaty of guarantee, **57**: 297, 417,n1;
   Bryce on League of Nations and, **58**:
   139; and woman suffrage, **58**: 535; **60**:
   155,n1; WW on French security treaty
   and, **58**: 602; and peace treaty, **59**: 58;
   and mandates, **59**: 137, 146; and
   League of Nations, **59**: 282,n1,2, 285,
   398, 471, 524n1, 528-29, 647; and publication of peace terms, **59**: 419, 471;
   Republican opposition to League of
   Nations Covenant and peace treaty,
   60: 41n1, 568,n2; attitude toward
   League of Nations Covenant, **60**: 42;
   WW on being too late to amend Covenant, **60**: 100,n1; Penrose elected Finance Committee chairman, **60**:
   113,n2; Tumulty on WW submitting
   treaty to, **60**: 145; Lodge's charges of
   peace treaty leak to Wall Street leads
   to Hitchcock Resolution, **60**: 156, 198,
   242, 242-44, 245-47, 249, 290, 299,
   536; WW on not being forced to present
   unsigned treaty to, **60**: 197; Lamont
   and, **60**: 201, 202-203, 379, 380, 382-
   83, 389, 536, 538; **61**: 68; Morrow on
   opposition to treaty, **60**: 202; issue of
   peace treaty publication and Johnson
   Resolution, **60**: 242,n1, 244, 247, 298,
   328,n1, 374,n1, 486; Johnson and

Hitchcock resolutions passed, **60**: 287, 288, 290; and publication of peace treaty, **60**: 328,n1, 329-30,n1; and Knox Resolution, **60**: 376-78, 612-13; and anti-Wilson forces in and relationship to Italy, **60**: 531; WW reply on publication of peace treaty, **60**: 570-72; Lodge on option open to regarding League of Nations Covenant, **60**: 571-72; WW on Knox resolution, **60**: 609; Tumulty on importance of WW meeting with his supporters in, **60**: 611; WW on, **60**: 621; resolution on investigation of massacres of Jews in eastern Europe, **60**: 640,n1; Burleson on telegraph strike and return of lines to private ownership, **61**: 10; and issue of treaty ratification, **61**: 33-34, 541-42; and Root's reservations concerning treaty, **61**: 66,n3, 232; and issue of treaty adoption without reservations, **61**: 115-16; differing views on treaty ratification, **61**: 137; various suggestions for WW's strategy for treaty adoption, **61**: 185, 186, 569-70; **62**: 16-20; **63**: 499; **65**: 81-82, 152; WW and Constantinople, **61**: 215-16; WW on treaty ratification and, **61**: 241, 247, 251-52, 247, 437, 439; and French security treaty, **61**: 312, 622; Willert on Republican senators on Covenant, **61**: 347,n1; and Johnson Resolution on U.S. troops in Siberia, **61**: 353,n2, 579-82; WW unsure whether to address joint session or just Senate, **61**: 370, 376, 383, 386; Eliot on WW addressing, **61**: 373; WW to address just Senate, **61**: 388, 397; Yost's suggestions for gaining support for League of Nations in, **61**: 399-400; WW delivers peace treaty to, **61**: 424-25, 457, 506; text of WW's address to, **61**: 426-36; comments on WW's speech to, **61**: 417, 444-45, 445-46, 459, 475; and draft resolution on League of Nations Covenant, **61**: 490-91, 491-92; resolution requesting information on alleged Japanese-German alliance, **61**: 495; resolution requesting information on Shantung settlement, **61**: 510; and WW's recommendations for permanent rank of general and admiral, **61**: 517,n1; WW's strategy in meeting with Republican senators, **61**: 561-62; sentiment on peace treaty in, **61**: 564; and Sundry Civil bill, **61**: 568n1; Norris urges WW to communicate with entire Senate, **61**: 569n1, 570; Lodge on treaty in Senate, **61**: 597; speculations on treaty vote, **61**: 618-19; Spencer presents reservations to WW, **61**: 619-22; and issue of treaty reservations, **62**: 3-4, 11-13, 67-69, 538-39, 614; **63**: 198,n1,2,3,4, 444, 444-45, 586; and French security treaty, **62**: 5, 27-29; Metzger on past treaty ratifications, **62**: 35-40; Hines

on railroad legislation and, **62**: 77; and treaty ratification and international labor conference, **62**: 132; requests documents from WW and WW's response, **62**: 151, 208-209, 534, 611-12, 624; and prices and cost of living, **62**: 307-309, 310-12; hearings on Bolshevik propaganda, **62**: 446,n5, 447; response to WW's suggestions on cost of living, **62**: 490-91,n1; and WW's *Constitutional Government*, **62**: 632,n14; and WW's speeches on western tour, **63**: 6; predictions on treaty approval by, **63**: 235; and police situation, **63**: 295; and Armenia, **63**: 304,n1; and Federal Trade Commission and Hoover report, **63**: 425; rejection of various amendments to treaty, **63**: 482,n2,4; Shantung amendment defeated, **63**: 482,n4, 576; WW on rejection or ratification of treaty, **63**: 499; effort to compromise on Article X, **63**: 529-31; Burleson on improved situation in, **63**: 535; Hitchcock's predictions on amendments, **63**: 571; reports of possible adjournment opposed by WW, **63**: 572; vote to override veto of Volstead bill, **63**: 601n1; Reparation Commission chairmanship and, **64**: 12,n2; Glass accepts seat of T. S. Martin, **64**: 41-42, 52, 60; Lansing fears appropriations will be withheld if U.S. continues activities in Europe, **64**: 67; action of leads to decision to withdraw U.S. delegates from Paris, **64**: 100, 102, 118-19; WW's draft statement on Germany's protocol obligations affected by action of, **64**: 118,n2; and Mexican situation, **64**: 120-21,n1; WW on foreign affairs advisory power of, **64**: 152; and bill for international conference on communications, **64**: 190; fight for Democratic leadership in, **64**: 192, 194, 273, 274,n1; and Cummins and Esch bills, **64**: 195n1; WW denies request of to send Morgenthau's report to, **64**: 198,n1; WW on referendum on League and, **64**: 199-202, 248, 258-59; WW inquires about effect of resignation of senators from specific states and Palmer answers query, **64**: 202-203, 214-15; and resignation of Hapgood as Minister to Denmark, **64**: 234,n2; Long's candidacy for seat in, **64**: 350; and Esch-Cummins bill, **64**: 467n1, 468; and possible shelving of treaty, **65**: 7; issue of extraterritoriality in Siam, **65**: 21; and repatriation of troops in Haller's Army, **65**: 43; Straus urges WW to accept reservations, **65**: 47-48; Hitchcock urges WW to meet with Simmons on Lodge reservations, **65**: 48; Burleson on hope for acceptable modification of Article X if WW writes letter, **65**: 56-57; WW's letter to Hitchcock refusing to compromise on reservations, **65**: 67-71; Lodge's changed

United States Congress (*cont.*)
reservation to Article X, **65**: 80, 81,n1;
WW urges Simmons to support unified
Democratic stance against reserva-
tions, **65**: 82; and Versailles Treaty, **65**:
108, 109,n1; **67**: 228, 351-52, 608-10,
610-11, 616-18; WW on defeat of treaty
in, **65**: 116; McKellar's suggestions for
treaty ratification, **65**: 120; Newberry
conviction and appeal, **65**: 120n2; Tumulty on treaty strategy of Democrats,
65: 122; WW on his course of action regarding treaty, **65**: 123-24; Hitchcock
on sending treaty back to Senate with
interpretive reservations, **65**: 150-51;
WW on "double dealing" of some senators, **65**: 179; religious leaders urge
WW to return treaty to Senate and accept it with any reservations acceptable to other nations, **65**: 184; Davis'
suggestions for WW's resubmision of
treaty with interpretive reservations,
and WW's negative reply, **65**: 224-25,
246,n1; and defeated bonus bill for veterans, **65**: 243,n1; WW on reasons
treaty defeated, **65**: 243; WW on Knox
resolution, **65**: 247; issue of separate
peace, **65**: 257,n1,2; vote on legislative,
executive and judicial appropriations
bill, **65**: 265n2; Armenia, **65**: 288n4,
320-23, 323-24, 351n2; **66**: 427; passes
Knox resolution, **65**: 328n3; WW on
question of returning treaty to, **65**:
348; **66**: 341-42, 390-91, 402; Cummings and WW on opposition to treaty
by, **65**: 350; and corrupt practices bill,
65: 354,n2; approves Army Reorganization bill, **65**: 355,n1; fate of budget
bill, **65**: 363n1; WW on vice-presidential candidate being able to lead, **65**:
397; and McCall nomination to Tariff
Commission, **66**: 8,n1, 10; and WW's
veto message of extension of Section 10
of Clayton Act, **67**: 12-13; and WW's
veto of revival of War Finance Corporation, **67**: 18-22,n3; and Yap controversy, **67**: 54; and army recruiting
issue and veto override, **67**: 97-98,n1,
118n2; WW's veto message of Milk
River Valley Gun Club bill, **67**: 112-
13,n1; and Emergency Tariff bill, **67**:
121n2; WW on German reparation to
Belgium and other Allied financial obligations, **67**: 144-46; WW's comment
"the Senate threw me down before and
I don't want to fall down by myself
now," **67**: 208, 211; and war-ending
resolution, **67**: 313n1; and Ford-Newberry case, **67**: 316-17, 323-24,n1; and
Treaty of Berlin, 1921, **67**: 399,n2, 412,
418, 419, 421-22, 422n4; WW's unpublished statement on Democrats who
voted for Treaty of Berlin, **67**: 428; WW
on men who misled, **67**: 430; E. P.
Davis mentions running for, **67**: 458,
471, 481; N. H. Davis on Washington

Conference and, **67**: 538; and anti-
lynching bill, **67**: 570; on Four Power
Treaty, **67**: 577,n1; and Treaty of
Bogotá, **67**: 581,n2; The Document condemns, **68**: 6, 217, 537; WW on Cummings running for, **68**: 90, 92-93; and
tariff bill, **68**: 97,n3; Dodge on members of, **68**: 115; McAdoo on political
prospects, **68**: 146-47; 1922 election results, **68**: 179n1; N. H. Davis on leadership in, **68**: 242; sends WW greetings
on his birthday, **68**: 247, 258; WW on
birthday greetings of, **68**: 259-60; N. H.
Davis on introducing legislation that
U.S. enter League of Nations and
WW's response, **68**: 273-74, 274; and
Borah amendment, **68**: 278n2; and situation in regarding League of Nations
and Permanent Court of International
Justice, **68**: 306-307; Gerard against
ratification of Turkish commercial
treaty and WW's response, **68**: 431-32,
440, 499-500, 504; suggestion of WW's
candidacy from N.J., **68**: 454, 458, 463,
588; WW's suggestions for N.J. seat in,
68: 459, 591-92, 595; *see also* under
names of individual committees, such
as Foreign Relations, Committee on;
Versailles Treaty
United States Constitution, **53**: 248, 267;
55: 76, 273, 295; **56**: 67, 84, 120n2, 228;
58: 475; **59**: 610; **60**: 376, 377; **61**: 399-
400, 588, 621; **62**: 343, 632n14; **63**: 235;
64: 30, 200, 278, 279, 281; **65**: 337; **68**:
538; and war-making power, **64**: 30,
39, 278, 329; WW on, **60**: 612-13; **61**:
251-52; and woman suffrage, **61**: 464;
65: 445,n2, 450,n2; **67**: 563,n1; Van
Dyke on League of Nations and, **61**:
475-76; W. A White compares Covenant and peace treaty to, **61**: 506n1;
and issue of presidential disability, **63**:
547,n1, 561, 562; and senatorial appointments, **64**: 214-15; and Article X,
64: 287n1; Grey on, **64**: 355n1; WW
charges Lansing with violating, **64**:
383; Lansing answers WW's charges,
65: 388; Lansing on discussions with
Tumulty and Grayson on WW's disability and, **64**: 455; Tumulty's suggestions on Eighteenth Amendment, **65**:
132-34; and treason,   **65**: 206; and
budget bill and presidential powers,
65: 358, 362-63; Republican platform
on, **65**: 418n3; and Ohio cases and
Nineteenth Amendment, **65**: 445n2;
League of Nations plank and,   **65**:
482n1; Burleson   on   Eighteenth
Amendment, **65**: 510n1; Cox on treaty
and, **65**: 523n1; Nineteenth Amendment and Tennessee, **66**: 30n1, 35; on
whether President has power of a magistrate, **66**: 116, 117; and war declaration power, **66**: 183
United States Court of Claims: appointment to, **61**: 482,n1

United States Employment Service, **53**: 24n2; W. B. Wilson on financial crisis of, **55**: 291-92, 447, 478; and Employment Sunday, **57**: 447

United States Food Administration: *see* Food Administration (U.S.)

United States Food Purchasing Board, **53**: 15n1

United States Grain Corporation: *see* Grain Corporation

United States Liquidation Commission, **56**: 193, 234-35; **57**: 495-98; **58**: 406, 407, 591; **65**: 214n1

United States Mail Steamship Co., **66**: 366,n1; **67**: 124n1, 125

United States Marine Corps, **60**: 613, 614; WW reviews brigade, **62**: 241,n1, 270-71, 291

United States Merchant Marine: *see* Merchant Marine

United States Naval Academy, **61**: 369,n1; WW writes dedication for yearbook, **66**: 325,n1

United States Navy, **53**: 47-48, 386; **60**: 18, 614, 615; and three-year program, **53**: 73, 282, 311,n1, 395n1; **54**: 281-82, 303, 411,n1, 501; and General Board's recommendations for peace conference, **53**: 312,n1; WW on Britain and, **53**: 314-15, 321; building program causes controversy with Britain, **57**: 91-92, 142, 143-44, 178, 179-80, 215, 216-17; Benson memorandum on naval policy, **57**: 180-88; first transatlantic flight, **57**: 447n1; **59**: 576; **60**: 44,n1; WW on continued work of Fosdick's group and, **57**: 459; Benson receives Distinguished Service Medal, **57**: 579, 628; and Adriatic crisis, **58**: 169, 408-10, 426; **63**: 556-57, 557,n2; and withdrawal of troops from Russia, **58**: 319-20; **60**: 241; Glass on urgent need for appropriation for dependents of servicemen, **58**: 330; and disposition of enemy ships and, **58**: 456-57; on retaining vessel at Archangel, **61**: 505-506; WW's recommendation for permanent rank of admiral, **61**: 517,n1; and General Leasing bill, **61**: 535; and proposed Interallied Commission of Inquiry on Greek atrocities in Turkey, **61**: 629-30,n1,2; and oil legislation, **62**: 46-49; fuel oil supply, **62**: 78-79, 617-19,n2; and Armenia, **62**: 460n1, 480-81; **65**: 536-37, 548-49; and Sims' articles on, **62**: 460,n1, 546-47,n2; WW on employment for returning servicemen, **64**: 80, 109; and Mexican situation, **65**: 246-47, 252; and Jones bill, **65**: 278; Roosevelt's resignation as Assistant Secretary, **65**: 544; and International Communications Conference, **66**: 57; and medal for chaplains, **66**: 120-21, 129-30; and Armistice Day, **66**: 151,n1,2; Huse's concern over "Bolshevik" ships in Baltic Sea, **66**: 207,n1;

and Gatewood case, **66**: 222-23; Daniels' report on, **66**: 452-53,n1; WW approves revised regulations of, **66**: 508, 511-12, 520, 527

United States Navy and Marine Bases, Domestic (Coletta), **62**: 460n1

United States Navy in the Pacific, 1909-1922 (Braisted), **62**: 460n1; **65**: 284n1

United States Office of Public Roads: *see* Public Roads, Office of

United States Policy and the Partition of Turkey, 1914-1924 (Evans), **66**: 394n1; **68**: 431n2

United States Railroad Administration: *see* Railroad Administration

United States Relief Administraiton: *see* Relief Administration, (U.S. proposed)

United States, Revolutionary Russia, and the Rise of Czechoslovakia (Unterberger), **62**: 82n2

United States Shipping Board, **53**: 107, 331, 396n1, 454, 480n1; **54**: 394, 395, 432; **55**: 398n1, 442n1, 534; **56**: 160, 161, 190; **59**: 120; **60**: 138; **61**: 278n7; **62**: 79, 517-18; **64**: 390; and European relief plans, **53**: 14, 59, 223, 234; **68**: 81n2, 107n1, 167,n1, 388n1; and contract adjustments, **53**: 47, 131, 253; and International Mercantile Marine Corporation, **53**: 112, 195-96, 209n1, 214, 261,n1; **55**: 171; suggestions for new head of, **53**: 704; Colby resigns from, **55**: 302; and Norwegian ships, **55**: 462; Hoover on lack of cooperation in relief effort, **58**: 202, 203; and tonnage for food relief, **58**: 269; and issue of building foreign ships in U.S. shipyards, **58**: 498; Gay suggested as appointee to, **59**: 121, 121,n2, 185,n1; McCormick on Hurley and, **61**: 134; and Hurley's resignation, **61**: 439-40, 440-41; and need for passenger-carrying vessels, **61**: 479-80; and steamship business of Panama Railroad Co., **62**: 8-10, 97; and disposal of German passenger ships now used as troop ships, **62**: 226-27; and disposal of plants and materials, **62**: 226, 249, 465-68; and coal to Italy, **62**: 448-49, 468; Payne on existing legislation regarding ships, **62**: 528-29; Lane on world oil supply and U.S. shipping needs, **62**: 617-19; and France's ships, **63**: 366-69; and Czech troops in Russia, **63**: 395; and *Imperator* controversy, **64**: 7-10, 33-34, 212; and appointments to, **64**: 205; Payne resigns from, **65**: 20, 64; R. U. Johnson on Italy's views of, **65**: 93-94; Benson accepts chairmanship of, **65**: 270n2; and Jones bill and Merchant Marine Act, **65**: 278, 351n1; newly formed, **65**: 467,n2; Alexander wishes to be appointed to, **66**: 7, 195-96; WW rejects McKellar's suggestion for, **66**: 175,n1; and coal situation, **66**: 206; WW's appointments to, **66**: 252,n1;

United States Shipping Board (*cont.*)
WW on Marburg's refusal to serve on, **66**: 273; and Hoboken piers, **66**: 425-26, 464-67; and statement for The Document, **67**: 593, 595; **68**: 8-9, 220, 541; and Morse case, **68**: 73,n2

United States Steel Corporation, **57**: 348n2; **61**: 407n1, 512n4; **62**: 581,n1; **63**: 30n1, 66, 148, 149; John Skelton Williams on, **62**: 518-22,n2; Gary on labor situation and, **62**: 596-601

United State Sugar Equalization Board: *see* Sugar Equalization Board

United States Supreme Court, **58**: 561; **60**: 206; **62**: 35; and *Schenck v. U.S.*, **55**: 462; and Debs case, **56**: 618; **58**: 605,n2; **65**: 209; **67**: 98; and prohibition, **59**: 76n1; and presidential disability, **64**: 562-63; and Elk Hills case, **64**: 354; Pinchot on oil cases and, **64**: 354-55; and Newberry appeal, **65**: 120,n2; and freedom of speech cases, **65**: 204-205, 206; and Ohio cases and woman suffrage, **65**: 445,n2; Palmer on judicial power and powers of magistrate, **66**: 115-17; WW on Clarke's retirement and Sutherland appointment, **68**: 127-28,n1; Clarke on cases and relationship with Brandeis, **68**: 130-31; McAdoo's views on, **68**: 148; and Pennsylvania mining case, **68**: 277n1; Cobb on prohibition and, **68**: 304

United States Tariff Commission: *see* Tariff Commission (U.S.)

United States Treasury: *see* Treasury (U.S.)

United States Trust Company of New York, **68**: 386n1

United States *v*. Anderson, **65**: 206

United States *v*. Doremus, **68**: 131,n4

United States *v*. Lanza, **68**: 304,n1

United States *v*. Midwest Oil Company, **62**: 46

United States *v*. Victor Berger, **65**: 206

United States Wheat Corporation (proposed): *see* Wheat Corporation

United War Work Campaign, **57**: 459; **67**: 74-75, 87-88, 96-97, 97

United Zinc and Chemical Co. *v*. Britt *et al.*, **68**: 131,n5

Universal News Service, **54**: 60; **62**: 627

Universal Postal Service, **54**: 434, 496, 499

University of Chicago Law Review, **55**: 347n1; **66**: 92n1

Unknown Prime Minister: The Life and Times of Andrew Bonar Law, 1858-1923 (Blake), **57**: 6n7

Unmailable: Congress and the Post Office (Fowler), **66**: 92n1

Unterberger, Betty Miller, **53**: 463n1, 556n4; **62**: 82n2

Upper Silesia, **59**: 186, 329, 416, 615, 627; **60**: 20, 21, 24, 43, 72, 80-81, 106, 130n4, 230, 297, 314, 423; **62**: 272, 415; **66**: 225-27; **68**: 77; American delegation on, **60**: 54-59, 67-68; House on, **60**: 82-83; Council of Four on, **60**: 84-92; and peace terms, **60**: 130,n5; and Leobschutz, **60**: 139, 480; Seymour on German counterproposals on, **60**: 139; Paderewski on Poland and, **60**: 156, 157-59; R. H. Lord on German counterproposals on, **60**: 183-85, 187; Commission on Polish Affairs on, **60**: 189-92; and plebiscite issue, **60**: 380, 404-406, 411-18, 421, 447, 468, 478, 553-56; committee reports and Council of Four, **60**: 411-15, 415-18; Council of Four's revision of peace treaty, **60**: 436,n1; and Czech frontier issue, **60**: 468, 478; amendments to committee's report on, **60**: 558-60, 562, 563; troops for occupation of, **60**: 602, 622, 628; and Poland, **61**: 187; WW on, **63**: 13-14, 98, 186-87

Upper Silesia: The Dilemma of the Powers (Coar), **67**: 463-64,n1

Upshaw, William David: on cotton prices, **57**: 511-12,n1, 578

Upton, Harriet Taylor (Mrs. George), **68**: 332,n2

Urbana, Ohio, **63**: 3n5

Urgent Deficiency bill, **58**: 330; **59**: 478,n1; **61**: 356; **63**: 608

Urofsky, Melvin Irving, **57**: 348n2; **67**: 319n1

Uruguay, **54**: 114-15, 264; **58**: 187, 198; **67**: 23,n1; on U.S. in Dominican Republic, **66**: 360; Colby to visit, **66**: 430,n1

Ussuri Cossacks, **53**: 184,n1

Ustrogov, Leonid Aleksandrovich, **53**: 630,n9; **57**: 420n1; **61**: 637,n3; **62**: 592,n9

Utah, **68**: 96

Utica, N.Y.: and WW Foundation, **67**: 555; Colby cancels speech in, **67**: 561

Vágó, Béla, **56**: 241n3

Vaida-Voevod, Alexandru, **60**: 418n6

Valdes, Alamiro Huidobro, **53**: 347n1

Valenciennes, France, **56**: 251

Valentine, Joseph F., **65**: 20

Valentino, Pietro Arone di, **55**: 300,n1, 301

Valera, Eamon de: *see* De Valera, Eamon

Valkenburg, Edwin Augustus Van, **61**: 373

Valley Forge Historical Society, **67**: 175

Valona, Italy, (now Vlona, Albania): *see* Paris Peace Conference —Valona

Van, Turkey, **65**: 74, 309, 321, 322

Vanadium Corporation of America, **66**: 288n1

Vance, James I., **65**: 86

Van den Heuvel, Jules Norbert, **58**: 237,n1

Vanderbilt, Cornelia, **68**: 566

Vanderbilt, Cornelius, **68**: 205

Vanderbilt, George, **68**: 566
Vanderbilt, William Kissam, **58**: 56,n4
Vanderbilt University, **67**: 285,n1
Vanderlip, Frank Arthur, **62**: 287, 315; **68**: 57,n1, 61, 548; on Europe's postwar economic problems, **60**: 147,n3, 149-50; speech to Economic Club, **60**: 202; and peace treaty leak investigation, **60**: 330,n2, 434; Houston on suggestions of, **68**: 62, 63; Glass on reserve banking schemes of, **68**: 78-80; WW thanks Glass for comments, **68**: 80
Vanderlip Reviews Genoa (New York *World*), **68**: 57,n1
Van der Poel, Jean, **68**: 437n3, 453n1
Van der Vat, Dan, **61**: 57n8
Vandervelde, Emile, **57**: 319,n1; **58**: 237,n1, 416
Van Dyke, Henry, **55**: 199,n1; **62**: 615-16; **67**: 182, 434; memorial poem of, **56**: 280-81,n2; **66**: 347-48; **68**: 352, 459-60, 462; on League of Nations, **61**: 475-76, 533,n1; gives up church pew, **68**: 519,n1
Van Egroo, G., **59**: 232,n3
Vanguard of Nazism: The Free Corps Movement in Postwar Germany, 1918-1923 (Waite), **54**: 93n4; **56**: 90n4
Van Hoesen, Henry Bartlett, **67**: 182
Van Horn, Sir William (Cornelius), **61**: 397-98,n2
Vanity Fair, **54**: 384n3; **68**: 450
Van Karnebeek, Herman Adriaan, **64**: 407n1
Van Kleek, Mary Abby, **63**: 57,n3
Van Lear, Eleanor Chambers (Mrs. John Findlay), **62**: 601,n3, 602
Vannutelli-Rey, Count Luigi, **60**: 467,n3, 478
Van Oss, Salomon Frederick, **59**: 245,n2; **60**: 566; on interview with WW, **60**: 250-55
Van Pelt, Hugh G., **65**: 45,n4
Vanzetti, Bartolomeo, **53**: 343n1
Vardaman, James Kimble: and Democratic senatorial primary, **68**: 93-94,n2,3 128n1
Varela, Don Francesco Tudelay, **55**: 297,n4
Varela, Jacobo, **65**: 338n2; **66**: 25,n2, 410,n1
Vargas, Manuel, **67**: 132
Vasoncellos, Augusto Cesar de, **54**: 374n11
Vatican, **54**: 258-59; on psychological moment for peace, **53**: 16-18; Benedict XV hopes WW will visit, **53**: 242; Tumulty urges WW to visit, **53**: 421; WW's visit to, **53**: 606-607, 625; WW on opposition to League of Nations by, **60**: 389; and German missionary property, **60**: 471-72, 479-80, 548,n3, 577-79, 594-95; *see also* Roman Catholic Church
Vatrzyki, Poland, **59**: 262
Vauclain, Samuel Matthews, **61**: 177n2

Vaughn, Henry, **68**: 583
Veblen, Oswald, **67**: 182
Veglia (now Krk, Yugoslavia), **66**: 447,n3; *see also* Paris Peace Conference—Veglia
Velleman, Antoine, **64**: 97-98,n1
Venable, William Webb, **55**: 297,n4
Venezia Guilia, **58**: 589,n3; **61**: 575
Venezuela, **56**: 170n1; **58**: 198
Venice, Italy, **57**: 342
Vénisélos, Eleuthérios Kyrios, **54**: 116, 208; **55**: 3, 6, 44, 45, 71, 118, 124, 140, 500-501,n2; **56**: 102, 170n1, 177, 300, 302, 335; **57**: 221, 224, 225, 262-63, 265, 350, 352, 545n2; **58**: 241, 317-18, 332-33, 339, 345, 477, 478; **59**: 11, 208, 299, 349, 468, 493; **60**: 133, 266, 546, 635; **61**: 189, 216, 567; **63**: 60, 61, 166; **64**: 300, 449; **65**: 64, 65, 114, 302; **66**: 47; **67**: 10, 11, 105n3; on sending Greek troops to Turkey, **54**: 402-403, 426; **58**: 510, 511, 512, 513, 514; on request to send Greek troops to the Ukraine, **54**: 402-403; and Greece's territorial claims, **54**: 463, 473n1; and League of Nations Commission, **54**: 509, 546; and Plenary Session, **55**: 178n2, 195, 196; WW on, **55**: 266, 315; on Greek troops landing at Smyrna, **59**: 22, 23, 24, 25; on Smyrna and Dodecanese Islands, **59**: 39, 42, 43, 44, 45, 46, 59; WW on, **59**: 40; **66**: 411n1; at Council of Four meeting, **59**: 265-66, 270n5, 271, 319; **60**: 170; Westermann on Greece's territorial demands and, **59**: 595-96; infractions of articles on minorities, **60**: 595, 596; thanks WW for efforts on behalf of small nations, **61**: 461; and Greek atrocities in Turkey, **61**: 629n1; and Thrace, **62**: 141, 238, 319-21, 327-28, 553, 603; **64**: 157-64; pact with Great Britain on Thrace, **62**: 238; WW's message to, **63**: 391; to meet with WW, **68**: 23,n2; photograph of, *illustration section*, **54**
Venzon, Anne Cipriano, **66**: 82,n1
Veracruz, Mexico, **65**: 246-47, 252,n1
Verchneudinsk, Russia, **62**: 86n5
Vergennes, Charles-Gravier, Comte de, **55**: 242
Verhandlungen der Verfassunggebenden Deutschen Nationalversammlung Stenographische Berichte, **59**: 84n2, 136n2
Vermes, Gabor, **53**: 7n3
Vermont: D. R. Stuart on "Democratic" anecdotes from, **68**: 1104
Vernon, Katharina Tappe (Mrs. Ambrose White), **68**: 459,n2
Verone, Maria (Mrs. Georges Lhermitte), **57**: 218,n1
Versailles, France: discussed as peace conference site, **53**: 4, 143; WW visits, **53**: 403; mentioned as seat for League of Nations, **57**: 224

Versailles Treaty: and preamble, **64**: 46, 46-47, 48; WW on, **64**: 65; **65**: 263, 348; WW calls meeting with Hitchcock, **64**: 71; and German ratification and exchange of ratifications with Allied Powers, **64**: 101,n1; draft of WW's statement on German protocol on, **64**: 118,n2; Ashurst on 1920 campaign and, **64**: 263; Lansing compares WW's and Bryan's position on, **64**: 267-69; WW on reasonable interpretations of treaty, **64**: 278-82; Tumulty on WW's opportunity to act on, **64**: 287; editorial comments on, **64**: 287,n1,2; R. S. Baker on, **64**: 326-27; issue of withdrawal of because of Adriatic proposal, **64**: 367; Straus on negative effect on treaty of WW's Adriatic response, **64**: 443; Davis' concern over U.S. representation on commissions created by, **65**: 60; Polk on Turkish treaty and, **65**: 76-77; Grayson on WW's reaction to defeat of, **65**: 149; France on Germany's violations of, **65**: 157; Allies' concern over enforcement of when France acts independently, **65**: 173; discussed at Cabinet meeting, **65**: 212; Senate situation on Armenian mandate and, **65**: 324; WW on, **65**: 348; and Bryan, **65**: 424; R. S. Baker organizes WW's documents on, **67**: 89; Hines on river shipping decision under, **67**: 93; on German obligations to Belgium, **67**: 145; various comments on failure to ratify, **67**: 227-29, 268-69, 324n1, 423,n1, 430; editorial supports ratification of, **67**: 313n1; question of location of original copy, **67**: 351-52, 354-55, 357; N. H. Davis on discussion with Lord Bryce on, **67**: 375-78; Straus on meeting with WW on plans to insure ratification, **67**: 607-10; Boeckel on strategy for ratification, **67**: 616-18; Lowell on ratification plan, **67**: 610-11

fight for ratification: Hitchcock's substitute reservations, **64**: 3, 28-30, 238; Tumulty's proposed letter to Hitchcock on dangers of reservations and delaying ratification, **64**: 15; and Article X, **64**: 28-29,n2, 43, 47, 48, 283, 287,n1, 446, 450; Lodge reservations, **64**: 37-38, 38-41, 45-50, 58-59, 288-95; Underwood's strategy, **64**: 42, 69-70; with exception of interpretations, WW not willing to make any compromise, **64**: 43-44; Hitchcock interview with WW on, **64**: 43-45, 46, 47; Senate controversy intensifies, **64**: 45-50, 71-72; WW urges vote against Lodge resolution of ratification or will withdraw treaty, **64**: 45, 48, 50, 56, 58; Hitchcock's draft letter opposing Lodge resolution of ratification, **64**: 51; Britain distressed over reservations, **64**: 53; Hitchcock's strategy for compromise, **64**: 59, 70,

93-94, 203, 244; Senate votes on treaty, **64**: 63-64,n2,3, 64,n3, 526-27, 528; Ashurst on votes on Lodge resolution of ratification, **64**: 63-64; House's strategy for treaty passage in, **64**: 89-90, 96; N. H. Davis on, **64**: 104-105; fate of Lodge resolution on for termination of the war, **64**: 126n1; responsibility rests with Senate, not WW, **64**: 126, 148-49, 187; WW will not agree to Lodge reservations, **64**: 165-68; comments on WW's uncompromising attitude toward, **64**: 183, 190, 192-94,n1, 267-69, 321, 327,n1; WW's draft of public letter challenging specific senators to resign, **64**: 199-202; WW's advice to Hitchcock, **64**: 206; Tumulty advocates WW adopt Hitchcock's substitute reservations as compromise plan, **64**: 238, 276-77; and Jackson Day message, **64**: 247-48,n1, 250-52, 252-55, 257-59; Houston on interpretive reservations not being objectionable, **64**: 251-52; Bryan on, **64**: 261n1; Cobb on need for compromise, **64**: 270n2; bipartisan committee meets, **64**: 276,n1, 283-84, 311-12, 312-13,n1, 328n2; WW on reasonable interpretations, **64**: 278-82; WW accepts Hitchcock's reservations, **64**: 329; Burleson and Hitchcock review WW's list of senators who hindered ratification of treaty, **64**: 336-37, 338-39; and Grey's letter, **64**: 355n1, 381,n1; comments on effect of Grey's letter, **64**: 365, 381,n1; and Taft reservation, **64**: 387-88,n1, 405, 410-11; Glass on Taft reservation and searches for WW's reactions to reservations, **64**: 410; Warner updates Lansing on treaty situation, **64**: 410; R. Crane suggests Masaryk send message on need for ratification, **64**: 466, 479-80; Dr. Park on effect of WW's letter to Hitchcock, **64**: 526; WW indicates refusal to accept Lodge reservations, **65**: 7; editorial history of letter to Hitchcock refusing to accept compromise and stressing importance of Article X, **65**: 7-10, 11-14, 25-28, 30-35, 49-55, 66, 67-71; R. S. Baker and House discuss strategy for approval of, **65**: 41; Straus urges WW to accept reservations in order to save, **65**: 47-48; rumor that WW will accept reservations to Article X, **65**: 81-82; WW views reservation to Article X as nullification of treaty, **65**: 82; rejected by Senate, **65**: 108, 109,n1; WW on defeat, **65**: 116, 243; McKellar's suggestions for, **65**: 120; and Gerry's reservation on Ireland, **65**: 120n1; WW on his course of action, **65**: 123-25; comments on WW's action regarding, **65**: 140-41; Hitchcock on sending treaty back to Senate with interpretive reservation, **65**: 150-51; WW on Hitchcock's strategy, **65**: 152; religious leaders urge

WW to return treaty to Senate and accept with any reservations acceptable to other nations, **65**: 184-85; N. H. Davis' suggestions, **65**: 223-25; Dodge's suggestions, **65**: 235; WW on reasons for treaty defeat, **65**: 243; WW refuses to return treaty to Senate with acceptable reservations, **65**: 247,n1; and issue of Knox resolution and separate peace, **65**: 257,n1; House on his strategy and on WW's, **65**: 274-75; WW's model plank on unqualified ratification of, **65**: 319; WW's veto of Knox's separate peace resolution, **65**: 328-29,n2; and WW's League of Nations plank, **65**: 437; and Cox's reservations, **65**: 523,n1; *see also* Paris Peace Conference—German Treaty

Versailles Palace: WW visits, **61**: 118; treaty signing at: *see* Paris Peace Conference—German Treaty; Hall of Mirrors

Versailles Twenty Years After (Birdsall), **56**: 499n3; **57**: 25n9

Versailles Treaty and After (R.S. Baker), **68**: 482,n1

Verviers, Belgium, **57**: 393

Vesnić, Blanche Ullman (Mrs. Milenko R.), **53**: 721,n3

Vesnić (Vesnitch), Milenko R., **53**: 700, 721,n3; **54**: 421n7; **55**: 5, 6, 43, 44-45, 46, 68, 69, 71, 88,n1, 118, 123; **56**: 170n1, 172, 176, 228, 302, 614; **57**: 220, 224, 225, 231, 249-50, 426, 500, 558; **58**: 161-64, 354, 374, 508; **59**: 221-22; **60**: 23, 133, 222, 268, 419-20, 485, 565, 643; **61**: 50-51, 54, 57-58; **63**: 465; **65**: 94; **66**: 531; League of Nations, **54**: 426,n1, 464, 483, 496, 545, 546; on Klagenfurt Basin, **60**: 122-29, 232-33, 361,n1, 428-29; on arms limitation, **60**: 169-70

veterans: and WW's State of the Union Message, **66**: 488-89

Viatka, Russia, (now Kirov, U.S.S.R.), **57**: 461, 589; **59**: 465; **61**: 164, 165, 166

Vickrey, Charles Vernon, **62**: 248,n1,2; **65**: 234,n4

Victor Emmanuel (of Italy): *see* Vittorio Emanuele

Victoria (Queen of England, Empress of India), **61**: 15

Victoria Alexandra Alice Mary, Princess: *see* Mary (daughter of George V)

Victoria Patricia Helena Elizabeth ("Princess Pat"), **53**: 594,n11

Victoria University, **56**: 122n1

Victors Divided: America and the Allies in Germany, 1918-1923 (Nelson), **56**: 12n1; **59**: 401n4, 402n5; **60**: 14n14, 489n2; **65**: 115n1

Victors in World War I and Finland: Finland's Relations with the British, French and United States Governments in 1918-1919 (Paasivirta), **58**: 404n2

Victory at Sea (Sims), **62**: 460,n1; **67**: 242n4

Victory at Sea. I. When Germany was Winning the War (Sims), **62**: 546-47,n2

Victory Chimes and Carillon Association, Inc., of New York, **64**: 345n1, 346

Victory Liberty Loan: *see* Liberty Loan

Victory loan bill and Act, **55**: 297-98; **66**: 61

Vie Feminine, La, **54**: 91n1

Vienna, Austria, **53**: 7, 8, 127, 649; **54**: 184; **56**: 314, 315, 326, 327, 328, 329, 329-30, 461; **58**: 205; **60**: 139, 643; talk of occupation of, **57**: 102

Vienna, Congress of (1815): *see* Congress of Vienna

Vienna, University of, **56**: 257

Viereck, George Sylvester, **66**: 248,n1, 249,n1

Viertel Jahrshefte fur Zeitgeschichte, **58**: 308n1

Vigliotti v. Commonwealth of Pennsylvania, **68**: 334,n1

Villa, Francisco (Pancho), **55**: 352; **61**: 487; **65**: 462, 487

Villa, Giovanni, **53**: 326,n6

Villach, Austria, **59**: 85, 95, 578; **60**: 36, 198, 362; **61**: 196

Villach-St. Veit Railway, **61**: 42

Villanuova (Villa Nova), Rhodes, **58**: 355,n4, 434

Villard, Oswald Garrison, **53**: 289; **54**: 397n7; **56**: 103, 127, 340, 466,n3; **61**: 373; WW on, **61**: 509,n3; **66**: 170n1; **67**: 37n1; **68**: 315n1

Villian, Raoul, **57**: 176n3

Vilna (Wilno), Lithuania (Poland), **53**: 611n1,2; **54**: 33; **59**: 411, 446; captured by Bolsheviks, **65**: 527n1

Vincennes Park, **59**: 186

Vincent, Edgar, 1st Baron D'Abernon, **66**: 46n7

Vincent, George Edgar, **53**: 302,n3

Vincent, Jesse G., **53**: 308,n1

Vincent, John Heyl, **65**: 423,n1, 424n1, 432

Vindictive, H.M.S., **61**: 6,n9

Vinel (Venel), General, **53**: 640,n4

Vinikas, Matthias J., **66**: 21n1

Vinnichenko, Volodmir Kirillovich, **54**: 33,n7

Vinson, John Chalmers, **67**: 484n1

Vinson, Robert Ernest, **66**: 369n1

Vio, Antonio, **56**: 565,n5

Virginia: and woman suffrage, **61**: 538; **62**: 462; and vacant Senate seat, **64**: 24, 41-42, 52; state Democratic convention, 1920, and League of Nations plank, **65**: 292, 293-94,n1; 331,n1, 333, 427, 482n1; and platform, 341n1; Democratic party in, **68**: 143,n1,2

Virginia, University of, **68**: 185-86; WW to serve on honorary centennial committee, **66**: 234, 258; WW on endowment fund effort, **67**: 138-39,n1; and centennial of, **67**: 263,n1, 265, 275,

Virginia, University of (*cont.*)
310; WW solicited for donation to, **67**: 281,n2; proposed move of medical school, **67**: 299,n1, 495,n1, 498,n1,2, 501, 559; and Wilson & Colby announcement, **67**: 344; plaque on WW's room at, **67**: 498,n1,2, 501; WW recommends Axson as faculty member at, **67**: 549; WW's debating career at, **68**: 134n1; WW's fraternity at, **68**: 291,n1
Virginia Bill of Rights, **55**: 319
Viral Encephalitis (A. B. Baker), **58**: 615n18
Vis Island: *see* Lissa Island
Visconti, Ruth T., **65**: 401n1
Visocchi, Achille, **61**: 109,n6
Vistula River, **53**: 38; **56**: 93, 94, 268, 471, 472, 560; **57**: 452, 572, 596; **61**: 273
Vittorio Emanuele II (of Italy), **53**: 605,n1; **63**: 517,n4; **64**: 407
Vittorio Emanuele III (of Italy), **53**: 345, 390, 439, 444n2, 449, 459, 589, 595-97, 600,n1, 601, 607, 608n1, 639, 696, 697-98; **54**: 134; **56**: 86; **58**: 239; **59**: 64n3, 561, 601; **63**: 270, 382, 465, 486, 516, 517, 524, 547,n4; **65**: 196; **66**: 323n2, 542; **68**: 255,n2; grants amnesty for political and military offenses, **55**: 301; urges WW to accept Tittoni's proposals, **63**: 297-98; R. U. Johnson on meeting with, **65**: 300-301, 303; photograph of, *illustration section*, **53**
Viviani, René-Raphaël, **53**: 384, 459; **68**: 111,n2
Vix, Ferdinand, **56**: 182n1, 242,n2, 276, 277, 332, 414,n10, 415, 461, 464, 474, 487; **57**: 77, 108, 169
Vladivostok, Russia, **53**: 152, 227, 631; **56**: 185; **62**: 478, 515; and zemstvo, **55**: 303; **59**: 148, 281; and Czech troops, **61**: 165, 287; Graves on, **62**: 86, 87-88; Japanese occupation of, **65**: 284n1, 391-92, 515, 516; Japanese on reasons for troops in, **66**: 51
Vlona: *see* Valona
Vlore, Albania, **66**: 45n6
vocational education, **60**: 151; and disabled soldiers, **61**: 568,n1; WW on veterans and, **66**: 488-89
Voldemaras, Augustinas, **59**: 18,n10
Völgyes, Iván, **53**: 7n3; **56**: 182n1
Volkermarkt, Austria, **60**: 36
Volosca (now Opatija, Yugoslavia), **58**: 83; **60**: 138; **63**: 617n1; **64**: 172, 370; and Adriatic settlement, **66**: 365
Volskii, V. K., **56**: 389,n2
Volstead, Andrew, **63**: 562n1
Volstead Act, **68**: 18; suggestion of amending, **65**: 132-34; WW on repeal of, **65**: 347n4; and Bryan, **65**: 424; WW and Glass on, **65**: 435-36; Tumulty on repeal of, **65**: 452-55; Burleson presents alleged plank of WW's on, **65**: 510n1; The Document on, **68**: 218-19, 310, 539; Cobb on, **68**: 304; Brandeis on, **68**: 334-36; Brandeis statement

mentioned, **68**: 336, 337; *see also* prohibition
Volstead bill, **59**: 76n1; **63**: 562n1, 571, 582, 590, 608; WW's veto of, **63**: 601
Voltaire, François-Marie-Arouet **66**: 442
Volunteer Act (1914), **66**: 58n1
Volunteer Army and Allied Intervention in South Russia, 1917-1921 (Brinkley), **54**: 372n7
Von der Goltz, Gustav Adolf Joachim Rudiger, Count, **61**: 86,n5
Von Retuer, Ludwig: *see* Reuter, Ludwig von
Von Steuben, S.S., **54**: 554; **55**: 434; **58**: 141
Von Wachendorf, Herr, **57**: 590
Vorarlberg, Austria, **53**: 7; **59**: 535; **60**: 642
Vorschlage der Deutschen Regierung fur die Errichtung eines Volkenbundes, **59**: 243,n1
Vosnjak, Boqumil, **58**: 111,n1
Vosuq od-Dowleh, Mirza Hasan Khan, **59**: 318,n1
Voter's Choice in the Coming Election (Eliot), **66**: 164,n2, 290,n3
Voyages de M. le Marquis de Chastellux dans l'Amérique Septentrionale dans les années 1780, 1781 & 1782, **67**: 333,n2
Vreeland, Alice May Brown (Mrs. Williamson Updike), **53**: 22; **67**: 524,n2
Vreeland, Williamson Updike, **53**: 22; **67**: 182, 524
Vrooman, Carl Schurz, **67**: 139-40,n1, 139n1, 140
Vyborg, Finland (now Russia), **61**: 455n1

W. R. Grace and Company, **55**: 398n1
Waddington, William Henry, **61**: 94
Wade, Harry Amyas Leigh Herschel, **54**: 33,n5, 200; **56**: 167n3
Wadsworth, Eliot, **53**: 302,n2
Wadsworth, James Wolcott, Jr., **56**: 339; **61**: 372; and treaty fight, **64**: 200-201, 337; **65**: 576n1; and army recruiting, **66**: 528,n1, 532
Wadsworth-Kahn bill, **65**: 576n1
Wagenknecht, Alfred, **67**: 99,n2
Wagner, Charles C., **53**: 319,n2; **57**: 468,n1; **63**: 557,n1, 558; **64**: 324,n1; photograph of, *illustration section*, **55**
Waite, Robert George Leeson, **54**: 93n4; **56**: 90n4
Walcott, Charles Doolittle, **65**: 105-106,n1; **66**: 469-70,n1, 471
Wald, Lillian D., **54**: 397n1; **58**: 140-41,n1, 142; **62**: 530; on Shillady incident, **62**: 527-28
Waldman, Eric, **54**: 93n4
Waldrep, Tom C., **64**: 466,n1
Waldron, John Milton, **63**: 268,n1; **64**: 522,n1
Wales, Henry, **60**: 28n12
Walfish Bay, South Africa, **54**: 296-98
Walker, Sir Herbert, **62**: 287

Walker, Seth M., **66**: 30,n1, 54n1; on woman suffrage amendment, **66**: 35

Wall, Joseph Frazier, **67**: 242n3

Wall, Louise Herrick, **68**: 164n1

Wallace, Hugh Campbell, **54**: 125,n1; **57**: 351, 353, 531-32, 581, 627; **58**: 3,n2, 331, 482; **60**: 157, 546; **61**: 178, 327, 624-25; **63**: 588; **65**: 89, 198,n1, 305,n1, 542-43; **66**: 86n1, 86, 180, 225, 496; **68**: 135n1; appointed ambassador to France, **53**: 693, 710; **56**: 194, 308; on reaction of French press to WW's Adriatic statement, **58**: 96-97; and WW-Poincaré dinner invitation episode, **61**: 112, 113, 114, 115, 180; suggests resolution honoring Foch, **63**: 301,n1; as unofficial observer, **64**: 148, 156, 156-57, 261, 261,n2, 382; and Adriatic question, **64**: 178, 260-61,n1, 263-66, 323, 340, 341-42, 342, 371, 450-51; and Turkish treaty, **64**: 261,n1, 345, 361, 372,n1, 373, 411; on Anglo-French Adriatic proposal, **64**: 298-305, 314-15, 318-20; Yugoslavia and Adriatic question, **64**: 331-35, 340, 341-42; **65**: 259,n1, 315; receives WW's note on firm Adriatic position, **64**: 398; instructions for Hungarian treaty negotiations, **64**: 446, 447, 448, 464-66; and French invasion of Germany, **65**: 159, 162, 163, 167, 170-73; WW on and San Remo Conference, **65**: 197, 213; on U.S. representation on European commissions, **67**: 33, 34-36; and French unknown solider ceremony, **67**: 131, 133; and fund-raising efforts for WW's S Street home, **67**: 137n3; and Yap controversy, **67**: 147, 153-56

Wallace, Mildred Fuller (Mrs. Hugh Campbell), **57**: 351,n2, 531, 581, 627; **60**: 157, 546; **61**: 327; **65**: 198,n3, 200

Wallace, William, **53**: 486,n2; **56**: 396,n5; **57**: 372

Wallachia, **55**: 373

Walloons, **57**: 392, 394

Wall Street, **60**: 568n2; **64**: 328n2, 494; Tumulty's fears concerning, **66**: 215, 216; WW on *New York Times* and, **67**: 301; peace treaty leak investigations, *see* United States Congress—Senate

Wall Street Journal, **68**: 119n2

Walsh, David Ignatius, **53**: 82; **56**: 398; **57**: 446; **63**: 445, 483; **67**: 37n1; and treaty fight, **64**: 200-201, 337; vote on reservation to Article X, **65**: 81n1; and League of Nations plank, **65**: 482n1; as "betrayer," **65**: 489,n1

Walsh, Francis Patrick, **55**: 422, 469; **57**: 419, 426, 427, 534,n1; **60**: 38, 298; **61**: 512n2; **63**: 118,n2; **66**: 263n1; resignation of, **53**: 215, 705n1; on Debs case, **56**: 245, 310; and Irish issue, **56**: 486,n1; **58**: 505,n2, 585-87, 588; **62**: 324-26; requests Paris Peace Conference investigate Irish situation, **60**: 239,n1; meets with WW, **60**: 383-87;

awaits outcome of Borah Resolution, **60**: 544; on Article X and Ireland, **63**: 389; and MacSwiney appeal, **66**: 88-89, 91

Walsh, John J., **65**: 545,n3

Walsh, Richard John: and WW's essay, **68**: 342, 353, 357, 368, 369

Walsh, Thomas James, **53**: 188; **55**: 262-63, 263, 280, 297n2; **57**: 446; **58**: 505,n2, 585-87, 588; **60**: 331, 431; **61**: 550-51; **64**: 273, 338; **67**: 70,n1, 522; **68**: 33n2; on Irish situation, **53**: 299-300, 306; **56**: 398; **61**: 512; supports WW, **60**: 568,n1; on Article X, **62**: 262-63; on WW's no-compromise statement, **64**: 192n1; and bipartisan meeting on reservations, **64**: 283; and Hitchcock's copy of text of Lodge reservations and, **64**: 291, 292, 293, 294; and Democratic caucus on treaty, **64**: 384; on Lansing's dismissal, **65**: 4; treaty vote, **65**: 109n1; WW and Cummings discuss, **65**: 345, 349,n7; code name for, **65**: 350; and Armenia, **65**: 436n2; and fight for Resolutions Committee chairmanship, **65**: 445, 470-71; and Treaty of Berlin, 1921, **67**: 418,n1; and Teapot Dome scandal, **68**: 119n2; and WW Foundation, **68**: 249n2

Walter, Herr (of Germany), **57**: 590

Walter Lippmann and the American Century (Steel), **60**: 202n1

Walters, Harry, **56**: 400

Walters, Henry, **53**: 112,n2; **57**: 233, 382,n23

Waltham (Mass.) *Free Press Tribune*, **68**: 418

Waltraute, S.M.S., **55**: 432

Walworth, Arthur, **53**: 544n1; **58**: 618n33

Wanamaker, Rodman, **67**: 128

Wandycz, Piotr Stefan, **54**: 33n6, 481n2; **65**: 527n1,2,3; **66**: 46n7, 225n2

Wang Cheng-t'ing (C. T. Wang), **54**: 293,n3; **57**: 426,n1; **58**: 553, 553-54; **61**: 289,n1; photograph of, *illustration section*, **58**

War, Department of, **53**: 53, 131, 253; **55**: 537; **56**: 83, 160, 161, 190; and food relief program, **53**: 59, 60, 75; not issuing new commissions, **53**: 101-102; Lea on, **53**: 262-64; and changes in treatment of military prisoners, **53**: 307n2; and enlistment of Polish troops, **53**: 605; and carpenters' controversy and National War Labor Board, **54**: 472, 519; sale of surplus trucks, **55**: 303-304,n1; and Mexican situation, **61**: 610-11; Palmer on cost of living and, **62**: 172; and Shipping Board on disposal of German ships, **62**: 226-27; Baker on effect of treaty delays on, **62**: 261; and Fort Leavenworth incidents, **62**: 545n3; and repatriation of Polish Americans in Haller's Army, **64**: 389-90; and appointment of Assistant Secretary, **65**: 227-28, 557-58; and Jones bill, **65**: 278-

War, Department of (*cont.*)
83; and water-power legislation, **65**:
447; N. D. Baker on sale of surplus to
Poland, **66**: 146; WW on Benson's request for Hoboken piers and army supply bases needed by, **66**: 464-67; and
Aeronautic Commission of Control, **66**:
536,n4; and army recruiting issue, **67**:
97n1
*War and Society in East Central Europe,
Essays on World War I: Total War and
Peacemaking, A Case Study on Trianon* (Kiraly, Pastor, and Sanders,
eds.), **56**: 462n11
Warburg, Felix, **53**: 251n1
Warburg, Max Moritz, **56**: 523n1, 585;
60: 263,n9, 315; suggestions on how to
get Germany to sign peace treaty, **60**:
178,n2, 179
Warburg, Paul Moritz, **55**: 248; **56**:
523n1; **60**: 330,n2; **68**: 405,n4
War Cabinet (Great Britain): *see* Imperial War Cabinet
War Cabinet (War Council), **53**: 56, 70,
150, 166, 205,n1, 604
War Cabinet (U.S.) (super cabinet) (proposed), **63**: 635, 636
War Camp Community Service, **57**: 459
war chests, **67**: 87-88, 96, 110
war crimes and war criminals, **64**: 364-
65,n1, 382; Lansing on, **64**: 381-82; former Crown Prince Friedrich Wilhelm
on, **64**: 397; and Britain's demands for
William II, **64**: 407,n1; WW on, **64**:
408; and German trials, **65**: 100,n1,
157; *see also* William II (of Germany)
Ward, Alan Joseph, **60**: 249n2; **61**:
183n2; **67**: 52n1
Ward, Geoffrey, **67**: 386n2
Ward, Sir Leslie, **54**: 384,n3
Ward, Mary Augustus Arnold (Mrs. Thomas Humphrey), **54**: 305,n5
Wardwell, Allen, **54**: 181n6; **62**: 447,n8
Ware, Moses, **67**: 553
War Emergency Division (Dept. of Justice): termination of, **60**: 115n7
War Emergency Fund (National Security
and Defense Fund): and Committee on
Public Information, **55**: 351, 447; **65**:
374, 375,n1, 442-43,n2,3; and Shannon
Copper Co. loss, **66**: 128,n3
Warfield, Solomon Davies, **55**: 247-48,n1
War Finance Corporation, **55**: 409n4,
536; **58**: 596, 597; **59**: 161, 177, 284; **60**:
26n11, 279, 539-40, 542, 543; **62**: 500,
502; **66**: 445,n1; **67**: 25n2,3, 70; and
ability to make monetary advances,
62: 81,n1; Glass on financial situation
and, **63**: 200, 203; and appointments
to, **64**: 205; issue of revival of, **66**: 36,
37, 60-62, 530; **67**: 16-17, 18-22, 27-28,
192, 193; farmers' organization requests hearing about, **66**: 224
war guilt clause, **61**: 74,n2
War Industries Board, **53**: 11-12, 14, 48,
253, 279, 705n1; **55**: 90, 188; **62**: 20n1;

65: 214n1; and issue of discontinuation
of, **53**: 124, 131-32, 201-202, 206, 229-
31; Baruch's resignation from, **53**: 132,
249-50; and steel prices, **53**: 205n1;
resignation of Price-Fixing Committee, **53**: 413-14; and Arizona copper situation, **66**: 126, 127; and Baruch, **66**:
288-89, 374; reunion of, **66**: 499; and
copper price fixing, **67**: 177-78
*War Industries Board: Business-Govern-
ment Relations During World War I*
(Cuff), **53**: 205n1
War Labor Board: *see* National War
Labor Board
War Labor Conference Board, **66**: 263n1;
and telegraph industry, **56**: 404n1
War Loan Organization, **57**: 471-72, 509
War Lords (Gardiner), **54**: 634n2; **55**:
466; **66**: 411n1
War Minerals Act, **53**: 131, 230
Warnemunde, Germany, **53**: 8
Warner, Charles Damuth, **64**: 428,n1
Warner, Hoyt Landon, **68**: 130n2, 131n8,
168n1, 178n1
War of the Pacific (1879-1883), **66**:
210,n2
war profits tax, **53**: 282; **54**: 501-502; **55**:
333-34,n1
War Prohibition Act, **59**: 76,n1
War Rajah, H.M.S., **59**: 67
Warren, Alice Edith Binsse (Mrs.
Schuyler Nielson), **66**: 274,n4
Warren, Charles, **63**: 623-24,n1; **68**:
521,n4, 522
Warren, Francis Emroy, **61**: 372, 492,
622; **62**: 5,n5; and treaty fight, **64**: 94,
200, 202, 337
Warren, Howard Crosby, **65**: 572,n11
Warren, Schuyler Nielson, Jr., **66**:
275,n5; **68**: 50,n1, 166, 284; on inter-
Allied indebtedness and WW's response, **68**: 106, 107; on organization of
nonpartisan group advocating U.S.
entry into League of Nations and WW's
response, **68**: 155, 156, 157, 158, 162,
163-64, 168,n1, 171
Warren, Whitney, **53**: 358-59
Warrin, Frank Lord, Jr., **56**: 223,n2,
396,n6; **57**: 467n2; **58**: 445
War Risk Insurance Bureau, **55**: 537-38;
56: 83, 397; appropriation bill, **58**: 330;
and Urgent Deficiency bill, **59**: 478n1
Warsaw, Poland, **56**: 92, 93, 122, 123,
133; **65**: 527n1; **66**: 9n1; and Jews, **55**:
372; **59**: 411
Warsaw Commission: *see* Inter-Allied
Commission to Poland
*War-Time Journal of a Georgia Girl,
1864-1865* (Andrews), **67**: 75-76,n1
War Trade Board, **53**: 14, 65, 100, 131,
229, 230, 253, 279, 331; **55**: 351; **56**:
161, 373, 553; **59**: 160; **60**: 114, 290n1;
61: 440, 513, 564n4; and cotton, **53**: 79,
149, 202; and Russian Bureau, **53**:
257,n3; WW on priorities of export, **53**:
281; and Russia, **54**: 259,n1, 261, 412,

413; and pork prices, **55**: 306, 307-308, 343, 362, 393, 396, 483; Glass on prices and, **55**: 361; and resumption of trade with Germany, **62**: 423-24; and chemical imports, **68**: 300

War With Germany: A Statistical Summary (Ayres), **53**: 275n2

War With Spain in 1898 (Trask), **56**: 531n5

War Work of Congress (H.C. Lodge), **65**: 257,n2

Washington, Booker Taliaferro, **54**: 176; **56**: 437

Washington, George, **53**: 521; **54**: 197; **55**: 419, 482; **59**: 450n2; **60**: 41n1, 245; **61**: 517n1; **63**: 375, 406; **65**: 415; **66**: 28, 280, 292, 330, 346n1; **67**: 76, 128, 135, 162, 183n1, 533n1, 566; **68**: 66, 488; and Sulgrave Manor, **66**: 115n1, 543,n1; Farewell Address, **55**: 312n1; **67**: 220, 358, 358-59; WW on not making movie about, **67**: 557,n1

Washington, Patty W., **67**: 534; **68**: 514,n1

Washington, Thomas, **66**: 223,n2

Washington, D.C., **53**: 4; **67**: 505,n1, 513; suggestion for congressional representation from, **53**: 251n1; parade for returning soldiers in, **55**: 36, 37, 294; revenue bill makes city "dry," **55**: 237-38; WW on, **55**: 311, 482; race riots in, **61**: 357n1, 576n2, 610; **62**: 21-22, 234,n1; WW's arrival in, **61**: 401; **63**: 533; and cost of living in, **62**: 174, 176, 215; bills to prevent profiteering in, **62**: 491n1; police situation in, **63**: 149-50, 150, 264-65, 295, 296; WW on threatened police strike in, **63**: 302; Rent Commission formed, **63**: 562n2, 571; Wilsons decide to settle in, **66**: 291,n2; WW on street names, **66**: 306; photograph, *illustration section*, **63** Washington (state): "slacker raids" in, **60**: 115n6

Washington and His Colleagues: A Chronicle of the Rise and Fall of Federalism (Ford), **53**: 340,n1

Washington: Capital City, 1879-1950 (Green), **67**: 505n1

Washington Daily News: alleged interview with EBW, **67**: 479n1, *Washington, D.C. Herald*, **55**: 341n1; **63**: 265; Rogers on H. Hoover and, **66**: 169,n1, 492n1

Washington Monument, **65**: 405

Washington National Cathedral (Mount St. Albans), **68**: 429, 430; Freeman and WW on building plans, **68**: 395-96, 396; and WW's burial, **68**: 579-84

Washington Naval Conference: *see* Conference on the Limitation of Armament

Washington Post, **56**: 551n1; **57**: 232; **58**: 51-51; **59**: 450n2; **61**: 492n2, 518n1, 627n1; **62**: 6n, 92n, 114n, 162, 169, 432n,n3, 596; **63**: 265, 273n2, 274n2, 545n, 546n1, 550n, 553n, 556n, 557n1, 561n, 573n, 575n, 577n, 582n, 587n2;

64: 32n, 100n, 138, 149n2, 187n, 192n1, 511n1; **65**: 71n3; **66**: 17n, 39,n2, 238,n1, 506n1, 506n5; **68**: 24, 155

Washington Sees a Gentler Wilson (*New York Times*), **68**: 57n4

Washington Sends Replies to League (James), **67**: 402n1

Washington Star, **56**: 187; **60**: 299, 378; **62**: 197; **63**: 265; **65**: 495n2; **66**: 519n1; **68**: 57n1, 61, 234,n1, 239

Washington Times, **62**: 227n1, 627; **63**: 265; **67**: 363, 364

Waskow, Arthur Irwin, **61**: 357n1, 576n2

Watch Tower and Tract Society: *see* Jehovah's Witnesses

Waterloo, Belgium, **61**: 11

Waterlow, Sydney Philip Perigal, **60**: 511,n2

water-power legislation, **65**: 398,n1, 447-48, 449; Houston on, **68**: 270

Waters, Henry Jackson, **63**: 611; **64**: 64n1

Waterways Commission (created by Newlands Act), **65**: 448

Watford, Colonel, **59**: 241,n1

Watkins, Thomas Hamer, **53**: 356,n2

Watson, David Robin, **59**: 173n1; **60**: 118n1

Watson, Edwin Martin, **54**: 278,n1, 305,n3

Watson, Emory Olin, **66**: 120-21,n1, 129-30, 378n3

Watson, James Eli; **63**: 5; **67**: 316,n3; **68**: 278n2, 346n2; meets with WW on treaty, **62**: 29,n1, 92-93, 114; and WW's health, **64**: 135-36; and treaty fight, **64**: 200-201, 336; and Article X, **65**: 48

Watson, Thomas, **53**: 537

Watson, Thomas Edward, **65**: 219-20,n1,2

Watson, William, **67**: 105n3

Watt, William Alexander, **54**: 366,n5

Watter, Count Theodor von, **65**: 157n1

Watterson, Henry, **59**: 451,n1; **68**: 475, 591,n5; WW on introduction to memoirs of, **54**: 389,n2

Wattles, Gurden Wallace, **63**: 94n3

Watts, William Carleton, **58**: 495,n6; **65**: 284n1

Ways and Means Committee (House of Reps.), **55**: 334n1; **64**: 340; **67**: 121n2, 191, 484, 485n5; and McCall, **66**: 8

Weatherford, Willis Duke, **62**: 106-107,n2

Weaver, James Bellamy, **63**: 76,n1

Weaver, Zebulon, **55**: 367,n1

W. E. B. Du Bois: Propagandist of the Negro Protest (Rudwick), **54**: 126n1

Webb, Sidney, **53**: 8

Webb-Pomerene Act, **53**: 78,n2

Weber, Eugene, **59**: 195n4

Webster, Charles R., **68**: 545-46,n1, 546-47

Webster, Daniel, **54**: 63; **55**: 460-61, 462; **68**: 202; WW on, **59**: 528; WW's admiration for oratory of, **65**: 145

Webster, James Edwin, **65**: 258,n1, 262; **67**: 491,n7, 494

Weck, René de, **54**: 233,n1

Weeks, John Wingate, **55**: 449; **61**: 469,n1; **63**: 625; **67**: 432,n2, 442; **68**: 346n2; and Muscle Shoals project, **68**: 448,n1

Weeks, Robert S.: WW sends photograph to, **65**: 491, 501

Wei, Suntchou, **57**: 426; **58**: 229

Wei, Wen Pin, **56**: 183

Weihaiwai, China, **63**: 314, 323, 330, 412, 413, 471-72

Weimar, Germany, **60**: 618n3

Weimar Coalition and Ruhr Insurrection, March-April 1920: A Study of Government Policy (Angress), **65**: 155n1

Weinstein, Edwin Alexander, M.D., **56**: 556n2; **57**: 146n4, 240n2; **58**: 276n1, 607, 611,n1, 612, 613, 617n26, 624, 626, 639; **59**: 574n1; **61**: 374n3; **62**: 628,n1; **63**: 539n1; on WW's neurologic illnesses, **58**: 630-35

Weiser, Charles W., **67**: 279-80

Weiss, André, **61**: 83,n3, 85

Weizmann, Chaim, **53**: 572, 717; **54**: 231, 258, 347; **58**: 555

Weld, Sylvia Parsons (Mrs. Rudolph), **68**: 414,n3, 415

welfare legislation: Tumulty on, **65**: 478

Welles, (Benjamin) Sumner, **66**: 179,n2, 367, 506,n4; on Dominican Republic, **66**: 359,n1, 360-64

Wellesley College, **68**: 452n2

Wellington, Arthur Wellesley, 1st Duke of, **56**: 316, 321

Wells, Charles E., **58**: 612n5, 615n17; **62**: 629n4

Wells, H. G. (Herbert George), **53**: 331; **66**: 343n2; **67**: 433, 437

Wells, Thomas Bucklin, **66**: 163-64,n1, 170, 171; **68**: 392-93

Wells Fargo Express Company, **65**: 463

Wemyss, Sir Rosslyn (Erskine), **53**: 325; **54**: 30,n1; **55**: 3, 16, 17, 21, 40, 112; **56**: 338, 430, 489; **57**: 92, 104; **58**: 547, 548, 581-84

Wends, **60**: 23,n3, 268

Wentz, Daniel Bertsch, **55**: 398,n2

Wertheimer, Mr. (German correspondent), **64**: 364

Wertz, Edwin Slusser, **67**: 100-101,n5

Wescott, John Wesley, **64**: 232-33

We Shall Be All: A History of the Industrial Workers of the World (Dubofsky), **65**: 187n3

Wesleyan University, **64**: 514,n1; **65**: 251n2

West, James Edward, **66**: 282n1

West Carnifex, S.S., **56**: 574n3

Westcott, John Howell, **53**: 129, 235; **67**: 182, 411, 412, 494; on inscription found in Nice, **67**: 482

Westcott, John Howell, Jr., **53**: 129,n1, 235; **67**: 411,n3

Westcott, Marian Bate (Mrs. John Howell), **67**: 411n2, 412, 482,n2

Westcott, Mary Dunton, **67**: 482,n1

Westenhaver, David Courtney, **67**: 101

Westermann, William Linn, **53**: 349,n5, 350, 356; **54**: 490,n2; **56**: 155; **57**: 312-13, 468; **59**: 373,n1; **60**: 492; **61**: 105; **64**: 163n6; **65**: 502, 532; on Palestine, **57**: 326,n3; on settling Syrian issue, **57**: 443-44; on mandates formed from Ottoman Empire, **58**: 206, 207-10; on Ottoman Empire, **59**: 349; interviews WW on Anatolia and Asia Minor, **59**: 374-76; on Greece's territorial claims in Asia Minor, **59**: 595-96; memorandum on Near East, **61**: 127, 127-29, 332; on signing of peace treaty, **61**: 328-32; and Turkish-Armenian border dispute, **66**: 65, 110, 350, 357; photograph of, illustration section, **57**

Western Democrat (Mullen), **67**: 312n1, 321n1

Western Political Quarterly, **56**: 98n1

Western Telegraph Company of Great Britain, **66**: 219-22, 514; and landing of foreign cables on U.S. shores, **65**: 518-19

Western Theological Seminary (Pittsburgh), **67**: 335

Western Ukraine Republic (Western Province of the Ukrainian National Republic), **58**: 505n4; Colby on, **68**: 110-11, 118, 119, 121, 134, 140-41; WW on, **68**: 113, 114, 135-36, 142; Colby sails for London concerning, **68**: 152

Western Union Telegraph Company, **53**: 248; **56**: 403; **58**: 51, 303; **61**: 10; **67**: 3; and strike, **60**: 378; McAdoo on, **66**: 219-22, 235-36; WW on, **66**: 224, 250, 500; Colby on controversy over cable, **66**: 399-401; Cabinet on cable issue, **66**: 413, 484; Davis on consistency of position on, **66**: 513-14, 544

Westfalen, S.M.S., **55**: 23, 427; **56**: 28; **58**: 127

West Indies, **61**: 435

Westminster Seminary, Philadelphia, **68**: 519n1

West Prussia: Lord on German counterproposals on, **60**: 185-86, 197

West Virginia: WW urges ratification of 19th Amendment by, **65**: 36; coal situation in, **65**: 335-37; and coal strike, **66**: 445-46,n2

West Virginia State Federation of Labor, **65**: 337

Westphalia, **54**: 246; **58**: 226

Wetherill, Samuel Price, Jr., **66**: 275,n11

Weyand, Louis, **64**: 431; **65**: 16

Weygand, Maxime, **54**: 7, 239, 541; **55**: 11, 95, 102; **56**: 14, 352, 413, 455, 490, 527; **57**: 75, 76, 290, 291, 400, 401, 494; **58**: 288, 545; **59**: 592; **60**: 599, 600, 601; **61**: 33n2; and issue of transport of Polish troops, **56**: 88, 142, 143, 144, 145,

145-46, 409, 496, 497, 527-28; and equipping Rumanian army, **56**: 307; on plans if Germany refuses to sign treaty, **59**: 7, 8, 9; sent to Poland, **66**: 46,n7
Weyl, Walter Edward, **61**: 538,n1; notes of WW press conference, **61**: 240-45,n1
Weyman, Stanley, **66**: 442; **67**: 105n3
Whaling, Thornton, **67**: 473,n1
Wharton, Arthur Orlando, **62**: 570; **65**: 189n1
What I Remember (Fawcett), **55**: 145n4
What May Happen in Germany (Coar), **67**: 463-64,n1
What Really Happened at Paris: The Story of the Peace Conference 1918-1919 (House and Seymour, eds.). **56**: 351n1, 530n4; **67**: 24n2, 57n1; N. D. Baker on, **67**: 296
What the Senate Costs the Country (New York *World*), **62**: 180,n1
What Wilson Did at Paris (R.S. Baker), **63**: 609n2; **64**: 320,n1, 325,n5, 335; **66**: 521,n1, 522, 533; **67**: 16,n2
wheat, **53**: 254, 603, 604; and prices, **55**: 252, 360; **57**: 472-74, 475, 578; **59**: 77; **61**: 499, 549,n1, 612, 613; decision to continue functioning of Grain Corporation, **56**: 281-82, 372, 426; Redfield on prices, **56**: 619-20; Barnes to head Grain Corporation, **57**: 375, 475; Barnes' proposals regarding, **62**: 51-57; and prices and cost of living issue, **62**: 94-95, 104-106, 159, 168, 171-72, 198, 200; **66**: 36,n3; Hoover on, **62**: 124, WW on prices, **62**: 212; and shipments to Poland, **64**: 4-6, 12-13; and shipments to Armenia, **64**: 13-14; WW on imports and exports of, **67**: 191, 191-92
Wheat Act (March 4, 1919), **59**: 192,n1
Wheat Administration, **59**: 206n1
Wheat Corporation (proposed), **56**: 282
Wheat Guarantee Act (March 4, 1919), **62**: 180,n1
Wheeler, Clayton L., **64**: 322n1
Wheeler, Eleanor Josephine McPartland (Mrs. Howard Durgee), **55**: 456,n3; **56**: 64; concern over cancellation of war contracts, **53**: 18-20, 47
Wheeler, George Wakeman: on suggestions for WW's League of Nations strategy, **61**: 459, 460
Wheeler, Howard Durgee, **55**: 456,n1; **56**: 63-64
Wheeler Newspaper Syndicate, **55**: 341n1
Wheeling Steel and Iron Company, **57**: 385
Wheelwright, Jere Hungerford, **63**: 56,n2
When a Man Comes to Himself (Wilson), **68**: 370,n1
When the Cheering Stopped: The Last Years of Woodrow Wilson (Smith), **58**: 636,n9; **67**: 137n3
Whipple, Sherman Leland, **53**: 186-87, 261, 587; **54**: 125, 396, 432; **67**: 339; **68**:

81,n2, 82, 83, 96,n1, 190; and Norwegian ships, **55**: 357,n2; suggested for Attorney General, **55**: 193, 222; **60**: 115-16; WW on, **68**: 83,n1
Whistler, James Abbott McNeill, **61**: 489,n1
White, Charles Thomas, **62**: 627
White, David, **62**: 617n2
White, Edward Douglass, **66**: 191; suggested for International Court of Justice, **60**: 431, 432; as judge of William II, **61**: 396,n2; and Panama-Costa Rica dispute, **67**: 382n5, 384
White, Emily Vanderbilt Sloane (Mrs. Henry), **68**: 320,n2
White, Grace Hoffman (Mrs. John Jay), **58**: 140-41,n1
White, George, **65**: 551,n1; **66**: 173; **67**: 302, 390,n1; **68**: 577; on visit with WW, **67**: 308; issue of resignation of, **67**: 321n1, 325, 339-40, 349-50
White, Henry, **53**: 185, 318, 321, 336, 344, 358, 357, 368, 384 385, 391, 401, 411,n1, 573, 707; **54**: 4, 62, 127, 264, 404, 489, 556; **55**: 152, 154, 187-88, 234; **56**: 124, 396, 429, 435; **57**: 35, 52, 312, 332, 496; **58**: 3, 138, 255, 312, 379, 410, 521, 534; **59**: 68, 156, 285, 397, 398, 480-81, 524, 546, 594, 603; **61**: 46, 105, 111, 115, 117, 128, 178, 332, 347-48, 477, 526-27, 623-24, 629,n1; **62**: 11, 264, 319, 404; **63**: 91, 537, 606; **64**: 472; **65**: 108, 141; **66**: 330; **67**: 69, 291; appointed peace commissioner, **53**: 147,n1, 167, 195, 243; on urgency of food appropriations passage, **53**: 692; and Greece's request to send troops to Turkey and the Ukraine, **54**: 402-403, 426-27; on Belgium and reparations, **55**: 200; on Bullitt mission to Russia, **55**: 540n1; on Rumanian delegation, **57**: 136-37; on abolition of secret sessions and other suggestions, **57**: 301-302; on newspapers and French security treaty, **57**: 416-17, 430; and Kiel Canal, **57**: 457, 567-68; on Austria presenting her position in Paris, **58**: 205; and Japanese claims and settlement, **58**: 232, 320, 327, 328; on German delegates' credentials, **58**: 424-25; on Montenegro, **59**: 178; on Sultan not residing in Constantinople and mandatory issue, **59**: 395-97, 444; on Denmark, **59**: 472; on German counterproposals, **60**: 70, 71; on somebody taking notes for WW, **60**: 285, 286; on Senate resolution of Ireland being heard at Paris Peace Conference, **60**: 375; on Upper Silesia, **60**: 402, 404, 405; on Serbian and Yugoslav atrocities in Albania, **60**: 530; WW answers on Albania, **60**: 564-65; and WW-Poincaré dinner invitation episode, **61**: 115, 132, 180, 188, 189; WW on, **61**: 180; **67**: 440; at Versailles signing ceremony, **61**: 324; on replacing his son as minister to

White, Henry (*cont.*)
  Siam, **61**: 348; on trade with Bolshevik Russia, **61**: 482-84; meets with Tittoni and rejects his Adriatic proposal, **61**: 551-54; on Bulgaria and Greece, **61**: 566-68, 588-93; on Italian situation, **61**: 575-76; on proposed blockade of Soviet Russia, **62**: 14-16; and disposal of German and Austro-Hungarian ships, **62**: 146; and Shantung settlement, **62**: 150, 151, 208; EBW praises, **62**: 155-57; on Bessarabia, **62**: 206-207; and Thrace, **62**: 510; and Adriatic question, **62**: 575, 605,n3; and Bullitt testimony, **63**: 337n1; WW interested in buying house of, **65**: 513-14; declines to serve on Åland Island Commission, **65**: 531,n1; and Lord Robert Cecil's visit, **68**: 320, 344, 346n2; photograph of, *illustration section*, **53**; **58**
White, John Beaver, **53**: 15, 60
White, John Campbell, **55**: 187,n1; **61**: 348,n3; **65**: 108,n1; **66**: 87n1
White, John Philip, **63**: 56,n1; and Coal Commission, **64**: 206, 209n1; **65**: 95,n2
White, Julian Leroy, **62**: 157,n9
White, Lawrence Grant, **53**: 639,n1; on WW's conference with Bissolati, **53**: 641-44
White, Margaret Stuyvesant Rutherford (Mrs. Henry): portrait of, **62**: 157,n8
White, Sam, **68**: 572
White, Sanford, **53**: 639n1
White, Sebastian Harrison, **63**: 490,n1, 500
White, Sir Thomas, **58**: 416, 493-94, 517
White, William Allen, **58**: 241-42, 327, 490-91; **59**: 70; **64**: 62,n2; **66**: 246n2; **68**: 148,n5, 452n2, 495; on Russia, **56**: 544, 545;on WW's achievements and on partisan politics concerning League of Nations Covenant, **61**: 506-507,n1; and WW Foundation, **68**: 249n2
White, William Charles, M.D., **58**: 449,n3
White Against Red: The Life of General Anton Denikin (Lehovich), **59**: 550n2
White Armies of Russia: A Chronicle of Counter-Revolution and Allied Intervention (Stewart), **54**: 93n5; **60**: 95n2; **63**: 588n1
White Book on war responsibilities: *see Is Germany guilty? German White-book concerning the Responsibility of the Authors of the War*
White Chief: James Kimble Vardaman (Holmes), **68**: 93n3
White Eagle, Red Star: The Polish-Soviet War 1919-1920 (Davies), **53**: 611n1; **65**: 527n1,3; **66**: 46n7
Whiteman, Harold B., Jr., **53**: 544n1
Whitlock, Wlla Brainerd (Mrs. Brand), **61**: 172
Whitley, John Henry, **55**: 91n1
Whitley Councils, **55**: 91n1
Whitley Councils Scheme (Seymour), **55**: 91n1

Whitley plan, **58**: 605
Whitley Report, **55**: 91,n1
Whitlock, Brand, **53**: 552-53, 712; **54**: 495, 550; **56**: 521-22; **57**: 422; **58**: 593; **60**: 358,n2; **61**: 3, 29, 34; **62**: 6, 252, 253; **65**: 330; **68**: 452n2, 521, 522; appointed ambassador to Italy, **60**: 56, 192, 358, 485; **61**: 134, 177-78, 290, 386; WW on appointment of, **60**: 360; T. N. Page on, **61**: 9,n2; on WW's Belgian tour, **61**: 105-106; WW thanks, **61**: 172-73; sends WW Whistler's book, **61**: 489; on King Albert's proposed visit to U.S., **61**: 609; photograph of, *illustration section*, **61**
Whitlock, Ella Brainerd (Mrs. Brand), **53**: 553,n1; **61**: 172
Whitmarsh, Theodore F., **53**: 15, 59; **54**: 105; **55**: 253, 358, 360; **57**: 376
Whitney, George Washington Tapley, **67**: 182
Who's Who in America, **53**: 113n1; **68**: 134n1
Whyte, Margaret Emily Fairweather (Mrs. Alexander Frederick), **67**: 46,n4
Wiart, Adrian Carton de: *see* Carton de Wiart, Adrian
Wichita, Kan., **56**: 404n1; WW cancels trip to, **63**: 520, 522-23; WW's message to people of, **63**: 524
Wickersham, George Woodward, **53**: 441,n2; **60**: 330n5; **61**: 178,n1; **64**: 64n1; **65**: 148,n1, 184,n4; **66**: 141n2, 246n2, 542n1; **67**: 607; on League of Nations, **63**: 222-23,n1; **68**: 162,n2, 178n1, 273, 274, 282; WW on conversion of, **63**: 248; and second Industrial Conference, **63**: 611
Wichersham Answers League Obstructionists (*New York Times*), **63**: 223n1
Wiener, Franz: *see* Croisset, Francis de
Wiesbaden, Germany, **58**: 45; **60**: 60n7
Wiesner, Friedrich von, **56**: 614,n2
Wilberforce, Robert, **68**: 106, 107
Wilberforce University, **68**: 106
Wilbur, Charlotte D., **67**: 91,n1
Wilbur, Ray Lyman, **66**: 246n2
Wilde, Louis J., **63**: 370,n1, 371, 382
Wilder, William Royal, **65**: 246, 572,n7, 574, 575; **67**: 458
Wile, Frederick William, **67**: 72n1
Wiley, Louis, **68**: 11; praises WW, **66**: 188,n1, 327; WW thanks, **66**: 199, 338; requests tribute to Ochs from WW, and WW's response, **68**: 524, 525
Wilhelmina, Queen of The Netherlands, **55**: 219-20
Wilkerson, James Herbert, **68**: 129,n1, 148
Wilkins, William J., **66**: 379,n1, 382
Willard, Belle Layton Wyatt (Mrs. Joseph Edward), **56**: 585,n2
Willard, Daniel, **63**: 607,n3, 613,n1
Willard, Joseph Edward, **56**: 585; **60**: 192; interview with Alfonso XIII, **56**: 392

Willard, Mary Elizabeth, **56**: 585,n2
Willert, Arthur, **61**: 347,n1
William II (of Germany), **53**: 487, 576; **55**: 504; **59**: 554, 627; **60**: 545; **61**: 313, 323; **62**: 442; **67**: 226; abdication of, **53**: 63n1; and The Netherlands, **53**: 130,n2, 138; proposed trial before international tribunal, **53**: 324,n2; WW on guilt and, **53**: 364; George V on, **55**: 228; comments about responsibility and punishment for the war, **56**: 269, 530n4, 616; **57**: 122, 123, 124, 125, 126, 127, 128, 131-32, 146,n4, 149-50, 308-309, 319, 331, 405, 631; **58**: 278,n3, 295, 416, 503; **60**: 475-76; and China, **57**: 625; effect of WW's health on making decision on guilt of, **58**: 624-25, 627, 633, 634; Germany's treaty reservations concerning, **61**: 69, 70, 74-75; Council of Four on, **61**: 150; 334-35, 340; delivery of by Holland, **61**: 157, 194-95, 199, 200-201, 204-205, 218, 257-58, 258-59; Grayson on Smuts and, **61**: 304,n3; Bethmann Hollweg accepts responsibility for war instead of, **61**: 334-35, 340; possible extradition of to Great Britain, **61**: 395-96,n1; Pope Benedict XV against proposed trial of, **62**: 26-27; WW answers Pope Benedict on, **62**: 371; and penalties, **62**: 318; and war crimes, **64**: 382, 407,n1
William Allen White's America (Johnson), **68**: 148n5
William E. Borah and American Foreign Policy (Maddox), **68**: 278n2
William F. McCombs: The President Maker (Lyons), **67**: 306n1
William Francis Joseph Charles, Archduke, **54**: 32,n4
William Jennings Bryan (Coletta), **67**: 532n2
William and Mary College, **55**: 444; WW receives honorary degree from, **62**: 42n2; **63**: 463; Grayson thanks Dodge for contribution to, **65**: 341-42
William Morris Hughes, A Political Biography (Fitzhardinge), **54**: 351n3
Williams, Archibald, **57**: 466
Williams, C. D., **67**: 212
Williams, David C., **67**: 614n1
Williams, Dixon C., **68**: 149,n6
Williams, Edward Thomas, **56**: 153,n2; **58**: 144, 214, 229, 253, 327; on China's claims, **57**: 626-27; **58**: 46, 70-73; on meeting between Lansing and Chinda on Japan's claims, **58**: 165-68
Williams, Elizabeth Dial Webb (Mrs. John Sharp), **54**: 555,n1; **67**: 454,n1, 455; **68**: 294,n1
Williams, Enoch: protests Anthracite Coal Commission award, **66**: 75, 106, 107
Williams, George Weems, **59**: 38,n2
Williams, Henry Winslow: proposed draft of Senate resolution on League of Nations Covenant, **61**: 489-91,n1, 491-92

Williams, Jay Jerome, **54**: 60; **62**: 626
Williams, John R., **65**: 506n1
Williams, John Sharp, **55**: 198, 270, 325, 326, 412; **60**: 245n8, 245-46,n10, 330, 417, 462-63, 469, 596; **62**: 336; **64**: 156,n2; **65**: 482; **66**: 166-67, 368; **67**: 166; **68**: 93n2, 292; and woman suffrage, **53**: 244, 717; **54**: 56, 90,n1, 274, 555, 555-56; **55**: 37; and Armenia, **55**: 65-66; **62**: 116, 241, 259-60; **63**: 304,n1, 464, 466; **65**: 351n2; and vote on Ireland being heard at peace conference, **60**: 249n2; congratulations and some advice for WW, **61**: 410-11; on WW's address to Senate, **61**: 444-45; appointment suggestions for U.S. Court of Claims, **61**: 482,n1; questions WW at Foreign Relations Committee meeting, **62**: 339, 340, 348, 353, 354-55, 360, 362, 363, 368, 369, 383; and Foreign Relations Committee's minority report, **63**: 198,n1; and Mexican situation, **64**: 120; and Democratic caucus on treaty, **64**: 384; and Armenian mandate, **65**: 351n2; on WW's health and campaigning, **66**: 147-48; **67**: 399n2; on being in crowd that cheered WW and WW's response, **67**: 454-55, 455; and Four Power Treaty, **67**: 518, 525-26, 577n1; WW's farewell to on leaving Senate, **68**: 293-94
Williams, John Skelton, **54**: 429; **61**: 496,n2; Republican opposition to appointment of, **54**: 485,n1; on steel trust and cost of living, **62**: 517-22, 526; suggested for Railroad Labor Board, **65**: 44; on WW's nephew's job performance, **66**: 38,n1, 39, 40-41, 42; WW thanks for job evaluation, **66**: 42; Houston on, **66**: 445
Williams, Joyce Grigsby, **63**: 606n1
Williams, Maie Hewitt (Mrs. John R.), **65**: 506n1
Williams, Samuel Wells, **66**: 79,n1
Williams, Talcott, **67**: 607
Williams, William Reid, **65**: 557-58,n2; **66**: 237-38,n1
Williams College, **53**: 307; **58**: 428n1; and Garfield, **64**: 181n1; and Wilson & Colby announcement, **67**: 344
Williamson, Norris Charlescraft, **65**: 294,n1
Williamstown, Mass., **53**: 437
Willing, Mr. **67**: 359
Willis, James F., **58**: 278n3; **64**: 364n1; **65**: 100n1
Willis, John S., **66**: 175,n2
Willoughby, Westel Woodbury, **54**: 194,n2; **56**: 270n5; **61**: 635,n2; **66**: 246n2
Wilmington, Del., **55**: 410
Wilmington (N.C.) *Star*, **67**: 488
Wilno, Poland: *see* Vilna, Poland
Wilson, Agnes Williamson (Mrs. William Bauchop): death of, **66**: 228,n1
Wilson, Alfred McCalmont, first cousin once removed of WW, **68**: 387,n4

Wilson, Arnold Talbot, **57**: 247,n4; **58**: 172,n1
Wilson, Ben, **56**: 283
Wilson, Charles Stetson, **66**: 358,n1
Wilson, Edith Bolling Galt (Mrs. Woodrow), **53**: 22, 68, 85, 166, 181, 184, 189, 204, 292, 309, 310, 314, 315, 318, 319, 320, 336, 344, 345, 346, 368, 369, 384, 385, 391, 420n1, 432, 436-37, 450, 458, 459, 467, 468, 470, 473, 491, 496, 510, 511, 522-23, 527, 534, 537, 538, 540, 546, 547, 553, 584, 586, 605, 609, 613, 615; **54**: 5, 35, 61, 62, 104, 126, 134, 150, 170, 217, 227, 237, 304-306, 307, 309, 428, 489, 552; **55**: 36, 41, 65, 66, 265, 266, 269, 281, 283, 308, 309, 409, 410, 440, 531; **56**: 2, 62, 81, 125, 163, 311, 338, 350, 355, 408, 421, 428, 428-29, 439, 440, 540, 542, 585, 586, 588; **57**: 51, 60-61, 67, 140-41, 239, 284, 306, 316, 331, 333, 351, 390, 420, 476, 478, 503, 513, 530, 533, 576, 580, 581, 585; **58**: 3, 4, 48, 54, 103, 104, 112, 170, 171, 172, 176, 187, 188, 216, 244, 245, 275, 277, 331, 367-68, 421, 422, 428, 429, 430, 462, 463, 500, 503, 530, 535, 594; **59**: 3, 35, 39-40, 48, 124, 161, 162, 186, 207, 247, 248, 249, 254, 289, 321, 371, 410, 420, 479, 530, 554, 605, 606, 625; **60**: 4, 19, 44, 116, 157, 204, 249, 292, 300, 333, 334, 388, 435, 532, 545, 546, 547, 569, 574; **61**: 22, 29, 33, 35, 61, 114, 135, 172, 179, 231, 302, 303, 327, 354, 355, 369, 374, 378, 383, 385, 397, 400, 409, 416, 459, 482n1, 518n1, 551, 562; **62**: 102, 185, 270, 271, 303, 336, 423, 456, 516, 626; **63**: 165, 167, 526, 558, 559, 575, 578n1, 585, 608; **64**: 12n3, 42, 44, 50, 57, 61, 71, 87, 130, 227, 229, 237, 245, 274, 320, 325, 345-46, 350-51, 353, 355, 405n, 420, 428, 467, 473-74, 480, 488-89, 495, 511n1; **65**: 37, 94, 217, 235, 291, 297, 432, 514; **66**: 50, 79, 92, 171, 193, 195, 216, 222, 235, 251, 310, 329, 330, 333, 388, 434, 521, 526, 536, 545; **67**: 6, 23, 83, 134, 152, 174, 201, 202, 205, 215, 229, 234, 236, 244, 251, 305, 321n1, 325, 333, 342, 351, 357, 375, 392, 411, 434, 441, 458, 459, 470, 481, 494, 504, 510, 530, 554, 557, 562, 564, 565, 575, 605; **68**: 33, 42, 43, 64, 69, 72, 84, 85, 87, 99, 102n2, 109, 115, 116, 117, 126, 127, 128, 137, 140, 144, 150, 151, 156, 169, 180, 191, 198, 201, 222, 227, 274, 279, 281, 283, 286, 290, 292, 293, 294, 304, 311, 325, 326, 329, 332, 339, 346, 352, 355, 363, 372, 374, 384, 385, 386, 392, 396, 401, 407, 423, 427, 430, 433, 442, 458, 465, 472, 504, 507, 510, 514, 517, 519, 524, 526, 531; and Morgenthau's book, **53**: 3; takes walks with WW aboard ship, **53**: 321, 327, 341; WW's affection for, **53**: 356-57; Seymour's description of, **53**: 377; on arrival in Brest and Paris, **53**: 396-99; **55**: 487; her

rooms in Murat Palace described, **53**: 429-30; sends her family Christmas greetings and news of her activities in France, **53**: 400-501; on activities in London, **53**: 591-95; on Italian trip and activities, **53**: 611-13; Benham's impression of, **54**: 218; and Gobelin tapestry, **54**: 306; on reception after WW's speech to French Chamber of Deputies, **54**: 487-88; voyage to and arrival at Boston, **55**: 204, 205, 218, 226; departs for France, **55**: 442; activities aboard ship, **55**: 456, 465, 471, 489, 490, 491; WW's dependence on, **55**: 466; on WW's appearance after conference with House, **55**: 488n2; visits battlefront, **56**: 194 visits Red Cross Tent City, **56**: 525; King Albert of Belgium visits, **56**: 555, 556; as nurse to WW, **57**: 145, 235; **63**: 527, 528, 549, 619, 621; meetings with Queen Marie of Rumania, **57**: 190, 193, 241; asks House for explanation of his comments to Steed, **57**: 532n2; Grayson on, **59**: 79; on Sonnino's reaction to Vénisélos presence at Council of Four meeting, **59**: 319; bunion problem, **59**: 477, 526, 528, 577, 578, 621; **60**: 3-4; on somebody taking notes for WW, **60**: 285-86; on tour of Belgium, **61**: 3, 6, 11, 12, 14; I. Hoover on WW's health and, **61**: 112n1; her wedding band and WW's signet ring, **61**: 179; and Poincaré dinner invitation episode, **61**: 180, 188, 189; and WW's daily walks aboard ship, **61**: 370; on increase of Red Cross fund from sale of wool from White House sheep, **61**: 505; concern over WW's proposed speaking tour, **61**: 543; personal thoughts to Henry White, **62**: 155-57; on western tour with WW, **63**: 4, 31, 32, 63, 65, 94, 95, 96, 122, 168, 169, 239, 273, 308, 382, 419; reception in Portland, **63**: 276; on meeting with Mrs. Hulbert, **63**: 419n1; and decision to cancel remainder of trip, **63**: 519; trip exhausting for, **63**: 523; N. D. Baker offers to help lessen WW's work load, **63**: 534; and WW's stroke, **63**: 539n1; and WW's health, **63**: 552n1; **64**: 232-33, 503, 507, 509, 509-10; **65**: 90, 332-33; and Adriatic crisis, **63**: 557, 558, 617; entertains WW by reading, **63**: 561, 636; **65**: 342; **67**: 517; **68**: 197; furnishes WW with news, **63**: 574; informs Mrs. House of WW's condition, **63**: 580-81; House's concern about news of him being withheld from WW by, **63**: 587-88; on reasons for not telling WW of House's return from Paris, **63**: 592; and visit of Belgian royalty, **63**: 603,605, 606n1; and Craufurd-Stuart affair, **63**: 606n1; conduit for WW, **63**: 609, 615; **64**: 4, 6, 10, 12n3, 14, 16, 37-38, 42, 50-51, 52n1, 53, 58-59, 61, 72, 88-89, 90, 95-96, 97, 100, 103,

104n1, 119, 145, 147, 156, 166, 167, 179n1, 180n1, 190, 198, 202, 203, 204, 206, 218, 228, 230n1, 232, 233-34, 235, 242, 243, 244, 246, 274, 276-77,n1, 282-83, 297, 330, 330n1, 332, 335-36, 342n2, 346, 352-53, 366, 389, 391, 405, 448, 457; **65**: 24, 28, 40, 48, 56, 82, 117, 119, 122, 128-29, 134, 143, 146, 175, 183, 194, 215, 270n2, 372, 395, 396, 398, 400, 453, 554, 564; **66**: 33, 38, 81, 102-103, 112, 122-23, 153n1, 170, 173n1, 189, 234, 253, 298-99, 306, 317, 371, 383-84, 401, 410-11, 420, 469-70, 531; **67**: 119, 141, 142, 167, 188-89, 189, 241, 278, 282, 284, 285, 286-87, 393, 559-60; **68**: 322n1, 521, 522; on WW being unable to study Adriatic question at this time, **63**: 617; appears tired and worn, **63**: 619; R. S. Baker on, **63**: 619, 621; **67**: 82, 93, 237, 244, 256, 289, 360, 585, 586, 617; and House, **63**: 621; **64**: 347, 348; marriage announcement to WW, **63**: 624-25; at time of WW's stroke, **63**: 633-664; during WW's illness, **63**: 637, 637-38; influence during WW's illness, **63**: 638; and Queen Mother of England, **64**: 28; greets Prince of Wales, **64**: 31; thank you from Prince of Wales, **64**: 36-37; Thanksgiving Day, **64**: 93; Lansing on political decision making and, **64**: 124; notes on WW's meetings with Hitchcock and Fall on Mexico, **64**: 130-31, 133-35; and draft of WW's statement on treaty, **64**: 199n1; and railroad situation, **64**: 222,n1, 223,n1; Lansing on role of during WW's illness, **64**: 231; House on discourteous treatment of Lord Grey by, **64**: 239; relationship with Lansing, **64**: 243; C. R. Crane's advice to, **64**: 262; and Lansing's resignation, **64**: 270, 416, 417,n3; **65**: 21-22; mentioned as WW's adviser, **64**: 270; R. S. Baker on, **64**: 320-21; R. S. Baker's offer to help WW with compromise position, **64**: 326-27; to R. S. Baker on having the "right spirit" of the treaty, **64**: 335; House on treaty position of, **64**: 348; and WW's decision to resign, **64**: 362n1; **66**: 436; **67**: 568; draft letter to Glass on Taft reservation, **64**: 405; C. R. Crane offers vacation home to, **64**: 425; Grayson on care of WW by, **64**: 499; vetoes divulgence of WW's physical condition, **64**: 507n1, 510; **67**: x; on WW's stroke, **64**: 507n1; told of diagnosis of WW's illness, **64**: 510; accompanies WW on motor rides, **65**: 41, 42, 67, 86; **68**: 249, 378, 380; House suggests R. S. Baker see on treaty, **65**: 41; Pershing thanks for flowers, **65**: 108; relays news of treaty rejection to WW, **65**: 108; thanks Long for offer of vacation home, **65**: 110; and Egan's book, **65**: 122,n2; if WW unavailable, religious leaders press for

meeting with, **65**: 184, 185; ends WW's first Cabinet meeting since illness, **65**: 186,n1, 187; sends sample stationery and affection to WW, **65**: 287; words of love and encouragement for WW, **65**: 324, 376; to receive pin cushion from Salvation Army, **65**: 332; code with Cummings, **65**: 348, 481; Cummings on, **65**: 349; 349; Geddes on, **65**: 369; and objection to Marshall's taking over, **65**: 384; issue of renomination of WW, **65**: 400, 435, 492n1, 493-94, 498; and granting of Seibold interview with WW, **65**: 401n1; Seibold on, **65**: 406; and General Barnett's replacement, **65**: 430n1; asks H. White if his house is for sale, **65**: 513-14; Swem on influence on WW, **65**: 550; takes ride with WW, **66**: 15; WW on her way of folding letters, **66**: 29-30; nurse impertinent to, **66**: 36; Hawkins on during WW interview, **66**: 154, 155, 165-57; and White House sheep, **66**: 185; dines with and discusses with Cummings WW's role and feelings about campaign, **66**: 189-91; unable to change WW's position on use of Root material, **66**: 230; and plans for home in Washington, **66**: 291,n2, 345n2, 354; returns House's clothes, **66**: 379-80l; tender care of WW, **66**: 435; R. S. Baker on, **66**: 435, 438; on R. S. Baker's draft article on WW, **66**: 446-47; Dodge on seeing WW and, **66**: 449; R. S. Baker informs he will not print his article on WW, **66**: 450-51; R. U. Johnson on, **66**: 481; decision to buy S Street house, **66**: 519,n1; Jessie on, **66**: 534; love for WW, **67**: 5; and WW's Nobel Prize money, **67**: 52; and house plans, **67**: 84, 127; Swem on encouragement given WW by, **67**: 103; congratulates K. Trask on her forthcoming marriage, **67**: 106-107; attends theater with WW, **67**: 111, 381; WW's valentines to and love for, **67**: 133, 371, 536, 545; and WW's bad portrait, **67**: 143; and delegation from Harvard's WW Club, **67**: 158-59; Axson's news for and thoughts of, **67**: 172-73, 310; R. S. Baker on his book and, **67**: 184; and the Hardings' visit to White House, **67**: 189-90; Houston on, **67**: 200; Tumulty praises, **67**: 202; and inauguration day activities, **67**: 208, 209, 210, 211, 212; in new home, **67**: 212; and Mrs. Harding, **67**: 237; Cummings on, **67**: 270; on WW's break with House, **67**: 289-91,n3; and decoding of House's personal message, **67**: 293-94; receives students from Princeton, **67**: 311; McAdoo's concern for health and burdens of, **67**: 356; R. S. Baker on her care of WW and beauty of, **67**: 360; and likeness of WW for WW Foundation certificate, **67**: 369-70, 372; and Armistice Day activities, **67**: 401, 449-53, 453n1;

Wilson, Edith Bolling Galt (*cont.*)
Nell on belated birthday greetings to, **67**: 429; in tears at ovation for WW, **67**: 451; Dodges look forward to seeing, **67**: 470, 471; E. Helm's praise of, **67**: 477, 479; and alleged interview with *Washington Daily News*, **67**: 479,n1, 492,n1; and crowd from local WW Foundation, **67**: 523; WW's physical therapist on, **67**: 612; appears with WW before crowd, **68**: 38; WW's dedication of proposed book to, **68**: 39-40; Tarbell on, **68**: 45, 47; WW on vacation plans and, **68**: 59; and Jefferson Day dinner brouhaha, **68**: 60; E. P. Davis on, **68**: 65; WW on strain on, **68**: 75; and WW's improvement, **68**: 146; and R. S. Baker's *World Settlement*, **68**: 150-51, 176, 480; WW's love for, **68**: 238, 315, 412, 415; McAdoos send love to, **68**: 240; Axson on during Christmas and WW's birthday celebration, **68**: 255, 256, 257; Dodd on, **68**: 259; exchanges valentines with WW, **68**: 288; in NYC for Lord Robert Cecil's speech, **68**: 310, 315,n1, 317, 383; arranges visit with WW for Lord Robert Cecil, **68**: 320; involved with decision on WW's essay, **68**: 342-44, 344-45, 347, 347-48, 353-54, 356, 356-67, 370; Lord Robert Cecil on, **68**: 345; "breaks down" trying to help with WW's essay, **68**: 348n1; and *Collier's* request to publish WW's essay, **68**: 368; devotion to WW, **68**: 383; at Harding's funeral, **68**: 400, 401, 402; attends theater, **68**: 404; on activities during her vacation in Massachusetts, **68**: 408-11, 412-13, 413-14, 415, 416-17; love for WW, **68**: 408, 409, 410, 413, 417; keeps track of days since WW was stricken, **68**: 410; Hamlin on positive impression left by, **68**: 418-19, 420; and trust fund for WW, **68**: 442-43, 444; stays with Norman Davises, **68**: 450,n1, 461; at Armistice Day demonstration, **68**: 469, 470; on the McAdoos' visit, **68**: 480; and Knott offer, **68**: 483, 501; and WW's birthday, **68**: 509; and Mrs. Hulbert, **68**: 527; and C. H. McCormick's attempt to reconcile WW and House, **68**: 528-29, 529; and reception for Democratic National Committee, **68**: 531-32; has the grippe, **68**: 544; and WW's last illness, **68**: 549, 550, 552, 555, 556, 557, 559, 562, 564, 565; and Coolidge's concern over WW's health, **68**: 552; consoled by clergy, **68**: 558; and WW's death, **68**: 566, 573; invites Coolidge to WW's funeral, **68**: 574; requests Lodge not attend funeral, **68**: 574; has flowers sent to army hospitals, **68**: 575; at WW's funeral, **68**: 582, 583, 583-84; Kerney on devoted sheltering of WW by, **68**: 596; photograph of, *illustration section*, **58**; **61**; **65**; **67**; **68**

Wilson, Edmund: offered but declines appointment, **65**: 245,n1, 317,n3
Wilson, Edmund, Jr., **65**: 245n1
Wilson, Edwin Clinton: WW's first cousin once removed: WW's condolences to, **68**: 387-88,n1
Wilson, Ellen Louise Axson (Mrs. Woodrow), **60**: 647; **63**: 632n1; **64**: 516; **65**: 243; **66**: 320; **67**: 173n4, 256, 307n2; **68**: 76n2; 556n3; Grayson on, **64**: 485; and placement of her picture during WW's illness, **64**: 490; and Berry Schools, **67**: 456; and Mrs. Peck, **68**: 527
Wilson, Florence, **64**: 275
Wilson, George Grafton, **54**: 512n3; **56**: 212,n3
Wilson, Henry Braid, **53**: 397,n2; **61**: 400; **62**: 460n1
Wilson, Sir Henry (Hughes), **53**: 326,n3, 498, 560,n2; **54**: 244, 499, 538; **55**: 112, 180; **56**: 259n1, 326, 327, 409, 456, 583; **57**: 75, 76, 103, 104, 460; **58**: 315, 435, 436-37, 438, 441, 507, 545, 580; **59**: 21, 139, 140, 277, 330, 331, 333, 592, 632; **60**: 300, 303, 304, 589, 617; **61**: 33n2, 274; **68**: 301,n9; requests U.S. troops be sent to Murmansk and Archangel, **55**: 28; on meeting with Foch on peace terms, **55**: 212-13,n1; and Greek troops to Turkey, **58**: 511, 512, 514; concern over rapid withdrawal of U.S. troops, **58**: 572; on landing Greek troops at Smyrna, **59**: 22, 23, 24, 25, 26; and Syria, **59**: 336, 340, 341, 343, 345; at Council of Four on Hungarian-Czechoslovak conflict, **60**: 312-14,n1, 315-16; on Rhineland army of occupation, **60**: 364,n2
Wilson, Ida Gordon (Mrs. John Adams), **68**: 387,n3
Wilson, Janet Woodrow (Mrs. Joseph Ruggles), mother of WW, **53**: 424; **55**: 473; **66**: 252; WW visits birthplace of, **53**: 537, 538, 541; and Carlisle, England, **64**: 184
Wilson, John Adams, first cousin of WW, **64**: 320, 490
Wilson, John Harden: congressional victory of, **55**: 448,n1, 457, 458
Wilson, Joseph Ruggles, father of WW, **53**: 32; **58**: 147; **59**: 248, 255; **63**: 417; **64**: 515; **66**: 252, 277n1, 306,n2; **67**: 75, 76, 307, 567-68; WW on, **59**: 162; **60**: 489n1; **63**: 624; **64**: 517; and Daniel Webster's speeches, **59**: 528; and Oglethorpe University, **65**: 86,n2, 89, 117, 382; and oratory, **65**: 145; as professor at Southwestern Presbyterian University, **66**: 134,n4
Wilson, Joseph Ruggles, Jr.: brother of WW, **60**: 645,n5; **67**: 403-404; arrives at White House, **63**: 549; and WW's last illness, **68**: 554, 556, 558, 564, 569, 577; and WW's death, **68**: 566

Wilson, Justina Leavitt (Mrs. Halsey William), **62**: 225,n1
Wilson, Kate Wilson (Mrs. Joseph R., Jr.), **68**: 577,n8
Wilson, Margaret Woodrow, daughter of WW and EAW, **53**: 21, 68, 213, 262, 344, 384, 397,n5, 399, 501, 612,n1, 615; **54**: 134, 400, 410, 522, 550,n1; **55**: 440; **56**: 62, 81, 81,n1, 311; **57**: 61; **58**: 277, 331; **60**: 335, 381, 532, 546, 569; **61**: 3n1, 12, 22, 61, 106, 173, 188, 302, 385, 551; **62**: 185, 227n1, 303, 516; **63**: 549, 619; **64**: 57, 93, 320, 325; **65**: 243; **66**: 266, 300, 320; **67**: 163, 174, 270, 411, 428, 485, 605; **68**: 38, 115, 256, 275,n2, 326, 443, 506; notified of WW's canceled trip, **63**: 521; and visit of Belgian royalty, **63**: 603, 606; asks Mrs. Reid for human interest stories for WW, **63**: 575-76; greets Prince of Wales, **64**: 31; and WW's health, **64**: 503, 507, 510; and Brown-King wedding, **66**: 506n1; and inauguration day, **67**: 209; Dodd informs of revising parts of forthcoming book on WW, **67**: 75-77; WW's concern over publication of letter from doctor, **67**: 483; career of, **68**: 296, 373, 386, 391, 391-92; Lord Robert Cecil on, **68**: 345; WW's concern over promoting prize fight, **68**: 386; sends news of her activities, **68**: 422-23; WW happy to hear from, **68**: 427; congratulates WW on Armistice Day speech, **68**: 471; WW sends requested greetings for success of child welfare program, **68**: 478-79; Sophie Loeb on, **68**: 492; and WW's birthday, **68**: 509; at WW's bedside during last illness, **68**: 549, 550, 554, 556, 558, 562, 564, 565; and WW's death, **68**: 566, 573; at WW's funeral, **68**: 582
Wilson, Oliver, **62**: 623,n1
Wilson, Philip St. Julien, **54**: 391n2
Wilson, Trevor, **53**: 575n1
Wilson, William Bauchop, **53**: 118, 273; **54**: 409-10, 521; **55**: 91; **57**: 376, 387, 447, 450; **60**: 41, 248,n1, 568; **62**: 250; **63**: 56, 554; **64**: 64, 193; **65**: 24, 187n5, 212; **66**: 3, 217n1, 254-55, 281, 498; **67**: 9, 109, 150; **68**: 576; on selection of peace commissioners, **53**: 154-55; on importance of Employment Service, **55**: 291-92, 447, 478; on need for appropriation for National War Labor Board, **57**: 510, 578; on electric railways, **59**: 287-88, 320; on immigration issues, **60**: 432-33; on international labor conference, **62**: 95-96, 131-33, 162-63; and appointments, **62**: 224, 314, 436, 437; on conference on labor and capital, **62**: 582, 583-84, 623,n1; on importance of treaty ratification for business and labor, **62**: 584-86; on nationwide campaign to interpret WW's statement to railroad shopmen, **63**: 53, 54; compares railroad and coal situations, **63**: 54-55; on Women's Bureau, **63**: 56-57; **66**: 520; and coal strike, **63**: 593, 598; **64**: 147, 154, 166, 167, 207-208; **65**: 544,n2, 545, 553,n1, 554, 558-62, 566, 568-69; and second Industrial Conference, **63**: 611; and First International Labour Conference, **64**: 98n1; and Mooney case, **64**: 145,n1; rumor of resignation of, **64**: 166, 167, 184-85; draft letter to H. M. Robinson, **64**: 206n1; on not linking end of federal control of railroads with new bill, **65**: 16-19; on cause of railroad strike, **65**: 187n4; and "Palmer raids," **65**: 187,n5; draft of letter to Anthracite Wage Scale Committee, **65**: 312-13,n1,2; on anthracite coal situation, **65**: 314, 352-53; on appointments to the Anthracite Coal Commission, **65**: 353,n1,2; **66**: 66-69, 75, 76-77; on U.S. representation on International Commission on Emigration and Immigration, **65**: 360-61, 569-71; on coal situation, **65**: 568-69; **66**: 10-11,n1, 27n2; on Jones bill, **66**: 60; on differences between anthracite and bituminous coal settlements and WW's reasons for not reconvening Joint Scale Committee, **66**: 104-108; on Arizona copper situation during wartime, **66**: 125-28, 132; WW's condolences to, **66**: 228; issue of reinstatement of outlaw strikers, **66**: 262-63, 546; and Gowen case, **66**: 265; sends WW his speech during campaign, **66**: 346,n1, 249; on U.S. representative on International Commission on Immigration and Emigration, **66**: 475-77; and Martens case, **66**: 504; question of amnesty for Debs, **66**: 533-34, 535; Cabinet farewell, **67**: 199; on not approving immigration bill, **67**: 178-80; on O'Callaghan case, **67**: 37-38, 48-51, 52,n1; praises WW, **67**: 186; and short-lived appointment to Canadian Commission, **67**: 196,n1; photograph of, *illustration section,* **67**

WOODROW WILSON

Morgenthau dedicates book to, **53**: 3; impression of as an intellectual machine, **53**: 24; offered honorary degree from Oxford, **53**: 27-28, 161,n1, 162,n1; **59**: 552-53,n1; receives congratulations on war's end, **53**: 32, 34, 46, 46n1, 46-47, 50, 53-54, 126-27, 204, 246; on armistice acceptance, **53**: 34; addresses Congress on peace terms, **53**: 35-43; remarks to state food administrators, **53**: 52; State of the Union message, 1918, **53**: 73, 217, 251n1, 274-86, 301, 305,

Woodrow Wilson, cont.
310; Thanksgiving Proclamation, **53**: 95-96; curtails all but necessary appointments, **53**: 160-61; Red Cross appeal, **53**: 202-203; Baruch's praise of, **53**: 209; remarks to B'nai B'rith, **53**: 239,n1, 239-40; teller of stories and anecdotes, **53**: 332-33, 343, 366, 392, 424, 425, 552; and indemnity issue, **53**: 563; WW's appeal for a Democratic Congress mentioned, **53**: 401; London *Times* interview, **53**: 422-30; Christmas message, **53**: 491; on European food crisis, **53**: 578-79; suggestion that WW return to Boston, not N.Y., **53**: 625-26, 698; **54**: 58; proclamation on T. Roosevelt's death, **53**: 634, 635; indignation over French and British claims, **53**: 707-708; first "Paris draft" of League of Nations Covenant, **53**: 655; address in New York on behalf of Red Cross mentioned (January 18, 1918), **54**: 102, 103n7; proposes Clemenceau as president of Paris Peace Conference, **54**: 127, 129-30; second "Paris draft" of League of Nations Covenant, **54**: 138-48; address to French Senate, **54**: 155, 155n2, 156-57; acknowledges biography by H. W. Harris, **54**: 159,n3; annoyed at France's insistence that he visit devastated areas, **54**: 175, 178; meets with Gardiner, **54**: 175-78; entertains orderlies, chauffeurs, and guards, **54**: 237, 305-306; Cork and Dublin, Ireland, offer freedom of the city to, **54**: 256,n1, 399,n1, 552; **56**: 96; presents draft of Covenant to Plenary Session, **54**: 265-68; League of Nations speech, **54**: 271, 278, 304, 382, 406; remarks to working women in Paris, **54**: 257n2, 271-73, 307; remarks to French Protestants, **54**: 282-83; remarks in Paris to League for the Rights of Man, **54**: 309-10; and Watterson's memoirs, **54**: 389n2; address to French Chamber of Deputies, **54**: 464-67, 488, 489; and Romanes Lecture, **54**: 468-69; unable to visit home of Marquis de Lafayette, **54**: 518; offered many honorary degrees, **55**: 3, 89, 116; Fourteen Points cited, **55**: 30, 31, 32, 33; plans for parade for returning soldiers in Washington, D.C., **55**: 36, 37, 94; on anti-Wilson propaganda and French press, **55**: 66, 88, 94, 120, 153, 266, 489-90; and Number 13, **55**: 120, 156; sends autographed photograph to French dignitaries, **55**: 149,n1; holds press conference before leaving Paris, **55**: 161; catches a few winks of sleep during Syrian pact's recitation, **55**: 162; address to Third Plenary Session of peace conference presenting League of Nations Covenant, **55**: 164-78; wishes to discuss League of Nations with foreign affairs committees of Congress, **55**:

Woodrow Wilson, cont.
184; voyage to and arrival in Boston, **55**: 185, 205-206, 218, 218-19, 221, 222, 223, 224, 225, 226, 229, 231, 235-37, 238-45; new residence and servants in Paris, **55**: 193, 223, 230-31, 246, 256-57, 327; statement on departing from France, **55**: 196, 197; on assassination attempt on Clemenceau, **55**: 209; on not calling extra session of Congress, **55**: 222, 254, 295, 296, 297-98, 409; congratulates *The Hatchet* on its first anniversary, **55**: 224,n1; on inscription on Lafayette monument, **55**: 232; trip from Boston to Washington, **55**: 237-38, 254; dinner and meeting on League of Nations with congressional foreign affairs committees, **55**: 268-76; news reports of meetings at the Capitol, **55**: 295-98; greetings for Chamberlain, **55**: 298; on League of Nations being part of peace treaty, **55**: 320, 531, 532; denies making statement on Ireland, **55**: 324-26; and amnesty issue, **55**: 338, 344-47, 365-66; talk of third term, **55**: 340; **59**: 74-75; **60**: 41n1, 112-13; **61**: 374, 506n1, 577; **65**: 71n3, 117-19, 123, 382, 383, 400, 426, 427-28, 435, 438-39, 438-40, 457-59; **68**: 425, 541-43, 588-90; address to Governors and Mayors Conference, **55**: 389-91; condemns group of senators who have obstructed necessary legislation, **55**: 408-409; leaves Washington for New York, **55**: 409-12; meets with Irish Americans, **55**: 411-12, 443; address at Metropolitan Opera House on League of Nations, **55**: 413-21, 447; departure for France, **55**: 442; R. S. Baker on, **55**: 464-65; **58**: 419; arrives at Brest, **55**: 487; development of break with House, **55**: 488,n2; **60**: 492; **62**: 525,n1, 573-74,n1, 574, 576, 633; **67**: 289-91,n3; arrives in Paris, **55**: 497; and issue of Senate ratification of peace treaty, **56**: 58,n4, 66-67, 69, 97-98; on not permitting T. Roosevelt to lead volunteer division in France, **56**: 87; on transport of Haller's Army, **56**: 133, 134, 135-36, 138-40, 141, 144; French society of workmen name their association after, **56**: 183,n2,3; visits French battlefront, **56**: 194-200, 244; and White House sheep, **56**: 204; **57**: 428; concerns over civilian staff wives being in Paris, **56**: 235; House on, **56**: 335, 517; **58**: 483; gives Daniels tour of Paris White House, **56**: 338; as decision maker, **56**: 338; confrontation with Clemenceau, **56**: 349-50, 351, 353, 353-54, 365-68, 434; talk of going home, **56**: 354, 540, 580, 581, 583; receives medal from French Academy of Moral and Political Science, **56**: 428,n2, 440; a day's schedule, **56**: 441; **57**: 426-27; and French bill for WW's traveling expenses, **56**:

Woodrow Wilson, cont.

444, 513,n1, 547-48; **57**: 374; WW's anger over Steed's formula for Saar Basin, **56**: 517n1; Whitlock forwards Belgian medal to, **56**: 521-22; asked to attend first lecture for U.S. Army personnel at The Sorbonne, **57**: 36-37; Tumulty's advice to take "dramatic action," **57**: 37, 60; plans to leave Paris if no progress on peace negotiations, **57**: 50-51, 53, 61; summons *U.S.S. George Washington,* **57**: 63-65,n1, 68, 69, 70, 140; visited by two peasants from Galicia, **57**: 237-38, 290; annoyed at tardiness of Queen Marie of Rumania, **57**: 241-42; statement on summoning German delegates to peace conference, **57**: 336; Adriatic question and Italian claims, **57**: 343-45, 542-44, 549,n5, 551, 552-53, 559-60, 575-76, 611, 613; **58**: 4, 5-8, 15, 27, 48, 56, 57, 58, 91; **59**: 96-97; **64**: 458-63; receives medal from Belgian workers, **57**: 422; made honorary citizen of San Marino, **57**: 426; on Employment Sunday, **57**: 447; message to Italian people on third anniversary of Italy's entrance into war, **57**: 493,n12; relationship with House, **57**: 508, 532,n2; on construction of his speeches, **57**: 577; Serbian woman knits socks for, **57**: 585; presented with picture by French workers' organization "La Wilsonienne," **58**: 111,n3; on Hoover's request that wives of relief workers be permitted to come to Paris, **58**: 136; and secret treaties, **58**: 145; tribute from French General Confederation of Labor, **58**: 164,n1; Robinson's story on labor clause shows WW's writing ability, **58**: 174n1; Clemenceau on, **58**: 186; remarks to Plenary Session on changes in League of Nations Covenant, **58**: 199-202; and controversy over Shantung, **58**: 229, 244-45; talks of making U.S. tour, **58**: 364; Japanese settlement causes sleepless nights, **58**: 421; presented with wild flowers by French woman, **58**: 422; angered over France's changes in Covenant, **58**: 430-31; and French security treaty, **58**: 489-90, 490; **62**: 27-29; waves to guards each morning, **58**: 535; message to Congress, **58**: 560, 602, 603, 605-606; **59**: 76, 78, 79, 123, 124-25, 190, 283, 286, 289-97, 367; remarks at Sir Thomas Barclay's dinner, **58**: 598-600, 627, 634; changes in handwriting, **58**: 607, 608-10; **59**: 574n1; **61**: 376n1; address to Academy of Moral and Political Science, **59**: 4-6; reply to Germany's objections to peace treaty, **59**: 28,n3; break with Herron, **59**: 68,n2; Scheidemann on, **59**: 84n2; portrait sittings for official Paris Peace Conference painting, **59**: 315, 350; asked to write article on League of Nations, **59**:

Woodrow Wilson, cont.

316; **60**: 112; on Lloyd George-Clemenceau conflicts, **59**: 321, 368; on Lloyd George's proposal for U.S. mandate in Asia Minor, **59**: 339; on "all fours," studies maps, **59**: 420, 647-48; conversation with Lloyd George and Clemenceau on Italy, **59**: 492-94; remarks on Brazil's new president, **59**: 520-22; message to American people on Memorial Day, **59**: 571; on Article X of Covenant, **59**: 604; takes part in Memorial Day ceremony at Suresnes Cemetery, **59**: 605-10; 621, 621-22, 624; speaks to Plenary Session on small nations and minority rights, **59**: 626, 628-30, 644, 645-46; Grayson promotes relationship between Balfour and, **60**: 3; late for meeting at St. Germain, **60**: 19; discusses treaty with American delegation, **60**: 45-71; his wishes for Princeton University, **60**: 119; and relationship with Lloyd George, **60**: 144; portrait by Orpen, **60**: 249, 333, 432, 489; **61**: 45; description of Paris residence of, **60**: 250-51; commitment to formation of League of Nations, **60**: 252-53, 254-55,n8; gives autograph to Van Oss, **60**: 255; seating plan for Council of Four meetings, **60**: 285; urged to have somebody take notes for him at Council of Four meetings, **60**: 285-86; replaces wreath at Lafayette's grave, **60**: 286, 291-92; offers help to automobile accident victims, **60**: 292; annoyed at delays at Council of Four meetings, **60**: 300, 333; and photograph of "Big Four," **60**: 333; and hot weather, **60**: 382; interview with Walsh and Dunne on Ireland, **60**: 383-87; praises Lamont, **60**: 382, 389, 399; speech of Sept. 27, 1918, quoted, **60**: 444; quotes from speeches used to show legal basis for the peace, **60**: 455-57; plans for proposed U.S. speaking tour, **60**: 537, 538, 568n5, 610; **61**: 34, 246-47, 350, 373, 386, 475, 489, 542, 562, 565, 602n2, 622, 641, 642-43; **62**: 5, 7, 507n1, 587, 626-27, 633, 636; on not delaying treaty signing, **60**: 558, 559, 563; Lloyd George's accusation of "loading dice against Germany," **60**: 559, 563; talk of need for return to U.S., **60**: 572; adamant on presenting treaty to Germans when promised and on having time to review revised text and covering note, **60**: 573-74; furious over Foch's leaving because he was "tired of waiting," **60**: 582-83; plans to return to U.S. when Germany signs treaty, **60**: 609, 618, 621; greetings from his Princeton class, **60**: 610; leaves for Belgium, **60**: 613; Cardinal Mercier on "Wilsonian Peace," **61**: 13, 22; receives honorary degree from University of Louvain, **61**: 22-23,n1, 31,

Woodrow Wilson, cont.

129; R. S. Baker on WW as orator, **61**: 30; controversy over refusal of Poincaré's dinner invitation, **61**: 112-14, 115, 132, 133, 136, 173, 178, 180, 189-91; and rearrangement of furniture, **61**: 112n1; sleep habits, **61**: 112n1; receives honorary degree from University of Prague, **61**: 136-37; 347; press conferences with American correspondents, **61**: 235-38, 240-45, 246-52, 417-24; plans for arrival in U.S., **61**: 291, 371, 376, 377; statement on signing of peace treaty, **61**: 292-93; at treaty signing ceremony then departs for U.S., **61**: 302-306, 328, 333, 354; signs treaty with EBW's pen, **61**: 303; signs autographs at Versailles, **61**: 323, 324-25; seal for treaty signing, **61**: 324; statement upon leaving France, **61**: 350; aboard *George Washington* returning to U.S., **61**: 354, 355-54; receives honorary degree from University of Geneva, **61**: 356-57; works on message to Senate, **61**: 356, 360-61, 362, 363, 369, 370, 385-86, 386-88, 388, 397; address to fellow passengers aboard *George Washington*, **61**: 378-82, 383; to address Senate, **61**: 397; welcome in New York City, **61**: 401; address in Carnegie Hall, **61**: 401-404; congratulatory notes to, **61**: 407, 410, 411; text of address to Senate, **61**: 426-36; comments on address to Senate, **61**: 425, 444-45, 445-46, 459; holds reception-discussion after Senate address, **61**: 437-38; acknowledges letters on his Senate address, **61**: 462-63; new availability to congressman, **61**: 474-75; Whitlock sends Whistler's book to, **61**: 489,n1; invitations to and meetings with Republican senators on treaty, **61**: 492-93,n2, 516-18, 541, 548,n1, 561-62, 569-70, 593-95, 599-602, 619-22; on increase of Red Cross fund from sale of woool from White House sheep, **61**: 505; and payment for bronze wreath in memory of *Otranto* victims, **61**: 508,n1; remarks to Czech soldiers, **61**: 518-19; and testimonials to wartime volunteers, **61**: 540; illness may postpone trip west, **61**: 578; invites Albert to visit U.S., **62**: 6; commitment to treaty ratification without reservations, **62**: 16-20; presents French security treaty to Senate, **62**: 27-29; meets with Republican senators on treaty, **62**: 43-45, 90-94; suggests "World War" as "official" name, **62**: 69; tribute to Princeton men in class of 1917 who gave lives in war, **62**: 102; on Cardinal Mercier's visit to U.S., **62**: 111,n3; statement on Shantung settlement, **62**: 170, 171; address to Congress on cost of living mentioned, **62**: 171, 179n2, 180-81, 196, 198; message to Hines on railroad cri-

Woodrow Wilson, cont.

sis, **62**: 192-93; urges railroad workers return to job and negotiations to begin, **62**: 194-95; and Senate's request for documents from, **62**: 208, 219,n2, 534, 535; message to Senate regarding documents on Shantung settlement, **62**: 208-209; address to joint session of Congress on cost of living, **62**: 209-19; on revision of *The State*, **62**: 225; how he learned of Plumb plan, **62**: 227n1; reviews marine brigade, **62**: 241,n1, 270-71, 291; on New Era Movement, **62**: 251; vetos repeal of daylight-saving law, **62**: 304-305,n1; and Lord Rectorship of Glasgow University, **62**: 331-32; **63**: 395-96; conversation with members of Foreign Relations Committee, **62**: 339-411; Fall's memorandum on treaty and WW's reply, **62**: 411-15, 417-19; and Pittman reservations, **62**: 432n3; message to librarians, **62**: 436,n1; on responsibility issue, **62**: 449,n1; on Admiral Sims' writing plans, **62**: 460; statements on railroad crisis, **62**: 472-76, 496-98; on story that WW kept Cleveland from attending Princeton "faculty meeting," **62**: 479-80, 526; news report on position of no wage increase for railway shopmen, **62**: 489-93, 493-95; on proposed German translation of *George Washington*, **62**: 564-65,n1; receives honorary degree from William and Mary College, **62**: 588; **63**: 463; Labor Day message, **62**: 595-96; and scandal involving army colonel,**62**: 610-11; Lansing on labor views of, **62**: 612; deaf to treaty changes, **62**: 613-14; his interpretive reservations, **62**: 621; confident of acceptance of treaty, impatient with delay, **63**: 17-18; on his remarks at Sursenes Cemetery, **63**: 181, 197; message to First Division, **63**: 274; regrets that he is unable to welcome Pershing, **63**: 295; to receive the Prince of Wales, **63**: 297,n1; answers San Francisco Labor Council's questions, **63**: 303-304; Albert wishes to bestow honors on WW and other officials, **63**: 307-308; reaction to Bullitt testimony, **63**: 338n4; on origins of the war, **63**: 359-60; first test of "voice phone," **63**: 369-40; cannot accept foreign decorations by Albert, **63**: 392; Tumulty's strategy and suggestions for WW's speeches, **63**: 397-99; Albert's visit, **63**: 515, 526, 532; to be informed of Senate vote on reservations, **63**: 586; visit from Belgian royalty, **63**: 602-606; presents Albert with set of *History of the American People*, **63**: 603; Thanksgiving Proclamation, **63**: 613-15; sends election congratulations to Coolidge and Edwards, **63**: 615,n1; commitment to early literary work, **63**: 624; I. Hoover on author-

Woodrow Wilson, cont.

ship of WW's Annual Message to Congress, **63**: 638; Armistice Day statement, **64**: 7; with exception of interpretations not willing to make any compromise on treaty, **64**: 43-44, 55, 65, 165-66, 187, 385; Lansing on personal animosity of Republican senators against, **64**: 54-57; White House sheep, **64**: 57n1; R. S. Baker on House-WW relationship, **64**: 62; and draft of Annual Message to Congress, **64**: 72, 73-87, 106-16, 123; House offers strategy for treaty passage, **64**: 89; draft of statement on protocol concerning treaty, **64**: 118,n2; Lansing on WW's ability to perform duties, **64**: 123-25; statement on coal stiuation, **64**: 153-54,n1, 154-55; relationship between Lansing and, **64**: 179, 243; made citizen of Carlisle, **64**: 184; chair at Davidson College named after, **64**: 191-92,n2, 213; questions effect of a U.S. senator's resignation in certain states, **64**: 202-203; appoints Bituminous Coal Commission, **64**: 206-208; Christmas, **64**: 211; hoped for vacation in Bermuda, **64**: 214,n1; issues Executive Order for half days for government employees, **64**: 218; proclamation ending federal control of railroads, **64**: 226-27; birthday wishes from George V, and WW's thank you, **64**: 230, 231; birthday wishes from King Albert and WW's thank you, **64**: 230; Princeton University sends his desk to, **64**: 246-47; Jackson Day message, **64**: 247-49, 257-59; advocates direct referendum on treaty, **64**: 248, 254; and election of 1920, **64**: 267; refuses to endorse candidate for Democratic minority leadership, **64**: 274,n1; letter to Hitchcock on reasonable interpretation, **64**: 278-82; R. S. Baker on futility of situation of, **64**: 321-22; and Nobel Peace Prize, **64**: 342; **65**: 40; **66**: 477-78, 492-93, 501, 504-505, 523-24, 531, 536, 543; **67**: 51-52, 365; and numerous requests to support fund raising "schemes," **64**: 345-46; requests all documents be delivered in sealed envelopes, **64**: 351; effect of Grey's letter on, **64**: 362,n1; decision to resign, **64**: 362,n1; **66**: 436; **67**: 568; decision to withdraw Versailles Treaty if Anglo-French Adriatic proposals are accepted, **64**: 380, 402; on calling of Cabinet meetings by Lansing, **64**: 383, 384; on Lansing's resignation, **64**: 417n3; emotional reaction to Cummings' speech, **64**: 428; Grayson on inauguration memories, **64**: 485-86; and public opinion on entry into war, **64**: 487; remarks in1918 at a stag dinner at 10 Downing Street, **64**: 490-92; on essays to be published, **64**: 514-15; willing to assist W. M. Daniels in Princeton Uni-

Woodrow Wilson, cont.

versity position, **64**: 514; and drafting of letter to Hitchcock of March 8, 1920; **65**: 7-10, 11-14, 25-28, 30-35, 49-55, 66-71; House returns unused funds to, **65**: 75, 80; various comments on letter to Hitchcock, **65**: 76, 80, 84,n1, 84-85, 89, 140; thanks House for unexpected funds, **65**: 80; and honorary degree from Oglethorpe University, **65**: 89-90, 382; reaction to news of treaty rejection, **65**: 108-109, 109,n1, 124; Tumulty's suggestions for WW's announcement on not seeking third term, **65**: 117-19; ready for impeachment fight, **65**: 124; admiration for oratory of Daniel Webster, **65**: 145; issue of name on ballot in Georgia primary, **65**: 145-46,n1; on Foch and French invasion of Germany, **65**: 159; and 1912 nomination, **65**: 189n2; request for article from and WW's refusal, **65**: 218,n1; concern over cutting down of trees in park, **65**: 219, 250, 258, 262; Lloyd George's alleged personal attack on discovered to be unfounded, **65**: 221, 231-32,n1; reads only Baltimore *Sun*, **65**: 230; reasons for not subscribing to Princeton's endowment fund, **65**: 246; and Zionism, **65**: 248,n1; statement to Oregon Democrats urging support of League of Nations, **65**: 263-64; House on statement to Oregon Democrats, **65**: 274; Lodge-WW conflict, **65**: 274; and dedication of memorial amphitheater at Arlington National Cemetery, **65**: 289,n1; on Democratic National Convention of 1920 and candidacy, **65**: 291; unable to supply Cushing with letters from Sir W. Osler, **65**: 296; supports Salvation Army's fund appeal, **65**: 297; message to Anthracite Wage Scale Committee, **65**: 312-13; and White House sheep, **65**: 317-18,n1, 332, 354; and model plank on unqualified ratification of treaty, **65**: 319; on Congress accepting Armenian mandate, **65**: 320-23; Memorial Day message, **65**: 325; various comments on veto message of Knox resolution, **65**: 328-29, 331, 335, 339-40, 341; acknowledges his supporters, **65**: 343; chooses amusing code names, **65**: 350; veto of budget and auditing bill, **65**: 362-63; on the preservation of his letter to Oglethorpe University, **65**: 393; on Republican platform, **65**: 396; not up to writing greeting on statue to be given to France, **65**: 397,n1; on vice-presidential candidate, **65**: 397; work routine of, **65**: 406-407; on Republican convention, **65**: 415-16; on referendum on League of Nations, **65**: 416, 417; on not wanting to influence Democratic party on candidate choice, **65**: 419, 420; Southern Baptists request letter

Woodrow Wilson, cont.
of introduction for European mission, **65**: 321-23; sends letter to be auctioned by Chautauqua, **65**: 423,n2, 424,n1; asked to help in kidnapping case, **65**: 425; denies National Institute for the Blind request for letter, **65**: 430, 432-33; support for at convention opening, **65**: 471,n1; Democratic party sends resolution of appreciation, **65**: 472-73; votes received in *Literary Digest* poll, **65**: 474n2; grateful for message from convention, **65**: 489-90; attitude toward possible nominees, **65**: 498-99; and Pulitzer's request for column for New York *World*, **65**: 501n1; receives suit of cartridge cloth from N. D. Baker, **65**: 502; asked to be editorial contributor to *The Independent*, **65**: 504-505; statement on meeting with Cox, **65**: 525; declines writing offer of Buenos Aires newspaper, **65**: 530-31; declines offer to lecture at Rice University, **65**: 553,n2; gives valuable books to library of Princeton University, **65**: 572; receives title change to Professor of Jurisprudence, **65**: 572; on Princeton's reunion problems, **65**: 573, 575; Cummings on Colby's attempt to renominate, **65**: 579-81; touring car being repaired, **66**: 15; on EBW's way of folding letters, **66**: 29-30; and *U.S.S. Mayflower's* practice trip, **66**: 30,n1, 58; cannot commit himself to public speeches at Philadelphia Academy of Music, **66**: 40; does not wish to become a "Mr. Butt-in-sky", **66**: 40; and Selective Service Act of 1917, **66**: 58,n1; wishes to be consulted on all things growing out of treaty, **66**: 82; annoyed at drivers who pass his automobile, **66**: 103,n1; inquires if he has powers of magistrate, **66**: 103; offered and accepts first medal to be given to Army and Navy chaplains, **66**: 121, 129-30; contributes to Democratic campaign, **66**: 122,n1; receives request for stay and pardon for prisoners, **66**: 132-33,n1; asked to endorse "College for Memphis campaign," **66**: 134; and Armistice Day Proclamation, **66**: 151,n1,2, 204-205; on not making his income tax public, **66**: 157; EBW and Cummings discuss position in campaign, **66**: 190-91; Tumulty's statement for on dangers if Republicans elected, **66**: 214-16; unable to fulfill requests for statements on League of Nations, **66**: 223,n1; will not permit Tumulty to show that Root's proposed changes were incorporated in Covenant, **66**: 230; Pershing sends specially inscribed copy of final report to, **66**: 231,n1; and Univ. of Virginia, **66**: 234, 258; **67**: 138-39, 263, 265, 495, 559; urged to help with campaign, willing

Woodrow Wilson, cont.
but has conditions, **66**: 250; and Cox's invitation to New York meeting, **66**: 253, 257; statement on Article X and on moral obligations of U.S., **66**: 277-80; and Boy Scouts fund-raising drive, **66**: 282,n1; endorsement of Cox, **66**: 290-91; wishes to keep his papers and not turn them over to Library of Congress, **66**: 292-93,n3; greets White House crowd, **66**: 316; Thanksgiving Proclamation, **66**: 345, 351-52; and proposed statue at Univ. of Texas, **66**: 369,n1,2; and reproduction of Kipling's "If," **66**: 386, 456, 479; Rice Institute requests one of WW's honorary diplomas, **66**: 410-11, 420; **67**: 235; and Masonic Order, **66**: 421; suggestions for State of the Union Message, **66**: 431, 436, 445, 448, 452,n1, 453-56,n1; mention of lecture given at Brown University, **66**: 467; sends photographs for his portrait rather than having sitting, **66**: 469-70, 471; State of Union Message, **66**: 484; Glass on Lodge at White House, **66**: 494-95; statement on Chinese famine relief, **66**: 495-96; asked to be trustee of Church Peace Union, **66**: 502-503; invited to Brown-King wedding, **66**: 503; birthday congratulations, **66**: 524; message to Congress mentioned, **66**: 525, 530; wishes to keep his personal and Trenton file, **67**: 39,n1; involvement with R. S. Baker's *Woodrow Wilson and World Settlement*, **67**: 15, 27, 71-72, 93-94, 360-61; annoyed at Tumulty's request for condolence letter, **67**: 30; on his ordeal at Paris Peace Conference, **67**: 40,n4, 44, 69; elected second vice president of American Historical Association, **67**: 64, 514, 518-19, 534; fondness for limericks, **67**: 71; Bok on WW lecturing on League of Nations, **67**: 72; Dodd on disposition of papers of, **67**: 76-77, 282; on plans for Harding inauguration and luncheon, **67**: 83; denies Debs pardon, **67**: 102n8, 157; on lucky number, **67**: 105, 115, 125; receives ovation at theater, **67**: 111-12; concern over telling lie to Tumulty, **67**: 117; search for desk used aboard *George Washington*, **67**: 124-25, 128, 146-47; on Greek language, **67**: 125; photographed with Cabinet, **67**: 126,n1, 138; denies request to have photographs taken, **67**: 128-29,n2; wit of, **67**: 128; Creel says WW "must" write, **67**: 141; acknowledges tribute from women, **67**: 143; reaction to bad portrait of himself, **67**: 143; I. Hoover compares to other Presidents, **67**: 150; Colby endorses joint law pratice with WW, **67**: 160-61; Long on as professor at Princeton, **67**: 164-65; receives answer on removal of articles from White House, **67**: 187-88; has

Woodrow Wilson, cont.

tea with Hardings, **67**: 189-90; news accounts of departure from White House, **67**: 205-14; decision not to attend inaugural, **67**: 211; rides from Capitol to new home and receives ovation, **67**: 212-14; Cobb's estimate of, **67**: 216-29; invited to lecture at Rice, **67**: 235-36; does not comment on Cardinal Gibbons' death, **67**: 243; contributes to fund for Professor Jellinek, **67**: 247, 248; admitted to N.Y. bar, **67**: 248, 260, 261,n1, 262, 329, 331-32,n2; messsage to Democrats of Akron, **67**: 255; asked to write on Foch and declines, **67**: 267, 270-71; emotional reaction to question on League of Nations, **67**: 269; on his valet's service, **67**: 273; sightseers constantly waiting for, **67**: 295; on Ochs and *New York Times'* editorial policy, **67**: 301; report of G. White visit to, **67**: 308-309; meets with Mullen on Democratic party, **67**: 321n1; and Newberry case, **67**: 323-24; admitted to District of Columbia bar, **67**: 328-29, 330; submits witticism for book, **67**: 341,n1,2; joins New York County Lawyer's Association, **67**: 346; sends copy of Versailles Treaty to Hughes, **67**: 351-52; unable to fulfill autograph requests, **67**: 362; first time at law office, **67**: 370-71; Dodge on WW's reply to Germany on Armistice note, **67**: 374,n3; policy of silence, **67**: 386-87, 401,521, 528, 529, 531, 533, 554-55, 555-56; receives honorary degree from University of Cracow, **67**: 392, 400; unpublished statement on Treaty of Berlin, **67**: 394-95; a normal day's routine, **67**: 395-98; Armistice Day participation, **67**: 400-401, 402, 432, 438-39, 439-40, 442, 451-53, 452,n1, 456, 461; cheering crowd brings tears to WW's eyes, **67**: 449-53; children's delegation presents flowers to, **67**: 450-51, 453, 457; Davidson College weekly to be dedicated to, **67**: 473, 474,n2; on Morley's writings, **67**: 476; inscription on WW found in Nice, **67**: 482; on alleged interview with EBW by *Washington Daily News*, **67**: 492,n1; plaque on dorm room at University of Virginia, **67**: 498,n1,2, 501; on his secret of "success," **67**: 499, 502-503; greeting to soldier who introduced himself to, **67**: 508,n1; asked to endorse fund raising for Presbyterian colleges in Missouri, **67**: 519; demonstration by local WW Foundation endorsing, **67**: 521-23; endorses Berea College's fund-raising campaign, **67**: 539,n2; on *Mere Literature,* **67**: 551; on reasons for not publicly endorsing anti-lynching bill, **67**: 571; on his preferred form of being addressed, **67**: 572; on not giving autographs, **67**: 572; and unveiling of statue of T. Roosevelt, **67**:

Woodrow Wilson, cont.

577-78, 579, 584, 587; and Lincoln Memorial dedication, **67**: 580; and plans for Versailles Treaty ratification, **67**: 608-10; makes brouhaha over Tumulty's concocted telegram to Jefferson Day dinner, **68**: 3, 10, 11, 11-12, 14, 14-15, 51, 59-60; Colby on supporters, **68**: 36-37, 38; Jameson answers on European attitude toward newly formed U.S. government, **68**: 65-67; and 1922 Armistice Day proceedings and speech, **68**: 91-92, 186-87; receives Order of White Eagle from Poland, **68**: 177, 183; on dissolution of law partnership, **68**: 213-14; and visit with Clemenceau, **68**: 226-28; concern over public perception of his involvement in Democratic party and 1924 election, **68**: 234-35,n1; birthday activities, **68**: 247-49; Senate resolution on his birthday, **68**: 247; exchanges with Brandeis over "What Is Progress" article, **68**: 277, 279, 280; and Non-Partisan League of Nations Association, **68**: 286n1; Princeton Unviersity Library issues bibliography of works of, **68**: 308,n2; Baruch on J. C. Nugent's speech on, **68**: 373-74; receives many ovations and demonstrations at theater, **68**: 375-76, 382-83, 404; occasional rumors of his death, **68**: 379-80; and participation in Harding's funeral, **68**: 399-400, 401, 401-402; on his photograph, **68**: 411; meets with Brennan on 1924 campaign, **68**: 425-26; suggestion that he run for Senate from N.J., **68**: 454; sends limerick to Lloyd George, **68**: 457; radio address on Nov. 10, 1923, **68**: 466-67, 593; addresses pilgrims on Armistice Day, **68**: 467-71; requests his report on social reorganization of Princeton University, **68**: 477; albums from Czechoslovakia, **68**: 481; R. S. Baker on interview and WW's response, **68**: 482, 494; Davis on a manifesto for 1924 campaign, **68**: 486-91; Fosdick and WW on WW's educational plan, **68**: 492-94; elected president of American Historical Association, **68**: 522-24; C. H. McCormick, Jr., on trying to reconcile House and, **68**: 528-29, 529-30; receives Democratic National Committee, **68**: 531-32; notes and passages for an acceptance speech, **68**: 541-42; notes and passages for a third Inaugural Address, **68**: 542-43; changes C. R. Webster's death sentence to life in prison, **68**: 545-46,n1; fight for Federal Reserve bill, **68**: 585-87; Kerney's last interview with, **68**: 588-97; *see also* Council of Four; Paris Peace Conference; Wilson & Colby; Woodrow Wilson Clubs; Woodrow Wilson Foundation; photographs of, *illustration sections* **53, 54, 55, 56, 58, 59, 60, 61, 63, 65, 67, 68**

Woodrow Wilson, Appearance and Impressions, cont.

APPEARANCE AND IMPRESSIONS

53: 66, 321, 322, 349, 357, 377, 423-24, 460; **54**: 106,n1, 440; **56**: 518; **59**: 245, 286; **60**: 196, 491; **61**: 363, 487; **66**: 316; **68**: 481; analysis of WW's smile, **53**: 424; photographed with one cuff up, **53**: 569; Cecil on, **54**: 152, 514; Cambon on, **54**: 235-36; two soldiers who were photographed with WW give their impressions, **54**: 237; Seymour on, **54**: 383, 384; tired, **55**: 162, 298, 412; **56**: 178-80, 337, 542; **57**: 195, 286; **58**: 229; **59**: 158; **60**: 78, 252; as he leaves Paris, **55**: 196; at Washington press conference, **55**: 295; looks rested, **55**: 448, 490; R. S. Baker on, **55**: 463, 489; **57**: 68; **59**: 245-46, 286, 317; upon emerging from conference with House "He seemed to have aged years," **55**: 488n2; during confrontation with Clemenceau, **56**: 351; "growing grayer and grimmer," **56**: 577, 578; wears golf cap, **58**: 422; Inquiry members' opinion of, **59**: 158-59; House on, **59**: 449, 624, 644; Balfour on statesmanship and intellect of, **59**: 477-78; Grayson on character analysis of, **59**: 625; Van Oss on smile of, **60**: 251, 252, 255; Lloyd George on, **60**: 303; **68**: 456; House on Orpen portrait of, **60**: 363; attire on Belgian tour, **61**: 5-6; in new straw hat, **61**: 34; I. Hoover on, **61**: 112n1; **63**: 633-35; twitch in eye, **61**: 112n1; Thompson on, **61**: 246; Lansing on stubborn expression of, **62**: 258; during meeting with Foreign Relations Committee, **62**: 335; Jessie on resemblance of her new son to, **63**: 167,n4; Mrs. Hulbert on, **63**: 419n1; at work, when dictating letters, **63**: 514; extraordinary concentration, **63**: 514; Rappard on, **63**: 626, 629, 630, 631; Hitchcock on after stroke, **64**: 45n1; Hitchcock and Fall on, **64**: 131, 132; R. S. Baker on, **64**: 360; **66**: 435, 438, 441-42; **67**: 237-38, 360, 361, 585; in wheel chair wearing sweater and old golf cap, **64**: 420; grows beard during illness, **64**: 489; labor leaders on visit with, **65**: 5; during motor rides, **65**: 42, 67; Egan on newspaper photographs of, **65**: 121; at first Cabinet meeting since illness, **65**: 186n1, 188; Daniels on, **65**: 270; as he reviews circus parade, **65**: 290; Peter on, **65**: 338-40; Polk on, **65**: 343; Cummings on, **65**: 344; **66**: 331; **67**: 268-70; **68**: 88; Geddes on, **65**: 369; Seibold on, **65**: 404, 408-409, 413-14; meeting with Cox and Roosevelt, **65**: 520n1; Hawkins on, **66**: 153, 158; pro-League Republicans on, **66**: 273, 374; Tumulty on, **66**: 292n2; after election, **66**: 320; EBW on R. S. Baker reworking some

Woodrow Wilson, Appearance and Impressions, cont.

comments in draft article, **66**: 446-47; Dodge on, **66**: 526; Dodd on, **67**: 39-40, 43-44, 76n3; Cox on, **67**: 94n1; at theater, **67**: 111, 381,n1; at meeting with Harvard's WW Club delegation, **67**: 158-59; at last Cabinet meeting, **67**: 176n1, 203; Cobb on, **67**: 216-29; loneliness of, **67**: 256, 289; R. S. Baker compares to E. M. House, **67**: 290-94; Mullen on weariness, disillusionment, desolation of, **67**: 321n1; as sworn into District bar, **67**: 328-29; two years after stricken, **67**: 395-98; Redfield recalls wit and humor of, **67**: 403-404; in tears over ovation, **67**: 449, 451; before cheering crowds, **67**: 450, 523; during Armistice Day procession, **67**: 452; Hankey on, **67**: 462n2; improvement, **67**: 560; Jameson on, **68**: 26; before group of women supporters, **68**: 36-39; Tarbell on, **68**: 45, 47-48; inflexibility of, **68**: 48; Cummings on, **68**: 88; at 1922 Armistice Day demonstration, **68**: 187-88; on his 66th birthday, **68**: 249, 250, 257; T. Roosevelt on, **68**: 252n2; tired, **68**: 255; photograph of in Paris compared to appearance on 66th birthday, **68**: 257; as he leaves theater, **68**: 375-76; Oulahan on improvement of, **68**: 381-82; during Harding's inauguration, **68**: 398; at Harding's funeral, **68**: 401-402; at 1923 Armistice Day speech outside his home, **68**: 468, 469, 469-70; Kerney on, **68**: 590, 592-93; as a lonely man, a dreamer, **68**: 591

APPOINTMENT SUGGESTIONS, APPOINTMENTS, AND RESIGNATIONS

resignation of McAdoo, **53**: 58, 74, 150-51, 151; Sharp resigns as Ambassador to France, **53**: 80-81, 441-42, 463, 693; **54**: 57; and woman for a reconstruction commission appointment, **53**: 117; Baruch resigns from War Industries Board, **53**: 132, 249-50; accepts W. H. Page's resignation, **53**: 203-204; accepts Walsh's resignation from War Labor Board, **53**: 215; accepts Garfield's resignation, **53**: 307,n1; Glass appointed Secretary of the Treasury, **53**: 441,n1, 587; suggestions for and appointment of Attorney General, **53**: 587; **54**: 31-32, 52, 125, 410, 428-30, 485; **55**: 36, 193, 206, 222, 263-64. 276-77, 294, 339, 412; suggestions and appointment of Director General of Railroads, **53**: 646-48, 704, 710; N. H. Davis appointed U.S. Finance Commissioner at Spa, **53**: 691; resignation of Gregory, **53**: 705, 706, 715; resignation of Davison as president of Red Cross, **53**: 707; Wallace named Ambassador to France, **53**: 710; **55**: 194;

Woodrow Wilson, Appointments and Resignations, cont.

H. Hoover appointed Director General of Relief, **53**: 714; **54**: 277; V. C. McCormick resigns as Democratic National Chairman, **54**: 56,n1, 61; resignation of War Industries Board's Price Fixing Committee, **54**: 52; Tumulty on, **54**: 393; and John Skelton Williams as Comptroller of the Currency, **54**: 485,n1; **55**: 412; and Attorney General of Porto Rico, **55**: 158-59, 264-65; Hapgood appointed Minister to Denmark, **55**: 185, 194, 439,n1; **56**: 101, 191,n1; **59**: 512,n1; judgeship in Missouri, **55**: 206-207; Colby resigns from Shipping Board, **55**: 302,n1; resignation of McIlhenny from Civil Service Commission, **55**: 330,n1; WW requests Civil Service Commission resignations, **55**: 330,n3; on judgeship in Chicago, **55**: 340,n1; Creel resigns from Committee on Public Information, **55**: 363,n1; accepts resignation of Assistant Attorney General, **55**: 394; Galloway and Civil Service Commission, **55**: 460, 478; **56**: 280; **57**: 348-49; **58**: 260-61; and U.S. Minister to Czechozlovakia, **56**: 112,n1; **57**: 374; and U. S. Minister to Poland, **56**: 123-24,n2; **57**: 285, 373; suggestions for mideastern commission, **56**: 155-56, 179, 200, 310; and Interstate Commerce Commission, **56**: 194,n1; consul to Prague appointed, **57**: 95,n1; House's suggestions, **57**: 334; resignation of Judge Barney, **57**: 630,n1; Gompers and labor conference, **58**: 204; minister to Finland appointed, **58**: 404n2; T. N. Page resignation, **58**: 448-49; **59**: 517; **60**: 135-36; **61**: 559-60; **62**: 561; House on WW's enthusiasm for only two appointment suggestions, **58**: 482; on appointment of Gay to Shipping Board, **59**: 121,n2, 121, 160, 185,n1; and Reparation Commission, **59**: 161; **61**: 493, 520-21, 544, 582, 609,n1; Bullitt resignation, **59**: 232-33, 314; Grayson on events leading to Palmer's appointment as Attorney General, **60**: 115-16,n4,6; House's suggestions for Page's replacement, **60**: 192; Whitlock appointed Ambassador to Italy, **60**: 192, 358, 360, 485, 566; **61**: 290; Fosdick appointed Under Secretary of League of Nations, **60**: 290n5; Page offers to stay on if needed, **60**: 327-28; suggestions for proposed commission on Jews in Poland, **60**: 358,n2, 601; WW and House on suggestions for lawyer for International Court of Justice, **60**: 431, 432; House unaware of new appointment to Italy, **60**: 494,n1; Hurley resigns, **60**: 568; **61**: 439-40, 440-41; Hoover remains as Food Administrator, **61**: 133; Lansing and

Woodrow Wilson, Appointments and Resignations, cont.

McCormick discuss appointments, **61**: 134; on making Pershing Chief of Staff, **61**: 293; H. White on his son in diplomatic service in Siam, **61**: 348n3; American Federation of Labor requests Burleson's removal, **61**: 364-65; Gibson appointed Minister to Poland, **61**: 365n1; and first Belgian Ambassador to U.S., **61**: 385; WW considers Polk for ambassadorial position, **61**: 396; and F. B. Harrison's resignation, **61**: 478,n1; and U.S. Court of Claims, **61**: 482,n1; no nepotism in appointments, **61**: 482; Taussig's resignation, **61**: 514, 550, 617-18; power to make appointments to international commissions, **61**: 519, 520, 522,n2; T. W. Page appointed to Tariff Commission, **61**: 617,n2; Taussig interested in position of Ambassador to Germany, **61**: 618; Fine suggested for secretary of Federal Reserve Board, **61**: 625,n1; and proposed Interallied Commission of Inquiry, **61**: 629-30,n4; Reinsch's resignation and selection of successor, **61**: 631-36; **62**: 147, 260, 282; Cobb rejects WW's offer of press information position, **61**: 644-46; N. H. Davis suggested as Assistant Secretary of Treasury, **62**: 70; and appointment of Mary Anderson in Labor Department, **62**: 97,n9, 314-15, 436, 437; Redfield's proposed resignation, **62**: 103-104, 115, 266, 586; **63**: 52,n4, 573-74,n1,2; Hoover's resignation as Food Administrator, **62**: 125; and interim Reparation Commission, **62**: 143-44, 236-27, 550; Galloway resignation, **62**: 164, 251; Gertrude Barnum suggested for Labor Department, **62**: 167, 224; new chairman of Shipping Board, **62**: 226,n1; and Ambassador to Italy, **62**: 252-53; McCormick mentioned as possible successor to Redfield, **62**: 266; suggestions for Minister to China, **62**: 283-84; Garrett resignation, **62**: 435,n1; issue of Americans for commission on Saar Valley and Danzig, **62**: 451; successor to Dulles, **62**: 551,n1; Baruch resigns from Advisory Committee of Council of National Defense, **62**: 554,n1; on resignation of T. N. Page, **62**: 561; WW asks Rathbone to be financial adviser with peace commission in Paris, **62**: 634; Women's Bureau, **63**: 56,n1, 57,n4; request for Negro delegates to first Industrial Conference, **63**: 268; and Industrial Conference, **63**: 300,n1, 336, 609-12; Tumulty suggests WW's illness prevented request for Lansing's resignation, **63**: 338n4; and Lane, **63**: 552,n1; and appointments for transportation commissions as designated by treaty,

Woodrow Wilson, Appointments and Resignations, cont.

63: 606-607, 613,n1; second Industrial Conference, **63**: 618; **64**: 64,n1; Glass resigns to take Senate seat, **64**: 41-42, 50, 52, 103; Phillips suggested as Minister to Netherlands, **64**: 41, 103, 119; McCormick declines Secretaryship of Commerce, **64**: 95; Talcott and district judgeship, **64**: 97,n1, 215-16, 322,n1; appointment of Secretary of Commerce, **64**: 142,n1,2; rumors of W. B. Wilson's resignation, **64**: 166, 167, 184-85; Lansing responds to WW's charges and resigns, **64**: 179, 255-56, 385, 385-86, 388-89, 398, 404, 405, 408-10, 414, 415-19, 432, 433; resignation of Garfield, **64**: 181, 181-82, 185, 186; House on Alexander's appointment, **64**: 185; Tumulty submits list of vacancies, **64**: 204-205; and Bituminous Coal Commission, **64**: 206,n1; Daniels on, **64**: 216; **65**: 186-87; and reappointments to Hague Tribunal, **64**: 216, 273; on delegates to international conference on communications, **64**: 228,n1; secretaryship of Interior offered to Jones, **64**: 232; resignation of Hapgood as Minister to Denmark, **64**: 233-34; Fosdick resignation from League Secretariat, **64**: 274, 286, 306, 310; Palmer on judicial appointments and age factor, **64**: 296-97; and some "terrible" appointments, **64**: 296; WW and Lansing on several diplomatic appointments, **64**: 296, 316-17, 322, 366, 407-408; resignation of Fletcher, **64**: 310, 397; Houston's resignation and new appointment, **64**: 330, 349; R. U. Johnson appointment to Italy, **64**: 343-44, 346, 474; **65**: 93-95; resignation of Close, **64**: 344; appointment of Minister to Switzerland, **64**: 350-51, 352, 353, 383-84, 398, 413, 414, 451-54; Leffingwell willing to defer resignation, **64**: 373-74, 374; Robinson regrets he canot accept Secretaryship of Interior, **64**: 392-93; and appointment to Greece, **64**: 414,n2; Tumulty's suggestions for Lansing's successor, **64**: 419; Cummings on not getting an appointment, **64**: 427-28; Payne as Secretary of the Interior, **64**: 448; Colby as Lansing's replacement, **64**: 464,n1, 472-73; McCombs as Ambassador to France, 1913, **64**: 523, 524n1; Morgenthau appointed Ambassador to Mexico, **65**: 20, 121, 138-39, 140; Payne resigns from Shipping Board, **65**: 20, 64; concern over Britain's appointment of Geddes, **65**: 43-44, 55-56; suggestions and nominations for Railroad Labor Board, **65**: 44-45, 189,n1; Phillips resigns as Assistant Secretary of State, **65**: 47, 63; Norris resigns from Farm Loan Board, **65**: 63; suggestions for diplomatic posts,

Woodrow Wilson, Appointments and Resignations, cont.

65: 85, 87-88; and U.S. representative on Reparation Commission, **65**: 92-93; Hines recommends appointment of Fuel Administrator, **65**: 98; and position of Solicitor of State Department, **65**: 107, 229, 238, 245,n1, 317,n3; suggestions for vacancies in State Department, **65**: 107, 108, 153, 180, 181, 225-26, 229; and Texas circuit court appointment, **65**: 109; H. H. Gardener appointed to Civil Service Commission, **65**: 115-16; postmaster in Nashville, **65**: 119; Jay appointed Minister to El Salvador, **65**: 125, 426; Davis resigns as Assistant Secretary of the Treasury, **65**: 147, 381; and U.S. representative to international woman suffrage congress, **65**: 151-52,n1; Mrs. Summers suggested for State Department permanent position, **65**: 185,n1; and Polk's resignation, **65**: 196-97, 197, 230-31, 352, 355, 397-98; and Egyptian post, **65**: 202,n2, 215, 232; decision not to appoint Edwin B. Parker, **65**: 214, 218-19; Hines approved as arbitrator in German river fleet distribution, **65**: 217,n1,2; resignation of and suggestions for Assistant Secretary of War, **65**: 227-28, 557-58; Meeker resignation, **65**: 248-50; Droppers suggestions for replacement, **65**: 251,n1, 260, 260-71, 271, 317; suggestions for Teschen Commission, **65**: 255-57, 272; resignation of Minister to Honduras and suggestions for successor, **65**: 260-61, 316-17, 317, 357-58, 361; and Director General of Railroads, **65**: 296-97,n7; and Davis to Spa Conference, **65**: 330-31; members named to Anthracite Coal Commission, **65**: 353,n1,2; Long's resignation, **65**: 377-78, 381; and International Joint Commission, **65**: 378,n3,4; WW on resignation of chief clerk of White House staff, **65**: 393; and Third Assistant Secretary of State, **65**: 444,n3; and chairman of Federal Power Commission, **65**: 448, 449; and international communications conference, **65**: 479; and Aland Islands Commission, **65**: 526, 531,n1; **66**: 212,n1, 229, 230-31, 253, 263, 265, 304; Roosevelt's resignation as Assistant Secretary of Navy, **65**: 544; **66**: 77; Chief Justice of Customs Court of Appeals, **65**: 546n1; **66**: 6, 531-32; and B. M. King for Forest Service, **65**: 530,n1, 567,n1; Cummings suggested for Cabinet post, **66**: 7-8; and Shipping Board, **66**: 7, 252,n1, 273; talk of Alexander's resignation and Cummings as replacement, **66**: 7, 196; and Tariff Commission, **66**: 8-9,n1, 10; approves Woodbury as Assistant Secretary of Navy, **66**: 55, 56, 91; fate of Garrett nomination as judge

Woodrow Wilson, Appointments and Resignations, cont.

in Tennessee, **66**: 60,n2, 386,n1,2; WW asks for and receives opinion of delaying date of appointments, **66**: 117-18, 138; possible resignation of J. W. Davis, **66**: 144, 150; issue over J. H. Chitwood in Virginia, **66**: 167-68, 172-73; WW rejects McKellar's suggestion for Shipping Board, **66**: 175,n1; Colver resigns from Federal Trade Commission, **66**: 241,n1; and Canadian Boundary Commission, **66**: 333-34; **67**: 168,n1, 196,n1; Colby and WW on whether to appoint a Minister to Bulgaria, **66**: 358, 367; and Supreme Court, **66**: 392; Sharp on purchasing diplomatic residences abroad, **66**: 431-32; suggestions for International Commission on Immigration and Emigration, **66**: 477; Morgenthau appointed mediator of Armenian situation, **66**: 490, 517-18; and Chinese Famine Relief Committee, **66**: 491, 495; Woolley resigns from Interstate Commerce Commission, **66**: 505,n1; and Women's Bureau, **66**: 520; and Wisconsin judgeship, **67**: 14, 22; and Interstate Commerce Commission and Woodbury, **67**: 25,n1, 29; and J. W. Davis' resignation, **67**: 36, 60-62; Swem on WW's "petty prejudices" on, **67**: 67-68; concern over proposed Oklahoma appointments, **67**: 70; and special request for civil service position, **67**: 113,n1; recommendation for Railroad Labor Board, **67**: 121,n1, Tariff Commission and Kirby, **67**: 166-67, 168-69, 171-72; at last Cabinet meeting, **67**: 175-76,n1; Lane on resigning, **67**: 614; and peace commissioners: *see* Paris Peace Conference—commissioners

CABINET

53: 444, 604; **55**: 251, 254, 266; **63**: 54, 556, 606; **64**: 3, 50, 57, 274, 366; Daniels records meetings, **53**: 65, 135; **63**: 555, 559-60, 598; **64**: 141, 166, 222; **65**: 186-87, 212, 230, 270-71, 298, 351-52, 380, 381; **66**: 4-5, 25-26, 39-40, 60, 78, 159, 341-42, 380, 413, 445-46, 484, 504; **67**: 9, 25-26, 70-71, 90-91, 109, 124; McAdoo's resignation from, **53**: 58, 74; N. D. Baker on his remaining in U.S. and, **53**: 183; Gregory's resignation from, **53**: 715; and prohibition and brewing industry, **54**: 59,n1, 193-94, 216, 227; and prices, **55**: 90, 306; House on geographical representation in, **55**: 193; Lane as candidate for Red Cross Director General, **57**: 330, 422; and price controversy between Railroad Administration and Industrial Board, **57**: 377, 387; Lansing calls meeting to consider WW's disability,

Woodrow Wilson, Cabinet, cont.

63: 542; **64**: 383, 384, 385-86, 388-89, 398, 404, 405, 408-10, 418, 444, 454-58, 496; and WW's disability, **63**: 555, 562, 585-86; on Russia, **63**: 589; **65**: 247, 445; on coal situation, **63**: 598; **64**: 141, 153n1, 166, 167; and second Industrial Conference appointments, **63**: 618; WW's attendance at during his illness, **63**: 637; and WW's message to Congress, **63**: 638; **64**: 16,n1; proposed history of women in war work, **64**: 3; and *Imperator* controversy, **64**: 8; Glass resigns from Treasury, **64**: 52, 60; McCormick declines Secretaryship of Commerce, **64**: 95; Alexander appointed Secretary of Commerce, **64**: 142,n1,2, 185;rumors of W. B. Wilson's resignation, **64**: 166, 167; Lansing resignation, **64**: 179, 255-56, 404, 408-10, 414, 432, 433; and railroad situation, **64**: 183-84, 222n1, 222, 223, 224; WW offers Secretaryship of Interior to Jones, **64**: 232; secretaries of Treasury and Agriculture appointed, **64**: 330,n1, 330, 331; Houston's resignation as Secretary of Agriculture to become Secretary of Treasury, **64**: 349; Lane's resignation, **64**: 373-74, 374; **67**: 614; Robinson regrets he cannot accept appointment to, **64**: 392-93; Tumulty on Lansing's successor, **64**: 419,n1; Cummings on his not being appointed to, **64**: 427-28; physicians on WW's ability to attend meetings, **64**: 435, 527; rumors of N. D. Baker's resignation, **64**: 436; Payne appointed Secretary of the Interior, **64**: 448; B. Colby appointed Secretary of State, **64**: 464,n1, 472-74; Dr. Park on WW's health and secret meetings of, **64**: 527; mention of Lansing's calling meetings of, **65**: 22, 139-40; Payne appointed Secretary of the Interior, **65**: 64; complaints of WW not meeting with, **65**: 79; Grayson urges WW to meet with, **65**: 179; holds first meeting of since illness, **65**: 186,n1, 187,n3; discusses "Palmer raids," **65**: 187,n4; Lansing inquires about meeting of, **65**: 188; Colby on tonic effect of WW's contact with, **65**: 222; Houston on meeting of, **65**: 238; on Jones bill, **65**: 270; **66**: 60; third-term Cabinet members, **65**: 382; Seibold mentions meeting of, **65**: 413; Tumulty on taking up Retirement Act with, **65**: 478; WW's attitude toward members on their return from the convention, **65**: 511n2; WW seeks advice of on lifting ban on brewing, **65**: 576; possible appointment of Cummings to, **66**: 7-8, 195-96; wishes to have mail censorship issue discussed at, **66**: 99; Alexander's resignation hoped for, **66**: 195-96; farmers' organization requests hearing with, **66**: 224; debate on whether to send

Woodrow Wilson, Cabinet, cont.

treaty back to Senate, **66**: 341-42; on Western Union cable issue, **66**: 413, 484; on reparations and tax on German exports, **67**: 109,n1; unwilling to accept resignations, **67**: 109; time for resignation letters, **67**: 124; photograph taken, **67**: 126,n1, 138; WW's first meeting with in Cabinet room since illness, **67**: 138; letter of farewell from, **67**: 150, 199; bids farewell at last meeting of, **67**: 175-76,n1; practice of retiring members to replace table and chairs, **67**: 187-88; receives gift of chair, **67**: 330, 365, 366; and Wilson & Colby announcement, **67**: 343; proposes a Secretary of Transportation, **67**: 431, 559, 591; **68**: 7, 219, 539-40; N. D. Baker on lack of confidentiality in, **68**: 164-65; WW on leaks in, **68**: 286; photograph of, *illustration section*, **67**

FAMILY AND PERSONAL LIFE

62: 99; news from Jessie, **53**: 21-22, 68-69, 212-13, 436-37; **54**: 107-108; **55**: 216-17; **58**: 428; **62**: 42,n2, 101, 303; **63**: 166-67; **67**: 107-109, 615; **68**: 149-50, 338; and insurance settlement for WW's burned hand, **53**: 159, 205; F. B. Sayre not going to Europe with The Inquiry, **53**: 213,n2; one of WW's favorite stories, **53**: 343; EBW and WW's relationship, **53**: 357, 366; **54**: 218; **58**: 367, 368; shyness gives impression of austerity, **53**: 358; food preferences, **53**: 358, 447; sleep habits, **53**: 369; punctuality of, **53**: 422; **54**: 522; **55**: 296; **58**: 170, 171; Grayson on WW's routine day and personal traits and habits, **53**: 446-48; love of children, **53**: 447, 461; family relationship to McAdoo prevents Secretary from being peace commissioner, **53**: 468; and Carlisle, **53**: 524, 537-38, 541; birthday, **53**: 526-27; lucky number, **53**: 694; **59**: 158-59; **66**: 440-41; **67**: 105, 115, 125; dislikes walking, **54**: 217; on Margaret's visiting Paris, **54**: 410; praise and love from the McAdoos, **55**: 204-205; becomes grandfather again, **55**: 234,n1; E. P. Davis reports on WW's new grandson and WW's thanks, **55**: 265-66, 304; wants to hold on to property in Ontario, **55**: 282; keeps the McAdoos informed of his activities, **55**: 283, 395; sends regards to M. A. Hulbert through her son, **55**: 304; and Yates memorial fund, **55**: 387; **56**: 191, 553; **57**: 98; visits Jessie and newborn grandson, **55**: 410; A. Blaine on her deceased son's personal feelings for WW, **55**: 440-41; reminisces on teaching, **55**: 442-43; likes to tease, **55**: 443-44; enjoys puns, limericks, and puzzles, **55**: 465-66; **58**: 147; R. S. Baker on, **55**:

Woodrow Wilson, Family and Personal Life, cont.

466-67; **59**: 368; **61**: 383, 416; wishes he had a good picture of his mother, **55**: 473; on cities to retire to, **55**: 482; answers inquiry into death of McAdoo's son-in-law, **56**: 125; superstitious, **56**: 128; recalls studying geography during his boyhood, **56**: 347-48; House on, **56**: 350; **60**: 373; does not discuss business at meals, **56**: 437, 440; Jessie asks for WW's help on establishing Y.W.C.A. programs in Russia, **57**: 60-61; incidents at Princeton, **57**: 353; **61**: 361-62; longs for silence, **57**: 427-28; on his father, **58**: 147; **60**: 489n1; **63**: 624; **64**: 517; **68**: 52-53, 257; rearranges furniture, **58**: 276,n1, 276 (2 references); **59**: 245; on student days at Princeton, **59**: 40; Seymour on attitudes of, **59**: 158-59; maternal ancestors, **59**: 190,n3; receives volume and copy of portrait of his ancestor Robert Wodrow, **59**: 190; on summers spent bicycling in Scotland, **59**: 247-48; attributes story to his father, **59**: 248, 255; concern over EBW's foot infection, **59**: 477; on Yates' death, **59**: 526; writes news to Jessie, **59**: 526; unable to attend class reunion at Princeton, **59**: 604-605,n1; and taxes, **59**: 604; **60**: 247, 331; **61**: 116; nervous before and after speeches, **59**: 621, 622; Balfour on sense of humor of, **60**: 204; makes toast to peace and League of Nations, **61**: 135; House on Poincaré invitation episode, **61**: 179; WW's signet ring, **61**: 179; aides surprise with mechanical toys, **61**: 231; hand trembling from excitement when signing treaty, **61**: 324; arrival at the White House, **61**: 401; the Pettys repay loan, **61**: 543, 624; news to Cousin Lucy, **61**: 551; takes two-day cruise aboard *Mayflower*, **61**: 562-63; receives autographed book by Canby, **61**: 568,n2; thanks E. P. Davis for verses and book, **62**: 102; goes to theater to relax, **62**: 115; renews financial commitment to Nacoochee Institute, **62**: 164; greetings from old friend and classmate, **62**: 469,n1; birthday greetings to Jessie, **62**: 516; looks forward to seeing old friend in San Francisco, **62**: 554; Chambers confides in, **62**: 601-602; regrets missing head of his boyhood school, **62**: 624-25,n1; grandson's christening postponed, **63**: 167; Jessie on resemblance of her new son to, **63**: 167,n4; on his ancestors, **63**: 282; last meeting with Mrs. Hulbert, **63**: 419,n1; description of WW at work, **63**: 513-14; emotion on canceling trip, **63**: 519; daughters notified of trip cancellation, **63**: 521; family all arrive at White House during illness, **63**: 549, 550; Margaret asks Mrs. Reid for human in-

Woodrow Wilson, Family and Personal Life, cont.

terest stories to tell WW, **63**: 575-76; receives Belgian royalty in his sickroom, **63**: 602-606; announcement of marriage to EBG, **63**: 624-25; observes Thanksgiving, **64**: 93, 97; college life at Davidson, **64**: 191-92; birthday greetings from Queen Mother Alexandra, **64**: 235; discusses with Grayson future use of notes for memoir, **64**: 324-25; birthday greetings to grandson, **64**: 451; examples of sense of humor and wit, **64**: 488-90; Grayson on WW and EAW's picture, **64**: 490n1; temperament of, **65**: 6; on Bryn Mawr's endowment fund, **65**: 79, 359; honorary degree from Oglethorpe University, **65**: 86, 117; unable to sit for portrait, **65**: 105-106; Long offers vacation home to, **65**: 110; responds to nephew's query on girls' schools, **65**: 211, 220; on Margaret's fear of dark, **65**: 243; on raising children, **65**: 243; wishes he could join his Princeton friends, **65**: 258,n2, 262; EBW and WW's affection for each other shown through sending of sample stationery, **65**: 287; McAlpin reaffirms loyalty to WW, **65**: 327, 333; thought of train travel a nightmare, **65**: 342; Puritanical strain evident, **65**: 349; EBW's love of, **65**: 376; **67**: 5-6; **68**: 383, 405, 409, 410, 413, 417; sends photograph to his broker, **65**: 491, 501; on royalties from *The State*, **65**: 503,n1, 509; on buying a house and thoughts of his future, **65**: 506; on being hopeless and on people having lost interest in him, **65**: 511; interested in buying H. White's house, **65**: 513-14; suggests B. M. King for appointment, **65**: 530, 567; nephew seeks job promotion, **66**: 38, 39, 40-41, 42; tempted by offer of Harlakenden, **66**: 57,n1,2, 71,n1; answers grandson's letter, **66**: 79-80; niece Jessie Dyer appeals to for loan and WW declines, **66**: 80-81, 99; plans vacation in Grasmere, England, **66**: 92, 134-35, 192, 245; Congressman Park makes walking cane for, **66**: 117, 129; Bok presents his autographed autobiography to, **66**: 131-32,n1; plans with architect for retirement mansion, **66**: 217-18, 232-33, 242, 291,n2, 305, 344-45,n2,3, 354-55,n1,2, 393, 410, 458, 470, 510-11, 518-19, 535,543, 545-46; **67**: 7-8, 30-31, 47-48, 84-85, 86-87, 105, 136; **68**: 105, 276,n1; answers questionnaire from Pelman Institute, **66**: 251-52; attempt to locate furniture commissioned and paid for years ago finally ends, **66**: 257,n1, 300-301, 338, 339, 379, 385; real estate owned in Canada, **66**: 257n1; as inspiration for Hall's book, **66**: 290; decision to settle in Washington, **66**: 291,n2; writes to

Woodrow Wilson, Family and Personal Life, cont.

Nell, **66**: 302, 332; Nell's encouragement after election, **66**: 315; McAdoo on support and encouragement shown by, **66**: 318-19; Axson reassures Jessie of WW's love and health, **66**: 319-20,n1; Jessie sends love and invitation to visit, **66**: 329-31; "passion for privacy," **66**: 346; and Kipling's "If," **66**: 352-53,n1, 369; and desk used on *George Washington*, **66**: 366, 370; can only own one home, **66**: 368; keeps picture of Nell, **66**: 409; enjoyed Thanksgiving turkey, **66**: 421; Brown-King wedding, **66**: 503, 505-506,n1; niece Jessie on Nobel Peace Prize award and family news, **66**: 503-504, 519; birthday luncheon, **66**: 506n1; decision to buy S street house, **66**: 519,n1; love and thanks from Jessie, **66**: 534; and Aunt Felie, **67**: 11, 16; thanks McAdoo for birthday greetings, **67**: 14; granddaughter thanks for Christmas gift, **67**: 18; responds to granddaughter's note, **67**: 22-23; responds to McAdoo on family, **67**: 22; R. S. Baker on relationship between EBW and, **67**: 82; contributes to Beach gift fund, **67**: 91, 123-24; guest list for housewarming, **67**: 105n3; EBW reveals love for in letter to K. Trask, **67**: 106-107; suggests law partnership to Colby, **67**: 107,n1; and granddaughter's poem, **67**: 108-109, 125; friends buy Pierce-Arrow for, **67**: 116-17,n1, 148, 156-67, 167, 167-68, 186,n1; visits new home and prepares for move, **67**: 127; arrangements for Nobel Prize money, **67**: 131-32; valentines to EBW, **67**: 133, 545; friends' fund-raising effort for S Street house, **67**: 137,n3, 148-49, 157; and law practice with Colby, **67**: 160-61, 161; ancestry of, **67**: 170, 171; Axson's news and thoughts on WW and EBW, **67**: 172-73; Jessie's praise and good wishes in new home, **67**: 188; arrives at new home, **67**: 206; liquor, **67**: 214, 312,n1; **68**: 107, 143, 167, 506; eager to have Jessie see new home, **67**: 231; unable to attend christening of grandson, **67**: 267; unable to attend reunion of "Witherspoon Gang," **67**: 277, 281, 300, 302-303; University of Virginia solicits for donation, **67**: 281,n2; and automobile accident claim, **67**: 303,n1, 385, 388; and EAW's grandfather, **67**: 307,n2; McAdoo's concern for EBW's health and burdens, **67**: 356; receives rare copy of Washington's Farewell Address, **67**: 357-59; love for EBW, **67**: 371; Dodge's invitation and reminiscences, **67**: 373-74; birthday greetings to Jessie, **67**: 385; a normal day's routine, **67**: 395-98; life style and finances, **67**: 398; news of Harpers and West-

Woodrow Wilson, Family and Personal Life, cont.

cotts, **67**: 410-11, 412; Jessie's desire to see WW, **67**: 427-28; on arrangements if entire Sayre family visits, **67**: 428-29; Nell's news and thanks for birthday greeting, **67**: 429-30; cheering crowd brings tears to WW's eyes, **67**: 449-53; and Berry Schools, **67**: 456-57, 459, 503-504, 507-508; news from E. P. Davis, **67**: 458; E. Helm on WW and EBW, **67**: 477; concern over publication of letter from doctor, **67**: 483; Webster on death of Bob Henderson and memories of "Witherspoon Gang," **67**: 491; favorite color and flower, **67**: 519; and Cousin Jessie Brower, **67**: 536; recommends Axson as faculty member at University of Virginia, **67**: 549; Jessie on son Woodrow, **67**: 553, 554; Nell on love for WW and on her move to California, **67**: 562; sends love and welcome to McAdoos, **67**: 565; **68**: 75; letters to grandchildren, **67**: 566; contributes to Near East Relief, **68**: 25, 465; dedicates proposed book to EBW, **68**: 39-40; decision not to leave Washington for summer vacation, **68**: 58-59; McAdoo sends family news, **68**: 72-73, 122-24, 145-46, 221, 222, 239-40; asks Professor Stuart for help with Greek, **68**: 101; inquires after C. H. Dodge's health, **68**: 112-13; delighted with news of McAdoos, **68**: 129; 151-52, 229, 243, 267-68, 510; writes to Jessie on election results, **68**: 180; sends Christmas gift to Eleanor, **68**: 238; birthday greetings from WW Foundation, **68**: 245-46; shows Grayson mail and flowers received on birthday, **68**: 250-51; WW's "old Princeton Chair," **68**: 250; the McAdoos send birthday greetings and book, **68**: 254, 260-61; Grayson's memorandum of two visits to S Street by Stockton Axson, **68**: 255-58; 1922 birthday dinner, **68**: 256; memories of blind soldier in France, **68**: 256; birthday toast to his mother-in-law, **68**: 266,n1; thanks McAdoos for book, **68**: 267; WW and EBW exchange valentines, **68**: 288; and college fraternity, **68**: 291n1; concern over Margaret's career plans, **68**: 296, 373, 386, 391; love for EBW, **68**: 315, 412, 415; R. S. Baker sends check from syndication of *World Settlement*, **68**: 321; encourages F. B. Sayre to take position in Siam, **68**: 351-52; cannot solicit friends for WW Foundation contribution, **68**: 355, 357; excited by planned visit from Jessie, **68**: 366-67; weekly demonstrations at theater exit, **68**: 375-76; refused to be member of fashionable country club, **68**: 376,n3; Oulahan on house of, **68**: 378-79; privacy of, **68**: 378; daily routine of, **68**: 380; on death of cousin John A. Wilson, **68**: 387-88;

Woodrow Wilson, Family and Personal Life, cont.

EBW keeps WW informed of her activities during her vacation in Massachusetts, **68**: 408-11, 412-13, 413-14; EBW's love for, **68**: 408, 409, 410, 413, 417; on getting along without EBW, **68**: 413; Hamlin on delight of EBW's visit, **68**: 418-19; Margaret on her activities and WW's response, **68**: 422-23, 427; on island he owns in Lake Rousseau, Ontario, **68**: 424; sends check for Japanese earthquake relief, **68**: 424,n2; friends establish trust fund for, and WW thanks, **68**: 438-39, 440-41, 441-42, 442-43, 444, 445, 526, 534; friends present with new Rolls-Royce on his birthday, and WW thanks, **68**: 443, 509, 513-14; subscribes to numerous magazines, **68**: 449-50; unable to attend ceremony at his boyhood church, **68**: 450-51,n2; Fosdick on WW's desire to return to educational field, **68**: 451,n1; Margaret congratulates WW on Armistice Day speech, **68**: 471; WW on his emotional breakdown during Armistice Day speech, **68**: 472; mention of his not supporting McAdoo for presidency, **68**: 476,n3; Sophie Loeb sends thanks and praises Margaret, **68**: 492; and California property, **68**: 503, 510, 532, 545; Nell thanks WW for gifts and sends family news, **68**: 505-506; birthday greetings to, **68**: 507-508, 508, 511, 512, 516; thanks Jones brothers for friendship and generosity, **68**: 517-18, 518; Long on Grayson's intimate knowledge of, **68**: 527-28; and Peck affair, **68**: 527; favorite limericks, **68**: 533-34, 595; S Street house, *illustration section*, **67**; photographs, *illustration section*, **68**

FOREIGN POLICY

See under the names of the individual countries, such as Great Britain and the United States

HEALTH

53: 695; **57**: 284; cold, **53**: 305, 314, 318, 327, 343, 376; **54**: 126, 150; **55**: 217-18, 457; **56**: 406, 408, 428, 429; **63**:46; **68**: 26, 36, 42, 45, 47, 48, 88, 151, 236, 285, 356, 402, 531, 532; very tired, **53**: 319, 321; **54**: 489, 521-22; **55**: 201, 298; **56**: 353, 355, 429; **57**: 239, 316; **60**: 120, 569; **61**: 112n1, 231, 543; twitching eyelid, **53**: 358; fatigue and strain on, **54**: 4, 473; **58**: 48, 168, 367, 368, 419; **59**: 574,n1; **63**: 397, 446; fighting over mandatory issue taxes mental resources, **54**: 334; E. Benham on strain on, **55**: 66; rests in room aboard ship, **55**: 202; Grayson examines, **55**: 410; sore throat and fever, **55**: 462; sore

Woodrow Wilson, Health, cont.
gum, **55**: 462; vascular accident of 1906 leaves one eye almost blind, **55**: 465,n2; good health of attributed to Grayson, **55**: 465; nonsmoker, **55**: 466-67; stays in bed all day, **55**: 471; WW on his ailments, **55**: 473; jokes that his health related to gases generated by Republican senators, **55**: 473; sleeps late aboard ship, **55**: 486; recovered from sickness, **55**: 495; exhaustion, **55**: 538; nose abscess, **56**: 85, 102; automobile jolt causes cut on head and headaches, **56**: 199, 337-38; nose and throat treated, **56**: 525; Grayson on WW's being "violently ill," **56**: 556-57,n2; "influenza," and recovery, **56**: 556n2, 577, 580, 584, 585, 558; **57**: 3-4, 50, 51, 62, 67, 145, 235, 304, 312; **68**: 257; improving by "letting off steam," **57**: 51; Jessie's concern over, **57**: 60; Rawnsley's concern over, **57**: 98; Grayson on precautions during recovery, **57**: 98, 101; EBW as nurse, **57**: 145, 235; and decision on punishment of William II, **57**: 146,n4; working too hard has effect on, **57**: 194; irritable when ill, **57**: 240,n2; exhaustive typical day, **57**: 304-305, 426-27; advised to stay away from crowds and tells story on that subject, **57**: 389; Grayson orders laxatives, **57**: 477; Grayson on, **57**: 580-81; **58**: 248, 368, 536; **60**: 573; **63**: 64, 123, 211n5, 276; rumors of ill health, **58**: 54; Grayson requests urotropin, **58**: 146,n1; problems reflected in delivery and speech to Plenary Session, **58**: 199n1; possible daze, **58**: 278n3; does deep breathing exercises, **58**: 535; changes in handwriting, **58**: 559,n1, 608-10, 625-26, 629,n91, 630; **61**: 544n2; **63**: 636; **64**: 105-106, 125, 486, 492; **65**: 244; speech to dinner guests seems disoriented, **58**: 562,n1, 598-600,n1, 627; Grayson fabricates report to put WW's remarks in a reasonable context, **58**: 562n1; seems relieved and cheerful, **58**: 601; editors' commentary on, **58**: 607-11, 638-40; neurologic illness at Paris, **58**: 607-40; memory failures, **58**: 612-13, 632; **59**: 574n1; **62**: 629-31, 636; effect of hypertension, **58**: 612, 614, 636, 637, 638; supposed influenza, **58**: 615-19, 639; headaches, **58**: 616,n20; **59**: 321; **60**: 120; **63**: 3, 32, 152, 275, 340, 397, 446, 489, 523, 574, 620, 639, 640; ophthalmologic history, **58**: 630-31; mixed dominance and, **58**: 637; Senator Gerry on, **59**: 124; morning walks, **59**: 288-89, 453; poor vision, **59**: 453; Grayson urges extra rest, **59**: 477; twitch on left side of face, **59**: 574,n1; query if WW was treated by psychiatrist, and negative reply, **60**: 569, 573; tired, **60**: 120, 569; fatigue from Belgian trip, **61**: 33; Lloyd George

Woodrow Wilson, Health, cont.
on long recovery of, **61**: 44; I. Hoover on changed mental attitude and behavior after illness in Paris, **61**: 112n1; Montenegro presents Grayson with medal for keeping WW healthy, **61**: 239; rests, **61**: 356; looks well, **61**: 363; and badly written shorthand, **61**: 368n5; morning walk aboard ship, **61**: 374; indications of lack of proper blood supply to head, **61**: 446,n1; noticeable contraction in back of neck, **61**: 446,n1; EBW on, **61**:543; **62**: 156; appears well when reviewing Czech troops, **61**: 569; small stroke on July 19, 1919, **61**: 569, 578-79; **62**: 628-29; good wishes from his pastor, **61**: 595,n1; address to Congress indicates extent of stroke, **62**: 209n1; and decision to make cross-country tour for League of Nations, **62**: 507n1; dementia, **62**: 628, 629,n4, 637; neurologic illness during summer of 1919, **62**: 628-38; and increased obstinacy, **62**: 630-31, 632,n4; impairment of brain function, **62**: 634-35; twenty-year period before speaking tour of 1919, **62**: 637; second phase after large strokes, **62**: 637; Grayson insists WW conserve his strength, **63**: 96, 309; Grayson's concern over WW's needed rest, **63**: 237; alleged effect of I.W.W. "silent demonstration" in Seattle on, **63**: 238n1; cough and coughing spells, **63**: 275, 446, 527; Grayson refuses to permit WW to speak at fairgrounds in Oregon, **63**: 275; first physical indication of break, **63**: 338n4; speaks at Berkeley reportedly against wishes of physician, **63**: 340n1; Grayson's concern over, **63**: 370, 446, 488-90; nervous condition apparent, **63**: 467; takes walk for an hour to stretch legs, **63**: 488-89; asthmatic attacks, **63**: 489, 539; face-muscle twitching, nauseated, seriously ill, "stroke warning," **63**: 518-19, 567, 579, 640-41, 641; trip cancellation, **63**: 518-21, 522, 523; news article on Grayson's plans for WW's rest on return to Washington, **63**: 527-28; fairly good night on train, **63**: 531; Grayson on WW's restless night and discomfort due to train speed, **63**: 532-33; Grayson emphatic about strict rest for WW, **63**: 533; get-well wishes, **63**: 534, 535, 535-36, 536, 548, 549, 580; news reports on improved condition, **63**: 536-37, 552-53; official bulletin on, **63**: 536; Polk inquires about, **63**: 536; Grayson's analysis of situation, **63**: 537-38; bulletins indicate no change, **63**: 538; Grayson gives Garfield account of WW's condition, **63**: 538-39; specialists called in, **63**: 539, 544-45, 546,n1, 551, 553, 634; suffers stroke, **63**: 539n1; Tumulty's grief, **63**: 539; Lansing on WW's condition and effect on running of govern-

Woodrow Wilson, Health, cont.
ment, **63**: 540-41, 542, 571; news reports and bulletins on, **63**: 543-45, 549-50, 550-51, 555-56, 560-61, 561-63, 563-64, 568, 572, 574-75, 576-77, 577-78, 581, 586-87, 590; **64**: 511,n1; and nervous exhaustion (neurasthenia), **63**: 545, 642; illness during Paris Peace Conference, **63**: 546,n1, 551n1; **64**: 492-93; on "stroke" of 1906, **63**: 551n1; Grayson reports to Cabinet on, **63**: 554; Long relays Grayson's report to Lansing on, **63**: 558-59; unable to resume duties for some time, **63**: 560, 561; rumors, **63**: 563-64, 564-67, 586, 608; **64**: 494-95, 511n1; retinal lesion, **63**: 567-68; Grayson on mental alertness of WW, but rest cure a priority, **63**: 569-71; prostate gland affliction, **63**: 572,n1, 577-78, 578-79,n1, 580, 581-82, 620; **64**: 499, 506; **65**: 298-99; **67**: 237; upsetting news kept from, **63**: 580; issue of who acts for WW during disability, **63**: 585; House concerned over information about himself being withheld from WW, **63**: 587-88; signs bills, but still required to rest, **63**: 587; improvement visible, **63**: 608; Lansing on WW's Thanksgiving Proclamation as reflection of severe illness, **63**: 619; R. S. Baker on, **63**: 619-22, 622; Grayson on left facial drag or looseness, **63**: 620; R. S. Baker on secrecy concerning, **63**: 620; Grayson stopped some early remedies, **63**: 622; had rest before western trip, **63**: 632-33; I. Hoover on, **63**: 632-38, purchase of special wheelchair from Atlantic City, **63**: 636; hypertension, **63**:639; Park on, **63**: 639-46; **64**: 525-29; eye problem, **63**: 641; leaves sickbed for wheelchair on Armistice Day, **64**: 6, 32; comments on continued improvement, **64**: 31, 37, 105-106, 307, 325, 351, 435, 495; goes outdoors, **64**: 32-33, 37, 50, 57, 100; spirits rise after visit from Prince of Wales, **64**: 32; not weakened but strengthened against his opponents, **64**: 44; Hitchcock on, **64**: 45n1, 133; issue of ability to perform duties, **64**: 52, 123-25; press speculates ill health reason for Hitchcock's failure to see WW, **64**: 99-100; Fall and Hitchcock agree on WW's ability to meet country's emergencies, **64**: 131; uses right hand, **64**: 131; and retort to Fall's prayer for, **64**: 133,n1; Grayson on Fall-Hitchcock visit and, **64**: 135-39; Fall on, **64**: 139; Lansing on, **64**: 139-40, 229, 231, 269, 385, 415-16, 417, 453-54; House on, **64**: 183; walks about room, negates rumors of paralysis, **64**: 187; Polk on, **64**: 227; EBW on, **64**: 232-33; contracts viral infection, **64**: 325, 351, 362n1; recovers, spends time outside, **64**: 361; R. S. Baker on, **64**: 365;

Woodrow Wilson, Health, cont.
Dr. Young's interview on, mentions diagnosis of cerebral thrombosis, weather only factor keeping WW from public appearances, says Young, **64**: 394-96; weight gain, **64**: 395; Dr. Dercum on, **64**: 403, 433-34, 435, 500-507; **65**: 90; publication of cerebral thrombosis diagnosis incenses WW, **64**: 403; WW's reaction to Dr. Young's interview on, **64**: 403; Dr. Bevan on diagnosis of WW's illness, recommends WW's resignation, **64**: 432-33; restless night, coughing spell, **64**: 472; health during first year of presidency, **64**: 497; Grayson's unpublished statement on WW's health history, **64**: 497-99; neuritis, **64**: 497; **65**: 409; in Paris, **64**: 497-98; phlebitis, **64**: 497n2; hernia operation in 1904, **64**: 407,n2; cerebral-occular accident in 1906, **64**: 497,n3;; diagnosis of paralysis, **64**: 503,n9; decision to issue general statements on WW's health, **64**: 507n1, 510; diagnosis by Drs. Park and Toole, **64**: 507n11; Park on aftermath of stroke, **64**: 525-29; editorial comments on Lansing incident and relationship to, **65**: 3-7; takes motor rides, **65**: 67, 86, 90, 110-11, 201, 243; idea of his taking advantage of illness to avoid Cabinet meetings, **65**: 79; looks robust, **65**: 80; Dercum's suggestions for continued improvement, **65**: 90; R. U. Johnson on, **65**: 93; unable to sit for portrait, **65**: 106; effect of presidential campaign of 1920, **65**: 124; uses cane, **65**: 125; House on, **65**: 140; depression, **65**: 149, 244, 512, 514, 552; **66**: 170, 320; **67**: 268, 270; effect of treaty defeat on, **65**: 149; WW asks about his ability to continue as President, **65**: 179-80; various comments on at first Cabinet meeting, **65**: 186,n1, 187, 188; cough, nervous, **65**: 244; talks slowly, **65**: 270; Swem on, **65**: 291, 521, 550; **67**: 103-104; EBW on WW's fighting spirit, **65**: 332-33; M. Peter questions WW's isolation, **65**: 340; Grayson's personal account of improvement in, **65**: 342-43; weight gain, **65**: 342, 413; Geddes on, **65**: 369; eye examination, **65**: 380; WW on his health as "uphill work," **65**: 383; House and McReynolds question WW's ability to serve, discuss issue of WW's resignation, **65**: 384; on his illness, **65**: 409; neuritis, **65**: 409; restless nights and concern over lungs, **65**: 481; nervous restless, asthmatic attack, **65**: 488, 529; **66**: 451; Roosevelt and Cox's observations on, **65**: 520n1; Cox on, **65**: 523-24; on his personal interest in foreign policy, but feels he's no longer of service, **65**: 531; uses as excuses not to meet with Socialist delegates, **65**: 550n3; I. Hoover on, **66**: 15; nurse dis-

Woodrow Wilson, Health, cont.
missed, **66**: 36; Lloyd George on, **66**: 43; prescription for eruption on chest, **66**: 55; exercise, **66**: 102; Creel on, **66**: 133n2, 170; Murray on, **66**: 133; J. S. Williams on WW conserving his health, **66**: 147-48; EBW on, **66**: 193; nervous about seeing people, **66**: 216-17; Grayson advises him to resign, **66**: 217,n1; answers Pelman question-naire, **66**: 251-52; on his own illness, **66**: 252, 504; on suffering from nervous exhaustion, **66**: 252; mention of retar-dation of progress, **66**: 274; Axson on, 66: 319-20; **67**: 309-10; R. S. Baker on, **66**: 435, 438, 440; **67**: 71, 237-38, 245, 284, 300-301, 360, 585; EBW on R. S. Baker reworking some comments in draft article, **66**: 446-47; Grayson and Tumulty on, **66**: 451; nervousness, **66**: 451; often breaks down and weeps, **66**: 451; Grayson persuades WW not to de-liver message to Congress in person, **66**: 456-57; Dodge on, **66**: 526; W. E. Dodd on, **67**: 68; various comments on improvement of, **67**: 71, 148, 308, 360, 397-98, 401, 585; loss of initiative, **67**: 103-104; ventures out in cold, **67**: 111-12; Harding on participation in inau-guration and, **67**: 149; and last Cabinet meeting, **67**: 175-76,n1; uses cane, **67**: 175, 205, 206, 208, 329, 381, 450; mem-ory lapse on Yap possibly due to small stroke, **67**: 195n4; uses wheelchair at Capitol, **67**: 207, 210; attack of nervous indigestion, **67**: 245, 246, 434-35, 436, 436-37; importance of exercise, **67**: 245, 310, 395; **68**: 397; Bolling on im-provement, **67**: 247, 336, 354, 357, 362, 410, 413, 427, 470, 501; rests con-stantly, **67**: 256; on his slow improve-ment, **67**: 281, 423, 442, 495, 507, 510, 532, 536; advanced planning to avoid fatigue during Washington bar admis-sion ceremony, **67**: 318; mentally keen, **67**: 321n1; uses only one hand, **67**: 360, 423, 430, 443, 582, 585; improve-ment evident, **67**: 370-71, 381-82, 440; walks unassisted, **67**: 370, 380-81, 397-98; difficulty with stairs, **67**: 439, 442; **68**: 58; unable to attend opening of Washington Naval Conference, **67**: 444; and reasons for not accompanying unknown soldier to grave, **67**: 448; Bal-four and Grayson on, **67**: 516-17; Dr. Mayo's advice, **67**: 535, 542; depression gone, **67**: 542; issue of recommended resignation, **67**: 568; painful to write, **67**: 572; physical therapist on, **67**: 611-14, 618-19; skin condition, **67**: 612; double vision, **67**: 613; sleep habits, **67**: 613; WW confides in therapist on, **67**: 613; unable to attend Democratic Na-tional Committee dinner, **68**: 33; frail and on cane, unable to make speech, recites limerick, **68**: 36-39; compares

Woodrow Wilson, Health, cont.
his own to F. D. Roosevelt's, **68**: 39; de-cision not to take vacation from Wash-ington, **68**: 58-59, 65; looks heavier, **68**: 88, 249, 382; WW and others on slow improvement, **68**: 94, 129, 143, 146, 227, 325, 356, 370, 428, 479-80; on his own lameness, **68**: 117, 400; state of mind shown by comments on people he disliked, **68**: 134n1; Harding's wishes for WW's improvement, **68**: 152; stands without cane, **68**: 187, 249; una-ble to stand erect, **68**: 188; Sullivan on WW's peace program and, **68**: 223n2; and issue of another term, **68**: 234n1; and Senate resolution on WW's birth-day, **68**: 247; small stroke in April 1919 mentioned, **68**: 257,n7; on becoming crank on subject of, **68**: 286; types with one hand, **68**: 298; and Creel's di-lemma concerning publication of WW's essay and concern for, **68**: 342-44; Lord Robert Cecil will not comment on, **68**: 344; on his own and J. H. Clarke's, **68**: 361; walks with difficulty and limp, **68**: 375, 377; mental health, **68**: 377-78; Oulahan on improvement, **68**: 377-78, 383; involvement of EBW, **68**: 383; ad-vises Cobb to take a rest, **68**: 384; Har-ding's consideration for shown by or-ders for Grayson, **68**: 398-99; and par-ticipation in Harding's funeral, **68**: 399-400, 401; electric massage, **68**: 409; EBW keeps track of days since WW was stricken, **68**: 410; EBW on his taking walk every day, **68**: 413; links fate of League of Nations to, **68**: 422; physically unable to condense Bar-uch's article, **68**: 431; Fosdick on crip-pled body of, **68**: 451n1; thanks Swan-son for partridges, **68**: 463

LAST ILLNESS AND FUNERAL

68: 553-60, 561-66, 579-84; Bolling on last illness, **68**: 548-50; press told WW has digestive attack, **68**: 549, 551, 552; news bulletins on, **68**: 553, 559; kidney failure, **68**: 554, 559; last days of, **68**: 561-66; death of, **68**: 566-70, 571-72; throng kneels in silent prayer, **68**: 570-71; Coolidge offers assistance to WW's family, **68**: 573; EBW invites Coolidge to WW's funeral, **68**: 574; EBW re-quests Lodge not attend funeral, **68**: 574; service at home, **68**: 575; tribute and prayers by Beach and Freeman, **68**: 578-79; photograph, *illustration section*, **68**

LETTERS OF PRAISE AND SUPPORT

66: 268-69, 272, 280, 280-21, 281-82, 289-90, 297, 296-97, 299, 299-300, 305, 306, 312-13, 313-14, 314, 314-15, 317n1, 318, 328, 329, 336, 343-44, 346n1, 347-48, 357n1, 378-79, 391-92,

Woodrow Wilson, Letters of Praise and Support, cont.
433, 450, 469, 474-75, 487, 483, 524-25, 536; **67**: 3-4, 4-5, 17, 17-18, 26-27,n1, 29, 29-30, 42, 57-58, 58-59, 123, 135, 151, 161-62, 164-65, 166-67, 170, 172-73, 181, 181-82, 183,n1, 186, 187, 199-200, 200-201, 201-202, 202-203, 204, 232-33, 240-41, 262-63, 266, 402-403, 454-55, 514-15, 528, 564, 573-74; **68**: 289, 313-14, 352, 440-41, 467, 485, 508, 511, 526; WW's acknowledgements of, **66**: 325, 331-32, 338, 346, 349, 354,368, 388, 393, 471, 499, 535, 539, 540; **67**: 29, 169-70, 171, 196, 197, 198, 230, 233n2, 233, 234, 247

LITERARY REQUESTS

Creel becomes agent for, **66**: 33-34, 64-65, 81, 121, 170, 171; Harper & Brothers' continued interest in publishing WW's works, **66**: 64-65, 163-65, 170, 171; on "no personal memoirs," **66**: 121, 387; on writing elementary history of U.S., **66**: 242; writes dedication for Naval Academy's yearbook, **66**: 325,n1; cannot make commitment for future writing, **66**: 354, 420; denies news reports that he's writing diplomatic history of the war, **66**: 370-71,n2; Doran seeks world rights, **66**: 417; R. S. Baker proposes writing book on events at Paris from the American point of view, **66**: 521, 521-23, 532-33, 533; Creel on, **67**: 141-42, 241-42, 243-44, 249, 254-55; **68**: 353-54, 356-57; will not write history, **67**: 158, 176n1, 246; Dodd and, **67**: 163-64, 283; will not prepare discourse for Rice Institute pamphlet, **67**: 246-47; denies request for book on life of Jesus, **67**: 259,n1; writes foreword to book of Ormond's lectures, **67**: 335-36,n1, 348-49; plans and notes for books, **68**: 39-42; WW essay, "Road Away From Revolution", **68**: 322-24, 325-26, 342-44; EBW's involvement with decision on essay, **68**: 344-45, 347-48,n1, 356; and Foley's book on League of Nations from WW's speeches, **68**: 349-50, 250, 351,n2, 355, 408; on decision to publish essay with *Atlantic Monthly*, **68**: 354, 363-64,n2, 369, 387; *Collier's* offer to publish essay, **68**: 368; essay to also be published in book form, **68**: 370, 371, 374; declines offer to write on ethics, **68**: 387,n2; WW on *Harper's* request for literary piece, **68**: 392-93; text of "Road Away From Revolution," and comments, **68**: 393-95, 395, 402-403, 406, 407, 410, 427; and *Louisville Post's* proposal, **68**: 483-84; on Davis' manifesto involving writing WW unable to do, **68**: 494-95; Kerney's offer declined by WW, **68**: 498, 499, 594; request from

Woodrow Wilson, Literary Requests, cont.
theological seminarian for his thesis, **68**: 500-501; and R. S. Baker as biographer, **68**: 524-25, 544; WW promises R. S. Baker exclusive access to his personal papers, **68**: 547

OPINIONS AND COMMENTS

Hunger does not breed reform; it breeds madness and all the ugly distempers that make an ordered life impossible, **53**: 42; on conquest, **53**: 42; **61**: 23; on peace, **53**: 52, 239, 336-37, 532; **60**: 455-57; participates in peace conference, **53**: 96-97, 286; on William II in The Netherlands, **53**: 138; on reparation, **53**: 351; **60**: 68, 319; **56**: 247-48, 290, 292, 296, 357, 357-58, 359-60, 364-65, 365, 367-68, 370, 452-53, 499,n3; **60**: 68, 319; Tell me what is right and I'll fight for it, **53**: 352, 356, 365; on cabinet form of government, **53**: 364-65; on League of Nations, **53**: 420; **58**: 599; **63**: 232; **67**: 521-22; **68**: 36; on his reception in Paris, **53**: 421; The best induction into education was to feel the pulse of humanity which had beaten from age to age through the utterances of men who had penetrated to the secrets of the human spirit, **53**: 461; The task of those who are gathered here, or will be presently gathered here, is greatly simplified by the fact that they are masters of no one; they are the servants of mankind, and if we do not heed the mandates of mankind we shall make ourselves the most conspicuous and deserved failures in the history of the world, **53**: 462; on mission of peace conference, **53**: 541, 549, 598; **54**: 265; **63**: 341; This fine correlation of the two things of duty and of right is the equipoise and balance of society, **53**: 550; on friendship, **53**: 550, 551; **61**: 435; and formation of association of nations, **53**: 552, 598; **54**: 266, 465; **59**: 609; **60**: 41; on Lloyd George, **53**: 589; **58**: 332; **60**: 329, 492, 533; **67**: 376n1; The only use of an obstacle is to be overcome. All that an obstacle does with brave men is, not to frighten them, but to challenge them so that it ought to be our pride to overcome everything that stands in the way, **53**: 598-99; on Mazzini, **53**: 614; on Columbus, **53**: 615-16; Force can always be conquered, but the spirit of liberty never can be, and the beautiful circumstance about the history of liberty is that its champions have always shown the power of self-sacrifice, have always been willing to subordinate their personal interests to the common good, have not wished to dominate their fellow men, but have wished to serve

Woodrow Wilson, Opinions and Comments, cont.

them. That is what gives dignity, that is what gives imperishable vitality, **53**: 619; on Montenegro and Serbia, **54**: 18-19,n5; and woman suffrage, **54**: 56; **61**: 464; **62**: 615; **65**: 295; on Russian problem and Bolsheviks, **54**: 102-103,n7; **56**: 247, 254, 328-29; **59**: 29, 29-30, 31, 301-302; **63**: 73; on press publicity at peace conference, **54**: 158; on importance of early peace, **54**: 242; the real strain of the war has come where the eye of government could not reach, but where the heart of humanity beats, **54**: 265; on self-determination, **54**: 267, 466; A conference of peace settling the relations of nations with each other, would be regarded as going very much outside its province if it undertook to dictate to the several states what their internal policy should be, **54**: 271; on the League of Nations being part of the peace treaty, **54**: 354; and Irish problem, **54**: 381; **55**: 474, 480-81; **60**:304; **61**: 291, 438, 439; must carry on work in private, **54**: 550-51; on German arms reductions, **55**: 12, 14, 15-16; on renewing Armistice for short period, **55**: 56; on freedom of seas as nonissue, **55**: 160, 162; on treaty, **55**: 175, 177; on public opinion destroying intrigue, **55**: 175, 414; Many terrible things have come out of this war, gentlemen, but some very beautiful things have come out of it. Wrong has been defeated, but the rest of the world has been more conscious than it ever was before of the majesty of right. People that were suspicious of one another can now live as friends and comrades in a single family, and desire to do so, **55**: 177; on W. S. Churchill's Russian initiative, **55**: 208; on direct election of senators, **55**: 228-29; on the hope and confidence vested in the U.S., **55**: 240-45; Speaking with perfect frankness in the name of the people of the United States I have uttered as the objects of the great war ideals, and nothing but ideals, and the war has been won by that inspiration, **55**: 241; on party loyalty, **55**: 310-11; The wrong opinion is generally better organized than the right opinion, **55**: 311; on contempt he feels for opponents of the League of Nations, **55**: 322-24; **59**: 608; **64**: 43; I do not mean to come back until it's over over there, and it must not be over until the nations of the world are assured of the primacy of peace, **55**: 417; The only place a man can feel at home is where nothing has to be explained to him. Nothing has to be explained to me in America, least of all the sentiment of the American people, **55**: 419; on the

Woodrow Wilson, Opinions and Comments, cont.

Covenant, **55**: 419; on more employer-employee partnerships, **55**: 471-72; on education, **55**: 473-74; compares British to Americans, **55**: 474-75; on Rhineland (the left bank), **55**: 479-80; **57**: 296-98; **58**: 584; **60**: 59-60, 277; on sentencing of Jehovah's Witnesses, **55**: 482-83,n1; on Gen. Wood, **55**: 486-87; on mideastern questions, **56**: 112-13, 113-14, 116; on delays caused by French delegates, **56**: 164-65, 312, 524, 541, 542; on need for food relief, **56**: 190; on submarine cables, **56**: 214-15, 218, 218-19; on his style of oratory, **56**: 249; on being removed from office during a crisis, **56**: 285; and withdrawal amendment for League of Nations, **56**: 301-302; on peace conference delays, **56**: 313; **57**: 130; on Saar Basin, **56**: 451-52; **57**: 128-29, 161-62, 162-63, 163-64; on Hungarian situation, **56**: 461-62; on war crimes and responsibilities and punishments for, **56**: 531-32; on Fiume and Adriatic, **56**: 563-64; **57**: 90, 484-85, 487; **60**: 211-12; on Monroe Doctrine amendment to Covenant, **57**: 255-56, 266-67; on Japan's racial equality amendment, **57**: 263-64, 264, 268-70; on individual delegates taking credit for work accomplished, **57**: 388; on prohibition, **57**: 429; on W. H. Page, **57**: 509; on Liberty Loan, **57**: 509-10; on Orlando, **57**: 513, 575, 576; on Japan's claims and China, **57**: 605-607; **58**: 18, 19, 245-46, 272-73; **59**: 479, 503-506, 507, 552, 574; **60**: 270-72; **61**: 170-71; **62**: 603-605, 619-20; **66**: 367; on Adriatic question and Treaty of London, **58**: 18, 19; on claims regarding German ships in U.S. ports, **58**: 37, 38; on publicity of peace terms, **58**: 61-62, 62-63; on secret treaties, **58**: 111, 112; fears for Paris Peace Conference, **58**: 112-13; on submarines, **58**: 127; The treaty which ends so terrible a war must unavoidably seem harsh towards the outlaw who started the war, but when the details are read and understood I believe that the impression will be largely removed, **58**: 205; on German sentiment toward himself, **58**: 332; on French people, **58**: 332; on labor program of peace treaty, **58**: 364; When I leave public life I don't want to be under contract, as I have been all my life. I want to be free, **58**: 504; on international law, **58**: 599; on German scholarship, **59**: 5,n2; **60**: 209, 215; on political science, **59**: 5; The greatest freedom of speech was the greatest safety, because if a man is a fool, the best thing to do is to encourage him to advertise the fact by speaking, **59**: 5; on Germany's objections to the treaty,

Woodrow Wilson, Opinions and Comments, cont.

59: 12; on medical specialist versus general practitioner, **59**: 79; on his father as his best teacher, **59**: 162; on German treaty, **59**: 187-88; on mandates, **59**: 207n1, 344-45; **61**: 363-64; **62**: 235, 257, 316, 579; on Jews and minority rights in Poland, **59**: 218, 219, 220, 221; on American commercial and industrial legislation supporting reconstruction, **59**: 293; I fear being misquoted, if interviewed: and if I talk freely, I do not know how to be discreet, **59**: 317; on women's fashions, **59**: 454; on Treaty of London as "infamous bargain," **59**: 479; It is better to separate the question of Asia Minor from the question of the Adriatic. For the peace of the world, I believe that Italy must remain outside of Asia Minor, **59**: 493; on need to return to U.S. as soon as possible, **59**: 552; Our thoughts and purpose are now consecrated to the maintenance of the liberty of the world and of the union of its people in a single comradeship of liberty and right, **59**: 571; These men did not come across the sea merely to defeat Germany and her associated powers in the war. They came to defeat forever the things for which the Central Powers stood, **59**: 607; We must not close our eyes to the fact that in the last analysis the military and naval strength of the Great Powers will be the final guarantee of the peace of the world, **59**: 629; I have no desire to soften the treaty, but I have a very sincere desire to alter those portions of it that are shown to be unjust, or which are shown to be contrary to the principles which we ourselves have laid down, **60**: 67, 78; The most fatal thing that could happen would be a break between the Allied and Associated powers, **60**: 68, 80; on Germany signing peace treaty, **60**: 71, 78; on Great Britain and treaty, **60**: 71; on club system at Princeton, **60**: 118-19; on English college system compared to American, **60**: 118-19; on attitude of "the Three," **60**: 286; on Clemenceau, **60**: 329; **61**: 370, 374-75; on 1920 election, **60**: 381; on Warren G. Harding, **60**: 381; I wish that I could make plain to you all that I feel. You cannot realize how difficult has been the task that has been set for me to do and how it has hurt me inside to realize that I have not been able to carry through to completion the entire program which I outlined, **60**: 387; would rather Germany didn't sign rather than weaken terms of treaty, **60**: 488; on blockade, **60**: 495, 499, 533, 534, 565, 621, 639; on the peace treaty, **60**:

Woodrow Wilson, Opinions and Comments, cont.

532-33 534; **61**: 108, 243-44, 250-51, 251, 292-93; on aversion for Germany, **60**: 553; compares Lloyd George to T. Roosevelt, **60**: 570; on destruction of Ypres, **61**: 5,n6; on King Albert, **61**: 16; I believe that Belgium and her part in the war is in one sense the key of the whole struggle, because the violation of Belgium was the call to duty which aroused the nations. The enemy committed many outrages in this war, gentlemen, but the initial outrage was the fundamental outrage of all, **61**: 17; The League of Nations is an inevitable consequence of this war. It is a league of right, and no thoughtful statesman who lets his thoughts run into the future could wish for a moment to slacken those bonds, **61**: 18; on the desecration of the University of Louvain, **61**: 21; on true scholarship, **61**: 23; on Poincaré, **61**: 114; on Senate adopting entire treaty without reservations, **61**: 115-16, 116, 137; on accomplishments of treaty, **61**: 236-37; on Shantung settlement, **61**: 237, 242, 249-50, 603; on Fall Resolution, **61**: 240, 247; on American people being misled about League of Nations and treaty, **61**: 245, 246-47, 251; on executive treaty-making powers, **61**: 251-52; on Germany and League of Nations membership, **61**: 254; on future relations with Italy, **61**: 307, 308, 309, 346; on not making public notes of the conversations in Council of Four, **61**: 336, 337, 338; and Allied warning to Italy, **61**: 342-46,n3; on amnesty issue, **61**: 351-52, 352; on lifting prohibition when demobilization completed, **61**: 351, 352; I have found one can never get anything in this life that is worthwhile without fighting for it, **61**: 354; on American universities, **61**: 363; on government ownership of railroads, **61**: 366; on his timing for entering the war, **61**: 371; on college athletics, **61**: 374; on the Fourth of July, **61**: 378-79, 380, 382; on the Armistice and new freedom for the world, **61**: 380; U.S. is champion of liberty throughout the world, **61**: 380; on naturalized citizens, **61**: 381; on laws of freedom, **61**: 382; on his mistake on South Tyrol, **61**: 387-88; The League of Nations was the practical statesman's hope of success in many of the most difficult things he was attempting, **61**: 433; There can be no question of our ceasing to be a world power. The only question is whether we can refuse the moral leadership that is offered us, whether we shall accept or reject the confidence of the world, **61**: 436; on nepotism, **61**: 482; on reasons for not

Woodrow Wilson, Opinions and Comments, cont.

writing tributes to individuals, **61**: 541,n2; on Article X, **61**: 595; refuses to compromise on reservations, **61**: 600, 601; on wheat situation, **62**: 57; on Thrace, **62**: 141-42; The world must pay for the appalling destruction wrought by the great war, and we are part of the world. We must pay our share, **62**: 216; on Anna H. Shaw, **62**: 225; I will withdraw the French treaty rather than consent to see the Turkish Empire divided as spoils!, **62**: 235; on legal *v.* moral obligation, **62**: 361-62; on his knowledge of secret treaties, **62**: 364-67,n27; **63**: 28, 39, 137, 261, 359; on Rumania, **62**: 427; disgusted with conduct of Europe, inclined not to have U.S. join League of Nations, **62**: 428-29; Foreign affairs certainly cause a man to be profane, **62**: 429; on keeping reservations out of articles of ratification, **62**: 433; on League bureaus, **62**: 455; Demands unwisely made and passionately insisted upon at this time menace the peace and prosperity of the country as nothing else could, and thus contribute to bring about the very results which such demands are intended to remedy, **62**: 497-98; on Wilson Dam, **62**: 515; on proposed cross-country tour, **62**: 516; on amnesty and Spargo's memorandum, **62**: 555, 559; This treaty is not merely meant to end this single war. It is meant as a notice to every government which in the future will attempt this thing that mankind will unite to inflict the same punishment, **63**: 8-9; on revolution, **63**: 12-13; on nationalism, **63**: 33; The seed of war in the modern world is industrial and commercial rivalry, **63**: 45; on isolation, **63**: 79; on "Germanism," **63**: 113; on idealism, **63**: 113, 189; on progressivism, **63**: 127, 216; on ethnic diversity of America, **63**: 139-40, 280; on hyphenated Americans, **63**: 140, 143, 320-21, 469-70, 493, 501; In order to live tolerable lives, you must lift the fear of war and the practice of war from the lives of nations, **63**: 144; on radicalism, **63**: 177; on U.S. decision to enter war, **63**: 181-82, 191, 213, 233-34, 293, 312, 347, 401, 430, 468; on the world's confidence in America, **63**: 184; on economic conditions, **63**: 189; on police strikes, **63**: 196, 302; The only thing in the world that is unconquerable is the thought of men, **63**: 282; The only thing that makes the world inhabitable is that it is sometimes ruled by its purest spirits, **63**: 321-22; The only effective force in the world is the force of opinion, **63**: 345, 360; This treaty is nothing else than an

Woodrow Wilson, Opinions and Comments, cont.

organization of liberty and mercy for the world, **63**: 357; Stop for a moment to think of the next war, if there should be one. . . . I ask any soldier if he wants to go through any hell like that again. That is what the next war would be. And that is what would be the destruction of mankind. And I am for any kind of insurance against it and the barbarous reversal of civilization, **63**: 495; My clients are the children; my clients are the next generation, **63**: 511; will give his life for the treaty, **64**: 43; on isolationism, **64**: 79, 109; on representative government as way to reform, **64**: 116; on following the Constitution regarding Mexican situation and Senate subcommittee, **64**: 152; on various articles of treaty, **64**: 329-30; on Geddes, **64**: 484; on men who have turned against him, **64**: 488; on friendship between U.S. and Great Britain, **64**: 491-92; on Article X, **65**: 9, 12, 26, 31, 53, 70, 82; on conflicts between democracy and imperialism, **65**: 26-27, 32-33, 52-53, 69, 70; on imperialistic designs of nations other than Germany, **65**: 52, 69; on H. Hoover, **65**: 149; **66**: 497; **68**: 305; on dead treaty, **65**: 152, 212; on "double dealing" of some senators, **65**: 179; on Mexico's choice for Ambassador to U.S., **65**: 201, 202,n1; on coeducation, **65**: 220-21; The Democratic party has now a great opportunity to which it must measure up. The honor of the nation is in its hands, **65**: 264; and calling meeting of League of Nations Assembly in Geneva, **65**: 501, 503-504; on Gore, **66**: 3; on direct communication, **66**: 71; reaction to order to send U.S. ship to Danzig, **66**: 78; on prerogatives of presidential office, **66**: 89; cannot endorse denominational colleges, **66**: 151; on election being referendum on League of Nations and Versailles Treaty, **66**: 175-86,n2, 181-83; on T. Roosevelt, **66**: 175; I am ashamed to have taken the advice of those insincere men who are not trying to help but to embarrass and inhibit, **66**: 184; on Josephine Berry, **66**: 228, 229; on Christian education, **66**: 229; on Harding's "invention" concerning France, **66**: 246; on not answering Root's charges, **66**: 249; on Jefferson Davis, **66**: 369; on memorial gateway with his statue at Univ. of Texas, **66**: 369,n1,2; on Lodge, **66**: 479, 484; on democracy, **66**: 485; on why he would not write about what happened at Paris, **66**: 533; on his birthday, **67**: 9; on immigration, **67**: 9; on Robert E. Lee, **67**: 28; on O'Callaghan case, **67**: 52; on Lansing and his book, **67**: 60; You university

Woodrow Wilson, Opinions and Comments, cont.

men must keep up the fight. These ideas must win. If you stand together and continue to preach them and write them, men will listen to you; they can not help doing so. If I only knew how best to help, it would be the one work of my remaining years to aid in this cause, **67**: 69; on new house, **67**: 91; on shorthand, **67**: 127; on Foch, **67**: 270-71; on Minor, **67**: 275; on Democratic party, **67**: 279-80, 280; **68**: 63; on Memorial Day, **67**: 279; on Harvey, **67**: 289; on not moving University of Virginia's medical school, **67**: 299,n1; on duty of the nation, **67**: 424; on advancing commercial development, **67**: 430-41; on preventing revolution, **67**: 431-32; on transportation coordination, **67**: 431; on "America First," **67**: 443, 589-90; **68**: 5, 215, 535-36; on Dodd for president of University of Missouri, **67**: 509; on not breaking his silence, **67**: 602, 602-603; asked to support teaching of evolution in schools but declines, **67**: 536,n2, 537,n1,3; on making movie about George Washington, **67**: 557; on Nortoni, **67**: 563,n2; on not moving educational institutions, **67**: 567-68; on newspaper profession, **67**: 574; on J. A. Reed, **67**: 578, 579, 586; **68**: 24; The Presidency is what the incumbent makes it. If he is a small and compliant man it is a small office; if he is a real leader, it is an office of leadership. There is nothing dangerous about the office. The only danger is the man you put into office, **67**: 605; compares office of U.S. President to that of British Prime Minister, **67**: 605; on presidential possibilities and qualifications, **67**: 605-607; on third term, **67**: 605; on Republican policy of isolation, **68**: 6, 215, 536; on strategy for Long to defeat Reed, **68**: 12; on "mind your own business week," **68**: 23, 24; on Newberry case, **68**: 46-47; We have made the world safe for democracy. The world would not permit today that any small nation should be seized, agree that it has the right to work out its own destiny; but democracy is in danger from interior revolution, it must learn to preserve itself, **68**: 47; on selection of candidates, **68**: 63-64, 71; on characteristics of European public men, **68**: 77; on need of right kind of men in public office, **68**: 90-91, 92-93; on Hardwick, **68**: 93; against cancellation of war debts, **68**: 107; on evolution, **68**: 121,n2; on Sutherland, **68**: 121, 127; on importance of entering public life, **68**: 128; on American Bar Association, **68**: 129; on Bruce, **68**: 134-35; on failure of churches to support U.S. in League of

Woodrow Wilson, Opinions and Comments, cont.

Nations, **68**: 144-45; on E. Colby, **68**: 163; Nothing can restore to us the international leadership which we lost by failure to ratify the Treaty of Versailles, or put us in the rightful attitude of frank cooperation and joint responsibility with the rest of the world, except our entrance into the League on the same footing and terms with all the other members, **68**: 170, 189; I think I am justified in saying that I am perhaps the only public man in the world who does not need to be interpreted to anybody, **68**: 175; on difference between armistice and peace, **68**: 186; on League of Nations being Democratic party issue, **68**: 189; The world has been made safe but democracy has not yet made the world safe, **68**: 192, 323, 394; on Sullivan, **68**: 227; on Pasteur, **68**: 229; on his birthday resolution from Senate, **68**: 251; on Mussolini, **68**: 251-52; on difference between "sarcasm" and "irony", **68**: 256-57; against nonpartisan action for League of Nations, **68**: 276; on college fraternities, **68**: 291,n1; on Ku Klux Klan, **68**: 298; on preservation of Monticello, **68**: 321; on capitalism, **68**: 322-23; on A. Meiklejohn, **68**: 388-89, 390; It has been true of me all my life that it was impossible for me to write to order—even my own order. I must always wait for the subject and the impulse, **68**: 392; on building the Washington Cathedral, **68**: 396; As I see it the greatest fight of all lies immediately ahead of the liberal forces of this country and of the world—the fight to conquer selfishness and greed and establish the rule of justice and fair play and universal cooperation, **68**: 445; on Lord Birkenhead, **68**: 448; on candidates from N.J. for Senate, **68**: 459, 592, 595; on Armistice Day, **68**: 466-67; on "peace without victory," **68**: 515; tribute to Cobb, **68**: 520; on justice, **68**: 543; on C. Coolidge, **68**: 553; on Senate, **68**: 589

RECREATION

53: 447; **67**: 309; reads aloud, **53**: 3; **54**: 309, 431,n1, 433; takes walks, **53**: 321, 322, 327, 332, 336, 346; **55**: 202, 207, 308-309, 456, 471, 474, 481, 531; **56**: 3-4, 103; **57**: 513; **59**: 288-89, 321, 370, 453, 527; **60**: 114, 299, 381, 545; **61**: 370, 374; **63**: 32; views movies aboard ship, **53**: 327, 343, 358, 370, 371; **55**: 207, 443, 448, 456, 457, 465, 474, 490; **61**: 363, 370, 378, 383, 385, 397, 398; singing, **53**: 344; **55**: 491; **61**: 383, 398; enjoys musical comedy aboard ship, **53**: 366; reading, **53**: 369; **65**: 342, 411;

Woodrow Wilson, Recreation, cont.
66: 102; plays Canfield, **53**: 369; **54**: 309; **55**: 442; **56**: 164, 408; **57**: 450, 478, 576; **58**: 4; **59**: 3, 48, 369, 606; **60**: 157, 334; **61**: 45; golf, **53**: 552, 577, 592, 706; **55**: 479, 489; **56**: 439-40; **57**: 304; **64**: 492; **65**: 551; **67**: 524; **68**: 425; attends opera, **53**: 614; **54**: 305,n7; **56**: 62,n4; thanks Fairbanks for movie projector, **54**: 53; Poincaré refuses WW's invitation to attend theater, **54**: 76-77, 104; takes automobile rides, **55**: 36, 66, 367, 538; **56**: 428-29, 542; **57**: 146, 239, 284, 316, 450, 478, 513, 580; **58**: 170-71, 176, 216, 244, 245, 331, 422, 535; **59**: 39-40, 78, 124, 161, 186-87, 248, 253, 254, 289, 371, 419, 420, 453, 479, 528, 553, 554, 577, 606, 625; **60**: 3, 19, 43, 116, 203, 204, 249, 286, 292, 300, 334, 388, 435, 567, 574, 612; **61**: 33, 44, 45, 69, 78, 187; **63**: 92, 423, 523, 533, 536; **65**: 41-44, 67, 86, 90, 110-11, 201, 244, 342; **66**: 102, 340, 442; **67**: 238, 250-51, 265, 289, 306, 308, 396, 419, 425, 469, 586; **68**: 57,n4, 404, 416, 425, 596; reminiscences of visit to Yorktown, Va., **55**: 444-45; enjoys games and puzzles, **55**: 465-66; plays shuffleboard aboard ship, **55**: 471, 481, 490; Grayson reads R. S. Baker's stories aloud to WW, **55**: 491; love of music, **56**: 62; Grayson tells stories of O. M. James to, **56**: 348-49; limericks, **56**: 440; attends theater, **57**: 502-503, 533,n4, 581; **59**: 627-28; **63**: 636; **67**: 111, 268, 380-81, 397, 435, 440, 571, 586; **68**: 57,n4, 404, 416, 425, 596; relaxes at Baruch's country residence, **58**: 170-71; laughs at cartoons of himself, **58**: 245; visits Barbizon, **58**: 422, 427; **59**: 248-49; at Longchamps racetrack, **58**: 535, 536; **59**: 124; shows less enthusiasm for normally satisfying activities, **58**: 614; attends theatrical performance given by U.S. troops, **59**: 207; on summers spent bicycling in Scotland, **59**: 247-48; enjoys watching people, **59**: 453-54; motors to Fontainebleau, **59**: 477; EBW reads to, **63**: 561, 636; "talking machine": entertains WW, **63**: 561; I. Hoover on period between return from Paris and western trip, **63**: 632; wheelchair rides outdoors, **64**: 57; sings hymns with family in 1913, **64**: 487; sings "Old Nassau," **64**: 487; watches Grayson's son have pony ride, **65**: 194; motors with G. Grayson, **65**: 244; reviews military parade, **65**: 289n1; enjoys watching circus parade, **65**: 290-91; and movies, **65**: 342, 348, 349, 380, 384-85, 400, 404, 411-12, 514; **66**: 102, 435, 438-41; **67**: 71, 82, 103, 150, 397, 530;interest in theater, **65**: 404; on exercise, **65**: 410; rides in horse-drawn carriage, **66**: 15; unable to attend special theatrical production, **66**: 112-13; receives motion

Woodrow Wilson, Recreation, cont.
picture equipment, **67**: 368,n1; is read aloud to, **67**: 517; **68**: 380; attends theater and receives reception, **68**: 425; subscribes to numerous magazines, **68**: 449-50; auto rides cease, **68**: 551, 559 photograph of, *illustration section*, **58**; **65**; **67**; **68**

RELIGION

63: 282; **68**: 324, 395; Thanksgiving Proclamation, 1918, **53**: 95-96; attends church, **53**: 376; **55**: 36,n1, 66, 201, 367; **56**: 428; **59**: 247-48; **63**: 93, 273, 423; on Providence, **53**: 530, 575-76; on belief in God, **54**: 282; R. S. Baker on, **55**: 467; unable to attend meeting of Society of Sunday Schools of France, **56**: 64,n1; reads Bible, **57**: 513; **67**: 397; **68**: 257; questions Pershing on, **59**: 253-54; refers to sermon by H. Black, **59**: 254; observes Sabbath, **61**: 65; **63**: on comfort of, **64**: 488; turns to when treaty rejected, **65**: 109n1; Southern Baptists' request for letter of introduction for European mission denied by, **65**: 421-23, 430; cannot endorse denominational colleges, **66**: 151; on Christian education, **66**: 213, 229; endorses Hebrew Union College's fundraising tour, **66**: 261, 265-66; Dodd on, **67**: 75-76; always says grace, **67**: 396; denies request for message for men in ministry, **67**: 503, 507; unable to endorse fund raising for Presbyterian college in Missouri, **67**: 519, 524; declines to lecture on Christian missions, **67**: 529-30,n2; on Christian Science, **68**: 68-69,n1; and his illness, **68**: 370; sends message on consecration of Bishop of Washington, **68**: 420-30; leaving church in Paris, photograph of, *illustration section*, **54**

THE DOCUMENT

67: 588-601; **68**: 5-9, 215-21, 535-41, and Brandeis' involvement with, **67**: 319-20,n1, 443, 472, 475, 506, 506-507; **68**: 405, 413; first mentioned, **67**: 319-20,n1; WW on, **67**: 430-32, 443, 506-67; WW's suggested introductory paragraph, **67**: 435-36, 437; Colby and, **67**: 437, 556, 575-77, 579; **68**: 4, 13, 17-19, 28, 34; and Houston on taxation, **67**: 476-77, 484-87, 499-501; WW's revisions of Houston's taxation statement, **67**: 499-501; WW thanks all who have worked on, **67**: 515-16; **68**: 19, 56, 71-72, 325; H. J. Ford on railroads and, **67**: 550,n1; on farmers, **67**: 566-67, 582-83, 583-84; **68**: 252-54; text of, **67**: 599-601; Baruch on, **68**: 4; text sent to Brandeis and Colby, **68**: 5-9; "America First," **68**: 5, 215, 309, 535-36; and Chadbourne, **68**: 19-20, 28-29, 33; calls

Woodrow Wilson, The Document, cont.
conference on, **68**: 26-27,n1, 27; asks
Houston and Davis to rephrase parts
of, **68**: 32; Davis and Houston contribution to, **68**: 42, 43, 49, 51, 53-55, 172,
237, 241, 242, 244, 244-45; addition to
on executive right to places on floor of
Congress, **68**: 105-106; draft of, **68**:
215-21; WW on Houston's contribution, **68**: 260; Houston continues to re-
fine, **68**: 269-73; WW wishes to review
with Baruch and Cobb, **68**: 294,n1,
294-95, 295-96; Davis works on redraft, **68**: 296, 302-303, 311, 317-19;
suggests resolution on party policy, **68**:
297-98,n3; revisions of, **68**: 308-10; evolution of statement on prohibition, **68**:
315, 334-36, 336, 337, 338; and N. D.
Baker, **68**: 534-35, 544,n1; final draft,
68: 535-41; and R. S. Baker, **68**: 544n1;
see also under names of individual contributors such as Brandeis, Louis
Dembitz, Davis, Norman Hezekiah,
and under specific topics such as agriculture

TRIP TO EUROPE

House and WW plan for, **53**: 44, 69, 70;
invited to stay at Buckingham Palace,
53: 85, 109, 491; offered home of Prince
Murat in Paris, **53**: 154, 180-81; plans
for his sailing to France, **53**: 190, 193,
221, 229, 240; begins voyage from
Washington, **53**: 305; reaction to Congress' opposition to trip, **53**: 313; sendoff from Hoboken, **53**: 313-15; activities aboard *U.S.S. George Washington*,
53: 318-19, 319-21, 321-22, 327, 332-
33, 336-40, 340-41, 341, 343, 343-44,
348, 348-49, 350-52, 353-56, 356-57,
357-58, 364-65, 365-66, 366-67, 367-
68, 369-70, 370-71, 371-72, 375-76,
377-78; plans for stay in Paris, **53**: 344-
45, 345-46; arrival, reception and
speeches in Brest, **53**: 378-79, 380-81,
396-97; arrival, reception and activities in Paris, **53**: 382-84, 384-85, 386-
87, 389-91, 391-92, 398, 399, 403-404,
404-405, 405, 410, 417-18, 421, 458,
458-60, 461-63, 467, 488; receives degree from University of Paris, **53**: 345,
458, 459-61, 461-63; hospital visit to
wounded Americans, **53**: 467, 469;
spends Christmas with Pershing and
troops in Chaumont, **53**: 404, 502-505,
505-507; leaves France for England,
53: 508-509; arrival in Dover, **53**: 509,
569; arrival in London, **53**: 509-
12, 592; meetings, receptions, and
speeches in London, **53**: 519-22, 522-
24, 525, 526-29, 530, 531-33, 533-34,
535-36, 592-95; unofficial visit and
speech in Carlisle, **53**: 537-41; visit and
speeches in Manchester, **53**: 539-41,
543-46, 548-49, 549-52; returns to Lon-

Woodrow Wilson, Trip to Europe, cont.
don, **53**: 546-47; leaves England to return to Paris, **53**: 569, 570; departs for
Italy, **53**: 578, 589; arrival, activities,
and speeches in Rome, **53**: 595-97, 597-
99, 599-600, 600-601, 602-603, 605-
607, 608-609; visits the Vatican, **53**:
606-607; activities and speeches in
Genoa, **53**: 613, 614, 614-15, 615-16;
arrival and remarks in Milan, **53**: 613-
14, 616-20; arrival and address in
Turin, **53**: 620-21, 622-24; Tumulty on
changed attitude in U.S. toward WW's
trip, **53**: 625; return to Paris, **53**: 634;
photographs of, *illustration section*, **53**;
see also Paris Peace Conference

TOUR OF BELGIUM

61: 10-16, 34; address to Parliament, **61**:
12-13, 16-20; remarks at a luncheon,
61: 16; greetings by Cardinal Mercier,
61: 21-22; remarks at Louvain, **61**: 21;
remarks at University of Louvain, **61**:
22-23; remarks at Brussels City Hall,
61: 23-24; remarks at dinner in Royal
Palace, **61**: 25–26; R. S. Baker on, **61**:
28-30; thanks King Albert and Queen
Elisabeth, **61**: 33; Whitlock on, **61**: 105-
106; thanks Whitlock, **61**: 172-73; King
Albert thanks WW, **61**: 355; photograph of, *illustration section*, **61**

VETO MESSAGES

of extension of application of Section 10
of Clayton Act, **67**: 12-13,n1; of revival
of War Finance Corporation, **67**: 18-
22, 27-28; of Milk River Valley Gun
Club bill, **67**: 112-13; of bill to cease
army recruiting, **67**: 117-18; of Emergency Tariff bill, **67**: 191-94

WESTERN TOUR
(activities, events, speeches)

64: 276n1, 277; **66**: 147; first appearance, **63**: 3; preparation and delivery of
speeches, **63**: 6; address in Columbus,
Ohio, **63**: 7-18; remarks in Richmond,
Indiana, **63**: 18-19; address in Indianapolis Coliseum, **63**: 19-29; addresses
in St. Louis, **63**: 33-42, 43-51; welcome
in Kansas City, **63**: 63-64; complains of
heat in Kansas City Auditorium, **63**:
64n1; in St. Joseph, Missouri, **63**: 64-
65; arrival and activities in Des
Moines, **63**: 65-66; address in Kansas
City, **63**: 66-75; address in Des Moines,
63: 76-88; wants only absolutely urgent mail forwarded, **63**: 92, 120, 151;
arrival in Sioux Falls, **63**: 95; rides on
rear platform, **63**: 95; on train, **63**: 96-
97; address in Omaha, **63**: 97-107; address in Sioux Falls, **63**: 107-17; address in Minneapolis Armory, **63**: 123-
24,n1, 131-38; address in St. Paul, **63**:

Woodrow Wilson, Western Tour, cont.
124, 138-48; address to joint session of
Minnesota legislature, **63**: 125-31; arrival and address in Bismarck, **63**: 152-
62; remarks in Mandan, North Da-
kota, **63**: 162, 163; plans for California
tour, **63**: 164; reception and activities
in Billings and Helena, **63**: 168-69; address in Billings, **63**: 170-80; address
in Helena, **63**: 180-97; stay in Coeur
d'Alene and Spokane, **63**: 210-11; address in Coeur d'Alene, **63**: 212-21;
speech in Spokane, **63**: 224-34; activities in Tacoma and Seattle, **63**: 236-40;
I.W.W. "silent demonstration" in Seattle, **63**: 238,n1, 240; speeches in Tacoma, **63**: 240-41, 241-52; remarks and
address in Seattle, **63**: 253-54; 254-64;
meets with labor leaders in Seattle, **63**:
273,n2; activities in Portland, **63**: 274-
76; automobile accident, **63**: 275-76,
277; addresses in Portland, **63**: 277-83,
283-94; arrival and activities in
Oakland and San Francisco, **63**: 308-
10, 340; address to Associated
Women's Clubs of San Francisco, **63**:
311-22; address in Civic Auditorium,
63: 322-23, 323-36; luncheon address
in San Francisco; **63**: 341-50; address
in Berkeley, **63**: 350-52; address in
Oakland, **63**: 352-61; first test of micro-
phone, **63**: 369-70; arrival and activities in San Diego, **63**: 371-82, 382-88;
arrival and activities in Los Angeles,
63: 396-97, 423; speeches in Los Angeles, **63**: 400-407, 407-18; arrival and
activities in Sacramento, **63**: 426; remarks in Sacramento, **63**: 426-27; address in Reno, **63**: 428-41; activities
and speeches in Ogden, Utah, and Salt
Lake City, **63**: 446n2, 447, 448, 448-63;
arrival and address in Cheyenne, **63**:
467, 467-82; arrival, activities, and
speeches in Denver and Pueblo, **63**:
487-88,n2, 490-500, 500-513; walk on
Colorado plateau, **63**: 488-89; description and schedule of typical day, **63**:
513-14; cancellation of remaining
speeches, **63**: 519-20, 522-24; sends
message to people of Wichita, **63**: 522,
523, 524; on return trip to Washington,
63: 526, 527, 531-32; back in Washington, **63**: 523-33; Lansing on reasons for
opposing, **64**: 55; Grayson on, **64**: 488;
Foley on printing excerpts of WW's
speeches on, **66**: 152; Cummings and
WW discuss, **66**: 195 photographs of
WW during tour, *illustration section*,
63

Western Tour—Themes

The end of American isolation, **63**: 36,
79, 112, 115, 138, 155-56, 173, 189,
215, 279, 291-92, 334, 401-402, 407,
415-17, 448, 456-57, 480

Woodrow Wilson, Western Tour, cont.
The treaty an American document, **63**:
66-67, 72, 77, 82, 98, 184-85, 281,
311, 342, 401
The treaty a nonpartisan document, **63**:
19, 26, 49-50, 97-106, 130-31, 221,
228-29, 247-48, 288-89, 374-75, 386,
417-18, 494, 499-500
The treaty a world settlement, **63**: 7, 72,
131-32, 154, 171, 184-85, 212, 225,
344, 351
The treaty a humane document, **63**: 15-
16, 34, 97, 137, 173, 262, 351, 354,
356-57, 371-73, 380, 458; the Magna
Carta of Labor, **63**: 14-15, 78-79, 99,
110, 127-28, 137, 146-47, 246, 261-
62, 356, 373, 497, 502; the mandate
(trustee) system a protection of in-
digenous peoples, **63**: 15-16, 111-12,
435, 458; the redemption of the
rights of new and weak nations, **63**:
10-11, 24-25, 34-35, 187, 259, 291,
329, 335-36, 374, 379-80, 403; the
protection of women and children,
suppression of traffic in drugs, etc.,
63: 16, 137, 262, 357
*The necessity of American leadership in
League to prevent future wars,* **63**: 9,
17-18, 28-29, 37, 47, 78-79, 107-108,
113, 115, 116-17, 134, 145-46, 155,
157-58, 160-62, 172, 179-80, 180-81,
217-18, 234, 248-49, 284, 292, 312,
334-35, 348, 350, 360-61, 382, 384,
386-87, 405-406, 410, 418, 433-34,
448, 469, 474, 478, 494-95, 498, 510-
12
*Defense of various provisions of the
Covenant:* the Monroe Doctrine, **63**:
49, 85-86, 103, 192-93, 230-31, 247-
48, 287-88, 318-19, 322, 327, 376,
403, 429-30, 431-32, 450-51, 475; the
Shantung settlement, **63**: 28, 40, 83-
84, 94-95, 104-105, 123-24, 193-94,
237, 314-17, 329-32, 411-13, 436-40,
460-61, 470-74, 496, 507; voting in
the Assembly (six votes for the British Empire), **63**: 231-32, 309-10, 320-
21, 328-29, 377-78, 414-15, 435-36,
476-78, 491-92, 504-506; the right of
withdrawal, **63**: 102-103, 179, 190-
91, 226-27, 288, 319-20, 326-27, 440-
41, 449-50, 475
*The League of Nations and collective
security:* Article X the heart of the
covenant for peace, **63**: 22, 40-42, 84,
101, 158-59, 191-92, 214, 226, 227-
29, 316-18, 331-32, 345, 403-404,
432-33, 451-52, 459-60, 475-76, 478-
80, 506, 507-508, 509; Article XI and
the peacekeeping machinery of the
League (procedures for settlement of
international disputes), **63**: 20-21,
23-24, 37-38, 48-49, 67-68, 86-87,
100, 109, 114-15, 135, 142-43, 158,
176, 194-95, 218, 245-46, 255-57,
345-47, 380-81, 386-87, 409, 482,

Woodrow Wilson, Western Tour, cont.
492,494, 503; (boycotts), **63**: 23, 38-
39, 49, 68, 87, 100, 135-36, 257-58,
346, 409-10; the League as insurance against future war, **63**: 101-
102, 146-47, 175-76, 195, 225, 227-
28, 359-60, 380-81, 409-10, 459-60,
481-82, 495, 512-13
On reservations and changes, **63**: 102-
104, 105, 160, 171, 185, 219-20, 231,
262-63, 290, 291, 379, 392, 451-54,
479-80, 498, 510
Reservations to Article X, **63**: 158-59,
452-54, 478-80, 480-82; *see also* Article X the heart of the covenant for
peace, above
Opponents of the League, **63**: 25-26, 29,

Woodrow Wilson, Western Tour, cont.
43, 72-73, 105, 228, 289, 325, 351,
352, 402-403, 408, 428-29, 449

WRITINGS

approves revision of *The State*, **53**: 45;
George Washington translated into
French, **53**: 261-62; remarks that he'll
be an historian again, and publishing
offers, **55**: 323, 340, 456,n2; on not ab-
breviating his *History of the American
People* for general use, **55**: 341,n1, 484;
unable to write article for *Everybody's
Magazine*, **55**: 392,n1; *see also* The
Document; The Road Away from Revolution

End of Woodrow Wilson entries

Wilson & Colby, **68**: 380; first suggestion
of, **67**: 107,n1; Colby endorses idea of
joint practice, **67**: 160-61; verbal announcement of law partnership made
from White House, **67**: 190; WW on his
law partner, **67**: 234; admission to N.Y.
bar, **67**: 248, 250, 256-57, 259, 260,
261,n1, 262, 331-32,n2, 336, 343; Bolling and Colby on plans for practice and
preparation of office, **67**: 250, 320-
21,n3, 325, 336-37, 337-38, 347-
48,353-54, 357; and J. S. Seymour, **67**:
257,n2; Colby on first British client for
firm and WW's response, **67**: 277;
Axson on WW's health, **67**: 310; WW's
admission to District bar, **67**: 318, 320,
329; and Merrill case, **67**: 320, 325,
338-39, 342-43; printed announcements of law practice, **67**: 337-38, 372;
Colby on WW joining N.Y. bar association, **67**: 340, 346; WW's mailing list
for announcements, **67**: 343-44; plans
for New York office, **67**: 347; offices to
open, **67**: 361; WW's first time at, **67**:
370-71; and Burson case, **67**: 379-80;
statement refutes political rumors
about, **67**: 381-82; receives check from,
67: 401, 402; letterhead choices, **67**:
420, 425; Colby's concern over law
practice and WW's response, **67**: 472,
475; WW on Costa Rica and, **67**: 548;
denies defending Pelletier, **67**: 556,n2;
and Nortoni, **67**: 563; and Ecuador, **67**:
571; **68**: 56, 74, 111-12, 113-14, 114;
and Colombian project, **67**: 581,n2,
582; and Flatt-Badger case, **68**: 81-83,
83; and Western Ukraine Republic
case, **68**: 110-11, 119, 134, 135-36, 140-
41; and Teapot Dome scandal, **68**: 119-
20,n2; Colby's concern about, **68**: 125,
199-200; Colby on Sinclair case, **68**:
125; consideration of closing Washington office, **68**: 199; WW on dissolution
of, **68**: 202, 213-14; Colby on dissolu-

tion of and public announcement, **68**:
211-12; press release on dissolution of,
68: 231,n1; WW thanks Colby for his
press release on dissolution of, **68**: 232;
termination of partnership, **68**: 234n1,
238
*Wilson: Campaigns for Progressivism
and Peace, 1916-1917* (Link), **68**:
405n2
*Wilson: Confusions and Crises, 1915-
1916* (Link), **68**: 587n6
Wilson: The New Freedom (Link), **61**:
469n1; **62**: 5n6; **63**: 66n7, **65**: 398n1;
66: 157n6; **68**: 78n1, 585n4
Wilson: The Road to the White House
(Link), **65**: 189n2
*Wilson: The Struggle for Neutrality,
1914-1915* (Link), **57**: 453n4; **66**: 39n5
Wilson, the Third Term and the Treaty
(*Springfield* [Mass.] *Republican*), **60**:
41,n1; **65**: 118,n2
Wilson Clubs: *see* Woodrow Wilson Clubs
Wilson Dam, **62**: 437,n1; WW on, **62**: 515;
68: 448n1
Wilson Denied Cable Tribune Did Not
Have (*New York Tribuen*), **54**: 96,n2
Wilson for Lasting Peace (Grasty), **57**:
67,n5
Wilson-House Break is Near (Hills), **62**:
573-74,n1
Wilsonian Maritime Policy (Safford), **53**:
110,n1; **65**: 270n1, 351n1, 467n2
Wilsonienne, La (society), **56**: 183,n2,3;
58: 111
Wilsonism (Dodd), **68**: 259,n2
Wilson Order Will Keep Up Bread Prices
(*New York Herald*), **61**: 549,n1
Wilson sees Russia by Steffens' Eyes
(*New York Tribune*), **56**: 551n1
Wilson Will Fight League Foes Any-
where (Philadelphia *Public Ledger*),
55: 253,n1
Wimer, Kurt, **56**: 98n1; **64**: 199n1
Winans, Richard M., **64**: 496n1

Winchell, Horace Vaughn, **65**: 77
Winchester, Alice Goodwin (Mrs. Caleb Thomas), **65**: 251,n2
Winchester, Caleb Thomas: death of, **65**: 251n2
Windau (Ventspils), Latvia, **60**: 474n21, 482, 498, 500; **61**: 87
Windham Papers (Rosebury), **68**: 67
Windhoek, South-West Africa, **54**: 252n3
Wingo, Otis Theodore, **55**: 297,n4
Winnetka, Ill., **66**: 256
Winnington-Ingram, Arthur Foley, **53**: 529,n7
Winship, North, **53**: 613-14,n1; **54**: 259,n2
Winslow, Lawrence Lanier, **53**: 573-74
Winslow, Lanier & Company, **67**: 379
Winterfeldt, Hans Karl Detlof von, **53**: 5,n1, 33; **54**: 238,n2, 241, 414
Winton, George Beverly, **61**: 551,n1, 548
Wirbel, Henri, **53**: 502,n1
Wire Control Board, **57**: 530n1; **61**: 503n1, 504, 539
wireless telegraphy: and peace terms, **56**: 38; and censorship, **56**: 245, 372-74; **57**: 423; and return to private ownership, **58**: 106, 145-46, 176, 215, 243, 365-66
Wirt, William, **66**: 116-17
Wisconsin: supports League of Nations, **55**: 158,n1,2; appointment of judge in, **67**: 14, 22
Wisconsin, University of, **53**: 349n5, 350n1; **59**: 403n2; **61**: 329n3; **64**: 425n2; **65**: 502; **68**: 175n2, 367n1, 388n1
Wisconsin Steel Company, **57**: 384,n31
Wise, Edward Frank, **60**: 511; **61**: 314,n8; on Rhineland occupation, **60**: 501,n1, 502, 503
Wise, Louise Waterman (Mrs. Stephen Samuel), **68**: 87,n1
Wise, Stephen Samuel, **54**: 5, 6, 90, 195; **55**: 368, 386; **58**: 602; **59**: 553; **65**: 183,n3; **67**: 105n3, 487-88, 490; **68**: 94, 248, 249n2; on plight of eastern European Jews, **55**: 368-81; **66**: 108-109, 356-57; on Palestine, **55**: 381-85; on minority rights, **59**: 516; Jews and Gibson's appointment to Poland, **61**: 365,n1; requests WW send message to Zionist Organization of America, **65**: 248; WW answers on eastern European Jews, **66**: 110, 368; and WW Foundation work, **67**: 533-34,n1; on comments in London on League of Nations, **68**: 87; on anti-Semitic demonstrations in Rumania, **68**: 333,n1
Wiseman, Carol, **66**: 45n6
Wiseman, Florence Marjorie Hutton Sams, Lady, **53**: 593,n7
Wiseman, Sir William, **53**: 72, 226, 409, 414, 507,n2; **54**: 386, 556; **55**: 195; **56**: 4, 5, 56, 539; **57**: 71, 142, 503, 534; **58**: 104, 138, 331, 360, 382; **66**: 303; **67**: 294; **68**: 112; and House, **53**: 394-96, 400, 418, 419; on League of Nations,

54: 151, 459, 460, 461; suggested as ambassador to the U.S., **54**: 304; on U.S. recognition of British protectorate of Egypt, **57**: 464-66, 467; House suggests for Distinguished Service Medal, **58**: 138,n2; and Irish issue, **59**: 104, 106; on WW's strategy with Republican senators and outlook for treaty ratification, **61**: 541-43, 561-62; on Mexican situation, **62**: 155,n1; concern over Senate action on reservations, **64**: 53; WW on not sending to Mexico as U.S. representative, **66**: 312
Wissenschaft und Kriegsmoral: Die deutschen Hochschulleher und die politischen Grundfragen des Ersten Weltkrieges (Schwabe), **53**: 121n1
Wister, Owen, **59**: 398,n1
Wiswall, Frank Lawrence, **67**: 261n2
With De Valera in America (McCartan), **61**: 183n2
Witherspoon Gang, **67**: 491,n1, 493
Witos, Wincenty, **66**: 10,n2, 88
Witt, Cornelis Henri Wilhelm de, **54**: 282n1
Wittpenn, Caroline Bayard Stevens Alexander (Mrs. Henry Otto), **67**: 350-51,n1; and WW Foundation beginnings, **67**: 271n1, 327n6
Wittpenn, Henry Otto, **67**: 350n1
"Wobblies": *see* International Workers of the World
Wodrow, Robert (1679-1734), **59**: 190,n3,4
Wofford College, **67**: 260
Wohl, Robert, **60**: 118n1
Wolcott, Josiah Oliver, **54**: 397n1; **55**: 263; **62**: 18; and woman suffrage, **54**: 229, 274
Wolf, Lucien, **59**: 219,n8
Wolf, Simon, **53**: 239n1, 259-60; **55**: 438n3; on anti-Semitism, **66**: 102, 130n1
Wolfe, Manson Horatio, **58**: 497,n1,2
Wolff, Harold, **62**: 637n24
Wolff, Theodor, **60**: 311-12
Wolff Brothers, **61**: 373
Wolf-Vukovic, Filip, **59**: 125n1
Woll, Matthew, **62**: 97,n8; **65**: 20
Woman Citizen, **67**: 434,n2
Woman's Hardy Garden (Ely), **67**: 481,n1
woman suffrage, **53**: 23, 24, 217; **56**: 191,n1; **59**: 203; **66**: 346n1; WW continues to try to gather support for, **53**: 244, 277, 287, 711, 717; **54**: 56, 274, 281, 302; **55**: 37, 368; "liberty bonfires," **54**: 90,n1; as international issue at Paris Peace Conference, **54**: 133; **55**: 145-47, 183-84;; WW meets with French group on, **54**: 133, 262; Tumulty on, **54**: 228-29, 519, 555, 555-56; **58**: 273-74, 605; amendment defeated, **55**: 94; and Senator Harris' vote, **58**: 273-74, 364, 535, 601, 606; **59**: 47, 120,n1; and Texas, **58**: 497-98,n2; **59**: 203,n1; WW on, **59**: 296; **62**: 462, 615;

woman suffrage (*cont.*)
68: 155; House of Representatives passes amendment on, **60**: 155n1; Senate passes amendment on, **60**: 155,n1, 204; WW congratulates Mrs. Catt on Congress' adoption of amendment, **60**: 247; death of Anna Howard Shaw, **61**: 376-77, 377; and Alabama, **61**: 464, 479; and Georgia, **61**: 480-81; Hale works for passage of amendment on, **61**: 537-38; WW tribute to Anna H. Shaw, **62**: 225; creation of League of Woman Voters, **64**: 396,n1; New Jersey ratifies 19th amendment, **64**: 396n1; and Oklahoma, **64**: 466n1; WW urges ratification by West Virginia, **65**: 36; U.S. representative suggested for international congress on, **65**: 151-52; and Louisiana, **65**: 163-65, 294-95; and Delaware, **65**: 351; Hawke *v.* Smith decision, **65**: 445n2; and Tennessee, **65**: 445,n2, 460; **66**: 30n1, 35, 54,n1, 54-55; Frierson on states' power concerning amending process, **65**: 450,n2; and North Carolina, **65**: 450, 473; Overman on reasons for not supporting amendment on, **65**: 466-67; and Roberts, **65**: 468; Brandeis on, **67**: 563,n1; Mrs. Simonson on, **68**: 264; John Sharp Williams on, **68**: 292
Woman's Committee: discontinuation of, **55**: 299-300
Woman's Suffrage Association of Louisiana, **65**: 294
women: suggested for peace commissioners, **53**: 114-15, 125-26, 129, 216-17; and a proposed reconstruction commission, **53**: 117, 118; WW's praise of war work and sacrifices by, **53**: 277, 618; **54**: 272-73; mention of WW's meeting with, **54**: 91, 138, 257,n2, 307; D'Estournelles de Constant wishes WW to thank, **54**: 256n1,2; WW's remarks to working women in Paris, **54**: 271-73; and League of Nations, **55**: 6, 9, 122, 145-47, 172, 175-76; **56**: 303; **57**: 43, 218-19, 236; **58**: 190; and census bill, **55**: 281,n1; and war work, **55**: 299-300; request to appear before League of Nations Commission, **56**: 223, 374; and International Labour Commission's recommendations, **56**: 231; and labor laws, **57**: 528n3; support for WW's Adriatic statement and League of Nations, **58**: 140-41,n1; and labor clauses, **58**: 174, 200, 362; Taft's criticism of WW's reply to women's peace group, **59**: 450n2, 478n1; and labor, **60**: 150, 151; **64**: 98n1; delay in transportation home of, **60**: 644-45; and equal pay, **61**: 38; and peace treaty signing ceremony, **61**: 118; and Labor Department appointments, **62**: 97n9, 167, 224, 314-15; and Democratic National Committee, **62**: 587; and labor unions and proposed inter-national labor conference, **63**: 56-57, 58-59; WW on, **63**: 140; proposed history of war work of, **64**: 3,n1; and appointment to Civil Service Commission, **65**: 115-16; suggested for appointment to Federal Trade Commission, **66**: 241n1; praise of WW, **67**: 135,n1; WW acknowledges tribute from, **67**: 143; many in procession going to WW's new home, **67**: 213; and WW Foundation, **67**: 271n1; **68**: 264-66; and Democratic politics in Maine, **67**: 302n2; supporters of WW, **67**: 450; WW praises Democratic, **68**: 33-34,n2, 155; demonstration before WW's home, **68**: 36-39; Tarbell on League of Nations and, **68**: 46; first senatorial candidate from Mississippi, **68**: 93,n3; activities of in Democratic party, **68**: 155, 156-57, 157; Clarke on League of Nations movement and, **68**: 159, 161, 184; N. H. Davis on public issues and, **68**: 182
Women of America! (leaflet), **62**: 566n1
Women Workers of America, **57**: 426
Women's Big Conference (Barrett), **68**: 36n1
Women's Bureau (Dept. of Labor), **62**: 97n9; **63**: 56-57; **66**: 520
Women's International Conference for Permanent Peace (May 1919), **59**: 117,n4, 450n2
Women's International League for Peace and Freedom, **58**: 141n1; **67**: 42,n1, 43
Women's International League for Peace and Freedom, 1915-1965: A Record of Fifty Years Work (Bussey and Tims), **58**: 141n1; **59**: 117n4
Women's Pan American Congress (Baltimore): *see* Pan-American Conference of Women
Wood, Henry Alexander Wise, **59**: 372n2, 451n1, 452; **61**: 373
Wood, Leonard, **68**: 528; WW on, **55**: 486-87; **58**: 531; **65**: 372; **67**: 447; mentioned as presidential candidate, **64**: 325; and campaign spending, **65**: 354n2; surgery and subsequent lameness, **65**: 403,n3
Wood, Levi Hollingsworth, **61**: 398-99,n1, 480; **62**: 126,n1; **67**: 37n1
Wood, Robert Elkington, **53**: 60,n1
Wood, Spencer Shepard, **55**: 235,n1
Wood, Waddy Butler, **66**: 519n1, 534
Woodbridge, Jeanie Wilson Woodrow (Mrs. Samuel Isett), **62**: 616n1
Woodbridge, Samuel Isett: and Shantung settlement, **62**: 616-17,n2
Woodbury, Gordon: appointed Assistant Secretary of Navy, **66**: 55, 56, 91, 207,n1; and Interstate Commerce Commission, **67**: 25,n1, 29; praises WW and WW thanks, **67**: 29, 32
Woodbury, Levi, **66**: 55,n2
Woodhull, Alfred Alexander, **65**: 572,n2
Woodman, Francis Call, **54**: 255-56, 262

Woodrow (family name): *see* Wodrow

Woodrow, Felexiana Shepherd Baker (Mrs. James) (Aunt Felie), **67**: 11n1, 16, 171

Woodrow, Fitz William McMaster, first cousin once removed of WW, **68**: 556,n2, 576

Woodrow, James, uncle of WW: and Oglethorpe University, **65**: 86,n2, 117, 382; **67**: 78, 170n1

Woodrow, Marion, first cousin of WW, **67**: 170n1, 171

Woodrow, Thomas, maternal grandfather of WW, **53**: 524, 537, 538, 541

Woodrow Wilson (*Daily Princetonian*), **67**: 306,n1

Woodrow Wilson (*New York Times*) **67**: 183n1

Woodrow Wilson (Walworth), **58**: 618n33

Woodrow Wilson: A Medical and Psychological Biography (Weinstein), **56**: 556n2; **57**: 146n4, 240n2; **58**20: 276n1, 607, 611n1, 613n11, 617n26, 631n1; **59**: 574n1; **61**: 374n3; **62**: 628n1; **63**: 539n1

Woodrow Wilson and Colonel House: A Personality Study (George and George), **58**: 618n30

Woodrow Wilson and Far Eastern Policy (Curry), **57**: 626n3

Woodrow Wilson and His Work (Dodd), **65**: 432,n1; **66**: 165,n2; **67**: 39, 40n4, 297, 446, 456

Woodrow Wilson and the American Diplomatic Tradition: The Treaty Fight in Perspective (Ambrosius), **61**: 66n3; **62**: 308n1; **63**: 482n4; **64**: 276n1, 328n2; **65**: 292n1, 328n2

Woodrow Wilson and the Mexican Interventionist Movement of 1919 (Trow), **62**: 155n1; **64**: 120n1

Woodrow Wilson and the Service He Has Rendered His Country and Humanity (Holt), **67**: 187,n1

Woodrow Wilson and Woman Suffrage: A New Look, (Lunardini and Knock), **58**: 364n1

Woodrow Wilson and World Settlement (R. S. Baker), **55**: 488n2, 531n1; **56**: 393n1, 563n3; **62**: 607n1; **66**: 537n1; **68**: 223n2, 259,n2, 281-83, 326, 523; *see also* Baker, Ray Stannard

Woodrow Wilson: An Interpretation (Cobb), **67**: 234,n1

Woodrow Wilson: An Intimate Memoir (Grayson), **56**: 556n2; **62**: 507n1, 629n3; **63**: 539n1; **65**: 109n1

Woodrow Wilson and His Work (Dodd), **67**: 39, 40n4, 297, 446, 456; **68**: 258,n1

Woodrow Wilson and World War I, 1917-1921 (Ferrell), **66**: 58n1

Woodrow Wilson As I Know Him (Tumulty), **63**: 338n4, 547n1; **64**: 417n3; **66**: 292n2; **67**: 414,n2; **68**: 259n2, 591,n6

Woodrow Wilson Award, **67**: 334, 543-44,n3

Woodrow Wilson Clubs (National Council of Woodrow Wilson Clubs), **67**: 257-58, 259-60, 260, 271, 273-74, 285-86, 288, 326-28; at Harvard, **66**: 409, 409-10, 467-69; **67**: 158, 258, 263-65, 267, 318n1, 326, 327, 328; formation and organization of, **67**: 253,n1, 285, 318-19; at New York University, **67**: 271, 275; WW advises keeping appeal separate from Foundation drive, **67**: 275, 276; WW accepts honorary presidency, **67**: 286, 288; of Portland, Maine, **67**: 302; Princeton University, **67**: 306,n1, 311, 315, 334; and contribution list from Democratic National Committee, **67**: 324, 344-35; concern over WW Foundation's fund raising at colleges, **67**: 386; Stuart on not competing with WW Foundation, **67**: 415-17; delicate position of WW regarding WW Foundation and, **67**: 425-26

Woodrow Wilson Democracy, **68**: 44,n1, 44, 50,n1, 106, 157n1, 173, 284

Woodrow Wilson, Jan Smuts, and the Versailles Settlement (Curry), **53**: 515n1

Woodrow Wilson Foundation, **67**: 327n6, 393-94,n1, 487,n1, 547,n1, 572, 585; **68**: 15n2; and Mrs. Kruse, **67**: 250n1; beginnings of, **67**: 271,n1, 273-74, 327n6; **68**: 264-66; WW on name of the Fund, **67**: 341-42, 348; WW on, **67**: 341-42, 531; first use of word "foundation," **67**: 346; WW's reasons for opposing word "Foundation," **67**: 348; issue of competition with WW Clubs, **67**: 352, 353, 386, 415-17; search for best portrait of WW for certificates, **67**: 369-70,n1,6, 372; origination of idea for, **67**: 393, 399-400, 565; I. T. Jones on, **67**: 408-10; WW's position of silence on, **67**: 417-18; delicate position of WW regarding WW Clubs and, **67**: 425-26; sends birthday greetings to WW and WW thanks, **67**: 497, 504; **68**: 245-46, 511, 513; Cambridge Division, **67**: 520,n1; mass meeting and march launches Washington campaign, **67**: 521, 522-23; Toy on success of, **67**: 526-27,n4; Spargo on, **67**: 528; and Rabbi Wise, **67**: 533,n1; Bok on, **67**: 535; comments on awards to be given by, **67**: 543-44, 545-47, 548-49; greetings to WW on fifth anniversary of entrance into war and WW's response, **67**: 603-604, 604; WW thanks F. D. Roosevelt for work on, **68**: 39, 246; birthday greetings to WW and WW's thanks, **68**: 245-46, 511, 513; F. D. Roosevelt on success of, **68**: 245; delegation visits WW on his birthday, **68**: 247, 248-49, 250; charter and organization of, **68**: 249,n2; monies received, **68**: 249; WW asks who had original idea for, **68**: 262;

Woodrow Wilson Foundation (*cont.*)
Holt on originator of, **68**: 264; receives check from family of deceased soldier, **68**: 266; trustee installation ceremony, **68**: 284-85, 285-86,n1, 288, 355; WW will not solicit friends for contributions, **68**: 357; luncheon in celebration of WW's birthday, **68**: 508, 509-10; Redfield to speak at, **68**: 508; nominations open for prize, **68**: 509, 510

Woodrow Wilson, Revolutionary Germany and Peacemaking, 1918-1919: Missionary Diplomacy and the Realities of Power (Schwabe), **55**: 458n1; **56**: 530n4; 44n1, 308n1; **59**: 68n3, 554n2, 579n1

Woodrow Wilson: Revolution, War, and Peace, (Link), **58**: 635n20

Woodrow Wilson, the League, and America's Present Duty (speech, Dodd), **67**: 355,n7

Woodrow Wilson's Case for the League of Nations (Foley), **66**: 152n2; **68**: 330n1, 351,n2, 411n1

Woodrow Wilson's Dollar Diplomacy in the Far East: The New Chinese Consortium 1917-1921 (Matsuda), **65**: 259n1

Woodrow Wilson's Eloquence (Wescott), **64**: 232n2

Woodrow Wilson's Neuropsychologic Impairment and the Paris Peace Conference (Weinstein), **62**: 628n1

Woodrow Wilson's Pierce-Arrow: The Story of the President's Car Exhibited at His Birthplace (Woodrow Wilson Birthplace Foundation), **67**: 166n

Woodrow Wilson's Place in History (Smuts), **67**: 26-27,n1

Woodrow Wilson's Plan to Enter the League of Nations through an Executive Agreement (Wimer), **56**: 98n1; **64**: 199n1

Woodrow Wilson Was Well Prepared for Leadership (Whaling), **67**: 74,n2

Woods, Hiram, Jr., **65**: 258,n2; **67**: 277, 300

Woods, Lawrence Crane, **67**: 306, 307-308, 334-35, 340-41; praises WW, **66**: 433-34,n1, 447

Woods, Lawrence Crane, Jr., **67**: 306,n2, 311, 315, 334, 340

Woods, Rebekah Wilson Campbell (Mrs. Lawrence Crane), **66**: 434,n2; **67**: 306,n5, 335

Woods, William Seaver, **61**: 541,n1

Woodson, Urey, **68**: 426

Woodward, Sir (Ernest) Llewellyn, **61**: 157n9; **62**: 254n2

Woodward, William, **65**: 318n1; **66**: 185

Woolley, Clarence Mott, **55**: 308,n1, 336, 357; **56**: 553,n1; and price controversy between Railroad Administration and Industrial Board, **57**: 374,n1, 376,n3, 381, 384, 387

Woolley, Mary Emma: and WW Foundation, **68**: 249n2, 355,n1, 365

Woolley, Robert Wickliffe, **53**: 24; **54**: 260, 261, 413, 429, 521; **58**: 274,n3; **59**: 148-49,n1; **64**: 445,n1; **65**: 274, 275; **68**: 577; on Democratic party and campaign organization, **66**: 173-74; on election results and praise of WW, **66**: 313-14; WW thanks for letter of support, **66**: 325; WW accepts resignation of, **66**: 505,n1; and WW's veto of extension of application of Section 10 of Clayton Act, **67**: 12n1

Woolsey, Lester Hood, **61**: 522,n2; **65**: 107, 231

Worden, Montana, **63**: 168,n1

Work, John McClelland, **55**: 92n1

Workmen and Peasants Rebel (*New York Times*), **62**: 445n3

Works of John C. Calhoun (Crallé, ed.), **53**: 267n2

World Court: *see* Permanent Court of International Justice

World Peace Foundation, **53**: 82,n2

World's Court League, **55**: 278

World's Student Christian Federation, **66**: 144,n1; **67**: 407-408, 413, 422

World's Work, **55**: 290n1; **60**: 146,n2; **62**: 460,n1, 546-47,n2;   **67**: 242n3,4,5,6; **68**: 498; and *World Settlement*, **67**: 241, 242,n6, 249

World Tomorrow, **53**: 307n2

World War: and false armistice, **53**: 21; number of U.S. troops sent abroad, **53**: 200, 275; losses of U.S. men at sea, **53**: 275n2; and foreign loans, **53**: 441-42, 477-80, 691

aftermath: and War Industries Board, **53**: 11-12, 201; H. Hoover on expanding functions of Belgian Relief Commission, **53**: 14-15; and cancellation of war contracts, **53**: 18-20, 47-48; and WW and postwar reconstruction program, **53**: 24, 62, 67, 94; Clarkson on use of local and state councils of defense, **53**: 97n1; War Cabinet (U.S.) on issues, **53**: 150; Gompers on, **53**: 217-20, 220; France on U.S. representatives remaining on inter-Allied councils, **53**: 497; and U.S. Treasury representatives in Paris, **53**: 626-27, 691, 715-16; origin of the name, **61**: 611; *see also* European relief

Armistice: Germany's reaction to, **53**: 4-5; plans for publication of, **53**: 26-27; Germany accepts, **53**: 27, 33, 34; reaction of Congress to, **53**: 35; WW's address to Congress on, **53**: 35-43; military terms, **53**: 36-38; and naval conditions, **53**: 39-40; duration of, **53**: 40-41; and Australia, **53**: 44; Lodge on, **53**: 82,n1; Bullitt on signing peace only with representatives of German Constituent Assembly, **53**: 122; Italy's

abuse of, **53**: 208; N. D. Baker on returning to normal conditions, **53**: 252-53; WW on economic and industrial readjustment in U.S., **53**: 278-79; and International Armistice Commission, **53**: 627n1; battle deaths and war costs, **63**: 221, 243-44, 349, 349-50; WW on start of, **63**: 372-73, 430-31

atrocities: torpedoing of ships, **53**: 275n3; and proposed trial of William II, **53**: 324n2; Poincaré on, **53**: 386n1; Grayson on visit to Belgium, **61**: 4-5

World War Foreign Debt Commission, **68**: 434n1

World Zionist Organization, **61**: 461n1

Wormser, Georges Marcel, **60**: 9,n2, 10

Worthington, Frank: on interview with WW, **53**: 573-76,n1

Worthington-Evans, Sir Worthington (Laming), **53**: 77,n1

Wrangel, Count Anton Magnus Hermann, **57**: 251,n3

Wrangel, Petr Nikolaevich, **65**: 288n3

Wrentmore, Clarence George, **60**: 201

Wrentmore, Margaret McFarland (Mrs. Clarence George), **59**: 204,n2; **60**: 199, 201

Wrentmore, Salena Elizabeth, **59**: 204n1

Wright, Chester Whitney, **56**: 283,n1

Wright, Joshua Butler, **53**: 594n9; **56**: 396,n4; **65**: 254,n1; **66**: 144,n1; **67**: 61; **68**: 573, 580

Wright, Louise, **66**: 222-23

Wright, Maude Wolfe (Mrs. Joshua Butler), **53**: 594,n9

Wright, Theodore, **53**: 394,n1

Wroblewski, Wladyslaw, **68**: 183n2

Wuchang Hankow Bar Association, **60**: 101n1

Württemburg, **60**: 585, 587, 588, 618n3; **65**: 101

Wu T'ing-fang, **66**: 102,n1

Wyndham, Sir Percy Charles Hugh, **59**: 263,n8, 265

Wyoming, **53**: 636,n1; **61**: 535; and Teapot Dome scandal, **68**: 119,n2

Yager, Arthur, **55**: 264,n2; **59**: 122,n1; **66**: 25,n3

Yakutsk, Russia, **62**: 87

Yale, William, **58**: 327n5

Yale Law Journal, **66**: 314,n1, 315n2, 483n2

Yale University, **53**: 348n1,3; **61**: 568n1; **62**: 82n2, 314n1; **65**: 217n1, 238n2; **67**: 285, 458n4; **68**: 126,n1 and football rivalry with Princeton, **61**: 373; and Wilson & Colby announcement, **67**: 344

Yamagata, Prince Aritomo, **57**: 607,n7

Yamakawa, Tadao, **58**: 346,n3

Yamanaka, Itsuro, **61**: 189n8

Yangtse (Yangtse Kiang) River, **58**: 131

Yangtse Valley, **58**: 132-33

Yap Island, **54**: 381-82, 400,n1; **55**: 24; **57**: 358, 455, 554; **58**: 297, 300, 346, 353; controversy over Japanese mandate for, **66**: 308, 458-64, 493, 496; **67**: 53-55, 58, 79, 147,n1,2, 154-56, 194-95,n1,4, 462n2

Yates, Emily Chapman Martin (Mrs. Frederic), **54**: 488; **55**: 282,n2, 387; **56**: 191, 553; **59**: 526; **68**: 428-29

Yates, Frederic, **54**: 488; **55**: 282; death of, **54**: 488n1; **55**: 282n3, 387; **56**: 191, 310; **59**: 526; **64**: 490n1; and memorial fund, **57**: 98

Yates, Halsey Edward, **56**: 334,n4

Yates, Louis A. R., **56**: 12n1

Yates, Mary, **54**: 488; **55**: 282n2, 387; **59**: 526

Yatsu, N.Y., **58**: 626n74

Yerevan: *see* Erivan

Yiddish language, **55**: 372; and Polish Jews, **61**: 89-92, 273

Yi Sung-man: *see* Rhee, Syngman

Yitang, Wang, **55**: 424

Yokohama, Japan: earthquake in, **68**: 424n1

Yorck, S.M.S., **55**: 432

York, Alvin Cullum, **62**: 42,n2

York Dispatch, **55**: 440,n2

Yorktown, Va.: WW's visit to, **55**: 444-45

Yost, Casper Salathiel, **61**: 481; suggestions for gaining Republican support for League of Nations, **61**: 399-400,n1

Youdenitch, General: *see* Yudenich, Nikolai Nikolaevich

Young, Allyn Abbott, **53**: 367,n1, 378, 381; **56**: 58,n1; **58**: 120; **59**: 171; **65**: 139,n1; on Fiume, **56**: 607-609; **57**: 432-33, 456; photograph of, *illustration section*, **57**

Young, Evan Erastus, **67**: 8,n1

Young, Hugh Hampton, M.D. **63**: 578-79,n1, 580, 581, 582, 643; **64**: 32, 489, 506; **65**: 3,n1, 4, 5; interview on WW's stroke, **64**: 394-96, 403, 425, 432

Young, James, **55**: 297,n4

Young, Milton, **68**: 535

Young, Owen D., **64**: 64n1; and second Industrial Conference, **63**: 611

Young, Riley S., **55**: 158n2

Young, Virginia, **67**: 350

Young Americans, Democratic League, **66**: 262,n1, 414,n1; of Maine, **67**: 302n3

Young Fiume (organization): *see* Giovine Fiume

Young Men's Christian Association (Y.M.C.A.), **53**: 707; **54**: 5n2, 557; **57**: 459; and Jessie Sayre, **57**: 60-61; and relief funds, **67**: 85-86

Youngstown, Ohio: and Ida Clarke, **68**: 139

Young Turks, **60**: 612; **65**: 306

Ypres, Belgium: WW's visit to, **61**: 4, 5; photograph of, *illustration section*, **61**

Yser Canal, **61**: 29

Yser River, **61**: 4n3; photograph of, *illustration section*, **61**

Yudenich, Nikolai Nikolaevich, **59**: 20,n13, 196; **63**: 588n1

Yugoslavia: **57**: 112, 368, 466; **58**: 6, 12, 15, 17, 39, 76, 92, 359n1, 509; **59**: 82, 83n3, 85, 119-20, 125, 166, 167, 613; **60**: 134,n7, 146, 577n5, 582n5, 607, 643; **61**: 55, 206; **67**: 461n1; **68**: 62; and Adriatic Question and Fiume, **53**: 56, 224, 226, 294, 296, 338, 649; **54**: 19, 20, 50, 112n3, 124, 134, 148-49, 170, 197-98, 233, 388; **55**: 85, 85, 87-88, 243, 305; **56**: 393n1, 472, 490,n1, 556, 562-65,n3, 567-72, 607-609,n1; **57**: 337, 338, 340-41, 344, 432-33, 467n2, 499-502; **58**: 88, 89, 160, 239n4, 396, 452, 588, 589-90; **59**: 34, 96-97, 201, 241, 551, 552, 553, 555, 556 556-59, 569, 569-70, 645; **62**: 456, 574-75, 604, 620; **63**: 82, 188, 205, 207-208, 209-10, 298, 365, 366, 465, 525; **64**: 168-79, 264-66, 376, 465; **65**: 37-39, 45-46, 259n1, 303,n10, 315-16, 322, 364-65, 367, 377, 388-89; and Jews, **55**: 380; and Italy, **53**: 43,n1, 123-24, 128, 167, 303,n10, 315-16, 433, 434, 435-36, 459, 466, 564, 643, 696; and Steed memorandum on Adriatic, **53**: 444-46; and Montenegro, **53**: 638n1, 640, 700, 703; **58**: 161-64, 268; **59**: 178n2; and Jews, **55**: 380; 620,n1; Smuts on, **57**: 171-73, various comments on Italian claims and, **57**: 369-70, 434-35, 477, 541, 545, 549, 613, 614; Benson on deportation of Yugoslavs by Italy, **57**: 442-43; issue of recognition of, **58**: 150, 236; and boundary issues, **59**: 60-63, 405-406; **60**: 16,n1; and reparations, **59**: 74n1, 305n13, 384n1, 391; **61**: 100, 101; Day on Fiume and, **59**: 171; WW on plebiscite and, **59**: 329; and Carinthia and, **59**: 403-405, 501-502, 631,n2; D. W. Johnson on Klagenfurt Basin and, **59**: 406-408; and prisoners of war, **59**: 425, 426; Bliss on fixed military strength for, **59**: 428-32; and Italy, **59**: 505; on title of Austrian delegation, **59**: 587-88; and minority rights and Austrian treaty, **59**: 629-30; Italy on recognition of, **59**: 631-32, 634, 635; and Klagenfurt Basin, **60**: 22, 34, 121-29, 232-33, 262, 267-69, 361, 640; **61**: 41-43, 50-56, 57-59; on clauses on minority rights in peace treaty, **60**: 97,n8; Lloyd George wants changes in peace treaty regarding, **60**: 120; and arms limitation, **60**: 169-70; Council of Four on Adriatic question and, **60**: 213; results of plebiscite in Fiume favor, **60**: 293-94; and Hungary, **60**: 312-14,n1; **64**: 447; advance and occupation of Klagenfurt by, **60**: 261-62, 394, 628; and Albania, **60**: 530, 565; **66**: 308; and and Italy, **61**: 196, 552; D. W. Johnson on

Adriatic question and, **61**: 227-30; and frontier issue, **61**: 279; and Sudbahn, **61**: 280, 317-21; Vénisélos on, **64**: 162; and Albania, **64**: 177; Anglo-French Adriatic proposals, **64**: 298-305, 313-16, 318-20, 331-35; Lansing and Wallace on U.S. course of action on Adriatic proposal and, **64**: 398-402, 459-63; Anglo-French reply to WW on, **64**: 437-39; and "Wilson line" boundary, **65**: 373,n1; issue of representation at Spa Conference, **65**: 459, 477; children fed in, **65**: 469; issue of representation at Spa Conference, **65**: 459, 477; children fed in, **65**: 469; and Italy and former Austrian naval squadron, **66**: 26n1; and Balfour and inter-Allied indebtedness, **68**: 106n1; *see also* under names of spokesmen for, such as Pasić, Nikola P.; Vesnić, Milenko R.

Yugoslavia at the Paris Peace Conference: a Study in Frontiermaking (Lederer), **53**: 638n1; **55**: 88n1; **59**: 125n1; **62**: 574n1; **65**: 469; **66**: 364n2

Yugoslav National Council at Zagreb, **53**: 43

Yuan Shih-k'ai, **53**: 140

Za-Baikal Railway, **53**: 146

Zaghlul, Sa'd, **56**: 122n2, 154n1; **61**: 8,n1

Zagreb: National Council at, **53**: 43,n1, 123n2; *see also* Agram

Zaharaff, Sir Basil, **60**: 349,n1

Zangezur, Armenia, **65**: 287

Zaouditou, Empress of Ethiopia, **61**: 406n1, 470, 471-72, 472, 603

Zara, Croatia, **53**: 446, 640,n2, 643; **54**: 51, 112n3; **57**: 483, 488, 511, 611, 612; **58**: 14, 81, 82, 83, 163, 358, 450, 452, 590,n8; **59**: 71, 82, 83n3, 86, 96, 125, 201, 242,n2, 249, 552, 553, 565, 569, 570; **60**: 138, 211, 213, 217, 266, 308, 310, 311; **61**: 171, 228, 552, 553-54, 575; **62**: 456, 575, 603, 604, 605, 620; **63**: 91, 206, 207-208, 465, 617n1; **64**: 170, 172, 264n4, 265, 299, 300, 301, 302, 305, 333; bases of arrangement, **59**: 557, 558, 559; and D'Annunzio invasion of, **64**: 517n2; and Adriatic settlement, **66**: 364, 365, 377

Zavoiko, Vasili Steoanovich, **64**: 390-91,n2

Zayas y Alfonso, Alfredo, **66**: 84, 124; **67**: 24n1, 26,n4

Zebouni, Jean, **57**: 426

Zeebrugge, Belgium: WW visits, **61**: 6-7,n,9, 20; photograph of, *illustration section*, **61**

Zeitoun, **54**: 517

zemstvo, **55**: 403

Zenzinov, Vladimir Mikhailovich, **59**: 156,n4

Zerbst, Frederick G., **62**: 422,n1

Zerkowitz, Emil, **56**: 241,n2

Zervos, Skevos, **58**: 355-56,n1

Ziegfeld, Florenz, Jr., **54**: 227,n2

Zimmern, Alfred Eckhard, **53**: 331,n2
Zinov'ev, Grigorii Evseevich, **54**: 92n2;
  62: 205,n2
Zionism, **57**: 326n3; **58**: 400; WW and, **53**:
  260, 543, 572; **54**: 231-32, 258, 432-33;
  55: 381-85, 386, 438; **59**: 373, 413; **61**:
  44, 128, 178, 442n1, 443; **62**: 608; **64**:
  358, 449; **65**: 248,n2; **67**: 388; **68**:
  100,n1,2, 485; Balfour on Palestine
  question and, **56**: 203-204; Frankfurter
  on, **58**: 555-56; Rev. Matthews on, **62**:
  456; WW on, **62**: 609; **65**: 248,n2

Zionist Organization of America, **62**:
  609n1; **65**: 248, 334,n1; **68**: 100n1
Zolger, Ivan, **55**: 88n1
Zonguldak, Turkey, **59**: 91n5
Zorn, Andres Leonard, **55**: 225,n3
Zurich, University of, **58**: 382n5
Zwischen Compiègne und Versailles:
  Geheime amerikanische Militärdiplo-
  matie in der Period des Waffenstill-
  standes 1918/19: Die Rolle des Ober-
  sten Arthur L. Conger (Epstein), **58**:
  308n1